D1480635

For Reference

Not to be taken from this room

The New York Times
Film Reviews
1975-1976

The New York Times
Film Reviews
1975-1976

The New York Times & Arno Press/New York 1977

Copyright © 1975, 1976 The New York Times Company

Copyright © 1977 The New York Times Company

Library of Congress Catalog Card Number: 70-112777

ISBN 0-405-10657-2

Manufactured in the United States of America by Arno Press Inc.

Contents

79655

Foreword

In 1970, THE NEW YORK TIMES FILM REVIEWS (1913-1968) was published. It was a five-volume set, containing over 18,000 film reviews exactly as they first appeared in The Times.

The collection was accompanied by a sixth volume, an 1,100 page computer-generated index, which afforded ready access to the material by film titles, by producing and distributing companies, and by the names of all actors, directors and other persons listed in the credits.

Further volumes appeared in 1971, 1973 and 1975 reproducing the reviews that were printed in The Times during the years 1969-1970, 1971-1972 and 1973-1974; the present volume carries the collection through 1976. The same type of index as originally conceived was incorporated into the 1969-1970, 1971-1972, 1973-1974 and the present volume.

New compilations will be published periodically to keep the collection constantly updated.

BEST FILMS

Articles listing the best and award-winning films published in The Times appear at the end of each year's reviews. These include the awards of the Academy of Motion Picture Arts and Sciences and the "best films" selections of The New York Times and the New York Film Critics.

The New York Times
Film Reviews
1975

COMEDIANS (Komödianten), directed by G.W. Pabst; screenplay (German with English subtitles) by Axel Eggebrecht, Walter Von Hollander and Mr. Pabst, based on the novel "Philine" by Olly Boeheim; music, Lothar Bruhne; director of photography, Bruno Stephan; editor, Rudolf Griesbach; produced by Bavaria Films; distributed by Trans-World Films. Running time: 111 minutes. At the First Avenue Screening Room, First Avenue near 61st Street. This film has not been rated.
Karoline Neuber............Kathe Dorsh
Philine Shroder............Hilde Krahl
Duchess of Weissenfels ....Henny Porten
Duke of Kurland.........Gustav Diessl
Armin.................Richard Haussler
Johann Neuber.........Friedrich Domin

By VINCENT CANBY

"Comedians" (Komödianten), made by the late G. W. Pabst in Nazi Germany in 1941, is of primary interest to students of Pabst and German war films in general. It's not great Pabst and it's not even of much political and social importance, being overshadowed by Pabst's less innocent "Paracelsus," made two years later.

"Comedians," which will be shown at the First Avenue Screening Room at noon and midnight today and tomorrow, is a straightforward if highly melodramatic biography of Karoline Neuber (1697-1760), the actress-manager who is credited with having created the foundations for the classic German theater by tossing out the clowns, requiring rigorous rehearsals, playing French classics in German translation, and even supervising the private lives of her players. Thus, says an opening credit card, she provided a theater tradition that would make possible the works of Germany's own great playwrights.

The film is fusty romance on the "Stage Door" theme that theatrical success demands absolute negation of private life. The actors behave in a broadly operatic manner though they are seldom allowed to sing. One small scene stands out: the performance of a chamber opera at the court of the Duchess of Weissenfels. It is delicate, mannered, charming and much less overblown than the movie that contains it.

A major disappointment is Pabst's big orgy scene when Karoline and her troupe visit St. Petersburg. Josepf von Sternberg did this sort of thing much better in "The Scarlet Empress."

Somehow Pabst's vision of Russian high-jinks lacks sincerity. There is much spilled wine, dancing on table tops and grabbing at young women but less passion and abandon than you'll see at the Metropolitan Opera on almost any Saturday afternoon in the season.

1975 Ja 3, 13:2

Film Forum Program

SINGLE FRAME DANCE, a collection of eight short films: "Clearview," direct by Brian Wood, 28 minutes; "Apalachee," directed by James Herbert, 12 minutes; "Watching for the Queen," directed by David Rimmer, 11 minutes; "Canadian Pacific," directed by Mr. Rimmer, 10 minutes; "Michigan Avenue," directed by James Benning and Bette Gordon, 6 minutes; "Tom's Film," directed by Linda Klosky, 73 seconds; "Meiosis," directed by Marguerite Carter, 5 minutes; "Single Frame Dance," directed by Lenny Horowitz, 10 minutes. At the Film Forum, 88th Street, west of Broadway.

"Single Frame Dance," the collective title for this week's Film Forum show, is a program of eight shorts, 73 seconds to 28 minutes long, each an exploration of single-frame editing. This is the process by which time can be brought to a stop or so speeded up that three months can be refined into 10 minutes of screen life, as David Rimmer does in his lovely time-lapse landscape movie, "Canadian Pacific."

Most of the films in the program are of less interest as film art than as exercises in a very particular film technique. The exceptions are the Rimmer films and one by James Herbert called "Apalachee," made by rephotographing original footage, frame by frame, to create a painterly visual image quite unlike anything you've probably ever seen on film.

The program opened at the Film Forum yesterday and will run through Sunday night. It will be repeated Jan. 9 through. 12. Showings are at 8 P.M. VINCENT CANBY.

1975 Ja 3, 13:4

BROTHER OF THE WIND, directed by Dick Robinson; screenplay by John Mahon; produced by Mr. Robinson and Mr. Mahon; executive producer, G.M. Ridges; narration written by John Champion; director of photography, Rod Allin; music, Gene Kauer and Douglas Lackey; supervising film editor, John Joyce; editor, John W. Levins; distributed by Sun International Productions, Inc. Running time 87 minutes.

At the Guild Theater, 50th Street west of Fifth Avenue, UA East Theater, First Avenue at 85th Street, Cinema Village, 12th Street east of Fifth Avenue, Olympia Theater, Broadway at 107th Street, and other theaters. This film has been rated G.
Sam Monroe ....Dick Robinson
Narrator ....Leon Ames

By VINCENT CANBY

"Brother of the Wind," which opened at four Manhattan theaters yesterday, is perfect escapist entertainment for those animal-loving, city-bound children who count themselves lucky if they can own a hamster. It's about wildlife in the Canadian Rockies, particularly about the growing pains of four timber-wolf puppies that are raised (and then returned to the forest) by Sam Monroe (Dick Robinson), a fine, stanch, white-bearded mountain man who looks a good deal the way Santa Claus might if he got more exercise.

Mr. Robinson, who directed and co-produced the movie, is the only character in a film that is concerned with introducing us to nature's various systems of checks and balances. The film's style is direct, simple, often beautiful and mostly free of the sort of anamorphosizing clichés that one usually finds in such movies.

The wolves share the camera's attention with, among other things, deer, bear (black, grizzly), salmon (going upstream), coyote, elk, weasel, muskrat, duck, mountain lion and raccoon. The animals are terrific, the landscapes spectacular and the photography first-rate. More important is the way that "Brother of the Wind" demonstrates the survival-of-the-fittest law with such gentle tact.

Leon Ames provides the soundtrack narration that is meant to be the old man's musing monologue.

1975 Ja 9, 49:1

GUEST VIEW

ALFRED KAZIN

Can Today's Movies Tell The Truth About Fascism?

When the Israeli athletes were murdered at the Olympic games in Munich, Jean-Luc Godard thoughtfully pronounced: "The Palestinians were right with their basics, but not their external conditions. They didn't realize the world was just watching a looking-machine —the television—and the killings didn't have the effect they wanted." Godard is too come-and-go a "Maoist," in the conversational French style (and knows too much about movies), to believe that a movie about a political happening is anything but just another movie. There's nothing like movies, but there's not too much to movies. "Visuals,"—movies and television—are by now such a powerful, too-powerful, omnipresent, seductive impersonation of the "real" that they are like newspapers— a surface daily life presents. (Over and over again.) "The eye sees more than the heart knows," said William Blake. It sees more than it ever did. It sees more than it knows what to do with. How to tell the difference between the unending news show on film and "reality"?

World War II, for example, is by now the longest running movie of all time. Thanks to so much film, it is as big a myth to most people as the Civil War.

Alfred Kazin's latest book is "Bright Book of Life: American Novelists and Storytellers from Hemingway to Mailer."

The film opens on the Nuremberg rallies so "marvelously" staged and shot by Leni Riefenstahl in the mid-thirties, cuts to the frowning face of Hitler at the Olympic games, cuts to the marvelous action shots of Stukas and tanks making Blitzkrieg! over "helpless" Poland. Then there are the cinema vérité shots of Churchill brooding against the rubble of Coventry Cathedral. There are the German newsreels of Russian girl partisans hanged side by side on a portable gallows, Jews milling helplessly in the few streets left them in the Warsaw ghetto.

● ● ●

Who can forget the famous Russian shot of Red Army men rushing to each other across the snow at Stalingrad to celebrate their encirclement of the German Army? This famous scene was actually staged for the cameraman who had not been present the first time. But what of it? I am a World War II buff, (bitter joke), and the pseudo-real thing can still make me shake and rejoice as I did in 1943 when I first saw the Stalingrad scene in Anatole Litvak's propaganda film for the Army, "The Battle of Russia."

Now we have a new generation, very different times. Lately, it seems to me, this unending movie called World War II has become too glib and easy a subject for young European filmmakers bored with actualities like the Middle East, the Common Market, inflation, the current lack of De Gaulles and Churchills (and Hitlers). France, for example, is not yet in a full-fledged depression, but it is certainly depressed. Italy is in such a state that people laugh when they read that tons of undelivered mail were recently *sold* as waste paper. The Germans, as Maximilian Schell tried to say in "The Pedestrian," seem to have an uneasy conscience in prosperity— and there are powerful people all over the world, many of them now filmmakers, who can never forget what it was like to be a child under the Nazi occupation.

•   •   •

Where in this stalemate, this endless paralysis and frustration of war-time hopes, are the revolutions promised by the glorious liberation in 1945 from Hitler, Mussolini, Laval, Franco? Whatever happened *after* "anti-fascism"? Did the Dietrich Bonhoeffers die on a Nazi gallows for the *Wirtschaftswunder?* Where is an end, in our hearts and lives, to the bitterness of the "final solution," the heaped up bodies at Coventry, Dresden, Leningrad, Hiroshima?

The answer, I guess, is that peace can be "boring," that depressions are a lot more frightening than bombs. D. H. Lawrence said that World War I was "sensational delight posing as pious idealism." No one who sees what a permanent lift was given to sado-masochism by Nazism can wonder that the favorite pornography, the mother of all pornography, is cruelty in a wartime setting. The favorite time for melodrama about killing on a *big* scale, lots of naked bodies, is always 1939-1945; the favorite setting is Belsen, Auschwitz, and other such places in your favorite horror comics. The worst horror comic is a current movie called "The Night Porter," which proves that a Jewish girl can love her S.S. tormentor even if he did rape her. Hitler has had his revenge. Credit for bringing this film to America belongs to Joseph E. Levine.

The truth about craven, violence-fascinated humanity is that World War II is the most endlessly "dramatic" as well as, or because it is, the most hideous of all modern subjects. We who lived through it can never get over it, but boast that "we had the last good war." The young, who have had to grow up everywhere on the leavings of this war's cruelty, occasionally envy its old-fashioned assault on pure evil.

Movies and war go together. Has World War II become *nothing* but a movie? Movies created so lopsidedly powerful a visual presence, moving in just one direction alone, that it makes me despair to think how few World War II films are anything but trifles. In the last few weeks I have seen almost a dozen recent European films that in one way or another depend for subject matter on The Age of Fascism (1922-1945). One of these is exceptionally honest—Michel Mitrani's "Black Thursday" (Les Guichets du Louvre), a film about that unspeakable day in Paris, July 16, 1942, when the Jews were rounded up by *French* police and *French* Fascist *milice* to the indifference of the general population.

One is subtly ambitious—Louis Malle's "Lacombe, Lucien"—which I take as the attempt of a very intelligent but not altogether well-informed Frenchman (Malle was 13 when the war ended) to explain away the undeniable collaboration of so many Frenchmen with the Nazi terror in the person of a young farm boy who, turned down by the resistance, becomes a Gestapo agent.

My overwhelming impression about most of the "new" directors who now describe Nazism and Fascism is that their films are about Europe today. They seem to arise from a political and intellectual vacuum, a disgust with Europe's inability to move from the class inequalities and injustices that have so maddeningly been perpetuated along with the traumas and guilts of the Hitler age.

•   •   •

The "respectables" in France said, "Better Hitler than Leon Blum," in Germany pretended not to know who was burning in the ovens of Treblinka, in Italy abetted Mussolini's most ridiculous schemes for conquest until he proved that he could not take over Greece on time, much less make his phony "revolution." But these people are still running French business, German cities

and German universities, while in Italy it no longer matters *what* you did under Fascism, the current system being such a joke.

Lena Wertmuller, the exciting Italian woman director who made "Love and Anarchy" (and "The Seduction of Mimi"), was 17 when Mussolini was hung by the heels in Milan. She is still an "anti-Fascist" in "Love and Anarchy," an Italian radical altogether frustrated by "the system" (post war) she mordantly portrayed in "The Seduction of Mimi." She shows that there was no "anti-Fascist resistance," just a few lonely martyrs who were easily picked off by the all-enveloping Fascist network *before* the war. The Italian bourgeoisie accommodated itself very comfortably to Fascism. As Camus said about the French, their main delights were fornication and the daily press. Wertmuller's poor isolated anarchist would-be hero, all shy and pockmarked and probably a virgin, must take refuge in a *brothel* while he plans his lunatic assault on Mussolini. (Of course, it never comes off, and he is murdered in his cell by the Fascists. This is the *one* scene out of all these recent films that conveys to the children of the postwar world what the daily horror was like for opponents of Mussolini and Hitler.)

•   •   •

Louis Malle, in my estimation a totally superior cinema mind, nevertheless seems to me in "Lacombe, Lucien" caught in a not altogether deliberate apologia for the French who "fell" into collaboration with Hitler. I admire Malle's directorial gifts and I love his quietly strategic kind of mind—he really thinks like a chess player of genius: he surrounds you with moves you have not yet thought of, but should. The question: why did so many Frenchmen participate in the crime against their own people, in the crime of the century? The answer: life is a matter of inertia, and evil is banal.

What troubles me about "Lacombe, Lucien" is that so many people are convinced that it all happened in just that way. The brutish peasant boy who liked shooting down birds, who was bored with washing floors in an old age home, who asked to join the Resistance but was turned down, becomes a French Gestapo man and is somehow an epitome of the essential ethical neutrality of the French during the war.

Movies are really insidious, they please us so easily. They are one of the great drugs of our time, as irresistible as sex and liquor. I am an addict, but at times I do cry out against my chains. I sit in a darkened theater, looking at "Lacombe, Lucien" among people who cannot help being seduced by Malle's intelligence into thinking his film "truth." "Lacombe, Lucien" is subtle, resourceful, above all clever in the clinches. We see every side at once—the peasant boy's stolidity dominates the film, assaults us with its "irrefutable" but unchangeable human stupidity. But the underlying premise is false. People do live and move and torture one another from *conviction.* Alas, people mean what they do.

There were plenty of *cynical* collaborators in France during World War II, but they had a philosophy of cynicism, sometimes called French common sense. It was this "common sense" that outraged Camus as editor of Combat during the war, when he described a charwoman who would not cut a prisoner's bonds even when the Gestapo had left him for the night. "I'm not paid for that!" said the charwoman. Balzac, Maupassant, Flaubert classically dealt with this bourgeois malady—found in all classes. But films, though they can terrify and move me beyond words when I see Jews being rounded up among Parisians placidly going off to lunch (as in Michel Mitrani's "Black Thursday"), simply cannot deal with the moral complexity, the moral actuality, of a world dominated by totalitarian terror. (There haven't been any good Soviet films for years.) The fact is that the people who survive when their neighbors are dragged off just don't believe in loving their neighbors. They don't even believe in having neighbors.

"Black Thursday" is not so brilliant and subtle a film as "Lacombe, Lucien." But the "looking machine," as Godard called it, does get to our nerves as it shows the *flics* stealing up on Jews in every alley.

•   •   •

Michel Mitrani's "round-up" of the Jews in "Black Thursday" is better on the indifferent cynicism of these

French police than on the amazement and despair of the Jewish victims obediently walking into the Paris busses that will take most of them to death. The main point the film makes is that the Germans were not needed on that Thursday.

"Black Thursday" turns, very touchingly, on the attempt of a non-Jewish student to warn Jews in time. He fails to arouse them to their danger. We see him vainly trying to reverse their pitiful obedience to authority, their illusions that only "work" in Germany is required of them. A young Jewish girl, who for most of this dreadful Thursday, does go along with the student, finally leaves him, just as she is about to get past the gates of the Louvre to the Left Bank and to freedom. Her mother and sister were arrested and she turns back to join them.

Mitrani makes the most honest and the most compassionate judgment on Jewish "obedience" to the Nazis. In the end, it was the decision not to abandon one's family that ultimately destroyed so many Jews who might have escaped. But equally important is the fact that most Jews could not *believe* in the full horror hanging over them. They believed the Nazi promises of "work" as a guarantee of freedom. They still believed in legality, in civilization, and this is why they perished. How convey this to a more cynical postwar generation that has lived through Vietnam and worse? But the Jewish faith in the "world," an illusion fundamental to our understanding of the helpless participation of the Jews in their own Holocaust, cannot be conveyed in Mitrani's film, brave in detail and urgent as it is.

Another new film about Jews under the Nazi yoke in France, "Les Violons du Bal," seems to me just an autobiographical self-indulgence on the part of the director, Michel Drach. This is a soft, pretty picture of a Jewish mother and her gorgeous little Jewish son that in the end robs the film of all its implicit terror. The end is ridiculous. Mother and son manage to slip under the barbed wire into Switzerland, and a benevolent Swiss guard looks down on them and croons, "Now you are free." A lot could be said about the falseness of this scene, for the Swiss were as gentle to "illegal emigrants" as one of their bank tellers would be to a pauper. But let us not get into that intractable monster, real History. Back to the movies. Back to the "looking machine."

1975 Ja 12, II:1:3

'Les Violons du Bal', at top, presents 'a soft, pretty picture of a Jewish mother and her gorgeous little son' escaping the Nazis. But history, says the author, was not so kind. Above, the reality of Jews being rounded up in the Warsaw ghetto during World War II.

BROKEN TREATY AT BATTLE MOUNTAIN, directed by Joel L. Freedman; narration written by Tom Schachtman; photography, Chuck Levey; editing, Walter Katz, Stephen Gyllenhaal and Sarah Stein; produced by Mr. Freedman and Mr. Gyllenhaal; distributed by Soho Cinema, Ltd. At the Whitney Museum of American Art, Madison Avenue and 75th Street. Running time: 60 minutes.

"Broken Treaty at Battle Mountain," the documentary being shown through Tuesday in the New American Filmmakers Series at the Whitney Museum of American Art, generates a narrative excitement that is not often found in nonfiction films given to exploration of issues.

This is the story of a small group of Western Shoshone Indians who live in Nevada's Battle Mountain Indian Colony. Unlike most of their neighboring fellow Indians, they are traditionalists, people who want to retain their culture and their lands. The land in question consists of 24 million acres, about one third of Nevada, and they contend that the treaty they concluded with the United States in 1863 did not make any concessions to the nation that had come upon them.

They have refused compensation and are threatened by Government policy, which permits thousands of trees on the land to be torn down,

trees that the tribe's religion regards as sacred and that also provide food.

Joel L. Freedman, producer and director of this 70-minute color film, spent two years making it. He has told it as a story of a small, menaced people, depicting their way of life, their problems, their humor, their aspirations, much of it in their own words, although Robert Redford narrates the script by Tom Schachtman.

Chuck Levey's photography dramatically focuses on faces and foliage, following the Indians from the quiet of their colony to a dramatic climax in the Indians' confrontation with the Indian Claims Commission and depicting the relentless uprooting of the trees by a huge chain pulled between two tractors.

"Broken Treaty at Battle Mountain" has much to say to anyone who is concerned with big against small, with preservation against "progress" and it says it well. The story does not end with the film. These Western Shoshones are still in litigation and seeking public support; the film should go a long way toward finding it. After the Whitney run, it goes to Quad Cinema next Wednesday.

RICHARD F. SHEPARD

1975 Ja 16, 49:1

MACON COUNTY LINE, directed by Richard Compton; screenplay by Max Baer and Mr. Compton, based on a story by Mr. Baer; produced by Mr. Baer; executive producer, Roger Camras; editor, Tina Hirsch; director of photography, Daniel Lacambre; music, Stu Phillips; distributed by American International Pictures. Running time: 89 minutes. At neighborhood theaters. This film has been rated R.

Chris Dixon	Alan Vint
Wayne Dixon	Jesse Vint
Deputy Reed Morgan	Max Baer
Jenny	Cheryl Waters
Hamp	Geoffrey Lewis
Carol Morgan	Joan Blackman
Deputy Bill	Sam Gilman
Lon	Timothy Scott
Elisha	James Gammon
Luke	Leif Garrett
Gurney	Emile Meyer
Augie	Doodles Weaver

By VINCENT CANBY

When a movie like "Macon County Line" comes into town nine months after it has opened elsewhere in the country, having already earned more than $8-million, the primary impulse is to ask why. What does it mean?

"Macon County Line," which arrived at neighborhood theaters yesterday, apparently means that rural melodrama—the kind that

realizes our worst nightmares—is still sure-fire box office if it is vivid and violent enough and if it's pitched at a mentality that finds road-sign reading an intellectual labor.

Like Phil Karlson's "Walking Tall," another national phenomenon, "Macon County Line" is set in the back-country American South, a region that is becoming as essential to a certain kind of pop

American melodrama as Transylvania is to the vampire movie.

•

In these melodramas, the rural South is a place of unrelieved bigotry, cruelty and violence. Travelers from other parts of the country either are crooks who teach the natives new ways to misbehave or they are innocents, like those in "Easy Rider," who wander too close to the edge of the civilized world and fall off it. It was one of the few credits to "Billy Jack," set in the Southwest, that it showed the South to have no corner on evil.

Also like "Walking Tall," based on the life of Buford Pusser, the late Tennessee sheriff, "Macon County Line" is said to be a fictionalized account of something that actually happened. There, however, the similarity ends. Mr. Karlson is a talented, canny director who knows his medium. Richard Compton, who directed "Macon County Line," has studied the medium but he doesn't seem to trust it. After the first 30 minutes, there isn't a scene or a revelation that the director (and co-author) hasn't so laboriously set up that a bright 10-year-old couldn't predict all the subsequent events.

That, of course, could be one reason why the movie has proved so popular. It affirms our belief in our own witless superiority.

The screenplay was written by Mr. Compton and Max Baer (late of "The Beverly Hillbillies"), who also produced the film and very creditably acts a leading role. As Deputy Reed Morgan, Mr. Baer plays a beefy, bigoted sheriff whose Confederate sympathies (he wears a small rebel flag on his sleeve) are somehow made to seem responsible for the griefstricken rampage that highlights the film.

The story, placed in the mid-nineteen-fifties, concerns two young men from Chicago, brothers about to be inducted in the Army who, in the course of a final spree across the country, are mistaken for a pair of murderous psychotics. That's all there is: vagrant viciousness and coincidence. It's about nothing more than casual error.

Yet the film is not without its moments of primitive fascination, which result, I suspect, from the spectacle of watching innocent people hopelessly if arbitrarily trapped.

•

"Macon County Line" also benefits from its performances by the professionals who play the leads, including Mr. Baer, and by the nonpros who play the supporting roles, random country folk, characters like waitresses and filling-station attendants whose awkwardnesses carry peculiar conviction.

Alan Vint and Jesse Vint, brothers in real life, display an easy, intelligent self-as-surance as the ill-fated tourists from Chicago, and Cheryl Waters is surprisingly affecting as the good-hearted bar girl who has the misfortune to be picked up by the brothers. The written roles seem merely outlines for characters, but these three young performers gives them individual and identifiable substance.

1975 Ja 16, 49:1

Gidal's 2 Silent Films Explore Light, Shapes

TWO FILMS BY PETER GIDAL: FILM PRINT, running time, 40 minutes; ROOM FILM 1973, running time, 52 minutes. At the Film Forum, 256 West 88th Street. Through Sunday and Jan. 23-26, 8 P.M.

Two silent films characterized by intellectual and visual repetitiveness form the program that opened yesterday at the Film Forum.

"Film Print" and "Room Film 1973" are works by Peter Gidal, an avant-garde American film maker. The former, an exploration of perception, consists of motion pictures of still photographs. The camera moves in to examine the contents of rooms, nosing jerkily into light, texture and objects, producing flattened images twice removed from reality before it pulls back to reveal that it is taking pictures of a picture. Once is a surprise; twice is amusing; but 40 minutes' worth becomes a descent into abysmal tedium.

Mainly by comparison, "Room Film 1973," which is in color, is an improvement. It is a murky, granular journey around a room broken by occasional incursions of light. At its infrequent best, it suggests a voyage through a vast, dark universe where objects loom as features of uncharted planets.

LAWRENCE VAN GELDER

1975 Ja 17, 17:1

Nicholas Ray Subject of 'Stranger Myself'

I'M A STRANGER HERE MYSELF, directed by David Helpern Jr.; produced by James C. Gutman; written by Myron Meisel, Mr. Gutman and Mr. Helpern; narrated by Howard da Silva; director of photography, Austin de Besche; editors, Richard Bock and Frank Galvin; distributed by October Films (Cambridge, Mass.). Running time: 61 minutes. At the First Avenue Screening Room, near 61st Street. This film has not been rated.
WITH: Nicholas Ray, John Houseman, Francois Truffaut, Natalie Wood and others.

By VINCENT CANBY

Jean-Luc Godard called him the camera. An admiring student describes him as a con artist. He himself says that when he read the laudatory analyses of his work by French film critics he didn't know who they were talking about. He is Nicholas Ray, the fine, often troubled film director who is the subject of the feature-length documentary "I'm a Stranger Here Myself," which will be shown at the First Avenue Screening Room at noon and midnight today and tomorrow.

The film is a fascinating footnote to contemporary motion picture history. It's too affectionate to be critically definitive, but it captures a lot of the contradictions in the life and career of this man who manages to seem most elegant and ascetic when he most needs a shave and a fresh cigarette, who is simultaneously old and young, totally sincere and just occasionally full of bananas.

•

Mr. Ray may well be his own most complex, riveting hero. He's a romantic with a fiercely realistic view of things.

After a solid apprenticeship in the New York theater, Mr. Ray moved to Hollywood in the nineteen-forties, managing to make several classics ("In a Lonely Place," "Rebel Without a Cause" and "Johnny Guitar") while playing the role of one of the town's most dependable contract directors. He then more or less disappeared in the sixties, his fortunes declining and falling with a couple of big-budget made-in-Spain blockbusters ("King of Kings," "55 Days at Peking").

"I'm a Stranger Here Myself," which he describes as the working title of every project he's ever worked on, examines Mr. Ray and his career from the vantage point of the two-year hitch (1972-1973) he put in teaching at Harpur College at the State University of New York at Binghamton. Intercut with sequences showing Mr. Ray directing his students in the production of an ambitious experimental feature are interviews with John Houseman (identified by the director as one of the two most important influences on his career, the other being Elia Kazan), Natalie Wood (who co-starred in "Rebel Without a Cause") and François Truffaut, who eloquently describes his admiration for "Johnny Guitar."

The film also makes use of clips from various Ray films "Johnny Guitar," "Rebel Without a Cause," "In a Lonely Place," "They Live by Night") to back up these points, and though the clips are fairly extensive, they have a way of undercutting the things said. Snippets from movies, even good ones, are seldom substantial enough to carry the weight of this sort of analysis.

•

Most fascinating and moving are the Binghamton sequences: the director badgering his leading lady for being late to a wintry midnight location (she has a round, pretty unfinished face and an unfinished star's temper), theorizing about acting, recalling some of the great names he has worked with, pausing in a frozen half-crouch as he studies the set-up for a shot, pretending with all his heart to be making the next great Ray film. That's not meant to be pejorative. Pretense, illusion and monumental self-assurance are part of the drive of genius.

Howard da Silva provides the mostly straightforward narration for the film, which was made by two talented young men named David Helpern Jr. (director) and James C. Gutman (producer). Auston de Besche was director of photography. They are up to the demands of their subject who, at 63 years old, is still one of the most irascible, original men making movies.

1975 Ja 17, 20:1

'Paperback Hero,' Tale of Living a Fantasy

PAPERBACK HERO, directed by Peter Pearson; screenplay by Les Rose and Mr. Pearson; photography, Don Wilder; editor, Kirk Jones; music by Ron Collier and Gordon Lightfoot; produced by James Margellos and John F. Bassett; released by Rumson Film Distributors, Inc. At the Festival Theater, 57th Street at Fifth Avenue. Running time: 87 minutes. This film is classified R.
Rick .... Keir Dullea
Loretta .... Elizabeth Ashley
Pov .... John Beck
Joanna .... Dayle Haddon
Big Ed .... Franz Russell
Burdock .... George R. Robertson
Julie .... Margot Lamarre

By RICHARD F. SHEPARD

"Paperback Hero," the new film at the Festival Theater, is about a swashbuckling young Walter Mitty who is actually living out his fantasy and making a botch of it. It is a pictorially vivid, often engrossing motion picture that sets you ruminating on what it is really all about after you've seen it rather than while you are looking on.

In a small town in Saskatchewan, the kind of place where the local beer hall functions as the sole cultural center, Rick Dillon, handsome, strong fellow, hard drinker, brawler, woman chaser and star of the local hockey team, has also decided to play the role of a marshal of the Old West. He wears the 10-gallon hat, totes a gun, sports a star and is the very image of television's Marshal Dillon.

At first the town laughs with him, then it laughs at him, although respect is what Rick really craves. After all, what are his options? The hockey team, the only arena in which he stands out—he works as a clerk in a store for a living—is being closed down. He has an offer to go elsewhere to work as a building janitor, although he would like to work in "management."

But life here has to be a dull dead end, and Rick becomes more the marshal, bringing the story to a sad, ludicrous, flamboyant finale. Real life just does not let one live in dreams without going through normal channels.

Keir Dullea makes a fine, heroic nonhero. He is the very essence of the swaggering, not overbright clod who goes through all the motions of a wild one but who is really small potatoes. He has charm and humor, but it is all canned in the way of a cardboard hero of film — or paperback novel.

Elizabeth Ashley, who is currently starring with Mr. Dullea on Broadway in "Cat on a Hot Tin Roof," has a difficult assignment, as Rick's sexy but serious, honest and loving girlfriend, and she brings to it a passion and understanding that nicely offset the stridence that envelops the story.

Under Peter Pearson's direction, the town, Delisle (population 700) and its environs also achieve star status. The cameras pan over the flat dullness of it all, emphasizing the flat-country vastness and isolation of the place, a fit setting in which one man's lonely trauma becomes the community's spectacle. The eruptions of the marshal and the glamour of hockey, erupting in a riot, make all kinds of sense on this stage. "Paperback Hero" is a simple but intriguing movie that says much if you are willing to listen.

1975 Ja 20, 23:3

'Men's Lives' Looks at Male Mystique

By RICHARD F. SHEPARD

"Men's Lives," the documentary that opened yesterday at the Bleecker Street Cinema's Filmmakers Showcase, explores the masculine mystique in a competitive society.

The film was made in their native Midwest by Will Roberts and Josh Hanig, who worked two years on this first venture, starting when they were students in Antioch. It is an interesting, even entertaining look at how males grow into men, mostly aggressive-minded men, and what values rub off on them as they do so.

•

The thesis is formed by interviews with men, boys, some women, too. And the ones who are doing the speaking are not psychologists or professional social observers. They are factory workers, teachers, coaches, athletes, students, and each presents his perspective articulately.

A town barber, with the sensitivity of a good analyst, describes what his customers tell him and makes sage comment. Girls describe how they feel in relationship to the role of men. The result of all this is to give you a new view of yourself and your world.

Because so much of masculine behavior seems to hinge

so much on competition, there is some confusion, perhaps, about which, if either, led to which. It would be worthwhile to follow up "Men's Lives" with a look at masculinity in noncompetitive societies, wherever they are.

●

Also on the bill is "Janie's Janie," about a welfare mother in New Jersey, white and separated from her husband. In her own words, this working-class woman tells how, after being dominated by father and husband, she was able to develop her own personality. It's an absorbing account, filmed by Geri Ashur and Peter Barton.

1975 Ja 22, 24:5

4 Experimental Works by Sidney Peterson

Four experimental works by Sidney Peterson, made in San Francisco between 1946, when he began film making, and 1949, when he retired, constitute the Whitney Museum of American Art's current film program, titled "The Lead Shoes." The program, which opened yesterday, will run through Tuesday.

The films owe a great deal to the surreal collaborations of Luis Buñuel and Salvador Dali, especially the first film on the program, "The Potted Palm," which marked the joint debut of Mr. Peterson and James Broughton as serious avant-garde film makers. Adolescent sexuality, the fear of death and terrible guilt are the themes of what turns out to be a mostly humorous piece, full of comic juxtapositions of rather banal images.

"Clinic of Stumble," made by Mr. Peterson in 1947, is a lovely, comically solemn dance film composed of superimposed images. "Mr. Frenhofer and the Minotaur" (1948) and "The Lead Shoes" (1949) are examples of surreal film making that depend increasingly on literary associations and the use of language on the soundtrack, often nonsensical.

The program's total running time is 83 minutes.

VINCENT CANBY.

1975 Ja 23, 27:3

THE ALGERIAN WAR, a French documentary with English commentary, by Yves Courriere and Philippe Monnier; music by Francois de Roubaix; written by Mr. Courriere; distributed by European Film Exchange. At the First Avenue Screening Room, at 61st Street, today and tomorrow at noon and midnight. Running time: 155 minutes. This film has not been classified.

By RICHARD F. SHEPARD

France's long war in Algeria, a struggle that nearly brought down the Republic, seems so ancient that it comes as a shock to realize that it only took place from 1954 to 1961: The world has moved too quickly since then.

"The Algerian War," a 1973 French documentary of what seems to be mostly old news film with special commentary and music, recalls the conflict at length—two hours and 35 minutes, to be exact —in its current showing at the First Avenue Screening Room. It does not have the dramatic impact of "Battle of Algiers," but, even in just recounting the bloody history, it fills one with horror, as history always does, when one sees the missed opportunities and the suppression of the sensible to the passions of the purists, on both sides.

"The Algerian War" traces the inexorable violent path of struggle, showing the extremists, the moderates, the mass of people who were drawn into battles they might rather have remained out of.

Made by Yves Courriere and Philippe Monnier, with a commentary in English, the film is a balanced account of brutality, heightened by a blaring background of patriotic songs and frenzied chanting. It is one of a number of films being shown in a series of documentaries at the theater.

1975 Ja 24, 19:1

French Import Lacks Drive of British

By VINCENT CANBY

"Love at the Top," which opened yesterday at the 68th Street Playhouse, is a 1973 French comedy that dimly recalls a number of nineteen-fifties English comedies about the rise and rise of cynical young men possessing—and possessed by—ambition. There is one major difference: The English comedies, films like "Room at the Top" and "Nothing but the Best," were essentially concerned with the English class system and how to beat it.

●

"Love at the Top" has no such nourishing drive. It's about nothing more than what it seems. It's the story of a timid bank clerk (Jean-Louis Trintignant) who, under the direction of a second-rate novelist (Jean-Pierre Cassel), who conceives brilliant real-life plots, becomes one of the richest, most powerful men in Paris through a complicated series of liaisons with beautiful women and their protectors.

Michel Deville ("Benjamin," "The Bear and the Doll") is one of those directors whose work is never more than competently stylish, and most of that stylishness is the kind that can be bought as easily as furniture, by hiring the right actors, cameramen, set designers and so on.

The Cast

LOVE AT THE TOP (Le Mouton Enrage), directed by Michel Deville; screenplay (French with English subtitles) by Christopher Frank; produced by Leo L. Fuchs; director of cinematography, Claude Lecomte; music, Saint-Saens; a French-Italian co-production of Viaduc Productions (Paris) and Trac (Rome), distributed by Peppercorn-Wormser, Inc. Running time: 105 minutes. At the 68th Street Playhouse, Third Avenue at 68th Street. This film has been rated R.
Nicholas .... Jean-Louis Trintignant
Roberte .... Romy Schneider
Fabre .... Jean-Pierre Cassel
Marie-Paula .... Jane Birkin
Flora .... Florinda Bolkan
Lourceuil .... Georges Wilson
Berthoud .... Henri Garcin

In addition to Mr. Trintignant and Mr. Cassel, the cast includes Romy Schneider, as a badly used housewife, and Jane Birkin, as a sunny-natured streetwalker. They have true style, but it can't upgrade the movie much.

There is even something second-rate about the title that the film's distributors have chosen for the American release. The original French title, which was also that of the Roger Blondel novel on which it's based, is "Le Mouton Enragé" (The Mad Sheep). That's hardly a zinger in translation but it's better than the warmed-over associations of "Love at the Top."

1975 Ja 27, 18:1

GALILEO, directed by Joseph Losey; screenplay by Barbara Bray and Mr. Losey, from Charles Laughton's English version of the German play by Bertolt Brecht; produced by Ely Landau; executive producer, Otto Plaschkes; original music by Hans Eisler; additional music, Richard Hartley; director of photography, Michael Reed; editor, Reginald Beck; an American Film Theater production presented by the Ely Landau Organization and Cinevision, Ltd. Running time: 145 minutes. At selected theaters. This film has been rated PG.
Galileo Galilei .... Topol
Cardinal Inquisitor .... Edward Fox
Priuli .... Colin Blakely
Ballad Singer's Wife .... Georgia Brown
Ballad Singer .... Clive Revill
Court Lady .... Margaret Leighton
Old Cardinal .... John Gielgud
Sagredo .... Michael Gough
Cardinal Barberini/Pope .... Michael Lonsdale
Fulganzio .... Richard O'Callaghan
Ludovico .... Tim Woodward
Angelica Sarti .... Judy Parfitt
Federzoni .... John McEnery
Cardinal Bellarmin .... Patrick Magee
Virginia .... Mary Larkin
Andrea (boy) .... Iain Travers
Andrea (man) .... Tom Conti

By VINCENT CANBY

Last year the American Film Theater seemed hellbent on bringing us culture even at the risk of boring us to death, which it almost did with the exceptions of "The Homecoming," Alan Bates's performance in "Butley" and its pick-up of the National Theater Company's production of "Three Sisters." Things look a lot better this year on the basis of the initial presentation of the film theater's second season here.

The opening attraction is one of Bertolt Brecht's most fascinating, most abrasive, most accessible plays, "Galileo," directed by Joseph Losey, a man who knows more about film and more about Brecht than possibly any other film director at work today. "Galileo," which was shown at selected theaters yesterday, will be repeated today at matinees and evening performances.

●

It's apparent from the opening credits of the film—a view of the movie set as seen from the rafters of the soundstage—that Mr. Losey knows exactly what kind of "filmed theater" he wants to achieve, and how to achieve it. There's no nonsense about "opening up" the Brecht play to make it look like a movie. The sets—stylized, glossy, new, with perspectives foreshortened—

are always sets, not some bleary-eyed set-decorator's attempts to recreate realistically the look of 17th-century Italy. Nor—because the camera has become a character—is there the claustrophobic feeling of a theater piece that has been merely recorded.

One never for a moment forgets that this "Galileo" is a stage piece, yet the awareness has the effect of enhancing our perceptions of what is being said and done. Everything takes place in a world where the sun is subject to man's laws, where the wind has been turned off and where every sound that is heard is important. Nothing is by chance. The laws that govern this world are as much anathema to the realist cinema as Galileo's were to the Roman Catholic Church.

Mr. Losey has experimented with this style before, in "King and Country" in 1967, but it is more fully and beautifully realized in "Galileo," whose first American theatrical productions he staged in California and New York in 1947.

There is one problem with the film, and it is a major one; the casting of Topol in the title role as the contradictory physicist who first challenged the church through his discoveries, recanted when faced with torture by the Inquisition, then lived out his days engaged in surreptitious research that finally became his most monumental work.

In spite of Brecht's impatience with the theater of emotion, and with identification by the audience with a character in ways that

From left: Michael Lonsdale, Vernon Dobtcheff, Patrick Magee and Topol

confuse dialectics, his Galileo is a marvelously complicated, fallible, identifiable character, so much so that to attempt to play him in a fashion that might be described as winning is to put frosting atop frosting.

Topol remains the kind of actor I thought he was in "Fiddler on the Roof"—all resonant voice, calculated gestures, surface mannerisms, most of which seem designed to convince the audience that he's a lovable fellow who, at worst, has moments of being crotchety. What's worse is that although he's a big man he imparts no sense of intellectual heft.

•

In a key scene in which Galileo debates his discoveries with the cardinals in Rome, one hears only words. They roll out of his mouth like one long strand of spaghetti. It's as if he didn't want to alienate those of us in the theater by appearing to know more than we do.

Thus much of the toughness and wit of the Brecht script are lost when Topol is on screen. Just how good the production might have been with another actor is seen in two magnificent scenes in which Topol doesn't appear. The first is that hugely theatrical scene in which the Pope (Michael Lonsdale) is being robed for an audience and trying not to give in to the Inquisitor's arguments to do something about Galileo. The other—Mr. Losey's boldest cinematic conception—is set on what could be a theater stage, when Galileo's followers nervously await word whether the master has recanted.

With the exception of Topol, the cast is superb, full of actors who really do appear to be able to think. It includes John Gielgud and Margaret Leighton in what are virtually walk-ons and, in the larger roles, Mr. Lonsdale, Edward Fox (the Inquisitor), and John McEnery and Tom Conti as two of Galileo's most loyal associates.

Topol is not easily acceptable but the rest of the production has exceptional style and intelligence, the sort of things one should be able to expect from the American Film Theater.

1975 Ja 28, 26:1

Jason Miller Has Lead in Real-Estate Drama

By NORA SAYRE

Those who choose to see Robert Mulligan's "The Nickel Ride" must be prepared to work very hard and then be defeated in trying to follow the plot, since this action picture resists an earthling's comprehension. In fact, it's the most confusing movie I've seen since several reels got mixed up during a Greek film of radiant obscurity. At any rate, this heap of murk opened yesterday at several neighborhood theaters.

The movie appears to be a drama of real estate. Jason Miller plays a neighborhood fixer who is attempting to lease a warehouse for the storage of stolen goods; however, the deal is delayed, and he's threatened by the minor hoods who are his clients. His role is a study in worry: the angst rarely leaves his deep-set lemur's eyes. We watch him worrying in profile, in full and three-quarter face, standing or sitting or lying down, in daylight and darkness, on the phone, in his office and out of doors. All in all, he seems more vulnerable to an anxiety attack than to an assailant's bullet.

The Cast

THE NICKEL RIDE, directed and produced by Robert Mulligan; written by Eric Roth; director of photography, Jordan Cronenweth; film editor, O. Nicholas Brown; music, Dave Grusin; released by 20th Century-Fox Film Corporation. At the Cine Malibu, 59th Street between Second and Third Avenues; Cinema Village, 12th Street, east of Fifth Avenue; East 86th Street, between Second and Third Avenues and Roosevelt, 145th Street and Seventh Avenue.

Cooper	Jason Miller
Sarah	Linda Haynes
Paddie	Victor French
Carl	John Hillerman
Turner	Bo Hopkins

•

Although much of the narrative is unfathomable, the audience knows almost everything that's going to happen, since we're warned by a series of triumphant movie clichés—including one of the silliest prophetic dreams that's been filmed of late. Throughout, there are little lulls that promise immediate violence. And when someone buys a rabbit's foot it means that he'll have bad luck; when a character resolves to go straight and leave "the business" it's obvious that he'll be shot; when a couple plan a vacation we know that they won't take it. The movie also employs the maddeningly ancient device of a live man talking to a dead one—without realizing that he's wasting his wisdom on a corpse.

•

"The Nickel Ride" is handsomely filmed in bleak pastels, but the numerous close-ups manage to stress the slowness of the action, and quick cuts can't dispel the tedium. Bo Hopkins has some good moments as a chatty sadist with a face full of ominous grins; nodding his head in malicious innocence, he's given to bursts of inane chuckles. Linda Haynes is desperately bland as Mr. Miller's girlfriend, although her lines don't help: she has to say (of the woods) "So crisp and green!" and "I'm a big girl!" when her lover conceals his worries from her, and "Oh, business, business, business!" when he doesn't.

What with the references to characters we haven't met and to events we never see and to the good old days that will never come again, one wonders if the director actually wanted to make a different picture. If only he had.

1975 Ja 30, 26:4

THE STREET FIGHTER, screenplay by Koji Takada and Steve Austin; photography by Kenji Tsukakoshi; martial arts direction, Masafumi Suzuki; produced by Toei Company, Ltd.; released by New Line Cinema. At the 59th Street Twin 2, east of Third Avenue; the Cinerama Theater, Broadway at 47th Street, and the 86th Street Twin 2, west of Lexington Avenue. Running time: 92 minutes. This film is classified X.

Terry Tsuguri	Sonny Chiba
Ratface	Gerald Yamada
Sarai	Doris Nakajima
Shad	Tony Cetera

Like the late Bruce Lee in the slew of bloody capers he dominated, Sonny Chiba, a Japanese newcomer to the karate school of Oriental cinema, now is proving he too can handle all the bad guys and gals from Hong Kong to Tokyo—in "The Street Fighter," which landed, gushing gallons of synthetic gore, in local houses yesterday. If nothing else, this Japanese-made, English-dubbed import illustrates that its inane violence deserves the Xrating with which it has been labeled.

Mr. Chiba, a stocky, muscular type, who has mastered a combination of Chinese boxing and the grunts, groans, grim stares and balletic hands-and-feet mayhem of karate, is immersed in a plot as complex as chop suey. Basically he's battling Yakuza gangsters who have joined with the Mafia to kidnap a gorgeous oil heiress—and, incidentally, he has also incurred the enmity of another karate champ, whose brother he has killed and whose sister he has ruined.

Obviously the story is not the thing here. And Mr. Chiba is not so much a hero as a rough citizen who appears to savor the bloodletting and the killing karate chops. He even rips the genitals from a would-be rapist and the throat from another adversary to indicate his love of this bloody contact sport.

"I think we're in trouble," observes Gerald Yamada, his clownish sidekick, at one point in the murderous goings-on. It's an understatement for everyone concerned, including viewers.

A. H. WEILER

1975 Ja 30, 26:4

MR. RICCO, directed by Paul Bogart; screenplay by Robert Hoban, based on a story by Ed Harvey and Francis Kiernan; produced by Douglas Netter; music, Chico Hamilton; director of photography, Frank Stanley; editor, Michael McLean; an M-G-M production, distributed by United Artists. Running time: 108 minutes. At Forum Theater, Broadway at 47th Street, and other theaters. This film has been rated PG.

Joe Ricco	Dean Martin
George Cronyn	Eugene Roche
Frankie Steele	Thalmus Rasulala
Irene Mapes	Denise Nicholas
Jamison	Cindy Williams
Katherine Fremont	Geraldine Brooks
Purvis Mapes	Philip Thomas

In "Mr. Ricco," a very bad urban melodrama directed by Paul Bogart, Dean Martin plays a brilliant San Francisco criminal lawyer much as if brilliant San Francisco criminal lawyers modeled their behavior on successful television personalities such as Mr. Martin.

Everything about the character Mr. Martin plays, a man named Ricco, looks like displaced Southern California: the tan, the hair-set and even the boredom, which suggests the fellow wants to get back to that old gang of his in the Polo Lounge as quickly as possible. When the TV personality isn't being directly evoked, the movie relies on reversals that are inside jokes for about 60 million people. Mr. Rico drinks nothing but milk (he has an ulcer) and is such a terrible golfer he uses his dog to cheat for him.

The story is about the search for someone who we are meant to believe is a black militant leader turned cop-killer. It doesn't hold much water. It's such a clumsy movie it makes all the actors look dreadful, which may or may not be the fact.

"Mr. Rico" opened yesterday at the Forum and other theaters.

VINCENT CANBY

1975 Ja 30, 26:4

ALICE DOESN'T LIVE HERE ANYMORE, directed by Martin Scorcese; screenplay by Robert Getchell; produced by David Susskind and Audrey Maas; director of photography, Kent L. Wakeford; editor, Marcia Lucas; distributed by Warner Bros. Running time: 113 minutes. At the Sutton Theater, 57th Street east of Third Avenue. This film has been rated PG.

Alice Hyatt	Ellen Burstyn
David	Kris Kristofferson
Tommy	Alfred Lutter
Ben	Harvey Keitel
Flo	Diane Ladd
Bea	Lelia Goldoni
Audrey	Jodie Foster
Vera	Valerie Curtin
Donald	Billy Green Bush
Rita	Lane Bradbury
Mel	Vic Tayback

By VINCENT CANBY

Alice Hyatt (Ellen Burstyn) would seem to be up a creek. She lives in semi-urban New Mexico, married to a human slug who drives a soft-drink truck and who is so alienated from their 12-year-old son, Tommy (Alfred Lutter), that when we first see the family together it seems as if the father is no more than a particularly unpleasant, demanding boarder. Suddenly and fortuitously everything changes. Donald, Alice's husband, is killed in a highway accident and Alice must take charge of her own life, which, until this time, she has always left in the care of others.

Martin Scorcese's "Alice Doesn't Live Here Anymore," which opened yesterday at the Sutton Theater, is the fine, moving, frequently hilarious tale of Alice's first lurching steps toward some kind of self-awareness and self-sufficiency.

The story moves across the American Southwest as Alice and Tommy, their belongings stuffed into their station wagon, set off on the journey back to Alice's home town of Monterey, Calif. The geography is familiar and mostly flat, strewn with motels, drive-in restaurants, taverns, service stations and diners—the bright, shiny artifacts of America's mobile optimism.

The interior landscape of the film is something else again. It's a Krazy Kat world where it's difficult to tell the difference between night and day, between robust laughter and hysterical tears, where the brick that hits you in the head may cause a slight concussion but may also knock some sense into you. The experience is scary but if you keep your wits about you, as Alice ultimately does, the chances are that things will work out. You'll get a slight purchase on survival, on life.

"Alice Doesn't Live Here Anymore" seems especially remarkable because it was directed by the man who first smashed into our consciousness with an entirely different kind of movie, "Mean Streets," a male-dominated melodrama about life in New York's Little Italy.

•

"Alice Doesn't Live Here Anymore" is an American comedy of the sort of vitality that dazzles European film critics and we take for granted. It's full of attachments and associations to very particular times and places, even in the various regional accents of its characters. It's beautifully written (by Robert Getchell) and acted, but it's not especially neatly tailored.

It begins rather badly, with an unnecessary sequence showing Alice as a little girl, and then jumps forward to Alice's home life with her slob husband, played at such a high pitch you're not sure that Mr. Scorcese and the actors will be able to sustain whatever it is they are about. You don't know at first. It's a comedy that creeps up on you, somewhere near the Arizona state line, as Tommy begins to get on Alice's nerves by threatening to be carsick.

At the center of the movie and giving it a visible sensibility is Miss Burstyn, one of the few actresses at work today (another is Glenda Jackson) who is able to seem appealing, tough, intelligent, funny and bereft, all at approximately the same moment.

•

It's Miss Burstyn's movie and part of the enjoyment of the film is in the director's apparent awareness of this fact, as in a sequence in which Alice is making a little extra money by singing and playing ersatz cocktail-piano in a roadside tavern. Alice is

Kris Kristofferson and Ellen Burstyn

never going to bring show business to its knees, but the beer drinkers love her and Mr. Scorcese circles his camera around her as lyrically as if she were Ida Lupino knocking the customers dead in "Road House."

Of equal but less spectacular importance are the supporting players, including the men. Although this is a movie that takes women seriously, and although it is essentially the chronicle of Alice's liberation, Mr. Scorcese has not shortchanged the actors, especially Harvey Keitel, as a small-town sadist who traps Alice for a while; Kris Kristofferson, as the comparatively gentle rancher who wins her, and Alfred Lutter, as her son who, when the chips are down, is not at all bad.

Two other performances must be noted, those of Diane Ladd and Valerie Curtin as waitresses in a diner where Alice works. Their marvelous contributions in small roles are a measure of the film's quality and of Mr. Scorcese's fully realized talents as one of the best of the new American film makers.

1975 Ja 30, 28:1

'70 Chabrol Work Has Virtues, Difficulties

LA RUPTURE (The Breakup) was shown at the 11th New York Film Festival. The following excerpt is from Vincent Canby's review, which appeared in The New York Times on Oct. 5, 1973. The film is being shown at the Playboy Theater, 110 West 57th Street.

Claude Chabrol has reportedly described his 1970 melodrama, "La Rupture"

The Cast

LA RUPTURE (The Breakup), directed by Claude Chabrol; screenplay (French with English subtitles) by Chabrol, based on a novel by Charlotte Armstrong; produced by Andre Genoves; director of photography, Jean Rablier; editor, Jacques Gaillard; music, Pierre Jansen; a Belgian-French-Italian co-production by Les Films la Beetle, Furo International and Cinevog Film. Running time: 125 minutes.
Charles Regnier ....Jean-Claude Drouot
Helene ....Stephane Audran
Paul Thomas ....Jean-Pierce Cassel
M. Regnier ....Michel Bouquet
Mme. Regnier ....Marguerite Cassan
Charles Regnier ......Jean-ClaudeDrouot
Mme. Pinelli ....Annie Cordy
M. Pinelli ....Jean Carmet
Elise Pinelli ....Katia Romanoff

(The Breakup), as belonging to his Fritz Lang period, which may be one of its virtues as well as one of its difficulties.

At least I find it difficult to sit comfortably through a movie in which innocence and virtue are so hopelessly imperiled that it takes nothing less than a fairly arbitrary plot device to straighten things out.

●

Perhaps one *should* be impatient with a film that opens with a brutal sequence in which a father beats up his wife and attempts to smash the brains of his 4-year-old son. Later on, the film treats us to the spectacle of a retarded teen-age girl, who has been kidnapped and drugged by the villain, being shown pornographic films and seduced by the man's mistress.

"La Rupture" is the story of a woman trapped in such circumstances that even her decency and trust can be used as weapons against her.

When Hélène, played by the extraordinarily gifted Stéphane Audran, attempts to leave her husband, a part-time writer and full-time junkie, her wealthy father-in-law attempts to discredit her morals in order to obtain custody of his grandson. The father-in-law, played by Michel Bouquet, employs Jean-

Pierre Cassel to frame Hélène, but the attempts are so clumsy that the film, though emotionally harrowing, is plausible only as an arid statement about the possibility of evil.

Within this frame, which I found difficult to accept, "La Rupture" contains some true Chabrol achievements, especially the sense of locale (Belgium, which is seen as the suburb to the rest of the world), and the performance by Miss Audran. About halfway through the film, she delivers a monologue about Hélène's marriage that is one of the most moving things I've seen this year. It may be difficult on any realistic level to accept Miss Audran as the barmaid she is supposed to be, but the stunning quality of her beauty and personality become a kind of personification of Chabrol's cool concerns, which, otherwise, have no recognizable human shape.

There is also another problem with the frame of the film; the disadvantages and indignities are piled so thickly on the poor heroine that one knows early that the film is obliged to offer her vindication. Otherwise it has no shape. That her vindication is achieved at a high price isn't surprising or touching enough to transform the melodrama of "La Rupture" into tragedy.

1975 Ja 31, 20:2

NOTHING BY CHANCE, executive producer, and narrator, Hugh Downs; produced and directed by William H. Barnett; narration written by Richard Bach; director of photography, Flemming Olsen; film editor, Fred Heinrich; music, Lee Holdridge; a Ravlin Productions, Inc., and Creature Enterprises, Inc.; film distributed by R. C. Riddell & Associates. Running time: 93 minutes. This film is classified G.

At the Fine Arts Theater, 58th Street between Park and Lexington Avenues. WITH Richard Bach, Jack Brown, Chris Cagle, Stu Macpherson, Spence Nelson, Glenn Norman and Steve Young.

"Nothing by Chance," playing at the Fine Arts Theater, is a pretty documentary about flying that comes a cropper by trying too hard to flog too much nostalgia and significance out of what is essentially a summertime barnstorming jaunt in a pack of old planes. The group of dedicated pilots and parachutists is headed by Richard ("Jonathan Livingston Seagull") Bach.

Filmed in color as the members of the self-proclaimed Great American Flying Circus, established 1922, hopscotched across middle America, landing in pastures and stubble fields to sell rides at $3 to small-town residents, it is at its best in the air.

It is then that this film needs none of the forgettable narration written by Mr. Bach and delivered with furry smoothness by Hugh Downs to sell the romance of flying the brightly colored little 1929 biplanes or the equally impressive glories of the countryside below.

But when the participants come to earth and labor, at times painfully, to wrench mystique and profundity out of flying, planes and the Grant Wood people its cameras favor, "Nothing by Chance" lapses into tedium.

None of the talk can make it more than what it is—a simple valentine to a bygone era, full of bright color and shallow sentiment.

LAWRENCE VAN GELDER

1975 Ja 31, 25:2

NATIVE LAND, directed by Paul Strand and Leo Hurwitz; songs and narration by Paul Robeson; music, Marc Blitzstein. Running time: 85 minutes. At the Whitney Museum of American Art, Madison Avenue and 75th Street. Through Tuesday.

By RICHARD F. SHEPARD

When "Native Land" was first shown here in 1942, Bosley Crowther, then film critic of The New York Times, said, "Manifestly, this is one of the most powerful and disturbing documentary films ever made, and certainly it will provoke much thought and controversy."

"Native Land," now being shown in the New American Filmmakers Series at the Whitney Museum of American Art, is still a powerful film, though one would have to recall the years it was made, 1938 to 1942, to realize that it was disturbing then.

●

This is an impassioned sermon on behalf of civil liberties and respect for the Bill of Rights. Under the direction of Leo Hurwitz and Paul Strand, the film consists of re-enacted scenes of violations of rights that were made known to a Senate committee in 1938. The stories are bridged by documen-

tary shots of workers, farmers, plain people. They are done in brilliant style but today give one the impression of seeing Works Progress Administration murals come alive.

There is so much to say about "Native Land" in all respects, as a treat for the eye (Mr. Strand did the camera work), as an important bit of film history, as an example of what liberal and leftist circles were concerned about in the late nineteen-thirties. It is often heavy with pomposity and propaganda, but it is no less fascinating for all that.

Paul Robeson narrates the commentary written by David Wolff, and his rich voice is loosed in song along the way. Marc Blitzstein's music is in keeping with the general pattern, in which the camera spells out every word and thought—flags flying, shots looking up at Thomas Jefferson, earth being put on the grave of a worker slain by the police at a lawful gathering.

The scenes depict ordinary people who suffer because they stood up to forces of evil: the farmer beaten for having spoken his mind at a grange meeting; the union members dismissed as a result of industry's espionage and intimidation activities; a small shopkeeper driven out of town for having helped union members; sharecroppers, black and white, slain for having prayed together at a church.

●

The camera and script catapult you from happiness to despair, as the plain people, enjoying the small things in life, are assaulted by forces that are bigger than the law. Throughout, "Native Land" reaffirms its faith in the American dream and, in keeping with the post-Pearl Harbor days in which it made its debut, links the fight against fascism at home with the struggle against the Axis.

This is a time-capsule film that tells you much about America during those years of strain.

1975 F 1, 19:1

FILM VIEW

VINCENT CANBY

Terrific, Tough-Talking 'Alice'

Martin Scorsese, the young New York director whose "Mean Streets" was such a smashing New York film, has done it again. He hasn't made another New York film, but he's made an equally riveting, entertaining movie that seems all the more original because it is so different from his last one, at least in its immediate concerns.

"Alice Doesn't Live Here Anymore" is essentially a comedy. It's also essentially a movie about the American southwest—New Mexico, Arizona and California, which is just about as far as you can get from New York's Little Italy without going on a ramble to Baja California. "Alice Doesn't Live Here Anymore" is not about the great wide open spaces but about the more or less urban southwest and the people who live as much of their lives in automobiles—getting to and from work, supermarkets, shopping centers, roadside taverns, diners and bowling alleys—as they do in their small-down-payment subdivision houses equipped with color television and other transistorized aides to more homogenized living.

Don't be put off by reports that "Alice Doesn't Live Here Anymore" is a woman's picture, which makes the movie sound as if it were going to be terribly solemn and humorless, and perhaps even a little chauvinistic about women's rights. Dramatized Gloria Steinem. It's not. It's a clear-eyed, tough-talking, often boisterously funny comedy about women *and* men, seen from the point of view of a woman, Alice (Ellen Burstyn) who, at 35, suddenly finds herself widowed and the sole support of her 12-year-old son, Tommy (Alfred Lutter), who is self-possessed, foul-mouthed, a walking, talking headache and, in times of crises, capable of great common sense.

"Alice Doesn't Live Here Anymore" is the story of Alice's sometimes bungling struggle toward self-awareness and self-sufficiency after having spent almost half her life as the legal consort of a guy who drives a soft-drink truck, a caricature slob of such crude grandeur that he'd seem a bit much in a comic strip.

This character, who, fortunately, is gotten rid of with dispatch, and the prologue that opens the film, are the movie's only questionable decisions, but since they both come at the beginning, "Alice Doesn't Live Here Anymore" has the distinct advantage over most films by growing on you, by getting better and better as it goes along until, at the end, you look back over it with some of the wonder and pleasure with which you might suddenly acknowledge an unexpected friendship.

Friendship is one of the operative words of "Alice Doesn't Live Here Anymore," as it was in "Mean Streets," though in the earlier film friendship had associations with an old world code of honor, with duty, with ancient allegiances.

●　　　●　　　●

All sorts of very American friendships are demonstrated in "Alice Doesn't Live Here Anymore," including the friendships that really aren't. At one point when Tommy asks Alice why she had ever married his father, since Tommy assumed that because they fought all the time she didn't love him, Alice says she married him because "he was a good kisser." Which shuts Tommy up for a bit. It also points the way to Alice's future problems with men. As they don't bother to know her, to find out whether or not they really like her before getting her to bed, so is she inclined to a kind of myopia about men. "I don't know how to live without a man," she says tearfully towards the end of the film in a scene that is simultaneously funny and very sad. What Scorsese and Robert Getchell, who wrote the screenplay, obviously know is that she's also saying that she doesn't know how to live *with* a man, at least in any kind of harmony.

Until that moment the men in her life have been false friends—roles that she has helped cast. Like the charming, sweet-talking roadside cowboy (stunningly played by Harvey Keitel from "Mean Streets") who picks her up in a bar and turns out to be a suburban sadist. The exception is the rancher she ultimately falls in love with, a gentle, unflappable man (played by Kris Kristofferson) who, like Alice, has to learn a thing or two about peace between men and women who aren't necessarily slaves. They become friends as well as lovers.

"Alice Doesn't Live Here Anymore" is almost a catalogue of friendships: the friendship of Alice and her son, living in impossible intimacy in motel rooms as they drive across the country from New Mexico towards California, bored with each other, worried, antagonistic, and then erupting in friendship in a hysterical water fight instead of violence. There's the friendship of Tommy and the weird little girl who befriends him in Tucson and who sounds as if she's memorized Phyllis

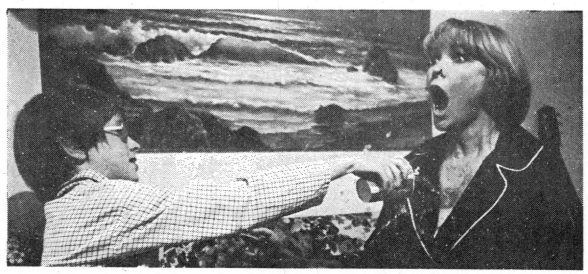

Alfred Lutter treats Ellen Burstyn, as his mom, to a Coke.

Diller's vocabulary. Most important, there are the friendships that Alice makes with her fellow waitresses, splendidly played by Diane Ladd and Valerie Curtin, when she settles down for a while with a job in a diner.

● ● ●

Behind the wisecracks and truly riotous comedy in these scenes there emerges, very movingly, an awareness of another kind of friendship, the friendship between women who may be, much of the rest of the time, in fierce competition.

The entire film is beautifully cast and acted but the plum role is that of Alice. It could well turn out to be the plum role of the entire year, and Miss Burstyn never misses the eccentric beat that distinguishes it—that makes Alice such a hugely appealing character who is both banal and very rare. They don't write many roles like this anymore (they never did, as a matter of fact); roles that allow actresses to extend their range without resorting to the easy melodramatics of madness, alcoholism, nymphomania or some other anti-social sport. Miss Burstyn is terrific.

1975 F 2, II:13:3

RAFFERTY AND THE GOLD DUST TWINS, directed by Dick Richards; written by John Kaye; director of photography, Ralph Woolsey; film editor, Walter Thompson; music, Artie Butler; produced by Michael Gruskoff and Art Linson; released by Warner Bros. At the Beekman Theater, Second Avenue and 65th Street. Running time: 92 minutes. This film is classified R.

Rafferty .... Alan Arkin
Mac .... Sally Kellerman
Frisbee .... Mackenzie Phillips
Vinnie .... Alex Rocco
Alan Boone ...... Charlie Martin Smith
Billy Winston ...... Harry Dean Stanton
John Beachwood .... John Mclaim

By RICHARD F. SHEPARD

Somewhere along the line they'll probably have an Oscar category for movies about footloose, mature men who lead roving lives of light larceny and carefree carousing while taking care of young girls — middle teens and under — who are the brains of the outfit.

One entry for this genre will be "Rafferty and the Gold Dust Twins," now at the Beekman. In this case the fellow has two girls, one a looker of consent age and the other a sulky 15-year-old who has escaped from an orphan asylum and is the one who does the thinking.

●

The film is set into the framework of an auto trip from Los Angeles to Tucson, Ariz., the route on which Rafferty, a boozy driving-test examiner, played by Alan Arkin, is taken, at gunpoint to start, by the girls played by Sally Kellerman, the older, and Mackenzie Phillips, the younger. The escapades that line the route make the story.

Dick Richards, the director, keeps things moving at a fair and funny pace, and John Kaye's episodic script covers its fragility with so many little adventures, gimmicks and cameo characterizations that you won't mind the lack of substance. Mr. Arkin, instead of being a happy, lively, carefree fellow, is a refreshingly dour carefree type to whom things happen rather than a man who generates action.

●

Miss Phillips, as the hostile youngster, is marvelously uptight, angry at the world but secretly (you can tell from obvious little vignettes) longing for familial love. Miss Kellerman makes a suitable sultry road companion.

An ancient car, unkempt and unkept, with broken doors, no muffler and no safety, but lots of energy, practically co-stars, and does very well, too. If nothing else, "Rafferty and the Gold Dust Twins" passes the time pleasantly enough — and several belly laughs and lots of chuckles—and leaves you with the feeling that out of such things come television series.

1975 F 3, 32:1

PAGE OF MADNESS, a 1926 silent Japanese film produced and directed by Teinosuke Kinugasa; script by Yasunari Kawabata; director of photography, Kohei Sugiyama; music, "Modern Bamboo Flute" Ensemble, a Shin Kankaku-Ha Eiga Renmei production. At the Quad Cinema, 13th Street between Fifth and Sixth Avenues. Running time: 60 minutes.
WITH: Masao Inoue, Yoshle Nakagawa, Ayako Iijima, Hiroshi Nemoto and Misao Seki.

Fantasies and hallucinations mount and mingle and dissolve throughout Teinosuke Kinugasa's "Page of Madness," a silent film set in an insane asylum that was made before "The Cabinet of Dr. Caligari" was ever shown in Japan. The print was believed to be long lost until a few years ago, when the director — who once studied with Eisenstein, and is mainly known in this country for "Crossways" (1928) and "The Gate of Hell" (1953)—found a copy in his garden shed. That discovery is well worth celebrating, and the movie is at the Quad Cinema III.

The film centers on an elderly janitor whose wife (who drowned their baby) is a patient in an asylum where the inmates riot briefly. He encourages her to escape, but she recoils in fright and anger from the outside world. While much of the film reflects the distorted consciousness of the mad, there's an equal stress on the sufferings of their sane relatives—those who have to accept the abnormal as the norm. The old man's marvelously sensitive face records the impact of all the lunacies that surround him, while an eerie, metallic soundtrack evokes chaos in the mind.

The movie's visual excitement springs from the extraordinary range of imagery: Again and again, faces are seen through real or imaginary bars, while water—gushing through gutters or splashing in a sink—recalls the drowning of the baby. When a crazed young woman dances wildly alone in her cell, we see the drums that she thinks she hears.

●

Some patients struggle in the arms of nurses, while others lie or sit in trances; at moments, their laughing frantic faces challenge the chilly doctors who control them. Toward the end, the film itself seems to go deliberately berserk, in a style that conveys the contagion of madness. Meanwhile, this hypnotic work has a contemporary intensity and sophistication, even though it's almost 50 years old.

NORA SAYRE

1975 F 4, 26:4

REPORT TO THE COMMISSIONER, directed by Milton Katselas; screenplay by Abby Mann and Ernest Tidyman, based on the novel by James Mills; director of photography, Mario Tosi; film editor, David Blewitt; music, Elmer Bernstein; produced by M. J. Frankovich; released by United Artists. At the Criterion Theater, Broadway at 45th Street, 86th Street East Theater, at Third Avenue and the UA East Theater, First Avenue and 85th Street. Running time: 112 minutes. This film is classified PG.

Beauregard (Bo) Lockley Michael Moriarty
Richard (Crunch) Blackstone Yaphet Kotto
Patty Butler .... Susan Blakely
Captain D'Angelo .... Hector Elizondo
Thomas (Stick) Henderson ..... Tony King
Lieutenant Hanson ...... Michael McGuire

By NORA SAYRE

Festooned with liberal intentions gone awry, Milton Katselas's "Report to the Commissioner" suggests an awkward mating of "Serpico" and Watergate—a coupling that's rapidly established when police officials exclaim, "We have the biggest scandal the department ever had!" and "I want a report—I don't want a cover-up!" Apparently, some policemen are impure. The movie, which concentrates on a young rookie cop (Michael Moriarty) who becomes a fall guy for two of his ambitious colleagues, was adapted from James Mills's novel, and it opened yesterday at neighborhood theaters.

Amid the garbled discussions of ethics, the movie's main problem is its characterizations: the good citizens are simply too good—and the bad too bad—to be (even faintly) believable. Also, the dialogue by Abby Mann and Ernest Tidyman strains to be hyperhip in a style that's now old-fashioned, especially where the language of young drug addicts or blacks is concerned. In fact, if critics got a dime for every "groovy" in this picture, we might be able to hold our next award meeting in Bermuda.

Mr. Moriarty's role—as a dangerously naive, idealistic police trainee—requires him to be pudgy-minded: you might say fatheaded. He's the kind of incompetent who would make a mess of Monopoly, let alone a narcotics assignment. But this very fine actor can't and doesn't do his best with lines like "What am I doin' here anyway, walkin' around on this planet?" Wearing an eternal fuzzy smile, he uses a quavery adolescent voice that hits some high notes for agitation; otherwise, he mumbles far too much. Susan Blakely has a nearly impossible part as an undercover agent; perhaps she's meant to be a fearless contemporary woman, but she comes off as blithely suicidal. And the talents of two particularly gifted actors, Hector Elizondo and Yaphet Kotto, are wasted on one-note characters.

Athrob with benign principles, the movie offers a ponderous critique of machismo, and police brutality is dutifully condemned. However, the potential suspense and excitement of the narrative are throttled by long scenes that seem designed to slow the viewer's pulse.

A final complaint: the movie fails to use New York as pictures such as "Klute" or "The Taking of Pelham One Two Three" or a host of others have done; the opportunities offered by the city's character are ignored, and "Report" might as well have been filmed in White River Junction. Still, there's a shoot-out in Saks Fifth Avenue near what appears to be the loungewear department. Due to the ineptitudes of this movie, you may never feel quite the same about Saks again.

1975 F 6, 25:1

A BRIEF VACATION, directed by Vittorio de Sica; screenplay (Italian with English subtitles) by Cesare Zavattini; photography, Ennio Guarnieri; music, Manuel de Sica; released by Allied Artists. At the Little Carnegie Theater, 57th Street east of Seventh Avenue. Running time: 106 minutes. This film is classified PG.

Clara .... Florinda Bolkan
Husband .... Renato Salvatori
Luigi .... Daniel Quenaud
Ciranni .... Jose Maria Prada
Gina .... Teresa Gimpera

By NORA SAYRE

The late Vittorio de Sica's sympathy for and identification with those who are desperately dependent on their deadening jobs and gaunt wages emerges strongly in his last movie, "A Brief Vacation," which opened yesterday at the Little Carnegie. The movie revolves around Clara (Florinda Bolkan), a young factory worker who's exhausted by the job that barely supports her surly, disabled husband, their three children, her lazy brother-in-law and his senile mother.

Awakening to broken plumbing, the nagging relatives who regard her as a money machine, and the anxiety of being late to work, she struggles against the accumulative fatigue of the days behind and the months ahead, along with her helpless anger against a poverty that seems insoluble and a social system that's stacked against the poor. There's a gentle but profound pessimism here that harks back to de Sica's earlier work. This movie is in no way as painful as "The Bicycle Thief" or "Umberto D," but the characters do mean it when they say it's a rotten world.

When it's discovered that Clara is tubercular, she's sent to a mountain sanatorium, where she's refreshed and renewed by good care and then by a love affair. It's ironically clear that her daily life was so bad that illness and convalescence are preferable to health. Surrounded by kindness, she gains a confidence that she never had before, dicovers her own independence, and finds herself nourished by a new awareness. But she's left with the prospect of losing her nascent freedoms.

The movie is rich with small revelations about ordinary experience, as when two strangers who are potential lovers discuss the difficulties of their jobs—which is an unusual scene for a first meeting in a movie, or when someone who rarely has the chance to be alone savors the luxury of solitude. "Vacation" also explores the friendship and mutual support among sick people, the awkwardness between relatives who haven't met for awhile—the close-ups that reveal uneasiness are particularly good—plus the ravages of destructive family relationships

And de Sica excelled at incongruities: the ludicrously free associations that occur during moments of deep emotion, as when a woman remarks that there's no butter in butter cookies and then immediately weeps from the fear that her lover will reject her, or when another woman (who attempted suicide) says that she had a vision of baked lasagna after she shot herself

●

Clara, who began as a dingy, despairing woman begrimed by the world, goes through subtle physical changes as she comes alive. De Sica resisted the spectacular overnight flowering that might have tempted another director, and his sensitivity to women's feelings is impressive. The only flaw in this modest, touching film is that the adoring young man whom Clara loves is simply too good to be true: He's merely a device, and has no character at all.

"A Brief Vacation" doesn't evoke de Sica's major works, and the emotional impact isn't on a par with that of "The Garden of the Finzi-Continis." But the director's personal warmth is unwavering throughout, and the film makes an honorable ending to his career.

1975 F 10, 20:1

Pianist, 89, Subject and Star of Documentary

At this late date it is obviously idiotic to "discover" Arthur Rubinstein's virtuosity. The 89-year-old pianist has been enthusiastically proving himself all over the world for more than 70 years. But "Arthur Rubinstein — Love of Life" succeeds in turning the rare trick of revealing an extraordinary human being as well as an amazing artist. The documentary, which was made in 1968 and won an Academy Award, had its belated theatrical premiere here yesterday at the Festival.

Francois Reichenbach and S. G. Patris, the directors, and Christian Odasso, the photographer, were obviously fortunate in having a photogenic and multilingually articulate performer to focus on. And what would first appear to be an episodic, somewhat haphazard approach evolves as a personal memoir and musical document that speaks volumes without touching on every detail of a long and outstanding career.

•

In combining vintage black-and-white clips and home movies with the film's superb color footage, the producers follow Mr. Rubinstein along a concert tour that includes Iran, Paris and Israel. If these stops include only excerpts from rehearsals and recitals, an intimate, heartfelt and vigorous musicianship is still evident in every area of the classics played—Beethoven, Chopin, Brahms, Falla.

But the producers have not merely recorded a musical dossier. Mr. Rubinstein, man and boy, is recalled by himself (in English and French mostly) in sometimes serious, sometimes humorous reflections. These intermittent interruptions of the music recall, among other things, early struggles in Berlin as well as successes in Carnegie Hall in 1944 and other points in a worldwide itinerary. They also unveil a contented family life in Paris, Beverly Hills, New York and Marbella. "My kids have learned to be happy," Mr. Rubinstein notes to the accompaniment of appropriate scenes.

"Arthur Rubinstein" may vividly illustrate a psysiological phenomenon through extreme close-ups on his hands in action. But the 89-year-old master also puts the love of his life in close-up when he says "One must play what one feels with all one's heart." And, he adds with obvious relish, "but one must be born with talent." Both the indestructible talent and the rare man are strikingly served in 'Arthur Rubinstein."

A. H. WEILER

The Program

ARTHUR RUBINSTEIN—LOVE OF LIFE, directed by Francois Reichenbach and S. G. Patris; photography, Christian Odasso, edited by Catherine Mouvin; music, Beethoven, Chopin, Brahms, Villa-Lobos and Liszt; produced by Francois Reichenbach and Bernard Gavoty; a Midem Production; distributed by New Yorker Films. At the Festival Theater, Fifth Avenue at 57th Street. Running time: 91 minutes. This film has not been classified.

WITH the Israel Philharmonic Orchestra directed by Maitre Inbal; the Paris Orchestra directed by Paul Klezki.

1975 F 10, 20:4

SHAMPOO, directed by Hal Ashby; screenplay by Robert Towne and Warren Beatty; director of photography, Laszlo Kovacs; editor, Robert Jones; music, Paul Simon; produced by Mr. Beatty. At the Coronet Theater, Third Avenue at 59th Street. Running time: 112 minutes. This film is classified R.

George .... Warren Beatty
Jackie .... Julie Christie
Jill .... Goldie Hawn
Felicia .... Lee Grant
Lester .... Jack Warden
Johnny Pope .... Tony Bill
Lorna .... Carrie Fisher

By NORA SAYRE

Disappointment comes in all weights and flavors, but the brand that's generated by Hal Ashby's "Shampoo" is a bit harder to swallow than some. It's the disappointment that occurs when you look forward to a particular combination of talents—and the ingredients don't mesh. The movie, produced by Warren Beatty and written by him and the immensely gifted Robert Towne, begins with a reminder of "Carnal Knowledge" (sexual gurglings in the dark), and contains some echoes of Robert Altman's work—mainly in the use of overlapping dialogue. But the jokes are so leaden and the characters so broad that this glossy farce never levitates: it's harmless and heavy, like a dead mastodon. "Shampoo" opened yesterday at the Coronet.

•

Mr. Beatty plays a Beverly Hills hairdresser who's ardently pursued by many jealous women. Boyishly awkward, mumbling and gesturing in a traditionally inarticulate style, the actor is devoid of gumption: he's supposed to be keen on women and sex, yet he seems quite pasive and unenthusiastic. It's surprising that he didn't give himself a livelier role. Much of the time, he seems to be acting against his lines: his manner contradicts the words he utters.

Julie Christie, as an old-fashioned kept woman, is querulous and brittle; at moments, she squeals with anger. She appears to be a depressive, but we never know why. She and Mr. Beatty perform together without any of the attractive tensions that seeped through "McCabe and Mrs. Miller." Goldie Hawn has little to do but reprach Mr. Beatty for his giddiness—she even has to tell him that he's "incapable of love," a phrase we thought had been retired—and her nimble sarcasm is wasted. Lee Grant brings grace to a thankless part as a devouring rich woman. Carrie Fisher makes a deft, cool debut as a hostile adolescent: somehow, the daughter of Debbie Reynolds seems more at ease in the movie than most of her hip senior colleagues.

The most puzzling figure is Jack Warden as a tycoon who's married to Miss Grant and supporting Miss Christie. He's made to be so lumpish and ridiculous that we can't imagine why either woman would give him her time between haircuts—and it's hard to see why such a person was included in this movie. But perhaps he was invented to make Mr. Beatty appear dazzling. The two men have a long embarrassing scene in which Mr. Beatty grows rueful about studhood, and the mood becomes bewilderingly moralistic.

"Shampoo" is set on the election eve of 1968, but there's no apparent reason for reviving the nineteen-sixties beyond putting Miss Hawn in a miniskirt. Jaunty references on the radio to Saigon and the Paris peace talks, strobe lights, bits of the Beach Boys and "Sergeant Pepper," don't evoke the period any more than lines like "Lindbergh's landed!" or "Let's Remember Pearl Harbor!" serve to recreate earlier decades in other nostalgia flicks. Meanwhile, joints are circulated as carefully as if they were archeological artifacts. Again, snippets of Nixon's victory speech and his promises of "an open Administration" could have been rich with irony—if they hadn't been inserted in such a labored way.

Amid all the ho-hos about hairdressing, and the limping gags about hairdressers being homosexual, Mr. Beatty's own hair is beyond reproach. However, after he restyles the heads of Miss Christie and Miss Hawn, both cease to look as spectacular as they did before: the locks are dowdy. The lapse in their coiffures seems like an image for this picture: the intentions were appealing, but the set went awry, and the comb-out didn't work.

1975 F 12, 47:1

JANIS, a documentary about Janis Joplin directed and edited by Howard Alk and Seaton Findlay; produced by Crawley Films; released by Universal Pictures. Running time: 96 minutes. This film is classified R. At Cinema I, Third Avenue and 60th Street.

To witness "Janis," the documentary about the late rock singer Janis Joplin, is to confront the realization that one is not so much in the presence of biography or homage as of psychiatric case history.

Although the film that opened yesterday at Cinema I might have served as the occasion for a retrospective appraisal of the brief career of this performer, who died in October, 1970, of an overdose of heroin, considerations of the quality and durability of her artistry become subordinate to awareness of the agonizing psychic wounds that were the wellsprings of her talent.

The naked emotion—full of tantrums, railing and unconcealed pain—that erupted through her throat in the torn voice that was her trademark and the gift she squandered on her public is by itself sufficient to suggest the extraordinary extent of her suffering.

But this evidence — in scenes of Miss Joplin singing, among others, such songs as "Ball and Chain," "Tell Mama" "Kozmic Blues," "Cry Baby" and "Move Over" in places such as Monterey, Woodstock, Frankfurt, Calgary and Toronto, with groups such as Big Brother & The Holding Company, the Kozmic Blues Band and the Full Tilt Boogie Band—is buttressed by a series of interviews.

These interviews are apparently routine, but time and again they serve to reveal a deeply injured little girl whose only adequate focus of energy, communication and emotional feedback was offered by singing. The most telling of these interludes in "Janis" occurs when Miss Joplin, garbed to a freaky turn, goes back to her home town, Port Arthur, Tex., to attend the 10th annual reunion of her high school class.

Although her design is obviously to flaunt success among the people who ostracized her, it is clear that instead of enjoying a triumph, she is being compelled to rake emotional scar tissue. A doctor, she recalls, once told her mother that unless Janis straightened up, she would be in jail or a mental institution by the time she was 21.

Miss Joplin was 27 when she died.

As film, "Janis" is conventional documentary composed of performance clips and interviews. As case history, it is a poignant film.

LAWRENCE VAN GELDER

1975 F 13, 43:3

FEMALE TROUBLE, directed, written and photographed by John Waters; editor, Charles Roggero; a Dreamland production, distributed by New Line Cinema. Running time: 95 minutes. At the RKO 59th Street Twin I, 59th Street east of Third Avenue. This film has been rated X.

Dawn Davenport .... Divine
Earl Peterrson .... Divine
Donald Dasher .... David Lochary
Donna Dasher .... Mary Vivian Pearce
Taffy Davenport .... Mink Stole
Ida Nelson .... Edith Massey
Concetta .... Cookie Mueller
Chicklett .... Susan Walsh
Gater .... Michael Potter

When, at age 16 or so, Dawn Davenport (Divine) doesn't get the cha-cha heels she wants for Christmas, she wraps the Christmas tree around Mom's neck, tells Dad he knows what he can do with himself, then stalks out of the house and is quite happily raped by a passing motorist, a slob of heroic proportions also played by Divine, a 200-pound-plus female impersonator.

Thus begins "Female Trouble," the story of Dawn's search for stardom that opened yesterday at the 59th Street Twin 1 Theater. The movie was directed, written and photographed by John Waters, the Baltimore film maker responsible for "Pink Flamingos".

A lot of people would say that Dawn goes from bad to worse, but it's just one of the dozens of often predictable reversals in "Female Trouble" that Dawn sees herself as going from good to better, finally winding up in the electric chair for murder, an occasion she proudly describes as "the page one of my life."

•

"Female Trouble" is regional camp of very limited appeal, a movie that celebrates tackiness in a way that was revolutionary and sometimes very funny in the sixties when Andy Warhol and Paul Morrissey did it. Now it seems almost provincial, though I realize that too could be interpreted as a plus by people who are willing to work very hard to rationalize small laughs.

Divine, who looks like a hippo in drag even when he's not in drag, may not be an untalented comedian, though it's impossible to tell in a movie in which the second-rateness of everything is the point. In the Warhol-Morrissey films such as "Trash" and "Women in Revolt," the wit and the idiosyncracies of the performers (Holly Woodlawn, Jackie Curtis, Candy Darling) had the effect of reversing the reversals, so that the films were funnier (and more serious) than was immediately apparent.

Mr. Waters's actors work hard to achieve some of that same quality, but with one exception they never achieve it. The exception is an actress named Mink Stole, who occasionally displays a fine madness as Dawn's 14-year-old daughter who doesn't look a day less than 30.

VINCENT CANBY

1975 F 13, 43:1

THE STEPFORD WIVES, directed by Bryan Forbes; screenplay by William Godman, based on the novel by Ira Levin; produced by Edgar J. Sherick; executive producer, Gustave M. Berne; music, Michael Small; director of photography, Owen Roisman; editor, Gene Callahan; a Fadsin/Cinema Associates production, distributed by Columbia Pictures. Running time: 115 minutes. At Loew's Tower East Theater, Third Avenue near 72d Street, Loew's State 2, Broadway at 45th Street, and other theaters. This film has been rated PG.

Joanne	Katharine Ross
Bobby	Paula Prentiss
Walter	Peter Masterson
Carol	Nanette Newman
Dale Coba	Patrick O'Neal
Charmaine	Tina Louise
Dr. Fancher	Carol Rosson
Ike Mazzard	William Prince

By VINCENT CANBY

The comic possibilities existing in "The Stepford Wives," at least as indicated in the screenplay that William Goldman has adapted from Ira Levin's novel, seem to have been mowed down during the actual production of the film as if they were as unsightly as crab grass.

The humor that remains in the movie, which opened at theaters here yesterday, is preesnted with such facetiousness one almost feels embarrassed to watch. You want to tell the actors to take it easy, since it's apparent that Bryan Forbes, the film's director, didn't.

●

The movie is an adaptation of another tale by Mr. Levin ("Rosemary's Baby") about a woman in distress, this time a dauntless, grown-up quite sophisticated Nancy Drew-type named Joanna (Katharine Ross), a reasonably happy wife and mother who wants to express her individuality through professional photography.

Joanna is no more nuts than Rosemary was, and when she begins to suspect that something is wrong in Stepford, the upper-crust little Connecticut town to which she and her husband have just moved, you know that she's probably onto something. There are clues everywhere.

For one thing, as Joanna points out, most suburban wives in these circumstances would be a trifle bored. They might be expected to philander, drink, join garden clubs or even to play too much bridge. But not the wives of Stepford. Most of them are model drudges, doting on husbands (their own), children, cooking and floor-waxing.

Joanna, who, in her own words, "messed around with women's lib in New York," fails utterly when she tries to organize a women's consciousness-raising group. Instead of beefing about their lots in life, the women sit around discussing various detergents with the intensity of television creatures whose only interest in life is to rid the world of rings-around-the-collar.

At first Joanna has a couple of allies in Bobby (Paula Prentiss), a tall, gawky wife with immense distaste for tidy kitchens, and Charmaine (Tina Louise), the baby-doll wife of a TV executive. Then, Bobby and Charmaine join the ranks of the perpetually happy homemakers. Good grief! Domestic bliss suddenly becomes as pernicious as anemia.

The basic idea of "The Stepford Wives" is more satiric than sinister but Mr. Forbes treats it with what might be described as broad solemnity. There are laughs here and there, most of them provided by the liberating presence of Miss Prentiss, whether in her guise as loudmouth or an automaton.

●

Miss Ross, too, is an interesting actress, but her predicament seems nearly always funnier than dangerous, which is not the way the movie is meant to be taken. An actor new to me, Peter Masterson, plays Miss Ross's husband with a gravity and a desperation that, under other circumstances, would probably be affecting.

Science-fiction fans may well be disappointed when they realize that the so-called mystery of Stepford is very reminiscent of the fine Ray Bradbury story about a husband who found a unique way of running out on his wife. More than that a critic is not allowed to say.

1975 F 13, 43:1

HUMAIN, TROP HUMAIN (Human, Too Human), a documentary feature in French (with English subtitles) directed by Louis Malle; produced by Mr. Malle and NEF; director of photography, Etienne Becker; editors, Suzanne Baron, Reine Wekstein and Jocelyne Riviere; distributed by New Yorker Films. Running time 77 minutes. At the First Avenue Screening Room, First Avenue near 61st Street. This film has not been rated.

By VINCENT CANBY

Louis Malle's "Humain, Trop Humain" (Human, Too Human), which will be shown at the First Avenue Screening Room today and tomorrow at noon and midnight, is a provocative, vivid, complex, original movie that should not be missed by anyone remotely interested in Mr. Malle, in films or in the set of modern civilization.

I say that right away because I'm not at all sure I can adequately evoke the special fascination of this film by simply describing it. "Humain, Trop Humain" is a 77-minute documentary made in the summer and fall of 1972 in the Citroën automobile assembly plant in Rennes and at the annual automobile show in Paris. It is divided into three parts, though it has no visible seams between the sequences.

Part One is a kind of introduction to the assembly plant, during which Mr. Malle's cameras study the larger, more familiar movements of assembly-line production, beginning with some flat steel plates that end up as a four-wheeled vehicle. Part Two is the Paris auto show, a sequence that is as funny as something by Jacques Tati and a little sinister, too, in the way it casually records the fanaticism and the faith of the public.

●

Part Three returns to the assembly plant where, this time, the cameras begin to share the experience of the workers, particularly those engaged in small, precise repetitions of tasks that, contrary to the liberal beliefs of the nineteen-twenties and thirties, do not dehumanize the workers so much as comfort them with familiar duties. The limiting territory and repeated tasks create order in what otherwise would be a chaotic universe.

In saying that, I realize that I'm making the film seem judgmental. It's not, but it wants us to rethink those earlier attitudes toward modern industrial processes that made it chic as well as humanistic to be aghast at what we have wrought in the last 100 years.

●

If these processes were as debasing as Charlie Chaplin suggests in "Modern Times," Mr. Malle seems to be saying, then the entire system would have come apart a long time ago. It hasn't yet come apart. The workers that Mr. Malle shows us don't look like robots, nor do they look like a happy chorus in one of those early, gung-ho Soviet films about the joys of surpassing production quotas. Mr. Malle is wondering why.

In the Malle filmography, "Humain, Trop Humain" comes after "Murmur of the Heart," a witty, genuinely feelingful comedy about the usually breast-beating, guilt-ridden subject of incest, and before "Lacombe, Lucien," an unsentimental look at French behavior during the Nazi occupation of France.

Though it is a documentary, it shares with these films a firm disinclination to accept easy or popular answers. Like Mr. Malle's remarkable series of television films on India, "Humain, Trop Humain" begins at a new beginning. It says: Forget what you've been told and have read. This is the way it looks and the way it may be. Think about it.

"Humain, Trop Humain" is, in addition, a film of stunning images, a lot as beautiful as any that Jean-Luc Godard captured in his later Marxist films. Some also are very funny, and there are some for the die-hard film buffs, such as a shot of an automobile chassis slowly sinking into a vat of viscous gray liquid—a nod, I suspect, to "Psycho" and that old film master Alfred Hitchcock.

1975 F 14, 28:1

HENRY MILLER ASLEEP AND AWAKE, directed by Tom Schiller, 35 minutes; BUKOWSKI, created and produced by Taylor Hackford; Richard Davies, co-director and cinematographer, 60 minutes. At the Whitney Museum of American Art, Madison Avenue and 75th Street.

By NORA SAYRE

Filmworthy as a circus or a dolphin or your favorite child, Henry Miller is emerging as a natural for the screen. Last year, we had Robert Snyder's fine documentary on the writer, made in 1969; now, Tom Schiller's "Henry Miller Asleep and Awake" (1973) yields another highly enjoyable visit with this scribacious person. The film at the Whitney Museum of American Art, will run through Tuesday.

●

Awakening with a flurry of sleepy grunts, Mr. Miller leads the camera to his bathroom, where he fingers his features to see if they're still there, and then proceeds to give us a tour of the pictures and photographs on the walls. The result is "a voyage of ideas." Musing on various Buddhas, Blaise Cendrars, Hieronymous Bosch, several Japanese writers, Hesse, a stone carving by Jung, women he found attractive, Gurdjieff and Gauguin, he makes his enthusiasms contagious.

His jovial monologue includes reflections on his tendency to hear "celestial music" in airplanes, the relationship between Zen and sex, the fact that "most writers don'[illegible] (because they spend so much time alone), and the question of identity, which "harasses" him. Recalling a youthful day when he saw a face that wasn't his own in a subway gum machine, Mr. Miller describes a recurrent nightmare in which a similar hallucination drives him mad. (Few can talk so cheerfully—even gleefully—about despair.) At 81, he also exults in his loathing of New York, and marvels that he's still sane—after his early poverty, "the monsters and the misery" that he knew. Meanwhile his pleasure in the present should raise anyone's morale.

Also on the program is Taylor Hackford's and Richard Davies's extraordinary "Bukowski." You rarely see such raw or intimate emotions in a documentary as those revealed in the cinema verité portrait of the 52-year-old poet Charles Bukowski. Cataracts of hostility pour out of this bitter yet sometimes genial man, and it's unusual to encounter someone as hostile who's also likable.

●

A misanthrope, a very old-fashioned sexist, a person who seems to revel in disgust, who hates his past and his heredity, he seems to cling to the role of a primitive as a form of self-defense. As the two women in his life speak freely about their problems with him, you experience some disturbing moments of feeling like an emotional voyeur; yet, from the way that both participate, they don't appear to have been manipulated by the film makers.

There are also some exciting excerpts from a public reading by Mr. Bukowski; his work comes over very well on screen. Though he and others emphasize that he isn't "like" his poems, the momentum of his most casual remarks does evoke his poetry. Throughout, a sardonic humor punctuates the pessimism. He seems to recoil from success and yet to want it but he implies that it's too late in his life for him to feel rewarded or threatened. Certainly, he and Henry Miller are well-paired on this program: both are defiant survivors.

1975 F 16, 65:1

3 ANTHROPOLOGICAL FILMS, directed by David Hancock (camera) and Herbert Di Gioia (sound); produced [illegible] Miller for the American Universities Field Staff; with English subtitles. AFGHAN NOMADS: THE MALDAR, [illegible] minutes; WHEAT CYCLE, 16 minutes; NAIM AND JABAR, 48 minutes. At the Film Forum, 256 West 88th Street, today and Thursday through next Sunday, 8 P.M.

A series of three pensive, extraordinarily beautiful ethnographic documentaries by David Hancock and Herbert Di Gioia convey the rhythms and the rigors of primitive agricultural life in northern Afghanistan. (The films are part of a series produced for the American Universities Field Staff, concerning the effect of modernization on the lives of country dwellers.) Clearly, the film makers put their subjects at ease; one senses a rapport between these rural people and the camera. The program appears today and Thursday through next Sunday at the Film Forum, 256 West 88th Street.

"Afghan Nomads" follows the Maldar tribe on its search for grazing areas for its herds; the wanderers have already traveled 250 miles. The stress is on the necessity—and the impossibility — of owning land, especially irrigated land, but these people are far too poor to do so. As their figures recede into the dusty folds of the hills, we realize the effort and the patience essential to their long journeys. "Wheat Cycle" revolves around the annual production of the wheat crop, as hired laborers reap and thresh and harvest. Again, there's an emphasis on the meticulously hard work required.

"Naim and Jaber" yields a touching glimpse of the lifelong friendship of two adolescent boys. They know what a struggle it will be to earn a living, and that education will be crucial to employment. They leave their town to visit the capital of the province, Mazar-i-Sharif, where the older goes to school, and the younger hopes to be admitted. Both seem very bright and alert; their elation at exploring the city is exhilarating to watch. A discouraging official interviews the young applicant, who's crushed on learning that he doesn't qualify for his friend's school. He takes the disappointment bravely, but both are very distressed at the prospect of being separated. All of these films show a sensitivity and a respect for individuals whose ways of life are in transition—and whose future is beyond their control.

1975 F 16, 65:1

FILM VIEW

WALTER GOODMAN

'Shampoo': Is It a Farce or a Freak Show?

"**S**hampoo" showers us with signals. An opening line on the screen notifies us that the time is election eve, Nov. 4, 1968—ah, the resonances of that date—and we are never allowed to forget it. See the Nixon-Agnew posters . . . see Nixon-Agnew on those TV sets, playing away with obtrusive unobtrusiveness in every house we enter . . . see Huntley-Brinkley doing their election-night routine . . . hear the returns. Clearly we are being prepared for something more stimulating than a rinse.

What can be the relationship between the 1968 election and this tale of the involvements of a hairdresser-cum-community-stud—Warren Beatty, looking suitably harassed as he commutes on his Triumph cycle between salon and boudoir "in Technicolor on location in Beverly Hills, California"—with three stylishly got-up women? Before grappling with this question, let's meet the cast. There's the sweet, dim, affectionate young thing— Goldie Hawn, doing the turn for which she seems to have been born and which she will keep doing until liberated by age. There's the hairdresser's gorgeous now-and-again sex-partner—Julie Christie, making moues for all she's worth—who is at the moment the mistress of a rich businessman—Jack Warden, puffy and grotesque in orange hair—who is considering setting up the hairdresser in a shop of his own at the instance of his (the orange-haired businessman's) wife—Lee Grant, giving the film's only interesting performance—who, you guessed it, is having an affair with the hairdresser.

It's the stuff of farce, with couples coupling all over the place, in steam rooms, on floors, even in bed, with discoveries and close calls, with mix-ups and bustle aplenty and other ingredients indigenous to the form. All that is wanting here is style—but in farce, of course, style is all. Without it, we have a freak show; the characters become ridiculous at best, the audience is asked to find amusement in the antics of actors whom it is impossible to accept even as movie-real, much less to sympathize with, much less like. Julie Christie and Warren Beatty make a super-sexy pair—but pair of what? This is the old Hollywood starworld of the beautiful non-people, nowadays showing they are with it by their bounteous use of non-beautiful four-letter words.

The most promising farcical moment, the big scene of the movie sure to be advertised by word of, pardon the expression, mouth, comes at a Nixon celebration party, when Julie, overwhelmed with an urge to perform a very personal service upon Warren, announces her intention most colloquially and then proceeds to the job in the presence of her patron and his wife, Warren's sometime bedmate. But the episode is presented in such a labored fashion that what ought to be hilarious confusion becomes just confused.

Whatever the talents of director Hal Ashby, who did "The Last Detail," "Harold and Maude" and "The Landlord," they evidently do not encompass farce. In "Shampoo" Ashby shows that he has a good memory for a couple of decades of cinematic clichés. He gives us an unnecessary motor race and some obligatory slow motion, but he misses most of the opportunities offered him. For example, when the cuckolded husband remarks to his wife that he suspects that the cuckolding hairdresser is a "fairy," the gag is dissipated by the limp directorial hand.

Granted, Ashby gets little aid from a script which propels characters in all directions in hope of churning up some fun and, heaven spare us, some significance. That Robert Towne, who wrote the unusually complex and literate screenplay for "Chinatown," should take credit for this frank effort to repeat the success of "The Graduate," to which it bears an uncanny resemblance, is

Hairdresser Beatty and customer Christie

mystifying, until we note that his co-writer was the producer-star Warren Beatty.

The whole commotion ends, by scriptwriters' fiat, with all parties reassessing their values and the poor hairdresser, that sexual object, left lonely on a hill. Now, the resolution of even a farce ought to be justified by something that has gone before. Here, with no rhyme and less reason, the story is allowed to sink into a slough of sentimentality. When Warren earnestly tries to explain the irresistible appeal of good-looking women, when Goldie says she wants babies, when Jack Warden announces he is not pleased with either Nixon or Johnson and expresses the wish for a better future for all, one wants to wash these people out of one's hair.

But to get back to Nixon-Agnew, their presence in the movie must be received as a message. Mr. Beatty and his co-workers want to say something to us, or think they want to. What can it be? Not just a running joke surely? To see and hear our former President and Vice President talking about punishing immorality and bringing the country together is funny, in an uncomfortable way, but not very sustaining. (One cannot discover from this movie, incidentally, that it was Hubert Humphrey who ran against Nixon in 1968, and there is no mention of Vietnam. Can the film's peculiar discretion be related to the report that Warren Beatty is now associated with the candidacy of Senator Henry Jackson, who was a ferocious hawk in 1968 and is now

Walter Goodman is the assistant editor of the Arts and Leisure section.

Vincent Canby is on vacation.

courting Humphrey's good will?)

My suspicion is that the concocters of "Shampoo" believed that they were making a social comment of a sort—a highly conventional sort as it turns out. The businessman-husband listens incessantly to stock quotations on the radio of his Rolls-Royce. A banker refuses to give the hairdresser a loan—mutually incomprehensible life styles, get it? (By the way, are Los Angeles banks open on Election Day?) Also, the businessman's wife makes a speech about how big campaign contributors are out to make deals for themselves and are not really concerned for the welfare of the nation. Wow! Also, this woman's daughter (who, naturally, enjoys a quickie with the hairdresser) hates her; that must be significant. And I fear to carry forward the implications of the fact that this rich Beverly Hills family eats lox and chopped liver.

The hairdressing salon symbolizes the glittering vanities of America, doesn't it? And when the son of the salon's seemingly effeminate proprietor is reported killed in a car accident, that must signify Reality intruding, mustn't it? And how about that big party with pot and strobe lights and Beatles numbers and beards and skinny-dipping, in contrast with the stuffy Nixonian dinner which is broken up by a bomb scare? The two faces of America, right? (The pot party scene may be taken as an intended parody of yesterday's breathlessly admiring film treatments of the alleged Youth Culture or as an unconscious self-parody of this trendy movie itself, where the generation gap is symbolized by the difference between a limousine and a sports car.)

•   •   •

Perhaps, after all, there is truly an intimate connection between "Shampoo" and the politicians who took over Washington in 1968. One mark of the Nixon Administration, typified by that very Agnew whose image pursues us through this film, was a show of high purposefulness masking the lowest of backstairs doings. The Vice President delivered lectures on deportment and pocketed envelopes containing cash money. In its pretensions to Meaningfulness, its dumb little lectures, its shrewd mindlessness, its show-biz exploitation of any subject from sex to politics that promises to be box-office, "Shampoo" pays tribute to the kind of public behavior it aspires to judge.

1975 F 16, II:1:1

Sailing Film Is Awash With Wholesomeness

By NORA SAYRE

Healthy family pictures can be as hard to judge as the health of any given family. "The Dove," directed by Charles Jarrott and produced by Gregory Peck, is probably far too wholesome for most of the families I know, although there may be a radiant audience lurking just outside the realms of my acquaintance. The movie, based on the actual experiences of Robin Lee Graham, a 16-year-old who spent five years sailing around the world alone, opened yesterday at neighborhood theaters.

"The Dove" is superbly filmed by Sven Nykvist, who has shot many of Ingmar Bergman's movies. From Fiji to the Australian outback or the Galápagos Islands, the stunning evocations of landscape and seascape make you wish that this were a straightforward travel film, bereft of actors. Joseph Bottoms, as the young sailor, smiles too much in the first half of the movie; after that, he cries too much. His initial

The Cast

THE DOVE, directed by Charles Jarrott; screenplay by Peter Beagle and Adam Kennedy, based on the book by Robin Lee Graham with Derek Gill; director of photography, Sven Nykvist; film editor, John Jympson; music, John Barry; produced by Gregory Peck; released by Paramount Pictures. At neighborhood theaters. Running time: 105 minutes. This film is classified PG.
Robin Lee Graham........Joseph Bottoms
Patti Ratteree...........Deborah Raffin
Lyle Graham..............John McLiam

overwhelming sunniness turns the viewer into a sadist: You're glad when his cat gets killed or grateful when a shark appears in the ocean. Deborah Raffin, as his winsome girlfriend, is rarely allowed to stop laughing and wagging her head; the two grin and glow at each other until you yearn for a catastrophe.

An excellent storm near Madagascar provides some welcome abrasion. However, when Mr. Bottoms is later becalmed, someone should have prevented him from reciting "The Ancient Mariner." Still, the wet-sneakers crowd might enjoy this movie, and it's a privilege to tour the world with Mr. Nykvist.

1975 F 20, 38:2

SCORPIO RISING, by Kenneth Anger; FLAMING CREATURES by Jack Smith; RITE OF LOVE AND DEATH, by Yukio Mishima, Japanese with English subtitles, At the First Avenue Screening Room, at 61st Street. Total running time: two hours.

By NORA SAYRE

It's always fascinating to re-encounter experimental works after some years have passed—to see them outside the period that seemed to frame them. I first saw Kenneth Anger's "Scorpio Rising" in 1965, and it's pleasing to report that it holds up very well. The movie is playing today and tomorrow at the First Avenue Screening Room, and anyone who missed what was once called the underground should catch it.

"Scorpio," made in 1963, mocks the motorcycle cult and the voluptuous toughs who worship their machines. Blue-tinted shots of Marlon Brando in "The Wild One" and pin-ups of James Dean alternate with glimpses of Cecil B. De Mille's silent "King of Kings," and a Walpurgis party where genitals are plunged through a cardboard skeleton and mustard is squirted in a man's navel. The rock sound-track is hilarious: "Wind Up Doll," "She Wore Blue Velvet," "Baby, You're Torturing Me" and "I Will Follow Him" pound away throughout the proceedings, and there are flashes of some admirable abdomens. However, a few too many death's heads are included.

Oddly enough, the references to the nineteen-fifties, which seemed dated and rather ponderous in 1965, don't make the film appear old-fashioned now. Admittedly, one then saw it in an unfortunate context—draped in the mystique of the underground, when a number of inferior films employed some similar imagery, such as the juxtaposition of Christ and hipsters, or close-ups of all-purpose skulls. But after a decade's education in put-ons, one can savor the impudent freshness of "Scorpio" today.

•

Jack Smith's "Flaming Creatures" (1963) has aged—but so has the print, hence it's hard to fully imagine what the impact would have been in 1966, when the film was judged "indecent, lewd, and obscene," and the theater that showed it was closed by the police. (Also, I suspect that this print may have been cut.) Now, this lighthearted pantomime of a group-grope seems almost as genteel as your in-laws' home movies. Since many of the participants are male transvestites, some in quasi-Victorian costume, it's occasionally startling to see a real breast. Though the turn-ons are elderly, they're still amusing, and the film has acquired a historical interest.

"Rite of Love and Death" (1968) produced, directed written and performed by the late Yukio Mishima, was

based on his fine short story "Patriotism," which concerns a young lieutenant who committed suicide in 1936—rather than fight against his friends and fellow officers who had failed in a military coup against the Government. Both the story and the film are intensely romantic about death, but the strength of the prose version springs from anticipation as the man and his wife prepare to kill themselves. However, the silent movie is mannered, creaky and unintentionally comic—a warped recording of "Tristan and Isolde" dispels the soberness that was intended.

1975 F 21, 13:1

FILM VIEW

VINCENT CANBY

What's So Good About Bad Taste?

The recent opening of "Female Trouble," directed, written and photographed by John Waters, the Baltimorean who made "Pink Flamingos," prompts the following defense of Bad Taste, which might otherwise get a rotten reputation after being refined with such effective recklessness by master practitioners on the order of Lenny Bruce, Mark Twain, Mel Brooks, the successive staffs of the Harvard Lampoon, Woody Allen and a man whose name I never learned. He was at a recent cocktail party, listening to a woman talk about making one's own mulch, one of the ingredients of which, she said with discretion, was dog poop. Good heavens.

The man bore two repetitions of the phrase and then, impulsively, corrected the woman. Terse. Blunt. To the point. Everyone laughed, including the woman, who said that she thought her use of his phrase would have been in bad taste.

There are times when Bad Taste is the only acceptable mode of behavior, but Bad Taste should not be wasted on the dumb. It's one of the most important weapons in the continuing struggle for social betterment, in revolutions against political tyrannies and in sudden, spur-of-the-moment deflations of the pompous. Bad Taste, properly timed, has also been known to cure hiccups.

"Female Trouble," like "Pink Flamingos," trades on the good reputation of Bad Taste and then perverts it. It's a comedy that takes nothing seriously at first and then asks us to take it seriously at the end. The movie stars Divine, a mammoth female impersonator who is a grotesque extension of the fantasies of all little boys who grew up in the forties and fifties wanting to be Marlene Dietrich or Mae West. "Female Trouble" is the story of the rise to celebrity of Dawn Davenport, played by Divine, a parody of every Joan Crawford character who lammed out of a small town to seek fame and fortune in the big city—climaxing when the ecstatic Dawn is electrocuted for murder, an event she describes as "the page one of my life."

"Female Trouble" tries very hard to be in Bad Taste. Its women, real and fake, are horrors. Its men are frauds or dim-witted studs. Its tackiness is intentionally epic. The color has a garishness one associates with poorly developed eight-millimeter stock which is part of the Bad Taste it means to cultivate. There is a good deal of method behind the film. Too much. The problem is that the method eventually shows—in a speech towards the end when Dawn, who thinks of herself as an arch criminal, links her life of crime with the exploits of some of our more notorious mass murderers and assassins.

Mr. Waters makes the fatal mistake of attempting to explain his mini-minded drag show on the grounds that it's really where America is at.

Silly pretensions of that sort, openly admitted, are a wooden stake through the heart of Bad Taste, which survives only by being heedless.

Bad Taste of merit never seeks to justify itself. It

13

doesn't mind if we try, but it's too busy to worry about explanations. Bad Taste isn't easy.

• • •

.I can remember fondly about half of "Blazing Saddles" where Mel Brooks's evocation of Bad Taste was mostly in the form of rude, four-letter expletives. An essential part of Mr. Brooks's comedy has always been a mixture of determined rudeness and corny old gags that, when carefully pinched and pulled, suddenly seem brand new. Though it is more rude, "Blazing Saddles" isn't as funny as "Young Frankenstein" because the shock value of the words diminishes as the comic pattern is repeated. "Young Frankenstein" has its share of good Bad Taste gags, but the comedy is less dependent on random Bad Taste inspirations than on its genuine affection for the form that it parodies.

A certain amount of cruelty is always evident in Bad Taste of any worth. Ralph Bakshi's "Heavy Traffic" is absolutely terrible to almost everybody—blacks, Jews, women, midgets, policemen—but the effect is less to deny the value of everything than to make us reconsider the values that have been lost or twisted out of shape.

Some of the same sort of effect is gotten by Billy Wilder in two of his best Bad Taste movies, "Kiss Me, Stupid" and "The Fortune Cookie," unsentimental, uproarious comedies about petty greed and doomed-to-fail ambitions. Robert Downey's movies are not consistent, but their best moments sometimes attain heights of monumental Bad Taste and involve such things as incest, loathsome children, bestiality, physical handicaps. Mr. Downey, I suspect, would suffer a major amputation rather than justify these concerns, as Mr. Waters does.

• • •

Woody Allen, the best comic filmmaker at work today, is no stranger to the world of Bad Taste, especially its cruelties, though they are less apparent in his films than in the work of other directors. This, I think, is principally because the character he plays, though usually a rat, is as often victim as perpetrator.

Mr. Allen also has a fondness (which he shares with Mr. Brooks) for the kind of gags that once were simply racy but have been elevated to the status of true Bad Taste by various concerned, consciousness-raising groups. Remember the swishy robot in "Sleeper" and the huge, 40-foot-tall female breast that ravaged the countryside in "Everything You Ever Wanted to Know About Sex. . . ."?

The problem with Bad Taste is that it doesn't stand still. It varies from hemisphere to hemisphere, from country to country, state to state, family to family, person to person, day to day. One's tolerances change. I remember, as a very young man, being outraged at the things Westbrook Pegler used to write about Mrs. Roosevelt. Now I think I'd probably be delighted. Not that my admiration for her is less, but my appreciation for the kind of balancing impudence or outrage, which Bad Taste represents, is more.

1975 F 23, II:17:1

JACQUES BREL IS ALIVE AND WELL AND LIVING IN PARIS, directed by Denis Heroux; produced by Claude Heroux; co-producers, Paul Marshall and Cinevideo, Inc.; screenplay by Eric Blau; director of photography, Rene Verzier; editor, Yves Langlois; music conducted and orchestrated by Francois Rauber; an American Film Theater production presented by the Ely Landau Organization and Cinevision, Ltd. Running time: 98 minutes. At selected theaters.
WITH Elly Stone, Mort Shuman, Joe Masiell, Jacques Brel and others.

By VINCENT CANBY

"Jacques Brel Is Alive and Well and Living in Paris," the American Film Theater's second presentation of the season, has less importance as a movie than it has as a public service for those people who somehow managed not to see the Off Broadway stage show during its nearly five-year run at the Village Gate.

Maybe not. Maybe the people who did not see the

original show chose not to. In that case they may now choose not to see this very fancified film version, which opened at selected theaters here yesterday and will be given two more performances today.

•

The movie, directed by a young French - Canadian named Denis Heroux, tries very hard to recreate the sense of intimacy and spontaneity of the plotless show, which is actually 26 Brel songs performed by Elly Stone, Mort Shuman, Joe Masiell, a chorus and by Mr. Brel himself, who makes a fine and much too brief appearance in the film to sing one song.

Mr. Heroux, with the obvious cooperation of Eric Blau

Jacques Brel

and Mort Shuman, who conceived the original show and wrote the English translations of Mr. Brel's French lyrics, has transformed what was essentially a concert into an extravaganza of surreal images that keep messing things up. The images are vivid and disconnected to one another (good) but they inevitably wind up being visual translations of the lyrics (bad). It's a rather classy variation on the format employed by the old "Hit Parade" television show, though it's seldom as witty.

I should admit that I've never been a Brel maniac. Some of his songs are most engaging, ("Timid Frieda," "The Taxi Cab," "Amsterdam" and "Carousel"), and some make one long for the lyrics of Rod McKuen as comic relief. Mr. Brel is something else as a performer, which is apparent here when he comes on after intermission to sing his own "Ne Me Quittes Pas."

The song is not great, but the performance is—deadpan and pseudo-world-weary in the cabaret tradition of chansonniers, and Mr. Brel was one of the best until he decided officially to retire from performing to devote his full time to composing. Which was too bad.

Other people take Mr. Brel's songs too seriously. Or, to put it another way, they lack that touch of redeeming ham that can sometimes make charming and even moving a truly rotten lyric about love or death or war or some other little flea in mankind's ear.

•

Mr. Brel, you see, is inclined to write about rather large subjects, and the movie treats them so portentously it doesn't hesitate to give us a crucifixion scene. The song is "Sons of . . ." in which Miss Stone mocks Jesus for the world's ills, seriously, I think.

Furthermore, the camera isn't always kind to the performers with the exception of Mr. Shuman, a burly, comic man with a fine voice and an aggressive way of singing that turns criticism into nitpicking. Miss Stone, a small, Giulietta Masina-type with a voice big enough to stop a clock at 300 yards, and Joe Masiell, who might be described as the romantic lead, are continually being caught

in the act of hard-selling songs that ought to erupt with feeling.

What's worse—if not for me but for people who take the Brel lyrics to heart—is that a lot of the lyrics are difficult to hear and understand. Sometimes it's the fault of the orchestrations, but more often it's the fault of all those images and the changes of scenery and costumes. They get in the way of possible listening pleasure.

1975 F 25, 31:1

BOSS NIGGER, directed by Jack Arnold; screenplay by Fred Williamson, produced by Mr. Arnold and Mr. Williamson; distributed by Dimension Pictures. Running time: 87 minutes. At neighborhood theaters. This film has been rated PG.
Boss Nigger ....Fred Williamson
Amos ....D'Urville Martin
Mayor ....H. G. Armstrong
Jed ....William Smith
Clara Mae ....Carmen Hayworth
Miss Pruitt ....Barbara Lee

By VINCENT CANBY

"Boss Nigger," the black Western that opened in neighborhood houses yesterday, is the kind of unpretentious, ramshackle movie that can be a pleasant surprise if you stumble upon it without warning. To anticipate it with pleasure is to put a hex on it, however. Such anticipation is a burden that movies of this sort immediately collapse under. You've got to discover them yourselves, which means that writing about them becomes a discreet form of public disservice.

•

"Boss Nigger" stars Fred Williamson, one of the more popular of the new crop of black actors. He also wrote the screenplay and co-produced the movie with Jack Arnold, who directed it. Unlike most leading actors, black or white, Mr. Williamson seems to possess a genuine sense of humor that hasn't yet been systematized —like Burt Reynolds's—as part of a public personality. I have no idea whether Mr. Williamson is witty or not, though his movie is.

In "Boss Nigger" he plays a bounty hunter who, with his black sidekick (D'Urville Martin), finds he has to take over the law office of a frightened frontier town in order to collect a debt. The West is that timeless West where it's always 1870, but the complications of the plot suggest the kind of West where Roy Rogers used to ride in the nineteen-forties: the villains are immediately identifiable, the heroes incredibly noble as well as bullet-resistant, and coincidence is a fundamental narrative device.

•

The wit of the film is in Mr. Williamson's performance, which is an immensely self-assured parody of the Man

With No Name played by Clint Eastwood in Sergio Leone's films. Though the screenplay gives the supposedly comic lines to Mr. Martin, it's Mr. Williamson who is responsible for most of the good humor, ambling through the movie, doing the old Eastwood act of squinting, shooting and being irresistible to women with less effort than it takes most other men to select a tie.

Most black Westerns either ignore race or make it the fundamental point of the movie. "Boss Nigger" somenow manages to do both quite successfully. There's a lot made of the bigotry of the small Western town in which the black sheriff operates, but the effect of Mr. Williamson's Eastwoodesque performance has less to do with his color than with details observed and gently sent skyhigh.

1975 F 27, 30:2

WHO DOES SHE THINK SHE IS? directed by Patricia Lewis Jaffe and Gaby Rodgers, 60 minutes; HAVE A SEAT by Randall Fullmer, 3 minutes. At the Whitney Museum of American Art, Madison Avenue and 75th Street.

By NORA SAYRE

"Who Does She Think She Is?," by Patricia Lewis Jaffe and Gaby Rodgers, cuts pleasingly between the fantasies and the daily life of the novelist and playwright Rosalyn Drexler, one of our most inventive and least predictable wits. (I like Norman Mailer's reflection that "At her best, she writes like a cross between Henry Miller and Ronald Firbank.") The film opened yesterday at the Whitney Museum of American Art and will run through Tuesday.

In the mundane world, we watch Miss Drexler singing at Reno Sweeney, cooking "a weird omelet" for her son, chatting about marriage with her painter husband in his studio—she says that 27 years of monogamous marriage "embarrasses" her— discussing her early career as a wrestler (Rosa Carlo, the Mexican Spitfire), participating in a women's sexuality conference, questioning the editors of Screw, inspecting her own paintings, trading jokes and reprimands with her daughter (she inquires tenderly when her offspring's unemployment insurance will run out), and ordering friends out of her apartment because this movie's being shot.

She says that nonviolence appeals to her "because I'm a violent person" (but her husband disagrees). And she describes how she began writing as a child: Since she couldn't stop her parents from arguing, she wrote down their mutual accusations and then "presented them with a court record." Indignantly, they tore it up, which taught her "that writing has an effect and is disposable."

Miss Drexler asserts that "a little repression is interesting, because that's what you build your fantasies on." Here, her own fantasies take the form of charades: masquerading as Colette (whom she hugely admires) and spoofing "Chéri" with the aid of a young actor, or being a bank president who reluctantly opens an account for a snake. She's also interviewed by Jack Kroll of Newsweek, who explains that "her essential insight is that people and things are completely insane, and she speaks from inside the whale."

While you'll learn more about and from Miss Drexler by reading her books (I particularly relish "To Smithereens") than you will from this genial little movie—which may prove too elusive for those who don't know her work — it makes a very diverting visit with the writer. And surely no one can say "shut up" more pleasantly than she can.

1975 F 27, 32:1

THE HISTORY BOOK, a series of seven animated films produced by Jannik Hastrup and Li Vilstrup for the Danish Government Film Office, distributed by Tricontinental Film Center. Running time: 116 minutes. At the Film Forum, 88th Street west of Broadway. These films have not been rated.

By VINCENT CANBY

"The History Book" is the collective title for nine short educational films, made primarily for children, which dramatize a Marxist interpretation of the last 500 years of history. The technique of the films, a combination of various kinds of animation with live-action footage (newsreels, interviews), is imaginative and entertaining. The content is something else—judgmental, didactic and so selective that one might never understand that the Soviet Union had several allies in World War II.

All Marxist interpretations of history are inclined toward simplification, at least in their easy attributions of the cause for every effect. However, a Marxist interpretation of history aimed at small new minds, which have short attention spans, is close to ridiculous when it tries to ignore such things as the Protestant Reformation and the social needs supplied by capitalism, which are quite as important as the economic needs.

The series was originally produced by Jannik Hastrup and Li Vilstrup for the Danish Government Film Office. The English-language version, which has seven of the nine original films, can be seen today through Sunday at the Film Forum, where it will be repeated March 6-9.

"The History Book" is for film - buff, style - is - content grown-ups and nonaligned children.

1975 F 28, 15:1

A Realistic Appeal for Rights of Labor

By A. H. WEILER

Women's liberation, or better still, universal liberation from industrial injustice, is emphatically served in "Coup Pour Coup," which had its premiere yesterday at the First Avenue Screening Room. The French feature made in and around Rouen in 1971 and dealing with a garment-factory strike is labeled "a fiction film." It is as realistic as a forceful documentary. And if "Coup Pour Coup" is prolabor and shouts its pleas for justice with the fervor of Soviet agitprop films of the past, it nevertheless presents a strong case, even if passionately slanted.

•

Despite subtitles, "Coup Pour Coup" calls for further explanation. According to program notes, it is a collective effort involving about 100 people, including some "60 unemployed working women, film makers and actors and actresses," who were paid the same $300 a month fee and who collaborated on the filming and dialogue.

In shooting the film in a manner that was "a metaphor for the story of the film," the producers have achieved striking naturalism both in their simple story line and from their unprofessional cast. Essentially, "Coup Pour Coup" traces the stultifying effects of the assembly line on these women, some of whom do double duty as mothers after work. Inadequate pay, a hard-driving

---

The Program

COUP POUR COUP (Blow for Blow), a French film produced by Marin Karmitz with Cinema Services, Paris, and W.D.R., Cologne; United States distributor, Red Ball Films. At the First Avenue Screening Room, at 61st Street. This film has not been classified.

---

management, lip-serving union officials and the dismissals of two workers finally serve to provoke a strike and a sit-in take-over of the plant, a revolt that leads to ultimate victory and the meeting of their demands.

Although it is impossible to differentiate actor from authentic worker, the "performances" are, by and large, properly rough-hewn and seemingly ad lib. The old woman who reminisces about her strike experience in 1936 seems to be as real as the young, harried sit-in mother who rails at her husband's inability to handle their youngsters.

•

Perhaps the seizing of the plant owner, whom the workers plague "blow for blow" with the indignities they have had to endure, is a bit melodramatic. But the cast appears to project truth as well as passion and understanding of their newly found cama-

---

raderie in their resistance to hired thugs and the police, their cynical put-downs of union leaders and in the help from friends, farmers and other workers who have joined them in sympathy strikes.

"Coup Pour Coup" does not list credits for either a writer or a director, but if the collaborators here have fashioned a tract, they have also invested it with a good deal of human drama.

1975 Mr 3, 37:3

Abstract Expressionist Work Is at Whitney

By VINCENT CANBY

Stan Brakhage's "The Text of Light," which opened at the Whitney Museum of American Art yesterday, is 70 minutes of meditation upon color, an abstract expressionist work made by photographing light of varying intensities, refracted through heavy glass. To report that the heavy glass is, in reality, an ashtray may be a disservice since the effect of the film is lyrical, disconnected to identifiable objects or even time and space.

Seventy minutes is a bit long for this kind of film, which is not, after all, a canvas you can return to at your own speed and mood. The demands of the film—that you sit there until it's through with you—set up tensions that, at first, work

---

The Program

THE TEXT OF LIGHT, a film by Stan Brakhage; distributed by the New York Filmmakers Cooperative. Running time: 70 minutes. At the Whitney Museum of American Art, Madison Avenue at 75th Street. This film has not been rated.

---

against the liberating intentions of abstract expressionism.

However, if you can pass through the first 15 or 20 minutes without fidgeting, it's rather like breaking through the sound barrier. There is beauty and serenity in Mr. Brakhage's world of constantly changing colors and shapes. Sometimes they fill the screen like volcanic eruptions; at other times they merely punctuate the black background, suggesting lazy, radioactive caterpillars looking for rest.

"The Text of Light," which will be shown daily at the Whitney through next Tuesday, is one of the most cheerful and engaging in the series of nonrepresentational films the museum has been showing recently.

1975 Mr 6, 46:2

AT LONG LAST LOVE, directed, written and produced by Peter Bogdanovich; music and lyrics by Cole Porter; director of photography, Laszlo Kovacs; music arranged and conducted by Artie Butler; editor, Douglas Robertson; distributed by 20th Century-Fox. Running time: 115 minutes. At Radio City Music Hall, Avenue of the Americas at 50th Street. This film has been rated G.
Michael Oliver Pritchard 3d .. Burt Reynolds
Brooke Carter .... Cybill Shepherd
Kitty O'Kelly .... Madeline Kahn
Johnny Spanish ...... Duilio Del Prete
Elizabeth .... Eileen Brennan
Rodney James .... John Hillerman
Mabel Pritchard ...... Mildred Natwick

By VINCENT CANBY

"At Long Last Love," which opened yesterday at Radio City Music Hall, is Peter Bogdanovich's audacious attempt to make a stylish, nineteen-thirties Hollywood musical comedy with a superb score by Cole Porter but with performers who don't dance much and whose singing abilities might be best hidden in a very large choir.

It's a movie compounded of nerve and a lot of cinematic intelligence, which is no substitute for fun. "At Long Last Love" is almost entirely devoid of the kind of wit, vigor and staggering self-assurance with which real musical comedy performers — people like Fred Astaire, Ginger Rogers, Ethel Merman, Clifton Webb, Nanette Fabray, Charlotte Greenwood, Jack Buchanan—could turn a leaky rowboat of a show into the Ile de France.

"At Long Last Love" never quite sinks, but then it never leaves the pier. It may be some measure of my own feelings toward it that, at the end, I was exhausted. I'd been wanting it to work and had been straining to enjoy the good things that came along.

In the forefront of the good things are the Cole Porter songs, more than a dozen (most of them complete with their verses), some so beautifully integrated into the story that no seams show. I also liked the intentional vacuousness of Mr. Bogdanovich's screenplay, which is about what used to be called a madcap heiress who loves a playboy millionaire, who loves a wisecracking Broadway star who, in

---

turn, loves a charming Italian roué. There's also a comic valet and a no-nonsense ladies maid.

Then, too, there are some great art deco sets representing posh New York hotel suites, an elegant country club and a Long Island mansion with a foyer bigger than the Hall of Mirrors at Versailles. They are the frankly fake artifacts out of our Great Depression movies, settings made for Fred and Ginger and Eric Blore.

But there are no Fred and Ginger to inhabit them. Instead there is, most prominently, Cybill Shepherd as the madcap heiress, and casting Cybil Shepherd in a musical comedy is like entering a horse in a cat show. She's beautiful and lithe and has great lines but she's the wrong species. She's too big. She'd look terrific on a tennis court or playing golf but she's too literal to seem anything except gross in these fairy-tale surroundings.

When she attempts to sing, she also attempts to "act" the lyrics, and there is no sense of fantasy. The bluntness and naiveté that made her so appealing and so right in "Daisy Miller" are simply abrasive here.

The other performers have an easier time, especially the indestructibly funny Madeline Kahn, who plays the Broadway star, and Eileen Brennan, who plays the ladies maid, a role that manages to evoke performances by both Patsy Kelly and Helen Broderick. Duilio Del Prete, as the Italian roué, is a macho Erik Rhodes who signs passably, and John Hillerman is nicely stuffy as the valet who puts great store on social form.

The problem that Mr. Bogdanovich set himself in "At Long Last Love"—and which he never solves—is how to top these evocations of the past for our current pleasure. Because the past is always right, it may be that "At Long Last Love" would have seemed as vapid as it does even if it were an immensely

Burt Reynolds and Cybill Shepherd

clever film, which it isn't.

●

The film's most pleasant surprise is Burt Reynolds as the playboy millionaire, a performance that doesn't invite comparisons with any except earlier ones by Mr. Reynolds. He sings reasonably well. He dances. He plays the comedy lightly and earnestly, with low-key good humor of the kind that everyone else (except Miss Kahn) lacks.

Best of all is the Cole Porter score and it's to the director's credit that we can at least understand all the lyrics. But this joy is not unalloyed: You keep remembering how they sound when done by Frank Sinatra, Ella Fitzgerald or Ethel Merman.

1975 Mr 7, 22:1

'Daughters, Daughters!' Falls Short of Style

By VINCENT CANBY

"Daughters, Daughters!" is an Israeli comedy that becomes bleak when it means to be bittersweet and sentimental when it means to be robust. I suspect the reason it keeps falling short is that its central character is a man whose self-absorption is more cruel than comic.

Sabbetay Alfandari (Shai K. Ophir) is a rich, middle-aged businessman, a tyrant around the house, a man obsessed by the fact that he has eight daughters and no sons. He's terrible to his wife, to his daughters, to his young mistress. In a last desperate effort to get a male heir he resorts to magic and succeeds in making both his wife and his mistress even more miserable.

"Daughters, Daughters!," the official Israeli entry at the 1974 Cannes Film Festival, treats its male chauvinist pig too seriously to allow us laughs at his expense. We are, instead, appalled, mostly because Mr. Ophir is an actor of such heaviness that he never seems to be kidding, nor does his plight seem especially important in the context of the real-life Israel we see around him.

Like "the House on Chelouche Street," which was also directed by Menahem Golan, "Daughters, Daughters!" is a film that fails to

The Cast

DAUGHTERS, DAUGHTERS!, directed by Moshe Mizrahi; screenplay (Hebrew with English subtitles) by Mr. Mizrahi and Shai K. Ophir; produced by Menahem Golan; director of photography, Adam Greenberg; executive producer, Yoram Globus; editor, David Hoenig; music, Alex Kagan; distributed by Steinmann-Baxter Company. Running time: 88 minutes. At the 68th Street Playhouse on Third Avenue. This film has been rated P.G.

Sabbetay Alfandari........Shai K. Ophir
Bianca ....Zaharira Harifai
Joseph ....Yossef Shiloah
Esther ....Michal Bat-Adam

find a distinctive tragic comic style. What charm it has depends entirely on the performances, particularly on that of Zaharira Harifai, a big, handsome, expansive actress who transforms the wife into a woman of real comic pathos.

"Daughters, Daughters!" opened yesterday at the 68th Street Playhouse.

1975 Mr 10, 40:2

THE WRONG DAMN FILM, directed, written and produced by Carson Davidson; music, Arnold Eidus; director of photography, Richard Françis; editor, Mr. Davidson; distributed by Mr. Davidson. Running time: 84 minutes. At the First Avenue Screening Room, at 61st Street. This film has not been rated.

Alex Rounder........Barry Bostwick
Donna Compere... ...Barbara Dana
Agent Bradford
Businessman Wilton....Keene Curtis
Salesman Hughes
General Hatfield

By VINCENT CANBY

"The Wrong Damn Film" opened yesterday at the First Avenue Screening Room and the management should be scolded. Over the last year and a half the theater has built up a solid reputation as as a showcase for difficult but deserving films of quality that more commercial theaters would not touch.

The only reason I can imagine that any commercial theater might not touch "The Wrong Damn Film" is that it's terrible. It's a witless political satire padded out with the kind of weak sight gags that most film makers forget by the time they reach the age of eight—when it's no longer seems funny to make a man dive backward out of a swimming pool by reversing the motion of the film through the projector.

"The Wrong Damn Movie" was produced, directed, written and edited by Carson Davidson. He's also distributing it himself. It looks like a vanity project.

1975 Mr 11, 26:1

FUNNY LADY, directed by Herbert Ross; screenplay by Jay Presson Allen and Arnold Schulman, based on a story by Mr. Schulman; produced by Ray Stark; director of photography, James Wong Howe; music written by John Kander and Freb Ebb; additional songs by Billy Rose; editor, Marion Rothman; a Rastar production, distributed by Columbia Pictures. Running time: 140 minutes. At Loews State 2 Theater, Broadway at 45th Street, Orpheum Theater, 86th Street near Third Avenue, and Loews Tower East Theater, Third Avenue near 72d Street. This film has been rated PG.

Fanny Brice ....Barbra Streisand
Billy Rose ....James Caan
Nick Arnstein ....Omar Sharif
Bobby ....Roddy McDowall
Bert Robbins ....Ben Vereen
Norma Butler ....Carole Wells
Bernard Baruch ....Larry Gates
Eleanor Holm ....Heidi O'Rourke
Fran ....Samantha Huffaker

By VINCENT CANBY

"Funny Lady," wherein Ray Stark, the producer, and Barbra Streisand, his star, continue the Fanny Brice story they began in "Funny Girl," looks like a somewhat aged mirror-image of the first film. Everything that happens to Fanny, including the crises that prompt her to burst into song, as well as the new songs she bursts into, are calculated to repeat the responses evoked by "Funny Girl." If you have a good thing going for you, you obviously don't junk it.

●

In "Funny Lady" Fanny is a little older and a big Broadway star of the depressed nineteen-thirties, but her private life is a mess. Stardom is a hollow thing for poor Fanny. Her luck in men is still terrible. No sooner has she been dumped for the umpteenth time by

Barbra Streisand

Nick Arnstein, again played by Omar Sharif, than she becomes involved with and marries pint-sized song writer-producer Billy Rose, played by tall, athletic James Caan in the casting non sequitur of the decade.

Billy, like Nick, bristles at being referred to as "Mr. Brice." He also wears garish pajamas, a habit that, when combined with his own ambition for fame, makes their marriage an impossibility. It isn't long before Fanny is singing the blues again. And again and again.

As long as Miss Streisand as Fanny is singing the blues, or singing anything else, "Funny Lady" is superb entertainment, but the minute she stops the movie turns into a concrete soufflé. It's heavy and tasteless. Also, in attempting to be understanding to all its real-life characters (or to their memories), the movie is so bland that it makes little sense. Moments meant to be dramatic are embarrassingly bad.

●

The score includes a lot of fine old standards written by the late Mr. Rose ("Me and My Shadow," "More Than You Know," "Paper Moon") and a bunch of new songs by John Kander and Fred Ebb. Mr. Kander and Mr. Ebb are talented composers (they did "Cabaret" among other things) but I had the feeling that they wrote their score for "Funny Lady" with a gun at their heads, being told to come up with song-by-song equivalents to the great "Funny Girl" numbers by Jule Styne and Bob Merrill.

To match "Don't Rain on My Parade" from "Funny Girl," they have written "Let's Hear It for Me." For "Who Are You Now?" they've written "How Lucky Can You Get?" Herbert Ross, who staged the musical numbers in "Funny Girl" and directed everything in "Funny Lady," even repeats staging tricks from the first film, including a helicopter sequence. There's nothing intrinsically wrong with this, I suppose, but it makes "Funny Lady" predictable and it works against the star in unintended ways.

●

When Miss Streisand takes over a good song or tears into a revue sketch, there should be the sense of discovery we always get with unique performers. Our awareness of the calculation that went into this film diminishes even its good moments.

Miss Streisand looks sensational most of the time and is so forceful that even a good strong actor like Mr. Caan seems sort of feeble.

Nostalgia note: James Wong Howe, the great old Hollywood cameraman who did such films as "The Thin Man," "Yankee Doodle Dandy," "Sweet Smell of Success" and "The Rose Tattoo," was the cinematographer for "Funny Lady," which is as full of microscopically loving close-ups as a nature film about the life of a queen bee.

1975 Mr 12, 30:1

THE OTHER HALF OF THE SKY: A CHINA MEMOIR, written and produced by Shirley MacLaine; directed by Claudia Weill and Miss MacLaine; photographed by Miss Weill; edited by Aviva Slesin and Miss Weill. At the Whitney Museum of American Art, Madison Avenue and 75th Street. Running time: 74 minutes.

By A. H. WEILER

Shirley MacLaine adds a professional, if not fulfilling, credit to her Renaissance woman status as film star, author, producer and political activist with "The Other Half of the Sky," the documentary she wrote and produced as head of the women's group that visited China in 1973. The documentary was screened yesterday at the Whitney Museum of American Art.

The record of those three weeks in April and May—and 2,000 miles of travel—is picturesque, authentic and sincere but unfortunately no more inclusive of all points of view than those of the comparatively few, uniformly contented, industrious Chinese who appear on film.

Although this "China Memoir" is not explicit as to why the Mao Government invited Miss MacLaine and the "regular American women" she chose for the junket, as well as the "regular Chinese" and the English-speaking guides they met, all were charming and natural. Included were a Texas housewife (Pat Branson), a black Mississippi activist (Unita Blackwell), a Navajo (Ninibah Crawford), a California psychologist (Phyllis Kornhauden), a Bostonian (Margaret Whitman), a Puerto Rican sociologist (Rosa Marin) and a 13-year-old Californian (Karen Boutilier).

The trip—shot in appealing color by Claudia Weill, who led the distaff technical crew—jumps kaleidoscopically in visits to Canton, Shanghai, Hangchow and Peking. But the film evolves as a generally eye-catching spectrum of happy people in such places as homes, farms, day-care centers, city communes, schools, hospitals, the Great Wall, the ballet and Peking's May Day celebration, which was apparently appreciated by the inquisitive tourists and their cooperative hosts.

●

If this curious group concentrated on "the other half of the sky" achieved by the liberated Chinese women, it also focuses on some unusual vignettes of mainland life. Included among these is a Caesarian delivery filmed in intimate, clinical detail in which the mother is anesthetized by acupuncture and is even fed a meal during the painless operation. Also, there's a discussion of social and political issues with Teng Ying-chao, which unfolds as a rare and effective close-up of Premier Chou En-lai's wife.

Nowhere, however, is there an indication of crime, poverty, deprivation or unhappiness among China's 800 million people. And some of the Chinese seriously questioned by Miss MacLaine and the others, gently point out that artistic, musical and literary creativity must conform to Maoist principles.

While it is not noted on screen, Miss MacLaine told reporters on the eve of her journey that "in China, the equality of women is an official fact. In America we haven't achieved it. I'm curious to see how it all compares."

The comparison in "The Other Side of the Sky" is not entirely conclusive. It is an interesting, sometimes fascinating, if one-sided picture of the East that is still fairly mysterious.

1975 Mr 13, 45:1

THE GREAT WALDO PEPPER, directed and produced by George Roy Hill; screenplay by William Goldman, based on a story by Mr. Hill; director of photography, Robert Surtees; editor, William Reynolds; music, Henry Mancini; distributed by Universal Pictures. Running time: 107 minutes. At the Rivoli Theater, Broadway at 49th Street;

Bo Svenson and Robert Redford

Murray Hill Theater, 34th Street near Third Avenue, and 86th Street East Theater, 86th Street near Third Avenue. This film has been rated PG.
Waldo Pepper..................Robert Redford
Axel Olsson......................Bo Svenson
Ernst Kessler....................Bo Brundin
Mary Beth..................Susan Sarandon
Newt..........................Geoffrey Lewis
Ezra Stiles............Edward Herrmann
Dillhoefer......................Philip Bruns
Werfel..........................Roderick Cook
Patsy..................Kelly Jean Peters
Maude..........................Margot Kidder

By VINCENT CANBY

Goggles, gallantry and white silk scarves flying from the cockpits of ancient biplanes. George Roy Hill's "The Great Waldo Pepper," which opened at three theaters yesterday, is set in the nineteen - twenties and is about stunt flying when airplanes were truly dangerous, when they expressed a pilot's eccentricities, and when he could feel the immediate force of the air he was flying through. It's set in that long-ago time before airplanes had become flying bus terminals.

The film is about self-confident, nervy Waldo Pepper (Robert Redford), a former World War I pilot who, Snoopy-like, dreams of the glory he was denied during real combat and then, in a Pirandellian twist, realizes it at long last in Hollywood, where dreams are manufactured by the yard.

"The Great Waldo Pepper" is a most appealing movie. Its moods don't quite mesh and its aerial sequences are so vivid—sometimes literally breathtaking—that they upstage the human drama, but the total effect is healthily romantic. It's the kind of movie that enriches dreams even though its story seems sort of strung-out, like a first draft, and includes moments that slip into bathos.

As much as the movie is carried by its marvelous aerial sequences, it is made moving by Mr. Hill's passion for flying and his generosity toward the fanatics who bounced around the country after World War I, picking up small change while risking their lives at air circuses or running sightseeing tours from cleared cornfields.

It's this passion and generosity that make "The Great Waldo Pepper" seem a more

important, a more personal film than either of his two earlier smash hits, "Butch Cassidy and the Sundance Kid" and the phenomenally profitable "The Sting." You get the feeling that in this film, as well as in his "Slaughterhouse - Five," he has put himself on the line.

The faults of the film are real. The character of Waldo Pepper doesn't seem either mad or possessed enough to support the movie's ending. I'm not sure whether this has to do with the way the role is written or with the way Mr. Redford plays it, which is as a cheerful, fundamentally decent rogue, not too different from any number of other conventional adventure heroes. But Waldo Pepper should be different, someone who is probably as nasty as he is poetic, if the drama is to make sense.

The subsidiary characters are, with one important exception, more interesting. They include Waldo's good-natured, indestructible stunt-pilot pal, played by Bo Svenson, Margot Kidder as the girl to whom Waldo returns after every accident, Susan Sarandon as a small-town girl who gets a star-complex when she joins the flying circus, and Edward Herrmann who plays Waldo's designer-friend who has the crazy dream of building a monoplane.

The exception is Bo Brundin, who plays the former German ace who, in the postwar years, is reduced to tank-town stunting to make a living. His life has been all downhill since the momentous morning when, over a French countryside during the war, he shot down four Allied pilots in a matter of seconds. Again it may be that the role is awkwardly written—I have no way of being sure—but Mr. Brundin doesn't seem to help it.

For most people in the audience I suspect that the flying sequences will be enough, and they are, in a

word, smashing — outside loops, wing-walking, midair transfers, and crack-ups that can be believed when seen.

1975 Mr 14, 24:1

THE PRISONER OF SECOND AVENUE, directed and produced by Melvin Frank; screenplay by Neil Simon; director of photography, Philip Lathrop; film editor, Bob Wyman; music, Marvin Hamlisch; released by Warner Bros. At the Sutton Theater, Third Avenue and 57th Street. Running time: 98 minutes. This film is classified PG.
Mel Edison.................Jack Lemmon
Edna.........................Anne Bancroft
Harry Edison..................Gene Saks
Pauline.................Elizabeth Wilson
Pearl.....................Florence Stanley
Belle.......................Maxine Stuart
Man Upstairs...................Ed Peck
Charlie.....................Gene Blakely
Psychiatrist..............Ivor Francis

By A. H. WEILER

If Neil Simon's adaptation of his 1971 Broadway hit, "The Prisoner of Second Avenue," which arrived at the Sutton yesterday, is less than an overpowering study of a married couple driven to distraction by the irritations and indignities of local middle-class living, it still scores valid points, both serious and funny. This time, the largely farcical kind of Manhattan madnesses Mr. Simon observed in his 1970 film, "The Out-of-Towners," have the impact of reality that has been humanely dulled by injections of relevant comedy.

•

Comparisons are odious, but it should be noted that the play hasn't been changed appreciably in its transition to the screen. And, if Melvin Frank's direction is polished but not innovative, he is ably aided by a cast headed by Jack Lemmon and Anne Bancroft, who project forcefully natural characterization that are as realistic as the authentic Second Avenue and other New York sites caught by the color cameras.

As in the original, New York is hardly a wonderful town for Mr. Simon's principals. Mr. Lemmon is frustrated and anxiety-ridden because of the faulty air-conditioning and inconsiderate neighbors in his high-rise apartment house, among other things. And, his fraying nerves aren't helped much when he is dismissed by his faltering firm. As a jobless ad executive, he cannot be blamed for railing at an unemployment office clerk. And he shouldn't be criticized for banging on fragile walls, cursing the neighbors, who douse him with water in retaliation, and developing neuroses inflamed by enforced idleness and visits to a noncommittal psychiatrist.

If Anne Bancroft, as his truly loving helpmate who resolutely gets a job to support them, becomes tense and confused to the point of paranoia, she, too, can't be faulted for her rising fears when she loses that job and must decide whether to accept financial help from her husband's concerned, if questioning, relatives.

Mr. Lemmon, no stranger to Mr. Simon's work ("The Odd Couple," "The Out-of-Towners"), and Miss Bancroft are simply an unromanticized, believable team as recognizable in their comic and serious give-and-take as many of New York's scrambling millions. And they get sturdy, pointed support from Gene Saks, as Mr. Lemmon's well.-to-do, plain-speaking but doting older brother and Elizabeth Wilson and Florence Stanley, as his careful sisters, among others.

•

They aren't involved in

Greek tragedy or in commonplace television situation comedy. Mr. Simon is serious about a theme that isn't earth-shaking and he understandably cloaks its gravity with genuine chuckles that pop up mostly as radio news bulletins such as the flash that a Polish freighter has just run into the Statue of Liberty. And, with a cast whose members appreciate what they're saying and doing, the gnawing problems of "Second Avenue" become a pleasure.

1975 Mr 15, 18:1

FILM VIEW

VINCENT CANBY

Not So Bad, Not So Good

Bad movies by ambitious no-talents are easy to write about, either with pious indignation and outrage or with venom of the sort that always sells more papers than affection ever did. The most difficult films to criticize are the ambitious movies that fail in parts, that are neither bad nor good, neither smash hits nor dismal flops, in spite of the intelligence and talents of the people involved. It's especially tough if you think you can see evidence of the talent and intelligence throughout the particular film.

You find yourself writing sentences that start "It's a failure even though . . ." or "On the other hand . . ." Sentences that begin with "on the other hand" are as boring to write as they are to read. They mean that nobody—neither the writer nor the reader—is going anywhere. Everyone sits around on dead-center being glum and registering tactful pain.

It was that sort of week recently when, in a very short period of time, I saw Peter Bogdanovich's "At Long Last Love," producer Ray Stark's "Funny Lady," a sort of retread of "Funny Girl" directed by Herbert Ross, and George Roy Hill's "The Great Waldo Pepper." With the possible exception of "Funny Lady," none of these three is bad, but only one, "The Great Waldo Pepper," could be called likeable. Because they are movies that might be easily dismissed except by special interest groups (Burt Reynolds fans, Barbra Streisand fans, Robert Redford fans), I feel an almost suicidal need to defend them, sort of, without once saying "on the other hand. . . ."

"At Long Last Love" is a 1930-ish Hollywood musical comedy, beautifully and wittily set, costumed, decorated and scored (with more than a dozen songs by the late Cole Porter) and starring Cybill Shepherd and Burt Reynolds who have, between them, four left feet and who sing with a gallantry that reminds me of small children taking their first solo swim across the deep end. They've been taught the fundamentals but haven't yet attained ease or style.

Miss Shepherd may be the most magnificent example of American WASPdom in movies today, a quality that served her well in both Bogdanovich's "Daisy Miller" and Elaine May's "The Heartbreak Kid." As a madcap heiress, circa 1935, in "At Long Last Love," she is merely waspish. She is not unlike Ginger Rogers in this respect, but when Ginger was lured out on the dance floor by Fred Astaire, the pouting and peevishness disappeared and we suddenly could recognize the voluptuous intelligence Fred had been courting all that time.

There are no comparable revelations in "At Long Last Love." Everyone tries very hard but when you notice that performers like Madeline Kahn and

Eileen Brennan are trying, you know that something is decidedly wrong, not with them but with the material—the pacing, the lines. Only Burt Reynolds comes through with honors, playing Bogdanovich's idea of Depression Hollywood's idea of a playboy millionaire with just the right mixture of comic fervor and detachment.

Bogdanovich, a very good film critic before he became a director, has an academic sense of humor. He appreciates the techniques of physical (slapstick) humor, and knows how to employ them, as he did in "What's Up, Doc?" but romantic comedy eludes him, partially because it's wrongly cast.

●　　　　●　　　　●

If there's a Beverly Hills in the sky for thoughtful sons-in-law then Ray Stark has certainly earned himself a corner lot with a heated swimming pool through his devotion to the memory of his late mother-in-law, Fanny Brice.

"Funny Lady" continues what a press release refers to as "the saga" of Miss Brice, begun in "Funny Girl," with all of the solemnity and attention to ritual that you might expect in the dramatization of a Norse legend. Herbert Ross was the director and Jay Presson Allen and Arnold Schulman wrote the screenplay but one suspects that the real auteurs of "Funny Lady" were Miss Streisand, Mr. Stark and the millions and millions of dollars earned by the original film, which has been copied even down to the new songs (by John Kander and Fred Ebb) and a lot of the lighting and camera angles.

Omar Sharif reprises his role as Nicky Arnstein and James Caan plays Billy Rose who, in middle years, treated Fanny as badly as Nicky did in her youth. Poor Fanny. She has terrible taste in men. She also has an unreliable eye for detail. In the film she keeps calling Billy Rose a hustling little creep and other phrases that refer to his small stature, though Caan clearly towers above her. The drama is absurd but a lot of the musical numbers, particularly the comic ones, are first-rate.

"The Great Waldo Pepper" is more than just likeable. It's hugely appealing even as you become aware that it seems to be a movie in search of itself. The original story by director George Roy Hill (screenplay by William Goldman) is about a former World War I pilot named Waldo Pepper (Robert Redford), who barnstorms around the middle west in the late twenties trying to make a living and fabricating legends of his wartime exploits. How he finally achieves glory makes for a fascinating twist, but by the time the movie reaches this point you get the feeling it's been dawdling between the beginning and the end.

"The Great Waldo Pepper" seems sort of unfinished, like a Broadway show that needs more time on the road. A lot of the dawdling is made up of spectacular aerial sequences that are as good as anything you've probably ever seen about the early days of flying. The characters and characterizations by good actors (Redford, Bo Svenson, Margot Kidder) are more or less functional.

"The Great Waldo Pepper" is a lot less smooth and classy than two other Hill films that starred Redford ("Butch Cassidy and The Sundance Kid" and "The Sting") but it exhibits an affection for—and generosity toward—fanatics (in this case, fliers) that make it not only very appealing but probably the most personal film Hill has ever made.

1975 Mr 16, II:17:1

Bill Owen, left, and Alan Bates

IN CELEBRATION, directed by Lindsay Anderson; screenplay by David Storey, based on his stage play; produced by Ely Landau; executive producer, Otto Plasckes; editor, Russell Lloyd; director of photography, Dick Bush; an American Film Theater production, presented by the Ely Landau Organization and Cinevision, Ltd. Running Time: 131 minutes. At selected theaters. This film has been rated PG.
Andrew Shaw .... Alan Bates
Colin Shaw .... James Bolam
Steven Shaw .... Brian Cox
Mrs. Shaw .... Constance Chapman
Mrs. Burnett .... Gabrielle Daye
Mr. Shaw .... Bill Owen

By VINCENT CANBY

David Storey's "In Celebration," the American Film Theater's third offering in its current subscription season, brilliantly demonstrates what the A.F.T. is supposed to be up to: presenting films that preserve the quality and excitement of superior theatrical performances of plays we might not otherwise be able to see.

"In Celebration" is an early play by Mr. Storey, the English novelist ("This Sporting Life") and playwright who has been represented on Broadway by "Home" and "The Changing Room." Although "In Celebration" has been done by the Arena Stage in Washington, it's never been seen in New York, an oversight now corrected by this fine, spare screen adaptation, directed by Lindsay Anderson with most of the cast he directed in the play's original Royal Court production in London.

●

The film, which was given two performances at selected theaters here yesterday, will be repeated twice today.

"In Celebration" is a family play that recalls most immediately O'Neill's "Long Day's Journey Into Night" though the spectacular passions of the O'Neill characters appear muted in Mr. Storey's work. The passions are there, certainly, but they are inhibited as much by love as by class attitudes. Also, they lack the furious poetry with which the Tyrones of "Long Day's Journey" expressed themselves while tearing into one another.

The outbursts of Mr. Storey's characters are in no way cathartic. They reveal ancient wounds, which, seen briefly, are scratched again in passing. New scabs form on old scars and everyone tries to ignore the pain.

The setting is a coal mining town in the north of England and the occasion is the wedding anniversary of a wiry, 64-year-old miner named Shaw (Bill Owen) and the girl above his station he married 40 years earlier after getting her in trouble. Mrs. Shaw (Constance Chapman) is a model wife and mother, the principal mover behind the three sons who went to the university, moved out of the working class and now, each in a different way, feel disconnected from their environments.

Andrew (Alan Bates), the eldest, has thrown over his career as a lawyer to become an abstract painter of no great drive or talent. Colin (James Bolam) is a successful labor negotiator for a large automobile company. Colin is a fastidious man. He talks in upbeat clichés but he clings to his self-confidence with desperation, as if it were the only life-preserver around. Steven Shaw (Brian Cox), the youngest son, is on dead-center, the father of four children and a writer with a block the size of the Tower of London.

In the course of the reunion, Mr. Storey presents a family portrait that is immensely moving and sad. The cramped, neat little row house, recently refurnished by the affluent Colin, hides skeletons everywhere. Resentments fester but only Andrew, played with edgy flamboyance by Mr. Bates, comes close to exposing them. Andrew remembers his mother bragging of having once studied "human hygiene," then he adds: "There are no alien bodies in this house."

●

They are all alien bodies, Mr. Storey seems to be saying, but through no conscious fault of anyone. Mrs. Shaw, played by Miss Chapman with a kind of near-sighted innocence, may well be the villain even though there's never been any malice in her.

Mr. Anderson, who directed the film version of "This Sporting Life," has succeeded in making a very complete, full-bodied film of Mr. Storey's play without being tricky or intrusive. When the camera ranges beyond the Shaw parlor, the principal battleground, there is always a point to the movement. Mr. Anderson has also gotten terrific performances from everyone, especially Mr. Bates, Miss Chapman and Mr. Cox, as the most troubled of the Shaw sons.

Toward the end of the film, "In Celebration" recalls Chekhov. More things have been said than anyone wants to acknowledge. In spite of this, life will go on more or less as before. There is a major difference between Chekhov and Mr. Storey, however. There is no brighter tomorrow for the Shaws. It's already arrived—and it's no less bleak than yesterday.

1975 Mr 18, 30:1

A MAN, A WOMAN AND A KILLER, created by Richard A. Richardson, Richard R. Schmidt and Wayne Wang; directed by Mr. Schmidt and Mr. Wang; filmed, edited and produced by Mr. Schmidt, with Lura S. Janda as executive producer. At the Bleecker Street Cinema, 144 Bleecker Street. Running time: 78 minutes.

Dick	Richard A. Richardson
Ed	Edward Nylund
Z	Caroline Zaremba

By A. H. WEILER

Despite a provocative title, "A Man, a Woman and a Killer," which had its premiere yesterday at the Bleecker Street Cinema, is, at best, an only mildly interesting series of soul-searchings. As a first feature recently completed on the West Coast by a 30-year-old Californian, Richard R. Schmidt, with the cooperation of a relatively unknown small team, the convoluted comedy-drama rarely rises above an over-all look of unresolved improvisations.

The film, a program note explains, "presents itself as a gangster story," which actually becomes the portraits of "three lives searching through the script to find their own identities." Much of the script is projected through the "writings" of one of the actors, Richard A. Richardson, and much of this dialogue is, for no especially effective reason, repeated as subtitles.

Mr. Richardson, lanky, laconic and square-jawed, is, we discover after many circuitous reflections, a Vietnam veteran who has knocked around and "always wanted to make a film" but whose "writings" and performance hardly sparkle. Caroline Zaremba, a pretty, if somewhat wan brunette given to posing and sudden bursts of laughter is, we learn, finding her identity through her all-too-recent discovery of Mr. Richardson in the making of the film. And, Edward Nylund, a benign 60-year-old man enlisted to play the "killer," is cheerfully involved because "I'm the only older person they knew."

But despite their obvious sincerity, their identities remain vague and unimpressive and "A Man, a Woman and a Killer" emerges as a largely static and undramatic film about the making of a film.

1975 Mr 18, 32:1

LENNY BRUCE WITHOUT TEARS, a documentary directed, written and produced by Fred Baker; continuity and narration written by John Parson; editor, Edward Deitch; narrated by Mr. Baker; distributed by Fred Baker Films, Ltd. Running time: 78 minutes. At the Bleecker Street Cinema, 144 Bleecker Street. This film has not been rated.

By VINCENT CANBY

What the world needs now is not another Lenny Bruce film on the order of Fred Baker's documentary, "Lenny Bruce Without Tears," which opened yesterday at the Bleecker Street Cinema. There is nothing very wrong with the movie, but there's not much of interest in it unless, by some curious combination of coincidences, you've missed all the other Lenny Bruce films, the kinescopes of his TV appearances, the books, the newspaper and magazine articles and reminiscences, the recordings of his nightclub routines.

"Lenny Bruce Without Tears" is a competent compilation of familiar Bruce material. There are interviews with Mr. Bruce, recording of some of his routines, some material from his appearances on the old Steve Allen Show (which you may have seen already), plus interviews with people like Malcolm Muggeridge, Kenneth Tynan, Jean Shepard, Paul Krassner and Mort Sahl.

Still the most interesting Lenny Bruce film around is the filmed record of his nightclub routine, made shortly before he died in 1966. It was called simply "Lenny Bruce" when it was first released in 1967 and retitled "The Lenny Bruce Performance Film" for its recent re-issue.

Lenny Bruce is a footnote to American social history. Movie like Mr. Baker's are footnotes to a footnote.

1975 Mr 19, 59:1

Excess and Excitement and Many Decibels

By VINCENT CANBY

Ken Russell makes movies the way another man might design a ride through a funhouse. He deals in headlong but harmless plunges from giddy heights, abrupt changes of pace, joke turns, anachronistic visual effects, ghouls that pop out of the dark, all accompanied by sound of a force to loosen one's most firmly rooted back teeth.

The method is spectacular but it has seemed wickedly foolish in movies like "The Music Lovers" (about Tchaikovsky), "The Savage Messiah" (about Gaudier-Brzeska) and "The Devils" (an adaptation of Huxley's "The Devils of Loudun"). Now at long last the man and his method have found a nearly perfect match in subject matter, "Tommy," The Who's rock opera written by guitarist-composer Pete Townshend.

●

"Tommy" can take being fiddled with, and Mr. Russell's "Tommy" virtually explodes with excitement on the screen. A lot of it is not quite the profound social commentary it pretends to be, but that's beside the point of the fun. "Tommy," which opened yesterday at the Ziegfeld Theater, is mad, funny, irreverent, passionately overproduced, very, very loud and full of the kind of magnificent physical energy that usually wrecks a movie by calling attention to performance.

"Tommy" is a solemn tale

The Cast

TOMMY, directed by Ken Russell; screenplay by Mr. Russell, inspired by the rock opera by Pete Townshend; additional musical material by John Entwistle and Keith Moon; produced by Robert Stigwood and Mr. Russell; executive producers, Beryl Vertue and Christopher Stamp; music director, Mr. Townshend; directors of photography, Dick Bush and Ronnie Taylor; editor, Stuart Baird; distributed by Columbia Pictures. Running time: 110 minutes. At the Ziegfeld Theater, 54th Street west of the Avenue of the Americas. This film has been rated PG.

Nora Walker	Ann-Margret
Frank Hobbs	Oliver Reed
Tommy	Roger Daltrey
Pinball Wizard	Elton John
Preacher	Eric Clapton
Uncle Ernie	Keith Moon
Specialist	Jack Nicholson
Group-Capt. Walker	Robert Powell
Cousin Kevin	Paul Nicholas
Acid Queen	Tina Turner
Young Tommy	Barry Winch
Priest	Arthur Brown
Sally Simpson	Victoria Russell

that must not be taken too seriously. It's an elaborate put-on about the terrible victimization of a small boy who is traumatized deaf, dumb and blind when he sees his stepfather murder his real father. Young Tommy then goes on to become the pinball champ of the world and, eventually, after he miraculously regains his senses, the new messiah who preaches salvation through pinball playing.

●

Mr. Russell's style, which had the effect of literalizing the artistic impulse in "The Music Lovers" and "The Savage Messiah," seems to liberate Mr. Townshend's rock score and lyrics, which are sometimes in embarrassingly dead earnest.

"Tommy" is composed of excesses. Bad jokes or heavy-handed satire are redeemed by everyone—director, production designer, orchestrators, actors—going too far, which is, after all, what the original "Tommy" is all about: a world inhabited by people too jaded to react to anything but overdoses.

The performers are extravagantly fine, particularly Ann-Margret who, as Tommy's mother, ages 20 years in the course of the film (largely through the increased application of blue eye shadow) and sings and dances as if the fate of Western civilization depended upon it. She is tough, vulgar, witty and game. The Who's lead singer, Roger Daltrey, plays the grown-up Tommy with a drive that matches Ann-Margret's while successfully simulating show biz innocence. Oliver Reed is, correctly, almost a cartoon as the opportunistic stepdad. He also sings quite nicely.

●

The movie, which has the structure of a vaudeville show, is laced together with specialty bits, some of which are simply jokes (Jack Nicholson playing a vacuous Harley Street medical specialist) and some of which are production numbers as riveting as rock can be at its best. These include a sequence in which Tina Turner shows up as The Acid Queen who attempts to cure the catatonic Tommy, and others with Elton John, as the Pinball Wizard defeated by Tommy, and Eric Clapton, as the Preacher who presides over a Lourdes-like shrine devoted to the healing powers of St. Marilyn (Monroe).

As I said, it's all fairly excessive and far from subtle, but in this case good taste would have been wildly inappropriate and a fearful drag.

1975 Mr 20, 48:1

THE YAKUZA, produced and directed by Sydney Pollack; screenplay by Paul Schrader and Robert Towne; story by Leonard Schrader; director of photography, Okazaki Kozo; film editors, Thomas Stanford and Don Guidice; music, Dave Grusin; released by Warner Bros. At the Criterion Theater, Broadway at 45th Street and the Beekman Theater, Second Avenue at 65th Street. Running time: 123 minutes. This film is classified R.

George Tanner	Brian Keith
Harry Kilmer	Robert Mitchum
Tanaka Ken	Takakura Ken
Wheat	Herb Edelman
Dusty	Richard Jordan
Eiko	Kishi Keiko
Tono	Okada Eiji
Goro	James Shigeta
Kato	Kyosuke Mashida

Beware "The Yakuza." This movie, which opened yesterday at the Criterion and Beekman theaters, is a cinematic hybrid that crosses American stars, writers and a director with a popular Japanese film form. To come upon it unsuspecting is a little like opening an Almond Joy wrapper and finding inside the arrangement of fish, rice and seaweed known as nori maki.

The effect is surprising; the contents prove, upon examination, not unattractive; but the product as a whole has a potential for evoking revulsion or ridicule from anyone whose mind clenches at the exotic or whose heart is firmly set upon an Almond Joy.

●

Yakuza are Japanese thugs, who, in their most romanticized form, are latter-day samurai with a touch of Robin Hood thrown in. As a group, they are comparable to the Mafia, with warring factions, overlords, a boss of bosses and a formal code of behavior.

"The Yakuza" is a movie about obligation—of American to American, of Japanese to American and of American to Japanese. It is also, in keeping with its genre, a movie of bloody gunplay and swordplay, of death and dismemberment unreeled with such momentum that the expectant and horrified mind's eye is sent hurtling repeatedly past the audacious brinksmanship of the editing into unseen but imagined freshets of gore.

Out of a sense of obligation, Harry Kilmer (Robert Mitchum) agrees to help and old friend, George Tanner (Brian Keith), whose daughter has been kidnapped by a yakuza boss who believes that Keith has cheated him on a gun deal. To accomplish his undertaking, Mitchum is compelled to enlist the aid of Tanaka Ken played by Takakura Ken), a former yakuza and a moral relic who is obligated to Mitchum despite long-standing enmity.

What follows is predictably combative, reaching a breathtakingly tense climax as Takakura, armed with a sword and backed by a gun-toting Mitchum, takes on a swarm of adversaries.

Although admirable for its understated contrast of hoary ritual with modern trappings, "The Yakuza," written by Paul Schrader and Robert Towne ("Chinatown") and with Sydney Pollack ("The Way We Were") as producer-director, is also didactic. It is slowed by the need to instruct its audience in the way of the yakuza; it is marred in its early exposition by some impenetrable Japanese-accented English; it is burdened by the attenuation of an unexciting love interest (which Mitchum's character freely admits being too old for); and a couple of formidably important revelations are simply dropped in, as though no one had the time to plot them properly.

●

To some extent this movie pays the penalty for breaking ground with a new audience.

But its merits as an action film strongly dosed with exotic culture and subculture are offset by obvious flaws. Neither fans of Almond Joy nor of nori maki are likely to be wholly satisfied by "The Yakuza," but those who don't mind sampling both won't go away famished.

LAWRENCE VAN GELDER

1975 Mr 20, 48:1

THE FOUR MUSKETEERS, directed by Richard Lester; screenplay, George MacDonald Fraser, based on Alexander Dumas's novel "The Three Musketeers;" director of photography, David Watkins; film editor, John Victor Smith; music, Lalo Schifrin; produced by Alexander Salkind; released by Twentieth Century-Fox Film Corporation. At Loews State 2, Broadway and 45th Street and Loews Cine, Third Avenue at 86th Street. Running time: 103 minutes. This film is clasified PG.

Athos	Oliver Reed
Mme. Bonancieux	Raquel Welch
Aramis	Richard Chamberlain
D'Artagnan	Michael York
Porthos	Frank Finlay
Rochefort	Christopher Lee
Louis XIII	Jean Pierre Cassel
Anne of Austria	Geraldine Chaplin
Duke of Buckingham	Simon Ward
Milady	Faye Dunaway
Cardinal Richelieu	Charlton Heston

"What could be better than The Three Musketeers?" the ads ask, and then go on to answer, "The Four Musketeer." I agree.

Richard Lester's "The Four Musketeers," which opened yesterday at Loew's State 2 and Cine Theaters, is the concluding and (to my way of thinking) better half of the two part film Mr. Lester introduced last year as "The Three Musketeers." Everything about the film — including the cast — is the same only lighter, funnier, less burdened by exposition, though there are still large remnants of the old Dumas plot to be got through.

The Queen of France (Geraldine Chaplin) is still carrying on with the English Duke of Buckingham (Simon Ward) who is warring with Anne's husband, Louis XIII (Jean Pierre Casse). The King's loyal Musketeers spend a great deal of their time saving pretty Anne's reputation from exposure by the ambitious Cardinal Richelieu (Charlton Heston), who is always the villain of the piece though his vision of France is positively De-Gaullean.

Even the romantic criss-crossing of loyalties seems funnier in this second film, perhaps because one doesn't spend too much time worrying about who is doing what to whom or why. It doesn't matter.

"The Four Musketeers" is beautifully light-headed, the sort of movie in which Raquel Welch (as the Queen's seamstress) gets herself kidnapped by what is, in effect, a pile of watermelons. It's a movie that asks the questions: How do you blindfold a one-eyed man who already wears an eye-patch on his bad eye? Vertically?

The 17th-century settings are grand and occasionally almost surreal, as when we watch the King and Queen picnicking in a field of daisies, listening to a portable pipe organ, while several rebels hang by their necks from a nearby tree.

The time is seasonless, as in any good fairy tale, winter one day and midsummer the next. The funniest, most stylish performances are those of Mr. Heston as the wicked Cardinal, and Faye Dunaway as Richelieu's most accomplished spy, though everyone else is also in top form, including Michael York as D'Artagnan and Miss Welch as his accident-prone mistress.

One of these days "The Three Musketeers" and "The Four Musketeers" will make a terrific double-bill.

VINCENT CANBY.

1975 Mr 20, 48:1

AND NOW MY LOVE, directed by Claude Lelouch; screenplay by Mr. Lelouch and Pierre Uytterhoeven; director of photography, Jean Collomb; editor, Georges Klotz; music by Francis Lai; released by Avco Embassy Pictures. At the Fine Arts Theater, 58th Street between Park and Lexington Avenues. Running time: 121 minutes. This film is classified PG.
Sarah, her mother, her grandmother, ... Marthe Keller
Simon .... Andre Dussolier
Sarah's father, camera operator, Sarah's grandfather .... Charles Denner
Sarah's Italian girlfriend .... Carla Gravina
Simon's friend .... Charles Gerard
Gilbert Becaud .... Himself

By A. H. WEILER

As a somewhat cynical French romantic in love with love and with movie cameras, Claude Lelouch first clicked here in 1966 with "A Man and a Woman." He scores with "And Now My Love," which arrived at the Fine Arts yesterday. This exploration of how an attractive young pair of Parisian strangers come to be smitten at first sight evolves as a tender dissection of the couple and of the two generations that preceded them. It makes the improbable fairy-tale ending realistic and persuasive.

"And Now My Love" is, in fact, more sweeping than its French title, "Tout Une Vie," implies in the succession of lives exposed to illustrate the family backgrounds of the hero and heroine, who are fated to meet only at the film's end. If the director was a mite self-indulgent with his camera in "A Man and a Woman," "The Crook," and "Love Is a Funny Thing," he has used it this time for constructive and illuminating effect.

The past, he strongly indicates, impinges on the present. So, with speed, humor and appreciation of vintage movie making, we're introduced to the respective grandparents by way of pre-World War I silent but sub-titled black-and-white footage, then to the couple-to-be's Jewish parents, who've met after being freed from Nazi concentration camps.

Thus, the parallel inspections of preceding generations add substance to the film's contemporary personalities. Sarah, the daughter of the concentration-camp survivor, is as troubled as her doting father. When she falls in love as a teen-ager with the pop singer Gilbert Becaud, her opposite number, Simon, is being jailed for stealing some Becaud records.

Their careers proceed along trying paths to maturity; she goes from bored dilettante to conscientious social awareness, and he from convict to work with porno and commercial films and, eventually, to recognition as a rising movie maker.

But Mr. Lelouch is not just spinning a chronology. Included in his kaleidoscopic inspection are pertinent observations on the spinning social scene. And the implications of ideologies and the future being spelled out by scientists also serve to develop believable human beings.

Screen: Boring 'Arnold'

ARNOLD, directed by Georg Fenady; screenplay, Jameson Brewer and John Fenton Murray; director of photography, William Jurgenson; film editor, Melvin Shapiro; music, George Duning; produced by Andrew J. Fenady; released by American International Pictures. At neighborhood theaters. Running time: 95 minutes. This film is classified PG.
Karen .... Stella Stevens
Robert .... Roddy McDowall
Hester .... Elsa Lanchester
Jocelyn .... Shani Wallis
Evan Lyons .... Farley Granger
Minister .... Victor Buono
Governor .... John McGiver
Constable Hooks .... Bernard Fox

"Arnold," now playing at neighborhood theaters, is a movie that mixes the merry with the macabre and produces not laughter and chills but boredom and embarrassment.

Briefly, it is the story of a corpse, who, believing himself freed of marriage by the feat of dying—after all, his wife is not a wife now but a widow—arranges his marriage to his mistress. She is to receive the bulk of his considerable estate if she will simply remain always at his side. He has a sit-up casket that plays tape cassettes.

The mistress has no such ideas, and a succession of murders ensues.

Aside from being technically sloppy and grossly illogical, "Arnold" is the sort of movie that relies on bird-droppings and double-entendre for humor.

Its chief interests lies in the opportunity it offers for renewing acquaintance with some old favorites — Elsa Lanchester as the corpse's dotty sister, Stella Stevens as the corpse's bride, Shani Wallis as the widow, Roddy McDowall as the bride's lover, and Farley Granger as the lover of the widow and the bride.

All of them have seen better days.

LAWRENCE VAN GELDER

1975 Mr 22, 36:1

In their portrayals of the major characters over the years, a slim, blond, photogenic Marthe Keller and an intense Charles Denner project the anxieties, sorrows and joys of people making the best of changing worlds. André Dussollier is natural and appealing as Simon, whose instincts remain decent despite a rough road to success. They are profession-ally supported by, among others, Mr. Becaud and Charles Gérard as Mr. Dussollier's jailmate and friend.

Mr. Lelouch, of course, gives amour its due in "And Now My Love," but this is not nearly so impressive as his perceptive, often touching portraits of three eras and their principals.

1975 Mr 22, 36:1

FILM VIEW

VINCENT CANBY

Who Says They Don't Make B Movies?

About halfway through a movie called "Deranged," its hero, a slightly retarded country fellow named Ezra, picks up a piece of fried chicken, smears it daintily with peanut butter and takes a large healthy bite. The audience the other day at the 42d Street Lyric Theater laughed at and cheered this gesture, clearly appreciating the consistency in Ezra's bizarre behavior. Ezra, you see, is no ordinary eccentric. In addition to liking peanut butter on his fried chicken, he has missed his dead mom so much that he has brought her home from the cemetery and set her up in a bedroom so they can chat, "Psycho"-fashion, with Ezra doing both voices.

"Deranged," which most people reading this will probably never have heard of until now, is a surprisingly funny horror film that eventually falls apart—but not before it had convinced me of the truth of a suspicion that's been lurking in the back of my mind for some time now:

The movies we used to call B pictures aren't dead. They're alive and lurking about the country in various flamboyant disguises. You may not find them in any posh Eastside house belonging to Reade or Rugoff but they keep turning up at theaters like the Cinerama, Penthouse and Forum on Broadway, and on double-bills in neighborhood theaters where they come and go with weekly regularity.

Still the best place in New York to see B pictures—that is, today's equivalents of yesterday's B pictures—is 42d Street, most frequently at the Lyric and Harris theaters, those seedy but gallant holdouts against porn, where, in the bright twilight of orchestra and balcony, time seems to have stood still. People snore, move about furtively, snap bubble gum, talk to each other and back to the screen. Time seems to have stood still because, for these audiences, movies haven't yet become a big deal. They aren't intimidating.

Today's B pictures are considerably different from the ones we grew up with in the pre-television era. They are not so innocent. The language is rough and the violence absurdly overstated. Their plots are thick but their concerns are limited. There are no B-picture comedies today like M-G-M's old Hardy family series. Instead of presenting us Ann Rutherford as a model of young American womanhood, today's B picture may offer Pam Grier, the black beauty who tears up urban landscapes and maims much of the male population to the thorough delight of candy-bar munchers of all ages.

The B pictures of today can be black exploitation melodramas, horror films, westerns, or, very occasionally, melodramas on the order of "Macon County Line," movies that pretend to have some social content while exploiting either sexual or racial fears. B pictures always are action-adventure movies that combine the basic elements of two or more specific genres since audiences tend to overlap. If the movie is woolly and wild enough, the black/white audiences couldn't care less what color the characters are.

One of the most financially successful of the recent B's is "Abby," a hilariously unabashed, black parody (almost scene for scene) of "The Exorcist." The victim—the title character—is the young wife of a black minister in what may be Louisville, Ky., who is suddenly possessed by the devil that her father-in-law, William Marshall, while on a dig in

Africa, lets out of an ancient box. Poor Abby. When the devil takes hold, all hell breaks loose, but what's worse is that her eyebrows grow alarmingly bushy and she starts saying rude things to any man around. Carol Speed, the actress who plays Abby, was an inspired choice since, in the scenes in which she's supposed to be demure and saintly, it's very apparent she has the slightest suggestion of a mustache on her upper lip. The members of the audience with whom I saw "Abby" loved it for what we always knew the original Billy Friedkin film to be—a fancified B picture compounded of a good deal of technical expertise and even more hot air.

Some other typical B's include:

"Rape Squad," wherein a very pretty but very butch rape victim gets her sister-victims together to form a vigilante group that successfully terrorizes would-be rapists and traps the young man who has been causing them all such anguish. Rape is a serious problem but "Rape Squad" is much more interested in showing us (1) women being humiliated (by the rapist), and (2) men being humiliated (by the rape squad). It has something for everybody who doesn't think much.

"Seizure," an ambitious horror film made in Canada by a young New York director named Oliver Stone. Its cast includes a lot of good New York actors, including Jonathan Frid and Anne Meacham, and its plot (about three mysterious strangers who take over a house-party, Manson-style) has enough gore to keep a 42d Street audience polite. The screenplay includes two or three too many twists but there is some genuinely funny, waspish dialogue. Mr. Stone, a graduate of the N.Y.U. Film School, is now writing an original screenplay with Robert Bolt ("A Man for All Seasons").

● ● ●

"Boss Nigger," a black Western starring Fred Williamson as a bounty hunter who, Clint Eastwood-style, makes himself the sheriff of a bigoted little frontier town in order to collect a debt. In addition to starring in the movie, Williamson wrote the screenplay and coproduced. The narrative line is as simple and straightforward as an old Roy Rogers Western, but the wit and cool are strictly contemporary. It's fun because it's no-big-deal.

"The Beast Must Die," an English horror film with a difference: black Calvin Lockhart plays the monomaniacal tycoon who invites an ill-assorted group of guests to his country estate in order to find out which one of them is a werewolf. Like so many English horror films, the movie looks much better than it is. The 42d Street audience liked Lockhart's lordly manners and his rudeness to his white guests. They also guffawed when Calvin says to his wife, "One of our guests is a werewolf" and she answers, with perfect sense: "Then why did you invite them?"

B pictures of the sort I'm describing are not to be confused with movies made for television, which are, most of the time, too polite, too slick, too carefully structured (for commercial breaks, if nothing else) to satisfy the true B picture audiences. Most movies made for television are, when you study them, about events first, people second. The B pictures one sees in theaters—maybe because they are so often raw and raunchy—frequently have the touch of life.

1975 Mr 23, II:15:1

False Art of the Propaganda Film

By WALTER GOODMAN

In most lands around the globe, propaganda is a monopoly of the state. In this country, however, the most notable examples of the

Walter Goodman is the assistant editor of the Arts and Leisure section.

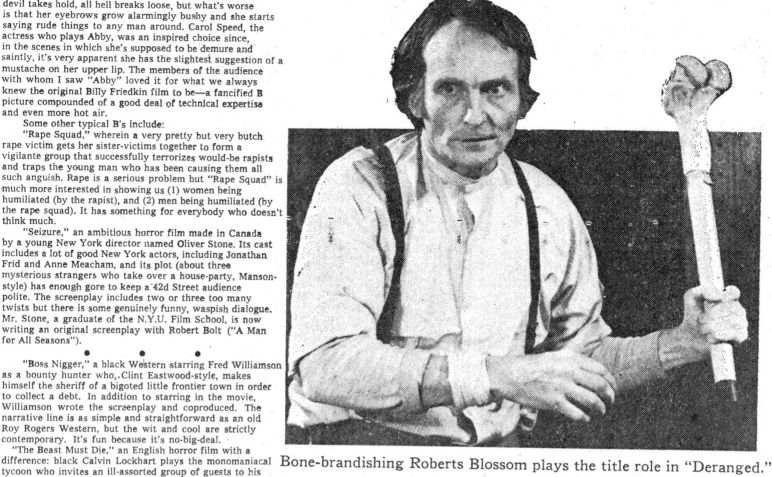

Bone-brandishing Roberts Blossom plays the title role in "Deranged."

craft, such as the three current films discussed below, come from the state's adversaries. When Shirley MacLaine takes a camera crew to China or Jane Fonda takes one to North Vietnam or when Peter Davis, who made the TV documentary, "The Selling of the Pentagon," sets out to do a film about the war in Southeast Asia, no-

body expects a testimonial to U.S. foreign policy. Yet works of propaganda—works whose primary design and overriding effect is the promotion of a case or cause, usually without the intention being made explicit—often send forth messages that their creators did not intend and in the process draw attention to the creators' set of mind and guiding impulses.

"The Other Half of the Sky: A China Memoir"—currently at the Whitney and to be shown April 15 on Channel 13—is the account of a three-week visit to China in the spring of 1973 by a group of American women selected by Shirley MacLaine. In addition to the actress herself, they included a 13-year-old from California and an elderly Bostonian, a talkative black activist from Mississippi and a talkative white admirer of George Wallace from Texas, a psychologist from San Francisco, a sociologist from Puerto Rico, a Navaho. Co-directed by Miss MacLaine and Claudia Weill, and made with the cooperation of the Chinese, it is a good-humored, sappy sort of travelogue, agush with handholdings, huggings and kissings.

The most arresting se-

quence, for those who can bring themselves to watch it, is the delivery of a baby by Caesarian section to a woman who remains conscious from start to finish; it's done with needles. The most instructive scenes are those in which the women from America, inquiring into the state of Chinese women now that they have attained "liberation," learn that the word signifies marrying a man with the correct political attitudes and then taking a job to the specifications of the state. Except for a show of dismay when a resident commissar explains that if a Michelangelo were to appear in the New China, he would have to be reeducated to the service of The People, Miss MacLaine, who wrote as well as produced this film, seems entirely gratified with the way things have been going since China's liberation, a word she employs without irony. Today, she reports the peasants "are the masters of the country." (Miss MacLaine plays fair; she speaks her own most fatuous lines. Madame Chou En-lai, making a guest appearance, probably had her lines written for her at headquarters.)

In one quite touching scene, a woman tells of how her feet were bound under the old regime. For some reason, the concern of these filmmakers over bondage stops at the ankles. Miss MacLaine seems enthralled by a society in which all small boys are taught that their mission in life is to join the People's Liberation Army and fight the American imperialists. Despite her best efforts in behalf of her hosts, this "Memoir" lends chilling support to George Orwell's observation, made in 1939, that "It may be just as possible to produce a breed of men who do not wish for liberty as to produce a breed of hornless cow."

Now, one knows from Miss MacLaine's public record that if she discovered that American children were being "programed"—to use the word that the Boston woman applies to what she is seeing of Chinese education before she is subdued by a layer of cant from the psychologist; that they were subjected to paramilitary training from a very tender age; that their most intimate relationships were being manipulated by the state for the state's interests; that they were being taught to worship a man-

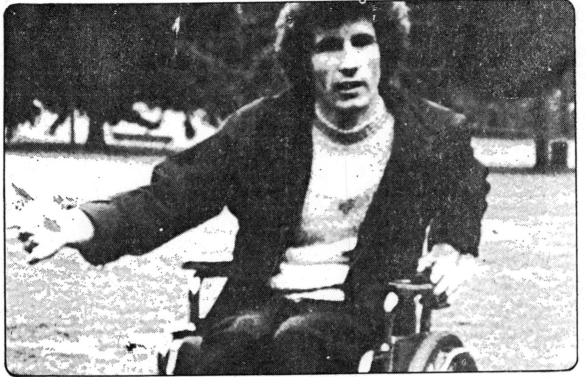

Ed Hausner/The New York Times

Paralyzed Vietnam vet in "Hearts and Minds"—powerful images and cheap shots

god and to repeat, by rote and in unison, tag ends of an ideology· which they can scarcely comprehend — she would be among the first to protest. Yet what she would condemn in her own country is counted an achievement when it is done to the Chinese. Can this be anthropological relativism, or the latest thing in radical racism? Is Miss MacLaine mischievous or only simple? We may leave the question open. It is clear enough that her film advances a cause in the guise of a "memoir"—which fits our shorthand definition of propaganda.

•

Although Jane Fonda never states right out that she is acting as a publicist for North Vietnam, her film allows no doubt on that score. "Introduction to the Enemy" is a refreshing movie in the sense that it makes no pretense to critical judgment. It delivers its political line straight, right from the mouths of party functionaries. Sponsored by the Indochina Peace Campaign, an organization evidently committed to the Vietnamese revolutionary cause, it features Jane Fonda and Tom Hayden smiling their way around the country, along with Haskell Wexler's pictures of beautiful children, bombed-out towns, beautiful children, workers making bicycles out of the remains of an F-104 fighter and beautiful children. (It is

a revelation to observe how subdued our native firebrands become once they find themselves in a congenial dictatorship.) To fully appreciate a movie such as this or Miss MacLaine's "China Memoir," one must come to it persuaded that the presence of beautiful children in a country is evidence of a regime's benevolence. The high spot of this show is a Frisbee match between Fonda-Hayden and a host of beautiful children.

America has never been bereft of publicists for the totalitarian mode. There have always been people around ready to exhibit to us the scrubbed faces of youths in Mussolini's Italy, in Hitler's Germany, in Stalin's Russia. Generally, they were motivated by a combination of allegiance to a doctrine and affection for the Fatherland or Motherland. Not so the Misses Fonda and MacLaine. Their celebrations of Oriental police states are prompted less by worship of Mao and Ho, I believe, than by their opposition to American activities in Southeast Asia. They show us the benign face of the enemy in hopes that it may compel us to look into ourselves.

•

Peter Davis's remarkable film "Hearts and Minds," which opens in New York today, is more directly about America. In Davis's description, his film, which combines interviews, battlefield shots and scenes from civilian life here, "is an attempt to understand what we have done and what we have become. It is more psychological than political, and it is not a chronology of the war so much as a study of people's feelings."

"Hearts and Minds" is rich in powerful images, not easily shaken off: The former pilot making an unbearable connection between the napalm he dropped and his own young daughter. The old Vietnamese woman, trying in her bewilderment to explain the destruction of her life by the bombs; the unbudging camera, whirring in the background, stays focused on her for perhaps 30 long seconds as she tries to grasp her own condition—"I'm so unhappy." Clark Clifford, former Secretary of Defense, recounting his efforts, as a rational man, to come to terms with the insatiable demands of an irrational military machine. Walt Rostow, a planner of our Vietnam adventure, bursting forth in exasperation at being asked why we got involved in Vietnam—"Are you really asking me this goddam silly question . . . pedestrian . . . sophomoric . . .!"

The Rostow sequence, which has drawn attention as a result of his efforts to have it deleted, displays the mentality, sometimes called tough-minded, which managed to escalate Vietnam into a catastrophe. Yet as the film went on, I found myself somewhat uneasy about this scene. We do not see Rostow's interrogator; we can't be certain whether some provocation, a gesture, a facial expression, a turn of phrase, may have prompted his outburst. Perhaps none of this would have occurred to me had it not been for other jarring elements, messages which force the producers' opinions on the viewer in a most clumsy way: A fragment of a remark by President Eisenhower suggesting that the United States was in Vietnam for the tin and tungsten; the camera searching out names of U.S. firms in

Saigon—Coca Cola, Esso, Chase Manhattan; the breaks for commercials by a dissident South Vietnamese priest who speaks exclusively in Vietcong slogans; a staged appearance by the late Ho Chi Minh having his beard plucked by small children, reminiscent of pictures of an avuncular Joe Stalin receiving bouquets from tots in Popular Front times.

Whereas the MacLaine and Fonda films are run-of-the-mill sales pitches, "Hearts and Minds" is the product of talented filmmakers caught between clashing impulses—to produce a work of art or to advance a political argument. The most grating instance of the director undermining his own material comes after a long, heartbreaking scene of a SouthVietnamese boy hugging his father's picture at the father's graveside, sobbing, sobbing. (Here, again, we become conscious of the unrelenting camera; we want it to turn away out of pain or embarrassment but we also need to watch; the camera holds on, creating a high and affecting tension.) Cut to General William Westmoreland, former leader of our forces in Vietnam, saying "The Oriental doesn't put the same high price on life as does the Westerner." All right, the point is made—but at what cost? Westmoreland, a man who has clearly learned during his years in the military bureaucracy to utter inanities in a weighty manner, is an easy mark. In using the boy's tragedy to score off the general, the filmmakers show no faith in either their material or their audience; it's like putting an exquisite painting into a showy frame, the better to peddle it to the philistines.

Now, General Westmoreland, we must understand, is speaking not for himself, but as representative of one side of America, also exemplified by slaughter-the-Japs clips from World War II Hollywood movies and personified by the returned POW who gives talks to Middle American audiences on how to whip the gooks and by the former pilots who describe their bomb-dropping as "a technological expertise thing," or as a happy memory—"I dinged them . . . I felt good." The film makes a causal connection between this manly state of mind and scenes from a college football game: an up-and-at-'em minister telling his parishioners how much God cares about the game; a half-crazed coach attacking his boys with exhortations to win; the empty-faced cheerleaders, the

Why do our radicals celebrate foreign police states?

beefy players colliding like tanks, the howling fans. Well, there is something to all of this—the violence of the football field transmitted to the battlefield. But it's much too simple, much too easy, laid on much too heavily; life is cut to the propagandist's measure. The insistence of the makers of "Hearts and Minds" on dividing America into two camps—Daniel Ellsberg, I.F. Stone, the peace marchers, the draft evaders, the young amputees coming to the bitter realization that they have had their futures shattered for no purpose; versus Westmoreland, Rostow, the jingoist POW and his open-mouthed audiences—works against their more subtle revelations.

In a deeply moving sequence, the father of a man who was killed in a helicopter crash explains quietly, as much to himself as to the interviewer, why he still feels his son's death was in a worthwhile cause, why he still trusts President Nixon, as his wife, hardly listening, touches gently a model plane, presumably her son's. How many times he must have told himself his loss cannot have been for nothing; how many times she must have fondled that plane. The humanity of this moment exposes the crudeness of the football field analogy.

•

The final shot—a confrontation between Loyalty Day marchers and pickets for peace—caps the film's self-betrayal. Its makers ignore their own best evidence and resort to a trite image, simplified to the point of distortion. The difficult truth is that the great majority of Americans belong to neither of these parties. When these filmmakers focus on human beings, they give us moments of depth and beauty; when they force a tendentious thesis upon us, they diminish their film. Even if they had resisted the temptation to score elementary points, "Hearts and Minds" would still have been propaganda—but it would have been something much more as well. Peter Davis and his colleagues may have had their hearts in the right place, but they did not trust the minds of their audience. ∎

1975 Mr 23, II:1:1

HEARTS AND MINDS, a documentary directed by Peter Davis; produced by Bert Schneider and Mr. Davis; editors, Lynzee Klingman and Susan Martin; director of photography, Richard Pearce; a Rainbow Pictures presentation, distributed by Warner Brothers. Running time: 112 minutes. At the Cinema 2 Theater, Third Avenue near 60th Street. This film has been rated R.

An American soldier in South Vietnam

By VINCENT CANBY

Power is virtually the first word heard in Peter Davis's epic documentary, "Hearts and Minds," and power, real and mythical, is what the film contemplates in as many tones and moods as you might expect in superior fiction.

"Hearts and Minds," which opened yesterday at the Cinema 2, recalls this nation's agonizing involvement in Vietnam, something you may think you know all about, including the ending. But you don't. Just as television's presentation of the war made it seem small, orderly and comprehensible, to fit the physical dimensions of the television set and the programing schedules of the television industry, "Hearts and Minds" deals in disorderliness, contradictions and historical perspectives that are often shadowy, subject to any number of interpretations.

•

Mr. Davis, who made the award-winning television documentary, "The Selling of the Pentagon," makes no attempt to justify the American involvement in Vietnam, which, it's obvious, he believes to have been a disaster. "Hearts and Minds," however, is so various, so full of associations that go beyond the war, that the film does a lot more than preach to the committed.

Some sympathetic, liberal critics—listening to their own well-meaning, must-be-fair-to-everyone consciences—have expressed sorrow that Mr. Davis has occasionally loaded his dice, that he has allowed himself to make points cheaply by, for example, cross-cutting between a pious Gen. William C. Westmoreland talking about the cheapness of life in the Orient and a small Vietnamese boy's sobbing at a gravesite. This is correct as far as it goes, but to dwell on it is to miss the more profound meaning of an extraordinary movie, which may well be the true film for America's bicentennial.

"Hearts and Minds" is not about General Westmoreland, nor the succession of United States Presidents and their advisers who sought desperately and probably sincerely to understand Vietnam. Rather it's about the generations of attitudes, wishes and beliefs that these men represented. It's about the power the country inherited.

Mr. Davis uses old newsreel footage as well as new material that he shot in Vietnam, in this country and in France. He also uses clips from old Hollywood movies and dozens of interviews with peasants and policymakers, with American civilians and fighting men, some of whom survived as physical wrecks and some of whom returned home more convinced than ever of America's mission to save the world from what J. Edgar Hoover and Lyndon B. Johnson pronounced "Comun-ism."

An interview with Clark Clifford, the former Secretary of Defense, at the beginning of the film sets what I take to be the theme when Mr. Clifford recalls the extraordinary economic, military and industrial power the United States found itself with at the end of World War II. The film then goes on to examine the nearly suicidal effects of that power when it was explained, justified, defined and, in particular, when it was wielded as something that had been God-given rather than as something inherited through one of the most marvelous accidents — the unplanned conjunction of people, place and time—in recorded history.

I don't think the film means to knock American achievements but only to point out that a certain lack of perspective, of modesty, perhaps, can be close to fatal.

"Hearts and Minds" has a lot to say about an average American's education and, indeed, about his ability to re-educate himself as conditions change. At one point Daniel Ellsberg remembers having looked at Vietnam in gung-ho World War II terms, when it was possible easily to distinguish the good guys from the bad, to see a war clearly in terms of territory won and lost. Vietnam was something terrifyingly new to the World War II people. The origins and the issues were not neat and tidy.

This is what "Hearts and Minds" so vividly recognizes in a collage of scenes that, though blunt and often harrowing, eventually demonstrate something that I. F. Stone once said about the survival of the Vietnamese people through years of bombing. Their incredible survival, said Mr. Stone, has re-established "the primacy of man in the age of technology."

"Hearts and Minds" is a tough film but it is no mere rehash of sad events. It is always aware of the primacy of man when man's given even half a chance.

1975 Mr 24, 38:1

DONKEY SKIN (Peau d'Ane), directed by Jacques Demy; screenplay (French with English subtitles) by Mr. Demy, based on a story by Charles Perrault; photography, Ghislain Cloquet; music, Michel Legrand; produced by Mag Bodard; United States distributor, Janus Films. At the Regency Theater, Broadway between 67th and 68th Streets. Running time: 90 minutes. This film has not been classified.
Peau d'Ane .... Catherine Deneuve
Prince .... Jacques Perrin
Blue King .... Jean Marais
Fairy Godmother .... Delphine Seyrig
Red King .... Fernand Ledoux
Red Queen .... Micheline Presle

"Donkey Skin," the French film that opened yesterday at the Regency, is billed as a fairy tale for all ages.

A fairy tale, indeed, it is based on the "Peau d'Ane" of Charles Perrault, the man who gave us "Cinderella." But classic fairy tales, as we all know but sometimes forget, are stories full of violence, cruelty, bloodshed and perversion.

This one pivots on incest, and while incest is by definition, a family pursuit, there are some who might want to think twice before taking the children to "Donkey Skin." The caveat having been sounded, let it be said as swiftly as possible that "Donkey Skin" is a gently charming, opulently beautiful and slyly humorous retelling of the old story set down by Charles Perrault.

It's the one about the happy and handsome king (Jean Marais) and the beautiful queen (Catherine Deneuve) who, instead of a goose that lays golden eggs, have a donkey that litters his lavish stall with gold and gems. One day, illness strikes the queen, and on her deathbed she extracts a promise from the king: He will never remarry until he has found a woman as beautiful as she. Eventually he looks toward his own daughter (also played by Catherine Deneuve), who is not altogether repelled by the idea.

Fortunately for the conventions, she has a fairy godmother (Delphine Seyrig) who, being endowed with the power of magic, has no difficulty managing to keep an eye on the welfare of her charge and another on the main chance.

There's no sense giving away the rest. But just for the record, it does no harm to say that no one will come out weeping from "Donkey Skin."

Now, not only are there a king and a queen and a gold-en-haired princess and a very well-preserved fairy godmother; there are also the customary attractive prince, another king and queen, two castles, living statuary, the standard forest equipped with magic cottage, and for those who insist on the truly enchanted, a magnificent gilded coach, a talking, seeing rose, a crone who spits frogs and a ring assigned the role played by the shoe in "Cinderella."

And, oh, yes, those who have never seen a purple cow and never hope to see one should be put on notice that there are red and blue horses (to say nothing of people) around. Film buffs will appreciate the film's decorative homage to Jean Cocteau.

There is all of this, and music, too, because "Donkey Skin" is the concoction of the people who previously collaborated on "Umbrellas of Cherbourg" and "The Girls from Rochefort" — Jacques Demy, as director and screenwriter, and Michel Legrand, in charge of the music.

Musically, "Donkey Skin" won't wipe out memories of "My Fair Lady." But taken as a whole, with its airiness, piquancy and lavishness, "Donkey Skin" is a most agreeable confection.

LAWRENCE VAN GELDER

1975 Mr 24, 39:1

ROSEBUD, directed and produced by Otto Preminger; screenplay by Eric Lee Preminger with additional dialogue by Marjorie Kellogg, based on the novel by Joan Hemingway and Paul Bonnecarrere; music, Laurent Petitgirard; director of photography, Denys Coop; editors, Peter Thornton and Thom Noble; distributed by United Artists. Running time: 126 minutes. At the Plaza Theater, 58th Street east of Madison Avenue, and Paramount Theater, Columbus Circle. This film has been rated PG.
Larry Martin .... Peter O'Toole
Sloat .... Richard Attenborough
Hamlekh .... Cliff Gorman
Fargeau .... Claude Dauphin
Senator Donnovan .... John V. Lindsay
Lord Carter .... Peter Lawford
George Nikolaos .... Raf Vallone
Lady Carter .... Adrienne Corri
Kirkbane .... Amidou
Hacam .... Yosef Shiloa

By VINCENT CANBY

Talent and Nerve continue to wrestle for Otto Preminger's soul. When Talent wins, Mr. Preminger makes good, tough commercial films —"Such Good Friends," "The Man With the Golden Arm," and "Anatomy of a Murder." When Nerve triumphs he may come up with "Skidoo" or something like his latest, "Rosebud," a suspense melodrama of such ineptitude, lethargy and loose ends that only someone with his arm being twisted would take credit for it.

•

Though there is some action in the film, and a lot of moving around, "Rosebud" consists principally of exposition, spoken by people with accents so thick that only Mr. Preminger might understand them, about a group of Arab terrorists who have kidnapped five rich girls and hold them for a ransom I'm not sure is ever defined.

The exposition takes place in Paris, the south of France, Corsica and Israel, but which scenes are set where is one of the film's lesser mysteries. The people we hear most often are a tattered Central Intelligence Agency man (Peter O'Toole), who masquerades as a Newsweek correspondent; a renegade Englishman (Richard Attenborough) who has turned Muslim and is planning his own holy war against Israel and Communist-leaning Arabs, and a nice, clean-cut Israeli intelligence officer (Cliff Gorman).

Some of the other speakers include actors of the stature of Claude Dauphin, Peter Lawford and Raf Vallone, and one former Mayor, John V. Lindsay, whose discomfiture seems no greater or lesser than that of his colleagues.

Mr. Lindsay plays a United States Senator, the father of one of the hijacked girls, a man whose manner of looking worried is to look elegant. Mr. Lindsay thus is reduced to displaying haberdashery, which, as those of us know who've seen him sing and dance in local Inner Circle shows, is a waste of one of the city's natural resources.

The screenplay was written by Eric Lee Preminger, the director's son, with additional dialogue by Marjorie Kellogg, the author of "Tell Me That You Love Me, Junie Moon." Their consistently idiotic work includes the following bit of dialogue about Rosebud, which is the name of the yacht on which the kidnapped girls disappear: "Rosebud," says someone, "that's a strange name for a yacht. What's it mean?" "I'm not sure," is the reply, "I think it has something to do with a movie."

This "Rosebud," which opened yesterday at the Plaza and Paramount Theaters, is pure camp.

1975 Mr 25, 24:1

Kesey Work at Whitney Sad Souvenir of 60's

By VINCENT CANBY

"The Merry Pranksters," which heads the new film program at the Whitney Museum of American Art, is a sad, wan, hung-over souvenir of the mid-nineteen-sixties—that time when so many sons and daughters of America's well-heeled middle-class were dropping out and turning on that it seemed theoretically possible Marx's dreams would come true by default.

The members of America's bourgeoisie weren't going to be wiped out in revolution. They were going to disappear into their own LSD-expanded consciousnesses.

•

Well, the big drop-out never came. The highs are now over, and reporters who are paid to spot trends in several thousand words or less are now writing pieces about the renewed popularity of booze among the young. The country clubs of the nation are apparently safe. For a while, anyway.

"The Merry Pranksters" is a 55-minute record of the first lap of a cross-country bus trip taken by Ken Kesey, the West Coast novelist and acid guru, and his band of followers in 1964. The official title of the film is "Intrepid Traveler and His Merry Band of Pranksters Search for a Cool Place, Part I." It is, according to the Whitney program notes, the first installment of what is expected to be 20 one-hour films about that trip. I wouldn't want to bet that we'll ever see the others.

"The Merry Pranksters"

THE MERRY PRANKSTERS, a documentary directed by Ken Kesey and Ken Babbs; distributed by the Archive Institute (Pleasant Hill, Ore.). Running time: 55 minutes. At the Whitney Museum of American Art, Madison Avenue near 75th Street. This film has not been rated.

says nothing and everything. It's a desperately dopey home movie, officially directed by Mr. Kesey and Ken Babbs, terribly photographed and full of people doing and saying things that strike them as hugely funny but aren't to anyone who hasn't dropped a little LSD.

One long segment shows us some nice looking, shaggy-hair kids decorating their old school bus with psychedelic designs in Day-Glo paint. At another point the kids run around the side of the highway wearing funny hats of the sort one usually asociates with conventioneers. When you are on the outside of this dream peering in, the dream looks like a particularly unmemorable class picnic.

There is nothing in the film that conveys any sense of what it was like to be part of Mr. Kesey's dream. For that one has to go back to Tom Wolfe's "The Electric Kool-Acid Tet" (1968), written in Mr. Wolfe's special Day-Glo prose that caught the tempo, madness and humor of the Kesey adventures in inner space.

Also on the program is Robert Nelson's seven-minute short, "Grateful Dead," which attempts to find visual equivalents to the Grateful Dead's music. The movie has a built-in problem: When it succeeds, it's redundant; when it fails, it's a waste of eyesight. One might more profitably be reading a good book.

1975 Mr 27, 37:1

SHEBA, BABY, directed by William Girdler, screenplay by Mr. Girdler, based on a story by Mr. Girdler and David Sheldon; produced by Mr. Sheldon; editors, Henry Asman and Jack Davies; distributed by American International Pictures. Running time: 90 minutes. At the Cinerama Theater, Broadway near 58th Street, and RKO 86th Street Twin 2 Theater, 86th Street near Lexington Avenue. This film has been rated PG.

Sheba .... Pam Grier
Brick .... Austin Stoker
Pilot .... D'Urville Martin
Andy .... Rudy Challenger
Shark .... Dick Merrifield

"Sheba, Baby," which opened yesterday at the Cinerama and 86th Street Twin 2 Theaters, is a moderately entertaining B picture in the mode of "Foxy Brown" and "Coffy," though somewhat less violent. It's about a beautiful black private eye named Sheba who goes home to Louisville in an attempt to save her father, a kindly money-lender, from the mob that wants to take over his business.

Pam Grier, who also starred in "Foxy Brown" and "Coffy," plays Sheba in a most unusual way. Although she's no great shakes as an actress, she gives the impression of being as intelligent as she is beautiful.

The film was shot mostly in and around Louisville under the direction of William Girdler, who also directed another Louisville-located black melodrama, "Abby." From what one can see at the sides of the frame and in the background, Louisville looks serene and prosperous.

VINCENT CANBY.

1975 Mr 27, 37:1

BRANNIGAN, directed by Douglas Hickox; screenplay by Christopher Trumbo, Michael Butler, William P. McGivern and William Norton; story by Mr. Trumbo and Mr. Butler; editor, Malcolm Cooke; music, Dominic Frontiero; produced by Jules Levy and Arthur Gardner; released by United Artists. At the Penthouse, Broadway and 47th Street, the 86th Twin I, at Lexington Avenue, the 59th Street Twin 2, east of Third Avenue and neighborhood theaters. Running time: 111 minutes. This film has been classified PG.

Jim Brannigan .... John Wayne
Commander Swann .... Richard Attenborough
Jennifer Thatcher .... Judy Geeson
Mel Fields .... Mel Ferrer
Larkin .... John Vernon
Gorman .... Daniel Filon

Brannigan happens to be, among other things, an Irish-oriented euphemism for a drunken brawl and the name John Wayne goes by in "Brannigan," which erupted like a donnybrook in local theaters yesterday. But there's little in "Brannigan" to dispel the nagging notion that after more than 200 largely Western adventures shot over 45 years, he is still the indestructible cowpoke despite a Chicago detective's badge and the contemporary London locale. The results are no more convincing than a standard shootout on a Hollywood set.

"Brannigan," it should be noted, generates a suspicion of self-parody since, it will be recalled, our hero also played a police lieutenant in last year's "McQ." But as a cop, he again is the rough, if tiring, hombre, who's quick with his gun and fists, hates bad guys as much as rustlers and relishes taking them on singly or in gangs.

•

This time he's the veteran dispatched to London to extradite a top racketeer for the Windy City's grand jury. As the fugitive mobster, John Vernon is blatantly obvious despite Savile Row clothes and the rich life in Mayfair. But he's surrounded by sordid types, like James Booth, who kidnap him, and a double-dealing lawyer blandly played by Mel Ferrer. Of course, there's John Wayne simultaneously contending with a tenacious hit man, Daniel Pilon, imported to get him and Richard Attenborough, as Scotland Yard's smoothest sleuth, in pursuit of the rackets chief.

If we're exposed to an improbable blitz of gun battles, bombings, car chases, a saloon slug fest and Judy Geeson, as Wayne's pretty, British detective aide, we're also guided on a colorful Cook's tour of such landmarks as the Garrick Club, Piccadilly, Tower Bridge and the Thames docksides. Unfortunately, Mr. Wayne's first film trip to London doesn't appear to have been necessary. He and his busy company only serve to make "Brannigan" a commonplace crime caper.

A. H. WEILER

1975 Mr 27, 37:1

THE MIDDLE OF THE WORLD (Le Mileu du Monde), directed by Alain Tanner; screenplay (French with English subtitles) by John Berger and Mr. Tanner; photography, Renato Berta; editor, Brigette Sousseller; music, Patrick Moray; executive producers, Yves Gasser and Yves Peyrot; production companies, Action Films, Citel Films, a New Yorker Films release. At the 68th Street Playhouse, Third Avenue. Running time: 115 minutes. This film has not been classified.

Adriana .... Olimpia Cariisi
Paul .... Philippe Leotard
Juliet .... Juliet Berto

"The Middle of the World" ("La Milieu du Monde") was shown last year at the 12th New York Film Festival. The following excerpt is from Nora Sayre's review, which appeared in The New York Times last Oct. 7. The film is being shown at the 68th Street Playhouse, Third Avenue.

While most American movies continue to dodge the relations between the sexes, some of the European directors are surging ahead in that area.

Alain Tanner, who made "La Salamandre" and "Le Retour d'Afrique," brings an extraordinary sensitivity to one pair's experiences in "The Middle of the World." A married engineer who's running for Parliament in Switzerland becomes obsessed by a waitress whom he glimpses at a railroad cafe. He pursues her, they revel in their sexual affinities, he loses the election (but doesn't care), he wants to marry her, and she leaves him.

Among the film's many virtues is the tranquil build-up to passion. The engineer is served, almost stolid. Then, his excitement becomes exciting, and the urgency of their intimacy produces some of the more erotic scenes I've seen of late—even though they are briskly edited.

Meanwhile, the woman—who is gentle, earthy, affectionate—wonders if they will change each other. He's boyish and playful when they are together, while she grows more remote—mutely rejecting the materialistic life and the swank technology that he cherishes.

Throughout, the movie stresses the concept of "normalization"—whereby contact between the economic classes, or countries such as the United States and the Soviet Union, or the sexes, is acceptable "as long as nothing changes" in the power structure. The movie takes a profound, though subtle, stand against treating women as objects; it really is a feminist statement.

Both of these people are very likable, because of the sympathetic performances of Olimpia Carlisi and Philippe Leotard. Yet the director's attitude toward his male character is much sterner than mine would be—even though his feelings have no dimension beyond the sexual. But the woman has been so passive, so inexpressive of herself, that neither her lover nor the audience can guess what she's like. In fact, the movie's one flaw is that her character is so undeveloped.

However, it was also Mr. Tanner's intention to keep his characters somewhat elusive, so that the spectator might flesh out each portrait. And in its pensive way, this is a very radical movie. By portraying inequality so quietly, the theme has all the more impact—and the film goes on echoing in your mind well after you have seen it.

1975 Mr 29, 10:5

HOMO EROTICUS, produced and directed by Marco Vicario; story and screenplay (Italian with English subtitles) by Piero Chiara and Mr. Vicario, from an idea by Mr. Vicario; director of photography, Tonino Delli Colli; film editor, Sergio Montanari; music, Armando Trovajoli; released by Universal Pictures; produced by Atlantica Cinematografica-Rome Productions and Rotfeld-Paris Optimax Films-Paris Productions. At the Eastside Cinema, Third Avenue between 55th and 56th Streets. Running time: 92 minutes. This film is classified R.

Coco .... Rossana Podesta
Michele .... Lando Buzzanca
Achille .... Luciano Salce
Carla .... Sylva Koscina
Marchesa Trescorie .... Adriana Asti
Dr. Mezzani .... Bernard Blier
Signora Mezzini .... Ira Furstenberg
Amelia .... Angela Luce
Ambrogio .... Sandro Dori

By A. H. WEILER

"Homo Eroticus," an Italian farce filmed in 1971 that arrived at the Eastside Cinema yesterday, is, like the Leaning Tower of Pisa, unusual but unlikely. The film's basic idea may be scientifically possible, but as a lighthearted attempt to detail the amours and trials of a young man endowed with extraordinary genitalia and drives, it doesn't kid sex so much as leer at it.

As the title and English subtitles make plain, "Homo Eroticus" focuses largely on the dark and handsome Lando Buzzanca and his effect on the women and men of Bergamo. Let's just say that our contemporary Casanova is more than equal to his rare anatomical attributes. Up to a traumatic point, that is, which leads to a fairly happy ending.

Mr. Bazzanca is athletic, if nothing else, as the peasant who has fled from his native Sicily and quickly adjusts to the romantic needs of Bergamo's society women and their maids. And he cannot be faulted for rushing from boudoir to boudoir and economic improvement, since the affluent women, including Rossana Podesta, Sylva Koscina and Adriana Asti, are revealingly photogenic even if they do not expose much character.

In having him speed through a succession of affairs and double entendres, Marco Vicario, the producer-director, and his associates are not guilty of a crude, pornographic approach. Their "Homo Eroticus," which occasionally may be funny and a voyeur's dream, is essentially a small joke that doesn't really need all this amplification.

1975 Mr 29, 10:5

FILMS BY ROBERT BREER: FORM PHASES I, 2 minutes; FORM PHASES II, 3 minutes; UN MIRACLE, 30 seconds; RECREATION, 2 minutes; CATS, 2 minutes; A MAN AND HIS DOG OUT FOR AIR, 3 minutes; HOMAGE TO JEAN TINGUELY'S 'HOMAGE TO N.Y.', 10 minutes; BLAZES, 3 minutes; HORSE OVER TEA KETTLE, 6 minutes; PAT'S BIRTHDAY, 13 minutes; FIST FIGHT, 11 minutes; PBL NO 2, 1 minutes; 69, 5 minutes; 70, 5 minutes; GULLS AND BUOYS, 6 minutes; FUJI, 8 minutes. March 27-30 and April 3-6, 8 P.M. At the Film Forum, 256 West 88th Street.

If the spirits of Piet Mondrian and Saul Steinberg took possession of the imagination of Walt Disney and set up shop on Sesame Street, the result would likely be the films of Robert Breer.

These films—15 of them, ranging in length from all of 30 seconds to 13 minutes — are the substance of "Robert Breer: A Selected Retrospective," the 80-minute show now at the Film Forum.

And a delight it is, full of the lively inventiveness of an artist whose works are marked by uncommon vigor, expansive imagination, sharp insight and welcome humor.

The range is imposing—animation and live action, color and black-and-white, sound and silent, abstraction and representation, collage, montage, cartoons and calligraphy—all harnessed to a talent that bends film to its

service with the panache of a first-rate conjurer.

●

And, like an exceptional performer, Mr. Breer knows when enough is enough. In 30 seconds he has his way with Pope Pius XII as juggler. It takes him about a minute to sketch the sorry history of black-white relations. His animated images tend to pass before the idea at a

hectic pace. Forms become objects; objects, forms. In this context, "Pat's Birthday," a 13-minute live-action film made in 1962 with Claes Oldenburg, seems snail's paced. Yet it, too, is lighted with humor and perception. "Robert Breer: A Selected Retrospective" is a show with rarely a dull moment.

LAWRENCE VAN GELDER

1975 Mr 29, 18:1

Has Martin Scorsese Gone Hollywood?

Anthony Crickmay

His "Alice" isn't up to "Mean Streets."

By STEPHEN FARBER

More than ever before, the movie studios are terrified to try anything new. They want to repeat past successes, and they have found a new generation of filmmakers willing to oblige them. During the sixties young directors dreamed of becoming the American Bergman or Fellini. Today's young filmmakers are more likely to emulate Peter Bogdanovich, the film-buff-turned-director who has built his career on clever reproductions of the genre movies of the thirties and forties.

When second-hand schlock is at such a premium, even

Stephen Farber is a free-lance critic based in Los Angeles.

the most talented filmmakers have a difficult time retaining their integrity. In contemplating the career of Martin Scorsese one cannot help feeling a measure of concern. Scorsese's "Mean Streets" conveyed an original vision; his new film, "Alice Doesn't Live Here Anymore," also reveals flashes of originality, but a great deal of the urgency is gone. Since Scorsese is one of the most promising directors of his generation, his evolution deserves close scrutiny.

Scorsese began work as an editor, and directed two minor films ("Who's That Knocking at My Door?" and "Boxcar Bertha") before "Mean Streets" clearly established his talent when it was released in the fall of 1973. A corrosive study of small-time hoods in New York's Little Italy, "Mean Streets"

was plainly drawn from Scorsese's own experience, and it violated all the rules of Hollywood entertainment. The movie had rough edges, repetitious passages, a bit too much belligerent masculine camaraderie, but it was electric and unforgettable; the characters were created with a ruthless insight that indicated the emergence of an unconventional artist.

Despite ecstatic reviews, "Mean Streets" turned out to be a box-office flop; evidently it was too disturbing for most audiences. But "Alice Doesn't Live Here Anymore" (from a slicker, more commercial script by Robert Getchell) recently opened to good business, as well as to extraordinary, if unmerited, critical acclaim. A road picture set in New Mexico and Arizona, "Alice" has some of the same energy as "Mean Streets," the same feeling for people. After dissecting the masculine world of "Mean Streets," Scorsese has tried to stretch himself and make a movie about a contemporary woman.

The attempt is admirable but unsuccessful. Despite some pungent scenes and all-around fine performances (particularly from Diane Ladd as a tough-talking Tucson waitress and Harvey Keitel as a sadistic factory worker), "Alice" is a distinct disappointment. Following the example of many of his contemporaries, Scorsese has capitulated to Hollywood; this time he has revived all the conventions of pop romance that he seemed to have repudiated in "Mean Streets."

The film has probably been overrated because it is almost the only current movie with a juicy role for an actress. But critics have described "Alice" as a far more radical and controversial feminist film than it actually is. In many ways the new film is *less* sophisticated than the romantic comedies of the thirties and forties that starred Rosalind Russell, Jean Arthur and Katharine Hepburn. Although those movies may have ended with an affirmation of marriage, they concerned professional women — journalists, advertising executives, actresses, sometimes even lawyers or psychiatrists —who could survive quite effectively on their own. By contrast, the heroine of "Alice" admits that she does not know how to live without a man.

When her husband is killed in an accident, Alice (Ellen Burstyn) takes her 12-year-old son (Alfred Lutter) and hits the road in pursuit of the singing career that she had abandoned for marriage. But since she has no singing

talent, we know that her attempt at independence is doomed. Her career is only a pipe dream, and when she falls in love with a gentle, warmhearted rancher (Kris Kristofferson), her odyssey is over. Her future will most likely be limited to a job at the neighborhood bar, and a home on the range. Thus, Alice can hardly be considered representative of women with more complicated aspirations.

However, the characterization of Alice can at least be discussed seriously. The more disturbing problem with the movie is the jaunty, artificial tone that keeps undermining the intended realism. Robert Getchell's Broadway-cute dialogue is terribly leaden. Every character talks like a reject from a Neil Simon comedy; even the kids sound like standup comics with an endless supply of one-liners. The repartee between Alice and her wisecracking young son ("How did I get such a smartaleck kid?" "You got pregnant.") is not drawn from life, but from papier-mâché movies like "A Thousand Clowns" and "Paper Moon."

"Alice" is highly movie-conscious; it opens with a parody of "The Wizard of Oz," and there are references to other movies as well—Alice Faye singing "You'll Never Know" over the titles, a clip of Betty Grable in "Coney Island." At first it seems as if Scorsese may be attempting a satiric commentary on Hollywood myths, an investigation of the ways in which popular culture conditions women. But the movie ends as a simple celebration of Hollywood fantasies. The climactic scene in which Alice and the rancher argue across a crowded diner, and eventually fall into each other's arms as the customers applaud, is a deliberate *homage* to the fake happy endings of the thirties. Although dressed up to look modern, "Alice" is just another Technicolor advertisement for cotton candy romance.

In the midst of all the clichés and screwball comedy routines, a few moments have the intensity of "Mean Streets." The scene in which Harvey Keitel bursts into Alice's motel room in a murderous rage is a standout, brilliantly acted and directed. But this hair-raising scene only underscores the slickness and contrivance of the rest of the movie.

"Alice" contains a number of stylistic inconsistencies, some of which were also visible in "Mean Streets." On the one hand, Scorsese seems to be aiming for a new kind of movie naturalism; he uses real locations and encourages the actors to improvise. At the same time, he has a very sophisticated, self-conscious visual style; his elaborate camera movements and editing effects, and his operatic use of music, clash with the semi-documentary approach of many scenes. An artist can work in either a naturalistic or expressionistic style, but Scorsese veers uncomfortably from one to the other in the same film.

This stylistic schizophrenia is symptomatic of a more profound tension in Scorsese's temperament. At his best he is an intransigent artist committed to unvarnished truth on the screen; but, like Peter Bogdanovich, he is also a film buff with a taste for Hollywood showmanship and an abiding affection for kitsch. Scorsese is going to have to come to terms with those conflicting impulses before he makes too many more movies.

His own inner conflicts are undoubtedly exacerbated by the commercial pressures of working in Hollywood. A director needs big-grossing films in order to survive in the business, and so after a couple of failures, he half-consciously begins to court success. This compromise will be less painful if a part of him is secretly attracted to the synthetic style of Hollywood schlock. Like other maverick directors, Scorsese should think about making more films outside the industry. Both "Who's That Knocking at My Door?" and "Mean Streets" were independently financed, and last year Scorsese made an affectionate, exuberant documentary about his parents, "Italianamerican," that was on every level a more original and memorable film than "Alice." To see him waste his talents trying to salvage a shallow TV-style script like "Alice" is depressing.

Scorsese has reached an important turning-point in his career. He has done one shattering, uncompromisingly personal film that lost money, and he has done an enjoyable but hokey Hollywood comedy that is a box-office hit. Now he has to decide which kind of success he wants. Unfortunately, the critics who have praised "Alice" so extravagantly may seduce him into believing that both films have the same value. The truth is that Scorsese needs to get back to the fierce, abrasive quality of "Mean Streets." With "Alice Doesn't Live Here Anymore" Scorsese has demonstrated that he can make a jazzy, crowd-pleasing commercial movie. Somehow it seems a hollow victory. ■

1975 Mr 30, II:1:1

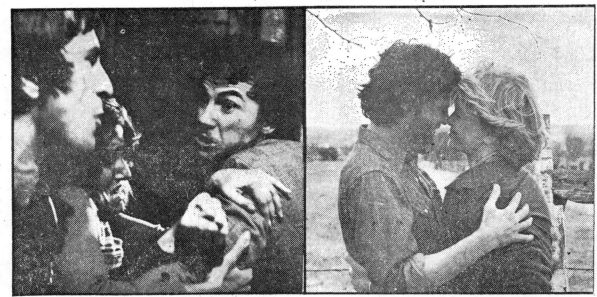

Scorsese followed the shattering "Mean Streets" with the hokey "Alice."

FILM VIEW

VINCENT CANBY

When Too Much Is Just About Right

"Tommy," Ken Russell's screen elaboration of The Who's rock opera written by Pete Townshend, is the movie that proves that there are times when much too much may be just about right, when overindulgence approaches art, when to allow oneself to become the victim is to triumph as the victor. The movie that pretends to be blasphemous is an all-out Christian assault on the senses. Salvation is the message but "Tommy" couldn't care less about appealing to reason. It doesn't want to convert men's minds. It wants to paralyze them. It pounds you, insults you, mauls you, and drills holes into your eardrums — in case salvation turns out to be a matter of physical implantation, something the missionaries never thought of.

With the exception of "Women in Love," which was a fairly decent, simplified, scaled-down version of the D.H. Lawrence novel, all of Mr. Russell's previous films have struck me as gargantuan mistakes, the work of a manic window-dresser who thinks he has a Hot Line to Freud, and whose movies mostly recall the disciplines of Olson and Johnson. In "The Music Lovers" (about Tchaikovsky), "The Devils" (suggested in part by Aldous Huxley's "The Devils of Loudun"), "The Savage Messiah" (about Gaudier-Brzeska), and even in "The Boy Friend" (in which Mr. Russell sank Sandy Wilson's small, witty show under a production as big and heavy as Australia), the director has pursued his muse with all of the grace of a trainer attempting to retrieve a drunk elephant.

Mr. Russell hasn't changed his method with "Tommy," but for the first time he has found a property that not only fits his style but also excuses it from the kind of rational scrutiny that was so withering to the other films. "Tommy" is to movies what a juke box is to furniture. It's not something you'd want to live with every day but it's kind of fun when you go out.

●　●　●

Mr. Townshend's rock opera—so called, I suppose, because there's no dialogue that isn't sung, though I'm not sure that qualifies it as opera — is a very loose morality tale about a little boy named Tommy who's struck deaf, dumb and blind when he sees his stepfather murder his real father who was supposedly lost in World War II. For satirical purposes that aren't of the heaviest weight, Tommy grows up to become the pinball champion of the world and, after miraculously recovering his senses, the messiah of a new religion that promises salvation through proper pinball-playing.

Mr. Russell is still calling upon Freud for help. The film gives every indication that what Tommy saw the night he was traumatized was not the murder of his father but simply his stepdad and mum having a go in the privacy of their bedroom. The old Primal Scene problem. Which actually makes more sense, if sense is what you're after in "Tommy" — though it shouldn't be. The story of Tommy's fall, rise and fall is merely the excuse for Mr. Russell to present Mr. Townshend's score (more than 24 songs) in a way that illuminates the concerns of the concerned youth of the nineteen-sixties, and that sends up those concerns at the same time. The members of The Who have taken trade ads to thank the director for bringing them into films, but I'm not sure they shouldn't sue, that is, if they take the warmed-over philosophical content of "Tommy" as seriously as they take the music, which is exciting and genuinely original.

The targets of "Tommy's" satire are — are you ready? — materialism, greed, parental laziness, medical quackery, organized religion, celebrity, television, fickleness, and lots of other things in passing, including the perversity of dirty old uncles left in the charge of helpless nephews.

"Tommy" is not the extravagant entertainment it is because of the delicacy of its feelings or the brilliance of its intellect but because of the way it captures the spectacular tastelessness of an era. It may be the most overproduced movie ever made, but there is wit and reason in this. It is the last word in pop art. It's for tastebuds that have been worn away by too many hamburgers, too many French fries, too many Cokes. Everything, including the sound level, is too much. But even this works in an odd way. The victim of the movie is as much the person sitting in the audience as it is Tommy.

This, of course, would be intolerable were it at all solemn, but "Tommy" is like a roller-coaster ride. It bursts with energy even when it seems in poorest taste: a Lourdes-like scene in which Tommy's mother (Ann-Margret) takes Tommy to the shrine of St. Marilyn (Monroe) where the world's halt and blind seek cures and take communion of Scotch and Seconals; a ghastly and funny scene in which a champagne-sodden Ann-Margret finds herself up to her chin in chocolate syrup that has burst forth into the room from a commercial on the TV screen; a hypnotically vivid scene in which Tina Russell, as The Acid Queen, attempts to cure Tommy by turning him on, though the dreams Tommy has have less to do with him than with Mr. Russell's fondness for outrageous decor and special effects.

As "Tommy" may be the perfect vehicle for Mr. Russell's kind of overstatement, Mr. Russell may be the perfect director for Ann-Margret's particular kind of performing energy. While she was terrifically appealing and funny in "Carnal Knowledge," no other film she has been in has as fully utilized her insatiable appetite for singing, dancing and generally raising the roof as "Tommy." She is as sensational as she intends to be.

Roger Daltrey plays (and sings) the grown-up Tommy with a lot of the same verve, and with the kind of comic, mock innocence that keeps the Christ-figure from being as dopey as it is essentially. For the first time in years, Oliver Reed shows signs of life as Tommy's opportunistic stepdad. The specialty bits by Eric Clapton, Elton John, Keith Moon and Jack Nicholson are equally effective.

"Tommy" is not the sort of movie you may ever want to see again, but it's an unforgettable souvenir of a time in our history when the only adequate dose was an overdose.

1975 Mr 30, II:13:1

Roger Daltrey: an appealing "comic, mock innocence"

Marvin Lichtner from Lee Gross

PIROSMANI, directed by Georgy Shengelaya; screenplay (Russian with English subtitles) by Mr. Shengelaya and Erlom Akhvlediani; director of photography, Konstantin Apryatin; editor, M. Karalashvili; music, V. Kukhianidze; produced by Gruzia Film Studio. Running time: 85 minutes. At the Museum of Modern Art, 53d Street, west of Fifth Avenue.
Niko Pirosmanashvili .... Avtandil Varazi

By VINCENT CANBY

"Pirosmani" the Russian film that opened the Museum of Modern Art's fourth annual New Directors New Films series yesterday, is a fine, firm, gentle consideration of the life and work of the Georgian primitive painter Niko Pirosmanashvili, who was born in 1862 and died in 1919, an alcoholism and poverty victim.

I use the word consideration instead of biography since the movie is not interested in factual details. Rather it attempts to reconstruct the feelings experienced by the alternately determined and tortured artist as reflected in his work—straightforward portraits of village elders, scenes of wedding celebrations, idyllic pastoral scenes, functional, four-feet-on-the-ground pictures of cows used to identify a dairy shop.

A lot of "Pirosmani" recreates the special look of the Pirosmanashvili paintings. One is often conscious of fore-shortened, perspectives and of the texture of things that someone untutored might find difficulti r boring to paint—large expanses of wooden floors, of earth of no especially marked color. Pirosmanashvili, like other primitives, delighted more in small details fastidiously reproduced, which is something the film does in the photography and in the narrative strucure.

Georgy Shengelaya, the 38-year-old Georgian director whose second feature this is, makes no attempt to analyze or explain the artist in conventional ways. Instead the film seems to glide across the artist's life seeing odd though not-so-random details, some more psychologically important than others. It has the manner of the

artist whose attention at has own wedding was sidetracked by the look of his wife's hands, the shape of the fingers outlined against the cloth of her dress. He sees some things with rare clarity, and reacts to them, while other matters, including his poverty and alcoholism, are ignored as if invisible.

"Pirosmani," which will be shown again at the museum tomorrow evening, is one of the few films I've ever seen that respects the mystery of the creative process and sidesteps melodrama. The manner of the film is detached, almost shy, like the artist himself as played by Avtandil Varazi.

Mr. Shengelaya attempts to show us the world as seen by the painter, though he never presumes to go inside the artist's mind to the extent of making connections between things seen and actions taken.

As a result we, in the audience, have to form our own connections, which, in the long run, makes "Pirosmani" much more moving and involving than films that give us too much information and reduce the artist to the dimensions of case-history.

"Pirosmani" gets the New Direcors/New Films off to such an auspicious start that I can only wonder why the film, which was made in 1971, has taken so long to reach this country. It represents new film making of particularly high and demanding order.

1975 Ap 5, 34:1

CHAC, directed, written and produced by Rolando Klein; director of photography, Alex Phillips Jr.; editor, Harry Keramidas; music, Victor Fozado and Elizabeth Waldo; a Cientifilm Aurora production. Running time: 95 minutes. At the Museum of Modern Art, 53d Street west of Fifth Avenue.
Diviner .... Pablo Canche Balam
Cacique .... Alonso Mendez Ton
Mute boy .... Sebastian Santis
Father .... Pedro Tiez

'Chac," is officially identified as a Panamanian film though it was made in

Mexico by a young Chilean-born film director, Rolando Klein, who studied cinema at the University of California at Los Angeles. The film itself is equally eclectic, a sort of Museum of Natural His-

tory movie about Mayan culture, put together with all sorts of slick, elaborate, sophisticated film techniques.

The camerawork is as glossy as a layout in the National Geographic and the

movie, though sincerely intended, just a bit patronizing towards the Mayan descendents it means to appreciate. The film was shown yesterday at the Museum of Modern Art in the New Films-

New Directors series and will be shown there again this evening at 6.

Though the movie's glossy, picturesque look has the effect of denying the depth of the director's interest in the primitive culture he is studying, Mr. Klein does show real ability in obtaining simple, direct, unselfconscious performances from his Indian actors. They all perform with that kind of natural absorption that often elludes amateurs, including those women secretly photographed in supermarkets touting their favorite brand of detergent.

"Chac" has a story of sorts. It's about the members of a contemporary Mayan tribe who, when their own shaman fails to produce rain, seek the help of a possibly evil hermit called the Diviner. Mr. Klein incorporates many Mayan legends into the movie and gives us what ultimately has the effect of a fairly posh, all-expenses-paid weekend in the primitive Yucatan. VINCENT CANBY

1975 Ap 5, 34:3

GENERAL IDI AMIN DADA, a documentary feature directed by Barbet Schroeder; produced by Jean-Pierre Rassam and Charles-Henri Favrod; executive producer, Jean-Francois Chauvel; director of photography, Nestor Almendros; editor, Denise de Casabianca; a production of Mara Film, TV Rencontre and Le Figaro. Running time: 90 minutes. At the Museum of Modern Art, 53d Street west of Fifth Avenue.

Barbet Schroeder's feature-length documentary "General Idi Amin Dada" is one of those "authorized" profiles that couldn't be more revealing even if it had been put together in secrecy. The subject of the film, who has been Uganda's dictator since he took power in a coup d'état in 1971, is not the sort to use bushels to hide lights that would embarrass other men.

"General Idi Amin Dada," which was shown Saturday and Sunday as part of the Museum of Modern Art's current New Directors/New Films series, was made by Mr. Schroeder and his associates, including the celebrated cameraman, Nestor Almendros, in Uganda early last year with the enthusiastic cooperation of the general, who has no fear of making a fool of himself.

•

To think that General Amin does make a fool of himself, as you sit there watching the movie, which often seems to be funny, is simply a way of insulating yourself to one of the movie's principal points: that modern Africa, lurching toward useful identity, still has a long way to go before it achieves it. In the meantime, extraordinarily complex characters like General Amin bumble along creating lethal chaos along with some measure of self-esteem.

The only fault I'd find with the film, which, according to Mr. Schroeder, was largely directed by the general and afterward submitted for his approval, is that it will seem to be funny, colorful and quaint to sophisticated audiences. Here's a sequence of the general racing some younger associates across his swimming pool and, of course, winning. In another he is reminded of his wild telegrams to the heads of other governments (including former President Richard M. Nixon), which strike him (and us) as hugely comic, if only because they are so rude.

General Amin, who sees himself as the father both of his country and of black Africa, boasts, struts, plays the accordion, acts as tour guide through a game reserve, lectures his cabinet on hard work and cautions Uganda's doctors not to drink too much.

Behind it all one sees the general's megalomania, his cruelty, his wit and his charm.

Mr. Schroeder, who made what may be the definitive film about young European drop-outs of the nineteen-sixties, "More," never intrudes upon the general in this straightforward documentary. The film is virtually a self-portrait—both terrifying and sorrowful.

VINCENT CANBY

1975 Ap 7, 40:1

TIBET PATHS OF CESSATION, directed by Robert Fulton, 55 minutes; **IMAGES OF ASIAN MUSIC,** directed by Peter Hutton; distributed by Canyon Cinema Cooperative, 29 minutes. At the Whitney Museum of American Art, Madison Avenue and 75th Street. April 6-8 and 10-15.

By A. H. WEILER

As avant-garde film makers in good standing, Robert Fulton and Peter Hutton, respectively represented by "Tibet/Paths of Cessation" and "Images of Asian Music," which arrived at the Whitney Museum yesterday, obviously are fascinated by peaceful people and places in a tormented world. But if their focus on strange horizons is generally fascinating, their stylized, personal approach to their subjects is often diffuse and confusing.

Despite its poetic title, "Images of Asian Music" is an entirely silent black-and-white record of Mr. Hutton's experiences as a seaman and in Thailand, which is never identified as such, made in 1973-74. He is, as he illustrated in his well-received 1972 short, "In San Francisco," a dedicated film diarist. His footage is largely disconnected and haphazard, but it nevertheless evokes mood and feeling about brooding seascapes, isolated temples, thick, palm-studded jungle vistas, misty rivers and varied Asians.

"Tibet," the more ambitious and effective subject, shot in color, black-and-white and sound footage last year, is perhaps more specialized in its treatment of its landscapes and people. A viewer is presented with shots of the towering, cloud-garlanded Himalayas, of peasants in villages and mountain meadows of leathery-faced sherpas, chanting holy men, schoolchildren and, as a repeated figure, a bald, wrinkled, kindly sage who is apparently the teacher of local and visiting seekers of spiritual contentment.

But as he made evident in his artistic 1972 short, "Running Shadow," Mr. Fulton does not confine himself to a simple travelogue. He circuitously uses successions of superimposed images, montages, speeded-up sequences, native and English dialogue and a quickly moving camera to give his film both reality and a sense of mystery and charm. Like "Images," his "Tibet" could use fuller explanations, but it manages to be both memorable and eye-catching.

1975 Ap 7, 40:1

A SIMPLE EVENT, a Persian film with English subtitles; written and directed by Sohrab Shahid Saless; produced by Sohrab Shadid Saless for the Central Film Office of the Iranian Ministry of Culture; executive producer, Kasem Radjiniya; photography, Naghi Massumi; editing, Kasem Radjiniya. Running time: 80 minutes. This film has not been classified. At the Museum of Modern Art, tonight at 6.
WITH Ana Mohamad Tarikhi, Habibollah Safarian, Hedayatollah Nawid.

By A. H. WEILER

"A Simple Event," the Iranian entry in the Museum of Modern Art's New Directors/New Films series, which was shown last night and will be repeated tonight, is an altruistic but all too simple saga. Sohrab Shahid Saless, a documentary director who made his feature film debut with "Event" in 1973, has again achieved a documentarylike authenticity. But his overlong, sometimes repetitious examination of a small-town family vitiates a potentially powerful drama and loosely veiled implications of the seemingly hopeless life in the Persian hinterland.

His unspecified, reportedly nonprofessional, principals are an obedient, if badgered, schoolboy; his fisherman father, and his ailing mother. Unfortunately, their lives are matters of mere survival in unchangingly drab surroundings, perceived through largely unemotional reactions to the normal and occasional abnormal situations with which they are faced.

The English subtitles are understandably sparse, since the cast is, at best, taciturn and hardly articulate. One empathizes with the dutiful boy who keeps running from school, where he is constantly criticized, to fetching the fish to stores, to home and silent, meager meals, to bed and back again to the same rounds. And a viewer is momentarily touched by his mother's sudden death and lonely funeral and his father's sympathetic, if unsuccessful, attempt to buy him a new suit.

But the automatonlike father, who is given to work, drink and sleep, as well as the worn mother and their sad-eyed youngster, emerge as merely pitiable figures on an unrewarding, distant but mostly placid landscape. They deserve compassion but, like the tragedy of isolation, poverty and helplessness, they remain vague and largely unresolved in this "Simple Event."

1975 Ap 8, 33:1

THE ENGAGEMENT OF ANNA, directed by Pantelis Voulgaris; screenplay (Greek with English subtitles) by Mr. Voulgaris and Menis Koumantareas; director of photography, Nikos Kavoukidis; editor, Dinos Katsouridis; produced by Mr. Katsouridis. Running time: 82 minutes. At the Museum of Modern Art, 53d Street west of Fifth Avenue.

Anna ....Anna Vagena
The Lady ....Smaro Veaki
Thodoros ....Kostas Rigopoulos
Kosmas ....Stavros Kalaroglou

By VINCENT CANBY

Anna (Anna Vagena) is a fine sturdy woman in her early 20's. Her eyes are large and dark, and she would be beautiful if given half a chance, but she denies herself all chances of beauty by dressing and moving with genteelly sef-effacing slovenliness.

Anna is the maid of all work in the middle-class Athens household where she has lived since she came to the city from her country village 10 years earlier. Anna is a gem. She is almost one of the family, and when the members of the family set about to arrange a marriage for her, she seems hurt, as if they didn't want her.

But that is just the beginning of "The Engagement of Anna," the exceptionally wise and moving Greek film that was shown at the Museum of Modern Art yesterday as part of the New Directors/New Films series. It will be shown again at the museum this evening at 8.30.

•

It's a bit difficult to describe the unique quality of "The Engagement of Anna." It's a political film in which politics are never mentioned, and its mood is furious, although, until somewhere near the end, no one ever acknowledges his anger.

"The Engagement of Anna" was directed by Pantelis Voulgaris in 1972 when he was 32. As far as I can find out, it's his first fiction feature, although he demonstrates the sort of marvelous narrative control many much older directors never achieve.

Mr. Voulgaris's method is in knowing just how much information to reserve. The camera eye never boggles at obvious points. It doesn't slip into easy close-ups to force our attention. It maintains instead a kind of respectful distance from the action, which gives the film a deceptively serene look. Indirection is as much the director's manner as it is the manner by which Anna is finally humiliated when the family frightens away her suitor.

Mr. Voulgaris builds his film so carefully and quietly that it's only toward the end that one recognizes it to be a horror story not only about the members of one bourgeois family but also about the system that certifies them. Mr. Voulgaris, according to the museum's biographical notes, spent some months in prison last year before the overthrow of the government of the colonels. It's no great wonder.

•

"The Engagement of Anna" tells what seems like a very small story, about how the (probably sincere) love of the family for Anna, depicted in scenes of genuine tenderness, so quickly turns cruel and selfish when the family's order and ease are threatened. Conspiring in Anna's downfall—and a lifetime sentence of domestic servitude—are her peasant mother and her own feelings of guilt—social, sexual and religious.

No one in "The Engagement of Anna" is even remotely aware of revolution, but that is what the film is calling for, in a voice that is so polite that you hear the real anger of the words only afterward.

1975 Ap 8, 32:1

THE PASSENGER, directed by Michelangelo Antonioni; screenplay by Mark Peploe, Peter Wollen and Mr. Antonioni, based on a story by Mr. Peploe; produced by Carlo Ponti; executive producer, Alessandro Von Normann; director of photography, Luciano Tovoli; editors, Franco Arcalli and Mr. Antonioni; a Metro-Goldwyn-Mayer production, released by United Artists. Running time: 119 minutes. At the Baronet Theater, Third Avenue at 59th Street. This film has been rated PG.

Locke .... Jack Nicholson
Girl .... Maria Schneider
Rachel .... Jenny Runacre
Knight .... Ian Hendry
Stephen .... Stephen Berkoff
Achebe .... Ambroise Bia
Hotelkeeper .... Jose Maria Cafarel
Robertson .... Chuck Mulvehill

By VINCENT CANBY

To be alone in the middle of an African desert at high noon, without shade and miles from any reminders of a recognizable world, is bad enough. The one thing worse is then to be ignored by the only other presences that cross the scene, an Arab and a camel that, through the distant heat haze, look to have been fused into a single creature.

As the camel-riding Arab passes close by, he nods without interest to the frantic Locke (Jack Nicholson) and continues toward the opposite horizon. Space has become time. Locke is so far out of it he could be dead.

This is the beginning of Michelangelo Antonioni's

dazzling new film, "The Passenger." Not long afterward, Locke is dead, at least legally.

•

Locke is a successful English - born, American - bred television reporter, the kind whose fame gives pop importance to any story he wishes to cover. At the start of "The Passenger," Locke is nearing the end of his rope. He is looking for the hideout of an African guerrilla group, but each time he thinks he's found it, it turns into a mirage.

The initial sequence of "The Passenger" is a metaphor for Locke's life — his failed marriage, his dissatisfaction with his job. Locke is cornered in an interior landscape that is as vast and arid as the Sahara. When a stranger, an Englishman about Locke's age, dies suddenly of a heart attack at the desert hotel where he's staying, Locke assumes the dead man's wardrobe, name, passport and appointments book, as casually as he might borrow some ties.

"The Passenger," which opened yesterday at the Baronet, is primarily a superior suspense melodrama about Locke's efforts to become the man he knows nothing about but whose life, he assumes, must have had more meaning than his.

In the manner of any number of lesser melodramas of this type, "The Passenger" has an insatiable appetite for geography and local landmarks. It moves from Africa to Britain to Germany and, finally, to Spain. It deals in coincidences, which, in "The Passenger," are as important as they are in "Oliver Twist" though a lot more provocative.

"The Passenger" is probably Mr. Antonioni's most entertaining film. It could also become his most popular, partly because he is using commercial forms of the sort he twisted out of shape in "L'Avventura" and that he ignored completely in "La Notte," "The Eclipse" and "Red Desert."

It most resembles "Blow-Up," which, like this new film, contains a never fully resolved mystery. "The Passenger," however, never indulges itself in nonsense to equal that earlier film's ballless tennis game. One of the things that makes "The Passenger" so compelling is its absolute fidelity to observable fact, though that is not to say it's meant to be realistic.

As the film progresses, as Locke learns more and more about the man whose identity he has taken on, "The Passenger" becomes filled

Maria Schneider and Jack Nicholson

with details that have the effect of dozens of small mirrors, reflecting back to Locke the life he never led but might have. His journey through Europe, in the company of a beautiful, liberated architecture student (Maria Schneider), the kind of girl most easily found in movies (I suspect), becomes less a quest for truth than a suicide mission. Mr. Antonioni has turned the suspense melodrama inside out.

You should be prepared to go along with him when, somewhere in the middle of the film, Locke explains to the girl why he has been trying to avoid the people who are pursuing him—his wife and his London employer. The girl shrugs. "People disappear every day," she says. Locke answers, "Every time they leave a room."

They do and they don't, which is, I think, the most ambiguous thing you have to worry about in this Antonioni film. The screenplay was written by Mr. Antonioni, Mark Peploe and Peter Wollen, the film critic and author of "Signs and Meaning in The Cinema," so I suppose it demands all sorts of interpretations.

•

The structure is not so esoteric, though, that it must be read with a pony. It invites us into a strange world, but without the intimidation that has so often been evident in other Antonioni works.

I realize I've said very little about the performances but that's because it's difficult to separate them from the end result. Mr. Nicholson, the most flexible of major American actors, seems suddenly to be an Antonioni creation with an American accent. He's an Antonioni concept of alienation who also happens to be a most particular person.

No other performer in an Antonioni film, except Jeanne Moreau in "La Notte," has so gracefully submitted to Mr. Antonioni and survived intact. If Miss Schneider is less remarkable it may be because the girl is more a device than a character.

1975 Ap 10, 46:1

BAR SALON, directed by Andre Forcier; screenplay and dialogue (French with English subtitles) by Mr. Forcier and Jacques Marcotte; produced by Jean Dansereau; director of photography, Francois Gill; editor, Mr. Gill; a co-production of Les Films Andre Forcier and Les Ateliers du Cinema Quebecois, Inc., Running time: 84 minutes. At the Museum of Modern Art, 53d Street west of Fifth Avenue.
Charles Methot .... Guy L'Ecuyer
Cecille Methot .... Lucille Belair
Michele Methot .... Madeline Chartrand
Robert .... Jacques Marcotte
Larry .... Gelinas Fortin
Louisette .... Michele Dion

By VINCENT CANBY

When André Forcier's "Bar Salon" begins, it looks very much like a respectably tough neo-realist film about a small group of French Canadians who live on the brink of a poverty that never quite kills as it corrupts.

Charles Methot (Guy L'Ecuyer) is a paunchy, middle-aged patron of a Montreal neighborhood bar going slowly into bankruptcy. His daughter Michele (Madeleine Chartrand) works in a fish store during the day, tends bar at night and sleeps with her fiancé, Robert (Jacques Marcotte) a taxi driver, whenever it pleases her. For a touch of domestic melodrama Mme. Methot (Lucile Belair) is about to have a hysterectomy.

"Bar Salon" is a far cry from melodrama, however. It's not even as neorealistic as its drab settings or its purposely dingy black and white photography would have you believe. By so accurately catching the surface details of his characters' lives, Mr. Forcier has somehow managed to create an intense awareness of interior worlds that are not realistic at all.

Charles Methot, who bickers with his daughter and largely ignores his wife, is a romantic. At one point he makes the momentous decision to leave his family and run off with a go-go dancer who, though not exactly in her prime, promises him some of the love and excitement he's been denied all these years.

This affair goes badly, winding up as a sort of failed joke. Charles returns to the fold. Michele finally marries Robert with all of the ritual due a temple virgin. Robert gets drunk at the reception, and when Charles's older brother leaves the party, also very durnk, he keeps asking Charles, "You're sure you won't forget me?"

"Bar Salon," which was shown yesterday at the Museum of Modern Art in its New Directors/New Films series, will be repeated there tomorrow evening at 6.

It's a finely controlled, low-key film that knows that to say a lot about characters is sometimes to say nothing. I've described more of what might be called plot than usual because plot is not important. It is simply the plan of the things that *happen* while we are brought into the film's experience by filling in the omissions, mostly the whys and the hows.

"Bar Salon" is the third feature by Mr. Forcier, who made it last year at the age of 31. According to the museum's program notes, Jean Vigo is the director whom Mr. Forcier most admires but the young director sees the world in his own terms. The view is compassionate, comic and unafraid.

1975 Ap 12, 14:4

A PRIVATE ENTERPRISE, directed by Peter K. Smith; screenplay by Mr. Smith and Dilip Hiro; director of photography, Ray Orton; editors, Mr. Smith and Charles Rees; music, Ram Narayan; a production of the British Film Institute Production Board. Running time: 78 minutes. At the Museum of Modern Art, 53d Street west of Fifth Avenue.

Shiv .... Salmaan Peer
Ashok .... Marc Zuber
Uncle Ramil .... Ramon Sinha
Chandra .... Shukla Bhattercharjee
Chandra's father .... Yehye Saeed
Penny .... Diana Quick

"A Private Enterprise," the first feature film to be directed by Peter K. Smith, a 39-year-old Englishman, is a sympathetic comedy about somebody whose values are almost hopelessly second-rate.

Shiv (Salmaan Peer), its hero, is a young Indian engineer who works in Birmingham as a laborer but dreams of making his fortune manufacturing and selling plastic toy elephants.

Shiv is less naive than madly hopeful. The elephants he wants to market are of a vulgarity that reduces shopgirls to helpless giggles. When a snobbish English girl picks him up on the train, he is the last one to realize that to her he is just another exotic ornament, a higher-class version of one of his elephants.

"A Private Enterprise" has the shape of comedy but its tone, ultimately, is sorrowful, not unlike the Anglo-Indian comedies of James Ivory and Ismail Merchant. Shiv is not a tragic character. He's a befuddled one, trying unsuccessfully to fit into a society that doesn't want him.

•

The film is small, precise and, at crucial moments, beautifully funny, as when a radical Indian friend quotes Chairman Mao to the backsliding Shiv. "A Private Enterprise" was shown at the Museum of Modern Art yesterday in the New Directors/ New Films series. It will be given a second screening there tonight at 8:30.

VINCENT CANBY

1975 Ap 12, 14:4

WEDDING TROUGH (Vase De Noces), directed, produced, edited and photographed by Thierry Zeno; screenplay by Mr. Zeno and Dominique Garny. Running time: 82 minutes. At the Museum of Modern Art, 53d Street west of Fifth Avenue.
The man .... Dominique Garny

"Wedding Trough" is a movie about a young man who lives on a farm. Since "Wedding Trough" is supposed to be an avant-garde movie, the young man has no name and very little expression in his face. He does, however, have some chickens, some ducks, some turkeys and a large cheerful sow who goes "oink, oink" as she forages for food and the soundtrack plays Monteverdi.

When we first see the young man he is trying to fit the head of a doll over the head of a pigeon. The pigeon will have none of it. The young man sets the pigeon free. Later the young man chops off the head of a chicken. The chicken runs around without it for a while, then collapses. Still later the young man has sex with the sow while she continues her search for food. The sow knows it isn't love, even before the young man hangs their three piglets, murders her and becomes hugely preoccupied with his own excrement.

"Wedding Trough," which was screened yesterday at the Museum of Modern Art in its New Directors/New Films series, will be repeated there Monday.

It is experimental film-making of the most ordinary, unstimulating sort. It's the first feature by a 24-year-old Belgian director whose pseudonym is Thierry Zeno and whose idol, apparently, is Pier Paolo Pasolini at his worst. "Wedding Trough" may be about things other than those events shown on the screen but I doubt it.

VINCENT CANBY

1975 Ap 12, 14:5

'Mirror' by Tarkovsky Is Unorthodox and Popular

By JAMES F. CLARITY
Special to The New York Times

MOSCOW, April 12—"Mirror," a new film by Andrei Tarkovsky, the controversial and unorthodox Soviet director, is delighting, puzzling, disapping serious Muscovite movie enthusiasts.

The film began showing in two theaters here this week and instantly became the talk of moviegoing intellectuals because, they say, nothing quite like "Mirror" has ever been made before by a Soviet director. Scores of people have been clamoring for tickets in the last few days.

Some Muscovites who have seen the film predict that it is sure to be attacked for its unorthodoxy by the ideologically oriented critics of the official press. But in the first round of published reviews, in which some of Mr. Tarkovsky's fellow film makers evaluated his new work, there is much praise, tempered with criticism of some parts of the film.

Unconcerned With Abuse

In the way he has created "Mirror"—using techniques familiar to viewers of Federico Fellini and Ingmar Bergman pictures, but not to many Soviet moviegoers—Mr. Tarkovsky seems to make it clear that he is unconcerned with the abuse he has taken for some of his earlier films. "Andrei Rublev," the grim, realistic story of the 15th-century Russian monk and icon painter, was banned in this country for several years, although it won a Cannes Film Festival prize in 1970. Mr. Tarkovsky's science-fiction film, "Solyaris," was criticized a few years ago as being too arcane and whimsical for the average audience to understand.

"Mirror," a Mosfilm production, is not at all easy to understand, in the sense that it does not have the traditionally recognizable plot structure that

is rarely tampered with by Soviet directors. There are flashbacks, slow-motion dream scenes, newsreels and a mixture of color for some sequences and black and white for others.

The camera work of Georgi Rerberg on hazy countryside scenes and prolonged still-life shots of, for example, spilled milk or a spot of moisture evaporating on a shiny wood table fascinated viewers who saw the picture the first night it was shown here. Several Russians discussing the film later in the evening argued for various interpretations of various scenes, but all agreed that parts of the movie produced a shock of self-recognition.

Soul of One Man

As far as it can be summarized, the movie follows the course of the soul of one man, who narrates but is rarely seen on the screen. His relationship with his wife, his mother and his children and the society around him develops in events connected in his mind. How this connection is translated to the screen is what puzzles or delights the viewer, as he watches the hero's wife doubling in his mind as his mother.

There are symbolic birds and fires and winds and rainfalls, and newsreels of a bullfight in Spain, Chinese agitators taunting Soviet soldiers at the border and Soviet soldiers tramping through mud. Stalin peers for a split-second from a poster into a print shop where a mistake might have been made. The hero's wife seems to long for him, but she kills him metaphorically by beheading a large white rooster.

"Mirror," according to the criticism of several of Mr. Tarkovsky's fellow directors, will narrow his audience in the Soviet Union. It could increase his audience and his prestige in the West, if the Soviet authorities permit the film to be shown abroad.

1975 Ap 13, 58:6

FILM VIEW

VINCENT CANBY

'Shampoo' Could Be the Year's Best Comedy

I t's only April but Hal Ashby's "Shampoo," which opened in February, remains the American film comedy of the year to date— a witty, furtively revolutionary, foul-mouthed comedy-of-manners cast in the fairly conventional frame of a story about the comeuppance of a small-town Casanova.

In this case the small town happens to be very rich Beverly Hills, Calif., and the Casanova is a hairdresser named George, played by Warren Beatty with intense, exuberant self-absorption that has the effect of making him just that much more appealing to women. Even the ones who should know better are ready to abandon everything—family, career, semantics—in the company of George. Like Jill (Goldie Hawn), a would-be actress of some taste and intelligence who makes no effort to correct George when he says "I'm at the epitome of my life" or worries "I've been cutting too much hair recently. I'm losing my concepts."

George is a great comic character, partially because the role is beautifully written by Robert Towne and Mr. Beatty (who share the screenplay credit) and partially because he's played by Mr. Beatty, who turns out to be one of the handful of actors today (Jack Nicholson and Walter Matthau are two others) who can make outrageous self-interest plausibly funny in a way that escapes many professional comedians, including Bob Hope.

George's womanizing should not be over-interpreted. It's simply a part of the total movie that regards the American scene on the eve of the 1968 election with jaundiced hindsight. Though he could be successfully (and creepily) analyzed, George is a Casanova who should be taken at face value in the frame of the film. When asked how he happened to become a hairdresser, he explains that he just likes women and he likes to make them happy in every way he knows how. When at the end

Why couldn't Beatty keep Christie?

Jill wants to know how many of his clients he's slept with, he says, at first sheepishly and then angrily, refusing to apologize, "All of them." At the end of the day, says George, "I feel good."

•   •   •

"Shampoo" gets some mileage—though not as much as it might have tried for had it been less disciplined—out of the fact that most male hairdressers, according to popular belief, are homosexual. The fact that George isn't, and isn't in a quite spectacular way, may be one of the more revolutionary things in the film. It is also, ironically, one of the more disturbing elements to people who feel that "Shampoo" maligns hairdressers who are homosexual. The liberal reasoning being that had a macho Beatty played a gay hairdresser there would have been a breakthrough but that, as it is, "Shampoo" is still employing stereotypes, especially in its presentation of George's swishy associates at the beauty salon. Maybe so, but that sort of interpretation quickly gets one so bogged down that one loses sight of the movie's great gusto and candor.

The world of "Shampoo" is largely populated by other citizens who, like George, are so busy pursuing their own ends that they can't see the nature of the society they're living in. It may be argued, very persuasively, that by setting "Shampoo" around the 1968 election, the director and the writers are overstating the obvious. I must say that I totally disagree. The television clips that Mr. Ashby shows us—the victorious Spiro Agnew talking about the spiritual strength of the nation and Richard Nixon going on in his most spurious down-home manner about bringing the country together—still stagger me. Was it just seven years ago? What could have happened? Were the last years of the Nixon Administration some ghastly accident?

It was just seven years ago and it did happen and they weren't an accident.

"Shampoo" is about a lot of quite nice, myopic people going to hell in a handcar and not noticing. Not paying attention. Thinking they're happy when they're miserable. It does not—if I see it correctly—attempt to fill in the causes for the effects, that is, the events of the early nineteen-seventies. It's not that simple or didactic a film.

Instead it recalls a state of mind that still exists today. If "Shampoo" is to be faulted, it's on the grounds that George's comeuppance (which is, after all, the cautionary point of all Don Juan literature) can, by association, make the collapse of the Nixon Administration appear more cathartic for the national well-being than may actually be the case. Time will tell.

•   •   •

Until "Shampoo" I've always had a couple of major reservations about each of Hal Ashby's films but this one works so well in its mixing of moods that I'm prepared to upgrade both "The Landlord" and "The Last Detail," though "Harold and Maude" will probably forever escape me. The common denominator of all his films is the excellence of the performances. Mr. Ashby casts his films as carefully as he directs them. Remember Beau Bridges, Diana Sands, Lee Grant and Pearl Bailey in "The Landlord," and Jack Nicholson and Randy Quaid in "The Last Detail"?

The performances in "Shampoo" are equally precise, a practical result of good casting for the right material. At the end of "Shampoo" I was struck by how much we knew of the characters, by the variety of associations we have with them, even though the screenplay, like most good screenplays, never indulges in the kind of character exposition that we take for granted in written fiction. "Shampoo" is all present tense but there is no awareness of missing pasts.

In addition to Mr. Beatty and Miss Hawn, the first-rate cast includes Julie Christie, looking simultaneously splendidly chic and a bit vulgar, as George's one possibly true love, now a kept woman; Lee Grant, as one of George's more voracious clients; Jack Warden, as Miss Grant's husband, and keeper of Miss Christie, and Carrie Fisher, the 17-year-old daughter of Debbie Reynolds and Eddie Fisher, as a pretty, pudding-faced girl who seduces George on his journey to nowhere.

I have one more slight reservation about "Shampoo." We now have movies about bank robbers who get away with the loot. Isn't it about time that guys like George be allowed to wind up as happy and satisfied as they and we wish they could be?

1975 Ap 13, II:15:1

ALMA, directed by Zelito Viana; screenplay (Portuguese with English subtitles) by Mr. Viana, Eduardo Coutinho and Antonio Carlos de Birto, based on the novel "Os Condenados" by Oswald de Andrade; director of photography, Dib Lufti; editor, Eduardo Escorel; music, John Luciano Neschling; produced by Tadito Val Quinfans and Alvara Freire for Mapa Films, Ltd. Running time: 90 minutes. At the Museum of Moden Art, 53d Street west of Fifth Avenue.

Alma	Isabel Ribeiro
Joao	Claudio Marzo
Mauro	Roberto Bataglin

By VINCENT CANBY

Alma (Isabel Ribeiro) is a whore who thoroughly enjoys her job. She's not pretty in any conventional way. Her figure is too lean to fulfill Earth Mother fantasies. There's something else about Alma that appeals to men, a streak of recklessness that seems almost mad. Alma couldn't care less about the consequences when her wealthy lover finds out that she's got another fellow on the side. It's simply back to the brothel and let's-have-a-party.

Alma, the title character in Zelito Viana's beautiful, haunting new Brazilian film, hasn't always been a whore. But after she was strictly brought up by a puritanical grandfather, she was ruined by a local São Paulo roué. "Alma" is the story of another man's obsessional love for her, and Alma's total inability to respond to it. Alma wants excitement, even if it means getting beaten up now and then. João (Claudio Marzo), an uptight office worker, keeps trying unsuccessfully to save her, which is his way of getting beaten up.

"Alma" is less about sadomasochism, however, than about a series of fatally interlocking dependencies. These, I suspect, might well give the film political implications in Brazil that we here could easily miss.

Mr. Viana, the film's 37-year-old director, has set the movie in the late nineteen-twenties and early thirties, which affords the production designer certain opportunities for visual spectacle. It also gives the director the chance to meditate upon the social structure of a country where, as wealth feeds upon poverty, despair prompts the unlikeliest hopes. No matter how repressed he is, poor João couldn't pursue his doomed love for Alma without her wholehearted cooperation.

•

"Alma" is the third feature directed by Mr. Viana, who has been associated with Brazil's Cinema Novo also as a producer and writer. It is impeccably set and photographed and performed — principally by Miss Ribeiro and Mr. Marzo — with such restraint that its few moments of abandon (whorehouse frolics) seem much more shocking than they are by any standards except those created by the director.

"Alma" is a very thoughtful, mature film, one of the best in the Museum of Modern Art's current New Directors/New Films series. It was shown at the museum yesterday and will be shown again tomorrow evening at 6.

1975 Ap 14, 41:1

ONCE UPON A TIME IN THE EAST (Il Etait une Fois Dans l'Est), directed by Andre Brassard; screenplay (French with English subtitles) by Mr. Brassard and Michel Tremblay; director of photography, Paul Van Der Linden; music, Jacques Perron; editor, Andre Corriveau; produced by Les Productions Carle-Lamy, Ltd. Running time: 100 minutes. At the Museum of Modern Art, 53d Street, west of Fifth Avenue.

Helene	Denise Filiatrault
Pierrette	Michelle Rossignol
Lise Paquette	Frederique Collin
Carmen	Sophie Clement
Sandra	Andree Montomorency
Hare-Lip	Amuelette Garneau
Maurice	Denis Drouin
Hosanna	Jean Archambault
Cuirette	Gilles Renaud

Lise Pacquette, a waitress in Montreal's seedy East End, is very young, pretty and pregnant, but with no man in sight. When she tries to borrow money from the loan company to pay for an abortion, she explains that she wants a new stereo. Her application is turned down.

Pierrette is older but equally unhappy. Her man has left her for a younger woman, so she drinks too much. Old Mme. Lauzon receives word that she has won a million trading stamps. At first she is skeptical and cross. Then she becomes almost unhinged with excitement.

•

Hosanna, an aging transvestite who never successfully hides a five o'clock shadow, spends all day preparing for a drag ball where he'll appear as Cleopatra. Cuirette, Hosanna's roommate who fancies leather and chains, makes fun of Hosanna unmercifully.

Everybody in "Once Upon a Time in the East" (Il Etait une Fois Dans l'Est) dreams an impossible dream that is bound to come to no good end.

More to the point of the film, everybody has a big scene, one of those front-and-center moments when he or she can attempt the movie equivalent of stopping the show. But movies, being movies, don't stop. Thus, would-be show-stopping moments tend to collect, to bunch up, like too many people trying to attract the attention of a single taxi on a rainy night.

You've never seen as much acting as goes on from the start to the finish of André Brassard's French-Canadian film, which was screened Saturday at the Museum of Modern Art, as part of the New Directors/New Films series, and will be screened there again tonight at 8:30.

"Once Upon a Time in the East," based on a screenplay by Michel Tremblay and Mr. Brassard, has its origins in plays written by Mr. Tremblay and staged with great success in Canada by Mr. Brassard. An English translation of one episode of this film was done on Broadway last fall under the title "Hosanna."

•

Mr. Brassard and Mr. Tremblay have tried very hard to make a coherent film of all these actors doing what they do so well, but I, for one, could never forget that everyone was simply acting.

"Once Upon a Time in the East" has more busy moments than affecting ones. The characters all seem to be related to one another or, at least, to know one another, but there is very little sense of community in the movie. It's like a Broadway tribute of some sort, composed entirely of big moments from other shows.

VINCENT CANBY

1975 Ap 14, 41:1

DON'T CRY WITH YOUR MOUTH FULL (Pleure Pas la Bouche Pleine), directed by Pascal Thomas; screenplay (French with English subtitles) by Mr. Thomas, Roland Duval and Suzanne Schiffman; director of photography, Christian Bachmann; executive producer, Claude Berri; editor, Helene Plemianikov; music, Michel Choquet; produced by Renn Productions and Les Films du Cheflieu-O.R.T.F.; released by New Yorker Films. Running time: 116 minutes. This film has not been classified. At the Paris Theater, 58th Street west of Fifth Avenue.

Annie	Annie Cole
Father	Jean Carmel
Mother	Christiane Chamaret
Grandmother	Helene Dieudonne
Uncle	Daniel Ceccaldi
Aunt	Claudine Paringaux
Sister	Friquette
Alexander	Bernard Menez
Frederic	Frederic Duru

"Don't Cry With Your Mouth Full" was shown last year at the 12th New York Film Festival. The following excerpt is from Vincent Canby's review, which appeared in The New York Times on Sept. 28. The film is being shown at the Paris Theater, 58th Street west of Fifth Avenue.

Annie (Annie Colé) is in her mid-teens and of a physical ripeness so strong it seems to create an invisible force around her, like a magnetic field. Annie is aware of this and she enjoys it, but she is too sweet-spirited to turn that force into a weapon. Annie inhabits an idealized provincial landscape where everything is in bloom and where the only aggressions are of natural origin—and over and done with as quickly and as harmlessly as a summer thunderstorm.

Annie is the heroine of Pascal Thomas's bucolic, lazily funny, gently bawdy French film, "Don't Cry With Your Mouth Full" (Pleure Pas la Bouche Pleine"), which is about one summer in Annie's life, set in a small town that would seem to be somewhere southwest of Paris, and not too far from the sea. It's the kind of town where there's no great differentiation between village and countryside.

•

The film's focus is Annie, whom Miss Colé plays with marvelous, un-self-conscious humor. Miss Colé is a very pretty young woman but she's not an idealized beauty. She always seems to have small bruises on her arms and legs, as if on the few occasions when she pulled herself together to practice a more elegant walk, she has bumped into chairs and tables.

Her Annie is a delightful character, and the men in her life are no match for her. The men are Frédéric (Frédéric Duru), a nice country boy who, if pressed, would rather win a cross-country bike race than roll in the haystack with Annie, and Alexandre (Bernard Menez), the town lothario, a handsome young man with a hawklike nose that inevitably reduces all his man-of-the-world mannerisms to their comic components.

•

All the performances have a slightly mad, comic purpose, which may be one of the reasons Mr. Thomas's work is compared to that of Renoir and Truffaut. Although "Don't Cry With Your Mouth Full" is a finely disciplined film, which doesn't seek the easy laugh or ask for gratuitous sentiment, it never suggests the dark void beyond the sunlight, something that distinguishes the work of Renoir and Truffaut and sets their films apart from all others.

This is not something that can be tacked onto a film or inserted into it, as an isolated gesture, like the scene in which Annie's father, doubling as undertaker, must dress the nude body of an old woman for burial. The scene is fine in itself, but it's not enough to enrich the somewhat too sunny nature of the movie with the sort of intimations that separate good films from great ones.

1975 Ap 14, 41:1

CROSS SECTION: AN AMERICAN FILM PROGRAM, consisting of four short films: **JEFFERSON CIRCUS SONGS,** directed by Susan Pitt Kraning; produced in a summer film workshop sponsored by the Urban Arts Program and the Walker Art Center of Minneapolis; running time, 20 minutes; **THE PLAINT OF STEVE KREINES as RECORDED BY HIS YOUNGER BROTHER JEFF,** directed by Jeff Kreines; running time 47 minutes; **HOMAGE TO MAGRITTE,** directed and produced by Anita Thacher, with additional photography and sound by Larry Loewinger; running time, 10 minutes; **8½ X 11,** directed and produced by James Benning; running time, 33 minutes. At the Museum of Modern Art, on 53d Street west of Fifth Avenue.

The selection committee for the Museum of Modern Art's current New Directors/New Films series was obviously hard put to find American entries. There is no other way to explain this disappointing program of four shorts under the umbrella title, "Cross Section: An American Film Program."

It may be an American film program, but it is hardly a cross-section of American film making. Almost any week one can see better, more representative American films at the Whitney Museum of American Art and the Film Forum.

It is also unfair to the makers of these films to include their well-intentioned, modestly interesting work in a show otherwise devoted (with one or two exceptions) to the work of talented professionals from abroad.

The program, first screened on Saturday, will be repeated at the museum tomorrow night at 8:30.

VINCENT CANBY

1975 Ap 14, 41:4

SUSAN: APRIL TO JUNE, directed by Linda Jassim; camera by Christine Burrill. Running time: 23 minutes. And **METHADONE: AN AMERICAN WAY OF DEALING,** produced, directed and edited by Julia Reichert and James Klein; photographed by Alicia Weber; music, Bill Conway; distributed by Methadone Information Center. Running time: 62 minutes. At the Whitney Museum of American Art, Madison Avenue and 75th Street. Through Tuesday.

By A. H. WEILER

As illustrations of a national blight, "Methadone: An American Way of Dealing" and "Susan: April to June," the documentaries that arrived yesterday at the Whitney Museum of American Art, evolve as professional and provocative inspections of a terrible problem. But in presenting bleak facts and avoiding panaceas for the addicted or superficial notions about a dope-driven prostitute, they manage to shed light and a tiny ray of hope into the dark corners of our malignant drug scene.

"Methadone" may scientifically probe into its material, but it does so with its humanity showing. And Julia Reichert and James Klein, who focused their cameras on the only methadone clinic in Dayton, Ohio, and the collective self-help, RAP, Inc., center in Washington, stress that methadone is still highly controversial therapy and that RAP might be that sought-after alternative.

●

As a sociological study, the record is the afflicted's record. They speak for themselves — mostly black and some white junkies—in discussions of their introduction to drugs, their abilities to lead normal lives and conflicting debates on methadone therapy. Since this is implicit criticism of methadone, the film is counterbalanced by sessions inside the RAP center.

The emphasis here is on community living and working in a drug-free society in which therapy involves self-knowledge through delving into personal root causes of addiction coupled with political and academic education toward achieving a cure and a productive life. That glimmer of hope is implied even if a complete solution to the problem isn't indicated.

●

If the life-style of "Susan" seems short and episodic by comparison, it is effective in its unerotic, clinic approach to its subject. In Linda Jassim's staccato color vignettes, the 23-year-old bleached-blonde, somewhat pudgy Santa Monica, Calif., hooker enslaved in the oldest profession because of her expensive habit is an intelligent, if pitiable, woman, who is given unromanticized but empathetic treatment as she makes the rounds from street to police station to a state hospital and, presumably, rehabilitation.

While "Susan" and "Methadone," which, a program note by the producers says was "a radicalizing experience," are not shocking, they both project arresting, sobering views of a still unconquered scourge.

1975 Ap 17, 48:3

CAPONE, directed by Steve Carver; screenplay by Howard Browne; produced by Roger Corman; music, David Grisman; director of photography, Vilis Lapenieks; editor, Richard Meyer; distributed by 20th Century-Fox. Running time: 101 minutes. At Loews

State 2, Broadway at 45th Street, and Loews Cine Theater, Third Avenue at 86th Street. This film has been rated R.

Al Capone	Ben Gazarra
Iris Crawford	Susan Blakely
Johnny Torrio	Harry Guardino
Frankie Vale	John Cassavetes
Frank Natti	Sylvester Stallon
Jake Guzik	Peter Malone
Big Jim Colosimo	Frank Campanella
Anton Cermak	Royal Dano

By VINCENT CANBY

"Capone" reduces the gangster film to its single essential, the gun fight.

This gun fight goes on more or less nonstop after the title character is established as a poor but ambitious Brooklyn boy, at the beginning of the film, unti just before the end wher we leave the syphilitic Scar face Al (Ben Gazarra), nutty as a fruitcake by his Florida swimming pool, ranting about the Bolsheviks.

●

The weapons and the combatants change but everything remains basically the same. As old friends, such as Big Jim Colosimo (Frank Campanella), are mowed down, new ones, such as Frank Nitti (Sylvester Stallone), take their place. The movie requires a certain prior knowledge of the Chicago gang wars of the nineteen-twenties, which really aren't dramatized. Rather they are illustrated in a series of bloody tableaux, sometimes by anonymously driven vintage cars that pursue one another through Hollywood studio streets like robots possessed.

'Capone' which opened at Loews State 2 and Cine Theaters yesterday, was produced by today's King of the B's, Roger Corman, and written by Howard Browne, the two men who earlier collaborated on "The St. Valentine's Day Massacre," which covered pretty much the same turf.

This one, however, was directed by Steve Carver, who deals with the subject energetically, directly and completely without sentimentality, which is one of this unpretentious movie's small but remarkable virtues.

Some of the other virtues are the performances—by Mr. Gazarra, who plays Al with the kind of boldness that risks giggles; Harry Guardino, as the gentle-natured gangster, Johnny Torrio, and Sylvester Stallone, as a new-style gangster who succeeds Al when the latter is nabbed on income tax evasion. John Cassavetes makes a token appearance as a New York mobster early in the film.

"Capone" is not great but it moves with cold efficiency, which is its style whether you like it or not.

1975 Ap 17, 48:6

FILM VIEW

VINCENT CANBY

Antonioni's Haunting Vision

As if he were a member of some privileged order, Michelangelo Antonioni is allowed to see things the rest of us cannot. In his stunning new film, "The Passenger," he shares that privilege with us. His camera's eye is a laser that transforms everything it sees into a more precise definition of the thing represented—objects, people, movements, landscapes. Yet the definition of the thing represented—and this is the rub—becomes increasingly ambiguous the closer Antonioni's camera gets. The same thing happens when you say the same word over and over again so often that finally only the sound is left. We return to essentials.

This is one of the haunting effects of "The Passenger," a suspense melodrama, a story so basically conventional that it isn't until you're at least half-way through it you realize it's a magnificent nightmare, and that you are on the inside looking out. More effectively than any other film he has made, "The Passenger" translates Antonioni's concern with the quality of contemporary life into non-esoteric film terms. Even more successfully than in "L'Avventura" and "Blow-Up" he achieves a balance between psychological substructure and intellectual superstructure, the weight of which capsized "Zabriskie Point," his last film, even before it had left the dock.

"Zabriskie Point" was a collection of handsomely illustrated, neo-radical ideas, a meditation on America not of the first interest, for which a love story of sorts had been concocted, but it was a narrative that had no life of its own.

"The Passenger" is a fascinating tale of flight and pursuit that moves non-stop across the screen. Its intellect is more apparent in the way it looks (the best movies are what they look like) than in anything that anybody says. It's there in the beautiful opening sequence, which I will try to describe, and in the extraordinary closing sequence, which I won't, not only because it would be giving the story away but because it's the sort of cinematic tour de force that must be discovered for oneself.

This ending has some of the breathtaking quality of the ending of Bunuel's "Tristana," though the two sequences have nothing specifically in common. Neither sequence is particularly fancy, but each in its way rediscovers a narrative device unique to films.

The opening sequence of "The Passenger" is pictorial exposition of special order: a man (Jack Nicholson) is searching for someone or something through North Africa, on the outskirts of cities, in rural villages. He is scarcely acknowledged. People look through him, or away. In a cafe two black men help themselves to his cigarettes and turn back to their own affairs. Later a small Arab boy materializes and leads him and his Land Rover into the desert. There the boy motions the man to stop. The boy gets out of the car and disappears. The man can see nothing but desert and some distant mountains. No place for the boy to escape to. The dry heat and the seeming clarity of the desert light at high noon make him a little giddy.

Then, in the distance, there appears an Arab atop a camel riding leisurely across the sands. The man waves to the Arab and calls. The Arab and his camel pass close by. The Arab nods to the man, but distantly, as if he were on a ship whose course was being directed by others. The Arab goes on his way at the same unbroken pace. The man climbs back into the Land Rover, turns on the engine and quickly allows himself to get stuck in the sand. He gets out once more and kicks the half-buried tire. It is the last straw. It's also his own bloody fault. At last he's reached the end of the line.

The man is a television news personality named Locke, English-born, American-bred, the sort of reporter, one gathers, who's more of a celebrity than the people he reports on. Locke has been on a wild goose chase to find and interview a group of African guerrillas.

Locke returns to his fleabag hotel in the desert on foot. You suspect that he might be a Maugham character doomed to an exotic end in civilization's outpost. Not so. When a passing stranger, an Englishman about Locke's age, weight and height, dies suddenly of a heart attack at the hotel, Locke makes a choice. He assumes the man's identity. Locke picks up the man's name, passport, wardrobe and appointments book, and then sets out to discover who he now is.

Thus begins "The Passenger," which follows Locke on his search from North Africa to England to Germany to Spain. In the course of his travels he meets a pretty, calm, unflappable girl (Maria Schneider), who is known only as The Girl. The Girl is an architecture student but she exists only to help and comfort Locke. As much as he has known what the end of his search must be, he has known about the girl even before he meets her in Barcelona. Earlier, in London, he had seen her sitting on a park bench and they had recognized each other.

Antonioni doesn't spend too much time convincing us of the desperation of Locke's life that would make him so easily assume another's identity. He has been unhappily married, we are told, though the wife (Jenny Runacre) is hardly a harridan. We are also told he is fed up with his career, freezing on film those moments of history that never truly tell the entire story. He has been in the business of reducing to comprehensible terms—to television merchandise—events that may be incomprehensible in their complexity. Wars, revolutions, and the like. Locke wants out but unlike most of us who might have that dream from time to time, he gets the opportunity.

In Germany, where Locke goes to keep one of his new identity's appointments, he meets two representatives of an African terrorist group who give him $50,000 and thank him for obtaining the guns, though they are disappointed he couldn't get anti-aircraft equipment.

Gee, says Locke, in effect. "I'm sorry about the anti-aircraft guns. I hope it won't be too much of a drawback." It's the first important thing Locke has said in his assumed role, and it's funny because it's so obviously inadequate.

Later Locke learns far more forcefully the inadequacy of his masquerade. There has been, however, a recognizable nobility in his search for the truth.

"The Passenger," which was written by Mark Peploe, Peter Wollen (author of "Signs and Meaning in The Cinema") and Antonioni, is open to all sorts of solemn interpretations, a lot of them involving the use of the word "alienation," which may be the most boring word to gain wide currency in criticism in the last 20 years.

Once you leave the film's narrative level to ponder its other meanings, you are on your own. "The Passenger" shouldn't be scrutinized and deciphered like a top-secret NATO message. It's a poetic vision. Its images, as perfectly illuminated as a night landscape by a flash of lightning, suggest all sorts of associations, from "The Odyssey" to other movies, including pot-boiling, multinational coproductions about Interpol agents.

Locke, a role that Jack Nicholson assumes with such grace and ease that one almost forgets he's an actor, comes out of the barren world of earlier Antonioni films, but unlike earlier Antonioni characters he makes a decisive choice that sets him apart from his predecessors, who were too busy just trying to cope to make decisions of such magnitude. In his way Locke is a much more committed, much more revolutionary character than the pea-brained radical in "Zabriskie Point." He's also a much more appealing character than the photographer in "Blow-Up," a man who remained always outside his pictures.

"The Passenger" marks Antonioni's triumphant passage from the concerns of the nineteen-fifties and nineteen-sixties, when we seemed to be standing still, to those of the nineteen-seventies, when events have given us the guts to choose, perhaps to move on.

1975 Ap 20, II:1:1

American Film Theater Presents Genet Work

By VINCENT CANBY

"Everything that comes out of the kitchen is spit," says Madame to Claire, her maid. "Get out and take your mucous with you."

Madame is dressing for an evening on the town. She reviles Claire as she orders her about, fetching jewels and clothes. Madame insults Claire and Claire grovels with pleasure. When Claire has attempted to add a bit of polish to Madame's patent leather shoes, Madame sneers, "Do you think I find it pleasant to know that my foot is shrouded by veils of your saliva?" And Claire answers humbly, "I wish Madame to be lovely."

When the alarm clock suddenly rings, the two women clutch each other. Madame says, "Hurry. Madame will be back . . . It's over already and you didn't get to the end."

The end is the end of the ceremonial masquerade enacted by Claire and Solange, the title characters in Jean Genet's "The Maids."

•

Whenever Madame is out of the posh apartment, Claire and her older sister Solange take over the premises for an elaborate ritual in which each takes turn playing Madame while the other sister plays the maid who is not herself: When Claire is Madame, Solange is Claire. The end they never get to is Madame's death by strangulation.

This time, Solange (Glenda Jackson), who seems to be the stronger of the two, blames Claire (Susannah York), and Claire says rather wistfully, "We waste too much time with the preliminaries."

The Cast

THE MAIDS, directed by Christopher Miles, screenplay by Robert Enders and Mr. Miles, based on the Minos Volanakis translation of Jean Genet's French play; produced by Mr. Enders; executive producer, Bernard Weitzman; editor, Peter Tanner; director of photography, Douglas Slocombe; a Robert Enders Films in association with Cine-Films, Inc., presented by the American Film Theater. Running time: 10 minutes. At selected theaters. This film has been rated PG.

Solange	Glenda Jackson
Claire	Susannah York
Madame	Vivien Merchant

The American Film Theater's film version of Mr. Genet's one-act play has been somewhat literalized by being "opened up" for the screen by Christopher Miles, the director. Madame's elegant digs now are recognizably across the Place Vendôme from the Paris Ritz. Nothing much has been added by this information, nor by our being presented a sort of dumb-show behind the opening credits that tells us that Claire and Solange have written anonymous letters resulting in the arrest of Madame's young lover, a character who never is seen in the Genet play.

Though nothing much has been added by this mildly cinematic treatment, it is more important that nothing has been lost. The film, which was shown at selected theaters yesterday and will be shown again today, is a fine, vivid recording of what seems to have been a smashing theater production of the play in London last year with Miss Jackson, Miss York and Vivien Merchant (as Madame).

The film preserves the essential quality of the play, which is that of a series of performances designed not to tell a story or convince us of narrative truth, but to speculate on illusion, on the relationship between the looks of things and the reality. As is the inevitable case with Genet, illusion is the only reality, and reality is a lie or, you might say, an illusion.

•

In his preface to the Grove Press paperback edition of "The Maids," Jean-Paul Sartre has a good deal of ponderous fun going over this conundrum, which, at this point in history, seems a little schoolboyish and suggests nothing of the very real excitement of "The Maids" in performance.

It is the surface of things that makes "The Maids" spellbinding (even through an arbitrary intermission that has been stuck into the one-act play). The film is carried by the furious interplay between Miss Jackson's Solange and Miss York's Claire, when they are playing what they call their "scene," and then between the two maids and Madame, who renders Solange and Claire effectively impotent by her casual kindnesses, by her insistence on recognizing as tokens of love the presents they have given her in hatred.

Although "The Maids" is composed of role-playing, it is not a drama of identity as Antonioni's "The Passenger" is. Solange, Claire and Madame do not possess hidden hearts to be uncovered as by peeling artichokes. Each is a reflection of the other's wishes. Solange and Claire exist only in terms of the sado-masochistic relationship that binds them to each other and to Madame, who is, in turn, their creation.

The three actresses have a superb time giving life to this wild riddle, missing none of the sometimes caustic, sometimes matter-of-fact humor that Sartre never takes time to ponder in his preface, but which is essential to Genet's work and to this film.

1975 Ap 22, 41:1

TEN LITTLE INDIANS, directed by Peter Collinson; screenplay by Peter Welbeck, based on the story by Agatha Christie; produced by Harry Alan Towers; director of photography, Fernando Arribas; editor, John Trumper; music, Bruno Nicolai; released by Avco Embasy Pictures. Running time: 98 minutes. At Loews Astor Plaza, 44th Street west of Broadway, and other theaters. This film has been rated PG.

Hugh Lombard	Oliver Reed
Vera Clyde	Elke Sommer
Ilona	Stephane Audran
Raven	Charles Aznavour
Judge Cannon	Richard Attenborough
Blore	Gert Froebe
Dr. Armstrong	Herbert Lom
Elsa Martino	Maria Rohm
General	Adolfo Celi
Martino	Alberto De Mendoza

By VINCENT CANBY

"Ten Little Indians," the latest remake of the Agatha Christie story, looks less like a movie than a movie deal, the kind that gets put together over drinks at the Carlton Hotel bar during the Cannes Film Festival.

Somebody says he can get the screen rights to the true story of Omar Khayyam if somebody else can get a couple of "bankable" English actors. Another conferee promises to buy the French distribution rights in advance if there are some French stars in the film too. Italian, German and Ruritanian rights are disposed of in the same fashion. The basic financing is promised by still another party who keeps all his money in Iran and who requires that the film be shot there.

So far, so good. Then, at the last minute, the producer loses his rights to the Khayyam screenplay and shoots, instead, the Christie story. "What the hell," he may say to his startled cast, "all we have to do is change some of the lines, update the costumes and cancel the order for the bread and the wine."

•

"Ten Little Indians" is an international movie mess of the sort that damages the reputations of everyone connected with it, including Charles Aznavour, Richard Attenborough and the incomparable Stephane Audran. It was directed by Peter Collinson, who has made some bad movies in the past but nothing to compare with this lethargic, seemingly post-synchronized version of Miss Christie's great old story. You probably remember the plot about 10 people invited to an isolated house party in the course of which, one by one, each is systematically murdered.

For reasons that I suspect could have to do only with the picture's financing, the setting has been changed from England to what the production notes call "the fabulous Shah Abbas Hotel" in Isfahan, Iran. For reasons that apparently have to do with Mr. Collinson's concept of menace, and how to create a sense of it, most of the movie seems to have been shot by a camera 14 inches above the floor, or maybe by a cinematographer who is only 14 inches tall. After about an hour of this, you know how the world looks to a miniature poodle.

•

Oliver Reed, an able English actor, moves through the film like a cruise director on a sinking ship. He pretends to a cheerfulness that has absolutely nothing to do with the story or with the quality of the movie being made. He slaps Mr. Attenborough on the back and gives Herbert Lom an encouraging squeeze on the arm. Playfully he pats Elke Sommer's bottom. Nothing helps. They—and we—know they are in the middle of a disaster.

For the record: the same Agatha Christie story has been filmed twice before, in 1945 by Rene Clair with a cast that included Walter Huston and Barry Fitzgerald, and in 1966 by George Pollock with, among others, Fabian and Hugh O'Brian.

1975 Ap 24, 43:1

HEAVEN AND EARTH MAGIC FEATURE, an animated collage by Harry Smith. Distributed by the New York Film-makers Cooperative. Running time: 62 minutes. At the Whitney Museum of American Art, Madison Avenue at 75th Street.

Because it's been some time since Harry Smith's "Heaven and Earth Magic Feature" has been available to the public on a regular basis, the Whitney Museum's current booking should not be missed by anyone interested in this classic American avant-garde film.

The Whitney has on view the 62-minute version of the black-and-white animated collage, which is sometimes shown in shorter segments and sometimes with additional ones.

"Heaven and Earth Magic Feature," which Mr. Smith made between 1950 and 1961, should be first approached as a marvelous delirium, then deciphered (as much as you may want) afterward. Using cut-out figures from turn-of-the-century catalogs and old engravings, the film tells a kind of story, though I'd be hard put to describe it.

•

More important, Mr. Smith creates a truly mad, mad world in which people, animals and objects seem to be in constant combat, always in imminent danger of being reduced, grossly enlarged fragmented, transformed into something else, or consumed entirely (though never for long).

Surreal is a rather stuffy way of describing this world that turns on a set of mysterious physical laws that have a high slapstick content. A cutout of a face, finished except for the eyes, finally receives just one, which, though large, is one less than necessary. The single eye, tossed onto the face by the film's ubiquitous master of ceremonies, lodges in the middle of the forehead, reproachfully.

•

The film's busiest object is a furious mallet that is always popping up at opportune moments to fracture an image, maybe an egg, maybe the arms on a dressmaker's dummy. Syringes and hypodermic needles fly around the screen, sometimes on their own, sometimes in the service of recognizable humans, who delight as much in withdrawing vital essences as in injecting nasty foreign substances.

Delicately drawn birds, cows, dogs, cats, horse skeletons push in and out of the film frame. Pharmacists' mortars look like giant cauldrons. Sometimes the film's jet-black backgrounds are alive with manic saws, pliers, jugs, Rube Goldberg-like machines. In this world, an umbrella may be used as a means of propulsion.

If you have never seen "Heaven and Earth Magic Feature," here's a bit of advice: don't read the program notes until afterward. Make up your own mind and then have a go at Mr. Smith's explanation of his exuberant work.

VINCENT CANBY

1975 Ap 24, 43:1

TOUCH AND GO, directed by Philippe De Broca; screenplay (French with English subtitles) by Jean-Loup Dabadie; producers, Alexandre Mnouchkine and George Danciners; director of photography, Rene Mathelin; music, Michel Legrand; produced by Columbia Films, Les Films Ariane (Paris) and Vides (Rome); distributed by Libra Films. Running time: 110 minutes. At the D. W. Griffith Theater, 59th Street west of Second Avenue. This film has not been rated.

Lorene	Marlene Jobert
Valentin	Michel Piccoli
Basil	Michael York
Paul-Emile	Louis Velle
Woman	Didi Perego
Officer	Hans Verner
Mate	Amidou

By VINCENT CANBY

Philippe De Broca's 1971 French comedy, "Touch and Go," has two funny things in it—a small, single-engine airplane that seems to be so feeble it can only fly downhill and the sight of that same plane a little later, minus its wings, bumping along a desert highway. It's an airplane with gumption.

The rest of the film is Mr. De Broca at his most sappy and sentimental.

"Touch and Go," which opened officially at the D.W. Griffith Theater after playing a series of previews there, is set mostly in Italian-held North Africa during World War II and is about the supposedly suspenseful and comic flight to safety of a bird-brained English officer (Michael York) and a cheerful French black marketeer (Michel Piccoli), with the help of the pretty wife (Marlene Jobert) of the local Swiss consul.

The film has none of the wit or the slight touch of cynicism that in the past has redeemed such De Broca films as "The Five-Day Lover," "That Man From Rio" and even "King of Hearts." "Touch and Go" leaves a trail of feeble gags across its desert landscape, the refuse of a movie hoping to be saved.

In France the film was called "La Poudre D'Escampette," roughly translated as "French Leave."

1975 Ap 25, 24:1

WEST COAST FILMS: CYCLES by Jordan Belson and Stephen Beck, 11 minutes; TESTAMENT by James Broughton, 20 minutes; HIMALAYAN PILGRIMAGE by Jo Carson and Ward Sellars, 16 minutes; DUNE by John Knoop, 13 minutes; SKYEBOAT FOR BISCUIT by Beverly O'Neill, 3 minutes; LAST OF THE PERSIMMONS, 6 minutes, and SAUGUS SERIES, 18 minutes, by Pat O'Neill. At the Film Forum, 256 West 88th Street. Through Sunday, and next Thursday through Sunday, at 8 P.M.

By A. H. WEILER

The work of Western avant-garde movie makers, which has been appearing here seasonally over recent years, again is marked by vitality and independence, if not consistent effectiveness, in the program of seven short subjects that opened yesterday at the Film Forum. And once again, the West is simply an all-inclusive locus, and not the inspiration, for the vigorous thrusts at creativity exhibited by these film makers.

Oddly enough, the West Coast is a physical facet of James Broughton's "Testament", the most striking (and longest) subject in the collection. The veteran movie maker uses San Francisco and other California locales as backgrounds for his remembrance of things past. More important, however, is the fact that he combines purposefully childish poetry, slapstick and symbolism, shots of himself, his children and his California forbears, and clips from his early films such as "The Bed" and "Nuptiae" to develop a self-critical, charming and funny autobiographical portrait.

On the other hand, the Jordan Belson-Stephen Beck "Cycles" fuses film and a television synthesizer to fashion abstract scenes suggesting celestial, planetary and other moving forms that captivate and mystify a viewer. If Pat O'Neill's "Last of the Persimmons" is a cute film and an animated glimpse of that fruit, his more ambitious "Saugus Series" is academic rather than emotional in its impact. Its succession of vignettes of intercut abstractions and montages is largely interesting as an adept exercise in filming techniques.

The shortest entry, Beverly O'Neill's "Skyeboat for Biscuit," is just an idyllic moment at a pond set against the skirl of bagpipes. But John Knoop's "Dune," which courses along varied, sandy terrains and also skips to an air balloon floating above, projects imaginative images of strange and sometimes surreal shapes that stick in memory.

Although the Jo Carson-Ward Sellars "Himalayan Pilgrimage" traverses a visually exciting, distant area, its experimental approach merely titilates the eye. Its quickly flashing and jumping views of truly exotic people, places and language are photographically expert and unusual, but they make one hunger for the simpler, more informative illustrations of the normal travelogue.

The images in this current

consignment from the West may vary, but they make an attractive and fascinating package.

1975 Ap 25, 24:3

A Reincarnation Tale at Twin Theaters

By A. H. WEILER

"The Reincarnation of Peter Proud," which emerged on the screens of the Cinerama, 59th Street and 86th Street Twin Theaters yesterday, illustrates, perhaps more than anything else, that ghosts—even modern ones—needn't be convincing. Despite a sincere, polished treatment, this delving into the dark, sex-ridden, tragic previous life of Peter Proud generates clouds of suspense but no solid solution to the riddle of reincarnation.

"Suppose you knew who you had been in your previous life . . . what then?" the film's blurb enticingly asks. The answer, now that the results are in, would be to let bygones be bygones.

•

J. Lee Thompson, who directed in a properly moody style, and Max Ehrlich, who wrote the script from his novel, adhere to the trappings of current parapsychology, dream research and the like to give their mystery a scientific patina. But it isn't science as much as a persistent nightmare that drives Peter Proud, a young college professor, to seek surcease from his bad dream.

The trip takes him from his California campus to an upper-class suburban Massachusetts town of his nocturnal, frightening visions, where he discovers that, in the nineteen-forties, he had been Jeff Curtis, World War II hero, the father of an infant daughter, and who was

The Cast

THE REINCARNATION OF PETER PROUD, directed by J. Lee Thompson; written by Max Ehrlich; director of photography, Victor J. Kemper; film editor, Michael Anderson; music, Jerry Goldsmith; produced by Frank P. Rosenberg; a Cinerama release; distributed by American International Pictures. At the 59th Street Twin 2 Theater, east of Third Avenue and the 86th Street Twin 2 Theater, west of Lexington Avenue. Running time: 104 minutes. This film is classified R.

Peter Proud	Michael Sarrazin
Ann Curtis	Jennifer O'Neill
Marcia Curtis	Margot Kidder
Nora Hayes	Cornelia Sharpe
Dr. Samuel Goodman	Paul Hecht
Jeff Curtis	Tony Stephano
Dr. Frederick Spear	Norman Burton

murdered by his anguished wife for his callous indiscretions.

It should be noted that Peter Proud is plagued enough to fall in love and have an affair with a now grown, beautiful daughter of the late, unlamented Jeff Curtis—a sort of incest, once

removed—and to pursue his investigation to a macabre and fatal ending.

•

Michael Sarrazin is fairly sensitive and generally subdued as Peter Proud, a name, he admits lightly, that sounds like a nursery jingle. Margot Kidder does well by the unlikely roles of the young wife and the anxiety-filled hard-drinking mother whose murderous secret is finally exposed. And Jennifer O'Neill, as the surviving daughter, and Cornelia Sharpe, as Mr. Sarrazin's college pal, are genuinely confused by the mystery that distracts their lover.

Peter Proud, in short, utters a logical mouthful about this "reincarnation" when he tells the worried Miss O'Neill. "If I tried to explain, you'd think I was insane."

1975 Ap 26, 14:1

FILM VIEW

VINCENT CANBY

On Fragmenting Cinema Narrative

"The Middle of The World," Alain Tanner's fine new Swiss film about the love affair of a upwardly mobile Swiss engineer and a beautiful, profoundly self-aware Italian emigrant, covers exactly 112 days, a couple of dozen of which (identified by screen calendar cards) are dramatized in the film without apparent regard for their narrative importance.

Paul (Philippe Leotard), comfortably married and the father of one child, meets Adriana (Olimpia Carlisi) near the start of his campaign for public office. Paul and his backers hope to win the campaign by stressing that "ideologies are a thing of the past," and that what is needed in this day and age "are competent organizers and technicians who can solve the complex problems of an industrial society."

Paul would seem to be a sure thing. He is a competent organizer and technician and his only ideology is a healthy confidence in his ability to succeed. It's this confidence as much as anything else that first amuses and then enchants Adriana, whom he meets on one of his speaking engagements. Paul does not take Adriana under false pretenses. She knows he is married and in the midst of a political campaign that makes any possibility of scandal that much more dangerous. When they fall in love, it's something that neither one of them had expected. Paul offers to set up Adriana in a more comfortable apartment with an income so that she won't have to work—which she refuses. When he loses the election, his confidence is untouched and he offers to divorce his wife and marry Adriana. She turns him down and walks out on him.

At the railroad station just before her departure Adriana's best friend, another waitress, questions Adriana about her decision. Was it to save Paul's career? Was she paid to leave? Was Paul lousy in bed? Did Paul want to have what the friend discreetly calls "abnormal sex"? Was it because Paul was not Italian? Adriana smiles. It was none of these things.

Rather, it is suggested, it has to do with what the film refers to from time to time as the concept of "normalization," that desperate balance between opposing countries, between classes and between individuals that allows for free exchange provided that nothing changes. A narrator tells us that Paul's hopes did not allow for change. When Adriana leaves, the narrator comments: "Their hopes were normalized."

I've allowed myself to describe the events of "The Middle of The World" in enough detail to infuriate everyone who won't go to see "Hamlet" the second time because he knows the end. I'm convinced that the film wouldn't interest such people anyway. The fascination of "The Middle of The World" has less to do with what happens than with Tanner's style and the extraordinary amount of ground he manages to cover with such elliptical ease.

Carlisi: Why does she walk out?

"The Middle of The World" is in many ways a more fully realized demonstration of what may now be identified as the new kind of cinema narrative Tanner used in his "La Salamandre" (1972), and which (not so coincidentally, I suspect), was written by Tanner in collaboration with John Berger, the English critic and novelist who also collaborated with the director on "The Middle of The World."

I hesitate to identify any film as representing a new kind of anything. A letter will inevitably turn up in a week or two making a most convincing argument that what was described as new was done by Griffith or somebody else 50 years ago.

"The Middle of The World," like "La Salamandre," recalls a number of Godard films from the early 1960's. It contains no Godardian monologues, no conscious gimmicks but, like Godard's films, it always maintains a certain distance from its characters. The tone is cool. It is full of facts, explanations and definitions. It never pretends to go inside its characters heads but, instead, takes them at face value. This doesn't mean that we are to believe what its characters say. Rather, it is up to us to differentiate truth from falsehood or self-deception.

As did Godard in those 1960's films ("Vivre Sa Vie," "Bande A Parte," among others), Tanner very carefully places his characters in social-political contexts as well as psychological ones, not necessarily by involving the characters directly in the world around them, though Paul is running for political office in "The Middle of The World," but by exercising the storyteller's prerogative to feed us all information he thinks pertinent. He does this sometimes bluntly, through a narrator or through title cards, sometimes by simply cutting arbitrarily to a subsidiary plot. In his new film Tanner periodically cuts to a landscape, not because a character is passing through it but because the look of the landscape is the screen equivalent to punctuation in prose. Realism—the realistic detail—is put into the service of poetic truth.

Tanner is not alone among the world's filmmakers in following the way pointed by Godard (but not pursued by him) to free the narrative cinema from the strict rules that have been in effect for half a century. The recent New Directors/New Films series at the Museum of Modern Art included four films from as many countries that demonstrate in different ways this willingness to alter conventional narrative forms without doing away with them entirely: "The Engagement of Anna" (Greece), "Alma" (Brazil), "Bar Salon" (Canada) and "Pirosmani" (Russia).

The narrative may be fragmented, as in "The Middle of The World," requiring the viewer to make a lot of the connectives himself, or it may become so condensed that one small, seemingly very particular story suddenly bursts with associated meanings. This is the case with "The Engagement of Anna," directed by 32-year-old Pantelis Voulgaris, which begins as the gentle, sad tale

of a middle-class Athens household and concludes as a call to the barricades, though politics are never once mentioned.

"The Middle of The World" and these other films I've (probably loosely) described as a new kind of narrative cinema share a respect for our intelligence that amounts to tact. To enjoy them we must be able to do a certain amount of work. This is nothing less than bold when most films—theatrical and television—spend so much time spelling out the responses they want us to think we've come upon independently.

1975 Ap 27, II:1:1

The Sorrow and the Pity

By DAVID DENBY

What does a director of proven ability have to do to get his work respected by the men who finance movies?

Marcel Ophuls, who in 1971 made "The Sorrow and the Pity," a universally acclaimed documentary study of the French people under the Nazi Occupation—and a commercial success as well—has just had a remarkable new film on the Nuremberg trials and their aftermath taken away from him and mutilated or possibly destroyed after completing 95 per cent of the work on it. What started as a most promising project, made under conditions of virtually complete freedom, has turned into a nightmarish mess of charges and counter-charges, stolen reels of film, threatened lawsuits, and personal anguish on all sides.

quantities of ego and perhaps a strain of intellectual charlatanism to awe financiers and moviegoers into accepting their extravagant demands on patience and common sense. Ophuls has the ego but not the saving touch of bull, and he's certainly no diplomat. A formidable compound of obstinacy and intelligence, philosophical insight and compassion, he has shown an uncommon gift for dramatizing the personal dimensions of our century's most agonizing political and moral crises.

Ophuls, 47, son of the great German romantic Max Ophuls, grew up in Hollywood during his father's American exile, and has always wanted to make musicals and light comedies, but people keep asking him to make documentaries because he's so good at it. Two years ago, after completing "A Sense of Loss," a modest, extremely moving portrait of the battered people of North-

Are the moneymen mutilating his masterpiece?

Stories of intense conflict between moviemakers and moneymen go back at least as far as the days of D.W. Griffith, and the present instance is an illuminating case study of that continuing conflict. What gives special importance to this story is the subject and quality of the film and the extraordinary talent of Marcel Ophuls.

It's been said that great film directors need immense

David Denby is a freelance film critic.

ern Ireland, he launched another project on the colossal scale of "The Sorrow and the Pity": a film about war crimes and the question of national guilt, featuring interviews with surviving Nazi war criminals, witnesses and prosecutors; cultural life in Germany during the postwar de-Nazification period; and an examination of how the principles set down at Nuremberg have fared in such places as Algeria and Vietnam — especially Vietnam. Tying all this together would be the ideas and personality of Tel-

ford Taylor, General of the Army (retired), Chief U.S. Counsel at Nuremberg, now professor of law at Columbia, and the author, in 1970, of "Nuremberg and Vietnam: An American Tragedy." Ophuls titled his project "The Memory of Justice."

Last Dec. 18, in London, Ophuls showed his backers a film of four hours, fifty-eight minutes; afterward, he cut 20 minutes, making "The Memory of Justice" roughly the same length as "The Sorrow and the Pity." That was the last time Ophuls worked on his film. The nasty details will follow, but first let me describe what Ophuls has accomplished in "The Memory of Justice."

•

The film I saw (Ophuls is making his case by showing a duplicate of the original uncut workprint to a few persons at a time on an editing machine in New York) was undoubtedly a remarkable work, perhaps as fine as "The Sorrow and the Pity." Again Ophuls has created a complex mixture of cultural/political history and individual experience, again a film that is rich in personal glory, degradation, wit, madness and generosity. Drawing heavily on footage of the Nuremberg trials (from which Goering emerges as a brilliantly saturnine and nihilistic intelligence), he creates the framework for a superb set of interviews, encounters and moments of reflection. "The Sorrow and the Pity" made a heroic attempt to answer one of the century's most heartrending questions: Why, in times of stress, do so few people act honorably? With great compassion and not a trace of self-righteousness the film sought to understand the acquiescence that makes totalitarianism possible. Here Ophuls takes his inquiry a step further. How is it possible to judge a nation's or an individual's conduct? Is a victorious nation's judgment of a defeated one necessarily hypocritical? In particular, has America's participation in the Nuremberg trials been rendered meaningless by the cruelty of its behavior in Vietnam?

The film is a passionate dialogue between the instinct of moral accusation and the sentiment of forebearance. Ophuls begins by investigating how the Nazis themselves have reacted to judgment. By and large, their inplacable self-esteem had led them to reject it or deflect it into a corner. Eighty-two-year-old Admiral Karl Doenitz, the genius of U-boat warfare and Hitler's successor, shakes his wattles and insists that the Navy never discriminated against Jews; Professor Dr. Rose, a gray, withdrawn man who conducted medical "experiments" at Dachau, blandly assures Ophuls that his work was humanitarian in purpose; and so on. There's a prevailing inabilty to make simple connections, which protects people from moral doubt.

Only Albert Speer accedes to the judgment passed on him, and Speer, in the totality and ease of his self-reproach, is beginning to sound glib. Rejecting Andy Warhol's favorable opinion of his architectural designs for Hitler, he remarks, "Long before the Jews were murdered, it was all expressed in my buildings." Speer's dry, emotionless remorse, so elegantly contained, becomes eerie, disconnected, and my own moral bloodlust wasn't satisfied until Ophuls asked whether a speech Speer made late in the war had not resulted in some "lazy" foreign workers being sent to concentration camps. Speer admits it did.

Why does Ophuls bother with these tired old war criminals? Well, they remain as fascinating as ever, particularly when seen out of uniform, stripped of their exotic-erotic glamour. However satisfying emotionally, Ophuls appears to be saying, it is no longer intellectually defensible to regard Nazism as the unique definition of evil. Nazism was an experience inside the human condition, not some supernatural outbreak of demonic behavior. Without excusing Nazism in any way, he has made it less abstract and fantastic, and therefore more comprehensible.

In a gesture of profound simplicity and wisdom, he implicates himself—a Jew from an anti-Nazi family—in the historical process he's judging. We see a group of undergraduates at Princeton (where Ophuls teaches) gathered around his editing table, talking to his German wife, Regine. A student asks if she knew anyone in the Hitler Youth, "I was in the Hitler Youth," she replies and describes the pressures on families whose children did not join. And elsewhere we learn that Ophuls's father-in-law was an officer in the Wehrmacht. This sense of the filmmaker within history, a form of vulnerability, is the very opposite of the superior attitude of those who made the cheaply accusatory "Hearts and Minds."

•

Clearly, Ophuls wants to demystify the German people, something which

hasn't yet been done in American movies, where Germans are invariably portrayed as monstrous or comical (what would Mel Brooks do without his Germans?). A group of men and women in their late forties, teenagers during the war, are photographed in a nude sauna bath, trying to shed their inhibitions and evasions along with their clothes as they talk about their ambivalent relations with Germany's remaining Jews.

In another scene, college students of today debate whether they have the continued obligation to pay reparations to war victims.

After examining the judged, Ophuls, who is nothing if not dialectical, turns his eye on the judges, searching out traces of hypocrisy. Yes, the Allies also committed crimes. Wing Commander James Rose, former head of RAF intelligence, recalls his tragic inability to convince the British high command that Dresden should not be bombed. An excruciating "March of Time" newsreel, congratulating the GI's for buying the company of Berlin frauleins with only a chocolate bar, serves to point up American postwar arrogance. And there's that familiar, frightening failure to connect one area of experience with another: Lord Hartley Shawcross, the suave, upperclass British prosecutor at Nuremberg, sits in front of his fire in 1973 and calmly advocates civilian bombing as a measure to make wars less likely; the French prosecutor, Edgar Faure, fudges the question of torture in Algeria.

Just when we are despairing of the whole notion of judgement, Ophuls brings in Telford Taylor to assert that you must "impose principles" even if you fear you might in the future give way to evil yourself. In the substantial concluding section, which examines America's descent into evil in Vietnam, Taylor's distinction between planned genocide (Auschwitz) and sadism under pressure (My Lai) prevails over Daniel Ellsberg's simple-minded assertion that the Nazi high command was no worse than the American leadership in Vietnam. Ophuls, we feel, would continue to support such distinctions even at the edge of the grave. For if human history is seen as complete filth—one period and episode as utterly vile as the next, from the Crusades to Vietnam—then there is no defense against total cynicism, no particular reason to resist totalitarianism. Ophuls's attempt to view our recent history with some

'I've seen a terrific film—and it's being remade.'

measure of lucidity is itself a stand against despair.

•

A gigantic project, heaven knows, and it took three sets of producers to get it off the ground. In the summer of 1973, the BBC and Polytel International of Hamburg put up some seed money, but a private company was needed to guarantee completion. The two backers and Ophuls approached Visual Programme Systems of London, a medium-sized, scrambling outfit that had produced "Performance," "That'll Be the Day" (a rock film), and "Swastika." Ophuls was familiar with the directors of VPS, Sandy Lieberson (an American) and David Puttnam (an Englishman), who had earlier unsuccessfully tried to interest him in a full-scale film version of Albert Speer's "Inside the Third Reich."

"I liked them both but I was wary," Ophuls says now. "During our talks on the Speer project David Puttnam had openly identified with Speer's opportunism as a young man. He was so insistent about it that I finally had to assert my film would be anti-Nazi. Also, I was afraid of flashiness and radical chic: their favorite director was Ken Russell. But you always put such doubts aside at the beginning of a production, you're so eager to begin."

VPS came in, and the budget was set at roughly 130,000 pounds; the two companies would air the film in their own countries, VPS would control theatrical rights. With Puttnam and Lieberson serving as executive producers, Ophuls, as producer-director, was given complete control over the material during production but not the right of final cut. Should irreconcilable differences arise, the executive producers were free to remove him and make what changes they liked, providing no other director's name appeared on the credits. Naively, Ophuls thought he was safe. For who would release a four-and-a-half hour film without a director's name on it?

•

After shooting 135,000 feet and compiling 15 hours of archive material, a total of 90 hours of film, Ophuls began

to edit and was ready with the first 3½ hours last July. Before the screening for his backers, he was slightly apprehensive: he had been "emotionally unable" to interweave the Nazi and American scenes as originally planned; during the shooting the German material had become more and more exciting and he had stayed with it in the belief that the film would be more alive if its final structure remained open. In a memo to VPS he wrote: "This is too big an issue, too important a subject to be treated on the basis of theatrical equations (Auschwitz-Napalm or Hitler-Nixon). Auschwitz and Treblinka are the sources of our slow descent into hell. And I'm convinced, now, that this must first be shown, in detail, before we can go on to show Nuremberg's inherent flaws, or draw attention to other more recent atrocities . . ."

Lieberson and Puttnam were dismayed, not only by the film's political direction and balance (they wanted a more central attack on America in Vietnam), but also by its discursive sobriety and "grayness." In a long detailed memorandum Ophuls replied to their objections. For instance, he quoted Puttnam's desire for a less "cumbersome" approach, something more "fascist" (in the sense of dynamic, exciting). His response was abrasive and perhaps unforgivable. Declaring that many recent movie successes were based on a "tacit alliance" between "antihumanistic" movie producers and "fascist tendencies" in the audience, he wrote, "I'm just not talented enough to compete with Sam Peckinpah. If I were to swim in his direction, down the river instead of up, I would drown among the sharks."

Along with all the impatient and arrogant irony, one hears in these remarks the anguish of an artist dependent for support on people who haven't any idea of what he's up to. When Puttnam complained that the film was bad because it was a *personal* essay, Ophuls wrote, "Such criticism of my work is worse than useless. It's like telling a tap dancer he should take the metal edges from his shoes, because they make such an unpleasant noise."

Over and over, and with increasing despair, he asked VPS how they could have expected anything else from him but a film that was leisurely, complex in structure, highly personal. Refusing to make major changes after the July screening, he suggested that he be fired immediately. Why finish the film only to go through the same conflicts over the final cut? VPS refused (an act they now regret), but threatened him with breach of contract for being late and over budget. Ophuls admitted that both charges were true but claimed that VPS had caused a two-month delay by failing to pay promptly for archive material. During this time, the editing facilities and salaried editors remained idle. After a nasty stalemate lasting several weeks, the BBC and Polytel intervened with votes of confidence for Ophuls and some extra money, and work was resumed.

Puttnam and Lieberson seem never to have encountered a director as serious and intransigent about his work, and it bothered them. "What does Ophuls *want?*" Lieberson asked me plaintively, when I telephoned him recently in London. "We went a long way with this guy, but he's crazy." And Puttnam complained of Ophuls's inexhaustible will to argue: "He's unpleasant, unconstructive, unwilling to listen to criticism, and deeply boring."

In reply, Ophuls says, "I plead guilty to being nasty, opinionated, hard to get along with. However, since I've had more experience with these issues, I have the right to make my views prevail. Also, I don't consider the commissioning of a film an act of charity, and so I'm not endlessly grateful to my backers for the mere opportunity to work. They expect that gratitude though, and they're furious when you don't give it."

All of this personal vindictiveness reached its climax last Dec. 18, when Ophuls screened the complete version. The reaction was hostile: "boring" from Puttnam and "My butt hurt" from Gunnar Rugheimer of the BBC. Two days later, tempers somewhat settled, the men got together to negotiate their differences at the Hotel Ritz Bar, but this time the relationship collapsed for good. When Puttnam threatened to cut a full hour for the American market, Ophuls blew up and walked out. However, while Ophuls claims he meant only to leave the meeting, the executive producers concluded, or chose to conclude, that he had left the film.

Puttnam freely admits he threatened to cut the film without Ophuls's approval but insists that Ophuls quit the project at the Ritz Bar. The event remains unclear. In any case, within a half hour after Ophuls's departure, Puttnam, Lieberson, and Rugheimer had marched into the director's editing room, announced to the astonished editors that further work on the film was cancelled, and seized the cutting copy (workprint). Two weeks later another man—Lutz Becker, who had worked for VPS before on "Double-Headed Eagle" and "Swastika"—was busy recutting the film.

Never having received a formal dismissal (only a threatened suit for bringing in the film eight minutes too long, a problem he was willing to rectify) Ophuls maintained that he was still the producer-director, but there was little he could do to regain control. Too broke to hire a lawyer and take VPS to court, he returned to Princeton in despair in late January.

This might have been the end, but the story suddenly took a new and rather romantic turn. In early March, unbeknownst to Ophuls, a friend sympathetic to the director's version of "The Memory of Justice" hid in the London building where the film was being edited, entered the workroom in the middle of the night, and carried off duplicate copies of the workprint and soundtrack. In the morning the loyalist took the first boat-train to Paris and from there fled to the United States, turning the film over to a grateful Ophuls. "This became my only salvation," he says. "The only way I can fight for my version and protect myself against slander."

Apart from the silly complaint that the film is "boring," VPS has told me and other persons making inquiries that "The Memory of Justice" is "technically incompetent" and "incoherent." These descriptions are false. In addition, not content to take one film away from Ophuls, VPS & Co. are trying to justify their decision by taking his earlier work away, too. David Puttnam (and another of the backers who refused to be quoted by name) is circulating the allegation that Ophuls "was not responsible for the best things in 'The Sorrow and the Pity.'" Ophuls has threatened a libel suit against anyone making such charges publicly.

●

What will remain of the intellectual fiber of "The Memory of Justice" when Lutz Becker is finished recutting it? I asked to see the new version, but Sandy Lieberson told me it wasn't ready, and when I called Becker he wouldn't talk to me until he had checked with Lieberson and Puttnam. He then called back from London and insisted he was "protecting Marcel's conception." But, according to Becker, Puttnam, and other sources close to the production, the film has been cut by over an hour and considerably reshuffled, and all traces of Ophuls's questions, family history—in short, the quality of personal inquiry that made it unique—have been removed. The German sections have been reduced, the Vietnam sections beefed up with newsreels. In general, less talk, more action. And there will be no director's credit, only a line saying "Adapted by Lutz Becker."

This must be the oddest credit in the history of show business. *Adapted from what?* A documentary exists in only one form—the one given it by the director and editor after months of labor. Conceivably what emerges can be as personal and definitive as a film by Bergman and should be respected in the same way. Of course, Becker's "adaptation" might be good, too, but I'm not engaged in a pie-tasting contest here; I've already seen a terrific film, and it's being remade.

Despite the constant fuss over documentary, very few people have the freedom and desire to create documentary art. "The Sorrow and the Pity" was so moving, in part, because Ophuls threw off the usual limitations and boldly asserted new powers and privileges for an abused and very tired old movie form. "The Memory of Justice" is a continuation of that work. If the film is mutilated or buried, it signifies momentary defeat for a talented and courageous filmmaker and a full step backward for the art of documentary. ■

1975 Ap 27, II:1:4

An Office Party Begins Well but Collapses

By VINCENT CANBY

Is Switzerland a metaphor for the perfect world that most of us would want to escape from if it were ever achieved? Have the Swiss, after centuries of effort supported by an accident of geography, found themselves no longer living in a precarious balance of neutrality but on a dead center in the middle of an unbudgeable, maddeningly vacuous calm?

These questions are brought to mind indirectly by Claude Goretta's fine, delicately realized Swiss comedy, "The Invitation," which opened yesterday at the Regency. "The Invitation" seems to be about nothing more or less than an office party that begins idyllically and goes to pieces, the way office parties do when some of the guests drink too much, make passes at the wrong people, say the true but inopportune thing and then spend the rest of the year trying to forget.

●

Nothing truly terrible happens during this all-day party, and a lot of what happens is extremely funny. Yet there is throughout the film a sense of lives running out without ever having been lived, of disappointment that becomes so acute it is less sad than menacing.

One shouldn't insist on reading too much into "The Invitation" but, like another beautifully made Swiss production, Alain Tanner's "The Middle of the World," "The Invitation" is so perfectly precise that it inevitably draws one into territory beyond the frame of the film itself. It is fiction of a high order.

The party that occupies virtually the entire movie is not your ordinary, run-of-the-mill Christmas orgy, or anything like it.

The host is Remy Placet (Michel Robin), an office drone, a tall, shy, aging bachelor who looks like a salamander walking on its hind feet. A fastidious man, he seems to be composed of flesh over cartilage. You can imagine his bending a leg double without even breaking it.

●

When Remy's beloved old mother dies, he sells their small house in the city, which happens to be on hugely valuable property, and buys a country estate to which he bids his fellow office workers in thanks for their sympathy at his bereavement.

Presiding over the revels is Emile (François Simon), the butler hired for the day, a man whose kindness and discretion suggest both the discipline of a religious order and the manner of a man given to periodic bouts in some indescribable debauch. Emile has looked beyond the borders of Switzerland but he tries not to be condescending to those less fortunate than he.

As the party disintegrates, as Maurice (Jean-Luc Bideau), the office Romeo, becomes increasingly unruly, and as the younger girls become increasingly giggly, and as Miss Emma (Neige Dolsky), the office spinster, goes temporarily loony on rum and orange juice, the serene Emile becomes the last voice of reason. But reason can't answer every need, which may or may not be one of the points of the film.

●

"The Invitation" has a supple, seamless quality that I associate with the best short stories. It appreciates its characters' eccentricities but it neither exploits nor sentimentalizes them. By some curious means I don't quite understand, it manages to seem simultaneously banal and mysterious, commonplace and poetic.

The performers display the uniform excellence of players who have worked long and well together in a repertory company. You'll recognize several of them from Mr. Tanner's "La Salamandre" and "Charles — Dead or Alive," which, a couple of years ago, first alerted us to the news that something important was happening in Swiss film making.

The Cast

THE INVITATION, directed by Claude Goretta; screenplay (French with English subtitles) by Mr. Goretta and Michel Viala; executive producer, Yves Gasser; director of photography, Jean Zeller; editor, Joelle van Effenterre; music, Patrick Moraz; produced by Citel Films, Group 5, Swiss TV and Planfilm; distributed by Janus Films. Running time: 100 minutes. At the Regency Theater, Broadway at 67th Street. This film has not been rated.

Maurice....................Jean-Luc Bideau
Emile....................Francois Simon
Alfred....................Jean Champion
Simone....................Corinne Coderey
Remy....................Michel Robin
Aline....................Cecile Vassort
Helene....................Rosine Rochette
Rene....................Jacques Rispal
Emma....................Neige Dolsky
Pierre....................Pierre Collet
Mme. Placet....................Lucie Aveney
Thief....................Roger Jendely

1975 Ap 28, 34:4

MONTY PYTHON AND THE HOLY GRAIL, directed by Terry Gilliam and Terry Jones; written by Graham Chapman, John Cleese, Mr. Gilliam, Eric Idle, Mr. Jones and Michael Palin; executive producer, John Goldstone; producer, Mark Forstater; editor, John Hackney; director of photography, Terry Bedford; songs by Neil Innes, with additional music by De Wolfe; a Python Pictures, Ltd., production, distribution by Cinema 5. Running time: 90 minutes. At the Cinema 2 Theater, Third Avenue near 60th Street. This film has been rated PG.

WITH: Mr. Chapman, Mr. Cleese, Mr. Gilliam, Mr. Idle, Mr. Jones, Mr. Palin, Connie Booth, Carol Cleveland, John Young and others.

A foolish constancy is the hobgoblin of little minds and of some movie critics (who may or may not have little minds) when writing about the films of comedians.

In his own day, poor old W. C. Fields was always being rapped for not making movies that were as funny, from start to finish, as his adoring critics found bits of them to be. I'm afraid that once or twice I've gone so far as to suggest that a certain film by Woody Allen or Mel Brooks hasn't been consistently funny, that is, that there were some parts that weren't as funny as other parts. However, as any surveyor of anything will tell you, you can't have a high spot unless you have a low one from which to survey it.

●

All of which is a round about way of saying that "Monty Python and the Holy Grail" has some low spots but that anyone at all fond of the members of this brilliant British comedy group—which more or less justifies Sunday night television in New York—shouldn't care less.

"Monty Python and the Holy Grail," which opened yesterday at the Cinema 2, is a marvelously particular kind of lunatic endeavor. It's been collectively written by the Python troupe and jointly directed by two of them (Terry Gilliam and Terry Jones) so effectively that I'm beginning to suspect that there really aren't six of them but only one, a fellow with several dozen faces who knows a great deal about trick photography.

Unlike "And Now for Something Completely Different," which was a collection of sketches from "Monty Python's Flying Circus," television show, "Monty Python and the Holy Grail" is what is known on Broadway as a "book show."

It has a story with an approximate beginning, an approximate middle and it ends, or perhaps I should say that it stops after a while. To be more specific, it's the Python troupe's version of the legend of King Arthur and the search for the holy grail, with no apologies at all to Malory though it manages to send up the legend, courtly love, fidelity, bravery, costume movies, movie violence and ornithology.

Graham Chapman plays Arthur, the film's major continuing character, with the earnest optimism of a 19th-century missionary, who's doomed to fail but refuses to acknowledge the fact. The other members of the Python team turn up in a variety of roles—Round Table knights, snobbish French aristocrats, irritable serfs, mythical monsters and, in one case, as a noble son named Alice who tries to turn the film into an operetta.

●

The gags are nonstop, occasionally inspired and should not be divulged, though it's not giving away too much to say that I particularly liked a sequence in which the knights, to gain access to an enemy castle, come up with the idea of building a Trojan rabbit. When Arthur calls retreat, he simply yells: "Run away!" And the morale of Sir Robin, the least successful of the Round Table knights, isn't helped by a retinue of minstrels who insist on singing about his most embarrassing defeats.

I have no idea whether Mr. Gilliam and Mr. Jones have seen Robert Bresson's rather more austere film, "Lancelot of the Lake," which was shown at last year's New York Film Festival, but there are times when "Monty Python and the Holy Grail" seems to be putting on Mr. Bresson unmercifully. The dour lighting and landscapes that are so important in the Bresson film are tossed into this comedy without apparent thought for the havoc they do "Lancelot." Mr. Bresson's emphasis on what you might call the sound of knighthood (clanking armor, horses' hoofs) is also hilariously parodied, as well as the violence of the age, on which the Python people have the last bleeding word.

Everyone interested in Mr. Bresson would do well to stay away from "Monty Python and the Holy Grail" until after they see "Lancelot." The comparison, which may never have been intended, is nevertheless lethal to the work of the great French director.

VINCENT CANBY

1975 Ap 28, 34:4

ALOHA, BOBBY AND ROSE, directed and written by Floyd Mutrux; producer, Fouad Said; executive producer, Edward J. Rosen; director of photography, William A. Fraker; editor, Danford B. Greene; a Cine Artists International production, distributed by Columbia Pictures. Running time: 89 minutes. At the Columbia 2 Theater, Second Avenue near 64th Street. This film has been rated PG.
Bobby .... Paul Le Mat
Rose .... Dianne Hull
Buford .... Tim McIntire
Donna Sue .... Leigh French
Rose's Mother .... Martine Bartlett
Moxey .... Robert Carradine

By VINCENT CANBY

"Aloha, Bobby and Rose," which opened yesterday at the Columbia 2 Theater, is a sentimental, noisy, very bad movie about a young Los Angeles couple whom Floyd Mutrux, the director and writer of the screen play, describes as star - crossed though they seem less starcrossed than accident-prone.

Bobby (Paul Le Mat) and Rose (Dianne Hull) get into trouble when a clerk is fatally shot while Bobby is pretending to stick up a liquor store. The only tragic thing in a film like this is the quality of stupidity the characters are forced to exhibit in order to keep the plot going.

•

Although the story is contemporary, the film opens with Artie Shaw's classic "Begin the Beguine" playing on the soundtrack. Thereafter, the director does his best to stir up a little nostalgia for what actually is last week. "Aloha, Bobby and Rose" wants to have it eight different ways at once.

The film is full of what seem to be witting references to that harmless nineteen-sixties binge, "American Graffiti," which also starred Mr. Le Mat. Much of "Aloha, Bobby and Rose" was photographed in and around Los Angeles, in its streets, drive-ins and filling stations, a lot of the time at night. William A. Fraker, a very good cameraman with the right director, over-indulges a fancy for shooting directly into headlights, sunrises and sunsets, resulting in more halos than you would ever see at a convention of saints.

In claptrap of this order it's impossible to judge fairly lead performances that are so much a part of the method of the film. In subsidiary roles Tim McIntire and Leigh French are appealing as a pair of good-natured, free-spending Texans who, briefly, befriend dim-witted Bobby and dopey Rose.

1975 Ap 30, 24:1

STORY OF A LOVE AFFAIR (Cronaca Di Un Amore), directed by Michelangelo Antonioni; screenplay (Italian with English subtitles) by Mr. Antonioni, Daniele D'Anza, Silvio Giovaninetti, Francesco Maselli and Piero Tellini, based on a story by Mr. Antonioni; producers, Franco Villani and Stefano Caretta; director of photography, Enzo Serafin; music, Giovanni Fusco; produced by Vilani Film; distributed by New Yorker Films. Running time: 102 minutes. At the Cinema Studio, Broadway at 66th Street. This film has not been rated.
Paola .... Lucia Bose
Guido .... Massimo Girotti
Fontana .... Ferdinando Sarmi
Detective .... Gino Rossi

By VINCENT CANBY

The years haven't been kind to "Story of a Love Affair" ("Crònaca Di Un Amore"), Michelangelo Antonioni's first feature, made in 1950, but they have at least given it historical importance in view of the highly personal, hugely better films he made afterward, from "L'Avventura" to "The Passenger."

With hindsight one can see here, the beginning of a style that this idiosyncratic Italian Marxist would go on to develop into what became virtually a genre all its own—the film about people disconnected from each other and the world around them. I doubt that if we saw "Story of a Love Affair" today, without the benefit of hindsight, we would do much more than snicker between extended yawns.

•

The story and much of Mr. Antonioni's treatment of it recall the kind glossy soap-opera movie that was immensely popular in Europe a quarter of a century ago, before Europeans discovered the edifying joys of television drama. It's about the impossible love of a poor auto salesman (Massimo Girotti) and his former sweetheart (Lucia Bose), who has married a rich Milan textile manufacturer and moved bag and baggage into the upper classes, where she's lonely but very happy to be overdressed.

The pair, who had earlier parted full of guilt when they did nothing to prevent the accidental death of Mr. Girotti's fiancée, are reunited, first in fear, then in love, when Miss Bose's husband starts looking into her past. The fact that the affair is renewed as a result of the husband's groundless suspicions is an irony that is not to be taken lightly in a film that is completely without intentional humor.

"Story of a Love Affair," which opened yesterday at the Cinema Studio, has a number of easily identifiable Antonioni moments, some quite fine, such as the scene in which the lovers are reunited after seven years, and another, photographed in the stairwell of an office building, when the pair ascend from one floor to the next only to reach an absolute impasse in their relationship.

•

The trouble with the film is not that their problems are mini. To paraphrase Claude Chabrol, there are no small problems, only small films. In a better movie we might be able to take seriously Miss Bose's inability to cast aside her life of luxury, and Mr. Girotti's inability to see her for the bore she is. But "Story of a Love Affair" is tacky. It seems to share Miss Bose's fascination for high society, which, as shown in the movie, means playing bridge all afternoon and throwing fur coats on floors.

1975 My 1, 49:1

ANTHROPOLOGICAL CINEMA. Three documentaries, CHOREOMETRICS I (1974), designed and edited by Alan Lomax and Forrestine Paulay, running time: 40 minutes; MICROCULTURAL INCIDENTS IN TEN ZOOS (1971), produced and narrated by Dr. Ray L. Birdwhistell and photographed and edited by Jacques D. Van Vlack at the Eastern Pennsylvania Psychiatric Institute, running time, 34 minutes, and LEARNING TO DANCE IN BALI (1939) by Margaret Mead and Gregory Bateson, running time, 19 minutes. At the Whitney Museum of American Art, Madison Avenue and 75th Street. Through May 6.

By A. H. WEILER

"Anthropological Cinema" couldn't be more scientific as a general title for the three documentaries that— like graduate courses — opened recently at the Whitney Museum of American Art. If these studies are not precisely entertainments, they cleave to the definition of anthropology as the science of man and illustrate professional findings that are tributes to the researchers and films as a teaching tool.

As the latest and, perhaps, the newest anthropological calibration, "Choreometrics I," which was completed last year, is, according to program notes, both a word coined by Alan Lomax and his method for measuring relationships between dance and work patterns in the world's cultures. The noted folklore and song archivist, in association with Forrestine Paulay and Irmgard Bartenieff, dance specialists, as well as dozens of film sources and animated maps, has made his inspections of workers and dancers, from dervishes to square dancers and from Africans to Chinese to Eskimos and to South American Indians, a pictorially fascinating record.

Dr. Ray L. Birdwhistell, who worked with Jacques D. Van Vlack in making "Microcultural Incidents in Ten

---

Zoos" as an obvious lecture for students of psychiatry, is impressively straightforward in his presentation. The family groups visiting zoos from San Francisco, to London, Paris, Rome, Peking and Hong Kong, project body movements, gestures and the like that abet and enlarge his clinical on-screen and off-screen narration on social behavior.

•

As the oldest and perhaps most historic subject in the

---

collection, the Margaret Mead - Gregory Bateson "Learning to Dance in Bali," finished in 1939, is an episodic, black-and-white focus on native instructors and their young and mature pupils involved in the uniquely graceful hands, body and facial movements of Balinese terpsichore. It is a silent, somewhat sketchy record, but like the two accompanying verbal studies, it speaks volumes for man and his cultures.

1975 My 3, 41:3

FILM VIEW

VINCENT CANBY

A Joyously Indestructible Movie Returns

Among Great Moments in film history (the Odessa Steps sequence from "Potemkin," the last scene of "City Lights" and the montage that describes the failing marriage in "Citizen Kane," to identify just a few of the more obvious ones), there are at least half a dozen in a film that won no major Academy Awards and wasn't even listed on many Ten-Best lists for the year it came out (1952).

The film is the extraordinarily exuberant, always youthful, joyously indestructible musical, "Singin' in The Rain," which opens a special one-week return engagement at Radio City Music Hall Thursday, beginning what I hope will be a whole new lease on its theatrical life.

"Singin' in The Rain" has never been very long away from us. It turns up periodically on television and it's a fixture in any repertory program devoted to the Golden Age of the American film musical from the early forties to the mid-fifties. Yet the film cannot be fully appreciated in any abbreviated, chopped-up form on the small screen, nor in the kind of washed-out and scratched prints one so often has to put up with at repertory theaters.

I doubt that "Singin' in The Rain" could be fatally damaged except by fire or a shredding machine. Probably no film can rise above shabby surroundings with such panache, but that is no reason to penalize it, to deny it the gilt presentation that last year was given to "That's Entertainment," the compilation film that so cheerfully exploited the interest accumulated by 25 years of M-G-M musicals. "Singin' in The Rain" is the original capital investment on which "That's Entertainment" was based. It deserves to be seen in its own surroundings if possible— in a movie palace.

•   •   •

Although I haven't kept careful record, I think that I've probably seen "Singin' in The Rain" more times than I've seen any other film, probably five or six times since it first came out. I've seen it in fancy first-run theaters, in dumpy last-run theaters, on a 16-millimeter projector in the apartment of friends, in a shoebox-shaped theater in Paris with French subtitles. Most recently I watched it as I sat hunched up and freezing in a peculiarly air-conditioned New York screening room. The drafts from the ventilators were so strong I had to cup my hands around the match to light a cigarette. There were times when I thought the room was going to snow.

Nevertheless, nothing diminishes the pleasures of this remarkable film. Although it's no longer quite the discovery

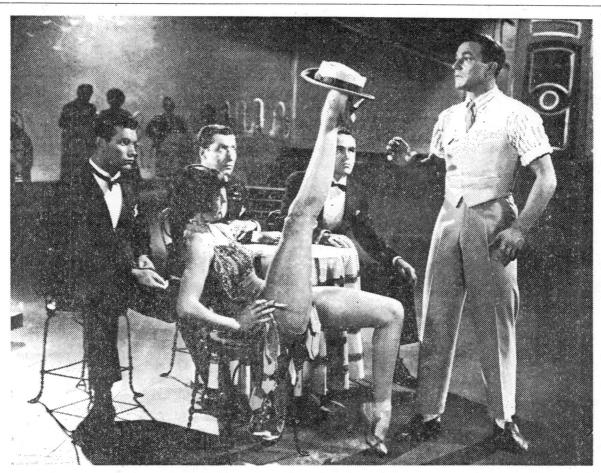

Charisse and Kelly in a classic production number from "Singin'
in the Rain." The film has at least five other Great Moments.

it once was, it has the freshness of a live performance
in the theater, which, I suppose, is another way
of saying it seems unique.

As so often happens with something unique, it's rather
easier to describe what it isn't than what it is. "Singin'
in The Rain" is not thematically important ("Fiddler on
The Roof"). It's not a carefully prefabricated sequel to
something else ("Funny Lady"). It's not a laboriously
studied evocation of an earlier kind of film ("At Long Last
Love"), nor a recycled Broadway musical ("Oklahoma!"),
nor even a recycled Broadway musical that was recycled
from a movie that was recycled from an earlier
Broadway play ("Mame").

"Singin' in The Rain" is an original and I'm as
hesitant to attempt to analyze it as I would be to take a
clock apart. I'm not sure I'd be able to get all the pieces
back in the right places. The most important thing is that
it works just as well today as it did 23 years ago. Maybe
better. Today we see it in the fairly barren context
of contemporary musical films, of movies that cost so
much to make that the possible disinterest of the Pakistani
audience has a bearing on what exactly goes into the film.

I suspect that if Betty Comden and Adolph Green,
who wrote the screenplay for "Singin' in The Rain (as well
as one of its funniest songs, "Moses Supposes"), were to
present a producer with the same screenplay today he'd
find its wit recklessly, dangerously parochial. "Singin'
in The Rain" is boy-meets-girl in a Hollywood teetering on
the brink of the sound revolution in the late twenties,
but it is pure musical comedy, alternately romantic and
farcical, and the only nostalgia it prompts is for the
nineteen-fifties, if only because movies like this could be
made then.

Technically it's about a Hollywood star (Gene Kelly),
the unknown actress he loves (Debbie Reynolds), his
long-time sidekick (Donald O'Connor) and his wickedly
bird-brained leading lady (Jean Hagen) who refuses to
believe Kelly when he says he loves Miss Reynolds. "That's

ridiculous," says Miss Hagen. She adds with the marvelous
illogic that propels the film, "Everyone knows you're in
love with me."

This is more or less the plot, but "Singin' in The
Rain" is demonstrably about high style and irrepressible
spirit, which are apparent in the writing, in the performances,
in the direction by Kelly and Stanley Donen, and in the
score by Arthur Freed and Nacio Herb Brown. By the time
"Singin' in The Rain" was made, "Oklahoma!" had made
the "integrated musical" the only kind of musical that critics
could take with true seriousness. Being integrated meant
not only that songs had to grow logically out of the
story but that they also had to be glum occasionally,
perhaps illustrated with at least one ballet sequence most
often introduced as a dream.

•　　•　　•

"Singin' in The Rain" is integrated, but it's not all
that integrated on the face of it. There is, towards the end,
an absolutely classic production number, "Broadway
Rhythm," in which Gene Kelly, with the assistance of
Cyd Charisse, describes for a movie producer the production
number that will conclude the film-within-the-film. It
could be argued this number doesn't have to be in the
movie, but that is to overlook the excitement and wit of
the number that make it an integral part of the film we've
been watching.

I won't give away the film's five other Great Moments
in case you'll be seeing it for the first time, though one of
them has to do with the title song, and you may have
already seen it in "That's Entertainment." It bears re-seeing,
as does the entire film. Enjoying "Singin' in The Rain" has
nothing to do with nostalgia or with sentimentality. It
is, simply stated, a Hollywood masterpiece.

1975 My 4, II: 15: 1

Karen Black and William Atherton watching a movie in "The Day of the Locust"

THE DAY OF THE LOCUST, directed by John Schlesinger; screenplay by Waldo Salt, based on the novel by Nathanael West; produced by Jerome Hellman; director of photography, Conrad Hall; music, John Barry; editor, Jim Clark; distributed by Paramount Pictures. Running time: 144 minutes. At the Cinema 1, Third Avenue near 60th Street. This film has been rated R.

Homer	Donald Sutherland
Faye	Karen Black
Harry	Burgess Meredith
Tod	William Atherton
Big Sister	Geraldine Page
Claude Estee	Richard A. Dysart
Earle Shoop	Bo Hopkins
Miguel	Pepe Serna
Mary Dove	Lelia Goldoni
Abe	Billy Barty
Adore	Jackie Haley
Mrs. Loomis	Gloria Le Roy
Mrs. Johnson	Madge Kennedy
The Gingos	Margaret Willey
	Florence Lake
Audrey	Natalie Schafer
Helverston	Paul Stewart
Ned Grote	John Hillerman
Director	William C. Castle

By VINCENT CANBY

Detail: A middle-aged man, coatless, sits in a canvas deck chair in a small, untended garden. It is hot and sunny but not really bright. The man stares at a large lizard, which stares back. When an orange falls from a tree, the noise it makes as it hits the ground suggests that the earth deep within is hollow.

Detail: A young woman, whose blonde prettiness is drugstore chic, watches the movie screen with the rapt attention of someone expecting a miracle. Suddenly she sees herself on the screen, transformed, as one of a group of harem girls in old Baghdad. For a brief moment she is the center of everything. Then it's over. Says the young woman to her escorts as she leaves the movie theater: "They ruined it."

Detail: A cockfight in a suburban garage late at night. One of the handlers, a middle-aged dwarf, picks up his bleeding, dazed bird. He strokes it. He licks the blood from its neck. Tenderly. Then he sends it back into the ring to be butchered.

Detail: An androgynous child of, perhaps, 12, with peroxide hair, dressed in short, Buster Brown pants and shirt, knocks on a window to get the attention of the man within. The man turns. The child does a grotesque imitation of Mae West's "Come up and see me sometime."

The place is Los Angeles in the late nineteen-thirties, when the Hollywood movie studios were booming and when California was still the promised land, filling up daily with more and more young hopefuls, with aging con artists, with Okies, the old and the ill who wanted to die in the sun. It is the setting for the huge, in many ways remarkable film that John Schlesinger has made from Nathanael West's small, classic novel, "The Day of the Locust."

•

"The Day of the Locust," which opened yesterday at the Cinema 1, is less a conventional film than it is a gargantuan panorama, a spectacle that illustrates West's dispassionate prose with a fidelity to detail more often found in a gimcracky Biblical epic than in something that so relentlessly ridicules American civilization.

In its scope, in its fascination with second-rateness as a way of life, in the boldness with which it dwells on shabby details, the film reminds me of murals that used to turn up from time to time in early Franklin D. Roosevelt-era post offices. Having been commissioned by the Works Progress Administration, furious, politically committed artists would produce views of American life that seemed to eat away at the walls of the buildings meant to contain them.

"The Day of the Locust" is like this. It is a Hollywood epic that uses Hollywood sleaziness as a metaphor for nothing less than the Decline of the West. The movie is far from subtle, but it doesn't matter. It seems that much more material was shot than could be easily fitted into the movie, even at 144 minutes.

•

Its narrative focus is uncertain. Are we seeing the story through the eyes of Mr. Schlesinger, the film's director, or of Tod Hackett (William Atherton), the young Yale graduate and apprentice scenic designer who moves through the film participating in events but not doing much about them? What Tod doesn't see, Mr. Schlesinger doesn't hesitate to show us. The film's pivot, Homer Smith (Donald Sutherland), a creepy, sexually repressed accountant from the Middle West, remains a mysterious cartoon of a character throughout.

Yet the film works without wasting time on these usual psychological underpinnings, in the way that mural art can. It is reality projected as fantasy. Its grossness—its bigger-than-life quality — is so much a part of its style (and what West was writing about) that one respects the extravagances, the almost lunatic scale on which Mr. Schlesinger has filmed its key sequences: a soundstage disaster (when a set representing the Waterloo battlefield collapses during the filming of the film within), and the climactic riot, when a Hollywood premiere turns into an event on the order of the Crucifixion.

•

In such a panoramic movie the performers have a way of being reduced to being the functions of the director and the screenwriter (Waldo Salt). The characters don't change. They don't become something else during the course of the film. They already are what they always will be. This is tough on actors, but Mr. Schlesinger has used this beautifully, with one possible exception.

This is a movie that has been ideally cast as much as it is acted—by Mr. Sutherland, Mr. Atherton, Burgess Meredith (as a rummy old vaudeville hoofer), Geraldine Page (though her sequence is superfluous), Jackie Haley (as the androgynous child) and Billy Barty (as a mean-tempered dwarf). Only the figure of Karen Black, playing the bit-player, the tough, doomed to-fail aspirant to stardom, softens the film with something like pathos. "The Day of the Locust" doesn't need it.

1975 My 8, 48:1

MANDINGO, directed by Richard Fleischer; screenplay by Norman Wexler, based on Kyle Onstott's novel and Jack Kirkland's play; producer, Dino De Laurentiis; executive producer, Ralph Serpe; director of photography, Richard H. Kline; music, Maurice Jarre; editor, Frank Bracht; distributed by Paramount Pictures. Running time: 127 minutes. At the Criterion Theater, Broadway at 45th Street, and R.K.O. 86th Street Twin 1 Theater, 86th Street near Lexington Avenue. This film has been rated R.

Maxwell	James Mason
Blanche	Susan George
Hammond	Perry King
Agamemnon	Richard Ward
Ellen	Brenda Sykes
Mede	Ken Norton
Lucrezia Borgia	Lillian Hayman
Doc Redfield	Roy Poole
Cicero	Ji-Tu Cumbuka

———

The illustrated ads for "Mandingo," which opened at two theaters yesterday, sort of remind you of the ones for "Gone With the Wind," what with the old plantation house in the background, the suggestion of crowds caught up in great events, flames, lovers pictured in tempestuous embrace.

There's a difference, though. The "Mandingo" ads show two pairs of lovers, and both are what the pornography trade calls "mixed combos," a black man with a white woman, and a white man with a black woman.

"Mandingo," based on the novel by Kyle Onstott and directed by Richard Fleischer, is steamily melodramatic nonsense that purports to tell what life on the old plantation was really like, though its serious intentions are constantly denied by the camera's erotic interest in the techniques of humiliation, mostly with sex and violence.

James Mason is the master of Falconhurst, a slave-breeding plantation in what seems to be antebellum Louisiana. Perry King is his crippled heir who prefers the company of a young black slave woman (Brenda Sykes), who talks like a Bryn Mawr graduate, to his neurotic white wife (Susan George), who talks a thick, movie-Southern dialect and who attempts to even the score by taking a young black stud (Ken Norton) as her lover.

To accomplish this, Miss George intimidates Mr. Norton by saying that unless he goes to bed with her willingly, she will tell her husband that the slave "riped" her, which is her way of saying "raped."

The movie has been handsomely photographed in a number of impressively decaying old Southern houses, and it is acted with ludicrous intensity by Mr. Mason, Mr. King, Mr. Norton, Miss Sykes and Miss George. I assume they had no choice.

VINCENT CANBY

1975 My 8, 49:1

THE SECRET (Le Secret) directed by Robert Enrico; screenplay (French with English subtitles) by Mr. Enrico and Pascal Jardin, based on the novel "Le Compagnon Indesirable" by Francis Ryck; director of photography, Etienne Becker; music, Ennio Morricone; distributed by Cinema National Films. Running time: 100 minutes. At the Paris Theater, 58th Street west of Fifth Avenue. This film has not been rated.

David	Jean-Louis Trintignant
Julia	Marlene Jobert
Thomas	Philippe Noiret
Claude	Jean-Francis Adam
Greta	Solange Pradel

David (Jean-Louis Trintignant) is in a fix. He has learned something "no one is allowed to know." When we first see him, in and behind the opening credits of the French film "The Secret." David is strapped to an operating table and water is dripping onto his forehead with maddening regularity. David is being tortured. By whom? What for?

The suspense is terrific for approximately seven and a half minutes. After that you may want to make a rude noise or ask for your money back.

"The Secret," which opened yesterday at the Paris Theater, proves that anybody, including Robert Enrico, who directed this film, can come up with a promising beginning for a suspense melodrama. It's the middles and the ends that cause all the problems.

"The Secret" is the sort of movie that arbitrarily withholds information. It also depends on its characters to make unlikely, possibly lunatic decisions to string out the running time.

Furthermore, it leaves its actors high and dry, looking totally foolish. In addition to Mr. Trintignant, these include Philippe Noiret and Marlene Jobert, who play a married couple that befriend the possibly crazy David. They hide him in their country house near Carcassonne. They give him a gun with which he can better terrorize them, in between those moments when his pathetic story of conspiracy prompts them to attain new heights of idiotic charity.

Like most people who go to movies, I'm as willing as the next person to suspend belief. Not this time.

VINCENT CANBY

1975 My 9, 19:1

STILLS, a program of six short films: "PASADENA FREEWAY STILLS," by Gary Beydler, 6 minutes; "HAND HELD DAY," by Mr. Beydler, 6 minutes; "AQUATENNIAL," by Linda Klosky, 33 minutes; "I-94," by Bette Gordon and Jim Benning, 3 minutes; "PRODUCTION STILLS," by Morgan Fisher, 11 minutes; "SUBJECT," by Ken Feingold, 5 minutes. At the Whitney Museum of American Art, Madison Avenue at 75th Street.

———

"Stills," the collective title for the Whitney Museum's current program of six short films, meditates at length on the relationship between the still picture and motion pictures, a subject that may be of more interest to philosophers than to film buffs or even to film makers at this point.

Each of the shorts is a variation on the fact that a series of still pictures, when shuffled, creates the illusion of motion within the eye. Thus, someone might say, there is no true motion. But is anything ever truly *without* motion? These are questions I flee.

VINCENT CANBY

1975 My 9, 19:3

THE HAPPY HOOKER, directed by Nicholas Sgarro; screenplay by William Richert, based on the book by Xaviera Hollander with Robin Moore and Yvonne Dunleavy; executive producers, Dennis Friedland and Marlene Hess; producer, Fred Caruso; music, Don Elliott; director of photography, Dick Kratina; editor, Jerry Greenberg; distributed by the Cannon Group. Running time: 96 minutes. At the Plaza Theater, 58th Street west of Park Avenue, and other theaters. This film has been rated R.
Xaviera Hollander	Lynn Redgrave
Yves St. Jacques	Jean-Pierre Aumont
Madelaine	Lovelady Powell
Carl Gordon	Nicholas Pryor
Mrs. Gordon	Elizabeth Wilson
J. Arthur Conrad	Tom Poston
Fred	Conrad Janis
Chris	Trish Hawkins

By VINCENT CANBY

"The Happy Hooker," which arrived yesterday at the Plaza and other theaters, is not to be confused with "The Life and Times of Xaviera Hollander," the pornography film that played the World Theater some months ago. "The Happy Hooker" is not pornographic.

The movie is a cheerily amoral New York comedy about greed and lust in the land of opportunity. It's based on the book of the same name by Miss Hollander, who was once named Secretary of the Year in her native Netherlands and then went on to become one of Manhattan's most successful madams, written in collaboration with Robin Moore and Yvonne Dunleavy.

In the title role the film has the enormously talented Lynn Redgrave - slim, chic and irrepressibly comic as a young woman who strides confidently up the primrose path to wealth and ill fame.

●

I haven't read the book, so I have no idea how the movie's Xaviera compares with the original. I suspect that this one is the result of the happy collaboration of Miss Redgrave, William Richert (the producer of "Derby"), who wrote the screenplay, and Nicholas Sgarro, who directed the film. Individually and collectively they've had the good sense to put on instead of put down.

Miss Redgrave's Xaviera isn't one to fret about bygones or missed opportunities. She has the resilience of Little Orphan Annie with

none of the fabricated innocence. She's a woman who always listens to herself. Early in her career, when a man she thinks she loves walks out on her, leaving her with an envelope full of large bills, she says the hoary old obligatory line rather huffily: "You make me feel like a whore." As soon as she has said it, however, you are aware that she realizes, with wickedly shrewd self-perception, that this is her call in life.

Moralists may object to the fact that the film steers carefully clear of any of the seamier aspects of big-time prostitution. We are given the impression that Xaviera refused to pay for police protection and that she did so because of her scruples. When thrown in the overnight lockup with a bunch of tough streetwalkers, Xaviera's girls are as shocked as debutantes forced to hitchhike to the ball.

"The Happy Hooker" doesn't deny degradation so much as it airily ignores it in the interests of comedy.

The film, which never quite gets around to Xaviera's deportation from this country in 1972, is told in flashbacks cued by her arrest and arraignment for running her brothel. Her memories are uncluttered by feelings of remorse. At one point she tells us with Miss Redgrave's touch for comic solemnity: "True, I'd gotten myself into a business that wasn't very romantic, but because I liked it, I was able to bring something special to it."

Mr. Sgarro has brought something special to the film by surrounding Miss Redgrave with some of New York's best actors, including Elizabeth Wilson, Lovelady Powell, Nicholas Pryor, Tom Poston, Conrad Janis and Trish Hawkins, with an assist from abroad by Jean-Pierre Aumont. Among other things, the film is a fine advertisement for local talent.

Having been derived from such unlikely subject matter, "The Happy Hooker" is doubley surprising. It's a witty work. Lynn's mother and father need not be embarrassed.

1975 My 9, 22:2

WINDOW WIND CHIMES PART ONE by Vincent Grenier, 27 minutes; THE DESPERATE AND THE DEEP by George Kuchar and the students of the San Francisco Art Institute, 21 minutes; NUDES (A SKETCHBOOK) by Curt McDowell, 30 minutes. At the Film Forum, 256 West 88th Street. Through Sunday and May 15 through 18.

By A. H. WEILER

The trio of short subjects by members of California's film making avant-garde that opened Thursday at the Film Forum as successors to a similar Western collection displayed there last month focuses on aspects of the human condition in occasionally satiric but often uneven style.

If, as the program notes point out, these films were influenced by George Kuchar, who, with his twin, Mike, was the Bronx enfant terrible of the underground before migrating to San Francisco, they expose a personal approach that may need polish but is rarely boring.

More importantly, Mr. Kuchar is represented by "The Desperate and the Deep" and his mastery of his special métier of kidding cinema clichés again is evident in this travesty of a bickering husband and wife and their square son and other voyagers aboard a doomed ship bound for Egypt.

This silly antic, shot with purposely crude backgrounds and outrageously stilted performances and dialogue in what seems to be a dimly lit fish tank, is neither deep nor desperate but as funny as such previous Kuchar lampoons as "Sins of the Fleshapoids" and "Hold Me While I'm Naked."

On the other hand, Vincent Grenier's titularly vague "Window Wind Chimes Part One" is honest, if not gripping, in its close inspection of a man-woman relationship, that is enacted by Mr. Grenier and his wife (courtesy of the program notes), Ann-Knutson. The succession of gentle, seemingly ad lib, confrontations, involving jealousies, friends, food, loveplay and the like within the confines of a small apartment are naturalistic but evolve

as largely unfinished bits and pieces.

The dozen vignettes in Curt McDowell's "Nudes," including one of Mr. Kuchar enjoying a sylvan retreat, are equally intimate and, mainly, sexual sketches. If these miniatures of his friends tend toward the homosexual, their over-all effect, especially in

sensitive studies of an ethereal "Barbara," a mother and child in "Jenny and Jamie" and the erotic fantasy in "Melinda," illustrate a determined drive for artistry evidenced, if not entirely achieved, by all the films in this interesting package.

1975 My 10, 18:5

FILM VIEW

VINCENT CANBY

A Marvelously Foolhardy 'Day Of the Locust'

When you get to southern California you've gone about as far as you can go. Another few steps and you walk into the Pacific. Southern California is the far edge. It's where the continent runs out. It's America at the end of the dream, which is what Nathanael West's small, classic novel, "The Day of the Locust," is all about. It's also the unrelenting theme of John Schlesinger's virtually epic film version of the novel about life on the seedy fringe of Hollywood in the 1930's.

One's first reaction on seeing this ambitious film is likely to be wonderment: has there ever before been a film of such manifest expense and physical scale, with so many extras and so much attention paid to set, costume and period (1938) detail, to celebrate a vision of such futility?

Karen Black: "Life on the seedy fringe of Hollywood"

I doubt it. Which is one of the reasons I admire what appears to be the built-in madness of the project. It's a film that took truly remarkable self-assurance to make. To hell with market research, with polls (and songs) that tell us audiences want to pack up all their cares and woes when they go to the movies. "The Day of the Locust" is like a DeMille version of "The Ten Commandments" in which everyone gets drowned crossing the Red Sea. It plays havoc with accepted myth.

"The Day of the Locust" is not one of the great films of all time but like the movie version of another classic novel that may well be unfilmable, "Catch-22," it's a fascinating companion piece to the original work. It's a big, annotated, illustrated guide that, if it does nothing else (and it does), should create a lot of new readers for West's indelible body of work, just four novels of which "The Day of The Locust," published in 1939, the year before West's death, was the last and, to my way of thinking, the best.

West's novel is very short, very spare in style, but it is dense with details, which explains why the film that Schlesinger has made, from a screenplay by Waldo Salt, runs almost 2½ hours. You might think that a novel that is 140 pages long (in its paperback edition) should run only 90 minutes at most, but Schlesinger and Salt have chosen not to seek equivalents (if, indeed there are any) to West's prose style. They have, instead, made a film that uses the book as a blueprint for what becomes an elaborate movie structure. The triumph of the film is that it never seems embalmed, like Visconti's "Death in Venice," or merely evocative, like Clayton's "The Great Gatsby."

"The Day of the Locust" has a life of its own, so much so that I can accept the enthusiasm with which the filmmakers have transformed two of the novel's tersely surreal sequences into pieces of moviemaking spectacle that are the equal of anything to be seen in any of the recent batch of so-called disaster movies. A less intelligent adaptation would be wrecked by this kind of spectacle: a sequence in which a large portion of a movie set representing the Waterloo battlefield collapses while a film-within-the-film is being shot on a soundstage, and the novel's climactic sequence, a Hollywood premiere at Grauman's Chinese Theater that turns into an apocalyptic vision of the decline and fall of America and, possibly, of the entire western world.

These sequences work, I suspect, because the characters in "The Day of the Locust" are mostly seen at a dispassionate distance, without sentimentality. They cannot be upstaged by spectacle since their lives are parts of the same panorama, presented in the film from time to time, somewhat too literally, in the paintings being done by the film's principal observer.

I use the term principal observer since "The Day of the Locust" doesn't really have what could be called a hero. It has instead Tod (William Atherton), a clean-cut young Yale graduate who works at Paramount Pictures as an apprentice scenic designer. We see almost everything in the film through his eyes, which are those of a painter who is gifted with the intuitions shared by all artists.

Los Angeles, the home of Hollywood, the great dream factory, is where people come to die as their hopes wither away. Tod is fascinated by the spectacle but never a part of it. Like an anthropologist among some especially eccentric aborigines, he is tolerated but never really understood.

Among those who tolerate him are Faye Greener (Karen Black), a self-centered, hard-as-nails dress extra and part-time hooker who dreams of becoming a star; Homer Simpson (Donald Sutherland), a sexually repressed, middle-aged bachelor from a small midwest town; Harry (Burgess Meredith), Faye's boozy old father, a bitter, ex-vaudeville hoofer who sells his own "magical miracle solvent" door-to-door, whenever he feels well enough; Abe (Billy Barty), a nasty tempered dwarf who makes book, and Adore (Jackie Haley), a furiously evil, androgynous child actor.

They all are extraordinarily vivid, as is Geraldine Page who plays an Aimee Semple McPherson type of California evangelist in a sequence that is the invention of Schlesinger and Salt and, though effective as filmmaking, is the only part of the movie that seems totally superfluous. The movie has said just about everything there is to say about the nuttier aspects of southern California culture, circa the late thirties, without this sort of easy satire.

"The Day of the Locust" goes flatly literal occasionally, as if it didn't trust us to figure out that it is using Hollywood as a manic metaphor. There are times when it seems to want us to accept Faye Greener as a much more pathetic creature than she is, when the bridges between sequences have an elephantine clumsiness to them, and when other connectives have apparently been left on the cutting room floor. Yet it's such a marvelously foolhardy, one-of-a-kind movie that I'm amazed it ever got made at all.

1975 My 11, II:1:1

LULU THE TOOL, directed by Elio Petri; screenplay (Italian with English subtitles) by Ugo Pirro and Mr. Petri; director of photography, Luigi Kuveiller; produced by Euro International Films; executive producer, Uto Tucci; distributed by New Line Cinema. At the D. W. Griffith Theater, 59th Street and Second Avenue. Running time: 91 minutes. This film has not been classified.

Lulu	Gian Maria Volonte
Lidia	Mariangela Melato
Militina	Salvo Randone
Adalgisa	Mietta Albertini

By A. H. WEILER

"Lulu the Tool" is no more descriptive a title for Elio Petri's Italian social drama that opened yesterday at the D. W. Griffith Cinema than "La Classe Operaia Va in Paradiso" ("The Working Class Goes to Heaven"), the title under which it shared (with "The Mattei Affair") the grand prize of the 1972 Cannes Film Festival. But if neither tag is memorable, there is little doubt that the director-writer, whose convictions are Communist, has projected a cynical view of the worker's lot that is both fascinating and sobering.

Mr. Petri, who scored with his 1970 dissection of police authority in "Investigation of a Citizen Above Suspicion," has again joined Ugo Pirro in writing the script. With Gian Maria Volonte, the top cop in "Investigation," he points up the Kafkalike condition of "Lulu."

As a productive, fairly happy, if griping, hand in a northern Italian factory, Lulu, his hero, appears to have licked the stultifying effects of the assembly line by sticking to his lathe, thinking carnally about a well-endowed fellow worker, his incentive pay and his family. But there are forces he can't control. Include among these a complaining wife (Mariangela Melato) and the pleasures of the bed and a young son he is too work-weary to enjoy; a factory accident that costs him a finger, and, above all, a strike and the confusing dialectics of student activists and union leaders.

Mr. Petri, who called his film "propaganda for the working class" at Cannes, hews to that hard line. His activists are weakly defensive when confronted by an unemployed Lulu, his unionists seem to be self-serving, and a once-tough Lulu is terrified by the lucid flashes of doom prophesied by an elderly mental patient, gently played by Salvo Randone, who has been wrecked by the assembly line.

•

If our hero gets his chance for that fling (in his car) with that shapely virgin co-worker he's been ogling, it's a faintly comic and labored joust that's sadly disappointing for both. And, though the strike is won, it is strongly implied that the victory for Lulu, as the tool of capitalism, unions and activists, is unrewarding.

The focus, of course, is largely on Mr. Volonte, as the harried Lulu amid a company of unfamiliar players who seem to be at home in the factory and on the picket line. It is a varied, naturalistic and sensitive portrayal of a simple and vigorous man buffeted, frightened, anguished and perplexed by suddenly changing circumstances in his once comfortable bailiwick of the workers' world.

"Lulu the Tool" may not be an entirely original concept, since "Coup Pour Coup" ("Blow for Blow"), the 1971 French feature shown here in March, also illustrated a case against industrial injustice. "Lulu the Tool," of course, delivers the director's avowed "propaganda" forcefully, as the film's English subtitles make clear. But, more important, he has fashioned a swiftly moving, human and often disturbing drama.

1975 My 12, 39:1

CRIME AND PUNISHMENT, directed by Lev Kulijanov; screenplay (Russian with English subtitles) by Nikolai Figurovsky and Mr. Kulijanov, based on the novel by Dostoyevsky; director of photography, Vyacheslav Shumsky; a Gorky Studios production, distributed by Artkino Pictures. Running time: 200 minutes. At the Bijou Theater, 45th Street west of Broadway. This film has not been rated.

Raskolnikov	Georgi Taratorkin
Inspector Porfiri	Innokenti Smoktunovsky
Sonia	Tatyana Bedova
Dunia	Victoria Fyodorovna
Svidrigailov	Yefim Kopelyan
Marmeladov	Yevgeni Lebedev
Mrs. Marmeladov	Maia Bulgakova
Mrs. Raskolikov	Irian Gosheva
Luzhin	Vladimir Basov
Razumihin	Alexander Pavlov
Mrs. Aliona	Elizaveta Evstratova
Lizaveta	Liubov Sokolova

By VINCENT CANBY

Dostoyevsky's "Crime and Punishment" has been filmed at least five times since the 1927 silent version, and I haven't seen every version, but I can't imagine one more faithful to the full sweep of the novel than the 1970 Soviet adaptation that opened yesterday at the Bijou Theater.

It's a fine, brooding, beautiful movie, photographed in black and white and in CinemaScope, whose proportions (an image nearly three times as wide as it is high) suggest the oppressive weight of the poverty, hopelessness and despair that hang over Dostoyevsky's extraordinary collection of characters. It's the first time I can remember that doom has had a visible screen shape.

•

This "Crime and Punishment" runs three hours and 20 minutes, which makes certain demands on the audience. It also allows Lev Kulijanov, the director, and Nikolai Figurovsky, with whom he wrote the screenplay, to expand their adaptation far beyond the cat-mouse game that is the subject of most film versions.

Mr. Kulijanov's "Crime and Punishment" is much more than a psychological manhunt in which the cool, shrewd, benignly possessed police inspector, Porfiri, persuades the brilliant, half-mad Raskolnikov, a self-described "former student," to confess his murder of an old pawnbroker and her sister.

The movie teems with the subsidiary characters and subplots that give the novel its tumultuous life—Raskolnikov's genteel mother and his sister Dunia, the members of the quite mad Marmeladov family, including Sonia, the saintly streetwalker, Luzhin, the middle-aged councillor who courts Dunia, and Svidrigailov, the wealthy country gentleman and roué who tries to seduce Dunia and, when he fails, puts a bullet through his brain.

•

Most of the film versions of "Crime and Punishment" I've seen have been somber, but this one seethes with contradictory moods and emotions. Death scenes have no dignity to them. A funeral lunch becomes a brawl. Drunks talk common sense and Raskolnikov, at his most sane and philosophical, talks nonsense thoroughly confused with truth.

All the performances are fine, but the most easily identifiable are those of Georgi Taratorkin as Raskolnikov, whose tall, crooked silhouette, topped by his stovepipe hat, is the haunted symbol of the film, and Innokenti Smoktunovsky, as Inspector Porfiri.

Mr. Smoktunovsky, who was seen here in the Soviet "Hamlet" (1964) and "Uncle Vanya" (1972), is an especially elegant, witty actor. When he congratulates Raskolnikov on an article on the psychology of crime, which Raskolnikov wrote as a student, he says, "I love first efforts . . . so full of the heat of youth," and you are aware he's also talking about Raskolnikov's fruitless murder of the old pawnbroker.

•

The physical production beautifully evokes old St. Petersburg, its grubby streets and tenements, its canals, its parks that are forever cheerless to Dostoyevsky's people, no matter how sunny. Its houses are simultaneously full of drafts and airless. Raskolnikov is continually moving up and down dimly lit stairwells, but he is always cornered.

The English subtitles give the film a literary flavor that some audiences may object to. I can hear some outraged customers saying, "I didn't come to the movies to read, for God's sake." Yet they are completely in keeping with the nature of the film, which never denies its literary origins or their complexities.

1975 My 15, 48:1

BENEDICT ARNOLD, directed by Walter Gutman; story and narration by Mr. Gutman; photographed by Robert Cowan, Mike Kuchar and Mr. Gutman; distributed by New York Filmmakers Cooperative. At the Whitney Museum of American Art, Madison Avenue and 75th Street. Running time: 105 minutes. This film has not been classified.
Mrs. Benedict Arnold ... Susan Haviland
John Andre .... Peter Bartlett

By A. H. WEILER

Walter Gutman, a financial expert and patron of avant-garde film makers, obviously adores movies and, in recent years, made and appeared in a couple of underground, sex-oriented features, "Unwrap Me" and "The Grape Dealer's Daughter." And he proves he is equally devoted to historic figures in "Benedict Arnold," the documentary that arrived yesterday at the Whitney Museum of American Art. If the results are not definitive, they represent a serious, if rambling, study of a period and a man he considers more noteworthy and talented than just his most memorable label as our most memorable traitor.

As the director-writer and chief off-screen narrator who's also seen briefly, Mr. Gutman admits his long interest in the Revolutionary general and the fact that "the Bicentennnial year was a good excuse for the film." The movie, in effect, is a compilation of vintage paintings, a Cook's tour of famed Revolutionary sites and re-enactments with various off-screen narrators quoting from "a score" of letters by Arnold, his spy and co-conspirator, John André; his second wife, the former Peggy Shippen; Alexander Hamilton and others.

Fitting these missives to their settings obviously was a formidable, if not impossible task. But a fair degree of ancient authenticity is achieved in such New York locales as Fort Ticonderoga, Tappan, Lake Champlain, West Point and in Connecticut (with actors impersonating bewigged gentry) who figured in the Arnold saga. And, for example, one conjures up a good idea of the sumptuous, gay life at a fancy ball for Philadelphia's élite from a detailed commentary and still reproductions of the event.

Mr. Gutman, in short, does

not scoff at facts and adds his feelings about such facets of history as Arnold's military prowess before his involvement with the ill-fated André; his naval exploits, his success as a businessman, his antecedents, his wife and her relationship with André and his life after he fled to England. His appreciation of a complex Arnold and his coterie is sincere, if ruminative and occasionally repetitive. If it is no substitute for a biography such as James T. Flexner's "The Traitor and the Spy," it does serve to enliven history's pages.

1975 My 16, 22:4

IN SEARCH OF DRACULA, a documentary produced and directed by Calvin Floyd; written by Yvonne Floyd; photography, Tony Forsberg; music by Calvin Floyd; released by the Independent International Pictures Corporation. At neighborhood theatres. Running time: 86 minutes. This film is classified PG.
With: Christopher Lee

The vampire legend, which turned the bats from Bram Stoker's classic 1897 novel into big business for its many stage, screen and TV successors, is treated with the solemnity of a doctoral thesis in the partly dramatized documentary "In Search of Dracula," which descended on local theatres Wednesday. But with all respect to the research on the historic background of the bloodsucking undead, this "Dracula" is more scholarly than chilling and hardly a competitor of the late Bela Lugosi and other ersatz Draculas.

"In Search of Dracula," according to the film's distributors, was produced and directed by Calvin Floyd, an American working in Sweden. With the aid of Christopher Lee—the Dracula of a succession of British-made adaptations of the legend—as the off-screen narrator and on-screen Dracula, the film courses through Dracula country in Transylvania, Rumania, Hungary and Germany to trace authentic sites and Dracula facts and folklore.

•

Bram Stoker, in case you did not know, never set foot in Transylvania; bat fears and worship date back to antiquity, and the prototype for Dracula was Prince Vlad, a 15th-century Transylvanian who delighted in impaling his enemies with such cruelty that he was stamped a vampire.

There are contemporary fiends too, including the German who was the model for the film "M," starring Peter Lorre.

A cinema aspect is added to the current somber proceedings by excerpts from other vintage films such as F. W. Murnau's 1921 version of Dracula, "Nosferatu"; the 1930 Bela Lugosi "Dracula" and a couple of silent films featuring, respectively, Mr. Lugosi and Lila Lee, and that

noted vamp, Theda Bara.

As a veteran "Dracula," Christopher Lee is menacing in brief impersonations of the vampire and the vicious Vlad and in intoning varied facts and hearsay about stakes through heart, sex, religion and the real Dracula castle. "There are more things in Heaven and Earth than are dreamed in your philosophy," he warns classically. Dracula devotees aside, too many "things" are unearthed in this "Search."

A. H. WEILER

1975 My 16, 24:1

SHEILA LEVINE IS DEAD AND LIVING IN NEW YORK, directed by Sidney J. Furie; screenplay, Kenny Solms and Gail Parent; based on the novel by Miss Parent; produced by Harry Korshak; music, Michel Legrand; director of photography, Donald M. Morgan; editor, Argyle Nelson; distributed by Paramount Pictures. Running time: 112 minutes. At the Baronet Theater, Third Avenue near 59th Street. This film has been rated PG.
Sheila Levine .... Jeannie Berlin
Sam Stoneman .... Roy Scheider
Kate .... Rebecca Dianna Smith
Bernice .... Janet Brandt
Manny .... Sid Melton
Wally .... Charles Woolf
Agatha .... Leda Rogers

By VINCENT CANBY

Something disastrous happened to the heroine of Gail Parent's funny novel, "Sheila Levine Is Dead and Living in New York," on her way to the silver screen.

Sheila, the Jewish girl from Harrisburg, the college graduate with a degree in epic survival, has lost her wit, her self-perceptions, her lucky way of failing at suicide or, rather, of having a pushy mother who knows just when to call the cops.

The movie Sheila, played by Jeannie Berlin, is still a grade-A mess, but Miss Parent and Kenny Solms, who collaborated on tie screenplay, have turned her into a tired Jewish joke. This Sheila is so aggressively naive and dumb, when it suits the purposes of the comedy, that it's quite impossible to believe that even her family could stand her, to say nothing of the Mr. Right with whom the film provides her.

Miss Berlin, who was so good in her mother's "The Heartbreak Kid," plays Sheila with bovine gracelessness that, I suspect, is what was required by the script and by the director, Sidney J. Furie. She is permitted neither intelligence nor taste. We are asked to believe that Sheila, after living in New York for some time and traveling with fairly swinging friends, would try to attract her man by dolling herself up like Messalina.

Watching Sheila schlep from one arbitrary disaster to another in the course of the movie is not funny, and it's not moving. It is mere exploitation. It's also a total waste of the talents of Miss Berlin and Roy Scheider, who

plays the handsome, sensitive, unmarried doctor who is the answer to the dreams of every Jewish girl and her mother. In this kind of fiction, anyway.

1975 My 17, 14:2

FILM VIEW

VINCENT CANBY

What Makes A Movie Immoral?

When I write about bad movies, I sometimes hear myself sounding like a Bible-thumping moralist, full of indignation that the world should have to put up with this latest piece of value-distorting, experience-diminishing, time-consuming junk. No matter how lofty or honorable a subject may be, a movie that is bad—clumsy, cliched, banal—does it a disservice.

Movies are about much more than their plots and the moral fiber of their characters. They are a mysterious combination of technical facility, emotional perception and artistic vision—to such an extent that it's possible to find a comedy like "Shampoo," about a group of completely amoral people, more important, more energizing, more moral, than something as well-intentioned but lifeless as "Sounder," in which the characters are identifiably heroic.

Good movies are movies that enhance our lives. They allow us to see things we may never have noticed before. They don't waste our time. They are, in effect, moral. Bad films—films I don't like—are immoral. At any rate, this is the roundabout way I justify my having found "The Happy Hooker" to be such an amiable and funny film, and essentially a moral one, while I reacted with varying degrees of moral outrage to several much more ambitious films—Otto Preminger's "Rosebud," Richard Fleischer's "Mandingo" and Floyd Mutrux's "Aloha, Bobby and Rose."

"Terror is the ultimate weapon," say the ads for "Rosebud," and one would expect that Mr. Preminger would at least take his ad writers seriously if not the expectations of his audience. "Rosebud" plays upon our memories of the terrorist activities of Palestinian fanatics in Munich, at the Tel Aviv airport, in the Sudan. We cart along to the theater all of our accumulated feelings of horror, frustration and impotency, and what do we find? A witlessly written screenplay in which most of the action is verbal (and almost unintelligible) about the kidnapping of the daughters of five of the richest and/or most influential men in the western world.

The movie's most peculiar revelation is the fact that the real villain is not a ruthless member of the Black September but a psychotic Englishman (Richard Attenborough), a converted Muslim (they are the worst, you know), who has designed the kidnapping as part of his campaign against Israel as well as against all Commie-loving Arabs. One can almost forgive this cop-out. After all, American movies depend on the international market so what could be more practical and topical than a movie about Arab terrorism that more or less avoids the subject? Instead it pins the rap on one nutty renegade representing absolutely nobody except himself.

What one cannot forgive is the movie's lethargy and the confusions of the plot (or maybe of the editing) that are so troubling that watching the movie is like being on a guided tour without the guide. Is that the coastline of the south of France? Israel? No, it's Corsica. Maybe.

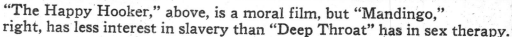
"The Happy Hooker," above, is a moral film, but "Mandingo," right, has less interest in slavery than "Deep Throat" has in sex therapy.

It's not too much to suggest that this waste of raw materials—film stock, acting talents like those of Peter O'Toole and Cliff Gorman, the wit and ability of Mr. Preminger—is immoral.

"Mandingo," based on the novel by Kyle Onstott, promises to tell us what life on the old plantation was really like. It rips away the Spanish moss to find more Spanish moss underneath. The film was shot on location in the south, in some magnificently decaying old mansions, and the camera work is not at all bad, but what the camera sees is enough to make you long for the most high-handed, narrow-minded film censorship. "Mandingo" has less interest in . slavery than "Deep Throat" has in sexual therapy. It is as silly as "The Little Colonel" but much more vicious. While the poor darkies are singing on the soundtrack, they are being beaten, humiliated, denied, raped and murdered on-screen, with the kind of fond attention to specific details one more often finds in the close-ups employed in pornographic films. This one is strictly for bondage enthusiasts.

"Aloha, Bobby and Rose" makes a suicidal attempt to find beauty and romance in the most barren reaches of contemporary American life. The setting is Los Angeles and Bobby and Rose, its ill-fated lovers, go from bad to worse when a liquor store clerk is accidentally killed after Bobby, whose sense of humor is not terrific, pretends to hold him up.

Bobby and Rose are a far cry from Henry Fonda and Sylvia Sidney in "You Only Live Once." They are no more important than the local architecture. They are a filling station in love with a drive-in hamburger stand (actually Bobby is a mechanic and Rose is a waitress) caught up in a half-hearted urban renewal project. That's the impact of the film. The movie allows its characters no life of their own. They are dehumanized robots acting out the arbitrary wishes of the filmmaker.

In this context, "The Happy Hooker" seems like Restoration comedy. The movie was directed by Nicholas Sgarro and adapted by William Richert from the book by Xaviera Hollander, the Manhattan madam, with Robin Moore and Yvonne Dunleavy.

It doesn't exactly glorify high-priced prostitution but it makes it clear that for Xaviera, played with great verve by Lynn Redgrave, prostitution was something she had a natural flair for. She cares. She's not frivolous. Or, as she says in one of the film's nicer, mock-solemn lines, "Making people happy is a difficult job."

The film makes no moral judgment about Xaviera, nor does it attempt to explain her. Would anybody attempt to explain the talent of Mark Spitz? Or Barbra Streisand? Talent is not something to be explained. It just is.

"The Happy Hooker" follows Xaviera's career from the day she arrives in this country, a former Secretary of The Year in her native Holland, and is jilted almost immediately by her stuffy, mother-dominated fiance. There are no great problems to be hurdled so the film more or less concentrates on Xaviera's resilient way with difficult men, like the business tycoon (Tom Poston), who is driven mad with desire as she does a reverse strip-tease (that is, as she puts her clothes back on) while reciting the day's stock market report.

"The Happy Hooker," beautifully acted by Miss Redgrave, Elizabeth Wilson, Mr. Poston, Lovelady Powell, among others, is a first-rate satire, a light-hearted send-up of a very special kind of capitalism.

1975 My 18, II:19:1

'French Connection II' Is Very Different

By VINCENT CANBY

Popeye Doyle is not dead. He's alive and treacherously hooked on heroin and pursuing drug dealers (on foot, pantingly) through Marseilles in "French Connection II," John Frankenheimer's fairly stylish spinoff from Billy Friedkin's enormously successful 1971 original, "The French Connection."

Gene Hackman's Popeye Doyle, the hard-nosed, quick-tempered, narrow-minded New York police officer, was just about the only identifiable human amid all the spectacular wreckage in the first film.

Popeye hasn't gone soft or genteel in "French Connection II." If anything, he appears to have become a bit more of a magnificent boor as he charges around the Marseilles waterfront, belting a lot of the bad guys (as well as a few of the good ones by mistake), wondering dimly why no one understands good English and behaving, in general, like an upper-class Frenchman's nightmare of an American tourist run amok.

Although the producers of "French Connection II" would like to emphasize that this is an entirely new film, with no real connection to the first one, they aren't above associating the two through the title and the use of the central character, whose individuality depends more on Mr. Hackman than it does on the material supplied by the screenwriters.

The two films *are* exceedingly different. The Friedkin picture was as much a hallucinogenic portrait of life in that New York half world shared by the police and criminals as it was a superior suspense melodrama. "French Connection II" is nowhere near so complex, though it's still entertaining.

In these further adventures of Popeye Doyle, the American detective is the entire

The Cast

FRENCH CONNECTION II, directed by John Frankenheimer; screenplay by Robert and Laurie Dillon and Alexander Jacobs; produced by Robert L. Rosen; director of photography, Claude Renoir; editor, Tom Rolf; distributed by 20th Century-Fox. Running time: 118 minutes. At the National Theater, Broadway near 43d Street, Trans-Lux East, Third Avenue at 58th Street, and Murray Hill Theater, Third Avenue at 34th Street. This film has been rated R.
Popeye Doyle .... Gene Hackman
Charnier .... Fernando Rey
Barthelemy .... Bernard Fresson
Raoul .... Jean-Pierre Castaldi
Miletto .... Charles Millot
Old Lady .... Cathleen Nesbitt

subject of the film. Marseilles, its inhabitants and its ways of life provide the exotic backgrounds and raw materials for the movie's various specialty numbers, principally chases in which Popeye and his French counterparts attempt to nab drugdom's Mr. Big, the character played by Fernando Rey, who disappeared at the end of "The French Connection." The concerns of "French

Connection II" are not much different from those of old Saturday-afternoon movie serials that used to place their supermen in jeopardy and then figure ways of getting them out. The difference is in the quality of the supermen and in their predicaments.

Popeye is a colorful and interesting — though hardly noble — character, and when the Marseilles drug people kidnap him, forcibly create a heroin habit in him, and then release him, you have a very special kind of jeopardy that the film and Mr. Hackman exploit most effectively. The perverse intensity and the anguish in these sequences recall some of Mr. Frankenheimer's best work in "The Manchurian Candidate" and "Seconds."

The supporting cast includes Bernard Fresson, as Popeye's worried French associate, and Cathleen Nesbitt, as an ancient charwoman in the hotel where Popeye is held prisoner. In one brief, beautiful scene, the old woman, herself a ravaged addict, tenderly advises the drugged American not to rave and shout, while at the same time she is stealing his watch.

1975 My 19, 24:4

THE MAN IN THE GLASS BOOTH, directed by Arthur Hiller; screenplay by Edward Anhalt, based on the play by Robert Shaw; producer, Ely Landau; executive producer, Mort Abrahams; director of cinematography, Sam Leavitt; editor, David Bretherton; presented by the American Film Theater. Running time: 120 minutes. At selected theaters. This film has been rated PG.
Arthur Goldman ...... Maximilian Schell
Miriam Rosen .... Lois Nettleton
Judge .... Luther Adler
Charlie Cohn ...... Lawrence Pressman
Jack Arnold .... Henry Brown
Moshe .... Richard Rasof
Rami .... David Nash
Uri .... Martin Berman
Rudin .... Sy Kramer
Dr. Weisberg .... Robert H. Harris
Samuel .... Leonidas Ossetynski
Churchill .... Lloyd Bochner
Schmidt .... Norbert Schiller

By VINCENT CANBY

Arthur Goldman (Maximilian Schell), who appears to be in his late 50's but says his age is beyond recall, is a Nazi concentration camp survivor who, after the war, came to the United States to amass a fortune only slightly less large than his guilt complex.

At the start of "The Man in the Glass Booth," the American Film Theater's production that opened yesterday at selected theaters, Arthur is acting most strangely. He paces the terrace of his New York penthouse, alternately joking with his male secretary and sneering at him. He issues enigmatic orders and peers through a telescope to see Nazi uniforms down below on Fifth Avenue and his old father, long-since dead in a Nazi oven, selling pretzels on the corner of what seems to be Fifth and 57th Street.

The enigmatic orders he has given his secretary are

the clue to about the only mystery that remains in this clumsy film version of Robert Shaw's 1968 Broadway play. Arthur Goldman is carefully setting himself up to be unmasked as a notorious Nazi war criminal who murdered thousands of Jews. In the second act Arthur allows himself to be kidnapped by Israeli agents and whisked off to Israel, where he admits everything, though his subsequent trial goes terribly awry.

Mr. Shaw's name has been eliminated from all the credits of the film because—according to American Film Theater sources—he objected to Edward Anhalt's screenplay, which removed most of the ambiguity surrounding Arthur Goldman's real identity.

In the play, as in Mr. Shaw's novel, I'm told, one is never sure whether Arthur Goldman is a messianic Jew, obsessed with the idea that he can somehow absorb German guilt and Israeli hatred, or a most crafty ex-Nazi who had deliberately arranged false evidence that will eventually acquit him of his old crime.

In the film, which is the fifth and last in the American Film Theater's second season of subscription presentations, there is no doubt at all. Arthur is really Arthur Goldman, which reduces the drama to mere recitation of its overly theatrical, none-too-searching dialogue. The movie that tells us too much about Arthur also tells us too little about his agony.

Mr. Schell rants and colorfully carries on, with all of those sudden shifts in mood and pace that are supposed to make a role interesting to

the actor and the public alike, but this performance makes one aware of little except surface mannerisms. Without substantial material to guide it, the actor's energy escapes without doing anything, like heat lost up a chimney.

Arthur Hiller has directed the film in a sober, straightforward manner that assumes the screenplay has more on its mind than it actually has. "The Man in the Glass Booth" is the sort of movie that wouldn't have been damaged at all by a few superfluous touches. They would give us something more to think about.

1975 My 20, 46:4

THE FORTUNE, directed by Mike Nichols, screenplay by Adrien Joyce; produced by Mr. Nichols and Don Devlin; executive producer, Hank Moonjean; director of photography, John A. Alonzo; music conducted and adapted by David Share; editor, Stu Linder; distributed by Columbia Pictures. Running time: 95 minutes. At the Coronet Theater, Third Avenue near 59th Street. This film has been rated PG.
Freddie .... Stockard Channing
Oscar .... Jack Nicholson
Nicky .... Warren Beatty
Mrs. Gould .... Florence Stanley
Chief Detective ...... Richard B. Shull
John The Barber .... Ton Newman
Photographer .... John Fielder

By VINCENT CANBY

Though it is set in the nineteen-twenties, Mike Nichols's very funny, manically scatterbrained new movie, "The Fortune," is an epic version of those old two-reel comedies that I associate with Saturday afternoon moviegoing in the thirties, with stars like the Three Stooges, Vera Vague, Ernest Truex and Charlie Chase.

It's a marvelous attempt to recreate a kind of farce that, with the notable exceptions of a handful of films by Blake Edwards and Billy Wilder, disappeared after

World War II.

The characters in "The Fortune" are motivated by greed first and lust second, usually when it's inconvenient. They think big but act small, often the victims of their own short tempers. Nobody is permanently injured—neither physically, by going to sea in a leaky trunk, nor emotionally, by learning that one's lover has been plotting murder all the while.

"The Fortune," which opened yesterday at the Coronet, has the short focus and the comic self-absorption of two-reelers in which all of the world's problems might be reduced to the difficulties inherent in moving a piano from one room to another.

Nicky (Warren Beatty), who uses mounds of Vaseline on his hair and wears a Ramon Novarro mustache, and Oscar (Jack Nicholson), a failed embezzler who often looks like one of the Stooges, are attempting something much more grand than piano-moving, though they are always interrupted by problems as petty as a doorway that's too narrow.

In the screenplay by Adrien Joyce, which is less important as a coherent narrative than as the frame for a collection of comedy routines, Nicky and Oscar are out to separate Fredericka Quintessa Bigard (Stockard Channing), known to them as "the mouse-bed heiress," from her family and then from her money. This involves Oscar's marrying her (because Nicky, who is supposed to be her lover, is already married to someone who remains a long distance off-screen) and then transporting her from New York to Los Angeles, where the pair attempts to murder her.

Stockard Channing, Warren Beatty and Jack Nicholson

Farces about attempted murder can be a little bit nervous-making when the intended victim is as appealing as Miss Channing. a Nichols discovery of major importance. She's a fine-grained, robust, comic talent who keeps the film in proper balance by being just as intently lunatic as her two co-stars.

Miss Channing's Freddie, speaking in a horsy, upper-crust accent, delivers lines filched from True Romances with a gravity that's as funny as anything in the film. "The scales have dropped from my eyes," she says primly as she listens to Nicky and Oscar fighting over her future inheritance. Or, with a deep sigh as the two men ignore her to pursue some other minor point: "Je n'existe pas."

Mr. Beatty's role is less flamboyant than Mr. Nicholson's, but he plays straight with determined comedy style. Mr. Nicholson is nothing short of superb, being the obligatorily dense member of the con-artist team, the sort of man who, after being arrested for a murder he doesn't realize he hasn't committed, immediately adopts police jargon to oblige his captors. "Then," he says helpfully, "we carried the victim out of the house and put her in the pond," which happens to be a bird bath.

Though it's only 95 minutes long, which is virtually a short subject these days, "The Fortune" does have sequences that sag, and there are moments when it's obvious that farce is not exactly the native art of any of the people involved. One occasionally is aware of the tremendous effort that has gone into a particular effect, though that doesn't spoil it for me. The endeavor is nobly conceived in an era that has just about abandoned farce in favor of parody, satire, situation and/or wisecrack comedy, all of which Mr. Nichols already can do with—perhaps—too great an ease. "The Fortune" will probably be compared to "The Sting," because of the overlapping of the eras and the con-man theme. Incorrectly, though. "The Sting" is an adventure. "The Fortune" is farce of a rare order.

1975 My 21, 49:1

THE RETURN OF THE PINK PANTHER, directed and produced by Blake Edwards; screenplay by Frank Waldman and Mr. Edwards; music, Henry Mancini; director of photography, Geoffrey Unsworth; editor, Tom Priestly; presented by Jewel Productions and Pimlico Films, distributed by United Artists. Running time: 113 minutes. At the Rivoli Theater, Broadway at 49th Street, 86th Street East Theater, 86th Street near Third Avenue, and the Eastside Cinema, Third Avenue at 55th Street. This film has been rated G.
Inspector Clouseau........Peter Sellers
Sir Charles Litton...Christopher Plummer
Claudine Litton.........Catherine Schell
Chief Inspector Dreyfus....Herbert Lom
Colonel Sharki.............Peter Arne
Chief of Police.........Gregoire Aslan
General Wadafi.........Peter Jeffrey
Cato...................Burt Kwouk

By VINCENT CANBY

In Paris, Inspector Clouseau (Peter Sellers), illustrious hero of "The Pink Panther" and "A Shot in the Dark," pounds the pavement as a common gendarme. Demoted. Kicked downstairs. Stripped of his prerogatives to interfere with the more important affairs of justice. But talent will out.

Strolling one day along an avenue on his beat, Clouseau comes upon a blind organ grinder and his monkey outside a bank. Clouseau has a long and profoundly solemn exchange with the organ grinder about the business arrangements the man has with the monkey (or "minkey," as Clouseau pronounces it).

All the while, through the bank window, we witness the hold-up that Clouseau, with his usual preoccupation with the nonessential, doesn't see. When the bank manager runs out to the sidewalk calling for help, he's the one that Clouseau clubs, not the organ grinder who was, of course, the lookout.

●

Blake Edwards's "The Return of the Pink Panther" brings back Inspector Clouseau in the superbly awkward figure of Peter Sellers—riding, walking, falling, driving, slipping and stumbling to success. His dignity is challenged from time to time, but his faith in his nonexistent deductive powers remains unshaken.

Clouseau is the very special slapstick triumph of Mr. Sellers and Mr. Edwards. He's not stupid in any ordinary sense. He simply allows himself to be too easily distracted by details of secondary importance. He's like a child who has just learned to read. No set of instructions on an aspirin botle would be without interest to him.

When Clouseau is at hand, innocent objects become potential weapons of destruction, often his own. It has something to do with the intensity of his distraction. You can imagine him getting fatally entangled in a ball of yarn.

"The Return of the Pink Panther" is not to be muddled with "Inspector Clouseau," the feeble Bud Yorkin spinoff with Alan Arkin in the title role, made in 1968. It is, rather, a glorious throwback to the two 1964 Sellers-Edwards collaborations, "The Pink Panther" and "A Shot in the Dark."

"The Return of the Pink Panther," which opened yesterday at three theaters, is again introduced by the marvelous Richard Williams cartoon character who upstages all of the title credits and is, in effect, everything that Clouseau is not — urbane, witty, sly, quick-witted, graceful.

When Clouseau suavely salutes a passing lady by raising his billy club, he misses his hat and hits his eye. This time Clouseau is saved from the injuries that can be suffered on the street by the disappearance of the fabled Pink Panther diamond, the national treasure of the emerging, mythical Middle Eastern country of Lugash. They are the same diamond and the same country that Clouseau saved in the first film.

Should you want to analyze the screenplay by Frank Waldman and Mr. Edwards, which probably isn't wise, you'd find it bears a distinct likeness to Alfred Hitchcock's "To Catch a Thief." Clouseau is called in to solve the new theft by the grateful government of Lugash, while the prime suspect, Sir Charles Litton (Christopher Plummer), the retired jewel thief, joins the case to clear his name. Sir Charles, known as the notorious Phantom, is repeatedly referred to by Clouseau as Sir Charles Phantom, the notorious Litton.

●

Somewhat complicating matters are the presences of Clouseau's superior, Chief Inspector Dreyfus, hilariously played by Herbert Lom with the fury of the demonically possessed; Sir Charles's wife, Claudine (Catherine Schell), who seems to be enjoying herself no matter how outrageous the circumstances of the slapstick, and Cato (Burt Kwouk), Clouseau's Oriental servant, who sometimes hides in the refrigerator, the better to surprise his employer with an unexpected karate chop.

The screenplay is funny but even better are the sight gags that are a kind of inventory of everything Clouseau has been unable to master in his long, irrelevant career —monkeys, magnifying glasses, vacuum cleaners, sauna baths, door bells, dance floors, false mustaches, knee-hole desks and four-wheeled vehicles, all kinds and models.

When Clouseau takes the wheel, the vehicle is inclined to balk, like a donkey, or to give up, to fall apart, as if suddenly stricken with an acute case of engine fatigue.

1975 My 22, 32:1

THE EIGER SANCTION, directed by Clint Eastwood; screenplay by Hal Dresner, Warren B. Murphy and Rod Whitaker, based on the novel by Trevanian; producer, Robert Daley; executive producers, Richard D. Zanuck and David Brown; director of photography, Frank Stanley; editor, Ferris Webster; music, John Williams; a Malpaso Company film, distributed by Universal Pictures. Running time: 128 minutes. At the Forum Theater, Broadway at 47th Street; Beekman, Second Avenue at 65th Street, and 34th Street East Theater, 34th Street near Second Avenue. This film has been rated R.
Jonathan Hemlock.......Clint Eastwood
Ben Bowman..........George Kennedy
Jemima Brown.........Vonetta McGee
Miles Mellough.........Jack Cassidy
Mrs. Montaigne.........Heidi Bruhl
Dragon...............Thayer David
Freytag.............Reiner Schoene
Meyer...............Michael Grimm
Montaigne.........Jean-Pierre Bernard
George.............Brenda Venus
Pope...............Gregory Walcott

"The Eiger Sanction" is a long, foolish but never boring suspense melodrama about a college art professor named Jonathan Hemlock (Clint Eastwood), who has a passion for French Impressionists and mountain climbing and an underground reputation as the best assassin in the international spy business.

At the start of "The Eiger Sanction," which opened at three theaters yesterday, Jonathan is lured from the campus by his former employer, a man named Dragon, the head of a secret United States Government agency called CII (pronounced "See-Too," not "See-Eye-Eye"), to assassinate a couple of men in Switzerland who earlier had assassinated a CII man. Jonathan agrees so that he can buy a newly "hot" Pissarro and receive Internal Revenue Service approval of all the other stolen masterpieces in his private collection.

Jonathan isn't above murder-for-pay or underwriting art thieves but he draws the line when a pretty student offers to sleep with him in order to get a B-minus in his course. Jonathan is that sort of guy: vaguely scrupulous.

"The Eiger Sanction" is full of people with divided loyalties and peculiar names that recall the somewhat fresher inventions of Ian Fleming. It moves around this country and in Switzerland as if it had a Eurailpass good for the world. I suspect that one shouldn't inspect the plot too closely, but it passes so quickly most of the time you don't notice it.

One of the film's two major sequences is set in the American West, where Jonathan goes to freshen up his mountain climbing techniques and where he murders an old enemy by leaving him to starve in the middle of Monument Valley. This is patently silly. Everybody knows you couldn't starve to death in Monument Valley. You'd be rescued before sunset by a Hollywood movie crew.

The other major sequence —and it's a stunning one if you've been able to sit through everything else—is an attempt to scale a Swiss mountain peak known as the Eiger. Jonathan has gone on the climb because one of the other members of the expedition is the second assassin he's after. Which one is it? He doesn't know but you can possibly guess by reading the cast list carefully. What is more important than mystery is the spectacle of the climb, which looks difficult and very beautiful.

The rest of the movie is the kind of tongue-in-cheek nonsense that Mr. Eastwood, who also directed the film, laboriously intended. Supporting the star are George Kennedy, as an old mountain-climbing buddy who calls Jonathan "old buddy" all the time; Vonetta McGee, as Jonathan's black girlfriend who also hustles as a courier, and Jack Cassidy, as a swishy courier who owns a dog called Faggot.

VINCENT CANBY

1975 My 22, 32:1

CORNBREAD, EARL AND ME, directed by Joe Manduke; written by Leonard Lamensdorf; director of photography, Jules Brenner; film editor, Aaron Stell; produced by Mr. Manduke; released by American International Pictures. At the Penthouse Theater, Broadway and 47th Street, the 59th Street Twin II, east of Third Avenue, and 86th Street Twin II, west of Lexington Avenue. Running time: 95 minutes. This film is classified PG.
Blackwell...............Moses Gunn
Sarah..............Rosalind Cash
Atkins.............Bernie Casey
Leona.............Madge Sinclair
Cornbread...........Keith Wilkes
Earl...............Tierre Turner
One Eye.............Antonio Fargas

"Cornbread, Earl and Me," which opened yesterday at the Penthouse, 59th Street Twin II and 86th Street Twin II theaters, is so much a tract for virtue that a feeling of guilt becomes inescapable in pointing out its shortcomings as a movie.

After all, it's not every day that we get films that persist in extolling truth and decency even while making a bloody display of the unfairness of life. And judging by the warm-weather fare of the recent past, it isn't likely that this spring and summer will offer too many films that — like "Cornbread"—can appeal to youngsters on a wholesome ethical plane while telling a story that bears some resemblance to life, and death, on real city streets.

●

Part urban tragedy, part courtroom melodrama, "Cornbread" is the story of Cornbread Hamilton a black teenage basketball star about to leave his less-than-ideal neighborhood for college and obviously destined for a big-money professional career. The boy, however, is shot down by the police, who are pursuing an apparent psychopath, who has just left a woman all but dead.

It's an all-too-familiar case, one in which the patrolmen involved — one white, one black — speak of something shiny, perhaps a gun, in the running youngster's hand. And it is one in which police superiors bring very real pressures to bear on adults and children in an effort to make certain that no contradictory evidence is offered after Cornbread's parents retain a lawyer to clear their dead son's name.

●

Inasmuch as this is a movie that reinforces one's commitment to truth-telling, it must now be said that what detracts from it is a certain unevenness in the acting and a slapdash air about the climactic inquest that contrasts unfavorably with the careful and occasionally slow-moving construction of the early part of the film.

Making his movie debut as Cornbread is Keith Wilkes, a pleasant personality but unlikely to win as an actor the accolade that he has just won for his feats with the Golden State Warriors of the National Basketball Association—rookie of the year.

LAWRENCE VAN GELDER

1975 My 22, 34:1

FILMS BY ROBERT POLIDORI: MUREMUR DIPHTHONG, 38 minutes; **SCANNED,** 20 minutes; **GENETIC CODES,** 25 minutes. At the Whitney Museum of American Art, Madison Avenue and 75th Street. Through Tuesday.

The Whitney Museum of American Art set a precedent yesterday in presenting its first program of silent, photographic slides and film frames under the general title "Genetic Codes." A collection of three studies made by Robert Polidori, dwelling largely on the examination of a succession of stills, it is a tribute to the producer's devotion to his special field but is something less than exciting for, say, a standard moviegoer or, perhaps, a film buff.

In "Genetic Codes," which is related to science, Mr. Polidori, a 24-year-old New Yorker who seems to favor exotic titles, used a movie camera to capture and then "reanimate" in varying shades of color and light, individual frames of outdoor greenery, parts of a house and an occasional, passing human figure. He is a mite more direct, if less artistic, in his longest offering, "Muremur Diphthong," which focuses on the doors, ceiling, lights, windows sills, corners and walls of a variety of rooms.

●

If "Genetic Codes" and "Muremur Diphthong" purposely concentrate on facets of mostly static objects, "Scanned" achieves an almost total immobility in its close views of a series of cards showing an assortment of hand-drawn pencil lines. It's debatable, of course, if slides constitute *motion* pictures, but Mr. Polidori's "Scanned," like his two other more complex observations of still life, illustrate unusual, polished skills.

A. H. WEILER

1975 My 22, 35:2

THE WIND AND THE LION, directed and written by John Milius; produced by Herb Jaffe; music by Jerry Goldsmith; director of photography, Billy Williams; editor, Robert L. Wolfe; a Metro-Goldwyn-Mayer film, distributed by United Artists. Running time: 119 minutes. At Radio City Music Hall, Avenue of the Americas at 50th Street. This film has been rated PG.

Raisuli	Sean Connery
Eden Pedecaris	Candice Bergen
Theodore Roosevelt	Brian Keith
John Hay	John Huston
Gummere	Geoffrey Lewis
Captain Jerome	Steve Kanaly
The Bashaw	Vladek Sheybal
William Pedecaris	Simon Harrison
Jennifer Pedecaris	Polly Gattesman

By VINCENT CANBY

"The Wind and the Lion," which opened yesterday at Radio City Music Hall, is an elaborate, expensive-looking, ludicrously jingoistic historical-adventure that comes out so firmly in favor of Teddy Roosevelt's "Big Stick" policy, 70 years later, that it could also be a put-on.

Written and directed by John Milius, who made "Dillinger" a couple of years ago and who wrote the screenplay for John Huston's "The Life and Times of Judge Roy Bean," this new film may be the most sappy movie ever made, as well as one of the shrewdest. It's also fairly funny in camp ways that I'm sure are completely intentional.

●

Based on a true incident, "The Wind and the Lion" is the story of Roosevelt's sending the Marines—without invitation—into Morocco in 1904 to rescue an American widow and her two children who had been kidnapped by the last of the Barbary pirates—a desert chieftain named Raisuli.

"The world must respect American private property and its citizens," shouts Teddy (Brian Keith), who needs a hook for his 1904 Presidential campaign, while John Hay (John Huston), his Secretary of State, looks worried and says, "Theodore, you're dangerous."

What Hollywood usually refers to as "the human drama" is played out by Candice Bergen as the American widow, Mrs. Eden Pedecaris, and Sean Connery as Raisuli, the courtly desert brigand who often sounds as if he'd taken a degree in fortune-cookie philosophy at the University of Edinburgh.

Mr. Milius's screenplay cuts back and forth between Morocco and the United States to draw parallels between Roosevelt (the wind) and Raisuli (the lion), whose sense of manhood eventually dazzles Mrs. Pedecaris, though she was a bit piqued early in her abduction when he beheaded a couple of tribesmen in her vicinity.

The movie eschews any overt signs of a romantic attachment between the widow and her captor and details, instead, the sort of mutual respect that doesn't get in the way of the glorification of machismo, both on an international and personal level.

Brutality is beautiful, war is wonderful and men who carry big sticks (big swords, big guns, big anythings) are to be feared and thus respected, Mr. Milius seems to be saying. He says it so broadly, in fact, that he plants the suspicion that he is making fun of his own Hollywood reputation as a gun-loving Hollywood eccentric.

●

In the midst of all this nonsense, Miss Bergen is nothing less than a subversive precence. She seems to be suppressing giggles at a lot of the lines flying around her head. Two samples: "Ignorance is a steep hill with perilous rocks at the bottom" and, "I'll see you again, Mrs. Pedecaris, when we both are like golden clouds on the wind."

The physical production is handsome enough and one sequence (the landing of the Marines to invade a peaceful Morocco) is exceptionally effective, but so brutal it will mystify children who should be the film's major supporters.

The appearance of this film when the Mayagüez incident is still so fresh is fitting. "The Wind and the Lion" is a paean to opportunism of awesome proportions, and if interest in it is stirred up by the current headlines, it is not inappropriate.

1975 My 23, 22:1

THE NUER, directed by Hilary Harris and George Breidenbach, 75 minutes; **ORGANISM,** directed by Hilary Harris, 20 minutes. At the Film Forum, 256 West 88th Street. Through Sunday and May 29-June 1, 8 P.M.

By A. H. WEILER

It is gratifying but not surprising that "Organism" and "The Nuer," the double bill at the Film Forum that focuses on a feverish New York and comparatively placid, isolated Ethiopian villagers, respectively, brilliantly illustrate Hilary Harris's artistic personal style and technique. As the director of a wide variety of documentaries over the last 25 years, including the Oscar-winning "Seawards the Great Ships," he again proves that documentaries are not synonymous with trite travelogues or dull pedantry.

This is strikingly true of the recently completed "Organism," which imaginatively relates our town's activity to the flow of organisms within the human body. In using time-lapse photography (shot in good part from the 80th floor of the Empire State Building) he has speeded up street traffic and life in parades, the stock market, etc., to project a powerful comment on our frenzied urban society.

●

But in meshing these eye-catching shots (captured in arresting colors) with superb microphotographic footage of the movement of cells within the bloodstream and the like, coupled with an authentic anatomical offscreen narration, he has achieved parallel pictorial effects that are both pointed and poetic.

While "The Nuer," which was co-directed by Mr. Harris and Harry Breidenbacr in 1970 for the Film Study Center of Harvard University's Peabody Museum, is a straightforward record of that Ethiopian cow-herding tribe, its empathetic inspection of their folkways makes for an equally arresting observation of the human experience.

Their view of "The Nuer" reveals a lanky, largely happy, simple people whose physical and spiritual lives are lovingly intertwined with their humpbacked cattle from birth to death.

Children at play, an old man ruminating about the past, a girl pounding corn in a mortar, a smallpox victim, a boy being inducted into manhood in a bloody ritual or a mother kissing her baby are vignettes of primitive but benign culture that are treated with nonintrusive, dignified appreciation.

Both the bucolic, distant "Nuer" and a frenetic New York are worlds apart in place and pacing, of course. But under this highly professional guidance, they are graphically educational and excitingly visual journeys.

1975 My 23, 24:1

Sordid Career of Thug Shown Dutifully

By VINCENT CANBY

Louie (Lepke) Buchalter was a bad little boy who stole things and lied. He was bound to come to no good end, as the film called "Lepke" so dutifully shows, but before he arrives at that point, the electric chair, he makes a lot of money, marries a sweet, orthodox Jewish girl named Bernice, and kills a number of men intentionally.

There are some people in this world who could imagine worse lives and I suspect, it's for them that this dour, witless movie is intended. "Lepke," which opened yesterday at the Loews State 2 and Cine Theaters, covers most of Lepke's life, from the delinquent years of his adolescence in Brooklyn through the delinquent years of his adulthood in Brooklyn, as the head of the outfit called Murder, Inc.

The cast of characters includes such other "name" hoods of the nineteen-thirties as Lucky Luciano, Albert Anastasia and Kid Twist Reles, all of whom have turned up in earlier, better gangster films. This one is different only in that it gives the Jewish side of the underworld story.

"Lepke" was produced and directed by Menahem Golan, the Israeli film maker ("Kazablan"), mostly in and around Los Angeles. A mature Tony Curtis plays Lepke as well as the limited concerns of the screenplay allow. Vaughn Meader, the impressionist once so closely identified with the Kennedy-era Camelot, appears briefly as the late Walter Winchell, while Milton Berle plays Lepke's father-in-law, a man who apparently puts on old-man make-up in the morning the way some women wear lipstick and eyeshadow. It doesn't make Mr. Berle look convincingly old, just spongy.

1975 My 24, 12:1

The Cast

LEPKE, directed and produced by Menahem Golan; screenplay by Wesley Lau and Tamar Hoffs, based on a story by Mr. Lau; executive producer, Yoram Globus; director of photography, Andrew Davis; an AmeriEuro production, distributed by Warner Brothers. Running time: 110 minutes. At the Loew's State 2 Theater, Broadway at 45th Street, and Loew's Cine, Third Avenue near 86th Street. This film has been rated R.

Lepke	Tony Curtis
Bernice	Anjanette Comer
Kane	Michael Callan
Gurrah	Warren Berlinger
Anastasia	Gianni Russo
Luciano	Vic Tayback
Mr. Meyer	Milton Berle
Walter Winchell	Vaughn Meader

'Children of Rage,' on Conflict in Mideast

CHILDREN OF RAGE, directed by Arthur Allan Seidelman; screenplay by Mr. Seidelman, based on a story by Mr. Seidelman and Ana Laura; produced by George R. Rice; director of photography, Ian Wilson; editor, Paul Davis; music, Patrick Gowers; an Emessee production, presented by Stirling Gold. Running time: 106 minutes. At the Fine Arts Theater, 58th Street west of Lexington Avenue. This film has been rated PG.

David Shalmon	Helmut Griem
Leyla Saleh	Olga Georges-Picot
Omar Saleh	Richard Alfieri
Ibrahim	Simon Andreu
David's father	Cyril Cusack
Abdullah	Robert Salvio
Yaacov	Simon Ward

By VINCENT CANBY

If a movie could be made by a computer, it might look like "Children of Rage," a fastidiously well-meaning, completely lifeless film that attempts to dramatize the Israeli-Palestinian conflict in what producers call human terms.

It's about a selfless Israeli doctor who sneaks off to minister to Palestinian refugees in a camp in Jordan, the young Palestinian woman who loves the doctor, and her younger brother, who becomes a terrorist out of frustration. The movie was directed and written by an American, Arthur Allan Seidelman, whose characters are mouthpieces for the various Palestinian and Israeli, conservative - through - liberal positions.

"Children of Rage," which opened yesterday at the Fine Arts, is totally lacking in the kind of idiosyncratic detail that forever separates cinema from mere picture-taking.

1975 My 29, 29:2

FILM VIEW

VINCENT CANBY

New Comedies –Serious, Farcical, Slapstick

Despite all indications that next year will be a very lean, very conventional movie year, 1975 is turning into a bumper year for comedy, the toughest, riskiest kind of movie there is. Mel Brooks got things off to an early start before Christmas with "Young Frankenstein," which is still going strong and becoming something of a cult film among the very young. I don't mean just teenagers. I also mean the very, very young, the four to 10-year-olds who respond to Brooks's affection for rude sounds and words, peculiar names (and more peculiar pronunciations), sight gags, running gags and even the double-entendre, the rhythm of which is accessible to kids even when they miss the redeeming dirt.

In addition to "Young Frankenstein," we have Hal Ashby's "Shampoo," the most ambitious "serious" comedy of the year to date, and "The Happy Hooker," in which Lynn Redgrave cheerily tends to the sexual fantasies of all sorts of maladjusted men in the most affluent of all societies. It's as if Genet's "The Balcony" had been rewritten for a television sit-com audience, which isn't a terribly bad idea.

•   •   •

The English comedy collective that calls itself Monty Python's Flying Circus is represented by "Monty Python and The Holy Grail," which may be one of the year's most successful comedies because although it pretends to be slapdash, it's anything but uncalculated. The low points have absolutely no effect on the highs. The movie works the other way around. The brilliance of its best flights of fancy, combined with the striking, authentic beauty of the physical production, makes even the occasional so-so gags look good. Terry Gilliam and Terry Jones, the two members of the Python company who co-directed the movie, are not inconsiderable, untutored filmmakers. Like Woody Allen, they appear to know a good deal about how movies are made. The spectacular battle scene that more or less concludes the film (which really just peters out) is virtually a how-to guide for filmmakers who want to shoot a spectacular battle scene without missing any cliches, the sort that have been made obligatory through the years by "Ivanhoe," "El Cid" and dozens of other solemn epics.

•   •   •

Also like Woody Allen, the members of the Python company, who are jointly responsible for the screenplay, are poets of free association with a special fondness for transforming the mundane into the monstrous. The beast that guards one of the secrets of the grail is a white rabbit. He's small but mean. To gain access to an enemy castle, King Arthur's knights build a Trojan rabbit (though they forget to climb inside it). Rabbits are important in this world. So are objects like the Holy Hand Grenade of Antioch. Here is a film that asks "Do cocoanuts migrate, like plumbers?" "What is the correct spelling of the word pronounced 'ni-GIT'?" (Ans.: k-n-i-g-h-t). "Is it possible to chop down the mightiest tree in the forest with a herring?"

The two newest comedies of the year are exuberant farces of the sort we seldom see anymore—Mike Nichols's "The Fortune," set mostly in Southern California in the 1920's in a landscape of crummy bungalows, two-lane highways, nosey landladies and dumb cops, and Blake Edwards's "The Return of The Pink Panther," which restores Peter Sellers to his finest role, that of Inspector Clouseau, the Parisian detective first met in the two 1964 Edwards-Sellers collaborations, "The Pink Panther" and "A Shot in The Dark."

•   •   •

In "The Return of The Pink Panther" Inspector Clouseau is no wiser but he is older, and even more imperturbable, never aware of dangers of his own making that lie in wait for him in every automobile, refrigerator, swimming pool and sauna bath. Clouseau has the self-assurance of a mad genius and the patience of a saint but his deductive powers would fit into the ear of a flea.

In this latest adventure Clouseau is called in by the government of Lugash, an emerging, mythical Middle Eastern nation, to recover the fabled Pink Panther diamond, which figured in the first Clouseau film. He botches things beautifully, not because he is stupid but because he is so easily distracted by non-essential details, such as a doorbell that comes apart in his hand. Other men would say to help with it and leave the doorbell, but Clouseau always stops to pick things up or put them away.

"The Return of the Pink Panther" is low physical comedy—slapstick—of the kind largely ignored by contemporary American filmmakers. Watching it is like taking a long, wild sail off a banana peel and landing a couple of hours later, softly and unharmed, exhausted from laughing.

"The Fortune" is very funny and also fascinating since it's such a departure from anything that Nichols has done before in film. The only thing it comes close to is the ending of "The Graduate"—the shambles of the interrupted wedding, which many people felt did not easily attach to the rest of the film. "The Fortune," written by Adrien Joyce (who wrote "Five Easy Pieces"), is all farce, the tale of three quite different but equally matched nitwits, a slick con artist (Warren Beatty), his seedy sidekick (Jack Nicholson) and the New York heiress (Stockard Channing) whose fortune they covet. Characters in farces should not be held accountable for base motives and terrible deeds. Farce is a land without consequences. To enjoy "The Fortune" one must forget that we've come to associate Nichols, as well as his two male stars, with various comedies much concerned with consequences. Both "Carnal Knowledge" and "Shampoo" are morality movies. "The Fortune" is not.

It's a feature length film in the manner of a two-reel comedy. It's about blundering and then coping with subsequent disasters, all harmless. It's joys are not easily analyzable, like the point of most jokes, but they are vivid. They include watching Miss Channing, slightly hungover after spending the night at sea, drunk, in a steamer trunk, climbing out the next morning, being puzzled for a fraction of a second, and then pulling herself together for the hitch-hike back to town. They also include listening to Nicholson describe his embarrassment when, as a little boy, he had to go to the drugstore to buy "mouse blankets" for his mother.

"The Fortune" is a marvelous, uncharacteristic stunt, and Nichols pulls it off with style. He has also presented us with a fully-developed comic actress of unique quality. Stockard Channing is a new star, a young woman who somehow recalls Ethel Merman, Kay Kendall and Barbara Harris without losing her own very odd, very appealing identity.

Comedy is doing well, indeed. All this and, within a couple of weeks, Woody Allen's "Love and Death."

1975 Je 1, II:15:1

POSSE, directed and produced by Kirk Douglas; screenplay by William Roberts and Christopher Knopf, based on a story by Mr. Knopf; executive producer, Phil Feldman; director of photography, Fred J. Koenekamp; music, Maurice Jarre; editor, John W. Wheeler; a Bryna Company production, distributed by Paramount Pictures. Running time: 94 minutes. At neighborhood theaters. This film has been rated PG.

Howard Nightingale............Kirk Douglas
Jack Strawhorn...............Bruce Dern
Wesley ....Bo Hopkins
Hellman ....James Stacy
Krag ....Luke Askew
Pensteman ....David Canary
Pepe ....Alfonso Arau
Mrs. Cooper.........Katharine Woodville
Mr. Cooper...............Mark Roberts
Mrs. Ross................Beth Brickell

By VINCENT CANBY

"Posse," directed and produced by Kirk Douglas, who is also the star, is a genial, sometimes witty Western about a Texas marshal, Howard Nightingale (Mr. Douglas), who stakes his campaign for the United States Senate on the capture of a notorious outlaw named Strawhorn (Bruce Dern). Although it's a film of action, "Posse" is also something of a morality movie—and a very curious one at that. "Posse" clearly favors the outlaw, who doesn't hesitate to shoot to kill almost anybody, over the marshal, who is politically ambitious and thus evil.

It's one of the ironies of this country, where tremendous ambition is as essential as money in the achievement of political success, that we should automatically consider ambition to be a sin. It's as if we wished that Presidents could be brought by storks.

•

Mr. Douglas and Mr. Dern have a high old time of it, shooting it out on horseback, foot and, once, on a hijacked train. Mr. Douglas's talents as a director have clearly improved since his maiden effort, last year's "Scalawag," but then the screenplay (by William Roberts and Christopher Knopf) is also much better. This is Saturday afternoon entertainment that needn't be ignored at night.

1975 Je 5, 48:1

LANCELOT OF THE LAKE (Lancelot du Lac), directed by Robert Bresson; screenplay (French with English subtitles) by Mr. Bresson; produced by Jean-Pierre Rassam and Francois Rochas; director of photography, Pasqualino de Santis; editor, Germaine Lamy; music, Philippe Sarde; a French-Italian co-production of Mara Films/ORTF/Laser Productions/Gerico Sound; released in the United States by New Yorker Films. Running time: 85 minutes. At the Art Theater, University Place and Eighth Street. This film has not been rated.

Lancelot ....Luc Simon
Guinevere ......Laura Duke Condominas
Gawain ....Humbert Balsan
King Arthur......Vladimir Antolck-Oresek
Mordred ....Patrick Bernard
Lionel...........Arthur de Montalembert

"Lancelot of the Lake" was shown last year at the 12th New York Film Festival. The following excerpt is from Vincent Canby's review, which appeared in The New York Times on Oct. 1. The film is being shown at the Art Theater, University Place and Eighth Street.

It's said that at one time or another every film director yearns to make a spectacle, one of those multi-million-dollar epics with lots of horses, costumes and extras, the sort of film that has to be directed from a raised platform with an electronic voice-magnifying system. To the extent that "Lancelot of the Lake" has horses, costumes and extras (a few), and to the extent that it's inspired by some of the tales in Malory's "Morte d'Arthur," it may be called Robert Bresson's spectacle, but it's unlike any conventional film spectacle you've ever seen.

•

"Lancelot of the Lake" is about the last days of King Arthur's Round Table when, after the bloody, fruitless quest for the Holy Grail, the knights return to a fading Camelot and fall out among one another.

The age of chivalry is over, but no one knows why. Arthur suspects that God has been provoked. He urges his knights to forget their enmities and to better themselves.

Lancelot, who once was

allowed a vision of the Grail, thinks God is punishing them all for his being Guinevere's lover. When he asks her to release him from his vows to her and to surrender to God, she refuses. "If I surrender," she says, "it will be to you, not God."

Although Mr. Bresson ("Diary of a Country Priest," "Au Hazard, Balthazar," "La Femme Douce," etc.) is not especially interested in visual spectacle, he has made a stunning-looking movie that often pares down spectacle to what seems to be an irreducible minimum. Virtually an entire tournament is photographed with the camera's eye focused between the horse's hoofs and midsection.

Mr. Bresson once said that the true calling of cinema "is first to be exact, and then to be interior—rather than exterior or decorative."

"Lancelot" could never be called decorative, but it is sometimes breathtaking in its exterior details, which is not the same as being realistic. The concluding sequence of the film, after chivalry's final upheaval, is one of the most beautiful and strange the director has ever done:

A riderless horse charges aimlessly through a twilight forest as the world's last knight, wounded and dying, staggers slowly toward the bodies of other armor-clad knights. It looks simultaneously mysterious, like the remains of the civilization on another planet, and banal, like a pile of damaged gasoline pumps.

What's missing from the film is any urgent interior meaning, and this it may be because of the distractions of the exterior details. It may also be because the conflicts that rage within Lancelot—between duty and desire, courtly love and physical love—simply aren't complex enough to bring out the best in Mr. Bresson.

●

As usual in a Bresson film, the actors are unknowns or nonprofessionals, chosen by the director for their faces and their willingness to be drilled into that state of somnambulance by which he is best able to create his interior visions.

Laura Duke Condominas is a lovely, young, girlish Guinevere, who is both passionate and demanding. Luc Simon also looks right as a Lancelot who is no longer young, and whose trials have given a firm set to ascetic features that, in youth, would have seemed soft.

1975 Je 5, 50:1

THE ABANDONED CHILDREN, a documentary in Spanish with English subtitles by Danny Lyon, 63 minutes; IN THE STREET, filmed by Helen Levitt, Janice Loeb and James Agee, 15 minutes. At the Film Forum, 256 West 88th Street. Today through Sunday and Thursday through next Sunday, 8 P.M.

By A. H. WEILER

Some of the world's poor and disenfranchised may live in the shadows of anonymity and official apathy, but "The Abandoned Children," a new documentary on Colombia's homeless young, and "In the Street," a vintage short on Harlem's barrio, which arrived at the Film Forum yesterday, project them into a glaringly sharp spotlight. The films' points of view may be vague on occasion, but they constitute pictorial records that tug at the heart and stir the mind.

Danny Lyon, the 32-year-old film maker and still photographer responsible for "Children," who was represented here in 1973 by documentaries on New Mexican Indians and others, again seems to be less concerned with polished technique than with an obvious empathy for his pitiable principals. Filmed last year in eye-catching color, reportedly in Santa Marta, his subjects are, mostly, a group of boys who personalize the will to survive.

The off-screen narration and subtitles call for fuller explanations, but it is clear that the children have been abandoned or simply left their families to join one of many groups of hardy derelicts who beg for the scraps they eat, wheel and deal, sleep, play and wander through the raucous streets or beach or stream they call home.

●

If the film tends to digress on variations on similar themes or for vignettes of teen-age prostitutes, it does expose its largely laconic children in sequences that often speak louder than words. Ranging in age from preteen, pixieish Joselin to dour, teen-aged Ivan, crudely chanting songs about their tribulations, they are seen sleeping on the steps of the city's cathedral or under the compassionate gaze of the Christ figure in its vaulted interior; snagging leftovers from a restaurant or nibbling chicken claws roasted on a city lot; playing games and building sand castles.

In illustration of their seeming aimlessness, one blond boy says flatly that he didn't know his father and that he came to the city on a train. The authorities, the narrator explains, ignore these "thousands" of youngsters because of their numbers and the expense involved to arrest and/or support them. The documentation of their errant life-style may be diffuse, but it strikingly illustrates, as Mr. Lyon states in a program note, "the absolute lower end of survival on the yardstick of human existence."

●

"In the Street," oddly enough, is having its first theatrical showing since it was produced in 1952 by Helen Levitt, Janice Loeb and the late James Agee, who, in 1948, collaborated on the memorable drama of a troubled Harlem boy in "The Quiet One." The East Harlem they picture in "In the Street" is benign "theater and battleground," especially in the vitality of the carefree Latin and black children pelting one another with flour sacks or gazing pensively from tenement windows. They too, like the adults strolling about or chatting on dilapidated stoops, are rambling but historic and eloquent reminders of survival and poverty.

1975 Je 6, 14:1

DEATH RACE 2000, directed by Paul Bartel; screenplay by Charles B. Griffith and Robert Thom; director of photography, Tak Fullmoto; music, Paul Chihara; film editor, Tina Hirsch; produced by Roger Corman; released by New World Pictures. At the 59th Street Twin I, east of Third Avenue, the Cinerama Theater, Broadway at 47th Street, and the Lyric Theater, 42d Street between Broadway and Eighth Avenue. Running time: 80 minutes. This film is classified R.
Frankenstein .... David Carradine
Annie .... Simone Griffith
Joe .... Sylvester (Sly) Stallone
Myra .... Louisa Moritz
Jane .... Mary Woronov

"Death Race 2000," now playing at three theaters, is an Orwellian vision of the American future, if you believe that Orwell was afflicted with blurred perception and an inclination toward the adolescent in satire.

Set in the year 2000, in a generally docile and economically humbled United Provinces of America ruled by a paternal and Francophobic Mr. President and a Bipartisan party, the film centers on the great annual American sporting event—a coast-to-coast road race in which the chief ingredients of victory are speed and a willingness to score points by running people down.

●

Women are worth 10 points; the elderly, who are sometimes placed out in the road by hospital personnel in observance of Euthanasia Day (which seems to coincide with race day) are worth 100.

Five teams, each composed of a man and a woman, and each appropriately costumed and with an appropriately arrayed car, compete. Among the contestants are a Calamity Jane, in a car equipped with deadly steer's horns; Machine Gun Joe Vitebo, whose car has guns and a knifeblade protruding from its foreparts; and the enigmatic, charismatic and heroic Frankenstein (David Carradine), a creature garbed in zipered black leather and black cape whose car seems to be the result of a mating between Dracula and a stegosaurus.

Frankenstein's navigator, Annie, has been planted in the race by a resistance movement led by her grandmother, a woman named Thomasina Paine.

"Death Race 2000," a Roger Corman production with a screenplay by Robert Thom ("Wild in the Streets") and Charles B. Griffith ("The Wild Angels") has a good time belaboring the easy targets—spectators, sportscasters, victims and the sort of clergy who have a benediction for anything.

When it comes to political satire, however, "Death Race 2000" finds the going tougher. In the end, it reveals itself to have nothing to say beyond the superficial about government or rebellion. And in the absence of such a statement, it becomes what it seems to have mocked—a spectacle glorifying the car as an instrument of violence.

— LAWRENCE VAN GELDER

1975 Je 6, 17:1

FILM VIEW

WALTER GOODMAN

Why 'Faithful' Adaptations Fail

An appreciation of literature is an excellent quality, in movie people as in the rest of us, and their occasional efforts to translate literary works to the screen must be welcomed as a sign of grace. Yet a pair of ambitious efforts along these lines, now showing in New York, serve to demonstrate how esteemed books can prove snares for the virtuous moviemaker.

Lev Kulijanov, who directed and collaborated on the screenplay for the Soviet cinema's latest "Crime and Punishment," was reported in the publication Soviet Film to have "set himself the task of bringing Dostoevsky's novel to the screen in as faithful a version as possible . . ." Now, faithfulness to Dostoevsky does offer rewards. Notably, the meetings between Raskolnikov and Inspector Porfiri, brilliant passages in the book, become brilliant scenes in the film, owing mainly to Innokenti Smoktunovsky, whose police inspector is at once guileful and candid, knowing and puzzled, unctuous and sincere, dissembling and likeable, as he leads Raskolnikov to make the confession which that odd young man needs to make for his soul's sake. Indeed, the performance of Smoktunovsky (who at moments resembles Ralph Richardson) is so subtle, so many-sided, so contemporary that it exposes the period-piece quality of much of the rest of the film.

And a period-piece it in large part is. After all, if one is to be as faithful as possible to Dostoevsky, then one must retain all the sub-plots, including the big scene between Raskolnikov's sister Dunia (pallidly played by pretty Victoria Fyodorova, who made the papers here some months ago when she came over to meet her father, a retired U.S. Navy admiral) and her passionate admirer—cynical, sinister Svidrigailov. Cynical, sinister Svidrigailov has lured Dunia to his apartment and locked all the doors. "Where's the key?" she cries. "Open the door!" He refuses. She accuses him of having killed his wife: "You killed her, you villain." He replies: "If I did it, it was for you." She calls him a blackguard. She pulls out a small pistol: "Don't stir, I'll shoot." He stirs. She shoots. Well, that's Dostoevsky.

● ● ●

There are more fundamental problems. How is Raskolnikov's over-heated state of mind or soul to be captured—his ever-changing moods, his bouts of delirium, his obsessions, his self-searchings and self-torture? A difficult job, handled by the director and his leading player, Georgi Taratorkin, with crazed looks, disappearing eyeballs, sweatings, tremblings, wrenchings of the collar and that sort of thing. The psychological ambience of Raskolnikov's St. Petersburg is conveyed by tiny rooms, long narrow alleyways, hallways and staircases, splotched walls and sharp contrasts of dark and light. These devices are effective in the early scenes, but after a time—the picture

---

Walter Goodman is assistant editor of the Arts and Leisure section. Vincent Canby will return next week.

How to capture Raskolnikov's delirium?

runs or strolls 3 hours and 20 minutes—the effectiveness inevitably lessens; I found myself becoming conscious of the devices instead of succumbing to the mood they were supposed to create. The director is inordinately fond of the dramatic flash of light, the sudden sound, the picturesque setting. The anonymous characters, in their assorted costumes and beards, who move along his picturesque streets seem to have been collected from a provincial touring company.

In the end, Kulijanov's attempt to reproduce on film the unbearably high-pitched sensibility that imbues Dostoevsky's pages turns into artificiality. His notion of faithfulness was too orthodox. To be true today to the spirit of a compelling but not always convincing 19th-century novel such as "Crime and Punishment," he would have had to depart from many of its particulars.

"The Day of the Locust," too, is full of nightmarish elements, and John Schlesinger, who directed the film version, evidently responds to Nathanael West's baleful vision of the crop of lunacy being cultivated in Southern California. With only a couple of lapses (notably a revival meeting which becomes a display of star pyrotechnics by Geraldine Page), Waldo Salt's screenplay is quite faithful to the original. But West's work, though remarkable in its way, is not a full-bodied novel; it's more a series of vaudeville turns, with the relations between characters elusive, the characters themselves rather free-floating. In capturing this aspect of the book, Schlesinger and Salt have succeeded in capturing its weakness. They were more at home with "Midnight Cowboy," where they did not have to live up to an author's reputation.

Perhaps, had their ambitions been smaller this time out, their movie would have been more of a piece, and kinder to the novel. The words in Schlesinger's "Locust" may be mostly West's, but the creation is Hollywood's; this movie is at odds with itself. Schlesinger, I believe, strove for fidelity to West, but he seems to have been forced or tempted by the resources available in moviedom to distort the book's inimitably intimate quality. Despite the authentic language and scenes, the movie is outsized, misshapen. West's work, like F. Scott Fitzgerald's, is masterful within a small frame. But Hollywood cannot abide small frames. A picture like "Locust" is a multi-million

Kahn and actor-director Wilder

dollar deal, and the big screen calls forth big scenes. Everything must be expanded, blown up out of all proportion; the star power must be turned on; the director, however respectful he may wish to be toward his raw material, has to show what he can do—and John Schlesinger can do quite a lot. So West's spare dialogue and succinct episodes are outfitted as production specials and a good, modest story sinks beneath the trappings of an opera.

Two paragraphs in the early pages of "The Day of the Locust" epitomize the special tone of the book. As Tod Hackett, the young artist who serves as the reader's eyes in Hollywood, walks along Vine Street one evening, he sees the following:

"A great many of the people wore sports clothes which were not really sports clothes. Their sweaters, knickers, slacks, blue flannel jackets with brass buttons were fancy dress. The fat lady in the yachting cap was going shopping, not boating; the man in the Norfolk jacket and Tyrolean hat was returning, not from a mountain, but an insurance office; and the girl in slacks and sneaks with a bandanna around her head had just left a switchboard, not a tennis court.

"Scattered among these masquerades were people of a different type. Their clothing was somber and badly cut, bought from mail-order houses. While the others moved rapidly, darting into stores and cocktail bars, they loitered on the corners or stood with their backs to the shop windows and stared at everyone who passed. When their stares were returned, their eyes filled with hatred. At this time Tod knew very little about them except that they had come to California to die."

It is evident throughout the film that Schlesinger and Salt are trying to convey this vision of seething madness, but they never manage to get it across in Tod's and West's matter-of-fact manner. Maybe that literary trick is beyond the resources of the moviemaker. Whatever the reason, when the climactic scene of the burning of Los Angeles occurs, it becomes a showpiece, an extravaganza, a tour de force of the special effects folks, uncertainly related to what has gone before. Like the movie of "Crime and Punishment," the movie of "The Day of the Locust" is impressive in its parts but finally unpersuasive.

•   •   •

Here I have been chiding the men who took on Dostoevsky and West for their literal sort of deference to the originals—yet if they had taken gross liberties with books that I treasure, I should certainly have faulted them for that. Grappling with such works is a difficult business, and the old, hard truth applies—good intentions have never been good enough.

1975 Je 8, II:17:1

Animals in Movies—The Abuse Gets Worse

By T.E.D. KLEIN

"Pit 'em," Earle said.

Juju climbed again, cutting and hitting so rapidly that his legs were a golden blur. . . . He broke one of the red's wings, then practically severed a leg.

"Handle them," Earle called.

When the dwarf gathered the red up, its neck had begun to droop and it was a mass of blood and matted feathers. The little man moaned over the bird, then set to work. He spit into its gaping beak and took the comb between his lips and sucked the blood back into it . . .

"Pit 'em," Earle said.

The lines above, from Nathanael West's "The Day of the Locust," describe the preliminary rounds of a cockfight. Both birds have been fitted with "gaffs" — three-inch steel spurs, sharp as needles, fastened to their legs. Midway through the fight the "big red" loses the top half of his beak. The struggle ends when Juju, the smaller bird, drives a gaff through the other's eye, into the brain.

●

Like dogfights, bullfights, and other barbaric spectacles, cockfights have been outlawed throughout the United States since about the turn of the century. Not many New Yorkers would pay to see one. Yet that's exactly what they're doing when they line up for Paramount's "The Day of the Locust," which opened here May 7—right in the middle of Be Kind to Animals Week. For, in a misguided attempt to remain true to the West novel, director John Schlesinger has staged a genuine cockfight, complete with blood, spurs and a bird that dies twitching at the actors' feet while the camera lovingly records every detail.

Such self-indulgence in the name of "realism" is totally unnecessary. Hollywood has effectively staged cockfights before—most memorably in "The Cincinnati Kid" and "Ace Eli and Rodger of the Skies"—but they've been simmulated. "No birds were hurt, injured, or killed," says Harold Melniker of the American Humane Association, whose office worked with the filmmakers. "The only

T.E.D. Klein is a freelance writer.

The cockfight in "Locust"—spurs, blood and a dying bird

Mary Ellen Mark from Lee Gross, Inc.

trouble with simulation is that it requires a little extra time and money."

But time and money are luxuries in this industry, especially in the precarious world of the small-time independent producers—two of whom, sensing the exploitation value of chicken blood, are about to cash in on the trend with forthcoming films of their own: both "Supercock," shot in Manila, and "Born to Kill," shot in Georgia, will feature real cockfights.

Inexcusable in any circumstances, such practices are even more so in a $6-million movie from a major studio. Yet Vincent Canby lauded "Locust" for its fidelity to the original novel, and Pauline Kael praised actor Billy Barty for "the tenderness in his handling of the wretched, mutilated bird." All of the critics seemed to overlook the fact that, unlike Donald Sutherland's bloody death at the hands of a mob, the bloody death of the fighting cock was *real.*

Perhaps they just didn't care. Last summer, in a Village Voice column whose flip title—"On Being Beastly to the Beasties"—matched the tone of his prose, critic Andrew Sarris waxed poetic over the deaths of "all those marvelously expressive rab-

bits in 'The Rules of the Game,'" and suggested that animals killed in films "should have felt honored to be called upon to contribute their ephemeral lives and bodies to such immortal works of art." There is, of course, a precedent for this ghoulish aesthetics: watching a group of Ethiopian horsemen blown up by an Italian bomb, Mussolini's son compared the sight to "a budding rose unfolding." Presumably the horsemen shoud have felt honored.

Like the critics, directors have long considered animals expendable in the cause of art. In a 1974 article for the Arts and Leisure section, I cited a few such examples from the likes of Sam Peckinpah, Dennis Hopper, Alexandro Jodorowsky, and others: rabbits roasted in the sun, sheep with throats slit, mice crushed beneath boots, horses made to fall by means of "trip wires," often with enough force to break their legs—or necks.

The piece drew a furious two-page reply from Robert Redford, who justified the killing of an elk and buffalo in "Jeremiah Johnson" on grounds that the animals were "diseased and earmarked for an early death." If that's true, let's hope his friends stay healthy.

The same year the Motion Picture Association of America received an unprecedented 1,400 letters decrying animal abuse. Its president, Jack Valenti, agreed to a much-publicized meeting with the heads of four humane societies, at which he spoke of the M.P.A.A.'s determination "to abolish inhumane treatment of animals" and urged filmmakers to let American Humane Association personnel supervise the filming of animal scenes. Unfortunately, compliance with the resolution was left strictly voluntary.

Recently two state legislators—New York assemblyman Leonard Stavisky and California state senator David Roberti—have introduced bills making it a misdemeanor to show films for which animals were killed or mistreated, and industry spokesmen have reacted with predictable cries of government interference; like Valenti, they prefer appealing to the "conscience" of those involved. But Paramount's "The Day of the Locust," with its arrogant disregard for law as well as for the M.P.A.A. pledge, illustrates the futility of such appeals. "They never consulted us at all," says the American Humane Association's Harold Melniker.

During filming of Paramount's "Jonathan Livingston Seagull," dozens of birds were reportedly killed by caustic bleaches and hair sprays, others were crippled by control cords, and some 88 suffered eye injuries; the same studio's "Posse" employs trip-wires, as do two other major films involving horses: Columbia's "Bite the Bullet" and MGM's "The Wind and the Lion."

It has become increasingly obvious that animal abuse is no longer confined to shoestring American productions and foreign films. Assuming the industry is permitted to maintain its present hypocritical standards of "self-regulation," we can look forward to the next logical step: a major studio's biography of Shakespeare, complete with real bear-baiting. ■

1975 Je 8, II:17:1

LE CHAT ("The Cat"), directed by Pierre Granier-Deferre; screenplay (French with English subtitles) by Mr. Granier-Deferre and Pascal Jardin, with dialogue by Mr. Jardin, based on the novel by Georges Simenon; executive producer, Raymond Danon; director of photography, Walter Wottitz; music, Philippe Sarde; distributed by Joseph Green Pictures. Running time: 88 minutes. At the 68th Street Playhouse, Third Avenue at 68th Street. This film has not been rated.

Julien .... Jean Gabin
Clemence .... Simone Signoret
Nelly .... Annie Cordy
Doctor .... Jacques Rispal

By VINCENT CANBY

It began years ago as love, when he was a young, virile factory worker and she was a beautiful acrobat. They married, moved into a pretty little house on the edge of Paris, and then slowly, carefully over the decades, they refined that love so successfully that it now exists only as obsessive hate.

Their house stands isolated, one last habitation in a desolate field of urban renewal. In the same way Julien (Jean Gabin) and Clemence (Simone Signoret) have effectively cut themselves off from the world around them by an almost total preoccupation with their civil war.

•

When they go shopping together, they walk at a distance, never speaking, occasionally exchanging angry glances. Mealtime is much the same. While Julien fries his onions and adds a soupçon of wine to his tripe, Clemence, on the other side of the kitchen, gasps at the horrid, vulgar smell, and just as fastidiously as Julien, she prepares her mussels. They eat at the same time, at separate tables, and sleep in the same room, the same hours, in separate beds.

Loathing as fixated as theirs is miraculous. It has transformed banal objects and gestures into infuriating insults. Each listens for the other's footstep, his breathing, the clearing of a throat, and they track each other around the house like Indians in the Amazon jungle. In the evening, after supper, they sit in the parlor, in chairs facing each other, Julien reading Zola's "Le Terre" and Clemence crocheting. If she talks, he answers by written note flicked into her lap.

•

"Le Chat" ("The Cat"), based on the Georges Simenon novel published here in 1967, is about the last months of that marriage. The title refers to Julien's pet, but it also refers to him. It's a most curious, vivid, unusual film and, considering the subject matter, it's an unexpectedly entertaining one. It wouldn't be quite accurate to describe it as invigorating in any conventional sense of the word, but there is a good deal of excitement in watching these two marvelous professionals, Mr. Gabin and Miss Signoret, having at each other with such passion and wit.

"Le Chat," which opened yesterday at the 68th Street Playhouse, was made in 1971, and I suppose it's taken so long to get here because it might be considered depressing. Two old people who hate each other, who wants that? A lot of people, I suspect, who long to see a film that so minutely explores its limited territory that the territory becomes as large and varied as a new continent.

Mr. Gabin and Miss Signoret are precise and perfect in their performances, and though the character of Clemence has been made more robust and more sexually hungry in the film, the actors work with lean, spare manners that suggest the quality of the Simenon prose.

This is also true of the look of the film and of its direction by Pierre Granier-Deferre, whose work is new to me. The only false note is provided by lumpy flashbacks designed to inform those members of the audience who are retarded that Julien and Clemence were once deliriously in love, which is information we might have been given much more gracefully in any number of other ways. We never do know exactly what happened to that love to turn it inside out, but that doesn't matter. We accept the transformation as one of the common mysteries of life, which, like the weather, can be charted though never adequately explained.

1975 Je 9, 43:5

LOVE AND DEATH, directed and written by Woody Allen; produced by Charles H. Joffe; executive producer, Martin Poll; music, Prokofiev; edited by Ralph Rosenblum; director of photography, Ghislain Cloquet; a Jack Rollins and Charles H. Joffe production, distributed by United Artists. Running time 89 minutes. At the Sutton Theater, 57th Street east of Third Avenue, and Paramount Theater, Broadway at 61st Street. This film has been rated PG.

Boris	Woody Allen
Sonja	Diane Keaton
Mikhail	Feodor Atkine
Rimsky	Yves Barsacq
Don Francisco	Lloyd Battista
Dimitri	Brian Coburn
Ivan	Henry Czarniak
Mother	Despo Diamantidou
Countess Alexandrovna	Olga Georges-Picot
Natasha	Jessica Harper
Father Andre	Leib Lansky
Young Boris	Alfred Lutter 3d
Father	Zvee Scooler
Napoleon	James Tolkan
Anton	Harold Gould

By VINCENT CANBY

Boris Grushenko (Woody Allen), the most reluctant Russian patriot ever to take up an arm against Napoleon, sits in his prison cell awaiting execution. At the instigation of his wife, Sonja (Diane Keaton), the sort of young woman who likes to debate moral imperatives, Boris had plotted the assassination of the French general and gotten caught.

Boris, like Sonja, is of philosophical bent. As death approaches, as it has been doing throughout his life, Boris muses: "Every man has to go sometime . . . but I'm different. I have to go at 6 A.M. It was 5 A.M., but I have a good lawyer."

"Love and Death," which opened yesterday at the Sutton and Paramount Theaters, is Woody Allen's grandest work. It's the film (as he said somewhere) that God tried to stop, a sweeping, side-splitting spectacle of Europe at war, of clashing armies and of Boris's puny attempts to remain neutral, if not to evade the draft. At the height of one battle, Boris hid in the muzzle of a cannon.

Diane Keaton and Woody Allen

"Love and Death" is Woody's "War and Peace," written in English by Woody Allen, which may or may not be a nom de plume for the late Constance Garnett, and filmed on locations where it all did not happen, in Hungary and France. It's Woody's homage to Tolstoy, Kierkegaard, Eisenstein, Groucho Marx, Bob Hope and maybe even Robert Z. Leonard. It looks terrific. You might say that it looks like a million, except that is probably a million or so less than it cost.

Besides being one of Woody's most consistently witty films, "Love and Death" marks a couple of other advances for Mr. Allen as a film maker and for Miss Keaton as a wickedly funny comedienne. Miss Keaton here plays a warped kind of Natasha. At first she is married to a rich, elderly, odiferous herring merchant while happily carrying on with most of St. Petersburg's available males, and then, after a brief widowhood, she becomes Boris's wife, who loves him as if he were a brother.

•

"Sex without love is an empty experience," she solemnly tells Boris when he first makes advances. Boris ponders that a moment and suggests, "But as empty experiences go, it's one of the best."

The professional Woody Allen character, compounded of equal parts of optimism and pessimism, leavened by cowardice and a ready access to fractured philosophical jargon and literary allusions, has never before been as completely utilized as he is in "Love and Death." If Woody's early films had the flavor of his nightclub monologues, this new one suggests the parodies he writes for The New Yorker magazine, fully expanded to film form and annotated with movie references.

•

"Love and Death" evokes not only "War and Peace" but also "The Brothers Karamazov," especially in the mystical experiences that Boris has been prone to all his life. The first time was when he was a boy of 12 (played by Alfred Lutter 3d of "Alice Doesn't Live Here Anymore") and met Death, whom he prodded to answer one key question: Are there any girls? Woody's vision of the Grand Inquisitor is a guy who wears a white sheet and goes about the daily routine in a methodical, conscientious way, sort of like mankind's gardener.

Most prominent in the large supporting cast are Olga Georges-Picot, as a sultry countess who, briefly, fals head over heels in love with Boris; James Tolkan, who plays Napoleon as if Napoleon were Roman Polanski, and Jessica Harper, as a mopy society girl who doesn't want to get married, just divorced.

1975 Je 11, 48:1

REFLECTIONS (DRY SUMMER), directed by Ulvi Dogan and Ismail Metin; screenplay by Necati Cumali and Jim Lehner; photography by Ali Ugar and Peter Palian; edited by Ulvi Dogan and Stuart Gillman; music by Manos Hadjidakis; music edited and supervised by Tarik Bulut; produced by Mr. Dogan; released by Hittite Films. At the Bleecker Street Cinema, 144 Bleecker Street. Running time: 90 minutes. (This film has not been rated.)

Hassan	Ulvi Dogan
Ossman	Errol Tash
Bahar	Hulya Kotch

Eleven years after it won the grand prize at the Berlin Film Festival against such competition as "The Pawnbroker," Ulvi Dogan's "Reflections," also known as "Dry Summer," began evening showings yesterday at the Bleecker Street Cinema.

A somewhat choppy looking black-and-white film in Turkish with English subtitles, "Reflections" is one of those earthy, lusty, rustic melodramas played out on parched earth under hot sun to the accompaniment of the "Never on Sunday" ensemble and Ravi Shankar.

What troubles "Reflections" is the incomprehensively submissive behavior of one of the principal characters and the fact that Mr. Dogan — having assembled the ingredients of tragedy— contents himself with a lesser conclusion.

As actor, Mr. Dogan plays the role of Hassan, the younger, more intelligent and more decent brother of a crude, powerful farmer named Ossman, who incurs the wrath of his neighbors by limiting and then cutting off the supply of water from his land to theirs.

Ossman's behavior is at least consistent with his manifestation of the sort of provocatively destructive paranoia exhibited by Humphrey Bogart as Fred C. Dobbs in "Treasure of Sierra Madre." But the film lacks any explanation of why Hassan, the younger brother, lets Ossman make the central decisions in his life— like going to jail for a killing he did not commit.

So, while generating a considerable amount of tension and conflict—between Ossman and the farmers, between Ossman and Hassan, and between Ossman and Hassan's wife, Bahar—"Reflections" leaves one feeling that much of what happens could have been avoided.

As director, Mr. Dogan is given to neatly framed shots, to acting styles that should have seemed dated even in 1964, to the kind of symbolism that shows a sexually deprived woman fondling candles and embracing poles and a predictability that signals our final view of Ossman long before it appears.

LAWRENCE VAN GELDER

1975 Je 12, 30:1

NIGHT MOVES, directed by Arthur Penn; screenplay by Alan Sharp; produced by Robert M. Sherman; editor, Dede Allen; director of photography, Bruce Surtees; music, Michael Small; distributed by Warner Bros. Running time: 100 minutes. At the Loews State Theater, Broadway at 45th Street, Trans-Lux 85th Street Theater on Madison Avenue and other theaters. This film has been rated R.

Harry Moseby ....Gene Hackman
Ellen ....Susan Clark
Paula ....Jennifer Warren
Ziegler ....Edward Binns
Marty Heller ....Harris Yulin
Nick ....Kenneth Mars
Arlene Iverson ....Janet Ward
Quentin ....James Woods
Marv Ellman .... Anthony Costello
Tom Iverson ....John Crawford
Delly Grastner ....Melanie Griffith

Arthur Penn's "Night Moves," the director's first film since the epic "Little Big Man" five years ago, is an elegant conundrum, a private-eye film that has its full share of duplicity, violence and bizarre revelation, but whose mind keeps straying from questions of pure narrative to those of the hero's psyche.

Over the years we have come to expect our private eyes to be somewhat seedy and second-rate, beer-drinking loners with their own secrets to hide. But that seediness, as well as the decency that lurked beneath, has always been in the service of the genres. One never worried about Philip Marlowe's mental health; one does about Harry Moseby's. In fact, Harry is much more interesting and truly complex than the mystery he sets out to solve.

•

This is the only way I can explain my mixed feelings about "Night Moves," which opened yesterday at Loews State 2, the Trans-Lux 85th Street and other theaters. Harry Moseby (Gene Hackman), his wife Ellen (Susan Clark) and the assorted characters he encounters in the film seem to deserve better than the quality of the narrative given them.

I can't figure out whether the screenplay by Alan Sharp was worked on too much or not enough, or whether Mr. Penn and his actors accepted the screenplay with more respect than it deserves.

When we first meet Harry, he is taking on a classic missing-persons case. It's to find the nymphomaniac daughter of a once beautiful Hollywood actress. The daughter, who is only 16, has been competing with Mummy for boyfriends.

The girl also stands to inherit the trust fund from which Mummy now gets a sizable income. Why does Mummy seek the return of the child, whom she clearly detests?

The plot thickens, but in the wrong ways. Harry discovers his wife is having an affair, and we learn that Harry had a terrible childhood, that he has trouble facing things squarely (as a knight moves in chess?), and that for one reason or another, he wants to face things squarely in this particular case. It'll prove something, you see.

•

In addition to the performances of Mr. Hackman and Miss Clark, "Night Moves" features two others of note, by Jennifer Warren, as a beautiful, enigmatic drifter Harry meets in the Florida keys, and by Melanie Griffith, as the not-so-missing person. They all are more or less realistic, believable characters.

However, they are forced to behave and react in the completely unbelievable ways demanded of private-eye fiction, when people we know to be sensitive and caring can walk away from a new corpse as casually as if it were a minor social indiscretion. After a while it just seems absurd.

VINCENT CANBY

1975 Je 12, 30:3

NURITH, directed by George Ovadia; screenplay by Ada Ben Nachum; photography by Yechiel Ne'eman; music composed by Boaz Sharabi and Shaike Paikov; music arranged and conducted by Albert Piamanta; edited by Avi Lifshitz; produced by Arie Films, Ltd.; distributed by Cinemagic Productions, Inc. At the Quad IV Cinema on 13th Street (between Fifth Avenue and the Avenue of the Americas) and the Utopia Theater in Queens and the Graham Cinema in Brooklyn. Running time: 90 minutes. (This film has beeen classified PG).

Moshe ....Sassi Keshet
Shoshana ....Yona Elian
Nurith ....Tova Katzav
Father ....Jack Cohen
Moshe's Mother ....Tova Pardo
Stepmother ....Adi Kaplan
Ilana ....Rachel Furman
Three Troubadours ....Arie Elias, Yaacov Ben-Sira, Ezra Dagan

The most modern and pleasant thing about "Nurith," an incredible Israeli movie that opened yesterday at the Quad IV and other theaters, is its driving, bouncing pop music.

But if one had to judge the state of Israeli technology solely on the basis of "Nurith's" screenplay and the kind of heavy-handed direction that permits meaningful winks and jump-cuts to obvious thoughts, the assumption would have to be that the Israeli army is equipped with flintlocks.

The story—and what a story it is—concerns two attractive lovers, Moshe (Sassi Keshet) and Shoshana (Yona Elian). Her father doesn't want her to marry him because he's too poor. His mother wants him to marry Ilana (Rachel Furman), a rich girl who can help him. Shoshana and Moshe plan, nevertheless, to marry. She becomes pregnant.

Before they can be wed, he is killed in an accident—or so she believes. She commits suicide—or so he believes.

•

She has his baby. He lets Ilana foster his career as a pop singer. Shoshana looks in vain for work. Just after being turned away by Ilana's housekeeper, she is knocked down by an auto and blinded. The three stooges from the car — Chanuka, Ringo and Shmil — adopt her and her daughter, Nurith, and they all wander around singing.

Years later, Nurith meets Moshe by accident. Out of love for the child and not knowing that it is Shoshana he is helping, he pays for the operation that restores her sight.

Shoshana, Nurith and the three stooges decide to go to thank Moshe (who has changed his name after becoming a star) on the day he is marrying Ilana.

To reveal what happens next would be unfair to Ada Ben Nachum, who did the screenplay. But the temptation is powerful.

LAWRENCE VAN GELDER

1975 Je 12, 30:4

MURPH THE SURF, directed by Marvin Chomsky; screenplay by E. Arthur Kean, based on a story by Allan Dale Kuhn; director of photography, Michael Hugo; edited by Howard Smith; production designed by James Vance; music composed and conducted by Phillip Lambro; executive producer, Caruth C. Byrd; produced by J. Skeet Wilson and Chuck Courtney; released by American International Pictures. At neighborhood theaters Running time: 101 minutes. (This film has been classified PG).

Allan......................Robert Conrad
Jack Murphy.................Don Stroud
Ginny Eaton................Donna Mills
Sharon Kagel..............Robyn Millan
Max "The Eye"............Luther Adler
Avery.......................Paul Stewart
Arnie Holcomb.............Morgan Paul

and

THE DESTRUCTORS, directed by Robert Parrish; written by Judd Bernard; director of photography, Douglas Slocombe; edited by Willy Kemplen; music by Roy Budd; produced by Judd Bernard; a Kettledrum Films—P.E.C.F. Production; released by American International. At neighborhood theaters. Running time: 89 minutes. (This film has been classified PG).

Deray.....................Michael Caine
Steve Ventura............Anthony Quinn
Brizard......................James Mason
Lucianne................Maureen Kerwin
Calmet..................Marcel Bozzuffi
Brizard's Mistress......Catherine Rouvel
Briac....................Maurice Ronet
Marsac..................Andre Oumanksy
Rita...................Alexandra Stewart

By A. H. WEILER

The theory that crime isn't always the stuff of trenchant movies is scenically illustrated in "Murph the Surf" and "The Destructors," the adventures that crashed into local theaters yesterday. If there is a gloss of sincerity in these depictions of antiheros in action here and abroad, it is overshadowed by successions of explosive capers in Miami and New York and Paris and Marseilles that loom a good deal larger than the tough but doomed characters they attempt to dissect.

Proof that truth can be more fabulous than fiction is fairly evident in "Murph the Surf," which dramatizes some of the actual exploits of Jack Murphy and Allan Kuhn, the Miami beach boys — jewel thieves, that were capped by their highly publicized, ill-fated heist in October, 1964, of the Star of India sapphire and 23 other fabled gems from the American Museum of Natural History here.

Although the script stems from Mr. Kuhn's own story, the drives and mental make-up of the decidedly oddball principals still call for fuller explanations. As Kuhn, who served his time in prison and is now free, Robert Conrad appears to be too meticulous a mastermind to have allied himself with an apparently carefree, if fearless Murph the Surf (now incarcerated for life for other crimes) flamboyantly portrayed by Don Stroud.

If there is some service given to their relationship with Robyn Millan and Donna Mills, as their respective, attractive girls, and their motivations and life style, it is largely surface psychology that is not nearly as edifying as the action. Under Marvin Chomsky's merely workmanlike direction from the script centered on flashbacks from the major, daring heist to the preceding robberies and chases in Miami and the Bahamas, the escapades and the beauties of those resorts stick in memory more than the ill-defined principals.

•

"The Destructors," once reportedly titled "The Marseilles Connection," involves Anthony Quinn, as the harried American narcotics chief in Paris, in a variety of murderous machinations to eliminate James Mason, as the Marseilles kingpin of the international dope traffic. Mr. Mason, it turns out in a highly convoluted plot, has knocked off our hero's best agents, thus driving him to Maurice Ronet, as a seemingly helpful Parisian police inspector, and Michael Caine, as a professional hit man, womanizer and old friend, and others, to do the job.

If Paris's streets, bridges and Metro and the Marseilles waterfront never were lovelier, the script by Judd Bernard, who also produced, rarely delves deeply into the characters of his cast. Speed is the essence of director Robert Parrish's approach, which includes shootings, stabbings, car chases, payoffs and wisps of amour and sex between our hero and Alexandra Stewart and Mr. Caine and Maureen Kerwin, as our villain's pretty daughter, and even a brief appearance by former Presidential aide Pierre Salinger as a top embassy official.

It's ungallant to reveal who finally does the deed, but Mr. Mason is more casual than sinister. And Mr. Quinn is simply as muscular and disheveled as the film's complicated plot.

1975 Je 12, 30:6

NASHVILLE, directed and produced by Robert Altman; screenplay by Joan Tewksbury; executive producers, Martin Starger and Jerry Weintraub; director of photography, Paul Lohmann; music arranged and supervised by Richard Baskin; editors, Sidney Levin and Dennis Hill; a Jerry Weintraub production, presented by ABC Entertainment and distributed by Paramount Pictures. Running time: 159 minutes. At the Baronet Theater, Third Avenue at 59th Street, and Cinema II Theater, Third Avenue at 60th Street. This film has been rated R.

Norman .... David Arkin
Lady Pearl .... Barbara Baxley
Delbert Reese .... Ned Beatty
Connie White .... Karen Black
Barbara Jean .... Ronee Blakley
Tommy Brown .... Timothy Brown
Tom Frank .... Keith Carradine
Opal .... Geraldine Chaplin
Wade .... Robert Doqui
L. A. Joan ....Shelley Duvall
Barnett .... Allen Garfield
Haven Hamilton .... Henry Gibson
Pfc. Glenn Kelly .... Scott Glenn
Tricycle Man .... Jeff Goldblum
Albuquerque ....Barbara Harris
Kenny Fraiser .... David Hayward
John Triplette .... Michael Murphy
Bill .... Allan Nichols
Bud Hamilton .... David Peel
Mary .... Cristina Raines
Star .... Bert Remsen
Linnea Reese .... Lily Tomlin
Sueleen Gay .... Gwen Welles
Mr. Green .... Keenan Wynn
Jimmy Reese .... James Dan Calvert
Donna .... Donna Denton

By VINCENT CANBY

Robert Altman's "Nashville" is the movie sensation that all other American movies this year will be measured against. It's a film that a lot of other directors will wish they'd had the brilliance to make and that dozens of other performers will wish they'd had the great good fortune to be in.

It should salvage Mr. Altman's reputation in Hollywood as a director who makes movies only for the critics, and it could well be the highpoint in the careers of a number of its performers, who may never again be so ideally presented in roles that utilize their special gifts with such affection. What will Ronee Blakley or Henry Gibson or Lily Tomlin or Barbara Harris do for encores? It's a tough question but not an unhappy one.

"Nashville," which opened yesterday at the Baronet and Cinema II Theaters, is a panoramic film with dozens of characters, set against the country - and - Western music industry in Nashville. It's a satire, a comedy, a melodrama, a musical. Its music is terrifically important — funny, moving and almost nonstop. It's what a Tennessee granddaddy might call a real toe-tapper of a picture.

There are so many story lines in "Nashville" that one is more or less coerced into dealing in abstractions. "Nashville" is about the quality of a segment of Middle American life. It's about ambition, sentimentality, politics, emotional confusion, empty goals and very big business, in a society whose citizens are firmly convinced that the use of deodorants is next to godliness.

•

"Nashville" doesn't make easy fun of these people. It doesn't patronize them. Along with their foolishness, it sees their gallantry. At the beginning of the film when Henry Gibson as Haven Hamilton, Nashville's biggest male star, records "200 Years," a patriotic song in honor of the Bicentennial ("We must be doing something right/To last 200 years"), the movie is amused by the song's maudlin sentiments and rhyme schemes, and by Haven's recording-studio tantrums. But it also appreciates the song's stirring beat and the vast, earnest public for whom it will have meaning.

The film, which has an original screenplay by Joan Tewksbury, who collaborated with Mr. Altman in adapting "Thieves Like Us," has a well-defined structure, while individual sequences often burst with the kind of life that seems impossible to plan, though that may be to underrate Miss Tewksbury's contributions and those of the extraordinary cast. I have no idea where the director and the writer leave off and the performers take over.

Whoever is responsible, "Nashville" comes across as a film of enormous feeling. It's compounded of moments that tingle the spine, as when Lily Tomlin, who makes a spectacular dramatic debut in the film as a gospel singer and the mother of two deaf children, patiently draws forth a story from her 12-year-old son, in words and sign language, about a swimming test he's just passed.

At the end of the film Barbara Harris, as a perpetually disheveled, very unlikely aspirant to country and Western stardom, almost tears the screen to bits with a gospel version of a song heard earlier ("It Don't Worry Me") that concludes the narrative in a manner that is almost magical.

Ronee Blakley, a composer singer who came to Mr. Altman's attention when she attempted to interest him in some of her songs, dominates the film, as much as it can be dominated by any one performer, as Barbara Jean, Nashville's beautiful, fragile, country and Western princess—a rural girl who's hit it big and throughout the film, sinks deeper and deeper into emotional panic.

The stunning effect of her performance has as much to do with Miss Blakley's talents as singer-composer-actress and her particular beauty as with Barbara Jean's role in the events the film records.

•

"Nashville" is an immense collaboration, a timely coming together of all sorts of resources, including those of 25-year-old Richard Baskin, who arranged and supervised the music, much of it written by the people who perform it.

In addition to Miss Blakley and Mr. Gibson, this includes Karen Black, who wrote two songs and has a fine sequence as Nashville's No. 2 female star, and Keith Carradine, who plays a cad of a rock singer and who wrote two songs, "I'm Easy" and "It Don't Worry Me," which, with Miss Blakley's "My Idaho Home," are three of the film's best.

"Nashville" has some weak spots. Geraldine Chaplin turns up as a visiting British Broadcasting Corporation reporter of such gross idiocy she'd probably have trouble getting a job on a shopping guide. A couple of sequences in the middle of the movie just mark time, but usually everything works, to make "Nashville" the most original, provocative high-spirited film Mr. Altman has yet given us.

1975 Je 12, 32:1

Ronee Blakley and Henry Gibson

SATURDAY NIGHT AT THE BATHS, directed by David Buckley; written by Franklin Khedouri and Mr. Buckley; director of photography, Ralf Bode; edited by Jackie Raynal and Suzanne Fenn; produced by Mr. Buckley and Steve Ostrow. At the RKO 59th Street Twin I Theater. Running time: 102 minutes. (This film has been classified R.)
Michael .... Robert Aberdeen
Tracy .... Ellen Sheppard
Scotti .... Don Scotti

"Saturday Night at the Baths," which opened at the RKO 59ht Street Twin I Theater yesterday and was filmed at local sites, including the Continental Baths, which is favored by the homosexual crowd, is, like the baths, slightly steamy and enervating.

In making his movie directorial debut, David Buckley, one of the founders of Screw magazine, is grappling with one of the world's minor problems in focusing on an indecisive relationship among Robert Aberdeen, as a handsome, blond piano player; Ellen Sheppard, as his attractive, loving girl, and Don Scotti, his employer at the Continental, who also adores him.

The desires, and confusion displayed by these newcomers to the screen is earnest, if not convincing, even if some of their liaisons are raunchily explicit.

Mr. Buckley, who also collaborated on the script, appears to be making a valiant attempt to stress his understanding of the current sexual scene. But despite some glimpses of Judy Garland, Shirley Bassey, Carmen Miranda and Diana Ross impersonators, this gay life in the "Baths" is somewhat sad and pointless.

A. H. WEILER

1975 Je 12, 33:1

CORRECTION

In the review of "Saturday Night at the Baths" in last Thursday's Times David Buckley was incorrectly identified as a founder of Screw magazine. He served for a short time as its advertising director.

1975 Je 17, 35:7

FILM VIEW

VINCENT CANBY

'A Satire, a Melodrama, A Celebration'

Let's face it: Robert Altman's "Nashville" is a smash, a big, gaudy, panoramic movie whose style and substance are both a reflection of and a comment upon the country-and-western music with which it is so brilliantly scored. It's a film that takes off with the opening credits, which parody those late-night, hard-sell TV commercials that urge us to buy cut-rate record albums containing 106 of our all-time favorite golden oldies from 1973, and it never stops until the lights come up in the theater at the end.

It's a satire, a comedy, a musical, a melodrama. It's a pageant of celebration. It's also the most original and free-flowing film yet from this most eccentric, most sophisticated, most regional of American directors. Altman doesn't make movies as if he were a sight-seer. He makes them as if he'd lived in a place long enough to be bored in it and dreamed, unsuccessfully, of getting away.

"Nashville," which is about a couple of dozen characters directly or peripherally involved in the country-and-western music business, gives the impression of being virtually all musical performance (actually it's a series of related performances) that are mostly set in recording studios, the Grand Ole Opry, late night joints and barrooms, motel rooms and private homes.

Only the final sequence of the film, a political rally on behalf of a third party candidate for President, is set in a recognizable site, Nashville's remarkable replica of the Parthenon, originally built of plaster of Paris for the city's centennial and later rebuilt of sterner though no more convincing stuff when folks came to like Nashville's being called the Athens of the South.

It's in front of this curious, only-in-America structure that the film's climactic drama is played out, somewhat like the last stanza of an especially moving though maudlin country-and-western ballad, the sort that seeks desperately to raise accident to the status of tragedy.

"Nashville," which is Altman's first unequivocal hit since he made "M*A*S*H" five years ago, is another extraordinary chapter in the director's continuing history, of America seen largely through the stories of gallant losers ("Brewster McCloud," "McCabe and Mrs. Miller," "The Long Goodbye," "Thieves Like Us" and "California Split"). There is no grand design in these films, at least I hope there isn't since Altman is not at his best when he's being schematic.

Rather his concerns are most effectively expressed in stories about people who think they know exactly what they want. What they do is not as important as how they do it, and how they do it, in "Nashville," is not as important as their projections of themselves through the music of the film.

Just as there is a danger in over-selling a film as good as "Nashville," there is the possibility of over-interpreting material that is so rich in associations. It would be a mistake to attribute to the film too many mystical metaphors about the American Experience. "Nashville" makes a big point of recalling the fate of the Kennedy brothers, as well as the assassination attempt on the life of George Wallace, but the use it makes of these recollections is like that of the C & W balladeer.

They are purposely sentimentalized, even trivialized, which is the songwriter's way of making them comprehensible, so they conform to what we'd all like to think of God's Grand Plan.

The most stunning aspects of "Nashville" are the performances and the music, which has a good deal to do with the excitement the film generates, whether or not you have ever considered yourself a country-and-western fan.

I suspect that a major credit for the success of the film must go to 25-year-old Richard Baskin, who arranged and supervised the music, which includes his own songs as well as others by such "giants" of the music industry as Henry Gibson, Karen Black, Keith Carradine and, very especially, by Ronee Blakley.

•   •   •

Miss Blakley, a C & W composer-performer unknown to me, makes an enchanting film debut in "Nashville," singing her own songs as well as giving a delicate and funny performance as Nashville's biggest star, a fragile beauty who wears Mary Pickford hair-dos and dresses and who can rip into a lyric one minute and teeter on the edge of a breakdown the next.

I have no idea how to credit the superlative performances in the film except alphabetically and incompletely: Karen Black (as Miss Blakley's tough-as-nails rival for the queen's crown); Timothy Brown (as Nashville's biggest black star); Keith Carradine (as a totally self-absorbed rock star who is in Nashville to do some recordings; Robert Doqui (as a black waiter in love with an aspiring white C & W singer of absolutely no talent); Shelley Duvall (as a bird-brained

C & W groupie); Allen Garfield (as Miss Blakley's husband); Henry Gibson (as Nashville's biggest, though shortest, male singing star, very rich and self-satisfied, the sort of nouveau riche who would say ". . . and welcome to my lovely home"); Barbara Harris (as another aspiring C & W singer who is prepared to sell trucks if she fails, but who gets her chance to triumph at the end); Lily Tomlin (as the white leader of a black choir, a woman of great feeling and intelligence, which is communicated), and Gwen Welles (as the no-talent, would-be singer, who can't even carry off a strip-tease without bungling).

There are others, too, but there isn't space to give everyone a line. If any film's performances deserved a collective award, "Nashville's" do. There is one exception, and I'm not at all sure it's Geraldine Chaplin's fault since her role, as an idiotically gross BBC reporter, is the film's single miscalculation, so broad that it nearly destroys every scene she barges through, as, apparently, Altman and the screenplay by Joan Tewksbury required.

Movies involve an awful lot of complicated technology —and Altman's movies involve more than most. What makes "Nashville" so fascinating is its appearance of having been discovered as it happened, by great good luck, without terrific fuss and effort.

1975 Je 15, II: 1:7

'A Cascade of Greed, Cruelty, Hysteria'

By TOM WICKER

A neurotic country music star, recovering from some vague illness, sits on her hospital bed cropping her toenails and criticizing another singer who is at that moment performing as a substitute for her. In one corner of the room, her husband-manager, overweight and blustery, gorges himself greasily on a take-out order of Colonel Sanders' fried chicken. When the wife-singer grows too petulant, he licks off his fingers and combines bullying with cajolery to quiet her. Then he goes off to thank the substitute singer publicly, not because he or his wife is grateful, but because it's good business—it will *look* good.

Not a major episode, not a turning point in "Nashville," Robert Altman's new movie about the world of country music and politics—just one more scene in a two-and-a-half hour cascade of minutely detailed vulgarity, greed, deceit, cruelty, barely contained hysteria, and the frantic lack of root and grace into which American life has been driven by its own heedless vitality.

In another scene, a telescoped crunching of dozens of cars on one of those concrete rivers that flood our bulldozed cities—a scene as ponderously comic as cavorting elephants—foreshadows

Tom Wicker is an associate editor of The Times.

an automobile graveyard where the metal bodies in endless rusting stacks have been reduced to so many beetles squashed flat under mechanical feet.

In other scenes, we have already heard the infernal roar of the stock car races—a sound as ubiquitous in most of America as the twang of country music — drowning out a singer whose grotesque contortions while belting out an unheard song suggest the writhings of a culture that does not even know it is choking on exhaust fumes.

Meanwhile, an invisible Presidential candidate's arcane message is solemnly intoned in bits and pieces from a sound truck that weaves in and out of the picture, in and out of the life of Nashville. It is impossible to piece the message together, to know whether the candidate is good or bad, fraud or prophet, until, near the end of the film, his fleet of black limousines suddenly appears — silent, circling, ominous. Even then, it is not possible to see *who* it is in those limousines, who it is the Bremer-like assassin in the crowd must be waiting for. But the audience is waiting for a political assassination, expecting it out of its own experience more than from any suggestion in the movie.

In "Nashville," the audience does not get what it is waiting for. Altman will not let its easy expectation be rewarded, but offers instead an even darker per-

" 'Nashville' is my distorted view of American culture," director Robert Altman, left, told Tom Wicker. Above, Ronee Blakley, Henry Gibson and Barbara Baxley.

ception that informs and controls virtually every scene of "Nashville," despite its vivacity. I recently asked Altman if he had set out to make a commentary about American culture.

"It's my view—my distorted view—of the culture," he said. "But I don't have any philosophies. I don't have anything to say. I don't believe in propaganda. In 'Nashville' there's certainly not a definitive study of a culture. It's not supposed to be. It's not even supposed to be accurate. It's just an impression."

On the other hand, he concedes, "There's no way that things that impress me or do not impress me, things that I'm reflecting or seeing, don't have my attitude expressed in them. Anything that filters through you has got to come out in your shape."

Altman got the idea for "Nashville" when someone told him that William Price Fox's novel about country

music, "Ruby Red," was "flawed" in that it featured a fading country-music star. "But there's no such thing— they don't fade," Altman was told. He thought about it and decided that was true enough; country-music stars like Roy Acuff or Hank Williams can no more "fade" than the saints of a church; they and their songs stand for something that transcends their mere careers. Seeing this, Altman perceived too "that our political, our elected officials . . . are also hard to shake once they get up there. And their speeches are no different than the country-western songs—each new song doesn't really say anything. And that's pretty much how the thing started —the idea of making that comparison."

At least to hear him tell it, Altman primarily let this conception work itself out. For example, Geraldine Chaplin, who plays a British radio reporter tape-recording a documentary about Nashville, wrote much of her own

commentary. All the songs were written and sung for themselves by the more-or-less well-known actors—Karen Black, Henry Gibson, Keith Carradine, a newcomer named Ronee Blakley. The political campaign was conceived and written by the novelist Thomas Hal Phillips, who had helped Altman film "Thieves Like Us" in Mississippi. Even Altman is not entirely sure what the candidate is saying or stands for. When he hired the real-life Howard K. Smith to do a commentary on the filmed campaign, he told Smith to "say whatever you want about this man, because it didn't make any difference to me whether he was for him or against him, or in the middle of the road or how."

Not many who hear Smith's movie commentary will be sure, either, what he thinks of the unseen candidate—and after all, if one thinks back to say, L.B.J. in 1964 or Nixon in 1972, candidates who can't be pinned down, not to mention the commentators who can't pin them, are right in the mainstream of our politics.

•

Altman's method of working has a way of combining reality and fiction. When he needed a well-dressed crowd of supposed political contributors to attend a fund-raising smoker staged in the film, he found it was not easy to get 200 of "the kind of people we wanted" to work at low pay for two days. So in advertisements for men to play in the scene he said he would raffle off to one of them two free trips to Hollywood with a side trip to Disneyland.

"Well, they came in droves," he told me "and those people that showed up are the same ones that would have been there for the real thing." The scene features a striptease; when the shooting was over, one of the volunteer performers stood up and demanded a "big hand" for the actress who had taken off her clothes "because that wasn't easy what she did and, by God, I admire her." So everybody stood and applauded, art and life commingled.

"I try more and more to let the people making the film express their part in it honestly without necessarily knowing what the whole is," Altman said. "In other words, they don't have to know how it's going to come out. It's like working on a mural. Somebody's down at this end working on the horses, and somebody over here is working on the building, and probably the muralist himself is the only one who knows how it's going to go together, and yet he really doesn't know either. But he has an idea."

So in the end, for all the different sensibilities at work on different segments of the mural "Nashville," the whole comes down to Robert Altman's perception of American life. He chose to register that perception by linking the worlds of country music and politics, two vital threads of a culture desperately clinging to the idea of value while vulgarizing almost every particular value. Such a linkage could be exploited in art because it had meaning in life—it is not a melodramatic invention or a contrived world—and left Altman plenty of room for the inclusion of anything that might touch or be touched by that linkage.

Nothing, therefore, needs to be explained, because it exists in a world all too vividly recognizable. Geraldine Chaplin wanders around

Some faces from the "Nashville" crowd (clockwise from left): Barbara Harris, Keith Carradine and Shelley Duvall, Geraldine Chaplin, Lily Tomlin and Michael Murphy

a vast school bus park bubbling ineffectually about its symbolism, but the only thing that really needs to be said about the rows upon rows of buses is what Altman said of the squashed cars in the auto graveyard: "I had no comment to make about them at all. I mean other than the fact that they're there. That's a comment."

But far more is *there* in "Nashville" than merely the American mobility culture, with its autos obsolete and crunchable the day they're sold, its fast-food parlors, plastic motel rooms, take-out orders, transient sex and junk music. This is a culture in which old people are thrown aside as carelessly as Colonel Sanders chicken bones, patriotism and sentimentality salve the hideous wounds of progress, and madmen peer mildly from benign eyes just before they strike. The greatest reward in this world is prime time, the greatest achievement is visibility, the most profound corruption is not that of the con men but that of the conned, who march willingly into their delusions and falsities.

One more scene: A country rock husband-and-wife team are quarreling in their motel room. He suspects, correctly, that she is having an affair. She is sullen, hostile, unyielding. The room is littered with the remains of take-out orders, yesterday's beer cans, clothes dropped anywhere, life lived entirely in the moment. Underneath the stardom, the showbiz glamour, whatever talent there may be, the reality is squalor, betrayal, anger. But a knock on the door brings an offer of television exposure on behalf of the Presidential candidate and the husband and wife revert like puppets to their false, smiling fronts.

"But your movie doesn't condemn this culture," I said to Altman.

"Not at all."

"Only as it condemns itself."

"Yes."

The dark perceptions of "Nashville" are not, moreover, apocalyptic. The vitality of the culture is double-edged; dreariness and vulgarity and falsity affirm life if only by opposing death. In the end there is even an aspiring singer who gets an unexpected chance to go on and makes it big, while the country-music crowd, seen earlier as callous and threatening, joins in a rousing singalong—"You may say I ain't free/But it don't worry me."

These final scenes, confirming both the vitality and the heedlessness of American life, form what Altman

calls "a total negative and a total positive. You come out and you say, 'Jesus Christ, four minutes after the girl's gotten killed, they're out there singing as if nothing happened.' But, on the other hand, you say, 'Wait a minute, aren't those people fantastic? In the face of this disaster, they're going to go on.'"

That is more explanation than "Nashville" gives of itself, or needs. "We're not telling a story," Altman said. "We're showing." ∎

1975 Je 15, II:1:1

GUEST VIEW

EDMUND MORRIS

Does Teddy Roosevelt Really Deserve This?

My first reaction to John Milius's historical epic "The Wind and the Lion" was the same "Tchah!" of mild disapproval with which Candice Bergen, in the movie, views the decapitation of two Arabs. Why get hot under the collar at a film so engagingly ridiculous, so shrewdly aimed at adolescents? The latter were at the Music Hall in force when I attended a recent morning show, and the pop-popping of their bubble-gum soon became indistinguishable from the pop-popping of ammunition on the screen. They giggled at Sean Connery's matchless nostrils, looked on impassively as American soldiers gunned down Moroccans, and applauded when, after what seemed to me at least seven hours, the movie came to an end. Only then, as I watched them trooping happily out into Sixth Avenue sunshine, their heads full of phony history, did I begin to feel uneasy.

Why? After all, Shakespeare messed about with the facts as much as writer-director John Milius does in this movie. But the Bard's distortions are those of a magnifying glass: the essential truth of history looms larger. In "The Wind and the Lion," what looms large is a lie.

Billed as "a spectacular salute to the Bicentennial era," the movie purports to tell the story of a United States armed invasion of Morocco in 1904, and the subsequent rescue of an American citizen who was being held for ransom there. A publicity release states that while some aspects of the screenplay are fictitious, it is "well-grounded in authenticity," and its casting "reflects the respect that Milius has for history."

Well, let's see now. The part of the kidnapped Perdicaris, in real life a bald, fat, sixtyish gentleman, is given to Candice Bergen, who may be prematurely wizened, but is neither bald nor fat, and is by no means a gentleman. Cromwell Varley, the actual Englishman captured with Perdicaris, somehow becomes a pair of imperturbable child actors. Their abductor, Mulay Hamid El Raisuli, Lord of the Riff, Sultan to the Berbers, is played, with a rich Scottish accent, by old 007 himself. Minor parts proceed according to the laws of caricature: Germans wave monocles, American admirals chew cigars, Arab potentates fondle dates, and so on.

• • •

The only part which Milius treats with some "respect" is that of Theodore Roosevelt, the Lion to Raisuli's Wind. Brian Keith does what he can with the role, flashing his teeth to good effect, and even managing to make credible such lines as "Gentlemen, I'd like to be alone with my bear." However, TR comes off, on the whole, much worse for this treatment, since responsibility for the invasion is laid directly at his door.

In fairness to the 26th President, I think it should be said that the invasion, with all its coincidental resemblance to the Magueyez affair, never took place. TR did not order

Brian Keith as TR

a force of Marines ashore; he merely sent a cable demanding "Perdicaris alive or Raisuli dead." This was more to impress the 1904 Republican convention, which was considering his nomination for another term, than Raisuli, who, as TR well knew, had already released Perdicaris anyway. The whole matter was settled diplomatically; not a drop of blood was shed; and the President was triumphantly re-elected.

So much for the historical facts. As long as they are known, "The Wind and the Lion" can be viewed for what it is—a long, noisy, beautifully-photographed piece of nothing in particular. Whether you like it or not depends on how much bubble-gum you chew. For myself, the only reward for sitting through its 119 interminable minutes was a line Candice Bergen shrieks when her son becomes fascinated by one of Raisuli's more grisly trophies: "Get away from that tongue!"

Edmund Morris is currently writing a biography of Theodore Roosevelt.

1975 Je 15, II:17:7

JACQUELINE SUSANN'S ONCE IS NOT ENOUGH, directed by Guy Green; screenplay by Julius J. Epstein, based on the novel by Jacqueline Susann; produced by Howard W. Koch; executive producer, Irving Mansfield; music, Henry Mancini; director of photography, John A. Alonzo; editor, Rita Roland; distributed by Paramount Pictures. Running time: 121 minutes. At Loews Astor Plaza Theater, 44th Street west of Broadway, and Cine Theater, Third Avenue near 86th Street. This film has been rated R.

Mike Wayne.................Kirk Douglas
Deirdre Milford Granger....Alexis Smith
Tom Colt..................David Janssen
David Milford.............George Hamilton
Karla.....................Melina Mercouri
Hugh......................Gary Conway
Linda.....................Brenda Vaccaro
January...................Deborah Raffin
Mabel.....................Lillian Randolph

By VINCENT CANBY

A film review doesn't often involve the reader in the same way that the film involves its audience. One scans the review and that's it. The words stay on the page while the reader goes on to other things. There's been no emotional connection.

With this in mind, I've devised what may well be the world's first audience-participation film review, which, I trust, will approximate the impact of the movie itself. The review is a multiple-choice test, the answers for which will be found at Loews Astor Plaza and Cine Theaters, where the film opened yesterday:

"Jacqueline Susann's Once is Not Enough" is based on the celebrated novel by (Charles Dickens, Olive Higgins Prouty, Cotton Mather, Anaïs Nin, none of these).

It was adapted for the screen by Julius J. Epstein, whose late brother and collaborator was (Philip Epstein, Jacob Epstein, Joseph Epstein, Jason Epstein, Barbara Epstein, all five).

It was directed by a celebrated Englishman whose last name is a color (Redd Foxx, Guy Green, Kid Blue, Shirley Temple Black), the man who earlier gave us the celebrated ("Potemkin," "House of Wax," "House of Secrets," "The Little Colonel").

"Jacqueline Susann's Once Is Not Enough" is about Mike Wayne, played by Kirk Douglas, a down-on-his-luck Hollywood producer of (films, Kentucky Fried Chicken, tie clasps) whose daughter is named January because she was born in (pride, April, a trunk, none of these).

January, who is 19 years old, has an unnatural attachment for her father, a complex sometimes called (wholly natural, boring, kleptomania). When she returns to the States to visit him, she finds New York immersed in (a garbage strike, pollution, immorality, all three). January is shocked by Mike's lavish (life-style, new wife, hair-piece).

Mike has married Deirdre Milford Granger, played by Alexis Smith, for her money because Deirdre is (the fifth richest woman in the world, crazy about chicken, the best he can do), but Deirdre is secretly in love with Karla, played by Melina Mercouri, an elderly actress - recluse who wears a lot of (ouzo, kohl, lashes) around her eyes.

This kind of love is sometimes called (wholly natural, boring, kleptomania) and was once known as the love that (dare not speak its name, launched a thousand ships, was won on the playing fields of Eton).

January, in her turn, makes do with Tom Colt, played by David Janssen, who is (impotent, living at the Plaza, a Pulitzer Prize-winning novelist, all three) and has affection for David Milford, played by George Hamilton, a New York playboy who

(has a perpetual tan, uses hairspray, walks funny).

Like Mr. Hamilton, the movie seems to have been composed of (whole cloth, snips and snails and puppy-dogs' tails, press releases). It is (ludicrous, bad, terrible, horrendous). It's a film that seems to have been made (to warn motorcyclists not to drive fast, under a hair dryer, to make money look boring, to make money, all four).

1975 Je 19, 28:5

JAWS, directed by Steven Spielberg; screenplay by Peter Benchley and Carl Gottlieb, based on the novel by Mr. Benchley; produced by Richard D. Zanuck and David Brown; director of photography, Bill Butler; editor, Verna Fields; music, John Williams; live shark footage, Ron and Valerie Taylor; underwater photography, Rexford Metz; special effects, Robert A. Mattey; distributed by Universal Pictures. Running time: 124 minutes. At the Rivoli Theater, Broadway at 49th Street; Orpheum Theater, 86th Street near Third Avenue, and 34th Street East Theater, near Second Avenue. This film has been rated PG.
Brody .... Roy Scheider
Quint .... Robert Shaw
Hooper .... Richard Dreyfuss
Ellen Brody .... Lorraine Gary
Vaughn .... Murray Hamilton
Meadows .... Carl Gottlieb
Interviewer .... Peter Benchley

By VINCENT CANBY

If you are what you eat, then one of the sharks in "Jaws" is a beer can, half a mackerel and a Louisiana license plate. Another is a pretty young woman, a cylinder of oxygen, a small boy, a scout master and still more. The other characters in the film are nowhere nearly so fully packed.

"Jaws," which opened yesterday at three theaters, is the film version of Peter Benchley's best-selling novel about a man-eating great white shark that terrorizes an East Coast resort community, which now looks very much like Martha's Vineyard, where the film was shot.

It's a noisy, busy movie that has less on its mind than any child on a beach might have. It has been cleverly directed by Steven Spielberg ("Sugarland Express") for maximum shock impact and short-term suspense, and the special effects are so good that even the mechanical sharks are as convincing as the people.

"Jaws" is, at heart, the old standby, a science-fiction film. It opens according to time-honored tradition with a happy-go-lucky innocent being suddenly ravaged by the mad monster, which, in "Jaws," comes from the depths of inner space — the sea as well as man's nightmares. Thereafter "Jaws" follows the formula with fidelity.

Only one person in the community (the chief of police) realizes the true horror of what has happened, while the philistines (the Mayor, the merchants and the tourism people) pooh-pooh his warnings. The monster strikes again. An expert (an oceanographer) is brought in who confirms everyone's wildest fears, at which point the community bands together to hire an eccentric specialist (a shark fisherman) to secure their salvation.

If you think about "Jaws" for more than 45 seconds you will recognize it as nonsense, but it's the sort of nonsense that can be a good deal of fun if you like to have the wits scared out of you at irregular intervals.

It's a measure of how the film operates that not once do we feel particular sympathy for any of the shark's victims, or even the mother of one, a woman who has an embarrassingly tearful scene that at one point threatens to bring the film to a halt. This kind of fiction doesn't inspire humane responses. Just the opposite. We sigh with relief after each attack, smug in our awareness that it happened to them, not us.

In the best films characters are revealed in terms of the action. In movies like "Jaws," characters are simply functions of the action. They're at its service. Characters are like stage hands who move props around and deliver information when it's necessary, which is pretty much what Roy Scheider (the police chief), Robert Shaw (the shark fisherman) and Richard Dreyfuss (the oceanographer) do.

It may not look like much but it puts good actors to the test. They have to work very hard just to appear alive, and Mr. Scheider, Mr. Shaw and Mr. Dreyfuss come across with wit and easy self-assurance.

It's not their fault if they are upstaged by the mechanics of the fiction. That, too, is the way "Jaws" was meant to be. Mr. Spielberg has so effectively spaced out the shocks that by the time we reach the spectacular final confrontation between the three men and the great white shark, we totally accept the makebelieve on its own foolishly entertaining terms.

1975 Je 21, 19:2

FILM VIEW

VINCENT CANBY

Love, Death, God, Sex, Suicide and Woody Allen

"Hope," wrote Emily Dickinson, "is the thing with feathers," though to Woody Allen the thing with feathers is his nephew whom he's going to take to see a specialist in Zurich. But just in case hope really is the thing with feathers, or if enough people believe that hope is the thing with feathers (which could be the same thing), Woody has called his latest collection of notebook entries, parodies, plays and essays (from the early period) "Without Feathers," a title that, in typical Woody Allen fashion, comes up from behind something sacrosanct and puts a brown paper bag over its head.

Feathers are not especially appealing to Woody Allen. Being an urban fellow he must be all too familiar with pigeons, having been caught more than once in the musty whirr of their last-minute take-offs from and premature landings on city sidewalks. If a pigeon is hope, then Woody Allen knows that hopelessness can't be all bad, and is probably a lot more sanitary.

The rhythm of the usual Woody Allen gag is that simple. It was perfected by Bob Hope and Groucho Marx, men whose routines he studied as a boy much as other boys tried to get the knack of a curveball. For variation, Woody reprises the kind of Groucho Marx exchanges in which phrases that polite society uses as if they were bumpers—to get through social intercourse without actually touching—become through repetition and dislocation something like a moment in hell. When in "Love and Death," Woody's newest and grandest film, three characters get all tangled up in a round-robin saying "It's a great honor for me," "It's a great honor for me," we have a glimpse of the sort of awful stalemate that was pretty much the sum and substance

of Sartre's "No Exit." There are times when I suspect that Woody Allen is as wise as Sartre. I know that he is much funnier and can ask the very same questions.

"Love and Death" is the quintessential Woody Allen film-comedy to date, the uproariously unhappy life of Boris Grushenko, the cowardly scion of Russian landowners, a man who fought against Napoleon's invasion of the Motherland and then was sentenced to death for a crime he did not commit. It's not accidental that one of the funniest episodes in the film is the brave way Boris faces the firing squad, having just had the assurance of the Angel of Death, who materialized in his cell, that Napoleon would issue a reprieve. Boris is double-crossed, of course, but how many people do you know who get double-crossed by the Angel of Death? You and I, by friends all the time. Boris is special.

So is Woody Allen and a lot of what makes him special is apparent in "Without Feathers," published by Random House, a collection of 18 pieces, some better than others but all of which contain evidence of the cosmic concerns that separate Woody from the rest of the pack.

● ● ●

Like Bob Hope, Woody has a huge vocabulary of commonplace words that are meant to be automatic laugh-getters. Hope's gag vocabulary includes words like smog, girdle, freeway and the name of whatever President happens to be in the White House at the moment. Woody's includes shorts (men's undershorts), spats, herring, insurance salesman, gravy, plus a lot of other words that have the effect of reducing mankind's thorniest philosophical questions to the terminology of the fellow whose greatest interest in the world is how many miles he gets to the gallon. "There is no question that there is an unseen world," Woody reports

Woody, hiding out in a briefly idle cannon in "Love and Death"

In a piece called "Examining Psychic Phenomena." "The problem is, how far is it from midtown and how late is it open?"

Who but Woody would have the clear-eyed nerve to call a comedy intended for the mass market "Love and Death"? And make no mistake about it, "Love and Death" is about love and death. It's also about God, sex, suicide, the suffering of the human race (equated with a herpes blister), herring, a man who saved string, and the same young woman who appears throughout Woody's oeuvre but who has never been as thoroughly and comically realized as she is by Diane Keaton, who earlier co-starred with Woody in "Play It Again, Sam" and "Sleeper."

In "Love and Death" she is named Sonja and she is the beautiful cousin whom Boris loves for her mind as well as her body. She, as might be expected, has no idea that Boris loves her, being attracted instead to his brother Ivan, though she does like to engage Boris in discussions of things like free will and the existence of God.

There's a Sonja in almost every Woody Allen work. She's the tall, intellectually myopic, incredibly well put-together college girl whose lunatic self-assurance is a terrific aphrodisiac to Woody.

One of the most inspired pieces in "Without Feathers" is a private-eye parody, "The Whore of Mensa," which shows where Woody's fantasies lead him. It's about a call-girl operation specializing in "emotional experiences." "For fifty bucks," the private eye learns, "you could relate without getting close. For a hundred, a girl would lend you her Bartok records, have dinner, and then let you watch while she had an anxiety attack. For one-fifty, you could listen to FM radio with twins . . . ."

•   •   •

I shudder to think of all the graduate papers that will one day be written about the various forms that Sonja has taken throughout Woody's stories and films, as well as about his use of death as a manifest character (in "Love and Death" and the short plays, "Death" and "Death Knocks"), and about his preoccupation with Judeo-Christian mythology.

There is a lot of marvelous material here to be interpreted away to mere typewriter smears, which will be to ignore the most basic appeal of the public Woody Allen character, whether in print or on film.

He's a small, ratty fellow, incurably loud-mouthed, ever teetering on the edge of hopelessness, absolutely fascinated by women, mostly put-upon by everyone, and he's read enough books to want always to place himself in the context of the overall human condition. He's fascinated by knowledge, by its accumulation as much as by anything it may bestow, which doesn't seem to be very promising. Ever.

"Love and Death" is Woody's "War and Peace," a side-splitting spectacle, a tormented, hilarious love story, and a film comedy that is about as personal a work as any American star-writer-director has made since the days of Keaton, Chaplin and Jerry Lewis.

1975 Je 22, II:1:7

X-Rated Film Decadent in a Humdrum Way

By VINCENT CANBY

"Charlotte," Roger Vadim's new French film, is less about decadence than decadent itself in the humdrum way of a cantaloupe that's been around too long and gone bad.

It's essentially soft-core porn but it pretends to have a mind. It's about a supposedly intellectual writer, played by Mr. Vadim, who decides to drop his current project, a book called "Freud, Criminal of Peace," to write a study of a beautiful, well-born young woman named Charlotte, with whom he once had a brief affair and who was later brutally murdered. Among other indignities suffered by the victim, her eyes were gouged out.

There's no mystery about the killer, who is virtually a parody of decadence, a pretty, young, wealthy German fellow whose family connections are so high the police don't want to arrest him. When he first meets the writer at a Paris fashion show, he introduces himself by saying, "I kill time and girls."

Charlotte is played by a Finnish actress named Sirpa Lane, who has the sort of near-perfect figure we have all come to expect to see a lot of in a Vadim film.

Poor Charlotte, of course, is cursed, both by her near-perfect figure and by a brain that is the size of a squirrel's. Through flashbacks we see Charlotte going from bad to worse, with lots of fancy photographic effects, as she is torn between her love for her homosexual husband and the fascination of the sadistic German, who sometimes

The Cast

CHARLOTTE, directed, produced and written (in French with English subtitles) by Roger Vadim; music, Mike Oldfield; director of photography, Pierre William Glenn; editor, Victoria Spiri Mercanton; a Paradoxe/Sedimo/Claude Capra production, released by Gamma III Distribution Company. Running time: 100 minutes. At the Paris Theater, 58th Street west of Fifth Avenue. This film has been rated X.
Charlotte .... Sirpa Lane
Georges .... Roger Vadim
Eric .... Mathieu Carriere
Serge .... Michel Duchaussoy
Elisabeth .... Elisabeth Wiener
Guy .... Alexandre Astruc

uses lipstick and keeps searching for the ultimate experience. If you are at all familiar with fiction of this kind, you know what that means.

Mr. Vadim has never been a great film maker, though none of his earlier films, including "And God Created Woman" and "Les Liaisons Dangereuses," has ever been quite so absurd and facetious as this one. It opened yesterday at the Paris.

1975 Je 23, 33:2

ROLLERBALL, directed and produced by Norman Jewison; screenplay by William Harrison, based on his short story; director of photography, Douglas Slocombe; editor, Antony Gibbs; distributed by United Artists. Running time 123 minutes. At the Ziegfeld Theater, 54th Street near Avenue of the Americas. This film has been rated R.
Jonathan E. ....James Caan
Bartholomew..............John Houseman
Ella.........................Maud Adams
Moonpie......................John Back
Cletus.......................Moses Gunn
Mackie.................Pamela Hensley
Daphne................Barbara Trentham

By VINCENT CANBY

The world of the future that Norman Jewison envisions in "Rollerball" doesn't look much different from the one we know today. At first, anyway. Then we begin to read the images more carefully. Interior decorators favor a lot of white on white, an indication that soot, grime and your ordinary heel marks are things of the past. All women grow up to look like fashion models and then, miraculously, they don't grow another inch.

People spend their leisure time in front of television sets that have four screens—one big screen with three smaller ones at the top—instead of today's functional single screen.

What have Mr. Jewison, his screenwriter and his production designers wrought?

Quite simply, a perfect world, a world of the not-too-distant future in which, after some vaguely remembered "corporate wars," society is governed by a conglomerate of city-state industries. Illness, poverty, hunger, racial animosities, even (you must suppose) nail-biting have been eliminated.

More important, war is no longer known. In its place the corporations sponsor a continuous world series of a sport called Rollerball, which looks like a combination of the kind of roller skating you see in a roller derby, professional wrestling and pinball, and it's supposedly so brutal, vicious and exciting that it works off all aggressions and keeps between two and three billion people glued each week to their multivision TV screens.

All science-fiction can be roughly divided into two types of nightmares. In the first the world has gone through a nuclear holocaust and civilization has reverted to a neo-Stone Age. In the second, of which "Rollerball" is an elaborate and very silly example, all of mankind's problems have been solved but at the terrible price of individual freedom.

"Rollerball," which opened yesterday at the Ziegfeld Theater, is the story of one man's attempt to regain that freedom. He is Jonathan E. (James Caan), a sort of dimwitted, futuristic Private Prewitt, the captain and star of the Houston Rollerball team whose popularity—so think the conglomerate executives — undermines the complacency of the world's citizens. After all, as one executive points out, Rollerball was designed to demonstrate "the futility of individual effort."

•

Because of his huge personal popularity, Jonathan E. is asked to retire. When he refuses, for reasons that are more clear in the program notes than in the film itself, the executives keep changing the rules of the game until, theoretically, it will be possible to murder Jonathan in the course of one of the games.

The only way science-fiction of this sort makes sense is as a comment on the society for which it's intended, and the only way "Rollerball" would have made sense is a satire of our national preoccupation with televised professional sports, particularly weekend football.

Yet "Rollerball" isn't a satire. It's not funny at all and, not being funny, it becomes, instead, frivolous.

It's as if Mr. Jewison, and William Harrison, who wrote the screenplay, really believed that things like war, poverty and disease could be so easily wiped away and that something like Rollerball could be inflated into such an effective soporific. The Romans threw Christians to the lions, but that didn't keep the lower orders quiet for long.

•

Rollerball, as demonstrated in the movie, looks nowhere near as brutal as lion-feeding, or even the Indianapolis 500. Rather, it seems to be as carefully planned as a third-rate pro wrestling match. That, of course, could be one of the points of the film, though I doubt it. Mr. Jewison spends far too much time on the graphic details of the various Rollerball contests to mean for us to find them nothing more than a melodramatic swindle.

The film has two interesting sequences. In the first, which suggests Fellini's imagination, the guests cap a fancy dinner party by going onto the lawn and playing with a hand-sized atomic gun that incinerates whole trees in an instant. In the second, Jonathan E. journeys to Geneva to question Zero, the world's most important computer tended by a sweet, fussy, forgetful old man, who is played by Ralph Richardson in a way that brightens the entire film for a few brief moments.

Everyone else, including Mr. Caan and John Houseman, who plays a leading Houston executive, is more solemn and serious than the movie ever merits.

1975 Je 26, 34:1

THE DROWNING POOL, directed by Stuart Rosenberg; screenplay by Tracy Keenan Wynn, Lorenzo Semple, Jr. and Walter Hill, based on the novel by Ross Macdonald; director of photography, Gordon Willis; film editor, John Howard; music, Michael Small; produced by Lawrence Turman and David Roster. Released by Warner Bros. At Loew's State 2, Broadway and 45th Street, and the Tower East Theater, Third Avenue and 72d Street. Running time: 108 minutes. This film is classified PG.

Harper ....Paul Newman
Iris Devereaux ....Joanne Woodward
Broussard ....Tony Franciosa
Kilbourne ....Murray Hamilton
Mavis Kilbourne ....Gail Strickland
Schuyler Devereaux......Melanie Griffith
Gretchen ....Linda Haynes
Franks ....Richard Jaeckel
Candy ....Paul Koslo
Pat Reavis ....Andy Robinson
Olivia Devereaux ....Coral Browne
James ....Richard Derr
Elaine Reavis........Helena Kallianiotes

By A. H. WEILER

Perhaps Paul Newman, the battered but unflappable private eye of that engrossing 1966 thriller, "Harper," who was created (as Lew Archer) by the acclaimed crime novelist Ross Macdonald, has become tired of red herrings and ill-usage in "The Drowning Pool," which was exposed yesterday at Loews State 2 and Tower East.

Even if he isn't weary, this second time around for Harper is a lackluster work-out despite its colorful settings, occasional tension and a cast that includes Joanne Woodward (Mrs. Newman). As a convoluted caper it generates action rather than character and surface mystery rather than meaning.

•

Under Stuart Rosenberg's muscular but pedestrian direction, the script, adapted from the author's 1950 novel, transports our hero from his native California to present-day New Orleans and its bayou environs. He answers the plea of a former flame (Miss Woodward) to protect her from an anonymous blackmailer and realistic charges of infidelity.

However, before you can say jambalaya, our confused sleuth is being manhandled by rough cops headed by Tony Franciosa and up to his revolver in oddball entanglements. These include Miss Woodward's man-hungry, nymphet daughter (Melanie Griffith); her wealthy mother-in-law (Coral Browne), who's promptly murdered; a blackmailing chauffeur (Andy Robinson), who also is soon dispatched; her homosexual husband (Richard Derr) and a weird, grasping oil baron (Murray Hamilton) surrounded by snarling pit bulldogs and tough flunkies, who will stop at nothing, including the use of that titular drowning pool, to grab the late old lady's potentially oil-rich estate.

Of Course, Mr. Newman's Harper survives beatings, traps and a variety of enticing offers with quips, charm and inherent decency projected in underplayed, workmanlike style. If his performance is not outstanding, it is a shade more convincing than the characterizations of the other principals, who emerge as odd types and not as fully fleshed, persuasive individuals.

•

Miss Woodward is simply an ill-fated, well-dressed, languid, if anguished, deep Southern society woman. Tony Franciosa, complete with corn-pone accent and Manchu mustache, is largely awkward as the top cop who's more than casually attached to her and her sexily errant daughter. Murray Hamilton is roughly flamboyant as the oily but villainous oilman. And bits by Miss Griffith (featured in the current "Night Moves") and Linda Haynes as a naive but helpful hooker, are momentarily captivating.

Unfortunately, the performances and such authentic facets as Cajun talk, bayous, New Orleans and an imposing, white-pillared, antebellum mansion set amid wide lawns and ancient live oaks, serve only to make "The Drowning Pool" a mildly interesting diversion.

1975 Je 26, 34:1

COOLEY HIGH, directed by Michael Schultz; written by Eric Monte; director of photography, Paul Vom Brack; edited by Christopher Holmes; music by Freddie Perren; produced by Steve Krantz; released by American International Pictures. At the Cinerama Theater, Broadway at 47th Street and the 86th Street Twin II Theater, west of Lexington Avenue. Running time: 107 minutes. This film is classified PG.

Peach ....Glynn Turman
Cochise ....Lawrence-Hilton Jacobs
Mr. Mason ....Garrett Morris
Brenda ....Cynthia Davis
Pooter ....Corin Rogers
Willie ....Maurice Leon Havis
Tyrone ....Joseph Carter Wilson

"Cooley High," which opened yesterday at the cinerama and 86th Street Twin II theaters, is the black "American Graffiti," a clear-eyed, funny, loving and deeply touching re-action of adolescent life on Chicago's near North Side in 1964.

Though it parallels "American Graffiti" most closely in offering a joust with the police that sends their patrol car skyward on a forklift and also in providing an epilogue that explains what fate held in store for its principals, "Cooley High" is in its own right a superior film.

•

Impressively written by Eric Monte and directed with an almost unwavering sense of pace by Michael Schultz, "Cooley High" pulsates with the careless exuberance of youth and captivates with characterizations and incidents presented not for the sake of nostalgia but out of the kind of understanding that cherishes and makes peace with the past.

In addition to settings and actions that never shy from the truth, "Cooley High" is blessed with an exceptionally good cast. Performances of genuine merit are turned in by Glynn Turman as Preacher, who reads poetry and history for pleasure, yearns for a career as a Hollywood writer and has the worst grades in two states; by Lawrence-Hilton Jacobs as his suave pal, Cochise, the basketball star; and by Garrett Morris in a brief role as one of their teachers at the Edwin G. Cooley Vocational High School. Cynthia Davis makes an attractive debut as the girl of Preacher's desires.

The catholicity of "Cooley High's" recreations, focusing on Preacher and Cochise as they move among their contemporaries and their families, run from class-cutting excursions, make-out sessions in hallways, joyrides in a stolen car, dice games, a fight at a 25-cent party, hanging out and dancing at the local rib joint, rip-offs of whites and blacks, and a monster-movie matinee that ends in a gang brawl, to the thrill of winning a scholarship, the travails of having siblings, the exquisite joys of first love and the shock and sadness of untimely death.

"Cooley High" is good history, good entertainment and good art.

LAWRENCE VAN GELDER

1975 Je 26, 35:1

BITE THE BULLET, directed and written by Richard Brooks; director of photography, Harry Straeding Jr.; music, Alex North; editor, George Granville; a Persky-Bright/Vista production, distributed by Columbia Pictures. Running time: 131 minutes. At Radio City Music Hall, Avenue of the Americas at 50th Street. This film has been rated PG.

Sam Clayton ....Gene Hackman
Miss Jones ....Candice Bergen
Luke Matthews ....James Coburn
Mister ....Ben Johnson
Norfolk ....Ian Bannen
Carbo ....Jan-Michael Vincent
Mexican ....Mario Arteaga
Reporter ....Robert Donner
Lee Christie ....Robert Hoy
J. B. Parker ....Paul Stewart
Rosie ....Jean Willes

By VINCENT CANBY

Richard Brooks's "Bite the Bullet," which opened yesterday at Radio City Music Hall, is a big, expensive Western that doesn't contain one moment that might be called genuine. In spite of all the care, the money and the hardships that apparently went into its production, the movie looks prefabricated, like something assembled from other people's earlier, better inspirations. It's a collage of characters, events, emotions and bits of business that might have been collected over the years in an alphabeticized file cabinet.

This is a fairly astonishing thing to have to say, considering Mr. Brooks's credits, which include a good, straightforward "In Cold Blood," a Western as slickly entertaining as "The Professionals," and a number of sincerely appreciative if plodding adaptations of works like "The Brothers Karamazov," "Lord Jim" and "Elmer Gantry." "Bite the Bullet" is an original, and it's as hollow as a drain pipe.

It's the story of what is meant to look like a grueling, 700-mile cross-country horse-race some time after the turn of the century, though exactly from where to where, and during what time of year, are never specified. One assumes that the film is intended to be a salute to the courage and endurance of the men who participated in such contests, as well as to the kind of gutsy outdoor fiction it's supposed to represent.

It fails on both levels. Its gutsiness is about as convincing as the ho-ho-ho laughter of the chorus in "The Student Prince," while its dramatization of courage is little more than perfunctory. Even worse is the film's total lack of excitement and suspense, although about three-fourths of the running time is devoted to the race itself.

•

The scenery is often spectacularly beautiful. Among the actors who get in front of it are Gene Hackman, James Coburn, Candice Bergen, Ben Johnson, Ian Bannen and Jan-Michael Vincent, who are some of the contestants in the race. Mr. Vincent plays a brash, gun-toting kid about whom someone says, quite seriously, "A boy looking for a reputation is the most dangerous thing alive."

Mr. Brooks also includes in his screenplay—as his own invention—a fine old Down East tourist joke that has been in the public domain for decades if not a century or two.

It's a small impropriety but it's a temptation that any writer with more talent and less chutzpah would have resisted.

1975 Je 27, 22:1

BENJI, directed and written by Joe Camp; director of photography, Don Reddy; music by Euel Box; edited by Leon Seith; animals owned and trained by Mr. and Mrs. Frank Inn; produced by Mr. Camp; released by Mulberry Square Productions. At the Guild Theater, 33 West 50th Street. Running time: 89 minutes. This film is classified G.

Cindy ....Cynthia Smith
Paul ....Allen Fiuzat
Dr. Chapman...................Peter Breck
Henry ....Christopher Connelly
Mary ....Patsy Garrett
Riley ....Tom Lester
Mitch ....Mark Slade
Lieut. Samuels...............Herb Vigran
Linda ....Deborah Walley

"Benji," which frisked into the Guild Theater yesterday with the boundless cuteness of, say, a "Lassie," is the simple story of a mongrel named Benji who saves a preteen brother and sister from three youthful kidnappers and winds up a member of the children's grateful household. It should be noted that a packed preview audience of youngsters and their parents were not too restless watching these juvenile adventures written, produced and directed by Joe Camp.

Cynophobes are warned, however, that Benji, a diminutive, bright-eyed, brown, shaggy bundle of energy and a veteran of movies and television, notably this "Petticoat Junction," series, dominates his human supporting players. If Benji, like his rudimentary story, is improbable, he's a good deal more lovable than Cynthia Smith and Allen Fiuzat, as the kids who adore him; Patsy Garett, as their understanding housekeeper; Peter Breck, as their father, and Deborah Walley, Tom Lester and Mark Slade, as the somewhat silly, callow kidnappers. A. H. WEILER

1975 Je 27, 25:1

OUR MOVIE COMEDIES ARE NO LAUGHING MATTER

By JOHN SIMON

Is there something new and wonderful happening in American film comedy? Great claims have been made for the year 1975, ushered in with Mel Brooks's "Young Frankenstein," and now celebrating its summer solstice with Woody Allen's "Love and Death." In between, the enthusiasts point a sanguine finger at Blake Edwards's "The Return of the Pink Panther" and Mike Nichols's

John Simon writes on the arts for New York, The New Leader, The Hudson Review and Esquire.

"The Fortune." One swallow, we know, does not make a summer; do four films constitute a bumper year of American movie comedy?

The first thing to strike me about this quartet is that none of the films is truly a comedy. "Love and Death" is a curious olio of nightclub patter, revue sketches and one-liners, most of them quite funny but uneasily stitched together. What comes out resembles a movie only as something midway between a crazy quilt and a potato sack resembles a suit of clothes. Now, there is nothing intrinsically wrong with that: like anything else, film can accommodate a great many forms or lacks of form of a madcap, one-shot, sui generis kind. But there is a grave problem with "Love and Death," hilarious as much of it may be. This

sort of film wears thin too easily; laughter that is largely pointless becomes in the end exhausting. This does not necessarily happen within a single Woody Allen film, which, kept wisely short, can generally squeeze by without our realizing until later that we have been exercising our jaws in a vacuum—that we could have gotten roughly the same effect from laughing gas, sneezing powder or a mutual tickling session with a friendly prankster. As a result, we approach the next Allen film with increased trepidation.

But for the more discriminating viewer a certain, as it were, postcoital depression sets in even earlier: say, midway through the film. It is in the nature of gags not to be all as funny as the best of the lot: a set of perfectly matched jokes is

infinitely harder to come by than a necklace of perfectly matched pearls. To avoid inevitable letdowns, the jokes, however, have a remedy unavailable to pearls. They can be helped by what they are strung on: plot, character, existential implications. These strings, in comedy, should be visible; unlike in necklaces, they have their impact to make. What put "Sleeper" above Allen's other films so far is that it really was about something besides gags—about what was wrong with present-day society revealed in terms of a grimly caricatured but all too plausible future.

In "Love and Death," however, the joke is everything; if it misfires, we promptly begin to wonder what it is that we have been laughing at, anyway. The film starts out as a vague

satire on Russian novels (do we need that?), but soon scatters toward all kinds of targets, from anti-Semitism to Jewish sexuality (or lack of it), from pretentious pseudophilosophical chitchat to village idiots, from take-offs on Ingmar Bergman to attempted plots against Napoleon Bonaparte's life. Overworked and unsupported, the gag begins to sag. "Love and Death," says the title, and we think that the film may work its way up to some comic insights into these two big subjects or, better yet, about how they interrelate. Yet while it boasts gags galore about both, it has nothing much to say about either, let alone about the two of them together.

•

This is particularly saddening because Woody Allen is more than merely funny: at his best, he exhibits a penetrating intelligence—indeed, intellect—well beyond the mental means of our run-of-the-mill farceurs. Such intelligence can uncover, ridicule, and perhaps help laugh out of existence genuine evils, and a little, a very little, of this elixir survives even in the anomic laugh-fest of "Love and Death." But the movie stoops far too often to such things as a facile sight gag about a convention of village idiots which, when you come right down to it, yields laughter that leaves you with a bad taste in the soul.

The other three items in our great comic revival are not really comedies but farces. Now, a farce operates through total exaggeration, which is all right as long as we know what is being exaggerated and why, and as long as we can feel some sense of recognition or relevance at the core of our laughter. In this fundamental respect "Young Frankenstein," modest as its aims are, works best of the three. It is principally a funny send-up of the horror-film genre, first by spelling out absurdities to which most of us have at one time or other paid emotional tribute; and, secondly, by bringing to the surface things latent in the genre that have not dared to become conscious: the intense sexuality masquerading as horror, and the secret double identity of the only superficially monstrous monster as object of our lust as well as of our repressed empathy. I am not saying that a person who laughs loud at the film's jokes must be fully aware of these implications, but I do think that, consciously or unconsciously, the unifying undercurrent of hidden meanings made all

but manifest helps make the laughter steadier and happier.

With "The Return of the Pink Panther" and "The Fortune," we come to the most typical abuses of farce: ways of turning the principal characters into bigger idiots than any audience can conceivably contain. Such movies offer their spectators the edifying experience of feeling superior to the sheer imbecility of the screen personages, and so lets them feel justifiably entrenched in any crassness of their own, which must now look, by comparison, like divine wisdom. In "Panther," there is also a desperate attempt to make all kinds of put-out-to-pasture jokes race again, or to make short-distance jokes run many miles on a soggy track, or simply to make jack-in-the-box gags leap at you out of every nook, cranny, or closet until you become totally slap-unhappy.

Granted, there are tried old formulas that work even here, particularly since Peter Sellers is still a grand jester —as when, sitting at the edge of a swimming pool, he leans backward to follow the form (physical, not technical) of a pretty diver until he himself ends up immersed; or, again, when dapperly crossing a dance floor, he runs into the flying hand of a cavorting young woman, and promptly lands on his back.

But how sorry the more extended, less split-second gags tend to be! I am not even going into the patently poor construction of the movie, which has two half-baked plots that never mesh into a whole: one concerning Christopher Plummer as a master jewel thief trying to get at the bottom of the one theft he did not commit, and another concerning Sellers as the bumbling Inspector Clouseau not really tracking down the stolen diamond but dodging his police chief, sparring with his Chinese butler, or trying to seduce Plummer's glamorous wife.

I *am* talking about the sheer old-hat idiocy of it all. Take the following sequence of shots. Sellers-Clouseau arrives at the Swiss resort where Schell has lured him. He jumps into a taxi and commands the driver to "Follow that car!" The driver promptly leaps out and starts running after Schell's car. The sense of déjà vu worsens as Sellers asks a passer-by whether he knows the way to the Palace Hotel; "Yes," says the man, and walks on. As Sellers arrives at the Palace, he is crossed by the cabbie still chasing after that now emptily returning car—a panting rather than running

Woody Allen: "Pointless and exhausting"

gag, if ever there was one. Stepping into the Palace lobby, after another superannuated gag with a revolving door, Sellers is accosted by a smooth-talking, suitably accented fellow who asks him successively whether he may have his coat, hat, gloves. Sellers suavely obliges, taking him for a hotel employe, only to have the man—a thief — disappear with the surrendered garments.

This is not merely ancient; it also depends, like most of the film's comedy, on stupidity and incompetence. Indeed, the overwhelming majority of the gags and routines in the film depends on Clouseau's or someone else's abject stupidity and incompetence. Yet this is even more disturbing in the case of Mike Nichols's profoundly unsatisfactory and unlikable "The Fortune." Here a petty married crook (Warren Beatty) needs an even pettier but unmarried crook (Jack Nicholson) to marry an heiress (Stockard Channing) for him. The time is the twenties, and Beatty must get her off to California, away from her powerful father, but the Mann Act makes transportation of women across state lines for immoral purposes a dangerous business — hence the marriage of convenience. A rather far-fetched premise, this—by Adrien Joyce (scenarist also of the vastly overrated "Five Easy Pieces" and the impossible-to-underrate "Puzzle of a Downfall Child"), but let that pass.

Having arrived in Los Angeles, both men vie more or less successfully for the heroine's favors until she discovers that they mostly want her money, which she then vows to donate to charity. The men decide that the only solution is to kill her and split the fortune between them. The main part of the film concerns their fumbling and comically foiled efforts to do away with the heiress. Now, funny movies about the queasy subject of unmurderable victims do exist—they go back at least as far as "The Ladykillers." Here, however, the jokes are al. based on the phenomenal dumbness and clumsiness of the three principals, and are not, by and large, funny enough. That is fatal. What gets killed is not the heiress but our sympathy for the characters: if they are that stupid, we begin to feel, they don't deserve to live, and, forthwith, the film has made misanthropists out of its viewers.

Do not make the mistake of assuming that all farce capitalizes on human stupidity. Think back on the great theatrical and cinematic farces, and you will recall that their humor lies in making fun of stupidity only coincidentally, and concentrating on such more amiable human foibles as lechery, eccentricity, mendacity, absent-mindedness, snobbery, laziness and the like, and that the characters amuse us by the outrageous ways in which they outsmart one another. In "The Fortune," all they can do is outstupid one another. Thus the would-be killers are birdbrained enough to think the heiress can drown in a birdbath; she, in turn, clambering out of a closed trunk accidentally washed ashore by the ocean, refuses to believe the police when they later tell her that her husband and lover tried to kill her.

Murderous or suicidal idiocy is not an apt subject for laughter (as outwitted murderous cleverness can be), and Nichols makes his film even sleazier when he allows a nocturnal shot of Beatty and Nicholson slinking away from the beach where Miss Channing may have been drowned by them to take on (in John A. Alonzo's excellent photography) an unearthly loveliness. This sort of dissociation of sensibility is a further demonstration of callousness, of moral tone-deafness. Whether one laughs at these characters out of smug superiority or deadly contempt, the laughter is equally unwholesome and, I repea_, turns against the laugher.

Go and see "The Return of the Pink Panther" and "The Fortune" if you must, go ahead and laugh at them if you can, but do not tell me that they make for an *annus mirabilis* of cinematic comedy. ∎

1975 Je 29, II:1:1

FILM VIEW

VINCENT CANBY

Sci-Fi: From Sports to Sharks

If a man's science-fiction is a measure of his imagination, then "Rollerball" suggests that Norman Jewison's is about the size of a six-pack of beer and a large bag of pretzels. "Rollerball," which Jewison directed and produced, is a pot-bellied Saturday afternoon nightmare about the not-too-distant future—"perhaps sooner than we are able to imagine in today's confusing and uncertain circumstances," say the film's gloomy production notes.

It's set in a world where all physical and material problems have been solved—poverty, genocide, pollution, over-population, hunger, pestilence, housing, garbage disposal—by a cartel of huge, benign corporations that keep the populace in somnambulant order by the sponsorship of what is meant to be a terrifying but fascinating spectator sport called Rollerball.

Rollerball, we are asked to believe by Jewison and William Harrison, who adapted his Esquire short story for the screen, has taken the place of war. It has the same fascination for the citizens of this utopia that professional football and basketball have for a large number of television-oriented Americans today, and that soccer, bull-fighting, cock-fighting, baseball, maybe flea-racing, have for populations elsewhere. The same only more so.

A lot of things, however, keep getting in the way of the film's portentousness, not the least of which is Rollerball itself.

It's possible to get away with vague, cryptic allusions to some vicious new sport in written fiction. It's something else to demonstrate that sport as Jewison tries to do, a task as difficult, and as guaranteed to end in deflation, as trying to convince a film audience that the scenes they see from the fictitious hit play within a film truly are from a hit play. They always look a bit silly, and so does Rollerball, which appears to be about as vicious as the old roller derbies I remember starring Ma Bogash, with a little bit of the sincerity of professional wrestling mixed in, plus a couple of touches taken from the playing of a pinball machine.

But even if one accepts Rollerball as being as fascinating, dangerous, exciting and hypnotic as it's supposed to be, the film raises other questions without providing answers satisfying enough to make us want to suspend our disbelief.

When the film opens, we learn that after some vaguely referred to "corporate wars" of the future, every major city of the world became responsible for a single industry (energy, food, transportation, luxury, etc.) and is represented in the continual worldwide Rollerball competition by its own team. Houston, Texas, the energy city, has the current world champions captained by an eight-year veteran known only as Jonathan E. (James Caan).

Jonathan E. is a combination of Joe Namath, Walt Frazier, Pelé, Knute Rockne and Robert Redford, and he has become so popular with the two to three billion people who watch Rollerball on their multi-vision TV screens every week that the executives of the Houston corporation, with the backing of those of the other major cities, think it time that he retire. After all, the executives reason, Rollerball was promoted to demonstrate "the futility of individual effort." Jonathan E.'s success and terrific popularity are undermining their hold, or so we are asked to believe. "Rollerball" is the story of Jonathan E.'s supposedly heroic fight against the system.

•   •   •

As I watched "Rollerball," I kept having the odd feeling that I was watching a film whose effect—probably unintentional—was not dissimilar to the purpose of Rollerball within the film, that is, to deflect our attention from the real problems of our lives. This isn't escapism. It's muddle-headed romanticism. It's a guilty, boozy reverie that might issue from the brain of a guy who feels he spends too much time on weekend afternoons sitting in front of the television set when he should be out cutting the grass.

Only someone comfortably loaded with beer, secure in the knowledge that there's more in the refrigerator, and not especially worried about the next payment on the car and the house, or even about nuclear war, could so blithely imagine as a nightmare a world in which all the world's real ills have been solved and the big issue is a man's right to be himself. To drink as much beer as he likes. I haven't read Harrison's original story but I would imagine, even from the piety of the Jewison film, that it must have been a satire on the tremendous popularity of televised sports events.

The film contains no hints that it's supposed to be funny except for a brief sequence in which Ralph Richardson turns up as the genial, fussy, completely ineffectual caretaker of Zero, the computer-of-computers in Geneva, where Jonathan E. goes for answers much as ancient Greeks traveled to Delphi. To the old caretaker's embarrassment, Zero, quite literally a pool of memory, balks by going all bubbly and pink.

With the exception of Richardson, none of the actors has much to do except keep a straight face, which is the only thing to be said of both Caan and John Houseman, who plays a dour, villainously paternal Houston executive. There are several very pretty young women in the film, all of whom look alike (perhaps by design) and all of whom are playthings of the system, which sums up the film's attitudes towards women's lib.

"Rollerball" has been R-rated reportedly because of the violence of its Rollerball scenes. Yet if you are like me, and have difficulty in believing that roller derby players are ever half as badly hurt as they pretend to be, this rating may strike you as being unnecessarily prudish.

A much more entertaining and even witty example of science-fiction is "Jaws," Steven Spielberg's film version of Peter Benchley's best-selling novel about the great white shark that, briefly, attempts to eat his way through all the summer residents of the fictional Amity, L. I.

The special effects are astonishingly good and the sharks and shocks carefully calculated to scare the wits out of you when you least expect it. Everyone connected with the film, including actors Roy

Scheider, Robert Shaw and Richard Dreyfuss, appear to have known exactly what this kind of movie is meant to do, and they haven't loaded it with a lot of spurious symbolism. There's a bit of gore now and then but it's Grand Guignol stuff.

1975 Je 29, II:15:7

ESCAPE TO WITCH MOUNTAIN, directed by John Hough; screenplay by Robert Malcolm Young, based on the book by Alexander Key; executive producer, Ron Miller; produced by Jerome Courtland; director of photography, Frank Phillips; music, Johnny Mandel; editor, Robert Stafford; a Walt Disney production, distributed by Buena Vista. Running time: 97 minutes. At the Festival Theater, 57th Street near Fifth Avenue, Fine Arts Theater, 58th Street near Lexington Avenue, RKO 86th Street Twin 2 Theater, 86th Street near Lexington Avenue, and other theaters. This film has been rated G.

Jason .... Eddie Albert
Aristotle Bolt .... Ray Milland
Deranian .... Donald Pleasence
Tia .... Kim Richards
Tony .... Ike Eisenmann
Sheriff Purdy .... Walter Barnes
Mrs. Grindley .... Reta Shaw

By VINCENT CANBY

"Escape to Witch Mountain" is a Walt Disney production for children who will watch absolutely anything that moves. The setting is the spectacular coast around Monterey, Calif., and the story is about two orphans, Tia and Tony, whose extrasensory perceptions make them valuable to rich, eccentric old Aristotle Bolt, who lives in a castle and wants them to dope the stock market and find oil.

The children, played nicely enough by Kim Richards and Ike Eisenmann, spend a good portion of the movie escaping from the greedy adults, including Ray Milland and Donald Pleasence, but it's no contest since the children, at will, can make cars fly, pistols leap and dogs turn on their masters. It's not very scary, but neither is it very exciting.

Eddie Albert plays a crusty, kindly old bachelor who befriends the children and doesn't turn a hair when, at the end, they fly off in their own space ship.

"Escape to Witch Mountain" opened yesterday at theaters around town on a double bill with a reissue of "Cinderella."

1975 Jl 3, 21:1

Vicious 'Bucktown'

BUCKTOWN, directed by Arthur Marks; screenplay by Bob Ellison and Mr. Marks; executive producer, Ric R. Roman; produced by Bernard Schwartz; director of photography, Robert Birchall; editor, George Fosley Jr.; music, Johnny Pate; distributed by American International Pictures. Running time: 94 minutes. At the RKO Penthouse Theater, Broadway at 47th Street, and other theaters. This film has been rated R.

Duke .... Fred Williamson
Aretha .... Pam Grier
Roy .... Thalmus Rasulala
T.J. .... Tony King
Harley .... Bernie Hamilton
Chief Patterson .... Art Lund
Steve .... Tierre Turner

"Bucktown" is really bad. It's a black exploitation film that manages simultaneously to be both silly and vicious, though its two leading performers, Fred Williamson and Pam Grier, display

enough of their own private wit to save the movie from seeming to be quite the mess it is.

The setting is a small, vice-ridden black community apparently incorporated under the name of Bucktown. Its citizens are mostly black. Its Mayor is black, but its white, five-man police force runs things so corruptly and effectively that only Mr. Williamson, who returns home to attend his brother's funeral, can straighten matters out. He imports five black brothers to do the job but they, in turn, become more corrupt than the honkies.

"Bucktown" opened yesterday at the Penthouse and other theaters.

VINCENT CANBY

1975 Jl 3, 21:1

FILM VIEW

VINCENT CANBY

What to See If You Can't Get Into The Hits

Drawing by Bill Plympton

By this time you must already know whether or not you can live another minute without seeing "Nashville," "Love and Death," "The Fortune," "Jaws" and "The Return of The Pink Panther." The chances are this summer that you won't be able to get in to see "Nashville" on your first couple of attempts. There'll be lines and somebody with you will say to-hell-with-it-I'm-not-going-to-stand-in-line-for-any-damn-movie and you'll go next door, or down the highway, and you'll pay good money to see something you've only vaguely heard of. The following is a consumer's guide to nine such films, a couple of which are worth seeing, a couple of which are not at all bad, and the rest of which are to be avoided with varying degrees of resolution if not panic. They are listed in alphabetical order:

"Bite The Bullet," written and directed by Richard Brooks ("The Professionals," "In Cold Blood," "Elmer

Gantry," etc.), is all about horses but it may be the most mechanical picture of the year, a cheerless Western about a 700-mile horse race that takes place in the early 1900's. It's a contest that tries the endurance of the horses, the riders and anyone in the audience who expects that a movie of this sort should have at least one or two seemingly spontaneous, entertaining moments. Dial-A-Joke is more spontaneous. Julia Child putting glaze on a ham is more entertaining. The scenery is sometimes very beautiful —mountains, deserts, plains—and the weather is invariably interesting. The race's contestants are played by Disneyland-like robots cannily designed to make you think they are Gene Hackman, Candice Bergen, James Coburn, Jan-Michael Vincent and Ben Johnson. Don't you believe it.

• • •

"Bucktown" is a foolish, rather nasty black exploitation melodrama. It stars Fred Williamson, the best of the new black superstars, as a Big City fellow who returns home to a place called (and apparently incorporated as) Bucktown to attend the funeral of his blood brother, the owner of a bar-and-grill who has been murdered by the white cops. Bucktown, which is located about halfway between Kansas City and Oz, is so riddled with vice it would make Gomorrah look like Salt Lake City. When Fred tries to clean up the mess by importing some black brothers, the brothers turn out to be just as vicious as the honkies. There may be a point here but it is a very tiny one. Supporting Fred in his anti-litter campaign is Pam Grier, who in her own films ("Coffy," "Foxy Brown," "Sheba Baby") plays the Fred Williamson role. Here she's just a sex object. Did I say "just"?

"Charlotte" is a French movie written and directed by Roger Vadim, who now appears to be the most notable victim of the porn revolution. Unlike Radley Metzger, his American counterpart, Vadim can't make the transition to hard-core pornography after having learned his discipline making stylish soft-core stuff like "And God Created Woman" and "Les Liaisons Dangereuses." "Charlotte" is a very mid-sixties movie about a bored, rich, sexy kid named Charlotte who has tasted every sensation but death, which, as she learns, doesn't serve seconds. Sirpa Lane plays Charlotte and Vadim plays a writer who is investigating Charlotte's premature withdrawal from life. Bunk.

"Cooley High" has been accurately described as a black "American Graffiti," a comedy about growing up resourceful in 1964 in a Chicago whose skyline is dominated by the Hancock Building, which wasn't completed until somewhat later. Derivative material, perhaps, but it is nicely acted by a lot of young black actors, including Glynn Turman and Lawrence-Hilton Jacobs.

"The Drowning Pool" returns Paul Newman to the screen as Harper, the impeccably-tailored, Ross MacDonald private-eye he first played in "Harper" in 1966. It takes place in and around New Orleans and the oil-rich bayou country, which is home for a lot of odd-ball characters played with gusto by Joanne Woodward, Murray Hamilton, Tony Franciosa, Coral Browne, Melanie Griffith and Richard Jaeckel. No need to analyze it, just enjoy it for the intelligent escapism it is.

"Escape to Witch Mountain" is a particularly silly Disney movie about a couple of children whose magical powers stem from their birthplace, which turns out to be another planet. As child actors go, Kim Richards and Ike Eisenmann aren't hard to take, but the movie is an overdose of Novocain. Shrewd parents will arrange to drop their children at the theater and pick them up afterwards.

"French Connection II," a spin-off from Billy Friedkin's "The French Connection," takes Popeye Doyle (Gene Hackman) to Marseilles where the hardhearted, brutally self-assured New York City cop gets his comeuppance, as well as the Mr. Big who escaped at the end of the first film. John Frankenheimer, the director, and Hackman succeed in suggesting all sorts of things about law-enforcement, the drug trade and Americans abroad that attractively flesh out the fairly conventional narrative.

"Jacqueline Susann's Once Is Not Enough" is soft-core porn for those senior citizens who are interested in what it looks like when Melina Mercouri and Alexis Smith make love. That is, to each other. Possibly the title is ironic.

• • •

"Night Moves," directed by Arthur Penn, is, technically speaking, a private-eye melodrama but Penn ("Little Big Man," "Alice's Restaurant," "Bonnie and Clyde," etc.)

is so interested in people and in the places and times they inhabit that "Night Moves" becomes something much more complex than a mere succession of story revelations. Its hero, Harry Moseby, beautifully played by Gene Hackman, is an uptight, failed mess of a California investigator, a man whose wife is cuckolding him and whose entire life is a trail of unresolved situations. The case that Harry takes on at the start of "Night Moves" is a conventional private-eye mystery, but the people in the film aren't conventional, and eventually the people and the plot seem to be out of touch with each other. They aren't really, of course, but that's the only way I can explain the curious feeling of disconnection I felt about a film that is simultaneously fascinating and a little absurd.

1975 Jl 6, II:9:1

Disney Comedy Brews Superhuman Formula

By VINCENT CANBY

"The Strongest Man in the World" is a Walt Disney comedy based on the old magic-formula story that's served the company well through thick ("The Absent-Minded Professor") and thin ("The Computer Wore Tennis Shoes"). The new film, which opened at theaters throughout the city yesterday, is nowhere near as funny as the first but a lot better than the second.

The setting once again is Medfield College, where the students look old enough to be junior executives on Wall Street, and behave like grade-schoolers. This time the magic formula is for a liquid that so fortifies a person that he has superhuman strength. In less time than it takes to tell it, the formula becomes the object of frantic competition between two breakfast-food companies, and the thing that will save the job of Medfield's nutty Dean Higgins, played by the late Joe Flynn.

•

"The Strongest Man in the World" has a lot of cheerful things in it, including a scene in which Dean Higgins must upbraid the school fat boy for always eating in class. "All this bag rattling and cracker crunching has got to stop," says the furious dean, which makes one long for a world in which cracker crunching might be the paramount problem.

Also reassuring are the appearances of Eve Arden and Phil Silvers, as the chiefs of the rival breakfast-food companies whose industrial spy networks recall the worst bungling of the Watergate burglars.

For a film designed for very young children, the movie contains one appalling scene that is meant, I assume, to be funny. When a couple of villains prepare the hero for hypnosis, they use acupuncture. They nail a long pin into the young man's skull, which may or may not give some members of the audience ideas. Vincent McEveety, the director, may not have been on the set that day.

1975 Jl 10, 19:1

The Cast

THE STRONGEST MAN IN THE WORLD, directed by Vincent McEveety; screenplay by Joseph L. McEveety and Herman Groves; produced by Bill Anderson; director of photography, Andrew Jackson; music, Robert L. Brunner; editor, Cotton Warburton; a Walt Disney production, distributed by Buena Vista. Running time: 92 minutes. At the Festival Theater, 57th Street west of Fifth Avenue, Fine Arts Theater, 58th Street west of Lexington Avenue, and RKO 86th Street Twin 2 Theater, 86th Street near Lexington Avenue, and other theaters. This film has been rated G.

Dexter .... Kurt Russell
Dean Higgins .... Joe Flynn
Harriet .... Eve Arden
A. J. Arno .... Cesar Romero
Krinkle .... Phil Silvers
Harry .... Dick Van Patten
Dietz .... Harold Gould
Schuyler .... Michael McGreevey

SHOOT IT: BLACK SHOOT IT: BLUE, written and directed by Dennis McGuire, from the novel "Shoot It" by Paul Tyner; director of photography, Bob Bailin; editors, Norman Gay, Sarah Stein and Bruce Witkin; music, Terry Stockdale; produced by The Shoot It Company; presented by Harbour Properties Associates; released by Levitt-Pickman Film Corporation. Running time: 93 minutes. This film is classified R.

Herbert G. Rucker ......Michael Moriarty
Lamont ....Eric Laneuville
Ring ....Paul Sorvino
Garrity ....Earl Hindman
Stacy ....Linda Scruggs
Buddy ....Bruce Kornbluth
Sal ....Anthony Charnota
Teacher ....Fred Burrell

and

SUPER SPOOK, directed by Anthony Major; screenplay by Ed Dessisso, Leonard Jackson, Bill Jay, Tony King and Anthony Major; based on an original idea by Mr. Major; director of photography, Jim Walker; film editor, Sandy Tung; music by Rheet Taylor; produced by Ed Dessisso; released by Levitt-Pickman Film Corporation; a Syn-Frank Enterprises, Inc., presentation. Both at neighborhood theaters. Running time: 103 minutes. This film is classified R.

Super Spook ....Leonard Jackson
Hi-Yo ....Bill Jay
Sgt. Sandwich ....Tony King
Rev. Ignatius Dooley Tile ......Bob Reed
Bag Woman ....Virginia Fields
Bag Woman Daughter ...Marcella Lowery
Big. D ....Sam McKnight

As disparate approaches to seriousness and clownish crime and punishment, respectively, "Shoot It: Black Shoot It: Blue" and "Super Spook," the double bill that arrived at local houses yesterday, rate high for their cooperative, independent efforts. But if the good intentions of both troupes are obvious, the results are varying disappointments.

•

Call "Super Spook" a good deal less than persuasive as comedy or a lampoon of the black private-eye movie. Filmed in Harlem by a black team headed by Anthony Major, director, these antics are slavishly dedicated to the crack, "If 'Shaft' can't, 'Hammer' won't, the 'Spook' will," delivered by Leonard Jackson, as its fumbling, titular sleuth. He's a good-natured buffoon, as are the others in an athletic cast, including Bill Jay, the lover-bad guy who rips off a numbers bag woman. But their genial, raunchy, muscular capers quickly become as tiringly repetitious as a succession of burlesque skits they seem to resemble.

No comparisons are intended but "Shoot It" is, naturally, stern, often provocative fare. In tackling the cold-blooded killing of a black mugger by a white policeman, director-writer Dennis McGuire, who shot the feature in and around Kansas City, is perhaps too perplexingly involved with racial antagonisms, clashing personalities and a young, black film student who has surreptitiously recorded the crime and ensuing events in a movie to be used in a $1-million suit against the errant policeman.

If the principals and their dialogue are naturalistic, their drives and character are, on occasion, shadowy and unconvincing. Among them are Linda Scruggs, as a rich flower girl who denounces our harried hero after a desultory affair, Eric Laneuville, as his young moviemaker-nemeses, and Paul Sorvino, as the square, white lawyer handling the case for the slain man's widow.

•

However, Michael Moriarty (following such fine roles as those in "Bang the Drum Slowly" and the Tony Award-winning stint in "Find Your Way Home") gives a realistically underplayed performance as the handsome but biased and beleaguered, ill-fated policeman gnawed by rising doubts and guilt. If the somewhat ill-defined causes, effects and points of view tend to flaw "Shoot It," it nevertheless emerges as provocative, if not fully satisfying social melodrama.

A. H. WEILER

1975 Jl 10, 19:1

RACE WITH THE DEVIL, directed by Jack Starrett; screenplay by Wes Bishop and Lee Frost; executive producer, Paul Maslansky; produced by Mr Bishop; director of photography, Robert Jessup; editor, John Link; music, Leonard Rosenmann; distributed by 20th Century-Fox. Running time: 89 minutes. At neighborhood theaters. This film has been rated PG.

Roger ....Peter Fonda
Frank ....Warren Oates
Alice ....Loretta Swit
Kelly ....Lara Parker
Sheriff .................R.G. Armstrong

"Race With the Devil," the title of the film that opened yesterday at neighborhood theaters, tell the whole story more or less.

It starts when a couple of pals, played by Peter Fonda and Warren Oates, partners in a San Antonio motorcycle shop, set out with their wives for a vacation in Aspen, Colo. The first night out, camped off the highway in their $36,000 mobile home, they become the accidental witnesses to a local witches' rite, a human sacrifice. Thereafter "Race With The Devil" turns into a highway chase film as the vacationers try desperately to outdrive if not outwit the witches, who include farmers, policemen, service-station attendants, truck drivers and senior citizens.

This is a ridiculous mishmash of a movie for people who never grew up, which is not so say it's for children. One would think that Mr. Fonda and Mr. Oates had better things to do, but perhaps not. American movie production is in a bad state.

VINCENT CANBY

1975 Jl 10, 19:3

THE WORLD'S YOUNG BALLET, a documentary of international ballet competition, directed by Arkadi Tsineman; script by Pyotr Abolimov, Boris Starshov and Arkadi Tsineman; narration in English by Boris Lvov-Anokhin; camera by Anatoli Kaznin, Mahmud Rafikov and Gleb Chumakov; released by Artkino Pictures, Inc. At the Bijou Theater, 45th Street west of Broadway. Running time: 70 minutes. This film has not been classified.

With: Loipa Arauio, Azari Plisetsky, Peter Schaufus, Maria Duddal-Nielsen, Lyudmila Semenyaka, Natalya Kasatkina, Vladimir Vasiliev, Nina Sorokina, Yuri Vladimirov, Francesca Zumbo, Patrice Bart, Mikhail Baryshnikov, Fukagawa.

"The World's Young Ballet," the Russian documentary that opened at the Bijou yesterday, is a vivid, if black-and-white, illustration of artistry that ignores geographical boundaries. Although this record of the 1969 ballet competition in Moscow's Bolshoi Theater that drew entries from 20 countries is fragmentary, it projects striking impressions of the talent of potential heirs to the golden slippers of even the likes of Rudolf Nureyev and Dame Margot Fonteyn.

If they haven't reached the magnitude of such stars, some appear to be on their way. Mikhail Baryshnikov, who, of course, has since defected and is now with the American Ballet Theater, is eye-catching as a dancer and actor in his award-winning performance in "Vestris." And Japan's Fukagawa seems to be his strong competitor in fluid leaps and turns.

While there is a mere glimpse of Helgi Tomasson, the American entrant now with the New York City Ballet, the film's international cast is ably represented. Ludmila Semenyaka, a petite ballerina from Leningrad, shows versatility in a gold-medal stint in both "Giselle" and in "We," a charming pas de deux in modern, jazz style. France's Francesca Zumbo and Patrice Bart combine difficult Indian, modern and classical idioms in Maurice Bejart's "Bakti." And Cuba's Loipa Araujo and her Russian partner, Azari Plisetsky, delicately glide through the classic, if standard, "Swan Lake" pas de deux.

If the long parade of dancers is a mite confusing, Boris Lvov-Anokhin's American-accented narration is helpful. And a viewer is given some offstage peeks at rehearsals, at the judges including the famed retired prima ballerina Galina Ulanova and such activities as anxious competitors in the wings and a tour of Leningrad's ballet school.

This "Ballet" is, of course, largely for special tastes. But even if Arkadi Tsineman's direction is somewhat disjointed and weighted in favor of the Soviet contingent, his documentation, even in excerpts, is captivating proof of the worldwide wealth of dedicated dancers.

A. H. WEILER

1975 Jl 10, 19:1

CLEOPATRA JONES AND THE CASINO OF GOLD, directed by Chuck Bail; written and produced by William Tennant; based on characters created by Max Julien; director of photography, Alan Hume; editor, Willy Kemplen; music, Dominic Frontiere; a Run Run Shaw/William Tennant production, distributed by Warner Bros. Running time: 96 minutes. At the Criterion Theater, Broadway at 45th Street, Apollo Theater, 125th Street near Eighth Avenue, and 86th Street East Theater, 86th Street near Third Avenue. This film has been rated R.

Cleopatra Jones .... Tamara Dobson
Dragon Lady .... Stella Stevens
Mi Ling .... Tanny
Stanley Nagel .... Norman Fell
Matthew Johnson .... Albert Popwell
Melvin Johnson .... Caro Kenyatta

By VINCENT CANBY

"Cleopatra Jones and the Casino of Gold" is a trashy black exploitation movie, but its six foot two inch star, Tamara Dobson, who plays the title role, forestalls all criticism by coming on like one of nature's androgynous wonders.

No one in his right mind would attempt to criticize a mountain peak, a sunset or hurricane. Miss Dobson is a large, beautiful, overwhelming presence whose real sexuality is denied by her movie role (that of a karate-chopping narcotics agent) and by costumes that seem to have been designed for a female impersonator.

The setting is Hong Kong. The adversary is the Ms. Big of the international drug trade, a lesbian known as Dragon Lady, a character that the irrepressible Stella Stevens plays for something more than the little it's worth.

The film, which opened yesterday at the Criterion, Apollo and 86th Street East Theaters, is a sequel to "Cleopatra Jones," the 1973 film that was defended in some quarters as being an example (though admittedly a fantastic one) of how black brothers and sisters might get together to clean up the hometown neighborhood. In this expansionist nonsense, the hometown neighborhood has been reinterpreted to include a British Crown Colony.

1975 Jl 12, 16:4

KAMOURASKA, directed by Claude Jutra; screenplay (French with English subtitles) by Mr. Jutra and Anne Hebert, based on the novel by Mrs. Hebert; directors of photography, Michel Brault, Francois Protat and Jean-Charles Tremblay; editors, Renee Lichtig, Francois London, Madeleine Guerin and Suzan Kay; music, Maurice LeRoux; produced by Cinepix (Montreal/Paris); distributed by New Line Cinema. Running time: 119 minutes. At the 68th Street Playhouse, Third Avenue at 68th Street. This film has not been rated.

Elisabeth d'Aulnieres ...Genevieve Bujold
Georges Nelson ....Richard Jordan
Antoine Tassy ....Philippe Leotard
Jerome Rolland .... .Marcel Cuvelier
Aurelie ....Suzie Baillargeon
Madame d'Aulinieres .....Huguette Oligny
Madame Tassy ....Camille Bernard

By VINCENT CANBY

Claude Jutra's "Kamouraska," which opened yesterday at the 68th Street Playhouse, is a French-Canadian melodrama that is too fastidious and tasteful in some of its parts to qualify as pulp fiction, but too sentimental and foolish to be tragic or even romantic.

When the film's illicit lovers misbehave to the point of murder, you don't respond to the grandeur of their passion. You think, instead, that they have dangerously short fuses. What's worse, they are careless. No wonder their lives are blown to bits.

The time is the late 19th century, and the setting is rural French Canada. Elisabeth (Genevieve Bujold), a pretty, virginal child of good family, brought up by her widowed mother and maiden aunts, is married off to Antoine Tassy (Philippe Leotard), the young, vigorous lord of Kamouraska, a remote but rich estate that overlooks the St. Lawrence River and even includes some of its islands.

●

The neighbors remark—as neighbors are wont to remark in this kind of movie—that Elisabeth and Antoine make a handsome couple and Elisabeth's first weeks at Kamouraska are blissful. Then, helas, the dream turns into a nightmare.

Antoine has terrible table manners. He slurps his food. He eats with his fingers and never, never uses a napkin. He drinks too much, uses gross language and takes his pleasure from Elisabeth in the thoughtless manner of a live-in rapist. But that's not all. Antoine is also certifiably nuts.

One night, he scrambles out of bed and tearfully confesses his sins as a drunkard and fornicator, all the while banging his head against a mirror that finally shatters. The next day, when Antoine stands mute in the living room, deep in catatonia, his mother is no help to Elisabeth. "All he needs is a little black coffee," she says with confidence — which is where the movie and I began to lose touch with each other.

"Kamouraska" was adapted for the screen by Mr. Jutra, the director (whose "My Uncle Antoine" was shown here in 1972), with Anne Hebert, who wrote the original novel. It's a number of stories awkwardly ellipsed into one—the story of Elisabeth's desperate attempts to get away from Antoine, of her romance with Georges Nelson (Richard Jordan), a moony country doctor, of their various plans to murder Antoine and of Elisabeth's later marriage to a rich, cranky, sick old man who, despite Elisabeth's trial and apparent conviction for complicity in the murder of one husband, depends on her to fetch his life-sustaining medicine.

Mr. Jutra is an able director, and he has a much more than able cast of players, but none of them are able to give emotional urgency to material that depends so heavily on our believing in these characters and sharing their sense of sin and guilt. Perhaps the form of the film, which is fractured into bits of time, works against a convincing, cumulative impact. The flashbacks and flashforwards have the effect of distancing us from the events, which is all right in social comedy but is fatal to this kind of headlong melodrama.

It's not enough that the film looks very good with all its moody landscapes and snowscapes, its fine country houses and its awareness of the seasons. The characters, too, look absolutely right, especially the mad Antoine of Mr. Leotard, who was so fine in Alain Tanner's "The Middle of the World."

Miss Bujold is a skilled, sometimes wonderfully surprising actress, but like Mr. Jordan, who gave an especially good supporting performance in "The Friends of Eddie Coyle," she is pretty much mired in the requirements and conceits of second-rate gothic fiction.

1975 Jl 14, 21:1

Modest Disney Effort on Bill with 'Bambi'

The Cast

THE BEARS AND I, directed by Bernard McEveety; screenplay by John Whedon, based on the book by Robert Franklin Leslie; narration written by Jack Spiers; produced by Winston Hibler; director of photography, Ted D. Landon; music, Buddy Baker; a Walt Disney production, distributed by Buena Vista. Running time: 89 minutes. At the Festival Theater, 57th Street west of Fifth Avenue; Fine Arts Theater, 58th Street west of Lexington Avenue; RKO 86th Street Twin 2 Theater, 86th Street near Lexington Avenue, and other theaters. This film has been rated G.

Bob Leslie ....Patrick Wayne
Chief A-Tas-Ka-Nay ....Chief Dan George
Commissioner Gaines ....Andrew Duggan
Oliver Red Fern ....Michael Ansara
John McCarten ....Robert Pine
Sam Eagle Speaker ....Val DeVargas

By VINCENT CANBY

First things first: "The Bears and I" is not the no-holds-barred story of Goldilocks as told to Gerold Frank.

It's a modest Walt Disney production about a young American Vietnam veteran who goes into the Rockies to find himself, which he does while bringing up three orphaned bear cubs, and settling a territorial dispute between an Indian tribe and the Parks Commission. The film opened yesterday at neighborhood theaters on a double bill with a reissue of Disney's "Bambi."

Patrick Wayne, son of John, plays the Vietnam veteran with the vigor and intelligence of a man who would never mistakenly buy Brand X. He's all-American. Chief Dan George plays the wise old Indian chief much as the late Maria Ouspenskaya used to play wise old maharanees—mostly by moving slowly and seldom changing expression.

The scenery is spectacularly beautiful, and the three bears enormously playful, even when grown up. The scene in the film, quite early on, in which the bears' mother is shot by a hunter, is so discreetly handled that children hardly notice it. However, one pragmatic little boy at the Festival Theater yesterday did notice it, and piped up to ask rather loudly, "Where's their father?"

1975 Jl 17, 21:1

THE HOUND OF THE BASKERVILLES, directed by Sidney Lanfield; screenplay by Ernest Pascal, based on the story by Sir Arthur Conan Doyle; a 20th Century-Fox production; distributed by the Film Group, Inc. At the D. W. Griffith Theater, 59th Street and Second Avenue. Running time: 80 minutes.

Sir Henry Baskerville....Richard Greene
Sherlock Holmes ....Basil Rathbone
Beryl Stapleton ....Wendy Barrie
Dr. Watson ....Nigel Bruce
Dr. James Mortimer.......Lionel Atwill
Barryman ....John Carradine
John Stapleton ....Morton Lowry

and

SHERLOCK JR., directed by Buster Keaton; written by Jean Havez, Joseph Mitchell and Clyde Bruckmann. Produced by Metro Pictures. Distributed by the Film Group, Inc. At the D. W. Griffith Theater, Second Avenue and 59th Street. Running time: 46 minutes. With: Mr. Keaton, Katheryn McGuire, Ward Crane, Joseph Keaton, Horace Morgan, Jane Connelly, Erwin Connelly, Ford West, George Davis, John Patrick and Ruth Holley.

By RICHARD EDER

The first bit in a program of Sherlock Holmes nostalgia at the D. W. Griffith Theater is an old filmed interview with Sir Arthur Conan Doyle. Stout, mustached and affable, the 68-year-old author made it clear what some people had always suspected: it was Watson who invented Holmes. In any case, Sir Arthur was mainly interested in talking about psychic research.

People wanted to know what happened to the generation of young Englishmen who died in World War II, he said. "Are they dissipated into nothing," he inquired, patting his dog, "or are they still the grand fellows we used to know?"

It wasn't Sir Arthur's ghosts that made a success of haunting: it was his stories. "Sherlock Holmes" is on Broadway, tourists still go on forlorn searches up Baker Street, Gene Wilder is filming Holmes's younger brother in London and Lord Olivier will tackle Moriarty this fall.

The centerpiece of the Holmes's film program is the 1939 Darryl F. Zanuck production of "The Hound of the Baskervilles." It isn't a great picture. It isn't even a great mediocre picture, but it is a good mediocre picture, and perhaps they made better mediocre pictures in those days than they do now.

Dartmoor, the funereal setting for "The Hound," may be partly painted backdrop but they roll in enough studio fog to do "Wuthering Heights twice. Basil Rathbone and Nigel Bruce play Holmes and Watson with comic exaggeration. It is a serious kind of comic exaggeration. It lets you watch it. It doesn't spoof itself: it doesn't wink at you and tell you that it's really just as sophisticated as you are and knows it is making a fool of itself down there on the screen.

The hound is just a large ugly dog, but it manages to be quite as frightening as the mechanical floor waxer in a white shark suit that plays the lead in "Jaws," and a lot less gory.

And then there are the phrases. "Mr. Holmes, you're the only man in all England who can help me." "I'm in mortal fear Sir Henry's life will be snuffed out." "They were the footprints of a gigantic Hound." "Watson, keep your eye on that hansom." "That's what I hate about his moor, there's always something strange." And, of course: "Oh Watson, the needle."

It's like the tunes—singable with a life of their own—that pop out of Gilbert and Sullivan.

Some of the audiences leaves after "The Hound," and the usher urges them back to their seats. He's right: the last picture in the program is a 45-minute Buster Keaton classic.

"Sherlock Junior" is not really a Sherlock Holmes picture. It is about a movie projectionist (Keaton) who wants to be a detective, courts a girl, is thrown out after a rival steals her father's watch and lays the blame on him, falls asleep while projecting a picture and dreams himself into the picture. There he becomes Sherlock Holmes, frustrates the scoundrels and wins the girl.

If it's not quite the masterpiece that "The General" or "The Navigator" is, it is still first-rate Keaton. That is, it is both disciplined and wild. The major part of the picture, where in his dream he literally walks down the aisle, climbs into the screen and joins the plot as Holmes, is full of marvelous chases, escapes and battles with exploding billiard balls.

But the quieter bits are even better. For example, he sweeps out the theater and finds in the debris two or three dollar bills that will allow him to buy candy for his girl. The customers return one by one to claim them. One is an old woman who comes up weeping. With agony he yields up the dollar bill to her. She takes it and yields her handkerchief to him.

1975 Jl 22, 23:1

THE APPLE DUMPLING GANG, directed by Norman Tokar; screenplay by Don Tait based on the book by Jack M. Bickham; director of photography, Frank Phillips; edited by Ray de Leuw; music by Buddy Baker; produced by Bill Anderson and Walt Disney Productions; released by Buena Vista Distribution Co., Inc. At the Festival Theater, 57th Street at Fifth Avenue; Fine Arts Theater, 58th Street and Lexington Avenue and the RKO 86th Street Twin 2 Theater, at Lexington Avenue. Running time: 100 minutes. (This film has been classified G).

Russel Donavan ....Bill Bixby
Magnolia Dusty Clydesdale ..Susan Clark
Theodore Ogelvie ....Don Knotts
Amos ....Tim Conway
Col. T. R. Clydesdale ....David Wayne
Frank Stillwell ....Slim Pickens
Bobby Bradley ....Clay O'Brien
Clovis Bradley ....Brad Savage
Celia Bradley ....Stacey Manning

By RICHARD EDER

Walt Disney started by making movies in which animated drawings played the parts of people or animals who stood for people. Later he turned to making movies in which people or animals play the parts of animated drawings.

They bound, they double-take, they simper when moved and quack when angry. Their disasters—crashes, plunges through space, explosions—are weightless.

"The Apple Dumpling Gang," the fourth Disney production to open here this month, is a fair example. It is about a Wild West cardsharp named Donavan who agrees to take delivery of some valuables for a friend, only to find that the valuables are three orphan children.

●

The three children are hellions, of course, and darling to boot. The gambler doesn't boot them, this being Disney Productions: he takes them in with the tough-talking but golden-hearted assistance of a woman stagecoach driver. Adventures occur, including the children's discovery of a giant gold nugget and the efforts of two wildly incompetent bandits to take it away from them.

Donavan, played by Bill Bixby, models his sputtering but doomed resistance to the tide of Disneyish good feeling on Donald Duck. The bandits, Don Knotts and Tim Conway, are clearly Disney skunks. The children are chipmunks except for the youngest, played by Celia Bradley. She is a little blond girl who creeps into Donavan's lap and says such things as "I love you, Mr. Donavan." She is probably Dumbo.

●

It is as cheerful and indistinguishable as rice pudding. It even has the two-and-a-half raisins that a quality-control office somewhere inside Disney Productions seems to allow its pictures. One, for example, when a bandit tries to rope the gambler and gets tangled up in his own noose. "Maybe we can head him off at the pass," he suggests without any conviction. "Mmm-hmm," his partner answers after a long silence.

It will keep the children away from poison ivy, and t will probably amuse them, though at a preview most of the laughing was done by a father whose two daughters sat in amiable silence. It won't hurt them, anyway, though after four Disney pictures in one month it may be necessary to hit them a bit if they show signs of crawling into your lap.

1975 Jl 24, 17:3

'Beyond the Door' . . . Exorcism

By A. H. WEILER

"Beyond the Door," which opened yesterday at the National and Trans-Lux East, reminds us once again that, in some movies, at least, the devil's work is never done. This case, involving a young, pretty San Francisco matron possessed by a demon during a decidedly weird pregnancy, serves only to conjure up a pallid successor to the likes of "Rosemary's Baby" and "The Exorcist," as well as last year's equally imitative "Abby."

As the work of Oliver Hellman who, the distributors report, is making his theatrical feature-film directorial debut with "Beyond the Door," it is more puzzling than shocking. And the script, which the distributors say is based on a true story, could do with some elaboration.

Gynecologists might note that Juliet Mills's gestation is the speediest on record. Not only is her term alarmingly abbreviated but it's also accompanied by other startling changes. There are ominous

sounds and a few furies around to slam doors, open drawers and, above all, to change her into a howling hag with basso voice shouting some raunchy dialogue and with wretching enough to scare the daylights out of her two kids and her terrified, record-producer husband.

For reasons understood only by qualified necromancers, it seems that Richard Johnson, who once was her boy friend and appears to have been killed in an auto accident, had made a pact with evil forces. And it is he who shows up to take a hand

in the exorcism she desperately needs.

Under the circumstances, the bearded Mr. Johnson; Miss Mills, who is levitated during one of her manufactured seizers, and David Colin Jr., as her agitated husband, cannot be faulted for merely acting distraught. An amused moviegoer might agree with the observation of one of the unbilled principals, who says, "How can you be scared of something that doesn't exist?"

1975 Jl 24, 17:4

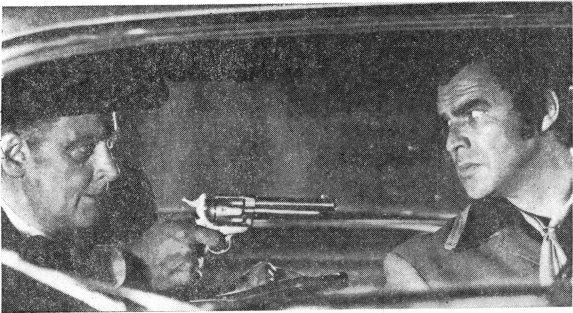

Art Carney, left, and Burt Reynolds

'W. W.' Is Pleasant Summer Surprise

By VINCENT CANBY

Even if you don't think you're ready for another variation on the one about the traveling con artist and the orphan who melts his slush-cold heart, you may find John, G. Avildsen's "W.W. and the Dixie Dancekings" an unexpectedly pleasant surprise. It's a skylarking sort of movie, full of the good humor and naïve optimism with which you start out on an all-day picnic on the hottest day of the year.

"W.W. and the Dixie Dancekings," directed by the man who made the schizophrenic "Joe" and the sentimental "Save the Tiger," is a small-scale, ebullient period (1957) comedy, set in and around Nashville and its country music business, though it has less in common with Robert Altman's epic "Nashville" than with Peter Bogdanovich's folksy "Paper Moon." It opened yesterday at Loews State 2, Loews Tower East and other theaters.

The film, based on an original screenplay by Thomas

The Cast

W.W. AND THE DIXIE DANCEKINGS, directed by John G. Avildsen; screenplay by Thomas Rickman; executive producer, Steve Shagan; produced by Stanley S. Canter; director of photography, Jim Crabe; music, Dave Grusin; distributed by 20th Century-Fox. Running time: 91 minutes. At Loews State 2, Broadway at 45th Street; Loews Tower East, Third Avenue at 72d Street, and other theaters. This film has been rated PG.

W.W. .... Burt Reynolds
Deacon .... Art Carney
Dixie .... Conny Van Dyke
Wayne .... Jerry Reed
Junior .... James Hampton
Butterball .... Richard Hurst
Leroy .... Don Williams
Mel Tillis .... Mel Tillis
Elton Bird .... Sherman Lloyd
Country Bull Jenkins .... Ned Beatty

Rickman, is about a debonaire, somewhat eccentric holdup man named W.W. (Burt Reynolds), about his 1955 black-and-gold Oldsmobile hardtop, one of Oldsmobile's golden anniversary specials, and about the Dixie Dancekings, a third-rate, five-piece, country band he adopts and, through one awkward ploy and another, guides to Grand Ole Opry stardom.

A certain part of this lunge to stardom is financed by W.W. through a series of holdups of S.O.S. gasoline stations, part of the S.O.S. empire owned by a nutty

Nashville fundamentalist named Elton Bird (Sherman Lloyd), who looks upon the robberies as the work of the devil. To stem this wave of sin, Elton calls in an old associate, an equally nutty fundamentalist who goes by the name of Deacon (Art Carney).

One of the charms of the movie is the casual way it seems to discover its story while it wanders from one minor crisis to the next. Mr. Avildsen's manner here is soft sell. It's a tall story, unhurriedly told, which allows the actors, particularly Mr. Reynolds and Mr. Carney, to work some very funny variations on rather conventional roles.

•

The overpublicized Reynolds machismo is apparent all right, but in this film it fails from time to time, as when he attempts to rob "the Southland's first drive-in bank" and succeeds only in wrecking the physical structure.

The film's supporting roles are very well cast, largely, it seems, by Nashville country music personalities who are

unknown to me. These include Conny Van Dyke, who plays Dixie of the Dixie Dancekings, a steely sort of virgin with a heart of gold, and Jerry Reed, who plays one of the Dancekings. Ned Beatty, who appears as Country Bull Jenkins, a country music star, is the only member of the cast who is also in "Nashville" (as the fast-talking lawyer).

Mr. Carney isn't around a lot of the time, but he is very funny when he is, especially in a radio broadcast in which he exhorts the audience to be on the lookout for the devil—the true devil, not a metaphoric one —driving that old black-and-gold 1955 Olds. He reminds his listeners that while the devil can change his shape, Oldsmobiles can't.

1975 Jl 24, 18:1

Rod Steiger Stars as an Irish Assassin

By VINCENT CANBY

A lot of us may have wanted to throw a bomb on occasion but only a few of us have ever set about the task seriously. A bomb thrower is thus different from you and me. Some aspect of his feeling must remain forever mysterious to us, as if he were the sole survivor of an airplane crash. We can speculate on how the wires inside his head are crossed, yet we'll never know for sure.

"Hennessy," which opened yesterday at the Radio City Music Hall, may be aware of this and doesn't speculate much at all about the emotional state of its hero, Hennessy (Rod Steiger), who sets off from Belfast to London to blow up the Queen, the royal family, the members of the British Cabinet, the House of Lords and the House of Commons at the state opening of Parliament.

The movie does give Hennessy a reason to be angry with Britain. He has just seen his wife and daughter accidentally machine-gunned to death by a British soldier during a demonstration against the continued British presence in Northern Ireland. Hennessy has a reason, all right, but reasons and feelings are not what "Hennessy" is all about. It is, instead, a sometimes clever, mostly mechanical suspense melodrama about how Hennessy fails in the nick of time.

The film was directed by Don Sharp ("The Face of Fu Manchu") and written for the screen by John Gay, who did the screenplay for "Sometimes a Great Notion."

Although it is about a political act, it is as carefully apolitical as an aspirin commercial. Hennessy, who, for the convenience of the story, is a demolitions expert, once had connections with the Irish Republican Army, but his plan to fragment Britain's power structure belongs to no one but himself.

Indeed, the movie makes a great point of the fact that as soon as word of the plan gets out, his former

I.R.A. associates are no less intent on stopping him than Scotland Yard. "If he should succeed," says one I.R.A. fellow with no irony whatsoever, "it would set us back 50 years."

Hennessy's assassination plans go along with remarkable ease almost up to the moment of the would-be fatal impact, when he has dressed himself up in the clothes and the identity of a kidnapped M.P. and wired himself with enough explosives to demolish everyone in the Lords chamber.

The suspense of the film

The Cast

HENNESSY, directed by Don Sharp; screenplay by John Gay, based on a story by Richard Johnson; produced by Peter Snell; executive producer, Samuel Z. Arkoff; director of photography, Ernest Steward; editor, Eric Boyd-Perkins; music, John Scott; distributed by American International Pictures. Running time: 103 minutes. At the Radio City Music Hall, Avenue of the Americas at 50th Street. This film has been rated PG.

Hennessy	Rod Steiger
Kate	Lee Remick
Inspector Hollis	Richard Johnson
Commander Rice	Trevor Howard
Williams	Peter Egan
Tobin	Eric Porter

Remembrances of 'B' Movies Past

By WALLACE MARKFIELD

Outcast gunfighters, Hamlet-like shamuses, father-loved boxers and housewives in heat were the key creations of those fine, mean, muscular movies that studio bosses used to lump under the designation of "B" (for Budget). Most critics treated B-movies with freezing contempt, cinéastes rarely gave

Wallace Markfield is a novelist who writes about popular culture.

until this moment has been fairly routine. The concluding sequence, however, is fascinating for the shrewd way in which the fictional footage has been intercut with the newsreel footage, which it perfectly matches. Unless you pay close attention, it does seem as if Elizabeth II looks up from the prepared text of her speech to glower benignly at the interruption caused by the two-footed bomb.

This is the only unique aspect of a movie that is otherwise a harmless time-waster. In addition to Mr. Steiger, who seems to be getting rounder with age, "Hennessy" features—without demonstrating — the talents of Lee Remick, as an I.R.A. widow, and Trevor Howard and Richard Johnson, as Scotland Yard fellows.

1975 Ag 1, 13:1

them a second thought and, to this day, only a few maverick film historians have bothered to discuss these quickie classics, which from the early forties through the

late fifties could always be caught in derelict metropolitan theaters located between penny arcades and tattoo parlors.

The very best of the B's were made on workhouse budgets under coolie conditions by the likes of Val Lewton, André de Toth, Rudolph Mate and Roy Rowland —modest, movie-wise, endlessly inventive craftsmen who would take a hopelessly hack assignment and turn it into 95 fast minutes of sharp detailing, understated performing and hard-nosed truth. They went after action, atmosphere and nervy, offbeat characterization, using their junk material, as the film critic Manny Farber has said, "to capture the unworked-over immediacy of life before it's been cooled down by art."

Right now, as for the last 20-odd years, hundreds of these shoestring miracles continue to show up on television and continue to be put down by daily and weekly guides as "quaint archaisms" or "just so much celluloid." To give readers a fair idea of what they're like and how well they've survived the small screen, I offer here, from TV's inventory of canned goods, 10 of my favorite forgotten B-jobs and a moment or two from each of the ten that has stayed with me for years.

1. "D.O.A." (directed by Rudolph Mate) gives Edmond O'Brien his one right role as a loner-loser dying with

each breath from a slow-acting poison meant for somebody else. He spends his last hours and energies hunting his not-quite murderer, encountering the bad, the worse and the implacably malign in a San Francisco whose benign, placid backgrounds vindictively counterpoint his mounting grief and rage. But "D.O.A." is no "Odd Man Out," no metaphor for the modern world; its power is derived from the central image of one chunky, sweating, absolutely desolated human and from the way it puts the spectator inside that human's skin and nerves. Case in point: the superb three-minute sequence when O'Brien, crazed by the doomful diagnosis he's just received, pounds down the steps of a hospital, yowls like a primate, then cuts and runs and keeps running till he blunders against a newspaper kiosk; along the front of this kiosk and in fat bunches on the counter are copies of Life magazine.

2. "Ramrod" (André de-Toth). In essence, the Western is a ballet with three basic choreographies: The Call-out, the Walk-out and the Shoot-out. "Ramrod," which pits an amiable, unscrupulous cattle baron against an amiable, unscrupulous saddletramp, works exquisite combinations and permutations with all three. Watch, above all, what may be the most quietly ominous and austere gunfight ever filmed: a shot of a man squatting awkwardly by a

stream; a shot of Joel McCrea taking small, stiff-legged steps to come up behind him; a shot of the man glimpsing McCrea's reflection in the stream and realizing death is inescapable; a shot of him trying to grin amiably; a shot of McCrea grinning cruelly back.

3. "The Prowler" (Joseph Losey). Van Heflin is a rogue cop, Evelyn Keyes a prurient, slightly pathetic housewife who makes faces at lawn-loving neighbors. Soon after doing what they like to do, they do what they have to do—murder her husband. But if "The Prowler" is discount "Double Indemnity," it's also a lot more comfortable with American places and objects, with the kind of sneaky, dangerous eroticism good tabloid melodrama needs. (Even in separate cars parked at a jammed freeway rest-stop Keyes and Heflin forge chains of intimate knowledge.) And the finale—Keyes in a $4-motel box suffering labor pains silently while Heflin moans—is as graphic and grueling as a battlefield amputation.

4. "The Gangster" (Gordon Wiles). Daniel Fuchs adapted his own novel, "Low Company," loading the script with lines that turn soda-jerks into small-time Falstaffs. ("Go wash your teeth and take care of your family.") It's a darkly-shot, bitter, poetic movie about people who measure out their lives with coffee spoons in a Coney Island luncheonette. One of these people is the gangster, Shebunka (Barry Sullivan). He has never used or wanted to use guns; as a result,

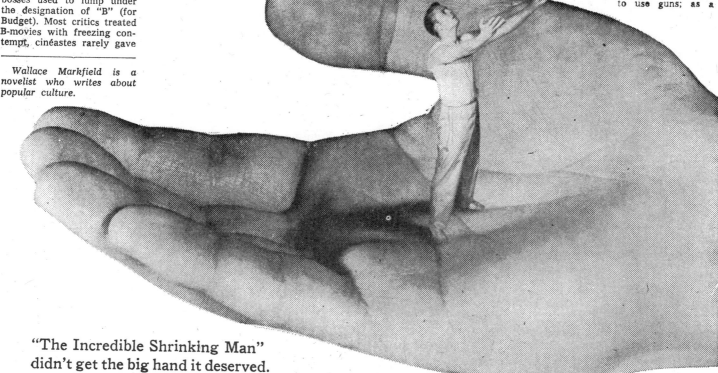

"The Incredible Shrinking Man" didn't get the big hand it deserved.

Culver Pictures

ruthless outsiders can push him easily, disdainfully out of his little empire of bungalow bordellos. ("Who do you know, Shebunka, and what have you got?") At the end he has nothing, not even his insistent self-pity; when gunmen wait off-camera to kill him, he holds out his arms and receives their bullets like a benediction. An immense compassion moves beyond cliché or campiness. I admire and honor as well the funny, forlorn humanity of Akim Tamiroff crooning to his new ice-cream machine and John Ireland looking and looking at his wife in her rump-sprung bathrobe and saying suddenly and mildly, "You know, I never had a good day with you."

5. "He Walked by Night" (Alfred Werker). Using the drainpipes of Los Angeles, Richard Basehart scuttles under the city to steal electronic gear; the stealing is precise and passionless, the thief as colorless as a glass of water. He has no traits, no idiosyncracies and, though we catch his name once, virtually no identity. We never know or care to know what he does and whom he sees

when he's not in the drainpipes, for the real achievement of this movie is in its acute presentation of someone who's managed to make society altogether irrelevant. Forget, therefore, the occasionally intrusive civic-minded narration and concentrate instead on those five minutes of brilliantly visual storytelling as Basehart, wounded, goes, not to a doctor, but to his own room—using his own surgical instruments and magnifying mirrors to remove the bullet himself.

6. "The Leopard Man" (Jacques Tourneur). Thirty-four years after its release, this thriller, about a psychopath who terrorizes a Mexican border town, may still be a bit ahead of its time. There's not a cheap trick in it, not an excessive shot or a single piece of cinematic rhetoric. The camera is logical and lucid, linking an image, an idea, to a character's perceptions, pulse rate, wave length. Thus, in a candlelight procession of hooded, keening penitents, it draws you moment by moment deeper into the guilt-ridden mind of the still-un-

known killer who walks among them. Various directors over the decades have tried aping this effect without even coming close; none, to my knowledge, has had the skill or nerve to take on the nightwalk: A tipsy señorita-swinger leaves the local hangout, heads home through back streets clicking castanets, wobbling on much-too-high heels. She fears her mother's wrath; the fear is magnified, resonated by sight and sound so that every pebble, bird, cloud partakes of abiding evil. Just as she reaches her door, a branch shakes, bends and, as her mother bolts the door against her, springs up. She screams, and her mother, mockingly, screams louder. At the height of her mother's screams, blood leaks under the door.

7. "Killer McCoy" (Roy Rowland). The story veers between ludicrous and lamentable. (Street-kid with sweet left hook; father with bottle problem; mobsters with big bet riding against the kid; trainer saying things like, "Kid, I'm throwing in the towel, the sponge, the stool.") But for once and for the last time, Mickey Rooney gets the chance to use a body as eloquent as Cagney's. You're best off, then, simply feeding on Rooney as he deals his drunken father the most poignant movie-slap ever put on film or parodies a flamenco dancer or relishes a rubdown, a shower, a frankfurter, a kiss. Try, especially, to catch him stroking his girl's hair with 8-ounce boxing gloves and see how long it is before

you find yourself forgetting about the gloves.

8. "Gun Crazy" (Joseph H. Lewis). A carnival marksperson (Peggy Cummins) and a deadeye hick (John Dall) turn Middle America into a pistol range. And while the round-faced apple-cheeked kill-happy kids chase around, we get a looney look at the country entering the fattening fifties. There's no message, really, or if there is one it's delivered by Cummins in a jolting line spoken while she's wandering around a treeless sun-drenched shopping center: "Hey, it hurts me here! Everything in these forty-eight states hurts me!" Yet the line is nearly lost under the blasting of horns, the idiot yells from a nearby fun house. Scene after scene abounds in similar tiny, tossed-away triumphs that are never underscored or overworked. Among these triumphs: a pump-jockey deliberately and with utmost delicacy cutting through the fan-belt of an out-of-state Cadillac; an expensively-dressed matron unloading the contents of a supermarket shopping cart, then the shopping cart, into her car; a pair of object-hungry young marrieds fondling pressure cookers in a department store and shivering orgiastically while a hold-up goes on.

9. "Jeopardy" (John Sturges). For its first 10 or 15 minutes, this one has the look of a low to medium-grade nail-biter. (Barbara Stanwyck and Barry Sullivan make camp between nothing and nowhere; Sullivan is pinned under the pilings of a jetty; and in hours the tide will cover his head.) Director Sturges loves, as a five-year-old cave dweller would and a Hitchcock sometimes does, the banal, beautiful reality of bumper jacks, tow ropes, lug wrenches, crowbars, joists, grapples. He loves, too, exploiting the plain, pure physicality of hard, marred men doing difficult jobs. Ralph Meeker is just such a man, the rescue operation just such a job, and both together wind the movie up like a tight spring; a rough equivalent to the last half hour might be watching the invention of the wheel.

10. "The Incredible Shrinking Man" (Jack Arnold) reduces, by means of special effects that are stamped on the retina, a good-sized, middle-class male into something a little less than the least of earth's creatures. In a way, this might be considered as a merely superb piece of science fiction; in the same way, Kafka's "Penal Colony" might be read as a plea for prison reform. I

'The B's went after action, atmosphere and offbeat characters'

Akim Tamiroff and John Ireland scuffle in "The Gangster."

Culver Pictures

mean that for me, at least, the movie's singularity and strength come from its quiet integrity, its stubborn refusal to rely on gimmickry — though just the battle against the spider or the scaling of the cellar steps or the whiney, peevish voice issuing out of a doll house could have easily carried the highest-priced sci-fi. While I don't know how to overpraise these sequences, I respect

even more that quiet closeup of Grant Williams studying his bed, registering thereby an eternity of sexless nights; that icey complaisance of his brother drawling, "Well, there must be certain . . . domestic problems"; that cheery masochistic mask of his wife's face while she sews and sizes the smallest of coverlets. As for the closing speech, I'll say only that it's worth committing to memo-

ry.

●

Just in case I come across as a cranky atavist or, worse, a nostalgia addict, I hasten to recommend "Murph the Surf" (Marvin Chomsky), a fairly recent release that seems to me to have something very much like the zest and velocity of my old B's. Though "Murph" was generally assigned to second-string critics and allocated two

sticks of type at the foot of most movie pages, I'll probably see it five times more for the sake of watching Don Stroud ignore the unbelievable cleavage of a blue-haired Miami Beach matron in favor of the believable seeded onion roll he is ravening. ■

1975 Ag 3, II:1:1

Rod Steiger seems to be able to assume the identity of the member of Parliament he has kidnapped. The performances match the mock solemnity of the material. The one thing about the film that gives it a little class is the extraordinarily effective, even witty way that the filmmakers have spliced their fictional footage with the newsreel footage. The light and color qualities are so beautifully matched that some wag somewhere is bound to nominate as the year's best supporting actress Queen Elizabeth II. If she doesn't have a percentage of the gross, she should have.

1975 Ag 3, II:11:1

FILM VIEW

VINCENT CANBY

On Being Entertained By Assassinations

If that alleged Central Intelligence Agency plot to assassinate Castro by sending him a gift-wrapped box of cigars had ever been implemented, how would the card have been signed? Simply "A Friend"? And why send Castro cigars at all when he—of all people—might reasonably be expected to have as many as he wants? Why not a Playboy calendar that had been treated with toxic ink? What is the C.I.A. thinking of?

Such are the thoughts that surface in the mind of a movie maniac while watching "Hennessy," this month's first assassination movie. "Hennessy" is one of those melodramas that you more or less tolerate for 90 minutes in order to see how things are set right in the concluding 10 or 15 minutes. It's about a demolitions expert, the title character played by Rod Steiger, a former I.R.A. man who lives in Belfast with his wife and small daughter, having renounced all political causes in favor of family ties.

When his wife and child are accidently machine-gunned to death by an English soldier during a demonstration, Hennessy goes quietly, systematically berserk. He books the first flight to London where he plans to blow up the Queen, the other members of the royal family, the Cabinet, the members of the House of Lords and of the Commons, by attending the state opening of Parliament formally dressed as a bomb in a gray suit.

"Hennessy," directed by Don Sharp, whose earlier films include "The Face of Fu Manchu" and "Bang, Bang, You're Dead," doesn't spend much time trying to convince us that Hennessy would do what he does. That's not the point. The wife and kid are gotten out of the way almost immediately, without distracting sentiment, and we are pretty much forced to accept Hennessy for what the film says he is. Nor does the movie want to get involved in anything as sticky as the political problems of Northern Ireland. The major part of the film is a contest between Scotland Yard and the Irish Republican Army people to see who can stop Hennessy first. Should Hennessy succeed in destroying what someone has described as "the whole power structure of the nation," one I.R.A. man says with no sense of irony whatsoever, "It will set us back 50 years."

Like "The Day of The Jackal" and "The Day of The Dolphin," "Hennessy" may be more accurately designated as a non-assassination movie. It's about the attempt to murder a real-life political figure, who we know never was assassinated. Thus we don't have to worry about whether or not the assassination is going to succeed, only about how it's going to fail. This has the effect of relieving us of any guilt we might feel about enjoying suspense at the possible expense of someone's life.

Assassination, however, remains a questionable,

slightly tawdry theme for an entertainment movie. At least in this time and place, for anyone who has lived through the nineteen-sixties. All of us have so many strong feelings about, and associations with, the assassinations of the Kennedy brothers, Martin Luther King, and the attempt on the life of Governor Wallace, that the moviemaker doesn't have to have much going for him in the way of talent to evoke our feelings. We're programed to respond, whether the movie deserves it or not, much as an atavistic fear of sharks has turned "Jaws" into a box-office sensation even in those communities where the most fearsome creature of the deep is a mud-puppy.

"Hennessy" exploits our feelings about assassination but it does so, I think, harmlessly. There was some small crisis of sorts in England when a major theater circuit refused to book the film, ostensibly on the grounds that the use of actual newsreel footage of the Queen opening Parliament might con some people into thinking she'd participated in a fictional venture.

There was also the fear that the movie might give ideas to some potential assassin. That probably will always be a problem with films that portray any kind of anti-social behavior whatsoever. Do assassins get their inspiration from assassination movies? Maybe. But chances are that any person who is going to become an assassin will succeed in becoming one even if brought up on a diet of nothing but Walt Disney films.

Perhaps somewhat more problematical than these movies about the aborted assassinations of the Queen, of General de Gaulle ("Jackal") and of former President Nixon ("Dolphin"), are films like "The Parallax View" and "Executive Action," which solemnly suggest the existence of assassination conspiracies, which is certainly a subject we should all think about, though they only grab our attention by graphically showing us assassinations successfully carried out. I suspect that they appeal to our blood lust more than they do to our intellect.

The only recent film that has touched on the subject of assassination with some intelligence, completely without exploitation, is Robert Altman's "Nashville," which, of course, is not really about assassination at all. "Nashville," an impressionistic, panoramic movie, makes no attempt to go inside the head of its deranged killer. We never know why the young man decides at the last minute to switch targets from the Replacement Party Presidential candidate to the country music star. We must fill in the gaps with our own speculation, based on the conviction that it's just outrageous and pointless enough, given the system of values, to be something that might happen.

"Hennessy" is another matter entirely. It's a conventional suspense melodrama exclusively concerned with the how, supported by a perfunctory why. A lot of the details of the how strain belief, such as the easy way

ONE OF OUR DINOSAURS IS MISSING, directed by Robert Stevenson; screenplay by Bill Walsh, based on the novel "The Great Dinosaur Robbery" by David Forrest; film editor, Peter Boita; director of photography, Paul Beeson; music, Ron Goodwin; produced by Bill Walsh; released by Buena Vista Distribution Co., Inc.; a Walt Disney Production. At the Festival Theater, Fifth Avenue at 57th Street; the Fine Arts Theater, 58th Street between Park and Lexington Avenues and the 86th Street Twin II Theater, west of Lexington Avenue. Running time: 97 minutes. This film is classified G.

Hnup Wan........................Peter Ustinov
Hettie..........................Helen Hayes
Quon...........................Clive Revill
Lord Southmere..............Derek Nimmo
Emily..........................Joan Simms
Fan Choy....................Bernard Bresslaw
Susan.......................Natasha Payne
Superintendent Grubs.......Roy Kinnear

Near the start of "One of Our Dinosaurs Is Missing" Derek Nimmo, an Englishman smuggling a secret formula out of China, is carried to the Tibetan border by an Abominable Snowman and dumped. "Thanks for the lift, old boy," he says.

It is hard to say whether this is funny in some absolute sense or only seems so because the rest of this Walt Disney picture—the fifth new one since the beginning of July, giving new meaning to the notion of a long hot summer—is so bleak.

●

Mr. Nimmo arrives in London and is pursued and captured by a Chinese agent, played by Peter Ustinov, and his gang. They are made up to look like men made up to look Chinese. Against this crew is ranged Mr. Nimmo's old Nanny—Helen Hayes—who recognizes him when he is hiding the formula in the neckbone of a dinosaur in the Natural History Museum.

Miss Hayes enlists the entire South Kensington nanny squad to help her, and the picture is full of stratagems, chases and battles as nannies and Chinese struggle for the formula and for Mr. Nimmo. At one point the nannies wrest the dinosaur from Mr. Ustinov's men and race it around the countryside in a red steam truck.

The plot is neither particularly good nor particularly bad. What makes the picture so bad is the mechani-

Helen Hayes and Peter Ustinov

cal and unbelieving way in which Mr. Ustinov, Miss Hayes and their troops grind it out. Slapstick whimsey demands real belief by its performers. The swindle this picture inflicts on the children who will go to see it is precisely that of some bored magician at a birthday party who doesn't bother to wear a clean shirt or prevent the cards from showing up his sleeve.

•

There was a time when the name Walt Disney promised much more and fulfilled at least some of the promise. So did the names Helen Hayes and Peter Ustinov.

The substance described in the formula, incidentally, is Won-Ton soup. As is the movie.

RICHARD EDER

1975 Ag 7, 39:1

KING LEAR, directed by Grigory Kozintsev; written by William Shakespeare; screen version written by Mr. Kozintsev; (Russian with English subtitles); Russian translation by Boris Pasternak; photography, Jonas Gricius; music, Dmitri Shostakovich; a Lenfilm Production; released in the United States by Artkino Pictures, Inc. At the Bijou Theater, 45th Street west of Broadway. Running time: 136 minutes. This film has not been classified.

King Lear	Yuri Jarver
Goneril	Elsa Radzins
Regan	Galina Volchek
Cordelia	Valentina Shendrikova
Fool	Otar Dal
Earl of Gloucester	Kiril Sebris
Edgar	Leonid Merzin
Edmund	Regimantas Adomaitis
Earl of Kent	Victor Emelyanov

By RICHARD EDER

When Shakespeare is put into the mouths of Russian actors, and when his scenes are cast on Russian landscapes, the effect is like hearing a familiar piece of music played by deeper-pitched, less wieldy instruments.

But if it is done well and with consistency, it can be a triumph. Five years after it was made, people here can see a Russian film version of King Lear that is close to triumphant. It has some extraordinary revelations as well as an occasional excessively operatic overtone, and mainly it is a "Lear" of freshness, tenderness and great momentum.

•

Shakespeare is somewhat bigger than the English language. The Germans have found things in him that the English tradition has not; so have the French, the Scandinavians, even the Italians.

There is no conceivable whole "Lear." Any particular English production will lose or shadow some things; any foreign version will lose even more — the language, obviously, first of all.

But the Russian—in this version by the late director Grigory Kozintsev, who also made a filmed Hamlet—can supply its own strengths. The Russian language, one would think, would be a problem, and certainly the flickering and sometimes badly synchronized English subtitles are a nuisance.

Yet, take the scene where Lear asks Cordelia what she can say about her love for him, after the sonorous speeches of her sisters. Valentina Shendrikova, a broad-faced young actress with the look of a suffering child, pushes out the three dry Russian syllables, each one seeming to constrict her more:

"Nichevo."

After that, "Nothing, my Lord" will never again seem quite adequate.

•

The Russian tradition allows a man to give a more physical expression to passions—it allows the women less—than would be credible on the English stage. So, for example, when Kent is banished for interceding for Cordelia, Yuri Jarvet as Lear can literally spit in his face. When the destroyed Lear is reunited with Cordelia he can lift a tear from her cheek and wet his lips with it. The gestures are stunning: in an English or American version they would not work.

Conversely, in the full mad scenes, the Russian style is excessive. Mr. Kozintsev is badly served by Shostakovich's musical accompaniment. A lamenting Russian chorus is just what isn't needed in the last collapsing act.

Mr. Kozintsev's Lear is less complex than the filmed version made at about the same time by Peter Brook. It may be less stimulating: I haven't seen the Brook. But it has its own strengths.

The main one is the Russian's decision to build the film around the image of wandering. He makes a Lear of journeys: the high-spirited, arrogant sally of Lear and his entourage to what he assumes will be a proper welcome at the castle of Goneril, his oldest daughter; the angry, near-desperate journey to Regan; his broken, mad wanderings afoot; the search of blinded Gloucester for a cliff to leap from.

•

Weariness is something concrete for Kozintsev: He films mud and bruised feet in the endless bleakness of the Russian landscape. He films homelessness, and makes this, quite as much as ingratitude, Lear's goad. When Lear lays his head upon stones to rest, the stones are cold.

Mr. Kozintsev also brings in the people—at times, in fact, he drags them in by their heels. When Lear is brought to shelter in a hovel it is full of homeless peasants. It suddenly strikes him that when it rains, poor people get wet: The force of that discovery is its own social comment. When Lear wanders, declaiming to Gloucester, dozens of poor people wander with them. The battle scenes are preceded or followed by hundreds of refugees struggling along with bundles and handcarts. And at the end, after all the death and destruction, the poor douse the embers with water and raise the charred beams.

The point: After all the problems of the high-born it is the common people who pay—and survive. It doesn't help much. It doesn't hurt much, either. It is a mannerism laid on; the equivalent of some of the super-Freudian trimmings that for a while were tacked onto Hamlet.

Yuri Jarvet, a thin, sweet-faced man, plays Lear as a vain intellectual in love with his own schemes, such as the one to divide his property according to his daughters' love. Mr. Jarvet's fall is not a grand one, but what he lacks in grandeur he makes up in pain. Even a vain man can suffer: he makes the suffering so moving that it is the motor of the whole film.

Of the others, apart from Cordelia, the most stirring performance is given by Victor Emelyanov as Kent. It is a coincidence that, playing the part of a man whose integrity and refusal to bow to authority lead him to exile, he should have such a pronounced physical resemblance to Aleksandr I. Solzhenitsyn.

1975 Ag 7, 39:3

BROTHER, CAN YOU SPARE A DIME?, a documentary directed and written by Phillipe Mora; produced by Sandy Lieberson and David Puttnam; a Dimension Pictures Release. At the Plaza Theater, 58th Street east of Madison Avenue. Running time: 103 minutes. This film is classified PG.

By RICHARD EDER

The evils of the present, so the theory goes, are caused by everything that happened in the past. Everything—not just the obviously bad things—is guilty. If the grass hadn't been so green, the sun so bright, the daisies so proud, Genghis Khan's grandmother might have said no.

Therefore, the green of the grass was really verdigris. The sun caused cancer. The daisies were hairy bullies of the meeker vegetable forms.

This may be a wretched view of history, but it allows for some pretty fashionable movie making. For example, it more or less links up the dizzying, sometimes brilliant disarray of film clips that make up "Brother, Can You Spare a Dime?," a documentary about the nineteen-thirties that opened Wednesday at the Plaza.

•

An old clip shows a pyramid of paper securities collapsing, and the great crash is on. The movie continues, drawing on documentaries, Hollywood pictures, stills and even home movies, to show dozens of disparate things as if they were all part of the same thing. There are malefic capitalists, strike-breaker gangs, a Communist orator, the Dust Bowl, Billie Holiday, Hollywood lushness, Dil-

A scene from "Brother, Can You Spare a Dime?"

linger's corpse, bread lines, Roosevelt and jitterbug contests.

The message follows in an epilogue. In quick succession we see Hiroshima, lunar landings, Johnson, Nixon, Ford, each displayed for the booing. Then the collapsing Wall Street pyramid reappears, this time in color.

Those jitterbuggers — they look pretty good, in fact — those skyscrapers, those beauty queens and rich folks' parties, Roosevelt fishing and the Kennedy boys leaving for Britain at the start of World War II: All are precursors of what the film takes for granted is our present rottenness and imminent collapse.

There is nothing wrong with asserting both of these sad things. But the movie doesn't assert. It signals, it uses shorthand—is 10 seconds of Nixon really equivalent to two chapters of the Book of Jeremiah?—it winks and cross-cuts us into belief. A Rolls-Royce, followed by a shot of a woman who can't afford to buy meat, followed by wild dancing. A Hollywood version of a Ku Klux Klan oath-taking followed by a clip of Buffalo Bill having a group of youngsters recite the Oath of Allegiance.

●

Propaganda films are a game that any number can play. The pity is that the techniques used by Philippe Mora — a French-born Australian, now living in Britain, who previously did film compilations on the Nazis' Germany — cheapen and sometimes frustrate his material.

And much of the material is magnificent. Furthermore, movies being what they are, it is possible to be moved and illuminated by the good things in "Brother" even while wishing that Mr. Mora would go for cofee. It is like touring a first-rate museum with a frequently—not invariably—insufferable guide.

The best things in "Brother" are the materials taken from documentaries, some not previously shown. Set beside these—and Mr. Mora does so frequently—the portions of Hollywood movies on the same subject seem farcial and unreal.

A fictional scene of hoboes riding the rails, good enough in itself, shrivels · when followed by an extraordinary newsreel clip of a state trooper telling a group of hoboes with some pity and shame that they will have to turn back.

●

There is a beautiful long sequence showing armed strike-breakers moving into steel pickets, first gently and tentatively, then with growing violence. There is an extraordinary, previously unshown jail interview with Giuseppe Zangara after his attempt to shoot Roosevelt.

●

There is another precious rarity: Billie Holiday, young

and in a plain black dress, singing a shivering version of "Jealousy Blues."

Perhaps the best sustained subject in the movie is the periodic reappearace of Roosevelt. The later Roosevelt, old, distinguished and foxy, is familiar enough, perhaps. To many people the clips showing him as a still youthful, still vigorous campaigner for his first term will be a revelation of just how rousing a man he could be, and why many of our fathers and grandfathers loved him in a way no American President has been loved since.

1975 Ag 8, 10:2

THE DEVIL'S RAIN, directed by Robert Fuest; written by Gabe Essoe, James Ashton and Gerald Hopman; director of photography, Alex Phillips Jr.; film editor, Michael Kahn; music, Al De Lory; produced by James V. Cullem and Michael S. Glick; released by Bryanston Distributors, Inc. Running time; 85 minutes. At Loews State II, Broadway and 45th Street, Loews Tower East Theater, Third Avenue and 72d Street and neighborhood theaters. This film is classified PG.
Corbis .... Ernest Borgnine
Dr. Richards .... Eddie Albert
Mrs. Preston .... Ida Lupino
Mark Preston .... William Shatner
Sheriff Owens .... Keenan Wynn
Tom Preston .... Tom Skerritt
Julie Preston .... Joan Prather

At the start of "The Devil's Rain," which opened yesterday at the Loews State II, Tower East and neighborhood theaters, the titles flash against a Hieronymus Bosch backdrop, and a muffled wailing is heard. "Let me out," voices cry. "Let me out." ↘

By the time this latest satanism epic ends, it is clear that the wailing is a bit of auditory ectoplasm. It is the accumulated sufferings of the audience at the previous showing that are giving tongue. "The Devil's Rain" is ostensibly a horror film, but it barely manages to be a horror.

●

The quality of writing, acting and direction give a general and routine witlessness to this movie about a devil-priest and his congregation of eyeless zombies taking revenge against a family whose forebears did them wrong some 300 years earlier.

In addition, though, it has a particular and specialized witlessness that, because it occurs in various other fright pictures around, deserves mention. The film is built upon—and collapses from—the contradiction between two crafts: camera work and special effects.

The special gimmick of "The Devil's Rain," its main attempted horror, is the physical transformation of the victim family as its members are captured and turned one by one into zombies. Their eyes are replaced by black holes, their flesh melts and runs at the slightest irritation, and when they are shot, orange and blue glue spurts out.

But the photography — its

sharp, precise color, meticulous focus, fine grain and zooming close-ups — sabotages the effects. The weave of the black cloth used to blot out the eyes shows up clearly. The stuff leaking from the bodies is foamily chemical. And when the coven is destroyed and the zombies and their master melt away, the interminable lingering of the camera on their dissolving faces only manages to make it evident that we are seeing wax or latex. It is as horrible as watching an egg fry.

If we are returning to the catchup school of scary movies, we would be better off with the grainy, black-and-white, underlit movies they used to make. That way we could imagine that the catchup was blood and the exposed brain something more than putty. The camera's lint-picking would not undermine things.

There isn't much else to say about "The Devil's Rain." Evil, as usual in Satan films, wins. Ernest Borgnine, whose mugging seems to have developed a minor camp cult —to judge from the authoritative giggling among part of the audience—plays the devil-priest. When his face is whooshed into the features of a satan-ram, you can hardly tell the difference.

Keenan Wynn, Eddie Albert and Ida Lupino also appear, with and without eyes.

●

At several of the same neighborhood theaters, a second film, "Dark Star," is be-shown. The Bryanston Film people, who are releasing it, had some trouble discovering just where but finally reported that it could be found as far south as 125th Street and as far north as Delancey Street. It will be seen and noted shortly. RICHARD EDER

1975 Ag 8, 11:1

SUPERVIXENS, directed, written, produced, photographed and edited by Russ Meyer; executive producer, A. James Ryan; music, William Loose; distributed by RM Films International, Inc. Running time: 106 minutes. At the Embassy Theater, Broadway at 47th Street, and other theaters. This film has been rated X.
Superangel
Supervixen .... Shari Eubank
Harry Sledge .... Charles Napier
Supersoul .... Uschi Digard
Clint Ramsey .... Charles Pitts
Martin Bormann .... Henry Rowland
Superlorna .... Christy Hartburg
Supercherry ..., ... Sharon Kelly

By VINCENT CANBY
The sexual revolution hasn't exactly rendered Russ Meyer obsolete, but since all restrictions have been removed from the manufacture of dirty movies, Mr. Meyer doesn't have much to tease us with any more. Mr. Meyer is the soft-core porn king of the nineteen-sixties who first hit the big money in the late fifties with "The Immoral Mr. Teas," about a wretchedly shy fellow who could see through women's clothing.

In his subsequent films, particularly "Lorna" and "Vixen," Mr. Meyer emphasized souped-up simulated sex and violence, with a preference for actresses whose breasts were so big they looked sore. He always went as far as the law allowed, and with such manic, idiosyncratic enthusiasm that he became something of a cult hero on campuses.

●

Although the law allows him to go much farther now, he doesn't. Maybe he simply isn't interested. The result is that "Supervixens," his latest film, looks sort of ritualistic, sort of perfunctory, made up of actions whose original meaning and purpose have been forgotten. It's full of the old Meyer preoccupations — insatiable women, impotent men, lonely desert landscapes in which the promise of sex is the only reliable compass. Yet something has been lost. Could it be innocence?

1975 Ag 9, 9:1

FILM VIEW
RICHARD EDER

Of Walt Disney, Russ Meyer And King Lear

There were times during these past hot weeks when it seemed that the main social usefulness of New York's movie theaters was to blow cool air out onto the sidewalks. If garbage is piling up on the streets, it's also piling up at the movies. The distributors must be cleaning out their basements.

This part of the summer has always been the dog-days, as far as releasing new movies goes. This year they come with an exceptionally thick cloud of fleas. A rash of Disney films, a rash of horror films, Russ Meyer adding, in "Super Vixens," another layer onto his monument to the female breast. Are these really movies? Do they have a human audience in mind? Are they talking to anyone?

They are, in fact, industrial films. Using a kind of portion-control, they administer their message—for the children industry, the horror industry, the sex industry—and stop. They have the approximate relation to real movies that an airplane pilot's take-off message has to real conversation.

●   ●   ●

Walt Disney Productions turns out such an enormous number of films that it would take a computer to plot their general trend, if any. The two most recently released —"The Apple Dumpling Gang" and "One of Our Dinosaurs is Missing"—are both examples of artificial delightfulness, relentlessly hammered in. Wielding a whimsy of iron, they marshal their young audiences through a fake meal of dishes labeled humor, sentiment, fantasy and suspense, each containing a little pink water. It would be like a children's tea party except that it's Walt Disney Productions that is doing the pretending, not the children.

Of the two, "Apple Dumpling Gang" is a little better

because it takes place outdoors, in the Far West, and horses are always nice to see in a movie. "Dinosaurs" is claustrophobic: one keeps watching Helen Hayes as a nanny archangel, and Peter Ustinov as a Chinese archfiend. Both succeed halfway: they are arch.

The Walt Disney pictures pretend to be good and aren't. The new horror films are a more contemporary kind of rip-off: they assert their badness and since you

have paid $3 or so to be there, you might as well get in on the joke so as not to look dumb.

In "The Devil's Rain," a bunch of goo-leaking zombies led by a Satanic minister takes over a family, and the horror effects—mostly dripping wax—seem almost deliberately bad. The dialogue is so awful that the audience laughs, in a we're-all-of-us-in-this-together-so-let's-enjoy-it way. It's a fraud. Only the members of the audience are in it together. The producer is somewhere else, counting his money.

In such famine conditions the Russians have come through with the movie equivalent of a shipload of wheat. Grigor Kosintsev's "King Lear" is straightforward, very beautiful and rather old-fashioned.

With Russian movies, straightforward and beautiful works are to be regarded warily. They tend to be elephantine and static like the furniture in some of the better Soviet hotels. But "Lear," cut sharply down to a little over two hours, has nothing whatever static about it. Kosintsev has put a Russian sensibility into Shakespeare's characters: the result is to remove some of the breadth and complexity and to establish the kind of highly-charged emotional unity that Lear often lacks on the English stage.

The old king's outsized and exaggerated obsessions are turned into Russian obsessions, and they no longer seem so exaggerated. For instance, his demand that his daughters compete for their inheritance by saying how much they love him is not the arbitrary, aberrant whim that it can seem in English.

This rough, provincial king is virtually a peasant. And there a tradition comes to life: the French or Spanish or Russian peasant who goes half-crazed when it comes time to bequeath his property.

Lear's court is a despot's court and there is a constriction about it reminiscent of scenes in "Ivan the Terrible." The courtiers, milling in a state room, go rigid when he is to appear. They are physically afraid of him. And when he enters, there is a hair-raising contrast between this fear and his manner: amiable, vain, with tousled white hair and a professorial look.

The texture of fear and power allows the protagonist, Yuri Jarvet, to keep an overwhelming authority in his tenderness, his vanity and his madness. It gives unusual force to small details: when Kent is banished and makes his way through the crowd of courtiers, their turning away is not simply courtly malice but animal dread of a wounded fellow.

Of course it is tedious, in a Shakespeare film, to have to follow subtitles, particularly when they are scratchy and have a tendency to wander up into the middle of the screen. Some of the acting is undistinguished, though not that of Lear, Cordelia, Kent and a Fool, physically ill from seeing too far. The driving, passionate style of the production, which works beautifully with the intimate scenes and those of political intrigue, deprives the mad scenes of subtlety and edge, making them simply howl.

But it is lovely and it moves, and it passes the test of any truly successful interpretation of Shakespeare: however often you have seen Lear, you are seeing it new.

Richard Eder is a film critic for The Times.

1975 Ag 10, II: 13:1

Let Us Not Praise 'Nashville's' Failures

By JOHN MALONE

Robert Altman's colorful, self-indulgent, overblown and vastly overpraised new movie, "Nashville," is basically like every other Altman film. It has the same strengths: some brilliant performances, moments of peculiar unnerving tension, an eye for realistic detail and a strong sense of place. And it has the same weaknesses; a story with more loose ends than you can count, a soundtrack deliberately designed to prevent you from hearing what the characters are saying to one another, a visual style that seems to have been learned at the knees of television news and quiz show cameramen, and, not least, a treatment of women that often borders on celluloid rape.

Altman clearly doesn't like or trust words very much. In all his films, he goes to inordinate lengths to make sure that huge chunks of dialogue are completely indecipherable. Several people will talk at once; background sounds are mixed in at such high volume that the voices of the actors are obscured or drowned out altogether; crucial exchanges take place in whispers just beyond the range of hearing. Altman often uses these devices with particular insistence in the early scenes of his films, when we are still trying to catch the names of the characters and figure out the relationships between them. The mess table sequences at the beginning of "M*A*S*H," for instance, during which the moviegoer is struggling to learn who's who in the medical unit, are a chaotic buzz of undifferentiated conversation, with names, jokes and insults flying back and forth far too fast to follow.

But in "Nashville," Altman outdoes himself. A multiple car crackup brings highway traffic to a halt. In various cars stopped behind the accident sit most of the film's major characters—a motley collection of country-western stars and their hangers-on, a couple of would-be singers, a television reporter, even a potential assassin. Several of these people we are en-

countering for the first time. But can we hear what they say—at least enough to find out something about who they are? Of course not. Most of their conversations are miked as though we were hearing them from outside the cars in which the characters are sitting. It is not until several minutes later, for instance, that we are allowed to discover that Barbara Harris is married to the old redneck whose truck she clambers out of in full

screech. Their argument inside the cab of the truck is totally unintelligible, and a vital chance to tell us a few specifics about these characters is thrown to the wind.

•

Altman's defenders excuse his peculiar use of the soundtrack by saying, "That's the way things really happen." Ah, yes, cinema verité and all that. But, in fact, Altman's use of the soundtrack does

The strip scene—a deliberate act of cruelty by Robert Altman?

John Malone is a novelist with a particular interest in movies.

not reflect reality at all. Anyone who has ever eavesdropped on people talking at another table in a crowded restaurant knows that it is possible to screen out the Musak violins, the anvil chorus of plates and silverware, even the words of your own dining companions, and to pick up instead the conversation behind you. But Altman deprives us of such genuine choice. He predetermines what we are going to hear. His "realistic" soundtrack is, in fact, just as artificial as that of any Harold Pinter film in which every word is crystal clear and the silences absolute.

But if it isn't "real," what is the point of Altman's manipulation of sound? The value of any work of narrative art must to some extent be measured by the artist's ability to clear away the distractions that in real life prevent us from grasping the significance of events. Altman not only fails to clarify matters for us, he goes to the opposite extreme, making it even more difficult for us to understand what is going on than it would be in actuality.

There might be some excuse for this exaggeration of real-life confusions if it were used with any consistency, to some discernible end. But Altman doesn't have that kind of discipline. His choices as to what we will hear and what we won't

seem arbitrary, almost spur-of-the-moment. He has not thought through the consequences of such choices. While miking most of the conversations from outside the cars during the "Nashville" traffic jam, he goes inside and renders with perfect clarity an exchange between Geraldine Chaplin and Lily Tomlin, during which we learn that Miss Tomlin's two children are deaf. Yet in a few minutes we will be able to see for ourselves that they are deaf, when she communicates with them by sign language. It would have been altogether appropriate, and more effective, if we had learned this particular fact by seeing rather than by hearing.

Altman allows us to hear Miss Tomlin's words when we don't need to, yet in the same scene denies us the words of Barbara Harris and her husband. And as a result, when Miss Harris finally has her moment of glory at the film's conclusion, we don't care nearly as much as we might because we know so little about her. She crops up in unexpected places and at odd moments throughout the movie, but she is never allowed to get out more than a few words without being interrupted. There is a joke in this, of course, but since we have been prevented from truly getting to know her, her eventual triumph lacks the

impact it deserves. Her magnificent singing in those final moments arouses our feelings to some extent, but not to a degree that is truly moving. If only she had been allowed a few lines of dialogue when we first met her in the front of her husband's truck, we might have cared much more.

Altman not only likes a busy, undifferentiated soundtrack—he also likes to pack as many distractions as possible into each frame. Rather than using the camera to comment upon or characterize the action, Altman, like a television news cameraman, just sets it up and lets things happen in front of it. It is left to the viewer to pick out the significant details from the purposeless clutter of any given shot. Of all contemporary directors, he is perhaps the only one who appears to have learned absolutely nothing from either Hitchcock or Welles, those two masters of the camera angle. The editing of his films is equally prosaic. In "Nashville's" concert sequences, we might just as well be watching "The Price Is Right," so mundane is the cutting back and forth between singer and audience, audience and singer.

The real measure of Altman's visual imagination, however, is taken in the "Nashville" traffic jam sequence. The initial pile up of cars is very well done. But from that point on, the

scene is a visual as well as an aural shambles. It has no pace, no rhythm, no real cinematic interest. Even the spatial relationships of the various cars in which the characters sit is not clear. This sequence must be especially disappointing to anyone who has ever seen Godard's "Weekend," in which the backed-up cars are filmed with extraordinary virtuosity, combining visual wit and social satire to ferocious effect.

Altman's visual style — which some critics dignify by calling it "documentary" —is apparently the result of deliberate choice. But when he does attempt something more complex, as in his disastrous "Images," he falls flat on his face. Is Altman's newsreel style really dictated by the god of "realism," or is it simply the best he can manage? Why should we praise an artist for turning his deficiencies into a manifesto? Aren't we really being conned?

If Altman's aural and visual techniques raise questions about his cinematic imagina-

'Altman's treatment of women often borders on celluloid rape'

tion, the treatment of women in his films is cause for a different kind of concern. He has a positive addiction to scenes in which jeering, leering men ogle naked women, or laugh at their physical discomfiture. In "M*A*S*H" there was the tormenting of "Hot Lips"; in "McCabe and Mrs. Miller" an entire litany of indignities was visited upon the town whores; in "The Long Goodbye" the naked young women exercising on their balcony were used as a running joke; and who could forget the hoodlum breaking a Coke bottle back and forth across the face of his mistress in that same film?

In "Nashville" there are two long key scenes in which the humiliation of two different women is depicted in loving detail. In the first of these, a pretty young singer (superbly played by Ronee Blakley) goes to pieces in mid-performance. She starts a song, but stops to tell an anecdote that is peculiar to the point of being "funny." We already know that she has been in a sanatorium, and now, clearly, she is falling apart again. Yet on the afternoon that I saw "Nashville," the audience greeted this entire scene with laughter.

Would the same audience laugh to see this happen at a live concert, featuring a real singer? More likely, they would be horrified. Is their laughter caused by a failure of craft on Altman's part, then, or are they responding to the director's own ambivalence toward his characters? Perhaps a little of both. Later there is another scene that also evokes laughter.

This time, a waitress who dreams of being a singer is forced to do a total strip tease before an all-male audience of political contributors. We could have been made to loathe this yelling, leering group of men. But instead Altman asks us to laugh at the waitress; his staging of the scene comes across as a deliberate act of cruelty. Although the screenwriter for "Nashville" was Joan Tewksbury, the emotional coloring of these two scenes is clearly Altman's own.

Because we are not encouraged to empathize with

The traffic jam—"a visual as well as an aural shambles"

these young women, but to laugh at them instead, the film as a whole is undermined. Why should we care that the waitress seems destined to turn into a small-time whore in pursuit of her false dream? And when Barbara Jean is assassinated, how can we be horrified? Her death almost seems like a release from torment. Moreover, the fact that we have been given no clues as to the motivation of the seemingly nice young drifter who shoots her adds to our confusion and further dilutes the impact of the film's climax.

Altman's treatment of women seems particularly dehumanized, but most of the men in "Nashville" are also prevented from engaging our emotions. Their humanity is further obscured by the distortions of the soundtrack and the newsreel-style cinematography. "Nashville," like all the director's films, never seems to move in the same direction for more than a few minutes at a time. Everything is improvised, scatter-shot, spur-of-the-moment. Nothing is carried through. There is no coherent vision, no controlling art. And ultimately the film's successful moments come to seem as accidental as its failures. ∎

1975 Ag 10, II:1:1

'Cooley High'—More Than Just a Black 'Graffiti'

By JACK SLATER

It is difficult to remember how it really was all those years ago, in my Cooley High, when Miss Stokes and Mr. Phillips and Miss Smith dominated our lives; when everything was "real sharp" or "real neat" or "cool," and 10th-grade boys wore their belts suggestively unbuckled, and girls applied hot irons and pounds of Dixie Peach to short hairdos. My Cooley High was Dunbar High

School of the 1950's in Dayton, Ohio. It was similar to the early sixties Chicago school portrayed in the new movie "Cooley High"—which is to say, it was all-black, isolated in one small corner of the city, untouched by black consciousness and almost casual about that wider, white world surrounding it.

Later, through the prism of civil rights, I would view Dunbar without generosity, as though it had been only a segregated school or only a sociological experience. But

"Cooley High" remembers more honestly and more clearly than I, remembers how it really was when we were young enough to see ourselves without sociology's help, without clichés, when our identity was largely a mixture of self-discovery, friendship and what we hoped to be.

•

"Cooley High" documents perhaps that last moment in modern American history—1964—when it was possible

Jack Slater is on the staff of The Times Magazine.

for young blacks to see their color as simply one of the components of their personalities. The civil-rights movement sweeping across the South in 1964 seems to have had little, if any, effect on the Northern teen-agers portrayed in the film, perhaps because the movement was then in Georgia, South Carolina, Alabama, Mississippi: We were overcoming there, we were on the offensive there.

•

So "Cooley High" altogether ignores the social and political significance of 1964 to explore instead the softer, warmer areas where young people really live. Concentrating on the exuberance, the aspirations, awkwardness, silliness, despair—and the culture—of urban black youths about to graduate from Edwin G. Cooley Vocational High School, the film is loosely held together by the friendship between two teen-agers, Preacher and Cochise. We are allowed to follow that friendship and each youth through dozens of bittersweet moments which include class-cutting excursions to zoos, 25-cent dancing parties, fights, a wine-drinking get-together, a breathtaking chase in a sto-

len car, the delicious taste of youthful, sexual love and, finally, early unexpected death. To be black and to watch "Cooley High" is to see one's vanished innocence —and beauty.

Because it takes a backward glance, the movie is now being called "a black 'American Graffiti,'" but it has, in my view, far more vitality and more variety than "Graffiti," which profiled bored, despairing youth in small-town America of the early sixties. No one in "Cooley High" is bored. Like the earlier film, however, "Cooley" does remind us, almost incidentally, of who we once were, reminds those of us who grew up black during the fifties and early sixties of the sense of self we managed to achieve during those years, before job-hunting became a futile exercise, before feeding our newly established families became a daily battle, before the knowledge slowly dawned that our children's education would be more of a mockery than the one we had received—before all of it (including the collapse of civil rights) forced us to caricature ourselves as victims — racial entities — alone.

•

But it wasn't only White America which forced us into caricature. When I was growing up at Dunbar High School, I remember, I used to read the poetry of Elizabeth Barrett Browning with the same passion as one of the teen-agers in "Cooley High." I also read Emily Brontë, over and over, like scores of other dreamy black youngsters. By the late sixties, however, with black nationalism rising in self-defense against the white nationalism which had always been present, no black high-school student would have been caught dead with a white woman's lovesick poetry or prose in tow. ("You trying to be different? Trying to be white?") By then, even James Baldwin and Ralph Ellison were viewed as "trying to be white." For we had already, voluntarily, leveled ourselves, constricted our scope and our interests to become, as writer James Alan McPherson suggests, not so much "the 'mass man' of sociological terminology" as "the 'right-on man' of black slang."

•

"Cooley High," then, returns us to that lost part of ourselves which once chose its own way—returns me, at least, to the time when and the Dunbar where

"When we were young enough to see ourselves without sociology's help"

it was possible to embrace Emily Brontë because she was "real neat," and also to the college where I preferred Virginia Woolf to Richard Wright, because she was the kind of writer I wanted to become. She was *my* way—or so I then believed. I had, after all, lived Richard Wright, and now I wanted to discover another sensibility.

It seems to me that "Cooley High" implicitly urges all of us to choose among the myriad of ways which illuminate all lives, white as well as black—choose and then discard them when they are no longer needed, if only to remain human and growing in a world which pushes us every day toward cliché. ■

1975 Ag 10, II:13:3

A PAIN IN THE A—— (French title, "L'Emmerdeur.") Directed by Edouard Molinaro. Screenplay by Francis Veber. Photography by Raoul Coutard. Music by Jacques Brel and Francois Gauber. Edited by Robert and Monique Isnardon. Produced by Georges and Alexandre Mnouchkine. Distributed by Corwin-Mahler. At the 68th Street Playhouse. Running time: 90 minutes. Rated PG.

Ralph .... Lino Ventura
Pignon .... Jacques Brel
Louise .... Caroline Cellier
Bellhop .... Nino Castelnuovo
Fuchs .... Jean Pierre Darras

By RICHARD EDER

Pignon is a gangling, frog-faced necktie salesman. His car is decorated with plastic flowers and a teddy bear whose eyes light up when the brakes are applied. He is a man of damp enthusiasms and uncoordinated passion and probably wears socks in bed.

Not surprisingly, his wife, who aspires to elegance, horseback riding and Paris-Match, has left him for the local psychiatrist. Pignon checks into the main hotel of the provincial capital and sets to work to kill himself.

The room next to him is occupied by Ralph, a professional assassin who has arrived on the opposite mission. He is to shoot a key witness in a corruption trial that is to take place in the Palace of Justice across the street. The crowded French farce "A Pain in the A--" ("L'Emmerdeur"), which opened at the 68th Street Playhouse yesterday, tells how the two men's efforts entwine hopelessly and are mutually frustrated.

•

Ralph, played by Lino Ventura, puts out a "do not disturb" sign and is assembling his rifle when water floods through the door crack. Pignon (Jacques Brel) has tried to hang himself, managing only to snap off the showerhead.

Furiously, Ralph helps the hotel bellhop extricate Pignon. The latter promptly directs the full force of his sticky fervor at the reluctant gangster, thrusting on him the role of spectator and rescuer at each successive suicide attempt. He involves him in a half-hearted campaign to get his wife to feel sorry for him and take him back.

Each time Ralph settles down to put his rifle together, Pignon intrudes spectacularly. Finally, in one tussle, Ralph's rifles goes off, the police open fire, and the would-be suicide and assassin are both jailed.

"I am very glad to have met you," Pignon tells his victim near the end. "I was very lonely these last three months." Trotting around the jail yard just ahead of his admirer, the efficient loner Ralph has clearly been given a life sentence of incompetent companionship.

•

Pignon is a character with enough originality and outrageousness to make this, potentially, a funny and biting picture. There are some fine moments. Pignon trots along on foot beside his wife on horseback, trying to win her back. He holds up some photographs of their new house. "But they're in color," he bleats, as she rides away without looking.

But "A Pain," though generally pleasant and often amusing, doesn't quite manage to be itself. One weakness is its French farce convention. It is packed so full of gags and reverses—many of them pretty worn out—that it becomes cloying. The French overeat, figuratively speaking, at their farces.

A bigger weakness, though, is that although Mr. Brel is a considerable singer, he is not the marvelous actor that is needed to make the sprawling improbability of Pignon take off. He drags Pignon around manfully but can't get him going on his own. Similarly, though less crucially, Lino Ventura, in a part Jean Gabin might have played, is meager and stolid.

1975 Ag 11, 33:2

THE LAND THAT TIME FORGOT, directed by Kevin Connor; screenplay by James Cawthorn and Michael Moorcock; director of photography, Alan Hume; editor, John Ireland; music by Douglas Gamley; produced by John Dark; released by American International Pictures. At neighborhood theaters. Running time: 91 minutes. This film is classified PG.

Bowen Tyler .... Doug McClure
Captain Von Schoenvorts .... John McEnery
Lisa Clayton .... Susan Penhaligon
Bradley .... Keith Barron
Dietz .... Anthony Ainley
Borg .... Godfrey James
Ahm .... Bobby Farr

"If I'm not mistaken," the German captain says as his submarine floats in the mysteriously tropical Antarctic bay, "that's a diplodocus."

Susan Penhaligon has been hard at work turning out moues of fear, hope, horror and resoluteness. Now she squeezes and produces an expression of scientific skepticism.

"A diplodocus?" she says.

Of course it's a diplodocus. Those were pterodactyls just now, and soon the place will be thick with tyrannosaurs and stegosaurs and other specimens from American International Pictures' carpentry shop.

•

"The Land That Time Forgot," a screen adaptation of a story by Edgar Rice Burroughs at neighborhood theaters is an initially agreeable picture about the discovery of a mystery realm where various stages of evolution coexist. Dinosaurs and cavemen. Ancient plant forms and more modern ones.

A German U-boat sinks a British transport ship during World War I. A boatload of survivors, including an American submarine expert played by Doug McClure, Miss Penhaligon as a biologist, and several British seamen, manages to seize the submarine when it surfaces and overpowers the crew. Later the crew, led by their gentlemanly Captain Von Schoenvorts (John McEnery), overpowers the overpowerers. Still later they are overpowered back again.

Amid all the confusion the U-boat drifts south and finds shelter in an undiscovered Antarctic island left warm by volcanoes. Friends by now, the submarine's occupants settle down to repair the vessel, fight off dinosaurs and explore the island. Erupting volcanoes and natives eventually destroy them, leaving Mr. McClure and Miss Penhaligon as the only survivors. They are last seen, dressed in yak suits, climbing the snowy north slopes of the island, determined, as Mr. McClure puts it, "to move forward into the greater mysteries."

•

Just as the much grander "Jaws" became less scary the moment its mechanical shark appeared, the early virtues of "Land" collapse once the island is reached and the traffic jam in artificial monsters develops.

There had been some good moments in the submarine, chiefly because of the sympathetic performance of Mr. McEnery as the neurotic but courtly captain. Possibly you have wondered how German U-boat commanders managed to sink all those ships when the visors on their caps were so very stiff, making it hard to look through the periscopes. The picture explains: each time the periscope goes up Mr. McEnery twists his cap around to the back. When it goes down he replaces it. There is something engaging about a movie that teaches.

"Land" answers another question, perhaps not conclusively. What does a tyrannosaurus say when he is gored by a triceratops?

"Ow!" RICHARD EDER

1975 Ag 14, 39:1

Mitchum Is Marlowe in New Version of Chandler's 'Farewell My Lovely'

By RICHARD EDER

FAREWELL, MY LOVELY, directed by Dick Richards; written by David Zelag Goodman, based on the novel by Raymond Chandler; director of photography, John Alonzo; edited by Walter Thompson and Joel Cox; music, David Shire; produced by George Pappas and Jerry Bruckheimer; released by Avco Embassy Pictures. At Loew's State I, Broadway and 45th Street and Loew's Tower East, Third Avenue and 72d Street. Running time: 97 minutes. This film is classified R.

Marlowe .... Robert Mitchum
Mrs. Grayle .... Charlotte Rampling
Nulty .... John Ireland
Mrs. Florian .... Sylvia Miles
Moose Malloy .... Jack O'Halloran
Brunette .... Anthony Zerbe
Billy Rolfe .... Harry Dean Stanton
Mr. Grayle .... Jim Thompson

Around the beginning of the nineteen-forties when Raymond Chandler wrote his thriller "Farewell My Lovely," Leopold Stokowski decided that Bach was too spare for contemporary ears and made a series of lush, big-sound transcriptions with the Philadelphia Orchestra.

Lush Bach is long out of fashion, but old movies are still getting the big-sound treatment. A new film version of "Farewell," directed by Dick Richards, opened yesterday at Loew's State I and Tower East. It has been touched up with a little contemporary sex and violence and more than a little contemporary cinematic self-indulgence.

It's as if someone had put pillow springs, power-steering and a tape deck into a classic racing-car. It is still handsome and it still goes, but it is a handsome mediocrity.

Mr. Richards has been less ambitious than Robert Altman, who two years ago translated another Chandler work, "The Long Goodbye," into personages and a setting totally of the seventies. "Farewell" is kept back in the forties; it is just that certain present-day movie mannerisms have been tacked on.

•

When Marlowe, the detective—played by Robert Mitchum—erupts into a brothel, the whores earn the picture its R rating by appearing naked. In the picture's most repugnant scene Mr. Mitchum is allowed to deal the fat old woman—admittedly, a villainess—a crunching and bloody blow in the face.

The camera can linger endlessly on yellow and brown interiors, on neon lights, on the technicolored dilapidation of back-alley Los Angeles. It is a movie interlarded with photography; about 15 excess minutes' worth.

Chandler plots can be confusing in the movies: people still argue about just what happened at the end of Howard Hawks's version of "The Big Sleep." "Farewell" deals with the efforts of Marlowe to track down a mysterious Velda, the lost love of a great, hulking ex-con who wants her back even though she hasn't written him all the years he was in jail.

Marlowe's search, which cuts across a swath of metropolitan corruption, is attended by elusive clues, red herrings—blood-red, usually—and a great many corpses. So much is unresolved along the way that the few violent minutes of elucidation at the end produce some confusion. If you are a critic you can refer to a synopsis. If you are a member of the audience you may have to read the book, or perhaps pay to sit through another showing.

The strengths of this movie are in Mr. Chandler and in the high quality of a lot of the acting. The author's lines, tough, funny and baroque, get full value. As in a 1945 version of the same book, with Dick Powell, there are substantial sections in which the narrator simply reads Mr. Chandler—in this case, with the camera wandering as he does it.

There are lines that stand out. When the ex-con, a virtual giant played with brutality and vulnerable charm by Jack O'Halloran, is asked what Velda is like, he replies:

"Cute. Cute as lace pants." His lips and neck quiver with the effort and triumph of finding a verbal equivalent for the delicate memory that torments his great bulk.

As a drunken widow, Silvia Miles plays a role that seems an overdone cliché until you realize that she is doing it with such subtlety that her lost beauty keeps flickering back. John Ireland, another fine and subtle actor, improves on his stock part as a cynical, tired and honest detective.

Robert Mitchum always takes getting to know in a role. He comes on too strongly at first: too stagey, too droopy an eye, an excessively dangling cigarette. But he settles into his part, his performance drops away and he moves through the picture with force, humor and unexpected humility. Inevitably you think of Bogart: he isn't Bogart but he is very good.

With Charlotte Rampling, long-haired and slinky, you think of Lauren Bacall: the imitation is both painfully intentional and painfully bad. Presumably the director noticed it; probably he ordered it. He should have stopped it. Miss Rampling has had some bad roles but she is beautiful and expressive and should have been allowed a more congenial way to play her part.

1975 Ag 14, 39:1

THE GREAT McGONAGALL, directed by Joseph McGrath; screenplay by Mr. McGrath and Spike Milligan; photographed by John Mackey; music directed by John Shakespeare and Derek Warne; produced by David Grant for Daritan Productions; released by Scotia American Films. At the Cinema Village, Fifth Avenue and 12th Street. Running time: 95 minutes. This film has not been classified.

Queen Victoria............Peter Sellers
William McGonagall......Spike Milligan
With Julia Foster, John Bluthal, Valentine Dyall, Clifton Jones, Julian Chagrin, Victor Spinetti and Charlie Atom.

By RICHARD EDER

The brand of humor devised 20 years ago by Britain's "Goon Show"—Spike Milligan, Peter Sellers and Harry Secombe—and revived more recently by "Monty Python's Flying Circus," has a shadowed, hallucinatory quality to it. Its wild associations are the kind that come as we drop off to sleep and just before we wake up.

It is particularly suited to the passive, divided attention with which we watch television. The non sequiturs, the outrageous inventions take form just outside the field of vision, loom up suddenly and just as suddenly switch to something else. Things blur; their sequence is obscure: The result is hilarity under ether.

It is hard to transpose this kind of thing to a movie. People have come to see it; they have paid admission; their attention is more sharply focused; the screen image is big, clear and detailed. A two-headed bearded lady can't lope by quietly in the background: she requires to be explained somehow.

If "Monty Python and the Holy Grail" worked, it is because the whirling lights were strung along a plot, rudimentary as it may have been.

Years after the Goons broke up, Mr. Milligan and their director, Joseph McGrath—both collaborated on the screenplay—have tried to put together a full-length Goon-style picture.

"The Great McGonagall," which opened yesterday at the Cinema Village, is endearing, and parts of it are lovely and hilarious. But it lacks enough of an organizing principle in its chaos to succeed as a movie.

It centers on the true figure of William McGonagall, an unemployed 19th-century Scottish weaver who imagined himself so passionately to be a poet that he in fact wrote verse and got it published. For instance, an ode to a cow:

The Hen it is a noble beast
The Cow is more forlorner
Standing in the rain
With a leg at every corner.

In no way can the plot be summarized. Things happen, one after the other: some belong to McGonagall himself, some to his dreams, some to his dying hallucinations. We struggle too hard — we shouldn't, perhaps, but we do —to disentangle dream from dream and reality from reality.

Mr. Milligan is the bearded, gentle McGonagall who pref-

aces every recitation of his verse with an inarticulate howl that allows everyone time to flee.

He sees, or imagines he sees, Queen Victoria at a theater variety show. He is invited, or imagines he is invited, to go to Balmoral Castle to read his poems. He goes, or imagines he does, and is turned away, or imagines he is.

The pace is frenetic, the level of reality shifts every two minutes, it is stuffed with visual absurdities, old jokes and take-offs. Some work, some exasperate. McGonagall dances with Queen Victoria—a monotonous, one-joke role played patiently by Peter Sellers—to an orchestra composed of Adolf Hitlers. He and Victoria and Prince Albert pump away at a steam calliope that projects dirty slides to the tune of "Amazing Grace."

McGonagall does Macbeth on stage, wearing a Band-Aid on his nose. With the vegetables hurled at him he gives a cast party. He locks the doors so the guests can't escape when he recites his poetry.

Finally, he lies on his death bed. The poet Tennyson and a man named King Theebaw of the Andaman Islands walk in carrying a decoration from the Queen. They strip to their Victorian underwear and climb decorously into bed with him while his wife serves cookies and tea.

McGonagall dies, and you are sorry. Despite his madness, his delusions, his bad poems, you miss him. He is a radiant failure. So, in a way, is his movie, with all bad jokes, carelessness and confusion.

1975 Ag 16, 10:3

FILM VIEW

RICHARD EDER

Has This Foreigner Done Right by Our Depression?

Aside from the anonymous obscene phone call, modern technology provides no potentially sneakier way of getting across a punchy message than film-editing. Take fat men. In real life they are not really funnier or more sinister than anyone else. But if you film a fat man walking on a crowded sidewalk, edit to make his gait halting and jerky, synchronize the jerkiness with, say, the percussive bursts in Rite of Spring, and freeze the frame at some point when his mouth is open, the fat man will be making a statement.

It won't be his statement. It will be the film editor's, except that the editor, particularly in a documentary, is taken by the public to be the midwife of reality, not its clandestine father. That is the way it was, the editor's film supposedly says.

Philippe Mora, a young filmmaker born in France, raised in Australia and living in London, took old documentary and other footage some time ago and arranged it into a portrait of Nazi Germany entitled "Swastika." He then decided, according to his distributors, to see "what things were like on the other side" during those same years.

• • •

The result, "Brother, Can You Spare a Dime?", is an idiosyncratic, absorbing and claustrophobic view of the 1930's in the United States. It is put together with newsreel stock, film archives, Hollywood product and some Douglas Fairbanks home movies. If the Germans had won World War II, given a little postwar cultural relaxation, they might have assembled such a film.

There may be some poetic justice lurking about here, but the main point is that considerable wariness must be used when confronting the product of a splicing machine and a pile of newsreels. All power corrupts, and there is a heady freedom in being able to weave, chop and pep up so much visual documentation.

Like some Victorian jewelers, Mr. Mora has used

priceless materials to construct a banal object. His message is a vague and marketable disgust, his method typified by a clip showing dressed-up people dancing while the sound track gives us "Brother, Can You Spare a Dime?" People look a lot more dignified suffering than partying, and it is not hard to use film footage to suggest that it was gross and evil of Americans to dance and go see silly movies while so many were out of work.

And still: the materials make the picture live, and critical objections founder on the fact that here is a chance to see some rare, lost and heartbreaking things. Part of the loss comes in wondering where we could ever find the idle, undirected camera time today to go out and record a new Dust Bowl, if there should be one. Distributor and exhibitor economics have killed the documentary newsreel, and television documentaries are too heavily planned to allow often the kind of tentative exploratory manner that made a high art out of our anonymous Depression newsreels.

The gray dust blows in these scenes, men and children hurry down clouded streets, cars with their headlights on churn across the Great Plains, railroad tracks gleam through the clogged winds, and a farmer, interviewed and asked what he is hoping for, grasps his child's shoulder and replies: "I'd like to see it rain. I mean, I have seen it. I'd like to have my son—he's 8 years old—see it."

And what can better capture the distance of the 1930's and the rush of time since than to hear a butcher interviewed about Roosevelt say that he'd listened to him "on the *rah*-dio"? So new was this fundamental artifact only 40 years ago that people hadn't even decided how to pronounce it.

One of the most curious effects in "Brother, Can You Spare a Dime?" is the continual cross-cutting between real-

FDR—an actor with conviction

life photography and bits of Hollywood pictures on the same theme. You see Paul Robeson self-consciously swinging a pick and declaiming "Water Boy," and immediately there are shots of a far more modest-looking Joe Louis chopping wood in his training camp. Scenes of crowds in New York streets give way to a view of passengers in an elevated subway and you know there is something unreal about it even before King Kong takes the train apart.

Actors, you realize, are far more natural, far less wooden, than people in real life. They have to be, of course: unless they are expressing what they are supposed to be, they have no justification for being there. Real people in real trains have no particular reason to look like themselves, especially when a stranger—the camera—is gaping at them.

Only when politicians come on is the line between Hollywood film and documentary film blurred. Roosevelt acted his own part with perfect conviction. Huey Long, in his earlier appearances, was a skillful, folksy speaker but he still had the stiffness of real life. In his last scene one's reaction is to wonder what actor in what fictionalized account of his life was playing him.

Like a bad ringmaster at a good circus, Mr. Mora keeps shooing his numbers out just when they have gotten started, and then substitutes his own sententiousness for their talent.

It's still worth going, but somebody should film Mr. Mora brushing his teeth. And dub in the sound of jackhammers.

Richard Eder is a film critic for The Times.

1975 Ag 17, II:11:7

COONSKIN, a partially animated feature directed and written by Ralph Bakshi; film editor, Donald W. Ernst; animation production manager, Don Selders; music by Chico Hamilton; produced by Albert S. Ruddy; a Bryanston Pictures Release. At the Trans-Lux East Theater, Third Avenue and 58th Street and the Bryan Theater, Broadway at 49th Street. Running time: 83 minutes. This film is classified R.
Samson, Brother Bear........Barry White
Preacher, Brother Fox....Charles Gordone
Pappy, Old Man ......Scat Man Crothers
Randy, Brother Rabbit.....Philip Thomas

By RICHARD EDER

In cartoon profile, the black woman has the mournful elongation of an African mask. She sits in the infested Harlem tenement rocking her baby and talking to herself. She is young and her life is gone.

Not long ago a cockroach named Malcolm had put in an appearance. First she swatted at him, then she got used to his jokes, then she began looking forward to him.

"Malcolm became a . . . friend," she says. And then Malcolm—whose cartoon is as line fuzzy and messed-up as his character—is packed and ready to move downtown. "Ain't it been good together Malcolm? says I," the desolate, dispassionate voice continues. But Malcolm is going where the walls won't fall on him, the buildings are heated and some junkie won't step on him.

The profile and the rocking resume. A rat tries to move in. She lets him have it between the eyes and the screen explodes blood-red. Her voice keens on:

"I don't wanta be hurt no more. You know what I mean."

"Coonskin," which opened yesterday at the Trans-Lux East and the Bryan, is a shatteringly successful effort to use an uncommon form—cartoons ad live action combined—to convey the hallucinatory violence and frustration of American city life, specifically black city life.

It is a rarity in contemporary American film-making: a picture that is lyrically violent, yet in no way exploits violence. It is a violence of denunciation not of complicity. The violence will be discussed and remembered: yet

for a start, it seems useful to point to the magical and laconic grief of the scene described above to give some measure of how much else Ralph Bakshi has been able to do.

It is Mr. Bakshi's third full-length animated feature. It could be called his masterpiece; but the progression has shown such extraordinary growth that he is clearly not ready for monuments.

"Fritz the Cat" was flashy and sardonic but didn't try for much more than that. "Heavy Traffic," an earlier attempt to portray urban life, was a much bigger picture, but sometimes it was diffuse and awkward and sometimes, tinny. "Coonskin" is much more powerful, better controlled and far richer.

"Coonskin" is two stories, one set within the other. The first is filmed with live actors: it tells of the effort of two Southern blacks to rescue a friend from jail. The prisoner waits through the night in the jailyard for the escape car to come. He is accompanied by an old convict who tells a story, an up-to-date version of Br'er Rabbit and the Tar Baby, to pass the time.

The fable is in cartoons, with live backgrounds and occasionally, for certain precise emotional effects, live characters woven in. It relates how Rabbit, a young sharpie, along with two companions — the righteous and slow-witted Bear and the unrighteous and wily Preacher Fox—go north to Harlem to make their fortunes.

It is a Harlem of violence and desperation and occasional beauty: a moon struggles through the sky as if against odds, and a trumpet solo keeps returning. Rabbit and his friends smash up the racketeer organization run by a phony preacher—who cavorts naked on a lit-up cross, rakes in money ostensibly for the black revolution, and is controlled by a languid white boss.

They take over the rackets, shoot up their enemies and grotesquely eliminate a white

policeman who preys on Harlem. They pump him full of heroin, dress him up as a transvestite, and turn him out to be sodomized and eventually shot down.

It is one of the hardest parts of the film: it is no longer denunciation, it is personal nightmare. So are some of the scenes showing Rabbit's biggest enemy, the Mafia. The Godfather is a soft, white, monstrous figure with a pack of murderous, homosexual sons. It is a brilliant, portrait of moral pestilence. Perhaps it is excessively brilliant, excessively inward.

Rabbit—the black hero who is violent and crooked because he is stepped on by greater violence and greater corruption—wins. His enemies get entangled in a new version of the Tar Baby.

The fable ends, and in the film's most triumphant and devastating moment, the live characters return. The old convict, the narrator, is sky-high with the victory of Rabbit.

"Man, what you laughing at —we're dead," says the young prisoner. It is daylight, and the car hasn't come. The film goes on, but in a way it has reached its conclusion. Nation's forget their chains singing about old or imagined victories.

1975 Ag 21, 44:1

RUSSIAN ROULETTE, directed by Lou Lombardo; screenplay by Tom Ardies, Stanley Mann and Arnold Margolin, based upon the novel "Kosygin Is Coming" by Mr. Ardies; photographed by Brian West; editor, Richard Marden; music by Michael J. Lewis; produced by Jerry Bick; released by Avco Embassy Pictures. At Loews Astor Plaza, Broadway and 44th Street. Running time: 93 minutes. This film is classified PG.
Shaver ....George Segal
Bogna ....Cristina Raines
Vostik ....Bo Brundin
Petapiece ....Denholm Elliott
Hardison ....Gordon Jackson
McDermott ....Peter Donat
Ragulia ....Richard Romanus

Premier Aleksei Kosygin is arriving in Canada to talk about disarmament. A hawkish K.G.B. faction decides to kill him. They grab a Latvian employe of the Central Intelligence Agency — a nasty man who ogles dirty pictures in the shower and confiscates children's hockey balls — stuff him full of explosives, and prepare to drop him out of a faked police helicopter right smack on Kosygin's head as he arrives at his hotel.

A body does, in fact, come plummeting from the sky. Conveniently, it lands right beside the police superintendent heading the security detail. It's not the human bomb — he detonates elsewhere — but the bearded, popeyed, furry-voiced chief plotter himself. "But he's K.G.B.," the superintendent protests. Plainly, he didn't pay attention during the first 90 minutes of the movie. "What is this?"

This is "Russian Roulette," which opened yesterday at Loews Astor Plaza. It is the latest of a genre, still without

a name, that sets out to be about how something didn't happen. Just a couple of weeks ago we saw how Queen Elizabeth wasn't blown up in Hennessey and before that there was how DeGaulle wasn't shot in "Day of the Jackal."

"Russian Roulette" concentrates on atmosphere—in this case, Vancouver's, with lots of drizzle and lovely views—and on subplots. I think this may be out of embarrassment that the main plot never really arrived. It's like a wake without a corps: rfreshments and pleasant company, but lacking a sense of occason.

George Segal is an uppity detective who, suspended for socking a superior, is nevertheless ordered to find and remove the Latvian from the scene. As an emigré, the Canadian authorities reason, he might be troublesome during a Soviet state visit. Little do they

suspect the plans the K.G.B. has for him.

Mr. Segal is endlessly thwarted and bumbling, though finally, after a lot of confused rushing about, he manages to knock out the K.G.B. and preserve Mr. Koygin and disarmament. Most of the time he is arguing with his girlfriend, played by Cristina Raines, or trying to buy her dinner.

It is cheerful and relaxing to have an incompetent detective in a movie: that is probably why you see them so often. George Segal could play the part in his sleep, and does.

The photography is lovely. Appreciating the photography in a movie is like noticing how good the bread is in a sandwich. Usually somebody has dropped the filling.

RICHARD EDER

1975 Ag 21, 44:2

FILM VIEW

RICHARD EDER

Playing a Savage Game With Disney's Toys

"**A**un aprendo," Goya scrawled under one of his late drawings. "I still learn." To make comparisons very far across the arts is ludicrous. But Ralph Bakshi, struggling to make animated cartoons speak tragically, has entered his equivalent of Goya's black period, still learning.

"Coonskin," a diabolical reworking of Br'er Rabbit and the Tar Baby into a parable of the black in America, marks another stage in Bakshi's effort to fashion a voice for agony out of Walt Disney's box of talking toys. The effort began with the tough social parody of "Fritz the Cat" and it continued with the tougher social protest of "Heavy Traffic." In "Coonskin" the protest has become nearly a howl and in places it slides from a social concern into personal nightmare. It is a work of brilliance and innovation.

There are limits to the dramatic weight an animated cartoon can carry, and sometimes Bakshi scrapes against those limits. But he does it so far beyond what we think of as the frontiers of animation that he has virtually staked out a new country or—to use a grittier scale— city block.

Animated cartoons, in their strengths and limitations, are analogous to puppet theater. The figures are empty. There is nothing to dwell on in the face of a puppet or the frame of an animated cartoon. Both achieve their effects in movement, in the relationship of the figures to each other. Puppets can carry tragedy but it is a didactic tragedy, a tragedy of action. The figures lack depth and the human ambiguousness we are accustomed to in theater and cinema. They accost us, they come without reverberations; but in compensation they have an abstract, unmodulated force. The same is true of animations.

Bakshi takes risks continually: with technique and with taste. In Coonskin, not only does he put cartoon characters against live Harlem backgrounds but he takes the more ticklish step of using live characters as well,

Brother Bear and Brother Rabbit in "Coonskin"

Richard Eder is a film critic for The Times.
Vincent Canby is on vacation.

'JAWS' AND 'BUG'—THE ONLY DIFFERENCE IS THE HYPE

By STEPHEN FARBER

In "Coonskin," Ralph Bakshi presents an angry parable of black America.

sometimes in alternation. For example, "Coonskin" begins with two black convicts, both played by live actors, waiting in a prison yard through the night for an escape car. The older man starts to tell a story and the cartoons begin with the enactment of that story: a hip rabbit, an upright but confused bear and a weak, backsliding fox go north, take over Harlem and smear their enemies—the police, the mafia—into a great tar baby. It is a glorious and hilarious victory.

The film then cuts back and we see the old live actor-narrator with the glory and the hilarity of his story still upon him. We also see that the sun is rising, the get-away car is hopelessly delayed and the prison escape is doomed. It is a tearing, desolating transition to which the change from animation to live action is perfectly suited.

At other points, where the cartoon figures appear together with live ones, the risk of failure is greater, but Bakshi makes them work, too. For instance, when a black stripper (played by a real woman) dances before a corrupt detective (a maddened, twitching cartoon), the film manages a biting switch. Instead of the stripper being depersonalized, it is the onlooker.

But Bakshi's biggest risks are in the matter of taste. Because cartoons have no softening human texture, their bite, their bitterness, is unrelieved. I suspect that not even "Coonskin's" greatest admirers can see it without experiencing some shock and distress. This is not intended as a condemnation of Bakshi: shock and distress can be legitimate esthetic effects. And in "Coonskin" they are overwhelmingly legitimate, though I have doubts in a few places; for example, in some of the more hellish mafia scenes, with a Godfather who would have given Hieronymus Bosch bad dreams, and his sadistic, transvestite sons.

It is the whites who are monstrous in "Coonskin." The blacks are smart, weak, violent, hopeful, crooked, enduring

and desperate. They are human: the whites are not. Mr. Bakshi — a Brooklyn Jew whose ancestors go back to Russia and India — is not denying humanity to white people. It is simply that "Coonskin" doesn't deal with whites in themselves. Bakshi's movie is about a segment of black experience as he can grasp it, one where the white man—policeman, redneck, city grafter—swims into view as someone who will make you poor, scared and sometimes dead. He is not saying that white people are nightmares in fact; but that they are nightmares for many blacks. At least that is his principal message; at a deeper level he gives expression to a tentative horror about life itself.

Of course, it is ironic that such a film should be attacked not by Italians or policemen or rednecks, but by a black organization. CORE has campaigned against "Coonskin" for nearly a year, delaying its opening and pressuring Paramount to withdraw as its distributor. The campaign argues that "Coonskin" is a savage and unfair caricature of the black community.

"Coonskin" clearly is savage, and a cartoon clearly is a caricature. But it seems stupid and blind not to see that Bakshi is making a most serious and difficult kind of artistic commitment in trying to capture black Harlem's human condition by heightening rather than softening its miseries. The propriety of a white man's doing so is another matter. In recent attacks on Bakshi the suggestion is that he has committed an act of social effrontery. He has, of course. It has always been an act of effrontery to twist human life into art.

1975 Ag 24, II:11:1

"Jaws" fever is turning into an epidemic. In its first two months of release in the United States and Canada, "Jaws" has already grossed $90-million, surpassing the box-office records of "The Sting" and "The Exorcist," and by the end of the year it could best "The Godfather" as the top-grossing film in movie history. The phenomenal success of "Jaws" is astonishing, because the movie—adapted from Peter Benchley's best-selling novel about a killer shark, and directed by Steven Spielberg—is nothing more than a creaky, old-fashioned monster picture, reminiscent of "Creature From the Black Lagoon," "The Beast From 20,000 Fathoms," and a whole rash of grade-B movies about giant ants, tarantulas, and rats on the warpath.

Although some critics have acclaimed "Jaws" as a movie milestone, it is strikingly similar to another monster movie in release this summer, William Castle's "Bug," about giant, incendiary cockroaches that overrun Los Angeles after an earthquake. Both "Jaws" and "Bug" belong to the Pavlov dog school of filmmaking; they treat the audience like laboratory animals wired to twitch whenever the electricity is turned on. In "Jaws," when the young scientist discovers a half-eaten corpse under water, or when the shark lunges out of the water to snap at a character's arm, everyone in the theater jumps at the same instant. "Bug" elicits exactly the same kind of mass squeals and gasps from its audiences when a cockroach begins nibbling a girl's ear, or sets another character's hair on fire. Everyone recognizes "Bug" as a cheap exploitation picture, but in the case of an $8-million exploitation picture like "Jaws," the expensive special effects camouflage the filmmaker's shoddy intentions.

The only significant difference between "Bug" and "Jaws" is in the size of the advertising budget. "Bug" was made on a shoestring, without name actors or the benefit of a pre-sold title, and so it was unceremoniously dumped in neighborhood theaters and drive-ins across

Stephen Farber frequently writes about film for The Times and other publications.

the country, with only the most perfunctory advertising. By contrast, the money spent on the promotion of "Jaws" was the largest pre-release advertising budget for any movie in the history of Universal Studios.

Audiences who think that *they* made "Jaws" a success are pitifully naive about the mass media. The campaign to sell "Jaws" began almost four years ago, before the novel was published. A story in The Times Magazine last year disclosed that Peter Benchley rewrote the novel several times at the direction of his editors, who were very conscious of fashioning a commercial property. One of the editors at Doubleday was quoted as saying, "You've got to think of the whole country as a child that climbs up on its daddy's knee and says, 'Tell me a story.'" When producers Richard Zanuck and David Brown bought the movie rights, they worked with the paperback publishers to batter that child into submission. Zanuck and Brown, along with members of Universal's publicity department, cunningly helped to circulate and promote the paperback in order to build the audience for the subsequent movie version. Carefully planned publicity throughout production of the movie —culminating with the lucky strike of a Time Magazine cover story and a bombardment of TV spot ads the week of the opening — ensured that the whole country would be "Jaws"-conscious.

When this kind of efficient publicity machine goes into full swing it is unsettling to realize how little free choice people actually have. They go to see "Jaws" because they have been conditioned to want to see it, and then they like it because they have been too intimidat-

ed to resist. The movie itself is the logical conclusion to the relentless ad campaign. The audience that has been pummelled by Universal's aggressive media blitz is then primed to respond to a scare show that works with the ruthless insistence of a cattle prod. Both the advertising and the film show the same manipulative contempt for the public.

Another disturbing thing is that so many normally discerning critics have jumped on the "Jaws" bandwagon; their delirious reviews are indistinguishable from press releases. Perhaps these critics are tired of being called snobs and elitists; they want to prove that they have not lost touch with popular culture. The critics probably could not have deterred the people who get their kicks watching dismemberments and mutilations, but they should have remained detached enough to point out the flaws in plot, characterization, acting, and direction.

"Jaws" consists of two separate stories, clumsily stitched together. The first half of the movie deals primarily with the conflict between the chief of police in Amity, L.I., who wants to close the beaches after the first shark attack, and the mayor and other businessmen, who are unwilling to jeopardize the summer tourist trade. Although the venality of the townspeople is really only a gimmick to keep the plot in motion, the glibness of Benchley's sociology and the infantile smugness of Spielberg's cynicism damage the film; the mercenary businessmen and the corrupt mayor are subhuman caricatures. In the most outrageous scene, logic breaks down completely: the mayor has succeeded in keeping the beach open, and the seashore

Jack Mitchell; Culver Pictures

Hitchcock's "Notorious" involved us emotionally with Grant and Bergman. It didn't need the gore of "Jaws."

is packed with vacationers who are nevertheless reluctant to go into the water. Yet the mayor, who knows the shark may be prowling nearby, walks among the tourists virtually prodding them into the ocean. Even on the movie's own terms, the action of the mayor makes no sense. It is the most glaring indication of the film's willingness to sacrifice character consistency for the sake of sadistic thrills.

The social issues raised in

the first half of "Jaws" are merely red herrings, and they are dropped as quickly as possible. The second half of the film turns into a conventional Saturday matinee adventure story: three men set out to sea to kill the beast from 20,000 fathoms. This section is derivative but at least relatively free of pretension. However, the basic problem with this sequence, as with the opening of the film too, is that the characters are such stock, paper-

thin figures. The salty, stubborn old fisherman (Robert Shaw)—part Captain Ahab and part Captain Hook —is the most tiresome stereotype. The wisecracking scientist (Richard Dreyfuss) is not much more credible. In typical Hollywood fashion he has been given cute, antic traits —like a lovable puppy—so as not to alienate the yahoos in the audience who still think scientists, being intellectuals, have pointed heads. The police chief (Roy Scheid-

"Both 'Jaws' and 'Bug' treat the audience like laboratory animals."

er) fears the water, yet he is the one who finally destroys the shark; in Hollywood's comic-strip mythology, cowards are always allowed an 11th-hour transformation.

The shallowness of these characterizations is aggravated by sloppy acting. Because he exercises some restraint, Scheider comes off best. Shaw bellows and blusters, while Dreyfuss — who showed great promise in "American Graffiti" and "The Apprenticeship of Duddy Kravitz"—mugs coarsely and relies on a manic cackle that is becoming something of an irritating tic. Since Shaw and Dreyfuss have both demonstrated their talents in the past, the blame for their overacting in "Jaws" must rest with director Steven Spielberg. In his first feature, "The Sugarland Express," starring Goldie Hawn and William Atherton as a fugitive couple pursued across the state of Texas by a squadron of police cars, Spielberg showed that he could direct traffic but not actors. He hasn't improved; he does wonders with the mechanical shark in "Jaws," but bungles all the scenes involving human beings.

The dramatic impact of "Jaws" lies in four or five grisly scenes — the water turning red as a child is attacked, a severed leg flying toward the camera, a mangled corpse discovered under water, the shark smashing the fisherman's boat and finally chomping Shaw until blood cascades from his mouth. These gruesome special effects are the only convincing details in the movie. Thrillers have always relied on shocks, but in superior melodrama the shocks come as the climax of a carefully constructed, credible suspense plot. "Jaws" is so shabbily constructed that audiences don't even pay attention during the quiet intervals; they're just waiting to see if the director can top the last spectacular death or dismemberment.

Critics who consider "Jaws" a classic suspense melodrama should be required to enroll in a crash course on Hitchcock, who taught that suspense depends upon believable characters and is greatly enhanced by atmosphere. In "Vertigo," for example, Hitchcock gives a lush, dreamlike quality to his images of San Francisco in order to make us share the hero's growing obsession with the supernatural. A television-trained director like Steven Spielberg has no real understanding of the visual possibilities of the film medium. The underwater scenes in "Jaws," which should have created the feeling of a dark, eerie, sinister universe teeming with mysterious animal and plant life, looked as if they had been shot in a swimming pool.

More important, the characters in "Jaws" are too colorless to inspire any sympathy or concern. In a truly classic suspense film like "Notorious," Hitchcock took the time to develop Ingrid Bergman's character and establish her vulnerability. Even today people seeing "Notorious" are so concerned for Miss Bergman's safety that they gasp when a bottle of wine topples off a shelf and smashes as she and Cary Grant furtively search a wine cellar. Later, a simple close-up of a poisoned cup of coffee is terrifying because we know that Miss Bergman is unsuspecting and completely helpless. Hitchcock involves us emotionally; he doesn't need blood and guts, crunching bones, and rotting corpses to make his audience respond. Unfortunately, most of the younger filmmakers lack the talent to make artful thrillers; they substitute shock for suspense, gore for psychological menace. "Jaws" illustrates the decline in movie story-telling.

Yet, because of the insistent publicity campaign, "Jaws" has become the entertainment "event" of the year. Maybe I am making too much of a sleazy horror movie, but I am concerned about the effect of this film on other films. The studios are looking for the magic formula for a commercial blockbuster, and since they are making fewer movies every year, they want to minimize risks. The giant success of "Jaws" may encourage them to keep aiming for the lowest common denominator; from now on it will almost certainly be a little harder to find financing for more modest and meaningful films. All the people connected with "Jaws" are going to be big winners in this year's box-office sweepstakes. The only losers are American moviegoers looking for a film experience that is somewhat more subtle and rewarding than two hours of shock therapy. ■

1975 Ag 24, II:1:1

WHITE LINE FEVER, directed by Jonathan Kaplan; screenplay by Ken Friedman and Jonathan Kaplan; produced by John Kemeny; executive producers, Gerald Schneider and Mort Litwack; director of photography, Fred Koenekamp; edited by O. Nicholas Brown; distributed by Columbia Pictures. Running time: 92 minutes. At the Columbia I and other Manhattan theaters. Rated: PG.

Carrol Jo Hummer ..Jan-Michael Vincent
Jerri Hummer ....Kay Lenz
Duane Haller ....Slim Pickens
Buck Wessle ....L. Q. Jones
Lucy ....Leigh French
Josh Cutler ....Don Porter
Pops Dinwiddie ....Sam Laws

By RICHARD EDER

The plot is inflated, the violence is inflated—though well-shot—there is a lot of blacktop highway and a great many roaring vehicles that swerve, crash and burn.

But "White Line Fever," a movie about truckers and racketeers, stands far above its own clichés. It has genuine excitement and a frequent beauty of style. It makes an occasional effort to treat a subject virtually unheard of in the movies nowadays, despite the recession; the pressure and bone-weariness of trying to earn a living. Finally, though the plot is often cardboard, it is inhabited by some real people who manage the ordinary human accomplishment—and the much rarer movie accomplishment — of intimacy.

●

"White Line Fever," which opened Tuesday at the Columbia I and other theaters in the mtropolitan area, is about a young man who get out of the Air Force, marries his sweeheart and goes into hock to buy a trailer rig. He wants to be a trucker, like his father: He finds that the business is dominated by a network of crooked businessmen, politicians and thugs.

Refusing to join in by accepting contraband cigarettes as part of his carpo, he is beaten up and blacklisted. He organizes a truckers' rebellion: He is shot at, beaten some more, framed on a murder charge, has rattlesnake planted in his truck an dis nearly burned to death with his pregnant wife.

He and his supporters manage to get rid of some of the crooks, and finally they organize a statewide truckers strike. It seems to be a victory, of sorts, but there are glimpses of higher-ups and still-higher-ups who seem to be doing as well as ever at the end. It is a life-like inconclusiveness.

The pace is fast, and the camera conveys beautifully the movement and danger in the big rigs. In a night scene, for example, the hurtling road is photographed from the cab at a steeper and steeper angle, giving the feeling that the blackness ahead is a wall.

The rarity in an action picture of this kind is the quiet and sensitive acting of the two principals Jan-Michael Vincent as the rebellius driver and Kay Lenz as his wife. They manage, tenderness quarreling and weariness as these things really are managed. They tie the melodramatics together.

1975 Ag 29, 14:1

THE WILBY CONSPIRACY, directed by Ralph Nelson; screenplay by Rod Amateau and Harold Nebenzal, based on a novel by Peter Driscoll; produced by Martin Baum; executive producer, Helmut Dantine; director of photography, John Coquillon; editor, Ernest Walter; distributed by United Artists. Running time: 101 minutes. At neighborhood theaters. This film has been rated PG.

Shack Twala .... Sidney Poitier
Keogh .... Michael Caine
Horn .... Nicol Williamson
Rina .... Prunella Gee
Persis Ray .... Persis Khambatta
Mukeriee .... Saeed Jaffrey
Van Heerden .... Ryk De Gooyer
Blaine Nierkirk .... Rutger Hauer
Wilby .... Joseph De Graf

By VINCENT CANBY

"The Wilby Conspiracy" is a sort of light hearted "Defiant Ones," played for a good many laughs as well as for suspense and of course social content in the Union of South Africa. It's about a black political activist (Sidney Poitier) and an apolitical white English businessman (Michael Caine) who become locked together by their need to escape from the Capetown police.

The film, which opened yesterday at neighborhood theaters, was directed by Ralph Nelson ("Lilies of the Field") and written by Rod Amateau and Harold Nebenzal. For a while—at the beginning when the film is establishing the reasons for the flight and pursuit that make up most of the film—it seems as if "The Wilby Conspiracy" is going to take itself seriously and solemnly as one of the first major American movies to come out firmly against apartheid.

It does take itself as seriously as the plot demands but never too solemnly, since "The Wilby Conspiracy" is, at heart, a good old chase melodrama, decked out in modern dress and in liberated racial attitudes. The best thing about the movie, flimed mostly in Kenya, is its performances, funny and hip and self-assured in the manner of television personalities working in front of loving audiences.

●

Mr. Caine and Mr. Poitier are never unaware that their material may not be the greatest, but that doesn't spoil their good spirits, and when a good line comes along they get maximum results without stomping on it or us.

Giving them excellent support, acting, in effect, as straightmen to the two leading comics, are Nicol Williamson, who is brilliantly wicked as the Cape Town security officer dedicated to the capture of the fugitives, and Saeed Jaffrey, who plays what is described as "a deeply committed Indian dentist," who attempts to assist the fugitives in Johannesburg. Mr. Jaffrey is gently, soberly funny, and it's no reflection on him when Mr. Caine says with some skepticism: "A deeply committed Indian dentist? That sounds like all the people I hate at cocktail parties."

"The Wilby Conspiracy" has a lot more plot than need be gone into here, some of it involving jet fighters, helicopters and Prunella Gee, as a pretty, liberated white South African lawyer, and Persis Khambatta, as a beautiful, perfidious Indian dental assistant, who, according to this film, should never be trusted with anything more lethal than a cotton swab.

1975 S 4, 31:1

RETURN TO MACON COUNTY, directed and written by Richard Compton; director of photography, Jacques Marquette; film editor, Corky Ehlers; music by Robert O. Ragland; produced by Elliot Schick; released by American International Pictures. Running time: 90 minutes. This film is classified PG.

Bo Hollinger..................Nick Nolte
Harley McKay.............Don Johnson
Junell ....Robin Mattson
Sergeant Whittaker.........Robert Viharo
Tom ....Eugene Daniels
Pete ....Matt Greene

and

THE WILD McCULLOCHS, directed and written by Max Baer; director of photography, Fred Koenekamo; editor, David Berlatsky; music, Ernest Gold; produced by Mr. Baer; released by American International Picteures. Both at neighborhood theaters. Running time: 93 minutes. This film is classified PG.

J. J. McCulloch...........Forrest Tucker
Culver Robinson...............Max Baer
Hannah McCulloch..........Julie Adams
Ali McCulloch............Janice Heiden
Steven McCulloch........Dennis Redfield
R. J. McCulloch..............Don Grady

By RICHARD EDER

Bonnie and Clyde did not die in vain. Go to a movie set in the thirties or forties or fifties. Let it begin with two or three funny, rebellious and attractive youngsters climbing into a car to conquer the world. It is going to end with the world squatting on them.

One of the troubles with "Return to Macon County" —besides a mindless plot and its gross imitation of the atmospherics of "American Graffiti"—is that no sooner do its young protagonists bebin to charm than the viewer begins to wait unhappily to see where the bullet holes will appear.

As it turns out the bullets —fired by the customary hate-choked rural policeman —smash the car but not the heroes. This spares us the final grisly convention of doomed-youth pictures. It doesn't spare us from sitting through most of the picture waiting for it.

"Return to Macon County," which opened yesterday at neighborhood theaters, is about two country boys who set out for California with their lovingly supercharged stock-car, determined to become champion racers. They pick up a hash-house waitress, an endearing pumpkin-faced girl played by Robin Mattson, who wants to get to California to be a movie star.

●

Besides being endearing, she is somewhere between fey and mad, and as dangerous as booby-trapped peanut butter. The two young racers think they're reasonably tough—they drag-race for money and sass police cars—but the waitress has the disconcerting habit of pulling out a revolver in moments of stress. "My Daddy gave it to me," she explains to her startled companions. "He says you meet some funny people."

The three tangle with some mean-spirited rival drag-racers, who improbably get on their trail with shotguns. They also cross a maniac policeman who, even more improbably, takes it upon himself to kill them. In fact he shoots their car full of holes, but it is the shotgun-wielding rivals who are in it at the time.

It is a pity about the car. It was boxy, cheerful and vivid yellow and it functioned serviceably, if un-originally, as a symbol of youth and hopefulness. It is one of the curious things about movies, in fact, that the yellowness of the car should serve to shore up this picture's frail virtues. A color itself can have an emotional value; as it does when the waitress tries on an old hat,

and its yellow arouses the same brash hopefulness already flaunted in the canary car.

Both the young men, played by Nick Nolte and Don Johnson, are very good. Mr. Nolte, in particular, conveys exuberance, a reasonable but not excessive violence, and vulnerability.

Robin Mattson is the picture's strongest asset, however. Her half-innocent explosiveness is skilfully conveyed: at first it captivates her partners, and finally it is too much for them. She has some wonderful moments: one of the best, when in the middle of fantasizing about the future with Mr. Nolte she looks at him, takes

in his boyish good looks, says matter-of-factly: "You're going to lose," and resumes the fantasy.

●

On the same double bill is a terrible picture called "The Wild McCullochs." A mawkish revival of nineteen-fifties melodrama, it tells about a rich father, a two-fisted, self-made man, who gives his children lots of nice clothes and opportunities but doesn't understand them. There is a great deal of weeping, a long, boring and *lovable* fistfight, and a family priest who wears a red wig and the kind of quaintness that was prohibited by Vatican Council II.

1975 S 4, 31:1

WOMEN'S PRISON U.S.A—RAPE, RIOT & REVENGE!

WHITE HOT DESIRES MELTING COLD PRISON STEEL!

CAGED HEAT!

What Do You Do at Midnight?
You See a Trashy Movie

By MICHAEL WOLFF

There is nothing to do.

That is how the distributors and marketing men explain the popularity of low-budget movies that play to predominantly young audiences exclusively at midnight.

"O.K., sure, most of these pictures are crummy, Neanderthal, boring, boring, boring, and no quotes on this," says an executive of a small New York film distribution company, as he hurries through Times Square to catch a distributors' screening "of some silly resurrection of Little Rascal clips, and another one of those rock and roll splice jobs." He shakes his head in vague disgust.

"So what do you want me to do," he continues, "go to confession or something? I admit already, these are worthless movies. Puerile. Dumb. Blah! Period! But that's not the point. You don't need Pauline Kael to tell you that the garbage stinks. The point is why am I going to make a million dollars gross this year off these things? It's like this— in New York, Chicago, Boston, Long Island, Philly, we've got these things playing all over. The kids, you know, the 18 to 25 crew, they just have nothing to do. Nothing. Zero! And they'll take anything. God, they must have jelly brains. Just see one of these films and you can bear me out on that.

Michael Wolff is a frequent contributor to the Sunday Times.

The New York Times/Larry Morris

"So it's easy to understand what we're doing, we're simply exploiting a generation of children raised on excitement —you know, all that sixties stuff—who are now wandering around thinking what the hell is there to do. We put these movies on at midnight, only at midnight, which makes them seem special, a conspiracy or something, really avant-garde. And every kid who owns a pair of blue jeans thinks he's gonna find the spirit of his generation in a midnight movie house. For-

"You don't need Pauline Kael to tell you the garbage stinks," says the distributor of films that play "midnight movie" theaters. Yet young people continue to line up each midnight.

get it; it's all crummy kink, banal camp, bad sex. Jesus, why am I complaining? For me it's a terrific cash flow."

●

The cash may flow as high as $35-million through the midnight houses next year. In New York there are several midnight theaters, including the Elgin, the Cinema Village, the Waverly and the 8th Street Playhouse. "It's a beautiful business to be in," says Jim Dudelson of New Line Cinema, the distributor of "Pink Flamingos," a midnight classic featuring a 300-pound transvestite who, in Dudelson's words, "is one of the really true gross-outs, but funny, very funny. Everybody, really everybody, is getting into midnights. Across the country midnight shows are one of the fastest growing theatrical ideas."

"What makes a midnight movie?" Dudelson muses, searching his desk for a poster-sized pin-up of Divine, the transvestite star. "You can't really put your finger right on it. Rock films are a sure product. And, of course, we've done fabulously with 'Pink Flamingos,' and then 'Mondo Trasho,' 'Multiple Maniacs,' 'Reefer Madness,' 'Sex Madness,' 'Cocaine Fiends.' But it's hard to say exactly what it is we look for. We've been doing sort of kinky humor; now I'm thinking about getting into a little softcore porn. The field is pretty open. You see a picture and it strikes you. Just the right kinkyness, or camp, or sex . . . or . . . well . . . awfulness for the midnight audience, people who want a little late-night kick."

The Cinema Village's midnight show, Sunday through Thursday, is now "The Texas Chainsaw Massacre," a low-budget, over-exposed, horror film which originally played in drive-ins. In the movie, a demented family in rural Texas makes its living by processing 'its chainsaw victims into Texas barbeque, which the family then sells in its roadside filling station. The victims are five hapless teen-agers who wander into the family's house—creaking door and all. Four of the teen-agers are promptly massacred—three by the chainsaw, one impaled on a meat hook. The fifth is caught, escapes, is caught again, escapes again. Most of the movie is dominated by a hulking chainsaw operator running pell-mell through the woods and over dirt roads waving his weapon inches away from the escapee's head. The "Jaws" of the midnight runs.

In a melancholy way, the people arriving just before midnight at the Cinema Village recall the young couples and groups of friends trailing down St. Mark's Place toward the Fillmore East five years ago. "Everybody's digging midnights," says a boy with a jean jacket thrown over his shoulder, a girl on his arm, and plastic flowers tied in his hair. "It's a scene to make, the funkiest thing since rock and roll."

"Remember the Joshua Light Show—you remember it, don't you?" says Martin Cole, a Long Island high school student. "Well I don't, I was too young for a lot of the really high things, but I think midnights are kind of like the Joshua, very . . . you know . . . visual, but with plot and all."

•

Later, inside the theater, joints are smoked and six-packs of beer consumed, but the response to "The Texas Chainsaw Massacre" is half-hearted. Finally, an impatient voice booms out, "So cut off her goddamn head already!"

"You saw 'Texas Chainsaw'?" says Wayne Cozart of Arista Theatres, the organization which owns and operates the Cinema Village. "The

whole thing? That's one I couldn't sit through. But midnight movies are what I would call goof films. You've had plenty to drink or smoke and you want to keep going. Let's face it—even in the Big Apple there's not that much to do these days."

The Tuesday midnight feature at the Elgin, "Caged Heat," does not set new standards of cheapness, violence or grossness, as most midnight movies seem determined to do. It is a film about women in prison that offers little more than some zippy music, a lot of bosom shots and a perverted prison doctor.

"That was a rip-off," says a young girl, standing under the Elgin's marquee after the film.

"Yeah, so did you have anything better to do?" replies a boy in blue suede earth shoes.

She shrugs. "Let's go to your place and see what's on the tube."

No one in the business of midnight movies seems exactly sure how the trend developed. Some credit "El Topo," the South American western featuring the random mutilation of thousands of pounds of animal and human flesh, as the pioneer film of the movement. Others give that honor to "Pink Flamingos," a showcase of human degradation. (Its distributor, New Line, points out that "Pink Flamingos" is in its 101st week in Philadelphia and its 36th week in Los Angeles, having played 56 weeks in New York. Made on a budget of $10,000, the quickie film has so far grossed $2.5-million.)

•

Midnight movies have also been regarded as an outgrowth of the cult films of

the sixties—films like Philippe DeBroca's "King of Hearts," or even the early Andy Warhol films. But midnight entrepreneurs deny any connection. "Cult films catered to a select, sophisticated audience," says Cozart. "Midnight movies have an altogether different audience, an audience that goes to see something which is really culturally bad."

Yet a compelling film does occasionally manage to slip into the midnight schedules. For example, "The Harder They Come," a startling, sometimes beautiful fantasy about a Jamaican music star, gained limited recognition in regular runs before it became a midnight hit. "For all its attractiveness," says Ralph Donnelly, who opened "The Harder They Come" at The First Avenue Screening Room before the theater turned to hardcore gay fare, "it is still too rough, too low-budget, to stay for long in a regular house. Midnight is frequently a time for films that are unmarketable anywhere else."

Another such film is "Snapshots," an eccentric and occasionally brilliant autobiographical film about the decadence of the sixties, now playing at the Waverly, a Walter Reade Theatre. "We could do better with something worse," admits a Walter Reade agent, "but someone liked the film, and it's really too peculiar to run in a regular slot, so we dumped it in a midnight."

But "The Harder They Come" and "Snapshots" are exceptions, not in keeping with a rule of movie-booking that sees the midnight hour as prime time for a generation looking for a little action, but too apathetic to wander far in its search. ■

1975 S 7, II:17:3

FILM VIEW

RICHARD EDER

Sometimes Violence Is Called For

How many Americans are going to end up as a shark's breakfast, turn into Satan robots, be dynamited by a Western policeman, gunned down by a Southern policeman, or have a Russian policeman topple from a skyscraper onto their heads? Or suffer any of the other inconveniences that make up Hollywood's notion of the human condition,

judging from the film product it has been extruding these past couple of months?

On the other hand, how many will lose their jobs or fear losing them, be unable to find new ones, grow weary or sick of the jobs they do have, see their lives constrict for lack of money or illusions? And who is making movies about it?

Hollywood's attitude toward the Depression was complex. There was denial and evasion but there was also a certain amount of facing up to it. A picture like "The Grapes of Wrath," released in 1940, of course treated the Depression directly. But even "Dinner at Eight"—generally thought of as a frothy masterpiece—has a bitter underlay of awareness that the world is dropping away. Lionel Barrymore, the host, collapses from the nightmare of combining hospitality with the knowledge that his business is in ruins.

Granted, the recession hasn't been around as long as the Depression, nor cut as deep. But it is the most seriously-felt national concern, and there is a good chance that it will continue to be for quite a while. The movies, however, ignore it, giving us, instead, variations of violent catastrophe.

•   •   •

In fact, movie violence—the way it comes through in a "Jaws," a Satan picture, or in "Russian Roulette" or "Super Vixens"—is a form of escapism. Real violence shapes life, limits it and produces, in an individual's or a society's efforts to cope with it, some of the most specific human values. What the so-called violent movies have been giving us is a trivialization of violence, a caricature of it. They treat it solely in terms of its physical movements, just as pornography treats sex: dehumanizing us, they allow us to escape from human burdens.

In terms of this trend toward dehumanization, "White Line Fever," the trailer-truck movie that opened here recently to widely unfavorable reviews, is oddly encouraging—though it is by no means a masterpiece. For one thing, it is a formula picture—that abused phrase actually denotes a movie in which the formula is mediocre and shows—or a mixture of formula pictures. It is partly an internal-combustion-engine formula picture (trucks instead of cars or motorcycles), partly a little-guy-gets-fed-up-and-lashes-out formula picture, and partly a plain blood-and-mangled-guts formula picture.

But it is better than it sounds. Surprisingly, the formulas are executed with considerable style, though at a time when stylish camera work and editing are used to gild some perfectly horrible pictures, that isn't saying very much. Much more important, the director, Jonathan Kaplan (who also helped write the script), dismounts from his formulas and walks around. He pokes holes in them. He puts people into them. Like many successful movies of the past, "White Line Fever" manages to triumph over noticeably carpentered plots. A few real people dress up the plasterwork immensely, especially when one can see them think, breathe, hesitate and get tired.

Kaplan's actors—Jan-Michael Vincent as the leader of a truckers' rebellion and Kay Lenz as his wife—help a lot. Perhaps they engage in the understatement of performers trained in television work, but in this case, with so much overstated plot and action, it is a helpful habit. At the end, Vincent, who has broken most of his bones but managed to get a state-wide strike going against the corrupt higher-ups, comes out of the hospital to be cheered by his followers. Kay Lenz's face stares from a window, strained, exhausted and suggesting that there is no ending.

•   •   •

Beyond this, though, "White Line Fever" does make a commendable, if modest, attempt to deal with real social problems. The movie is about poor people who have to work brutally hard for a living. For brief moments, at least, we can actually see and feel the economic pressures that make people act, or not act, or simply get fed up with acting. Kay Lenz is shown working in a bottling plant: the arduousness and boredom of the job are registered not so much there as afterward, at home, where the demoralizing force of her job carries over into her relationship with her husband.

The pressures that push Vincent out on the road, that make him fight his blackballing by the trucking organization, stem visibly from the need to support his pregnant wife and keep his mortgaged trailer-rig from repossession by the bank—and not merely from an abstract "machismo," as is the case in so many contemporary

Vincent in "White Line Fever"

American films.

The violent scenes in "White Line Fever," in fact, which have offended a number of critics, do not seem to me to be gratuitous. There has been a lot of talk and concern about the cult of violently taking the law into one's own hands, as exemplified in pictures such as "Death Wish" and "Walking Tall." But in an admittedly crude and insufficient form, the violence in "White Line Fever" is of an older, more respectable and more humane kind. It is the violence of social protest, of rebellion under intolerable pressure, when all authority is corrupted and there is no other redress.

Richard Eder is a film critic for The Times. Vincent Canby is on vacation.

1975 S 7, II:7:1

JUST BEFORE NIGHTFALL ("Juste Avant la Nuit"), directed by Claude Chabrol; screenplay (French with English subtitles) by Mr. Chabrol; based on the novel, "The Thin Line," by Edward Atiyah; produced by Andre Genoves; director of photography, Jean Rabier; editor, Jacques Gaillard; music, Pierre Jansen; a French-Italian co-production by Les Films la Boetie, Columbia Pictures and Cinéasi; distributed by Libra Films Corporation. Running time: 100 minutes. This film is classified PG.

Helen Masson	Stéphane Audran
Charles Masson	Michel Bouquet
François Tellier	François Perier
Jeannot	Jean Carmet
Dominique Prince	Dominique Zardi
Cavanna	Henri Attal
Bardin	Paul Temps

"Just Before Nightfall" was shown at the 11th New York Film Festival. The following excerpt is from Vincent Canby's review, which appeared in The New York Times on Oct. 9, 1974. The film is being shown at the Paris Theater, 58th Street west of Fifth Avenue.

Marriage is a joke, according to nightclub comedians who possess no great amount of imagination. Claude Chabrol, the French director who has a lot of imagination, goes substantially further in his elegant, witty "Juste Avant La Nuit." If an ordinary marriage is a joke, he says, what appears to be a perfect marriage may be a cosmic jest.

This is one way of describing "Juste Avant La Nuit," which is about the problems of poor Charles (Michel Bouquet), a successful Paris advertising man, the husband of the incomparable Hélène (Stéphane Audran), the father of two healthy, spoiled children, and the possessor of a suburban house so modern, so full of corners, split-levels and glass that any drinking except for medicinal purposes is impractical.

As the film opens, Charles is matter-of-factly throttling the life out of his beautiful mistress, the wife of his best friend, François (François Perier) who is also his architect. The soon-to-be-late mistress, an enthusiast of sado-masochism, has goaded Charles into strangling her, though she didn't mean for him to go all the way.

Did Charles intend to kill her? Probably not, though we are never sure. Charles gets away with murder easily enough. The only thing Charles cannot escape is his own need to be punished.

He must confess to Hélène, who is pained for a moment and, being the perfect wife, she consoles him. François is equally reluctant to be an instrument for retribution. "Listen," he says as if talking about a bit of bad luck on the golf course, "we've known each other for 25 years. What happened was a nightmare. Nobody is guilty in a nightmare."

"Juste Avant La Nuit," like so many Chabrol films, eventually becomes too schematic, but early on the scheme has so many ambiguous twists and turns that the film continues to provoke the memory long after one has left the theater.

The relationship between Charles and Hélène is especially complex. They maintain that precarious balance sometimes achieved by two loving, intelligent people who deny each other nothing except true intimacy. It is significant that although we see Charles in passionate connection with his mistress (murder, I assume, is passionate), there is never any hint of sex between him and Hélène. When such intimacy is denied, Chabrol suggests, the results can be disastrous. They can also be extremely entertaining.

On the scale of recent Chabrol films, "Juste Avant La Nuit" is somewhere below "La Femme Infidèle" and "Le Boucher" but above "La Rupture." This one is a comedy of a high, intelligent and dark order, full of scenes of charming domestic accord, casually punctuated by a close-up shot of a mouse making a fatal lunge at the cheese in a mousetrap.

1975 S 10, 37:4

SHARKS' TREASURE, written, produced and directed by Cornell Wilde; director of photography, Jack Atcheler; film editor, Byron Brandt; music by Robert O. Ragland; released by United Artists. At the DeMille Theater, Broadway and 47th Street, and neighborhood theaters. Running time: 95 minutes. This film is classified PG.

Jim	Cornel Wilde
Ben	Yaphet Kotto
Ron	John Neilson
Lobo	Cliff Osmond
Larry	David Canary
Johnny	David Gilliam

By RICHARD EDER

Call it Yaws. (cf. Webster's New International Dictionary: "Yaw . . . deviate from one's own course; move or cause to move erratically.")

There are plenty of sharks in "Sharks' Treasure," which opened yesterday at the De Mille and neighborhood theaters, but they are puny and don't pay proper attention. They move in circles, erratically.

Their distraction will be shared. Cornel Wilde, whose work as a director occasionally raised a spark of interest, has made a home movie. The home needs cleaning.

Mr. Wilde stars as a charter-boat captain who takes on a crew and finds sunken treasure near a Caribbean island. He poses in a brief, black bathing suit, lectures on the dangers of smoking and shows his fitness by doing one-hand push-ups.

A gang of homosexual convicts comes on board and ties up the crew. The leader, a big, bearded man, capers around the deck and alternately beats and caresses a small, blond convict. The small convict cries a lot.

Sometimes the camera mounts to the mast and films everything straight down. Either it is taking a correspondence course in cinema esthetics or it is trying to get out of the way.

Eventually Mr. Wilde and his crew untie themselves and manage to eliminate the convicts. By this time the sharks have long since left and if the audience is wise it will have taken the hint.

1975 S 11, 35:1

MITCHELL, directed by Andrew V. McLaglen; screenplay by Ian Kennedy Martin; executive producer, Benjamin Melniker; produced by R. Ben Efraim; director of photography, Harry Stradling; music, Larry Brown and Jerry Styner; editor, Fred A. Chulack; an Essex Enterprises, Ltd. production, distributed by Allied Artists. Running time: 96 minutes. At Loew's Astor Plaza, 44th Street west of Broadway, Loew's Cine, Third Avenue near Lexington Avenue, and other theaters. This film has been rated R.

Mitchell	Joe Don Baker
Cummins	Martin Balsam
Deaney	John Saxon
Greta	Linda Evans
Benton	Merlin Olsen
Mistretta	Morgan Paull
Tony Gallano	Harold J. Stone
Chief Pallin	Robert Phillips

By VINCENT CANBY

"Mitchell," starring Joe Don Baker as a hard-nosed Los Angeles detective named Mitchell, has a lot of over-explicit violence, some gratuitous sex stuff and some rough language, yet it looks like a movie that couldn't wait to get to prime-time television. Perhaps it's a pilot film for a TV series, or maybe it's just a movie that's bad in a style we associate with some of the more mindless small-screen entertainments.

Mitchell spends what seems to be the greater part of the film climbing in and out of automobiles, driving automobiles, chasing other automobiles, parking automobiles, and leaning against the body of automobiles that are temporarily at rest. Once he smashes a hoodlum's hand in the door of an automobile.

The climax, for a giddy change of pace, features a police helicopter in pursuit of a high-speed cabin cruiser. Automobiles sink when driven onto water.

Mr. Baker, who seemed an interesting character in "Walking Tall," has no character whatsoever to work with here. There is an effort —admittedly it's a frail one— to portray him as a dedicated loner, disliked by his colleagues because of his stubborn pursuit of justice, even when it means dispensing with search warrants. He is also briefly upset when a small, black prowler is shot to death, though the prowler was unarmed. In a film like "Mitchell," that's a flaming social conscience.

Martin Balsam has several good moments as a worried underworld figure, the man Mitchell trails throughout the film to find a cache of heroin. Mostly the movie is hypnotized by the mechanics of transportation, in the manner by which its plywood people get from one spot to another. What happens in-between is sawdust.

The movie opened yesterday at Loews Astor Plaza, Loews Cine and other theaters.

1975 S 11, 35:1

FILM VIEW

VINCENT CANBY

Truffaut's Clear-Eyed Quest

The films of François Truffaut are full of quotations—some of the disenchanted will say too full. The quotations are always relevant to the multi-levelled films Truffaut makes with such seeming effortlessness, yet they aren't essential to the primary pleasures. They are dividends. The quotations, which may be images as easily as lines of prose, are sometimes salutes to mentors and colleagues. Sometimes they are simply comic references and sometimes they mean exactly what they say.

There is one in "La Peau Douce" (Soft Skin, 1964) that illuminates all of Truffaut's films from "The 400 Blows" through his Oscar-winning "Day for Night," as well as the way he sees himself as a filmmaker. They are lines from Andre Gide's "La Séquestrée de Poitiers":

"I bring no doctrine, I refuse to give advice, and in an argument I immediately back down. But I know that today many are feeling their way tentatively, not knowing what to put their trust in. To them I say: Believe those who seek the truth, doubt those that find it, doubt everything, but don't doubt yourself."

More than any other qualities in Truffaut's work, his clear-eyed appreciation for the reckless quest, and his sympathy for the tentative gesture, keep his films surprising and fresh when films made more recently by other, supposedly talented directors, appear to have congealed in no-longer-popular, Lucite-like given truths. These qualities, I suspect, explain why, on a recent post-Labor Day Friday afternoon, the auditorium of the Carnegie Hall Cinema was filled close to capacity for a one-day rerun of "La Peau Douce" and "La Sirène du Mississippi" (Mississippi Mermaid, 1969), which were derided by most critics and were box-office failures when they were originally released here.

● ● ●

It also explains why many of us anticipate with so much interest his newest film, "The Story of Adèle H.," which will be the closing night (Oct. 12) entry at the forthcoming New York Film Festival. Through the thin and thick of contemporary fashions, Truffaut's films survive triumphantly. This is particularly true of "La Peau Douce."

The pairing of "Soft Skin" with "Mississippi Mermaid" might seem an unlikely program even to those of us who appreciated both films separately in their own times.

"Mississippi Mermaid," with Jean-Paul Belmondo and Catherine Deneuve, then France's two most expensive stars, is a romantic melodrama of the all-for-love school. It's an updated, relocated adaptation of a William Irish novel about a southern U.S. planter and his beautiful mail order bride who is not quite what she seems. In Truffaut's version, the setting is first Reunion Island in the Indian Ocean and then the metropolitan France of discothèques, rented villas and sleep cures. The story is about the revivifying effects of true love, even when that love may be of short duration and possibly fatal. "Mississippi Mermaid" is in scope and color and full of the kind of exotic details one doesn't usually associate with Truffaut.

"Soft Skin" is something else entirely, a small, black-and-white, minutely observed love story about the adulterous affair of a middle-aged, minor-league Parisian literary pundit and a pretty, much younger airline stewardess he meets on a brief trip to London. The triangle is completed by the pundit's wife, whom he still loves in a desultory fashion and who loves him with a fury he is too dense to understand until she appears at his bistro one morning and blows his chest apart with the family shotgun.

● ● ●

"Mississippi Mermaid" is the sort of melodrama Hollywood stopped making in the forties after it reached its peak in Germany with Josef von Sternberg's "The Blue Angel" in 1930 and in France with Jean Renoir's "La Chienne" in 1931. ("La Chienne," incidentally, will be a retrospective selection at this year's New York Film Festival.) "Soft Skin" has the shape of soap opera.

Yet the two films have profound and fascinating connections, each being an exploration of a man's attitude towards romantic love. In "Mississippi Mermaid," the planter character played by Belmondo, a fellow who has sought a safe, permanent love, is liberated when he chooses to follow the ephemeral. In "Soft Skin," the literary pundit, beautifully played by Jean Desailly, hedges. He refuses to acknowledge himself either to his wife or to his mistress, preferring to keep all his relationships ambiguous. Thus he is destroyed. Even without the shotgun blast that ends the film you realize he would have eventually destroyed himself anyway.

Both the planter and the pundit are projections of different aspects of Antoine Doinel, the Truffaut surrogate figure played by Jean-Pierre Léaud first as a boy in "The 400 Blows" and then in those deceptively comic films of courtship and marriage, "Love at 20," "Stolen Kisses" and "Bed and Board."

In the latter film, the last of the Doinel films Truffaut has said he will make, Antoine has become a bit of a bastard. His reckless quest (a disastrously funny affair with a beautiful Japanese girl) almost ruins his marriage and causes his wife real emotional damage. Yet the wife (Claude Jade), sweet as she is, is a heavy spirit compared to Antoine. Antoine, in his easily distracted way, pursues the ephemeral.

● ● ●

As in so many of Truffaut's films, in "Mississippi Mermaid" and "Soft Skin" we have variations on the most important war, a war between those who demand and desperately need to believe in the permanence of all things, and those who have had some fleeting glimpse of their impermanence, but who move blithely on, living on outside chances. These are the ones who continue to seek what in Gide was called truth. They doubt those who claim to have found it.

"Soft Skin," coming right after Truffaut's enormously lyric "Jules and Jim," was something of an affront to many of his admirers. It is anything but grand. Neither the pundit nor his mistress (played by the late Françoise Dorléac, Miss Deneuve's sister) is an especially appealing character, and the only person in the film who possesses true passion is the wife (played by Nelly Benedetti)—and the screenplay gives her very short shrift.

Yet it's an extremely complex, affecting film, composed of those hundreds of tiny, specific details (in particular, the practical difficulties of urban infidelity) with which Truffaut, working modestly within the frame of conventional films, turns out unconventional, highly personal works of art.

1975 S 14, II:13:1

TIDAL WAVE, directed by Shiro Moritani and Andrew Meyer (American version); screenplay by Shinobu Hashimoto, based on a story by Sakyo Komatsu; American dialogue by Mr. Myer; executive producer, Tomoyuki Tanaka; producer (American version), Max E. Youngstein; directors of photography, Hiroshi Murai and Daisaka Kimura; American photography by Eric Saarinen; editor, Michiko Ikeda; music, Masaru Sato; a Toho Company production, presented by Roger Corman and Max E. Youngstein, distributed by New World Pictures. Running time: 90 minutes. At the Cinerama Theater, Broadway at 47th Street, and other theaters. This film has been rated PG.

Warren Richards	Lorne Greene
Tanaka	Keiju Kobayashi
Fran	Rhonda Leigh Hopkins
Onoda	Hiroshi Fujioka
Prime Minister	Tetsuro Tanba
Reiko	Ayumi Ishida

By VINCENT CANBY

Those two inscrutable, indestructible American movie producers, Roger Corman and Max E. Youngstein, are joined together for the presentation at local theaters of "Tidal Wave," a Japanese disaster movie that has been re-edited to include American scenes and dubbed English dialogue for the American market.

"Tidal Wave" is occasionally very funny and perhaps of some cinematic interest since it is virtually a retrospective of all the accomplishments of Japanese special-effects technicians. Just about everything happens in a disaster movie — earthquakes, tidal waves, volcanic eruptions, fires, boys losing girls. All these things, with the exception of the boys and girls, are done with miniature sets the Japanese make so well. The sets and effects are clever though they never fool you. The cities that are destroyed in "Tidal Wave" would fit around your electric train.

Andrew Meyer, a young American director ("Night of the Cobra Women") with some cult following, is credited as the director of the American version, the focal point of which is Lorne Greene, who plays the United States representative at the United Nations. Mr. Greene isn't on-screen much. He appears from time to time to urge his United Nations colleagues to provide homes for the Japanese population, whose islands are sinking into the sea in the other part of the movie. Mr. Greene's voice is getting so sonorous these days you suspect he'd prefer to sing his lines.

It's not giving away a huge secret to say at the end of the movie the Japanese Government flees to the United States while the royal family is packed off to Switzerland. The import of that split decision may possibly be profound.

1975 S 16, 53:1

SWEPT AWAY (BY AN UNUSUAL DESTINY IN THE BLUE SEA OF AUGUST), directed by Lina Wertmuller; screenplay (Italian with English subtitles) by Miss Wertmuller; produced by Romano Cardarelli; cameramen, Giulio Battiferri, Giuseppe Fornari and Stefano Ricciotti; music, Piero Piccioni; a production of Medusa Films; distributed by Cinema V. Running time: 116 minutes. At the Cinema II Theater, Third Avenue near 60th Street. This film has been rated R.

Gennarino	Giancarlo Giannini
Raffaella	Mariangela Melato

By VINCENT CANBY

Summer. A blue Mediterranean seascape seen through sunlit mist. In the distance a handsome white yawl moves with the light breeze. On the soundtrack we hear some jazzy instrumental music that recalls the score of every Italian film about the sweet life you've ever seen, but there's a point to it in the film. It pollutes air that once was as pure as it looked.

As the camera nears the yacht, the music gives way to the bickering of the yacht's well-heeled passengers. The mood that from a distance had seemed so serene turns suddenly, abrasively indolent —and furiously funny. People who have nothing to do, no visible responsibility to anything except tan skin, angrily debate capitalism, Communism, consumerism, the role of the Vatican in Italian life, while complaining about a crewman's smelly T-shirt.

This is the beginning of Lina Wertmuller's most entertaining new Italian comedy, "Swept Away (By an Unusual Destiny in the Blue Sea of August)," which opened yesterday at the Cinema II Theater.

"Swept Away" is Miss Wertmuller's fourth film to be released in this country. It follows "The Lizards," which was shown in New York several years ago as part of a Festival of Women's Films, "Love and Anarchy" and "The Seduction of Mimi," and it's played by the two actors, Giancarlo Giannini and Mariangela Melato, who were so remarkable in the latter two films. It's also by far the lightest, most successful fusion of Miss Wertmuller's two favorite themes, sex and politics, which are here so thoroughly and so successfully tangled that they become a single subject, like two people in love.

●

The shape of the film is as artificial as a fairy tale or a cartoon strip. Raffaella (Miss Melato), the rich, beautiful, acid-tongued Milanese who has chartered the yacht, and Gennarino (Giannini), the swarthy Sicilian deckhand whose T-shirts offend her, are marooned for several weeks on the only Mediterranean island not yet occupied by German tourists. They are Popeye and Olive Oyl locked in passionate combat.

The way Gennarino folds his pants and shirt—quickly, neatly, according to careful training that has become habit, you know he is a man who believes all things have their place, including women, who belong in the house with the children. Raffaella is an intelligent, selfish, superficially liberated slob who has never picked up anything in her life if there was an outside chance someone else would pick it up for her.

He is a Communist with the dedication of a first-century Christian. She is a capitalist because, for her, the system has paid off. More important, he is a man and she is a woman, for which there is hell to pay on both sides.

●

"Swept Away" is the story of their tumultuous, slapstick courtship, his systematic humiliation of her (as she sees it) until, suddenly, she submits to her love for him and becomes in the process truly liberated. Feminists, I suspect, will debate a number of plot points as if Miss Wertmuller had set out to write a treatise and not to make a love story, some of whose meanings are not easily translated into feminist agitprop.

More easily apparent are the director-writer's concerns about the Italian society that bred these two people and turned them into the mixed-up, wrong-headed characters they are, capable occasionally of unexpected, if imperfect nobility. Her sympathies appear to be more with Gennarino than Raffaella, but that's a matter of politics, not sex, and he is, on the surface, a male chauvinist pig of a classic type.

"Swept Away" is less a film about ideas than about previous commitments, for which neither character can be held completely accountable. The enormous appeal of the comedy has to do with the way, briefly, each character, is able to overcome those commitments.

It also has to do with the performances of Mr. Giannini and Miss Melato, who tear into their roles with a single-minded intensity that manages to be both hugely comic and believable, even in the most outrageous of situations. They are the best things to happen to Italian comedy since Marcello Mastroianni and Sophia Loren squared off in the nineteen-sixties.

1975 S 18, 48:1

THE TOOTH OF CRIME, the Performance Group in a play by Sam Shepard; a film by Ken Kobland and James McCarthy; directed for the stage by Richard Schechner; produced for the stage by the Performance Group. Running time: 97 minutes. At the Whitney Museum of American Art, Madison Avenue and 75th Street.
Doc, Galactic Max .... Stephen Borst
Cheyenne .... James Griffith
Star and Ref .... Elizabeth LeCompte
Becky .... Joan Macintosh
Crow .... Timothy Shelton

"The Tooth of Crime" is nighttime opera, a black vision of a present-day phenomenon—the rise and fall of the stars of pop culture, suddenly famous and suddenly extinguished—as if it were the bloody and dangerous rite of some primitive tribe. It is the present seen as the barbarous prehistory of an inhuman future.

This hard and dazzling film, that repels and moves, opened this year's festival of New American Filmmakers at the Whitney Museum of American Art. For an opening it is both a forceful and a limited choice: forceful because of its contents, limited in that it is mainly a filming of a play by Sam Shepard as done two years ago at the Performing Garage in a production by Richard Schechner.

●

Mainly—but not entirely. It is not just the filming of a play, but the filming of a performance of a play. There is a difference. At the Performing Garage the audience sat on the stage, and its presence made a kind of chorus of passivity that heightened the tensions of what was going on. In the film this effect is *seen*: those dumb, alive, involved and aloof faces seem both to goad and drain the players.

Hoss is a creature swum up into the light and fighting desperately to hold his place in it. He is a warrior prince—the war is ambiguous: mainly Hoss is a rock superstar, living by the charts and holding sway over his territories against his rivals. But at times the imagery slips into that of car racing; and at other times it becomes that of the street gangleader.

He came up by rebellion, by a harder, more driving, more rending style that toppled the older stars. Now he is older, and in a prison of his success playing by the rules of his mysterious

"Keepers," getting word in his gilded and attended isolation of the incursions of younger and would-be stars, of newer rebels. He rages to be free, to regain the living style that has died on him to fight; but the Keepers lull him reassuring him of his invincibility, and his success has made him afraid.

Finally, one of the new breed—vicious, funky, effeminate, surreal, a new kink in the violent switchbacks of popular musical fashion—appears. They duel, the Keepers put their favor on the new man and Hoss is destroyed.

●

The main thrust of the fable is clear enough: the champion not as hero but as bear at a bear-baiting; nourished and sustained for a while, then displaced and discarded. It is, of course, an ancient theme but it finds life in its powerful and stylish interpretation, and in its devastating application of old myth to modern delusions.

There is confusion in the detail, however. The drugged, balletic movements, the procession of grotesques, the level of inhuman shriek in which most of the performance is conducted, make "Tooth" harder to sit through as a movie—where we, unlike the audience we watch, have no connection with the proceedings—than as a play. Furthermore Mr. Shepard's use of rock language, brilliant as it is, and the speed and ellipses in the delivery, make for many unintelligible moments.

Against this must be set the brilliant, heart-rending playing of Hoss by Spalding Gray. Mr. Gray is a presence of dignity, power and desperation. His remarkable and difficult achievement is to move back and forth between ritual stylization and sheer suffering humanity without a single false note.

It is a great performance and it makes up for much of the harshness and stylistic violence of this difficult but interesting film.

RICHARD EDER

1975 S 18, 49:1

BUG, directed by Jeannot Szwarc; screenplay by William Castle and Thomas Page, based on "The Hephaestus Plague" by Mr. Page; director of photography, Michel Hugo; edited by Alan Jacobs; produce dby Mr. Castle; released by Paramount Pictures. At Loews State 2, Broadway and 45th Street and Loews Cine, Third Avenue at 86th Street. Running time: 100 minutes. This film is classified PG.
James Parmiter ..... Bradford Dillman
Carrie Parmiter ...... Joanna Miles
Gerald Metbaum ...... Richard Gilliland
Norma Tacker .... Jamie Smith Jackson
Mark Ross .... Alan Fudge
Tom Tacker .... Jesse Vint

By RICHARD EDER

Movie companies have the right to make bad pictures and reviewers the right to say unkind things about them. Normally, that is that: The public buys tickets, or not, the producer makes money, or not, and not much

other harm is done. "Bug," which opened yesterday at Loews State 2 and Ciné, raises a different problem.

To put it by analogy: If a restaurant reviewer eats a poor meal, that's one thing. If he gets ptomaine poisoning, that's another. "Bug" is decidedly poisonous.

It is not simply a scary picture, nor simply a violent one. It is a cruel picture. Not necessarily because of the theme which is as improbable as, but not necessarily more harmful than, those of dozens of other pictures.

●

An earthquake releases from the depths of the earth a swarm of ash-eating beetles with the property of setting objects, people and animals violently on fire. Cars explode, people burn up, buildings are set ablaze. The beetles are badly adapted to surviving above ground until a mad scientist develops a new, resistant strain. There are horrendous explosions at the end, and as far as the viewer can tell—the narrative is pretty fuzzy—the new beetles swarm out to destroy the world.

So far, so bad. In the classical horror film the horror was somehow overcome at the end. Stakes were driven through the vampires. Civilization, in some fashion, fought back. In "Bug"—as in "Rosemary's Baby," an earlier film by the same producer, William Castle—evil won and civilization was not only ineffective, but also virtually compliant.

Horror pictures need upbeat endings as no other kind of movie does, precisely because they are pure fantasy. Who could stand a fairy tale in which the witch ate Hansel and Gretel and stayed in business?

But there is worse. The fear and loathing of small, crawling, barely visible creatures are a lot more basic and widespread than the fear, say, of white sharks. Spiders, mice, snakes—these are specific children's nightmares.

●

The movie does vile things with this susceptibility. A girl answers the telephone and a beetle hidden in the receiver sets her ear on fire. A housewife is thumbing through a cookbook and a beetle gets in her hair and sets her hair on fire. A cat plays with a beetle and is horribly burned to death. All this is done with highly competent special effects and relentless, unending screaming.

For some inexplicable reason "Bug" is rated PG. This means that parents should advise their children whether or not to go. Most parents will not be able to see "Bug" before deciding. This review urges them to decide no. "Bug" is sick, and literally sickening.

1975 S 18, 50:1

ALI THE MAN, with Richie Havens, directed by Rick Baxter; executive producer, Shintaro Katsu; music by Simon Stokes; released by CinAmerica Released, Inc. At neighborhood theaters. Running time: 55 minutes. This film is classified PG.

On the eve of his third bout with Joe Frazier, Muhammad Ali is still as much an enigma as a charismatic, enduringchamp ion to judge by "Ali the Man," which, with the previous "Ali the Fighter," arrived at the Penthouse yesterday. As a documentation of a long career that, according to Ali, includes 280 fights, it is a slick, surface, fragmented portrait that is not especially penetrating or memorable. It is largely the Ali the public already knows, a truly fascinating figure but one whose heart and mind are rarely exposed fully.

'Out of an amalgam of color footage directed by Rick Baxter, old black-and-white film dating back to the callow Cassius Clay of Olympics fame, and a Richie Havens recording session intercut into the action, the Muhammad Ali that emerges appears to be all things to all men. Ali's philosophies are represented in discussions with black kids in Harlem, in projecting his feelings about his Muslim faith and in his somewhat confusing attitude on violence in the ring.

This production, which ranged from Harlem to Tokyo,

as wel as stops at bouts and training camps in this country, also manages to focus on his wartime confrontation with the armed forces.

and the conflict between his faith and Army service that made the front pages, which unfortunately doesn't add to these old records. And, there's a good deal of highly stylized footage of Ali jogging through sylvan settings against the background of Mr. Haven's plaintive music ("don't let them try to keep you down"), as well as constant chatter by the champ, who, at one point, makes it comic when he says, "I hate fighters who talk too much."

Of course, there are clips for the fight fans too. A succession of knockout in slow motion, as well as prefight, stagy, vociferous clashes with such opponents as Jerry Quarry and Sonny Liston, are fleeting and, like much of "Ali the Man," it merely illustrates but doesn't really reveal a highly complex, controversial human being.

The associate attraction, "Ali the Fighter," the documentary of the first Ali-Frazier fight, which was released here in January, 1974, as "The Fighters," is highly recommended, however, both as an excellent fight film and as an incisive view of the principals and the fight game, which isn't a game at all.

A. H. WEILER

1975 S 18, 50:1

FILM VIEW

VINCENT CANBY

Epic Battle of the Sexes

All choices are political, Lina Wertmuller, the gifted Italian director, suggested here in an interview last February, and in none of her earlier films seen in this country has this thought been more wittily and exuberantly demonstrated than in her newest film, "Swept Away (By an Unusual Destiny in The Blue Sea of August)." You may notice that I didn't identify Miss Wertmuller as the gifted Italian *woman* director, though women directors in motion pictures are still so rare that the fact remains newsworthy. She is, before everything else, a first-rate director and screenwriter (she does her own screenplays), a talent of such independence and range that some details in her films give pause to her sisters in the feminist movement.

In the same interview referred to above, Miss Wertmuller said that she agrees with about 75 per cent of what the feminists are fighting for these days—and that seems just the sort of qualification that got Trotsky assassinated. Miss Wertmuller is deeply committed, but no party lines are going to dictate the shape of her work or stuff it with uplifting messages to be memorized like Chairman Mao's. The best films don't usually start with ideas that are then illustrated. Like Miss Wertmuller's, they have their origins in feelings and attitudes, in mysteries the explorations of which are the works they give rise to.

● ● ●

SEPTEMBER 21, 1975

Giannini and Melato in "Swept Away"—"a knockdown, dragout comedy that plays hell with party lines"

This is evident throughout "Swept Away," which is first and foremost a love story that takes the form of knockdown, dragout comedy. The lovers—the contenders, really—are the conventional poles apart, one being a man and the other a woman. They are also separated by birth (he's a Sicilian, she's a northern Italian), by class (he's a sailor, a member of the proletariat, she's rich, a member of the bourgeoisie), and by politics (he's a devout Communist, she's a raving capitalist).

In the kind of contrivance that works equally well in a fairy tale or a comedy of this kind (which is really a contemporary fairy tale), the pair is marooned on a deserted Mediterranean isle for several weeks with the predictable results, though how those results are achieved is not easily predictable.

Each of the four Wertmuller films seen here to date has to do with choices: "The Lizards," an examination of small-town Italian life that recalls Fellini's early films; "Love and Anarchy," about an anarchist's almost comically ill-fated attempt to assassinate Mussolini in the thirties; "The Seduction of Mimi," about a Sicilian Communist's war with the Mafia, and now "Swept Away." In this film the choices made by Gennarino (Giancarlo Giannini), the sailor, and Raffaella (Mariangela Melato), the rich woman who has chartered the yacht on which Gennarino is a deckhand, begin as being simply extensions of their social roles and then become almost hopelessly tangled by other considerations, including sexual and emotional ones, when they find themselves isolated on what must be the only island in the Mediterranean not yet occupied by German tourists.

Miss Wertmuller is much more a sociologist than either a socialist or a feminist. All her films have their roots in specifically detailed milieus that have direct effect on how her characters behave. To this extent her films are schematic and intimately connected with formal ideas, but there is so much spontaneous life in their execution that they transcend easy categorization. They can be pulled apart, their pieces labelled according to the rhetoric of any of several dogmas, but something ambiguous always remains. It's that ambiguous core that separates artists from—you might say—craftpersons.

Gennarino is everything that a male chauvinist pig has ever represented. He's intolerant of any women's rights. He's also the sort of man who will tick off the evils of capitalist society (Swiss banks, taxes, the quality of television programing) while systematically beating the hell out of the woman he really loves. Raffaella, beautiful, vain, mindless of others though certainly not stupid, is the Shrew Rampant. Their confrontation on the island begins with Gennarino's careful humiliation of Raffaella, progresses to her submission to him, and (in a development that may have the feminists screaming) blossoms into mutually passionate love.

Not since John Barrymore and Carole Lombard squared off in "Twentieth Century" have there been such epic physical battles of the sexes as in "Swept Away," and these are funny, not because either one of the combatants seriously brutalizes the other (they don't), but because they both emerge as people of such unexpected if imperfect nobility. This movie plays hell with party lines.

It is also full of beautiful things to look at, the dazzling light of Mediterranean summer and the extraordinary performances by Giannini, who played the title role in "Mimi" and the attempted assassin in "Love and Anarchy,'" and Miss Melato, who also illuminated those films. Miss Melato, memorable as the frizzy-haired prostitute in "Love and Anarchy," is such an interesting actress that it's almost impossible to associate that earlier performance with the wicked and witty patrician who is momentarily humbled here. Giannini, whom Miss Wertmuller occasionally photographs in fond, misty close-ups that recall Von Sternberg's treatment of Dietrich, may be on his way to becoming the Marcello Mastroianni of the seventies. He appears to be the kind of pliant, resourceful actor who (close-ups notwithstanding) doesn't intrude on a character. Even when the character's being most outrageous, the actor remains invisible within. It's one of the mysteries of good film acting.

"Swept Away" is the first major release of the fall season, and I hope it becomes the first major hit. Just as a reminder: don't confuse Miss Wertmuller's work with that of another, far more splashy, far less talented Italian director, Liliana Cavani, the woman who made "The Night Porter." They share little more than a country of origin.

1975 S 21, II:15:1

DOG DAY AFTERNOON, directed by Sidney Lumet; screenplay by Frank Pierson, based on a magazine article by P. F. Kluge and Thomas Moore; produced by Martin Bregman and Martin Elfand; editor, Dede Allen; director of photography, Victor J. Klemper; an Artists Entertainment Complex, Inc., production, distributed by Warner Brothers. Running time: 130 minutes. At the Cinema 1 Theater, Third Avenue near 60th Street. This film has been rated R.
Sonny ....Al Pacino
Sal ....John Cazale
Sheldon ....James Broderick
Moretti ....Charles Durning
Sylvia ....Penny Allen
Mulvaney ....Sully Boyar
Margaret ....Beulah Garrick
Jenny ....Carol Kane
Deborah ....Sandra Kazan
Miriam ....Marcia Jean Kurtz
Maria ....Amy Levitt
Howard ....John Marriott
Edna ....Estelle Omens
Vi ....Judith Malina
Angie ....Susan Peretz
Leon ....Chris Sarandon
Bobby ....Gary Springer

By VINCENT CANBY

"Dog Day Afternoon," which opened yesterday at the Cinema 1, is Sidney Lumet's most accurate, most flamboyant New York movie —that consistently vital and energetic Lumet genre that includes "The Pawnbroker" and "Serpico" and exists entirely surrounded by (but always separate from) the rest of his work. Mr. Lumet's New York movies are as much aspects of the city's life as they are stories of the city's life.

"Dog Day Afternoon" is a melodrama, based on fact, about a disastrously ill-planned Brooklyn bank robbery, and it's beautifully acted by performers who appear to have grown up on the city's sidewalks in the heat and hopelessness of an endless midsummer.

•

If you can let yourself laugh at desperation that has turned seriously lunatic, the film is funny, but mostly it's reportorially efficient and vivid, in the understated way of news writing that avoids easy speculation.

Each of the several principal lives it touches has been grotesquely bent out of shape. The director and Frank Pierson, who wrote the fine screenplay, don't attempt to supply reasons. The movie

John Cazale and Al Pacino in "Dog Day Afternoon"

says only that this is what happened. No more. This severely limits the film's emotional impact, though not its seriousness or its fascination. "Dog Day Afternoon" is a gaudy street-carnival of a movie that rudely invites laughs at inappropriate moments, which is in keeping with the city's concrete sensibility.

The incident on which the film is based was the attempt to rob a branch of the Chase Manhattan Bank on Aug. 22, 1972. The two bandits, one of whom was seeking money for a sex-change operation for a boyfriend, failed miserably, after they held the bank's employes hostage for 14 hours, appeared live on television, became the center of an impromptu neighborhood Mardi Gras, and negotiated for a jet plane to fly them out of the country.

Mr. Lumet's film is exclusively concerned with the robbery attempt and the time it occupied. Only briefly does the film move out of the bank and away from the lower-middle-class neighborhood of apartments over pizza parlors, barber shops and

barrooms. We occasionally see the neighborhood in a high, smoggy long-shot, the tar-paper shingles shimmering in the reflected heat.

Most of the time the film stays contained within the bank. This concentration in space and time is responsible for much of the film's dramatic intensity.

So too are the brilliant characterizations by the members of the large cast, including Al Pacino, as the (probably) more than a bit mad mini-mind of the holdup, a man with bravura style when he plays to the crowds outside the bank but apparently quite demented in his personal relationships.

He vows his love for his wife and children and especially for his boyfriend, whom he had "married" in a drag wedding some months earlier with his mother as a witness. On the other hand, the boyfriend, played with just the right mixture of fear, dignity and silliness by Chris

Sarandon, testifies that his would-be patron has tried to kill him on several occasions.

•

The other characterizations that one remembers are those of Penny Allen as the bank's efficient head teller, Estelle Omens as a woman teller of a certain age who objects to

profanity even under stress ("My ears aren't garbage cans"), John Cazale as Mr. Pacino's sidekick in crime, a man who doesn't smoke because "the body is the temple of the Lord," and James Broderick and Charles Durning as the chief representatives of the law. Of particular interest is Susan Peretz as Mr. Pacino's wife, in whom one sees the tangle of city distress, anger, sweetness and violence, which is one of the main things that "Dog Day Afternoon" is all about.

1975 S 22, 41:1

GIVE 'EM HELL, HARRY!, a film of a play; written by Samuel Gallu, directed by Peter H. Hunt, produced by Mr. Gallu and Thomas J. McErlane; film directed by Steve Binder, produced by Al Ham and Joseph E. Bluth; director of photography, Ken Palius; music by Milton P. Larsen; presented by Theatrovision. At the Ziegfeld Theater, Avenue of the Americas and 54th Street. Running time: 104 minutes. This film has not been classified.
Harry S. Truman . . . James Whitmore

By RICHARD EDER

It starts bumpily and against the grain. "Give 'Em Hell, Harry!" a filmed version of James Whitmore's monologue re-creation of Harry S. Truman, has a lot going against it.

Almost any stage show put flatly and squarely on camera gives a weakened, strained effect, like coffee made with used grounds. Filming a monologue imitation—a uniquely theatrical form—is especially chancy.

When a lone figure comes out on a stage to do something so seemingly impossible as juggle seven balls or imitate a courting elephant, the audience is at least briefly on his side. Its sympathy, its will to believe, can be quickly dissipated by a bad performance, but it is there for a while.

•

Films are different. We are skeptical when they try to address us. Movies have to wait a little. We only assent slowly to a face talking to

us from the screen; there has to be some preparation first. Perhaps that is why so many movies begin with long shots, aerial sequences, views of people going about their business and paying us no attention.

And here is Mr. Whitmore straight off, sitting at a desk and trying to make us believe he is Harry Truman. We know he isn't Truman; he doesn't even look very much like him. And whom is he trying to fool, with his noisy snuffling after each especially trenchant remark? Stage devices come unbuttoned in front of the camera.

And yet "Give 'Em Hell, Harry!," which is being shown for a limited run at the Ziegfeld Theater, works its way gradually past these problems. In the end, it captivates and even moves.

For one thing, Mr. Whitmore may suffer the disadvantage of playing a stage part on the screen, but it is a first-rate stage performance. It is clear why his show has been such a success onstage in Washington. If at the start he is an actor straining away to imitate Truman, by the end he is the man.

The script, put together by Samuel Gallu, is beautifully articulated and balanced. Mr. Gallu has taken a series of Truman confrontations—with General of the Army Douglas MacArthur, with Senator Joseph R. McCarthy, with the Ku Klux Klan, with the railroad unions, with a lawn mower back in Independence—and, using real quotations, friends' reminiscences and his own sensitive and restrained imagination, has made a portrait that is stirring as well as amusing.

Perhaps the main force at work among all the craftsmanship is the way that Truman's authenticity — his sense of his limits and his additional sense that these limits were also possibilities —keeps gnawing away at our awareness of what has happened since in American politics.

James Whitmore, as President Harry S. Truman, having fun with a premature headline

In a way it took Richard M. Nixon to make Truman appreciated. How else could the sight of Mr. Whitmore fishing in his pocket for a stamp to mail a letter convey such a dramatic pang, a sense of the coarsened Presidential ethics of more recent times?

1975 S 23, 30:1

THREE DAYS OF THE CONDOR, directed by Sydney Pollack; screenplay by Lorenzo Semple Jr. and David Rayfiel, based on the novel "Six Days of the Condor," by James Grady; produced by Stanley Schneider; director of Photography, Owen Roizman; music, Dave Grusin; supervising film editor, Fredric Steinkamp; editor, Don Guidice; a Dino de Laurentiis presentation, distributed by Paramount. Running time: 118 minutes. At Loews Astor Plaza, 44th Street west of Broadway, and Lowes Tower East, Third Avenue near 72d Street. This film has been rated R.

Turner .... Robert Redford
Kathy .... Faye Dunaway
Higgins .... Cliff Robertson
Joubert.................. Max Von Sydow
Mr. Wabash.................. John Houseman
Atwood .... Addison Powell
Barber .... Walter McGinn
Janice .... Tina Chen
Wicks .... Michael Kane

By VINCENT CANBY

Turner (Robert Redford) is not your stereotypical Central Intelligence Agency operative, the short-haired, buttoned-down kind we've seen testifying live on television from time to time. Turner's hair is fashionably long. He wears blue jeans and shirts without ties and he rides to work on a motorcycle. He's an eccentric link in the C.I.A. chain of command.

Turner's "work" is on Manhattan's upper East Side, in a handsome old brownstone identified as the American Literary Historical Society, which is a blind for an esoteric C.I.A. research center where agents read and feed into a computer pertinent details from contemporary novels, short stories and journals of all sorts. The aim: to find out whether pending C.I.A. operations may have somehow been leaked, and to pick up pointers on spy methodology that may have been fantasized by hack fiction writers.

•

Turner is a C.I.A. "reader," which, like the job of a reader at a movie company, is about as unimportant as a job can be while still qualifying its incumbent as a member of the team.

Yet in Sydney Pollack's "Three Days of the Condor," Turner, whose code name is Condor, comes close to wreaking more havoc on the C.I.A. in three days than any number of House and Senate investigating committees have done in years. (The film, based on James Grady's novel, "Six Days of the Condor," has compressed the story's time span, necessitating the modification of title.)

"Three Days of the Condor," which opened yesterday at Loews Astor Plaza and Tower East Theaters, is a good-looking, entertaining suspense film that is most effective when its being most conventional, working variations on obligatory sequences of pursuit and flight, and on those sudden revelations that can reverse the roles of cat and mouse.

As a serious exposé of misdeeds within the C.I.A. the film is no match for stories that have appeared in your local newspaper. Indeed, one has to pay careful attention to figure out just what it is that who is doing to whom in "Three Days of the Condor" and, if I understood it correctly, it's never as horrifying as the real thing.

In the screenplay by Lorenzo Semple, Jr., and David Rayfiel, Turner very early on stumbles upon the existence of a kind of super-C.I.A. within the C.I.A., after which his life is not worth a plug nickel. It doesn't do to analyze too closely the character Mr. Redford plays, that is, to ask why the bookish intellectual of the film's opening sequences would have joined the C.I.A. in the first place, or how he later manages so easily to become such a hotshot at tapping telephones and kidnapping very important persons.

•

The suspense of the film depends less on this kind of plausibility than on Mr. Redford's reputation (in a movie we accept the fact that he can do anything) and on the verve with which Mr. Pollack, the director, sets everything up. It also benefits from the presence of good actors, including Faye Dunaway (as the woman who befriends the fleeing Turner), Cliff Robertson, Max Von Sydow and John Houseman, though it's not a film to make particular demands on their talents.

At its best moments, "Three Days of the Condor" creates without effort or editorializing that sense of isolation—that far remove from reality—within which super-government agencies can operate with such heedless immunity. This point is implicit in the jargon the agents use. When a C.I.A. man speaks to Turner of "the community," he's not talking about a borough or a city or a state but about the brotherhood of intelligence people, who live in another dimension of time, place and expectation.

1975 S 25, 60:1

GREY GARDENS. Directed by David Maysles, Albert Maysles, Ellen Hovde and Muffie Meyer; photography, Albert Maysles and David Maysles; editors, Miss Hovde, Miss Meyer and Susan Froemke; produced by the Maysles brothers. At the New York Film Festival, Alice Tully Hall, Lincoln Center. Running time: 94 minutes.

Mother .... Edith Beale
Daughter .... Edith Beale
Handyman .... Jerry Torre
Birthday guest .... Lois Wright
Birthday guest .... Jack Helmuth
Gardener .... Brooks Hires

Set a movie camera down in a jungle clearing: Life is stood on end. The children caper and gesticulate or simply gape; the adults, a few paces back, pay whole-hearted attention or self-consciously pay none. There is authenticity, but there is also incitement. Part of what the camera sees it has created.

Something like this happens in "Grey Gardens," where the camera has been placed not in a backland settlement but in the decayed East Hampton, L. I., mansion of two lovely and tormented recluses. They are Edith Bouvier Beale, somewhere around 80, and her daughter Edie, in her mid-50's. They are the aunt and cousin of Jacqueline Onassis.

•

The two hidden and disabled lives, who have fashioned a littered, cat-infested carapace the same shape as themselves around themselves, are brought out for scrutiny by Albert and David Maysles, makers of some distinguished American documentaries.

The cycle of attachment and tension, the cramped routines in the large, crumbling house, the regular scratching and salving of each other's psychic wounds: all these elements of a two-part relationship are made triangular. The camera is there, the Maysles stand behind it, and the effect is like that upon moths in a dark room when a light is switched on outside. They are instantly at the window, fluttering their wings.

The stories of the two women come only blurrily to view in the film's 94 minutes of argument, reminiscence and halting, shifting monologues, which often go on simultaneously.

Mrs. Beale, who is bent and feeble—the camera is unsparing of her old sagging flesh, draped in a sort of towel—is witty, fierce and the center of the household. She was once a great society beauty, was divorced when Edie was a child, fell ill and some 25 years ago brought Edie back to stay with her.

Edie, who still has considerable beauty, seems the more deeply disturbed. She dresses in a strange costume that exposes most of her legs in black open-work stockings, keeps her head constantly covered with a tight hood and dances and sings disjointedly. She complains, sometimes confidentially to the camera, sometimes in brawling arguements, that her mother has chained her, driven away her lovers, ruined her life.

Mrs. Beale rejoins that if Edie has stayed it was because she really didn't want to do anything else. "You never fell for a man," she says. "France fell, but Edie didn't fall." But at another point, something else breaks through: "I didn't want that child taken away. I'd be entirely alone."

The camera picks up relentlessly the litter of the house, the cats and raccoons nesting, the motionless world where two women sprawl side by side on beds, eating ice cream and liver paste, singing, posturing, bickering.

And continually addressing the camera or rather, the microphone. They use it as a judge, an ally against each other and, in the case of Edie, as something more. "Darling David, where have you been all my life? Where have you been?" she calls out as she finishes a painful drum majorette routine. "All I needed was this man, David. David—I wish I'd had David and Al with me before this."

•

And all that comes back in response to this extraordinary unfolding by the two recluses is a quick view in the mirror of the Maysle's brothers, one at work on the camera, the other on the microphone. Or an occasional, perfunctory snatch of an answer delivered in the tone a doctor uses with a half-anesthetized patient.

There is no doubt about the artistry and devotion that the Maysles have used in recording the life in "Grey Gardens." There is no reason to doubt them when they say they love and admire the Beales. But the moviegoer will still feel like an exploiter. To watch "Grey Gardens" is to take part in a kind of carnival of attention with two willing but vulnerable people who had established themselves, for better or worse, in the habit of not being looked at. And what happens when the carnival moves on?

RICHARD EDER

1975 S 27, 21:2

CONVERSATION PIECE (Gruppo di Famiglia in un Interno), directed by Luchino Visconti; screenplay by Suso Cecchi D'Amico, Enrico Medioli and Mr. Visconti, based on an idea by Mr. Medioli; executive producer, Giovanni Bertolucci; director of photography, Pasqualino de Santis; editor, Ruggero Mastroianni; music, Franco Mannino; produced by Rusconi Film (Rome) and Gaumont International Sarl (Paris). Running time: 122 minutes. At the New York Film Festival at Avery Fisher Hall, Broadway at 65th Street. This film has not been rated.

Professor .... Burt Lancaster
Bianca Brumonti.................. Silvana Mangano
Konrad .... Helmut Berger
Lietta .... Claudia Marsani
Stefano .... Stefano Patrizi
Erminia .... Elvira Cortese
Mother .... Dominique Sanda
Wife .... Claudia Cardinale

By VINCENT CANBY

The choice of Luchino Visconti's "Conversation Piece" to open the 13th New York Film Festival last night can only be supported if one sees it as a tribute to the highly respected Italian director in recognition of his earlier work. This would include the neorealist "La Terra Trema" and "Rocco and His Brothers," as well as the elegant "The Leopard" and even the wildly operatic "The Damned."

"Conversation Piece" is a disaster, the kind that prompts giggles from victims in the audience who, willingly, sit through it all feeling as if they were drowning in three inches of water.

The movie was shown in Avery Fisher Hall at Lincoln Center. The 19 remaining selections of this year's festival will be screened at Lincoln Center's Alice Tully Hall during the next two weeks.

•

"Conversation Piece" continues to explore concerns that occupied Mr. Visconti in both "The Leopard" and in his later, much less successfull screen adaptation of "Death in Venice." The barbarians, the forces that represent social and political change and that acknowledge their physical passions, are attacking a citadel of the intellect, a place where reason has reigned at the cost of any possibility of love or commitment. It's one of Mr. Visconti's more dubious propositions that a person of taste and intelligence must always sleep alone in sterile splendor.

In "Conversation Piece" the citadel is the handsome old Roman palazzo owned by the Professor (Burt Lancaster), an aging, American-born, Roman-bred art historian who devotes his life to his books, his paintings by Old Masters, and his stereo recordings of Mozart. His life is turned upside down when his house is invaded by the real world as represented by a rich, pushy, overdressed marquesa, played by Silvana Mangano, the wife of a Fascist industrialist, her teen-age daughter (Claudia Marsani), her young German lover (Helmut Berger) and her daughter's lover (Stefano Patrizi).

The members of this rampaging horde of four are supposedly so vital and so fascinating that they are able to persuade the Professor to lease to them his upstairs apartment for a year, though to anyone watching the movie they seem less interesting than a group of ordinary, run-of-the-play dress extras. Part of it has to do with what they say and the way we hear it.

The screenplay is by Mr. Visconti and his longtime associates, Suso Cecchi D'Amico and Enrico Medioli and is said to be based on "an idea" by Mr. Medioli, which may well have once been a one-set play, the kind that has carefully timed entrances and exits and makes frequent use of the telephone to pass on information to us, if not people offscreen.

I suspect the screenplay was originally written in Italian, though the version shown last night is in English, with some of the actors (Mr. Lancaster, Miss Mangano and Mr. Berger, most likely) having post-synchronized their own lines in English, while other voices have supplied the English dialogue for the remaining characters. The result is a soundtrack that is not only lifeless but also often impossible to understand.

But then it is even worse when you can understand it. "Conversation Piece" is a movie made up of one part chit-chat ("May I use your telephone?"), one part unwanted confessions ("I threw myself into the student movement — deeper than most") and one part lumpy aphorisms ("The way of progress is destruction").

As in bad plays, everyone always means exactly what he says and never has to think a second before saying it. There is no feeling for the complexity of the mental processes, for the mysterious ways in which the mind works. This, of course, wouldn't be bad if these people had the wit and insight of George Bernard Shaw characters, but they don't.

•

As the invaders ultimately destroy the old professor, they also are the undoing of the German gigolo who, we are asked to believe, was once politically committed until ravaged by the bourgeoisie. Possibly some other actor could have handled this part, but Mr. Berger (who played the title role in Mr. Visconti's "Ludwig"), is such a lightweight he can function no more than as an ideogram for decadence.

Miss Mangano is grotesque in a grotesque role, while Miss Marsani, as her daughter, acts as if she'd seen too many "Gidget" movies.

Mr. Lancaster, fine old professional that he is, is awful, adopting that humble, "Birdman of Alcatraz" manner he uses when employed in what he apparently thinks is serious movie-making. "Conversation Piece" is the kind of fatuous film that the professionally pragmatic Burt Lancaster, the action movie hero, would snort at and leave in the middle of.

1975 S 27, 21:2

LA CHIENNE (The Bitch), directed by Jean Renoir; screenplay (French with English subtitles) by Mr. Renoir and Andre Girard, based on the novel by Georges de la Fouchardiere; directors of photography, Theodore Sparkuhl and Roger Hubert; editor, Marguerite Renoir; produced by Braunberger-Richebe, print owned by the Cinematheque Francaise. Running time: 100 minutes. At Alice Tully Hall at the New York Film Festival, Broadway at 65th Street.

Maurice Legrand .... Michel Simon
Lulu .... Janie Mareze
Dede .... Georges Flamant
Adele Legrand .... Madeleine Berubet
Alexis Godard .... Gaillard
Dagodet .... Jean Gehret

"This is neither a comedy nor a tragedy. It proves no moral at all. It's simply another story about He and She and The Other Guy."

So says, in effect, the master of ceremonies, the hand puppet that introduces Jean Renoir's 1931 classic, "La Chienne" (The Bitch), whereupon the camera moves across the apron of the miniature stage, through a cloth backdrop and into the world of real-life Paris.

•

Maybe it's not an absolutely real-life Paris. The city we see is familiar in all its physical characteristics, but it is lit by the unique combination of compassion, wit, amusement and surprise that this greatest of all French directors has brought to virtually every film he's ever made.

"La Chienne" will be screened as a retrospective entry at the New York Film Festival at Alice Tully Hall this afternoon at 3 o'clock and once again next Saturday at the same time and place. Of the seven festival films I've seen at this writing, it's the only one that can be recommended without reservation. It's fresh, funny, rude and gentle about the appalling consequences one faces if one has the gift of staying alive.

"La Chienne," which apparently has never been released here in an English-subtitled version, is Renoir's first full-length sound film. It's based on the novel by George de la Fouchardière that was also made into quite a different movie, "Scarlet Street," by Fritz Lang in 1945. The basic story lines of both films are approximately the same, but where the Lang is dark, violent and obsessive, the tone of the Renoir is contemplative and ironic. In spite of what the master of ceremonies says, "La Chienne" is a comedy in the best sense.

It's the not-really-so sad story of Maurice (Michel Simon), a painter on Sundays and a quiet, self-contained, somewhat comic figure of a bookkeeper the other six days. One night, Maurice, who is married to a perpetually furious shrew, meets a vulgar prostitute named Lulu (Janie Marèze). In the way of such tales, he falls desperately in love with Lulu and sets her up in a flat that is occupied mostly by Lulu and her pimp.

"La Chienne" is the tale of Maurice's degradation, his victimization and his ultimate liberation, first through love, followed by violence, then by that curious, benign second-sight that Renoir bestows upon charasters who have the courage to survive.

The late Mr. Simon' is superb as the bookkeeper who doesn't fit into any stereotype of henpecked husband. His Maurice is a man of many parts, including the will to indulge his pleasures and a remarkable resolution, when necessary. All of the performances are close to flawless, but it's Renoir's unseen presense one remembtrs most vividly, the man we saw on screen, and recognized immediately, when he introduced the vignettes of his last film, "The Little Theater of Jean Renoir."

VINCENT CANBY

1975 S 27, 21:4

FAUSTRECHT DER FREIHEIT (Fist-Right of Freedom), directed by Rainer Werner Fassbinder; screenplay (German, with English subtitles) by Mr. Fassbinder and Christian Hohoff; photography, Michael Ballhaus; editor, Theat Eymesz; music, Peer Raben; production company, Tango Film; executive producer, Mr. Hohoff; at the New York Film Festival, Alice Tully Hall, Lincoln Center. Running time: 123 minutes.

Fox .... Rainer Werner Fassbinder
Eugen .... Peter Chatel
Max .... Karl-Heinz Bohm
Philip .... Harry Baer
Father .... Adrian Hoven
Mother .... Ulla Jacobson
Hedwig .... Christiane Maybach
WITH: Peter Kern, Hans Zander, Kurt Raab, Irm Herman, Ursula Stratz, Elma Karlowa, Barbara Valentin, Bruce Low, Walter Sedlmyr, Evelyn Kunneki, Ingrid Caven, Marquard Bohn and Liselotte Eder.

By RICHARD EDER

There is no air in front of the camera. The outdoor scenes—damp green foilage, overstuffed German shop windows—seem shot indoors; the indoor scenes, in velvet boxes. Cars move noiselessly, their windows clean and closed.

Rainer Werner Fassbinder's work is highly prized in Europe and crosses the Atlantic each year to the New York Film Festival, where it tends to die. His entry this year, "Fist-Right of Freedom," is a movie that gives us social protest in terms of social dyspepsia. It is not really dead—it has, in fact, considerable drive and stylishness—but it excludes all life that is not within the very narrow intentions of its author. Its pores have been painted over.

•

Mr. Fassbinder denounces the injustices of civilization by laying more stress on the heartburn of rich than on the hunger of the poor. This is common enough with modern film makers. Visconti did it in "Conversation Piece," which opened the festival yesterday. So, in more complex and lively fashion, did Lena Wertmuller in "Swept Away by an Unusual etc . . ." which is playing here to full houses. It allows the film maker to explore decadence —always more fun than exploring scabies — while compiling revolutionary credits.

"FistRight is a full-suds treatment of the oldest weepy in the history of tears. Decades ago it was being parodied on the British music-hall stage:

She were poor, but she were honest,
Wictim of the squire's whim.
First 'e loved 'er, then 'e left 'er
An' she lorst 'er honest nyme.

Mr. Fassbinder does it with homosexuals, and he sets it in a modern Germany. His victim is the virtuous proletariat — as homosexual — taken up, used, destroyed and discarded by the gilded bourgeoisie — as homosexual.

Foxy comes on as the Talking Head in a traveling freak show. At the film's start the show is shut down, and Foxy buys a winning lottery ticket and picks up a middle-aged furniture dealer in a public lavatory. They go home and soon Foxy has paired off with Eugen, the languid, vulpine son of a factory owner.

Foxy is brash, violent, warmhearted and naive. At first he dominates, or seems to, but Eugen, with his world of wealth and savior-faire, gradually tames him. In fact Eugen's world is rotting away — image of capitalism — the family factory is broke, and Foxy is the golden goose to be plucked.

And he is plucked, painfully, relentlessly, in unsparing humiliation. Inevitably, the degradation is heightened by the style if not the fact of the homosexual setting. Mr. Fassbinder may not be explicit about it, but he has adjusted the emotional tone of his film to use homosexuality as a symbol of decadence. His characters mince, leer, flirt and favor pink.

It is a "Blue Angel" done in drag, and its political message hardly redeems it. As a performer, in the part of Foxy, Mr. Fassbinder creates a character of some charm, dignity and originality. He struggles in the elegant, seamless shroud devised for him by Fassbinder the author and Fassbinder the director, and it is hardly surprising that he succumbs.

1975 S 27, 21:4

F FOR FAKE, directed and written by Orson Welles; directors of photography, Christian Odasso and Gary Graver; production coordinator, Francois Reicheubach, editors, Marie-Sophie Dubus and Dominique Engerer; music, Michel Legrand; a S.A.C.I. production by Janus Film (Frankfurt) and Les Films de l'Astrophore (Paris). Running time: 90 minutes. At the New York Film Festival, Alice Tully Hall, Broadway at 65th Street. This film has not been rated.
WITH Orson Welles, Clifford Irving, Oja Kodar, Elmyr de Hory, Edith Irving, Francois Reichenbach, Joseph Cotten, Richard Wilson, Paul Stewart, Sasa Devcic, Gary Graver, Andres Vicente Gomez, Julio Palinkas, Christian Odasso, Francoise Widoff.

By VINCENT CANBY

"I'm a charlatan," says Orson Welles, looking very fit, his manner that of the practiced con artist who knows that if he confesses to everything, he will be held accountable for nothing. Or is it the other way around?

This is the beginning of Mr. Welles's latest film, "F for Fake," a charming, witty meditation upon fakery, forgery, swindling and art, a movie that may itself be its own Exhibit A.

The opening sequence is set in a fine old European railroad station, the kind with a peaked glass roof that romantics cherish, that Mr. Welles used in "The Trial" and that urban renewal people tear down. On a colder, snowy day, Anna Karenina might throw herself under some wheels here, but now it's sunny and warm. The mood is cheerfully skeptical.

•

Mr. Welles, the master of ceremonies, the credited director and writer as well as star of "F for Fake," welcomes us with some sleight of hand, turning a small boy's key into a coin and back again. "The key," says the charlatan, "is not symbolic of anything." The warnings keep coming, and you may be reminded of the late Old Gold slogan: "It's fun to be fooled, but more fun to know." Perhaps sometimes.

"F for Fake" is a documentary compounded of tricks, reversals, interviews with real forgers and re-creations of events that never happened. It's as much magic show as movie, a lark that is great fun even when one wishes the magician would take off his black slouch hat and his magician's cape and get back to making real movies. But did he really make this one? And is "F for Fake" not a real movie?

There are amused rumors to the effect that Mr. Welles did not actually direct a large part of "F for Fake." This part is an extended sequence set in Ibiza involving interviews with Elmyr de Hory, the well-publicized art forger, and Clifford Irving, who wrote Mr. de Hory's biography ("Fake") and later went on to make his own name by attaching it to Howard Hughes's.

The rumors are that these scenes were shot by François Reichenbach, one of the first practitioners of cinéma vérité, who himself shows up throughout "F for Fake," for which he receives credit as the production coordinator. "F for Fake" is so stylish in all its parts, in its editing and particularly in a final fiction sequence that, if it is a fake, it's a marvelous one, and to hell with the signature on it.

Which is one of the things that "F for Fake" is all about. Midway through the film, after we've listened to

Orson Welles in a scene from his film "F for Fake"

stories that may or may not be true about Mr. de Hory's sucess in supplying the art world with fake Matisses, Picassos and Modiglianis, Mr. Welles reminds us that there are no signatures on the cathedral at Chartres. Chartres needs no "experts" to authenticate its grandeur, he says. "Experts" are the villans of "F for Fake"—people who must tell us whether we should swoon when looking at a particular painting or turn up our noses in disgust.

Mr. Welles, who has been the subject of a lot of such expertise and takes a dim view of it, has a grand time with the film's final. This is the fanciful story of how Picasso was tricked by a ravishing Hungarian model, whose grandfather, an art forger, confesses on his deathbed to a furious Picasso that his dearest desire has always been to create "an entirely new Picasso period."

I have some minor reservations about "F for Fake." I don't share Mr. Welles's affection for either Mr. de Hory or Mr. Irving. Unlike the generous Mr. Welles, they are small potatoes. When Mr. Welles asks, "Doesn't it say something about our time that Cliff [Irving] could only make it through trickery?," my answer is no. It says more about Mr. Irving, who as far as I can tell, hasn't made it at all.

1975 S 28, 57:1

JEDER FUR SICH UND GOTT GEGEN ALLE (Every Man for Himself and God Against All), directed by Werner Herzog; screenplay (German with English subtitles) by Mr. Herzog; photography, Jorg Schmidt-Reitwein; editor, Beate Mainka-Jellinghaus; music, Pachelbel, Orlando di Lasso, Albinoni and Mozart; production, Werner Herzog Filmproduktion. At the New York Film Festival, Alice Tully Hall, Lincoln Center. Running time: 110 minutes.
Kaspar ....Bruno S.
Daimer ....Walter Ladengast
Kathe ....Brigitte Mira
Unknown man..............Hans Musaus
Circus director........Willy Semmelrogge
Lord Stanhope..........Michael Kroecher
Captain ....Henry van Lyck

By RICHARD EDER

The early tenor aria from "The Magic Flute" arches in a high arrow's trajectory over the opening shots: a boat moves on a blue river, a washerwoman on the bank looks up and regards us solemnly, and wind pushes the marsh grass in heavy waves.

It is impossible to know why these things move us, or why they prepare us for an experience out of the ordinary. Throughout "Every Man for Himself and God Against All" there are moments when we drift a bit outside of ourselves, in a kind of detached gratefulness that the person occupying our seat is being given so much.

Werner Herzog is a young German director with a rapidly growing reputation in Europe and, as yet, not much of a name here. "Every Man for Himself," which won this year's Grand Jury Prize at the Cannes Film Festival, should change that.

Mr. Herzog does not deal with small corners of reality; he riddles with universals. Like Ingmar Bergman, his concerns are more metaphysical than social, and again like Mr. Bergman, he explores them in ways that keep engaging our imagination, our intellect and our emotions.

His pictures are populated with freaks and deformities or people in freakish or deformed circumstances. Not, at least in his latest films, in order to dwell on these extremes—he is in no way exotic—but to focus on the main human condition, as a man might climb to the foothills at the edge of a city to see the city better.

"Every Man" is set on a real historical incident. In the early 19th-century a man appeared in a square in Nuremberg. He could not speak, he could barely stand, he had apparently been kept in some kind of dungeon. His identity was a mystery—the only clue was a paper he carried that gave his name as Kasper Hauser and asked that he be taken into service as a soldier.

He was taken in, taught to speak, to read and write, and then, in a fashion as mysterious as his first appearance, he was murdered.

This is Mr. Herzog's fable, allowing both a concrete and a philosophical exercise of the questions: Where do we come from? Why are we here? Where do we go?

A sound fable is not enough for a sound movie: "Every Man" is a superb movie because Mr. Herzog has managed to treat the fable in stunning human and dramatic terms. He has done so, in large part, through his use of a man identified only as Bruno S.—he is not a professional actor, and he has spent some time in mental institutions—as Kasper.

There is more than acting; there is a total, magical immersion of Bruno in the man who arrives in the world as a stranger, takes it in, tries to grasp it, judges it and is removed from it.

Kasper is seen first in his dungeon, grunting and playing with his only possession, a wooden horse. His keeper, a man in black—Mr. Herzog conceives God as a secret policeman — appears, jams boots on his legs, which are as soft and white as maggots, and carries him to the town square at dawn.

The world discovers Kasper and Kasper discovers the world. Nothing very dramatic happens until the end: The film is mostly a gentle, meditative and poignant discourse. The authorities send a tiny owl of a notary around after Kasper to record his actions and pronouncements, beautifully played by Walter Ladengast.

Kasper's extraordinary face, his eyes strained wide to see better, his whole posture suggesting a man trying to swallow, trying to grasp a world of strangeness, is the film's central image.

As he learns to speak, he learns to think. He wants to accept society but he cannot. "Every man is a wolf to me," he tells the professor, haltingly. His only struggle is to search for his own meaning: He has no ego. "Nothing lives less in me than my life," he says.

Scholars come to question him: he baffles and holds them off. He is trying to understand life, not the rules of life. He strains and strains; he dreams the beginning of a dream that may have the meaning he is looking for, but he can't manage to dream an ending.

The man in black reappears —"Wait here for me," he had instructed Kasper when he left him on the square— and strikes him down. Kasper dies, recounting the first half of his dream. an autopsy finds that his brain is deformed.

The notary society's representative, emerges, writing in his book. "We have found an explanation for this strange man; we cannot find a better one," he says with deep satisfaction. As he walks up the street and this beautiful cryptic and satisfying movie ends, we see that he is limping: He too is deformed.

1975 S 28, 57:1

CORRECTION

A dropped line in the review of the film "Every Man for Himself and God Against All" in The New York Times on Sunday. resulted in one actor's receiving praise meant for another. The praise was intended for Walter Ladengast, who played the role of a professor.

1975 S 30, 39:7

What the Sneaks Did for 'Smile'

By JOHN MALONE

One of the most promising entries to be shown in the New York Film Festival next month underwent a number of important changes last spring which were determined not in Hollywood but in Seattle, New York City and two small California cities—Riverside and Encino. The film is "Smile," directed by Michael Ritchie, whose previous films include "Downhill Racer" and "The Candidate." In each of the four cities where "Smile" was changed, it was given a sneak preview.

Sneak previews are shown in addition to a theater's regular attraction, giving that evening's patrons a chance to see two movies for the price of one. That is nice for the moviegoer—but what is the purpose of the sneak preview for the moviemaker? Are sneak previews merely a matter of testing the market, or do they have some creative use? To what extent do audience reactions influence the final shape of a movie when it is officially premiered weeks or even months later? Attempting to discover the answers to these questions, I talked with Michael Ritchie about the kinds of changes he had made in "Smile."

Like both "Downhill Racer" and "The Candidate," which dealt respectively with international ski racing and a political campaign, "Smile" takes an almost documentary look at an aspect of the world of organized competition, in this case a regional beauty contest for teen-age

John Malone is a novelist with a special interest in films.

These teen-agers left "Smile's" sneak-previewers smiling

girls. Because his films attempt to involve the audience with his characters' need to win; Ritchie feels that very careful editing is required to insure that moviegoers will not root so strongly for one particular character that they lose sight of the larger questions being raised about competitiveness. Sneak previews give him an opportunity to discover how well his intentions are coming across and to make adjustments accordingly.

Not all directors are as enthusiastic about sneak previews as Ritchie. Directors whose films are ultimately controlled by the studio for which they were made often dread them, since nervous studio executives may view the negative reactions of an audience as an indication that a film is in trouble and then proceed to lop out entire scenes and re-edit others in ways that distort the director's ideas. Even some directors whose contracts guarantee them control over the final cut of a film avoid sneak previews. Stanley Kubrick, for example, prefers to make changes only after a film has officially opened; in the three days following the New York premiere of "2001: A Space Odyssey," he cut the movie by 19 minutes.

Alfred Hitchcock, on the other hand, plans his films with such precision that the editing is virtually accomplished in the camera, and there is little or no extra footage to play around with. But Ritchie's documentary approach to his subjects is best served by allowing a certain leeway, and significant changes were made in "Smile," based on the reactions of preview audiences.

Ritchie did not make use of the rating cards that are sometimes distributed to audiences at sneak previews. He feels that the people who take the trouble to fill out such cards tend to be axgrinders and prefers to station three or four people around the auditorium and have them monitor the general audience response as well as pick up spontaneous individual comments. Ritchie himself, screenwriter Jerry Belson, and film editor Richard Harris attended all the sneak previews of "Smile." Conrad Hall, the cinematographer, was present at one of them.

"Smile" shows what happens when 25 teen-age girls descend upon Santa Rosa, California, to participate in the Young American Miss Pageant organized by the local Jay Cees. Much of the film deals with the beauty contest itself, including a series of classically inept talent acts. But the movie also de-

tails the emotional involvement in the contest of several of its organizers, especially Bruce Dern as a mobile-home dealer who serves as chief judge, and Barbara Feldon, playing a former contest winner who is more concerned with her duties as "mother hen" to the girls than she is with her own collapsing marriage. Because the moviegoer is asked both to laugh at and to sympathize with several of the characters, "Smile" presents special problems in terms of audience response.

The first preview was held in Seattle. A heavy snowstorm was in progress, and the small audience was, according to Ritchie, a peculiar mixture of "prostitutes, pickpockets, alcoholics, and stranded commuters." For the first 15 minutes, the refugees from the storm just sat and stared at the screen. But as bodily warmth returned, they began to enjoy themselves, and Ritchie and his cohorts were able to make at least a few judgments about the effectiveness of individual scenes.

A scene in which one of the girls discovers that the bandleader wears a toupee, for instance, wasn't getting the laugh Ritchie wanted. He says now that he simply "goofed" in filming that sequence; the camera angle he had selected obscured rather than heightened the visual joke. After the first three previews, the scene was taken out. On the other hand, the laughter of the Seattle audience indicated that the girls' no-talent talent acts were even more of a success than Ritchie had hoped for. He and his collaborators had filmed additional acts, but had left them out because they feared audiences would tire of them if too many were included. Before the final print was settled on, two of these sequences were added to the movie.

One scene was of particular concern to Ritchie. Barbara Feldon's husband, acted by newcomer Nicholas Pryor, gradually goes to pieces in the course of the movie. He has lost his job, is drinking heavily, and receives absolutely no comfort from his wife, either physical or emotional. After a violent argument with Miss Feldon near the end of the film, he disappears down a hallway to another room. Following her distraught husband, Miss Feldon discovers him with a gun in his mouth. She suggests, derisively, that this is no way to solve his problems. "You're right," he says, pulling the gun from his mouth and firing at her instead. The screen goes

blank.

In Seattle, this scene was greeted with a gasp. But Ritchie had expected laughter as well and had even hoped for applause — which was precisely the response elicited from a second preview audience, in Riverside, a town much like the community of Santa Rosa in the film. But in New York the scene once again drew only a large gasp. Ritchie thought he knew what the problem was: some kind of comic relief was needed in order to break the tension after the couple's argument in the living room. So Barbara Feldon was brought back in to record one more line of dialogue, to be added to the soundtrack just before she sees Pryor with the gun in his mouth. It has already been established that the woman played by Miss Feldon was more interested in the immaculate condition of her house and body than in any need of her husband's. The added line read: "If you're doing anything to mess up my clean rug . . ." Since Miss Feldon's back was to the camera as she moved down the hallway, no additional filming was required. At the subsequent Encino preview and at the Dallas Film Festival last April the gasp, the laughter and the applause all came just as Ritchie had wanted.

•

Obviously, the make-up of a given preview audience has a strong bearing on the kind of response a film will get. The Seattle preview was shown before an atypical audience, so that Ritchie found it necessary to discount its reactions to some extent. At the Manhattan preview, which I attended, the audience did not seem prepared for the kind of movie they were seeing. On this occasion, "Smile" was shown after "Lenny," which was then nearing the end of its run. The angry, manic, put-down comedy of Lenny Bruce's routines, as re-created by Dustin Hoffman, seemed to induce a certain cynicism and hostility in the audience, which was then directed toward "Smile." They tended to laugh at the characters rather than with them, responding most fully to the more hard-edged and satirical scenes and rejecting the film's warmer moments.

Ritchie later confirmed my impression that the reactions of the New York preview audience had been somewhat off-center. But that fact did not worry him particularly. "The purpose of making changes based on previews," Ritchie says, "is not to make the movie more palatable to

everyone, the way you'd test-market a breakfast cereal, but rather to make sure that your intentions have been fully realized." The warmest response at any of the preview showings came in Riverside, the community most like the Santa Rosa portrayed in the film, indicating to Ritchie that his own feelings about the characters in the film were coming across to this key audience.

•

The other previews were useful in more specific ways, prompting him to scrap two scenes that he felt simply weren't working. Other scenes were shortened, the editing tightened. Even with the addition of the extra teen-age talent acts, the overall running time was reduced by four minutes. Sections of the soundtrack were re-

mixed to bring dialogue into better balance with the musical score. And both Barbara Feldon and Dick McGavin, who plays the emcee of the pageant, were brought in to post-dub new lines of dialogue. None of these changes was major. Certainly they can't compare to the epic decision by director Frank Capra to throw out the first two reels of "Lost Horizon" after a disastrous sneak preview in Santa Barbara in 1937, a decision which he claims saved the film. But even the subtle changes Ritchie made in "Smile" demonstrate that while the sneak preview may be just a surprise double-feature for the moviegoer, it can be a significant creative tool for the moviemaker. ∎

1975 S 28, II:13:1

FILM VIEW

VINCENT CANBY

Quintessential New York Film

"Dog Day Afternoon" is not only the most accurate, most flamboyant of Sidney Lumet's New York movies, which include "Serpico" and "The Pawnbroker," it is the best film he's ever made, with the exception of "A Long Day's Journey Into Night," and that one had the advantage of the Eugene O'Neill play and three great roles superlatively acted by Ralph Richardson, Katharine Hepburn and Jason Robards.

"Dog Day Afternoon," which has a screenplay by Frank Pierson, is an original. The events are based on a real-life Brooklyn bank robbery and screen credit is given to P.F. Kluge and Thomas Moore for a magazine article in which they told the story of that robbery. Yet the point of view, the tone, the focal area of the narrative are the decisions of Mr. Lumet and his screenwriter, who were completely on their own. They had no pre-sold or tested literary sources to fall back on—which may not always be bad (Lumet's "Murder on the Orient Express" was a movie of much charm) but it has sometimes led the director into dimly lit states of pretension, as in "The Pawnbroker" and "Lovin' Molly."

"Dog Day Afternoon" is not cluttered with big themes that, more often than not, don't fit easily onto the movie screen. It's an action film in that almost everything it has to say grows spontaneously out of the confrontation of characters prompted by one bizarre event. This narrative method leaves a lot of psychological questions unanswered. Action movies, by definition, have no time for introspection, which is one of the reasons it took so long for critics to judge them seriously. For years movie critics only considered those movies "serious" that contained little self-conscious messages to be excised and quoted.

There are none in "Dog Day Afternoon," yet the film may be more "serious" than anything Lumet has done before. It's full of thoughts, feelings and questions about the quality of a certain kind of urban civilization. That sounds like a terrible load to drop onto any movie, much less one about a bank robbery, but these are the things about "Dog Day Afternoon" that continue to nudge the memory long after one has seen it, not the details of the attempted heist itself.

Lumet is so good with New York actors that it's difficult to tell whether "Dog Day Afternoon" has been well-cast or is exceedingly well acted. There are dozens of characters in the film and they all are so vividly performed that they avoid the kind of dramatic blurring you get in most movies with large casts. The success of the performers also has to do with the quality of Pierson's screenplay, which, with the exception of Sonny's frantic, overbearing mother, doesn't deal in the expected stereotypes.

Because "Dog Day Afternoon" is about an event and the behavior of its characters in the course of that event, Lumet keeps the time of the narrative to that

into that staid old building to shoot them all down in cold blood, made colder by the special ice pellets used — at least, that is one inference —by specially designed carnage-machines.

What was Robert Redford doing while his colleagues were being mowed down? He was out for lunch. Specifically, out to fetch lunch for his colleagues, it being his turn to go to the delicatessen. But, in order to avoid the rain, he ignores prescribed security regulations and bounds down the staircase and out the back door, which is closer to the deli; and anyway, it is time to establish him as a man of rather independent habits, who makes the boss of this super-secret C.I.A. front perpetually uneasy ("Are you sure you are quite happy working for us, Turner?") with that roaming, restless intelligence. (The

Al Pacino is "flawless" as a homosexual robber in "Dog Day Afternoon"

The real-life caper on which the film is based took place in Brooklyn on Aug. 22, 1972, when three young men (one became frightened right away and took the subway home) walked into a branch of the Chase Manhattan Bank shortly before closing time and pulled the stick-up. The men were amateurs. The police were alerted and surrounded the bank, thus beginning hours of negotiations during which the bandits held the employes hostage and made plans to obtain a jet to fly to a foreign country. (In the film, Sonny, the leader of the gang of two, a character played flawlessly by Al Pacino, asks his sidekick, Sal—John Cazale—what foreign country he wants to fly to, and Sal, after giving the matter some thought, answers, "Wyoming.")

This is a laugh in the film, and like so much of its comedy, the laugh is edged in cruelty, this time at the expense of the ignorant Sal. Yet this edge of cruelty, and the way the movie allows—and even encourages—the audience to laugh at desperate characters driven to lunatic endeavors, are as much the method of the film as its message. The film's New York is a cruel, desperate, lunatic place. I don't want to frighten moviegoers away from "Dog Day Afternoon" by mentioning things like messages; I only want to emphasize that it is a movie that knows what it's up to even when it's being ambiguous.

One of the most ambiguous aspects of the film is the character of Sonny who, it's revealed early on, is staging the hold-up to obtain money for a sex-change operation for his boyfriend, currently in Bellevue Hospital recuperating from a suicide attempt—which was his way of getting away from Sonny. Sonny's homosexuality is played straight, without tears, though he is also clearly on the brink of psychosis. We are told that he and Leon, the boyfriend, were "married" in a drag wedding earlier and that in the past he has terrorized both Leon, played by Chris Sarandon, and his legal wife, played by Susan Peretz.

The movie—to its credit, I think—makes no attempt to analyze Sonny. As Pacino portrays him, he has a great deal of bravura style and sidewalk wit when he makes his periodic forays outside the bank to talk to the cops and the Mardi Gras-like crowds, but he's obviously a fellow whose emotional problems are as outsized as the city's fiscal ones.

of the hold-up itself, 14 hours, and seldom allows the action to get very far from the bank and the Brooklyn neighborhood. In fact, the only times the film falters are when he cuts away briefly to scenes with Sonny's wife and parents at home, watching Sonny's show live on television. It looks as if Lumet wanted to explain Sonny in some way, which is patently impossible in this sort of film.

The movie's concentration of time and place adds terrific intensity to the melodrama, though it limits the psychological territory that can be covered. This, however, is a perfectly honorable artistic decision to have made and, indeed, it's a part of the content and style of this quintessential New York film. More than any other city I know, New York is a present-tense town, a place where the moment is everything, yesterday is prehistory and the future, when and if it comes, will be suddenly transformed into the now. Why fret about consequences? Take the easy way out and let those who come later do the worrying.

1975 S 28, II:13:7

Redford vs. the C.I.A.

By WILLIAM F. BUCKLEY Jr.

"Three Days of the Condor" has everything, and one thing too many, wherein alas lies its chic. But for the terminal protuberance, we would have an expertly directed, trimly jigsawed, adequately acted spy-suspense story which catches the viewer with the opening scene:

What can that mysterious man in the parked car be about, checking off the names, one by one, of the half-dozen people as they saunter into the "American Literary Historical Society" on Manhattan's East Side to begin a day's work? Why, what he is doing is making sure there's a full house, because at lunchtime, he and his accomplices are going

director, Sydney Pollack, is unwilling to blemish Redford's beautiful face with any of the scars of The Thinker, but makes the concession of having him, occasionally, wear glasses. He does not wear glasses when he makes love to Faye Dunaway, but then this is not a moment when his restless intelligence is his dominating concern).

Redford's job at the "American Literary Historical Society" is to apply his encyclopedic knowledge and omnivorous curiosity to the scanning of routine material in search of surreptitious enemy activity. He has recently come on an anomaly: A certain bestseller has been translated only into Dutch and Arabic. So what, you say? So you would never qualify to work for the C.I.A. because of your restless intelligence. Redford has sent down to Washington, through his superior at the Manhattan front, the datum, on which he frames a hunch which is mercifully unexplicated, and the lunch-hour carnage is the result. Redford had stumbled over an operation of international significance, and it is a lucky, lucky thing that it was his day to go to the deli and

William F. Buckley Jr. is author of the upcoming novel, "Saving the Queen," based on the adventures of a C.I.A. agent.

He picked a fine time to visit the deli.

that he used the back door, else he'd be stone-cold dead, along with the boss, the beautiful Oriental secretary, and all the others.

On bringing in the hot dogs and finding everybody dead, Redford decides he had better report the event to Washington, but he is good and scared, and so are you in his behalf, I'm telling you. So when he calls Washington, and is told by the bigger boss which alleyway to report to at exactly what hour, Redford says, No sirree, I'm not going to report to any alleyway to meet up with a perfect stranger. How do I know I'm not talking to the chief killer himself? It is therefore arranged that the unknown boss will be accompanied by an old friend of Redford's from another division of C.I.A. Recognizing his old friend, Redford will say to himself—and would even if he didn't have a restless intelligence—"That's my old friend all right, so the guy with him must be O.K."

But what happens is that as soon as the three men get together, the boss suddenly whips out a pistol and in the general shoot-out Redford's friend is killed, the boss is fatally wounded, and Redford knows he's in real trouble. So he kidnaps Faye Dunaway, a perfect stranger

of the kind Robert Redford would come upon, and over the next couple of hours the plot proceeds along its anfractuous way, and the viewer has a superb time as assassins come and go, and gets a true sci-fi thrill out of the display of intelligence hardware, of which my favorite is a machine that flashes a map showing the location of the telephone being used by the caller. However, Redford's restless intelligence at some point in his life put him on to everything anybody ever knew about telephones, and he manages to cross the lines of half the telephone trunks in the city and sits comfortably on a ganglion that makes a laughing stock out of the Central Intelligence Agency's telephone-spotting machine.

By now we all know that the Mr. Big who ordered the killings is very high up in government. Our government. Indeed, by the laws of compound interest, if the movie had endured another half an hour, one would have been satisfied only if the President of the United States, or perhaps even Ralph Nader, had proved to be the energumen behind it all.

●

Thus it goes, right to the smash ending, as unbalancing as Jimmy Durante's nose. The viewers would, at that point, have been left totally satisfied by a traditional double-agent theme—Mr. Big was really working for the Soviet Union; or, if that is not trendy enough for Pollack-Redford, a Chilean colonel. It transpires, however, that Mr. Big is a 100 per cent American who had to eliminate all those people at the "American Literary Historical Society" because they might have become privy to a contingent operation by following the lead turned up by Redford's restless intelligence.

Then, in a dramatic sidewalk confrontation, Mr. Junior Big explains to Redford that it is all high patriotism, working against a future national shortage of oil, and invites Redford to come back into the company and accept the requirements of orthodoxy in the modern world. But Redford says, taking off his glasses, No, never! This very day I have told everything to . . . the camera slithers up to a marquee above the two men who are talking and you see the logo of . . . The New York Times. The director failed only to emblazon under it, "Daniel Ellsberg Slept Here." Mr. Junior Big reacts like the witch come into contact with water. He snarls and shrivels away, and says, half-desper-

ately: "Maybe they won't print it!" But Redford has by now seeded the audience with his restless intelligence, and we all know that The New York Times will print it, and we shall all be free.

The film's production notes state: "Over a year ago, Stanley Schneider, Robert Redford, Sydney Pollack and Dino de Laurentiis decided to create a film that would reflect the climate of America in the aftermath of the Watergate crisis." "The climate of America" is a pretty broad term. They really mean: The climate of America as seen by I. F. Stone, Seymour Hersh, Susan Sontag and Shirley MacLaine. One recalls Will Rogers, returning from the Soviet Union where he had seen a communal bath. "Did you see all of Russia?" he was asked. "No," Rogers said, weighing his answer. "But I saw all of parts of Russia!"

Redford-Pollack-de Laurentiis have shown us the climate in all of parts of America. It sure is cold out there. ■

1975 S 28, II:1:1

●

PART 2 WALKING TALL, directed by Earl Bellamy; written by Howard B. Kreitsek; director of photography, Keith Smith; film editor, Art Seid; music by Walter Scharf; produced by Charles A. Pratt; distributed by Cinerama/American International; released by American International Pictures. At neighborhood theaters. Running time: 109 minutes. This film is classified PG.
Buford Pusser................Bo Svenson
Pinky Dobson...............Luke Askew
Carl Pusser.................Noah Beery
Ray Henry..................John Chandler
Obra Eaker.................Robert Doqui
Grady Coker................Bruce Glover
Stud Pardee................Richard Jaeckel
Ruby Ann..................Brooke Mills
John Witter................Logan Ramsey
Margeanne Stilson.........Angel Tompkins

A sequel to the dramatized true story of the late Tennessee sheriff Buford Pusser, "Part 2 Walking Tall," illustrates, if nothing else, that there's no point in dropping a good thing. If "Part 2" is less violent than "Walking Tall," which reportedly earned more than $10-million, it cleaves to good guys against the bad guys clichés with the doggedness of an uninspired TV shoot-'em-up.

●

The original writer-director team of Mort Briskin and Phil Karlson has been replaced by Howard B. Kreitsek and Earl Bellamy. And Bo Svenson has taken over for Joe Don Baker in the role of Pusser, who was killed in a car crash last year. The present cast and their accents do not appear to be out of place in the rural western Tennessee locales where "Part 2" was shot.

As the sheriff who is now recovered from wounds of the original bloodletting that killed his wife, Bo Svenson is a more sentimental, if not wholly restrained, lawman. But he is still the club-swinging, gun-toting giant determined to rid McNairy County

of those moonshiners headed by their rich but shadowy boss, Logan Ramsey.

If there are moments to indicate that the undaunted sheriff is a family man who dotes on his motherless kids (Leif Garrett and Dawn Lyn) and his mother and father (Noah Beery and Lurene Tuttle), these are merely breaks in the action involving a variety of attempts on his life through car tampering and ambushes by the likes of Luke Askew, Richard Jaeckel, John Chandler and Angel Tompkins.

The sheriff, using his club to smash cars and secluded stills, not heads, is a good deal more fortunate than his adversaries, who emerge as one-dimensional and obvious. A scene depicting the funeral of Pusser's faithful black deputy, Robert Doqui, is touching and, as the bloodied but unbowed sheriff, Mr. Svenson stands out as a decent, dedicated, if tough citizen worthy of sympathy. But for all of its basis in truth, "Part 2," which was filmed in color, emerges as a simple, largely unconvincing black-and-white melodrama.   A. H. WEILER

1975 S 29, 37:7

Study Recalls Inventor of the Zoopraxograph

By A. H. WEILER

The name may excite only historians while giving printers the megrims, but "Eadweard Muybridge, Zoopraxographer," at the Whitney Museum, deservedly brings Muybridge, the pioneer protographer and scientist, out of the past. While the documentation of his work and life pointedly states that he did not create motion pictures as we know them, it vividly illustrates his classic century-old studies of animal and human locomotion, which foreshadowed the birth of movies in the eighteen-nineties.

Muybridge is generally, if vaguely, known as the photographer who, in the eighteen-seventies, used a series of cameras and tripping wires to record the motion of a horse for Leland Stanford, the California railroad tycoon and horse fancier. But this is only one facet of Thom Andersen's film study of this dedicated researcher who died in 1904 at the age of 74 in his native England after having spent his creative years here.

Among other things in a complex life, Muybridge also helped develop the zoopraxograph, a machine that animated his photographic motion studies.

The technology of time and motion culled from Muybridge's encyclopedic collection and other sources is occasionally too academic. Yet the film manages to reveal an unusual, complicated, even mysterious man.

The Program

EADWEARD MUYBRIDGE, ZOOPRAXOGRAPHER, produced, directed and written by Thom Andersen; editor, Morgan Fisher; music, Michael Cohen; animation photography, Mr. Andersen, Don Baker, Bill Coffen, Mr. Fisher, Alan Harding and Marlyn O'Conner; released by New Yorker Films. At the Whitney Museum of American Art, Madison Avenue and 75th Street. Running time: 60 minutes.
WITH Sharon Hagen and Anje Bos.

We see shots of the patriarchal, white-bearded Muybridge as one of many nude "models" shown in "action." Also shown are a San Francisco devastated by the 1868 (not the storied 1906) earthquake, Yosemite National Park, Indians of the period and "motion" nudes (photographed at the University of Pennsylvania) for comparative studies of pathology.

Muybridge's pictorial records of animals and largely nude women and men were made with a scientist's disregard for Victorian mores. They also helped correct artists' misconceptions.

On the biographical side Mr. Andersen has not ignored Muybridge as the center of a scandal in the eighteen-seventies — he was judged not guilty after having killed his wife's lover.

According to the distributors, "Thom Andersen is a young man in his 20's who made the film last year for his master's degree in fine arts at U.C.L.A." It is a specialized but fascinating case history worthy of its subject.

The accompanying, 10-minute "Homage to Magritte" by Anita Thacher may not be as surrealistic as that noted artist's paintings, but its intercut and parallel images of roaring waves, beaches, placid skies and a pretty humming girl arranging flowers makes a pleasing and imaginative collage. It is unpretentious and satisfying.

1975 S 30, 31:1

BLACK MOON, directed by Louis Malle; screenplay by Mr. Malle with Ghislain Uhry and Joyce Bunuel; executive producer, Claude Nedjar; director of photography, Sven Nykvist; editor, Suzanne Baron; music, Diego Masson; produced by NEF (Paris) and Bioscop (Munich). Running time: 92 minutes. At the New York Film Festival at Alice Tully Hall, Broadway at 65th Street. This film has not been rated.
Lily ....Cathryn Harrison
Old Woman ....Theresa Giehse
Sister ....Alexandra Stewart
Brother ....Joe Dallesandro

By VINCENT CANBY

The time is early morning, midsummer. A fat badger noses its way across the macadam surface of an otherwise deserted two-lane highway. What would so fascinate a badger on the surface of a highway? The trail of a lost friend? The scent of an old hot dog? In the distance we hear a chorus of crickets and, close up, the sniffing of of the badger.

All is serene until a car appears in the distance. The self-absorbed animal pays no attention. It continues to sniff, to consider and to move a few more inches on.

You know what's going to happen. It does, swiftly, with a small thud. The animal is squashed. The car swerves to a halt and a pretty young woman with blond, Alice-in-Wonderland hair alights. She looks at the body, but there isn't much one can do. She gets back into the car and races off.

•

At this point, the beginning of Louis Malle's vivid fable of a film, "Black Moon," the girl suggests Lewis Carroll's Alice going down the rabbit hole in a sports car, falling into another dimension of experience. It's a world where, like Alice and sometimes like Goldilocks, she is successively ignored, threatened, bullied and laughed at, while she tries stoically to make order of things and only occasionally loses her temper.

"Black Moon" will be shown at the New York Film Festival at Alice Tully Hall tonight at 9:30 o'clock and again on Thursday at 6:15 P.M.

It's an uncharacteristically eccentric film to come from Mr. Malle. His best movies—"Le Feu Follet," "Murmur of the Heart," "Lacombe, Lucien" and the documentary "Humain, Trop Humain"—have, by the simplicity and precision of the film-maker's style, transformed the banalities of the real world into poetic visions. "Black Moon" is a poetic vision made to look so absolutely literal one doesn't question the validity of the images.

Alice/Goldilocks (the character's name is actually Lily) is running away from a ferocious, all-out war between men and women. We first hear the sounds of battle on the highway. Further on, the girl witnesses the execution of a dozen women soldiers by a male patrol. As she continues to flee, she comes across the body of an old shepherd hanging from a tree above his flock.

Finally she finds uncertain sanctuary in a handsome old farmhouse occupied by a batty, bedridden old woman who converses on a two-way radio across time ("What's that you say? Priam's dead? What about Helen?"), her mute son and her nonmute but equally enigmatic daughter.

The movie evokes the dream state without once resorting to the use of fuzzy filters, slow-motion photography or even lap dissolves. We see everything with the clarity with which Lily observes it, though, unlike Lily, our tendency is to interpret what we see rather than simply to accept it. If one can accept the images in this way, the movie has a liberating effect. If not, it's a diagramless crossword puzzle.

I'm not sure it's ever possible to respond to anything as literal as a movie composed of recognizable people, animals and objects, and not to wish to interpret the images in some fashion, at least part of the time. Thus, Lily's flight to me, seems to be out of a world of accepted, natural disorder (war) into a state where no laws yet apply, at least none that she understands. At the end it's as if she were at the beginning of comprehension and a new order.

"Black Moon" is baffling and beautiful and occasionally very funny. The cast includes a rather testy unicorn who can quote Lady Maceth and a large rat named Humphrey who talks in an unknown language to the old lady. There are flowers that moan when Lily lies on them and the recurring image of small naked children herding pigs. When Lily listens to a slug as it crawls over a log, it sounds as if a defeated army were making its way over a mountain.

•

"Black Moon" is dazzling to look at, for which Sven Nykvist, the cinematographer, is partly responsible. The cast includes Cathryn Harrison, who is Rex Harrison's granddaughter, as Lily, Joe Dallesandro (the mute son), Alexandra Stewart, (the daughter) and the late Theresa Giehse, to whom Mr. Malle dedicates the film, as the old lady. There is an order to this film, but we must supply it, each according to his needs.

1975 S 30, 31:1

ELEKTREIA, directed by Miklos Jancso; screenplay by Laszlo Gyurko and Gyula Hernadi (Hungarian with English subtitles); photography, Janos Kende; editor, Zoltan Farkas; music, Tamas Gseh; production company, Hunnia Studio. At the New York Film Festival. Running time: 76 minutes.

Electra	Mari Torocsik
Aegisthus	Jozsef Madaras
Orestes	Gyorgy Cserhalmi
Courtiers of Aegisthus	Maria Bajcsay, Lajos Balazsovits
Chrisothemis	Gabi Jobba

By RICHARD EDER

Miklos Jancso's version of the legend of Electra opens in the fog, sets out in all directions at once and never does find itself again.

"Elektreia"—the Hungarian title is "Szerelmem, Electra," which means "Electra, My Love," and better reflects its pastry-tray character—opens at Lincoln Center this evening, the seventh offering of the New York Film Festival.

"Elektreia" is played in a mixture of ballet, song and dialogue. Visually, it is erratic, with moments of great force and others of considerable silliness. Dramatically, it is weightless. Politically, it is schizophrenic. The libertarian points made in the first hour, when the Electra legend is retold, are lopped off in a mushy 15-minute coda that has the effect of an ideological sales tax.

•

Set on a muddy plain, with horsemen wheeling and maneuvering in the background, Mr. Jancso produces a stripped-down "Electra," in the sense that there is virtually no scenery besides the plain itself and a brick barn, and virtually no props. Also in the sense that many of the figures who mime the chorus wear no clothes.

Electra, played with wind-blown fierceness but not much effect by Mari Torocsik, is held in unwilling subjection by Aegisthus, who has killed her father, Agamemnon. She strides about reproaching Aegisthus for his bloody rule and warning him that her brother, Orestes, will come and kill him.

Aegisthus, whose portrayal by Jozsef Madaras is the one dramatic strength of the film, speaks of the need of rulers to be harsh, asserts that people live better under fear and blames Agamemnon for confusing his subjects by giving them freedom.

Perhaps the boldest bit of political satire, in a film made under Hungarian state auspices, comes in the scene of a feast day when Aegisthus's subjects, normally herded about by black-garbed men with whips, are entitled to speak freely.

"My wife bore me three sons this year," one man says.

"Money was worth twice as much this year," says another.

"This year I had good deams," says a third.

•

Mr. Jancso brings tragic tension to several confrontation scenes: the first between the prisoner Electra and the tyrant Aegisthus; the second between Orestes and the tyrant, he has overthrown. In each case the dialogue proceeds while the weaker person advances instead of retreating, and the stronger one retreats instead of advancing. It is a bold reversal, and works brilliantly.

Orestes shoots Aegisthus with a pistol, and he and Electra walk off. It would be kind to suppose that Mr. Jansco has walked off too. In any event, somebody left the camera running for another quarter of an hour.

Orestes and Electra shoot each other, fall dead, get up again, climb into a red helicopter. This hovers overhead while a voice tells about a firebird that gives the working classes strength and hope. The movie peters on out with masses of people dancing and the voice droning such phrases as: "Tomorrow is a new day," "A new world starts at last" and "Perhaps this, our great creed, shall someday be realized."

It is as if somebody had poured a great deal of water into a small and never very robust soup.

1975 S 30, 31:2

An Understated Swiss Comedy by Goretta

By VINCENT CANBY

The Cast

PAS SI MECHANT QUE CA ("Not Really That Bad"; English title: "The Wonderful Crook"), directed by Claude Goretta; screenplay (French with English subtitles) by Mr. Goretta; executive producers, Yves Gasser and Yves Peyrot; director of photography, Renato Berta; editor, Joele van Effenterre; music, Arie Dzierlatka; produced by Citel Films, Artco Films, Action Films and M.J. Productions. Running time: 112 minutes. At the New York Film Festival, Alice Tully Hall, Lincoln Center. This film has not been rated.

Nelly	Marlene Jobert
Pierre	Gerard Depardieu
Marthe	Dominique Labourier
Julien	Philippe Leotard
Pierre's father	Jacques Debary
Francois	Michel Robin
Drunkard	Paul Crauchet

Switzerland, Swiss film makers seem to be telling us, is a perfect Swiss movement that doesn't deliver the correct time. None of the best Swiss films we've been seeing here recently—"La Salamandre," "The Middle of the World" and "The Invitation," among others—could be easily categorized as social or political in content. They share a comically reserved manner that is hardly the thing for agit-prop. Yet each in its way is as deeply concerned about the quality of life as any of Godard's more revolutionary films.

Such a film is "Pas Si Méchant Que Ca" "Not Really That Bad"), the second feature by the extremely gifted Claude Goretta, whose first, "The Invitation," remains one of the most finely boned comedies to be released in New York this year. The new film will be shown at the New York Film Festival tonight at 6:15 and repeated there Friday at 9:30.

"Pas Si Méchant," which will be titled "The Wonderful Crook" when it is released here commercially, is not a comedy that will have you rolling in the aisles or tossing your hat in the air or even laughing all that much. Which may be a terrible thing to say about a comedy early in a review, but I suspect that audiences need a bit of preparation for this particular Swiss film.

It deals in small events, in details so practical that one is apt not to notice the comic attitude it wears. Its method is either carefully elliptical or understated. Indeed, even its overstatements are understated—and it is delightful.

"Pas Si Méchant" is the story of a not quite perfect son's coming of age in a perfect world. There is some irony in this, of course. He is Pierre (Gerard Depardieu), a happy-go-lucky fellow, married to a sweet, earthy girl and the father of a small child. Pierre works, though not very hard, in his father's small furniture factory, where everything is fashioned with care by hand, of wood that, his father says, breathes.

When Pierre's father is incapacitated by a stroke, Pierre must take over the factory and learns to his sorrow that it's such a financial failure it's on the edge of bankruptcy. To meet the payroll Pierre takes to robbing post offices and banks. Each month he packs up a load of furniture that has been ordered by bogus customers, drives into the country where he burns it, and then stops by a bank just before closing for a quick illegal withdrawal.

Something is obviously wrong when the kind of workmanship represented by this one factory can no longer be afforded, but then there is also something wrong with Pierre. Mr. Goretta apparently has a cheerfully open mind about bank robbing, which is one of the pleasures of the film, but not about Pierre, which is what gives the film its impact.

Pierre, as charming as he is, deceitfully implicates everyone he would protect, including both his wife, Marthe (Dominique Labourier) and the plucky young woman, Nelly (Marene Jobert), whom he meets in the course of a heist and who subsequently becomes his mistress.

Pierre has style and he displays a good deal of grace under pressure, but he's a crybaby too. With the best of intentions, he winds up failing everyone, especially Nelly, who has joined his life of mini-crime with her eyes wide open.

•

Mr. Goretta's direction looks deceptively simple. The characters and situations seem familiar at the start, yet little by little, scene by scene, you realize that the film is not simple at all, as when Pierre, rough-housing with his son, becomes just as excited and semihysterical as the child. In another scene the patrons of a corner bar watch an Italian immigrant worker dancing drunkenly with a vase of flowers, making everyone desperately uncomfortable. Obliquely we learn more than we ever thought possible.

Mr. Depardieu is very funny and complex in the pivotal role, which is not totally appealing, though the women's roles are. Philippe Leotard, the hero of "The Middle of the World," is fine in a supporting role, as is Michel Robin, the lonely bachelor of "The Invitation." A whole different subject is the superior quality of the ensemble acting in these new Swiss productions.

1975 O 1, 59:1

XALA, directed and written by Ousmane Sembene; photography, Georges Caristan; editor, Florence Eymon; production companies, Societe Nationale Cinematographique, Filmi Domireew, to be distributed by New Yorker Films. In French and Wolof, English subtitles. At the New York Film Festival. Running time: 123 minutes.

By RICHARD EDER

Dancing and jubilation in the seaside African capital, where coconut-icing skyscrapers loom over the shanties, the trees are gray with dust and the bougainvillea is like a terminal illness.

Africans in bright-colored togas move into the big building in the main square, order out the white men and remove the busts of Napoleon. Next scene: the Africans, in expensive European suits, sit around the table, the white men stand importantly behind as "advisers" and pass them briefcases stuffed with money, the black soldiers push back black crowds and rid the streets of unsightly beggars.

In a way, therefore, Osmane Sembene's cutting, radiant and hilarious film "Xala," which opens at the New York Film Festival this evening, is "Animal Farm" applied to Africa independence.

•

It is part fable and part satire, but it is much more: with the greatest fineness and delicacy, Mr. Sembene, the Senegalese writer and director who made this picture, has set out a portrait of the complex and conflicting mesh of traditions, aspirations and frustrations of a culture knocked askew by colonialism and distorting itself anew while climbing out.

Mr. Sembene sets his fable not among the new politicians but the new businessmen. The President and his cabinet are in fact the president and governing body of the Chamber of Commerce, but they represent the new élite of corrupt power and corrupt money combined.

The story centers on the downfall of El Hadji, one of the pillars of the chamber. El Hadji, a tall, aging man who wears his corruption as a flaring innocence, runs the town's import business. He brings in whisky, perfume, yoghurt and bottled water, which is used, among other things, to wash his white Mercedes-Benz.

El Hadji is taking a third wife, and the garden party to celebrate the marriage, attended by the cream of this clotted society, is a comic and mordant masterpiece. Cabinet ministers arrange deals among the whisky, two businessmen discuss plans for "le weekend" and wonder what the English word for it is, a new automobile for the bride arrives tied up in ribbons.

It is the series of quick scenes between El Hadji and his first two wives that adds humanity and social dimension, however. Adja, the first wife, is traditional African: a woman with dignity, presence and an angry acceptance of her displacement. The second wife, Oumi, is a fading sexpot, a modern African—of the nineteen-fifties, with no training whatsoever in acceptance.

Bitter rivals at the start, the two women are slowly pushed together by the new threat of the third marriage. In one splendid shot they sit side by side along the wall, bypassed, each holding a plate of food and a glass of Coca-Cola.

El Hadji is alone with his young bride and discovers—shatteringly — that someone has laid a curse (the "Xala" of the title) upon him. He is impotent.

It is a catastrophe: a public one. He consults the President, who sends him to his private witch doctor. El Hadji, in his Paris-made suit, sits in a bush hut being magicked, but to no avail. A second witch doctor is tried, with somewhat better results.

But the lion—he is a jackal, really, but the charity Sembene shows to his personages at the same time he is being ruthless with them allows El Hadji dignity as well as squalor — is wounded and must fall. He is implicated in a financial scandal and his fellow thieves at the Chamber of Commerce expel him.

•

Wife Number Two moves out, Wife Number Three is removed by her mother; Wife Number One remains with the stunned and broken El Hadji. His impotence, furthermore, is back upon him: the check he gave the second witch doctor bounced.

In comes a procession of crippled beggars that has been seen at various points during the film. El Hadji can become himself again — not himself as a profiteer but himself as a man and an African—if he will strip and let himself be spit upon.

He does, and the end comes with a visual and symbolic wrench. It is too sudden and didactic—furthermore, as is almost inevitable when it is a matter of relentless decline and fall—the movie has already begun to drag.

It is a fault but not a ruinous one: "Xala" is an instructive delight.

1975 O 1, 62:1

Corruption Triumphs in Story of Gambler

By A. H. WEILER

Although its plot is convoluted, "Framed," which arrived yesterday at Loews State 2 and other houses, is basically uncomplicated. Crime, it's obvious here, is not subtle. The writer-director star team of Mort Briskin, Phil Karlson and Joe Don Baker, who previously struck a bonanza with "Walking Tall," are now simply fighting gunfire with gunfire and beatings with beatings. "Walking Tall" may have dramatized the true story of a crusading, if violent, Tennessee sheriff, but "Framed" is not so much the business of justice triumphing as it is corruption and violence triumphant.

•

Our hero-gambler-nightclub-owner's luck is bad from the start when he wins a big bundle at poker. Almost immediately he runs into a murderous, if mysterious, ambush, a slugging match with a deputy he kills in self defense and a frame-up by the cops and shadowy political types that lands him in jail. But our tough boy takes no pushing around and, with the aid of a gangster big shot who admires his guts and gambling, he's out, muscles quivering and gun in hand, to get his framers and, of course, his loot.

The Cast

FRAMED; screenplay by Mort Briskin; from the novel by Art Powers and Mike Misenheimer; directed by Phil Karlson; produced by Mort and Joel Briskin; director of photography, Jack A. Marta; editor, Harry Gerstad. Presented by Paramount. At Loews State 2, 45th Street and Broadway, and other theaters. Running time: 106 minutes. This film has been rated R.

Ron Lewis	Joe Don Baker
Susan Barrett	Conny Van Dyke
Vince Greeson	Gabriel Dell
Sal Viccarrone	John Marley
Sam Perry	Brock Peters
Haskins	Roy Jenson
Bundy	John Larch
Morello	Warren Kemmerling
Andrew Ney	Joshua Bruant
Senator Tatum	Walter Brooke
Frank	Paul Mantee

As the indestructible gambler, Joe Don Baker convincingly combines a linebacker's physique and a laconic Southern talk to absorb a going-over that hospitalizes him and then engage in a succession of bloody clashes that dispatches a platoon of the rough opposition, including one whose ear he shoots off.

•

All this action is not that unusual, of course, but it does include some workmanlike performances by, among others, Gabriel Dell, as Mr. Baker's prison pal and a hit man; John Marley, as the gang boss who aids him, and Brock Peters, as an honest deputy. Conny Van Dyke, our hero's pretty girlfriend as well as singer and partner, who has been mauled and raped by the bad guys, may not be just plain folks but she is awfully logical when she says after one gory bout, "I just don't understand you."

1975 O 2, 47:1

THE LOST HONOR OF KATHARINA BLUM (Die Verlorene Ehre Der Katharina Blum), directed by Volker Schlondorff and Margarethe von Trotta; screenplay (German with English subtitles) by Mr. Schlondorff and Miss von Trotta, based on the novel of Heinrich Boll; executive producer, Eberhard Junkersdorf; director of photography, Jost Vacano; editor, Peter Przygodda; music, Hans Werner Henze; a production of Bioskop Film. Running time: 102 minutes. At the New York Film Festival, Alice Tully Hall, Lincoln Center. This film has not been rated.

Katharina Blum	Angela Winkler
Beizmenne	Mario Adorf
Werner Totges	Dieter Laser
Dr. Blorna	Heinz Bennent
Trude Blorna	Hannelore Hoger
Moeding	Harald Kuhlmann
Alois Straubleder	Karl Heinz Vosgerau
Ludwig Gotten	Jurgen Prochnow

By VINCENT CANBY

"The Lost Honor of Katharina Blum," based on Heinrich Böll's German novel that was published here in English this year, is a movie that looks as if it had been made out of steel. It is cold and bright and has dozens of lethal edges. It's very difficult to like even though it has things to admire. The film, a dramatized polemic about what it sees as the excesses of freedom in the democracy of West Germany today, makes its point, with tiny variations, as relentlessly as someone dealing in Revealed Truths.

The movie will be shown at the New York Film Festival this evening at 6:15 and again on Monday at 9:30.

Volker Schlondorff, the German director ("Young Torless," "The Sudden Wealth of the Poor People of Kombach," etc.), and Margarethe von Trotta, his actress-wife, with whom he has collaborated on his recent screenplays, including "A Free Woman," share both the writing and directing credits on this new film.

•

"The Lost Honor of Katharina Blum" is about the systematic victimization of a poor but proud young woman, who works as a housekeeper and waitress and who has the bad luck to pick up and take home from a party, for one night only, a young man who is suspected by the German police of being a terrorist. Katharina had never met the young man before, but circumstantial evidence makes it appear as if she had been his mistress for months.

In a period of several days, Katharina's privacy and, particularly, her honor are destroyed, first by the police, who terrorize her, and then by the yellow press, which creates in her name the image of a politicized Bonnie Parker, beautiful, heartless and on fire for the Communist cause.

Though Katharina is quite quickly cleared, her life has been ruined. When she decides to take a gun to the reporter who was instrumental in her downfall, someone piously declares that the shots Katharina fired were aimed not at the reporter but at the freedom of the press.

One of the difficulties with the way Mr. Schlondorff and Miss von Trotta handle their subject matter is that although everything happens in the course of the movie, it is completely without surprises. There are no unusual insights, no progressions of understanding. Paradoxically, this is not true of Mr. Böll's novel, though the book opens with the act of violence that the film saves until the end.

•

Mr. Böll tells Katharina's story mostly in terms of secondhand information—in official police reports and in the words of people who knew her, and only once in her own terms, and that's an official statement that continues to keep Katharina at a distance from the reader.

The film sees Katharina frontally, close up. The mystery of her passion and her resolve is maintained only by the carefully controlled, implacable performance of Angela Winkler, a handsome, dark-haired woman who looks a good deal like Susan Sontag—an unimportant fact, perhaps, but one that makes it difficult to believe Katharina as a waitress.

I'm not familiar with the German press, and it may be that it's as outrageous as the movie describes. "We have to help simple people express themselves," says a wicked reporter while he puts words into the mouth of Katharina's dying mother. The corruption portrayed by the film is so pervasive that one expects it to challenge us more. It doesn't. Instead it has the effect of numbing us. Its singleminded intensity nails the imagination to the floor.

This may be exactly what the film makers intended to do, but it's not the kind of movie that greatly interests me. "The Lost Honor of Katharina Blum" is less a drama than a neo-Brechtian demonstration of a known lack of principles.

1975 O 3, 41:1

Critic's Notebook: Puff and Circumstance at Festival

By RICHARD EDER

This city has a lot wrong with it, but pretentiousness is not one of its faults. Its ceremonials are homely ones: Macy's parade and painting the stripe on Fifth Avenue green are about as close as it comes to panoply. Grander efforts look a little silly and often come unstuck.

New York's Film Festival was comfortably in the tradition this year. It made its ceremonial entrance into Lincoln Center—over which pretentiousness does hover from time to time—and promptly fell on its face. It then picked itself up and has been rolling along cheerfully and quite successfully ever since.

Visconti's "Conversation Piece," the festival's grand opener, produced the effect of slow suffocation in a secondhand furniture shop with the heat turned up. Pushing out his lines, Burt Lancaster was like a guest at a banquet who is too polite to protest that he is being served successively eggshell soup, fried carpet and diced worm.

The audience was not too polite, however. It booed. Afterward, a Lincoln Center official, was asked if he was embarrassed. "Embarrassment I can take," he said, and pulled the back of his dinner jacket over his head. "But humiliation . . ."

●

But what good is a festival without a disaster? It would be like "Macbeth" without daggers. There is nothing like a round of booing to give an audience a sense of participation. And the audience at the New York Film Festival is a uniquely participating one: It may be angry, but it isn't alienated.

There is none of the womb-like passivity at Alice Tully Hall—where the films are shown—that one normally associates with going to the movies. At how many movie houses are the members of the audience sitting forward in their seats, mentally making the movie for themselves. How often do you get applause not during the film but during the credits, with the biggest hand given to the cameraman?

●

The festival also marks one of the few opportunities a film audience has to talk back. The discussions after the screenings, where the director and sometimes the stars are trotted out to answer questions, reveal less about the movie makers than about that municipal institution, the New York Film Buff.

Generally the questions are detailed and technical: Why a shot was made from a particular angle, why a certain actor moved his head at a certain time. The questioners were reshooting the movie.

Perhaps the archtypal buff question came at a press screening of Jean-Marie Straub's film based on the opera "Aaron and Moses" by Schonberg. It is an extremely static picture: The camera moves only slightly; the characters, hardly at all.

Why, the questioner wanted to know, had Mr. Straub allowed several members of the chorus to look around "in a nonritualistic, naturalistic way" toward the end of Act I? Mr. Straub, who has never been criticized for excess motion, looked stunned.

Some questions dealt with broader issues. One journalist walked into the lobby at the start of Louis Malle's "Black Moon." Was that badger she had just seen run over really killed? she demanded. Mr. Malle assured her that he did not kill badgers, and she went back inside.

●

After the Visconti, the entries picked up considerably. "The Wonderful Crook" by the Swiss director Claude Goretta was a touching and amusing story of the collapse of a man who tries to go in opposite directions at the same time: He runs a furniture factory and robs banks to make up his payroll; he has a wife to help him with the factory and a mistress to help him with the robbing.

It is a curious contrast, incidentally, to the current bank-robbing hit, "Dog Day Afternoon." The American film also has bungling bank robbers, and also deals brilliantly with their incompetence. But the Sidney Lumet film is about aberrants; Mr. Goretta's is about a normal man caught up in the aberrant course of modern society. As such it is far more socially relevant.

●

"Every Man for Himself and God Against All" by the German director Werner Herzog, a beautiful and piercing parable based on a personage who is suddenly dropped into civilization after spending all his life in a cave, seemed to me one of the best things at the festival, though it was not universally liked.

On the other hand I found Louis Malle's "Black Moon," which was generally well-received, too self-indulgent and undisciplined a collection of elegant bits and pieces to have any force as surrealism. It was a series of unresolved cadences, an orchestra perpetually tuning up with snatches of improvisations and never getting down to play.

●

One of the more interesting films still to come is "Milestones," a powerful — though extremely long — documentary that deals with a central if not overly discussed question about America. It explores what has happened to the lives and the outlooks of the young people who were involved in the social protest of the late nineteen-sixties and early seventies.

Another picture that is awaited with great interest is a new one by François Truffaut, "Adele H," dealing with the wandering life of a 19th-century Frenchwoman, a relative, as it happens of Victor Hugo.

●

The festival, whose choices are made by its director, Richard Roud, and a selection committee, is noncompetitive. It tends to be director-oriented. That is, it has concentrated on particular directors, bringing their work over year after year, even when the particular film is a less-than-brilliant specimen of that director's work.

This leads to some weak entries: the Visconti, the Malle and perhaps Orson Welles's "F for Fake," an amusing but minor work selected at least partly on the theory that anything by such a major figure must be of interest.

The disadvantages of such a method are obvious. But there is no systematic way of bringing new developments in foreign filmmaking into New York; no theater makes a steady educational effort of this kind.

Instead, pictures come in hit-or-miss fashion based inevitably on an estimate of their commercial chances. Mr. Roud and his committee provide a well-publicized showcase, once a year, to lay out what they consider to be important and viable in the art. Not all the selections are good: Some are terrible; and not all the good selections are picked up each year as a result of their reception at the festival. But some are —this year, for instance, the Herzog film, "Every Man for Himself" — and this alone would make the event totally worthwhile.

1975 O 3, 40:1

HEARTS OF THE WEST, directed by Howard Zeiff; screenplay by Rob Thompson; produced by Tony Bill; director of photography, Mario Tosi; editor, Edward Warschilka; music, Ken Lauber; a Metro-Goldwyn-Mayer production, distributed by United Artists. Running time: 103 minutes. At the New York Film Festival, Alice Tully Hall, Lincoln Center. This film has been rated PG.

Lewis Tater .... Jeff Bridges
Howard Pike .... Andy Griffith
A. J. Nietz .... Donald Pleasence
Miss Trout .... Blythe Danner
Kessler .... Alan Arkin
Stout crook .... Richard B. Shull
Polo .... Herbert Edelman
Earl .... Alex Rocco
Pa Tater .... Frank Cady
Lean crook .... Anthony James

By VINCENT CANBY

The early nineteen-thirties in Hollywood: sound is still a new toy, Clark Gable, Greta Garbo and Joan Crawford are virtually kids at M-G-M, and the Warner brothers are beginning to turn out those terrifically popular films about gangsters and G-men, and imposing historical personages who look like Paul Muni. Hollywood is approaching its Golden Age and Americans can't get their fill of the talkies, formerly referred to as photoplays.

That's one side of the old Hollywood. The glamorous side. The other side is the scroungy, tacky world of B-pictures — Westerns, war movies, raucous musicals, shot on shoestrings on backlots and in the nearby hills, by fly-by-night operators who make the major studio film makers look like Cellinis.

●

This is the eccentric world recalled with such affection and good humor by "Hearts of the West," the benign comedy directed by Howard Zeiff that will be shown at the New York Film Festival tonight at 9:30. The film, which will be shown again at the festival Tuesday evening at 6:15, will open its regular commercial run at the Sutton Theater on Wednesday.

"Hearts of the West," written by Rob Thompson, a brand-new Hollywood writer, is a kind of testimonial to innocence. There's not a truly nasty person in the movie, though it has its share of operators and con artists, each of whom fails with varying degrees of ineptitude.

The film tells the remarkable adventures of an Iowa farm boy named Lewis Tater (Jeff Bridges), whose father is called Pa Tater and who dreams of becoming a writer of Western novels like Zane Grey.

To this end Lewis goes west to pick up local color and winds up, instead, reluctantly being groomed as a Western star of B-pictures directed with a stunning hysterical lack of talent by a Mr. Kessler (Alan Arkin). When Kessler is shooting on location and running behind schedule, he likes to hear his "cowboys" sitting around the campfire at night yelling encouraging cowboy yells. It gives his reassurance.

"Hearts of the West" is full of delightful details—most notably, Mr. Arkin—but it is sometimes too innocent for its own good. It meanders in a way that would horrify any B-picture maker. It develops characters and situations and then doesn't do anything much with them, which is a luxury that even A-pictures have never easily afforded. And, in Lewis, it has a hero who must be two things at once—a comic dunderhead, a sort of a Merton-of-the-movies, to give the film comic drive, as well as straight man, to give it poignancy. It doesn't always work.

Instead, the film is carried by the consistent intelligence of its observations and the sweetness with which it tolerates ineffectual rogues, rascals and fanatics of a very parochial kind. These include a cowboy "extra" who says proudly of his own profile, "Reeks character, that's what they said," as well as Mr. Mr. Bridges's Lewis, who is always writing in his head. Suffering a setback in his Hollywood career, he bucks himself up by rewriting his life: "Living by his wits . . . he met the challenge of this womanless land."

●

The film is also consistently well played by Mr. Arkin and Mr. Bridges and the large supporting cast, including Blythe Danner, Andy Griffith, Donald Pleasence and by Richard B. Shull and Anthony James, who recall Twain's Duke and Dauphin as operators of a phony correspondence school for writers.

"Hearts of the West" may well be the kind of imperfect movie that is as much as it is just because of the ways in which it is imperfect. This was one of the charms of Mr. Zeiff's "Slither," and it could be that Mr. Zeiff's talent is one we must learn to appreciate without wishing it were more conventionally slick.

1975 O 4, 14:1

COMPANERO, directed by Martin Smith; executive producer, Stanley Forman; editor, Shelagh Brady; music, Victor Jara; released by New Yorker Films: Running time: 60 minutes. With: Victor Jara, Joan Turner, David Naden (narrator).

and

AUTOBIOGRAPHY OF A PRINCESS, directed by James Ivory; screenplay by Ruth Prawer Jhabvala; produced by Ismail Merchant; director of photography, Walter Lassally; editor, Humphrey Dixon; music, Vic Flick; a Merchant-Ivory production, distributed by Cinema 5. Running time: 60 minutes. At the New York Film Festival, Alice Tully Hall, Lincoln Center.

Cyril Sahib .... James Mason
The Princess .... Madhur Jaffrey
Delivery Man .... Keith Varnier
Papa .... Nazruh Rahman
Blackmailers .... Diane Fletcher,
Timothy Bateson, Johnny Stuart

By VINCENT CANBY

"The English florists simply do not know how to make a garland. I had to show them how to do it," the Princess (Madhur Jaffrey), daughter of a maharajah, complains daintily to her guest as she flutters about the tea table in her posh London town house. The princess affects the mannerisms and vocabulary of the English aristocracy and laments the passage of an India that weighed its princes in gold and sent its royal children to English boarding school where, after a few years they had no idea if they were English or Indian.

The occasion is a party for two marking the birthday of the Princess's late father. It's an annual occasion. The garland hangs over the full-portrait of the maharajah, whom her aging guest James Mason had served first as a tutor and then as a secretary of state.

The guest, whom the Princess calls Cyril Sahib, is a singular sort of man who, as he recognizes his own disappointments, tires politely to correct the Princess's statements about the past. Though she never quite understands him, he indulges her. She is the last link he has to the past.

James Ivory's 60-minute film, "Autobiography of a Princess," is a delicate, autumnal satire, funny at some moments' bitter at others, and illuminated throughout by the kind of appreciation for lost civilizations that is shared by all of Mr. Ivory's films about India, from "Shakespeare Wallah" through "Bombay Talkie."

●

It will be seen at the New York Film Festival this evening at 6 on a bill with "Compañero," a 60-minute film about Victor Jara, the Chilean folk singer who was one of the victims of the right-wing revolution that overthrew the government of the late President Salvador Allende in 1973. The two films have very little in common but it's a moving program.

By far the more interesting cinematically, is "Autobiography of a Princess," which is to conventional feature-length films what a novella is to a novel. It is a compact movie, dense with information and contradictory feelings.

Through the interplay between the Princess and Cyril Sahib, and with the aid of some home movies that the Princess shows, Mr. Ivory and Ruth Prawer Jhabvala, who wrote the screenplay, manage to bring three very curious characters to life.

James Mason in a scene from the film "Autobiography of a Princess."

They are the Englishman who went to India for a year and stayed, effectively, until he was drained of his life, the spoiled, silly Princess who is out of place in both India and England, and her father, "Dear Papa," who was obviously a tyrant though the Princess persists in thinking of him as some sort of libertarian.

"Why," says the Princess, "there were hardly any suttees."

"What about your great-aunt?" asks Cyril Sahib.

"That was different," the Princess replies crossly. "She loved her husband so much she didn't want to live without him."

There are awkward moments in the film. Mr. Ivory introduces a television interview with the Maharani of Jaipur and her son, which is funny and informative but doesn't match the quality of the fiction that he is spinning so economically with Miss Jaffrey and with Mr. Mason. The latter has one especially marvelous moment when he recalls his creeping awareness of the rot that was destroying his life in the final Indian years. "Those ceremonies," he says. "As the years went on the ceremonies blended together. I knew less and less.... All those crowds, and always the waiting, and the confusion about how the thing was to be done."

"Autobiography of a Princess" is a small, elegant, oblique film. "Compañero" is small, angry and straightforward, composed mainly of an interview with the late Mr. Jara's English-born wife, Joan Turner, who talks at length and in extremely affecting terms about her husband, his commitment to the revolution, his talent, and his murder in the Santiago soccer stadium two days after the coup.

The film was directed by Martin Smith, an Englishman, and the soundtrack carries Mr. Jara's voice singing the songs that made him such a popular figure in his own country.

1975 O 5, 60:7

Straub's Version of 'Aaron and Moses' by Schoenberg Is Uncompromising

By RICHARD EDER

At first, movies were silent images: Then sound was added. For some time now, the German director Jean-Marie Straub has been at work trying to remove the images.

In his latest film—it can't be called a movie because virtually nothing moves, neither the camera nor what it is photographing — Mr. Straub has come close to purging the screen of anything to see. At the same time, he will come close to purging the movie theater of anybody to watch.

Some kind of anchorite ideal is being approached here: a motionless screen in an empty theater with angry, monotone voices on the soundtrack reading out pamphlets to music.

Some people — more in Europe than here—fervently admire Mr. Straub for his aridity. Dryness in our still lush and overnourished civilization can seem a virtue. "Aaron and Moses," which will be shown at Lincoln Center this afternoon and Tuesday night as Mr. Straub's entry in the New York Film Festival, is one great Sahara.

It is a filmed version of the atonal opera by Arnold Schoenberg, whose work was attacked in its day for uncompromising severity and even now is rarely whistled. Schoenberg, considering himself no minor prophet, modeled Moses upon himself. In the opera his Moses stands for the gaunt, unadorned religious Idea, conveyed solely through words and without images. Aaron argues that a living people needs images—the Golden Calf, for instance —and other aids to be able to grasp and fulfill the Idea.

The opera is about the conflict. Schoenberg uses his technique to reinforce it: Aaron's tenor has musical phrases to sing; Moses' bass keeps to an atonal sung speech.

Mr. Straub too seems to identify with Moses the image-breaker. He uses his cinema techniques in an attempt to reinforce the musical effect sought by Schoenberg. The first section, where Moses is present, is almost without motion. Moses' opening, lasting nearly five minutes, is rendered by the camera's fixing itself on the back of the singer's head. When he enlists Aaron, a second lengthy scene is done with the two men performing simultaneously, the camera merely showing them face to face.

The Chosen People is represented by the Chorus of the Austrian Radio standing in a motionless block, like workers posing for pictures at a factory picnic. At times the screen goes blank or black for minutes on end, allowing the tiny light flaws skipping across to make up one of the film's visual high points.

When Moses is up on the mountain and Aaron is in charge, the figures move a bit more. The Golden Calf is set up, there is a bit of dancing and a tiny orgy. It is done in detached, drugged fashion, with deliberate pictorial dullness.

Dullness can be a statement, and in the case of Mr. Straub, whose control of his material is not in doubt, it obviously is. (The one major nondeliberate error is the subtitles. With so much emphasis on the singing and talking, and nothing much else happening, they assume a major importance. They are so bad, so Germanic, that sometimes it seems that this is a movie about present participles.)

The reason for making dullness into a statement is less clear. But it seems to amount to a radical rejection of the successive cinematic fashions that generally try to heighten or vary the image, not to deaden it.

Mr. Straub is making a minimal film, in other words, the equivalent of minimal painting. It is an antimovie and this would be fine except, maybe, for the people who go see it. Could they get in, perhaps, with antimoney?

1975 O 5, 60:4

'Exhibition' Looks at Pornography as a Career

There is no disguise like nakedness. This, among other things, cripples Jean François Davy's two-hour documentary about a French porno-film star and the emotional transactions that take place in the making of dirty movies.

Pornography itself is a counterfeit of sex. And the making of it involves an intended lying to the camera. Angles are faked, performances are faked, and, where the performances are genuine —as they are in many of the scenes of Mr. Davy's film —the emotions are faked.

And even the faking is unreliable. As the bodies of the performers in this documentary, entitled "Exhibition," saw away at each other, shadows of arousal, amusement, embarrassment and plain workmanly comradeship keep flitting by.

If Mr. Davy would leave it at that, his movie would be better. But he keeps lunging for the shadows and they evade him.

"Exhibition" has acquired all kinds of sociological and political veneer in becoming a fashionable success in France. This has allowed it to become the first hard-core film ever to get into the New York Film Festival. But whatever else Mr. Davy asks or tries to establish, what he mainly wants to know is whether performers in dirty movies find their work sexy.

Mr. Davy, with all his beard and intellectual camera and committed gear, is bamboozled precisely as the patrons of West 42d Street live-sex shows are bamboozled. Yes, the performers tell him, they are enjoying themselves. No, they tell him, they are shamming. And the action he films is equally elusive.

In a way it is something of a human triumph to see how sexuality can maintain its privacy even in such unlikely circumstances as a cinéma-vérité porno filming.

But it doesn't do much for a documentary whose intention is, so to speak, to photograph the giant squid and not merely the cloud of ink that its probing stirs up.

It is a pity, too, because in Claudine Beccarie, one of France's most successful pornography performers, Mr. Davy has found a personage of considerable complexity and wit. The most successful parts of the film come when he lets her keep her clothes on and simply talk—about her life, her family, her work.

The trouble is that Miss Beccarie's job is to lie to the camera with her body. And when it is her mind that she is exhibiting to the camera, the spectator cannot avoid feeling that he is getting the same mixture of apparent revelation and real concealment as when she strips.

1975 O 5, 60:4

FILM VIEW

VINCENT CANBY

Hits and Misses at the Film Festival

Are you really interested in arguing whether or not the New York Film Festival is necessary? I'm not. I do it under duress. Twelve years was nothing for an early Christian debate on a tiny point of dogma, but it's maybe nine or 10 years too much for a debate about a film festival when the circumstances and the selections of that festival change each year. It's like debating popsicle flavors. By the time one reaches any conclusion, the things have melted away.

The point is that we have a functioning film festival in New York. It exists. The New York Film Festival is as good as any of the non-competitive festivals I know of, better than those I've attended and, right now, more highly regarded by creative film people (directors, writers, actors) than any festival now operative, noncompetitive or competitive. The festival allows us to see a random sampling of mostly foreign films selected by a small group of people (sometimes only by one man) and, by and large, the ones that are worth seeing make up for the ones that aren't. One can even make a case for the ones that aren't: they give us additional perspective on the ones that are.

In the past the New York Festival has been mainly defended for calling attention to films we might not otherwise see. It still does that. More important now—in this place and time of dwindling production and increasing costs—is the festival's reminder to us that filmmaking need not be completely preoccupied by mass-market blockbusters designed to appeal and/or condescend to the largest possible audience. It does us good to have another kind of filmmaking recalled. Audiences dizzy with the New York beat of "Dog Day

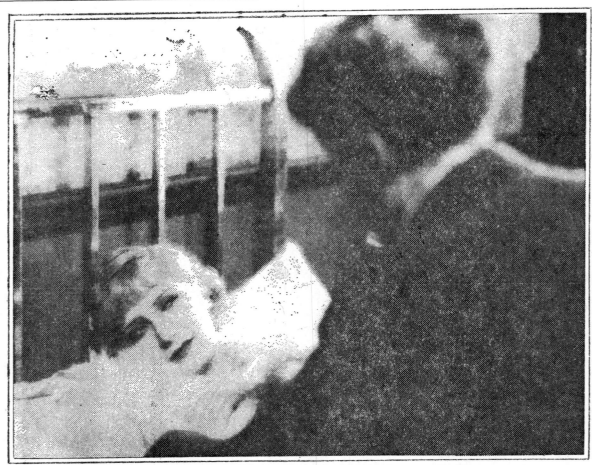

Renoir's 1931 "La Chienne" outshines many contemporary festival entries.

Afternoon," the carefully contrived suspense of "Three Days of the Condor" and the successful use of plastic in "Jaws" should be reminded that other sorts of pleasures and mistakes exist.

At this writing, I've seen eight of the 20 programs at the 13th New York Film Festival now in progress at Lincoln Center. So far there have been no revelations of unknown talents, no trends uncovered that wouldn't be stretching a point to make journalism. The following is a brief run-down on those eight films, some of which will obviously merit fuller discussion later. They are listed in the order in which they were seen:

"Conversation Piece," Luchino Visconti's English-speaking, Italian-made drawing-room drama about an aging art historian (Burt Lancaster) whose ivory tower (actually a Roman palazzo) is invaded by barbarians from the contemporary world. These are a Fascist industrialist's philandering wife (Silvana Mangano), her young German gigolo (Helmut Berger) who is portrayed, without any conviction at all, as a former student activist and Communist, her teen-age daughter whose name should be Gidget but isn't, and the daughter's boyfriend, a non-entity. Visconti seems concerned by the consequences of sexual passion and the current political scene in Italy but he demonstrates less grasp of these subjects than a visiting Eskimo might. The acting and the dubbed English soundtrack are ludicrous.

"La Chienne," Jean Renoir's 1931 classic (his first full-length sound film), which has never been released in this country with English subtitles. It's a beautiful, funny, wise movie about a middle-aged Parisian cashier (Michel Simon) who, hen-pecked by his wife, falls extravagantly in love with a cold-hearted prostitute. There are a murder, an innocent man convicted of that murder, and one of the most gallant, witty endings that Renoir ever conceived. Splendid.

*   *   *

"Fist-Right of Freedom" (that is not a typo for "First-Right" but is an awkward translation of German slang meaning that might makes right), another exercise in style by Rainer Werner Fassbinder, the prolific young German director ("The Bitter Tears of Petra Von Kant," "Merchant of Four Seasons," "Ali—Fear Eats The Soul"). The style, which gives the impression of a physical world from which all air has been removed, is more impressive than the subject matter: a poor working-class fellow, played by Fassbinder, a perfectly well-adjusted homosexual, is emotionally and economically exploited by his callous bourgeois lover and the lover's father and mother, who are rude in the way rich people used to be in Chaplin comedies. But this isn't meant to be funny.

"Grey Gardens," another fascinating example of "direct cinema" by Albert and David Maysles ("Salesman," "Gimme Shelter," etc.). This time they turn their camera on 79-year-old Mrs. Edith Bouvier Beale and her 56-year-old daughter, Edith, who live in epic squalor in a rundown, 28-room East Hampton "cottage." More than they ever have in the past, the Maysles in this film acknowledge their presense, which has a lot to do with what Mrs. Beale and Edie do and say. How can lives become so disconnected? The film's expression is impassive. Also a little cruel. Part of the fascination, of course, has to do with the physical resemblances one sees between the Beales and their niece/first cousin, Jacqueline Bouvier Kennedy Onassis.

*   *   *

"F for Fake," Orson Welles's funny, marvelous meditation upon fakery, forgery, swindling and art. It uses documentary footage, fiction footage, clever intercutting between ideas, between sequences, real people (Clifford Irving, Elmyr de Hory) and fictitious characters. Welles himself is the master-of-ceremonies and, he wants us to believe, the biggest con artist of them all. Don't believe it. On the same bill at the festival: "Arthur and Lillie," a 28-minute short about Arthur and Lillie Mayer, respectively 89 and 86 and both indefatigably young. It's delightful and very moving when Arthur and Lillie are allowed to speak for themselves and not treated as great moments in history.

"Black Moon," Louis Malle's beautiful gambol into surreal filmmaking, is also a financial gamble. It's a movie without an intelligible story, about a war between men and women, a lost young woman and the strange household where she seeks refuge. The images are precise, clear, poetic, baffling, and often liberating.

"Pas Si Mechant Que Ca" (Not Really As Bad As That), the second film by Swiss director Claude Goretta, is not as spectacular as his "The Invitation," but its rueful, reserved humor is a rare sort in movies. About a cheerful young man (Gerard Depardieu) who becomes a bank robber to pay the employes of his carpentry shop.

"The Lost Honor of Katharina Blum," the German screen adaptation of Heinrich Böll's furious novel about an innocent young woman's martyrdom as the result of what we used to call yellow journalism. It's an unrelenting film, well acted by Angela Winkler and directed by Volker Schlondorff and Margarethe von Trotta. For some reason, though, it has the effect of nailing the imagination to the floor, instead of sending it soaring into associated spheres.

1975 O 5, II:15:1

'Conduct Unbecoming'

Film of the Hit Play Is Taut and Polished

By A. H. WEILER

Like some wines, "Conduct Unbecoming" travels well. Barry England's play about a messy officers' mess in Victorian India was a hit in London before landing on Broadway five years ago, and it has lost none of its flavor in the British-made movie that opened yesterday at the Baronet. Dealing with a scandalous mystery exposed in a trial at a frontier army post, it is largely a suspenseful period piece that lovingly recalls and jibes at Hollywood's India as seen in the likes of "Lives of a Bengal Lancer."

Michael Anderson, the director ('Around the World in 80 Days," etc.) shot "Conduct" in Pakistan with enough scarlet-coated officers and mountainous backgrounds to satisfy the "Lancer" fans. But the play and Robert Enders's devoted adaptation are concerned mostly with dissecting officers who are not precisely gentlemen and their shibboleths of regimental pomp, ceremony and special codes of honor.

●

A newly arrived junior officer is accused of assaulting the pretty, flirtatious widow of the regiment's revered hero. The kangaroo tribunal wants to get the beastly matter over with quickly. The officers and the callow subaltern directed to defend him have inherited regimental traditions as sons of illustrious officers. But there's a twist. The accused has never wanted ny part of either defending the empire or army traditions, while his timorous but tenacious advocate sees them as shining ideals.

Of course, his persistent investigation reveals more than the innocence of his client and the actual culprit. It projects some expert play

The Cast

CONDUCT UNBECOMING, screenplay by Robert Enders; from the play by Barry England; directed by Michael Anderson; produced by Michael Deeley and Barry Spikings; director of photography, Bob Huke; editor, John Glen. A British Lion production released by Allied Artists. At the Baronet Theater, Third Avenue and 59th Street. Running time: 107 minutes. This film has been rated PG.

2d Lieut. Arthur Drake.........Michael York
Maj. Lionel Roach..Richard Attenborough
Col. Benjamin Strang......Trevor Howard
Capt. Rupert Harper.......Stacy Keach
Marjorie Scarlett..........Susannah York
Maj. Alastair Wimbourne...
.............................Christopher Plummer
2d Lieut. Edward Millington...
.......................James Faulkner
Regimental Doctor..........James Donald
2d Lieut. Richard Fothergill...
.......................Michael Culver
Pradah Singh ....Rafiq Anwar
Mrs. Bandanai........Persis Khambatta
Mrs. Strang ....Helen Cherry

acting that shatters those ideals. Yet it still clings affectionately to the colorful, if old-fashioned, views of the pig-sticking, drinking (but very proper) thin red line of resolute cavaliers who held those rebel tribesmen off at the Khyber Pass in 1878.

Michael York is genuinely appealing as the indomitable defender torn between his "bourgeois principles" of honor and integrity and the hollow men he sees mocking them. James Faulkner is properly cynical as the innocent defendant, and Susannah York is decorative and distraught as the allegedly wronged woman.

As the sole American in the cast, Stacy Keach is convincingly British in a strong stint as the trial's presiding adjutant, whose rigid beliefs are changed by the evidence. Trevor Howard, as the bewhiskered, beloved colonel determined to maintain the honor of the regiment he is soon to leave, and Christopher Plummer and Richard Attenborough, as senior officers contributing to its dishonor, effectively delineate both the hypocrisy and the fierce pride of their élite group.

In a nuclear age, "Conduct Unbecoming" may seem a somewhat quaint view of a romantic past. But its taut construction, mounting tension and polished performances make for a fascinating entertainment.

1975 O 6, 42:1

MILESTONES, directed, photographed and written by Robert Kramer and John Douglas; produced by Barbara Stone and David C. Stone. At the New York Film Festival. Running time: 195 minutes.
Mama...................Mary Chapelle
John, blind potter ....John Douglas
Erika ....Kalaho
Lou, with beard ....Lou Ho
Helen, film maker ....Grace Paley
Elizabeth, Heeln's daughter...
.......................Tina Shepherd
Karen, gives birth to Leila ....Sule Solf
Joe of Joe's Bar ....David C. Stone
Peter, released from prison ..Paul Zimet

By RICHARD EDER

If it had rained only 20 days, Noah and his passengers would have had to disembark and find a way to live in their same old water-logged country. The nineteen-sixties in America turned into the seventies. The waters of protest had seemed to rise pretty high, but when the New Left's ark grounded it was still somewhere in California.

"Milestones" is the most honest, complex and moving film exploration yet made of what has happened to the survivors of what came to be called the Movement: the young people who were radicalized by civil rights campaigning and the Vietnam war into forms of passive and sometimes active resistance.

●

The authors of "Milestones," Robert Kramer and John Douglas, are veteran radical film makers. They made a documentary in North Vietnam in 1969, and a year later Mr. Kramer wrote and directed "Ice," a fictional film about guerrilla warfare in the United States. Both men remain Marxist revolutionaries, at least in theory. But the marvel of "Milestones," which will be shown tonight and Saturday at Lincoln Center, is that it is not so much advocacy as a voyage of discovery, propelled by the author's own uncertainties.

It looks at the battered politics, the groping lifestyles, the search for meaning of a whole sector of society that has lost its revolutionary tactics and certainties but remains apart. One that lives turned inward, but uneasily, in a tangle of hope, futility, experimentation, apathy, valor and self-analysis.

The film's authors have taken more than 50 members of the Movement and shown them as they are living now: on communal farms, in burned-out squatters' premises, shared apartments, lofts, and on the road. They are experimenting with nudism, drugs, homoerotic groupings, crafts, farming, personal relationships of every conceivable size and shape, and even local radical politics.

There are dozens of sequences in which the characters talk, reminisce, discuss their problems, join and break up. The scenes are written—fictional to that extent—but they concern the real thoughts and experiences of those who enact them, and their authenticity is overwhelming.

The young prophets are older, the burnishment of

An actress in "Milestones"

five years ago—most came from a glossy upper middle class—now slightly blurred, their ideas tentative. They circle around the void left by their old commitments. The future is a bed they have slept in too long.

They are people trying to make decisions for a life whose rules they are devising at the same time. They are often tired, confused, incompetent.

There are more bright pieces in this mosaic than can possibly be mentioned. In a communal farmhouse, at sunset, a young man makes his farewells, saying vaguely "Maybe I'll visit a few middle-sized cities." Once on the road he remarks to his companion that he has had trouble relating to the friends he has just left.

A mother and her two grown daughters try to disentangle their past relationships. "You kids have a better relation to your feelings than I did. You trust them," she says.

A young man, just out of prison for helping military deserters leave the country, revisits his former comrades and makes them—all pulled slightly into their private worlds — uneasy. "There's something beautiful going on in Peter, but also he's frigid and brittle," one girl says.

Peter, the former prisoner, keeps reappearing, tentative, uncertain; a symbol of all those the film is about. He talks with a potter who finds

his workshop both a haven and a prison. He talks with his doctor father—both of them are marked and gentled by the bitter differences that flared between them in the past, but they are not really closer.

The movie is full of the children of these wandering souls. They are bright, brave, overstimulated, carried too long from place to place, kept up too late too often. They would be more assured in their gypsy life if their parents had more assurance about it themselves.

"Milestones" has some flaws. It lasts three hours and a quarter, though for most of the time it is so absorbing that only in the last half-hour—a childbirth scene that seems to me seriously misjudged—does the length really tell. The complex interweaving of its characters makes for some initial confusion. One or two of its scripted sequences seem stagy.

But there are so many affecting and instructive things in it—it is a deadening and unhealthy part of American life that there has been so little news from a sector from which formerly there was so much—and it is made with such a compassionate, hilarious and desolate eye that it must be seen.

1975 O 8, 24:1

INDIA SONG, directed and written (French with English subtitles) by Marguerite Duras; executive producer, Stephane Tchalgadjieff; director of photography, Bruno Nuytten; editor, Solange Leprince; music, Carlos d'Alessio; produced by Sunchild Productions and Les Films Armorial. Running time: 120 minutes. At the New York Film Festival, Alice Tully Hall, Lincoln Center. This film has not been rated.
Anne-Marie Streotter ....Delphine Seyrig
Vice Consul ....Michel Lonsdale
Embassy Attache ....Mathieu Carriere
Michael Richardson ....Claude Mann
Stretter's Guest.........Didier Flamand
Georges Crawn ....Vernon Dobcheff

By VINCENT CANBY

Marguerite Duras's new film is titled "India Song" but it might be more accurately called "Leprosy," since leprosy provides the film with its most vivid metaphors. "Lepers," someone explains early on, "burst like sacks of grain," almost happily or, at least, without pain.

So too bursts poor, elegant Anne-Marie Stretter (Delphine Seyrig), the promiscuous wife of the French Ambassador in Calcutta in the mid nineteen-thirties. Anne-Marie has what is variously diagnosed as leprosy of the soul and leprosy of the heart, which is a fancy way of saying she's bored out of her skull with her husband, with her lover, with all of her would-be lovers, and the members of Calcutta's diplomatic corps who live, like lepers, cut off from the life of the India that surrounds them.

●

Anne-Marie doesn't have the good grace to blow up on the screen, and thus add a touch of melodrama to the otherwise static "India Song." She simply walks into the sea, off-screen, her soul and heart having burst simultaneously. So it goes in this kind of romantic nonsense that isn't too different in essential content from the four-hankie movies of the nineteen-thirties and forties.

"India Song" will be shown at the New York Film Festival tonight at 6:15 and again Friday night at 9:30.

Miss Duras is a writer of fascinating novels and screenplays ("Hiroshima, Mon Amour") but I've yet to see a film directed by her that didn't seem a carefully thought out, overly intellectualized mistake. "India Song," based on an as-yet unproduced play commissioned by Peter Hall for the British National Theater, is no · content and all style, some of it quite beautiful.

Most of the so-called action takes place in a corner of the drawing room of the French Embassy in Calcutta, where we see Anne-Marie, usually in a stunning red evening dress, dancing with her lover, her suitors and finally with the mysterious French Vice Consul from Lahore (Michel Lonsdale), who has been sent to Calcutta in disgrace. One night he apparently had the bad manners to start shooting at the beggars and cats in the garden below his residence.

None of this information comes to us directly. There is, in fact, no synchronized dialogue in the film. Instead the images are attached to disembodied voices, mostly those of embassy guests but sometimes those of Anne-Marie and the Vice Consul, who tell us in gossipy terms the terrible scandals Anne-Marie has been involved in, as well as (near the start of the film), the bad end she came to.

•

The irritating thing about the film (which may well be consciously affected) is that the characters do seem interesting in a terribly distant sort of way. The movie looks and sounds like something shot underwater, that is, everything except the fine, schlocky, thirties musical score by Carlos d'Alessio, which gives the film a life that has been carefully drained from the individual performances. ♦

Miss Seyrig is marvelous to contemplate, as the camera does endlessly, reminding us from time to time of a somewhat patrician version of Rita Hayworth, back in the days when she was making stuff like "Gilda." "India Song," at its mushy center, isn't very different.

1975 O 8, 24:1

SMILE, produced and directed by Michael Ritchie; screenplay by Jerry Belson; director of photography, Conrad Hall; editor, Richard Harris; music editor, Ted Whitfield; distributed by United Artists. At the New York Film Festival. Running time: 113 minutes. This film has been classified PG.

A scene from "Smile"

Big Bob Freelander..........Bruce Dern
Brenda DiCarlo..........Barbara Feldon
Tommy French..............Michael Kidd
Wilson Shears..........Geoffrey Lewis
Andy DiCarlo............Nicholas Pryor
Robin..................Joan Prather
Doria..............Annette O'Toole
Maria Gonzales..........Maria O'Brien
Emile Eidleman..........Tito Vandis
Little Bob Freelander........Eric Shea

By VINCENT CANBY

Middle America is not exactly the fastest-moving target in the world. You don't have to be a sharpshooter to hit it. It just sits there like someone on a giant billboard, wearing an ear-to-ear grin, the eyes sparkling in anticipation of achieving some new plateau of pleasure, waiting to be defaced by anyone who has the price of a can of spray paint.

It's because Middle America is a pushover that Michael Ritchie's new comedy, "Smile," about an annual beauty pageant in Santa Rosa, Calif., is such a pungent surprise, a rollicking satire that misses few of the obvious targets, but without dehumanizing the victims. It's an especially American kind of social comedy in the way that great good humor sometimes is used to reveal unpleasant facts instead of burying them.

"Smile" will be shown at the New York Film Festival tonight at 6:15 and again on Saturday night at 9. No date has yet been set for its regular New York theater opening, though it has already played in several other cities around the country.

On its most general level, "Smile" is about a society in which optimism and positive thinking virtually amount to a political system, a guide to the making of choices, the principal goal of which is to have fun. A man who is on the brink of suicide is advised by his lifelong friend: "You've got to pull yourself together. Go out there and start having some fun." Fun is the operative word and, of course, fun is as illusive as a dim light in the dark. When you look at it directly, it disappears.

•

The pageant that is the center of "Smile" is fictitious, a statewide (California) Young American Miss contest that, one assumes, precedes the kind of national clambake that Bert Parks emcees annually. The film covers the four days of various trials in which the teen-age contestants are graded on poise, beauty, zest for living, talent and their concern for their fellow man.

They are coddled, threatened and frightened into fakery with such questions as, "Marie, can you tell me why you want to go into missionary work?" and "Why do you play the flute, dear? In your own words . . ."

The kingpin of the affair is a local Santa Rosa booster named Big Bob Friedlander (Bruce Dern), a live-wire automobile salesman who, in the course of this particular pageant, begins to lose the smile that, until now, he had been convinced was making America great.

This is no big dramatic deal. "Smile" is not a film of explosive revelations. The soul-searching we do is our own. It's a comedy composed of dozens of vignettes—about Big Bob, about the pageant coordinator, Brenda DiCarlo, a pretty, silly, edgy woman beautifully played by Barbara Feldon, about Brenda's suicidal husband, Andy (Nicholas Pryor), about the other officials of the pageant and especially about some of the contestants.

•

Unlike "Beauty Knows No Pain," a comic and rude short subject made several years ago about the training of some drum majorettes in Texas, "Smile" treats its beauty contestants without condescension. The girls are sometimes hugely funny and foolish, but they are also decent and appealing in their earnest efforts to be the Ann-Margrets of tomorrow.

Three young actresses stand out in these roles: Maria O'Brien as a pushy, driving contestant who sells her Mexican-American heritage for all its worth; Joan Prather, as the most levelheaded of the contestants, and Annette O'Toole, as the most desperate.

Jerry Belson wrote the excellent screenplay. "Smile," which is Mr. Ritchie's best film to date (better than both "Downhill Racer" and "The Candidate"), questions the quality of our fun, while adding to it.

1975 O 9, 52:1

FRENCH PROVINCIAL (Souvenir's d'en France), directed by Andre Techine; screenplay (French with English subtitles) by Mr. Techine and Marilyn Goldin; director of photography, Bruno Nuytten; editor, Anne-Marie Deshayes; music by Philippe Sarde; produced by Stephan Films. At the New York Film Festival. Running time: 91 minutes.
Berthe .... Jeanne Moreau
Hector .... Michel Auclair
Regina .... Marie-France Pisier
Prosper .... Claude Mann
Augustine .... Orane Demazis
Pedret .... Aram Stephan
Lucie .... Helene Surgere
Victor .... Julien Guiomar

By RICHARD EDER

Jeanne Moreau has a genius for the particular. She could be marched off for execution and her fretful gait, her expression, her silences would argue so strongly against any mere universal application of law that the firing squad would fall apart arguing.

In "French Provincial" the young director André Té-chiné has sent Miss Moreau trundling down a long, heavily furnished corridor of a movie about the multigenerational rise and fall of a French bourgeois family. By no subtle extension it argues through its particular provincial setting the decline and dissolution of bourgeois France.

Miss Moreau implants all kinds of cross-rhythms in Mr. Téchiné's ponderous though talented work, with its air of a nineteenth-century novel. She arrests the predictable playing-out of his cards; she enhances his uneven strengths.

"French Provincial," which will be shown tonight and tomorrow at Lincoln Center, is set around the fortunes of a family-owned foundry in a small French town. It was founded by Pedret, a young immigrant from Spain who by hard work and a driving vision built it up out of a simple smithy, and married the daughter of a prosperous local family as well.

•

This is told in flashback. Most of the film takes place when Pedret has become the family patriarch, running the business with his three grown sons and dominating the life of the town. One trenchant scene shows the family going to the local movie theater in the same hierarchial fashion that an English squire and his family would go to church.

Sturdy as one of his iron boilers, bearded and mystically devoted to the foundry, old Pedret represents for Téchiné the vitality the bourgeoisie once had. The three sons, in different ways, are the class in decadence.

There are two marriages. One brings in Régina, a cold, spoiled girl who nests in the family like a leech, and eventually runs off with an American soldier. The other brings in Berthe, the town laundry woman.

Berthe — Jeanne Moreau — is vital, passionate and strong. She has an affair with Hector, most likable of the three sons, and when the family intervenes, threatens to leave town.

Miss Moreau flickers fiercely, unpredictably, a hawk who lets herself be caught. Take one scene, for example. She has been snubbed by the family, and her laundry business is being boycotted.

We see her in her kitchen, making herself dinner. She beats the omelet, muttering banal phrases on the lines of "It will pass," "What's the difference?" She chops salad, she pours wine. Each action is like assembling a bomb. The bomb goes off. In a magnificent Moreanuvian reversal she suddenly sweeps out — abandoning omelet, salad and wine — goes to the foundry, and rallies Hector to defy his family.

Old Pedret can't afford to lose Hector, who is the works manager, so he pragmatically decides they must marry. The lesson: The bourgeoisie will co-opt members of the proletariat when necessary.

Berthe is new blood: when Pedret dies she takes over. Emotionally she is of the people—at the film's start she gets a job for Pierre, who will eventually lead the workers in strike against her—but she is pulled unwillingly away. Only during the war—when she drives a munitions truck for the resistance group run by Pierre—does some of the old emotional unity come back. As did France's.

•

The war ends. She, not Pierre, gets a medal. Pierre, the militant union man, is won over to the bland new European style of worker-management cooperation. But the foundry itself is going under, in competition with big multinational firms. Only American money can save it. It comes—with Regina and her American lover who also happens to be a big businessman. At the end we see Regina and the American making love under the portrait of old Pedret.

By this time the movie has collapsed under the increasingly coarse style that Téchiné adopts to symbolize his thesis of capitalist collapse. It isn't helped by the fact that his Americans, speak English with grotesque French and German accents and look something out of Krokodil.

Miss Moreau lies helplessly in bed. She can do no more to save the foundry: It will probably go on, but it won't be hers or even French. On the other hand, she has almost saved the movie.

1975 O 9, 52:1

MAHOGANY, directed by Berry Gordy; screenplay by John Byrum, based on a story by Toni Amber; produced by Rob Cohen and Jack Ballard; director of photography, David Watkin; music, Michael Masser; editor, Peter Zinner; distributed by Paramount Pictures. Running time: 110 minutes. At Loews State 2 Theater, Broadway at 45th Street, and Loews Orpheum Theater, 86th Street near Third Avenue. This film has been rated PG.

Tracy	Diana Ross
Brian	Billy Dee Williams
Sean	Anthony Perkins
Christian Rosetti	Jean-Pierre Aumont
Florence	Beah Richards
Miss Evans	Nina Foch
Carlotta Gavina	Marisa Mell
Wil	Lenard Norris

Berry Gordy, the Detroit music executive who successfully put Motown Records into the movie business a couple of years ago with "Lady Sings the Blues," has now directed his first film, "Mahogany," about a poor black girl from Chicago who becomes the toast of the international fashion world only to renounce it for the love of a poor but honest black politician who once cautioned her: "Success is nothing without someone you love to share it with you."

The length and breathlessness of that sentence describe the kind of movie that Mr. Gordy has made so slickly that Jacqueline Susann might have envied it. "Mahogany" is silly fiction—it's rdiculous—but it's been directed with undeniable energy and canniness, and with all of the cheap surface sophistication that money can buy.

•

Moreover, it has as its star Motown's biggest single natural resource, the incomparable Diana Ross, whose years as a singing Supreme must, I suspect, have something to do with the ease with which she has turned into such a dynamic film performer. Miss Ross plays the title role, which is the nickname given the struggling young fashion designer by the jaded homosexual photographer (played by Anthony Perkins) who transforms her into the world's most famous model.

It's not easy making a silk purse out of material like this. It defeated Joan Crawford several decades ago, but then Miss Ross has a couple of things that Miss Crawford was seldom allowed to display—a furious gutsiness and a ribald humor that, when they surface, make "Mahogany" a lot more entertaining than the material has any right to be.

Mr. Perkins is also an asset as the more than slightly bent photographer, a role that begins as a cliché but becomes increasingly idiosyncratic before it winds up as a cliché again. Mr. Perkins's strength as an actor helps to give shape to Miss Ross's performance.

Billy Dee Williams, who played opposite Miss Ross in "Lady Sings the Blues," is cast as the politician who eventually saves Miss Ross from the fleshpots of Rome. He's handsome and bland, a kind of black George Brent, though, on a couple of occasions with Miss Ross, he demonstrates a flair for comedy that movies like this can't tolerate for long. It shows up the sentiments of the rest of the film.

•

Mr. Gordy's style as a film maker is early CinemaScope, that period in the nineteen-fifties when 20th Century-Fox, the company that introduced CinemaScope, insisted on making every film into a travelogue. The scenes set in Chicago are full of Chicago scenery, and "when the movie goes to Rome, you might think you're back looking at "Three Coins in the Fountain."

Everything is photographed big and long, including an extended montage tracing Miss Ross's rise as an international model, and (what I take to be) an unintentionally hilarious fashion show, some of the clothes for which were designed by Miss Ross, whose designing talent might best be utilized in comic opera.

"Mahogany," which opened yesterday at the Loews State 2 and Orpheum Theaters, has two perceptive sequences (two more than ever crept into a comparable film based on a Susann novel). One is a rowdy, comic scene set in an unemployment office, and the other depicts the photographer shooting a high-fashion layout with models perched all over the facade of a Chicago tenement.

Two scenes and a couple of good performances don't make a movie, but Mr. Gordy is more aware of how movies are made than most directors who've devoted their lives to perfecting junk.

VINCENT CANBY

1975 O 9, 54:1

HARD TIMES, directed by Walter Hill; screenplay by Walter Hill, Bryan Gindorff and Bruce Henstell; Philip Lathrop, cinematographer; Roger Spottiswoode, editor; music by Barry de Vorzon; produced by Lawrence Gordon; distributed by Columbia Pictures. At neighborhood theaters. Running time: 97 minutes. This film has been classified R.

Chaney	Charles Bronson
Speed	James Coburn
Lucy	Jill Ireland
Poe	Strother Martin
Gayleen	Maggie Blye
Gandil	Michael McGuire
Jim Henry	Robert Tessier
Street	Nick Dimitri

The taciturn stranger looms out of the morning, puts the affairs of weak, fallible, decent people to rights, up-ends the bad guys, breaks a poor girl's heart but leaves her upper lip stiff, and goes as quietly as he came.

They don't make Westerns like that any more? Right. This isn't a Western.

"Hard Times" is a stylish, sharp, ingratiating movie about pick-up fighters who travel around with their managers staging high-stakes matches in warehouses, on piers and in fields just outside town. It opened yesterday at neighborhood theaters.

It takes place in New Orleans during the Depression and the one indulgence of its director, who has set it out in a series of refreshingly short, laconic sequences, is to stuff it with every conceivably symbol of the era. Ceiling fans turning slowly, black boys doing a buck-and-wing on the sidewalk, lots of vintage cars, everyone in suspenders, bar girls wearing hats: everything that could be there is there. It's a bit excessive, but it looks nice and it doesn't do any harm.

Charles Bronson, who looks more and more like Clark Gable left out too long in the sun, gets off a freight train. He shows his devastating skill in an impromptu fight, and is taken on by James Coburn, playing a shiftless, volatile but charming fight manager.

They take on the best New Orleans has to offer⅛ namely, a shaven-headed giant made out of concrete pilings, and they win.

Coburn gambles away his share of the winnings and goes in debt to the Mob&. He will be chopped up unless Bronson agrees to a last fight with a Mob-Imported professional.

Bronson, who says only about two dozen words throughout, and whose main conversational gambit is to go away, has been sulking in his bedroom, but agrees. He wins painfully, gives most of his prize money to Coburn and an opium-addicted doctor named Poe, boards another freight train, and leaves

Nothing more than thi: yet it moves well, its character, good and bad, are taut and springy, and it is frequently funny. The fight scenes are done with restraint, apart from the usual phony-sounding "thwacks" when the blow land. Why don't they try chimes for a change?

Jame Coburn manages an engaging quality of irascibility: he is part dolt but not completely. Charles Bronson screws his eyes up as if he were full of feathers, but he projects noble meant to do. Dr. Poe, played by Strother Martin, is fine.

RICHARD EDER

1975 O 9, 54:2

DARKTOWN STRUTTERS, directed by William Witney; screenplay by George Armitage; director of photography, George Armitage; film editor, Morton Tubor; a New World Pictures Release. At neighborhood theaters. Running time: 90 minutes. This film is classified PG.

Syreena	Trina Parks
Carmen	Edna Richardson
Miranda	Bettye Sweet
Theda	Shirley Washington
Mellow	Roger E. Mosley
Wired	Christopher Joy
Raunchy	Stan Shaw
Commander Cross	Norman Bartold

The idea of kidding black films is strained to the breaking point by "Darktown Strutters," which clattered aimlessly into local theaters yesterday. Both black spoofers and the white spoofed move witlessly on motorcycles through the Watts area of Los Angeles in an unsuccessful quest for fun.

But they are no less harebrained than the gnarled plot about a tough black attractive heroine, Trina Parks, and her efforts to find her mother and other blacks kidnapped for weird reasons by Norman Barthold—the conniving, rich, white Colonel Sanders-type fried-ribs magnate.

Naturally, Miss Parks is joined by wacky, bigoted police officers and other broadly burlesqued characters, including Uncle Tom servants and minstrel singers. Unfortunately, the sight gags and raunchy quips are not rib-ticklers, and the blatantly diffuse script, one-dimensional acting and artless directing only serve to make the frenetic business a lame, unfunny affair. A singing group in "Darktown Strutters" make a cogent point when it carols, "You get what you see."

A. H. WEILER

1975 O 9, 54:4

THE MASTER GUNFIGHTER, directed by Frank Laughlin; produced by Philip P. Parslow; Jack A. Marta, director of photography; William Reynolds and Danford Greene, editors; music, Lalo Schifrin; distributed by Taylor-Laughlin Distributing Company. At the Penthouse and other theaters. Running time: 120 minutes; this film has been classified PG.

Finley	Tom Laughlin
Paulo	Ron O'Neal
Chorika	Geo Anne Sosa
Eula	Barbara Carrera

"The Master Gunfighter" starts with a procession of riders filmed in slow motion on a Pacific beach. The camera speeds up after a bit, but the picture never does. It is long, stilted, self-conscious, badly acted and boring. Apart from that, there is little to recommend it.

Made by the people who made the vastly successful "Billy Jack" movies, it is a dim and grandiloquent account of how one group of the oppressed—a Mexican ranch family overtaken by the United States acquisition of California — massacres another group of the oppressed—the Indians.

It is done, of all reasons, to get hold of the Indians' gold in order to pay United States taxes. From the standpoint of the crack-brained brand of mystical individualism preached in the Billy Jack pictures, taxes would seem to be a wicked thing and one is to feel sympathy for the desperate lengths to which the Mexicans are driven as well as for the Indians.

Not too much sympathy, though. Up rides the Master Gunfighter—played by Tom Laughlin, who also played Billy Jack—and ends up massacring just about everyone in sight. He does it as much with a sword as with his 12-shooter revolver—even the revolver is exaggerated —and he does it reluctantly, sighing. With each sigh, about 17 people perish.

After avenging the dead Indians and preventing a second massacre he literally rides off into the sunset followed by his wife, who happens to be one of the few survivors of the Mexican ranch family.

The sword fighting seems to be patterned on stylized Japanese movements. The dialogue sounds as if someone had translated it from the Japanese, too. Some of the photography is arresting, but mostly it manages to make the splendid California coastline look stuffy.

RICHARD EDER

1975 O 10, 32:4

THE NEW YORK TIMES

Anna Prucanl on barge with a head of Karl Marx on prow

SWEET MOVIE, directed by Dusan Makavejev; produced by Vincent Maille; supervising producer (Canada), Richard Helman; executive producer, Helene Vaser; original music, Manos Hadjidakis; director of photography, Pierre L'homme; editor, Yann Dedet; no screenplay credit—dialogue in English and French (with English subtitles; a co-production of V. M. Productions (Paris), Mojack Films (Montreal) and Maran Films (Munich); distributed by Biograph Films. Running time: 95 minutes. At the D. W. Griffith Theater, 59th Street near Second Avenue. This film has not been rated
Miss Canada ....Carol Laure
Sailor from the Potemkin ....
           Pierre Clementi
Capt. Ann Planela ......Ann Prucanl
El Macho ....Sami Frey
Chastity Belt Lady ....Jane Mallet
Mama Communa ....Marpessa Dawn
Jeremiah Muscle ....Ray Callender
Mr. Kapital ....John Vernon
With Otto Muehl and members of the Therapie-Komune of Vienna

By VINCENT CANBY

"Sweet Movie," Dusan Makavejev's fifth feature film, which was the major scandal at the 1974 Cannes Film Festival, has finally arrived in New York (at the D. W. Griffith Theater) with approximately four of its more scatological minutes removed. The excision makes the film easier to sit through—less aggressively idiosyncratic — while the over-all work remains a courageous example of a personal kind of film making that, to me, leads nowhere.

"Sweet Movie," like Mr. Makavejev's "WR: Mysteries of the Organism," is a collage movie, with a structure that its producers describe as "open and nonauthoritarian . . . made up of nonverbal elements." This is a fairly intimidating way of saying that if you find it heavy-handed, obscure, unfunny, boring, self-indulgent and not terribly stimulating on any

level, there's something wrong with you, not the movie.

For a film so full of concern for the political and social sanity of man, "Sweet Movie" is, paradoxically, élitist. If one doesn't share Mr. Makavejev's knowldge of the history of Communism and Reichian psychology, much of it is incomprehensible.

What are comprehensible are the two intercut lines of visual action, both having the style of political cartoons. The first follows the farcical adventures of a Miss Canada (Carole Laure) who is married by Mr. Kapital (John Vernon), discarded by him when she objects to the manner in which he gets his sexual kicks, then is subjected to numerous fates worse than death and, when last seen, is being dunked in a vat full of chocolate syrup for a TV commercial.

The second, which is much more vivid, furious and compelling—is a political metaphor: a barge named the Survival, which carries a huge, papier-mâché likeness of Karl Marx on its prow, steams through the canals of a European city. Its captain (Anna Prucanl) stands on Marx's brow, luring innocents abroad. Her principal victim is a young, ever-optimistic sailor (Pierre Clementi) off the Potemkin, whom she eventually destroys.

As Mr. Makavejev has brilliantly demonstrated in his

earlier films — particularly "Man Is Not a Bird"—he can make films of comparatively conventional form if he wants to. Now he obviously doesn't want to. This independence of spirit is laudable, but when it involves the large amounts of money that apparently went into "Sweet Movie," it begins to seem dacadent. Too much money is being spent for the benefit of the few.

"Sweet Movie" rolls around in food—mostly sugar, eggs, milk, chocolate syrup — to such an extent that one's mind wanders from the intellectual concerns of the director to the logistics of the film making. When Miss Prucanl and Mr. Clementi make love in a bed full of sugar, one forgets the metaphor and starts to worry about how they got all that sticky stuff off after the scene was shot. On two occasions male actors urinate onscreen, once in a close-up. Is this real or were some sort of devices used?

When the audience begins to wonder how an effect was achieved instead of why it has been done, a film's claim to seriousness flies out the window. "Earthquake" and "The Towering Inferno" made no such claims. "Sweet Movie" does—and fails.

1975 O 10, 32:3

ROYAL FLASH, directed by Richard Lester; screenplay by George MacDonald Fraser, based on his novel; produced by David V. Picker and Denis O'Dell; director of photography, Geoffrey Unsworth; a David V. Picker presentation, distributed by 20th Century-Fox. Running time: 99 minutes. At the Coronet Theater, Third Avenue near 59th Street. This film has been rated PG.
Harry Flashman......Malcolm McDowell
Rudi Von Starnberg..........Alan Bates
Lola Montez............Florinda Bolkan
Bismarck ....
Duchess Irma............Britt Ekland
Kraftstein ....Lionel Jeffries
Old Rouse ....Roy Kinnear

By VINCENT CANBY

Harry Flashman is not quite a scoundrel. He is, rather, a hero who is thoroughly, irretrievably flawed. He lieslies and cheats. He's chicken-hearted. He's vain. When the going gets tough and the tough get going, Harry flees or, if all exits are closed to him, hides. When caught, he cries. Once, during a battle in the Crimean War, when his side was losing, Harry almost broke his neck trying to surrender. The thing about Harry is that whatever he does, he does hard.

As played with fine, manic intensity by Malcolm McDowell in Richard Lester's new comedy, "Royal Flash," Harry can't even smile straight. The corners of his mouth go up in the expected fashion but in the middle of it there's a misplaced leer. Ever optimistic, Harry keeps his leer at the ready, even though he's the sort who loses when playing strip poker with a girl.

Harry Flashman is good comic company and "Royal Flash," which opened yesterday at the Coronet, is good comic fun. The screenplay is by George MacDonald Fraser, based on his novel about the adventures of the young. English Army officer —part rogue, part twit—who romances Lola Montez and finds himself up to his neck in Bismarck's schemes to unite the German princely states.

Though "Royal Flash" is set in the mid-19th century, the manners and morals look very much like those of Mr. Lester's "The Three Musketeers" and "The Four Musketeers," the two films he made out of the Dumas novel with screenplays by Mr. Fraser.

If the seams between the gags are beginning to show in "Royal Flash," and if the pace seems occasionally a little less than breathless, it may be due as much to our expectations of—and our familiarity with—the Lester method as to any lack of invention on the part of the film makers.

Mr. Lester throws away more gags in "Royal Flash" than some comedy directors think up in an entire career.

Now and then you wish he'd take time to develop a routine a little more, to give it a classic beginning, a middle and an end, instead of rushing on to the next sequence. He is profligate with his talents, which is, of course, very much a part of the method of any Lester comedy.

Another part is the impeccable casting. Charlton Heston was never better in "Ben-Hur" than he was as Cardinal Richelieu in the "Musketeers" films. There are no plums of such size in "Royal Flash," though Mr. McDowell is very good, and actors like Alan Bates, Oliver Reed and Florinda Bolkan give the enterprise heft it might otherwise lack.

One typical Lester sequence: Lola Montez (Miss Bolkan) dances before Ludwig of Bavaria, who is enchanted with her, though not as history has told us, because of her shape or her beauty. Giggling with pleasure, he asks, "Are they real?" Being mad, Ludwig means the cardboard spiders that she uses as props in her dance. It's low-comedy and almost nonstop.

1975 O 11, 23:1

Screen: 'Lisztomania'

It's Ken Russell's Spangled Post-Beatles Rococo and Manic Look at Composer

By RICHARD EDER

Ken Russell blows up his colored balloons with ether: They bob prettily, and when they burst we pass out.

Lisztomania, which opened yesterday at the Ziegfeld, is the latest of his spangled flights of fancy. Fancy it is, but hardly a flight.

It is a tiny, potentially appealing weed of a picture, absurdly dragged down by a mass of post-Beatles rococo. For Mr. Russell, the shortest line between two points is a pretzel, preferably painted gold and doped.

It is a pity. For the first half-hour or so, Mr. Russelle's treatment of Franz Liszt and Richard Wagner as the pop stars of their day is manic and extremely funny. Then it relapse sinto a noisy bit of pretentiousness in the manner of its predecessor, "Tommy": full of flashing lights, satin spacesuits, chrome-lucite furniture and mock agony.

The opening scene with Liszt—played by Roger Daltrey, the star of "Tommy"— making love to a countess to the best of a rhinestone metronome is of limited appeal. But things improve when the count comes in. Liszt and his mistress are strapped inside a piano while

The Cast

LISZTOMANIA, written and directed by Ken Russell; director of photography, Peter Suschitzky; editor, Stuart Baird; music by Rick Wakeman; produced by Roy Baird and David Puttnam; distributed by Warner Bros. At the Ziegfeld Theater; running time: 105 minutes; this film has been classified R.
Liszt..............Roger Daltrey
Princess Carolyn.......Sara Kestelman
Richard Wagner.........Paul Nicholas
Countess Marie........Fiona Lewis
Cosima.............Veronica Quilligan
Olga.................Nell Campbell
Hans von Bulow........Andrew Reilly
Pope.................Ringo Starr
Count d'Agoult........John Justin

the count gleefully pounds out one of the noisier Liszt pieces. "Perhaps this will teach you not to bang on the piano," he chortles.

The next scenes show Liszt, rendered in Mr. Daltrey's best Liverpudlian accents, at the height of his pop-star success. One takes place in a crowded musicians' cafe. Mendelssohn is putting down an admirer: "Music, shmusic; i's a living." Rossini circulates with a tray of chicken. "Eat or you'll get sick," he tells Berlioz. Infantile, but it works.

So does Liszt's concert scene. The place is packed with 19th-century groupies. Liszt strikes a chord, and he's mobbed by hundreds of berserk yellow bonnets.

Then Liszt goes to Russia to look up one of his loves, the Princess Caroline, and the movie founders. There is a repulsive scene in her antechamber in which Liszt belts out a rock number while circled by some voracious-looking women. It culminates with a spidery Princess Caroline presiding over a feigned sexual mutilation involving an enormous plastic phallus.

Nothing improves after that. Richard Wagner appears as Liszt's arch-rival, a kind of Nazi Antichrist, with his own groupie cult. Liszt—by this time he has become a priest—is sent by the Pope —played by Ringo Starr—to destroy him.

Liszt breaks into Wagner's turreted castle and does him in by playing "Liebestraum" at him on a fire-belching piano. Before Wagner dies, however, he creates a Nazi Frankenstein's monster, and it takes Liszt, in a celestial rocket ship, accompanied by all his mistresses, to destroy it.

●

To the degree one chooses to find symbolism in all this, it is ludicrous. Equating Wagner's music with Nazism in this fashion is absurdly simplistic. It is even more absurd to set up Liszt's music as some kind of counterforce to Wagner's, let alone one that is capable of overbearing it.

Now it can be argued that Mr. Russell, with all his dazzle, is not intending, but aping symbolism. Or that he is not so much being pretentious as mocking pretention. Try mocking a quicksand by somersaulting artistically into it: The rate at which you sink is just the same, and only your closest admirers will be interested in pulling you out.

1975 O 11, 23:1

SIDECAR RACERS, written by Jon Cleary; directed by Earl Bellamy; director of photography, Paul Onorato; edited by Robert L. Kimble; produced by Richard Irving and presented by Universal. At local theaters. Running time: 100 minutes. This film has been rated PG.
Jeff Rayburn .... Ben Murphy
Lynn Carson .... Wendy Hughes
Dave Ferguson .... John Clayton
Carson .... Peter Graves
Ocker Harvey .... John Meillon
Pete McAlister .... John Derum
Rick Horton .... Peter Gwynne
Bluey Wilson .... Serge Lazareff
Bob Horton .... Paul Bertram

By A. H. WEILER

Australia may be photogenic, its young men may be daring, and speeding motorcycles can be thrilling, but "Sidecar Racers," which roared into local theaters Wednesday is merely scenic and noisy about its racers and their cycles. Aside from its uncommon views of the dangerous, Australian two-man sport of sidecar motorcycle racing, the film is familiar melodrama, no more exciting than its uninspired story and largely native cast.

The script by an Australian novelist, Jon Cleary ("The Sundowners," etc.) involves a visiting American, Ben Murphy, playing a onetime Olympic swimming champion as the sidecar passenger

who teams with an Australian cyclist, John Clayton, to win the big race. Naturally, there's also some offtrack romantic rivalry between them for Wendy Hughes, daughter of the other American in the cast, Peter Graves, playing a tire tycoon who makes a few token appearances before they all reach the finish line.

Even though there are clashes between some tough guys and our heroes and a couple of tragic crashes, "Sidecar Racers" leans heavily on its thunderous racing footage, which eventually becomes a mite redundant. Although the handsome, boyish Mr. Murphy chooses to give up both his chances of glory and the girl to the dark, properly resentful Mr. Clayton, they both emerge as sincere but slightly sophomoric figures. Miss Hughes, however, appears to be a spoiled, indecisive prize, hardly worth all their wrangling.

Under Earl Bellamy's pedestrian direction, Australia is colorful but hardly worth the trip, even in those rocketing racers.

1975 O 11, 24:1

Why
Stix
Nix
Big
Pix

By CHARLES HIGHAM

LOS ANGELES

Appearances can be deceiving, especially in Hollywood—a phenomenon which may explain a series of recent rose-colored reports suggesting that the movie industry is enjoying its biggest economic boom since the blissfully busy 1940's. While it is true that profits this past summer were up approximately 23 per cent over those of the previous summer, this rise is due entirely to the huge success of a very small handful of films, including "Shampoo," "Tommy," "White Line Fever,"

Charles Higham is the author of a number of books on the Hollywood scene.

Soviet Film Bares Workers' Problems

By CHRISTOPHER S. WREN
Special to The New York Times

MOSCOW, Oct. 11—A long argument about failures in building construction may not sound like the stuff from which prize-winning films are made, but a new Soviet movie is attracting audiences by adroitly exploiting just that subject.

The film is "The Bonus" and it won the main prize this year in the Eighth All-Union Film Festival in Kishinev, the capital of Soviet Moldavia. It tells of a team of construction workers who refuse a bonus and of the clash of interests that erupts when a Communist party committee summons the team leader to find out why.

Some perennial problems of the Soviet construction industry get candid airing, among them mismanagement and manipulation of production statistics.

"The Bonus" has tackled the familiar work production theme more realistically than its mock-heroic Soviet film predecessors.

Glorification of labor has long been mandated in official Soviet culture. "The working man is the principal hero of Soviet art," declared Pravda recently in an editorial praising films like "The Bonus."

Leader of Simple Honesty

The tradition has produced other recent works like "The Hottest Month," a film about steelworkers, and "Man From Outside," a play about an engineer. They have advanced the genre somewhat beyond the boy-meets-tractor clichés of the Stalinist era.

The success of the new Leningrad-made film is due in large part to a credible

performance by Yevgeny Leonov. He plays Vasily Potapov, the lumber team leader, whose simple honesty is as solid as his calluses.

The film itself is confined almost entirely to the office of a large construction site, where Potapov is goaded into disclosing why he and his 17 workers rejected their part of a bonus that was awarded the enterprise for having placed third in an industrial competition.

"It's not profitable," he blurts, and introduces a young cement pourer who lost 400 rubles in wages— more than three months of average pay—because cement was sometimes not available. His bonus amounts to only 40 rubles.

"You draw a salary," Potapov reminds the committee. "For you this bonus is a bonus. And for him it isn't. Because he is on a piecework basis, he has no cement and he is stuck. For him it is a handout."

In the recriminations that ensue, it is revealed that the construction enterprise could not meet its original production plan, but won the 37,000 ruble bonus by substituting a more modest plan and then overfulfilling it.

The enterprise's director, Batartsev, who is played by Vladimir Samoilov, tries to justify the incompetence and deception.

"The scales of construction in our country are huge, the problems very complicated," he says. "Do you understand?"

Potapov produces two red notebooks filled with calcula-

tions, provided by a disillusioned economist, to show that the initial plan could have been fulfilled. He proposes that the bonuses be collected and given back to the bank.

"It's somebody else's money and it should be returned," he insists. But the team leader is betrayed when it is learned that seven workers went behind his back and picked up their bonuses anyway. Potapov trudges from the office in silent defeat, the notebooks clenched in his fist.

But the party secretary, Solomakhin, who is portrayed by Oleg Yankovsky, insists that the meeting continue. "We love to mount the podium and say beautiful words about the working class," he says. "But when he came here, when he bared to us everything that has sickened him, we didn't recognize him."

"Do you know why these seven men took the bonus now?" Solomakhin asks the director. "Because they no longer believe. They don't believe Potapov can achieve anything, that it's possible to change anything at this construction site. Shall we prove it now?"

The committee votes to return the bonus, with the enterprise's director breaking a tie and thereby risking his career. The members file out into the night looking as beaten as the team leader.

The ending of the script, by Aleksandr Gelman, was perhaps ideologically predictable. But the audience in one Moscow theater seemed to enjoy the exposures of official frailty that preceded it.

1975 O 12, 10:4

"Benji" — and most sensationally—the jumbo-grossing "Jaws."

On the other hand, a surprisingly large number of highly touted movies have distressed their producers by just barely breaking even, or by flopping altogether; as a result, the current accent in Hollywood is very much on old-fashioned, uncomplicated escapism, and the new breed of movie moguls, swaying uncertainly in their swivel chairs, is even beginning to rethink the heretofore unquestioned value of stars.

No more striking example of a "surefire" winner-turned-loser can be found than Robert Altman's highly praised "Nashville." Based on the film's enthusiastic critical and public reception in New York, one might have expected it to surpass the box-office business of "Benji" — a low-budget "family movie" about a heroic dog. Yet Robert Altman's complex blend of country music and

social significance is proving something of a box-office fizzle, although it will presumably turn a small profit eventually.

As of this writing, the film, which was produced for slightly under $2.5-million, has made just over $3-million. This would seem to indicate that Paramount and ABC, the film's backers, had already raked in $500,000 in profits, but such is not the case. Because of the high price of distribution, exhibition and promotion, a movie must earn approximately two-and-a-half times the amount of its initial cost before it can begin to show a profit. As a result, "Nashville" won't become a money-maker unless or until it earns somewhere in the neighborhood of $6-million—which may take a long while in view of its lacklustre showing on Variety's weekly charts, compiled by Standard Data Corporation. (It should be noted that published

figures of film-completion costs and box-office returns are sometimes less than 100 per cent reliable, due to a variety of factors, such as additional distribution costs and tax write-offs. However, the Standard Data Corporation comes as close as possible to the hard financial facts.)

●

Mike Nichols, like Robert Altman, is a director whose recent films have failed to generate small-town excitement, despite an abundance of big-city hype. As a result, a fortune is precisely what "The Fortune" will not make for Columbia. It's been estimated that the period comedy, starring Jack Nicholson and Warren Beatty as a couple of con artists, needs to bring $8-million into the box office before it can turn a profit, but Variety's chart shows that it has earned just a bit over $2.5 during a 16-week period. "French Connection II" also failed to connect at the box office, as did the costly "Bite the Bullet," "The Drowning Pool" and "The Day of the Locust."

Executive reshuffles within the studios have added to Hollywood's jitters, and the pressures on the new chiefs to deliver commercial fare are intense. David Begelman, of Columbia, and Mike Medavoy, of United Artists, seem to be making the grade. Highly successful agents before becoming production chiefs, they are evidently favored by their superiors because they know agents' tricks and can see very clearly when a proposed package is being oversold. They can be particularly tough in the area of bargaining.

Former agents abound in the studio hierarchies, as a matter of fact. Ironically, the very commodity they once peddled—the major star—is the one many of them are now most reluctant to promote. "I used to come into a studio with a star as the chief item in a package, because I had to please my client," says David Begelman from behind his massive desk at Columbia. "Now I can see through a deal brought to me by an agent. I will never take any deal if the only thing going for it is a star name. In fact, I'll look with equal favor on a deal that doesn't have any stars in it at all. Of course, a star can put a picture into higher profits in some cases. But you have to start with a hot subject."

•

A year ago, this simply wasn't true; most scripts were tailored to the demands of particular "names." Now they're designed for gimmick novelty or for shock value. Ned Tanen, of MCA/Universal, says: "Look at the success of 'The Exorcist'! No stars! And of our own 'Jaws'! No stars. It's true that 'The Sting' made fantastic money, with Newman and Redford. But without that script—forget it. Look at 'American Graffiti.' No stars, but it made a tremendous amount of money for us."

•

What qualities account for Hollywood's recent hits—and failures? Everyone seems to agree that it is more important than ever before to grab an audience on the gut level — intellectual nuance and cinematic subtlety are risky attributes. "American Graffiti" provided instant identification for small-town youths; "Mandingo" — a plantation melodrama mixing miscegenation and sadism— had devastating reviews but

proved a powerful and very popular sexual turn-on (it has recouped its budget many times over). "Shampoo" provides a titillating glimpse of Beverly Hills high life; "Jaws," "The Towering Inferno" and "Earthquake" seized on mass paranoia and exploited it relentlessly.

Why do certain ambitious, meticulously tooled movies fail? Richard Sylbert, new head of production at Paramount, advances this theory: "The public finds their themes too remote; they can't identify with them or get involved with them. For instance, 'The Fortune' was a movie about two guys who want to kill a sweet, pretty young girl, for God's sake. Who can identify with that? And 'The Day of the Locust' is about these deadbeats, these depressing people. As for 'Nashville,' Altman did some interesting things with the soundtrack, but it's impossible for people in the midwest and the south to understand what's going on in it. It's too much the work of an outsider, an intellectual, looking in on Nashville. Audiences feel they're being condescended to."

The same criticism has been applied to Fox's "French Connection II." "It was depressing," says Columbia's David Begelman," "The first 'French Connection' was exciting, lots of action, lots of movement. But the second was drab and gloomy and pessimistic. Forget it."

It is becoming increasingly apparent that stars can do nothing to save a movie if the word-of-mouth is sour. Supposed superstars Jack Nicholson and Warren Beatty couldn't save "The Fortune," and Gene Hackman failed to draw crowds in five recent pictures in a row: "Zandy's Bride," "The Conversation," "French Connection II," "Night Moves" and "Bite the Bullet." And Paul Newman sank in "The Drowning Pool."

There are exceptions to the rule, however. "Columbia and 20th took a poll recently to see who was the most popular star," says Richard Sylbert. "The star was Barbra Streisand. They then took a poll to see who was the *least* popular star. The star was Barbra Streisand." But Sylbert admits that, like Niagara Falls, or Old Faithful, Miss Streisand is a uniquely American phenomenon most people will still pay good money to see.

"We're going chiefly for subjects," says Alan Ladd Jr., the man in charge at 20th Century-Fox. "Irwin Allen is going to do a volcano picture for us, and one about a circus. Mel Brooks is going

to do a picture called 'Silent Movie' that will be just that —a silent movie. The script is hysterical: back to the Keystone Kops."

Obviously, films of the future will not ignore the past. At MCA/Universal, "Gable and Lombard" and "W. C. Fields and Me" are designed to turn on the nostalgia freaks, and "The Seven Per Cent Solution" hopes to sail on the crest of the Sherlock Holmes revival wave. Twentieth's "Sherlock Holmes' Smarter Brother" has similar ambitions. Paramount will do its nostalgic best with "Swing Shift," about factory girls in World War II.

•

The best safeguard against box-office disaster may be disaster itself, as the makers of "The Poseidon Adventure," "Earthquake," "The Towering Inferno" and "Jaws" can testify. So it comes as no surprise that Universal has high hopes for "The Hindenberg," in which people are burned alive on screen (will George C. Scott and Anne Bancroft make it through the wreckage?). Paramount has "The Marathon Man," with Dustin Hoffman being menaced by Laurence Olivier, as a murderous ex-Nazi with dentistry training. Then there is always Irwin Allen's volcano, a vicarious lava-bath for which it might be a good idea to revive 3-D. And Universal doesn't seem to be kidding when it talks about "Airport 1977" and "Jaws II."

Nobody can seriously dispute the fact that art is taking a back seat to commerce in Hollywood these days, which is not to say that the two cannot ride side by side on occasion. It will certainly be interesting to see what comes of Paramount's plans for the film of E. L. Doctorow's "Ragtime," which the studio is entrusting to Robert Altman despite disappointment with his "Nashville." Paramount is also tackling F. Scott Fitzgerald's "The Last Tycoon," to be directed by Elia Kazan, as well as Richard Brooks' "Looking for Mr. Goodbar," based on Judith Rossner's distinctly downbeat novel.

•

At the other studios it's strictly business all the way, and business means creating a second wave of hits to follow those of the past season. Market research is in use at Universal, Columbia and Fox, with the plots of pictures, possible casting, and even advertising campaigns being pre-tested for

the first time in the history of the industry. David Begelman puts it this way: "We're not about to put a message in a bottle, toss it in the sea and hope that it will reach its destination."

But wouldn't it be funny if the public decided not to buy the message of "Jaws II"? ∎

1975 O 12, II:1:1

'It is more important than ever before to grab an audience on the gut level. Cinematic subtlety is risky.'

FILM VIEW

VINCENT CANBY

Two Films That Are Well Worth Adjusting To

About halfway through "Hearts of The West," Howard Zieff's new comedy about B-picture-making in the Hollywood of the early thirties, you realize that the film's leisurely pace is not, as you might have expected, a prelude to something else, a slow build-up to a boff. It is, instead, the method and style of the film. "Hearts of The West" drags its foot, like Tom Sawyer on his way to school on a fine spring morning. It's a movie composed almost entirely of asides, of little narrative detours and of subsidiary characters who may not have a great deal to do with the principal plot line.

Such a character is the hotel proprietor played early in the film by Marie Windsor, herself a reminder of B-pictures of the nineteen-forties and fifties. The character, who runs the Rose Hotel, a lonely fleabag at the edge of the Nevada desert, is on-screen only briefly, and she's not particularly important, but the combination of Miss Windsor's presence and the rather bizarre circumstances she's associated with makes us remember the sequence with more clarity and affection than we give much more spectacular things. This is the way the movie works.

•   •   •

Once you get the rhythm of "Hearts of The West," it becomes thoroughly delightful and the criticisms that can be aimed at it become academic. Something of the same sort could be said about three other comedies of recent years—movies that more or less disarmed critics but never were huge successes with the public: Mr. Zieff's first film, "Slither," Ivan Passer's "Law and Disorder" and Milos Forman's "Taking Off." Some movies succeed just because of the things that are wrong with them. At least, our expectations, shaped by years of convention, make certain things seem wrong when, actually, they are simply different approaches.

It's because of our expectations that we want Lewis Tater (Jeff Bridges), the hero of "Hearts of The West," to be a sort of Merton-of-the-movies dunderhead. Lewis, when we first see him on his daddy's Iowa farm, dreams of becoming a writer of Western novels, the new Zane Grey, to which end he goes west to soak up local color. En route Lewis becomes involved with a couple of charlatans who run what might be called an infamous writers' correspondence school and almost becomes a B-picture star. The trouble with our expectations of Lewis is that he really isn't a dunderhead. He's not exactly William Faulkner, but neither is he your average comic hero. More than anything else, he's a midwestern innocent, the sort of fellow who is overcome with emotion at his first sight of a palm tree that was not made out of paper.

"Hearts of The West," with an original screenplay by a new writer named Rob Thompson, dawdles. It gives its actors' time to embroider their roles at the expense of narrative drive. Not since "Catch-22" has Alan Arkin (whose role isn't all that large) had the opportunity to demonstrate his special manic genius as genially as he does here, playing a schlock movie director named Kessler, a fellow who directs a small, run-of-the-mill, Western-movie shootout as if he were C. B. DeMille parting the Red Sea. Almost equally good are Andy Griffith, as a cowboy actor-writer of no scruples, and Blythe Danner, as a script girl who has lots of them.

The thing about "Hearts of The West" is that it is so very nice it runs the same risk as nice people. It runs the risk of being called bland, which is to miss its wit and intelligence in the expectation of seeing a more conventional kind of film. It's not a perfect movie by any means, but its flaws may well be responsible for its virtues.

•   •   •

So too are those of James Ivory's 60-minute feature, "Autobiography of A Princess," which, like "Hearts of The West," was given its American premiere at the 13th New York Film Festival (closing tonight).

"Autobiography of A Princess" has a lot of things going against it. It's virtually a one-set movie with only three characters, one of whom is only seen in still pictures and a full-length portrait. It has a running time that one associates with television fare about hard-nosed policemen and super-cool policewomen. It introduces vital information uneasily, in the form of home movies and television interviews, shown as films within the film. And it really doesn't have anything resembling a plot. It is, rather, a fascinating disclosure of three fiercely different but interlocking lives:

The Princess (Madhur Jaffrey), the daughter of a maharajah, a woman with the brain-pan the size of a sparrow's; Cyril Sahib (James Mason) who, as a young man, had gone to India as the maharajah's tutor and then stayed on as his secretary of state and unrequited lover, and the maharajah himself, a spoiled, willful tyrant, long-since dead, whose birthday the Princess and Cyril Sahib celebrate in the film over tea and biscuits in the Princess's London town house.

As they watch films that recall the era of the British raj, the Princess tries to persuade her father's old friend to write a book about the maharajah and the good old days, while Cyril Sahib tries to point out, ineffectually, what a waste those days were, to all of them, most of all to the Princess and himself.

"Autobiography of A Princess" has awkward cinematic moments. It stretches Ivory's imagination to introduce into the film a TV interview with the Maharani of Jaipur and her son, who says that in spite of the government's actions in confiscating the properties and titles of the princes, "the peasants still love us." What has been the effect of the government action? "We've had to move into smaller houses and palaces."

This makes a social point, I suppose, but "Autobiography of A Princess" is most moving not as a social document but as revelation of a certain kind of lost soul—intelligent, contained, aware of his own failures but not quite undone by that knowledge—a character that Mason plays with superlative style.

"Autobiography of A Princess" has the effect of a fine novella, being just long enough and not too long. It couldn't have fit into any other form. Its odd length and limited setting force the writer (Ruth Prawer Jhabvala), the director and the actors to do things that one doesn't often find in films. We must adjust to it, but it's well worth the effort.

1975 O 12, II:13:1

THE STORY OF ADELE H. (L'Histoire d'Adèle H.), directed by François Truffaut; screenplay (French with English subtitles) by Mr. Truffaut, Jean Gruault and Suzanne Schiffman, from "The Diary of Adele Hugo," edited by Frances V. Guille; director of photography, Nestor Almendros; editor, Yann Dedet; music, Maurice Jaubert; a production of Les Films du Carrosse and Les Productions Arvistes Associes. Running time: 97 minutes. At the New York Film Festival, Alice Tully Hall, Lincoln Center. This film has not been rated.
Adele H. .... Isabelle Adjani
Lieutenant Pinson .... Bruce Robinson
Mrs. Saunders .... Sylvia Marriott
Mr. Saunders .... Reubin Dorey
Mr. Whistler .... Joseph Blatchley
Colonel .... M. White
Orderly .... Carl Hathwell
Hypnotist .... Ivry Gitlis
Madame Baa .... Madame Louise
Notary .... Sir Cecil de Sausmarez
Judge Johnstone .... Sir Raymond Falla
Dr. Murdock .... Roger Martin

By VINCENT CANBY

In 1863 Adèle Hugo, the younger daughter of the great French poet and patriot, Victor Hugo, ran away from home on the Isle of Guernsey where her father was living in exile to follow a young English officer, a Lieutenant Pinson, to his new post in Halifax, Nova Scotia. Lieutenant Pinson was probably not a bad sort, not worse than most, but he wasn't very serious.

It's thought that the young, inexperienced Adèle had most likely been Lieutenant Pinson's mistress for a short time on Gurnsey, and it's known that she wanted desperately to marry him, though her father disapproved. In any case, Lieutenant Pinson was not interested — a circumstance that Adèle was ill-equipped to understand or ever to support.

"The Story of Adèle H.," François Truffaut's profoundly beautiful new film, is about Adèle's journey, taken with measured steps, into a magnificent, isolating obsession, first to frozen Halifax and then, when Lieutenant Pinson is transferred to the West Indies, to Barbados, where Adèle sweeps through the tropical streets and alleys of Bridgetown talking to herself, wearing a heavy black cloak, and looking like some mad, benign witch of the north.

Unable to cope with the truth, and using her imagination and her feelings as carefully as someone writing a piece of fiction, Adèle created another world where she became Lieutenant Pinson's wife, where love was her religion (and no humiliation too great a sacrifice), and where she kept a coded journal, only recently deciphered. It is this journal that is the basis for Mr. Truffaut's most severe, most romantic meditation upon love.

"The Story of Adèle H." was shown last night at Avery Fisher Hall to close the 13th New York Film Festival, which, despite one spectacular disappointment and several others of a lesser order, has been one of the best festivals in recent years. Without question the Truffaut entry was the surprising highlight, even to one who has admired the French director's films over the years.

One of the fascinations of the Truffaut career is in

Isabelle Adjani in title role of "The Story of Adele H."

watching the way he circles and explores different aspects of the same subjects that dominate almost all of his films. However, "The Story of Adèle H.," impeccably photographed by Nestor Almendros ("The Wild Child"), looks and sounds like no other Truffaut film you've ever seen.

The colors are deep, rich and often dark, and the soundtrack is full of the noises that one associates with old costume films produced by M-G-M in its great days—carriages riding over cobblestones, pens scratching across vellum, servants arriving and departing with important messages, bells that tinkle over the doors of bookshops. More important, there is the fine background score by the late Maurice Jaubert (he died in 1940), who composed for Vigo and Clair among others. The film has the manner of a romance but it's a romance from which all the conventional concerns have been eliminated.

In the single-minded way in which the movie sticks to its subject, "The Story of Adèle H." reminds one of "The Wild Child." It's virtually a one-character film. It contemplates the classic beauty of Adèle, played with extraordinary grace by 20-year-old Isabelle Adjani of the Comédie Française, much as Catherine Deneuve was admired by the camera in "Mississippi Mermaid," and it appreciates the particularity of women in a fashion that recalls the erratic journey of Catherine to the crematorium in "Jules and Jim."

•

"The Story of Adele H."

is not a psychiatric case history, though all the facts seem to be there if one wants to accept it as such. Rather it's a poet's appreciation of the terrifying depth of Adèle's feelings, which, early on, drive her to lying to her family, to making life miserable for Lieutenant Pinson in Halifax (including canceling his engagement to someone else), to spying on him, happily, as he makes love to another woman. She's willful and spoiled and, the film understands, impossible to deal with. Yet the film makes us see both the madness and the grandeur of the passion.

It's this ability to allow us to see a subject from several different angles simultaneously that often proves most unsettling in a Truffaut film. Toughness and compassion get all mixed up. It's also this talent that separates his films from those of all other directors who are working in the humanist tradition today. "The Story of Adèle H." is a film that I suspect Jean Renoir would much admire. He understands such things.

1975 O 13, 36:1

LIES MY FATHER TOLD ME, directed by Jan Kadar; original story and screenplay by Ted Allan; director of photography, Paul van der Linden; editors, Edward Beyer and Richard Marks; music by Sol Kaplan; produced by Anthony Bedrich and Harry Gulkin; distributed by Columbia Pictures. At the Parsi Theater. Running time: 103 minutes. This film has been classified PG.
Grandfather .... Yossi Yadin
Father .... Len Birman
Mother .... Marilyn Lightstone
David .... Jeffrey Lynas
Mr. Baumgarten .... Ted Allan
Mrs. Tannenbaum .... Barbara Chilcott
Mrs. Bondy .... Mignon Elkins
Uncle Benny .... Henry Gamer
Edna .... Carole Lazare
Cleo .... Cleo Paskal

By A. H. WEILER

Childhood memories, like too many successive sundaes, can be nauseating. But "Lies My Father Told Me," the Canadian-made comedy drama that arrived at the Paris Theater yesterday, makes its bittersweet nostalgia pleasurable without cloying aftereffects.

Ted Allan's dramatization of remembrances of his own Jewish family in the Montreal melting pot of a half-century ago is brought appealingly alive with the aid of Jan Kadar's perceptive direction and some strong, natural performances.

Father, mother, relatives and neighbors are important but not nearly as central to this memoir as 7-year-old David Herman and his bearded, Tevyalike, junkman grandfather (Zaida). They form a mutual admiration society that also includes Ferdeleh, the ancient nag that draws grandfather's creaking wagon (along with a happy David on Sundays) through slum backyard alleys and rich wooded areas in quest of castoffs.

•

Grandfather's orthodox religious beliefs are transmitted to the loving youngster through parables and tall tales. If he accepts them and his Zaida on adoring, ingenuous faith, he is also confused and shattered by the reality of an irascible father, who is a failed inventor of creaseless pants and the like and is constantly seeking loans from the old man for pie-in-the-sky schemes.

Of course, the teeming neighborhood scene's varied characters touch on and color lead to the seriocomic demise the local young prostitute, a friend of the clients and local kids, who is stridently done by Carole Lazare; the boy's truly doll-like little confidante-playmate, Cleo Paskal, and a gently argumentative Marxist tailor, portrayed to the manner born by the film's author.

And there's a termagant housewife, played in vixenish style by Barbara Chilcott, whose complaints about grandfather's stable, its smells and the horse manure David spreads on her backdoor leads to the seriocomic denouement.

A properly distraught performance by Marilyn Lightstone of David's hard-pressed young mother illuminates the tension of maintaining allegiances to her son, husband and father. And Len Birman's portrait of the luckless would-be inventor-husband is both brash and pitiable.

•

Dominating the largely Canadian cast is the veteran Israeli actor Yossi Yadin, in a forceful yet tender delineation of the grandfather. His unwavering faith in ancient religious tenets is equal to his love of his grandson and his resigned but wise acceptance of his son-in-law's inadequacies. As the wide-eyed

grandson, a newcomer, Jeffrey Lynas, reflects love, innocence, sibling rivalry and the ultimate shock of his grandfather's death with childlike but genuine conviction.

The clashes between the grandfather and the father leave no doubts as to the boy's allegiance. And Mr. Kadar, the Czechoslovak director best known for his memorable "The Shop on Main Street," is equally pointed in his affection and professionalism. "Lies My Father Told Me" (actually the harsh truths the boy cannot understand or accept) may be somewhat sentimental and quaint in its Jewish rituals and traditions. But under Mr. Kadar's sensitive guidance, this journey back to lost youth modestly but touchingly reveals people as authentic as the settings in which they are captured.

1975 O 13, 36:1

LET'S DO IT AGAIN; directed by Sidney Poitier; screenplay by Richard Wesley; from a story by Timothy March; produced by Melville Tucker; director of photography, Donald M. Morgan; music by Curtis Mayfield. At the Criterion, Broadway and 45th Street, and other theaters. Running time: 110 minutes. This film has been rated PG.
Clyde Williams........ Sidney Poitier
Billy Foster .... Bill Cosby
Biggie Smalls .... Calvin Lockhart
Kansas City Mack..... John Amos
Beth Foster .... Denise Nicholas
Elder Johnson .... Ossie Davis
Bootney Farnsworth ... Jimmie Walker
Lee Chamberlin .... Dee Dee Williams

By RICHARD EDER

All that Sidney Poitier and Bill Cosby were trying to do was raise funds for the Temple of Chaka, their neighborhood lodge. The improbable and sometimes diverting trouble they get into doing it makes up the scenario of "Let's Do It Again," a black action comedy that opened Saturday at the Criterion and other theaters.

Borrowing $18,000 from the temple's building fund, and putting in a little money of their own, they set out for New Orleans to do some philanthropic betting—and fixing—on the local fight scene.

Taking their cheerful and spunky wives along—their parts are along the lines June Allyson used to play but gutsier—they settle on a weedy candidate named Bootney Farnsworth. Mr. Poitier hypnotizes Bootney into thinking of himself as a tiger, and he trounces the local mob's candidate.

This gets the two philanthropists the money they need for the temple, but it also gets two rival gangs after them. They are dragged back to New Orleans under orders to hypnotize Bootney for the crooks' benefit. This time they hypnotize the other fighter and once more come out ahead.

The action — chases, escapes out of windows, and lots of sneaking through hotel corridors—is familiar

stuff, but some of it is pretty funny. The movie's main strength is Bill Cosby, who looks like a starved sheep in wolf's clothing, and is shifty and woebegone at the same time.

•

Mr. Cosby wearing a tangerine suit with Bermuda shorts and pink sunglasses to impersonate a major mobster is hilarious, even better is his line, barked over a telephone to impress a minor mobster: "I understand you're 6 foot 2 and good-looking. How would you like to be 4 foot 2 and ugly?"

Mr. Poitier is no comedian but he makes an adequate straight man. Ossie Davis is a suitably incompetent fighter, all teeth and buckling knees.

1975 O 13, 36:1

CORRECTION

In a review of the film "Let's Do It Again" in Monday's New York Times, Ossie Davis was mentioned as playing the part of Bootney Farnsworth, a boxer. The role should have been credited to Jimmie Walker.

1975 O 15, 45:7

Guzzetti Documentary Is at the Whitney

By VINCENT CANBY

"Family Portrait Sittings" is an album of reminiscences that is as much about the processes of remembering as it is about the things remembered. The featured-length documentary, which opened a week's engagement at the Whitney Museum of American Art yesterday, is the work of Alfred Guzzetti, currently visiting associate professor of film at the State University of New York at Purchase.

The family remembered is the director's—four generations that include his great-uncle and his grandmother on his mother's side and his mother and father, as well as his own generation and his small son's. It's in a particularly American kind of recollection, composed of emigration, from the old country, resettlement in the new and the slow climb to middle American respectability that seems, perhaps intentionally, vaguely unsatisfactory and sad.

The film maker's mother sits beside his father on a sofa in a genteelly furnished Philadelphia row house and worries about her aggressiveness, which she denies as much as she defends. His father, asked if he believes in God, puzzles over the question and then answers, "I believe in something."

His great-uncle recalls making the decision to come

The Program

FAMILY PORTRAIT SITTINGS, a documentary directed, photographed and edited by Alfred Guzzetti. Running time: 104 minutes. At the Whitney Museum of American Art, Madison Avenue at 75th Street.

to America from Italy, and the night, many years later, when his brother died. The recollections are fragmented. Sometimes they are favorite family stories that have been told many times; sometimes they have the form of mild disputes.

In spite of the home-movie footage that Mr. Guzzetti intercuts with his interviews—recollections of weddings, birthday parties, confirmations—the effect of "Family

Portrait Sittings" is not very cheerful at all. It's a little like listening to a group of people in a bar trying ineffectually to define the distinction between a republic and a democracy. To remember the past is to attempt to give it meaning, and no one in "Family Portrait Sittings," with the exception of the great-uncle, succeeds to his own evident satisfaction.

I suspect that this is a major point of the film and why one comes away from it feeling slightly chilled and at a distance from the character. All the insights in the film belong to the director.

1975 O 16, 47:1

A Literary Sensibility at the Festival

By JOHN LEONARD

At the recently ended New York Film Festival, one movie not reviewed by the press was a five-minute short from Canada called "Thanks Giving." Directed by Ken Wallace, "Thanks Giving" was filmed from the point of view of a turkey plucked and ready for the oven, with two sad, knowing eyes inserted into its hindquarters. The turkey, seeking to escape its fate, heaves itself out of the kitchen, down the stairs, toward the front door, grunting all the while like three Martians looking for a fourth for sex. In the end, it looks up at the camera and is cleaved by an ax.

That turkey, it seems to me, was a surrogate for the literary sensibility.

One literary sensibility went to this year's festival to check out the brouhaha. He took with him the usual carpetbag of atavisms: a respect for coherence and the unities; an uncertainty about the human condition; a bookish culture; a belief that language is a good thing because, among other virtues, it makes rational comment and abstract ideas possible (unless, of course, it's the language of Richard Roud in the festival program notes).

The literary sensibility was immediately in trouble. The books in his mind kept getting in the way of the pictures on the screen. And many of the pictures seemed impatient with, even hostile to, books, abstraction, rationality, coherence and language itself. Some unspecified apomixis of erotism was supposed to be preferable.

Trouble at the Outset

Perhaps this should have whispered to him something shrewd about the nature of play, the evocative capacities of images that run around for a couple of hours, the etiolations of the ink-sucking page and just how much people are willing to work when

they sit down in front of an artifact. Nonetheless, this was an unhappy sensibility. He felt that he was personally being attacked by celluloid guerrillas, and those guerrillas weren't a lot smarter than some friends of his who stuck to their typewriters. He had heard it before, and better.

For example, in Luchino Visconti's 'Conversation Piece," Prof. Burt Lancaster has clearly dried up from too much culture (cf., "Clockwork Orange," "Straw Dogs" and any old John Wayne movie, or most books by D.H. Lawrence and any novel with scientists in it). In Werner Herzog's "Every Man for Himself and God Against All," Bruno S. must dies because he wants to relate to nature, and all those philosophers keep asking him epistemological questions he can't answer (cf., Kafka, Beckett and Jerzy Kosinski). In Louis Malle's "Black Moon," language causes al lthe anguish, and the only antidote is a return to basics, like myth and mother's milk (cf., Lewis Carroll, Ludwig Wittenstein, Marshall McLuhan and Susan Sontag.)

A literary sensibility, on seeing Orson Welles in "F for Fake" propose Clifford Irving as the hero-artist of our time, thinks of Gide's "The Counterfeiters," Mann's "Felix Krull" and Nabokov's "Pale Fire." On seeing Ousmane Sembène in "Xala" ridicule Léopold Senghor and the rest of the Senegalese black bourgeoisie, he thinks of Evelyn Waugh's "Scoop" and "Black Mischief." On seeing and seeing and seeing three hours and 15 minutes of "Milestones," during which Robert Kramer and John Douglas explain that the radicals of the nineteen-sixties are, you know, groping, dig it, in the seventies, he thinks of books by Kenneth Keniston, Mike Rossman, Sol Yurick, Marge Piercy and Harvey Swados.

On seeing Francois Truffaut's exploration of obsessive love, "The Story of Adèle H." he thinks of "Anna Karenina,, "Madame Bovary," "The Red and the Black" and "Of Human Bondage." On seeing Marguerite Duras's meditation on boredom and sensuality in the colonized Orient, he would like her to read E. M. Forster, André Malraux, Anthony Burgess and Paul Theroux. One Seeing "Smiles," an account of a teen-age talent contest, he recommends that Michael Ritchie see "A Chorus Line." On seeing "Aaron and Moses," Jean-Marie Straub's film version of the Schoenberg opera in which a pair of mainiacs stand around in the desert for 105 minutes hurling atonalities at each other, he wonders where the bar is.

A Vision

Such a sensibility belongs in the library, where the only things that move are lips, not at the New York Film Festival, where the only thing that doesn't move is Jean-Marie Straub. Such a sensibility asks of art an organizing perception, a hierarchy of values, a sense of humor. He obviously doesn't know how to groove. Along with Jorge Luis Borges, he is convinced that thinking and analyzing are not just anomalous acts; they are the normal respiration of intelligence. Jorge Luis Borges, however, never made a movie.

And so such a sensibility swoons, to construct in a dream the definitive festival screenplay. The part of Alice in Wonderland is played by Helmut Berger. She has been begat by Léopold Senghor or Clifford Irving on the corpse of Theresa Giehse. Suckled in a cellar in Halifax, or Calcutta by Burt Lancaster or Walter Ladengast. Liberated by Moses or a turkey. Adopted by Edith Bouvier Beale or Richard Roud. Unable to stop the Trojan War or consummate the Hungarian revolution. Losing a pompom competition or flunking out of a commune. Moving, dig it, to Santa Rosa, Calif., to get her head together, and do a stretch, as a checker in a super market.

Alice/Helmut lives on ripped-off packages of frozen Straub, sprig of Welles, eggplant of Sembène, saccharine of Duras, Spam of Visconti and cyanide of Herzog. Bagging these groceries, she contemplates the surreal parking lot, where all the cars muzzle one another's bumpers, wear hooded looks and seem to be aggressive—Sting Ray, Jaguar, Mustang, Cobra, Spitfire, Barracuda, Tempest, Fury, Bronco, Hurricane, Dart, Shark, Cyclone, Falcon and Wildcat. It's so angry and, you know, depersonalized, a downer, a cylinder bore, a Malle-de-mer.

One night, pulling back her bedcovers, she finds a spark plug. The next night, a fan belt. The nights after that, an ignition scope, a babbit bearing and a torsion bar. Something about her diet—the corrosion inhibiter or the pourpoint dépressant — doesn't agree with her viscosity index. Too much. Her box ratios are out of line, her crank case leaks, and, according to Jean-François Davy, there's a negative rotation in her exhaust valves.

How, then, to dissolve her existential funk? Well, there's suicide ("Conversation Piece," "India Song"), murder ("Thanks Giving," "Every Man for Himself and God Against All"), madness ("The Story of Adèle H."), motherhood ("Milestones"), Jehovah ("Aaron and Moses"), spit "Xala"), or breast-feeding a unicorn ("Black Moon"). Instead, she drinks three quarts of friction-proofing, breaks out in rivets and goes to the ninth circle of Alice Silly Hall.

1975 O 16, 48:1

4 Shorts at Film Forum Blend Charm and Naivete

By RICHARD EDER

The past never seems as frail and long gone as when it is asserting something about the future. It is the avant-garde that dies first.

The point is evoked with eerie precision at a collection of four short films being shown by Film Forum to inaugurate its new premises at the Vandam Theater in SoHo. The four, all made in the nineteen-fifties, were considered more or less experimental in their day. All are interesting and two, at least, are masterpieces. But seen now, with many of their varying techniques having become familiar, the stylistic effect is a blend of charm and naiveté.

In fact their real impact, and it has almost the force of shock, is not in their style but in their viewpoint.

All four are in some way about New York. What stands out is the buoyancy, the sheer optimism and exuberance that this city, 20 years ago, imposed even upon those who were out to set it on its collective ear. The pictuers will be shown today through Sunday and again next Thursday through Sunday.

If "On the Road" was the bible of the Beat Generation, the film "Pull My Daisy" was a kind of short breviary. With a voice-over narration by Jack Kerouac and the manic participation of Allen Ginsberg, Gregory Corso, Peter Orlovsky and others, it takes the more or less formal setting of a social call and tears it into shreds.

The setting is a loft somewhere south of Greenwich Village. Lofts were still symbols of freedom and boundlessness: bodies with needle marks or stab wounds hadn't begun to turn up in them. It was littered with clothes: litter was still a statement and not a universal condition. A Tiffany lamp hung in it: Tiffany lamps were still found in junkshops and hadn't made their way uptown.

For the Beats the seamless stability of American life was like a field just snowed on, in which almost any kind of caper would leave a significant mark. So in "Daisy" Messrs. Ginsberg, Orlovsky and Corso, laden with beer cans bounce into the residence of Milo, a seraphic brakeman, and his long-suffering wife.

The three poets are young, their hair is slept-in but short, and they sit on Milo's couch like ruffled owls while sabotaging the visit of the Bishop and his mother and sister. The bishop is only about 17: still, he manages such lines as "A strange and interesting evening" while the air is full of talk about "tortured socks" and a short oratorio about cockroaches.

This is Dada: maximum shock with a minimum of pain; the feeling that stones could be hurled through windows and nothing would really break. Like Dada from the nastier perspective of the late nineteen-twenties, it seems innocent and touching.

"Skyscraper," made by Shirley Clarke, is a short film classic; a funny, exciting and absorbing account of the building of a skyscraper from demolition to completion.

We see old facades coming down and a great hole gouged out by power shovels, and with a sudden sense of time-warp we realize that what we see as not being deprecated or condemned but celebrated. A lilting voice sings about "this island, light as wine." Change is presented as triumph not loss, and the city is a place of limitless energies and possibilities.

Using a dialogue between Murphy—a high-steel man who is the wisecracking, know-it-all New Yorker and totally capable of astonishment — and his boss, the entire process of building a skyscraper is laid out. The camera shows bedrock being hauled away—"They're taking New York to New Jersey," Murphy protests——foundations laid, steel uprights swinging into place.

The bare girders frame towering views of Manhattan. The facade is laid on and, curiously, as the building is finished it becomes less real. The irony is unmeant and is only seen now in retrospect. Because all tihs romance, guts and imagination, all this high-flying geometry went to produce the gimcrack banality of Fifth Avenue's Tishman Building.

The other two films are less thematic: they are poetic and affectionate explorations of the beauty of the city. "N.Y., N.Y." by Francis Thompson uses optical effects—multiple images, distortion, color-blurring — to find geometric patterns in the city's bones. A morning cup of coffee is serialized into infinity; bridge-girders zigzag, framing the sky like stained glass.

A much better picture, the best of the four, in fact, is Weegee's New York, particularly its Coney Island section. Made by the photographer Weegee, it follows the day and evening through a crowded Coney Island Sunday.

1975 O 17, 24:3

Wayne and Hepburn in 'True Grit' Spin-Off

By VINCENT CANBY

"Rooster Cogburn," which opened at three theaters yesterday, is a high-class example of the low Hollywood art of recycling—taking bits and pieces of old stories and characters and making from them other movies that can never be described as completely new or fresh.

For John Wayne, who has the title hole, "Rooster Cogburn" is a continuation of the part he played in "True Grit," the film for which he was awarded his first (and fully deserved) Oscar. For Katharine Hepburn the film recalls her marvelous characterization opposite Humphrey Bogart in "The African Queen." The role of Eula Goodnight, the pastor's spinsterish Bible-quoting daughter in "Rooster Cogburn," is a lighthearted spin-off of the earlier role, but the important word here is lighthearted, not spin-off.

Miss Hepburn has been too long glum in her recent films. It's good to see her looking as if she were having a lark for a change. Good causes ("Guess Who's Coming to Dinner") and art ("The Trojan Women") are all well and good, but too much of that sort o fthing can get even a good woman down. In "Rooster Cogburn," Miss Hepburn has a roaring good time—so convincingly that you come to accept the movie on its own terms. It's a cheerful, throwaway Western, featuring two stars of the grand tradition who respond to each other with verve that makes the years disappear.

In this new film you remember with immense pleasure instead of regret the Hepburn of the great Cukor films of the nineteen-thirties, forties and fifties. The comedienne has not disappeared, only the good roles.

Martin Julien's screenplay for "Rooster Cogburn," using the Rooster Cgburn character from "True Grit," is hardly high comedy, but it gives Miss Hepburn and Mr. Wayne a number of decently funny lines and situations that Stuart Millar, formerly a producer, directs with good-humored affection.

From the left: Gregory Corso, Larry Rivers and Jack Kerouac in "Pull My Daisy"

The Cast

ROOSTER COGBURN, directed by Stuart Millar; screenplay by Martin Julien, suggested by a character in Charles Portis's novel, "True Grit"; produced by Hal B. Wallis; director of photography, Harry Stradling Jr.; editor, Robert Swink; music, Laurence Rosenthal; distributed by Universal Pictures. Running time: 107 minutes. At Loew's State 1, Broadway at 45t hStreet, Loew's Cine, third Avenue near 86th Street, and Murray Hill Theater, 34th Street near Third Avenue. This film has been rated P.G.

Eula	Katharine Hepburn
Rooster Cogburn	John Wayne
Breed	Anthony Zerbe
Hawk	Richard Jordan
McCoy	Struther Martin
Judge Parker	John McIntire
Luke	Paul Koslo
Rev. Goodnight	Jon Lormer
Wolf	Richard Romancito

Like "True Grit," the new film is essentially an eccentric chase film: Rooster Cogburn, the pot-bellied, whisky-soaked, one-eyed old Federal marshal, is commissioned to track down a gang of desperados in the Arkansas territory. In the course of his journey he is more or less forced to take along the woman whose father has been murdered by the outlaw gang and a young Indian boy.

That's all the story there is, or need be. What makes "Rooster Cogburn" so pleasant s the quality of the encounters between the marshal and Eula, who, it turns out, is a crack shot and not above lifting a watch from the body of a dead bandit over whom she's saying a solicitous prayer.

Mr. Wayne, of course, has played this role before, and there are signs—when Miss Hepburn is off-screen—that it would run away from him were he left to his own devices. He mugs, pouts and gets very close to playing it in the cute manner of the very young and very old. When Miss Hepburn is with him, however, a sense of discipline is established that brings out the best in both of them.

It's rather like one of the film's better scenes: Rooster, Eula and the Indian boy have stopped on the trial to rest and Rooster has taken the opportunity to get drunk, at which point he starts using their food for target practice. "Shooting cornbread in a meadow," Eula reminds Rooster firmly, "is not taking us anywhere."

When Miss Hepburn is not around, "Rooster Cogburn" is shooting cornbread in a meadow. Fortunately, she's on the screen most of the time.

1975 O 18, 22:1

DOWN THE ANCIENT STAIRS, directed by Mauro Bolognini; screenplay (Italian with English subtitles) by Raffaele Andreassi, Mario Arosio, Tullio Pinelli and Bernardino Zapponi; based on a novel by Mario Tobino; director of photography, Ennio Guarnieri; a co-production of Italian International Film and Les Productions Fow Europa; released by 20th Century-Fox. At the Little Carnegie Theater. Running time: 101 minutes; this film has been classified R.

Prof. Bonaccorsi	Marcello Mastroianni
Dr. Anna Bersani	Francoise Fabian
Bianca	Marthe Keller
Carla	Barbara Bouchet
Tonio	Pierre Blaise
Francesca	Lucia Bose
Gianna	Adrianna Asti

By RICHARD EDER

Take an insane asylum whose staff members ask one another such questions as "What is madness?" and pretty much agree that sanity is only to be found inside the place. Stage a costume party where the inmates come as catatonic Pierrots, deranged Columbines and 15-foot giants and film it through gauze to drugged music. Let the star act at the party be a mime show where the actors, also inmates, sag sadly at one another.

If I haven't lost count, Mauro Bolognini has managed to mount a metaphor upon a second metaphor that is mounted, in turn, upon a third metaphor. All were exhausted to begin with: Is he trying to kill them? He shouldn't, because he will undoubtedly want to use them again.

•

"Down the Ancient Stairs," which opened yesterday at the Little Carnegie, puts Marcello Mastroianni in the role of Professor Bonaccorsi, chief psychiatrist at the asylum. It is a Mastroianni role in that he is the lover of the wives of the asylum's director and surgeon and of one of the nurses. It also works up the actor's bent for being gloomy about it, as a man might be gloomy between bouts of compulsive overeating.

Professor Bonaccorsi's satyriasis—he fondles the patients as well as his colleagues—is metaphysical. He is obsessed with insanity: with establishing that there is indeed a difference between himself and the patients. At the asylum he sets himself up as a kind of godlike figure, running everything, holding off everyone—staff and patients — with busyness and with a show, often a physical show, of love.

Into this closed world comes Anna Bersani, a young woman doctor played by Françoise Fabian. She resists Bonaccorsi's advances, she questions his methods. To nail down his insistence that there is a clear demarcation between the sane and insane, Bonaccorsi keeps searching for a physical determinant of insanity.

One day he finds it, or thinks he does. He peers through his microscope, he exults. Insanity is a hairy splotch, he announces, appearing on the blood cells. Dr. Bersani checks the experiment and finds it is flawed.

Bonaccorsi quits the hospital and gets on a train. But it is Italy of the nineteen-thirties, and the compartment is full of raving Fascists. Not only is there no difference between the inmates and the staff in the asylum, Bolognini suggests, but there is also no difference between the asylum and the rest of the world.

It is relentlessly weary stuff; an image so venerable, a paradox so frequently trotted out that it has lost all its original force.

Mr. Mastroianni, Miss Fabian and the actresses playing Bonaccorsi's mistresses perform routinely. The pace is leaden, the dialogue ridiculous.

1975 O 18, 22:1

What's New in Animated Films? Sex, Gluttony and Computers

By JOHN CULHANE

Ralph Bakshi revived public interest in animation as a medium for the seventies with a trio of controversial cartoon features: "Fritz the Cat," the first X-rated animated cartoon; "Heavy Traffic," the first portrait of the artist as a young drawing; and "Coonskin," which has been crusaded against by the Congress of Racial Equality as an animated racial slur.

Whether you love Bakshi's films or hate them—and you will have plenty of company in either camp—it must be admitted that the abrasive, innovative filmmaker has gotten audiences excited about the possibilities of animation in the seventies the way that Disney did in the thirties and forties with "Snow White," the first feature-length cartoon, and "Fantasia," his animated symphony concert.

So what else is new in this frequently neglected medium? Well, among other

John Culhane is a film historian and co-author of "Noah's Animals," a forthcoming animated television special.

The festival included 142 shorts from 17 countries.

things, a tug at the heartstrings by clay figures, a computer-assisted film about human beings, and the children's book illustrations of Maurice Sendak and Tomi Ungerer come to life. All this and more, as anyone who attended the Third International Animation Film Festival in New York at Columbia University can testify. Fred Mintz, director of the five-day festival which ended on Oct. 4, devised nine categories for the series, each defining a way in which animation can be used (for feature films, entertainment shorts, educational films, industrial films, films for children, films by students, television commercials, experimental films and computer films.)

Although there were no feature films in competition in this—the third—New York festival, audiences witnessed competition among 142 short films from 17 countries. Their techniques ranged from good old pencil and paper to clay to computer animation. Their subjects ranged from world hunger to the right of privacy to sexual fantasies.

•

This year's festival winners were chosen by an international jury that included the animation directors Feodor Khytruk (Russia), Marcell Jankovics (Hungary), and Miroslav Kijowicz (Poland); Louise Beaudet, director of the Cinémathèque Quebecoise in Canada; and Phil Kimmelman, who makes animated commercials in New York. The chairman of the jury was Frank Thomas of the Walt Disney Studio, one of the most important figures in the world history of animation who has helped bring to life such memorable characters as Bambi, the Lady and the Tramp, and the little rabbits in last year's "Robin Hood." Now, at 62, Thomas is helping to train the first post-Walt Disney group of young animators at the Disney Studio on the next Disney animated feature, "The Rescuers." When he was 24, Thomas achieved a breakthrough in animation toward the end of Disney's "Snow White" that most animators thought they would never see. When the dwarfs are gathered, sorrowing, at Snow White's bier, and Dopey breaks down and sobs in Doc's beard, members of the premiere audience actually wept. Cartoons had made audiences laugh for years, but never cry. For the first time in history, moving drawings had become—moving drawings.

It was a similar breakthrough that won for a film called "Whazzat?" the Grand Prix of this year's animation festival. Arthur P. Pierson of Chicago animated clay to retell an 11th-century Arabic folk tale about six blind men. In an amazing scene—amazing because it manages to communicate strong emotion with featureless clay figures and without dialogue—the six blind men try to cross a chasm. One of the little figures stretches itself across the chasm to make a bridge. Four of the others cross their pal (literally, not dishonorably), then wait on the other side for the last little guy to cross over. But he is immobilized by fear. So they hop up and down, urging him on. Finally, he tries, only to have the bridge collapse and leave him dangling over the chasm. Fortunately, the blind buddies on the cliff quickly haul him up and soon they are all jumping for joy.

"This is the first time that I've seen clay animation communicate an emotion," said Thomas. "Usually, you know what a character is doing; you may even know what it's thinking; but you do not feel any emotion. 'Closed Mondays,' another clay film, got the Academy Award for animation last year, and it was like that. But Mr. Pierson has a group of six little characters, and though they don't have specific personalities, they have a group personality. When they're happy, you feel happy; when they're curious, you feel curious; and when they're apprehensive, you feel apprehension. And to get that out of little clay figures—and a group of them—is either awfully lucky or pure genius."

The winner in the category of computer animation, "Hunger," by Peter Foldes, is another triumph but one which uses a very different technique. Hungarian - born Foldes, 51, is a brilliant draftsman who has long been successful in translating his stark line drawings into the dimension of movement; but the computer gives these drawings an inhuman, flowing motion that perfectly suits his terrifying transformations. Foldes has learned to use a computer as another animation tool—like a special kind of pencil. "Hunger" is the first fully animated figurative film ever made using computer techniques. Produced by the National Film Board of Canada, it was made with a digital computer at the National Research Council of Canada, utilizing the programs that N. Burtnyk and M. Wein have developed there.

In "Hunger," Foldes takes a Dantesque view of modern gluttony, showing the metamorphosis of a slim, handsome young man into a grotesque and obese old man. When the old man dies of over-eating, he is cast bodily into hell, where his flesh is devoured by the spirits of those who have starved to death. In effect, the computer "draws" all the tedious drawings in between the extreme poses of an action, leaving Foldes free to concentrate on the key drawings.

This year's student films reflected much more maturity and technical achievement than those entered in the first two festivals. The jury gave first prize to "Roll 'Em, Lola," a sexual fantasy conceived and animated by Fred Burns of the University of Southern California, in which two high-powered automobiles chase each other around the nude body of a giant woman in a four-minute-thirty-second feast for the Jung at heart.

The violation of the human right of privacy is the theme of "Walls Have Ears," the surreal film directed by Poland's Andrej Ryska which won the prize in the festival's experimental film category. A terrible, ear-shaped protuberance grows out of the wall and drives a man insane before it is sliced off by a razor blade—only to be replaced by a growth like an eyeball.

The best example of the increasingly scarce "story" car-

toon to be shown at the festival was "The Heron and the Crane," a wry, Chekhovian animal fable told by I. Norstein and R. Kachanov of Russia. Gag cartoons are also less in evidence at animation festivals since the major Hollywood studios closed their cartoon department in the fifties and early sixties. And yet, the Eastern European animators, who have only recently caught up with all the Popeyes, Tom and Jerrys and Roadrunners made during and immediately after World War II, are trying hard to revive the pure gag cartoon. The biggest bellylaughs of the festival were heard during a six-minute cartoon from Pannonia Film Studio in Budapest called "Let's Keep a Dog," which illustrated a number of arguments in favor of having a dog as a pet.

•

"Because it is faithful unto death" was Argument Number Seven, accompanied by the stereotype image of Man's Best Friend stretched out upon his master's grave. A comforting image until darkness falls, whereupon the dog suddenly leers, leaps up, and digs down into the grave for a bone. "Let's Keep a Dog" and "The Heron and the Crane" were the winners among entertainment films—the first in the six-minute and under category, the second in the category of shorts lasting more than six minutes.

The best commercial was clearly "Trans-Siberian Express" from Richard Williams Animation in London—a studio which received a special award for the general high quality of its entries. Except for a brief pitch for Count Pushkin Vodka at the end, the commercial devotes its two minutes of screen time to an accelerating montage con-

A computer helped make this film.

juring up a 10-day train journey from Moscow to Vladivostock. "This was staggering art work—real impact!" said jury chairman Thomas. "And it's hard to get outstanding art work on the screen as you go into animation—because to do a strong still drawing and then move it and keep that strength is very difficult." The art work was done by Playboy cartoonist Rowland B. Wilson; it was moved by 23-year - old English animator Russell Hall; and it was edited by Art Babbitt, the man who made the mushrooms dance in Disney's "Fantasia."

The problem of animating strong still drawings cropped up again in the category of children's film, where animated film versions of several respected children's books competed for the prize. "We on the jury asked ourselves is it primarily a film—or is it just putting the book's illustrations on the screen?"

'What was missing was the art of personality animation.'

---

said Thomas. "In the case of Maurice Sendak's 'Where the Wild Things Are,' we felt that the director, Gene Deitch, did not improve it by putting it on the screen. It was better as a book. "We gave the prize to 'The Beast of Monsieur Racine.' [Book written and illustrated by Tomi Ungerer; movie directed by Gene Deitch in Czechoslovakia for Weston Woods Studio, USA.] Deitch added elements of timing and staging that added a new dimension, which I think you have to do when you make a picture of a book, and it held up as a picture."

The trick is to keep the same style and plot content, while translating the written word into moving images with sound. This "The Beast of M. Racine" does admirably, telling the story of a Frenchman who won't sell his prize pears to anyone, but suffers the misfortune of having them eaten by a strange beast. However, he manages to capture the beast and boasts: "I lost my pears but I found a companion." Now, people want to buy his beast. "The beast is my friend," says M. Racine, "and friends are not for sale."

But when he tries to show off his beastly friend at the National Academy of Science, a hoax is revealed: two children have been playing a trick on M. Racine by dressing up in a beast's skin. Undaunted, M. Racine adopts the children — and soon has "a new crop of pears which he happily shared with his two young

friends." Summarized, it sounds goofy; visualized—as when M. Racine kisses his pears good night while crickets and frogs provide a little night music—it is charming.

•

What was conspicuously missing from this year's competition was the art of personality animation—the ability to create characters with specific individual personalities, to put the spark of life into moving drawings so that pen-and-ink personages like The Three Pigs, the Seven Dwarfs or Fritz the Cat emerge on screen.

There was only one such moment at the festival, and it occurred with an already established character. It happened during the showing of the animated title credits for the new Peter Sellers comedy, "The Return of the Pink Panther." Without a word of dialogue or a change of costume, the Pink Panther walked through the credits in six different ways—and evoked six different personalities: Groucho Marx, Mickey Mouse, Charlie Chaplin, Frankenstein, a ballet dancer and a cowboy.

To be sure, the animator for these lively "Pink Panther" credits was that veteran Bugs Bunny/Roadrunner animator, Ken Harris. But the director was the New Wave's Richard Williams, who won an Oscar in 1972 for a half-hour cartoon edi-

tion of Dickens' "A Christmas Carol," which brought the original 1843 John Leech illustrations to magical life. And now that Williams has financing for his full-length animated "Raggedy Ann," we may hope for a new flowering of personality animation in 1976. ■

1975 O 19, II:1:3

Brilliance Gone Berserk

By PETER G. DAVIS

Rage—that was my immediate reaction to "Lisztomania," Ken Russell's latest and most perversely self-indulgent "music appreciation" fantasy. Not simply because the film is trivial, irrelevant and unswervingly stupid, but because at one time Russell did make great movies about composers—stunning investigations of their lives and creative problems that looked far beyond the trashy, hopelessly sentimentalized biographical epics of Chopin, Liszt, Schubert et al that Hollywood churned out in the forties and fifties.

Take "A Song of Summer," for example, Russell's exquisitely sensitive study of Frederick Delius' painful last years, brilliantly perceptive in its detailed examination of an artist's techniques and sources of inspiration; taped for the BBC several years ago, the film is still aired from time to time on National Educational Television. Or even "The Music Lovers," which, for all its excesses, captured the tragic ironies of Tchaikovsky's career with wit, exuberance, compassion and—despite what many critics maintained—historical accuracy. More about these and other films later. "Lisztomania" would not be worth discussing at all if Russell had not in the past brought visual life to the elusive theme of musical creativity so successfully. What, one may well ask, went wrong?

For one thing, Russell has simply tried to pack too much into a 105-minute film. Liszt, Wagner, Hans von Bülow, and Cosima Wagner (not to mention Berlioz, Rossini, Chopin, Brahms, Mendelssohn, Schumann, George Sand and Lola Montez in "cameo" appearances) are all protean personalities — never in music history have so many complex individuals, each of them touched by genius, intermingled with such explosive impact, artistically and personally, as did this group in the mid-1800's. Their entangled lives perplex musicologists and historians to this very day—Liszt, himself, is still shrouded by such a bewildering haze of fact, fiction and contradiction that no one has yet even attempted a major study of his life and works. (Eleanor Perényi's recent "Liszt: The Artist as Romantic Hero" is a splendidly clear-eyed view of the man and his environment, but the book stops in 1861, 25 years before his death and after his life as a "romantic hero" was over, and contains little discussion of the music.)

Secondly, Russell's manner and method of embroidering the basic historical facts have become more idiosyncratic and stylized with each successive movie. For example, the 1968 film "A Song of Summer" uses a straightforward narrative technique to focus on a brief period in Delius's life. The scope is expanded for Russell's first commercially released film about a composer, "The Music Lovers," to encompass all of Tchaikovsky's mature life; while an orderly sequential plot dominates, a strong element of fantasy colors the action to italicize Russell's viewpoint.

In "Mahler" (made before Russell's "Tommy" but not yet shown in New York), pure fantasy has usurped half the film: we see Mahler on his last train trip to Vienna in the year of his death indulging in wild Freudian dreams about his past. And now "Lisztomania" is completely unreal, a phantasmagorical nightmare in which Liszt, Wagner and the rest are barely recognizable: they cavort with giant penises, mad-scientist paraphernalia and voodoo dolls through abstract palaces, Gothic castles and overdecorated concert halls.

Perhaps a fantastic treatment is the only practical way to present such larger-than-life historical figures within the temporal confines of a film. This technique at least frees the director from the difficult if not impossible task of devising both a smooth chronological sequence and a collection of credible characters, each of whom could easily serve as the basis of a four-volume biography. Instead of making a pithy statement on the nature of the hyperromantic 19th-century artist, however, the fantasy of "Lisztomania" is boringly unoriginal and devoid of perception.

The first part of the film takes great pains to draw the obvious analogy between adulation generated by Liszt in the 1840's and the screaming fan worship that greets today's rock stars. Using a real-life rock musician to play Liszt (Roger Daltrey of The Who) and an audience of swinging teeny-boppers dressed in 19th-century bonnets and gowns, Russell further flails at the notion with a heavy-handed "groupie" scene where all the leading composers of the day are briefly caricatured.

Perhaps Liszt was the first pop superstar. Well, what of it? Russell just leaves it at that—all the blowsy window dressing, childish sexual imagery and audience hysteria add nothing except frivolous embellishment to an unimportant side issue. In actuality, Liszt's dilemma was that of a man with too much talent, as a piano virtuoso, composer, teacher, impresario, lover, religious and social thinker. Gifted in all of these areas, he excelled in none except the first, a fact that never emerges from Russell's lame dialogue, Daltrey's flat acting and tons of gratuitous sex symbols and other visual garbage.

Wagner, played with leering overkill by Paul Nicholas, dominates the second half of the movie, which unexpectedly turns from pornographic farce to lurid science fiction. Wagner, according to Russell, was the first Nazi, a man who dreamt of creating a philosophy of art which, championed by a superman-hero, would lead Germany to world domination. To accomplish this, he must "steal" Liszt's music, which he does symbolically by growing fangs, chomping at his friend's neck and drinking the blood. Liszt is directed by the Pope (Ringo Starr—the one charmingly low-keyed performance in the film) to exorcise Satan from Wagner, who is finally crushed in the rubble of his Dracula-like castle, only to return as Hitler dancing on the ruins of Berlin in 1945. Liszt, now playing a harp in heaven with a chamber group consisting of his former loves and daughter Cosima, launches himself in a rocket of organ pipes and wipes out Wagner once and for all.

•

Picturing Wagner as a raving proto-Nazi is as much of a cliché as presenting Liszt as a posturing proto-rock figure. In each case Russell exaggerates the most insignificant aspects of both men's character, trivializing their lives and works in the process. To ignore the complexities of Wagner's thought and the profound non-political impact that his art has exercised over the past century is a perverse distortion of the facts.

Even when Russell is at his worst, one can generally count on his energy and keen visual sense. "Mahler," for all its flaws, has several scenes of striking pictorial power—Gustav as a child, for example, wide-eyed at discovering the music of nature in a Bohemian forest at night, caps his revelation with a wild midnight ride, bareback on a white stallion. That such an incident probably never occurred is beside the point—the moment is a poetical one that crystallizes a significant stage in Mahler's creative development. In "The Music Lovers," Tchaikovsky's desperate attempt to forget his failure at both heterosexual and homosexual relationships by throwing himself into an empty social and musical whirl is captured in a madcap carnival-like sequence of breathless vitality. A superficially similar scene in "Lisztomania," the exorcism of Wagner, is strained, stale and, worst of all, utterly meaningless.

It's depressing to contemplate the possibility that the road traveled by Russell from "A Song of Summer" to "Lisztomania" (along with his non-biographical movies such as "Women in Love," "The Devils" and "Tommy") represents the gradual "refinement" of the director's true artistic credo. It's as if Russell is now possessed by some demon and sorely in need of exorcism himself. In contrast to the clutter of "Lisztomania," the Delius film treats its theme simply and honestly, focusing directly on an unsentimentalized view of musical composition, not only as a disturbingly mysterious act but one involving long study of techniques, bouts of self-doubt and sheer hard work. The two composer-heroes of "Lisztomania," on the other hand, hardly seem concerned with music at all.

Music is very much the central issue of "A Song of Summer." Delius, like Wagner, was a difficult, unattractive personality. Blind, crippled, testy, irascible, selfish and insensitive to others, he nonetheless painfully dictated his last and most searching works to Eric Fenby, the selfless young English musician who had come to live with Delius and his wife in France to serve as the composer's amanuensis. Russell not only delves into the actual process of musical creation with analytical intensity, but also movingly depicts the growing human bond between a genius and his acolyte.

Furthermore, in the film's one flashback—Russell's most effective experiment with fantasy to date—we get an unforgettable glimpse at the source of Delius's spiritual

"Picturing Wagner as a Nazi is as clichéd as presenting Liszt as a rock figure."

inspiration. Just before he becomes totally blind, the composer asks to be carried up a mountainside on a litter to watch the setting sun. The arduous ascent, the jagged camera angles cutting from human faces to the faces of nature, the fading sun suddenly illuminating Delius's almost sightless eyes — these images are of such evocative power that one feels instinctively how the profound mystery of natural forces came to pervade all of Delius's music.

Needless to say, there is nothing remotely resembling this sort of keen investigation into the artistic mind in "Lisztomania." The reasons for Russell's gradual abandonment of sensitivity for sensation over the past decade can only be speculated upon. Possibly one contributing factor for the success of the Delius film is the participation of Fenby himself in preparing the script— he may well have acted as a corrective to Russell's indulgences.

Another, sadder explanation might simply be a bid on Russell's part for crass commercial acceptance. It's no secret that the director's films since "Women in Love" have not done well at the box office. ("Mahler," in fact, will probably never be generally shown in this country after its short, disastrous run in Los Angeles last spring.) "Tommy" reversed the trend —the cash-registers were bound to ring with the combination of The Who's immensely popular rock extravaganza and Russell's growing penchant for unrestrained vulgarity.

By imposing his dreary rock-and-roll analogies on "Lisztomania," by casting Daltrey as Liszt despite his limited acting ability, and by calling upon another popular rock musician, Rick Wakeman, to clumsily arrange the music of Liszt and Wagner as well as compose irrelevant songs of his own, Russell may have felt that a wide audience appeal was assured— not only among the rock-oriented youth but among morbidly curious adults eager to leer at his latest outrageous spectacle.

Indeed, it's difficult to regard the director's recent efforts as other than a simple case of selling out, especially since Russell himself, in an interview in The Los Angeles Times, confesses that he actually detests rock music. Next on Russell's musical docket are George Gershwin and Ralph Vaughan Williams. One shudders to think of sweet, portly old Vaughan Williams, played by Barbara Cook in drag, gathering Eng-

"A Song of Summer," Russell's film about Delius, was "exquisitely sensitive."

lish folksongs in the countryside for his new rock opera, pausing to have intercourse with sheep.

Whatever the answer to this sad decline of a major filmmaking talent, it seems incredible that the same man who conceived the brilliant "A Song of Summer" is also responsible for the banalities, tired bombast and cartoon characters of "Lisztomania."

It's even more incredible that Ken Russell should declaim, in an official press handout, that "Music comes from nowhere." He has already demonstrated, with penetrating artistry, that music comes directly from the hearts and minds of exceptional human beings. ∎

1975 O 19, II:1:4

FILM VIEW

VINCENT CANBY

It Was the Best Festival In Years

To repeat the question for what will be the last time this year: Is the New York Film Festival necessary? Well, this one was. This festival— the 13th—was the best in years. There were no upsets in the event that closed one week ago tonight, but the general level of the entries was high. There even were times when I was glad to have seen something I didn't like at all. The festival had its usual quota of stuff to avoid. That includes Miklos Jancso's "Elektreia," which I've avoided so far (having seen everything he's done in recent years, I feel I've earned that modest privilege), and Marguerite Duras's "India Song," which I didn't avoid (see below).

If the movies we saw at this festival are some measure of what filmmakers around the world are up to (and the festival doesn't seriously pretend to do that), it's apparent that American directors are the only people on the planet who still possess robust humor. Witness "Hearts of The West" and "Smile." It may be our lot to laugh our way towards Doomsday. Another totally spurious generalization, based on Rainer Werner Fassbinder's "Fist-Right of Freedom," Werner Herzog's "Every Man For Himself and God Against All" and Volker Schlondorff's and Margarethe von Trotta's "The Lost Honor of Katharina Blum": the angry young men of the 1970's are alive and well and living in Germany, though their films strike me as so cool and so carefully composed according to predetermined principles that I find it difficult to respond to them with the kind of wonder and surprise that less schematic work evokes.

The following is a brief rundown on seven festival films not previously covered here:

"Xala," Ousmane Sembene's gently angry fable about the rise and fall of a black middle-class businessman in a newly independent African state that looks like Sembene's own Senegal. The director's sophistication as a filmmaker never upstages the comic simplicity of his moral lesson, which is told directly, often with great humor, and without condescension. Mr. Sembene is the first black African filmmaker to win the attention of the international film distributors. Now he must win the attention of international audiences, which he deserves.

● ● ●

"Exhibition," this festival's only claim to a real "first." "Exhibition," directed by Jean-François Davy, who makes porn films in France, is the first film with hard-core pornographic sequences ever to be selected for showing at the New York Festival. It's Mr. Davy's dead-pan documentary about the private and professional life of Claudine Beccarie, France's answer to Linda Lovelace. Miss Beccarie looks a little like Linda. She has the same sweetness of face though she's not as accomplished a performer. As we get to know her in the film she seems to be one of society's victims (reform school at the age of 14) who is playing the role for every last dime she can hustle out of it. She also comes across as cold in bed, which definitely limits the film's erotic appeal. The personality revealed in the film—a personality that the festival program described as "fascinating and complex"—is, rather, tough and self-interested. If "Exhibition" is the first porn film you've ever seen, it could turn you off for life.

"India Song," Marguerite Duras's newest demonstration of her cinematic style that, like her content, is clever, beautiful and empty. This is the tale of a femme fatale, Anne-Marie Stretter (Delphine Seyrig), the wife of the French Ambassador in Calcutta in the thirties, a lady who suffers from the film's chronic metaphors about leprosy, which, we are told by the disembodied voices on the soundtrack, Anne-Marie has in both heart and soul. Anne-Marie is bored, bored, bored, as we are after two hours of mostly looking at one mirrored corner of a drawing room. Anne-Marie occasionally drifts past—stage right to stage left, stage left to stage right—in the arms of this or that suitor, who is also bored, bored, bored. It's different but not terrifically stimulating, like watching goldfish sleep.

"Milestones," co-directed by Robert Kramer ("The Edge," "Ice") and John Douglas, a report on the sixties political activists and where they are in the mid-seventies. This three-hour-plus movie goes on too long but that may be the only way that such a report on an entire generation could be made. Dozens of characters, who often seem to be playing themselves, pass through the film, talking about feelings, relationships, feelings, the good old days, feelings. Everybody feels the need for feeling and often feels nothing. Nobody ever calls attention to the need for thinking. In spite of the life-affirming birth scene that ends the film, disillusion, loss and quiet desperation are the film's tone. It's also full of a sense of spontaneous life, with moments that are very funny and very sad. The wisest character in the film is not really of the sixties at all. She's a woman with two grown daughters and she's played with fine spirit and wit by Grace Paley.

● ● ●

"French Provincial," the rise and fall of a French bourgeois industrial family, directed by André Téchiné and given consistent interest by the performance of Jeanne Moreau, as a pragmatic wash woman who marries into the clan and saves it (for a while). Mr. Téchiné's stylized tableaux are sometimes amusing and sometimes obscure, but Moreau always is marvelous.

"Smile," Michael Ritchie's cheerful recreation of a beauty pageant in Middle America (actually, Santa Rosa, Calif.). Its theme, more or less, is that if a smile is your umbrella, you're going to get wet. It's not difficult to satirize this sort of thing, but it's news when it's done with such intelligence and, for lack of a better word, kindness. Jerry Belson wrote the excellent screenplay and it's acted with great gusto by Bruce Dern, Barbara Feldon (one of the best comic actresses to come out of TV), Michael Kidd, and three extremely pretty young women, Joan Prather, Annette O'Toole and Maria O'Brien.

"The Story of Adèle H.," a beautiful, rigorous, very original film by François Truffaut, about the consuming yet magnificent obsession of Adèle Hugo, the younger daughter of Victor, who pursued her love for a young English officer from Europe to Halifax and then to the West Indies. When the officer refused to cooperate, Adèle created her own truths, as well as an extraordinary diary, on which this film is based. Isabelle Adjani, 20 and a classic beauty, plays Adèle. More on this unique film when it opens commercially in New York.

1975 O 19, II:13:7

HESTER STREET, directed by Joan Micklin Silver; screenplay by Miss Silver, adapted from "Yekl" by Abraham Cahan; director of photography, Kenneth Van Sickle; music, William Bolcom; editor, Katherine Wenning; produced by Raphael D. Silver; distributed by Midwest Film Productions, Inc. At the Plaza Theater; running time: 92 minutes; this film has been classified PG.
Jake.....................Steven Keats
Gitl........................Carol Kane
Bernstein..............Mel Howard
Mamie................Dorrie Kavanaugh
Mrs. Kavarsky..........Doris Roberts
Joe Peltner.........Stephen Strimpell
Fanny...................Lauren Frost
Joey.................Paul Freedman
Rabbi....................Zvee Scooler
Rabbi's Wife.........Eda Reiss Merin

By RICHARD EDER

There is nothing very original about "Hester Street" except its loveliness.

Literally, it is a small movie about the struggles and transformations of the Jews who settled in the Lower East Side and tried to reconcile the ordered values they brought along with the unmarked opportunities they found.

The immigrant theme, with its anecdotes, its incongruities, its mixture of comedy and pathos, has been played through any number of stories, novels, memoirs, films. How, then, can this film be so good?

Partly, it is because movies are performances as well as creations. The effect of seeing "Hester Street" is that of seeing a familiar play—"A Midsummer Night's Dream" as done by Peter Brook or "The Wild Duck" as done by Sweden's Royal Dramatic Theater—lit up by an intent and flowering mind.

●

Performance doesn't refer simply to the acting, though

Carol Kane in the role of Gitl

the cast of "Hester Street," which opened yesterday at the Plaza Theater, is superlative, and Carol Kane in the starring role is extraordinary. It refers to the whole framing of the picture by Joan Micklin Silver, its author and director: the rhythms, the acute selection of incident and character.

"Hester Street" tells of the comic and painful Americanization of Jake and Gitl, an immigrant couple from Russia. In the opening scenes Jake, who has come over alone, is adapting wholeheartedly although with an aim that is slightly askew. Played with vigor and humor by Steven Keats, Jake has found himself a tailoring job, a whole bed for himself—actually, he confesses to a friend, it's a couch, but he's still ahead of others who have to double up—and a girlfriend.

But then Gitl arrives and brings with her not only hideous complications for Jake's love life, but also the dress, the bearing, the language and the customs of the Russian ghetto that Jake has so exuberantly put behind.

They settle in: Jake, Gitl, their little boy, and a lodger. The lodger is a former rabbinical student named Bernstein who went into tailoring because he couldn't keep his mind off women, but nonetheless spends his evenings studying.

It is a series of battles, Jake pushing his wife to give up her shawls, her hair-covering, her Yiddish; her making adjustments at her own pace, and far too slowly for him. The marriage founders; Jake gets a divorce, financed by his girlfriend, and marries her. And Gitl in a beautiful reversal that is neither sudden nor unprepared, but flows out of her own slowly blossoming strength, comes out ahead.

The film is constructed on a series of sharp, brief incidents. There is Jake at Ellis Island meeting Gitl, who is arrayed — clothes, bundles, bags—like a whole history of the Diaspora. "For what purpose are you bringing this woman in?" an official asks Jake. "For the purpose she's my wife," he answers in a near-howl.

There is the owner of the tailor shop gloating at Bernstein's struggle with the unaccustomed manual work. "The peddler becomes the boss and the Yeshiva student sits by the sewing machine," he chortles. "Some country."

And in the lodgings, when Jake has stormed out in one of his rages, Bernstein and Gitl sit in mutual misery. "When we come over here," he tells her, "we say 'Goodbye, Lord, I'm going to America.' "

The camerawork, in black and white, is deliberately restrained, but there is a moment of pure virtuosity. The scene is in the country, the camera points through leaves at the sun, a piano rag jangles on the soundtrack, and suddenly the whole comically tormented group bursts through the trees and the glare for a picnic.

●

Some picnic. Jake determinedly plays American ball with his son; Gitl and Bernstein droop in Old Country poses against a tree. There is a pause in the athletics. "Jake," she asks—never having been past Delancey Street—"are there any gentiles in America?"

Beyond all the details there is the magnificent performance of Carol Kane as Gitl. Big-eyed, scared and inaudible at first, a spark of allure pops out here, a spark of anger there, until by the end of the picture she is a triumphant bonfire. Miss Kane manages the high acting feat of seeming to change size physically, expanding and shrinking as she is happy or miserable.

There is a defect in the picture, although it is not a major one. The street scenes are too fully packed with color: too many peddlers, too many mischievous children, too many barrows. It's like a stage set. Even the dresses hanging on racks seem instructed in their parts.

But it is the only point at which Mrs. Silver's fine balance between realism and fable slips a bit into storyteller artifice. For the rest, "Hester Street" is an unconditionally happy achievement.

1975 O 20, 44:1

BLACK CHRISTMAS, produced and directed by Bob Clark; screenplay by Roy Moore; director of photography, Reg Morris; editor, Stan Cole; music, Carl Zittrer; distributed by Warner Bros. Running time 100 minutes. At neighborhood theaters. This film has been classified R.
Jess.......................Olivia Hussey
Peter.......................Keir Dullea
Barb......................Margot Kidder
Mrs. Mack'.............Marian Waldman
Lieutenant Fuller..........John Saxon

"Black Christmas," which landed on local screens a year after its release in Canada where it was produced, is a whodunit that begs the question of why it was made.

The answer, is hard to come by. This moody depiction of the Christmas slayings of university sorority sisters and their housemother, among others, is as murky as the script, which dotes largely on obscenities that are no more pointed than the violence, dull direction and pedestrian performances.

Why this skulking psychopath is driven to making explicitly obscene phone calls in a variety of crazed voices to the girls before dispatching them remains a fairly foggy business. The slightly comic, alcoholic house-mother, Marian Waldman, and Margot Kidder, who is also a drunk and as blatantly outspoken as the killer, and Andrea Martin and Lynne

Griffin as the other victims, are obvious in perfunctory portrayals.

Olivia Hussey, as the pregnant, sole survivor, is properly confused and terrified by the bloody events. But Keir Dullea, the neurotic music student-lover she rejects, does little but rant about the prospective child she doesn't want and smash his piano in a fit of rage.

After several witless murders, John Saxon, the film's unflustered, if perplexed, detective, cynically asks a dumb cop, "Don't you think we ought to look into it?" Considering the ersatz tension and plotting, "Black Christmas" is hardly worth the efforts of all concerned.

A. H. WEILER

1975 O 20, 45:1

'Yessongs' Pays Homage to Rock Group

"Yessongs," now at the National and RKO 59th Street Twin 1 theaters, is another of those visually repetitive, aurally hyperactive documentary valentines to a rock group.

In this case, it is a group called Yes, which is worth remembering, because there is little else in this film to distinguish it from its predecessors.

Here the group, which is not without talent, simply goes from one number to another performed at several concerts where the audiences cheer in quadraphonic sound and are seen occasionally on poorly matched film of quality ranging from blurry to downright pointillist.

Other than providing close-ups of the performers, the film makes no effort to add any dimension to their work. It seeks neither to inform, nor reveal character nor expand the vocabulary of film. Its true purpose seems to be an exploration of the limits of revenue derivable from concert appearances.

It is, really, an illustrated recording that has tightly circumscribed its appeal to those who already know and like the music of Yes.

The movie, which runs about 75 minutes, is accompanied by a short called "Death of a Red Planet." This film by Dale Pelton is said to be the first to use ion lasers to create images. The technique may be new, but the colorful viscous images and the sense of extraterrestrial excursion are not.

LAWRENCE VAN GELDER

1975 O 20, 45:1

40 Soviet Films of 20's, A Mishmash at Modern

By RICHARD EDER

Morning, in a hideously cluttered one-room Moscow apartment. The man sits up in bed, in the most objectionable good humor. He takes the cat and lays it on his sleeping wife's face. Bony shoulders protruding from his underwear, he does his exercises and strips a leaf from a calendar with a grubby picture of Stalin on it. He stands in a washtub, showering under a trickle of water from the samovar hung overhead.

He sits down to breakfast, complains about the milk, tries to feed his wife the skin from it, gives it to the cat when she refuses, and is off to work, reminding her to be sure to scrub the floor. "His Majesty the Husband," she mutters.

What a distance from the crashing montage and steel-tipped ideologies of Eisenstein's "Ten Days That Shook the World" or Pudovkin's "The End of St. Petersburg." Yet "Bed and Sofa" was made in the same high moment of Russian film production. It is all but unknown to the general public; it is a subtle, funny and beautiful masterpiece of individual psychological, and it is the great revelation of the massive showing of Russian silent movies at the Museuc of Modern Art.

Between the beginning of thsi month and Nov. 18, some 40 Soviet films, made in 1926 and 1927 will be shown. Made available by the Pacific Film Archive, and selected by Jay Leyda, an expert on Soviet cinema, the films afford and unusual opportunity for New Yorkers to form an idea of a time when there was a certain freedom in the Soviet film industry, before sound drew down the word-by-word attention of the censors.

The occasion is frustrating, as well. The selection is vast, beyond the capacity of even the dedicated filmgoer to make a useful selection. Worse, since each film is shown only once or twice—and mostly in the afternoon or early evening—even viewers who know what they want to see will have difficulty getting to see it.

Worst of all, only about a quarter of the pictures have the titles translated into English. It is purely ridiculous to expect people to sit through a highly stylized performance of the first part of Kosintsev's "The Cloak" or the tedious montage of people at work in Vertov's "One-Sixth of the World" and depend on subtitles in Russian.

The museum would never hang pictures like this: all jammed together and labeled in Sanskrit. With its limited resources, the film department would have done better to select 8 or 10 films out of the 40, arrange them in some meaningful pattern, see that each was properly subtitled, and present the series five or six times to give people more of a chance to take it in.

Take "Bed and Sofa." It will be shown only once, on Nov. 3 at 5:30 in the afternoon. This is quite wrong. Considering all the exposure Eisenstein gets, this picture, which stands almost alone not only in the work of its author and director, Avram Room, but in the history of Soviet films, should be far more widely available.

In its intimacy, its humor, the warmth that is closely subordinated to a wry and disenchanted commentary on individuals and society—Soviet society, mind you—"Bed and Sofa" had no imitators in its own country. Something in it may be reflected, though there seems to be no direct link, in the kind of picture that was made in Czechoslovakia in the mid-nineteen-sixties.

Of the dozen or so other films I have seen—most are part of a gift made by the Soviet Union to San Francisco when it opened a consulate there several years ago—none is quite up to "Bed and Sofa." But Some are very interesting. Eisenstein, of course, is represented by "Ten Days" and "Potemkin." Pudovkin's "The End of St. Petersburg," made in competition with "Ten Days" to commemorate the 10th anniversary of the Bolshevik victory, has strengths—and an equally developed propagandistic style—of its own.

There is an appealing early version of "The Forty-First," the story of a woman Red Guard and a White Cossack officer who are shipwrecked together and become lovers, before being overtaken by the conflict. There is a collection of newsreel excerpts entitled "Fall of the Romanov Dynasty," notable among other things for a shot of the last Czar bathing nude. Other pictures provide examples of the work of such directors as Kulishov, Dovzhenko and Vertov.

1975 O 22, 39:1

Sellers Plays 6 Roles in Boultings Comedy

By VINCENT CANBY

The time is late spring, 1940. France is falling with a snicker. An aged marshal of the Army retreats from the front to his favorite Paris brothel, where he had left his corset when the blitzkreig began. The brothel is also the hideout for a dashing English twit, a Royal Air Force officer who uses the place as a base for underground operations. The brothel is visited by Hitler and later, when German officers keep disappearing from its bedrooms, the house is investigated by a pinch-nosed Gestapo chief, a former income-tax examiner.

The faces aren't familiar but the actor underneath all that plasticine is. It's none other than Peter Sellers in the Boulting brothers' new comedy, "Undercovers Hero," which may possibly be the most awkward title of the week, next to "The Night of Counting the Years," which has an excuse. It was translated from the Arabic.

In "Undercovers Hero," which opened yesterday at theaters around the city, Mr. Sellers also plays a Japanese prince and a president of France, a total of six roles, three more than he played in either "The Mouse That Roared" or "Dr. Strangelove," and five more than he played in "The Return of the Pink Panther."

The suspicion that he plays five more roles than are absolutely necessary in "Undercovers Hero" is both unfair and inaccurate. One could just as well argue that "Jaws" would be a more serious film without the shark. Multiple-role playing, so dear to the heart of revue comics (and Mr. Sellers is one of the best), is the entire point of this film, though whether by design or default,

The Cast

UNDERCOVERS HERO, directed by Roy Boulting; screenplay by Leo Marks and Roy Boulting; produced by John Boulting; music, Neil Rhoden; director of photography, Gil Taylor; editor, Martin Charles; produced by Charter Film Productions, Ltd., distributed by United Artists. Running time: 95 minutes. At the National Theater, Broadway at 43d Street, and othr theaters. This film has been rated R.

General Latour Major Robinson Schroeder Hitler Prince Kyoto President of France	Peter Sellers
Mme. Grenier	Lila Kedrova
Gen. Von Grotjahn	Curt Jurgens
Marie-Claude	Beatrice Romand
Alan Cassidy	Rex Stallings

I can't tell.

"Undercovers Hero" is an almost creepily witless endeavor, and one that should make you appreciate the true lunacy of the Blake Edwards-Sellers collaboration on "The Return of the Pink Panther." Roy Boulting, who directed and co-wrote the screenplay of the new movie, and John Boulting, who produced it, have made a sketch film with very few jokes and of such incoherence that they have an actor feeding us a lot of dumb voice-over narration in the vocabulary and cadences of former President Nixon. What could they possibly have been thinking of?

Two of the Sellers impersonations are amusing—the British officer who sounds like a frightfully grand idiot and the seedy Gestapo officer whose dark plans are forever being sabotaged by Curt Jergens, who plays a nice German officer. The other members of the cast include Lila Kedrova, as the brothel's cheery madame, and Beatrice Romand (of "Claire's Knee") as an innocent brothel slavey, a girl who dreams of one day of having her own career.

They don't do very much, as if they feared that if they did, Mr. Sellers would take their roles for himself. All of the Sellers impersonations are impressive, which means they may be technically good even when they aren't funny at all.

1975 O 23, 48:3

THE NIGHT OF COUNTING THE YEARS, written and directed by Shadi Abdelsalam; photography, Abdel Aziz Fahmy; music, Mario Nascimbene; editor, Kamal Abou-El-Ella; presented by Merchant Ivory Productions; distributed by New Yorker Films. At the Regency Theater, Broadway near 67th Street. Running time: 100 minutes. This film has not been rated.

Wanniss	Ahmed Marei
Brother	Ahmad Hegazi
Mother	Zouzou El Hakim
Uncles	Abdelmonem Aboulfoutouh, Abdelazim Abdelhack
Zeena	Nadia Loutfy
G. Maspero	Gaby Karraz
Ahmad Kamal	Mohamed Khairi
Badawl Bey	Ahmad Anan
Murad	Mohamed Nabih
Ayoub	Shafik Noureddin
Stranger	Mohamed Morshed

By RICHARD EDER

"The Night of Counting the Years," which opened yesterday at the Regency Theater, is said by its distributors to be the first Egyptian movie to be shown in the United States. It has some beautifully composed shots of the desert and the Nile, and a few moments where the drama inhabits the actors instead of giving them orders from far away, but it isn't a success.

It is set near the site of ancient Thebes, burial place of the Egyptian kings. A mountain clan, the Horrabat, has lived for generations by stripping artifacts and ornaments from a burial mound known only to itself, and selling them to dealers.

The head of the clan dies; his two sons, learning for the first time of the trade off which they have lived, refuse to carry it on. One is murdered by their uncles; the younger one, Wanniss, hesitates but finally notifies the authorities. Soldiers remove the sarcophagi to Cairo, and the Horrabat's way of life is at an end.

There are possibilities in the theme. It is a conflict between the down-to-earth traditions of the clan for whom the dead are their dead and—in a true Nilotic cycle—the source of their life; and the larger, impersonal concern of Cairo with preserving history.

Shadi Abdelsalam, the author and director, manages only once or twice to capture the proper human scale of the conflict. There is a scene where the graybeard uncles urge their followers to attack the procession of troops and bearers that is removing the sarcophagi. Nobody moves; the uncles start forward with their ancient rifles and then halt, aimlessly. A tiny, hopelessly bypassed community has just expired.

Most of the movie, however, is done with stupefying grandiloquence. Wherever the camera touches, it sticks and won't let go. Landscape, brooding close-up—and how they all do brood—interminable patterns of black-robed figures against the white sand: Every shot lingers and lingers.

The acting is heavy and hieratic, fogged with a pretentious mysticism. As Wanniss sulks about, trying to decide whether to serve the interests of his uncles or those of archeology, a mysterious stranger appears, hangs around for a while and vanishes; all to no apparent purpose.

"Follow, observe but do not question," one of the uncles says early on, as he shows the brother the burial crypt. The dialogue is mostly in this style, accompanied by portentous background music. "The Night of Counting the Years" often feels like years of counting the minutes.

1975 O 23, 48:3

'Artist's Spaces,' or 3 Shorts at Whitney

PURSUIT (1975), a film by Bruce Nauman and Frank Owen. Distributed by Castelli-Sonnabend Tapes and Films, Inc. Running time: 28 minutes.
PINE BARRENS (1975), a film by Nancy Holt. Distributed by Castelli-Sonnabend Tapes and Films, Inc. Running time: 32 minutes.
SWAMP (1971), a film by Nancy Holt and Robert Smithson. Distributed by Castelli-Sonnabend Tapes and Films, Inc. Running time: 6 minutes.
At the Whitney Museum of American Art, Madison Avenue and 75th Street.

By A. H. WEILER

The literal inspection of places and people that has been fascinating moviemakers ever since Edison is given contemporary, if not wholly effective, application in "Artist's Spaces," the slightly vague over-all title for the three documentary shorts that opened yesterday at the Whitney Museum of American Art.

A viewer may wonder, with some reason, about the connection between "Pine Barrens," which traverses New Jersey's desolate back country, "Swamp," its accompanying, previously released, 6-minute trek through a reedy marsh, and "Pursuit," a doggedly detailed observation of human locomotion reminiscent of Eadweard Muybridge's classic 19th-century studies.

"Pine Barrens" and "Swamp" are distantly related. But if "Swamp" merely evolves as a simple filming exercise done in 1971 by Nancy Holt and her late husband, Robert Smithson, Miss Holt's recently made "Barrens" is a sensitively evocative, polished picturesque record of a truly secluded corner of the American scene.

Its roving color camera has captured its thickly wooded areas, ponds, marshes and flat sandy terrain, and some of its facts

and legends are narrated off-screen by its rural citizens with the excited eye of a true discoverer. One misses seeing these natives who still cling to a brooding environment that is not too distant from Manhattan or Philadelphia and is as lonely and eerie as its loon's cry. But there seems to be a surfeit of people in "Pursuit" much before it runs its course. There is no doubt as to the dedication of its producers. But in their close-ups of a succession of men and women jogging or running (on a treadmill apparently) to he panting sounds of exertion, they make an obvious, prosaic commentary on the appearance and effect of physical activity that soon becomes merely academic.

1975 O 23, 49:1

ABDUCTION, directed by Joseph Zito; screenplay by Kent E. Carroll, based on the novel "Black Abductor" by Harrison James; produced by Mr. Carroll; director of photography, Joao Fernandez; music, Ron Frangipane and Robbie Farrow; editor, James Macreading; released by Venture Distribution Company. Running time: 100 minutes. At the Penthouse Theater, Broadway at 47th Street, and other theaters. This film has been rated R.
Patricia .... Judith-Marie Bergen
Dory .... David Pendleton
Frank .... Gregory Rozakis
Mr. Prescott ...... Leif Erickson
Mrs. Prescott ..... Dorothy Malone
F.B.I. agent ...... Lawrence Tierney
Angie .... Presley Calon
Carol .... Catherine Lacy
Michael .... Andrew Rohrer
Jake .... Andrew Bloch

By VINCENT CANBY

"Abduction," which opened at the Penthouse and other theaters yesterday, is bargain-basement movie-making of the least interesting sort, an ineptly produced ripoff of

the Patricia Hearst story. Though it's based on a novel that was actually written before the kidnapping, it seeks to exploit the real events in a manner that defames almost everyone, including the alleged kidnappers and their prey.

It's about a pretty girl named Patty Prescott, whose father owns most of California, and her abduction by a small group of radicals who want Patty's father to blow up a high-income housing project that had originally been designed for poor people.

Unless Patty's dad meets their demands, say the kidnappers, they will murder his daughter. In the meantime they seek to convert her to their play-school politics by sexual humiliation, first a rape by one of the men, then a seduction by one of the women, video tapes of which are sent off to dad to convince him—of what I'm not sure. After a certain amount of rapping as well as raping, Patty has thrown in with her abductors and is really getting into group politics and sex.

According to Variety, "Abduction" was originally planned as a soft-core porn film, but most of that footage has been left out. What remains is numb, cruel and mingy. The writing, directing and acting are so astonishingly below par that one wonders what Dorothy Malone and Leif Erickson, who play Patty's parents, are doing in the same cans of film with these other people.

1975 O 25, 17:1

FILM VIEW

VINCENT CANBY

New Movies With That Old Appeal

The dreams haven't changed, only the dreamers. If you squint your eyes as you look at three new, apparently very successful, commercial American movies you might think that World War Two had never happened, that Korea was simply an obscure name for Chosen, that the French were still playing in their compounds around Saigon, and that no scandals could possibly develop of a magnitude that would unseat both an American President and a Vice-President during the same Administration.

The films are Walter Hill's "Hard Times," which is set in New Orleans in the mid-thirties and is about pick-up fighters and the hustling world they inhabited, Berry Gordy's "Mahogany," the story of a poor shopgirl's rise to fame and fortune, which prove to be empty without

the man she loves, and "Rooster Cogburn," the continuation of the adventures of "True Grit's" boozy, pot-bellied old Federal marshal, directed by Stuart Millar and produced by Hal B. Wallis, who has been making movies since 1922.

The curious thing about these movies is not that they seem old hat. Rather it's that the dreams they represent are so durable and so flexible that with only a small amount of adjusting they can meet the needs of people who, you might have thought, had moved on to other interests. Pop tastes today aren't all that different from what they were 30 to 40 years ago—so much for the rock culture, the new morality, the cultural explosion, and television's impact on the attention spans of the young. Our movies haven't budged.

The most dramatic example of this timelessness is "Rooster Cogburn," a cheerful spin-off of "True Grit" that not only could have been made 35 years ago but it could have been made with the same actors, John Wayne and Katharine Hepburn, who were just as big at the box office then as they are today. In 1940 Hepburn had already won her first Oscar and had had two distinct Hollywood careers. John Wayne, Republic Pictures' most popular cowboy, was becoming respectable under the direction of men like John Ford ("Stagecoach" and "The Long Voyage Home") and Cecil B. DeMille, for whom he made "Reap The Wild Wind" in 1942.

The formula that is the heart of "Rooster Cogburn"—the confrontation of the male roughneck and the civilizing woman—was hackneyed even in 1943 when Wayne and Jean Arthur made something called "A Lady Takes A Chance." Theoretically, anyway, "Rooster Cogburn" could have been made 35 years ago but I doubt that we would have responded to it with the warmth we do today as we watch a man, who is 68 and whom we've known all our lives, give as good as he gets from a woman, 66, whose indomitability gives a special edge to the comedienne we now observe.

"Rooster Cogburn" is a throwaway Western and, as a comedy, it shouldn't be mentioned in the same breath with the great Cukor-Tracy-Hepburn "Pat and Mike," which ended with a proposal of marriage sealed with a hearty handshake. Yet it is both entertaining and reassuring: the survival of Wayne and Hepburn gives the rest of us something to aim for.

Bronson in "Hard Times"— godlike and taciturn

"Mahogany" is pretty silly any way you look at it but silliness has never been a major crime in movies. It often wins Academy Awards. What we have here is a slick update of the shopgirl dream, complete with all of the built-in guilts that so afflicted the upwardly mobile white heroines a couple of generations ago. "Mahogany" was directed by Berry Gordy, the Mr. Big of Motown Records, who took over the direction from Tony Richardson after production had started. I've no way of telling who contributed what but, as silly movies go, "Mahogany" is about as cannily constructed as they come.

With the unique Diana Ross, the ex-Supreme who is becoming a first-rate screen personality, as the poor but ambitious fashion designer, and with Billy Dee Williams, a sort of black George Brent, as the man she really loves, "Mahogany" is first and foremost a film fantasy for black audiences. I suspect that it must also be answering the fantasy needs of a lot of white audiences who want to be told again (and again and again) that life at the top is lousy "without someone you love to share it with you," which is one of the pithier quotes from the film.

A Diana Ross movie in which she is only allowed to sing one song behind the credits is fairly ridiculous to start with. That "Mahogany" is sit-through-able is a credit to Miss Ross's talents as both a comedienne and actress. If you can look around all of the fancy scenery (much of the film was shot in Rome) and around the haute couture, which is of a dreadfulness to make a circus designer envious, you can see Miss Ross itching to create a full-length, gutsy character, which she succeeded in doing in "Lady Sings The Blues." One sign of the passing times: in 1935 the man loved by the white heroine would have been a doctor, working in a slum; in "Mahogany" he's a black politician, working in the ghetto.

• • •

"Hard Times," the best of these films, is a terrific directorial debut for Walter Hill, a 34-year-old screenwriter whose credits aren't all that promising ("Hickey and Boggs," "The Getaway"). The movie recalls classic Westerns about godlike heroes who come out of nowhere, set things straight and then move on, as well as more mundane movies of the thirties about men working at their jobs. I think especially of Howard Hawks's "Tiger Shark," which had to do with tuna fishing. But "Hard Times" doesn't depend on these associations to keep you entertained.

It's a small, vivid, tightly constructed melodrama about the business of pick-up fighting, about men who (in the Depression) moved around the country fighting matches on piers, in warehouses, wherever a match could be arranged, boxing with bare hands, no holds barred, including kicking, whose purses came from the bets placed. Charles Bronson, who is to acting what a monolith is to sculpture, plays the taciturn fighter, James Coburn is the unreliable manager whose fortunes Bronson recoups, and Strother Martin is Coburn's pot-headed assistant, a junkie whose weakness is absinthe. They are all fine but Martin, who is also marvelous in a short sequence in "Rooster Cogburn," is the stand-out as a man who, you realize, has by miraculous effort managed to pull himself together just before you meet him. Whether by design or coincidence, he looks and sounds very much like Tennessee Williams.

1975 O 26, II:15:1

DISTANT THUNDER (Ashani Sanket), directed by Satyajit Ray; screenplay (Bengali with English subtitles) by Mr. Ray, based on the novel by Bibhuti Bhusan Bannerji; director of photography, Soumendu Roy; editor, Dulal Dutta; music, Mr. Ray; executive producer, Mrs. Sarbani Bhattacharya. Running time: 100 minutes.

Gangacharan	Soumitra Chatterji
Ananga	Babita
Chhuki	Sandhya Roy
Dinabandhu	Gobinda Chakravarty
Biswas	Romesh Mukerji

"Distant Thunder" was shown at the 1973 New York Film Festival. The following excerpt is from Vincent Canby's review, which appeared in The New York Times on Oct. 12, 1973. The film opened yesterday at the Beekman Theater, Second Avenue at 65th Street.

The Bengali countryside is almost heavy with color, with golds, yellows, umbers, and especially with the greens of the rice fields. The village is tranquil. Caste is observed. It is part of the order of things. Occasionally groups of airplanes are heard overhead, but they are as remote as the war that, according to a village elder, "the king is fighting with the Germans and the Japanese."

Aside from a shortage of kerosene, the war, at first, doesn't have much effect on the villagers in Satyajit Ray's fine, elegiac new film, "Distant Thunder" (Ashani Sanket), which has the impact of an epic without seeming to mean to.

It is the work of a director who has learned the value of narrative economy to such an extent that "Distant Thunder," which is set against the backdrop of the "man-made" famine that wiped out 5 million people in 1943, has the simplicity of a fable.

Though its field of vision is narrow, more or less confined to the social awakening of a young village Brahmin and his pretty, naive wife, the sweep of the film is so vast that, at the end, you feel as if you'd witnessed the events from a satellite.

"Distant Thunder" is about Gangacharan (Soumitra Chatterji), the only Brahmin in his village, a solemn and rather pompous young man who accepts the responsibilities as well as the privileges of caste. As teacher, physician and priest he looks forward to the material rewards due him. When Ananga, his wife, asks him if he really can ward off cholera through spells, for which neighboring villagers will pay him handsomely, he replies that, in addition to the spells, he will pass on to the villagers the practical information from his hygiene encyclopedia.

As the war-induced rice shortage becomes increasingly acute, the tranquillity of the village is destroyed. Lifelong trusts are betrayed. Civil order falls apart. At the same time, the famine prompts some remarkable instances of love and compassion. The self-assured Gangacharan, who wears black-rim spectacles and carries a black umbrella, is at first angry when his wife proposes that she go to work to earn rice for them. Then he says quietly: "If we have to humble ourselves, it's best we do it together."

As the scramble to survive humiliates some of Mr. Ray's characters, it ennobles others, including Gangacharan who, toward the end, has begun to question the social system that he has always accepted as given and right. In the context of the film, this is a revolutionary conversion, and a most moving one.

Mr. Ray has chosen to photograph the film in rich, warm colors, the effect of which is not to soften the focus of the film but to sharpen it.

1975 O 27, 21:4

THE DEVIL IS A WOMAN, directed by Damiano Damiani; screenplay by Mr. Damiani, Fabrizio Onofri and Audrey Nohra, based on a story by Mr. Damiani; produced by Anis Nohra; music, Ennio Morricone; director of photography, Mario Vulpiani; editor, Peter Taylor; a British-Italian co-production, distributed by 20th Century-Fox. Running time: 105 minutes. At the 68th Street Playhouse, Third Avenue at 68th Street. This film has been rated R.

Sister Geraldine	Glenda Jackson
Rodolfo	Claudio Cassinelli
Emily	Lisa Harrow
Father Borelli	Adolfo Celi
Monsignor Badensky	Arnoldo Foa
Monsignor Meitner	Rolf Tasna
Monsignor Salvi	Duilio Del Prete
Prince Ottavio	Gabriele Lavia
Bishop Marquez	Francisco Rabal

By VINCENT CANBY

You might imagine that anyone would have to be kidding to call a movie "The Devil Is a Woman" in this day and age. Not at all. "The Devil Is a Woman," the British-Italian co-production that opened yesterday at the 68th Street Playhouse, means to be quite serious.

It has nothing to do with the 1935 film of the same title — the great Josef Von Sternberg-Marlene Dietrich collaboration—nor is it about diabolism. That is, it's not about diabolism as movie buffs in the last half of this century have come to recognize the symptoms: rocking beds, vomit, levitating children and the voice of Mercedes McCambridge running off at someone else's mouth.

This "Devil Is a Woman" was directed by Damiano Damiani, an Italian director whose earlier credits are none too promising ("Arturo's Island," "The Empty Canvas"), but originally it may not have been quite so foolish as it now is. The film seems to have been so badly edited for its American release that it contradicts its own plot at key places. Also, some of the post-sychronized English dialogue is impossible to understand.

Behind this cracked facade one occasionally glimpses the traces of an interesting if overwrought intellectual drama of the kind that Europeans take more seriously than we do. The setting is a religious hostel-convent in Rome, a place that doesn't look much different from thousands of other Roman buildings on the outside but that on the inside suggests a series of sets that haven't yet been fully dressed for a Ken Russell movie.

Running the establishment is Glenda Jackson, playing a character named Sister Geraldine, a handsome, frosty-mannered nun who enunciates so perfectly she always sounds as if she were in a speech competition. Sister Geraldine is big on the possibilities of redemption through prayer, group therapy (called "community meetings"), chastity and various other forms of self-denial.

•

Because of this she neglects her duties at the convent to devote herself to the saving of a motley group of souls who have sought voluntary refuge in her art-deco hostel. Among them are a beautiful young Latin American woman who fingered her right-wing husband for assassination by associates of her left-wing lover; a young Roman prince whose family won't allow him to marry the girl he loves (his sister); a Cuban bishop who sided with Fidel Castro in the revolution, and a Polish monsignor accused of working with the Nazis against the Russians.

Into this atmosphere, which is never as charged as it's supposed to be, comes a youngish Italian journalist who has been commissioned by the Polish monsignor to write the monsignor's defense. The journalist, who goes around preaching reason and the therapeutic value of not brooding too much, nearly wrecks Sister Geraldine's world, but he's a lazy fox in the hen house. How Sister Geraldine triumphs is the foggy point of the film.

Neither Miss Jackson nor the other performers is especially convincing meeting the film's sometimes operatic requirements, including suicide, self-abuse (a priest's discreet term), fetishism and the like. Moral dilemmas are introduced, labelled and then passed over, like the fancy decor seen by the camera. Nothing is explored in depth. "The Devil Is a Woman" sort of scratches ideas as if they were minor itches.

1975 O 27, 23:1

Black Western Goes on in Fits and Starts

By VINCENT CANBY

"Take a Hard Ride," which opened at three theaters on Tuesday, is a black Western that has something of the ingenuousness of a story being made up by a child as he tells it to his friends. It goes on and on—it lurches, really — in little fits and starts of inspiration from dimly remembered earlier movies.

It's about an honest cowboy (Jim Brown), a cheerfully dishonest gambler (Fred Williamson) and a mute Indian scout (Jim Kelly) and their efforts to transport $86,000 across hundreds of miles of Western wilderness to the families to whom it belongs in Mexico. The trail is fraught with dangers, and busier than Eighth Avenue on a Saturday night. There's a gun waiting behind every bush and lots of incredibly good marksmanship by the stars, and incredibly bad marksmanship by the villains, which is the only way

The Cast

TAKE A HARD RIDE, directed by Anthony M. Dawson; screenplay by Eric Bercovici and Jerry Ludwig; produced by Harry Bernsen; director of photography, Riccardo Pallotini; music, Jerry Goldsmith; editor, Stanford C. Allen; a Bernsen-Ludwig-Bercovici production, distributed by 20th Century-Fox. Running time: 103 minutes. At the Cinerama Theater, Broadway near 47th Street, RKO 86th Street Twin One Theater, 86th Street near Lexington Avenue and Colosseum Theater, Broadway at 181st Street. This film has been rated PG.

Pike	Jim Brown
Kiefer	Lee Van Cleef
Tyree	Fred Williamson
Catherine	Catherine Spaak
Kashtok	Jim Kelly
Morgan	Dana Andrews
Kane	Barry Sullivan
Dumper	Harry Carey Jr.
Skave	Robert Donner

a movie like this keeps going. The villains include Lee Van Cleef and Barry Sullivan and are mostly white. The film was shot in the Canary Islands by an Italian director who calls himself Anthony M. Dawson, though his name is actually Antonio Margheriti.

Mr. Williamson works hard to achieve a light touch but all his efforts are immediately absorbed by Mr. Brown, whose impassive performance acts as a kind of blotter. The two have a long way to go before they give Paul Newman and Robert Redford any competition.

1975 O 30, 52:2

PLACES AND FANTASIES; a program of short subjects, including "Los Ojos" (2 minutes) by Gary Beydler; "Bridge High" (10 minutes) by Manfred Kirchheimer; "Venice, Etude No. 1" (8 minutes) by Ian Hugo; "Coney" (5 minutes) and "Screentest" (20 minutes) both by Frank and Caroline Ahlfors Mouris, and "Jefferson Circus Songs" (19 minutes) by Suzan Pitt Kraning. These films have not been classified. At the Whitney Museum of American Art, Madison Avenue and 75th Street.

By A. H. WEILER

"Places and Fantasies" essentially identifies the content of the six short subjects that opened a two-week engagement yesterday at the Whitney Museum of American Art. But if the collection expectedly illustrates the avant-garde's independent approach to movie-making, the films, made between 1961 and this year, not only reflect individualism but also range widely in effect.

Manfred Kirchheimer's "Bridge High" (1975), for example, catches the bridges, rivers, skies, skyline and sounds of New York with a moving camera in loving, if not especially innovative, black-and-white images. On the other hand, Ian Hugo's "Venice, Etude No. 1" (1961) is surrealistically arresting in its color vignettes of canals, piazzas and gondolas even though these constantly superimposed shots of that sinking art museum of a city tend to confuse, rather than stimulate, a viewer.

Conversely, Suzan Pitt Kraning's "Jefferson Circus Songs" (1973) is sheer fantasy but constitutes a most imaginative use of the make-believe genre. As a cheerfully churned mixture of animated figures and real kids involved in toyland play-acting, songs and the like, it achieves strikingly distinctive, if occasionally mystifying Alice in Wonderland results.

In utilizing a speeded-up filming process, Frank and Caroline Ahlfors Mouris's "Screentest" and "Coney," which were completed this year, project an unusual technique stylistically. "Screentest" becomes a bit redundant in recording the extracurricular acting, miming, designs and off-screen, analytical commentary of nine, seemingly homosexual, fashion

designers, decorators and amateur film makers. Their apparently ad lib diversions may be narcissistic, but this color documentation of their off-hours life styles has the impact of truth and reality.

The 5-minute, "Coney," reportedly cut down from two hours of film shot over a full year, is the first part of a projected trilogy on our famed, if decaying, playground. As a year-round kaleidoscope of amusements, beaches, boardwalk, patrons and businesses, it makes for a fleetingly eye-catching but dizzyingly compressed trip.

While "Los Ojos" (1974) may be dismissed as a simple exercise that focuses aimlessly on a young man's quickly moving eyes, there are variously fascinating, if not outstanding, examples of talent and artistry.

1975 O 30, 52:2

JOYCE CHOPRA, three short films by Joyce Chopra about women in America: GIRLS AT 12, CLORAE AND ALBIE, distributed by Education Development Center. MATINA HORNER: PORTRAIT OF A PERSON, distributed by Phoenix Films. Running time: 82 minutes. At the Van Dam Theater, through Sunday and Nov. 6-9.

By RICHARD EDER

When the eye that aims the camera is bloodshot the picture comes out pink. This isn't an absolute rule for documentaries but it happens pretty often: they impart emotion as much as they record it.

Joyce Chopra's three short films at the Van Dam Theater, treating in various ways the position of American women, are sensitive and sometimes inspired in their choice of material. With the attentiveness of a butterfly catcher she awaits and snares the absorbed gesture of a girl choosing clothes in "Girls at 12," or the bitter wit of a tired young black woman in "Clorae and Albie."

But when she bends this material onto a statement about how women are trapped and self-entrapped in our society, the result is often a clumsy irascibility. The anger, instead of flowing out of her images, is injected into them.

"Girls at 12" is the clearest example of this. It is at once the best of the three films and the one most distorted by the weight of ideology. The camera goes to live among a group of 12-year-old girls in a middle-class New England neighborhood. It accompanies them to school, goes to their slumber parties, listens to their gossip about their largely incorporeal boy friends, buys clothes with them and interviews them, their teachers and their parents.

The film focuses particularly on two girls. There is Mary Ann, cheerful and eva-

sive who may have a good mind—as shown by a sudden and short-lived spurt in her grades—but seems to flee the consequences of such an ability, preferring to submerge into the average. The other, Diane, is stronger, more individual: she darts back and forth between what is expected of her as a pre-teen-ager and what may become her own individual talents and interests.

The tremulousness, the aimlessness of the age—an equivalent though different tremulousness and aimlessness could be found in boys of the same age—becomes a statement about the traps that society sets for women. The girls' pastimes—gossip, mooching around with clothes, practicing cheer leading, cookie baking—take on the melancholy of a fattening pen in the stockyard.

This is reinforced by interviews with Diane's and Mary Ann's fathers, both of whom agree that though careers are possible, the normal thing is to get married. Behind the pastimes, the message goes, is an iron hand hammering out social straightjackets. Maybe so, but the effect is a manichean heavy-handedness: the Puritans abolishing maypoles or nailing skulls onto them.

"Most of the time I like to fool around," Mary Ann tells the minatory camera, her eyes sliding afay and returning. "I don't like being serious. Its boring to be serious. It gives me a headache." Joyce Chopra's lens is too near, not for comfort but for truth. No adult's face should come so close to a child's. Mary Ann is doing fine.

The shortest of the films, "Matina Horner: Portrait of a Person," is a portrait of the president of Radcliffe College. It is at its best outlining Professor Horner's work; studies showing that women students fear not only failure but—because of a social conditioning that makes it "wrong" to compete with men—success as well.

The film as portrait is less successful. In order to prove an Integrated personality it isn't necessary to show Professor Horner at her job, leading a group discussion with students, sitting rather suspiciously among a group of male colleagues and then to swing to a shot of her teaching one of her children to play the piano.

The third film, "Clorae and Albie," suits message to material more naturally. Two young black women from Boston talk about their lives. Both are talented and have been taken into higher-education programs for minority groups. Both have dropped out, feeling little relation between college education and their own real lives. Both are painfully moving uphill once more: one, supporting three children and trying to go to school; the other, trying to go into social work.

As Clorae and Albie talk, their portraits and that of the world they live in are sharply etched. Their feeling of double disadvantage—being a woman and black—comes through. The drawback is monotony: both women keep a certain reserve, a tendency to talk about very limited things and to express their feelings with throwaway lines.

Some of the lines are brilliantly caught, however. Albie went briefly to Marlboro College in Vermont before dropping out. "It was very lovely up there," she says drily. "Like there were 275 people and two blacks."

Clorae is feeding her youngest child with a mixture of affection and desperation. "I love 'em and all that," she tell Albie, "but if I lose me, I can't love nobody."

1975 N 1, 17:1

FILM VIEW

VINCENT CANBY

A Radical Film About Ex-Radicals

Toward the end of "Milestones," an idiosyncratic, epic new American film by Robert Kramer and John Douglas, two men walk along a highway on the edge of what seems to be Detroit. The empty urban landscape has the desolate look of something marked for a renewal that will never come. In the distance we see the silhouettes of downtown office buildings. One of the men has a mustache. The other is bearded to the point of being as fully maned as a lion. They wear jeans and windbreakers and talk about old friends, about family relationships, about the Movement, a collective noun for the once New Left.

The men recall the political ferment of the late sixties and early seventies—the demonstrations in Washington, the Black Panthers, the Chicago conspiracy trial. Suddenly one says, "It seemed like we were the center of things." Both men are still young but it's as if they were veterans of the Lincoln Brigade, 30 years later.

"Milestones," a vast mosaic of a movie, is very much about the survivors of America's radical left today, but it's a good deal more than a lamentation or a recollection of old causes. It's both sympathetic and optimistic. It's huge, long (three hours and 15 minutes), novelistic film about the mood and temper, the successes, failures and aspirations of a group of earnest, mostly white, mostly upper-middle-class Americans, now that front-page attention has turned elsewhere. Its characters—more than 50 of them—are fictionalized versions of the people who play them, some more fictionalized than others.

Grace Paley, the short-story writer, plays a filmmaker closely identified with anti-war work, the mother of two grown daughters, a serene woman who has successfully established contact with her own children as well as the world around her. David C. Stone, another Movement figure who produced "Milestones" with his wife, Barbara, plays (with a lot of edgy wit) a saloonkeeper whose commitment to radical causes has grown fatigued with time. John Douglas, the co-director of the movie, has a major role as a blind pottery-maker whose studio becomes the temporary refuge of old friends looking to find new styles of living in a very different time.

Dozens of other people work their way through the film, including an emotionally disconnected young man who has just been released from prison where he served time for helping Army deserters; a liberated young woman who has left her husband and two children for a life of her own ("I don't miss the children at all. As people, yes, but not as children"); members of communes, hitchikers, couples on the verge of splitting up, children who are moved back and forth from one parent to another, over-analyzed much of the time but often more full of common sense and spontaneity than their elders. Says one little boy

Filmmakers Kramer and Douglas

on a visit to an aquarium as he stares into a tank full of alewives: "It looks like fruit jello."

"Milestones" is interesting as a report on a political movement, made by two men who are intimately connected to that movement, but it is important for far more provocative reasons. Language, for one. Though it is probably unintentional, "Milestones" is virtually a meditation on today's spoken American language, which sounds as if it were becoming less and less adequate. With several notable exceptions, the people we meet can barely communicate in words, which is one possible reason why there is so much clutching of the person being talked to.

Character after character in the film speaks of the need to get in touch with feelings, but without a vocabulary, who's to be able to report when that connection has been established? There is a great deal of talk about states of mind that are "beautiful" and about attempts "to relate," but one suspects the speakers would be hard-pressed to define what they mean. When a young man says with complete sincerity, "I've been reading DuBois' life of John Brown and it blew my mind," one is tempted to laugh, except for the revelation that something fundamental is awry. Could it be that jargon, not the oppressive forces of the military-industrial complex, is what ultimately slowed, if not defeated, the Movement?

Watching this film you might be reminded of Jean-Luc Godard's "Le Gai Savoir," which was non-stop dialogue between Jean-Pierre Léaud and Juliet Berto about the need to purge the language, to reestablish definitions, in order to defeat the forces of "reaction." As long as we use the Establishment's vocabulary, Godard was saying in effect, we will never be free. One can go on to say, a radical who can't express himself isn't going to make many converts. To express ideas we first must think them, not just feel them.

"Milestones" is the third Robert Kramer film to be released commercially. It follows "The Edge" in 1968, about Movement disillusionment and a doomed assassination plot, and "Ice" (1970), which was a threat, a promise and a handbook of urban guerrilla warfare. Mr. Kramer's concerns are so particular, and his manner usually so humorless, that one doesn't easily recognize his talents as one of our most original and gifted young filmmakers. Like Godard he is so unrelenting in his political commitments that they sometimes obscure the beauty of what he's doing. Furthermore, the three-hour-plus running time of "Milestones" seems bludgeoning every time the film strikes a false note, which isn't often, or when the childbirth sequence, which ends the film, goes into its second 15 minutes of on-screen labor.

If you go prepared, however, you may possibly be able to recognize the work of an irrepressible filmmaker. Though "Milestones" is long and, at first, seems chaotic, it is as carefully arranged as a piece of music. It moves forwards and backwards, and sometimes sideways,

using images, emotions and, most frequently, words as themes. It bursts with unexpected life—in what people say even when they fumble, and in the way Kramer and Douglas catch the look of the American landscape, whether it's the northeast coastline in a snowfall, the western desert or the interior of a burnt-out New York tenement. It's the first important American political film since "Hearts and Minds."

1975 N 2, II:1:2

'Hester Street'— Overpraised and Overdone

By WALTER GOODMAN

You evidently don't have to be Jewish to love "Hester Street." Reviewers of diverse persuasions have found this film, set on the Lower East Side in 1896, sufficiently to their liking to provide copy for advertisements — "profoundly moving and beautiful," "beautifully wrought," "something to shout about," "a jewel of a film," "an unconditionally happy achievement," and more. The man from Playboy noted that it had sex appeal.

The story has to do with a young immigrant husband, a snappy dresser with an eye for the ladies, who is into an affair with a voluptuous schemer down the street when his innocent wife and son arrive from the Old Country. The dialogue keeps insisting that the married couple have been parted by the husband's determination to become a "yenkee," but that is only a harmless pretention of the filmmakers; nothing so complicated is afoot. The husband gets or is gotten by his sexy girlfriend; his wife connects with a pious scholar more akin to her in temperament. It could happen not only in America.

•

"Hester Street" was written and directed by Joan Micklin Silver, a newcomer who has already been elevated by one reviewer to the company of Elaine May "in this country's sparsely populated top rank of women directors." Her movie does have its engaging moments— an energetic old peddler producing a remarkable array

Walter Goodman is the Assistant Editor of the Arts and Leisure section.

of goods from his bundles, a transparent young lawyer bargaining for a divorce settlement, the scholar moving suspiciously through Central Park, inherently mistrustful of the American outdoors. But even at its best, Mrs. Silver's touch is neither light nor sure. Her street scenes are so packed with pushcarts and peddlers, horses and wagons, kids and commodities that the elements which ought to display the action instead displace it. We can be certain that if Mrs. Silver takes us up to a tenement roof, there will be sheets blowing on clotheslines. She seems to trust neither the imagination of her audience nor her own powers of marshaling it.

With her actors, a very mixed bag, she permits or encourages inordinate mugging. A number of their interchanges, notably one involving what looks like a pork sausage, are awkward

Carol Kane as the immigrant wife

to the point of self-consciousness. These are the sort of excesses to which new directors are likely to be specially prone, and we may hope for more restraint in her future films.

If Mrs. Silver has a way to go as a director, she has a much longer way to go as a writer. Her dialogue is thuddingly blunt —except when she drops in a Yiddish saying—and repetitive. Delivered in a melange of accents, some more authentic than others, it keeps pounding home obvious and unproductive points, such as the husband's obsession with becoming a "yenkee." The most affecting scenes, particularly between the young wife, played fetchingly by Carol Kane, and her scholar, are those in which little is spoken, although there are places in this movie where even reticence is over-stated.

I have been addressing myself to what seem to me some of the film's weaknesses, yet "Hester Street" is by no means without its rewards. The story is well paced to hold one's interest; there are evocative moments; and it gives audiences an opportunity to hear Yiddish spoken in a way different from the uses made of the language by Mel Brooks and Woody Allen.

Even if Mrs. Silver and her cast were more skillful, however, their film would still be undermined at its center by the spirit of condescension toward its subjects. The kindly disposed may call "Hester Street" a fable or, as one reviewer did, "a page from the album of our past." Others, however, may see it as a cartoon, a group of fairly engaging one-dimensional figures playing out their assigned roles in picturesque settings. Where else can the lovers meet but on a fire escape? Everything occurs on the surface; this is a plot without shadows; these are characters without shadings. (The exception, perhaps, is the scholar, but since he is given little to do except say his prayers and cast wistful looks at the young wife, there's no way of telling if anything more lies behind the beard.)

What can account for the flurry of praise from many, though by no means all, reviewers for so modest a work as "Hester Street?" Nostalgia? Haven't they had enough of that? Women's Lib? Were some of the favorable reviewers so pleased to come across a film in which the women manipulate the men or so eager to find a woman filmmaker to acclaim? Philo - Semitism? Having grown weary of puffing up black films of slight merit, have reviewers decided that it is time again to be kind to the Jews? Or does the favorable reaction have more to do with our bad old habit of patronizing "simple" cultures?

In the week that I saw "Hester Street," I was reading Isaac Bashevis Singer's new book of short stories, "Passions," which, like "Hester Street," is concerned with Jews and with sex. I'm afraid that was unfair to the movie.

Singer abjures nostalgia. We find in his pages that life was just as mysterious, people just as unpredictable in the ghettoes of Europe and America generations agc as they are in our sophisticated cities today. That is a lesson which anthropologists have in their way been trying to teach us for quite some time, that remote cultures are not as simple as they may seem, that it is simple-mindedness on our part to reduce them to cartoons. An elementary lesson, but one that must complicate matters for moviemakers. ■

1975 N 2, II:15:6

THE HIDING PLACE, directed by James F. Collier; screenplay by Allan Sloane and Lawrence Holben, based on the book by Corrie Ten Bloom and John and Elizabeth Sherill; William F. Brown, executive producer; Frank R. Jacobson, producer; director of photography, Michael Reed; editor, Ann Chegwidden; released by Wide World Pictures, Inc. Running time: 145 minutes. At the Hudson Theater, 44th Street west of the Avenue of the Americas, and other theaters. This film has been rated PG.

Beatsie .... Julie Harris
Katie .... Eileen Heckart
Papa .... Arthur O'Connell
Corrie .... Jeannette Clift
Willem .... Robert Rietty
Tine .... Pamela Sholto
Peter .... Paul Henley
Kik .... Richard Wren

By VINCENT CANBY

Wnenver someone in "The Hiding Place" says "God knows," he isn't expressing metaphorical despair. The character means exactly what he says. Because God *does* know, it's up to the Ten Boom family, a family of Dutch Christians living in Haarlem during the Nazi occupation, to rely on that knowledge to accept the terrible things that befall them after they are arrested for helping Jewish refugees.

"The Hiding Place," which opened yesterday at the Hudson and other theaters, is a pious movie about a evry specific kind of faith. It was produced—with no apparent expenses spared—by an adjunct of the Billy Graham Evangelistic Association. "The Hiding Place" is not the sort of film that explores philosophical alternatives. It demonstrates its ideas as dramatically as it's possible to do when there's no real contest.

●

This is not to say the Ten Booms aren't subjected to all sorts of tests, but their faith never wavers. This is a sad story, as well as a true one, based on a book written by Corrie Ten Boom, the only surviving member of the Ten Boom family, after she was released, through a clerical error, from the Ravensbrück concentration camp shortly before the end of the war.

The cast includes Julie Harris and Jeannette Clift, as the two middle-age Ten Boom sisters, Arthur O'Connell as their father, and Eileen Heckart as a tough inmate who befriends the sisters on their way to Ravensbrück. The material is not the sort to test the skills of the performers, whose Dutch accents sound quite Swedish on occasion.

The film was directed by James F. Collier on locations in the Netherlands and in Britain.

1975 N 6, 51:2

NO WAY OUT, directed by Duccio Tessari; with Alain Delon and Richard Conte; distributed by Cinema Shares International. Running time: 91 minutes. This film has been classified R. At the National, UA Eastside and UA 86th Street East Theaters.

Do not be deceived by the blurry stuff in the foreground. "No Way Out," made in Italy a couple of years ago and arriving now for no good reason, is about Italian interior design. It has black leather chairs. Lucite-topped tables, stainless steel clocks, white-veneer beds and orange-panel radio controls.

Partly obscuring all this excitement are a lot of people killing one another. They work for the Mafia and one of them, played by Alain Delon, decides to quit. As a result he and his former colleagues engage in mutual destruction.

People die by shooting, stabbing, strangulation, defenestration from a moving train and compacting in an automobile graveyard.

Stick with the furniture, though. It is colorful and well-photographed. It is far more expressive than Mr. Delon, Richard Conte or the rest of the bullet-studded cast. The film opened yesterday at the National, the Eastside and other theaters.

RICHARD EDER

1975 N 6, 51:2

THE SUNSHINE BOYS, directed by Herbert Ross; screenpaly by Neil Simon; produced by Ray Stark; director of photography, David M. Walsh; supervising film editor, Margaret Booth; editor, John F. Burnett; a Metro-Goldwyn-Mayer picture, distributed by United Artists. Running time: 111 minutes. At Radio City Music Hall, Avenue of the Americas at 50th Street. This film has been rated PG.

Willy Clark .... Walter Matthou
Al Lewis .... George Burns
Ben Clark .... Richard Benjamin
Nurse in sketch .... Lee Meredith
Doris .... Carol Arthur
Nurse .... Rosetta Le Noire
Mechanic .... F. Murray Abraham

By VINCENT CANBY

For 47 years Al Lewis (George Burns) and Willy Clark (Walter Matthau) had been one of the most successful of all vaudeville comedy teams when they retired 11 years ago, and it's been 12 years since they actually spoke to each other off the stage. Willy hates Al with a fine passion, while Al, as he puts it, doesn't hate Willy; he simply can't stand him.

At the start of Neil Simon's new film comedy, "The Sunshine Boys," a broadcasting genius has had the bright idea of reuniting Lewis and Clark in a TV special. The chaos that results—a lot of it epically funny and all of it cheerful—is the sum and substance of "The Sunshine Boys," which was directed for the screen by Herbert Ross and opened yesterday at the Radio City Music Hall, with the hall's annual Christmas show on the stage.

●

The kind of retirement each man has slipped into describes their differences. Al lives contentedly in New Jersey wtih his married daughter, napping the afternoons away and awaiting the arrival of his grandchildren from school. Willy, who is a widower like Al, remains in the middle of Manhattan, the better to pursue his career as a single, lives in the Ansonia Hotel, plays cards at the Lambs, and occasionally reads for TV commercial jobs he never gets.

Al's life is serene. Willy's life has become a continuum of grudges—against his nephew-agent Ben (Richard Benjamin), against door locks that never open the same way twice, against people who don't speak up and particularly against Al who, as Willy remembers it, "retired right in the middle of my career."

Willie and Al, their mutual dislike and their similar habit of asking questions that have just been answered, are all that "The Sunshine Boys" has to offer, but with Walter Matthau at the top of his most antisocial form as Willy with George Burns giving a keenly funny, brilliantly straight performance as Al and with Mr. Simon delivering some of his best one-liners, the movie is extremely easy to take.

It's only afterward you realize that two complex characters, as well as a unique personal and professional relationship, have been used up—wasted—in the interests of comedy no more substantial than the insults that Willy and Al throw at each other.

There's a moment toward the end of the movie when you get an inkling of the story Mr. Simon chose not to explore. It's during a run-through of Lewis and Clark's "doctor" routine—a recollection of the great Smith & Dale "Dr. Kronkhite" sketch—and we are suddenly aware of the stage know-how and the heritage these two old actors represent, though the characters we've seen so far have been fairly standard versions of a couple of ill-humored old men approaching senility.

●

Mr. Burns, now approaching 80, is old enough to be his co-star's father, but he works beautifully with Mr. Matthau, much in the manner in which he played straightman for so many years to his late wife, Gracie Allen. He looks and listens. He uses a minimum of gestures and, by appreciating the chaos he is witnessing, he gives comic importance to the entire enterprise.

Without apparent strain, Mr. Simon has opened up his Broadway play to include a lot of local New York color, including a beautifully illogical confrontation between Willy and a garage mechanic when Willy, on his way to an audition, mistakes a garage on West 43d Street with the East 43d Street advertising agency he's looking for. Mr. Matthau is so good playing old men, we may never know when he finally becomes one.

1975 N 7, 28:1

MR. QUILP, directed by Michael Tuchner; screenplay by Louis and Irene Kamp, based on Dickens's "The Old Curiosity Shop"; director of photography, Christopher Challis; music and lyrics by Anthony Newley; produced by Helen M. Strauss; an Avco Embassy Picture. Running time: 118 minutes. This film has been classified G. At the Guild Theater, 33 West 50th Street.

Daniel Quilp .... Anthony Newley
Richard Swiveller .... David Hemmings
Sampson Brass .... David Warner
Grandfather, Edward Trent .... Michael Hordern
Single Gent, Harry Trent .... Paul Rogers
Sally Brass .... Jill Bennett
Mrs. Jarley .... Mona Washbourne
Kit Nubbles .... Peter Duncan
Betsy Quilp .... Yvonne Antrobus
Nell .... Sarah Jane Varley
Duchess .... Sarah Webb

By RICHARD EDER

Dickens may be dead, but anybody trying to pirouette on his grave is going to get broken ankles. Applying musical comedy conventions to his work is like skimming the highlights off a Rembrandt and trying to sell them as a painting. Whether you find him moving or stupefying, Dickens is a grainy accumulation of detail—comic, grotesque, lachrymose—amounting to a complex but integrated whole. Like the man whose character was so strong that he had to change his shirt twice a day, Dickens reeks of himself.

"Mr. Quilp," a musical film by Anthony Newley that opened yesterday at the Guild Theater, is a boneless and tentative excursion through "The Old Curiosity Shop." It starts off fairly directly with the misadventures of Little Nell and her grandfather, but it lags farther and farther behind the mercilessly advancing plot. Soon all you hear are faint voices among the furniture, dwindling finally into the fog that directors pump into Dickens movies when they can't find their way out.

To say that "Mr. Quilp" is by Anthony Newley is technically inaccurate. The director is Michael Tuchner, and the screenplay, such as it is, was written by Louis and Irene Kamp. But it is clearly fashioned around Mr. Newley as Quilp, the fiendish Cockney entrepreneur who persecutes Little Nell and her grandfather. And Mr. Newley, who seems to be directing himself, also wrote the lyrics and the music.

This is part of the problem. Mr. Newley's lyrics—except for one that may finally put out of their misery the three most abused words in musical comedy: "somewhere," "sometime" and "somehow"—are often clever. There is a particularly good one where he catalogues himself as a walking horror who is "so crooked I have to screw my socks on."

But the music is virtually nonexistent. It runs up and down and goes nowhere. Music can do a lot for a musical. It helped "Oliver," the last Dickens musical around, quite a bit, and it would have been welcome in "Mr. Quilp."

●

Without it we are back to Mr. Newley, eyes rolling, teeth like old Gorgonzola, posturing and mugging and putting out his cigar—a crooked one, of course—in a cucumber sandwich. He is good up to a point, but he can't manage to decide whether he is pantomiming evil or portraying it.

When he is on, at least, the picture has a certain vitality. Otherwise it gets by on the pinched-back performance of Sarah Jane Varley as Little Nell, the immovable melancholy of Michael Hordern as her Grandfather and the plain immovableness of David Hemmings, who literally has nothing to do in the role of Richard Swiveller.

Bits of Dickens drift in. There are moments when the wanderings of Little Nell and Grandfather, joining first a traveling carnival and then a traveling waxworks, almost become a persuasive image of uprootedness. For the brief time she is on, Jill Bennett does a marvelously palpitating termagant whose feet would stamp except that they don't quite reach the ground.

Mostly, though, the picture is becalmed, treacly and about three-quarters of an hour too long.

1975 N 8, 22:5

Ingmar Bergman's 'Magic Flute'

Bergman (left) with Josef Kostlinger, who sings Tamino

By PETER G. DAVIS

Ever since Geraldine Farrar briefly deserted the Metropolitan Opera for Hollywood in 1915 to make a silent movie of "Carmen," opera on film has seemed a lost cause. Over the past 60 years many have tried, but few have succeeded. Something always goes wrong no matter what approach a director takes, whether filming an actual stage production or a cast of dubbed-over actors in a naturalistic setting. The results almost invariably turn out to be faintly ludicrous as the two media obstinately refuse to mix.

Now here comes Ingmar Bergman with his film version of Mozart's "The Magic Flute" to prove that it can be done. In order to appreciate what the Swedish director has accomplished here, consider the odds against a successful operatic movie and the sorry heap of failures that have accrued over the years.

Opera, traditional repertory opera at any rate, is essentially a frozen art form, specifically designed by composer and librettist to exploit the conventions and physical proportions of a stage. The

second act of "Die Meistersinger," for example, requires the audience to have a full view of the action at all times if the complex simultaneity of events is to be effective. Flexibility and intimacy, two principal assets of film, are relatively useless in this case, and hopping back and forth from one group of characters to another can only ruin Wagner's dramatic counterpoint.

Furthermore, few opera singers (or opera sets, for that matter) can survive the close scrutiny of the camera —from the 25th row in the house, an amorous yet slightly paunchy middle-aged tenor can at least be given the benefit of the doubt. Opera singers are also trained by necessity to project a larger-than-life image into the farthest reaches of the family circle; such acting simply looks ridiculous at short range. Substituting "straight" actors rarely works either, for the kind of timing and coordination required in opera is quite different from spoken drama.

All of these problems and more beset the numerous operatic films made since 1945. During the forties and

fifties, studios in Italy turned out a rash of war horses using "on location" movie-lot sets and a company of dreadful actors standing in for the voices of Caniglia, Tebaldi, Del Monaco and Gobbi. More recently, filmed stage productions have been preferred, and five years ago we saw a whole "festival" of them at Lincoln Center: Karajan's lumbering, clumsily directed Salzburg spectaculars and several from the Hamburg Opera stage, impromptu affairs with crude tennis-match camera work.

The trouble with all these movies is that they were made either by opera directors with little knowledge of the film medium or by film directors with little knowledge of opera. Bergman knows both areas and his sensitivity to the requirements of each can be seen everywhere in "The Magic Flute." Although his practical experience in producing live opera is not as extensive as that of Franco Zeffirelli and Luchino Visconti, Bergman has had distinctive success with the few projects he has undertaken. After seeing the director's staging of Stravinsky's "The Rake's Progress" in Stockholm, Robert Craft commented: "I

have never seen I.S. more moved by a performance of a work of his . . . Bergman's groupings manage to be natural without infracting the conventions of opera . . . [his] singers act—move their bodies, use their eyes—as we have never seen singers act before."

Bergman's love and understanding of the art is also evident in the way he has used music in his previous films. He had commissioned some of Sweden's most outstanding contemporary composers, sure in the knowledge that their individual styles would create precisely the correct mood—Karl Birger Blomdahl wrote the score for "The Naked Night," Lars Johan Werle for "Persona"— and the music of Bach subtly haunts the soundtrack of "Through a Glass Darkly" and "The Silence." Critics have often commented on the operatic flavor that pervades his lighter films, particularly in "Smiles of a Summer Night," which seems to be an exquisitely fashioned libretto to an unwritten Mozart-Da Ponte comedy of errors.

One of the most delicious aspects of the director's "Magic Flute," Mozart's fan-

tasy about the quest of Tamino and Papageno for Pamina, daughter of the Queen of the Night, in the mystic realm of Sarastro, is the constant reminder that we are indeed watching an opera. Instead of disguising or apologizing for the fact, Bergman makes a virtue of it, re-creating the theatrical atmosphere of an intimate 18th-century court production: The "opera house" is a replica of Stockholm's jewel-like Drottningholm Palace Theater. Drops, flying flats and curtains fall or roll into place swiftly before our eyes; the animals attracted by Tamino's flute are lovable cloth creatures; the three boys who watch over Tamino's journey to self-knowledge make their appearances in the most marvelous machine, a cranked-up baroque air-balloon. We even get a brief glimpse of the backstage through the wings: Papageno hurrying to make his first entrance on time or, during the short intermission, Sarastro studying a score of "Parsifal," the Queen of the Night taking drags from a cigarette under a no-smoking sign, Tamino and Pamina concentrating on a game of chess in their dressing room.

How easily this could have become mere gimmickry— but such touches only enhance and complement the child-like wonderment that masks the message of Mozart's profoundly humanistic fairy tale—that the love between men and women is the path to eternal wisdom. During the overture, Bergman shows us close-ups of faces in the audience, people of all races, colors and ages, listening to the music with rapt attention, always returning to one smiling small girl (the director's daughter). It is a beautiful, moving introduction to the opera (and how cunningly the changing pictorial images match the rhythmic pulse of the music), stressing what Bergman so accurately describes as the work's "childish magic and exalted mystery."

●

Although this is essentially a filmed stage production, Bergman is far too imaginative and sophisticated simply to follow the singers around a prescribed acting area. Occasionally the camera will back away to remind us of the proscenium and pit, but once a scene is under way, the viewer is allowed to enter the action which opens up with maximum flexibility and freedom of movement. The technique is somewhat reminiscent of Laurence Oliver's "Henry V," which begins as a performance at the

Per B. Adolphson

Opera on film seemed a lost cause until Bergman's "The Magic Flute."
Above, Tamino and Papageno with a trio of temptresses in the new movie

Globe Theater. Unlike that film, however, "The Magic Flute" never becomes wholly naturalistic and retains its props-sets-and-costume ambience throughout. In this way Bergman avails himself of the best of both worlds—real and make believe—and combines them with technical virtuosity and striking visual compositions.

The production of "The Magic Flute" occupied Bergman for an entire year. Although the soundtrack was recorded before the actual filming of the opera, the singers themselves rather than professional actors enact the roles—a wise decision which ensures seamless musical continuity and smooth synchronization. The cast is made up of Scandinavian singers, none of whom appear on the international operatic circuit (the opera, in fact, is sung in a Swedish translation), and from a purely musical point of view, the performance is one of solid professional competence rather than polished Mozartean stylishness. Only the most glamour-oriented opera buff would complain, however—such superbly integrated ensemble teamwork could never be achieved had Bergman sacrificed his vision for a parcel of superstars.

In the end it is Bergman's vision of the opera that dominates and transfigures this heartwarming, life-affirming film. Unlike what one sees on so many opera stages today, this production of "The Magic Flute" has been conceived by a man passionately in love with what Mozart wrote rather than what he thinks the composer should have written. The special techniques that Bergman has brought to his film realization would not, of course, work for every opera in the repertory. Nor, perhaps, would the director be as successful with an opera that does not mirror his own ideas so clearly. And any filmgoer with the experience of Bergman's other movies behind him will see how central the underlying concepts of "The Magic Flute" are to his thinking—the quests for perfect love ("Smiles of a Summer Night") and truth ("The Magician"), the mystery of death ("Through a Glass Darkly"), the celebration of innocence ("The Seventh Seal"—the peasant couple Jof and Mia are surely Bergman's own Papageno and Papagena).

As the sea of faces that opens this film suggests, "The Magic Flute" is an opera that addresses itself to everyone at almost every level. In sheer cinematic terms, what Bergman has accomplished is pure enchantment; as an interpretation of a masterpiece, the production catches the spirit of Mozart's world more truthfully than most stage presentations; as an example of opera's potential in this medium, it sets a standard that few would have dreamed possible. ∎

1975 N 9, II:1:1

FILM VIEW

By VINCENT CANBY

'The Sunshine Boys' Is Fun While It Lasts

If the members of the Academy of Television Arts and Sciences were really adventurous they would consider voting an Emmy to "The Sunshine Boys" as the best television film made for theaters this year. I'm overstating the case to make a point. "The Sunshine Boys," which I like, is the sort of movie that makes you grin almost continuously, laugh out loud on a number of occasions, and then, at the end, leaves you wondering if that's all there is. What have we been laughing at? A couple of quarrelsome old men trading one-liners. That's all. If the movie were immediately followed by a station break and Johnny Carson, one might be so distracted that the quality of the earlier entertainment would not be questioned. It-was-fun-while-it-lasted-and-what's-on-next?

Theatrical movies are no longer bracketed by other movies or even short subjects, at least most of the time. They unreel, isolated, in the dark of the theater, and when they're over, there's nothing left to contemplate except the movie itself and/or the quality of urban

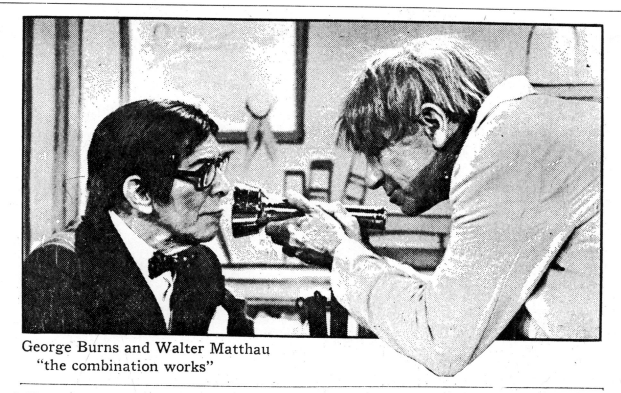

George Burns and Walter Matthau
"the combination works"

transportation that takes us home. If I sound mixed about "The Sunshine Boys," I mean to.

• • •

The film, directed by Herbert Ross and written by Neil Simon from his Broadway comedy, has a lot of attractive things to recommend it, more than enough, I'm sure, to make it a substantial box office hit and Simon's first film to duplicate or even exceed the success of the original Broadway play since "The Odd Couple." (I don't count the Simon screenplay for Elaine May's "The Heartbreak Kid," which was an adaptation of a story by Bruce Jay Friedman and still the best work Simon has done for films.) "The Sunshine Boys" has so much going for it that one keeps wanting it to be better, keeps waiting for Simon to make the breakthrough from a world described by gags into one that can acknowledge real feelings, as in "The Heartbreak Kid." But that, Simon has a perfect right to say, would be a different play.

"The Sunshine Boys" is about the disastrous attempts to reconcile two old-time vaudevillians, Lewis and Clark, for a one-shot repeat of their act on a television special. Having been a team for 47 years, the act split up 11 years earlier when Al Lewis (George Burns) retired or, as Willy Clark (Walter Matthau) puts it, "when Al retired in the middle of my career."

Willy, now in his early seventies, behaves most of the time as if he were much older. He's so befuddled that he can't remember how to undo the locks on the door of his rabbit-warren apartment at the Ansonia Hotel. He misreads instructions that direct him to an audition and blames his agent-nephew Ben (Richard Benjamin). He is cranky and mean-spirited. Most irritating to everyone around him is his way of asking a question that's just been answered.

Al Lewis is an entirely different sort of fellow. Al lives with his married daughter in New Jersey, naps in the afternoons and looks forward to visits from grandchildren who would drive Willy nuts. Al is cautious and fastidious, the sort of man who bundles up when he goes out on balmy days that might possibly turn cold. He's patient. He listens carefully, the way old people do when they have been accused of being forgetful. When Ben goes to New Jersey to persuade Al to do the TV show, the young man says he knows that Al hates Willy. Al thinks a moment and then qualifies the statement. "I can't stand him," he says sweetly, "but I don't hate him."

This has the design of a typical Simon wisecrack that could be said by almost any character in any Simon play, but it becomes a particular reference point for a particular character as it's delivered by Burns.

Now approaching 80 and having spent most of his career as straight man for his wife, the late Gracie Allen, Burns gives an astonishingly legitimate performance funny performance in "The Sunshine Boys." It entertains while it underscores our wish that Simon had given Al and Willy, or Burns and Matthau, a script with a little more heft to it.

Al and Willy are most appealing characters and Burns and Matthau are in top form, limited only by the shape of the comedy that is comprised of several encounters, each of which is essentially the same and ends with Willy having a tantrum and Al looking as surprised and innocent as only the guilty can.

There's a great deal more to such a relationship than Simon cares to explore, and I suspect that my disappointment with the film (slight but real) is a result of all the contradictions that Burns and Matthau succeed in suggesting within the Simon frame and the TV situation-comedy sensibility.

The casting of Burns with Matthau was a brilliant move and a risky one. Each might have made the other look foolish. Burns is old enough to be Matthau's father. He is truly old and yet he seems to be in marvelous shape. Matthau, with the help of make-up, looks not so much old as different, and in bad shape (which becomes a point of the script). Matthau is a dynamic actor, even when he's playing old men. Dynamism is his style.

• • •

Burns is from another, simpler acting era. Yet the combination works. The two men complement each other across the years. In Al and Willy's version of the Gallagher & Shean "Dr. Kronkeit" sketch you realize that it's Burns who's setting the rhythm for the two performances. Without Burns, Matthau's Willy comes very close to suggesting an outsized Mr. Magoo character. It's not that he bumps into things. He simply never listens. As Burns once paced Gracie Allen's jokes, so does he pace Matthau, sometimes giving him the lead, at other times gently drawing back so that Matthau must play to him.

The role that Burns plays was originally to have been played by the late Jack Benny. As much as I admired Benny I can't now imagine him in this role, having seen the quietly triumphant way that Burns handles it. Jack was one of the wittiest comedians we ever produced, even without the writers he always said he needed. His timing was unmatched by anyone in the business, but he was never a terrific actor. His public personality would have gotten in the way of this characterization. It was so pronounced that it would have gotten in the way even if it had been suppressed.

Burns has no such problems or, if he had, they are no longer apparent. Who or what is responsible? Herbert Ross, the director, I suspect, as well as Simon and Matthau, and, of course, all those years with Gracie.

1975 N 9, II:17:1

'Flute': Fable of Fun

THE MAGIC FLUTE, directed by Ingmar Bergman; opera by Wolfgang Amadeus Mozart, adapted for the screen by Mr. Bergman; in Swedish with English subtitles; produced by Mr. Bergman; director of photography, Sven Nykvist; conductor, Eric Ericson, with the Swedish State Broadcasting Network Symphony; distributed by the Surrosate Releasing Company. Running time 134 minutes. At the Coronet Theater, Third Avenue at 59th Street. This film has been rated G.
Sarastro ....Ulrik Gold
Tamino ....Josef Kostlinger
Speaker ....Erik Saeden
Queen of The Night ......Birgit Nordin
Pamina ....Irma Urrila
Papageno ....Hakan Hagegard
Papagena ....Elisabeth Erikson
Monostatos ....Ragnar Ulfung
Three Ladies ....Britt Marie Aruhn,
    Kirsten Vaupel, Birgitta Smiding
Three Youths ....Urban Malmberg
    Erland von Heine, Ansgar Krook
Two Priests ....Gosta Pruzelius,
Ulf Johansson

By VINCENT CANBY

It's grand opera. It's a Freemasonry fable. It was made for Swedish television and reportedly cost about $650,000, which would barely cover the expenses of a Hollywood motorcycle movie. It's based on a work with a magnificent score but with a libretto whose second act seems to have forgotten how the first act started.

Yet Ingmar Bergman's screen version of Mozart's "The Magic Flute," which opened at the Coronet yesterday, is an absolutely dazzling film entertainment, so full of beauty, intelligence, wit and fun that it becomes a testimonial not only to man's possibilities but also to his high spirits.

●

All of the best Bergman films have been about some aspect of love (often its absence), but "The Magic Flute" is virtually an act of it.

It is, first and foremost, Mr. Bergman's exuberant tribute to Mozart's genius, with full, amused recognition of the inconsistencies in the Schikaneder libretto. Mr. Bergman hasn't set out to interpret "The Magic Flute" but rather to present it as it originally was, bursting with the life of an exquisite stage production as it would look within the physical limitations of an 18th-century court theater.

This approach recalls the Laurence Olivier production of "Henry V," though there are marked differences. The Bergman "Flute" begins as if it were simply the record of a single performance of the opera on a golden summer evening in a theater set in a royal park. During the overture the camera scans the faces in the contemporary audience, all of whose members, with several obvious exceptions, look exceptionally, particularly Swedish. The recurring expression of the film itself is that of an enraptured little girl (said to be the director's daughter) as she watches the opera unfold.

As the overture ends and the curtain goes up, the camera slides over the footlights into a magical world of painted backdrops and other 18-century stage conventions. Unlike the Olivier "Henry V," the Bergman "Flute" never moves through the painted backdrops into a realistic world beyond. Though the film, after having established its stage conventions, enlarges upon them and, once or twice, abandons them when it suits the director's purpose, the Bergman production is virtually a hymn in praise of theatricality and the efficacy of art.

At the opera's intermission, the camera catches Tamino and Pamina, the opera's two young lovers, playing chess in a dressing room, while the evil Queen of the Night smokes languidly under a backstage "no smoking" sign. Mr. Bergman, who loves Mozart and the theater, has special fondness for the performers who work so hard for our joy.

●

"The Magic Flute" was first performed in a theater near Vienna on Sept. 30, 1791, just a few weeks before Mozart died. Though "Don Giovanni" is the grandest of Mozart's operas, "The Magic Flute" is the more ideally romantic, the work of a man who, while dying, was able to compose the kind of profoundly lyrical and witty music that almost convinces a lot of people—including me—that opera should begin and end with Mozart.

Mr. Bergman treats the odd Schikaneder libretto fairly straight, neither apologizing for it nor patronizing it. Tamino, the young prince who, in the first scene, is charged by the Queen of the Night with the rescue of her daughter from the wicked sorcerer, Sarastro, winds up by becoming a member of Sarastro's mystical priesthood, the members of which are the protectors of truth, beauty and wisdom. Somewhere near the end of the first act, the Queen of the Night has become the villainess of the piece, and "The Magic Flute" has turned into what was, in its day, quite bold propaganda for Freemasonry.

I hesitate to say even this much about the story of "The Magic Flute" since it gives no indication of the opera's phenomenal beauty and good humor. Reduced to its showbiz essentials, it's about the triumph of the perfect love of Tamino and Pamina, the daughter of the vengeful Queen of the Night, with the help of a little magic and a lot of steadfastness of purpose.

The aural quality of the production is superb. Mr. Bergman recorded the music before he began shooting the film, thus allowing the actors to lip-synch the lyrics (which are in Swedish, not German) instead of belting them out on-camera. The system works beautifully because of technological magic I don't understand and because the actors are lip-synching their own voices.

●

He has also found singers who both look and sound right, including his Tamino (Josef Kostlinger), who resembles a prince in a Maxfield Parrish mural, and a beautiful Pamina (Irma Urrila), who looks like a young Liv Ullman. He is especially fortunate, too, in his choice of a Papageno (Hakan Hagegard), who manages to be simultaneously robust and comic without ever being opera-silly.

The film is full of memorable moments, some moving, as in the first-act Pamina-Papageno duet, and some gravely funny, as when three little boys in a festively decorated 18th-century balloon caution Tamino to be steadfast, silent and wise, which are probably the three things that any three little boys you or I know would find most difficult to do. The camera, in close-up, never misses a gesture.

Make no mistake: This "Magic Flute" is no uneasy cross-breed of art forms. It's a triumphant film in its own right.

1975 N 12, 50:1

SPACE & TIME. Five short abstract films at the Whitney Museum of American Art. "Bringing Lights Forward" and "Vertical and Receding Lines" by David Haxton; "Silent Reversal", "Studies in Chronovision" and "Still Lives" by Louis Hock. Running time: 67 minutes. Through Nov. 18.

By RICHARD EDER

Art as wallpaper is all very well until the wallpaper covers all four walls and you can't get out.

Maybe this exaggerates the effect of the five abstract pieces that began a week's run yesterday in the Whitney Museum's Film Series. The Whitney provides a door, after all. But although leaving a movie is a response of some kind, it is not one strictly within the esthetic of movie-going.

●

A book can be shut and reopened; readers can look away from a page and return to it. With abstract painting, viewers can approach, recede, pause, walk along, come back. Time and intensity are totally within their their control.

Spectators' self-management is immensely important with abstract art. The reaction is so private, the rhythms to be caught so elusive and personal that you must be in charge of your own flight into and around it.

Movies don't allow this kind of autonomy. They are a guided tour of the most imperious kind. Transported at so many feet per minute and for so many minutes through the abrupt light flashes of Louis Hock's work, or the milky opaqueness of David Haxton, we are being literally railroaded through someone else's fantasy.

In the first of the Hock

Josef Kostlinger and Irma Urrila

works, "Silent Reversal," the railroading is gentle and, in any case, appropriate. Railroad trains—elevated railroad trains—shunt back and forth into a station. The rhythm of their movements, the shifting reflections in their glass windows, the motionless skyline behind, make a soft and haunting pattern. There is no sound, and that helps the effect. On the other hand, Mr. Hock creates the visual equivalent of a chittering soundtrack: a zigzag white band that follows along on top of the trains.

Mr. Hock's other two films are more strident. "Studies in Chronovision" plays jerkily with changes of light on objects and surfaces. "Still Lives" flicks 16 minutes worth of a road and parking lot at us, each frame followed by a blackout until our eyes are virtually goaded out of our heads. It is endless and intolerable.

Mr. Haxton has made two films with a single effect. He uses underlit negative: the result is a general whiteness into which smudgy figures disappear and reappear. In one, the figure is rearranging three lamps. In the second, the figure is stringing a rope to a frame. As the figure recedes it disappears.

It is restful, especially in contrast with the Hock film. The smudgy movements and the enveloping white make a pretty combination. But it is like looking through a particularly murky aquarium at fish we cannot identify and will never eat.

1975 N 13, 50:1

STARDUST, directed by Michael Apted; screenplay by Ray Connolly; produced by David Puttnam and Sandy Lieberson; director of photography, Tony Richmond; editor, Mike Bradsell; a Goodtime Enterprises production, distributed by Columbia Pictures. Running time: 107 minutes. At the Columbia 1 Theater, Second Avenue at 64th Street, and other theaters. This film has been rated R.
Jim MacLaine .... David Essex
Mike .... Adam Faith
Austin .... Larry Hagman
J. D. Clover .... Keith Moon
Colin Day .... Marty Wilde
Danielle .... Ines Des Longchamps

By VINCENT CANBY

Jim MacLaine (David Essex), an English rock star, is bored, bored, bored. He's the most popular entertainer in England and America. He has a sweet, pretty French mistress, a wife so noble that she won't take money from him, and good chums in the members of his group who call themselves the Stray Cats. But happiness does not buy happiness.

That seems to be the point of the terrible English movie, "Stardust," which opened yesterday at the Columbia I and other theaters. The film follows Jim's climb up the ladder to success with such solemnity you suspect it must be joking. "I'm tired of being locked up in planes and bathrooms, hiding from the people who've made me rich," Jim says in one of his bursts of annotated anguish. After all, he tells us without a flicker of a grin, all he's ever wanted to do was to write an opera deifying women.

•

Unfortunately for us he does write that opera, which is also referred to as a rock symphony, and from what we see and hear of it, it seems that Jim has been cribbing from Radio City Music Hall's Easter stage show when the Rockettes dress up like nuns. It's awful. It's also an immense success, viewed by some 300 million people around the world by satellite. From the proceeds of that venture, Jim buys a castle in Spain, where his unhappiness knows no bounds.

"Stardust" is the sequel to an earlier English rock film, "That'll Be the Day," which also starred Mr. Essex and told the story of Jim MacLaine from his grubby beginnings until he bought his first electric guitar.

Sometimes the story of Jim and the Stray Cats sounds as if it were meant to recall the rise of the Beatles. Sometimes it suggests the stories of other rock personalities. Mostly, though, it's just superficial claptrap, badly acted (except for Adam Faith, who plays Jim's manager), foolishly written and even more foolishly directed.

1975 N 13, 52:5

Fresh and Funny Films on Indonesia and Cuba

By RICHARD EDER

Two men meet at a party. The big one puts out his hand and booms: "I'm J. Peter Throgmorton. That's me." The small, sallow one puts out his hand and mumbles: "I'm Lycurgus Threep. That isn't me."

Michael Rubbo is a Canadian who makes Threeplike documentaries. His theme, as he goes from place to place, is the impossibility of getting at very much reality in any of them.

Most documentaries proclaim, stridently or politely: "This is it." or at least, "This is part of it." In his two funny fresh and mostly admirable films on Indonesia and Cuba, Mr. Rubbo's message is: "This isn't it."

The films are being shown by Film Forum at the Vandam Theater through Sunday and, again, Thursday through Nov. 23 at 8 P.M.

Mr. Rubbo photographs and asks questions and then asks himself what significance or truth or relevance can possibly be contained in what he has filmed or asked. He and his crew set down their camera in a jammed slum in Jakarta or a mental hospital near Havana. They interrupt life, slide off the realities and leave their footprints all around.

But most documentaries carefully conceal their footprints. Mr. Rubbo photographs his.

In the film on Indonesia "Wet Earth and Warm People," for example, where Mr. Rubbo is trying to encompass the vast, horrendous population-poverty cycle, we see him visibly lost on a swarming street, wondering what possible question or approach could even begin to make a dent.

Husky, copper-bearded, direct, he has that self-awareness so rare in both journalists and film makers. He knows his simple presence is enough to scare off the tenuous clues he is seeking.

"My cameraman looks like a small colonialist," he muses, standing beside a Landrover from which his crew is unloading equipment. "I look like one of the Dutch soldiers who used to be here."

He tries: he puts up a line of inquiry. For example he learns that the Jakarta authorities are trying to get rid of the swarms of pedicabs, their place presumably to be taken by taxis. This seems monstrous to him: the one available asset—millions of unemployed legs—to be replaced by expensive and polluting gasoline engines.

He goes about interviewing a pedicab driver, the Mayor, the Chief of Police; trying to ask why. The answers are vague, bland and polite. Gradually his question fades; so does his own certainty that it is a question to be asked.

•

So he lets his camera roam. There is a splendid sequence showing him projecting a film in a village: in the tropical, bug-ridden night the villagers stare big-eyed at a demonstration of how to build an igloo.

Even more surreal is the running relationship of good will and incomprehension between Mr. Rubbo and Indonesia's chief of police. Toward the end he shows the police chief and a few friends, decked out in bright-colored pareus, crooning "The Way You Look at Me" on national television.

"How much it's calculated is hard to say, but I do know he's trying to change the image of the police," Mr. Rubbo comments soberly. He doesn't mock the incongruousness of the scene. He wonders at it, and at his own wonderment. He doesn't spare his own foolishness, and out of it he has constructed a movie that has a beginning of wisdom.

"Waiting for Fidel," is stronger and tighter but basically it takes the same approach. It is about Cuba, in a way, but it is also about the difficulty in seeing Cuba for what it may be. Again, Mr. Rubbo holds his camera no higher than his own head; it is a perplexed, ambiguous head.

What he is filming, in fact, is a traveling argument. His trip to Cuba is taken in the company of two antagonists. One is Joseph Smallwood, a former Premier of Nova Scotia, a lifelong Socialist with a bubbling enthusiasm for the new Cuba. The other is Geoffrey Stirling, a self-made millionaire who is financing the trip and who wields a fierce suspicion of what he is seeing.

It is part holiday, part adventure, part inquiry, and it starts with a naive burst of enthusiasm. They have been promised an interview with Fidel Castro. And almost from the first shots it is clear to any journalist who has been promised the same thing that they are in the category of the middling honored visitor: They will get endless hospitality and no interview.

While they wait, they take strenuous guided tours around the island. They muse and argue about what they have seen: The fascination is in how little two shrewd and experienced men like Mr. Smallwood and Mr. Stirling really do see.

Mr. Rubbo likes the Cuban revolution, but he does not anchor the film to his liking. Perplexity is his instrument for measuring the world, and he never lets go of it.

•

There are disadvantages in the method: a certain blandness, a sameness. If Mr. Rubbo gets around to doing Lapland or Borneo, they may end up more alike than different. He will be standing before the camera in seeming disarray, saying: "This is Lapland (or Borneo). But it isn't."

But these disadvantages should not mask his accomplishment. Most documentaries are speeches to the audience or stories told to the audience. His come close to being a dialogue.

1975 N 14, 24:1

THE OTHER SIDE OF THE MOUNTAIN, directed by Larry Peerce; screenplay by David Seltzer, based on the book "A Long Way Up" by E. G. Valens; produced by Edward S. Feldman; director of photography, David M. Walsh; editor, Eve Newman; distributed by Universal Pictures. Running time: 103 minutes. At the Columbia 2 Theater, Second Avenue near 64th Street, and other theaters. This film has been rated PG.
Jill Kinmont .... Marilyn Hassett
Dick Buek .... Beau Bridges
Audra-Jo .... Belinda J. Montgomery
June Kinmont .... Nan Martin
Bill Kinmont .... William Bryant
Dave McCoy .... Dabney Coleman
Buddy Werner .... Bill Vint
Lee Zadroga .... Hampton Fancher
Dr. Pittman .... William Roerick

By VINCENT CANBY

Just a little more than 20 years ago Jill Kinmont, a 20-year-old California girl, was a sure bet for the United States Olympic ski team. Then, in the course of a trial competition in Utah, Jill took a fall, breaking her neck and becoming paralyzed from the chest down. "The Other Side of the Mountain," which opened yesterday at the Columbia 2 and other theaters, is the story of Miss Kinmont's fight to survive as a paraplegic and to find new purpose in her life. According to the film, Jill Kinmont's life really looked very much like a film in which one counts not the years but the lap dissolves, in which every important moment is underscored by a heavenly choir consisting of one voice (Olivia Newton-John's) that, on cue, intones depressing bits of lahrymose philosophy.

•

The life came first, but the movie seems to have less interest in Miss Kinmont than in the devices of romantic fiction that reduce particularity of feeling to a sure-fire formula designed to elicit sentimental responses. If you go to see "The Other Side of the Mountain," load up on handkerchiefs and leave your wits at home. Should you have even half a one with you, you'll be ahead of David Seltzer's screenplay at almost any plastic point.

I suspect that Larry Peerce, the director, knew exactly what he was doing in constructing this film the way he did. The audience it's aimed at likes to know in advance each new heartbreak, no matter how clumsily the hints are heaved at them. Such foreknowledge is reassuring and very much a part of the pleasure of weeper movies.

Knowing the kind of movie he wanted to make, Mr. Peerce has worked with a singleminded purpose to achieve it. He has an extremely pretty, efficient young actress named Marilyn Hassett to play Jill, and he has Beau Bridges to play the daredevil of a fellow—skier, motorcyclist, sky diver—who loves Jill through thick and thin. In a film like this, Mr. Bridges's appeaance s the sort of certificate of honor the audience looks for.

•

There are some beautiful ski scenes and some terrifying scenes in the hospital. The movie also contains a couple of moments of genuine feeling—all set in a Los Angeles center for the rehabilitation of the handicapped—that raise the over-all tone. Mostly, though, the inspiration one detects in "The Other Side of the Mountain" is the inspiration to make the kind of prefabricated romantic movie that every few years turns the American public into a bunch of blubbering idiots.

1975 N 15, 20:1

THE STORY · OF O, directed by Just Jaeckin; adapted by Sebastien Japrisot from the novel by Pauline Reage; camera supervision by Robert Fraisse; music by Pierre Bachelet; executive producers, Gerard Lorin and Eric Rochart; an Allied Artists release. Running time: 97 minutes. This film has been classified X.

O	Corinne Clery
Rene	Udo Kier
Sir Stephen	Anthony Steel
Pierre	Jean Gaven
Anne-Marie	Christiane Minazzoli
Therese	Martine Kelly
Maitre 2	Jean-Pierre Adreani
Commandant	Gabriel Gattano
Jacqueline	Li Sellgren

By RICHARD EDER

The proscribed becomes the permitted; the permitted becomes the prescribed; and the prescribed becomes a great bore.

A decade or two ago, "L'Histoire d'O" was a French underground classic. A year or two ago it was assigned reading at Yale and Wellesley. Now it is an expensive movie filled with elegant drapery and undrapery — the nudity is so fastidiously posed as to seem fully clothed—arcane sexual philosophizing and the same general relation to the erotic that pink has to red.

"The Story of O"—it opened yesterday at the Baronet with an English title and subtitles—is by Just Jaeckin, who also made that X-rated suburban marshmallow "Emmanuelle."

The theme of "O" was, in fact, a model for "Emmanuelle." It expounds sex as an élitist religon, with hierarchical initiations and a leaden ritual lightened by cruelty.

It is as far-fetched as "Emmanuelle" but less foolish, mainly because it is based on a book of some strength and subtlety. On the other hand it is less sensual. The book by Pauline Réage—said to be a pseudonym for a male member of the French Academy—is almost an abstraction. It is three peculiar syllogisms and a perverse hiccup looped onto the philosophic works of the Marquis de Sade.

The film, for all its rich photography and amber-lit bodies, is similarly abstract.

It is little more than an attempt to illustrate the book, with the bodies as colored plates.

The plot is a complex series of sadomasochistic transactions. O, played by Corinne Clery with fashion-plate beauty and numbness, is delivered by her lover to a series of sexual torments and humiliations held in a country house filled with other woman initiates and their male "instructors."

The whole thing is run for the benefit of a rich Englishman called Sir Stephen, and after a series of whippings and rape-seductions, O has her affections transferred to him. Once he is her lover, Sir Stephen hands her over to other men. In the process, O is transformed from postulant to initiator in her own right.

•

It is filmed with considerable discretion. Both the beatings and the sex scenes are done with more emphasis on facial expressions than bodily mechanics. Climaxes of pain or passion come precisely as Hollywood love scenes used to: signaled by swelling music and beating drums.

The restraint is a relief, in a way, but it doesn't do much for the monotony. There is some intellectual excitement in the book: the movie gives the effect of somebody reading the book out loud very slowly and with immense emphasis.

1975 N 15, 20:1

FILM VIEW

VINCENT CANBY

Bergman's 'Magic Flute': Funny, Moving and Sexy

THE most startling aspect of Ingmar Bergman's screen version of Mozart's "The Magic Flute" is the ease with which this enchanting fable of a film—simultaneously effervescent and haunting—fits so immediately into a filmography that includes such works as "The Hour of The Wolf," "Shame," "The Passion of Anna," "Cries and Whispers" and "Scenes From A Marriage."

"The Magic Flute," Mozart's last opera, contains some of the composer's most melodic, passionate and witty music, as well as a libretto by Schikaneder that doesn't always make the greatest of sense. It was first performed in a theater on the outskirts of Vienna on Sept. 30, 1791, only a few weeks before Mozart's death, and received reviews that on Broadway would mean a six-day run and quick oblivion. Goethe liked it but most of the professional critics felt that it was the sort of show that was carried by its special effects, all of which were fairly standard to the theater of the period.

Its book is schizophrenic. "The Magic Flute" begins as one kind of opera and ends as quite another. When the curtain goes up, Tamino, a prince, is being pursued through the forest by a serpent, who is subsequently destroyed by the handmaidens of the Queen of The Night while Tamino is in a temporary swoon. When Tamino comes to again, the handmaidens and the Queen of the Night herself, all equally taken by Tamino's good looks, dispatch Tamino to rescue Pamina, the Queen's daughter who has been abducted by a sorcerer named Sarastro. So far, so standard. The Queen of The Night is a woman wronged. Sarastro is an evil genius with a fondness for virginal princesses.

Yet everything suddenly changes: as Tamino learns, Sarastro is the high priest of a cult that serves art, beauty and wisdom. He is far from being a villain. He is the chief of chiefs of a mystic shrine. He had abducted Pamina to save her from her vengeful mother and in the knowledge that a perfect youth, such as Tamino, would come fetch her and, having passed the trials of air, fire and water, would carry on the leadership of the forces of light against those of the Queen of The Night (the forces of darkness).

It's necessary to go into plot in this detail because the plot is about as silly as the opera ever is. If you've ever heard the music, you know it transcends all contradictions, and when you've seen Bergman's sparkling film version, you won't even think about them. Those he doesn't reconcile aren't really worth worrying about.

I hesitate to freight Bergman's "The Magic Flute" with analysis that can dilute the pure joy of experiencing it. Bergman has cut some of its emphasis on freemasonry, and though he has eliminated the references to Isis and Osiris in Sarastro's arias, the film remains Mozart's opera in spirit

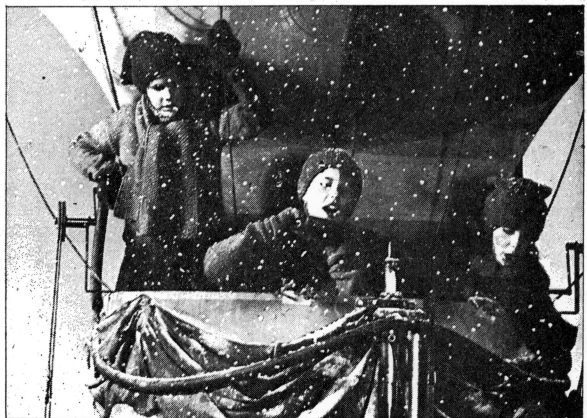

Per B. Adolphson

Bergman's boy-guides on an airborne "equivalent of a Mississippi raft"

as well as execution. The extraordinary thing is that without fiddling on Bergman's part the opera becomes the mythology, the prehistoric past, of Bergman's contemporary characters. The perfect love that is granted to Tamino and Pamina after they endure their trials is the perfect love that just eludes all Bergman's characters today. They fail, and make accommodations of one sort or another. Tamino and Pamina succeed, and seeing them succeed in "The Magic Flute" deepens our understanding of the losses suffered by those Bergman characters who are not so steadfast. "The Magic Flute" is not a parenthetical item in Bergman's career; it's a major achievement.

Cinematically, it's exquisite, as brilliant in its conception and discipline as Olivier's "Henry V," which comes quickly to mind since Bergman prepares us for the opera by setting it in a perfect replica of an 18th-century court theater, introducing us during the overture to the contemporary audience watching it, before gently sliding over the apron of the stage into the handpainted backdrops. Unlike Olivier, Bergman never fades into a real world beyond the backdrops. He preserves the stage conventions of the day, though he takes full advantage of those of film.

• • •

One of Bergman's most important decisions, and one that works under his direction, was to have the singers pre-record their voices and then lip-sync the lyrics while the film was being shot. The key to the success of this decision was in selecting singers who are not only actors but who also possess fine voices. They do, which allows us to react to the voices and the magnificent music without being put off by blank faces or by the kind of neutral, directionless quality of most post-synchronized soundtracks. This "Magic Flute" is aurally superb.

It's also hugely funny and, on occasion, most moving and—this may never have been said about "The Magic Flute" before—sexy. In Josef Kostlinger and Irma Urrila he has a Tamino and Pamina who not only can sing but who look untarnished—she's a young Liv Ullmann and he's a prince out of a Maxfield Parrish mural. Bergman also has an enormously robust clown in his Papageno (Hakan Hagegard) with the kind of fine voice that, on cue, can be believably romantic, as in the first act duet with Pamina, and later funny.

Comedy in grand opera is something we usually put up with, but in Bergman's "Magic Flute" it explodes naturally, whether in the Papageno-Papagana interludes, or in effects that Bergman has contrived in keeping with the spirit of the work. The three boys who guide and protect Tamino and Pamina have a high old time navigating around the stage in a marvelous 18th-century balloon, a sort of operatic equivalent of a 19th-century Mississippi raft. The wild beasts of the forest are actors in a magnificent teddy-bear (or teddy-dragon) costumes. When the singers come upon a particularly pious sentiment, they not only sing it but they haul down (or up) a title card on which the thought has been carefully spelled out for the benefit of those who may be hard of hearing.

Bergman's love for "The Magic Flute" is both protective and illuminating. He makes one quite startling addition to the text—the revelation that Sarastro and the Queen of The Night are father and mother to Pamina, which simply ties up one of Schikaneder's loose ends—but mostly he persuades us to appreciate the opera the way he does.

Not only do we see it, but we hear it, and we come out of the theater feeling years younger for it. What a piece of work is a man! Mozart, most especially. The demonstration of genius is a tonic. In one of the film's nicest moments, during the overture when the camera is cutting in tempo among the faces in the audience, we have a fleeting glimpse of Bergman himself. It's not a Hitchcockian gag. It's a declaration of the director's position and resolve.

Correction: As has been pointed out by several dozen readers so far, the comedy team known for its "Dr. Kronkhite" sketch was Smith and Dale, not, as I wrote last week, Gallagher and Shean.

1975 N 16, II:15:1

How to Make A Castro Movie Without Castro

By DAVID DENBY

Most film portraits of Cuba are inadequately detailed or ideologically blinkered. Indeed, it may be impossible to make a fully informed movie on the subject: the Cubans don't necessarily *want* to be seen accurately. But now, at least, the outsiders' obsession with Cuba has been captured on film. "Waiting for Fidel," which will play at the Film Forum in its new home at 15 Vandam Street in SoHo for two long weekends this month (Nov. 13-16 and 20-23), is a highly inventive and at times excruciatingly funny documentary about self-deception and the limitations of curiosity.

•

Produced by the National Film Board of Canada, it was directed by Michael Rubbo, an Australian-born, American-trained filmmaker in his 30's whose methods and works are controversial among film people in Canada and Australia; for reasons of Canadian diffidence and American arrogance, he is virtually unknown in this country. (One previous Rubbo film, "Sad Song of Yellow Skin," which played the Film Forum in early 1972 and received a rave from a Times movie critic, is by far the best film on Vietnam during the war years, I've seen. Why hasn't it been shown on public television?)

Rubbo may not have known what his film would be about when he began work because he never operates from preconceived strategies. Always present in the films as observer, narrator, participant, he goes out with the crew and has an adventure, finding his emphasis as he shoots. Unlike the standard American TV documentary, with its rigid billboarding of the entire topic in the first few minutes and its brisk point A, point B organization, Rubbo's films work toward their themes slowly, obliquely, through a deceptively casual accumulation of detail and incident. When he got to Vietnam, rather than chasing after generals and diplomats, Rubbo photographed some orphaned

David Denby is a freelance film critic.

streetboys, a prostitute's funeral, a group of eccentric Buddhist monks on an island in the Mekong Delta. At first puzzled by the selection of "marginal" subjects, I realized by the end that Rubbo had been working at the central issues all the time: the film captured the disintegration of Vietnamese social values under the pressure of war.

•

Having received a promise of an interview with Fidel Castro, Rubbo went to Havana last year with his crew and two Canadians—Geoff Stirling, a self-made millionaire who owns a chain of radio and TV stations, and Joseph Smallwood, former socialist Prime Minister of Newfoundland. The two men are like comic characters out of Dickens. Stirling is an up-to-date, Hollywood-style operator, complete with dark tan, lean body, arcane exercises (he stands on his head to "relieve the pressure on his organs"), and lessons from "Jonathan Livingston Seagull." Older, shorter, dowdier, Smallwood is a 30's type socialist (anti-Stalinist division), now out of power, ridiculed by New Left university students, a man who knows he'll never see his vision of paradise on earth—socialism and freedom combined—during his own lifetime.

•

Stirling, the liberal capitalist, has come to Cuba to find examples of the harmful effects of collectivism on human character, and to package the Castro interview commercially (he has money in the project). Smallwood, the old socialist, has come to admire Cuban achievements in housing and education and to make himself available for diplomatic overtures to the north. Lodged by the Cuban government in a sumptuous hacienda and plied with food and wine by a brace of servants, Rubbo, Stirling and Smallwood spend their time composing sample questions for Fidel and awaiting the great man's summons. Occasionally they make forays outside to argue with ("interview") some students, workers, mental patients, etc., but mainly they just wait, and wait . . . and that is the movie.

A joke? A way of making a film out of a non-event? It is certainly a joke, but in this case the "event" is the exploration of character. Clearly Stirling and Smallwood, like so many other ideologists contemplating Cuba, would rather argue the merits of capitalism versus socialism than actually encounter a functioning socialist state. Who needs knowledge when one's ideas are so clear? For the ordinary TV-documentary maker the trip would have been a fiasco without the Castro interview, but Rubbo had the intuition to keep shooting and to find his real subject and tone (absurdist comedy) in the "trivial" material others would have thrown out.

Almost all of Rubbo's films have combined exploration of an alien culture and mockery of the observer-explorer (including himself). Awkward, discursive, personal, his style may embarrass audiences accustomed to the smoothly impersonal, "authoritative" tone of network documentaries and foreign correspondents. To such viewers, Rubbo's self-exposure may look like self-indulgence.

•

Rubbo's style is a form of candor, a way of presenting the situation of filmmaking at face value. In "Wet Earth, Warm People" (also on the current Film Forum program), an examination of comtemporary Indonesia, Rubbo shows us several "unprofessional" sequences of people in Jakarta gathering around the crew and laughing, pointing, carrying on. When Rubbo's narration ruefully admits the impossibility of getting impoverished Asians to act "naturally" in front of Westerners carrying complicated equipment, we think he's merely granting the obvious. But then the relationship between filmmaker and subject becomes thematic: in one sequence Rubbo foolishly meddles in the life of a man in Jakarta thrown out of work by modernization; in another, he tries to show a movie in a remote village and winds up humiliating a local leader (a power generator fails); finally we realize that Rubbo's connection with technology, with its tremendous symbolic and actual importance in a country like Indonesia, is cutting him off from the very people he photographs. It's a chastening film.

•

Of course this combination of inward and outward probing has appeared before, at more ambitious levels of social investigation, among writers as diverse as Claude

Lévi-Strauss ("Tristes Tropiques"), Susan Sontag ("Trip to Hanoi"), and Erik Erikson ("Gandhi's Truth"), all of whom have begun their reports on alien cultures and ideas with an accounting of personal histories and vulnerabilities. One doesn't want to sound the trumpets too loudly, since Rubbo isn't nearly as sophisticated as these people, but he's part of the same process. Like them, he is attacking the complacency of conventional "observers" as a way of reasserting the right to observe. In "Waiting for Fidel," Michael Rubbo has made a minor classic of this self-conscious but necessary genre. ■

1975 N 16, II:15:7

THE EARTH IS A SINFUL SONG, directed and produced by Rauni Mollberg; screenplay by Mr. Mollberg, Pirjo Honkasalo and Panu Rajala, from the novel by Timo K. Mukka; photographed by Kari Sohlberg and Hannu Peltomaa; editor, Marjatta Leporinne. Distributed by Seaberg Films. Running time: 105 minutes. This film has not been rated. At the Eighth Street Playhouse.
WITH Maritta Vitamaki and Pauli Jauhojarvi.

Judging by the readily available evidence, films from Finland arrive here without about the same frequency as kind words from Moscow or Peking. So it is an occasion of more than ordinary note to record not only the arrival of such a film, but also the arrival of a good one.

"The Earth Is a Sinful Song" is the somewhat misleadingly lyrical title of this film, which opens today at the Eighth Street Playhouse. It is based on a novel set in Finnish Lapland in 1947-48 and concerns itself, in unusually intimate detail, with the lives of the inhabitants of a small, rustic community, and with particular emphasis on one family—an old man, his unhappy son, haggard daughter-in-law and teen-age granddaughter.

One is tempted to call these lives harsh and brutal. But that would be an urban judgment, passed upon people who exist so close to nature that the appearance of an automobile about midway through the film jars a viewer. No, these lives are simply different, stripped almost bare of what we like to call the amenities of civilibation. They have no luxuries. Hardship is omnipresent. Death comes among them frequently, taking people and animals. Pleasures are simple—an outdoor dance (where a drifter is killed); drink; religion; the sauna; and sex, indulged in and depicted with a minimum of fuss.

The seasons pass. Lives change. People grow up, grow older, die, are killed, are born. The cycle is ancient and eternal; the landscape is literal paradise and figurative hell. Rauni Mollberg, who wrote, produced and directed this film, which was shown at the festivals in Cannes, London, Edinburg, Berlin and Locarno, gives us stark lives and an impression of witnessing a documentary.

Events—a fatal calving, a reindeer roundup, an initiation into sex, a community religious service, even a party—tend to be joyless and devoid of sentiment. Mr. Mollberg seems to save his comment on life for the camerawork by Kari Sohlberg and Hannu Peltomaa. And what they seem to be saying, without incongruity, in scene after scene that dazzles the eye with the glory of nature or caresses the faces of strangers in a way that makes the heart care, is that the human animal is profoundly beautiful.

LAWRENCE VAN GELDER—

1975 N 19, 22:3

THE HUMAN FACTOR, directed by Edward Dymtryk; screenplay by Tom Hunter and Peter Powell; director of photography, Qusama Rawi; editor, Alan Strachen; music, Enrico Moriconi; distributed by Bryanston Films. At the Rivoli, Trans-Lux East, UA 85th Street and Loews 83d Street Theaters. Running time: 96 minutes. This film has been classified R.

John Kinsdale	George Kennedy
Mike McAllister	John Mills
Dr. Lupo	Raf Vallone
General Fuller	Arthur Franz
Janice	Rita Tushingham
Kamal	Frank Avianca
Pidgeon	Haydee Politoff
Taylor	Tom Hunter
Edmonds	Barry Sullivan

By A. H. WEILER

Vigilante justice, one of the oldest movie staples, is given improbable and gory treatment in "The Human Factor," which opened yesterday at local theaters. The idea of an intellectual's taking the law into his own hands is no newer than, say, last year's "Death Wish." But "The Human Factor," despite technological trappings, political innuendo and colorful Italian locales, evolves as a manipulated affair that is no more convincing than its lackluster direction, pedestrian performances and jerry-built script.

A modicum of tension is initially generated when George Kennedy, playing an American computer expert with NATO forces in Naples, discovers that the wanton slaughter of his wife and three children is the work of terrorists who, it is dimly indicated, will continue killing expatriate Americans at random if "political prisoners" aren't freed.

●

If our shocked hero deserves sympathy, it is diluted when, aided by a good deal of somewhat unbelievable computer sleuthing, he is able not only to unearth the gangsters but also to mow them down singly or en masse in bloodbath style. The gang members, led by Frank Avianca, who is also the film's producer, are a blatantly callous lot who stack the emotional cards in favor of Mr. Kennedy.

His drive for vengeance may be conceivable, but it's not entirely logical. Despite the pleas of John Mills, as his NATO scientific sidekick, to let the police do the dirty work, the highly intellectual Mr. Kennedy emerges in effect as a violent man who, under stress, doesn't seem to be much better than the murderers he systematically seeks out and destroys.

●

His characterization of a man racked by grief and hate is generally restrained and occasionally touching. But Mr. Mills as well as Raf Vallone, as the police inspector; Rita Tushingham, as Mr. Kennedy's colleague; Barry Sullivan, as an American Embassy official, and Arthur Franz, as the NATO general, are serious but perfunctory in largely surface stints.

In this case, "The Human Factor" is no more persuasive than its contrived and bloody melodrama.

1975 N 20, 50:4

ONE FLEW OVER THE CUCKOO'S NEST, directed by Milcs Forman; screenplay by Lawrence Hauben and Bo Goldman, based on the novel by Ken Kesey; produced by Saul Zaentz and Michael Douglas; director of photography, Haskell Wexler; additional photography by Bill Butler and William Fraker; music, Jack Nitzsche; supervising film editor, Richard Chew; editors, Lynzee Klingman and Sheldon Kahn; a Fantasy Films production, distributed by United Artists. Running time: 129 minutes. At the Sutton Theater, 57th Street near Third Avenue, and Paramount Theater, Broadway at 61st Street. This film has been rated R.

R.P. McMurphy	Jack Nicholson
Nurse Ratched	Louise Fletcher
Harding	William Redfield
Chief Bromden	Will Sampson
Billy Bibbit	Brad Dourif
Candy	Marya Small
Scanlon	Delos V. Smith, Jr.
Nurse Pilbow	Mimi Sarkisian
Dr. Spivey	Dean R. Brooks
Turkle	Scatman Crothers
Martini	Danny De Vito
Sefelt	William Duell
Cheswick	Sydney Lassick
Taber	Christopher Lloyd
Rose	Louise Moritz

By VINCENT CANBY

People like Randle Patrick McMurphy are foregone conclusions. You gather together at random any 12 men, and one of them will eventually surface as the group's Randle Patrick McMurphy, the organizer, the spokesman, the leading hell-raiser and free spirit, the man who accepts nothing at face value and who likes to shake up the system, sometimes just because it's there. The quality of Randle Patrick McMurphy depends entirely on the intensity of his opposition.

Before the start of "One Flew Over the Cuckoo's Nest," Milos Forman's film version of Ken Kesey's 1962 novel, Randle Patrick McMurphy (Jack Nicholson) was strictly small potatoes, his life distinguished by nothing except carelessness.

One assumes him to have been a quick-witted but none-too-bright fellow whose vanity, drinking, whoring and short temper have earned him a minor police record consisting mostly of assault-and-battery complaints, concluding with a conviction for statutory rape. The girl, who said she was 19, was only 15.

When we first meet Randle, he has served two months of his six-month sentence and has managed to get himself transferred to the state mental hospital for psychiatric observation, figuring that life in the loony bin would be easier than on the prison farm. It's the beginning of the end for Randle, but the ferocity of the system imposes on him a kind of crazy grandeur.

"One Flew Over the Cuckoo's Nest," which opened yesterday at the Sutton and Paramount Theaters, is a comedy that can't quite support its tragic conclusion, which is too schematic to be honestly moving, but it is acted with such a sense of life that one responds to its demonstration of humanity if not to its programmed metaphors.

●

Once in the bin, Randle becomes the self-proclaimed champion of the rights of the other ward patients, his adversary being Nurse Ratched, a severe, once-pretty woman of uncertain age who can be sympathetic and understanding only in ways that reinforce her authority. Nurse Ratched represents the System that all Randles must buck.

As played by Louise Fletcher and defined in the screenplay by Lawrence Hauben and Bo Goldman, the film's Nurse Ratched is a much more interesting, more ambiguous character than in Mr. Kesey's novel, though what we take to be her fleeting impulses of genuine concern only make the film's ending that much more unbelievable.

"One Flew Over the Cuckoo's Nest" is at its best when Mr. Forman is exercising his talents as a director of exuberant comedy that challenges preconceived notions of good taste. It's not too far from the mark to describe Randle as a sort of Mister Roberts who finds himself serving aboard the U.S.S Madhouse. It's to Mr. Forman's credit that the other patients in the ward, though suffering from all sorts of psychoses, are never patronized as freaks but are immediately identifiable as variations on ourselves, should we ever go over the edge of what's called sanity.

Mr. Nicholson slips into the role of Randle with such easy grace that it's difficult to remember him in any other film. It's a flamboyant performance but not so overbearing that it obscures his fellow actors, all of whom are very good and a few of whom are close to brilliant, including William Redfield (as an egghead patient who talks grave nonsense), Will Sampson (as a deaf-mute Indian) and Brad Dourif (as a young man with a fatal mother complex).

There are some unsettling things about "One Flew Over the Cuckoo's Nest." I suspect that we are meant to make connections between Randle's confrontation with the oppressive Nurse Ratched and the political turmoil in this country in the 1960's. The connection doesn't work. All it does is conveniently distract us from questioning the accuracy of the film's picture of life in a mental institution where shock treatments are dispensed like aspirins and lobotomies are prescribed as if the mind's frontal lobes were troublesome wisdom teeth.

Even granting the artist his license, America is much too big and various to be satisfactorily reduced to the dimensions of one mental ward in a movie like this.

1975 N 20, 52:1

NIGHT CALLER, directed and produced by Henri Verneuil; screenplay by M. Verneuil, Jean Laborde and Francis Weber; Jean Penzer, director of photography; editors, Pierre Gillette and Henri Lanoe; music by Ennio Morricone; a Columbia Pictures release. Running time: 91 minutes; this film has been classified R. At the National, the Selwyn 42d Street, Loews 83d Street I and RKO 86th Street Twin 2 Theaters.

Inspector Le Tellier	Jean-Paul Belmondo
Moissac	Charles Denner
Pierre Waldeck (Minos)	Adalberto-Maria Merli
Norah Elmer	Lea Massari
Germaine Doinzon	Rosy Varte
Doctor Lipstein	Roland Dubillard
Sabin	Jean Martin

By RICHARD EDER

Producers use Jean-Paul Belmondo like a security blanket, and they use him so often he is beginning to resemble one: the nub worn down, the creases gone limp.

Through some odd work with the trans-Atlantic scissors, the Franco-Italian production "Night Caller" by Henri Verneuil seems to be two completely different movies, neither of them up to much.

The overworked Mr. Belmondo is in both of them, and he even plays the same character in both, which saves changing suits. His name is Inspector Le Tellier, and he carries his great nose and jaw structure into battle against criminals and madmen, his misty eyes and bent smile one contemplative pace behind.

●

The main movie is about a deranged man with an artificial eyeball who calls women up and subsequently kills them. Inspector Le Tellier goes to work, but all of a sudden—amid screaming women, sinister black leather gloves and oppositely rolling eyeballs—he detours to catch a long-sought bank robber.

The 15-minute chase has Le Tellier chasing the robber by car through rush-hour Paris and then boarding the new blue-tiled express Métro line. In a final shoot-out the Inspector plugs the robber in a crowded subway car, dumping him for good measure into the path of an oncoming train.

This has absolutely no relation to the madman story. Perhaps it is an advertisement for the new high-speed Paris subways. On the old kind it wouldn't make much sense to have a lot of split-second dashing in and out since the doors open and close with dreamy slowness.

Back to the madman. There is this man who decides that women with free-ranging sex lives should be punished. He picks several. They all live in nicely furnished apartments where the phone rings loudly. The madman calls, threatens, and comes around two or three days later to strangle.

Le Tellier gets within striking distance of the killer once or twice. There is a long ledge-and-chimney-pot chase that ends inconclusively.

Finally, the madman throws a hand grenade into a porno-film theater and is off to hold the star hostage in her apartment. All the top Paris police authorities ask Le Tellier what is to be done. He has the answer. A helicopter lowers him outside the actress's window: he smashes the window and beats the madman to a pulp.

That is the end of the two movies. That is two movies out of the way for the price—and the length—of one.

1975 N 20, 52:2

The New Porno Movies: From X to Zzzzzzzz

By WALTER GOODMAN

The simultaneous appearance of five heavily promoted X-rated films in East Side movie houses represents an incursion in force by the pop-porn vendors into Drydock Country. Mild-mannered advance scouts, such as "Last Tango in Paris" and "Emmanuelle," have appeared before, but only in recent weeks has so sizeable a hard-core corps settled in. They carry classy passports. At the Fine Arts, straight from the New York Film Festival, is "Exhibition." At the Lido East, by way of the Cannes Film Festival, is "Sensations." At the RKO 59th Street Twin No. 1 is "The Naughty Victorians"; the Victorians are naughty to the music of Sir Arthur Sullivan. Opening Wednesday at Twin No. 2 is "The Story of Joanna." And at the Baronet is "The Story of O," adapted from the pseudonymous Pauline Réage's novel, or, as the advertisement has it, "masterpiece of bizarre love that stunned France."

Are these works different from those which occupy West 42d Street houses? Well, the titles are a bit different: no "Wet Teenagers" or "The $50,000 Climax" here. Although it is not easy at critical moments to tell a batch of intertwined limbs on the East Side from one on the West Side, the bodies on the East Side are perhaps marginally more attractive, and for now no use is being made here of animals, vegetables or fruit to help along the action. The East Side productions tend to be better gotten up, and so do the audiences. As for socially re-

Walter Goodman is the Assistant Editor of the Arts and Leisure section.

deeming value, I can't say I noticed more of that on the East Side than I have on any other side of town. Does Howard Cosell have redeeming social value?

Whatever the pretensions of the makers of films like "The Story of O" and "Exhibition," it is unprofitable to judge them by common criteria, such as the persuasiveness of the script or the quality of the acting; the squirmings and groanings all seem to have been learned at the same dramatic academy. The makers of these movies prefer to speak of them as "erotica" rather than "pornography," understandable when we recall that "erotic" has connotations of sexual love or at least desire, whereas "pornographic" calls up the French for call girl. That X-rated films are capable of arousing sexual excitement, many can attest. The main question for fans about the recent arrivals on the East Side is how effectively they are achieving their mission of arousal given their aspirations to be taken as something more than West 42d Street porn.

What makes "Sensations" something more is the unusual number of participants in the key scenes. Most porno movies are content with four or five principals. Here, an internationally incompetent cast of more than a dozen, their voices dubbed into facsimiles of English, wage an attack on sex in all its variety. After a dawdling start, the action, which takes place in swanky settings in Amsterdam (most X-rated movies have swanky settings), never falters. The gesture of a plot is too casual to relate; limbs and organs just have at each other because they are there, and we are given much too much of

some not very good things. The encounters are presented with all the charm of open-heart surgery, the grace of a tool and die factory, the elegance of a zoo. The sound effects may have been recorded at a beer-drinking contest. The show ends with the leading lady, wholesome Brigitte Maier, being devoured by her colleagues. It serves her right for associating with creeps.

Whereas "Sensations" gets right to the point, "The Story of O"—from the man who brought us "Emmanuelle"—is a devious sort of movie. Insofar as I could make out, it has to do with this swanky adult camp in the country where the women are not permitted to wear pants and the men are not permitted to take theirs off. That does not seem to impede relations, although one can't be sure because the camera lens, covered apparently by some gauze that should have been used to subdue the amplifying equipment, stays pretty much on the heroine's pretty face while the interesting things are evidently going on elsewhere. At these times, whether she is being whipped or pleasured, O's normally blank expression turns to one of discomfort, the point being, I believe, that pain and pleasure are ineffably connected, just like love and hate, bondage and freedom, power and submission, Swiss cheese and baloney. Young men in need of a turn-on—go West.

Or go just a little further East to see "The Story of Joanna," clearly inspired by "The Story of O." "Joanna" was written, produced and directed by Gerard Damiano, famed on the West Side for such accomplishments as "Deep Throat" and "The Devil in Miss Jones." He now affects the auteur role, starting off the credits with "A

Film by Gerard Damiano."

Damiano has his problems as a writer. His dialogue sounds as though it had been hastily translated from the Serbo-Croat: "How sad to spend one's whole life looking for that which does not exist." But he knows how to use a good body when he gets hold of one, and in Terri Hall he has gotten hold of a body good enough to keep the mind off her acting. Miss Hall plays Joanna, a girl who, like O, is made to suffer many indignities for the sake of love before receiving her reward.

Damiano is a chef of the close-up. He caters a buffet of tremendous tongues, prodigious penises, breasts like snow banks and buttocks like Moby Dick. He is also our foremost choreographer of portions of the body which do not customarily dance. I was specially taken with an intricately devised number between parts of Joanna and those of a friendly butler. Unlike "O," which is soft at the core, "Joanna" is the real thing.

In this new film, Damiano makes some use of chains and whips, items relied on by pornographers over many decades to stimulate jaded palates or whatever needs stimulating. Sado-masochism is enjoying a revival in some circles, and even so innocent a movie as "The Naughty Victorians" makes its gesture toward fashion. There are traces of wit in this tale of Jack, a schoolmaster who forcibly deflowers Alice, his sometime fiancée, in his swanky snuggery, "a private study for studying private things." The Gilbert and Sullivan music is fun, if a touch obvious. Well, there's a lot of shackling and unshackling as Jack and Alice proceed to wreak their will on Alice's maid, Molly. These three then take their pleasure of Lady Bunt (a standout for abysmal acting in a very competitive field) and her daughter Cicely. With the exception of Cicely, the women tend toward the dumpy, and poor Alice is flat-chested to boot. Someone ought to talk to the casting director.

Tastes do vary in these matters, and I can only report that it does not seem to me that women gain in appeal by being strung up like carcasses, even though they keep on their stockings and hats. Moreover, I discovered that I am squeamish about implements of torture and about physical abuse as an expression of love. Perhaps that is one reason why the scenes between women, which in the nature of things are relatively gentle and affectionate, seemed to me in

each of these films far more sexy than those of our heroines' incessant violations by their heroes. But the history of pornography suggests that we do not all suffer from the same inhibitions, and I must defer to the pros of porn when it comes to knowing their audiences.

The only movie among these five which altogether foregoes even a touch of S-M is "Exhibition," the first hard-core effort to be shown at the New York Film Festival. It takes the shape of a lengthy interview with shapely Claudine Beccarie, a star in France's erotic firmament. We learn that Claudine, now 30, enjoyed a conventional French childhood—raped at 14, several years in reform school, a stint in a Spanish brothel and a brief marriage —and holds to the precepts instilled by a middle-class up-bringing. She doesn't like perversions or vulgar talk. She doesn't care for the art of Linda Lovelace. She is now going with a young soldier, who also acts in erotic films, and they'd both love to have a baby girl. The interview is interspersed with scenes of Claudine at work; happily, her opinions do not get in the way of her art.

The interview is conducted by the film's director, Jean-Francois Davy. (Yes, it's "A Film by Jean-Francois Davy.") Entering Claudine's apartment, he says: "This is your home, your own little universe." He asks: "Do you always stock up on groceries?" He states portentously: "I'm going to ask you a tricky question." Pause. "Where do you stand ideologically?" (Claudine, who is most forthcoming about the type and quality of her orgasms, refuses absolutely to discuss a personal matter like politics.) After a few minutes of this, one is forced to conclude that Davy is either a nincompoop or a master of the put-on. If we give him the benefit of the doubt, there is fun to be found amid the flotsam packaged here. In one sequence, for example, Claudine interviews men who have just seen her in a movie. She asks one whether he recognizes her. He doesn't: "Who looks at faces?" She asks another whether he identified with the characters. He didn't: "At the circus, do you identify with the lion tamer?"

●

But to serious matters. "Exhibition" presents two main exhibitions. The first finds three well-fed young women and a dutiful man going through their acts under instructions from a director: "Frederick, change your position . . . Lower your leg . . . Your hand is in the way . . . Makeup, we need a kleenex." In the background a woman reads erotic passages and a zonked-out spectator watches with an air of fine indifference the fondlings and so forth taking place under his nose.

It is all very good humored; the audience is invited to join in kidding the sort of scene which, on the West Side, kids the audience. Sex is made to seem actually enjoyable, a revelation after "Sensations," and the people are likeable, in contrast to those in "O" or "Joanna." Had the rest of the movie come up to these few minutes, it would have made an offbeat light comedy. But sexually stimulating? Once the filmmaker put his tongue in his cheek, the effect struck me as more amusing than arousing. By the time Claudine's big masturbatory sequence came upon us, we had been made acutely aware of the presence, a yard or two off screen, of the director and his crew. All that splendid young woman's thrashings and moanings and clutchings of the bedclothes were being done, and overdone, to another's specifications. This was *cinéma sans vérité*. The forced realization that Claudine and I were not alone, that she was being directed and I was being manipulated, was enough to shrivel the libido.

Despite its over-all ineptitude, "Exhibition" suggests a sensible direction for X-rated movies. It holds out the possibility of real films which, while not hard-core as their be-all and end-all, would contain hard-core elements, permitting sex to be a part of art as it is a part of life. Gerard Damiano could be brought in to do the special effects. But the impresarios of porn are heading in a different direction. "Exhibition" is merely a rest stop in the ascent from the mild "Emmanuelle" to the impersonal, mindless "Sensations."

To see five such films within a single week is to emerge impressed both with the appeal of the human form even under adverse circumstances and with its limitations as a source of enjoyment for the viewer who is not quite a voyeur. None of the films is particularly long, yet each runs out of steam well before quitting time. It's not exactly that if you've seen one dirty movie you've seen them all, but the progressions do become predictable, the movements mechanical, the episodes repetitive; unless one is an incur-

able buff, interest must flag. Whips and chains may serve as audience restoratives for a while, but my guess is that animals, vegetables and fruit

will be putting in an appearance on the East Side any time now. ∎

1975 N 23, II:1:1

FILM VIEW

VINCENT CANBY

'Cuckoo's Nest' —A Sane Comedy About Psychotics

In a certain kind of sentimental fiction, mental institutions are popular as metaphors for the world outside. The schizoids, the catatonics, the Napoleons and the Josephines inside the hospital are the sanes, while all of us outside who have tried to adjust to a world that accepts war, hunger, poverty and genocide are the real crazies. It's the appeal of this sappy idea, I suspect, that keeps Philippe De Broca's "King of Hearts" playing almost continually around the country. In that film, you remember, the Scots soldier (Alan Bates) seeks asylum among the certified lunatics while World War I rages nuttily ouside.

It's a comforting concept, and a little like believing in Santa Claus, to think that if we just give up, if we throw in life's towel, and stop thinking rationally while letting our wildest fantasies take hold, that we'll attain some kind of peace. No fear. No pain. No panic. The world becomes a garden of eccentric delights.

The thing that distinguishes "One Flew Over The Cuckoo's Nest," Milos Forman's screen version of the 1962 Ken Kesey novel, is its resolute avoidance of such nonsense. Although the film is not without its simplicities and contradictions, its view of disconnected minds is completely unsentimental. I'm not at all sure that the terrifying events that Kesey describes so jauntily in his novel could take place, or would ever have taken place in any mental hospital 10 or 15 years ago, so one must accept the tale as a fictional nightmare of its time—the sixties. The mental hospital in "One Flew Over The Cuckoo's Nest" is, I suppose, a metaphor, but it is more important as the locale of one more epic battle between a free spirit and a society that cannot tolerate him.

There is always, of course, a certain sentimentality attached to this conflict, at least in our society. Twentieth-century Americans feel terrifically sentimental about—and envious of—non-conformists while knocking themselves out to look, sound, talk and think like everyone else. The only good non-conformist is the fictional non-conformist, or one who's safely dead. We apotheosize Yossarian while electing Presidents whose public images have been created in advertising agencies.

Randle Patrick McMurphy (Jack Nicholson), the fast-talking hero of "One Flew Over The Cuckoo's Nest," more or less has his non-conformism thrust upon him, out of bravado and ignorance and the demands of this sort of fiction. All that we ever know about Randle before he turns up in the Oregon mental hospital, where we first meet him and which is the scene of the film, is that he has been serving a six-month prison sentence for statutory rape. The girl was 15 though she had told him she was 19, he says, probably lying. After two months on a prison farm, Randle has gotten himself transferred to the hospital for psychiatric observation, figuring that the loony bin would be a softer touch than picking peas.

Once Randle is in the hospital, however, the world shrinks to the size of his ward, which is the private domain of a singularly vicious character named Nurse Ratched (Louise Fletcher), a woman of uncertain age who is capable of understanding and sympathy only when they

Jack Nicholson in "Cuckoo"— "a free spirit"

reinforce her authority.

The story of "One Flew Over The Cuckoo's Nest" is the duel between Randle and Nurse Ratched for the remnants of the minds of the other patients in the ward, a contest that starts out in the mood of a comedy on the order of "Mr. Roberts" and winds up, rather awkwardly, as tragedy.

"One Flew Over The Cuckoo's Nest" is indecently sentimental and simplistic if you take it as a serious statement on the American condition, which is much too complex to be represented by this mental ward. However, if you can avoid freighting it with these ulterior meanings—and Forman and his screenwriters have had the good sense not to bear down too heavily on them—"One Flew Over The Cuckoo's Nest" is a humane, loose-limbed sort of comedy containing the kind of fine performances that continually bring the film to explosive, very unsettling life.

Forman, the Czech director of "Loves of A Blonde" and "Firemen's Ball," has made one other American film, "Taking Off," in which the eye through which we saw the world was clearly that of an amused, sympathetic, sometimes appalled visitor. Perhaps because the locale of "One Flew Over The Cuckoo's Nest" is more particular than the middle-class and hippie milieus of "Taking Off," the new film betrays nothing except the director's concern for people who struggle to bring some order out of chaos. It's a struggle he finds supremely funny and sometimes noble, even when the odds are most bleak.

Jack Nicholson is something more than the star of "One Flew Over The Cuckoo's Nest." He is its magnetic north. His is the performance that gives direction to those of everyone else in the cast. I can't believe that a non-professional like Dr. Dean Brooks, who is actually the superintendent of the Oregon State Hospital (where the film was shot), could have been so comically speculative in a key moment had not Nicholson been setting the tone of the scene. Nicholson's flamboyance as an actor here is of an especially productive sort. It doesn't submerge the other actors. It seems to illuminate them. This is most noticeably true of Louise Fletcher, whose Nurse Ratched is much more interestingly ambiguous than the character in Kesey's novel, as well as of Will Sampson, another non-pro, who plays Nicholson's deaf-mute Indian sidekick, and Brad Dourif, as the ward's "kid" character.

There are some troublesome things in "One Flew Over The Cuckoo's Nest" that I'm not sure can be alibied by saying that it is, after all, a fiction and not a documentary. The ward that we see in the film is (most of the time) so spic and span that it seems to give the lie to horror stories we all know about the filth and overcrowding in so many mental hospitals. Also, can it be possible that shock treatments are (or were until recently) given out so arbitrarily as punishments, and could a single ward nurse ever have authorized a lobotomy without some second opinion?

These can be major factors in the way one responds to the film. But another is the extraordinary way that Forman has been able to create important, identifiable characters of psychotics, people who are most often represented in films as misfit exotics, creatures as remote from our experience as members of a Stone Age tribe in the Amazon.

1975 N 23, II:1:1

How Hollywood's Memory Plays Tricks on Us

By JAMES PARIS

The nostalgia craze is still with us. With the promise of forthcoming films dealing with the lives of stars (Clark Gable, Carole Lombard, W. C. Fields, John Barrymore, Clara Bow, Rudolph Valentino, Tom Mix, Sarah Bernhardt), to say nothing of Broadway revivals, a nostalgia book club, magazines and TV tributes to Hollywood's legendary past, it appears that we have a full-fledged nostalgia industry in our midst with no lay-offs in sight. What can account for it?

To start with, we might observe simply that with all the confusion, alienation and unrest in the present, Americans have a longing to return to the past—to an imagined past that is — where the world semed more comfortable, reassuring and manageable. So, naturally, Hollywood has been quick to cash in on these national yearnings by turning its attention backward. But questions arise: Just what in the past does Hollywood choose to re-create? And how does it go about doing it? In other words, how does Hollywood

James Paris teaches a course in film at Seton Hall University.

manipulate nostalgia? Two recent books dealing with Hollywood's past supply some useful guideposts for those seeking to understand these questions.

In "America in the Movies," a provocative examination of the American character as reflected in the films of the forties and fifties, Michael Wood points out that these films were not "as we often think, a full-scale flight from our problems, not a means of forgetting them completely, but rather a rearrangement of our problems into shapes which tame them, which disperse them to the margins of our attention." Our thirst for nostalgia, says wood, is not so much for mindless escapist fare as for films which allude briefly to our anxieties and then magically, sympathetically dispel them.

In "Movie-Made America," a well-researched study of "How the Movies Changed American Life," cultural historian Robert Sklar stresses the role of films in the reorientation of traditional values. Movies, he writes, were more iconoclastic than other forms of information and entertainment and they projected "a version of American behavior and values more risqué, violent, comic and fantastic than the standard interpretation of tradi-

tional cultural elites. It was this trait that gave movies their popularity and their mythmaking power."

Sklar demonstrates how, from the very beginning, movies presented "visions of alternative styles and behavior" and were as a result in constant conflict with the middle-class moral order. They did not become custodians of the nation's cultural heritage until the mid-1930's, when the Depression stimulated Hollywood to preserve traditional values, not undermine them. Before that, however, gangster movies ("The Public Enemy," 1931,) films of social realism ("I Am a Fugitive From a Chain Gang," 1932), and comedies subverting the social order ("Duck Soup" and "She Done Him Wrong," both 1933) "called into question sexual propriety, social decorum and the institutions of law and order."

●

It is good to remember this point, for when modern-day moviemakers decided to exploit the nation's nostalgic yearning, they did not go back to these vital, free-wheeling films; instead, they returned to later, more conservative modes—such as that of the screwball comedy —which were respectful of middle-class values. (Sklar observes that by celebrating "the sanctity of marriage, class distinction and the domination of women by men," screwball comedies "were never allowed to disturb the social order.")

Not knowing exactly which way to turn, contemporary Hollywood has been experimenting in various ways— with varying degrees of box-office success—to lure its runaway audiences with siren songs of the past. There have been revivals of the real thing, the "classic" movies themselves as well as compilation films made up of clips from old musicals ("That's Entertainment" and the upcoming "That's Entertainment, Too"). Films have been made expressly to allow us to wallow unabashedly in *je temps perdu* ("Summer of '42"), and a slickly contrived, highly romanticized view of the thirties reaped a fortune in the seventies ("The Sting"). Attempts have also been made to revive certain genres, such as the screwball comedy ("What's Up, Doc?") and the *film noir* ("Farewell, My Lovely"). The horror film (Mel Brooks' "Young Frankenstein") and the swashbuckler (Richard Lester's "The Three Musketeers" and its sequel, "The Four Musketeers") have been updated with a twist of camp.

All these films designed to satisfy our nostalgic inclinations turn out to be essentially conservative and reassuring. They do not attack the establishment, challenge society's values or subvert sacred institutions. On the contrary, each pledges allegiance to the "status quo." While "Farewell, My Lovely" may hint at political corruption, the wicked get what's coming to them in the end. The sex drive, too, is channeled into approved courses as "kookie" Barbra Streisand lands handsomely square Ryan O'Neal in "What's Up, Doc?" — and thereby confirms the audience's faith in marriage and domesticity. "That's Entertainment" supports the cherished notion that the past was truly magical and golden after all, and from the first shot of Frankenstein's murky castle ("Young Frankenstein") to the first note of the zesty Joplin music ("The Sting"), the audience is cued to sit back, relax, and enjoy these mindless, consoling trips to yesteryear.

Hollywood's backward steps indicate that for most people nostalgia is not so much a matter of setting as of tone. Robert Altman's "Thieves Like Us" and John Schlesinger's "The Day of the Locust" are both set in the 1930's, yet we would not call these pictures "nostalgic," despite the fact that they succeed masterfully in re-creating a sense of the past. They are too disturbing. It is the tone or attitude toward the material which makes so many current dramas soothingly nostalgic. The more a director can evoke a mythical past, a past carefully shorn of its upsetting aspects, the more successful he will be in attracting a fantasy-hungry public.

Hollywood's tendency to play it both ways is manifested in comedies as well. "Hearts of the West" posts a bill of Garbo in "Anna Christie" and expects us to believe we are in the 1930's, yet it employs language, attitudes and a sexual permissiveness which are right up to date. Hollywood, wishing to exploit our weakness for nostalgia without being considered old-fashioned, is turning out more and more of these uncertain hybrid films.

Is there a chance that American moviemakers will change their escapist ways and settle down to a serious exploration of our past? Possibly so, but first the movie-going public will have to demonstrate its desire to live in the present by hopping

down off the nostalgic bandwagon. In the meantime, make way for "Frankenstein at Middle Age" and "The Five Musketeers." ■

1975 N 23, II:15:1

RANCHO DELUXE, directed by Frank Perry; screenplay by Thomas McGuane; director of photography, William A. Fraker; editor, Sid Katz; music, Jimmy Buffett; produced by Elliott Kastner; distributed by United Artists. At the D.W. Griffth Theater, East 59th Street. Running time: 93 minutes; this film has been classified R.
Jack McKee .... Jeff Bridges
Cecil Colson .... Sam Waterston
Cora Brown .... Elizabeth Ashley
Laura Beige .... Charlene Dallas
John Brown .... Clifton James
Henry Beige .... Slim Pickens
Curt .... Harry Dean Stanton
Burt .... Richard Bright
Betty Fargo .... Patti D'Arbanville
Mary Fargo .... Maggie Wellman
Wilbur Fargo .... Bert Conway

By RICHARD EDER

"Rancho DeLuxe" is handsome, witty, apt and languid. It is so cool it is barely alive. First-rate ingredients and a finesse in assembling them do not quite make either a movie or a cake. At some point it is necessary to light the oven.

"Rancho," which opened yesterday at the D. W. Griffith Theater, is a kind of parody Western, a genre barely younger than the Western itself. And as long as Frank Perry, the director, and Thomas McGuane, the writer, are being wry about ranch owners who ride around in helicopters and ranch hands whose chores include vacuuming the rancher's Navajo rugs, they do extremely well.

●

All their characters are phonies, and this is fine. They are often very funny phonies. But the heroes—two fey and charming young rustlers who saw up other people's cows as an existential act—are infested with humorous self-pity.

Through them the portentous message creeps in: the West is dead and inhabited by maggots. Nothing happens to the message; it doesn't go anywhere. It is used as décor, dressing the set in a fashionable tone of lavender.

Affectations aside, there is a great deal that this picture does well. It relates the ill-starred but decidedly nontragic war between the two rustlers, Jack and Cecil, and the rancher, John Brown.

They begin by shooting a cow or two and sawing them up with a portable chainsaw. They go on to hold a prize bull for ransom—in a motel bedroom — and finally they attempt to steal a whole trailer-rig of cattle in partnership with Brown's ranch-hands.

Jack, played a bit too fatly and lovably by Jeff Bridges, is a rich boy who has left his wife and bums around with Cecil, a literate and spaced-out Indian.

Both of them move through a perpetual haze of self-parody. As they drive their pickup truck off from one cow-killing, one asks the other: "Do you believe in the tooth fairy?"

When Jack makes love to one of two sisters who hang out with them, he slips on a comic dog mask at the crucial moment.

Cecil, very well acted by Sam Waterston, makes jokes about being an Indian. "Let's burn and pillage," he suggests to Jack as the two sit around with nothing much to do.

They are blatantly inauthentic rustlers, and they know it. Their self-knowledge and their deliberate kookiness is their commentary—and the film's—on Western pretensions of retaining old values while in fact living off all the comforts and shortcuts of urban American life.

The film's other characters are just as inauthentic, but without self-consciousness, and this makes them much funnier. Brown, the rancher, wears lumberjack shirts and goes on about preserving "a West that's free." In fact he is a refugee from the hairdressing business back East and wears his cattleman image as a child wears a soldier suit.

His wife puts in game appearances at cattle shows, tries to seduce the ranch hands with war cries of "how about a little desire under the elms?" and longs to go back East. Their lavish ranch house is airless, and its picture windows frame the spectacular mountain scenery as if it were, in fact, no more than pictures.

Brown's two ranch hands are just as phony. One is a former appliance repairman, the other used to model hot combs. Their beautifully indirect inveiglement by Jack and Cecil into becoming their accomplices, played out in a bar, is the best scene in the movie.

As a decrepit and seemingly inept professional rustler-detective, hired by Brown, Slim Pickens for once has a strongly written comic role. He plays it with great effect, and Charlene Dallas, as his sluttish assistant, is almost as good.

Their earthy roles and acting styles do a lot to liven up a picture whose artfulness is marred by its own narcissistic excess.

1975 N 24, 28:1

DELUSIONS OF GRANDEUR (La Folie des Grandeurs), directed by Gerard Oury; screenplay (French with English subtitles) by Mr. Oury, Marcel Julian and Daniele Thompson; director of photography, Henri Decae; a co-production of Gaumont International (Paris), Mars Films (Rome), Coreal Produzione (Madrid) and Orion Film (Munich), distributed by Joseph Green Pictures. Running time: 85 minutes. At the Trans-Lux 85th Street Theater, at Madison Avenue, and Cinema Village Theater, 12th Street east of Fifth Avenue. This film has not been rated.

Sallustre .... Louis De Funes
Blaze .... Yves Montand
King .... Alberto De Mendoza
Queen .... Karin Schubert
Cesar .... Gabriele Tinti
Dona Juana .... Alice Sapritch

The refreshing thing about the frenetic comedy of Louis De Funes, one of France's biggest box-office stars, is that it seems to be adrift in time. Whether the setting is contemporary, as in "The Mad Adventures of 'Rabbi' Jacob," seen here last year, or 17th-century Spain, as in "Delusions of Grandeur," which opened at two theaters yesterday, Mr. De Funes seems always to be operating within his own tiny universe, out of touch with everything except his own ill humor, his greed and his schemes to cheat that inevitably fail.

Though his comedy is studiously untopical, it is far from being timeless in the manner of the truly great screen comedians—Chaplin, Keaton, Tati. Indeed, he is funny just because the character he has created seems so furiously petty. It's not simply that this character doesn't possess a generous bone in his body, he also has absolutely no awareness of this fact.

In "Delusions of Grandeur," directed by Gerard Oury in 1971, two years before he collaborated with the actor on "The Mad Adventures," Mr. De Funes plays a corrupt but supremely unsuccessful tax minister in the court of the King of Spain. Yves Montand plays the minister's roguish valet and the plot has some connection with Victor Hugo's "Ruy Blas"—though it's a very loose one.

The settings are splendid and the gags, some quite funny, are nonstop as Mr. De Funes maneuvers transparently to discredit the queen in order to win back the favor of the king.

Mr. Montand looks uneasy under these circumstances. He's a good comedian himself, but it must be trying to act with someone who mugs as outrageously as Mr. De Funes, who also is given the best of the cheerfully foolish lines. "Did you get my anonymous letter?" he asks the king at one point.

I also liked the pledge of a group of noblemen who are plotting to overthrow the king: "All for one and every man for himself."

VINCENT CANBY

1975 N 27, 45:1

THE ROMANTIC ENGLISHWOMAN, directed by Joseph Losey; screenplay by Tom Stoppard and Thomas Wiseman, based on the novel by Mr. Wiseman; produced by Daniel M. Angel; music, Richard Hartley; director of photography, Gerry Fisher; editor, Reginald Beck; distributed by New World Pictures. Running time: 117 minutes. At the Embassy 72d Street Theater, Broadway at 72d Street, and UA Eastside Cinema, Third Avenue at 55th Street. This film has been rated R.

Elizabeth Fielding ..... Glenda Jackson
Lewis Fielding .... Michael Caine
Thomas .... Helmut Berger
Isabel .... Kate Nelligan
Herman .... Rene Kolldehof
Swan .... Michael Lonsdale
Catherine .... Beatrice Romand
Annie .... Anna Steele
Miranda .... Nathalie Delon

By VINCENT CANBY

Lewis Fielding (Michael Caine) and his wife, Elizabeth

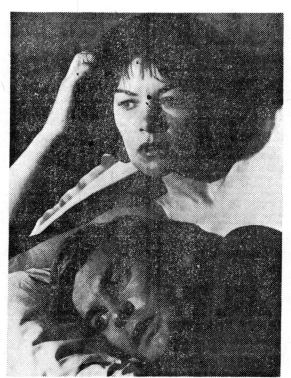

Helmut Berger and Glenda Jackson

(Glenda Jackson), think they have nothing when they have everything, which is just one of the curious reversals that keeps Joseph Losey's "The Romantic Englishwoman" interesting long after you've decided that something is decidedly wrong with it.

Lewis is a successful novelist and screenwriter. He and his wife have a handsome young son, a big, comfortable house in the country, access to other beautiful/successful people and no maid problems. Lewis and Elizabeth love each other too much or not enough?

•

When Elizabeth gets bored and runs off to Baden-Baden for a weekend, Lewis becomes obsessed with fantasies of her imaginary infidelities. The first two things Elizabeth does when she comes home, is to race to her bedroom, is to search for signs of Lewis's hanky-panky with the domestic help. This shared, obsessive fretfulness keeps Lewis and Elizabeth in a state of high, apparently pleasurable, sexual tension until Lewis has the bad taste to stage-direct their lives to simulate melodrama.

"The Romantic Englishwoman," which opened at two theaters yesterday, is about an unequal threesome —Lewis, Elizabeth and Thomas (Helmut Berger), a self-styled poet and gigolo who sometimes makes ends meet by smuggling heroin across national boundaries. When Thomas turns up in England after having met Elizabeth in Baden-Baden, Lewis invites the young man to live with them. Lewis has just begun to write a screenplay about a

woman, unhappy in her perfect marriage, who runs off to the Continent to find herself and in the process falls in love with another man.

"The Romantic Englishwoman" is an exceedingly elegant looking movie. It isn't just posh locales and handsome interior decoration that give this effect. The camera sees everything with a singular kind of appreciation for its high-priced mostly cold beauty. The camera is also obsessed with reflections of reality, which, I suppose, is one of the things the movie is meant to be about.

The film opens with a reflection of Miss Jackson's face in the train window en route to Baden-Baden. Scene after scene begins in such a way that one can't be quite sure whether one is seeing the real thing or a mirror image. When late in the film Elizabeth finally does fall in love with the gigolo, the question is raised, what has come first, the true passion or its reflection that is, Lewis's suspicions?

The screenplay, by Tom Stoppard (author of Broadway's "Travesties") and Thomas Wiseman, is full of the sort of auto-critique that seems designed to earn the film makers congratulations for the film they've made and forestall outside criticism. Early in the movie, when a producer asks Lewis to write a script about "the new woman," Lewis says with a sigh, "It sounds very boring. Why not turn it into a thriller?"

•

Mr. Losey and his writers have not turned "The Romantic Englishwoman" into a thriller. They've attempted to make an intelligent film

about intelligent people, and as long as Mr. Berger is kept off the screen, it is. Mr. Caine and Miss Jackson are interesting performers. When they are supposed to be thinking, puzzling things out, or caught up in feelings beyond their control, we believe it.

Mr. Berger is something else. It's impossible to know when he's supposed to represent fraudulence within the film or if he's simply being himself, a not very good actor defrauding the film of a performance.

He's a missing element and the movie, unequally balanced, goes off into a wobbly, out-of-control orbit as a result. When we should be moved or intellectually engaged, we are more inclined to snicker. Which is too bad, since "The Romantic Englishwoman" is in many other ways a film of feeling, tact and intelligence.

1975 N 27, 46:1

GRAIN FIELDS, four short films: "Apparent Motion" by Paul Sharits and "Lozenge Licking," "The Catalog" and "No Heroes" by Jon Rubin. Running time: 62 minutes. At the Whitney Museum of American Art.

If photographic expertise is its own reward, then the program of shorts inclusively titled "Grain Fields," which opened a week's run at the Whitney Museum yesterday, is a tribute to its two avant-garde movie makers. But as intricately technological treatments of the ingredients of raw film itself, their visual effects are momentarily interesting abstractions that unfortunately soon become redundant.

As the longest entry (30 minutes), the silent "Apparent Motion," which is the work of 32-year-old Paul Sharits, a member of the Center for Media Studies at the State University at Buffalo, lives up to its title by using superimpositions of particles of grain in raw film to create an illusion of variously shaped, colored spots in swarmlike, continuous activity. Although this motion is also made possible through specialized filming, printing and developing processes, the visual ends do not althougher appear to justify these scientific means.

Jon Rubin, a 28-year-old fellow in advanced visual studies at the Massachusetts Institute of Technology, has fashioned a snowfall of colored, pointillist-like animated particles in the silent, 10-minute, vaguely titled "Lozenge Licking." But a good deal more meets the eye in his equally silent, 16-minute, aptly labeled "The Catalog," a collection of images and people moving through changing colors and shapes by means of "photochemical processing" that are occasionally, if not constantly, arresting.

As the sole sound film in this package, Mr. Rubin's 7-minute "No Heroes" avoids such technical devices. But in focusing on the simple sight and sound of a babbling brook, this study, somewhat like the other shorts in the program, puts its idea across long before the film ends.

A. H. WEILER

1975 N 27, 46:2

THE DEVIL'S CLEAVAGE, directed and written by George Kuchar; director of photography, George Kuchar, with additional photography by Larry Huston and Mike Kuchar. Running time: 115 minutes. At the Film Forum, Vandam Theater, 15 Vandam Street. This film has not been rated.
WITH Curt McDowell, Kathleen Hohalek, Virginia Giritlian, Michele Gross, John Thomas, Mark Ellinger, Ilka Normile, Ann Knutson, Janey Sneed, Charlie Thomas, Barbara Linkevitch, and others.

By VINCENT CANBY

"People like us are the tripods that keep up the ceilings of motels," says Ginger Menninger, one of several heroines who lurch from one shattered dream to another in "The Devil's Cleavage," George Kuchar's metaphor-stuffed, sometimes solemnly funny parody of terrible movies. The film was presented by the Film Forum yesterday at the Vandam Theater, Greenwich Village, where it will be shown this weekend and next.

For those of you who may possibly have forgotten, or never knew, George Kuchar is one-half of the 33-year-old Kuchar twins (Mike is the other half) the underground film makers who have been turning out passionate paeans to Hollywood since they were toddlers in the Bronx. Among their early works: "The Naked and the Nude," produced when the twins were 15.

Since the brothers split up as a team some years ago, Mike has devoted himself to science-fiction works shot in livid color ("Sins of the Fleshapoids") while George has specialized in small, hysterical, black-and-white melodramas ("The Lovers of Eternity," "Corruption of the Damned").

"The Devil's Cleavage" is George Kuchar's' chef d'oeuvre, which is easy enough to say because it belongs to that tradition of commercial movie-making that automatically assumes that each new work is a chef d'ouvre until it flops at the box office. It's a thoroughly tangled two-hour soap opera whose several heroines all look like the overwrought, black-wigged Bette Davis in King Vidor's "Beyond the Forest," and all of whom long to be some place where they aren't.

Where they are appears to be, first, Honolulu, and then, perhaps, a small own in Oklahoma. I'm tentative only because the script is sketchy on such details. Also, you can never be quite sure in a

Kuchar film what is intended to be an ellipsis and what might somehow have been lost by mistake, or was never shot.

But then continuity is not important in a kind of narrative film making that has no patience with scenes that don't contain renunciations, rejections, rapes or big show-stopping monologues in which life may be compared to a box of Girl Scout cookies.

•

Movies like this often sound funnier than they are to sit through, especially when they are close to two hours long. Every form has its suitable length, and parody-camp of the Kuchar sort, when it goes on for 115 minutes, is like a 2,000-line limerick.

1975 N 29, 20:1

FILM VIEW

VINCENT CANBY

Now for a Look At Some Really Bad Movies

Maybe writing about good movies all the time isn't fair. It's a form of discrimination. It may also be short-sighted. If it's possible to reconstruct the interests, attitudes and values of a lost society from its garbage, then perhaps we should take a closer look at some of the junk that's passing through our movie theaters these days, often without benefit of reviews or advertising. Would you want a future historian speculating about your life on the basis of a mossy old print of "Ilsa, She Wolf of The SS"?

The following is a run-down on five such films, none of which was reviewed at the time of its opening. They sneaked in, the manner being less modest than surreptitious. Promoters of such films are well aware that they aren't dealing in things that will be hailed as gems by even the maddest movie nuts.

These five films represent a subculture that people who do their movie-going on Third Avenue are seldom aware of. Such films come into town to play a first-run engagement of one or two weeks at a grubby Broadway or 42d Street grind house, sometimes followed by a short circuit break, and then sail off to the hinterlands, often to make small fortunes in drive-ins where what goes on the screen is not of prime importance. The procedure is just as frequently the other way around, with the New York playdates following those elsewhere in the country when the New York City theater can't afford "Jaws" and knows that it has wrung the last possible buck out of a festival of Charles Bronson reissues.

• • •

"Ilsa, She Wolf of The SS": This could possibly be the worst soft-core sex-and-violence film of the decade —and the funniest. It's set in a World War II Nazi concentration camp built in a meadow that looks very southern California. You can almost hear the freeway traffic on the other side of the hill. Before the action starts, there is a message from the film's producer, Herman Traeger, noting that while some liberties have been taken in the interests of drama, the events depicted are basically true. Ilsa, the commander of the concentration camp, has what is usually called a warped mind, as well as breasts so large and unwieldy you suspect that the Nazis pioneered the use of silicone. Ilsa is a frosty-faced, sex-hungry martinet. To satisfy her various appetites, she takes male prisoners to bed at night, then has them castrated the following morning. "Once a man has slept with me," announces Ilsa in her top-heavy rhetoric, "he will

never sleep with another woman again." The castrations are carried out just below the camera's eye with a lot of moaning that apparently entertained the largely male audience with which I saw the film. Ilsa also tortures the female prisoners with cattle prods and gang-rapes carried out by the male guards. At the point I walked out of the theater, she was having an argument on the telephone with a superior officer whom she repeatedly addressed as "Hair Gain-hay-ral."

"Possibility, Zero": This is a conventional if tacky World War II action film that seems to have been made in 1972, if I read the Roman numerals in the credits correctly. Where it was made, I have no idea, though I suspect Italy or Greece. The star is Henry Silva ("A Hatful of Rain"), who speaks his own, post-synchronized English dialogue, while the supporting actors have obviously been dubbed by others. The plot —or what little I could get of it during the time I stayed with it—is about a commando raid on a remote Nazi installation containing (I think) a secret ray gun. It's a sort of tab version of "The Guns of Navarone" and for a while it thoroughly delighted me when I thought a lovely resistance fighter, who had managed to catch the eye of a German general, was intent on doing him in by poisoning his after-shave lotion. I was wrong, however.

"Torso": An English-dubbed, Italian-made suspense film, produced by Carlo Ponti, directed by Sergio Martino, starring Suzy Kendall. Those are fairly respectable credits but the movie, about a psychopathic killer who mutilates the bodies of beautiful young women, takes just as vicious a view of women as "Ilsa, She Wolf of The SS." There is a slight difference, though. These young women, who are supposed to be university students, all look like models, and behave that way. Hit over the head with a blunt instrument, a girl in this film inevitably collapses into a death-pose that would do credit to a Simmons mattress ad. "Torso" also features a lot of genteel female nudity and one gesture that fascinates me: whenever one of the lightly clad young women answers the telephone, she modestly draws her knees together. Because all three of the young Italian actors in the movie look alike, I still don't know who the killer really was, although I sat through the whole mess.

"Cry Rape": A truly puzzling film, originally German, I suspect, though the credits tell you little and the dubbed English dialogue even less. It's about two young men, one of whom looks a lot like Jack Nicholson, who kidnap a young woman who looks a lot like the early Bardot, take her to a gravel pit, and then spend the night raping her and fighting each other. There's just the slightest suggestion of a serious and interesting movie here as the young men role-play for each other's benefit. There's also one effective scene in which the men convince the girl that to report a rape to the police might be worse than to endure the act itself. The film, however, is more concerned in showing us her humiliation than in worrying about it.

"If You Don't Stop It. . . . You'll Go Blind": This movie would not warrant mention even in a story about junk movies except for two things. It has advertised itself as being funnier than "Blazing Saddles," which it isn't, and it presents as one of its "stars" and co-director, Keefe Brasselle, who gained some minor Hollywood fame in the fifties (acting in "The Eddie Cantor Story") and notoriety in the sixties (as a CBS producer when Jim Aubrey was a network chief). "If You Don't Stop It" is a collection of witless blackout sketches dealing with infidelity, wedding nights, impotence and masturbation, played by a small cast of not very talented actors. In its grand finale, which looks as if it might have been shot off-hours in a Las Vegas night club, Brasselle comes on-stage to sing and dance a production number that could only seem funny in Las Vegas. Its title: "Don't (deleted) Around With Love."

If these films tell us anything about our society, it's only that no matter how foolish the movie project, there's always somebody who is dim enough to finance it. When I saw these films, there were in every instance more people standing on the sidewalk outside the theater, looking at a TV monitor showing scenes from the film, than there were paying patrons inside. Which might well be a sign of hope.

1975 N 30, II:13:6

Jean-Louis Trintignant and Catherine Deneuve

ACT OF AGGRESSION (L' Agression), directed by Gerard Pires; screenplay (French with English subtitles) by Jean-Patric Manchette and Mr. Pires, based on the novel "The Shrewsdale Exit," by John Buell; produced by Alain Poire and Pierre Braunberger; director of photography, Silvano Ippoliti; music, Robert Charlebois; a co-production of S.N.E. Gaumont, Les Films du Jeudi, Les Films de la Seine (Paris) and Primex Italiana (Rome), distributed by Joseph Green Pictures. Running time: 94 minutes. At the Trans-Lux 85th Street, at Madison Avenue, and the Eighth Street Playhouse, west of Fifth Avenue. This film has not been rated.

Paul Varlin .... Jean-Louis Trintignant
Sarah .... Catherine Deneuve
Andre Ducatel .... Claude Brasseur
Escudero .... Philippe Brigaud
Helene .... Michelle Grellier
Patty .... Delphine Boffy

By VINCENT CANBY

"Act of Aggression," the French melodrama that opened yesterday at two theaters, is so bad that it makes a film as vicious as "Death Wish" look good.

Like the Charles Bronson character in "Death Wish," Jean-Louis Trintignant, the hero of "Act of Aggression," is a mild-mannered, middle-class businessman who is transformed into a killer ape after his wife and daughter have been brutalized by hoodlums. But where "Death Wish" exalted revenge, the French movie simply trivializes it with a plot that twists less easily than a dried noodle. Gerard Pires, the director, makes things even worse by employing the kind of flashy cutting and camerawork you might expect in a television commercial that's run amok.

Mr. Trintignant does a lot of driving of automobiles and looks quite understandably driven. Catherine Deneuve, who plays his sister-in-law, looks magnificent. She is not only one of the world's great beauties. She now possesses such substance and ease as an actress that she almost persuades us the movie couldn't possibly be as terrible as it is.

1975 D 4, 50:1

DOPE, a documentary photographed, edited and directed by Sheldon and Diane Rochlin. At the Whitney Museum of American Art, Madison Avenue and 75th Street. Running time: 90 minutes.

By A. H. WEILER

"Dope," the documentary on British and American denizens of the London drug scene, which had its local premiere yesterday at the Whitney Museum of American Art, was filmed in 1966 by Sheldon and Diane Rochlin, a peripatetic American husband-and-wife team. If its moment in social history is unspecified in its expressionistic, color footage, this penetration, if occasionally disjointed, record of our disengaged youth still appears to be a strikingly contemporary, sad and awesome commentary.

"Dope" may leave a gnawing need for further explanations, a point of view and identifications of the anonymous principals involved. But to the credit of the Rochlins, their dispassionate, cinéma-vérité treatment of their subject matter illustrates a personal commitment and a deep concern for the basically gentle, apparently rootless young people they realistically capture on film.

•

The depiction of constant injections of heroin or the use of other narcotics is not new on screen, but its pertinence here is still raw and shocking. But there is, more importantly, both a genuine feeling for a lost generation and, oddly enough, for togetherness in bits and vignettes of singles and couples in seedy flats living the strangely communal addict life of scroungers, marginal musicians, artists and the like.

While there is an absence of overt editorializing, there are intimations of addicts as friends and as devoted par-

ents of happy children, aware of their conflict with the Establishment. If, on occasion, some dialogue is distractingly superimposed on the action, it somehow projects both that conflict and the poignancy of the addict's uncertain existence.

An off-screen narrator, for example, colorfully relates the events leading to the death of a fellow addict, a loving husband and father, which he attributes to callous police and doctors, who, he says, thought his friend was feigning his terminal illness.

1975 D 4, 53:4

THE MAN IN THE TRUNK, directed by Georges Lautner; screenplay (French with English subtitles) by Francis Veber; director of photography, Maurice Fellous; music by Philippe Sarde; released by Gaumont International Films. Running time: 100 minutes; this film has been classified PG. At the Symphony and Waverly Theaters.

Francoise .... Mireille Darc
Captain Augier ....Michel Constantin
Major Bloch ....Jean-Pierre Marielle
Baggage Man ....Jean Lefebvre
Abdul ....Amidou
Mercier ....Robert Dalban
Ambassador ....Raoul Saint-Ives
The American ....Arch Taylor

By A. H. WEILER

Although "The Man in the Trunk," which was opened at local theaters yesterday, traverses wat appears to be most of the North African littoral, it doesn't seem to get anywhere in particular. Though it is nominally a French farce, it rarely generates a guffaw. And, as an extenuated chase involving an Israeli secret agent fleeing from irate Arabs (through that trunk mostly) in the unlikely company of a French intelligence officer, an Egyptian naval lieutenant and a leggy blond, Gallic charmer they all adore, it is a labored trip that isn't quite necessary.

Despite English subtitles that capture some of the nuances of the often idiomatic dialogue, one soon discovers that Mireille Darc is not so much the mysterious, smiling femme fatale but a simple, realist wo knows that the shortest route to her destination is through the boudoir. As her smitten swains, Jean-Pierre Marielle, (the harried Israeli), Michel Constantin (his blunt, befuddled French accomplice) and Amidou (the youthful, equally uncertain Egyptian) are athletic, if not convincing, in their ardor and their slightly comic, nationalistic quips.

Under Georges Lautner's uneven direction they seem to be running constantly through a succession of mild gags, while toting that trunk through hotel rooms, Libyan and Tunisian deserts and coastal waters. Unfortunately, most of that energy is wasted. Like its convoluted script, "The Man in the Trunk" takes us on a contrived, largely cheerless journey.

1975 D 6, 22:5

A Very Funny Film In Search of An Audience

"Rancho Deluxe," directed by Frank Perry and written by Thomas McGuane, the novelist ("Ninety-Two in The Shade"), is a most engaging, deliberately cool comedy about coping in the contemporary American West, specifically Montana, a magnificently scenic wasteland where the fight against boredom becomes nothing less than an affirmation of life. Beautifully acted by a cast headed by Jeff Bridges and Sam Waterston, the film is very funny and almost too smart for its own good. If it were a man, you'd call him a wisenheimer, until you understood that his cocky self-assurance—his complete inability to resist showing off—was fundamental to his living at all.

"Rancho Deluxe" is a small treasure, and one that apparently needs salvaging. Like two other recent American films, Howard Zieff's "Hearts of The West" and Michael Ritchie's "Smile," it is uncommonly bright and intelligent, as well as consistently entertaining, yet it seems to be having trouble finding its audience. According to the management of the D. W. Griffith Theater where "Rancho Deluxe" is currently playing in New York, the film's distributors weren't especially keen on spending the money required for an exclusive one-theater eastside opening since it had been shown elsewhere around the country and had not performed, which is trade argot for having done poor business. This may be scarier news than the huge profits being racked up by "Jaws."

Could it be that "Rancho Deluxe," "Hearts of The West" and "Smile" are the victims of the same circumstances that prompted the moneymen to finance them in the first place? The answer appears to be a very dreary yes.

As even the people who couldn't care less well know, American movie companies are making far fewer films these days than they did five years ago or even two years ago. The bonanza profits earned by several films, most recently "Jaws," "The Godfather" and "The Exorcist," have proved to producers all over again that there are pots of gold to be earned if only the right formula can be found.

"Jaws," "The Godfather" and "The Exorcist" seemed to signal the appearance of a new mass market, a single amorphous blob of hundreds of thousands of people, all of whom are alike to the extent that they shared a common interest in paying hard cash to see these particular films. This phenomenon has caused something of a counterrevolution in the Hollywood thinking of the late nineteenfifties and sixties, when producers and distributors had come to acknowledge that the old mass market had been fragmented by television competition into dozens of smaller markets that often could sustain their own low-budget films, given a little assistance from the spill-over from the other markets. The success of the black exploitation movies was a favorite case in point.

That thinking has now changed. The producers and distributors are well aware that there still are dozens of individual markets but they've also seen that, given the right picture, those markets can again be fused into a single whopper. Since intelligent producers never rely exclusively on proven formulas, they hedge their bets on the big-budget disaster films, private eye films and Mafia films by occasionally turning out comparatively inexpensive, off-beat works like "Rancho Deluxe," "Hearts of The West" and "Smile."

The problem today is getting those films into theaters, and being able to let them stay long enough to find an audience. The way the major film companies are now set up, they haven't the time, the patience or the money to waste on films that are problematical at the box office or, at best,

Charlene Dallas and Jeff Bridges in "Rancho Deluxe"

will only break even. The companies are geared for immediate results and big results and, given the huge costs of distribution, and the sort of mini-industry-within-an-industry that something like "Jaws" becomes, one can understand why.

It's not that these people don't appreciate movies like Ingmar Bergman's "The Magic Flute" or Joan Micklin Silver's "Hester Street." Appreciation has nothing to do with it. They are dealing in different commodities altogether. They're after big money and they haven't got the manpower to attend to films that don't immediately sell themselves.

What we are facing now is a Hollywood following the kind of trail that turned the Broadway theater into a boom-bust business able to sustain a few expensive, mostly conventional musicals and an occasional straight comedy or drama. Most of the interesting films will have to be produced and/or distributed by independents—Hollywood's equivalent to Off and Off Off Broadway. Mrs. Silver is distributing "Hester Street" herself while Carmen F. Zollo, a Manhattan importer of hides and skins, put up the money to acquire the American rights to "The Magic Flute."

In the meantime, "Rancho Deluxe" is in danger of being overlooked entirely, which would be a disservice to Mr. Perry, whose best film it is next to "Diary of A Mad Housewife," to Mr. McGuane, whose screenplay is full of the kind of antic eccentricities movies seldom employ, and to ourselves.

"Rancho Deluxe" can be faulted on several points that, to me, do not seem terribly important in view of the over-all film. Even though the results are often hilarious, the movie's schematicism is as predictable as a production of "Hamlet" in which all of the male and female roles are reversed.

"Rancho Deluxe" turns all of the old Western movie myths inside out. The old range is now ridden by helicopter and Lincoln Continental Mark IVs. Its two heroes, Mr. Bridges and Mr. Waterston, are cattle rustlers who drive around in a pick-up truck and carry a chain saw. The two nice town girls they date talk dirtier than Lenny Bruce. The ranch that is their principal target is owned by a bored couple from Schenectady (Clifton James and Elizabeth Ashley) who got their spread from the profits of a string of beauty parlors. Their two ranch hands were formerly an appliance repairman and an actor who demonstrated hot combs on TV. The land is breathtakingly lovely but the big sky overhead is flawed by a jet's trail.

There are lines in the film that you wish Mr. Perry and Mr. McGuane had resisted, but many more that make up for those lapses. The casting is exquisite, especially Slim Pickens as a crafty old fellow hired to catch the rustlers, and Charlene Dallas as his shy, physically spectacular niece who reminds one of the cowboys of Bambi.

The schematicism is there but the movie reaches out beyond the scheme to create a world inhabited by manic, completely unpredictable people who have homesteaded on the frontiers of sanity.

1975 D 7, II:17:1

SPECIAL SECTION (Section Speciale), directed by Costa-Gavras; screenplay by Jorge Semprun and Mr. Gavras; director of photography, Andreas Winding; editor, Francoise Bonnot; music, Eric Demarsan; produced by Jacques Perrin and Giorgio Silvagni; a co-production of Reggane Films-Artistes Associes (Paris), Goriz Films (Rome) and Janus Films (Frankfurt), distributed by Universal Pictures. Running time: 110 minutes. At the Beekman Theater, Second Avenue at 65th Street. This film has been rated PG.
Minister of Justice ...... Louis Seigner
Minister of the Interior . Michel Lonsdale
Admiral .... Ivo Garrani
Deputy General .... Francois Maistre
Attorney General .... Pierre Dux
State Prosecutor ...... Jacques Francois
President of the
Special Section ...... Claude Pieplu
Counsellor Linais .... Jean Bouise
President Cournet ...... Michel Galabru
Major Beumelburg ...... Heinz Bennent
Brechet .... Guy Relore
Bastard .... Yves Robert
Trzebrucki .... Jacques Rispal
Samplaix .... Bruno Cremer
Lawyer Lafarge .... Jacques Perrin

By VINCENT CANBY

Costa-Gavras's "Special Section" ("Section Spéciale"), which shared the best-direction award at this year's Cannes Film Festival, is the most severe, least hoked-up movie yet made by a director whose terrific flair for melodrama has occasionally seemed to obscure and exploit genuine political issues in "State of Siege," "The Confession" and, especially, in "Z."

"Special Section" could be the film that a number of critics have been urging Mr. Gavras to make, though now, it seems, we were wrong. Deny the director the techniques and devices of melodrama, which he uses so stunningly, and you may get a film that, like "Special Section," is full of fury but has neither great emotional nor intellectual impact. Perhaps Brecht could have pulled it off.

In "Special Section," which opened at the Beekman yesterday, Mr. Gavras and Jorge Semprun, his screenwriting associate, present the spectacle of supposedly honorable Frenchmen collaborating with and sometimes enthusiastically carrying out the illegal practices of the Nazi-dominated Vichy government.

The word spectacle best describes the form. "Special Section" is a film in which dozens of characters are used to illustrate an issue, rather than to speculate on its meaning or even to dramatize it in any depth. The characters come and go so quickly, sometimes with only the briefest of introductions, that you may have difficulty following the film without a printed program, even though the principal issue is clear enough.

In August of 1941, a young German naval cadet was assassinated in Paris. The outraged Nazis demanded reprisals, suggesting the execution of some of the leading Communists already held in French prisons. The Vichy government, suggesting that the Germans would execute 100 French hostages unless something was done quickly, obliged.

With the advice and cooperation of some of France's most prominent judges, the Vichy government promulgated a law that empowered "special sections" to the court of appeals to try citizens for crimes against the state that had already been adjudicated.

The miscarriage of traditional justice was further increased in that the law was made retroactive, so that a person could be held liable for prosecution for actions committed before the law made those actions crimes. Seven days after the German cadet was assassinated three Frenchmen, who had been held in prison for crimes that earlier commanded sentences no longer than five years each, were guillotined.

Throughout the rest of the German occupation, says a postscript to the film, these special sections functioned freely and, after the liberation, none of the judges was seriously penalized. Mr. Gavras and Mr. Semprun are clearly appalled that reasonable, intelligent, civilized men could so easily bend their ethics to fit the needs of the state. Ambition, opportunism, a misplaced sense of duty, each may have contributed to this behavior, they suggest, but that's about all.

This is such a fascinating subject that I don't quite understand how the film can be so cool and unmoving. Perhaps the Olympian point of view has something to do with it. The movie opens with a rather extended, very conventional sequence showing some young Parisians planning their terrorist tactics and then, after the assassination, the attention is shifted to the negotiations within the Vichy government to get the law enacted and to find men to carry it out.

Aside from the Minister of the Interior (Michel Lonsdale) and the aging Minister of Justice (Louis Seigner) there are scarcely any characters on the screen long enough to register anything except a political position. The movie becomes a series of conference room and corridor and courtroom confrontations, not unlike "Tora, Tora Tora," except that the arguments here are more interesting and the sets more handsome, though much of the acting is equally terrible.

It's curious that Marcel Ophuls's "The Sorrow and the Pity" was able to examine this same issue, and others like it, much more profoundly in the documentary form than Mr. Gavras can do with all of fiction's freedom. I suspect that he was determined not to make his subject sentimental or trivial by appealing to the emotions. Yet the film is neither complex nor witty enough to engage us on any other level.

1975 D 8, 42:1

ARTICULATION OF BOOLEAN ALGEBRA FOR FILM OPTICALS, a film by Tony Conrad. Running time: 70 minutes. At the Whitney Museum of American Art, Madison Avenue at 74th Street.

"Articulation of Boolean Algebra for Film Opticals," the film program that opened yesterday at the Whitney Museum, is a new Tony Conrad "flicker" film. It's a 70-minute assault on the eyes consisting of optically printed black lines and black rectangles alternating with clear film stock. At intervals the images speed up and slow down, as do the soundtrack noises, which often sound like a man jogging around an indoor track in sweat socks.

Mr. Conrad is a serious, highly articulate member of the avant-garde, but his films are more interesting to me in theory than in fact. By draining the image and the sound of almost all associations to things or ideas, he doesn't liberate the viewer's mind, he more or less forces it to wander.

VINCENT CANBY

1975 D 11, 59:2

Hack Writer Picks Up Woman on Riviera

By RICHARD EDER

It is winter on the Riviera, a time when the water turns beer-colored and cold and it costs less to put a movie crew up in the local hotels.

François, a clownish and sentimental hack writer, sees a waif-like blonde walking on the beach. She is possessed by an inalterable grief but he capers around her, lies down in front of her car and gets a smile or two.

The battle should be won. She agrees that he may come and see her at her villa. He strides in, tosses his coat onto a coatrack—it falls off, which is one of the amiable things about this picture—and the blonde, whose name is Peggy, seems prepared to receive him with friendliness.

But things aren't that simple. What François has picked up along with Peggy is a great load of trouble, and the movie's object is to keep the audience trying to decide just which kind of trouble he is in.

Peggy is attended by a whole bent posse: Mark, her lawyer; Mark's chauffeur and

The Cast

ICY BREASTS (Les Seins de Glace), directed by Georges Lautner; screenplay by Mr. Lautner from the novel by Richard Matheson; director of photography, Maurice Fellous; music, Philippe Sarde; distributed by Joseph Green Pictures. Running time: 105 minutes; this film has not been rated. At the 85th Street Trans Lux and the Cinema Village Theaters.
Marc .... Alain Delon
Peggy .... Mireille Darc
Francois .... Claude Brasseur
Jacqueline .... Nicoletta Machiavelli
Denis .... Flore Altoviti
Garnier .... Andre Falcon
Steig .... Emilio Messina
Albert .... Michael Peyrelon

Mark's goon. At least, they seem bent, and Peggy seems to want to get away from them. And when François tries to get her away, they

are successively chased by a black car, stuck in an elevator and assaulted in a pitch-black garage.

François naturally suspects that she is being held prisoner. When Mark, the lawyer, takes him aside and tells him Peggy is deranged and has murdered her husband, he looks at her elfin, freckled face—it is Mireille Darc's—and knows it is all a lie. Since Alain Delon, who has the crookedest straight face in the business, plays the lawyer, the suspicion is reasonable enough.

Except that the goon and Mark's brother both turn up stabbed to death after being closeted with Peggy. And the audience, if not François, knows that the movie's title is "Icy Breasts." It will be the reason many of them are there, in fact.

All in all, there will be no real doubt by the time this is two-thirds over as to who the real villain is. But it is one of those movies that are ridiculous without being altogether bad. One of its achievements is that emotional suspense remains for quite a while after intellectual suspense has fled.

The scene in the dark garage is genuinely scary. So is François's final tryst scene with Peggy in a mountain motel. And although Mr. Delon gives his customary performance as a patch of uninhabited film, both Miss Darc and Claude Brasseur are first-rate.

Miss Darc creates a character that without being really believable is effective. It isn't necessary to believe in ghosts to be scared by them. Mr. Brasseur is funny and messy and alive.

1975 D 11, 59:1

Experimental Work Is on Bill of 6 Shorts

By RICHARD EDER

Rudy Burckhardt films New York as a man might pick up shells and sea drift on the beach: Some bits because they're pretty or odd, some because they may come in handy and some because he happens to be stooped over anyway.

"City Pasture," the centerpiece of a group of short experimental works being shown this weekend and next at the Film Forum, is a collection of oddments whose thematic link is mainly that Mr. Burckhardt likes them.

As he collects, he talks to himself, or seems to. In fact the succession of fragmented scenes is accompanied by texts written by various poets, but the effect is a mumble. This is not a bad thing: Beachcombers are entitled to mumble, and if you are alone with them, and the sea and the weather are fine, there is no need to pay close attention.

Mr. Burchkardt's weather is pretty good, so it doesn't matter too much that some of

course without clubs, just for the exercise.

"Where There's Smoke" (Il-n'y-a pas de Fumée Sans Feu), which opened yesterday at the Cinema Studio, is about political corruption in a rich Paris suburb where to be mayor, apparently, offers such magnificent rewards (whether it's power, money or simply girls, the film never says) that the incumbent party resorts to bribery, blackmail and murder to stay in office.

Though Mr. Cayatte was once a lawyer, he doesn't acknowledge that there may be two sides to any question or that characters, like motives, may be mixed. "Where There's Smoke" is the story of the mostly successful efforts of the incumbent mayor to discredit his principal opposition, a clean-living young doctor (Bernard Fresson), by circulating a fake photograph showing the doctor's brave, loyal wife (Annie Girardot) participating in an orgy, which, if you've seen an Annie Girardot movie lately, is the last thing she would do.

The film in fact is less about political corruption and the lust for power than the technology of blackmail. The only sequence of interest in the movie shows how it's possible to fake a photograph, to place one person's head on the body of another, in such a way that even laser beams cannot detect the deception.

This may give you pause, if not quite making you stop and think.

1975 D 11, 59:1

WHERE THERE'S SMOKE (Il-n'y-a pas de Fumee Sans Feu), directed by Andre Cayatte; screenplay (French with English subtitles) by Mr. Cayatte; produced by Lucien Masse; executive producer, Jacques Bourdon; director of cinematography, Maurice Fellous; distributed by Libra Films Corporation. Running time: 112 minutes. At the Cinema Studio, Broadway at 66th Street. This film has not been rated.
Sylvie .... Annie Girardot
Olga .... Mireille Darc
Michel Peyrac .... Bernard Fresson
Morlaix .... Michel Bouquet
Ulrich .... Mathieu Carriere
Boussard .... André Falcon

By VINCENT CANBY

In the 1950's, André Cayatte, a French lawyer-turned-film-maker, made two films ("We Are All Murderers," "Justice Is Done") that received a good deal of favorable attention here. On the basis of everything he's done since, that acclaim seems to have been unwarranted.

Mr. Cayatte's newest film to be released in this country, "Where There's Smoke," virtually defines the pedestrian movie. It proceeds earnestly, step by step, from one obvious point to another, like a man walking around a golf

the objects he picks up are worthwhile mainly to himself. He follows the soft reflections in the city's plate-glass skyscrapers — fairly trite—but then he stands in some unidentified part of New York and films faces and feet, and they work.

He shoots a striptease routime by a male transvestite—one of the more futile occupations around, involving as it does the careful unrigging of a carefully rigged illusion —and then gives us an incredible stained-glass window. Almost instantly, you see it's not a stained-glass window but the orange sunset light striking Harlem brick. Lovely metaphor.

At the end, having poked

The Program

CITY PASTURE, a series of six short films: "City Pasture," by Rudy Burckhardt; "Evidence," by Alfred Guzzetti; "Playgrounds," by Allen Moore; "Trip," by Laszlo Papp and Istvan Ventilla; "Yaknetuma," by Jacob Burckhardt; "Postcards," by Andrew Lugg. Running time: 89 minutes. At the Film Forum, 15 Vandam Street.

his camera into the faces of pin-curled girls and bums drinking wine out of brown-bagged bottles, Mr. Burckhardt makes a graceful commentary on his own intrusive art. Three bums he is filming beat him and take his camera. A smal, bearded figure, he is last seen drinking from a brown paper bag himself, on humanity's side of somebody else's camera. It is staged, of course, but winning.

Of the shorter works, by other film makers, the best is "Yaknetuma," the near-ballet of a wispy Oriental girl addressing a grubby city block. She tries, various

things: dancing, splashing in a puddle, throwing flowers, taking off her clothes. Each brief sequence ends with her snatched from the frame: the dirty walls and muddy street remaining. Finally she simply walks off. It is casual, cocky, funny; the work of Rudy Burckhardt's son, Jacob.

Of the others, "Trip" is a vastly speeded-up view of a highway seen from a car. "Evidence" is a generally slowed-up version of much the same thing. They are not without grace and some emotion—movement without destination equals melancholy— but they are pretty minimal.

"Postcards" and "Playgrounds" both suffer from a fallacy common to experimental documentaries. Cows can dance, but it is not really what they are best at. The movie camera can be a paintbrush or distorting mirror— sometimes effectively — but usually there's a sense of strain.

"Postcards" puts a serio-comic intensity to work on various roadside commonplaces—motels, pizza parlors, factories — as if they were scenic wonders. The statement, whatever it is, exists only in the mind of the movie maker.

"Playgrounds" is more skillful. But the camera shoots slides, swings, seesaws at odd angles, in odd close-up, in odd lighting, making them look like artifacts from another planet. The children are frozen in profile against distorted skies. What is the author — Allen Moore — really trying to say about playgrounds and children? Nothing. Expressiveness obliterates the thing expressed.

1975 D 12, 53:1

FILM VIEW

VINCENT CANBY

You Don't Walk Out on Catherine Deneuve

Some thoughts on film acting: Two weeks ago I did *not* walk out on a particularly phony little French melodrama called "Act of Aggression." In fact I very seldom walk out on anything, no matter how bad. Sitting in the theater is one of the things a critic is paid to do and if someone has worked the better part of two years on a film, spending two hours watching it seems to be the least a critic can do. There are exceptions and, under ordinary circumstances, "Act of Aggression" would have been one of them. It's a souped up, sensationalized semi-whodunit about a French businessman (Jean-Louis Trintignant) who seeks to avenge the rape-murders of his wife and small daughter by a gang of bad-mannered motorcyclists.

The thing that kept me in the theater, as riveted as one can be by a terrible film, was the spectacle of Catherine Deneuve trying desperately and with wit to give some life to the venture. Now Miss Deneuve is one of the world's great beauties but she is never very close to the top of anyone's list of the world's great actresses. More than competent she is, and stunning to behold, even in a Chanel ad, but she never gets the kinds of notices that are heaped on Glenda Jackson, Ellen Burstyn and Jane Fonda.

Miss Deneuve was so effective within the dismal context of "Act of Aggression"—playing Trintignant's not terribly bereaved sister-in-law, a woman of intense sexuality and quick intelligence, qualities that appeared to be her contributions to the film—that I began to worry all over again about the manner in which critics treat film acting and actors.

• • •

Miss Deneuve has been marvelously effective in some fascinating films—Polanski's "Repulsion," Bunuel's "Belle de Jour" and "Tristana" and Truffaut's "Mississippi Mermaid"—but I don't think anyone has ever suggested that her performance alone had made any film worth seeing. I'm not about to know. "Act of Aggression" is unsalvageable. Given the right material, however, she appears to be growing into an actress of just such stature.
But will we ever know?

It's not, I think, a foolish question. All of us—critics as well as people who simply go to the movies because they like them—bring into the theater so many preconditioned responses that the way we react to the performances may have little to do with the performer or his talent.

From the point of view of the intelligent actor, movies must be the least rewarding experience there is, unless the actor has the clout to pick his associates and material and run the show. Bad lighting, an inappropriate directorial style, a cut-and-paste screenplay, lawn-mower editing, can make any good actor look imbecilic. Sometimes an actor stands away from the background. More often not. In those magical moments of fiddling around with material after it's been photographed, a performance that once made sense can be transformed into a double-talk joke.

Inappropriate—bad—casting is something we often blame on the actor when all he's trying to do is make a living. Take the recent work of Glenda Jackson, an actress who, for various reasons, is incapable of playing someone without brains and a good deal of spine. There's a certain amount of fun watching her in an over-ripe Italian tomato like "The Devil Is A Woman," playing a sexually hung-up nun, but the subterranean personality that shapes her every performance throws Joseph Losey's "The Romantic Englishwoman" off the track.

The film is interesting as long as it's about Miss Jackson and her equally intelligent though troubled husband, played by Michael Caine. They seem made for each other. They are peers. But when the movie introduces the idea that a woman like Miss Jackson could throw herself at the feet of a gigolo of Helmut Berger's weightlessness, the movie becomes a solemn, overdressed fraud. We lose patience with everyone, including Miss Jackson. She's still the actress she always has been but we blame her for having gotten into bad company.

• • •

The best film performers (and some of the most enduring) are the most pliant, though pliancy is not meant to be synonymous with versatility. Pliancy has something to do with talent and even more to do with the personality of the actor, the way he looks, his physical shape. Dustin Hoffman and Al Pacino are amazingly pliant actors, even though each one tends to evoke New York and there are times when all of us confuse the two.

Gene Hackman, who is a fine actor, appears to lack this pliancy. No matter what role he plays, the character seems to have some dread, Ibsen-like secret to live down from the past. His physical appearance is not pliant. This has nothing to do with his acting abilities but he seems unable to make us believe the character he's playing just happens to look like him. He overwhelms the role with a particular physical presence and brings to it a whole carload of psychological experiences we've come to identify with him from his other films.

Part of this may have to do with exposure. Hackman seems to have been on our screens non-stop all year and though the movies are different ("French Connection Two," "Night Moves"), Hackman isn't. Some actors

cannot accommodate frequent exposure. Hackman is one of them. So is Elliott Gould.

• • •

One who apparently is able to is Jack Nicholson, an actor who has a unique ability to sneak up on roles and occupy them so completely that, while you're watching him in "One Flew Over The Cuckoo's Nest," you're never associating him with, say, the spaced-out, white-suited lawyer in "Easy Rider."

The public personalities of actors, especially stars, are shaped as much by their high positions as by their films. Nicholson has had the good fortune to be in a variety of films that have seldom been stupid, if not always successful. His high position hasn't yet interfered with his career as it did with Marlon Brando's, once the most talented, the most pliant of them all. Paul Newman, Warren Beatty and Robert Redford are pliant actors. Burt Reynolds may be. Steve McQueen and Charles Bronson aren't.

Critics are fond of reporting that such-and-such supporting performer has run off with the acting honors in a film. It's nice to discover people and give praise when due but, let's face it, supporting people have a much easier time of it than the leads. They get on and off fast. Given the right material, they can create a vivid impression without risking much. Which may be one of the secrets of the success of Robert Altman's "Nashville," perhaps the best acted film of the year and one in which virtually everyone is a supporting actor—Henry Gibson, Ronee Blakley, Lily Tomlin, Barbara Harris, et al. Both Michael Ritchie's "Smile" and Frank Perry's "Rancho Deluxe" are similarly constructed.

Having gone on at this length, I should add that writing about film acting is, at best, perilous, at worst, nonsense. We can simply label performances "good," "fine," "gemlike," "lousy," or we can try to describe the performances. But describing a performance is like trying to describe the taste of broiled shad roe. You may be able to interest someone in trying it himself but until he does, the subject remains illusive.

1975 D 14, II:15:7

Why Couldn't This 'Lady' Have an Unhappy Ending?

By STEPHEN FARBER

LOS ANGELES
In movies the question of how to end a story arises more frequently than audiences may realize. A fascinating case in point is the recent radical alteration in the ending of the expensive sea adventure, "Lucky Lady," starring Liza Minnelli, Gene Hackman and Burt Reynolds, which opens in New York on Christmas day. The history of this film sheds light on the complex process of filmmaking and decision-making in Hollywood, the nature of popular storytelling and, quite possibly, the mood of the contemporary audience. Hollywood has always favored happy endings, but there may be times when the public is more desperate

Stephen Farber frequently reports on the movie scene.

for upbeat endings and less receptive to disturbing endings.

In 1973 Willard Huyck and his wife, Gloria Katz, the co-writers of "American Graffiti," wrote the original screenplay of "Lucky Lady," a romantic drama about two men and a woman smuggling booze from Mexico to California in the last year of Prohibition. The Huycks and producer Michael Gruskoff sold the script to 20th Century-Fox for $450,000. "The studio loved the script," the writers say, "and at that point no one objected to the ending." In this version, the two men were killed by Government agents and the final scene, some 10 years later, showed the heroine, Claire, now married to a rich but colorless businessman, remembering the romance of her lost youth.

A few months after the sale of the script Stanley Donen was hired to direct the film, and he worked with the Huycks on some changes in the script. Shooting began in Guaymas, Mexico, in February of this year, and because of the difficulties of shooting virtually an entire movie on the ocean, "Lucky Lady" went over budget; the final cost was $13-million. But the ending was shot as the Huycks had written it.

Since "Lucky Lady" was booked to open around the country at Christmas, Donen had only three months to edit the film. In October he began previewing the movie with the original sad ending, and at that point he became seriously concerned about the conclusion. He tried several different endings at subsequent previews, including a makeshift happy ending, which amounted to simply

Minnelli—Her lovers came back.

chopping off the last 10 minutes of the film. In mid-November, Donen, who had the legal right to do the final cutting of the film, decided that a new ending was needed. The Huycks at first protested but finally agreed to write a concluding scene in which the three leading characters are alive and together. By that time the studio also favored the idea of a happy ending. According to Donen, "Fox approved the new ending. Then I called Gene and Burt and read it to them. They loved it and agreed to do it without charging us anything." Since Liza Minnelli was in Rome filming "A Matter of Time" for her father, director Vincente Minnelli, Donen, Hackman and Reynolds flew to Rome and spent one Saturday in late November shooting the new ending.

Endings have troubled story tellers of every generation. Charles Dickens, for example, took a friend's advice and rewrote the ending of "Great Expectations" shortly before its publication. There have been a number of cases in film history where endings have been changed at the last minute. Frank Capra previewed five different endings of "Meet John Doe" in 1941. In one of the rejected endings, Gary Cooper actually committed suicide, but in the final released version he is rescued at the last minute; this ending, suggested by a fan who wrote Capra a letter, was shot after the film had already opened in six cities. More recently, Francis Ford Coppola tried out several different endings to "The Godfather, Part II" and did not make his final decision until three weeks before the movie opened.

In the case of "Lucky Lady," Stanley Donen explains that he always felt troubled by the ending: "When I first read the script, the ending touched me, but it also disturbed me, and I was not sure it would work. It left me with a feeling of dissatisfaction that I couldn't quite put my finger on. We discussed it but I couldn't come up with anything that I liked better. Then while we were shooting, the film changed tone. The Huycks had written the character of Mosely, the Coast Guard captain who pursues the heroes, as very menacing. I felt it wouldn't play that way, so I made him a buffoon, and said to the Huycks at the time, 'It's worrying me how funny this is becoming.'

"You see, the whole picture—with the exception of one battle scene in the middle—had become much fun-

"Lucky Lady" writers Huyck and Katz:
"People want films that won't tax them."

nier. And when it was cut and I saw it all put together, I said to myself, the ending is not integral to the movie. The film seemed to shift tone just to make people cry, to achieve a new sensation, not because it was inevitable in terms of the characters, but because I couldn't find a more adroit way of ending on a comic note. It was as if a play by George Bernard Shaw had an ending written by Clifford Odets."

I attended two previews of "Lucky Lady"—one with the original unhappy ending, and one with the makeshift happy ending. In both cases the audience reaction was enthusiastic. As the Huycks emphasized, "The audience was not storming the theater. It was a minority that objected to the ending."

"Previewing a film is like testing a play in New Haven," producer Michael Gruskoff points out. "At the six previews we had the reactions on the cards were 92 percent excellent or very good over all. But we found in looking more closely at the cards that about 20 percent of the people asked, 'Why did the two men have to die?' I always liked the original ending. I cried when I first read the script. And I still think people would have been touched by that ending. But now people walk out feeling entertained and happy. This is a business. You make movies to make money and entertain the public. We decided to give the people what they wanted."

Alan Ladd Jr., head of pro-

duction at Fox, adds: "Gene Wilder re-shot the ending to 'Sherlock Holmes' Smarter Brother' after a sneak preview. I always thought the original ending to 'Lucky Lady' would work. But the Huycks wrote and Stanley directed the film so well that the audience loved the characters and didn't want them to die. In Los Angeles and San Francisco the reaction was not that different when we tested the two endings. But we are aiming this film at a very broad audience. When you are making an all-family entertainment, you do not want to alienate any segment of the audience that would find the film too violent or too unhappy. I think people in the Midwest prefer a happy ending. I know kids prefer a happy ending. My kids asked me, 'Daddy, why did they have to die?' "

During the discussions after the previews, the Huycks argued to preserve their original ending. They explain that the ending was one of the strongest parts of their original conception for "Lucky Lady." "One of the first images in our minds when we began to work on the script was the ending," says Gloria Katz. "The idea of this woman remembering the two men she had loved. We worked backward from that. To us, the romance of the piece was in the idea of separation and loss."

Accordingly, the Huycks resisted. The prospect of changing their conception was painful, but they eventually went along with the

decision to rewrite the ending, and today Willard Huyck comments, "We understand why the decision was made. Everyone was very conscious of the fact that this was an expensive film." Cynics outside the industry may suspect that the filmmakers compromised their work in order to succeed at the box office. However, as one who was in a position to read the script and see both versions of the film, my own opinion is that the issue is more complex. The original sad ending introduced a harsh note of reality into a fantasy adventure, and it had a definite emotional force on paper and on film; but when I saw the film the shift from comedy to tragedy was jarring to me, as I suspect it was to many in the audience. Although the final version with the happy ending has less poignancy, the finished film is more of a piece, more consistent in mood.

When the Huycks saw the final version of the film last week, they decided that the new ending was successful in terms of the rest of the film. One lesson to be gleaned from their experience on "Lucky Lady" is that a script can be shot as written and still turn out subtly different in tone from what the writers intended. "A movie evolves," Gloria Katz admits now. "Stanley is a very good director, and he chose to emphasize the comedy in the script. If the movie had a different emphasis, the original ending might have worked better. Actually, when we saw the direction the film was taking, we added more comic dialogue while we were down in Guaymas. Given the film as it stands now, Stanley was right to change the ending."

Willard Huyck discusses another change in emphasis: "We always felt that 'Lucky Lady' was primarily the woman's story. To us the original ending made a comment about the choices a woman has to make. But instead of making it the story of this woman, Stanley has made it a story of three people. That's valid. It's just different from what we had originally intended. The audience loved the notion of a romance between three people. That is the audience's fantasy. We hadn't realized how strongly people would respond to that idea."

During the late sixties a significant number of movies with unhappy endings—"Bonnie and Clyde," "Easy Rider," "Midnight Cowboy," "Butch

Cassidy and the Sundance Kid," "They Shoot Horses, Don't They?" "Joe" and "Love Story" caught on with the public. Those films were made during the Vietnam War, when the country was inflamed by social protest, and although most of the films were not explicitly political they expressed the disillusionment of that era.

Today, in a period of political apathy and economic hardship, audiences seem to want to flee any confrontation with the real world. Gloria Katz reflects: "I think the audience's reaction to our original ending has a great deal to do with the temper of the times. Right now people want to see films that won't tax them at all. They want to block out any disturbance. They just want to be entertained." ■

1975 D 14, II:1:2

THE ADVENTURE OF SHERLOCK HOLMES' SMARTER BROTHER, directed and written by Gene Wilder; produced by Richard A. Roth; music, John Morris; director of cinematography, Gerry Fisher; distributed by 20th Century-Fox. Running time: 91 minutes. At the Little Carnegie Theater, 57th Street east of Seventh Avenue, and Loews Tower East, Third Avenue near 72d Street. This film has been rated PG.
Sigerson Holmes .... Gene Wilder
Jenny .... Madeline Kahn
Orville Sacker .... Marty Feldman
Gambetti .... Dom DeLuise
Moriarty .... Leo McKern
Finney .... Roy Kinnear
Lord Redcliff .... John Le Mesurier
Sherlock Holmes ...... Douglas Wilmer
Dr. Watson .... Thorley Walters

By VINCENT CANBY

"Unless I'm very much mistaken," says Sigerson Holmes (Gene Wilder), drawing the words out with care and smiling slightly, preparing to stun his audience with a grand new insight, " 'hadderd' is the Egyptian word 'to eat fat.' "

Sigerson is deciphering a coded message that has just been delivered to his tacky London flat in "The Adventure of Sherlock Holmes' Smarter Brother" and, of course, he's immediately off on the wrong track.

"The Adventure of Sherlock Holmes' Smarter Brother," which opened at two theaters here yesterday, is a charming slapstick comedy that honors Sir Arthur Conan Doyle's original creation as much by what it doesn't do as by what it does do. The film is a marvelously lowbrow caper but it makes no attempt to parody the great Sherlock himself, who is treated with cheerful if distant awe and respect, measured entirely in terms of Sigerson's ineptitude.

Sigerson Holmes, somewhat manic, capable of fits of intense, wrongheaded concentration, is the unique creation of Gene Wilder, who not only stars in the film but who also wrote and directed it.

It's correct to report that Sigerson is younger than his brother Sherlock (younger

Gene Wilder, left, and Marty Feldman

also than their brother, Mycroft, who does not appear in this adventure). He's also luckier and much, much blonder, but he is just a teeny-tiny bit dense, which is something he can never admit in his sibling fury.

Sigerson loathes Sherlock with a depth that is reserved only for the loathing that one brother cherishes for another. Yet that doesn't prevent Sigerson from hanging a shingle outside his door that reads "S. Holmes, Consulting Investigator," which occasionally catches a client who had intended to hire Sherlock.

Like "Young Frankenstein," the script for which was written by Mr. Wilder and Mel Brooks, "Sherlock Holmes' Smarter Brother" is full of affection and generous feelings for the genre it's having fun with. It never mistakes the conventions of the Sherlock Holmes world for jokes in themselves. It's not Victorian London nor Conan Doyle conceits that are funny. The humor is in the spectacle of Sigerson's solemnly demonstrating his inability to do absolutely anything right.

Always just offscreen, and sometimes briefly on, is the imposing presence of older brother Sherlock (played with nice style by Douglas Wilmer), who is the architect of the plot that Sigerson thinks he is solving by himself with some help from his equivalent of Dr. Watson. This character is a retired London detective named Orville Sacker who, as played by Marty Feldman, is just the Dr. Watson that Sigerson deserves—optimistic, wise-talking, obsequious and incurably nuts.

Mr. Wilder has surrounded himself with great comic actors and gives them all the opportunity to perform, especially Madeline Kahn, who may possibly be the funniest woman in films today. Miss Kahn plays Jenny Hill, who introduces herself as an actress ("I am simultaneously funny and sad"), but whose identities change from time to time, as befits a mystery.

In addition there are Leo McKern, as Professor Moriarty, still a ruthless villain but who, in Mr. Wilder's screenplay, doesn't know what to do with the decimal point in long division; Dom DeLuise, as a crazy Italian opera star with a misguided desire to succeed in espionage, and John Le Mesurier, as an aging British foreign secretary who has a letch for pretty nannies.

•

The film has a PG rating because—I suppose—of a few sexy gags of the kind that will go over the heads of the very young and will certainly not impair the morals of the kids who will understand them. "Sherlock Holmes' Smarter Brother" seems to be composed mainly of jokes that will delight the young while effectively recalling for the rest of us how hilarious it was to see a man lose his pants at a stuffy dinner party or the shambles that can be made of grand opera when the wrong people get on the stage.

Mr. Wilder, always a fine, very straight comic actor, here makes an impressive debut as a comedy director.

1975 D 15, 42:1

WOMAN TO WOMAN, produced, directed and edited by Donna Deitch. Running time: 48 minutes.
BEING A PRISONER, directed and edited by Suzanne Jasper. Running time: 28 minutes. Both films at the Whitney Museum of American Art.

Timeliness can have a great deal to do with the impact of a movie, especially if the movie is a documentary dealing with a well-publicized subject.

In the case of "Being a Prisoner" and "Woman to Woman," the two films that opened yesterday for a run through Dec. 27 in the New American Filmmakers Series at the Whitney Museum of American Art, the subject is

women—the role of women and women's views of women.

It is a subject that in recent years can scarcely be said to have been shielded from the light of inquiry and exploration. So much so that although both these documentaries are new, the level of consciousness they display seems dated and elementary, more suitable to films assembled in the last decade, at the outset of the latest recrudescence of feminism in America, than to 1975.

And since neither breaks new ground technically, although each has some delightful moments, they must be adjudged disappointments. The material—the plaints of imprisoned women in Suzanne Jasper's "Being a Prisoner" and the comments of prostitutes, housewives, artists, psychologists and others in Donna Deitch's "Woman to Woman" — is repetitious when taken in the light of all else that has been said on the subject.

Their virtue is that out of the tedium created by their insistence on restatement of problems comes an immense yearning for intelligent and durable solutions.

LAWRENCE VAN GELDER

1975 D 18, 62:2

THE MAN WHO WOULD BE KING, directed by John Huston; screenplay by Mr. Huston and Gladys Hill, based on the story by Rudyard Kipling; produced by John Foreman; director of photography, Oswald Morris; editor, Russell Lloyd; music, Maurice Jarre; a Persky-Bright/Devon picture, distributed by Allied Artists. Running time: 129 minutes. At Loew's Astor Plaza, 44th Street west of Broadway, and the Coronet Theater, Third Avenue near 59th Street. This film has been rated PG.

Daniel Dravot	Sean Connery
Peachy Carnehan	Michael Caine
Rudyard Kipling	Christopher Plummer
Billy Fish	Saeed Jaffrey
Kafu-Selim	Karroum Ben Bouih
District Commissioner	Jack May
Ootah	Doghmi Larbi
Roxanne	Shakira Caine

By VINCENT CANBY

The setting is India in the late 19th century when the British raj was in his glory. It is a time of mission and mystery and the white man's burden, of appalling poverty and of wealth often described as untold of. The cities teem with unruly humanity, with beggars, blind men, snake charmers, demented holy men, starving children. In the upland territories British soldiers guard the frontiers to places of which someone will say, quite seriously, "No white man has ever gone in there and come out alive."

In marvelous old movies like "Lives of the Bengal Lancers" and "Gunga Din," this world is very far removed and terribly romantic, as it still is in John Huston's highly entertaining new film, "The Man Who Would Be King," based on the short story by Rudyard Kipling. The film opened yesterday at two theaters.

•

The most pleasant surprise about "The Man Who Would Be King" is that although it is about as romantic and implausible an adventure as you're likely to see, it's not an anachronism. It's neither a silly update of an entertainment designed for pre-World War II Saturday-afternoon America, nor is it one of those films that are wise with hindsight about earlier eras, like John Milius's "The Wind and the Lion."

"The Man Who Would Be King" manages to be great fun in itself while being most faithful to Kipling, whose story, written in the 1890's, is a kind of raffish metaphor for the British colonial experience that did not end for another half century. But this really isn't what "The Man Who Would Be King" is about. It's a tall tale, a legend, of steadfastness, courage, camaraderie, gallantry and greed, though not necessarily in that order.

It's about two former English soldiers turned con artists, Danny Dravot (Sean Connery) and Peachy Carnehan (Michael Caine), who decide that Victoria's India is no longer big enough for them (and their growing reputations as blackmailers and forgers). They decide to carve out their own kingdom in Kafiristan, now a part of Afghanistan but then an undiscovered territory not visited by a known tourist or king since Alexander the Great.

Danny and Peachy are grand, old-fashioned adventurers with the gift of gab and a sense of style. Outrageously disguised as a holy man and his servant, they climb mountains and cross glaciers to penetrate the forbidden territory where, through luck and a series of coincidences, they realize their wildest dreams.

Danny gets himself crowned king and recognized as a god, the legitimate son of Alexander, and Peachy became chief of the armed forces and the treasure chamber. But while Peachy keeps his eye on the main chance, that is, an opportuni-

Michael Caine, left, and Sean Connery

ty to abscond with the gold, Danny begins to like the divinity business and to take his responsibilities seriously, which is their downfall.

•

Not in a very long while has Mr. Huston, who wrote the screenplay with Gladys Hill and also directed the film, been so successfully lighthearted and so consistently in command of his subject. Small-time frauds who get in over their heads have always appealed to him, and Danny and Peachy, as played by Mr. Connery and Mr. Caine, are two of his nicest discoveries — larger-than-life, robust, sometimes curiously prim but suddenly stalwart in the crises.

Christopher Plummer also gives the film weight in the role of the young Rudyard Kipling who, as a newspaperman in India, participates in the beginning and the end of the story. Supporting the stars are Saeed Jaffrey, as a sort of glib Gunga Din character, who always begins a tale of woe by saying "oh me, by jove, alas," as if it were one word, and Shakira Caine (Mrs. Michael Caine), who plays an exotic heathen beauty.

The movie, which was shot in Morocco, looks lovely and remote (how did we ever once settle for those black-and-white Hollywood hills?) and has just enough romantic nonsense in it to enchant the child in each of us.

1975 D 18, 62:1

THE KILLER ELITE; screenplay by Stirling Silliphant; directed by Sam Peckinpah; produced by Martin Baum and Arthur Lewis; executive producer, Helmut Dantine; photography by Phil Lathrop; edited by Garth Craven. Released by United Artists. At Criterion and Red Carpet Theaters. Running time: 123 minutes. This film has been rated PG.

Mike Locken	James Caan
George Hansen	Robert Duvall
Cap Collis	Arthur Hill
Laurence Weyburn	Gig Young
Yuen Chung	Mako
Miller	Bo Hopkins
Mac	Burt Young
O'Leary	Tom Clancy
Tommie Chung	Tiana
Amy	Katy Heflin

By RICHARD EDER

Sam Peckinpah knows how to make movies but perhaps he has forgotten why. At least that is the feeling given by this bag of mixed, often damp fireworks about the alienation of people who do dirty tricks for the Central Intelligence Agency and discover that the tricks as well as th dirt are on them.

"The Killer Elite," which opened yesterday at the Criterion and other theaters, resembles "Three Days of the Condor" so closely that it is as if Mr. Peckinpah had deliberately act himself to do flashier variations on the same theme.

•

The theme is the world as universal sell-out. The metaphor is a covert intelligence organization that does malignant things octensibly in a good cause. The protagonist is an individual who unwittingly falls afoul of one of the organization's plans, becomes its target and ultimately, after all kinds of mayhem, discovers its ends are as amoral as its methods, and walks out.

James Caan plays the role Robert Redford had in "Three Days." Since he is a better actor than Mr. Redford—sharper, more urgent—he is more convincing. Since Mr. Peckinpah is more talented than Sidney Pollack, who did "Three Days," his film has moments, at least, of greater brilliance.

Both pictures operate on the premise that the audience has brought along its eyes but left its head at home. Both are relentlessly far-fetched, presenting all the conceivable outrageousness of the clandestine world at the maximum, and without restaint. A work of art can't be credible when it makes everything happen that can happen.

Mr. Peckinpah is mannered and inventive, and these qualities both give the film its strengths and undermine it horrendously. Cleverness, for one thing, gets in the way of comprehensibility. The plot revolves around the efforts of a fanatical group of Japanese terrorists to kill an anti-Communist Chinese leader.

The attempt at the airport, with a spectacular slow-motion depiction of assassination by kungfu, is intercut with an indoor scene where the motives for all this are explained. The result is that the subsequent action is very hard to follow and it takes a long time to figure out which group of Orientals stands for what.

•

There is a confrontation scene between the leader of the clandestine group and his main assistant, who is working for the other side. The two men glower but don't confront: they talk about the stock market, instead. Perhaps this is stylish, but it is hopelessly obscure, and the film, which last 123 minutes, has already been going on for about 100.

On the other hand, Mr. Peckinpah uses his inventiveness to good purpose in the early part of the film. The protagonist has been grievously wounded by a fellow member of his organization. He sets himself to recover so he can avenge himself; his superiors vaguely discourage him.

In his painful hospital recovery—done with some of the director's bent for sadistic directness—each exercise, each effort to walk becomes another stage in the hero's progressive alientation from his organization.

There is a fine scene at the end where the anticommunist leader is being taken by sailboat to presumed safety on a line of mothballed Navy ships. The dead warships, in a massive gray line, wait: a stunning image of entrapment.

The climactic battle scene, aboard the warships, is ridiculously operatic, however. If a brief use of slow motion in the airport scene was effective, here it goes on endlessly. The notion of the various clandestine operatives standing around while the Chinese leader and his enemies fight things out with sabers is absurd: what is worse, the sight of it is absurd.

If there ever was a screenplay—the credits claim that there was—either it was feeble to begin with, or Mr. Peckinpah has gone galloping all over the lot with it. This director thinks he can do anything he wants, and he is nearly right: But he is a long way from his audience.

1975 D 18, 62:1

BARRY LYNDON, directed, written and produced by Stanley Kubrick; adapted from the novel by William Makepeace Thackeray; executive producer, Jean Harlan; production designer, Ken Adam; director of photography, John Alcott; editor, Tony Lawson; music adapted and conducted by Leonard Rosenman; aPeregrine production, distributed by Warner Bros. Running time: 185 minutes. At the Ziegfeld Theater, 54th Street west of the Avenue of the Americas, and Baronet Theater, Third Avenue near 59th Street. This film has been rated PG.

Barry Lyndon	Ryan O'Neal
Lady Lyndon	Marisa Berenson
Chevalier	Patrick Magee
Captain Potzdorf	Hardy Krugre
Nora	Gay Hamilton
Barry's mother	Marie Kean
German girl	Diana Koerner
Reverend Runt	Murray Melvin
Sir Charles Lyndon	Frank Middlemass
Highwayman	Arthur O'Sullivan
Captain Grogan	Godfrey Quigley
Captain Quin	Leonard Rossiter
Lord Bullingdon	Leon Vitali
Narrator	Michael Hordern

By VINCENT CANBY

"Barry Lyndon," Stanley Kubrick's handsome, assured screen adaptation of William Makepeace Thackeray's first novel, is so long and leisurely, so panoramic in its narrative scope, that it's as much an environment as it is a conventional film. Its austerity of purpose defines it as a costume movie unlike any other you've seen.

Yet in the brilliance of its images the film surrounds you—the way good 19th-century novels do — with characters, events and little discourses on the curious ways of a world in which folly is recognized as a legitimate form of self-achievement.

Don't be misled into thinking that "Barry Lyndon" is going to be a "Tom Jones" romp. The two films share a century (the 18th), one country (England) and the picaresque mode, but their concerns and styles are entirely different.

•

"Barry Lyndon," which opened yesterday at the Ziegfeld and Baronet Theaters, might be most easily described as an 18th-century comedy of manners, though that doesn't do justice to what Mr. Kubrick has attempted, which is coolly to examine a world as strange and distant in its way as were the future worlds of "2001" and "A Clockwork Orange."

Some people may have difficulty with its length (over three hours, and every minute necessary) and its deliberate pacing (which I find luxurious, like sinking into a fine long book). They make the film a rigorous experience unless you give yourself up to the director's method. Mr. Kubrick takes his own sweet time as he looks, examines, comments, enchants the eye frequently, but always remains a little distant. In a Kubrick film even genuine sentiments are so suspect that a scene that in any other director's film would be sentimental becomes almost malicious.

"Barry Lyndon" is about foolish, gallant overreaching. It's the story of the rise and fall of a poor, good-natured Irish opportunist, born Redmond Barry and later to take the name of Barry Lyndon, after his successful courtship of one of England's richest aristocrats, the widowed Lady Lyndon, a beautiful vaporous woman whose high station gives her the right to be boring. The film has a great deal to say about the privileges of class.

When we first meet Barry (Ryan O'Neal) he is a naive, headstrong young man without a bean but with a terrific crush on a female cousin, whose English suitor he shoots in a duel. This sends Barry off to the Seven Years War in Germany, first in the English Army, then the Prussian.

As is the fashion in such literature, no situation remains permanent, and Barry in the course of what the narrator describes as "a wandering and disconnected life," becomes, successively, a Prussian spy, a Continental gambler, a ladies' man and, finally, a husband to Lady Lyndon (Marisa Berenson). This in the not-so-mock piety of the film, is his undoing.

Mr. Kubrick has spent a fortune on the film, and it shows, not only in the care that's been taken in locations (England, Ireland and Germany), in the grand houses and in the battle scenes, but also in the photography of John Alcott.

•

One of Mr. Kubrick's boldest decisions was to make the film as beautiful as it is. Good movies should not be too beautiful. It's thought to be distracting if not a substitute for content. Yet the Alcott camerawork, which transforms scene after scene into something that suggests a Gainsborough or a Watteau, has the function of setting us apart from Barry's adventures, rather than tricking us into involvement.

Mr. O'Neal, who's on the screen throughout, is, I think, fine, too self-assured for his own good, growing increasingly reckless as the film progresses and, at the end, a surprised wreck. Among the supporting players Murray Melvin (as Lady Lyndon's resident priest), Marie Kean (as Barry's ambitious mother) and Diana Koerner (as a pretty German fortune of war) are superb. Marisa Berenson splendidly suits her costumes and wigs.

As in every Kubrick film, the musical score is special indeed, though no one element in this film can stand apart from the others. They all fit together. "Barry Lyndon" is another fascinating challenge from one of our most remarkable, independent-minded directors.

1975 D 19, 52:4

BUGS BUNNY SUPERSTAR, directed and produced by Larry Jackson; narration spoken by Orson Welles; featuring Bob Clampett, Tex Avery and Fritz Freleng; distributed by Hare Raising Films. Running time: 90 minutes. At the D. W. Griffith Theater, 59th Street west of Second Avenue, and Regency Theater, Broadway at 67th Street.

By VINCENT CANBY

"Bugs Bunny Superstar," which opened yesterday at the Regency and D. W. Griffith Theaters, is a 90-minute anthology film composed of 10 Warner Brothers cartoons produced between 1940 and 1948. Seven of the 10 star the pushy, incredibly self-assured rabbit whose voice, supplied by the great Mel Blanc, is as much a part of Bugs Bunny's public persona as his physique, which really isn't that much different from other rabbits you may have known.

Three ace Warner Brothers animation directors — Tex Avery, Bob Clampett and Fritz Freleng — come on the screen, none too briefly, to talk about how great it was in the old days on the Warner lot when it was just one big happy family. Orson Welles bridges the gaps with facetious narration that sounds as if it had been left on someone's Phone-Mate.

That's the bad news.

The good news is that Bugs and several of the other creations of Warner cartoonists are enduringly comic characters, as ebullient as any that the Disney organization created and always much more irreverent. This program includes two classics, "The Corny Concerto" (1943), a wickedly funny send-up of Disney's "Fantasia," and "Rhapsody Rabbit" (1945), in which Bugs and a mouse compete to see who can get through Liszt's Hungarian Rhapsodies first, with the least amount of piano left.

Of the other characters, my particular favorite is Henery Hawk, a young, intensely serious chicken hawk, who, in "Walky Talky Hawky," goes out to bag his first chicken under the near-fatal misunderstanding that dogs are chickens. Also on the program is another Warner classic, "I Taw a Putty Tat" (1948), in which Tweety Bird, the small yellow, peculiarly nude-looking canary, matches wits with Sylvester, the big, ragged, short-tempered cat who sounds like the late Bert Lahr.

Children, brought up on TV, should be dazzled by the slam-bang wit and the excellence of the animation techniques.

1975 D 20, 16:1

THE ADVENTURES OF THE WILDERNESS FAMILY, directed by Stewart Raffill; screenplay by Mr. Raffill; produced by Arthur R. Dubbs; music by Gene Kauer and Douglas Lackey; presented and distributed by Pacific International Enterprises Inc. Running time: 101 minutes; this film has been classified G. At the Guild and Embassy Theaters.

Skip	Robert F. Logan
Pat	Susan Damante Shaw
Jenny	Hollye Holmes
Toby	Ham Larsen

By A. H. WEILER

Togetherness should be synonomous with the holiday season, and "The Adventures of the Wilderness Family," which arrived at the Guild and Embassy Theaters yesterday is charmingly appropriate for the family and the season. Perhaps only curmudgeons over the age of 8 would find it unlikely that a black bear would take on a giant grizzly or that a devoted dog would hold off an entire wolfpack in defense of this family. But it's an ideally wholesome clan, and both wilderness and fauna are photogenic and endearing.

The family's season in the wilds, a program note indicates, stems from a true story of escape from illness, smog and other traumas of Los Angeles to the pioneer life in the lake-studded, forest high country of the Pacific Northwest. In this case, the youthful father and mother and their little boy and girl take to their new, gorgeously rugged terrain like Sioux. And before you can say Swiss Family Robinson, they've erected their own log cabin and collected a raccoon, a pair of cuddly, motherless bear cubs and a variety of problems.

Stewart Raffill, who directed from his own script, is a man to let the beauties of nature overwhelm him. Action is the key here. The children for example, innocently pick up a couple of cougar cubs, and so daddy and the family hound have to fight off the enraged mother. And, there's a rockslide and the little girl's sudden fever, which sends daddy down the rapids in search of a doctor. Also that wolfpack attack and that unfriendly grizzly.

Robert F. Logan and Susan Damante Shaw are fairly restrained, natural and attractive as the pioneering parents, as are Holly Holmes and Ham Larsen, as their wide-eyed, loving youngsters.

And, if they often seem to be minuscule figures against the striking uninhabited, wildlife-filled background of Utah's Uinta Mountains where the adventures were filmed, they do add appreciative bits.

1975 D 20, 16:1

"The Lost Honor of Katharina Blum," was shown at the 13th New York Film Festival. The following excerpts are from Vincent Canby's review, which appeared in the New York Times on Oct. 3, 1975. The film is being shown at the Cinema II Theater, Third Avenue and 60th Street.

"The Lost Honor of Katharina Blum," based on Heinrich Böll's German novel that was published here in English this year, is a movie that looks as if it had been made out of steel. It is cold and bright and has dozens of lethal edges. It's very difficult to like even though it has things to admire. The film, a dramatized polemic about what it sees as the excesses of freedom in the democracy of West Germany today, makes its point, with tiny variations, as relentlessly as someone dealing in Revealed Truths.

•

Volker Schlondorff, the German director ("Young Torless," "The Sudden Wealth of the Poor People of Kombach," etc.), and Margarethe von Trotta, his actress-wife, with whom he has collaborated on his recent screenplays, including "A Free Woman," shares both the writing and directing credits on this new film.

"The Lost Honor of Katharina Blum" is about the systematic victimization of a poor but proud young woman, who works as a housekeeper and waitress and who

has the bad luck to pick up and take home from a party, for one night only, a young man who is suspected of being a terrorist Katharina had never met the young man before, but circumstantial evidence makes it appear as if she had been his mistress for months.

In a period of several days, Katharina's privacy and, particularly, her honor are destroyed, first by the police, who terrorize her, and then by the yellow press, which creates in her name the image of a politicized Bonnie Parker, beautiful, heartless and on fire for the Communist cause.

Though Katharina is quite quickly cleared, her life has been ruined. When she decides to take a gun to the reporter who was instrumental in her downfall, someone piously declared that the shots Katharina fired were aimed not at the reporter but at the freedom of the press.

Mr. Böll tells Katharina's story mostly in terms of secondhand information—in official police reports and in the words of people who knew her.

The film sees Katharina frontally, close up. The mystery of her passion and her resolve is maintained only by the carefully controlled, implacable performance of Angela Winkler, a handsome, dark-haired woman.

I'm not familiar with the German press, and it may be that it's as outrageous as the movie describes. "We have to help simple people express themselves," says a wicked reporter while he puts words into the mouth of Katharina's dying mother. The corruption portrayed by the film is so pervasive that one expects it to challenge us more. It doesn't. Instead it has the effect of numbing us. Its singleminded intensity nails the imagination to the floor.

1975 D 20, 16:1

FILM VIEW

VINCENT CANBY

Kubrick's Latest Has Brains And Beauty

Some years ago when the movie industry was all there was and television was still some mad doctor's as yet uncommercialized evil scheme, Motion Picture Herald, the film trade journal, used to carry a full-page feature in which exhibitors would report their experiences with individual films. The page was called "What The Picture Did For Me," and it was often referred to as "What The Picture Did *To* Me." It was informative, hilarious

reading, full of outrage, sarcasm and small-town candor, and it was there, in the mid-thirties, I think, that one irate exhibitor commented on some highly regarded Hollywood bowdlerization of a classic novel: "Please don't send me any more pictures where the hero writes with a feather."

For the next 20 to 25 years Hollywood pretty much laid off the public-domain classics as material for costume pictures unless they also contained lion-eaten Christians, pirates, earthquakes, volcanos, shipwrecks or some other forms of gaudy come-on. There were occasional, very respectable exceptions—I think especially of the film version of "Pride and Prejudice" in 1940—but until Tony Richardson's uproarious screen version of "Tom Jones" in 1963, serious movies in which heroes wrote with feathers were extremely rare. They still are unless they're also funny and harmlessly dirty.

All of which is by way of expressing my admiration for what Stanley Kubrick has been able to achieve in his newest film, "Barry Lyndon," a leisurely, serious, witty, inordinately beautiful, premium-length screen adaptation of William Makepeace Thackeray's first novel, "The Memoirs of Barry Lyndon, Esq.," published in 1844 and set in the second half of the 18th century. Those are feathers that Barry Lyndon (Ryan O'Neal)—Irish adventurer, army deserter, gambler, fortune hunter, society's victim and most unrepentant sinner—signs his checks with.

• • •

One must be as staggered by the fact that Kubrick ever got this film financed (to the tune of a reported $11-million), and into the theaters in this comparatively rigorous form, as by the film itself, which has almost the breadth and maybe even more depth than the novel on which it is based. In this time of disaster films, Mafia melodramas and other cinematic short-cuts to visceral sensation, "Barry Lyndon" is unique, a long, chatty (in effect though not in fact), picaresque narrative that moves from Ireland to Germany and to England, paying scrupulous attention to historical and social detail as well as to minor characters, constructing a world of the past in as much vivid detail as Kubrick lavished on the future in "2001" and "A Clockwork Orange."

I would suspect that it was because of the box-office successes of those last two films that Kubrick had the clout with which to get "Barry Lyndon" made with such elegance, and in a length (three hours, four minutes, 44 seconds) absolutely necessary to the subject. I also suspect that the front-office people at Warner Brothers, which financed the film, might have had palpitations when they got their first look at what Kubrick had done, since "Barry Lyndon" is anything but a "Tom Jones" picture, as was anticipated by a member of the audience with which I saw the film.

It is sometimes very funny, and it has its moments of action, adventure and romance, but it is, more than anything else, a comedy of 18th-century manners, which may not be exactly what movie patrons—who were virtually kneed to attention by "A Clockwork Orange" and hypnotized by the cool perfection of "2001"—are expecting.

When you go see it, be prepared to forget your later commitments. Relax. Pick up the film's rhythm, which stimulates the discursive style of the 19th-century novel and finds, in its repeated use of the zoom lens, a visual equivalent of the kind of chapter headings with which Thackeray punctuated his novel ("Barry Bids Adieu to The Military Profession"). Time after time Kubrick starts a sequence in a tight close-up, then slowly zooms back to reveal a landscape that may be breathtakingly beautiful in itself but also contains hints of vital narrative disclosures to come.

The discursive style is further emphasized by the film's use of an off-screen narrator (the book is told in the first-person by Barry), an omniscient, friendly old voice (Michael Hordern) who often tells us about events before we see them, rather like someone relating a story over dinner, knowing that we aren't as interested in what happened as in the how and the why. The device has the effect of distancing us from the characters, turning them into curious specimens from another time zone, which, of course, they are. But it also has the effect of making suddenly, surprisingly moving, the events contributing to Barry's ultimate downfall, principally, I think, because until the last third of the film one can't be quite sure what Kubrick has been up to.

The film opens gracefully, gently, almost somnolently, as the narrator introduces us to the rundown circumstances into which Barry Lyndon, soon to be one of the most famous rakes in all Europe, was born in rural Ireland. We see the marvelous countrysides, photographed as they might have been seen by a Gainsborough or a Watteau, the colors romantically softened but the details peculiarly, sometimes antagonistically precise. Barry, in the person of Ryan O'Neal, is a handsome, totally blank page on which a character comes to be written, at first naive, smitten hopelessly with an older, comparatively well-placed female cousin, then thrown out into the world to make his fortune after killing his cousin's wealthy English suitor in a duel.

The film carefully picks up momentum as it follows Barry's adventures, first in the English army during the Seven Years War, then in the Prussian army when he's picked up after deserting the English. At the same time Barry himself firms up into a likeable opportunist, none-too-bright, really the kind whose early successes must inevitably lead to a kind of gallant over-reaching. The Kubrick pay-off comes with Barry's successful courtship of and marriage to a rich, highborn English widow (Marisa Berenson), an adventure that brings out the worst in the ambitious Barry Lyndon and, finally, some sense of the vulnerability of the boy of low station who aspired to mix with the nobs.

"Barry Lyndon" is not a warm film—Kubrick's never are—but it is so glorious to look at, so intelligent in its conception and execution, that one comes to respond to it on Kubrick's terms, which severely avoid obvious

laughs and sentiment with the exception of two or three scenes. The scale of the film is immense, even without its stunning battle sequences, and the casting is impeccable, especially in the supporting roles—Murray Melvin as the personal chaplain to Barry's "vaporous" wife, Leon Vitali as Barry's furious stepson, Diane Koerner as a German farm wife with whom Barry spends a short, idyllic time out of war.

Miss Berenson is not quite the foolish society frump that Thackeray created but her high fashion beauty is a good substitute. O'Neal has the most difficult time of it, being on the screen almost continuously, and one pays unnecessary attention at first to a slight brogue that seems to come and go. Yet eventually the apparent, cheerful blankness of an American movie star becomes a part of the texture of the character who uses people right up to the moment they have no further use for him. It's much more of an accomplished performance than he's likely to receive credit for.

"Barry Lyndon" is unlike any other period—or feather—film I can remember seeing, though it has close associations to both "A Clockwork Orange" and "2001." The emotions it evokes are not necessarily those evoked by identification with characters but by the final logical structure that governs the completed work. In the context of the general run of today's film-making, Kubrick has pulled off something that's most original and financially rash.

1975 D 21, II:1:7

'Cuckoo's Nest' Is Just An Adolescent Fantasy

By DAVID DENBY

Most people do their best to bury the emotions of late adolescence as they get older, so a movie that brings us back to the way we felt at 16 is a force to be reckoned with. If the movie also appeals to actual 16-year-olds, it's bound to be a hit.

Milos Forman's adaptation of Ken Kesey's novel "One Flew Over the Cuckoo's Nest" evokes powerful feelings of victimization and rebellion. Jack Nicholson's free-living redneck, imprisoned in a state mental hospital for "observation," leads a doomed revolt of the patients against a tyrannical nurse whose weapons include electro-shock treatment and lobotomy. The theater comes alive with communal memories of playing tricks on the teacher and horsing around after lights out, the awesome mysteries of conspiratorial friendship, loyalty, and hero worship. Yet there are elements in the movie's appeal that are rather squalid; it doesn't always say the benign things it thinks it is saying.

Written in 1960 and 1961, "Cuckoo's Nest," which became a prime text of the 60's counterculture, was imbued with the Freudian clichés and the anti-conformist bitterness of the late fifties. Kesey's great antagonists now seem like stock characters: on the one side, Nurse Ratched, destroying any signs of spirit in her male patients; on the other, Randle Patrick McMurphy, a proletarian version of the Rainmaker-Mr. Roberts redeemer figure who appeared in numerous fifties plays and movies.

Since the hospital and the nurse are largely unbelievable (how many nurses have this kind of power?), the book has been read by many as a parable of America's seemingly gentle but ultimately deadly suppression of its dissident spirits. However, Kesey sexualizes the struggle in ways that are peculiar and self-serving, compromising any such "political" or "social" interpretation. He is perhaps the first writer, in over 200 years to see insanity

David Denby is a freelance film critic.

in men as a form of moral weakness, (an attitude preserved in the movie), specifically a failure of masculine nerve. His surrogate McMurphy, using wildness and revolt as therapy, helps the frightened men defeat the woman in their lives and, by implication, defeat the "woman" in themselves. McMurphy is literally the bringer of heterosexual potency (Kesey's thunderbolt imagery suggests a hipster-Zeus descended from the Oregon forests), just as Ratched is literally the destroyer of potency.

Of course Kesey's revolt was only for men: his women are either "good chicks," willing to sleep with anyone the hero asks them to, or power-mad, castrating monsters. (It's strange that a book so hostile to conventional therapy should depend so heavily on Freudian ideas for its characterization.) A political book? More than anything else, "Cuckoo's Nest" expresses the fear of being under a woman's power, particularly a mother's power; perhaps only in America, with our tradition of macho - paranoid literature, could such a restricted, bizarrely misogynist fantasy be taken seriously as a statement about freedom and repression.

Screenwriters Lawrence Hauben and Bo Goldman have remained faithful to the novel's misogyny and to its hero-worshipping tone, and by discarding Kesey's first-person narration they've even dramatized the Ratched-McMurphy struggle even more directly. Yet despite Louise Fletcher's marvelous performance, the struggle seems fraudulent. Miss Fletcher gives us a genteel monster, a woman dangerously blind to her own anger and love of power, squelching her patients' manhood with the blandest of smiles. We understand the kind of vicious rectitude the actress is striving for, but the role as written still lacks the credibility and ordinary human complication that would allow it to escape the grips of Kesey's fantasy.

Watching Nicholson lead a revolt of the sons against this corrupt Big Mama, I looked for a touch of irony;

but although Nicholson is often funny in a scabrous way, he seems earnestly to believe that he's involved in a deadly struggle for freedom and human dignity. There's a touch of self-righteousness in his glowering hostility, and more than a touch of sacrificial piety—as if to say, "None of you is worth saving, but I'll do it out of noblesse oblige."

Milos Forman's direction is really good only in those quiet moments when the patients' infantile games and vague hostilities make us feel the pathos of time passing by. Like Kesey, the Czech director does not seem terribly sympathetic to the patients, and his lack of compassion probably helps at the box office. His penchant for grotesque comedy and for rubbing our noses in the sordid "reality" of nuthouse life seems designed to make the film a hip entertainment for kids. However, I don't think Forman's commercial acumen should be taken for some sort of dark comic insight. A paraplegic hacks at a punching bag from his wheelchair; wine is squirted into a catatonic's mouth and it dribbles onto his face and chest—are these really examples of Forman's celebrated "middle - European comic sensibility" that some people have been praising (with knowing references to Kafka), or just examples of stupid bad taste?

I have seen a number of serious films set in mental institutions, harrowing documentaries in which the filmmakers did not exploit the material. But I find something offensive in Forman's turning freaks into "good theater." When Peter Brook did this in his stage and movie productions of Peter Weiss's "Marat/Sade," the stylization and distancing devices alerted us to the didactic nature of the material, but in "Cuckoo's Nest" Forman has played for melodrama and "realism" and audience involvement, and people who are naive about acting and directing techniques are not likely to realize how thoroughly they've been manipulated. Isn't it a bit embarrassing that this supposed paean to freedom

and spontaneity is so coercively structured that when Nicholson finally jumps on Louise Fletcher and tries to strangle her to death, many people in the audience break into applause? I'm not sure that that's the kind of audience reaction a director should be proud of. Maybe it would be better if some of those buried adolescent feelings were allowed to rest after all. ■

1975 D 21, II:17:5

DISTANCE, directed, edited and photographed by Anthony Lover; screenplay by Jay Castle; produced by George Coe; distributed by Cine Bright. At the 68th Street Playhouse. Running ime: 93 minutes. This film has not been rated.
Elwood Horne .... Paul Benjamin
Greta Horne .... Eija Pokkinen
Larry Vincent .... James Woods
Joanne Morse .... Bibi Bosch
Jesse Horne .... Hal Miller
Mrs. Herman .... Polly Holliday

By RICHARD EDER

Sometimes "Distance" is awkward and sometimes it is misconceived, but it had a central virtue lacking in a number of more elaborate and—to use a horrible word —cinematic films around.

It wants to be made. It believes in itself, in its story, in its characters; and that belief pulls viewers into it. Sometimes they are pulled too hard, or in a certain embarrassment because the sequence is obvious or excessive or telegraphed in advance.

But self-belief is an arousing quality, especially at a time when an extreme of baroque weariness gives movies such as "Three Days of the Condor" or Sam Peckinpah's "Killer Elite" the hopeless feeling that they are meant for an empty theater.

"Distance," which opened yesterday at the 68th Street Playhouse, is set in a Georgia Army post in the mid-1950's. Its protagonist is Sergeant Horne, a black man whose natural force and ability have gone into building himself a shelter against the humiliations of being a Southern black of his time.

The Army gives Horne a place where his energy and intelligence can be channeled and protected. Not fulfilled, though: here the haven becomes the prison. He is too good for his job, too much a perfectionist, and he is held to the company of men to whom he knows he is superior: One of the film's many inspired touches is a scene where Horne drinks beer with his fellow-sergeants — easygoing, cynical white men. They drink from cans; he drinks from a glass.

The rigidity that is Horne's protection makes him a first-rate master sergeant, but it

has made a torment of his private life. He has brought over a German wife, played gracefully and touchingly by Eija Pokkinen. He loves her or has loved her—the failure of the film quite to define their relationship is a weakness—but he has gradually closed himself to her.

Her blond beauty, her gentleness and devotion are a lure and a goad. He needs to hurt her and be hurt by her. He burns like Othello, his fixation on his wife encompassing everything except the ability to see her as she is. He is his own Iago; he devises his own jealousies. There is no Cassio except for a young white recruit who has the most casual brush with Mrs. Horne. The ending is tragic, predictably, and almost predictable.

In fact, the tragic main plot is too pat and stagy, but it does have a use. It provides a gravely moving current that allows the film's real jewels—its freshness, its lovely characterizations, its splendid acting—to be set in something other than their own self-consciousness.

Perhaps the best part of the film is the subplot. The white recruit, a bright, languid young man played by James Woods, has an affair with a woman who sleeps with base commanders in order to be allowed to sell insurance to the troops

It is a splendid affair, in which both the recruit and the woman harden and soften, touch and withdraw. The young man's self-sufficiency is almost pierced, and the woman's defenses almost give way to hope. The acting of James Wood is admirable, but Bibi Besch, as the woman, gives the top performance in the picture and somewhere up among the best of the year.

As Sergeant Horne, Paul Benjamin provides force and passion, and some beauty. Less subtlety; but it is not Othello's function to be subtle.

This is the first full-length feature by Anthony Lover and George Coe. Their initial effort was a short, "The Dove," a charming and terribly funny takeoff on Ingmar Bergman, which is being shown along with "Distance."

There is no point describing it, other than to say that it's as if Bergman's symbols were holding a drunken cast party. The dove becomes a pigeon, prodigious at doing what pigeons are most noted for. Death plays badminton instead of chess. And so on.

1975 D 22, 44:1

THE STORY OF ADELE H., (L'Histoire d'Adele H.), directed by Francois Truffaut; screenplay (French with English subtitles) by Mr. Truffaut, Jean Gruault and Suzanne Schiffman, from "The Diary of Adele Hugo"; edited by

Frances V. Guille; director of photography, Nestor Almendros; editor, Yann Dedet; music, Maurice Jaubert; a production of Les Films du Carosse and Les Productions Artistes Associes. Running time: 97 minutes; this film has not been rated. At the Cinema I, Third Avenue and 60th Street.

Adele H.	Isabelle Adjani
Lieutenant Pinson	Bruce Robinson
Mrs. Saunder	Sylvia Marriott
Mr. Saunders	Reubin Dorey
Mr. Whistler	Joseph Blatchley
Colonel	M. White
Oderly	Carl Hathwell
Hypnotist	Ivry Gitlis
Judge Johnstone	Sir Raymond Falla
Madame Bea	Madame Louise
Dr. Murdock	Roger Martin
Notary	Sir Cecil de Sausmarez

"The Story of Adèle H." was shown at the 13th New York Film Festival. The following excerpts are from Vincent Canby's review, which appeared in The New York Times on Oct. 13, 1975. The film is being shown at the Cinema I, Third Avenue and 60th Street.

In 1863 Adèle Hugo, the younger daughter of the great French poet and patriot, Victor Hugo, ran away from home on the Isle of Guernsey, where her father was living in exile, to follow a young English officer, a Lieutenant Pinson, to his new post in Halifax, Nova Scotia Lieutenant Pinson was probably not a bad sort, not worse than most, but he wasn't very serious.

It's thought that the young, inexperienced Adèle had most likely been Lieutenant Pinson's mistress for a short time on Guernsey, and it's known that she wanted desperately to marry him, though her father disapproved. In any case, Lieutenant Pinson was not interested —a circumstance that Adèle was ill-equipped to understand or ever to support.

●

"The Story of Adèle H.," François Truffaut's profoundly beautiful film, is about Adèle's journey, taken with measured steps into a magnificent, isolating obsession, first to frozen Halifax and then, when Lieutenant Pinson is transferred to the West Indies, to Barbados, where Adèle sweeps through the tropical streets and alleys of Bridgetown talking to herself, wearing a heavy black cloak and looking like a mad, benign witch of the north.

Unable to cope with the truth, and using her imagination and her feelings as carefully as someone writing a piece of fiction, Adèle created another world where she became Lieutenant Pinson's wife, where love was her religion (and no humiliation too great a sacrifice), and where she kept a coded journal, only recently deciphered. It is this journal that is the basis for Mr. Truffaut's most severe, most romantic meditation upon love.

"The Story of Adèle H.," impeccably photographed by Nestor Almendros ("The Wild Child"), looks and sounds like no other Truffaut film you've ever seen.

The colors are deep, rich and often dark, and there is the fine background score by the late Maurice Jaubert (he died in 1940), who composed for Vigo and Clair among others. The film has the manner of a romance but it's a romance from which all the conventional concerns have been eliminated.

●

In the single-minded way in which the movie sticks to its subject, "The Story of Adèle H." reminds one of "The Wild Child." It's virtually a one-character film. It contemplates the classic beauty of Adèle, played with extraordinary grace by 20-year-old Isabelle Adjani of the Comédie Française, much as Catherine Deneuve was admired by the camera in "Mississippi Mermaid," and it appreciates the particularity of women in a fashion that recalls the erratic journey of Catherine to the crematorium in "Jules and Jim."

"The Story of Adèle H." is not a psychiatric case history, though all the facts seem to be there if one wants to accept it as such. Rather it's a poet's appreciation of the terrifying depth of Adele's feelings. She's willful and spoiled and, the film understands, impossible to deal with. Yet the film makes us see both the madness and the grandeur of the passion.

It's this ability to allow us to see a subject from several different angles simultaneously that often proves most unsettling in a Truffaut film. Toughness and compassion get all mixed up. It's also this talent that separates his films from those of all other directors who are working in the humanist tradition today.

1975 D 23, 15:2

HUSTLE, directed and produced by Robert Aldrich; screenplay by Steve Shagan; director of photography, Joseph Biroc, A.S.C.; Michael Luciano, editor; Frank de Vol, music; released by Paramount Pictures. Running time: 118 minutes; this film has been classified R. At the Loews State and other theaters.

Lieut. Phil Gaines	Burt Reynolds
Nicole Britton	Catherine Deneuve
Marty Hollinger	Ben Johnson
Sgt. Louis Belgrave	Paul Winfield
Paula Hollinger	Eileen Brennan
Leo Sellers	Eddie Albert
Santoro	Ernest Borgnine
Peggy Summers	Catherine Bach
Herbie Dalitz	Jack Carter
Gloria Hollinger	Sharon Kelly
Jerry Bellamy	David Spielberg

By A. H. WEILER

Burt Reynolds and Robert Aldrich, his director, who ran up a big score at the box office with their macho prison-football clashes in "The Longest Yard," are running just as tough and hard in "Hustle," which opened at Loews State and other theaters yesterday.

If this apparent tribute to the Raymond Chandler-Dashiell Hammett detective genre is slightly manipulated for effects, and if it strains a mite too much and too long for its cynicism, it still emerges as a fairly realistic inspection of flawed men's efforts to cope with an obviously flawed urban society.

As a disenchanted commentary on the contemporary scene, the script by Steve Shagan, remembered for "Save the Tiger," may not be an altogether novel view of the unending war between Los Angeles cops and the bad guys so dear to television and the movies.

But it is a perceptive and properly candid and disillusioning dissection of the sordid milieu inhabited by, among others, a case-hardened detective lieutenant who, for some valid reasons, tries to gloss over the apparent narcotics suicide of a soiled, driven girl despite the prodding of his black partner and the victim's anguished father.

●

As indicated, the plot is overly complicated by that implacable father's blindly angered insistence on doing his own investigation and a slew of clues pointing to a dangerously powerful, hooker-loving lawyer. There is, too, more than a suspicion of contrivance in the bittersweet romance between a high-priced, French call girl and the married but estranged sleuth torn between love and hate for his mistress's profession.

To the credit of the script, however, he and most of the cast behave as lifelike, fallible human beings. If Mr. Reynolds is a muscular, too wryly cute, amorously hung-up cop, he also evolves as an ill-fated man, whose innate integrity triumphs over the corruption in which he is immersed. As his black, appreciative partner, Paul Winfield also is a man governed by basic decency. As the call girl, Catherine Deneuve's blonde charms are obvious, but she does seem to have a heart of gold in her grasping for the honest love of Reynolds, her beleaguered sleuth-lover.

●

Eddie Albert and Ben Johnson are persuasive as the coldly suave, bigshot lawyer and the psychotic father, respectively, and Eileen Brennan is effective as the dead girl's pitiably errant mother forced into admitting some ugly truths.

There are, of course, some tangential shoot-outs and other rough police procedures, but Robert Aldrich's vigorous direction makes most of the action briskly pictorial and practical. Mr. Shagan's explicitly colloquial dialogue may be oversimplified in its moralizing about the good, old days, as against the crassness and hustlers of the present, but in "Hustle" we can empathize with the problems and frailties of small people trapped in a small, shoddy world.

1975 D 26, 37:1

'Black Bird' Certainly No 'Maltese Falcon'

THE BLACK BIRD, written and directed by David Giler; executive producer, George Segal; based on a story by Don Mankiewicz and Gordon Cotler; director of photography, Phillip Lathrop; music by Jerry Fielding; edited by Walter Thompson. Presented by Columbia Pictures. Running time: 98 minutes. At the Columbia I and II Theaters, Second Avenue at 64th Street. This film has been rated PG.
This film has been rated PG.

Sam Spade Jr.	George Segal
Anna Kemidon	Stephane Audran
Andrew Jackson Immelman	Lionel Stander
Effie	Lee Patrick
Wilmer	Elisha Cook Jr.
Litvak	Felix Silla

By RICHARD EDER

"The Black Bird" is an enchanting half-hour spoof of Humphrey Bogart and "The Maltese Falcon." Too bad it lasts over an hour and a half.

It is the problem with take-offs. A haunted house needs a house as well as a ghost. A movie needs legs as well as decoration. It's all very well to spring out at a party wearing a preposterous costume, but sooner or later you have to say something or at least help pass the sandwiches.

There is a lot to be happy with in the early parts of "Bird." George Segal is Sam Spade Jr. He has had a soft childhood—you can see it in his placidity and air of being put-upon—and is by no means the man his father was. A point that his secretary, a screaming fright named Effie, constantly dins into him.

●

Anyway he's stuck with his father's private-eye business, a waiting-room full of freaky clients he does his best to avoid, and the Maltese Falcon wrapped in a Miami Beach towel and stashed away in a file cabinet.

In marches a representative of the Knights Templar, an undernourished gentleman in an opera cape who offers him $300 to find the falcon and dies quickly. Spade, who wants no trouble, immediately tries to pawn the bird but he's only offered $14.50 and so, reluctantly, he begins to deal.

A sidekick turns up. He is Andrew Jackson Immelman—played by Lionel Stander—and the best thing in the movie. He is made of bricks, talks tough, refuses to hit women despite Spade's urging, reprimands him for calling policemen "pigs" and wears a bright green plaid suit.

●

Various rival would-be acquirers of the falcon arrive on the scene. Among them are four Hawaiian gangsters, a midget Nazi and an elegant woman (Stephane Audran) who lives in the silk-draped basement of a Greek Orthodox church.

Miss Audran is not cut out for this kind of romp: she always seems to be wearing her best clothes. But that's not the main trouble. Having assembled his carnival, David Giler, the writer and director, prods them down the endless corridor of a very narrow and winding plot. All of them are on the same level of preposterousness; there is no pace or variety and nothing much for them to do.

Delight turns to affection, which turns to tolerance, which turns to a wish that all these funny people would go home. Humphrey Bogart would have sent them home. George Segal is nice and charming and lovable, but he is no private eye: more of a private blink.

1975 D 26, 43:1

FRIDAY FOSTER, directed and produced by Arthur Marks; screenplay by Orville Hampton; director of photography, Harry May; editor, Stanley Frazen; music by Luchi de Jesus; an American International release. Running time: 90 minutes. This film has been rated R. At the Penthouse Thater, Broadway and 47th Street, and other theaters.

Friday Foster	Pam Grier
Colt Hawkins	Yaphet Kotto
Ford Malotte	Godfrey Cambridge
Bleak Tart	Thalmus Rasulala
Madame Rena	Eartha Kitt
Fancy Dexter	Ted Lange
Enos Griffith	Jim Backus
Rev. Noble Franklin	Scatman Crothers
Cleve	Tierre Turner

Times change. Christmas used to inspire great music or enduring sentimental literature. Now it brings us a pile of corpses and a movie equally full of holes called "Friday Foster."

Students of comic strips will need no introduction. Discriminating moviegoers will want none. Friday Foster, the black model turned photographer, began life in the so-called funnies; and, judging by this film, which opened Christmas Day at the Penthouse and other theaters, has not bettered herself artistically by changing media.

Condensing the plot of "Friday Foster" actually calls for the talents of an alchemist. But basically, Friday, on assignment from Glance magazine, finds herself in the middle of an attempt to assassinate "the black Howard Hughes." Then she finds herself stalked, even into the shower, by one of the would-be assassins. Her efforts to find out what's behind it all lead her to a plot against the nation's black leaders.

The action is faster than the calendar, so much so that it comes as a shock to discover that what seems like six days of running around actually takes place in the span from New Year's Eve to St. Valentine's Day.

Pam Grier plays the fearless Miss Foster. Yaphet Kotto, whom she calls her "main man" after bedding down with Blake Tarr, "the black Howard Hughes" (Thalmus Rasulala), and a United States Senator (Paul Benjamin), renders assistance as a private detective.

Among those who pass mercifully out of the picture as corpses are Eartha Kitt, who plays a fashion designer, and Godfrey Cambridge, who appears as an effeminate couturier.

This is one of those movies where everything and everybody looks a little too good—the clothes; the pimps; the hookers; the cars; the streets; the bosoms fleetingly bared; and even the blood, which looks as though it ought to carry a vintage.

Christmas used to bring us great feasts, too. Now it gives us mental and visual junk food.

LAWRENCE VAN GELDER

1975 D 26, 38:1

AARON LOVES ANGELA, directed by Gordon Parks Jr.; written by Gerald Sanford, produced by Robert J. Anderson, photographed by Richard Kratina; music and songs by Jose Feliciano and Janna Merlyn Feliciano Columbia Pictures. Running time 98 minutes. This picture has been rated R.

Aaron	Kevin Hooks
Angela	Irene Kara
Ike	Moses Gunn
Beau	Robert Hooks
Cleo	Ernestine Jackson
Willie	Leon Pinkney

A black Harlem boy loves a Puerto Rican Harlem girl. Montague and Capulet, but it doesn't come to grief. It comes to a lot of stickiness, a little violence and a few lovely shots of young people running through the open rubble sites of upper Manhattan. Drug dealers and white racketeers intrude but are handsomely foiled. Gordon Parks Jr. has very little movie here in "Aaron Loves Angela," and it is not helped by the underdeveloped acting of the two young leads. Moses Gunn as the black boy's disillusioned father is fine. There is some good background music by José Feliciano.

RICHARD EDER

1975 D 26, 46:4

LUCKY LADY, directed by Stanley Donen; written by Willard Huyck and Gloria Katz; produced by Michael Grushkoff; music composed and conducted by Ralph Burns, with songs by Fred Ebb and John Kander; director of photography, Geoffrey Unsworth; editors, Peter Boita and George Hively; a Gruskoff/Venture production, distributed by 20th Century-Fox. Running time: 118 minutes. At the National Theater, Broadway at 44th Street, and Trans-Lux East Theater, Third Avenue at 58th Street. This film has been rated PG.

Kibby	Gene Hackman
Claire	Liza Minnelli
Walker	Burt Reynolds
Capt. Aaron Mosley	Geoffrey Lewis
Christy McTeague	John Hillerman
Billy Webber	Robby Benson
Captain Rockwell	Michael Hordern
Mr. Tully	Anthony Holland
Rass Huggins	John McLiam
Dolph	Val Avery
Bernie	Louis Guss
Charley	William H. Bassett
"Ybarra"	Emilio Fernandez

By VINCENT CANBY

In Stanley Donen's "Lucky Lady," a Prohibition-era comedy about rum-running off the California coast, Liza Minnelli may remind you of the character played by Madeline Kahn in "Sherlock Holmes' Smarter Brother." Claire (Miss Minnelli) never says it, but everything about her performance reminds you of Miss Kahn's very funny, phony introductory line: "I'm an actress. I am simultaneously funny and sad."

Miss Minnelli's Claire is neither funny nor sad but an actress trying like hell to convince you that she is. The more she tries, the worse she gets. About halfway through the movie you feel like shaking her. You want to tell her to start over, to stand up straight, not to walk pigeon-toed and to wipe that silly-sad grin off her face. Waifhood is being abused.

●

As Miss Minnelli's performance is a mistake in make-believe, so is the entire over-produced, under-thought-out production. "Lucky Lady," which opened at two theaters yesterday, is, down deep, a nervous little sparrow of a movie that has been pumped up to the size of a peacock and outfitted accordingly. It's ridiculous without the compensation of being funny or fun.

This is difficult to understand, considering the people who are involved. Mr. Donen has directed some of our best musicals and comedies ("Singin' in the Rain," "Seven Brides for Seven Brothers," "Two for the Road," etc.) and he's a man of taste, but here, perhaps, taste is just what's wrong.

"Lucky Lady," written by Willard Huyck and Gloria Katz (who wrote "American Graffiti"), is about three down-on-their-luck losers, Claire, Kibby (Gene Hackman) and Walker (Burt Reynolds), who come together in a Mexican border town during the worst of the American Depression. Through some mysterious alchemy, they become immensely successful bootleggers and, even more surprising to them, a very happy ménage à trois.

Seediness should be the operative word if the film is to be funny or sad, yet Mr. Donen and Geoffrey Unsworth, the photographer, have chosen to shoot the movie as if it were a fashion layout for Vogue. Everything is lacquered with chic, even the old yacht, the Lucky Lady, with which the rum-runners begin their business. Seascapes and landscapes are the bleached, shimmery backdrops one associates with tall, bored yogurt-thin models. The film also contains a couple of art deco interiors so stunning they deserve marquee credit.

●

Thus upstaged by the scenery, the actors receive no help from their material, which is virtually nonexistent. The screenplay contains supposedly funny encounters with other bootleggers, the Coast Guard and one fairly spectacular sea battle, but there is nothing in the way of characterization other than what the actors bring to their roles. This is an impossible burden if you're Miss Minnelli and most at ease singing, or Mr. Hackman, whose comedy touch would punch a hole in the side of a battleship.

●

Mr. Reynolds comes off much better. He has a feeling for comedy, especially for the details that make vulgar second-rateness funny.

The failure of the ensemble acting is more a failure of casting than of talent, and perhaps three other actors, more suited to each other's moods and styles, could have made something interesting of the central three-sided relationship. Miss Minnelli, Mr. Hackman and Mr. Reynolds can't. They work and work and work, often intelligently, and you don't once believe them. They laugh frequently, but there's not a moment of spontaneous feeling in the whole film.

A theoretical case could be made for comic possibilities in having "Lucky Lady's" heroine and her two suitors settle down together happily ever after. One can imagine that Marlene Dietrich could have arranged some such thing with George Raft and Edward G. Robinson. In "Manpower" (1941) she was a presence to reckon with, but Miss Minnelli is neither interesting nor demanding enough to pull it off, even as a joke.

"Lucky Lady" is really an old-fashioned movie made out of new, cheap, synthetic materials.

1975 D 26, 47:3

THE HINDENBURG, directed by Robert Wise; screenplay, Nelson Gidding; based on a screen story by Richard Levinson and William Link and the book by Michael M. Mooney; director of photography, Robert Surtees; editor, Donn Cambern; special visual effects, Albert Whitlock; music, David Shine; special photography, Clifford Stine; special mechanical efects, Glenn Robinson, Andrew Evans, Frank Brendel and Robert Beck; a Robert Wise production, distributed by Universal Pictures. Running time: 109 minutes. At Loews State I, Broadway at 45th Street; Loews Orpheum, 86th Street at Third Avenue, and Murray Hill Theater, 34th Street at Third Avenue. This film has been rated PG.

Ritter	George C. Scott
The Countess	Anne Bancroft
Boerth	William Atherton
Martin Vogel	Roy Thinnes
Edward Douglas	Gig Young
Emilio Paietta	Burgess Meredith
Captain Pruss	Charles Durning
Lehmann	Richard A. Dysart
Joe Spah	Robert Clary
Major Napier	Rene Auberjonois
Reed Channing	Peter Donat
Albert Breslau	Alan Oppenheimer
Mrs. Channing	Joanna Moore
Mrs. Breslau	Katherine Helmond

As disaster movies go, "The Hindenburg" is so brainless and so peculiarly optimistic that it could have been the work of Ross Hunter, but wasn't. It is pricelessly funny at the wrong moments. It confirms portentiousness as school of cinematic art. It has George C. Scott, as a good German, saying through a mostly clenched jaw not long after the take-off, "I have an uneasy sense of disaster."

It has his wife complaining primly, "That song is going to make me *sick*," as if it were "Blue Suede Shoes" and not "The Horst Wessel Song." It has characters talking about "Hermann" (whose last name is Göring), and it makes completely implausible a perfectly plausible theory about the events that led up to May 6, 1937, when the German dirigible Hindenburg, the Titanic of all lighter-than-air craft, exploded and burned while landing at Lakehurst, N.J.

Yet I wouldn't have missed a single foolish frame of it. I sort of like disaster movies, even bad ones, for reasons that have to do with the special effects and with other things that probably go back to the prenatal state.

●

I'm also fascinated by dirigibles, those huge, cigar-shaped, rigid-framed (unlike the "soft" blimps of today) aircraft that Germany pioneered, gave a name to (Zeppelin, after the count who built them) and maintained successfully for so many years while ours, including the Macon and Shenandoah, kept cracking up.

If "The Hindenburg" does nothing else, and I'm not sure that it does, it may at least tease your imagination enough to research this curious chapter in aviation, the first most easily available source being "The Hindenburg," Michael M. Mooney's book, which provides the source material for the film. Like the Mississippi steamboat, the dirigible had a short, glorious, glamorous life and then suddenly expired. Very little of this sense, however, is conveyed by the film that opened at three theaters here yesterday.

"The Hindenburg" is far more schizoid than its three most notable predecessors "The Poseidon Adventure," "The Towering Inferno" and "Earthquake"). Unlike those films, which were total fictions, "The Hindenburg" is torn between known facts and the fictional narrative that sounds as if it had been manufactured in a Beverly Hills sauna.

According to Robert Wise, the director, Nelson Gidding, who wrote the screenplay and Richard Levinson and William Link, who slipped the other two the story idea, much as if it were a Mickey, the Hindenburg was sabotaged by a young German crew member who wanted to embarrass the Nazis. That part is plausible but the way this is dramatized makes you long for the sanity of "Take the Money and Run."

Remove the last 10 minutes of the film, which is the length to which Mr. Wise quite effectively stretches the actual disaster and original newsreel footage that lasted less than one minute, and "The Hindenburg" is just another, somewhat more tedious "Grand Hotel in the Sky" picture.

●

The cast includes just about everybody you didn't especially want to see in a movie right now, though Dana Andrews, Shelley Winters, George Kennedy and Helen Hayes are not in it.

Among those who are aboard are William Atherton (the saboteur), Gig Young, Burgess Meredith and Anne Bancroft, who fools around as a German countess named Ursula, which gives Mr. Scott the opportunity to say to her, when he catches her smoking in a potentially inflammable part of the ship, "Behave, Ursula, you know that's dangerous." The dialogue in this film may be as quietly loony as any you've heard all year.

VINCENT CANBY

1975 D 26, 46:1

WINSOR McCAY RETROSPECTIVE, a collection of shorts by a pioneer of American animated cartooning. Includes: "Little Nemo," "How a Mosquito Operates," "Gertie the Dinosaur," "The Sinking of the Lusitania," "The Centaurs," "Flip's Circus," "Gertie on Tour," and three films from the series "Dreams of a Rarebit Fiend." New American Film Makers Series, at the Whitney Museum of American Art. Yesterday through Jan. 6. Running time: 70 minutes.

By RICHARD EDER

Footpaths and dirt roads reach out to explore a new country and suddenly a highway is built and certain turnings are made obsolete. Movie cartooning was like that: some lovely directions were sealed off when Walt Disney made his particular style into a national monument.

One of the loveliest, strangest and most hallucinatory of these lost stretches of country can be seen at the Whitney Museum this week and part of next. They are showing 11 short cartoons by Winsor McCay, Disney's predecessor by 20 years and an artist who in contrast to the sunniness of Disney's best moments drew purely in moonlight.

●

In a sense McCay was an incipient artist who never developed fully the suggestions in his work. Partly it was because he was a pioneer. His cartoons are primitive; not in the sense of crudeness but, like the Italian primitives, in the limited techniques they could command.

But these limits are also freedoms. In the best of McCay's films one has a sense of sheer discovery. No canons exist, no conventions, and there is the sense that he may go almost anywhere and reach out for almost any emotion.

Some of the films shown at the Whitney may have a mainly historical appeal. The "Little Nemo" short, with its Harlequin protagonist, is not very interesting outside of some live filming in which McCay—who has an odd resemblance to Buster Keaton—re-enacts his early efforts to develop animation techniques.

Similarly, two "Gertie the Dinosaur" films are too limited in their development to mean very much; although there is a delicacy in the animation of Gertie, a wistfulness that Disney lost and struggled mightily to recapture.

It is in their capacity for unsettling fantasy, in their revelations of how much menace can be conveyed very directly by animation, that the McCay films are most gripping. Disney's magic, though sometimes scary, was always contained: McCay's approaches necromancy.

This comes through in three of the films, all part of a series entitled "Dreams of the Rarebit Fiend." They take the form of dreams that sprout from overeating. In one, "The Pet," the dream is of a puppy that has the faculty of growing bigger with every bite it eats.

It grows rhinoceros-size, then dinosaur-size; and finally devouring office buildings and trolley cars. It is a strange, gray, angular dog, a golem dog with white eyes.

Another, "The Flying House," is more complex, funnier and darker. Mortgagors try to seize a house: the husband installs a giant airplane engine and propeller in the attic and he, his wife and the house take off on an interplanetary flight. Finally, somewhere past the moon— from which they are evicted by a giant with a flyswatter — they are hit by a rocket and come tumbling to earth. This is not the wild but innocuous plunge that is a staple of cartooning; it is a real, nightmare fall by real, desperate people.

The most perfect of the lot, and one of the greatest cartoons ever made, is "The Sinking of the Lusitania." Done in 1918, with a clearly propagandistic intention, it conveys in absolutely singular fashion the horror of a great liner going down.

McCay's waves are like no other waves: they are endlessly marching mountains. His U-boat is a menacing profile, his Lusitania is a tortured profile. With the explosions, smoke and debris shoot from the liner like blood from an artery; the smoke from the funnels becomes dying snakes that ebb and collapse with the ship's life. Motionless faces—art, or the limits of his technique, or both?—bob in the water and a woman clutching a baby plummets through bubbles to the sea floor.

The power and beauty of this film would be enough to make it worth seeing the program. Perhaps they explain the peculiar nature of McCay's dead-end: like William Blake's it was too strange and personal to be generalized or to have children.

1975 D 29, 34:1

The Ten Best Films of 1975

ublishing Ten Best lists of anything is great fun as an annual game, but it's misleading. It asks people to take seriously the results of compromise, which is all very well and good at the peace table though it's a kind of sell-out in these remote dependencies of criticism.

Say that there are only 10 seats on the bus to immortality. Can one really be serious in suggesting that Martin Scorcese, who isn't dry behind the ears yet, deserves a place and that Arthur Penn and John Huston do not? Ridiculous, of course. Should Hal Ashby be saved from oblivion while John Frankenheimer is ignored? Certainly not. Is Woody Allen a greater filmmaker than Robert Bresson? (I'm thinking . . . I'm thinking.)

But that's pretty much the way that the list of the 10 best films of 1975 reads. It's full of compromises, and the deciding factor in almost every case has been, if not irrelevant, then at least very personal. Lina Wertmuller is not a greater director than Michelangelo Antonioni but for a couple of arbitrary reasons her "Swept Away" gets on the list and Antonioni's "The Passenger" just misses it. At this point in time, I have thought about "Swept Away" more often, with more feeling, than I have thought about "The Passenger," though the latter still seems to me to be one of Antonioni's most brilliant works.

This has been a bumper year for odd, offbeat comedies, most of which were American and most of which had serious flaws that were as much the reasons for their idiosyncratic appeal as the successful things they contained. Only one lunatic comedy makes the 10 best list this year, but that gives no idea of the pleasures that I, at least (and my mail tells me I may have been the only one), received from Mike Nichols's "The Fortune" and the manic performances of Jack Nicholson and Stockard Channing. I also think of Howard Zeiff's "Hearts of The West," Michael Ritchie's "Smile," Frank Perry's "Rancho Deluxe," Gene Wilder's "Sherlock Holmes' Smarter Brother," Blake Edwards' "The Return of The Pink Panther," as well as the English treasure, "Monty Python and The Holy Grail." At this very moment, late in the day, if someone told me that I could take a break from the typewriter to see either "The Return of The Pink Panther" or "Distant Thunder," I'd probably choose Peter Sellers instead of Satyajit Ray. "The Return of The Pink Panther" isn't a great film and "Distant Thunder" is, but greatness makes demands that have the force of obligations.

My choices of the 10 best films of 1975, listed in alphabetical order, are as follows:

"**Alice Doesn't Live Here Anymore**," directed by Martin Scorcese and written by Robert Getchell. The way film distribution works, this is last year's movie in Hollywood (which has already given Ellen Burstyn an Oscar for her performance) but a 1975 movie in New York, where it will be competing for the upcoming film awards. "Alice" is the alternately funny and harrowing story of a youngish widow in the southwest who has a 12-year-old son, a station wagon, not much money, and a desire to realize herself. Alice (Miss Burstyn) more or less lurches toward self-sufficiency in a series of adventures that describe the quality of a lot of middle-class American life. The film frees Scorcese ("Mean Streets") from the reputation of being a limited New York director, and offers superb performances by everyone in it, most notably by Miss Burstyn, Harvey Keitel, Alfred Lutter and Diane Ladd.

"**Barry Lyndon**," directed, written and produced by Stanley Kubrick, who also conned the money-men into putting up a reported $11-million for one of the most personal, severe costume movies ever made. The source material is Thackeray's first novel, which Kubrick has transformed into a dispassionate comedy of 18th century manners, breathtakingly beautiful but almost maliciously cool. As he did in "2001" and "A Clockwork Orange," Kubrick stands apart from his characters, forcing us to

make connections not to individuals but to an entire society. The cast is excellent (Ryan O'Neal in the title role) but the actors are primarily objects to be contemplated in Kubrick's extraordinary panorama. John Alcott's photography is Kubrick's principal collaborator.

"**Distant Thunder**," directed and written by Satyajit Ray. The story of India's "man-made" famine in 1943, when more than 5,000,000 people were wiped out, is examined in the experiences of rural villagers who comprehend nothing of war. As the scramble to survive humiliates some of Ray's characters, it ennobles others. The landscapes are beautiful, the mood deceptively tranquil, yet the concerns that motivate Ray are more angrily political than those of a much noisier, supposedly "political" filmmaker like Costa-Gavras. In Bengali with English subtitles.

"**Hearts and Minds**," directed by Peter Davis, winner of the Oscar as the best feature-length documentary of 1974. A fine, complex, admittedly biased meditation upon American power—military and economic, political and social—in the form of an examination of the United States's involvement in the Vietnam war. It's a collage of old and new newsreel footage, interviews with greats, near-greats and nobodies, with people who made policies, carried them out, fought against them or became their victims. As we become further removed from the war, I suspect that "Hearts and Minds" will reveal itself as one of the most all-encompassing records of the American civilization ever put into one film.

"**Love and Death**," directed and written by Woody Allen. It's about time. I mean Woody Allen films have been buzzing around these Ten Best lists for years, never making it because they were so full of jokes. Now Woody has had the good sense to make a movie set in Russia at the time of the Napoleonic wars. The characters still make jokes but they have serious, Russian-sounding names like Boris and Sonja and Mikhail and Rimsky. The film contains not just one Napoleon, which was enough for Tolstoy, but two Napoleons, and it has a character who really is Death, not someone in a rented sheet, and it has Diane Keaton, plus Woody in what flesh he has to offer. Let's be frank: Woody Allen is a greater film director by far than Bresson—Henri-Cartier Bresson.

"**The Magic Flute**," directed by Ingmar Bergman. Not since Olivier's "Henry V" has a work uniquely identified with the stage been so successfully transformed into a film. Bergman keeps the scale of the production almost small enough to fit into an 18th century court theater, which is the backdrop for a movie that seems to be eavesdropping onto a live performance. The Bergman touch has a Mozartean delicacy and edge. The sets are charming, the voices (Swedish, not German) belong to the people using them. The total effect: joyful and triumphant.

"**Nashville**," directed by Robert Altman and written by Joan Tewksbury. This is Altman's chef d'oeuvre, a practically perfect example of what this major American director is interested in, what he can do and how he does it. I'm afraid the film was so overpraised that some people were put off by expecting it to be more cosmic than it is, which is a satiric view of a certain segment of American life that is simultaneously foolish, vulgar, sentimental and gallant. The actors improvise, with Altman's encouragement, and they are wonderful, especially Henry Gibson, Ronee Blakley, Lily Tomlin and Barbara Harris. They all deserve awards, as does Richard Baskin, who was in charge of the music.

"**Shampoo**," directed by Hal Ashby and written by Robert Towne, under the over-all supervision of Warren Beatty who produced the film and is its star. A very funny and sometimes very scared look at the kind of good life a lot of Americans would live if given half a chance, "Shampoo" is "La Ronde" in southern California, with Beatty as a satyr disguised as a hairdresser. The glib, tough, desperate style of the film is a mirror-reflection of the lives it looks at. With Goldie Hawn, Julie Christie and Lee Grant.

"The Story of Adele H" (*L'Histoire d'Adèle H.*), directed by Francois Truffaut. A profoundly beautiful, single-minded movie about a love so consuming that eventually, it becomes an end in itself. It's the real-life story of Victor Hugo's daughter who followed her English lover to Halifax in 1863 and, when she was spurned, gave herself up to a kind of luxurious but fatal obsession that made a real love object unimportant. With 20-year-old Isabelle Adjani in the title role, Truffaut makes us see both the madness and the grandeur of the passion. Nestor Almendros was the cameraman. French with English subtitles.

"Swept Away by an Unusual Destiny in the Blue Sea of August," directed by Lina Wertmuller. Politics and sex. Sex and politics. Which comes first in a Lina Wertmuller film? It's impossible to tell in "Swept Away," a comedy that is so successfully integrated that one's first response is to the two marvelous, larger-than-life characters, a Sicilian seaman (Giancarlo Giannini), who is also a male chauvinist Communist pig, and a rich Milanese society bitch (Mariangela Melato). The film is the story of their stormy love affair as castaways in the Mediterranean, the forces that momentarily liberate them together and then draw them apart. A serious and super comedy. Italian with English subtitles.

The 10 runners up, in no particular order of preference: Antonioni's "The Passenger," Sidney Lumet's "Dog Day Afternoon," John Schlesinger's "Day of The Locust," Claude Goretta's "The Invitation," Lev Kulijanov's "Crime and Punishment," Robert Bresson's "Lancelot of The Lake," Robert Kramer and John Douglas's "Milestones," John Huston's "The Man Who Would Be King," John Frankenheimer's "French Connection II" and Arthur Penn's "Night Moves."

1975 D 28, II:1:3

Jack Nicholson

Isabelle Adjani

Kubrick who drew 28 for his direction of "Barry Lyndon."

41 Votes for Nicholson

In achieving his second consecutive victory as best actor, Mr. Nicholson registered 41 votes on the second ballot. He surpassed Al Pacino, who drew 26 votes for his characterization of the beleaguered bank robber in "Dog Day Afternoon."

Two ballots also were needed to name a winner in the best actress category when Miss Adjani took the honor with 44 votes.

Florinda Bolkan's portrayal of the struggling wife and factory worker in Vittorio De Sica's "A Brief Vacation" scored 29 votes.

Lily Tomlin also won handily on the second vote for supporting actress with a count of 49 to the 28 for Louise Fletcher, as the nurse in "One Flew Over the Cuckoo's Nest."

The selection of writing honors developed into the longest and closest contest, with the script for "The Story of Adele H" gathering 28 votes on the fourth ballot to nip the screenplay by the director Lina Wertmuller for "Swept Away" by two votes.

The supporting-actor category also required three ballots to determine the winner, Alan Arkin, whose 30 votes led the more than 20 contestants. Second in the voting was Henry Gibson's portrait of a country and Western singer in "Nashville" with 21 votes.

In a special resolution, the critics approved a letter to be sent to the Soviet authorities in Moscow and the Ukraine, protesting the jailing of Sergo Paradjanov, director of a noted drama, "Shadows of Our Forgotten Ancestors", and other Russian films.

Plaques will be presented to the winners at a reception at Sardi's Restaurant on Sunday, Jan. 25.

The voting critics were: Howard Kissel, Women's Wear Daily, chairman of the organization; Roger Greenspun, Penthouse; Judith Crist, Saturday Review/World; John Simon, New York magazine; Pauline Kael and Penelope Gilliatt, The New Yorker; Jay Cocks and Richard Schickel, Time; Joy Gould Boyum, The Wall Street Journal; Kathleen Carroll, Ann Guarino, Rex Reed and Jerry Oster, The Daily News; Bernard Drew, the Gannett Newspapers; Joseph Gelmis and Martin Levine, Newsday; Frank Rich, The New York Post; Frances Taylor, The Long Island Daily Press; Andrew Sarris and Molly Haskell, The Village Voice; William Wolf and Donald Mayerson, Cue magazine; Bruce Williamson, Playboy magazine, and Vincent Canby, Richard Eder, Howard Thompson and A. H. Weiler of The New York Times.

1975 D 31, 11:7

FILM CRITICS AWARD 'NASHVILLE' 4 PRIZES

"Nashville," the drama set against the background of the Tennessee city's celebrated country and Western music scene, won four of the eight awards in the 10th annual poll of the National Society of Film Critics. The 20 critics, representing newspapers and periodicals, voted the film the best of the year, named Robert Altman the best director and Henry Gibson and Lily Tomlin the best supporting performers.

The group, which cast its ballots at the Algonquin Hotel yesterday, cited Jack Nicholson as the year's outstanding actor for his performance as the inmate of a mental hospital in "One Flew Over the Cuckoo's Nest." Isabelle Adjani was voted the year's top actress for her portrayal of the obsessed girl in the French drama, "The Story of Adele H."

Writing honors were captured by Robert Towne and Warren Beatty for the comedy-drama "Shampoo," in which Mr. Beatty also played a stellar role. John Alcott was judged the year's outstanding cinematographer for his work on Stanley Kubrick's period drama-adventure, "Barry Lyndon."

The critics also voted a special award to Ingmar Bergman's "The Magic Flute" for "demonstrating how pleasurable opera can be on film."

Vincent Canby of The New York Times was elected chairman of the organization for the coming year, succeeding Penelope Gilliatt of The New Yorker magazine.

1975 D 30, 15:2

'Nashville' and Nicholson Get Film Critics' Awards

By A. H. WEILER

"Nashville," the comedy-drama involving a mixed gallery of people in that citadel of country and Western music, was judged the best motion picture of the year yesterday at the 41st annual meeting of the New York Film Critics. It also won two of the seven other awards.

The group also chose Robert Altman as the year's top director for his work on "Nashville" and Lily Tomlin, the comedienne who made her dramatic debut as the gospel singer-mother in that film, as the outstanding supporting actress.

In a decidedly unusual vote, Jack Nicholson, who won best actor honors last year for "Chinatown" and "The Last Detail," repeated his victory this year as best actor for his portrayal of a prisoner transferred to the state mental hospital in "One Flew Over the Cuckoo's Nest." He also received some votes for his role in "The Passenger."

Isabelle Adjani was voted the year's best actress for her characterization of the love-plagued heroine in the François Truffaut drama "The Story of Adele H." In closely contested canvassing requiring more than the normal two ballots, Alan Arkin was named the best supporting actor for his role of a director of Hollywood Westerns in the comedy "Hearts of the West," and the script of "The Story of Adele H," written by Mr. Truffaut, Jean Gruault and Suzanne Schiffman, was voted the year's best screenplay.

A Secret Ballot

Under the group's bylaws, canvassing is done by secret ballot with a simple majority deciding the winner on the first vote. Subsequent ballots permit each critic to award three, two and one points, respectively, to his three best selections.

The 28 critics, voting in person or by proxy and representing newspapers, magazines and other media, made their choices at the New York Newspaper Guild headquarters, 133 West 44th Street.

Although "Nashville" led Stanley Kubrick's "Barry Lyndon" by a vote of 12 to 5 on the first ballot, it took another poll in which 22 films competed for the honor, to decide the winner. Then "Nashville" garnered 45 votes to 30 for "Barry Lyndon."

Mr. Altman won his award on the second ballot by collecting 44 votes, against Mr.

The British Academy Awards for acting, presented yesterday by Princess Anne, all went to Americans: Ellen Burstyn and, as best supporting actress, Diane Ladd, both for "Alice Doesn't Live Here Any-

more;" Al Pacino for "The Godfather Part II" and "Dog Day Afternoon" and, as best supporting actor, Fred Astaire for "The Towering Inferno."

1976 Mr 18, 49:1

Nicholson Fame Official

By ROBERT LINDSEY
Special to The New York Times

LOS ANGELES, March 30 —In the moments after Jack Nicholson bounded off the stage of the Los Angeles Music Center last night, a grin on his face and a gleaming Oscar in his hands, one of the first things he said was: "God, isn't it fantastic?"

Hollywood had at last certified what many critics had been saying for some time— that Mr. Nicholson, who began acting in low-budget films here almost 20 years ago and scored his first major success in "East Rider" in 1969, had reached the top of Hollywood's acting hierarchy.

Mr. Nicholson won an award for best performances by an actor from the Motion Picture Academy of Arts and Sciences for "One Flew Over the Cuckoo's Nest." He was reported to have been bitter and disappointed after having been an also-ran in four other Oscar movies, including losses in the best-actor category during each of the last two years—for "The Last Detail" in 1973 and "Chinatown" in 1974.

The crowd seemed to be

on his side, too, for Mr. Nicholson received one of the loudest ovations of the night.

Race With Excitement

The 39-year-old New Jersey native, who frequently portrays an outsider bucking the system, as he did in "Cuckoo's Nest," "The Last Detail" and "Five Easy Pieces," seemed almost to race with excitement after collecting his award. "I'm shaken and surprised," he said, and then repeated it, and swore exuberantly.

In what has generally not been regarded as a vintage year for high-quality films, "One Flew Over the Cuckoo's Nest," a filmed version of Ken Kesey's novel about life in an Oregon mental institution, achieved what no other film had done since "It Happened One Night" in 1934.

It was selected not only as the best film of the year, but also won the top acting awards—Mr. Nicholson's antagonist in the film, Louise Fletcher, won the award for best performance by an actress in the leading role. Milos Forman was voted best director, and Lawrence H. Hauben and Bo Goldman won for their screenplay adaption of Mr. Kesey's novel.

George Burns, who is 80

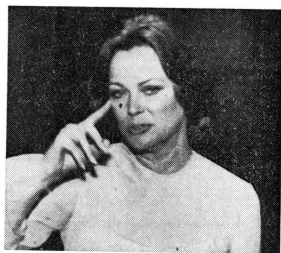

United Press International

Louise Fletcher using sign language to speak to her parents over television after receiving an Academy Award for best actress on Monday evening.

years old, won the award for best-supporting actor for The Sunshine Boys" and Lee Grant, in her third nomination in this category, won an Oscar for her supporting actress role in "Shampoo."

Reflecting the recent decline in film production here, only 227 motion pictures were eligible for the awards, down from 264 last year, and the lowest in many years.

At Hollywood social gatherings recently, it has been common for members of the Motion Picture Academy to admit that they were having difficulty deciding whom to vote for in some categories, not so much because of intense competition for outstanding performances, but what they perceived as being few performances meriting consideration for an Oscar.

Blaming mounting production costs rooted in inflation, and a recent renewed surge of high-wage demands by some top stars, most of the major studios have been making fewer and fewer films. "They all say they only want to make blockbusters," a well known film writer-director said during a conversation last night.

"They think they've found a secret formula—make just a few films that make a lot of money, and the heck with whether the critics like them or not," he said. "They think you can put it all in a computer—that if you have such a star, you can be sure it will bring in $64 million in rentals, and if you put in so and so, then you'll get $115 million."

Some Upturn Foreseen

This year, movie makers expect to see an upturn in film production, but still well below the volume of the late 1960's.

Curiously, "Jaws" which became Hollywood's top money winner only a few months after it reached the screen last year, collected only three Oscars for best original musical score, editing and sound. Although it was nominated for best picture, its director Steven Spielberg, was conspicuously absent from the list.

"Barry Lyndon," the Stanley Kubrick movie that many critics described as a beautifully photographed and executed but thematically thin tale of a likable rogue in 18th-century Europe, like "Cuckoo's Nest," won five Oscars. They were for cinematography, art direction, set decoration, costume design and best adapted-musical score.

Mervyn Leroy won the Irving G. Thalberg Award for his long career as a director, and Jules S. Stein, the long-time chief executive of MCA Inc., received the Jean Hersholt Humanitarian Award for his work in helping to combat eye disease. Mary Pickford, who has not made a motion picture since 1933, received, in a filmed presentation at her home in Beverly Hills, a special Oscar for her years of movie making.

Other awards follow:

Short Subject — animated: "Great," Grantstern Ltd. Bob Godfrey, producer.

Short Subject—live: Angel and Big Joe," Bert Salzman Productions. Bert Salzman, producer.

Sound: "Jaws," by Robert L. Hoyt, Roger Heman, Earl Madrey and John Carter.

Documentary feature: "The Man Who Skied Down Everest," a Crawley Films Presentation. F. R. Crawley, James Hager and Dale Hartleben, producers.

Documentary short subject: "The End of the Game," Opus Films Ltd. Claire Wilbur and Robin Lehman, producers.

Costume Design: "Barry Lyndon," Ulla-Britt Soderlund and Milena Canonero.

Art Direction: "Barry Lyndon," Ken Adam and Roy Walker; set decoration, Vernon Dixon.

Original Music Score: "Jaws," John Williams.

Original Song Score and Adaptation or Best Scoring, Adaptation: "Barry Lyndon," adapted by Leonard Rosenman.

Cinematography: "Barry Lyndon," John Alcott.

Editing: "Jaws," Verna Fielids.

Foreign Language Film: "Dersu Uzala," U.S.S.R.

Song: "I'm Easy" from "Nashville." Music and lyrics by Keith Carradine.

Original Screenplay: "Dog Day Afternoon," Frank Pierson.

1976 Mr 31, 26:4

147

The New York Times
Film Reviews
1976

A PROGRAM OF SHORT FILMS: "Rainbow Bridge" (Part One), by Vickie Z. Peterson, running time: 10 minutes; "Rainbow Bridge" (Part Two), by Miss Peterson, running time: 27 minutes; "State of Health," by Kent Hodgetts, running time: 18 minutes; "Glimpse," by Mr. Hodgetts, distributed by Serious Business Company, running time: 22 minutes. At the Film Forum, Vandam Theater, 15 Vandam Street. Total running time: 7 minutes.

By VINCENT CANBY

Two films each by Vickie Z. Peterson and Kent Hodgetts make up the new Film Forum program that opened yesterday. The program will run through Sunday and will be repeated next weekend.

Miss Peterson's films, "Rainbow Bridge" (Parts One and Two), are a series of abstract, geometric designs constructed mostly of images of the sea and close-ups of waves. The film maker uses these shots the way a nonrepresentational sculptor might use found objects, to create new images that are most beautiful when the original associations have been most effectively denied. It's not a labor for which I have particular sympathy.

In "State of Health" Kent Hodgetts examines his own body in frequently tight close-ups of the sort that transform a navel into a long-dead volcanic crater. In "Glimpse," a film made over the period of a year but that lasts only 22 minutes, Mr. Hodgetts focuses a stationary camera on an orchard seen through a window.

Lighting and seasons change while the film maker occasionally plays with the landscape by hanging a large metallic balloon in the foreground. Sometimes it swings back and forth. Sometimes it disappears. It is surrealism of the most ponderous, least liberating sort.

1976 Ja 1, 15:3

ABSTRACT FILMS BY HOLLIS FRAMPTON

By RICHARD EDER

The projector hums steadily. You notice it. You notice the red Exit and No Smoking signs. You notice the creaking of the elevator in some nearby cavern. You notice the dust in the beam of light traveling from the projection booth. You notice your own hair, your shirt collar, your fingernails, your unanswered letters. And after some 15 minutes of the Whitney Museum's latest experimental film program, about all you can do with what's on

the screen is notice it, in precisely the same way.

Week after week the Whitney's New American Film makers series presents new or little-known American work. It has the support of the National Endowment for the Arts, the New York State Council on the Arts and, to varying degrees, of an audience. Last week's retrospective on the early American cartoonist Winsor McCay was a sell-out; the programs devoted to abstract work are emptier.

The program by Hollis Frampton, which opened yesterday and will run through next Tuesday, falls into that abstract category, even though it uses recognizable filmed images. It fails in the category too, as much of the abstract experimental film work that I have seen seems to do.

Mr. Frampton's major piece is "Vernal Equinox." Against a constant dark background a red-haired woman, unclothed, stands, squats, moves a chair, tries to skip rope, drapes a scarf over her shoulders. The film records her movements and does variations on them. Frames are cut out, so each movement comes jerkily as if she were a robot with sand in the gears. Action is reversed, slowed, endlessly repeated.

Initially, there is a success. The human body moving can be abstractly as well as usably beautiful. The breaking-up of the movements by editing techniques increases the abstraction and in a way increases our ability to see.

But the film lasts 61 minutes, and this is a wild mistake. For one thing, however much abstracted—

"pixillated" is the word used by the detailed, confused and pretentious program notes—there is still a human figure to be dealt with.

Faces and bodies are powerful medicine in a film. For 10 minutes we might accept the abstraction. Over an hour we begin to conceive of the woman; she has a pleasant, squarish face, a pleasant, squarish body; she is benevolent but uninvolved. And the notion of her being a person collides completely with the notion of her caught in such minimal activity for the space of a full hour.

The use of a specific person makes a specific problem for "Vernal Equinox." But the problem of the time applies also to the second film-the half-hour "Summer Solstice" —and is much more general to abstract experimental films.

It is an absolute disregard for the medium—as much as if a painter didn't know how to mix oils;—for a film maker not to take account of time and its relation to what he is trying to do. Time is abused when the audience feels itself a prisoner or begins to notice the sound of the projector.

With the minimal kind of stimuli offered by abstract films, their duration, by and large, should be short. Most people will not want to look at a Maillol for a whole hour, let alone a Juan Gris.

1976 Ja 8, 26:1

How I Learned To Stop Worrying And Love 'Barry Lyndon'

By JOHN HOFSESS

While watching Stanley Kubrick's "Barry Lyndon," I recalled a story about a visitor to an art exhibit who, having studied each canvas with increasing perplexity, came up to the artist who painted the pictures and said, "I like your work—but I'm not sure exactly what it is you're trying to say." The artist replied, "If I could say it, I wouldn't have bothered painting it."

The same might be said of "Barry Lyndon": there isn't much for a verbally-oriented person to chew on. There's no conceptual or discursive aspect, no kernel of

John Hofsess is a Canadian film critic and the author of "Inner Views: Ten Canadian Filmmakers."

pop sociology or philosophical nutmeat. It isn't at all like "Nashville" or "Last Tango in Paris," where a knowing reviewer could write the kind of richly allusive, in-depth analysis that critics have long done for novels. Instead, "Barry Lyndon" throws down the gauntlet to those film critics who are really literary or drama critics in disguise and tests their ability to appreciate qualities of form, composition, color, mood, music, editing rhythms—among other cinematic qualities that generally do not greatly interest them. Words are a film critic's primary tools and when a movie doesn't lend itself to verbal translation—discussions about character, ideas, values, plot development, and so on—many critics are inclined to dismiss it as unimportant or as a failure.

Being a "word-man" myself, I well understood the discontent of certain reviewers with the film's lack of witty or memorable dialogue, its lack of provocative ideas, its lack of character development and an emotionally engaging central performance.

Film critics are supposed to write with the certitude of exclamation marks; unlike philosophers, they cannot build a reputation based on doubt. Yet, as my deadline drew near, I found myself turning into a question mark. How much easier my task would be, I reflected, if "Barry Lyndon" were like Kubrick's early films. They were graced by fine performances —one recalls Adlophe Menjou and Kirk Douglas in "Paths of Glory," James Mason in "Lolita" and, with special affection, Sterling Hayden and Peter Sellers in "Dr. Strangelove"—and occasionally they even produced quotable lines, like the ones in "Strangelove" about "preverts." They had definite subjects and were easy to talk about. In those days, one went to his films and came home with a message.

Beginning with "2001," however, as Kubrick began pushing inspiration and obsession to their outer limits, insisting on the primacy of a film experience that was essentially ambiguous and hard to explicate, one went

to a Kubrick film and came home floundering. Like it or not, your mind had been grazed by something original.

Not everyone liked it. When "2001" opened in 1968, it was greeted with derisive snorts from practically every major critic except Penelope Gilliatt. "A monumentally unimaginative movie," wrote Pauline Kael. "A major disappointment," said Stanley Kauffmann. "Incredibly boring," commented Renata Adler. "A regrettable failure," wrote John Simon, shrugging it off as "a shaggy God's story." "A disaster," said Andrew Sarris.

•

Bearing in mind the cold critical reception accorded "2001," I once asked Kubrick —shortly before the London opening of "A Clockwork Orange" — if he had ever learned anything about his work from reading film criticism. His response was a fast, firm "No."

"To see a film once and write a review is an absurdity," he said. "Yet very few critics ever see a film twice or write about films from a leisurely, thoughtful perspective. The reviews that distinguish most critics, unfortunately, are those slambang pans which are easy to write and fun to write and absolutely useless. There's not much in a critic showing off how clever he is at writing silly, supercilious gags about something he hates."

During a recent visit to England, I talked with Kubrick again at his home in Borehamwood, outside London. This time, of course, our main topic of discussion was "Barry Lyndon," and I had even arrived armed with an annotated edition of "The Luck of Barry Lyndon." Obviously, I was much better prepared to talk book than film.

"Quick!" Kubrick said to one of his assistants. "Hand me that Times article on 'Barry Lyndon,' so I can discuss Thackeray." The piece in question was a lengthy essay in the London Sunday Times describing in detail Thackeray's struggle to write the novel against a background of gambling debts and marital unhappiness. Kubrick's irony was playful but pointed. "The most important parts of a film," he said, "are the mysterious parts—beyond the reach of reason and language."

When I asked him about the apparent change in his films—from the early, more conventional dramas to the stylistic experiments of "2001" and later films, with their emphasis on images and music—Kubrick said, "There may be a change in the films but it doesn't mean there is any personal change in me. What happens in the film business is something like this: when a scriptwriter or director starts out, producers and investors want to see everything written down. They judge the worth of a screenplay as they would a stage play, and ignore the very great differences between the two. They want good dialogue, tight plotting, dramatic development. What I have found is that the more completely cinematic a film is, the less interesting the screenplay becomes. Because a screenplay isn't meant to be read, it's to be realized on film.

"So if my earlier films seem more verbal than the later ones, it is because I was obliged to conform to certain literary conventions. Then, after some success, I was given greater freedom to explore the medium as I preferred. There'll be no screenplay of 'Barry Lyndon' published, because there is nothing of literary interest to read."

Kubrick's point is well taken. There is a scene in "Barry Lyndon," for example, which in Kubrick's screenplay simply read, "Barry duels with Lord Bullingdon." Just that, nothing more. Yet

what finally reached the screen is one of the most stunning sequences in modern film. The scene runs about six minutes and if little happens in terms of actual content — three shots are fired and Barry is wounded in the leg by his stepson—a great deal happens in terms of style. It took six weeks— 42 working days—just to edit the sequence. To find the music — Handel's "Sarabande"—Kubrick listened to every available recording of 17th and 18th-century music that he could acquire, literally thousands of LPs. What he achieves in such moments of the film might be called cinematic gestalts—inspired combinations of words, images, music and editing rhythms, creating a kind of artistic experience that no other medium can convey.

Eventually, Kubrick may end up in a cul-de-sac, for he is following a similar line of development—using the "grammar" of the film medium—to that pursued by James Joyce and Vladimir Nabokov in fiction. There is no question that Joyce and Nabokov — more than any other writers in the 20th-century — brilliantly explored and expanded the limits of language and the structure of novels, yet both were led irresistibly and obsessively to cap their careers with those cold and lifeless masterpieces, "Finnegans Wake" and "Ada," more to be deciphered than read by a handful of scholars whose pleasure is strictly ratiocination. It is characteristic of such careers that people keep saying, "This time you've really gone too far! We liked your last film or novel—but that's it!" The price of growth is disaffection.

•

Two weeks after seeing "Barry Lyndon," I still hadn't formed a hard judgment of it. I kept wanting to add it to "add up" to something profound. But Victorian readers were equally dissatisfied with Thackeray's story about a young Irish rake on the make who develops an inordinate ambition to attain wealth, power and prestige, who gains the lot unscrupulously and then loses it with another turn of fortune's wheel. Readers complained bitterly that the story lacked a point, a purpose, and above all, the customary dosage of moral edification.

"I have no head above my eyes," replied Thackeray to these criticisms—a line that Kubrick could borrow to advantage. A second viewing of the film did not alter my lack of resolution. Then one night about another

week later, I played the soundtrack recording—Handel's "Sarabande," "Women of Ireland" by The Chieftans, and so on, and suddenly experienced a strong surge of emotion. Bits and pieces of the film—Redmond Barry's tremulous first love with his cousin Nora, the gaming tables banked in candlelight, the dueling sequence, among others—came rushing back to life, and I realized that they had become imperishable images in my memory, and that I was seeing a film and appreciating qualities in a manner quite new to me.

Like many other critics and filmgoers, I have grown so accustomed to films based on literary conventions and familiar structures, that to see a film which stretches one's awareness of what can be achieved in the medium seems prickly and puzzling. Kubrick's films have a way— at least with some people—of working on in the mind, of passing through all the stages from irritation to exhilaration. And curiously enough—for critics are supposed to be the most progressive and perceptive of filmgoers—it is the general public in this case, unencumbered by literary prejudices, that has done most of the leading in making "2001" and "A Clockwork Orange" not just films of immense popularity but of steadily growing stature.

It may be only half-true to say that the split over Kubrick's films is mainly between people who are verbally oriented and those who are visually oriented. Instead, the basic division seems to be between people who are fixed in their notions of what a film is or should be, and those of more flexible personality who are willing to respond to an esthetic experiment. Maybe the only abstract maxim that one can derive from Kubrick's new film is: "Openness is everything."

1976 Ja 11, II:13:1

ALL SCREWED UP (Tutto a Posto e Niente in Ordine), directed by Lina Wertmuller; screenplay (Italian with English subtitles) by Miss Wertmuller; produced by Romano Cardarelli; director of photography, Giuseppe Rotunno; music, Piero Piccioni; editor, Franco Fraticelli; a Euro International production, distributed by New Line Cinema. Running time: 105 minutes. At the Eastside Cinema, Third Avenue at 55th Street. This film has been rated PG.
Gigi .... Luigi Diberti
Marluccia .... Lina Polito
Carletto .... Nini Bignamini
Adelina .... Sara Rapisarda
Biki .... Giuliana Caiandra
Isotta .... Isa Danieli
Bagonghi .... Eros Pagni

Isa Danieli and Luigi Diberti

By VINCENT CANBY

It is late at night in the Milan tenement. Adelina, a pretty, conventional country girl newly moved to the city and quickly urbanized, finds herself fighting off the advances of her Sicilian fiance, Carletto. Carletto wants to marry Adelina but she thinks they should wait. After all, she has told him on more than one occasion, they haven't enough money for all those things he doesn't even know they need yet, like plastic flowers.

On this particular night, Carletto, a good sort really, has let his passion overcome his patience. He attacks. Frontally. They wrestle. He tugs at her bodystocking. She cries and kicks. He gets hopelessly tangled in underclothes. Finally they topple over in such a way that Adelina must decide — very quickly—whether to save her virginity or her new T Vset.

•

It's a crucial, hilarious moment, and one that is integral to the kind of social-political-sexual comedies that Lina Wertmuller, the brilliant Italian director, seems to have a corner on these days.

The scene is from "All Screwed Up," Miss Wertmuller's 1973 comedy that opened yesterday at the Eastside Cinema. "All Screwed Up," a wittessly slangy re-working of the Italian title (which is literally translated as "All in Order, Nothing in Place"), was made just after "Love and Anarchy" and just before "Swept Away."

In many details it seems less polished, less cohesive than either of those two films, but that may simply be because its narrative scope is broader and its concerns less delicately expressed. It's a noisy, angry, relentlessly paced comedy that leaves one exhausted. Miss Wertmuller is a risk-taker, which creates a certain amount of tension in the audience. Will she or won't she pull it off?

She sometimes underscores her points in blunt ways that would be avoided by a director more conscious — or more fearful—of the refinements of film criticism. She appears to be saying to hell with all that, as long as the point is effectively made. Watching "All Screwed Up"

is to be witness to a giant talent that won't be cut down to size by apprehensions of whether or not something is in good taste.

"All Screwed Up" is the often exuberantly funny tale about the often tragic adventures of a group of young country people who have come to Milan to make their fortunes. In addition to Adelina and Carletto there are Gigi, who drifts into a life of small crime (he becomes the sort of burglar who neatly folds the shirts as he ransacks a bureau drawer), Isotta, who becomes a street walker, and Sante and Mariuccia, who marry in bliss and, in two years, are something less than blessed with seven children (one set of twins followed by quintuplets).

•

Though the characters in the forefront are fully realized, Miss Wertmuller's fundamental interest is obviously in the society they inhabit, in the endless and usually fruitless pursuit of work and money and appliances. The film is not a polemic, however. It recognizes that there are no easy answers to social, political and sexual questions .Instead the film is fascinated and amazed that, given the odds against them, these people mnage to survive at all.

"All Screwed Up" juxtaposes contradictory scenes with occasionally breathtaking effect, as when Miss Wertmuller cuts from the silly, self-absorbed conversation of two young women to what amounts to a ballet by the workers in a slaughterhouse as they skin and grade sides of beef.

At her best, Miss Wertmuller combines these contradictory effects in a single scene: the beggars outside a butcher shop, when told they are disturbing the customers, answer logically that the meat is disturbing them. It is both too funny and too harsh. Sometimes the hysteria of the characters — so broadly acted they resist easy criticism—appears to envelop the film itself, but that, too, is part of the fascination of the film and what the director is up to.

There's no doubt about it now: Lina Wertmuller has become one of the major film talents of our day.

1976 Ja 15, 28:1

WHAT MAISIE KNEW, directed, written and photographed by Babette Mangolte. Running time: 58 minutes. With Epp Kolkas, Kate Manheim, Saskia Noordhoek-Hegt, and others.
SUB ROSA, directed and written by Michael Harvey; photographed by Mark Obenhaus. Running time: 12 minutes: With Kate Brockman. At the Whitney Museum of American Art, Madison Avenue at 74th Street.

The Whitney Museum's new film program, Babette Mangolte's 58-minute "What Maisie Knew" and Michael Harvey's 12-minute "Sub Rosa," are the sort of works designed to convince you that films are essentially a parasitic art.

Miss Mangolte displays a lot of nerve by invoking Henry James's subtle scrupulously complex novel about a rotten world as seen through the eyes of a resilient little girl. If Miss Mangolte's Maisie is the camera, as the director pretends in her program notes, then this little girl is prematurely bent. She sees the world through the viewfinder of an especially dull, film-school student whose friends don't mind making idiots of themselves. The film has nothing to do with James and everything to do with someone wanting to make a film but having no dependably talented impulse.

"Sub Rosa" is a not unendurable rip-off of Matisse's "Harmony in Red." A female model, in a red dress and red hat, sits in a red room, while the camera slowly moves around her as she quotes some of the master's musings about color ("Do you suppose red has a particular taste?"). I won't give away the ending.

VINCENT CANBY

1976 Ja 15, 30:1

OLD DRACULA, directed by Clive Donner; written by Jeremy Lloyd; director of photography, Tony Richmond; produced by Jack H. Wiener. Released by American International Pictures. Running time: 89 minutes. Rated PG. At Showcase Theaters in the Metropolitan area.
Count Dracula .... David Niven
Countess Vampira .... Teresa Graves
Maltravers .... Peter Bayliss
Angela .... Jennie Linden
Marc .... Nicky Henson

By RICHARD EDER

At the end of "Old Dracula," David Niven turns black. To explain why he turns black would give away the machinery of the plot. Probably the makers of "Old Dracula" care about the machinery, since they don't give us much else.

We do have David Niven as Count Dracula, proprietor of an up-to-date horror castle into which tours are booked. Besides paying for the castle's upkeep, the tourists are examined in their sleep to see if any has a particularly rare blood type. Dracula's wife died 50 years earlier of anemia, and a transfusion would bring her back. As Mr. Niven explains, it's no fun going to bed each morning in an empty crypt, especially one equipped with a matrimonial double coffin.

Does this seem funny? If so, "Old Dracula" will seem funny. If not, it will quickly turn tedious, although I liked the Mark Cross-style portable leather coffin that Dracula takes with him on his travels. It is hard not to have some affection for Mr. Niven: He is beginning to resemble a haunted house himself, but his lineaments remind us of better times even if his lines do not.

1976 Ja 15, 30:1

FILM VIEW

VINCENT CANBY

Uncovering Luis Bunuel's Mexican Treasures

In "Tristana," Luis Buñuel has Don Lope (Fernando Rey), an irascible old free-thinker in all matters that do not touch his private life, shout defiantly at a funeral party, "Long live the living!" The Museum of Modern Art is picking up that cry in its current retrospective of 21 Mexican films made by Buñuel between 1947, when Buñuel took up residence in Mexico, and 1966, which marked the beginning of the Old Master's second European period, the Golden Age in which he produced such masterpieces as 'Tristana" and "The Discreet Charm of the Bourgeoisie."

The ostensible peg for the retrospective is Buñuel's birthday—he will be 76 on Feb. 22—but it would have been enough, I think, to say with Don Lope, "Long live the living!" For Luis Buñuel is still very much alive, still residing in Mexico, which provided him with roots after he was exiled from Spain and had lived briefly in Paris and New York, and is still planning new films. That the Modern should be sponsoring this retrospective is most fitting. Buñuel worked there (none too happily, I gather, though he was thankful to be earning a living) from 1939 to 1943, adapting and editing documentaries. After that he worked in Hollywood, supervising the Spanish-language versions of major studio films. For another man, this period might have been the end of the briefly brilliant, three-film career composed of "Un Chien Andalou" (1928) and "L'Age D'Or" (1930), the surreal classics made in collaboration with Salvador Dali in France, and "Las Hurdes" (1932), a documentary shot in his native Spain.

For Luis Buñuel, as the MOMA retrospective clearly shows, these tours of duty in New York and Hollywood were merely temporary interruptions in a career that hadn't really gotten started yet and that was not, indeed, completely realized until the artist was in his sixties. In this respect Buñuel is unique among filmmakers: he survived through the thin and thick of the demands of commercial movies into maturity while still vital enough to take full advantage of the prerogatives of critical and box-office success.

• • •

For anyone familiar with and dazzled by Buñuel's early and late films, the MOMA retrospective is an absolute must. Except for a handful of films, Buñuel's Mexican output is largely unknown to us. More than half of the films were never released in this country, or were seen only in Spanish-language theaters.

For other moviegoers, the show is a mixed and rather demanding experience. Its full impact comes with an historical awareness of how the films are inter-related in time, of how themes once seemingly thrown away are developed later on. One might, with justification, dismiss as sentimental melodrama his "Daughter of Deceit" (La Hija Del Engano), made in 1951, if one were not aware of the extraordinary films that Buñuel had made under the same commercial film industry circumstances just before and just after—"The Young and The Damned" (Los Olvidados), made in 1950, and "Adventures of Robinson Crusoe," made in 1952.

"Daughter of Deceit" looks very much like a potboiler made for the Mexican and Latin American markets. It's a tearjerker about a good man who, when cuckolded, kicks out his unfaithful wife and places his infant daughter in the hands of foster parents and then turns into a ruthless, if very small-time, gambling czar. Most of the film is devoted to the man's later attempts to find his daughter, now grown up, interspersed with comedy routines and musical numbers of special tackiness. The movie means nothing by itself. In the context of Buñuel's entire career, it's a fascinating artifact. Don Quintan, the hero, is a low-comedy, Mexican cousin to the cracked Spanish moralists of Buñuel's later "Viridiana" and "Tristana."

Though it was made in Spain, "Viridiana" (1961) is included in the retrospective since it was a Mexican-Spanish coproduction. The retrospective also includes "The Exterminating Angel" (1962) and "Simon of The Desert" (1965), neither of which needs an introduction to American audiences.

The major revelation of the retrospective is the evidence it provides that Buñuel survived into his later, golden European age not by stooping to the demands of the Mexican film market but by embracing that market, by working within restrictions that would have hobbled a lesser artist. Make no mistake. The films in this retrospective are definitely Mexican. The production resources are not great and the leading actors and actresses all have a way of looking like Mexican re-treads of Hollywood stars of earlier decades. The acting is broad by any standards except Latin American. Buñuel's extraordinary accomplishment was that he was able to make films as idiosyncratic as he did, in spite of the limitations.

Some of the films in the retrospective are illuminated almost entirely by what we know—after the fact—of Buñuel's furious anti-clericism, his impatience with established order and with the sort of conventional morality that makes charity a virtue without taking issue with the circumstances that make charity necessary.

"El Gran Calavera" (The Great Madcap), Buñuel's second Mexican film, made in 1949, is charming enough, a comedy that recalls the populist work of Frank Capra in the thirties, but its interest to us today is in its relationship to "The Discreet Charm of The Bourgeoisie." It has the rather conventional frame of a story about a rich man who teaches his money-grubbing family the value of love and the peso, but Buñuel's attitudes toward his middle-class characters are just as merciless and—and this is the surprise—just as mellow as they were to be nearly 25 years later.

"Subida Al Cielo" (Mexican Bus Ride), 1952, is about the inhabitants of a small coastal village whose lives are generally serene since, the narrator tells us, the village is too poor to support a church and a priest. Nobody in the film suffers from guilt.

"La Ilusion Viaja En Tranvia" (Illusion Travels By Streetcar), 1954, is an uproarious low comedy about a streetcar motorman and a conductor who get drunk one night, steal a streetcar and then spend a frantic day trying to sneak it back to the barn. Almost every concern later to be identified as Buñuelian shows up in the course of the film, including religious frauds, a fondness for grotesque images (butchers hang their sides of beef and pigs' heads from the handstraps in the streetcar), and capitalistic minginess. An American tourist becomes frightened when she gets on the streetcar and is told it is free. She thinks it's a Communist plot.

Buñuel's Mexican version of "Wuthering Heights," called "Abismos De Pasion" (1954), is acted in a style that might be called Latin American-steamy, but it is far less romantic than William Wyler's version and its final scene, in which Heathcliff attempts to make love to the recently interred Cathy in her coffin, is pure Buñuel.

"Illusion Travels by Streetcar": An "uproarious low comedy" from Bunuel

Also pure Buñuel of a very high order is "Ensayo De
Un Crimen" (The Criminal Life of Archibaldo De La Cruz),
1955, a fine black comedy about a rich bourgeois man
whose emotional life was somewhat stunted when he was
a small boy and believed that he was responsible
for the death of his sexy nanny by simply willing it.

It's a fantastic film, and absolutely rational, as are all
of Buñuel's best works including "The Discreet Charm,"
in which dreams open one out of another like the sections
of a telescope.

Put end to end, Buñuel's films are a fantastic journey,
not into fantasy but into a kind of super-reality that isn't
necessarily realistic in the way of neo-realistic films.
His realism is poetic, open-ended, aware of essential
mysteries. The current retrospective, which ends Feb. 16,
is a rare opportunity to share that journey into what
Buñuel once described as "the marvelous universe of the
unknown." He wasn't describing outer space or some •
private world, but the society in which we live, work,
love and dream.

1976 Ja 18, II:13:1

A Neglected Film About Modern Marriage

By STEPHEN FARBER

One of the most intriguing
films of this season, Joseph
Losey's "The Romantic Englishwoman," was dismissed
by most critics and seems
to be on the verge of va-
nishing. Yet it deserves to
be added to the very small
list of provocative, memorable films—including Losey's
own "Accident," Stanley Donen's "Two for the Road,"
Richard Lester's "Petulia"
and John Schlesinger's "Sunday Bloody Sunday"—that
have managed to capture the
anxious, embattled style of
modern sexual and romantic
relationships.

One sign of a good director
is that he brings out the
best in his collaborators. Tom
Stoppard wrote the adaptation of the Thomas Wiseman
novel, and his savagely witty
dialogue enriches this comedy of manners about a
wealthy British suburban
couple and the German gigolo who disrupts their marriage. The verbal polish of
Stoppard's writing comple-
ments the elegant visual style
that Losey has achieved with
the aid of cinematographer
Gerry Fisher and production
designer Richard MacDonald.
In addition, the performances
by Glenda Jackson and
Michael Caine, as the husband and wife, are among
their most daring and richly
detailed.

Thanks to Losey's control,
the movie achieves surprising
dramatic intensity. In its acid
view of the subtle, almost
subliminal tensions of marriage, the sadistic gamesman-
ship, and the jockeying for
power, "The Romantic En-
glishwoman" recalls some of
Pinter's plays, as well as
Albee's "Who's Afraid of Virginia Woolf?" The three main
characters—Lewis Fielding,
a successful novelist and
screenwriter, his discontent-
ed wife Elizabeth, and Thomas (Helmut Berger), the adventurer who meets Eliz-
abeth in Baden Baden and
later turns up at her home
in England—are all seen in
the round. Losey refuses to
simplify the contest.

The romantic triangle constantly frustrates expectations. Lewis invites Thomas
into his household and actively encourages his wife's
adultery, partly because he
wants to introduce some danger into his placid bourgeois
existence, and partly because
he needs material for the
screenplay he is writing,
which happens to concern
a dissatisfied housewife. He
hopes that the emotional fireworks exploding in his own
home will spark his imagination. Like many modern
works of art, "The Romantic
Englishwoman" is about the
artist's self-absorption, his
coldness and voraciousness.

On the deepest level the film deals with the blurring of distinctions between fiction and reality. Like all writers, Lewis draws his novels and screenplays from his personal experience, but his experience is itself influenced and transformed by his own fiction and by a multitude of pulp romances that are the staples of our shared popular culture. Similarly, Elizabeth's fantasies of mystery and adventure—dramatized in the lovely but deliberately over-ripe opening scene in Baden Baden—are inspired by the movies she

has seen and by the romantic clichés she has absorbed. The film bitterly observes the moral consequences of this immersion in fantasy. Lewis and Elizabeth are so hypnotized — or tranquilized — by images from kitsch romance that they are incapable of taking any responsibility for their actions.

Perhaps "The Romantic Englishwoman" is too cerebral to attract a large audience, but I suspect that it will be around long after this season's flashier, more commercial films have been forgotten. ■

Stephen Farber is a freelance film critic.

1976 Ja 18, II:13:7

Hollywood and the God Question

By ANDREW M. GREELEY

The good religious film has eluded the American industry. To be sure, there has been no shortage of spectaculars ("The Ten Commandments," "King of Kings," and Joan of Arc in various manifestations), to say nothing of Biblical sexploitations ("David and Bathsheba," "Samson and Delilah"), tear jerkers ("Miracle of the Bells"), cloying chronicles of clerical culture ("Going My Way," "The Bells of St. Mary's," "Keys of the Kingdom," "Come to the Stable," "The Nun's Story"), ventures into the occult ("Heaven Can Wait," "The Exorcist"), and films with religious background for exotic effect ("Nashville," "A Woman Under the Influence"). American filmmakers have produced movies about religion, movies which use religion, movies which exploit religion to titillate or terrify, but no religious movies.

One need only visit the current series of Buñuel films at the Museum of Modern Art — especially "Nazarin," with its powerful depiction of the trials of a latter-day Christ figure—to get an idea of how foreign moviemakers, even the supposed atheists, have put Hollywood to shame. For further evidence of the European director's eagerness to come to grips with religion, consider Bergman's "The Seventh Seal," in which a knight returning from the Crusades

The Rev. Andrew M. Greeley is director for the center of the Study of American Pluralism at the National Opinion Research Center.

plays a fatal game of chess with death; Fellini's "La Dolce Vita," with its contrast between the sweet pleasures of high society and the corruption of death; Rohmer's "Ma Nuit Chez Maud," featuring a night-long discussion of Pascal's religious gamble —the argument that it's wise to bet on God, because you have nothing to lose if you're wrong and much to gain if you're right; Bergman's "Cries and Whispers," showing a family's desperate attempt to find meaning in the lingering death of a sister; and Buñuel's "Belle de Jour," dealing with the death and resurrection of a modern-day Magdalene.

Each of these directors makes films in which the fundamental religious issues are the very stuff out of which the story emerges. Their American counterparts seem afraid to raise such basic questions. Even in vintage Hollywood films about the clergy, one got the impression that Pat O'Brien, Bing Crosby, Spencer Tracy and Frank Sinatra—not to mention the young Jesuits in "The Exorcist"—were embarrassed to talk about religious beliefs. They may have uttered a few simple pieties, but if there was any religious agony in their lives, any struggle with doubt, any terror or hope, any experience of the transcendent, such phenomena never broke through their smooth, bland clerical exteriors.

The closest one gets to a saint in an American film is the Teilhard de Chardin-like exorcist or Jennifer Jones as Bernadette. To compare them with the very real and very moving Pierre Fres-

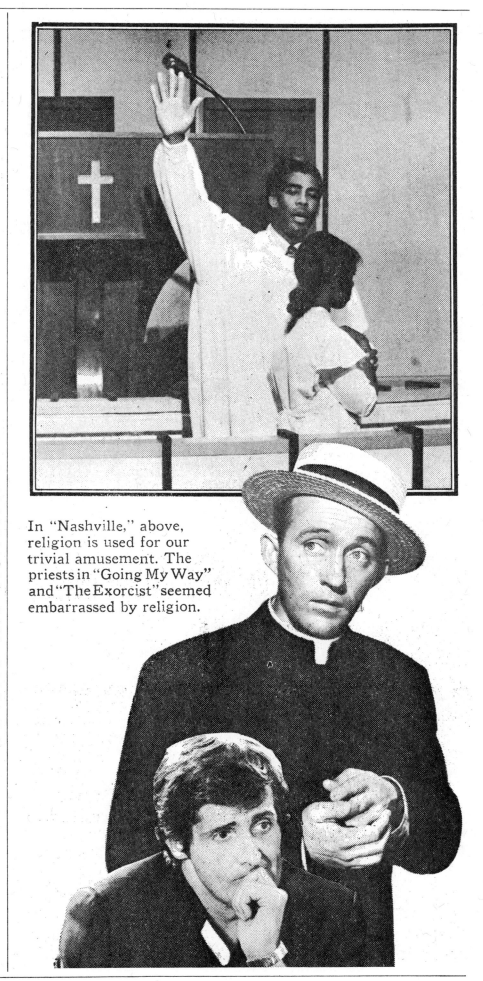

In "Nashville," above, religion is used for our trivial amusement. The priests in "Going My Way" and "The Exorcist" seemed embarrassed by religion.

nay in "Monsieur Vincent" is instructive. Fresnay understood the nature of sainthood: he knew that a saint is not somebody off on a pedestal, but somebody who is at ease with the world, somebody with an earthy confidence. Max Von Sydow and Miss Jones obviously had not the foggiest notion of what a saint is, and so they brought to their roles the complete immobility of plaster of paris statues.

Nor does it seem to be merely a matter of foreign filmmakers being technically superior to the American breed. Even when the Americans get a first-rate story and competent personnel, as in "The Fugitive," John Ford's version of Graham Greene's "The Power and the Glory," they seem as frightened about addressing themselves to the story's basic question of faith as they would be about telling obscene stories to a convent full of elderly nuns. The Greene classic was almost unrecognizable on the screen. One certainly got no suggestion of the agony or the degradation of the whiskey priest played by Henry Fonda; completely missing were the power and the glory of the priesthood which shone through the original work. Much more credible, it seems, is Spencer Tracy telling us there is no bad boy in "Boy's Town" or Deborah Kerr going to the lions in "Quo Vadis" en negligée.

Obviously, the European directors are not invariably true believers; they have no hesitation in portraying the clergy as human beings. The Lutheran ministers of Bergman's films are not really sure they believe anything. And the Italian nuns of Fellini or De Sica are often close to caricatures. The wicked ecclesiastical fashion show in "Roma" would have terrified American producers.

Nor are the Europeans necessarily on the side of traditional religion. Fellini and De Sica are Italian anti-clericals — potential death-bed converts. Buñuel's mysticism is profoundly Spanish, but one doubts that even the contemporary, rather progressive, Spanish church would want his films shown in Spain. Bergman wishes he could be an agnostic and suspects on occasion, most notably in "Through a Glass Darkly," that God is a spider. Even the vigorous and direct French Catholicism of Rohmer has the skeptical laicist flavor of Pascal at its core. Rohmer is not quite a Jansenist, just as Pascal was not quite one; but you suspect that he would not wait too long in line for a Papal au-

dience.

Still, European directors are not afraid to speak directly about the meaning of human life and the mystery of human death—which is what religion is supposed to be all about. It is not merely that Americans would handle such issues badly if they tried to explore them. Rather, they would not even think of dealing with them or of facing the questions which they raise.

Thus, the belly dance in front of the dresser with the Madonna's statue in "Nashville" does not have the same symbolic impact as the giant crucifix being flown over the sundeck in "La Dolce Vita." The former juxtaposes the sacred and the sexual for our trivial amusement; the latter challenges us to wonder about the depth of the ambiguities of human life. Similarly, the cut in "Nashville" from bearded country singer Keith Carradine in bed with his latest conquest to a stained glass Christ (in a Catholic church where the mass is still in Latin; it's been a long time since director Robert Altman has been to church, it would seem) may jar our sensibilities somewhat, but we know that we are supposed to be jarred and that spoils the effect. It is not quite the same thing as discovering, as the knight in "The Seventh Seal" does in the confessional, that his confessor is death. And we may be transiently shocked by an adolescent girl's masturbation with a crucifix in "The Exorcist," but it is not quite the same as the Dies Irae procession of the penitentes in "The Seventh Seal." The Americans trivialize the religious symbol when they do not prostitute it. The Europeans are brave enough to force us to face the anguish of life and death lurking in the symbol.

Nor will the European directors let us off with easy answers. One cannot think of a single American movie which approaches the ambiguous agnosticism of the dance of death across the sky in "The Seventh Seal," the deliberate blurring of the dream world and reality at the end of Buñuel's "Belle de Jour," or the bittersweet summer day of "Cries and Whispers." Only Rohmer is a confident believer (one might almost say, supremely self-confident); the others are not sure whether they believe or not. Still, unlike their American counterparts, these Europeans can talk about their agnosticism. They may not know whether there is a God or not, but they are sure that the question is one

worth raising. Only Martin Scorsese of the American Catholic filmmakers (Peckinpah, Altman, Coppola, Hitchcock) is able to drag in the God question for a few moments in "Mean Streets."

How come?

Why does a society with strong church affiliation and high levels of religious practice produce no deeply religious films, while countries where religion is in retreat and the church in trouble turn out filmmakers with an obsessive concern about religious issues? It certainly cannot be argued that Americans are religiously shallow; on the contrary, the pursuit of mysticism in the United States today would be unthinkable in Western Europe. Nor has America lacked religious thinkers who have agonized over the meaning of life. Emerson was not a Pascal and William James was something less than John of the Cross, but the two of them certainly represent a deep strain of religious concern which is part of the American cultural heritage.

I sometimes suspect that the reason is that the religious question (Is God mad? Is there graciousness in the universe? Are we alone? Is our hopefulness ultimately a deception?—phrase it your way) has not been considered intellectually respectable in the United States in the years since the advent of the film. The cultural elite which has dominated American life since the 1920's has been, for the most part, made up of first generation alienates from either pious Christian families (with a father or a grandfather, perhaps, a rigid but kindly clergyman) or strictly observant Jewish families. The alienation of prestigious literary figures like Dreiser, Steinbeck, Edmund Wilson, John Reed and Max Eastman was not so much anti-religious hostility as merely lack of interest. They were convinced that religion was not worth writing about. They and their successors, as the arbiters of American culture, effectively ruled out of court all serious agonizing over the meaning of human life. Moreover, one would be hard put to point out any lengthy discussion of the God question in the works of such intellectual heavyweights as Lionel Trilling or Sidney Hook, to say nothing of lesser gurus such as Mary McCarthy and Susan Sontag. Even theologians like Reinhold Niebuhr gained their reputations discussing the social gospel rather than strictly religious matters.

There has been no counter-elite tradition which you could argue for a minority

report. It may be hard to believe in God after you have read Sartre, but it is equally hard to reject the God question out of hand if you have grown up in an intellectual environment still presided over by the mystical genius of Blaise Pascal.

●

The divinity school and seminary faculties have been ill-equipped to respond to the bland agnosticism of the cultural elites—and until recently, Catholics have been too busy building churches and schools and organizing softball leagues to think much about God. Thus, when the cultural elites, of which the filmmakers are a part, say that the God question (the grace question, the meaning question, the hope question) is hardly worth asking, there is no one around to say, the hell it's not.

Indeed, after a brief flirtation with the pulpit-thumping Barth of neo-orthodoxy, the Protestant intelligentsia has returned to a mixture of social gospel and philosophical skepticism which leaves them open to pursue the latest political and cultural fads. Their Catholic counterparts, having been caught unprepared by the Second Vatican Council, are either speaking in tongues with Pentacostalism or parroting the cliches of the vulgar Marxism called liberation theology. Some of the more respected Jewish thinkers are insisting that after the Holocaust, the God question must be considered closed — as though there were not previous examples of genocide in human history (the potato famine in Ireland, for instance). In such a cultural environment, who could make serious religious films? And why would anyone want to?

So the American filmmaker uses religion as a stage prop or a grabber. He may be a skeptic, in which case he exploits religion with a wink of the eye. Or he may even be sincere; he may think that casting out devils or routing the Philistines in massive battle formations is what religion really is. After all, there's plenty of that in the Bible.

But the last thing in the world the American director does is permit his doubts and fears, hopes and ecstasy, horror and interludes of transcendence into his films. First of all, the questions involved in such experiences are regarded as not worth asking. Secondly, the director suspects that if he made people really think about them, he might scare the hell out of them, and they wouldn't come back to see his next movie.

Besides, in order to do that, he might have to think about the religious question himself. ●

1976 Ja 18, II:1:2

●

THE SLAP, directed by Claude Pinoteau. Screenplay by Mr. Pinoteau and Jean-Loup Dabadie. Photographer, Jean Collomb. Executive producer, Alain Poiré. Released by Silver Screen Productions. At the 68th Street Playhouse, Third Avenue. (This film has not been rated.) Running time: 104 minutes.
Jean .... Lino Ventura
Isabelle .... Isabelle Adjani
Helene .... Annie Girardot
Marc .... Francis Perrin
Remy .... Jacques Spiesser

By RICHARD EDER

There are sparks of humor and style in this new French film, but they gutter out like short birthday candles in thick frosting.

Like many weak movies whose virtues exist without redeeming them, "The Slap" starts out well. A study of an unquiet father and a daughter who is growing up and away from him, it quickly establishes its characters, their wry if unoriginal predicament and our interest in what happens to them. Unfortunately, nothing much does.

The father is a professor, a man whose considerable fire is banked by a determined conformity. His wife has left him years before; he keeps a respectable mistress, plays vigorous soccer on weekends, and takes care of his 18-year-old daughter.

●

Both father and daughter have the crises appropriate to their seasons. The father's repressed rebelliousness flares up when he sees a student beaten by two policemen. He scuffles with them, is arrested and threatened with disciplinary action by the education authorities, and submits his resignation.

His daughter wants to leave home and move in with her boyfriend, is forbidden to, rebels, submits, fails her exams, runs off with a new boyfriend. As the film plods along, with endless coming and going and telephoning and arguing and changing of minds, the two crises gradually erode.

The daughter's rebelliousness matures into real independence. The father's professional difficulties blow over, and by the end he has left his mistress and seems likely to take up again with his wife.

●

The director, Claude Pinoteau, has chosen two strong actors for his protagonists. As the professor, Lino Ventura manages stiffness dourness and moments of sudden sweetness that illuminate his complexity. His sour love for his daughter—he shouts her to her room in one flare-up, and the next morning brings her a solicitous cup of coffee in bed—is held firmly this side of sentimentality.

As the gawky, quicksilver, funny, fidgety daughter, Isabelle Adjani—who was the star of François Truffaut's "Adèle H."—also plays her part for what it is worth. Neither of the parts is worth a great deal, however. The characters are established, but they have remarkably little to do. About halfway through, the movie's slim vitality flickers out and never recovers. Mr. Pinoteau has set out pinwheels but failed to find a wind.

1976 Ja 19, 25:3

SEVEN BEAUTIES, directed by Lina Wertmuller; screenplay (Italian with English subtitles) by Miss Wertmuller; editor, Franco Fraticelli; director of photography, Tonino Delli Colli; music, Enzo Iannacci; distributed by Cinema V. Running time: 116 minutes. At the Cinema II, Third Avenue near 60th Street. This film has not yet been rated.
Pasqualino Frafuso .. Giancarlo Giannini
Pedro .... Fernando Rey
Commandant .... Shirley Stoler
Concettina .... Elena Fiore
Don Raffaele .... Enzo Vitale
Tofonno .... Mario Conti
Francesco .... Piero Di Orio
Mother .... Ermelinad De Felice
Carolina .... Francesca Marciano
Lawyer .... Lucio Amelio
Socialist .... Roberto Herlitzka
Doctor .... Doriglia Palmi

By VINCENT CANBY

"Seven Beauties," the fifth Lina Wertmuller film to be released in this country in less than two years, is the finest, most ambitious work yet made by this gifted Italian director whose films appear to be inspired by irreconcilable contradictions.

"Seven Beauties," which opened yesterday at the Cinema II, is a handbook for survival, a farce, a drama of almost shattering impact. It's a disorderly epic, seductively beautiful to look at, as often harrowing as it is boisterously funny, though it has a solid substructure of common sense and precisely observed details from life.

•

It's the story of Pasqualino Frafuso (Giancarlo Giannini), a natty, small-time, completely self-absorbed Neapolitan dandy who had some notoriety shortly before World War II as "the monster of Naples." Pasqualino, to defend his sister's honor, had murdered her pimp, then chopped up the body and mailed the pieces to different parts of Italy. Pasqualino is a character whom Brecht might have found fascinating. He is a survivor, possessed of what someone calls that "thirst for life" that outruns ideas and ideals.

Miss Wertmuller's screenplay opens after the collapse of the Italian front when Pasqualino has deserted from the Italian army while being shipped through Germany to the Russian front. Picked up by the Germans, he is sent to a concentration camp where, to stay alive, he sets out to seduce the camp's ferocious female commandant—an uproariously funny and thoroughly doomed campaign. Counterpointing this story are flashbacks that tell a parallel story of that earlier time in Naples when Pasqualino, at his murder trial, had sacrificed honor to stay alive.

As are all of Miss Wertmuller's films, "Seven Beauties is about choices, and the conditions that govern them. Though she states positions bluntly, she doesn't make films that are easily categorized for popular consumption as either optimistic or pessimistic. Pasqualino's survival is neither a triumph nor a tragedy, but simply the expression (as I take it) of the life force, whatever that may be.

The director is deeply committed to political action, which can alleviate intolerable social conditions, but her films are distinguished by an awareness that political action is always dependent upon the unpredictable human response. It's her awareness and her appreciation of this mystery that give her films their particular life.

They are also full of vitality and are marveously well acted. Giancarlo Giannini, superb as Pasqualino, receives especially effective support from Miss Stoler, Fernando Rey (as a fellow concentration camp prisoner), and Elena Fiore (as Pasqualino's elder sister, the would-be whore).

"Seven Beauties" deserves to be the first big hit of the new year.

1976 Ja 22, 42:1

Summarized in this fashion, "Seven Beauties" (which is Pasqualino's nickname in Naples) sounds more schematic than the eccentric, surprising, and compassionate film that Miss Wertmuller has actually made.

"Seven Beauties" is the work of a film maker at the peak of her energies, so full of ideas and images that she can afford to throw away moments that other, less talented directors would tediously emphasize.

•

Typical is a moment during Pasqualino's preconcentration camp wanderings in rural Germany when he sees in the distance a small group of soldiers escorting what looks to be a funeral party of well-dressed mourners. Slowly, methodically, the mourners stop, take off their clothes and offer themselves to their firing squad.

Pasqualino's companion, an Italian socialist, is outraged at Italy's complicity in the Nazi terror. Pasqualino shrugs, and it's Pasqualino who lives to return home, not the socialist.

Miss Wertmuller states political positions bluntly. When Pasqualino is convicted of murder, he is sentenced to 12 years in prison, while a political prisoner receives 28 years "for thinking." The female commandant (played by Shirley Stoler, the American actress) allows Pasqualino to make love to her, then sneers, "In Paris, a Greek made love to a goose . . . to eat, to live. That's why you'll survive . . . and our dreams for a master race [are] unattainable. . . ."

As are all of Miss Wertmuller's films, "Seven Beauties is about choices, and the conditions that govern them. Though she states positions bluntly, she doesn't make films that are easily categorized for popular consumption as either optimistic or pessimistic. Pasqualino's survival is neither a triumph nor a tragedy, but simply the expression (as I take it) of the life force, whatever that may be.

The director is deeply committed to political action, which can alleviate intolerable social conditions, but her films are distinguished by an awareness that political action is always dependent upon the unpredictable human response. It's her awareness and her appreciation of this mystery that give her films their particular life.

They are also full of vitality and are marveously well acted. Giancarlo Giannini, superb as Pasqualino, receives especially effective support from Miss Stoler, Fernando Rey (as a fellow concentration camp prisoner), and Elena Fiore (as Pasqualino's elder sister, the would-be whore).

"Seven Beauties" deserves to be the first big hit of the new year.

1976 Ja 22, 42:1

92 IN THE SHADE, written and directed by Thomas McGuane; executive producer, Elliott Kastner; photographed by Michael C. Butler; edited by Ed Rothkowitz; music by Michael J. Lewis. Released by United Artists. Running time: 93 minutes. At Showcase theaters. This film has rated R.
Tom Skelton .... Peter Fonda
Nicholas Dance .... Warren Oates
Miranda .... Margot Kidder
Goldsboro .... Burgess Meredith
Carter .... Harry Dean Stanton
Bella .... Sylvia Miles
Jeannie Carter .... Elizabeth Ashley

By RICHARD EDER

Thomas Guane's "92 in the Shade" is subtle and lively. Parts of its are overbrilliant, if anything, in that they compel our pleasure almost to the point of distracting. By the time it ends, we have unmistakably been entertained. Perhaps we have been mildly poisoned, as well.

Mr. McGuane, a novelist turned screen writer and director, has set his movie in the charter-boat, fishing-guide world of Key West, Fla. The blues and greens, the heat, the wilting paint hint at corruption. Under the film's humor and momentum there is also corruption. But the whole thing is so finely tuned, so edgily balanced that it's hard to say whether corruption is merely the theme or shades over into the viewpoint as well.

•

The film, which opened yesterday at Showcase theaters, uses a disarrayed and drifting child of plenty as its protagonist. Peter Fonda plays him as human desert planted with expensive flowers. He is selfindulgent and cold, disconnected and rich.

His name is Tom Skelton. His grandfather owns the bank, the police force and a vast supply of earthiness. iHs father has retreated semipermanently into a kind of outdoor crib — shades of "Baby Doll"—set out on the front porch. Tom takes candlelit bths with a bra-less schoodlteacher and suddenly decides that he is going to find something to do.

What he does is move his cloudy self-indulgence into a rough and real world, that of the boat captains who take tourists out fishing. They are hard, self-made men, at once competitive and clannish, and with no liking for a rich kid who tries to break into their business.

It is in its portrayal of these men that the movie moves from languid wit into something stronger. There is Nicholas Dance, a violent, primitive man with a rough code of honor which consists, as he puts it, in maintaining his "credence." There is Carter, cleverer, and quicker to see the threat to his struggling lifestyle posed by Tom.

Dance and Carter, in an act of half-playful, half-serious hazing, steal Tom's first client. Tom's detachment dissolves totally. He's never reacted to anything; now he overreacts viciously by burning Dance's boat. ·

Dance, played with marvelous strength and a kind of baffled sweetness by Warren Oates, tries to puzzle out the rights and wrongs. Egged on by Carter—another splendid performance by Harry Dean Stanton—he decides that even though he likes Tom and has wronged him, the reprisal is out of all measure.

To maintain his "credence," he warns Tom, he will shoot him if he continues to work as a fishing guide. Tom ignores him. He gets money from his grandfather and orders a boat built that is far grander than anything Carter or Dance have been able to buy. He takes out a tourist—sent to him by Carter, who wants to see him dead—and there is a showdown.

The showdown is more ironic than tragic. Quite coldly, in fact, this pseudo flower-child has used the old weapons of money and position—his grandfather's—to get his way. It is an ending with uneasy implications. Tom has been portrayed with charm as well as irony and there is an overwhelming desire not to see him shot dead. But it is he, fundamentally, who is the aggressor and the bully.

•

As in "Rancho DeLuxe," which he wrote, although he didn't direct it, Mr. McGuane captures the speech and style of young people who are funny and charming and empty and mean. "Ninety-two" maintains some of the disquieting ambiguity of viewpoint that weakened "Rancho." But it's a more satisfying picture.

The authenticity of Carter and Dance sets off the emptiness at the center of Tom, and gives us a focus to sense it. So does a line by Tom's invalid father who warns his son that, for Dance, the showdown is a matter of honor. "It's a matter of who gets to fish and who gets to cut bait," says Tom, shrugging the notion off. "You and your generation have a depraved sense of language," says his father retors.

1976 Ja 22, 42:1

3 Silent Gerson Shorts Begin Whitney Run

By A. H. WEILER

Art sometimes may be the end result of devotion to a specific style. And, the three short silent films by Barry Gerson, which began a week's run yesterday at the Whitney Museum of American Art, are stamped by a distinctly personal point of view on the interplay of images, color and movement. But if the man-made and natural subjects he lovingly focuses on do not have a shattering impact, they are notable for an unflagging concentration on familiar objects that eventually, if somewhat tediously, emerge as artful compositions.

Mr. Gerson, a 36-year-old New Yorker and a member

Giancarlo Giannini

FILM VIEW

VINCENT CANBY

An Epic Film About Honor and Survival

of the avant-garde, who was represented at the Film Forum here in 1972 with a variety of 4-minute "Window Studies," has not deserted this specialty. Both the 12-minute "Inversion" and the 32-minute "Celluloid Illuminations" are views, framed by windows, that evolve as placid, abstractlike studies. In "Inversions," which was

The Program

A PROGRAM OF THREE FILMS BY BARRY GERSON, "Inversion," "Translucent Appearances" and "Celluloid Illuminations." Total running time: 66 minutes. At the Whitney Museum of American Art, through Jan. 27.

shot in adjacent straight and inverted scenes, a green-and-white triangular-roofed house, blue skies and slowly moving side objects fitfully vie for attention.

•

In the more ambitious "Celluloid Illuminations," houses, beams, sky and water, with side panels of gradually changing colors, are captured in interestingly stylized geometric patterns. And, while the 22-minute "Translucent Appearances" is solely concerned with an unidentified waterfall that presumably is Niagara Falls, its varied aspects, from close-ups to raging torrent, amid accompanying, varying shades of color, make for intermittent, eye-catching imagery.

Like "Translucent Appearances," Mr. Gerson's work in this very special genre is often self-indulgent, but it projects honest, professional, personal and occasionally striking vignettes of normally mundane things.

1976 Ja 22, 44:4

At a crucial point in "Seven Beauties," Lina Wertmuller's epic new film about an Italian soldier's efforts to survive in a German concentration camp near the end of World War II, Pasqualino (Giancarlo Giannini), the soldier, determines that he might be able to save himself if he makes love to the camp's particularly ferocious female officer. As played by Shirley Stoler, the American actress ("The Honeymoon Killers"), this woman is a kind of Superbitch of Belsen. She's so large, so fleshy, so pink-skinned, so small-eyed, so utterly implacable, and so apparently without conventional sexual needs (it would seem to anyone in his right mind), that only a very desperate man would undertake such a doomed campaign. But Pasqualino is that desperate as well as slightly lunatic.

Though he is emaciated and his teeth are loose and though the looks he once had have long since turned grotesque, Pasqualino begins his seduction using the tricks that were successful in Naples. During morning inspections he winks at her ever so slightly. His lips make the tiniest suggestion of a kiss. When he chances upon her alone, he croaks out something that might have been a Neapolitan serenade. He is Mr. Magoo trying to flirt with a German tank. At first he is punished. He persists. Finally he is called in for a private interview, but he is impotent until he is given something to eat. Though the woman realizes what he is doing, though she knows that Pasqualino can't even look at her without feeling ill, she decides to use him as much as he uses her. Afterward she sneers at him: "In Paris, a Greek made love to a goose. . . . He did this to eat, to live. . . . And you, subhuman Italian larva, you found strength for an erection. That's why you'll survive and win in the end. You subhuman worms with no ideals or ideas. . . .'."

"Seven Beauties," which is Pasqualino's nickname in Naples, is not simply about survival. It's also about the "thirst for life" that, in effect, governs the choices Pasqualino makes, not only in the concentration camp but in his life in Naples, which we see in a series of

often hugely funny flashbacks. Pasqualino has neither an idea nor an ideal, but he wants to live, which he does with an exuberance that is both cockeyed and as mysterious as life itself. Miss Wertmuller never attempts to define this thirst for life, but in the ironic song that's sung behind the film's opening credits she inventories a lot of people who don't have it, including "the ones who have never had a fatal accident . . . and the ones who have . . ."

"Seven Beauties" is Miss Wertmuller's sixth feature film and her fifth to be released in this country in less than two years. It's also her second to be opened in New York in less than two weeks—her 1973 comedy, "All Screwed Up," having opened a week earlier. This artificial concentration of Wertmullers would be fatal to the work of a filmmaker less gifted than this brilliant, very original Italian director who has taken the social-sexual-political concerns of a lot of other filmmakers—including Fellini, Visconti and De Sica—and turned them into visions—both comic and poetic—unlike the work of anyone else.

"Seven Beauties" is Miss Wertmuller's "King Kong," her "Nashville," her "8½," her "Navigator," her "City Lights." It's everything she's ever been interested in to an extent that it could almost be a guide to her earlier films, if not a coda. Its method is comic though her concerns are profoundly serious. The physical production is seductively beautiful, even when the terrain is not, and the most important characters are either from southern Italy or Sicily, regions where the metaphorical contradictions —ones that the rest of us try to ignore in ourselves— comprise such an honorable way of life that people attempt to act them out.

• • •

In one of the several subplots in "Seven Beauties," Pasqualino tries to salvage the honor of his family by murdering the pimp who has turned his sister into a perfectly satisfied whore. However, since he shot the pimp in cold blood, without giving him a chance to defend himself, Pasqualino is advised by his Mafia benefactor to dispose of the body in an honorable way, by chopping it up and sending it by post to various parts of Italy. Pasqualino fails and, when arrested, desires to confess everything as his code of honor dictates, but his lawyer persuades him to plead insanity as the only way of escaping the death sentence. As he does later in Germany, Pasqualino chooses life above honor.

Why this choice when most people would clearly admire idealists who are prepared to sacrifice their lives for their beliefs? I'm not sure that admiration, or ideal acts, are the things that interest Miss Wertmuller most, or that she would think that idealists are terribly important in the long run of things. In "Seven Beauties" she makes no moral judgment about Pasqualino's impulse to live. It is, rather, a mysterious fact of societal life. She contemplates this impulse, turns it around, looks at all sides of it, not in the abstract but in terms of a particular, very vivid character, a fact that makes her work resistant to easy categorization. Because her characters have lives of their own, Miss Wertmuller's films do not fall neatly into prearranged political schemes, though there is no one today making films that are more essentially political than hers. Politics is making choices, and all of Miss Wertmuller's films are about the social and sexual conditions that govern them.

In "The Seduction of Mimi" Giancarlo Giannini plays a radical young Sicilian whose interest in the party immediately dims when he becomes a father and starts grooming his son to be a member of the consumer society. "Swept Away," Miss Wertmuller's most tumultuous comedy, is a love story in which the earlier lives of its lovers dictate their ultimate fate. Their choices were made before they ever met. Which is not to say that Miss Wertmuller's films are fatalistic. They are very much about the societies her characters inhabit—and the choices that keep those societies functioning.

• • •

Giancarlo Giannini carts off a corpse in "Seven Beauties."

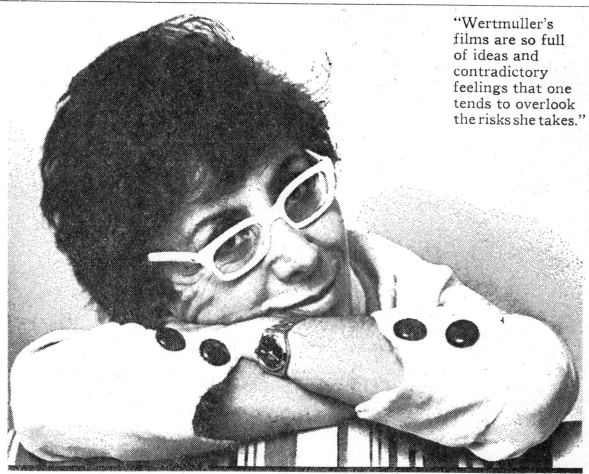

Nancy Crampton

> "Wertmuller's films are so full of ideas and contradictory feelings that one tends to overlook the risks she takes."

At the same time, there is the girl in the portrait who loves him, and whom he loves, but whose love—because of his blindness—he is too proud to accept. Love, pride and death contend, but the real struggle is between bathos and tedium.

"Scent" was well liked at last year's Cannes Festival, and Mr. Gassman won the Best Actor prize. In retrospect it is hard to see why. His performance has force, but his role is paper-thin. He is a comic lion in the early scenes. When matters become serious he is nothing but roaring.

1976 Ja 26, 28:4

HEDDA, directed by Trevor Nunn, screenplay by Mr. Nunn, based on the play "Hedda Gabler" by Henrik Ibsen; produced by Robert Enders; executive producer, George Barrie; director of photography, Douglas Slocombe; a Royal Shakespeare Company production, distributed by Brut Productions. Running time: 100 minutes. At the Fine Arts Theater, 58th Street east of Park Avenue. (This film has been rated PG.)

Hedda .... Glenda Jackson
Judge Brack .... Timothy West
Mrs. Elvsted .... Jennie Linden
Lovborg .... Patrick Stewart
Tesman .... Peter Eyre
Aunt Julie .... Constance Chapman
Bertha .... Pam St. Clement

By VINCENT CANBY

When we first see Glenda Jackson's Hedda Gabler in the opening credit sequence of the new film, "Hedda," she is standing on the deck of a Norwegian coastal steamer, her body straight and lean, her jaw firm and her eyes betraying no interest whatever. Hedda tolerates scenery. Fjords, mountains, autumn foliage are landscapes to be passed through as quickly as possible. That's all.

Standing on the deck, she is the steamer's figurehead. She could slice through a polar icecap without receiving a scratch. It's a striking image, and one that sets the style for the bright, cleanedge performance that follows.

"Hedda," which opened at the Fine Arts Theater yesterday, is Trevor Nunn's screen adaptation of the Royal Shakespeare Company stage production that he directed and toured in this country and Australia last year. It is very much a film, though, with a few exceptions at the beginning, it sticks to the single interior set of the Ibsen play.

●

Not having seen the stage production, in which Miss Jackson's interpretation caused a certain amount of controversy, I have no idea to what extent that interpretation has been modified, if at all. Her screen performance could hardly be called controversial, though it is certainly lively and—if you're like me—thank heaven for that. The pleasures of "Hedda Gabler" are not inexhaustible, especially when Hedda is played with the more conventional gestures of despair.

Miss Jackson's Hedda comes on with low-key fury,

This is especially true in "All Screwed Up," which, though it has just arrived in this country, was made after "Love and Anarchy" and before "Swept Away." It's about a group of young men and women who come in to Milan from the country to make their fortunes and get quickly caught up in the manic pursuit of work and money, for which no one of them is particularly fit. In a pricelessly funny key scene, the once-naive, sweet-spirited Adelina must quickly decide whether to protect her virginity or her new TV set, which has fallen on top of her while her fiancé is trying to rip off her bodystocking.

Miss Wertmuller's films are so full of ideas and contradictory feelings that one tends to overlook the risks she takes and the wizardry of her talent. She looks at the world not through the eyes of a neo-realist but of a poet, one whose occasional purple passages (the spectacular revolving camera movement that ends "All Screwed Up") are less exhibitionistic than they are visible extensions of the exuberance of her style.

An essential element in that style is Giancarlo Giannini, who has starred in all but one of her last five films, always as the southern Italian or Sicilian who embodies the contradictions that are the essence of comedy. Those contradictions have never been more movingly displayed than they are in "Seven Beauties." Giannini has a face as striated as the cross-section of a geological dig. The top stratum—the hair—is comic. On the next layer, the eyes, large and pale, are impassive. They record everything and say nothing. The mouth below does all the talking—the truth of which is often denied by general manner. The face, like the Wertmuller characters Giannini plays, doesn't appear to have been formed at one time, but to have accumulated through ages of experience.

It's the face of the survivor who knows instinctively that idealism is self-defeating, and that that sort of defeat can be transformed to triumph only in the post-mortems written by historians, fashions willing.

1976 Ja 25, II:1:4

SCENT OF A WOMAN, directed by Dino Risi, screenplay by Ruggero Maccari and Dino Risi, based on a novel by Giovanni Arpino, photography by Claudio Cirillo, edited by Alberto Gallitti, music by Armando Trovaioli. Released by United Artists. At the Paris Theater. Running time: 104 minutes. (This film has been rated R.).

Blind captain .... Vittorio Gassman
Ciccio .... Alessandro Momo
Sara .... Agostina Belli

By RICHARD EDER

"Scent of a Woman" is about a journey and a destination. The journey is funny, acid and intriguing. The destination is mawkish, melodramatic and interminable.

A young soldier is called to present himself at a house in Turin and place himself for seven days at the service of a retired captain, blinded in an explosion. The captain, played by Vittorio Gassman, is a handsome, vigorous man whose aristocratic arrogance suffers horribly not so much from the deprivation as the humiliation of his blindness.

●

He is bitter, sarcastic, domineering, and his handicap has inflated his native lechery to satyriasis. All these qualities are fully displayed in the curious train trip he sets out upon with his hapless traveling companion. The destination is Naples; they stop at Genoa and Rome.

The captain continually makes scenes. In the train, drunk, he insists on pressing whisky on a starchy old gentleman. When the latter only pretends to drink, the captain — whose other senses are almost sharp enough to compensate for blindness — slaps him and drives him from the compartment.

In Genoa, the captain embarks on a hilarious search for a prostitute. He can smell women, he tells Ciccio, his companion, but for proper choice needs a description as well. So he goes through Genoa sniffing and considering Ciccio's thumbnail descriptions until he meets a woman who seems to suit.

He requires assistance — hence Ciccio — but won't admit it. When he sits in a cafe he demands a newspaper as well as coffee. In Genoa, when a woman asks directions, he insists on giving them even though he can't see and doesn't know the city.

These things work well, and the relationship between the tormented captain and the good-natured, though sometimes rebellious Ciccio has humor and bite. It helps that the purpose of the journey is a mystery: Ciccio discovers a pistol and a portrait of a girl in the captain's suitcase.

The Rome sequence is a heavier replay of the adventures in Genoa. And finally they arrive in Naples. The journey is over, but the movie has a long, long way to go.

●

The captain is meeting another blinded officer, with whom he has a suicide pact.

Glenda Jackson and Timothy West

her manner so abrasive and openly sarcastic that it's difficult to see why men have tried to conquer her, unless it was simply the game and not the prize that was fascinating. She is intelligent. She's well-born. She's also lethal, which is so apparent from the start of Miss Jackson's performance that the interest is not in why she wrecks the lives around her, but how. This version of "Hedda Gabler" is all Miss Jackson's Hedda and, I must say, great fun to watch, though I don't think that I was moved for a minute.

Miss Jackson's technical virtuosity is particularly suited to a character like Hedda. Her command of her voice and her body, as well as the Jackson mannerisms, have the effect of separating the actress from the character in a very curious way. It's as if one were reviewing the other with rueful self-awareness. It's the drama critic in Hedda who describes as "a grotesque farce" her marriage to a dull pedant who doesn't come up to her ankles. Hedda is a terrific role—and Hedda knows it. She is willful, insatiable, articulate, but no more demanding of others than she is of herself.

One of the problems with the film is that none of the actors seem to have the resources needed to balance Miss Jackson's performance. Some of this is in Ibsen's play, of course. It's no con-

test from the beginning, when Hedda and her husband return from their honeymoon and she sets about goading her former lover into "a positive act" (suicide) and sparring with her husband's best friend, who could possibly become a lover.

Most effective is Timothy West, as the possible lover who is almost as ruthless as Hedda is. But both Peter Eyre, as her husband, and Patrick Stewart, as the former lover whose life and work she destroys, haven't the weight to make the contest with Miss Jackson especially interesting.

In this "Hedda," the women have the best moments. Jennie Linden is fine as the deceptively defenseless Mrs. Elvsted, who originally comes to Hedda's house for help and stays on to replace her. Miss Linden succeeds in uncovering the smugness underneath Mrs. Elvsted's helplessness, which then becomes a weapon as lethal as Hedda's arrogant demand for perfection.

The physical production is handsome, and Mr. Nunn is most successful in preserving the claustrophobic nature of the play without creating a static film. "Hedda" is an imaginative, intelligent film version of a play that I wasn't breathlessly waiting to see at this moment.

1976 Ja 26, 29:1

CALIFORNIA IMAGES, a program of two films including "Miracle," made by Ed Ruscha with Jim Ganzer, Michelle Phillips and Dana Derfus, and "The Desert People," written, produced and directed by David Lamelas with Carol Gary, Chris Holmes, John Voldstad, Michael Schwartz and Manuel Tomas Lucas. At the Whitney Museum of American Art.

By A. H. WEILER

"California Images," the collective title for "Miracle" and "The Desert People," which began a week's stand yesterday at the Whitney Museum of American Art, may be geographically precise but the films are substantively far apart, if equally provocative. As examinations of, respectively, a day in the life of an auto mechanic and the reactions of some young people to Papago Indians, they are fantasylike, if not wholly lucid, treatments of seemingly simple subjects that do manage to stick in memory.

In the 30-minute "Miracle," filmed last year, Ed Ruscha, the 38-year-old artist and prolific still photographer, projects the talent and whimsy noted in several of his exhibitions here in recent years. California may be the focus of "Miracle," but its focus is on Jim Ganzer, as the mechanic dedicated to rehabilitating a 1965 Mustang. He is a grimy, grease monkey who devotion causes him to forget his date with pretty Michelle Phillips and who is transformed into an immaculate scientist peering through a microscope for the finally successful solution to his problem.

"What are you doing," his pal, Dana Derfus, asks, "a heart transplant or a carburetor?" Mr. Ruscha, tongue-in-cheek and impish imagination exposed, seems to have had his heart in his minuscule, slightly vague but charming "Miracle."

David Lamelas, 28, a reported newcomer to the avant-garde movie scene, is good deal foggier and more startling in his approach to "The Desert People." His 49-minute study, made in 1974, appears to be a straightforward, if somewhat repetitious documentation of the opinions of five, young researchers returning by car to Los Angeles after having spent some weeks at a Papago reservation in Arizona.

These interviews, during the trip, with John Voldstad, Carol Gary, Chris Holmes, Michael Schwartz and, the most effective, with Manuel Tomas Lucas, an Indian, seem heartfelt and real. But, for reasons known only to Mr. Lamelas, the film and the characters' credibility are undermined by an unexplained, shocking climax in which they presumably plunge to their deaths when their car suddenly goes out of control and over a cliff.

His principals seem to be sincerely concerned with the culture and respected traditions of Papagos that have been ill-used in an imperfect, harsh world. But under Mr. Lamelas's professional juggling of fact and fantasy,

"The Desert People" evolves as an interesting but eventually enigmatic work.

1976 Ja 29, 26:2

THE AMERICAN SOLDIER, directed by Rainer Werner Fassbinder; screenplay (German with English subtitles) by Mr. Fassbinder; director of photography, Dietrich Lohmann; music, Peter Raben; distributed by New Yorker Films. Running time: 80 minutes. At the Film Forum, 15 Vandam Street. This film has not been rated.
Ricky..........................Karl Scheydt
Rosa...........................Elge Sorbas
Policeman......................Jan George
Policeman......................Hark Bohm
Mother.........................Eva Ingeborg Scholz
Hotel maid.....................Margarethe von Trotta
Brother........................Kurt Raab
Singer.........................Ingrid Caven
Pornographer...................Kathrin Schaake
Gypsy..........................Ulli Lommel
Franz Walsh....................R.W.Fassbinder

By VINCENT CANBY

"The American Soldier," which opened at the Film Forum yesterday, is an early (1970) film by Rainer Werner Fassbinder, the prolific and prodigiously talented young German director whose works are turning up in this country out of their chronological order. This is not necessarily a bad thing. It keeps all of us, including critics, on edge since it's not easy to categorize his work.

In the later Fassbinder films to be seen here, including "Ali—Fear Eats the Soul" and "Fist-Right of Freedom" (now being called "Fox"), Mr. Fassbinder appears to have settled—for the time being, anyway—on a rather rigorous style that is both understated in the way of cinema and exaggerated in the manner of epic theater.

His interiors are cages with walls instead of bars. His landscapes, even in a city, are eerily empty, which has the effect of foreshortening perspectives, making them seem unreal. His characters, including the ulcer-ridden Moroccan worker in "Ali" and the put-upon homosexual in "Fist-Right" have tumultuous private lives, but those private lives are always political parables — if you care to read them.

"The American Soldier" is not so ambitious a film, but it is extremely interesting and often bold. The great thing about Mr. Fassbinder is that he makes films quickly and moves on (more than 20 features in less than 10 years, I'm told). He doesn't fret about mistakes or rewriting. His late films, as well as the early ones like "The American Soldier," give the impression of having been created in a single burst of energy, not shot in bits and pieces over a period of time and then fitted together.

"The American Soldier" is a flamboyant but finally solemn joke that recalls early Jean-Luc Godard. Photographed in intentionally overlit black-and-white, it's the deadpan tale of a German-born gangster who returns home from

America to make a couple of "hits" on a contract from what appears to be the police.

The story is about as important as the name of the unit publicity man on your average, run-of-the-mill American disaster movie. "The American Soldier" is about people living lives styled after the highlights of American gangster movies, under the direction of a man who finds such movies both fascinating and funny. It's virtually an anthology of movie—learned attitudes and gestures that, in the world of this particular movie, give life meaning.

Ricky, the gangster, played by Karl Scheydt (who looks like a soft version of Charles Bronson), moves impassively through the film, knocking off assignments in the fashion of a distilled Alan Ladd, making love perfunctorily to women who go suddenly limp in his arms as if shot with curare, finally to be double-crossed by his employers.

The film has the cold eye of the political cartoonist, as well as the political cartoonist's eye for outrageous detail: Ricky's mom and brother, who are apparently conventional middle class types, have a pinball machine in the living room and swig their morning whiskies directly from the bottle of Ballantine's.

Mr. Fassbinder's achievement here is in avoiding obvious camp. The film has a languorous, dreamlike pace, a feeling of slow motion. "The American soldier is not —as was the Warhol-Morrisey "Heat"—a parody of a familiar subject, but a contemplation of one. It could be called "The American Gangster Movie, Theme and Variations."

1976 Ja 30, 18:1

MANSON, a documentary film by Robert Hendrickson; a Tobann International production, distributed by Marvin Films. Running time: 83 minutes. At the Bryan West Theater, Broadway at 49th Street, and other theaters. (This film has been rated R.)
WITH Charles Manson, Lynette Fromme, Vincent T. Busliosi and others.

By VINCENT CANBY

"Manson," the feature-length documentary now playing at theaters around town, is one of those rip-off movies that tut-tuts with shock at all the unpleasant details it feels it must give us in the interests of higher sociolog and the fast buck.

As its title indicates, the film is more or less about Charles T. Manson, one of the four convicted in what became known as the Tate-La-Bianca murders in California in 1969. There are bits and pieces of interviews with Manson, with some of the Manson "family" members who were not arrested in the two murder cases (including Lynette Fromme, who later gained her own notoriety) and with Vincent T. Bugliosi, the prosecuting attorney and author of the best-selling book about the Manson trial, "Helter-Skelter."

The producers attempt unsuccessfully to enliven the film by the use of split screens and kaleidoscopic effects, apparently meant to stimulate acid trips recollected in tranquillity, but none of it creates a point of view. This is old-fashioned Sunday-supplement journalism transplanted to the screen for no purpose I can think of, other than money.

1976 Ja 31, 20:4

The Brilliant, Brooding Films of Rainer Fassbinder

By DAVID DENBY

Lots of people are capable of turning out movies cheaply and quickly, but a fast-working movie *artist* is rare. One thinks of Chaplin, Keaton and Ford in their early years, and of such contemporary figures as Godard and Chabrol. Currently, the leading example of film-artist-on-the-run is the amazingly productive 30-year-old West German screenwriter, director and actor, Rainer Werner Fassbinder.

Fassbinder, who has been known to write a screenplay on an airplane trip, has completed 29 feature-length works (six were television films, three others were made on videotape) since 1969. He has also written a number of plays, staged revivals of theater classics (often in scandalous, updated versions), and acted in the theater and in his own and other people's movies. His manic productivity has caused a furor at film festivals and in film magazines, but commercial success has been slow in coming. In New York, greeted by wildly disparate reviews, his films have barely made a dent in their first-run bookings; however, a few of them (particularly the brilliant "Merchant of Four Seasons" and "Fear Eats the Soul: Ali") are beginning to click on the revival circuit.

Two examples of Fassbinder's output are currently on view: an "early" work, "The American Soldier" (1970), a deadpan parody of American gangster films, is showing at the Film Forum today and will be repeated next Thursday through Sunday; and the 1974 "Fox" (called "Fist-Right of Freedom" at the last New York Film Festival) opens a regular run today at the Waverly. "Fox" stars Fassbinder himself as a working-class homosexual in Munich and is the first serious, explicit but

David Denby is a freelance film critic.

'He shows the dark side of postwar Germany'

non-sensational movie about homosexuality to be shown in this country.

Fassbinder's working methods fulfill the fantasy of cinema students all over the world. As the director at various times of theater troupes in Munich and Frankfurt, he has developed some of his ideas on stage before putting them on film, and many of his former stage actors have worked with him repeatedly in his movies, shuttling back and forth between large and small roles in repertory-company fashion. At this point, Fassbinder and his actors and technicians form a group of friends and lovers so familiar with one another's strengths that they can put a movie together in a few months. Although the films often look gorgeous, they are made on very low budgets. Funding comes partly from producers, partly from Fassbinder's income from his more lucrative television work, and from an occasional government prize.

With his experimental attitude toward filmmaking, Fassbinder has tried just about everything, including adaptations of plays and novels, but most of his films—shot in the streets, bars, and apartments of contemporary Munich—are brooding stories of alienation and defeat, acrid reminders of the dark side of postwar German prosperity. One reason it's difficult to generalize about Fassbinder's work is that he changes his style before anyone can invent a vocabulary to describe the last thing he was doing. At various times, and in different combinations, the films have been marked by low-and high-camp estheticism, heavy Teutonic fatalism, Marxist indignation (influenced by Brecht's truculent tone and some of his distancing devices), and melodramatic excess in conscious imitation of the florid Hollywood weepers of the 50's.

"The American Soldier," the lesser of the two Fassbinder movies now playing, is a film esthete's dream of a gangster movie—all languorous gesture and sullen aggression. Its sensual, doomed hero (Karl Scheidt) lies around in a hotel room in a stunning white suit, swigging whisky from a bottle and making love to entirely submissive women, occasionally venturing out to kill someone in a preoccupied, listless manner until he himself is killed by corrupt policemen. The story isn't to be taken seriously, but some of Fassbinder's surly jokes are striking. In a police station we see a pregnant woman berating a policeman: "It's your child!" He begins slapping her, only to pause and salute another woman passing by, a higher-ranking officer, with his upraised palm.

Fassbinder's view of the world is harsh; he appears to be saying that domination and submission have been built into modern society, and with his bluntness of

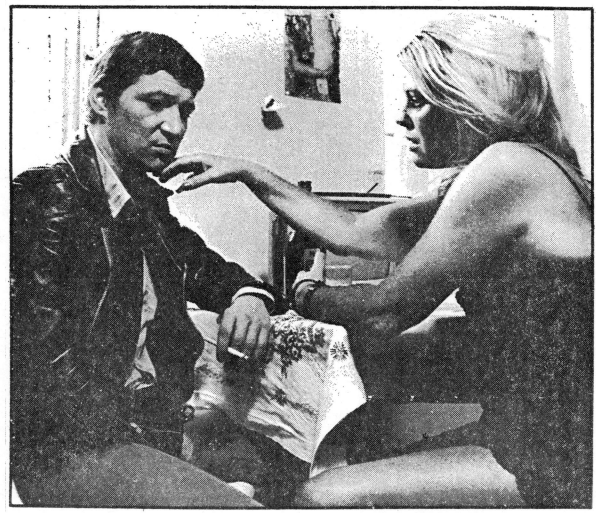

Director Fassbinder as a doomed homosexual in "Fox"

They Dumped a Good One on Skid Row

speech and characterization he gets to the point of triumph or humiliation much quicker than most directors. What puts off many viewers —and intrigues others—is the perversely campy style of his big emotional moments. Like so many young intellectuals who grew up at the movies, Fassbinder is half in love with banality, sometimes parodying the clichés of emotional expression by drawing them out until they become unbearably funny, at other times embracing them himself with rather unnerving directness. In Fassbinder's flamboyant updating of Brecht, the jokey soap-operatic moments pull you away from over-easy identification with the suffering characters and remind you of the "objective" political point being made.

In "Fox," one of Fassbinder's easiest, most naturalistic movies, homosexual power-ploys and rituals are depicted as a natural result of the class struggle. The hero, Fox (played by the director in an act of audacious self-exposure) is a working-class carnival entertainer and part-time hustler who wins a lottery fortune only to be systematically fleeced by a group of suave upper-middle-class men. The movie is a comedy about the pains of upward assimilation: Fox, hopelessly infatuated, submits to his lover Egon's ruthless schooling in the bourgeois fetishes of gourmet food, boutique clothes, and ghastly antique furniture— but poor Fox can't get his table manners right. Egon's parents, who need Fox's money to save the family business, don't object to their son's homosexuality, but the way Fox eats his cake at their table sends them up the wall.

This time it's Fassbinder's stinging coldness that forces us to concentrate on the political meanings: the working class will only be corrupted by trying to join the bourgeoisie; class solidarity is stronger than erotic loyalty; the oppression of the straight world isn't nearly as vicious as the way homosexuals exploit one another. Fassbinder's ideological view (and perhaps the absence of special pleading) has reportedly offended German homosexuals and may do the same here, but I think he is to be congratulated for refusing to yield to the pressures from Gay Lib militants for "progressive," helpful images.

Fassbinder films are undeniably irritating and a little strange; they are also completely alive, and it's to be hoped that he will soon find the large audience he deserves.   1976 F 1, II:1:3

I t is four-fifty on a Wednesday afternoon, inside the last house on the left as one staggers down 42d Street from Seventh Avenue toward Eighth. Outside there is snow that is turning to neon-lit slush even before it hits the sidewalk. Inside the light is almost as bright as on the street though the temperature is warmer. Two people on the opposite side of the balcony are arguing—crossly but lethargically. Each appears to forget from time to time what it is he finds insupportable in the other. Angola? Belfast? A rude smell? Two rows away from me a man, who has apparently been eating his lunch (or an early supper), starts to retch. With several other patrons in the vicinity, I look around, alarmed. Will I have to move? Leave entirely? No. The man doesn't get sick.

We are all relieved. Thankful for small favors. One's attention can stray back to the screen. There Elizabeth Ashley tries to explain to her husband, played by Harry Dean Stanton, why the expectant mother she now is needs a self-cleaning oven. It's a weirdly funny and brutal scene from what one sees and from what one can understand of the dialogue, which sounds as if it's being filtered through a loudspeaker with a frog in its throat. The cast also includes Warren Oates, Burgess Meredith, Peter Fonda, Margot Kidder and Sylvia Miles, all of whom appear to be giving quite manic, hugely original performances, though you can never be sure what they're saying. Or why.

The movie is "92 in The Shade," Thomas McGuane's adaptation of his fine, piercingly cool 1973 novel set in Key West about the confrontation between a spoiled, bored rich-kid, Peter Fonda, who can think but is fatally insensitive, and an eccentric commercial fisherman, Warren Oates, whose life is governed by tumultuous instincts, all of them self-destructive.

The film, which marks McGuane's directorial debut, is not great, perhaps, but it's very, very good. It's full of odd, headstrong, seemingly disconnected moments that only a novelist would dare, and it's a field day for its actors. I think of Elizabeth Ashley demonstrating the art of baton-twirling to a startled tourist in a sleazy, otherwise empty Key West saloon, or of Burgess Meredith arguing obscenely with his son, William Hickey, who has withdrawn from life into a crib-like, mosquito-netted bed on the front gallery of his Key West mansion.

The film touches a lot of bases but discreetly. It's as if everything is of peripheral importance, which is not actually true but a style of filmmaking that assumes the audience can make the necessary connections.

At the Anco 42d Street Theater, where I saw "92 in The Shade" on the first day of its New York City engagement, it was double-billed with Frank Perry's "Rancho Deluxe," an equally eccentric film, based on an original screenplay also written by McGuane. Why was such a movie playing its first run in such a theater, the color print looking pale and exhausted, as if it had been sitting up three nights running on the bus from Albuquerque?

It's not a long story, but a symptomatic one.

The Anco 42d Street Theater was just one of a handful of so-called "Showcase Theaters" in New York where the film opened that day, but without the benefit of a single line of advertising that I could find in any one of the city's three major newspapers. The only way to find out where it was playing was to call United Artists, the film's distributor, or to consult your local soothsayer.

How does a film project, about which some people thought highly enough to finance to the tune of $1,500,000, come to such a dim end?

Reached by telephone at his ranch in Montana, McGuane sounded philosophical. "It's a kind of

embarrassment," he said. Everyone connected with the film had worked for very little money because they liked the script, and were willing to go along with him, McGuane, a novelist, as the director. "It was made idealistically," he said. The producer, Elliott Kastner, had obtained the financing in England, which is where McGuane cut and scored the footage after completing photography in Key West.

The post-production period was touch-and-go, according to McGuane. The English backers were reportedly horrified when they saw the material he'd shot and eventually took the picture away from him, though they later gave it back and the film, as released, is the film he wanted to make.

The most curious thing about it, he went on to explain, was that United Artists "loved" it when they decided to take on the picture for U.S. distribution. But when the film opened in Los Angeles late last summer, the first reviews were murderous. The weekly Variety critic dismissed it as sophomoric and, in the same issue, went on to consider—in solemn terms and at much greater length—a homosexual porn film. What's worse, "92 in The Shade" did no business.

That's the key. "They (distributors) are like Indians in a canoe," said McGuane. They throw the baby into the water and if he swims, fine. If he sinks, they keep on paddling.

Elliott Kastner, who produced both "Rancho Deluxe" and "92 in The Shade," and is currently producing the multi-million dollar "The Missouri Breaks" (also written by McGuane) for United Artists, told pretty much the same story.

Ashley as an offbeat baton-twirler in the mistreated "92 in the Shade"

They, meaning the people at United Artists, gave the film a very good opening in Los Angeles, he said, but it died. Kastner admitted to having been "spastic" about the way United Artists had handled "Rancho Deluxe," but he felt they did their best with "92 in The Shade." He wasn't especially horrified by the Indian-in-the-canoe test. It is, in effect, sensible business judgment.

*   *   *

A United Artists executive was patient on the telephone, sounding like an elder statesman. It's all a matter of economics, he said. There once was a time, he said, when a company could take a chance on an off-beat, low-budget film, and "low-budget" meant a couple of hundred thousand dollars. Today a low-budget film can cost $1,500,000, and as much more to release it. If the film gives no signs of box-office life in its initial dates, the company saves money by not releasing it at all, or selling it directly to television.

The managements of movie companies are answerable to stockholders, not movie buffs.

All of which points a sternly inconclusive moral. Since, quite obviously, neither the director, nor the producer nor the distributor can be blamed when an interesting, worthwhile movie winds up playing first-run on Skid Row, the fault must rest with the public. If everyone stays home every night watching Mary Tyler Moore, "All in The Family" or reruns of "Upstairs, Downstairs," movies in 10 years are going to shrivel up to an annual output of a half-dozen big-budget, heavily promoted "Jaws" remakes. By that point Mary Tyler Moore will be doing "Electra" on TV, driving people out of the house at a time when there really won't be anything to see in the theaters.

I don't know the answer.

1976 F 1, II:13:1

Fassbinder Stars in a Work He Directed

"Fox and His Friends" was shown at the 13th New York Film Festival, under the English title "Fist-Right of Freedom." The following excerpts are from Richard Eder's review, which appeared in The New York Times on Sept. 27, 1975. The film is being shown at the Waverly Theater, Avenue of the Americas at Third Street.

There is no air in front of the camera. The outdoor scenes—damp green foliage, overstuffed German shop windows—seem shot indoors; the indoor scenes, in velvet boxes. Cars move noiselessly, their windows clean and closed.

Rainer Werner Fassbinder's work is highly prized in Europe and crosses the Atlantic each year to the New York Film Festival, where it tends to die. His entry this year is a movie that gives us social protest in terms of social dyspepsia. It is not really dead—it has, in fact, considerable drive and stylishness—but it excludes all life that is not within the very narrow intentions of its author. Its pores have been painted over.

Mr. Fassbinder sets his film in a modern Germany. His victim is the virtuous proletariat — as homosexual — taken up, used, destroyed and discarded by the gilded

The Cast

FOX AND HIS FRIENDS (Faustrecht der Freiheit), directed by Rainer Werner Fassbinder; screenplay (German, with English subtitles) by Mr. Fassbinder and Christine Hohoff; photography, Michael Ballhaus; editor, Theat Eymesz; music, Peter Ruben; production company, Tango Film; executive producer, Mr. Hohoff; at the Waverly Theater, Avenue of the Americas at Third Street. Running time: 123 minutes.

Fox	Rainer Werner Fassbinder
Eugen	Peter Chatel
Max	Karl-Heinz Böhm
Philip	Harry Baer
Father	Adrian Haven
Mother	Ulla Jacobson
Hedwig	Christiane Maybach

WITH: Peter Kern, Hans Zander, Kurt Raab, Irm Herman, Ursula Stratz, Elma Karlowa, Barbara Valentin, Bruce Low, Walter Sedimyn, Evelyn Kunncki, Ingrid Caern, Marquard Bohn and Liselotte Eeer.

burgeoisie — as homosexual.

Fox comes on as the Talking Head in a traveling freak show. At the film's start the show is shut down, and Fox buys a winning lottery ticket and picks up a middle-aged furniture dealer in a public lavatory. They go home and soon Fox has paired off with Eugen, the languid, vulpine son of a factory owner.

*

Fox is brash, violent, warmhearted and naive. At first he dominates, or seems to, but Eugen, with his world of wealth and savoir-faire, gradually tames him, in fact Eugen's world is rotting away — image of capitalism — the family factory is broke, and Fox is the golden goose to be plucked.

It is a "Blue Angel" done in drag,-and its political message hardly redeems it. As a performer, in the part of Fox, Mr. Fassbinder creates a character of some charm,

dignity and originality. He struggles in the elegant, seamless shroud devised for him by Fassbinder the author and Fassbinder the director, and it is hardly surprising that he succumbs.

1976 F 3, 24:1

NEXT STOP, GREENWICH VILLAGE, directed and written by Paul Mazursky; produced by Mr. Mazursky and Tony Ray; director of photography, Arthur Ornitz; music, Bill Conti; editor, Richard Halsey; distributed by 20th Century-Fox. Running time: 110 minutes. At the Cinema One Theater, Third Avenue near 60th Street. This film has been rated R.

Larry Lapinsky	Lenny Baker
Mom	Shelley Winters
Sarah	Ellen Greene
Anita	Lois Smith
Robert	Christopher Walken
Connie	Dori Brenner
Bernstein	Antonio Fargas
Herb	Lou Jacobi
Pop	Mike Kellin
Herbert	Michael Egan
Herb's wife	Helen Hanft
Mrs. Tupperman	Rashel Novikoff
Cop	Joe Spinnell
Doctor	Rochelle Oliver
Clyde	Jeff Goldblum

By VINCENT CANBY

Paul Mazursky is a film maker of breathtaking chutzpah. After the commercial (if not unanimous critical) success of "Bob and Carol and Ted and Alice," which he wrote (with Larry Tucker) and directed, he made the supremely self-important "Alex in Wonderland," which was about the problems of a young director who, having done a successful film like "Bob and Carol and Ted and Alice," cannot decide what to do next.

*

Unlike Fellini's great "8½" to which Mr. Mazursky made loving yet ultimately cheeky references, "Alex" had a good deal less to do with the problems of the con-artist (which is how Mr. Fellini saw himself) on dead-center than those of the non-artist who's run out of tricks.

"Next Stop, Greenwich Village," the new Mazursky film that opened yesterday at the Cinema One, is full of the same delusions of grandeur that motivated "Alex." Although it's a good deal easier to sit through than was "Alex," it's a big disappointment after "Blume in Love" and the no-nonsense satire and sentiment of "Harry and Tonto," written with Josh Greenfeld.

"Next Stop, Greenwich Village" isn't aggressively awful. It is inept but mostly it's just commonplace. It's white bread trying to pass as rye. It's as if Mr. Mazursky, in recollecting his youth as a nice young Jewish boy from Brooklyn, who seeks fame and fortune in Greenwich Village in the early 1950's, had passed those memories through a computer that had been programmed to transform everything into acceptable clichés.

His hero is Larry Lapinsky, (nicely played by Lenny Baker), who is less an artistic creation than a character pasted together from ones played earlier by Dustin

Hoffman, Richard Benjamin and Charles Grodin. Larry wants to be an actor, as Mr. Mazursky was with the Second City improvisational company and in the seminal Stanley Kubrick film "Fear and Desire."

Larry goes to acting class in the Village and pals around with other would-be theater types that have been cast according to a quota system. There's the handsome, WASPy-looking playwright (Christopher Walken), a young black man improbably named Bernstein (Antonio Fargas), who also doubles as the house homosexual, a pretty Jewish girl (Ellen Greene), a would-be suicide (Lois Smith), and so on.

Setting the tone for Mr. Mazursky's second-rate memoire is Larry's mother, a Jewish mom of the sort that only a writer-director with more nerve than talent could pass off on the public at this late date, post-Bruce Jay Friedman, post-Philip Roth.

*

Larry's mom is that mixture of horrendous, pushy, overprotective and dear that is often called a fat role, a term that Shelley Winters has taken so literally that you may not recognize her in the opening scenes. Miss Winters is funny at times. Just as often she's stupefying, and this may be the time to suggest that she's giving too much to art. Art can't take it.

Mr. Mazursky's screenplay is the clumsiest he's ever written, but the direction is sometimes even worse, or maybe nonexistent. The actors occasionally appear to be manufacturing their own exuberance, the way actors might do in an acting class when they attempt to create a mood out of thin air, or they all behave exactly alike. This has the effect of making the film's big Greenwich Village party scene look like a convention of sea gulls that have been beached during a storm. Everyone is pointing in the same direction.

1976 F 5, 24:1

FAMILY; CRAIG AND MARK; SINGLE PARENT, three studies of families by Hubert L. Smith. Total running time 100 minutes. At the Whitney Museum of American Art, Madison Avenue and 75th Street. Through Tuesday.

By RICHARD EDER

For each of these three films the camera was embedded week after week in the life of a California family. One of the families is happy, one is under stress, one is in distress. But for all their patience and honesty and, in the case of the last, something near brilliance, all three films are desolate. The desolation is partly extrinsic, as if camera and cameraman had been unable to avoid

casting a shadow upon the lives they were filming.

In cinéma vérité, where life is filmed supposedly without arrangement or overmuch self-consciousness, the camera makes the statement, "This is." It makes it in a peculiarly pure form; the unrehearsed gesture, the lack of an imposed pattern, the halting speech, all shore the statement up.

This is the power of the technique. The weakness is the implied corollary, "There is nothing else." What the camera does not see, it excludes.

This is not a criticism of the work of Hubert L. Smith, whose "Family," "Craig and Mark" and "Single Parent" are being shown at the Whitney Museum through Tuesday. It is a reflection that, with a structure as idiosyncratic and vulnerable as a family, the undeviating camera eye tends to capture frailty quicker than strength, and may even magnify the frailty of those things—a smile, a caress—that are in fact strengths.

*

"The Family" takes moments from the uneventful days of an intelligent, well-balanced and loving family of six—the father, who seems to be an economic researcher, the mother and their four children. They have breakfast, discuss the children's report cards, entertain friends and try to install a new lamp.

The camera focuses on forked moments—those in which there is both tension and tension overcome. The mother asks the daughter if she will stay in the rest of the afternoon. The daughter replies with a touch of crossness that she doesn't want to stay around the house all day. The father strokes the head of the younger boy and the boy pushes the hand away; the camera freezes on the interplay of hands. But it is unemphatic. The emphasis is more on links than no separations.

"Craig and Mark" takes a family trying to resolve a problem. The parents have seized on the idea of escaping from a confining routine by moving to the Colorado countryside and operating a general store.

Economic realities — the loss of the husband's paycheck—have begun to erode the idea. The film shows a series of discussions between the parents and the children, about allowances, the chores and staying out late. The question—to move or to stay —hangs over everything, and at the end it is talked out. The children are sharply, and probably briefly, disappointed. The parents' dejection at abandoning what the mother terms "a dream" is quieter and seems likely to be more permanent.

"The Single Parent" is the most recent of the three films, and the best. It is a portrait of Colleen, a young divorced woman, and her three small children.

The contained wrath and bitterness of Colleen, her alternation of almost brutal anger and devotion with the children, the burdens of running the house alone and her efforts to find a new relationship are done with economy and illumination. There are many beautiful moments—notably when the little boy, poker-faced until then, suddenly weeps inconsolably when Colleen scolds him; or a last scene when, buoyed up by a visit from a male friend, Colleen grabs her daughter and dances with her.

In 42 minutes Mr. Smith has given a sharp, moving portrait of a divorced woman that makes "Alice Doesn't Live Here Any More" look like soap opera.

1976 F 5, 27:1

PSYCHIC KILLER, directed by Raymond Danton; written by Greydon Clark, Mike Angel and Raymond Danton; produced by Mardi Rustam; cameraman, Herb Pearl. Released by Avco Embassy Pictures. Running time: 90 minutes. At the Criterion and 86th Street, East Theaters. (This film has been rated PG.)

Arnold .... Jim Hutton
Laura .... Julie Adams
Detective Morgan.............. Paul Burke
Dr. Gubner.............. Nehemiah Persoff
Anderson .... Aldo Ray

By RICHARD EDER

It takes a decent level of concentration to achieve that rare and profitable product, the movie that is so thoroughly and triumphantly awful that wave after wave of college students will return to sit through midnight showings in a rising haze of disconnection and other fumes.

Is "Psychic Killers," a movie about a madman who uses psychic energy to kill people, inspiredly bad or just plain bad? The signs go both ways.

At the start, amid a montage of microscope slides and electronic music aimed at showing we are at the heart of things, a quotation is flashed to the effect that the universe resembles a thought more than a machine. It is attributed to "Sir James Jean."

What happened to this eminent scientist's other Jean? Was it carelessness that reduced him from pluriform to singular? Or was it art that shrank Jeans?

•

The movie does move along with gleeful energy. A butcher is introduced into his own hamburger machine. A builder, dancing a tarantella on his building site, is crushed by a cornerstone inscribed with his own name. A mean nurse is scalded to death when the madman's psychic energy turns the hot-water lever all the way up.

There is a detective, who gets a pretty good straight performance from Paul Burke. This must be a mis-

take: It detracts from the integrity of the awfulness.

•

Full justice, on the other hand, is done by the performances of Jim Hutton as the madman and Nehemiah Persoff as the equally loony scientist who figures him out. Mr. Persoff models his performance on a man smelling something bad. Mr. Hutton mugs so horrendously that it becomes a mercy when the make-up man transforms his features into those of a decomposing corpse.

These things can be seen at the Criterion and at the 86th Street East Theaters.

1976 F 7, 9:1

TAXI DRIVER, directed by Martin Scorsese; screenplay by Paul Schrader; produced by Michael Phillips and Julia Phillips; music, Bernard Herrmann; director of photography, Michael Chapman; editors, Tom Rolf and Melvin Shapiro; distributed by Columbia Pictures. Running time: 112 minutes. At the Coronet Theater, Third Avenue near 59th Street. This film has been rated R.

Travis Bickle .... Robert De Niro
Betsy .... Cybill Shepherd
Iris .... Jodie Foster
Sport .... Harvey Keitel
Wizard .... Peter Boyle
Charles Palantine .... Leonard Harris
Tom .... Albert Brooks
Matto .... Vic Argo
Gun Salesman .... Steven Prince
Passenger .... Martin Scorsese
Personnel Officer .... Joe Spinell

By VINCENT CANBY

The steam billowing up around the manhole cover in the street is a dead giveaway. Manhattan is a thin cement lid over the entrance to hell, and the lid is full of cracks. Hookers, hustlers, pimps, pushers, frauds and freaks—they're all at large. They form a busy, faceless, unrepentant society that knows a secret litany. On a hot summer night the cement lid becomes a nonstop harangue written in neon: walk, stop, go, come, drink, eat, try, enjoy. Enjoy? That's the biggest laugh. Only the faceless ones — the human garbage — could enjoy it.

This is the sort of thing that Travis Bickle (Robert De Niro) might make note of in his diary. Travis, a loner who comes from somewhere else, drives a Manhattan cab at night. In the day he sleeps in short naps, pops pills to calm down, swigs peach brandy, which he sometimes pours on his breakfast cereal, and goes to porn films to relax. At one point he is aware that his headaches are worse and he suspects that he may have stomach cancer.

•

Travis Bickle is the hero of Martin Scorsese's flamboyant new film, "Taxi Driver," which opened yesterday at the Coronet. He's as nutty as they come, a psychotic, but as played by Mr. De Niro he's a riveting character inhabiting a landscape that's as much his creation as he is the creation of it.

"Taxi Driver" is in many ways a much more polished film than Mr. Scorsese's

Robert De Niro is the taxi driver; Martin Scorsese plays the role of the passenger

other major Manhattan movie, "Mean Streets," but its polish is what ultimately makes it seem less than the sum of its parts. The original screenplay by Paul Schrader, one of Hollywood's new young hopes (writers' division) imposes an intellectual scheme upon Travis's story that finally makes it seem too simple. It robs the film of mystery. At the end you may feel a bit cheated, as you do when the solution of a whodunit fails to match the grandeur of the crime.

But until those final moments "Taxi Driver" is a vivid, galvanizing portrait of a character so particular that you may be astonished that he makes consistent dramatic sense. Psychotics are usually too different, too unreliable, to be dramatically useful except as exotic décor.

Travis Bickle—the collaboration of writer, director and actor — remains fascinating throughout, probably because he is more than a character who is certifiably insane. He is a projection of all our nightmares of urban alienation, refined in a performance that is effective as much for what Mr. De Niro does as for how he does it. Acting of this sort is rare in films. It is a display of talent, which one gets in the theater, as well as a demonstration of behavior, which is what movies usually offer.

Were Mr. De Niro less an actor, the character would be a sideshow freak. The screenplay, of course, gives him plenty to work with. Until the final sequences, "Taxi Driver" has a kind of manic aimlessness that is a direct reflection of Travis's mind, capable of spurts of common sense and discipline that are isolated in his general confusion. Travis writes in his diary, "I don't believe that one should devote his life to

morbid self-attention," and then sets about to make a name for himself by planning a political assassination.

•

Travis is an accumulation of self-destruct mechanisms. He makes friends with a pretty, intelligent campaign worker, played by Cybill Shepherd (who here recoups the reputation lost in "At Long Last Love"), but wonders why she is shocked when he takes her to the porn films he likes so much. His mind is full of crossed wires and short circuits.

The point of the film

(which I can't talk about without giving away the plot), is, I feel, questionable, but the rest of it works. The supporting performances are fine, including those of Jodie Foster (whom I last saw as Becky Thatcher in "Tom Sawyer") as a teen-age hustler, Harvey Keitel as her pimp and Peter Boyle as a muddle-headed Manhattan cab driver.

You may want to argue with "Taxi Driver" at the end, and with good reason, but it won't be a waste of time.

1976 F 8, 36:1

FILM VIEW

VINCENT CANBY

Paul Mazursky's Profoundly Superficial Film

Novelists—some more than others—draw directly from the experiences of their own lives, from romantic and horrified projections of reality as well as from what actually happened. This is a tradition that is comparatively rare in films, if only because films are seldom one-man operations and are very expensive to make. The vision that a filmmaker produces is a mostly cooperative effort, shaped as much by the economic needs of the producer and the market as by the artistic concerns of the people involved.

There are exceptions. Though I know very little about the private life of Ingmar Bergman, it seems apparent that all of his recent films have in some way been Bergman's reflections on Bergman. Some of Federico Fellini's most interesting and occasionally his best films ("I Vitelloni,"

"8½," "Juliet of The Spirits" and "Amarcord") have made remarkably free use of the events that shaped his life into what it is and what it isn't.

Francois Truffaut's Antoine Doinel films ("The 400 Blows," "Love at Twenty," "Stolen Kisses," "Bed and Board") are lyrically autobiographical, while "The Soft Skin" appears to be Truffaut's dark equivalent of Fellini's "Juliet of The Spirits," the work of a man who admits to his wife that he is a heel and then goes on to blame her for having made him one.

Some few filmmakers are so entitled. The others should be enjoined by law. Instead of using their experiences, fears and fantasies as starting points for meditations, they simply regurgitate them, undigested, the way certain birds transport their food to their young. Maybe they aren't equipped to digest the material properly, or maybe they simply don't think it's necessary. They are like hangers-on of the New Journalism who no sooner live through something—*anything*—than they are delivering their copy to the editor. No remark, no action, is too petty or banal to be dumped into the wastebasket, thus to go unshared with the rest of us deprived souls.

These thoughts of food, regurgitation, New Journalism and experience-as-money-in-the-bank are prompted by the new movie, "Next Stop, Greenwich Village," Paul Mazursky's watery chicken-soup comedy that apparently draws on Mazursky's experiences when, in the early 1950's and a nice Jewish boy, he fled Brooklyn to become an actor in Greenwich Village. "Next Stop, Greenwich Village" has the form of a movie but it's a first-novel of such numbing banality that if it had been written first, it would certainly have wound up in his own reject file.

Mazursky is a tough man to handle critically. He is alternately witty and brilliantly sarcastic, then suddenly, soddenly sincere and self-centered, only to explode unexpectedly as a first-rate social satirist.

His background includes experience with the Second City troupe, as an actor in Stanley Kubrick's "Fear and Desire" as well as in "The Blackboard Jungle" and "Deathwatch," and as a writer (with Larry Tucker) of the Danny Kaye TV series and the films "I Love You, Alice B. Toklas," "Bob and Carol and Ted and Alice," (which was also his debut as a director) and "Alex in Wonderland." After "Alex," Mazursky and Tucker split and Mazursky went on to make what seemed to me to be his two best films, "Blume in Love" and "Harry and Tonto" (written with Josh Greenfeld).

Not knowing who was responsible for what in the Mazursky-Tucker partnership, I had assumed that its dissolution had freed Mazursky to realize his true talents as a filmmaker. "Next Stop, Greenwich Village" sends him back to square one. Like his biggest disaster, "Alex," which was the story of a young, successful Hollywood filmmaker who can't decide what his next film is going to be, it is "personal," but like "Bob and Carol" it is so profoundly superficial (is that possible?) that it has the air of something based not on life but on things other people have published, filmed or put on television during the last 10 or 15 years. It's second-hand.

Its hero is Larry Lapinsky, nicely played by Lenny Baker, who looks as if he'd been ordered from an agency that had run out of Dustin Hoffmans, Dick Benjamins and Charles Grodins. What's more dissappointing is that Larry himself is recycled from the characters those other actors discovered earlier with a true sense of surprise. When Larry moves to the Village, he leaves a home dominated by a Jewish mom type that should forever free us from further hauntings by Jewish moms. Shelley Winters, who is often funny and quite as often unbearable, doesn't act the role, she drives a wooden stake through its heart.

In the Village, Lenny belongs to a group of aspiring theatrical kids who seem to have been accepted on a quota system. There's one WASPy sort (a would-be playwright, played by Christopher Walken), a black fellow (Antonio Fargas), who also doubles as the house homosexual, a would-be suicide (Lois Smith) and a nice Jewish girl (Ellen Greene) who comes from a background much like Lenny's.

All of the performers are good and some are exceptionally good (Miss Smith, Miss Greene and Baker) but the film that Mazursky creates for them is less a recollection than a deja-vu, so awkwardly and obviously constructed that you want to cringe for the actors at the wrong moments. There are "timely" references to the Rosenberg spy case that make you suspect that no one in the movie can think, a suspicion that's confirmed by talk about art and poetry by people who haven't the vaguest idea what they're talking about. It would be all right if that were the point, but I don't think it is. Mazursky means us to find these muddle-headed people appealing, but they're passengers on a long subway ride. They're bores.

As there are in every Mazursky film, even the least inspired, there are some marvelous moments in "Next Stop, Greenwich Village." They include a funny and poignant scene in one of Larry's acting classes when he's struggling with a page of Clifford Odets' purple dialogue (from "Golden Boy"), and later a fantasy sequence when Miss Winters takes over the class. Best of all, however, are two scenes having to do with actors' auditions, both featuring a psychotically driven young man (Jeff Goldblum) who has a built-in self-destruct mechanism of such magnitude that the comic horror of his situation brings the film briefly to life.

Could it possibly be that Mazursky feels closer to this character, a nightmare grotesque, than he does to the film's blandly idealized hero? I suspect that Mazursky's real-life experiences were never as blah as the movies he makes from them. It's only that when he looks inside himself, he insists on recasting everything in terms of acceptable clichés.

1976 F 8, II:19:3

EMMANUELLE THE JOYS OF A WOMAN, directed by Francis Giacobetti, screenplay by Bob Elia and Francis Giacobetti from a novel by Emmanuelle Arsan; produced by Yves Rousset-Rouard; music by Francis Lai; photographed by Robert Fraisse. Released by Paramount Pictures. At Loews Orpheum and State Two. This movie has been rated X.

Emmanuelle	Sylvia Kristel
Jean	Umberto Orsini
Christopher	Frederic Lagache
Anne-Maria	Catherine Rivet
Ingrid	Caroline Laurence

By RICHARD EDER

Take an absurd hypothesis; that a whole genre of movies teaching people how to grow plants suddenly makes a breakthrough as movie entertainment, and as movie art. It would then be necessary to judge them from two different standpoints. Can you grow plants from them? And are they good movies?

Pornographic movies are somewhat the same. A reviewer, at least in a family newspaper, finds it easy enough to say whether they are good movies. Almost always not. But it is more embarrassing and more difficult to judge them on their utilitarian function; on what, after all, is the reason most people go to see them.

Embarrassing because one man's feet are another man's fetish, and movie critics probably have as strong a protective regard for their erogenous privacy as anyone else. Difficult for much the same reason: by what conceivable objective standard can it be said that a movie is or is not sexy?

•

With such partial disclaimers, consider "Emmanuelle the Joys of a Woman," which steamed into Loews Orpheum and State Two yesterday. It is a sequel to the first "Emmanuelle," a film that made a lot of money two years ago by putting together a mixture of soft-core pornography and soft-soap opera set to throbbing music in relentlessly exotic Far Eastern locales.

The new "Emmanuelle," like the old, is about a rich, liberated couple that practices multilateral sex as if it were a self-improvement cult. Emmanuellism is obviously trying to set itself up—for the pecuniary purposes of this movie—as a mystique. "Nothing is wrong if it feels good," the ads have been asserting.

The movie is every bit as fatuous as the philosophizing. The style is as romantic and quivering as the ripest work of the thirties: only the sex goes farther. Mustached gentleman, impeccably groomed, gargling his vowels, bends to bestow a kiss of homage upon tremulous heroine. Only it isn't her hand he's addressing.

It is a bad movie: repetitive, pretty, static. As for the plant-growing aspects, Sylvia Kristel has a sexy face and an expression that suggests all kinds of improper things. When she goes on to do these things they are less interesting: still, she is the movie's main asset and will probably make money for its owners.

1976 F 12, 41:3

GABLE AND LOMBARD, directed by Sidney J. Furie; screenplay by Barry Sandler; produced by Harry Korshak; director of photography, Jordan S. Cronenweth; editor, Argyle Nelson; music, Michel Legrand; distributed by Universal Pictures. Running time: 131 minutes. At the Loews State 1 Theater, Broadway at 45th Street; Loews Cine Theater, Third Avenue near 86th Street, and the 34th Street East Theater, near Second Avenue. This film has been rated R.

Clark Gable	James Brolin
Carol Lombard	Jill Clayburgh
Louis B. Mayer	Allen Garfield
Ivan Cooper	Red Buttons
Ria Gable	Joanne Linville
Dixie	Melanie Mayron
Noreen	Carol McGinnis

By VINCENT CANBY

'Gable and Lombard," which opened at three theaters yesterday, is a fan-magazine movie with the emotional zap of a long-lost Louella Parsons column. It's the somewhat reworked, no longer exclusive story of the Hollywood courtship and marriage of Clark Gable and Carole Lombard in the late 1930's and early 40's.

They meet for the first time at one of those screwball parties Hollywood was apparently noted for, an afternoon party where everyone is dressed in evening clothes. Clark refuses to wear what was then known as a "soup-and-fish." He's a rugged individualist. So is Carole, who arrives by ambulance and wrecks Clark's car. They fight. He threatens to spank her. She knocks him down with a punch to the jaw.

•

It's love, of course. At first it's a back-street kind of love (he's married), full of the tensions created by career conflicts, public relations duties and a benign Louis B. Mayer, the true king of M-G-M who doesn't want Clark's career damaged by scandal.

But it is also full of precious, golden moments, stolen—nay snatched—from the hurly-burly of Hollywood stardom. They go fishing together. They play practical jokes on each other and though the jokes don't seem very funny to us, we can be pleased that the funnybones of Gable and Lombard are in their ankles. They laugh a lot, and fight, and make up. Through all this we know what they don't know: that the fun-loving, life-loving, beautiful Carole is not long for this world. You might say that theirs was a love stalked by tragedy—that is, if you adopted the style of this film.

As written by Barry Sandler and directed by Sidney J. Furie, "Gable and Lombard" recalls not "Gone With the Wind," "Honky Tonk," "Twentieth Century," "Nothing Sacred" or "To Be or Not to Be," but clichés culled from the worst movies of that period. The actors don't help. James Brolin and Jill Clayburgh look a little like Gable and Lombard and a little more like Hamilton (George) and Lynley (Carol).

•

Of the two, Miss Clayburgh comes off better. She appears to be creating a character whenever the fearfully bad screenplay allows it. Mr. Brolin doesn't act. He gives an impersonation of the sort that makes you wonder if he can also do James Cagney and Edward G. Robinson.

Miss Clayburgh could be an interesting actress, but she's not a great one, nor is she a star, and there are always problems when small performers try to portray the kind of giant legends that Gable and Lombard were.

Because both Gable and Lombard are still very much alive in their films on television and in repertory theaters, there is difficulty in responding to Mr. Brolin and Miss Clayburgh in any serious way. They are stand-ins.

Jill Clayburgh plays Carole Lombard and James Brolin is Clark Gable in film about Hollywood in the '30's.

Life for actors often gets mixed up with the roles they play, but that's no reason why a movie about actors should get so' hopelessly mixed up with the movies the actors made. In "Gable and Lombard," Gable and Lombard "meet cute" (is that Anita Loos's phrase?) not once but a dozen times.

Although Carole swears a lot and makes a couple of obscene gestures in the course of the movie, both Gable and Lombard speak in the phrases of refined drivel that Lolly Parsons would have loved.

Life is okay, a philosophical Gable says at one point, "as long as you can look in the mirror and like what you see." "Listen," says the emotionally distraught Lombard, "I'm the No. 1 female star in America and I never said 'I love you' to anyone and meant it." My favorite, though, is delivered by Red Buttons, who plays Gable's pal at the time the actor begins to fall for Lombard: "First time a dame ever got to you?"

Turn on your telly for the real thing.

1976 F 12, 42:1

A Story of Revenge on a Longtime Friend

By VINCENT CANBY

Victor (Jacques Dufilho) is a widower, a small, nervous bullet-headed man with a furious temper. Anselm (Bernard Blier) is, like Victor, retired, but he's everything Victor is not—gentle, patient, kind, a slow starter. Victor and Anselm have been friends for 40 years, and for the last eight they have shared a tiny apartment in a middle-class quarter of Paris. It's not been easy.

When Anselm, who does the cooking, tells Victor they're having sausages and potatoes for lunch, Victor says crossly he doesn't like sausages and potatoes. "Last

The Cast

CHER VICTOR (Dear Victor), directed by Robin Davis; screenplay (French with English subtitles) by Mr. Davis and Patrick Laurent; music, Yves Lafaye; produced by Denise Petitdidier; distributed by Peppercorn-Wormser Film Enterprises. Running time: 102 minutes. At the 68th Street Playhouse, at Third Avenue. This film has not been rated.
Anselm .... Bernard Blier
Victor .... Jacques Dufilho
Anna .... Alida Valli

week you did," says Anselm. "This week I don't," says Victor. So it goes until one day at the corner pub, Victor, trying to teach Anselm manners in front of a lady, snatches Anselm's beret off his head, only to snatch off Anselm's toupee as well.

Victor doesn't know it, but that's the beginning of his end.

•

"Cher Victor," the French film that opened yesterday at the 68th Street Playhouse, is the story of Anselm's carefully plotted revenge on Victor, whom he drives slowly mad with suspicions that Victor's wife, dead eight years, had been unfaithful to her husband throughout their long marriage.

"Cher Victor" is not exactly a black comedy. It's rather more gray, which, I suspect, is just the tone that Robin Davis, the director, was seeking though the charm eludes me. It's a film of small details, methodically composed, which are sometimes funny in themselves, but which in the end have the effect of canceling one another out.

Victor is an unpleasant man, but his bigotry, selfishness and temper tantrums aren't maniacally funny in the way that those of Louis De Funes were in a film like "The Mad Adventures of 'Rabbi' Jacob." He's a difficult old crab, nothing more, neither horrendous nor horrendously funny enough to support the punishment he receives.

•

Anselm, too, fails to be particularly convincing. From the very beginning it is so apparent that here is a worm about to turn that one almost blames him for not controlling events better, but then there would be no film.

"Cher Victor" is very much a movie that calls attention to its modesty. In its gray sort of way, it seems pushy because though it's not really about anything, it asks for our attention. Mr. Dufilho and Mr. Blier don't overact. Instead they underact with the kind of deliberation that is just as gross as any amount of scenery-chewing.

Ultimately "Cher Victor" is less a reflection of life than an accumulation of stunts, including the casting of the now matronly, still handsome but hardly over-the-hill Alida Valli as the two old men's nutty neighbor who imagines herself once to have been a great opera star. Miss Valli and her two co-stars seem to be having so much fun acting and carrying on that I feel churlish to have to report that I found them all a good deal less than riveting.

1976 F 13, 19:1

NEW WOMEN/NEW FILMS I: EXPERIMENTAL AND PERSONAL FILMS. A program of short films by women. "Some Will Be Apples" by Phyllis Poullette-Macdougal and Kathleen Laughlin. "Jaraslawa" by DeeDee Halleck. "It's All About Time and No Time" by Rita Xanthoudakis. "In Memory of Roses" by Anne Murton. "Depot" by Susan Brockman. "Element" by Amy Greenfield. "Philadelphia Quartet" by Doris Chase. "Horizontal Transfer" by Madeleine Geklere. "Pastel Pussies" by Judith Wardwell. "Susan Through Corn" by Kathleen Laughlin. "Apple Tarte Aunt Jeanne" by DeeDee Halleck. At Film Forum, 15 Vandam Street, Feb. 12-15 and Feb. 19-22. Total running time: 86 minutes.

By RICHARD EDER

The Film Forum is showing a collection of short works under the title "New Women/ New Films," and by far the best of them is about a very old woman making pastry.

That's the kind of sentence onto which you might add, depending on your views, "ironically" or "appropriately" or "unfortunately" or—if your views are very bland— "curiously."

Blandly, then. "Jaraslawa" is a marvel. It is the equivalent of a 2-line poem: 10 minutes filming of a Ukrainian woman making dumplings and explaining how she makes them. A Ukrainian song accompanies her movements: During the explanations the frame freezes on her hands or her face.

The hands work with more than grace: with the rhythm and sureness of a natural process worn into them by 60 years of practice. The old face and its very slightly shifting expressions are a visual commentary on the hands' work. It is a musician listening to the music she makes.

•

Nothing else in the program approaches this. It is a weak program. This first of two selections of films by women is dedicated to what is labeled "experimental and personal" work.

The problem with the selections is not that they are too experimental, nor too personal, but that they are too private. Art that is the artist talking to himself or herself needs a force or a tension that commands overhearing. Not all keyholes invite looking through.

Thus, "It's All About Time and No Time," a five-minute musing by a woman painter about her life and other people's, approaches communication but doesn't break through. Not enough vitality.

"Some Will Be Apples" juxtaposes old photos of women doing menial or banal women's work with excerpts from the tentatively feminist writings of Zona Gale, a Victorian author. The message is simultaneously diffuse and obvious.

So it is in a much more complex, and rather affected film, "In Memory of Roses." A voice reads passages from a manual on rose-growing. Women and girls are photographed in nautral and posed groupings; snatches of nursery-rhymes and sententious pronouncement buzz through. The theme is entrapment and confinement, but it is frailly done.

"Element" is not frail, but it's even more private. A naked woman lurches and falls and writhes for 12 minutes in a mud wallow. The camera explores the writhings, the contours that mud adds to limbs, the reflections and textures that it imposes.

It can be viewed abstractly. It can be viewed symbolically. But pretty soon the question becomes: Why is this woman doing this? Or even: Is this where we have arrived — a woman rolling around in the mud and someone taking pictures of it?

Elephants have their ludicrous aspects but they always do elephantlike things and preserve their elephantine coherence. Armadillos and mayflies are never less than themselves. Why should people pretend to be mud snakes?

1976 F 13, 19:1

FILM VIEW
VINCENT CANBY

Disturbing 'Taxi Driver'

Several hours after I'd seen Martin Scorsese's new film, "Taxi Driver," last week, someone said to me with the kind of smugness with which pronouncements about the weather are made, "Well, it's the sort of film you either love or you hate. There's no middle ground." As I remember, my answer was non-committal but the more I thought about the remark, the more uneasy I became. There is — or should be — a very large middle ground surrounding this vivid and violent film, about a Manhattan cabbie who finds salvation through slaughter, made by one of our more talented young filmmakers ("Mean Streets," "Alice Doesn't Live Here Anymore"). Either to love or to hate it is not to pay attention to it. Rather it's to gulp it down whole, without chewing. Mindlessly.

With increasing frequency film critics, myself included, appear to be slipping into the use of hyperbole, the syntax of the copywriter who, in the interests of commerce, makes a complex world comprehensible by reducing everything to good or bad. More and more these days film critics are giving up the honorable, temperate middle-ground to occupy those polarized regions where everything's a hit or a flop, either the greatest thing since processed cheese or rotten bananas. It may be time that we attempted to retake the qualified middle, though not by making aggressive declarations to the effect, say, that " 'The Hindenburg' is junk and I loved it," which is just an aggressive way of straddling the same old fence.

As I suspect that certain kinds of advertising can create suspicion and cynicism of a general kind, the harmful effects of which cannot be measured, I think that our film criticism, especially the sort that means to support worthy projects, may ultimately be as damaging to the film industry as any number of awful films. Even before the opening of Lina Wertmuller's "Seven Beauties," which I believe is an extraordinary achievement, there were ads calling it a masterpiece. Ads for Paul

166

Mazursky's "Next Stop, Greenwich Village" (which I didn't like, though it is harmless) compare it to the work of a master director like Fellini. Is Isabelle Adjani, who gives a lovely performance in Truffaut's "The Story of Adele H.," actually the greatest actress of the year? I voted for her in both the New York Film Critics Circle and the National Society of Film Critics, but I get worried when I see those citations quoted in the ads. Most people who go to that film are being led to expect a legendary performance, a sort of Laurette Taylor feat, and it isn't.

Our eagerness to express enthusiasm, and the uses that producers make of it, can mislead the public. I'm sure that Robert Altman's "Nashville" eventually suffered from all of its terrific praise, in which I was a willing participant, because no film could possibly measure up to the expectations that we had created. "Nashville" is, after all, only a great movie. It is not a new religion. Is it too late to pull back a bit, not from "Nashville" but from the appearance that we are dealing in holy writ?

I hope that "Taxi Driver" is not thus oversold. Though it is much more flamboyant and much more elaborate technically than "Mean Streets," it is a smaller film. The screenplay, by Paul Schrader, is virtually a case history of a young man named Travis Bickle (Robert De Niro), a Vietnam vet who displays for us all of the classic symptoms of a first-class psychotic, though the people he meets find him only somewhat eccentric. Travis is every paranoid taxi driver you've ever met on your wildest nightmare ride. Unable to connect with anyone (he appears at times to be mentally deficient), he comes to loathe the inhabitants of the city to which he has been drawn, and in the way of those obsessed, he sees only his obsessions: the hookers, hustlers, pimps, freaks — the "garbage" — people who are successfully making out in a city that barely tolerates him. In time he decides that he can only make a name for himself by some spectacular act, namely the assassination of a prominent candidate for the Presidential nomination.

•   •   •

Until the penultimate sequence of the film, which is of a violent intensity that is not easily supported (for me, anyway) by what has gone before, "Taxi Driver"

is one of the most compelling portriats of a lunatic personality I've ever seen on film. De Niro, who played the simple-minded Johnny Boy in "Mean Streets," is superb. He manages to display both pathos and lethally dangerous charm as Travis goes about the city slowly and methodically preparing for his one-man Armageddon. As long as the film maintains its picaresque form — confrontations with assorted Manhattanites and tourists — it is a sort of crosstown epic, but when it demonstrates its more serious interests, in violence as a kind of catharsis, it goes suddenly schematic and didactic, but the scheme and the didacticism aren't up to the complex, contradictory observations of the rest of the film.

Both "Mean Streets" and "Alice Doesn't Live Here Anymore" had a great deal to do with friendship, with its responsibilities and with lives lived in community. "Taxi Driver" is about a life so special, so bent out of shape, that the effect of the movie is of a spectacular but grotesque circus. One of the problems may be that would-be Presidential assassins simply aren't very interesting characters, neither in fiction nor in fact. They are different from you and me. Their problems are not ours.

It's not necessary to identify with a character to find him fascinating but where Scorsese and Schrader go wrong in "Taxi Driver" is in attempting to make Travis Bickle in some way politically and socially significant. But he's not. He is an aberration, and the only way we respond to the character is in De Niro's display of himself as an actor of bravura unique among young American actors today. Nobody in the rest of the cast gets a chance to come near him, but there are some fine contributions, including those of Cybill Shepherd as a pretty, self-assured campaign worker who gives every indication of having a sense of the ridiculous, Harvey Keitel as an East Village pimp, and Jodie Foster as a pre-teen-age prostitute of terrifying self-assurance.

I can't truly say that I either love or hate "Taxi Driver," though it has some dazzling moments. It's a movie that one should discover for himself.

Lent is approaching and I'm seriously thinking of giving up adverbs and adjectives for one day each week of the Lenten period.

1976 F 15, II:1:5

De Niro—"a lethally dangerous charm"

Cassavetes Is Director of Bland Effort

By VINCENT CANBY

John Cassavetes's "The Killing of a Chinese Bookie," which opened yesterday at the Columbia I and II Theater, is like the last three of the director's films ("A Woman Under the Influence," "Husbands" and "Minnie and Moskowitz") in the way it resolutely refuses to come to a point strong or interesting enough to support the loving care that's gone into its production, particularly on the part of the actors.

Watching the film is like listening to someone use a lot of impressive words, the meanings of which are just wrong enough to keep you in a state of total confusion, but occasionally right enough to hold your attention. What *is* he trying to say? It takes a little while to realize that maybe the speaker not only doesn't know but doesn't even care to think things out. He hopes that if he continues to talk he may happen upon a truth as if it were a found object.

•

Though "A Woman Under the Influence" contained an impressive performance by

The Cast

THE KILLING OF A CHINESE BOOKIE, directed and written by John Cassavetes; produced by Al Rubin; supervising editor, Tom Cornwell; camera operators, Fred Elmes and Mike Harris; music conducted and arranged by Anthony Harris; released by Faces Distribution Corporation. Running time: 130 minutes. At the Columbia I and II Theaters, Second Avenue near 64th Street. This film has been rated R.

Cosmo Vitelli	Ben Gazzara
Mort Weil	Seymour Cassel
Flo	Timothy Carey
Phil	Robert Phillips
John-the-Boss	Morgan Woodward
Eddie-Red	John Red Kullers
Marty Reitz	Al Ruban
Rachel	Azizi Johari
Betty	Virginia Carrington
Mr. Sophistication	Meade Roberts
Sherry	Alice Friedland
Margo	Donna Gordon
Waitress	Trisha Pelham
Chinese Bookie	Soto Joe Hugh

Gena Rowlands as a truly mad housewife, the film never succeeded in establishing her in any convincing frame of family or society. She was one woman with her bag of tricks doing her show on a barren stage. The film lacked a consistent point of view, or perhaps it had as many as it had actors, director and cameramen. "The Killing of a Chinese Bookie" has nothing to compare with the spectacle of the Rowlands performance in "A Woman Under the Influence," but next to that earlier film it's virtually Bressonian in the rigidity of its purpose and style. It even has a story of sorts.

The story doesn't always make sense, but supporters of Mr. Cassavetes can argue that narrative coherence is not his bag. My suspicion is that either the film has been sloppily edited or that the director has no film idea on how to film the sort of sequences in which one actor with a gun stalks another actor with a gun in a dark garage. In the trade this is known as an action sequence and it quickly becomes rather too existential if you can't figure out who is stalking whom, or why.

"The Killing of a Chinese Bookie" is about Cosmo Vitelli (Ben Gazzara), the owner of a tacky nightclub on Hollywood's Sunset Strip, and Cosmo's troubles when the mob coerces him into carrying out a contract murder in order to pay off a $23,000 gambling debt. That's the story, but the film has less interest in story than in character, for which, in Mr. Cassavetes's vocabulary, you may also read actor.

Mr. Cassavetes's way of film making is to set up actors, whom he admires, trusts and finds endlessly fascinating, in situations in which they are as likely to philosophize about acting as about life. Acting—performance—is a legitimate metaphor for certain kinds of lives but by the end of "The Killing of a Chinese Bookie" you may rightfully expect more than you have actually received. This includes a lot of enigmatic snatches of Cosmo's nightclub shows, bits and pieces of intentionally awful sketches, as well as Cosmo's relationships to his "girls" and his emcee (a self-described "freak," played with good, self-contained desperation by Meade Roberts, the screen writer.

Perhaps because of the limitations imposed on Mr. Cassavetes by his screenplay, his actors are more restrained than they have been in his past efforts, though some of them are nice to see because they are familiar, especially Seymour Cassel (so good in "Faces" and "Minnie and Moskowitz") who plays a polite mobster.

•

Mr. Gazzara is also comparatively restrained, or perhaps inhibited, by the requirements of the particular character he's playing here.

It's a thoughtful, intelligent interpretation of a role that just may not have as much depth to it as he's ready to give it. Like the movie itself, it is, finally, bland.

1976 F 16, 28:1

WILL, I WILL . . . FOR NOW, directed by Norman Panama; written by Mr. Panama and Albert E. Lewin; director of photography, John A. Alonzo; music by John Cameron; produced by George Barrie. Released by 20th Century-Fox. At the Sutton Theater, Third Avenue and 57th Street, the Paramount, Broadway and 61st Street, and Loews Astor Plaza, Broadway and 44th Street. Running time: 107 minutes. This movie has been rated R.

Les Bingham .... Elliott Gould
Katie Bingham .... Diane Keaton
Lou Springer .... Paul Sorvino
Jackie Martin .... Victoria Principal
Dr. Magnus .... Robert Alda
Steve Martin .... Warren Berlinger
Sally Bingham .... Candy Clark
Dr. Williams .... Madge Sinclair
Maria .... Carmen Zapata
Dr. Morrison .... George Tyne
Miss Ito .... Koko Tani
Miss Donovan .... Sheila Rogers
Hildy .... Michele Clinton
Ted Davis .... Lou Tiano

By RICHARD EDER

In "I Will, I Will . . . For Now," a long, long comedy about a jittery modern marriage, Diane Keaton plays the part of a headache and Elliott Gould that of a loud noise. The film opened yesterday at the Sutton, Paramount and Loews Astor Plaza Theaters.

Miss Keaton rolls her eyes and looks miserable and appealing. Mr. Gould roars and wheedles and sulks and looks selfish and appealing. They are very rich, live in a sumptuous New York apartment, employ a humorous Spanish maid (Thelma Ritter used to do it Swedish), and have no recognizable worries.

They do have unrecognizable worries, of the carpentered sort Hollywood used to invent for Rock Hudson and Doris Day to thrash around with. In this case, a stale 1950's poundcake of a movie—the old doubletakes, smirks, shoulder shrugs are lifted carefully from their moth covers and hung upon us once more—has been given what will pass for a 1970's gimmick.

●

The couple's sex life is poor. He is quick and she is dead, or virtually. "You make love as if you were catching a Fifth Avenue bus," she says. "You make love as if you were playing chess," he says.

They have divorced each other, are unhappy, reunite —by contract arrangement rather than actual marriage —are still unhappy. A vampish upstairs neighbor lends him "The Joy of Sex" to improve things. He puts his back out following the instructions.

They go to an expensive sex clinic and there's a lot of underwear in the wrong beds, but no real sex. She still can't melt. "Give me a four-letter word for sexual intercourse," the clinic ringmaster asks her. "Love," she says.

●

I like that line, but not much else. Norman Panama, who directed and wrote a great many comedies over the last 30 years, a number of them successful, directed this one and helped write it. Neither job is well done. Nor is the acting, although

Paul Sorvino is mildly amusing in a supporting role until he chokes it to death. To cast Elliott Gould for repartee comedy is to mistake a camel for an antelope. "I Will, I Will" should make people happy that they don't make movies like that any more.

1976 F 19, 45:1

GREY GARDENS. Directed by David Maysles, Albert Maysles, Ellen Hovde and Muffie Meyer; photography, Albert Maysles and David Maysles; editors, Miss Hovde, Miss Meyer and Susan Froemke; produced by the Maysles brothers. At the Paris Theater. Running time: 94 minutes.
Mother .... Edith Beale
Daughter .... Edith Beale
Handyman .... Jerry Torre
Birthday guest .... Lois Wright
Birthday guest .... Jack Helmuth
Gardener .... Brooks Hires

When "Grey Gardens" was shown at the New York Film Festival last September, it was reviewed in The New York Times by Richard Eder. Following is an excerpt from the review:

Set a movie camera down in a jungle clearing: Life is stood on end. The children caper and gesticulate or simply gape; the adults, a few paces back, pay wholehearted attention or self-conciously pay none. There is authenticity, but there is also incitement. Part of what the camera sees it has created.

Something like this happens in "Grey Gardens," where the camera has been placed not in a backland settlement but in the decayed East Hampton, L. I., mansion of two lovely and tormented recluses. They are Edith Bouvier Beale, somewhere around 80, and her daughter Edie, in her mid-50's. They are the aunt and cousin of Jacqueline Onassis.

The two hidden and disabled lives, who have fashioned a littered, cat-infested carapace the same shape as themselves around themselves, are brought out for scrutiny by Albert and David Maysles, makers of some distinguished American documentaries.

●

The cycle of attachment and tension, the cramped routines in the large, crumbling house, the regular scratching and salving of each other's psychic wounds: all these elements of a two-part relationship are made triangular. The camera is there, the Maysleses stand behind it, and the effect is like that upon moths in a dark room when a light is switched on outside. They are instantly at the window, fluttering their wings.

Mrs. Beale, who is bent and feeble—the camera is unsparing of her old sagging flesh, draped in a sort of towel—is witty, fierce and the center of the household. She was once a great society beauty, was divorced when Edie was a child, fell ill and some 25 years ago brought Edie back to stay with her.

Edie, who still has considerable beauty, seems the more deeply disturbed. She dresses in a strange costume that exposes most of her legs in black open-work stockings, keeps her head constantly covered with a tight hood and dances and sings disjointedly. She complains, sometimes confidentially to the camera, sometimes in brawling arguments, that her mother has chained her, driven away her lovers, ruined her life.

●

There is no doubt about the artistry and devotion that the Maysleses have used in recording the life in "Grey Gardens." There is no reason to doubt them when they say they love and admire the Beales. But the moviegoer will still feel like an exploiter. To watch "Grey Gardens" is to take part in a kind of carnival of attention with two willing but vulnerable people who had established themselves, for better or worse, in the habit of not being looked at. And what happens when the carnival moves on?

1976 F 20, 15:2

'Grey Gardens': *Cinéma Verité* or Sideshow?

By WALTER GOODMAN

On Oct. 22, 1971, at the urging of some annoyed townsfolk, the Suffolk County police raided a house in East Hampton. There, in the house called Grey Gardens, they found two women, many cats, much litter and quite a few violations of local ordinances. What made the case more noteworthy than the usual recluse-in-messy-old-house story was the discovery that the inhabitants were related to Jacqueline Bouvier Kennedy Onassis. Seventy-seven-year-old Edith Bouvier Beale was the sister of Jackie's father, which, naturally, made Mrs. Beale's daughter, 54-year-old Edie, Jackie's cousin.

Among those attracted to the incident, in a professional way, were Albert and David Maysles, exponents of *cinéma verité*, or "direct cinema," as they prefer to call it, documentaries without a narrator or a musical score, filmed and recorded with lightweight portable equipment. The brothers Maysles had won a considerable reputation in recent years, especially with "Salesman," a generally admired study of four door-to-door Bible salesmen from Boston, and "Gimme Shelter," a controversial account of the Rolling Stones's 1969 tour of this country, which climaxed in a killing during a concert at the Altamont Speedway in California —a fortuitous denouement since it provided a climax for the movie. In 1973, they and three associates turned their talents upon the occupants of that rundown house in East Hampton. They made a film which is successful enough in their terms and distasteful enough in other terms to call their whole

Walter Goodman is the assistant editor of the Arts and Leisure section.

enterprise into question.

"Grey Gardens" consists of 94 minutes of almost nonstop, often simultaneous monologues by Mrs. Beale and Edie. Their talk runs on, meeting, crossing, diverging, breaking off now and then— once as they listen to a heartily inspirational radio sermon by Norman Vincent Peale— but never stopping for long. The talk is the blood of their relationship; while it flows, they seem not to feel so cut off from things.

The mother talks of her past happiness ("I had a perfect marriage, beautiful children, terribly successful marriage"); her singing career, remembered as brilliant; her fine husband and her talented accompanist. In the bed she shares with her cats and the cans and cartons of several days of food for them and for herself, she raises her arms, flabby and creased, and preens a bit, puts on a large hat out of another era, and sings, in poignant semblance of the voice and style she once boasted, "Tea for Two."

The daughter talks about her present unhappiness, about Mrs. Beale's rejection of her last suitor, about being forced by her mother to return to Grey Gardens from New York City more than 20 years before, and her resolve to leave again. "I think my days at Grey Gardens are limited," she says by rote. "My days are limited." She changes outfits, going from one odd costume to another. Her hair covered, her legs exposed well up the heavy thighs, she dances, much as she must have when she was a young girl with the prospect of entering Long Island society.

On the evidence of her scrapbook, Edie was a very attractive girl, and her mother, to whose portrait the camera keeps returning, was beautiful. Now, to judge from

the film, their days are spent in incessant banter, sometimes querulous, sometimes kidding, about whatever comes to mind, Edie playing and overplaying to the outsiders, Mrs. Beale dry and sharp:

Edie: She made me leave the Barbizon.

Mrs. Beale: Well, I thought you'd been in New York long enough. You were getting lines in your face.

Edie: But I was getting my audition—in 1952.

Mrs. Beale: Well, you didn't get it—you missed out.

Edie: I was just getting up what you call a little nerve when she said I had to come home. She started to high-pressure me to come back in March of 1952, and she kept it up until the end of July, and July 29th I checked out, got on the train and came back, and was never able to get back.

Mrs. Beale: It's very hot in New York on July 29th.

Why, in fact, did Edie return to her mother and to Grey Gardens? Why did she never marry or make any kind of career? What part did the long-gone Mr. Beale play in derailing these two lives? How did things manage to turn out as they did? No answers are forthcoming. Their quarrel is a litany, carried on without rancor, almost without interest. They are not listening very hard, having heard themselves so many times before, yet not wishing perhaps to disappoint the ingratiating outsiders. They talk on, drifting together in a place where the mists of the past meet the fumes of the present. As Edie says, "It's very difficult to keep the line between the past and the present. You know what I mean? It's awfully difficult."

I found the film sad, of course; who can fail to be saddened by the remnants of two lives expiring in a haze? But I felt angry, too. Would anyone have bothered with these people had they not been related to Jackie Onassis? The Maysleses were not out to ridicule the Beales, but the film presents them as a pair of grotesques. Why were they put on exhibition this way? Albert Maysles is quoted in publicity material as saying, "The essential thing about our work is not making believe but finding out." Although we see the women in pitiable circumstances and absurd poses, however, we find out remarkably little about how they got there. They have reached an accommodation; why not let them get by as well as they can now without this public display of their weaknesses, peculiarities, touches of wackiness?

To the practitioner of *cinéma verité*, evidently, such considerations are not compelling. The Beales agreed to be photographed. The contracts are in order, the women having been represented by a family attorney. They were paid for their cooperation and are due to participate in any profits. They are fair game.

For all the undoubted virtues of *cinéma verité* and forming for it and for its operator. She eyes the lens shrewdly; a parody of sexiness, she simpers, wiggles, tugs at her swim suit, carries on a seduction of the instrument before our eyes. She and the camera expose each other. How much the Maysleses themselves encouraged her displays, we cannot know — their muffled off-camera responses to Edie's questions and comments tend to be noncommital or condescending—but their very presence was clearly encouraging, if not inciting. "Darling David," Edie coos into the camera, "where have you

been all my life? Where have you been?" A scene of this woman in her 50's waving a small American flag as she does a drum majorette routine that may have seemed cute 40 years ago becomes a high spot of the movie. Is it the moviemakers' fault that their camera has this sort of effect on certain sorts of people? Are they not, after all, only observers of certain corners of life? "We believe in shooting life as it is being lived," their publicity material tells us. But would it have been lived in quite this way without them? Why were they in Grey Gardens anyhow? Why?

Can it be that these makers of documentaries whom we glimpse in a mirror, Albert's eye tight against the camera viewfinder, David's ears clamped in his headset, have stopped hearing and seeing their subjects as altogether human—as human, say, as themselves, and see them instead as . . . well, subjects, raw material for their productions? That, at any rate, would explain how direct cinema, with all its pretensions to art and high seriousness, has here been reduced to a form of tabloid journalism, not to say a circus sideshow.

The Maysleses have let it

be known that they love the Beales. "The truth couldn't possibly hurt them," said David at a New York Film Festival screening last fall, the implication being, first, that he has captured the truth and, second, that if he believed it would hurt the women, he wouldn't have made his film. Well, if my grip on things should one day become as uncertain as that of Edie Beale and I decide that it would be a good idea to take off my clothes in Times Square and do a tap dance, I hope that my friends will try to stop me rather than make a movie of the performance for my enjoy-

ment, their profit and the public curiosity.

It's certain that many viewers will find "Grey Gardens" sadly affecting, as I did—but perhaps some will be angered by it, too, as I was. The sagging flesh, the ludicrous poses, the prized and private recollections strewn about among the tins of cat food—everything is grist for that merciless camera. The sadness for mother and daughter turns to disgust at the brothers. ■

1976 F 22, II:15:1

FILM VIEW
VINCENT CANBY

Gable Never Made a Turkey Like This

I n the July, 1975, issue of "Film International," a magazine to be read under a hair dryer, Army Archerd, the Hollywood columnist, writes: "The plethora of upcoming pictures based on the lives of movie stars proves personal stories of celebrities are far more cinematic than roles they've played. And can another biofilm be in the making for a future date—'The Jack Lemmon Story'?"

If you read a little further in the article, you may hope not.

Archerd synopsizes his Lemmon biography by telling us about "Lemmon's drinking problem," describing some of the social gaffes Lemmon pulled while under the influence, until, at last, he won the Oscar for his performance

in "Save The Tiger." Archerd reports that "Jack's friends felt if he had not won the Oscar . . . his drinking would have become an insurmountable problem."

The winning of the Oscar, in effect, saved Lemmon and put him on the water-wagon.

Well, that certainly is a plot but I'm not sure it could be of much inspiration except to those people with drinking problems who are eligible to be voted cures by the Academy of Motion Picture Arts and Sciences.

I suspect that the reason Archerd thinks that Lemmon's story is a hot biofilm property is simply because it sounds like so many other terrible movies. The real-life stories of most movie stars are one thousand percent less interesting than even the worst roles they've played, especially

Were the Maysles brothers kind, or cruel, to their "friends," Edith Bouvier Beale and her daughter Edie?

after Hollywood wrenches life into the shape of bad fiction. If you can stand it, remember "The Jolson Story," "Jolson Sings Again" and "The Eddie Cantor Story."

Further proof is now provided by what must turn out to be one of the dumbest big-budget movies of 1976, "Gable and Lombard," which purports to be the story of Clark Gable and Carole Lombard who, according to the ads, "had more than love, they had fun." Maintain your skepticism, folks.

The movie was written by Barry Sandler and directed by Sidney J. Furie who, with the apparently enthusiastic help of the actors, James Brolin (as Gable) and Jill Clayburgh (as Lombard), make a blissfully witless assault on the reputations of two of the more remarkable stars produced by Hollywood in the nineteen thirties and forties.

The problem is not that Gable and Lombard were especially uninteresting off the screen, though even a reading of Warren G. Harris's carefully researched book, "Gable and Lombard," doesn't convince me that they are more worthy of being read about than William L. Marcy, President Pierce's Secretary of State, and Mrs. Marcy. Gable and Lombard were hugely popular movie stars when they fell in love and they were prevented from marrying for several years because his wife wouldn't divorce him. Finally they did get married and she was later killed in an airplane crash.

The movie, which presents these basic facts, is a fan magazine's idea of what Gable and Lombard were like, going through ludicrous situations that seem to have been collected from the worst movies of the period. Avoided is any idea that Gable was an extremely ambitious actor who, early on, hadn't been above performing stud duties to further his career. Instead he's presented as a sort of turf-kicking country bumpkin who had stardom thrust upon him. You don't believe that this Gable could have charmed a sleeping flea or won a supporting role in an amateur production of "Six Who Pass While The Lentils Boil."

Lombard is a shade more interesting in the film. She swears a lot and gives every indication that she likes sex, but when it comes down to fundamentals, she talks as if she'd been ransacking Vina Delmar's waste basket: "I'm the number one female star in the country and I never said 'I love you' to anyone and meant it."

Lombard and Gable, 1939

The movie means to convey some idea of what Gable and Lombard were like by having Brolin and Clayburgh behave as if "Gable and Lombard" were a distillation of all the movies they'd ever made, but it doesn't work. At best Brolin and Clayburgh are waxy, not very convincing look-alikes, so totally without charm that when, at one point, they engage in the kind of slapstick mayhem that recalls Lombard in "Twentieth Century" and "My Man Godfrey," one cringes in silent embarrassment.

At another point the film takes us onto the set of "Gone With The Wind" during the shooting of the scene in which Rhett Butler accompanies Scarlett out of the flaming Atlanta. If "Gable and Lombard" were just a tiny bit better, the effect of this curious piracy—featuring a sort of dumpy "Vivien Leigh"—would be to diminish one's fond memories of "GWTW." It doesn't do anything to memories though. "Gable and Lombard" has no relation whatsoever to those films we can still see almost any night of the year on television or in repertory theaters.

Gable worked extremely hard to cultivate the screen personality of comic, self-assured, nonchalant machismo that was infinitely adaptable, almost always the same and so long-lived that he was able to star in "Red Dust" in 1932 and its remake, "Mogambo," 21 years later.

In the thirties he was making four and five films a year. (Lombard was sometimes making as many as six films a year at that time.) I'm not sure whether the easy, well-defined but low-pressure Gable screen personality was the result of that heavy schedule or that Gable survived so long, so triumphantly, because he already had that personality in some form to start with. Whichever came first, the Gable of "It Happened One Night" (1934) is no more or less the master of the comic touch than the Gable of "Teacher's Pet" (1952). Brolin's weightless impersonation is an insult, but a small one.

Lombard made her fair share of turkeys in her much shorter career but none to equal "Gable and Lombard" in which Miss Clayburgh is forced (let's be kind) to play Lombard's screwball screen character in a movie that is otherwise as screwball as some awful Lloyd C. Douglas film.

At her best in "Twentieth Century," "My Man Godfrey," "Nothing Sacred" and "To Be or Not to Be," Lombard displayed the manic, self-absorbed intensity of the silent screen comedians with whom she got her start. That she was also an extremely beautiful woman, who projected intelligence, made her an unbeatable one-woman combination that was—and still is—rare. Only Maggie Smith, Paula Prentiss, Diane Keaton and the late Kay Kendall have been equipped to carry on.

● ● ●

"Gable and Lombard" has less to do with the Golden Age of movies, in which everything was always larger than life, than with the present television age, in which everything, including wars, assassinations, earthquakes, scandals of one sort and another, seem smaller than life, as if to fit on the little screen. "Gable and Lombard" doesn't even look like a theatrical movie. It could as easily have been a pilot film for a "Clark and Carole" TV series. It's not difficult to imagine how it might be done.

In the first segment Clark wants to go fishing but Carole, without Clark's permission, has bought a new mink coat that is due to be brought around for a fitting that morning. Can Carole fool Clark long enough to get the mink fitted? Will Clark cut off Carole's allowance? Tune in next week when, in segment two, Carole overhears Clark in his study rehearsing his lines for a love scene and thinks he is having an affair with the maid. Will Carole blow her stack? Will she attempt to make Clark jealous by pretending to be infatuated with the TV repairman? Tune in next week when, in segment three, Clark and Carole. . . .

1976 F 22, II:15:1

SALUT L'ARTISTE (Hail Artist), directed by Yves Robert; screenplay (French with English subtitles) by Jean-Loup Dabadie and Mr. Roberts; executive producers, Alain Poire and Mr. Robert; director of photography, Jean Penzer; music, Vladimir Cosma; a Gaumont International production; released by Exxel Film Gorup Inc. Running time: 96 minutes. At the Baronet Theater, Third Avenue near 59th Street. This film has not been rated.

Nicholas .... Marcello Mastroianni
Peggy .... Francoise Fabian
Clement .... Jean Rochefort
Elizabeth .... Carla Gravina
Zeller .... Xavier Gelin

By VINCENT CANBY

Nicholas (Marcello Mastroianni), the hero of Yves Robert's compassionate French comedy "Salut L'Artiste" (Hail Artist), is an actor who's never quite made it though he never stops working.

In the morning he'll be shooting a documentary at Versailles. At the lunch break he jumps into his car, still in his Louis XIV costume, and races into Paris for another job. In the evening he does a walk-on as an American gangster at the Chatelet Theater (walking on just long enough to get shot dramatically), after which he and a partner do an intentionally disastrous and funny magic show at a nightclub.

●

It's a giddy sort of life, full of excitement, good times, unreasonable rejections, sustained by expectations that the next assignment might very well put one over the top. With a daily schedule like that Nicholas hasn't time to worry, and when he does, he takes a Valium.

Mr. Mastroianni's Nicholas is one of his best performances in a long time—witty, self-absorbed, vain, unsentimental—qualities shared with the movie that contains it.

"Salut L'Artiste," which opened yesterday at the Baronet, is an affectionate salute to tentative failure. Mr. Robert, who was last represented here by "The Tall Blond Man With One Black Shoe," has been quoted as saying that actors aren't like other people since they have a tendency to separate themselves from life even while they are living it, to see everything as possible dramatic material.

That may be true, but I'm not sure that nonperformers don't spend a lot of the time doing the same thing, if not for the same reasons. All lives are lived on several planes of awareness simultaneously. There's a bit of actor in us all. I suspect that actors aren't really different. They're like everyone else, only more so.

Where a bank teller might have one job for 10 years, an actor like Nicholas might have 10 jobs in one week. Nicholas rushes through relationships in the same souped-up way, and though neither his wife (Carla Gravina) nor his mistress (Françoise Fabian) believes he has any real commitment to her, Nicholas would argue that his feelings and his commitments are as profound as anyone else's, and he's probably right.

Mr. Mastroianni's Nicholas is no grand vedette, no great star, no monumental talent seeking expression. The reason "Salut L'Artiste" is so moving and funny so much of the time is just that Nicholas is easily recognized. Nicholas keeps on going as if there were no biz like show biz, but life intrudes, which is responsible as much for the humor as for the poignancy of this film.

●

"Salut L'Artiste" is also nicely detailed and exceedingly well acted by the supporting cast, which includes Miss Fabian, as the beautiful mistress who is intelligent,

Marcello Mastroianni

understanding and furiously jealous of Nicholas's wife, and by Jean Rochefort, as Nicholas's best friend, an actor who, to the complete astonishment of Nicholas, decides to give up his career and go into product merchandising.

The friend is no less successful than Nicholas (if anything, he's a little more successful, having done a popular television commercial), and Nicholas is baffled as only one of God's faithful can be when a colleague turns suddenly to devil worship.

1976 F 23, 20:1

CATHERINE & CO., directed by Michel Boisrond; screenplay by Catherine Breillat and Leo L. Fuchs; produced by Mr. Fuchs; based on novel by Edouard de Segonzac; director of cinematography, Richard Suzuki. Released by Warner Bros. Running time: 99 minutes. At the Fine Arts Theater, 58th Street between Park and Lexington Avenues. This film has been rated R.
Catherine .... Jane Birkin
Francois .... Patrick Dewaere
Guillaume .... Jean-Claude Brialy
Moretti .... Vittorio Caprioli
Marquis de Puisargue.. Jean-Pierre Aumont
Thomas .... Mehdi

By RICHARD EDER

French sex farces aren't meant to be believable in themselves but, as with westerns, their success requires that they be performed with an air of belief. When Italians make westerns, it is the air of belief that is missing; so it is with most American efforts at sex comedies over the past three decades.

There isn't a lot that can be said in favor of "Catherine & Co.," which opened yesterday at the Fine Arts. It is sloppy, ill-shaped and very familiar. But it has a certain pleasure in itself, a wholeheartedness about its gimcrackery that arms us with patience, if not benevolence, and allows its funny parts—about two—to prosper mildly.

Catherine is an English girl, played by Jane Birkin, who comes to Paris with a vague offer of a job. The job gets vaguer and she has to find a way to sleep and eat. Her first device has some ingenuity: she sleeps, literally, with a succession of rich men. The literally lies in her ability to get them talking about their businesses with such enthusiasm and at such length that ardor is virtually forgotten.

When this gimmick runs out, she allows herself to be kept, in more traditional French-farce fashion, by four men. She treats them as investors rather than clients, however, and allows herself to be kept as a kind of Common Market effort in venture capitalism. It all pays off handsomely, and love, independence and prosperity are more or less equally served in the end.

Jane Birkin is not an actress of great subtlety or skill, but a mixture of coltishness and sensuality lets her keep the role more or less alive. As two of the lovers, Jean-Claude Brialy and Jean-Pierre Aumont are pretty dull. There is one good moment, though, where Mr. Brialy, with passion on his mind, proceeds down the front of Miss Birkin's dress, unbuttoning it, while she, with finance on her mind, follows, buttoning.

The best comic performance is that of a third lover, an Italian businessman played by Vittorio Caprioli. He bursts with passion, he lights up with passion, and it has been years since anybody has beamed such uncomplicated delight upon the screen as that which shines from Mr. Caprioli's round face as he trots upstairs after Miss Birkin.

1976 F 26, 23:1

NEW WOMEN/NEW FILMS, II: "Never Give Up: Imogen Cunningham," by Ann Hersey (1975; 29 minutes); "Chris and Bernie," by Bonnie Friedman and Deborah Shaffer (1975; 25 minutes); "Film for My Son," by Nadia Tesich-Savage (1975; 27 minutes). At the Film Forum, 15 Vandam Street, today through Sunday and next Thursday through Sunday.

By A. H. WEILER

The sensitive, steely fiber of several indomitable women is exposed with surgical finesse and a good deal of altruism in three short documentaries, collectively titled "New Women/New Films II," that are being served up at the Film Forum as successors to its previous, uneven, experimental "New Women/New Films I" program. The current "new women" are simply biographers who may not achieve unformly excellent results, but who do succeed in conmanding attention and in touching the mind and the heart.

Ann Hersey's 29-minute study of a famous photographer in "Never Give Up: Imogen Cunningham" projects a heroine who is endearingly human as well as heroic. Mrs. Cunningham, who will be 93 years old in April and has practiced her craft for 75 years, is anything but a dodderer in and around her picturesque, hillside home in San Franciso.

●

Gray-haired, rugged-faced and attired in a variety of hats and dresses, she is pictorially charming and memorably forthright in personal observations and credos, reminiscing on a career dating to 1901. Her fully enjoyed, fruitful life is illustrated by some of her painterly landscapes and nudes; portraits of such luminaries as Spencer Tracy and Cary Grant and a 1931 Martha Graham; studies of the father she adored ("he died at 98") and of her mother, husband and children and movie footage of Mrs. Cunningham as recipient of alumna honors at Washington University.

Of course, she is shown still taking shots with her Rolleiflex and, because of Miss Hersey's colorful evidence, a viewer is gratified to hear Mrs. Cunningham's cheerful assurance that she will "never give up."

●

"Chris and Bernie" two youthful, single mothers who are cooperatively bringing up a little boy and a girl in a house in a rural area, obviously are not noted citizens. But under the 25-minute professional inspection by Bonnie Friedman and Deborah they emerge as intelligent and self-reliant, if still troubled.

The failure of their marriages, their futures—one as a student nurse, the other as a carpenter—and their practical, loving approach to parenthood, are realistically reviewed in underplayed discussions and interplay with the youngsters whom they are determined to rear in a wholesome family environment. If the report occasionally is fragmentary and roughly edited, there is little doubt as to the courage and sincerity of Chris and Bernie.

In Nadja Tesich-Savage's 27-minute "Film for My Son," elusive moments in time as mementos for her little boy as she sees him are caught in an honest, bittersweet, if slightly home movie, style. The repartee, play and interaction between the bright, inquisitive 4-year-old and his filmmaker-mother and father in their Manhattan apartment and Riverside Park make for gentle but vivid reminders of a tender mother-son relationship. But it is clouded by her rather arty, repetitive reflections on her own happy and then traumatic childhood in a World War II-torn Europe. It seems doubtful they will stick in his memory.

Despite some flaws, these "new women," on and off the screen, are a tribute to the new feminism and also manage to captivate the eye and ear.

1976 F 27, 19:1

'Snuff,' Built on Rumor, Lacking in Credit

By JOHN LEONARD

"Snuff" is a contemptible movie now showing in Times Square. It is advertised as being so bloody that it could only have been made "in South America—where life is cheap." "Snuff" is also, in the slanguage of underground film freaks, a term denoting the actual murder, on camera, of a woman. The rumor among the freaks for months has been that several such movies were indeed made recently in Buenos Aires. "Snuff" seeks to capitalize on that rumor.

A number of articulate men and women, among them Representative Elizabeth Holtzman, Democrat of Brooklyn, Eric Bentley, Viveca Lindfors, Susan Brownmiller, Sol Yurick, Shelley Winters, Ellen Burstyn, Dave Dellinger, Gloria Steinem and Susan Sontag, object to the idea of murder as sexual entertainment. Understandably. If they did not, they would be moral cretins, like the people who made "Snuff," the people who distribute it—the Monarch Releasing Corporation, 330 West 58th Street—and the people who go to see it.

Eighty-two of these men and women have written to District Attorney Robert Morgenthau of Manhattan, asking him to close down the movie. Murder, after all, isn't free speech. Why should we tolerate a technicolored commercial for violence against women any more than we would tolerate such a commercial for genocide? Mr. Morgenthau doubts that he can do much.

Pickets Outside Theater

Meanwhile, a feminist lawyer and her friends the other day were wondering if they could take legal steps on their own. The trouble is that most of them hadn't seen "Snuff" and didn't want to. This, also, is understandable: To pay $4 to watch a young woman being dismembered, cinéma vérité, is to purchase your own humiliation. But if someone didn't see it, no one would know whether anything could or should be done about it, and, if so, how. Volunteers were required.

And so two yong women—one a professional film critic, the other an author of children's books—went in the company of a male friend to see "Snuff." Outside the theater, there were pickets, male and female, most belonging to activist homosexual organizations and most not having seen the movie, either. They were responding to the ad campaign. One sign said, "We Mourn the Death of Our Latin American Sister." One young man said, "They say that life is cheap. I take that personally. Is my life cheap?" He was suggesting a categorical imperative that would not have occured to the makers and distributors of "Snuff."

Inside the theater, there were escalators and buttered popcorn. It is a plush place — a perfectly respectable Schrafft's restaurant was torn down in order to confect it —in the Holiday Inn bordello style, with yards of synthetic velvet rope and machines for munching coins and playing games. The previous feature film at this theater was "Lucky Lady" with Liza Minnelli.

When one customer was asked about the etiquette of murdering women to make movies, he said, "If this is how somebody wants to end her life and make some money at the same time, what's the matter with it?" Before "Snuff" came on, there were "Woody Woodpicker" and "Pink Panther" animated cartoons.

"Snuff" begins with a young woman's being held down while one of her toes is sheared off. It ends with another young woman being held down while her hands and feet are sliced off, she is split lengthwise, throat to bowels, and, in a parody both of childbirth and autopsy, her intestinal tubing is triumphantly removed. In between, more men than women are murdered, but the killing of men is manly: a stabbing here, a gunshot there, no mutilation. "Snuff" does, though, honor equality of the sexes in one respect. Unlike "Last Tango in Paris," everybody keeps his and her pants on during sex. Bare breasts, buttered popcorn and blood are all that "Snuff" has to offer.

Well, not quite. Stupidity, too. The movie makers (there are no credits, nor should there be) must have gone to a tabloid correspondence school. They trick up the deliberations of their zombies with a muddy sound track about Nazis, furtive hints at Charles Manson, rhetorical pigsticking of the leisure classes, glowering—all sulky grunt—lesbian clinches and a sullen tribalism that would make the average caucus of Elks look ecstatic. The pretension stupefies.

All right. "Snuff," as if you hadn't guessed, is a hoax. Nobody gets vérité killed. "Marcus Welby, M.D." could have improved on the special effects. Afterward, the film critic and the author of children's books went off to dinner with the lawyer who wanted to enjoin. The author of children's books was relieved at having endured what was merely a hoax. The film critic pointed out that a similar dismemberment in the Andy Warhol-Paul Morrissey "Frankenstein" was much more obnoxious. The lawyer allowed that suing "Snuff" on the basis of false advertising would be counterproductive.

Does this report sound flattened-out, decorticated? Probably. The pornographic is an animated cartoon where somebody gets hurt and at least one dimension is missing. Having steeled oneself to bear witness—in the service of feminist or any other set of pieties—is one disappointed that the spectacle is not as outrageous as it was advertised? Having been brave, must one be bored? Does a counterfeit movie turn all our emotions into counterfeit, too? One hopes not. The fact that the murder in "Snuff" is counterfeit should have nothing to do with the fact that murder as sexual entertainment is pornographic.

Nor, alas, does either of these facts help us to determine which pornographic cartoon is liable, criminal, coercive, exempt from the absolutistic snuggles of the First Amendment. "Snuff" isn't murder, but is it shouting fire in a crowded theater? The flattening-out is an affectlessness. So many messages drum on the skull. Each makes the same noise, and some are more obscene than others. Commercials for rape and murder end up sounding like advertisements for the

"wings of man" and Preparation-H. We are reduced to "Mary Hartman, Mary Hartman," playing Ping-Pong with our brain, with the ears as paddles. One wishes that "Snuff" didn't exist. Since it does, one wishes that it were more egregious. Since it isn't, the genuine pornography is the static in one's mind.

1976 F 27, 21:2

FRENCH PROVINCIAL (Souvenir's d'en France), directed by Andre Techine; screenplay (French with English subtitles) by Mr. Techine and Marilyn Goldin; director of photography, Bruno Nuytten, editor, An-Marie Deshayes; music by Philippe Sarde; produced by Stephan Films. At the Embassy 72nd Street. Running time: 91 minutes.
Berthe .... Jeanne Moreau
Hector .... Michel Auclair
Régina .... Marie-France Pisier
Prosper .... Claude Mann
Augustine .... Orane Demazis
Pedret .... Aram Stephan
Lucio .... Helene Surgere
Victor .... Julien Guiomar

This film was reviewed by Richard Eder when it was shown at the New York Film Festival last autumn. Here is a shortened version of the review:

Jeanne Moreau has a genius for the particular. She could be marched off for execution and her fretful gait, her expression, her silences would argue so strongly against any mere universal application of law that the firing squad would fall apart arguing.

In "French Provincial" the young director André Téchiné has sent Miss Moreau trundling down a long, heavily furnished corridor of a movie about the multigenerational rise and fall of a French bourgeois family. By no subtle extension it argues through its particular provincial setting the decline and dissolution of bourgeois France.

Miss Moreau implants all kinds of cross-rhythms in Mr. Téchiné's ponderous though talented work, with its air of a 19th-century novel. She arrests the predictable playing-out of his cards; she enhances his uneven strengths.

"French Provincial," which opened yesterday at the Embassy 72 Street Theater is set around the fortunes of a family-owned foundry in a small French town. It was founded by Pedret, a young immigrant from Spain who by hard work and a driving vision built it up out of a simple smithy, and married the daughter of a prosperous local family as well.

This is told in flashback. Most of the film takes place when Pedret has become the family patriarch, running the business with his three grown sons and dominating the life of the town.

Sturdy as one of his iron boilers, bearded and mystically devoted to the foundry, old Pedrêt represents for Téchiné the vitality of the bourgeoisie once had. The three sons, in different ways, are the class in decadence.

There are two marriages. One brings in Régina, a cold spoiled girl who nests in the family like a leech, and eventually runs off with an American soldier. The other brings in Berthe, the town laundry woman.

Berthe—Jeanne Moreau—is vital, passionate and strong. She has an affair with Hector, most likable of the three sons, and when the family intervenes, threatens to leave town.

Old Pedret can't afford to lose Hector, who is the works manager, so he pragmatically decides they must marry. The lesson: The bourgeoisie will co-opt members of the proletariat when necessary.

Berthe is new blood; when Pedret dies she takes over. She guides the firm through the war and drives a truck for the Resistance. After the war the enterprise founders, badly in need of new funds. They come—with Régina and her new American lover, who happens to be a big-businessman.

By the time the movie has collapsed under the increasingly coarse style that Téchiné adopts to symbolize his thesis of capitalist collapse. As for Miss Moreau, she has taken to her bed. She can do no more for the foundry. On the other hand she has almost saved the movie.

1976 F 28, 14:3

INSERTS, directed and written by John Byrum; produced by Davina Belling and Clive Parsons; director of photography, Denys Coop; editor, Mike Bradsell; distributed by United Artists. Running time: 99 minutes. At the Criterion Theater, Broadway at 45th Street, 86th Street East Theater, 86th Street near Third Avenue, and UA Eastside Cinema, Third Avenue near 55th Street. This film has been rated X.
Boy Wonder .... Richard Dreyfuss
Cathy Cake .... Jessica Harper
Big Mac .... Bob Hoskins
Harlene .... Veronica Cartwright
Rex .... Stephen Davies

By VINCENT CANBY

Not yet 30, Boy Wonder (Richard Dreyfuss) is washed up as a Hollywood director. The year is 1930, and Boy Wonder is reportedly finished. Josef von Sternberg has told someone that he saw Boy Wonder panhandling on the Sunset Strip. Boy Wonder is not quite forgotten, though. Someone tells someone else, who tells Boy Wonder, that "that new guy at Pathe, Clark Gable," has said he'd like to work for Boy Wonder, which gives Boy Wonder a laugh. Boy Wonder is now making pornography films in a corner of the living room of his Spanish-style Hollywood mansion.

"Inserts," which opened at three theaters yesterday, is the story of 99 manic minutes in the life of Boy Wonder, during which a couple of leftovers from silent Hollywood—technology's rejects—meet and, figuratively speaking, rub shoulders with some hustling representatives of the new, talking Hollywood. The arena for confrontations

is Boy Wonder's living room, which, like Boy Wonder, the film refuses to leave.

"Inserts," which opened at three theaters yesterday, is essentially a stunt, a slapstick melodrama in the form of a one-act, one-set, five-character play. It is, however, a very clever, smart-mouthed stunt that, in its self-described "degenerate" way, recalls more accurately aspects of old Hollywood than any number of other period films, including "Gable and Lombard." It's not anything that "Inserts" says, but something to do with the dizzy pace, the wisecracks, the lack of sentimentality and, mostly, the characters, who could be shadowy parodies of once-living legends.

"Inserts" marks the directorial debut of John Byrum, the not-yet-30 screen-writer ("Mahogany," among other things), who, on the basis of this breathless stunt, not only knows how to write but also how to direct, especially when it comes to actors.

Mr. Dreyfuss must occasionally make plausible dialogue that's too self-conscious for the movie's good, but he gives a remarkably funny, tough and bristly performance as the Hollywood has-been who looks scarcely old

enough to vote. His chief adversary, a bootlegger on his way to becoming a Hollywood mogul, is played by an equally young but immensely talented English actor, Bob Hoskins, who suggests at least two real-life moguls that I can think of.

Veronica Cartwright, who looks a little like Maggie Smith, plays a former Hollywood star now reduced to drugs and porno-film parts, and Jessica Harper, who had a small but vividly funny role in Woody Allen's "Love and Death," plays a tiny, sweet-looking girl with a ferocious ambition to become an actress in "real movies"—and will do anythig to succeed. Stephen Davies, another newcomer, completes the cast as a young man who supplements his earnings as a Forest Lawn gravedigger by acting in Boy Wonder's porno-films, waiting for his star potential to be recognized and made legitimate.

Although "Inserts" has been rated X, it is not pornographic although it's a beautifully acted, tough-talking comedy that, at its wildest moments, manages to evoke the comedies of the late Joe Orton. It won't warm the heart, but its bleakness is almost buoyant.

1976 F 28, 15:1

FILM VIEW

VINCENT CANBY

Should Movies Have Messages?

"Even at their best, movies probably can never be more than entertainments for the child imprisoned in the oldest of us."

So writes Russell Baker, the New York Times columnist, in a recent piece questioning the sensibilities if not the sanity of the New York critics who were so taken by Lina Wertmuller's "Seven Beauties." Mr. Baker loathed the movie, which he describes as "a 'message' film." He's always been wary of messages in movies, he says, because, among other reasons, Stalin and Sunday-school teachers had a habit of slipping messages into stories.

I don't want particularly to defend "Seven Beauties" here. Though it's a film I admire tremendously, I do think that one of its faults is not that it has a message, but that it has too many. They aren't messages, really, they are associations that we make with the Wertmuller material, and sometimes they are quite contradictory. They are disorienting.

A second reading of the Baker piece suggests that it's not the existence of the "message" in "Seven Beauties" that bothers him as much as the repugnance of the message he has chosen to accept. He sees the movie—the story of a buffoon who stoops to anything to stay alive in a Nazi concentration camp—as "exalting human survival as the purpose of existence." In so reading the film Mr. Baker has, in effect, made something literal and sensible out of a work of art that can be interpreted with equal facility in several other ways, including Miss Wertmuller's, which, like Mr. Baker's, differs considerably from the way most of the New York critics saw the film. All of which proves nothing more than that artists are not always the best people to interpret their own work.

What is most interesting about the Baker piece is his feeling that "movies can probably never be more than entertainment for the child imprisoned in the oldest of us."

It's my suspicion that this conviction is responsible for much of the current anger, frustration and impatience with films being expressed today by so many people, especially in the over-40 age groups. Today's movies—not all of today's movies, just a tiny but important minority of today's movies—are hard on people who were brought up knowing that movies were supposed to be fun because they were a lesser form of literature that could be understood even if one didn't know how to read.

• • •

In pre-television days one went to the movies as a kind of reward, as a means to relax, having finished real, serious work, including all sorts of difficult, often boring, required reading. Movies were to be perceived in predictable ways. One could be sure that when one entered a dark, popcorn-scented movie house there was little chance of being hit in the face with Pascal's "Pensees." What ideas movies had were spelled out in pictures, which guaranteed they would never be very complex. Movies had beginnings, middles and endings, and unhappy endings were just as upbeat as the happy ones. Heroes never died in vain. In movies, life had shape.

Today's movies are different. They are not necessarily better, but they are decidedly different and that difference is alienating a lot of moviegoers who want movies to keep their old place. There's nothing worse than an uppity movie:

What the hell is "Claire's Knee" about anyway? Some guy with a thing about a knee and endless talk. The main thing wrong with "Nashville" is that it doesn't have a story and all the people in it are fools or con-artists. You can't even understand half the dialogue. What's so beautiful about "The Story of Adele H."? A movie about a rich, selfish girl who goes nuts over a guy who has made it very clear he doesn't love her? Take the fancy photography away from "Barry Lyndon" and what have you got? Just another costume picture, slower than most, about an 18th-century rogue who doesn't succeed—for more than three hours yet. It's no "Tom Jones," that's for sure.

"Seven Beauties?" Good grief! I don't go to movies to spend two hours in a concentration camp and get depressed. Why don't they make movies like they used to? (They do. It's called "Jaws," and it's not bad but there can be more to movies than jumping in your seat periodically.)

The New Movie is not new, of course. It's been around for years, regularly since the early 1960's, and there are as many kinds of New Movies as there are movies. Dramas, melodramas, comedies, satires, science fiction, love stories, made by such directors as Miss Wertmuller, Robert Altman, Stanley Kubrick, Ingmar Bergman, Michelangelo Antonioni, Jean-Luc Godard, Francois Truffaut, Federico Fellini, and sometimes by Mike Nichols, John Huston, Sam Peckinpah, Otto Preminger, Rainer Werner Fassbinder, Martin Scorsese, Francis Ford Coppola, John Cassavetes.

• • •

These directors are not all equally successful. Not since "Faces" have I been able to respond to a Cassavetes film with much interest. His "The Killing of a Chinese Bookie" is a disaster. Mr. Scorsese's "Taxi Driver" is a New Movie about which I have such mixed feelings that I could borrow a couple of phrases Mr. Baker attaches to "Seven Beauties." That is, "It is a parable of humanity in a society seen as bestial" and "I leave this movie unutterably depressed," though I'm not sure that says as much about the movie as about me, about my wishes, needs and capacities to look beyond the immediate images. No one can force you to look beyond the immediate image, and most of the time when you do look, there's nothing to see. But it's a big jump from that observation to say flatly that "movies probably can never be more than entertainments for the small child imprisoned in the oldest of us." It depends on the movie as well as on the imprisoned child who is looking.

New Movies can't be read like books or roadmaps.

One of the characteristics that the New Movies share is the seeming aloofness of the moviemaker to his characters, though if he were aloof he probably wouldn't have bothered to make the film. The New Movie is disorienting in that we can't always be sure of the writer/director's attitudes towards his material. He raises questions and doesn't attempt to answer them. The New Movie talks back to our prejudices without our knowing it.

Like the Old Movie, the New Movie feeds us all sorts

of information simultaneously through the eyes and ears, a process that keeps the mind busy while more information continues to pile in. Yet the New Movie's information is often contradictory, associative, incomplete. The mind has to work—and this, odd to say, can be terrifically entertaining. There are spaces to be filled in, judgments that we must make on our own. The New Movie considers something, perhaps discards it, considers something else, and moves on. It's not easily labelled optimistic or pessimistic.

No movie—New or Old—can be analyzed as if it were an editorial, at least, not if it's any good. If one has to make an association to the written word, a movie is closer to the poetic form, full of subliminal impulses, which is why the great ones delight both the child and the aging adult who imprisons him.

1976 F 29, II:15:1

Notes On Seeing 'Barry Lyndon'

By HAROLD ROSENBERG

The movies could make their maximum contribution to culture by following the lead of Stanley Kubrick's "Barry Lyndon" in recycling unread literature. Movies based on works that are still breathing — for example, "War and Peace," "Ulysses," "Death in Venice"—have the drawback of presenting themselves as replacements for the originals, and, since they are reproductions in a different medium, are likely to be regarded by the audience as distortions or vulgarizations. Only a graduate student in English, however, would be likely today to have read Thackeray's "Barry Lyndon." Why would anyone else take up time with this item of 19th-century pop entertainment? Years ago, Somerset Maugham, recognizing that such works are not being read, suggested that they ought to be reissued in versions cut down to their plot outlines.

Still, a cultured person should know something about "Barry Lyndon" as a work that constitutes part of his literary heritage, though this knowledge need not be detailed or complete.

Harold Rosenberg is The New Yorker's art critic. His latest book is "Art on the Edge."

Kubrick's "Barry" supplies exactly the right amount of familiarity—as much as a reasonably attentive reader would have been likely to retain. In short, the movie is a valid substitute for Thackeray's narrative, precisely because it is a "substitute" for something which the audience today doesn't have anyway.

But Kubrick's "Barry" is a lot more than a substitute for an all-but-forgotten tale. The movie also translates the printed page into art for the eye and the ear by coordinating the story with the paintings, music and landscaping of the period. The adventures of Barry, by this time commonplace and threadbare, are delivered in a faultless esthetic package. If the lead characters are poorly cast, the weakness of their acting is compensated for by their costumes and hairdos. The laggard unfolding of the plot permits one to lose oneself in countrysides that imitate paintings, in classically composed and toned interiors, in the placement and lighting of the figures. Kubrick's salvage job turns out to be a vessel filled with brand new 18th-century treasures. I could have watched "Barry Lyndon" for another two hours without the slightest interest in what was happening to its hero.

The American public today is avid for knowledge of the past, or something that passes for the past, including its art and fashions. Kubrick has done their homework for them. He has read the texts, scoured the picture galleries and art books, listened to the music and compared recordings. He has demonstrated that a confident movie director, not too eager to display his imagination, can be worth a hundred classrooms.

Think of the vein of potential film "properties" that has been opened up by Kubrick's "Barry": obscure novels by George Eliot, Owen Meredith, Disraeli, even Mel-

ville's "Israel Potter," to pull out of the air only a few titles. It gives the key to a treasury of livingrooms and parlors, duck ponds, battle formations, romance by the garden gate, fox hunts—all far more civilizing than the unshaven types in current movies who roll around in the grass with bears.

Original, up-to-date scenarios may be more exciting, but they are not certain to provide much in the way of education, since no one knows how long they will survive. Movies based on unread works by classical authors have the advantage of representing talents that have escaped extinction and thus belong in the common storehouse from which the minds of the living are obliged to draw. Regardless of the interest of the story, the story itself constitutes information that augments the spectator's knowledge. What he misses in pleasure, he makes up for in satisfaction at having earned a mental profit.

•

Moving pictures are not a good vehicle for original ideas. Images captured by the camera are not sufficiently detached from time, place and natural appearances to match the abstractness of words or mathematical signs. Movie directors sense the intellectual resistances of their medium and confine thinking in movies to references to ideas rather than attempts to develop or apply them. Even the most advanced European moviemakers rarely go beyond name dropping and idea dropping. Fellini, Antonioni, Truffaut relate themselves to thought by quoting, which is a species of scavenging. Avant-garde films stimulate the shock of recognition and generate an aura of profundity by mentioning Malraux or Croce or throwing in a shot of a "Merzbau." In short, like Kubrick's "Barry" they resuscitate the cultural past.

The act of reading a novel is not too dissimilar to that of watching a movie. One sits in a comfortable chair and lets the mind be carried by a stream of images as in a semi-dream. Reading or listening to poetry, or examining a painting, is of a different order; it calls for a heightened alertness. The mixing of media in the movies—dramatic dialogue, color photographs in motion, sound effects, music—produces an exact physical duplication of the novelistic daydream. It keeps the spectator/listener suspended in a universe of sensations, which may occasionally reveal something frightening—

Kubrick's film imitates paintings of the period: top, Gainsborough's "Duchess of Devonshire" and Dayes's "Queen Square, London"; bottom, scenes from the movie.

the whipping scene in "Barry"—but which does not threaten the witness lounging in his expandable seat.

●

Regardless of what educators do, the decline of read-

ing is likely to continue. Compared with multimedia relaxations, reading in the future will be preferred for entertainment by the kind of minority that in the past chose chamber music over grand opera. If accumulated

literary culture is not to die out with the large public, it must depend increasingly on translation into film.

Reworking old art is a major aspect of 20th-century creation — in painting and sculpture, it is perhaps the

dominant approach. Examples are Picasso's recomposed Velasquez paintings, Miró's Dutch masters and, most notorious, Duchamp's obscenely entitled Mona Lisa with mustache and goatee. The resurrected masterpieces

tend to contain elements of parody and camp, a way of compensating for the minority status of the fine arts today by flattering their public as insiders.

There is parody, too, in Kubrick's "Barry Lyndon": the dashing British army officer who falls in a faint when struck by a bullet made of dough. Also camp, as in Barry's marriage ceremony, with its robed priest dwelling on the theme of fornication, and in the beautifully composed funeral procession of Barry's son. On the whole, however, the handling of the adaptation is straight, with just enough caricature to disguise the sobriety of this essentially educational enterprise.

1976 F 29, II:1:1

FROM BEYOND THE GRAVE, movie in four episodes, directed by Kevin Connor, screenplay by Robin Clarke and Raymond Christodoulou based on stories by R. Chetwynd-Hayes; produced by Max J. Rosenberg and Milton Subotsky; director of photography, Alan Hume. Distributed by Howard Mahler Films. At Blue Ribbon Theaters. Running time 100 minutes. This film has been rated PG.
With Margaret Leighton, Donald Pleasence, David Warner, Ian Carmichael, Peter Cushing, Diana Dors, Ian Bannen and others.

By RICHARD EDER

In the decrepit antiques shop that links the four episodes of "From Beyond the Grave" the rule is: count your change carefully. Not because the cadaverous proprietor, a man with all kinds of spooky and disagreeable resources at his command, will cheat. But dreadful things happen to customers who try to cheat him. The movie, which opened yesterday at neighborhood theaters, demonstrates them.

John Collier used to write lovely short stories about this kind of thing, drawing odd and ironic genies out of his old bottles. The episodes in "Grave," based on stories by R. Chetwyn-Hayes, are crude and obvious. Each punch is telegraphed, each twist is a stranglehold. They overcompensate with blood for their lack of deftness. And the blood is rotten quality: dark, transparent stuff.

However, the producers have hired some distinguished and underworked British actors for several of the parts. In spite of the blood, none of the episodes goes much below a certain harmless tedium. And in one or two cases the actors bring in a real if momentary liveliness.

By far the best is "The Elemental," and the reason is the late Margaret Leighton. She is a medium brought in to exorcise a nasty spirit that has embedded itself in the stuffy left shoulder of a businessman, played by Ian Carmichael.

In yellow wig and dark glasses, Miss Leighton has—and bestows—a hilarious time wrestling the spirit all over a prim and proper Surrey cottage, filling the air with feathers, smashed crockery and outraged exclamations.

In "An Act of Kindness," Ian Bannen has some good moments as a long-suffering husband getting rid of his shrewish wife. As the wife, Diana Dors is also fine. I particularly liked her—after

her husband has stormed from the dinner table—uprighting the upset sauce bottle and continuing to chew.

The other two episodes, "The Gate Crasher" and "The Door" are pure stodge. If people still traveled much by railroad, "Grave" might be something to see between trains.

1976 Mr 4, 24:1

MAN FRIDAY, directed by Jack Gold; screenplay by Adrian Mitchell, based on "Robinson Crusoe," by Daniel Defoe; produced by David Korda; executive producers, Jules Buck and Gerald Green; director of photography, Alex Phillips; music and songs, Carl Davis; editor, Anne Coates; a presentation of I.T.C. and Keep Films in association with ABC Entertainment, distributed by Avco Embassy Pictures. Running time: 109 minutes. At Loews Tower East Theater, Third Avenue near 72d Street, and Loews Astor Plaza Theater, 44th Street west of Broadway. This film has been rated PG.
Crusoe .... Peter O'Toole
Friday .... Richard Roundtree
Carey .... Peter Cellier
McBain .... Christopher Cabot

By VINCENT CANBY

Some good people, including Peter O'Toole and Richard Roundtree, the stars, and Jack Gold, the director, have entered into a collaboration that brings out the worst in each of them. It's called "Man Friday" and it opened yesterday at Loews Astor Plaza and Tower East Theaters.

"Man Friday," written by Adrian Mitchell, is Daniel Defoe's "Robinson Crusoe" with a dopily raised consciousness—the story of the once-great, resourceful, 18th-century shipwreck survivor told from the point of view of his native manservant, Friday. In this version, Friday becomes a sort of exotic flower child who values fun, laughter, song and sex-without-guilt, while poor old Crusoe is an uptight, mean-spirited, self-righteous, Bible-quoting bigot.

The time is still the early 18th century, but the wit-lessness is strictly of the 1960's. While Crusoe (Mr. O'Toole) tries to teach Friday (Mr. Roundtree) the meaning of private ownership, money, sin, work and sportsmanship, Friday, just as unsuccessfully, attempts to liberate Crusoe from his hang-ups. This reversal of roles might possibly have stimulated George Bernard Shaw to an interesting idea or two, but it does nothing for Mr. Mitchell, whose screenplay is a spinoff from an earlier television script and a theatrical play.

The movie, which was photographed prettily in Puerto Vallarta, Mexico, seems to have been carefully aimed about two inches over the heads of an audience of 8-year-olds. There are some incidental songs in it that I can imagine being sung better by animated rabbits than by Mr. Roundtree. There is

also a lot of smug discourse, the tedium of which is occasionally relieved by ludicrous inspiration, as when Friday offers his body and his love to Crusoe when he finds his master flagellating himself for having had an "immoral dream."

•

Mr. O'Toole looks and sounds right, and he might have made a fine Crusoe in a film of fewer confusions and pretensions. Mr. Roundtree, whose first "Shaft" film had a good deal of style, has a terrible time trying to mime a primitive man's saintliness. Mostly he chooses to look baffled. He wrinkles his brow, cocks his head to one side and assumes a quizzical expression. The last actor to get away with this was Lassie.

1976 Mr 6, 22:1

'Snuff'
Is Pure
Poison

By RICHARD EDER

There is a patch of anti-matter on Times Square into which not only public decency disappears, but reality as well. It is a repulsive put-on film called "Snuff," and it is housed at the National Theater.

Everything about the film is suspect: the contents, the promotion and possibly even some of the protest that is conducted each evening outside the box office. Nothing is provable, nothing is believable, and although swindles are hardly new in show business, it's been a long time since such a peculiarly poisonous kind of swindle has come along.

On the face of it, "Snuff" is a horrendously written, photographed, acted, directed and dubbed bit of verdigris showing a group of devil-girls massacring people in Argentina or Uruguay—it's not clear which. The special effects are unsparing.

The main come-on—and put-on—of the picture, made by a group of people whose anonymity is deliberate, is a scene tacked onto the end. It depicts the director and the crew of a film-within-the-film getting so carried away

Richard Eder is a film critic for The Times.

that they dismember one of the actresses.

I didn't stick it out. When they took out scissors and cut off her fingers I put on my coat. By the time I'd buttoned the coat, they were applying an electric saw to her leg. By the time I was past a fascinated man on the aisle, an arm was off. I didn't turn around as I went up the aisle but I'm told a thorough job was done.

What brings people to the National Theater, what brought them to theaters in Philadelphia and Indianapolis where the authorities—in a move that could yet win censorship a good name—forced its departure, is less this final scene itself than the hype behind it.

Some months ago, word was spread, and picked up by several newspapers, that a movie had been made in which such a scene genuinely had taken place. It is still not clear whether "Snuff" was actually the original source of the rumor or whether the rumor was devised for some other cheapie lying on some shelf somewhere.

In any case, the "Snuff" distributor, Allen Shackleton, of the locally-based Monarch Releasing Corporation, is promoting his picture in a way to suggest that a real murder did occur in it. The

ads claim, for instance, that only in "Latin America, where life is cheap, could such a film be made."

Well, life is probably no cheaper in Latin America than in some parts of New York. It certainly is no cheaper than special effects. And special effects are most certainly cheaper than paying blackmail to any members of a crew who may have observed or even participated in such a thing. People who make this kind of garbage don't go in for unnecessary expense.

In the particular case of "Snuff," Mr. Shackleton is hermetically and profitably elusive about what happened. If it was true, he told a reporter from Variety, "I'd be a fool to admit it. If it isn't real, I'd be a fool to admit it."

It would seem that twisting illusion and reality for shock effect is proving a good thing for Mr. Shackleton, who says his usual specialty is "sexy little comedies, R-rated." He voluntarily rated "Snuff" as an X-film. "I thought young people might be damaged by seeing explicit violence," he said. He did not, he said, think it would harm adults.

"I would not personally seek it out for entertainment," he added.

1976 Mr 7, II:13:8

FILM VIEW
VINCENT CANBY

From 30's Porn
To 70's Corn

Four new films: two pretty good, and two duds. That's not bad for the February-March period when movie distributors, having given us their blockbusters for Christmas and still sitting on their Easter releases, assume that the only people going out want to see third-rate horror movies. Because these new films have little in common except sprocket holes, I'll make no attempt to find a trend. They are listed individually and in alphabetical order.

"Inserts," written and directed by John Byrum, is a slapstick melodrama set in Hollywood in 1930, about a once-successful young director, not yet 30, who stays in his living room all day making porn films for the stag circuit. It sounds terrible and it is a bit implausible. Why would anyone think that, say, a down-on-his-luck D. W. Griffith would make better porn loops than anyone else? We are also asked to believe that Boy Wonder, the name of this manic has-been who's played by Richard Dreyfuss, actually pioneered the use of the hand-held camera. But plausibility is not what's interesting about "Inserts."

The film is a one-set, five-character movie with the form of a tightly constructed one-act play that takes place in the time it uses to tell its story—99 minutes. It is mid-day and Boy Wonder is trying to finish the first

Dreyfuss in the x-rated "Inserts"

commitment of a six-picture deal he's made with a successful bootlegger who's branching out into blue movies. All he needs to do is to photograph the "inserts," the close-ups, but the work is complicated when the bootlegger (Bob Hoskins) and the bootlegger's fiancée (Jessica Harper) drop by to watch the day's shooting, when his leading lady takes a little too much heroin, and when his leading man (Stephen Davies), a part-time grave-digger, is called away to assist at the unscheduled burial of a friend.

"Inserts" is a stunt, but it's one that Byrum, a product of New York University Film School, pulls off with a lot of comic style. Though the subject is bleak, the movie's dizzy pace, desperately simulated sophistication and wisecracks recall a kind of comedy that Hollywood made in the thirties.

The cast is excellent, especially Dreyfuss, though he looks more like a pre-med student, exhausted from studying for his exams, than a former Hollywood boy wonder, and Miss Harper, a small, wistfully pretty, actress, who virtually carries off the last third of the film as she bulldozes Boy Wonder into using her for the close-ups needed to complete his film. She winds up, of course, using the young impotent genius for her own professional end.

"Inserts" is not itself pornographic but it has been rated X for all its nudity and graphically-photographed, simulated sex. Is that a contradiction?

"The Killing of A Chinese Bookie" is John Cassavetes's latest and in some ways most ambitious home-movie. It's also his worst, a hoked-up melodrama about the owner (Ben Gazarra) of a topless joint who must pay off a mob debt by carrying out a contract murder for which he's completely ill-equipped. No matter how indulgent Cassavetes's earlier films were, the improvisations of his actors bore a recognizable relation to characters caught in private dilemmas. The demands of the so-called story of "The Killing of A Chinese Bookie" do not allow for such improvisations, though that hasn't stopped the actors. Gazarra, who can be a fine performer, tries to act but often the camera isn't even looking at him. This one is only for people doing term papers on Cassavetes.

• • •

"Man Friday," directed by Jack Gold, is a terrible, consciousness-raised version of Defoe's "Robinson Crusoe" in which Crusoe (Peter O'Toole) comes to represent the worst aspects of a British colonial (capitalistic, bigoted, insensitive, joyless and guilt-ridden) while Friday (Richard Roundtree) is the voice of sweet reason whose method is alarmingly though primitively Socratic. I say alarmingly because two weeks on a desert isle with such a self-assured fellow would be enough to send any normal neurotic into catatonia, though this film would have us believe that Crusoe and Friday stuck it out for more than 10 years.

O'Toole speaks the idiot lines as if he wanted to believe them, while Roundtree acts as if he'd wandered off the set of Disney's "So Dear To My Heart." The movie

reinforces this notion with a couple of catchy songs that might as easily be sung by animated rabbits.

"Salut L'Artiste" (Hail Artist) is a funny, gently rueful portrait of the artist as a busy failure. The French film, directed by Yves Robert ("The Tall Blond Man With One Black Shoe"), is about Nicholas (Marcello Mastroianni), a Parisian actor who makes a decent enough living playing extras in films, doing walk-ons in the theater, acting in TV commercials and dubbing the voices of animals in cartoons. He is not a bad actor but he is doomed always to be a second-rater in a profession where not to make it big is not to make it at all. There's no such thing as building up small credit.

Robert's compassion for his characters doesn't cloud his comic view of them. Mastroianni has not had a better role in a long time. His Nicholas is selfish and self-aware, vain and desperate, at heart gallant. Françoise Fabian is his beautiful mistress, a woman who will put up with anything except infidelities with his wife (Carla Gravina), and Jean Rochefort is his sometime partner in a nightclub act. They all are fine.

1976 Mr 7, II:13:1

Avant-Gardist Toys With Past

By ROGER COPELAND

If one were to poll the film critics who write regularly for mass-circulation newspapers and magazines in this country, asking them to compile a list of significant new American filmmakers, they would probably agree on the names of Martin Scorsese ("Taxi Driver," "Mean Streets"), Francis Ford Coppola ("The Conversation," "The Godfather"), and Terrence Malick ("Badlands"). It is unlikely that the name of Ken Jacobs would appear on anyone's list, because most of the critics questioned would never have seen his work.

Yet, starting next Wednesday and continuing through Tuesday, March 16, the Whitney Museum will be showing a number of Jacobs' recent films as part of its New American Filmmakers Series. Are we talking here about two fundamentally different varieties of "New American Film"? The answer, I think, is yes.

Granted, filmmakers such as Scorsese, Coppola and Malick are relatively young, unmistakably talented, and much more independent of industry pressures than their Hollywood predecessors. They may stray a bit farther from conventional story-telling techniques than would an old-guard master like

Roger Copeland teaches a course in film esthetics at Oberlin College.

Howard Hawks; but their films remain fictional narratives, featuring professional actors who "impersonate" flesh-and-blood characters.

The Whitney, on the other hand, is interested in filmmakers whose work involves no such artifices—filmmakers whose efforts are more closely related to the modern paintings hanging on its walls. For a variety of reasons, many serious movie critics are willing to accept a higher degree of abstraction in painting than in film—a medium they view as inherently more representational because of the camera's built-in affinity for recording (rather than re-creating) the outside world. Of course, not all experimental films screened at the Whitney are painterly explorations of pure shape, color, and rhythm. Many are documentaries of one form or another, films that exploit the medium's potential for capturing an already existing reality in the most impersonal manner possible. But Ken Jacobs, one of the most innovative and influential avant-garde filmmakers, is constantly reminding us that no matter how life-like a cinematic image may look, it is ultimately the result of a beam of light projected onto a flat surface.

Strictly speaking, the 43-year-old Jacobs is not a "new" American filmmaker. His major work to date, "Tom, Tom, the Piper's Son," a 115-minute feature made in 1969, has frequently been shown at the Whitney,

though it will not be included in the museum's upcoming series of all-new films. Nevertheless, the film is worth discussing because it so well exemplifies some of Jacobs' major concerns and techniques. In "Tom, Tom," Jacobs rephotographs a short, 1905 silent movie while it is being projected on another screen. Thus, from the very outset, we are aware of watching projected light, rather than concrete substance. For the first 10 minutes, Jacobs simply runs the original film through in its entirety.

We chuckle at a charmingly silly, nursery-rhyme story about a young mischief-maker named Tom who steals a pig and is chased by townspeople through chimneys and haystacks, over fences and, finally, into a barnyard crammed with squawking ducks and geese. Eventually, the "captured" Tom is dragged up from a well, protectively clutching his pig.

The settings strike us as a fairly crude "representation" of the out-of-doors and this theatrical quality is intensified by the fact that the 1905 filmmaker's camera remains immobile, positioned in that proverbial "12th row, center" seat. The theatricality of the original film is most apparent in the opening fairgrounds tableau in which jugglers, acrobats, a woman tightrope walker carrying a hoop, candy-sellers, and wide-eyed spectators all mill around, perform, and hawk their wares simultaneously in one fixed space.

So far, "Tom, Tom" hardly seems the stuff of which important modern art is made, but just wait! Jacobs soon begins performing a dazzling series of "variations" on the 1905 original. He freezes individual frames and zooms in on minute details, thereby emphasizing the graininess of the film's texture and transforming recognizable, three-dimensional objects and people into flat, abstract shapes. He slows the film down and plays portions of it in reverse. Sometimes he tracks his camera back and away from the screen, thus creating a small rectangle of pulsating light surrounded by a vast, black abyss. On other occasions, he holds his camera still and jiggles the screen on which the original film is being projected. And, finally—lest anyone forget that what we are watching is a film (of a film!)—Jacobs even focuses his camera on the flickering projector bulb.

•

One reason the original footage appeals so strongly to Jacobs is that the fairground scene appears to have been modeled on the famous 18th-century painting, Hogarth's "Southwark Fair." In the course of Jacobs' re-filming, this sequence adopts a flat, grainy, pointilistic texture which lends it a remarkable likeness to Seurat's painting, "The Sideshow." Thus, on one level, Jacobs' film can be seen as a mini-history of painting from the 18th to the late 19th century. These painterly preoccupations are no mere accidents, for Jacobs studied painting under Hans Hofmann at The Art Students League before turning his attention exclusively toward film.

And, like most modernist painting, Jacobs' reworking of the original "Tom, Tom" demands to be looked at as a self-contained object, not as a sort of window on the world. In the course of the film, Jacobs destroys the three-dimensional, illusionistic space in which representational film and painting encourage us to become emotionally and imaginatively engaged.

Jacobs' films exist as a sort of perceptual training, a do-it-yourself kit for learning to see the world more lucidly. This becomes clear near the end of "Tom, Tom" when Jacobs replays the original film once again in its original form. This time we see it quite differently. We're more attuned to the "formal" richness which lies just beneath the representational surface, the "abstractness" of the middle portion becomes all the more meaningful because those richly textured dots of light are not seen as "arbitrary" figments of Jacobs' imagination, but are perceived rather as the underlying structure of the original images — something that was "there" all the time. Malraux once said that the post-impressionist still-life painters were more interested in "glorified color" than in "glorified apples." "Tom, Tom" is a film which glorifies light and shadow, form and texture.

Jacobs teaches film at S.U.-N.Y., Binghamton; and, on yet another level, "Tom, Tom" can be seen as an accelerated survey of film history. We begin with a "theatrical" film of the early 20th century; then Jacobs' manipulation of the original footage in part two corresponds to the "montage" experiments of Eisenstein and the Russians in the 1920's. And finally, the third section reminds us that many contemporary filmmakers — Welles, Rossellini, Miklos Jancso —have reincorporated the theatrical spaces of those early films.

It may appear from what has been said so far that Jacobs' films appeal to the eye and the brain in a rather cold, formal, unfeeling way. Not true. In fact, Jacobs' films exude a pathos all their own, deriving from the filmmaker's penchant for "found footage" (film originally shot by someone else and not "intended" for the uses to which it is eventually put). One of the new Jacobs' films to be shown next week at the Whitney, "Urban Peasants: A Study in Yiddish Structuralism," is actually a reworking of "home movies" shot in the Jewish section of Brooklyn in the 30's and 40's. We see families who know perfectly well how to pose before a still camera, but who are more than a little confused about what to do in front of a motion-picture camera. An extraordinary choreography emerges as three generations of Jewish life walk toward and away from a hand-held camera. The way in which the family members suddenly appear and disappear from the corners of the frame is strangely reminiscent of Fellini, yet we know that no such "effect" could have been intended.

The very fact that we know Jacobs is capable of "manipulating" the images the way he did in "Tom, Tom" makes us yearn all the more for the original footage in its most pristine state. But what we're really longing for is the past. Unlike the commercial purveyors of "nostalgia," Jacobs knows that the past cannot be recaptured; and consequently, this film, like most of his works, is pervaded by an almost unbearable sense of loss. Jacobs sees the cinema as the most mixed of blessings. In the hands of the Hollywood dream factory it can falsify and even destroy our sense of the past. But in the hands of a filmmaker like Ken Jacobs, it can, at the very least, poignantly remind us of what we've lost. ■

1976 Mr 7, II:13:4

'Seven Beauties'—A Cartoon Trying to Be a Tragedy

By JERZY KOSINSKI

"How did the world get like this? We all get killed and nobody says anything," philosophizes lady-killing concentration-camp inmate Pasqualino Frafuso (Giancarlo Giannini), in "Seven Beauties," the Italian filmmaker Lina Wertmüller's newest triumph. (Critics have called it everything from "a masterpiece" to "a monumental classic" to "a magnificent achievement" to "the Eureka film.")

The problem with the movie, and with its hero, is that both ask a false question. What they should be asking is, "How did I get like this?" because "Seven Beauties" seems to be a film about self-delusion. Wertmüller, like Pasqualino, never comes to grips with the misstated causes or destructive effects of this self-delusion.

Wertmüller might have made a more satisfying film if she had offered any insight into the formation of the character, and his times. Instead, she bombards us with familiar economic and political images such as war, poverty and Nazi persecution, arranged so that they seem to entrap and brutalize Pasqualino, an innocent man. The point is that the rogue Pasqualino, played winningly by Wertmüller's *homme fatale*, is no more an innocent

Jerzy Kosinski is the author of "Cockpit," "The Painted Bird" and other novels.

at the beginning of the film than he is a returned hero at the end: he's merely consistently engaging.

On screen Giannini is a pastiche of other actors' performances and various comic situations; he is a beloved Italian cartoon, the natty Neapolitan, in white suit and white hat, a carnation in his buttonhole, a cigarette holder clamped between his teeth. It's too easy to be inveigled by Giannini's presence into dismissing Pasqualino's morality. In fact, the character's personality seems almost to have been shaped to conform to Giannini's extremely marketable persona.

Wertmüller begins her film by introducing the protagonist as that *macho* Italian so ingrained in Western culture that we recognize and enjoy him on sight, and she is a capable filmmaker who knows how to milk a stereotype for maximum enjoyment, even in scenes of lurid brutality. No matter what

he does, Pasqualino is treated with indulgent good humor; considering the nature of his actions, humor seems an overly generous form of respect.

When Pasqualino's life is considered in the abstract, without benefit of Giannini's aqua eyes or Wertmüller's expert editing, we perceive it as being comprised of events which are intensely depressing evidences of power and manipulation. These events are revealed through a series of continuing flashbacks, which begin while Pasqualino and a comrade, both Italian deserters, wander through a forest in Germany, fleeing the Nazis.

Pasqualino's memories refer us to his pre-war days in Naples, where we see him as a small-time entrepreneur engaged in running a mattress-stuffing factory, an all-girl sweatshop, where he also is the self-appointed protector of his seven sisters and his mother. When he forbids an older sister to perform in a burlesque theater, and later forcibly extracts her from a whorehouse, it's more to save his own honor than hers. Consequently, it is his own dignity he seeks to preserve when he kills his sister's pimp-boyfriend, Totonne (Mario Conti), by sneaking into the man's room in the middle of the night, shooting him in his bed, dismembering the body, and shipping it in three suitcases to different places.

Denounced by his grieving sister as her lover's murderer, Pasqualino is apprehended

Pasqualino: Saving his sister's honor, or his own?

by the police. Insisting that he is "a man of honor" and that he killed Totonne solely to defend his dignity, Pasqualino confesses to his crime, is declared criminally insane, and sentenced to 12 years in an asylum.

•

Assigned to the women's ward as an orderly, Pasqualino continues his antisocial antics, including the violent rape of a restrained female patient. Subjected to electric-shock treatment, then pronounced "normal" by an older female doctor—yet another victim of his uncanny ability to charm women—he is offered a chance to fight with the Germans against the Soviets. He seizes it, but deserts with another Italian soldier, Francesco (Piero Di Orio), before the troop train reaches the Russian front. He and Francesco are soon caught and sent to a concentration camp, improbably run by a mammoth female commandant (Shirley Stoler), the very embodiment of Nazi cruelty and power.

It is in the commandant's office that Wertmüller makes her final great play for the audience's sympathy, turning Pasqualino from a lovable clown into a pitiable, abused "worm," a man who will do anything, even fornicate with the commandant, in order to survive. His reward is power: he is appointed Capo, the work boss of his stalag. His first responsibility is to select at random six men to be executed: his second, to shoot Francesco, the only person who even remotely qualifies as a friend. In both instances, Pasqualino complies with relative ease.

The film ends with Pasqualino's return to Naples, where even the sweet young girl he fancied before his imprisonment has become a whore. The war years have transformed Pasqualino from a lovable rogue into a brusque, cold cynic. No longer the passionate lover or the disarming clown, he solemnly announces to the whore that they must marry and produce children to defend themselves in the ongoing fight for survival.

Possibly Wertmüller intended the change in Pasqualino to teach us that man brutalizes man, making him antisocial and paranoid, convincing him that, since the enemy is everywhere, no one is to be trusted. In fact, let us recall again, Pasqualino is antisocial and brutal at the start of his story. He is, after all, commandant of the mattress factory, oppressing his female workers, restricting his sisters' person-

al freedom, curtailing their sexual preferences, and under the guise of preserving the family honor, exploiting them economically and emotionally.

Wertmuller's *simpatico* treatment of Pasqualino reverberates in the memory, contrasting with his more somber appearance at the film's end, but clearly, despite appearances, he is not significantly changed. He is a sexually dependent worm at the start and a pitiable abused worm at the end, and his metamorphosis is entirely superficial. What passes for remorse has less to do with past events than with the famous Giannini eyes — an ophthalmologist's dream, for "Seven Beauties" never reveals Pasqualino's character nor does it explain why he is what he is.

Just as Wertmüller exploits our preconceived notion of the Italian male, she tosses in another loaded image, the concentration camp, to summon up a guaranteed response in her audience. Since we accept the obvious truth that it was difficult to retain one's dignity and almost to retain one's sanity in the camps, how could we expect Pasqualino to be anything other than reduced by that experience? And since no one could survive the camps unchanged, his altered condition is a given, passed off as a surprise.

•

By building tension through culturally fostered audience responses, Wertmuller has not created a real character; all she has done was to design an abstraction. Pasqualino is a credible cliché, an egotist capable of self-awareness in only two modes: as a man of honor and as a lover. Yet, even these images are self-deceptions, because Pasqualino has energy but no real self-knowledge. For a man driven by honor, he behaves peculiarly: he kills an unarmed man, assaults the helpless, executes his friends, collaborates with the enemy, and, although women seem unable to resist him, the price of their adoration is inevitably subjugation. Only with the commandant are the roles reversed: the price of Pasqualino's sexual surrender is, also, oppression, and it is this very reversal which generates the scene's comic tension. The truth is that Pasqualino has always been a suitor, not a lover. It is only once, in the courtroom scene, that Pasqualino expresses anything akin to love. When he gazes at the sweet young girl he will eventually marry, we know we're in the presence of con-

ventional romance, but, even then, we sense no real feeling to back up the gesture.

For the most part, Pasqualino is defined by his sexual encounters in the most depersonalized fashion, as seducer, voyeur or rapist. The women with whom he becomes sexually involved are strangers, their faces hardly shown. They are seen only momentarily in flashbacks, and almost all of them are fashioned into grotesque creatures, as if to excuse Pasqualino's inability to love any of them. All we are told is that he is sexually prepared for his encounter with the Nazi commandant, when his deluded self-image as a lover makes him think he can instantly transform a Nazi murderess into a sex-starved girl with all the willpower of an eighth sister.

Even here, in an all-too-predictable, familiar, sadomasochistic scene which could easily have come from a porn magazine, Wertmüller makes Pasqualino's delusions go unchecked.

The commandant becomes a gross, engulfing Valkyrie, a female master who hates and emasculates men. Once again, Wertmüller gives us a cartoon character and a farcical situation which in no way extends Pasqualino or enriches us, but merely makes us hope for his victory over this Nazi. In short, Wertmüller's original use of the macho image pays off; we can't help but root for that earliest empty image to prevail. Because Wertmüller suggests the commandant is a lesbian, Pasqualino's inability to satisfy her doesn't damage his erotic self-image. Physically abused and verbally insulted, he still manages to come away with his macho intact. After he proves himself a man, the commandant lashes out at him: "You subhuman . . . Mediterranean . . . larva, you found the strength . . . for an erection. That's why you'll survive . . . and win in the end . . . You subhuman worms with no ideals or ideas . . . and our dreams for a master race . . . unattainable." Though the commandant's view of Pasqualino is accurate, the scene still manages to keep him *simpatico* by presenting him as a humiliated hero, and by having the truth told by a character too hideous to be believed.

In never showing us more than surface, by offering no insight into Pasqualino's character, Wertmüller omits the only possible grounds on which Pasqualino could be more than a "Mediterranean worm." We are given almost nothing of his emotional and

psychological history, little of his relation to the community. Instead, she tells us only that he is a simple man, a sex clown who believes himself in control of his existence, but who is swept away by events he cannot anticipate, understand or alter. By making him bigger than life in the comic strip sense, the film denies him any larger human dimension.

In the same way that Wertmüller gives bits and pieces of personality rather than a full character, she treats places and events clinically, building up serial images, presumably culminating in a full final impression. Ultimately, the images remain isolated fragments, interesting only as pictures, communicating no sense of historical or emotional reality. Wertmüller's concentration camp reality, for instance, is composed of barracks, compounds, latrines and barbed wires; the camp's prisoners are seen being beaten, hanged, whipped and shot. All are stock images, which have been exploited many times over. The only unusual touch comes as two prisoners wander among a courtyard full of corpses, playing a waltz on their violins, but this scene is a Grand Guignol artifice, not a meaningful symbol.

•

Thus, our ultimate choice of responses to the concentration camp is as limited as our choice of responses to Pasqualino: we see him only as destructive and ignorant of himself and of history, yet we know, indeed we hope he will survive, as the Nazi commandant declares, precisely because he has no ideals or ideas. Ultimately Wertmüller presents us with a man who has lost his only definitive characteristic, his comic mask, and has adopted the anarchist's view of the future: "Soon we will be killing each other for an apple." To this Pasqualino adds his own Mussoliniesque conclusion of life: "I want kids . . . lots . . . twenty-five . . . thirty. We've got to defend ourselves. There's got to be lots of us!"

Incapable of plotting anything other than self-defense, Pasqualino is actually no wiser or more ethical in the last scene than he was in the first. Although he had been exposed in the camp to political concerns by Francesco, and by the Spanish anarchist (Fernando Rey), he still cannot conceive of political solutions and has no concern for humanity in general. When we last see him, his new life in Naples and his

instinctive drive for *lebensraum*, his living space, are, if anything, more totally self-centered than before.

Pasqualino is, at best, a sexual manipulator, at worst a murderer, a Capo of history, but due to Wertmüller's cleverness and Giannini's appeal, what I suspect most viewers come to feel for him is a blending of pity and admiration. After all, he has endured his trials and emerged with an undaunted desire to live. Pity and admiration are a fairly conventional response to an abstract condition, to seeing people generally hurt by life, whereas, what we should feel in any film which portrays a character is concern for a particular life, which we have seen shaped and manipulated by specific circumstances and feelings.

Wertmüller's error is not only in trying to pass off a shell as a viable tragic character, in manipulating us into expending emotion on a vacuum. She turns Pasqualino into a ventriloquist's dummy worthy only of a few easy laughs, instead of true human attention. Such an attitude betrays more than a little contempt on her part, an elitist disdain that runs throughout a film dealing with the lower classes.

Given her undeniable talent, her vivacity, energy and sense of detail, Lina Wertmüller would seem to be one of the few contemporary directors who could have made an authentic film about the process by which a human being is turned into a caricature. Instead, "Seven Beauties" is about a caricature who remains a caricature, a poor fool who finally can be dismissed without much thought. At a time when television, popular literature and mass-market films continually crank out mediocre portraits of forgettable men and women, I regret that so gifted an artist as Wertmüller wasted this chance to create a character more worthy of our attention, and a film which would insist that a human being, any human being, cannot, indeed must not, be so easily dismissed. ∎

1976 Mr 7, II:1:4

VINCENT, FRANCOIS, PAUL AND THE OTHERS, directed by Claude Sautet; screenplay (French with English subtitles) by Jean-Loup Dabadie; Claude Neron and Mr. Sautet, based on the novel "La Grande Marrade," by Mr. Neron; produced by Raymond Danon; director of photography, Jean Boffety; music, Philippe Sarde; a co-production of Lira Films (Paris) and President Films (Rome), distributed by Joseph Green Pictures. Running time: 113 minutes. At the Regency Theater, Broadway at 67th Street, and D.W. Griffith Theater, 59th Street near Second Avenue. This film has not been rated.

Vincent	Yves Montand
Francois	Michel Piccoli
Paul	Serge Reggiani
Jean	Gerard Depardieu
Catherine	Stephane Audran
Marie	Ludmilla Mikael
Lucie	Marie Dubois
Julia	Antonella Lualdi
Colette	Catherine Allegret
Jacques	Umberto Orsini

By VINCENT CANBY

"Vincent, François, Paul and the Others," Claude Sautet's new French film, is about the sustaining friendship of three middle-aged, middle-class men whose lives in almost every other respect are failures.

Vincent (Yves Montand) is separated from his wife, losing his mistress and in the process of going quietly bankrupt. François (Michel Piccoli) is a society doctor whose wife sleeps around with his tacit, exhausted approval. Paul (Serge Reggiani), a successful newspaper writer, has been unable to bring himself to finish the definitive World War II novel for almost 20 years.

•

Every Sunday afternoon, Vincent, François, Paul, as well as a younger comrade named Jean (Gerard Depardieu), with their wives and mistresses, meet at Paul's country house. The friends drink, argue, play football, eat. Usually they reassure one another, but sometimes they explode in impotent rage. The failure of one is often intolerable to one or more of the others.

On the Sunday afternoon that opens "Vincent, François, Paul and the Others," the flames from a pile of burning leaves set a tool shed on fire. For a few minutes there is pandemonium in the yard. Someone remembers a cylinder of cooking gas in the shed. There is the danger of an explosion. Mothers pull their children away. One man goes into the shed and finds the cylinder (which turns out to be empty).

The fire is put out amid a lot of laughter and joking and good humor. At the same time we realize that something terrible could have happened — something irretrievable. The menace has been contained, at least for the moment.

Mr. Sautet, a director who is highly thought of in France, is a film maker about whom I have very mixed feelings. It's not only that he regards the bourgeoisie with solemnity unrelieved by any humor, but also that he seems as fascinated by the quality of their houses, the cut of their clothes, the make of their automobiles and the decibel range of their stereos as by the state of their emotional lives. Our envy of the good things of their lives competes with our sympathy and sometimes squashes it flat.

Of the three Sautet films I've now seen, "Vincent, François, Paul and the Others" is the most successful in keeping a decent balance between these interests. Though the director indulges his taste for fancy photography — romantic, shimmery images often shot through windshields or as mirror reflections—the film is haunted by a genuine feeling of menace barely contained, of love that's run out, of futility, which have the effect of defining the meaning of friendship. It's not love, but it's better than nothing.

Mr. Montand is fine in the key role, his face seeming to collapse from middle age to old age in the course of the film. Mr. Piccoli, too, gives a strong performance as the doctor, though we never know as much about him as Mr. Sautet thinks we do. As the youngest member of the group, Mr. Depardieu is forceful and funny, though we suspect that his life will not — ultimately — be much different from those of his friends: barren but well-upholstered.

Yves Montand

The women are largely décor since the film is, after all, about friendship not love, though Stéphane Audran has one superb scene. It's mostly one long, agonized reaction shot when Vincent, floundering from one false hope to another, asks her to reconsider their separation and divorce.

It's curious that friendship, something that is so important in all our lives, is so difficult to dramatize effectively. Perhaps that's because in our romantic way we assume it to be some lesser breed of relationship, one that, exécpt in war or on the football field, must always be suspect. In this ornate but thoughtful film, it is taken seriously.

"Vincent, François, Paul and the Others" opened yesterday at the Regency and D. W. Griffith Theaters.

1976 Mr 8, 32:1

CONFRONTATIONS, directed by Rolf Lyssy; written by Mr Lyssy and George Janett; photographed by Fritz Maeder; edited by George Janett; music by Arthur Paul Huber. In German with English subtitles. Released by New Yorker Films. At the 68th Street Playhouse, Third Avenue. Running time 115 minutes. This film has not been rated.

David Frankfurter	Peter Bollag
Wilhelm Gustloff	Gert Haucke
Frau Gustloff	Marianne Kehlau
Doris Steiger	Hilde Ziegler
Zvonko	Wolfram Berger
Rabbi Frankfurter	Michael Rittermann

By RICHARD EDER

Like Oran in Camus's "The Plague," Zurich is sick. It is sick with the sickness of history: apathy and disconnection while horrors take place all around. Just over in Germany, Hitler is putting together a formidable method out of madness.

"Here it is like living under the rim of a cheese dish," a Zurich Jew says, trying in vain to stir up his fellow Jews at a kosher restaurant. They are alarmed but calm; optimistic not from evidence but from need. They worry, they eat, they joke.

In "Confrontation," which is being shown at the 68th Street Playhouse, the Swiss director Rolf Lyssy films numbness virtually in physical form, as if it were architecture or statues.

Into this numbness of the normal comes the abnormal agent. He is Frankfurter, a Yugoslav Jew who leaves his medical studies in Germany when the pressures begin to build up and seeks a haven in Switzerland. He finds companions, a girlfriend and peace; or at least he would have peace if he didn't also have an extraordinary sensitivity to evil in the air. The evil is Nazism.

Frankfurter has a wasting illness that requires numerous operations. Mr. Lyssy preserves the ambiguity of the irony: Is Frankfurter's sensitivity a part of his illness, or is it sanity, and sanity a kind of illness in a sick world?

•

Frankfurter notices symptoms and is obsessed by them. He notices the headlines in a Zurich Nazi paper; he notices the swastika in the lapel of a passer-by. He retreats from his friends and from his studies, and one day he buys a gun, goes to the house of a local Nazi leader and kills him. He is arrested, tried and jailed.

Mr. Lyssy has made a highly intelligent movie but perhaps not a very successful one. He has adopted a flat and deliberately uninflected style, which has some hint of the work of Jean-Marie Straub. The sequences move rapidly, abruptly, bitten off at the end, and almost without transitions. This is effective, in fact; what does not work so well, and turns an original and disturbing film into something of a political pamphlet, is the long trial scene.

•

Mr. Lyssy wants to show the imperviousness of the mechanisms of society to genuine moral questions. He lays out in full the speeches of counsel—the state prosecutor, the Nazi lawyers representing the widow, the old defense lawyer who reads endlessly from articles about Nazism in an attempt to justify his client.

They are boring, they are mechanical, and they miss the moral point that is mutely reflected on the face of Frankfurter, magnificently played by Peter Bollag. It is not just evil that is banal, the film suggests, but good, or at least the narrow kind of good that society conceives itself as upholding.

The trouble is that this banality, this thickness is not merely stated or suggested. It plays on and on in the courtroom until we, like some of the courtroom public, feel like getting up and leaving.

Here too, of course, Mr. Lyssy makes his point; we show a callousness that could spawn new monsters if we, like those in the courtroom, get bored with the mumbled reading-out of Nazi atrocities. Except we are not in a courtroom; we are at a movie. Our moral obligations are vastly different. Our freedom is different.

•

It is too long, it is hard to take, and the ending pulls it out of shape. But on the way Mr. Lyssy accomplishes some remarkable things. There is a marvelous, laconic scene, for instance, showing Jews in an old-age home in Germany. Through the windows come the chants of a Nazi rally. The old men feebly discuss Hitler; is he a real danger or a momentary thing? Finally one patient says simply, "They'll elect him Chancellor." He collapses tiredly onto his pillow and suddenly the rambling conversation becomes tragic.

1976 Mr 9, 26:1

IMMORAL TALES (Contes Immoraux) four short films directed by Walerian Borowczyk; screenplay (French with English subtitles) by Mr. Borowczyk; music, Maurice Le Roux; produced by Anatole Dauman; distributed by New Line Cinema. Running time: 90 minutes. At the Fine Arts Theater, 58th Street between Park and Lexington Avenues. This film has been rated X.

TIDE

Julie	Lise Danvers
Andre	Fabrice Luchini

THERESE the PHILOSOPHER

Therese	Charlotte Alexander

ERSZEBET BATHORY

Erszebet Bathory	Paloma Picasso
Istvan	Pascale Christophe

LUCREZIA BORGIA

Lucrezia Borgia	Florence Bellamy
Pope Alexander VI	Jacopo Berinizi
Cesar Borgia	Lorenzo Berinizi

By VINCENT CANBY

Walerian Borowczyk's "Immoral Tales," the four-part French film that opened yesterday at the Fine Arts Theater, is a nice old-fashioned erotic film.

By saying nice and old-fashioned I don't want to be condescending to a film that featuers simulated sex and such undisguised fascination for the female nude. I mean to distinguish "Immoral Tales" from such hard-core nonsense as Gerard Damiano's "The Story of Joanna," whose essentially clinical appeal is ludicrously interfered with by the fake-fancy production values, and from souped-up, soft-core junk like Roger Vadim's "Charlotte" and Russ Meyer's "Supervixens," which are successively silly, vicious or vacuous.

•

Mr. Borowczyk, a Polish director who makes films in Poland and France, was first represented here by "Goto Island of Love," a pale gray, very arid political allegory, which was shown at the New York Film Festival in 1969. His "Immoral Tales" is a whole different thing, the work of a talented film maker who examines his obsessions as he enthusiastically, often solemnly, indulges them.

Mr. Borowczyk is fascinated by women, perhaps just a little afraid of them, and amazed by all of the erotic possibilities they present. "Immoral Tales" has almost nothing to do with love and everything to do with lust, and with the male-female transactions in which the female is usually dominant. She may not be the only game in town anymore but she is the best.

The four stories that make up "Immoral Tales" display a true Victorian gentleman's appreciation for the forbidden, especially when it takes a lot of trouble to get at. Not in years have you seen a film where so much time was spent pulling things up or down or in undoing buttons, bows, belts and ties of assorted purpose.

Mr. Borowczyk also shares with many European Roman Catholics an appreciation for the erotic attractions of Christian symbols. They are, indeed, so powerful in "Therese the Philosopher," the second of his four tales, that no thoughtful parent would allow an innocent daughter to enter a church even on a sight-seeing tour.

"Therese" is reportedly based on the true story of a young maiden in Normandy who in 1890 was, in the words of a local journal, "disgracefully raped by a vagabond." According to Mr. Borowczyk, the maiden in question had earlier been even more successfully abused by her own imagination fired by her readings from "The Stations of the Cross."

The film's first tale, "Tide," is a contemporary joke about a young man obsessed by his pretty young cousin's virginity, which, in a very particular way, he manages to take by so studying the tide tables that he successfully strands himself and his victim on a Normandy rock when the tides come in.

"Erzsebet Bathory," the third tale, is about the notorious 17th-century Hungarian countess who ravaged the countryside for young maidens in whose blood she took her beauty baths.

Though the one bath we see looks like tomato juice, the tale is elegantly set, costumed and represented (acted would be too formal a word to describe what the performers have done). Paloma Picasso, the late Pablo's daughter who plays the countess, has a magnificent figure and a face as fully beautiful as her father's drawings from his classical period.

"Lucrezia Borgia," the last tale, is also the most complex. It's a fantastic and satiric view of the family life of the Borgias—Lucrezia, her father (Pope Alexander VI) and her brother Cesar, the Cardinal, who join together to do saucy things behind the altar once services are over. That family knew how to stay together.

1976 Mr 11, 43:1

KILLER FORCE, directed by Val Guest; directed by Michael Winder, Mr. Guest and Gerald Sanford; produced by Nat and Patrick Wachsberger. Released by American International Pictures Inc. At DeLuxe Showcase Theaters. Running time: 100 minutes. This film has been rated R.
Webb .... Telly Savalas
Bradley .... Peter Fonda
Lewis .... Hugh O'Brien
Clare .... Maud Adams
Chilton .... Christopher Lee

By RICHARD EDER

This was a passable adventure picture about some crooks trying to smuggle diamonds from a formidable defended South African mine. Then someone hit it with a load of moral ambiguity, and it all caved in.

Twenty years or so ago there was a great fad for wine cookery. The idea floated over from Europe: the execution — literally — was thoroughly American. Pour wine, cheap wine, on any old mess. Pour it on TV dinners. The result was gourmet cooking.

Nowadays moral ambiguity—also Europe-born—has trickled down into cheap action films. It swamps them. It's all right to have a switch or two—a hero who turns out to be a skunk or a villain who is really working for the March of Dimes. But with much more moral complication than that, the attention is sidetracked from the action—the film's whole purpose in the first place—and focused relentlessly on the characterization. Since there isn't any, you sink.

For about half of its length, "Killer Force," which opened at Showcase Theaters yesterday, is a bumpy but entertaining story about a mine security agent, played by Peter Fonda, assigned to penetrate and foil the efforts of an outside gang to break into the mine camp and steal diamonds.

Mr. Fonda has a girl (Maud Adams) who loves him and a boss (Telly Savalas) who hates him. He has a mystery to crack: Someone inside the camp is working with the robbers.

There is some excitement at the start, and the security precautions at the diamond mine are interesting and perhaps authentic. Mr. Fonda's

tendency to languid skittishness is held in check for a while by a beard and a few good lines.

The unmasking of the inside man at the mine manages to be a surprise: Unfortunately, it also wrecks the movie's framework. It would be difficult to say who wins out in the end; the good guys or the bad. It would be even harder to care.

In the role of camp security chief, Mr. Savalas is a curiosity. His face is designed expressly for television. On a small box you miss nothing of his exaggerated features and expressions, even when the reception is bad. On a movie screen he looks like an enlargement.

1976 Mr 11, 43:1

FILMS BY KEN JACOBS: Lisa and Joey in Connecticut, January, 1965: "You've Come Back!" "You're Still Here!" (28 minutes, 1965); "Excerpts From the Russian Revolution" (31 minutes, 1969); "Urban Peasants: An Essay in Yiddish Structuralism" (filmed in the 1930's and 1940's, released 1975, 52 minutes) and "Nissan Ariana Window" (18 minutes, 1969). At the Whitney Museum of Modern Art, Madison Avenue and 75th Street. Through Tuesday.

By A. H. WEILER

As an esteemed avant-garde moviemaker and teacher (Harpur College), Ken Jacobs illustrates independence and a provocative personal style in the four films ranging from deceptively simple home movies to 3-D that opened at the Whitney Museum yesterday. That this is an uneven, occasionally self-indulgent program, does not essentially detract from the overall professionalism evident in the largely affectionate treatment of most of his subjects.

Having spent some 20 years at his craft, the 43-year-old film maker who most notably emerged from the underground with his 1969, feature-length variations on the 1906 short "Tom, Tom, the Piper's Son," again is most effectively evoking the past through solicitous usage of someone else's original material in the 1975 entry, "Urban Peasants: An Essay in Yiddish Structuralism."

●

Mr. Jacobs's personal home movie, the 1969 "Nissan Ariana Widdow," is an 18-minute color fragment by comparison. While this is also silent, his varied, uncluttered vignettes of his nude, pregnant wife and, later their infant daughter, classically capture often all-too-fleeting moments of togetherness.

The family also is the central theme of the silent, 1965 "Lisa and Joey in Connecticut." But it is slightly muddied by the intercutting of a vintage Mickey Mouse cartoon and a diffuse, jumpy concentration of objects and paintings in the home of the principals. His approach may

be arty but the love of the young mother, father and their little boy is both real and occasionally touching.

List the 3-D "Excerpt From the Russian Revolution" as an exercise that is more confusing than gratifying. It may be innovative. But the need for a moviegoer to use a plastic filter to view a continuous panorama of a snow-covered suburban landscape and middle-class homes to the off-screen accompaniment of an anonymous lady's dulcet description of the raptures of the boudoir from "The Sensuous Woman" is more monotonous than revolutionary. In this case, aural sex and minimal three-dimensional effects are palpably mismated.

1976 Mr 11, 43:1

ROBIN AND MARIAN, directed by Richard Lester; screenplay by James Goldman; produced by Denis O'Dell; executive producer, Richard Shepherd; music, John Barry; director of photography, David Watkin; editor, John Victor Smith; a Ray Stark–Richard Shepherd production, distributed by Columbia Pictures. Running time: 112 minutes. At the Radio City Music Hall, the Avenue of the Americas at 50th Street. This film has been rated PG.
Robin Hood .... Sean Connery
Maid Marian .... Audrey Hepburn
Sheriff of Nottingham ....Robert Shaw
King Richard .... Richard Harris
Little John .... Nicol Williamson
Will Scarlett ....Denholm Elliott
Sir Ranulf .... Kenneth Haigh
Friar Tuck ....Ronnie Barker
King John .... Ian Holm

By VINCENT CANBY

Robin Hood has grown somewhat stocky with age. His beard is graying. He's still vigorous, but physical combat now requires more effort, and the satisfactions of winning are fewer. King Richard the Lion-Hearted, always an ambiguous hero-figure, has gone quite mad, his

love of battle turned into simple, uncomplicated blood-lust. Maid Marian, abandoned by Robin when he took off with Richard on a Holy Land crusade, first tried suicide, failed, then turned to God. She is now Mother Jennet, the abbess.

Twenty years after the end of the legend we all remember, an exhausted Robin, accompanied by Little John, returns from his wars abroad to Sherwood Forest, which has discreetly overgrown in the way of an unused, untended Central Park. Though still not exactly a true wild wood, the old trees, the old clearings, the old hiding places have all but disappeared.

That's the story thus far. So begins "Robin and Marian," the curious and contradictory new film directed by Richard Lester and written by James Goldman, which completes a story that I'm not sure many people want completed. Being a mixture of adventure, spectacle, gag comedy, drawing-room comedy and romance, "Robin and Marian" is even more of a confusion of inspirations than Mr. Goldman's "The Lion in Winter," which was first of all a tightly constructed play.

Yet "Robin and Marian," which opened yesterday at the Radio City Music Hall, is ultimately most appealing as a story of mismatched lovers who found too little too late. I doubt very much whether Robin Hood-as-senior-citizen will hold much charm for purists, including children, but I found its love story moving enough to bridge those moments that don't work, when the bickering between Robin (Sean Connery) and Marian (Audrey Hepburn) sounds foolishly suburban

(She: "You didn't write." He: "I don't know how") and when the demands of a plot must be met. The film depends almost entirely on the presences of Mr. Connery and Miss Hepburn to generate responses that are not otherwise supported.

In his preface to the paperback edition of the screenplay, Mr. Goldman reports on an early lunch with Mr. Lester where the director, after highly praising the screenplay, said that he had not read it yet, but that he had been told about it. The idea of picking up the story of Robin and Marian 20 years later does sound good, but it's one of those good ideas that require a lot more work if it's going to be more than a gag. "Robin and Marian" never quite makes up its mind.

The opening is superb. Robin and Little John (Nicol Williamson) and a few tired soldiers are ordered by King Richard to take a desolate French castle for its nonexistent treasure. The landscape is barren. The ideals are gone. Even the catapult doesn't work properly. Mr. Lester's manner of debunking romantic myths is made up of equal amounts of cruelty and slapstick, which are often the same thing.

Once the film gets to Sherwood Forest, though, the contradictions become apparent. There is a lot of athletic rigamarole about saving Marian's nuns from the Sheriff of Nottingham (Robert Shaw) intercut with the reconciliation of Robin and Marian, whose 20-year religious habit isn't so strong that she cannot forget it almost immediately in a clover field.

Audrey Hepburn, Sean Connery and Nicol Williamson in "Robin and Marian"

Neither Miss Hepburn, whose last appearance was in "Wait Until Dark" in 1967, nor Mr. Connery is actually ready for a geriatric ward yet, but their screen presences—the intensity of the images they project — are such that we are convinced that their late-August love is important and final, something that I'm not sure Mr. Lester knows how to cope with.

The director is more comfortable debunking old myths than he is in implementing new ones, yet the last section of "Robin and Marian" is virtually the stuff of grand opera. That it succeeds is remarkable, and in succeeding, it makes the glib manner of a lot of the earlier business almost intolerable.

•

Mr. Williamson has a comparatively thankless role as Little John. He does what can be done but he is, by nature, too big and idiosyncratic an actor to be playing faithful-friend-to-the-hero. He would have been an interesting Robin. Mr. Harris does his best work in a long time as the mad Richard, and Robert Shaw makes a Sheriff of Nottingham who's more humane than is absolutely necessary. Denholm Elliott is wasted in the role of Will Scarlett.

"Robin and Marian" is a hybrid movie, one that seems embarrassed by its feelings; yet it works best when it admits those feelings, when it plays them straight.

1976 Mr 12, 26:1

THE FILMS OF BRUCE BAILLIE. Five short films made in the 1960's by the American avant-garde director. ALL MY LIFE, MASS FOR THE DAKOTA SIOUX, CASTRO STREET, QUIXOTE and VALENTIN DE LAS SIERRAS. At the Film Forum, 15 Vandam Street. March 11-14 and 18-21 at 7:30 P.M.

By RICHARD EDER

Bruce Baillie makes avant-garde films with the gifts of a painter and the objectives of a sign painter. A visual sensibility and a delicacy in balancing images founder in a determination to hammer these elements into sweeping and often crude social messages.

In five films, made in the 1960's and being shown this week and next at the Film Forum, Mr. Baillie gives evidence both of his talent and the distance by which it outruns his artistic judgment.

•

As for the talent, take the first of the five films, a tiny and beautiful piece entitled "All My Life." The soundtrack has Ella Fitzgerald singing the song that gives the film its name. The camera travels along masses of brilliant red flowers growing against a fence under a blue sky.

It is very simple, and it would simply be a pretty thing to watch except that

Mr. Baillie has struck upon a visual correlative of the singing that goes much further.

The flowers are wild and unkept, amid weeds and overgrown scrub, in the back lots of a slum somewhere on the edge of town. They are dusty flowers. It is obvious that there is broken glass and bits of rusty tin in the underbrush. Flaming red and a tenement roughness: Ella Fitzgerald has been remarkably seized and set to film.

The two major pieces in the program, "Mass for the Dakota Sioux" and "Quixote," show moments of the same lilting use of the camera. Both pictures are roughly similar: long assemblies of bits and pieces of American life, some seen plainly; others blurred, abbreviated or superimposed for complexity of mood. They are aimed in their whole at conveying a sense of emptiness, of cheapness, of violence, of futility.

"Mass" is done with more subtlety; and for the first third or so it promises to embody hauntingly the lament of Chief Sitting Bull that serves as epigraph: "No chance for me to live, Mother." But it goes on too long. There is a sameness and, by

now, a triteness in juxtaposing advertising slogans, battleships firing, politicians making speeches and high school parades and filming it darkly and blurrily to suggest oppression.

•

"Quixote" is much the same, but much longer. Forty-five minutes is excessive for this continual hammering of weighted images. And the weighting is even cruder. Mr. Baillie shoots a Rotary-style banquet and intercuts the diners' faces with views of pigs at a trough. Or he shows a high-school basketball game.

Now the movements in a basketball game, however little interest you take in the sport, are by any conceivable judgment buoyant, cheerful and often of considerable grace. Mr. Baillie edits and chops so it is all sharp elbows and gaping expressions. It becomes jerky and violent.

Similarly we see a horse on the ground, apparently dying. No, it is not dying; it is getting up. Projected at a certain speed and cut in a certain fashion life becomes death. Out of this, all possible messages can be made; and when they are, none commands belief or respect.

1976 Mr 12, 26:1

FILM VIEW

VINCENT CANBY

Robin's Back and Marian's Got Him

Nobody may have told us, but all of us probably have a pretty good idea of what happened to a favorite character after the curtain came down, the story ended, or the legend ran out. Little Orphan Annie, I'm sure, grew up to be the second woman ever admitted to the police force of Wichita, Kansas. She remained unmarried and though her relations with Daddy Warbucks had been cool during her teen years, she stood by him when he was tried and convicted on charges of mail fraud in the late 1950's. Her patience finally gave out when, two years after Daddy was released from Federal prison, she learned that he had invested her small annuity in a phony retirement village on Key Biscayne, Fla. Daddy died a month after his indictment was handed down. Annie is now a private investigator.

Some others? Well, the Hardy boys jointly held the Pontiac franchise in Southport, Conn., until Joe died of a coronary and Frank retired to Phoenix. Blanche DuBois, following her long hospital stay, took a job running a gift shop at Stone Mountain National Park. Dink Stover, a lush, lived his last years as a quarrelsome bore at the Yale Club in New York. Winnie The Pooh came apart in an automatic washer, unattended.

It is the firm conviction of screenwriter James Goldman ("The Lion in Winter") that Robin Hood and Maid Marian lived happily ever after in Sherwood Forest for no more than a year and that Robin, apparently bored by domesticity, then took off on a crusade to the Holy Land with Little John, both of them in the service

of the stalwart King Richard the Lion-Hearted.

At the beginning of the new film, "Robin and Marian," written by Goldman and directed by Richard Lester, 20 years have passed. Richard, now mean and somewhat mad, in love with battle for its own sake, is staggering home at the slowest possible pace accompanied by a small band of followers, including the still loyal but disillusioned Robin Hood and Little John. In a ridiculous siege of a castle undefended by one old man, Richard is finally killed, hit in the shoulder with an arrow thrown by the old man's hand. There is no further way that Robin and John can stall the inevitable. They return to Sherwood Forest and Nottingham and, of course, to Marian, better known now as sister Janet, the abbess.

"Robin and Marian" is a very appealing, contradictory sort of movie, a spectacle and a satire that is most winning when it is being most straight as a sombre love story. It hasn't the force of the two eccentric characterizations of Katharine Hepburn and Peter O'Toole that carried "The Lion in Winter," but it has the wit, strength and sheer presences of Sean Connery

Connery and Hepburn: more complex than Flynn and de Havilland

and Audrey Hepburn in the title roles, lovers who, as Goldman has written them, are part grand legend, part suburban statistics. Says Marian at one point, trying to keep the edge out of her voice, "But you didn't write." Robin (sweetly): "I don't know how."

How one reacts to this sort of demythologization, I suspect, depends entirely on how seriously or romantically one takes the legend of Robin Hood. The basic contradiction of the film is that Goldman and Lester want to play the legend two ways at once, for laughs and as one of history's great romances. The surprising thing is that they succeed as often as they do, and that they have made moving a last scene that might have been more appropriately scored by Verdi than by John Barry, the man who gave us the James Bond theme.

Satirical spin-offs of existing works are always easier to do than straight extensions of something as ephemeral as a legend. Thackeray had a fine old time with his

"Rebecca and Rowena," in which he set us straight about the married life of Ivanhoe, something that Scott had discreetly chosen not to do. Mel Brooks cheerfully carried forward two generations the chronicle of poor old Dr. Frankenstein, for marvelous effect. In each instance, the work, though satirical, was suffused with appreciation for someone else's material.

In writing the screenplay for "Robin and Marian," however, Goldman had—as far as I can tell—no particular work, no defining style, from which to take off. Was he thinking Ben Jonson, Alfred Lord Tennyson, Michael Curtiz or Walt Disney, all of whom have contributed to the Robin Hood legend? Goldman and Lester have had to create their own original material that has then been carried forward in their spectacular post-script.

●　　●　　●

There are moments when Lester's sense of realism, his choice of visual details, is at odds with Goldman's. Lester's view of 12th-century England is filled with images of cruelty and squalor, but the talk that goes on within these frames often sounds like Broadway drawing-room comedy. "Robin, are you ever going to grow up?" asks a petulant Marian. Lester's appreciation for the gag, curiously, works better: two knights, reaching for the same rock, crack their metal helmets together, or a soldier, part of a serious siege, gets a finger pinched in the catapult, which, as a topper, can't quite get the rock to the castle wall.

"Robin and Marian" is at its best, though, when it plays its love story without smart talk or gags, largely through Miss Hepburn's magnificent face, which time has touched just enough to make us aware of the waste that Marian's last 20 years represent. Why did Robin abandon Marian to go off on the crusade? Was he simply not serious? Was that first love not that great? The question is never answered satisfactorily. It may be that Robin actually means it when, early in the film, someone wonders if Marian might still be alive. Robin appears jolted. "Marian?" he says. "I haven't thought of her in years. . . ." The line gets a laugh but later, when we see the damage that the separation has caused, it's no longer quite so funny.

Connery's Robin is a fine old hulk of a man who is approaching the end of the road, his illusions gone, but still dependent on form and style to give his life meaning. "'The day is ours,' Richard used to say," Robin tells Marian towards the film's autumnal close. "And then it was tomorrow, but where did the day go?"

Lester and Goldman never try to convince us that Robin, Marian, Little John and the others have lost a kind of sylvan Camelot. Their world was never easy or perfect; more often it was cruel, arbitrary, without point. The strength of "Robin and Marian," which was once titled "The Death of Robin and Marian," is in its story about two former lovers who discover—in themselves and in each other—something new, more valuable than what had existed before. The characters that I still identify with Errol Flynn and Olivia de Havilland have become remarkably more substantial and complex with the years.

1976 Mr 14, II:1:1

Movie Madness

By WALTER GOODMAN

The subject of obsession is enjoying a flurry on movie screens around town, where obsessed persons of diverse era, gender and nationality are being carried inexorably to their appointed ends. The newest of these films, "Confrontation," focuses on a young Jewish medical student who is forced out of Germany in the mid-

1930's and works himself up to killing a Nazi bigwig in Switzerland — a real-life event.

Meantime, in another movie house, another character out of real life, Adele H., daughter of V. Hugo, is pursuing over continents a young soldier who won't give her the time of day. And elsewhere,

Walter Goodman is the assistant editor of the Arts and Leisure section.

"Confrontation"—too honest?

an entirely fictional, unmistakably mad New York City taxi driver is trying to make a connection of some sort with somebody, a loving connection if possible, a bloody one if need be.

Writers down the ages have been drawn to obsessed characters, through whom they might explore the underside of human nature, the odder twists of the human mind. Their appeal for contemporary filmmakers, I suspect, tends to be less profound and somewhat deceptive. Screenwriters and directors seem to believe that obsessed persons, driven by some uncontrollable force to carry out some extreme action, are much more exciting subjects for a screen treatment than more ordinary folk who pass their lives doing mainly unextreme things.

a credible movie madman. Raskolnikov on screen is apt to be reduced to rolling his eyeballs.

What, assuming that the screenwriter is not a Dostoyevsky of the cinema, are the moviemakers to do? Well, there are tricks of the director's and actor's trades which can be used to fill in for the deficiencies of a script—but, as the films currently on show demonstrate, these are not likely to be up to the job.

For example, if any actor could carry off the role of Travis Bickle, the driven taxi driver in Martin Scorsese's well received film, it would be Robert De Niro. He pumps so much intensity and nervous energy into the part that he almost compensates for the neglect of the scriptwriter, Paul Schrader, to

Filmmakers are having trouble getting deranged minds in focus

But the screenwriter who takes on the job of dealing with a deranged mind is confronted by a considerable challenge—how to explore an internal world through the use of external events. There may be a cautionary lesson in the fact that Dostoyevsky, the creator of those underground men who continue to haunt the modern consciousness, has not proved easy to translate to the screen. His sort of fevered investigations of feverish minds, done over many pages in which characters develop fitfully out of many moments of rationality and madness, passion and withdrawal, out of many introspective passages, are not available to the filmmaker. Whereas the novelist can work from inside out, the camera must rely on externals; considerable ingenuity is required to create

write it. We know little more about the man at the end of the movie than after the first few minutes, during which De Niro establishes, just by the way he glares into his rear-view mirror, that he ought not to have a chauffeur's license.

Instead of trying to probe behind De Niro's eyes, Schrader succumbs to what might be called the psychopathetic fallacy: if a character is presented as cracked in the first scene of a movie, then anything he does thereafter, no matter how peculiar, is permissible, since, after all, he is cracked and cracked people do peculiar things. But the case is exactly the opposite. Psychopaths in fact have fewer alternatives open to them than most people and behave in more, not less, predictable ways.

Since the thoroughgoing

madman is almost certain to be less complex and thus less interesting than the folks next door, strict fidelity to the clinical details of his madness would, in all likelihood, make for a tedious movie. Instead, we find Scorsese's taxi driver traveling not directly along the road down which his own devils would lead him, but being detoured by the moviemakers need to put on a lively show. When Travis gets out of his cab to court a pretty political campaign worker, everything turns fake, from his too charmingly forward approach to their too awkward date at a porno movie to their insipidly ironic final encounter. Travis's behavior is meant to express a reaching-out for human contact, but his actions can only be wholly believable to those who are willing to believe anything of a crazy man.

Scene after scene of this film, which captures so much surface realism, rings false, as the director's skills are employed repeatedly to distract us from the writer's failures. We are meant to conclude that Travis Bickle is driven to murder because he has been rejected in love. That case is not only imposed unsubtly, from without, but given the premise of the film, it's wasted effort since Travis, presented as nuts to begin with, is assumed to be capable of murder from the start. The big climactic scene of mayhem, in which he makes use of all the arms and all the martial arts in his repertory, as any TV fan might have predicted he would, is not out of character, but is so overdone for the sake of impact, that it becomes a parody of Charles Bronson in "Death Wish."

"Taxi Driver" has its rewards. In addition to De Niro's performance and a fine cameo appearance by Peter Boyle, there are cameraman Michael Chapman's steamy images of New York as hell city—the hookers and hustlers plying the summer streets, a busy taxi garage in the west 50's, cabbies hobnobbing at the Belmore cafeteria. But for reviewers to build up Scorsese's set pieces, compelling as they are, into a significant statement about the city or about the workings of a man's misshapen mind requires a willingness not only to accept but to abet.

Now, as suggested, the makers of "Taxi Driver" were faced with a dilemma. If they had not come up with some diversions, if they had been faithful to Travis's obsession, they would have turned out a film as boring

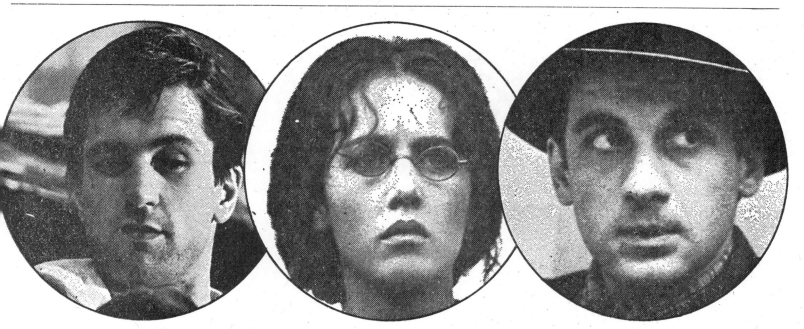

Three obsessed characters: De Niro in "Taxi Driver," Adjani in "Adele H.," Bollag in "Confrontation"

as "Adele H." Francois Truffaut steers his monomaniacal heroine safely past the whirlpool of artificially generated excitement only to leave her stranded on the rock of ennui. His visually stunning film shimmers in the memory. To watch Isabelle Adjani's face for a couple of hours is far from a painful experience—but except for viewers who share Truffaut's fascination with beauteous women possessed by dark impulses, it is not interminably irresistible.

Our heroine wanders through this gently flowing picture, becoming from sequence to sequence ever more dazed and disheveled. By the time she reaches the tropics on her journey from Nova Scotia, her gown is in frightful condition. A novelist might have explored the inner workings of Adele's progressive retrogression. The best Truffaut comes up with is to give the poor thing bad dreams, a sign of directorial desperation.

Constrained perhaps by the fact that he has taken it on himself to tell a true story, Truffaut resists the temptation to which Scorsese succumbs of having his subject do little numbers for the sake of our attention spans. Instead, he makes a gesture at "explaining" Adele's problems by tracing them, via those bad dreams, to her guilt over the death of a sister and to her relationship with her father, Victor Hugo. The latter effort will be persuasive only to those who believe that being the child of a great man is enough to account for any sort of craziness. Instead of setting up reverberations, the portentous but unrevealing

references to Hugo are distracting — dust in our eyes.

Of the three current films, only "Confrontation" makes a plausible try at explaining the obsession of its protagonist. David Frankfurter is not presented as irredeemably batty from scene one. Compared to Adele H. and Travis B., he is a model of mental health—yet, like them, he is driven to commit an extreme act. Why? The film engages that question, and so engages us. Watching a "normal" person take an "abnormal" path turns out to be more intriguing than watching mad people act mad.

We see, through the eyes of the Jewish student, the takeover of Germany by the Nazis and their impingement on his own life when he is hooted out of classes. Although the film of necessity relies on externals, here, unlike in "Taxi Driver," the events flow naturally out of the situations in which Frankfurter finds himself.

We can share his growing awareness of the brutal meaning of Nazism, his growing need to do something, his gradual focusing on a target. Director and co-writer Rolf Lyssy tells the story in a quiet way, without the fireworks of Scorsese or the lyricism of Truffaut. It's an old-fashioned sort of movie; and partly because of this, it has a sort of integrity missing in the other, more polished but less restrained films, an effort to be true to the real case from which the story is drawn, to get into the character who has been created out of that case.

One wants to believe in the student because he is

worthy of belief, yet the puzzle remains. What was special about him that while others shrugged or grumbled, he alone could be aroused to kill a man he had never laid eyes on? A key to his action, if one can accept it, is his conviction that he has a fatal illness. Yet even if that belief is added to the provocations we are shown, this extraordinary murder does not suit the David Frankfurter represented here. In Peter Bollag's listless performance he is placid to a fault, barely reacting to significant events. A succession of succinct, understated scenes, such as the one in which he sees a couple of stormtroopers push to the ground an elderly Jew, doesn't quite build to his murder of a man whom he has only read about in the newspapers. Whatever went on in David's mind has not been effectively transposed to the screen.

As if aware that his film's central question is not being convincingly addressed, Lyssy changes point of view midway. He moves abruptly outside the character and shows us David's trial for murder, evidently taken from official records and made up of formal charges of guilt, pleas of mitigating circumstances and some stagey courtroom business. It's a startling switch, and one's feeling of not being sure what the movie is about is heightened at the very end when the real David Frankfurter, now of advanced years and living peaceably in Israel with his family, is introduced in order to deliver a few words about the need to resist despotism. Having set out to chart the develop-

ment of an obsession, rather than merely present its symptoms, "Confrontation" finally settles for something easier. Still, it has given us matter to mull along the way.

Although "Confrontation" is more adult than "Taxi Driver" and more provocative than "Adele H.," it is not destined to attract the kind of attention lavished on those films. Rolf Lyssy is not a virtuoso, and virtuosity is what unleashes the big critical adjectives, even when it is used to conceal rather than reveal. The virtuosos behind the camera, like Scorsese and Truffaut, and some of their admirers in front of the screen seem so caught up in the process of moviemaking today, so infatuated with technique, that they are losing touch with the relatively normal lives out there which serious movies were once thought to illuminate or comment on or at least resemble. Our movie nuts may be in the grip of an obsession. ■

1976 Mr 14, II:1:1

MY MICHAEL, an Israeli film in Hebrew with English subtitles. Directed by Dan Wolman, written by Mr. Wolman and Ester Mor; produced by Shlomi Cohen; director of photography, Adam Greenberg; music by Alex Cagan. Presented by Alfred Plaine. At the Festival Theater. Running time: 90 minutes. This film has not been rated.
Michael .... Oded Kotler
Hanna .... Efrat Lavie
Aunt .... Dina Rollkof
Student .... Moti Mizrachi
Landlord .... Israel Segal
Duba .... Iliza Loria

By RICHARD EDER

To call "My Michael" a modest film is to exaggerate. It is downright imperceptible. This Israeli import, which opened yesterday at the Festival Theater, is made with seriousness and some skill.

Its depiction of a shut-in, obsessed marriage is a vehicle for exploring a fenced-in, surrounded quality in Israeli society. But we are more aware of the vehicle's own airlessness and monotony than of the landscape it is trying to take us through.

Based on the novel by Amos Oz, "Michael" is the story of Hanna, a young teacher who marries an archeology student in Jerusalem. The marriage is impetuous; neither has any money, and they move into a cramped apartment.

It is more than the apartment that is cramped, however. They are nice, educated young people; full of tolerance and good will. But life closes in on their marriage. She has a baby, he has to go on with his studies; time and space seem to dry up on them.

It is an arid, reasonable marriage. Michael, the husband, escapes into stolidity and a flirtation with a fellow student. Hanna fantasizes about being ravished and carried away. Not by pirates or airline pilots, but—this being Israel—by Arabs.

"What are we living for?" she asks her husband at one desperate moment before she drifts utterly away. "People don't live for anything: they just live," he replies.

Now all this could be a wry accusation that Israeli society lives amid Arabs while it avoids all psychological contact with them. The formal message is that such a posture has to be paid for by a loss of reality, by a drying-up of life. As a child, Hanna had two Arab children as her best friends; as an adult she dreams about naked bodies, black mustaches and—to pin down the nationality beyond doubt—checked keffiyehs floating out behind.

So costumed, the imaginary sequences are ludicrous.

Efrat Lavie and Oded Kotler in a scene from "My Michael"

But ludicrousness is not the problem with "My Michael." In fact, done as a slapstick comedy about an Israeli housewife with Arab fantasies, it might have been not only funny but pointed as well.

The problem is the film's deliberate attenuation; its deadpan development of married banality in a painfully banal style. Every possible soaper cliché is brought out: the announcement that she's pregnant; his sulky mopping of the floor while she sits, sulky and distended; his efforts to study while the baby cries; his flirtation; her sexual teasing of a young boy.

True, a number of these scenes are done with economy and charm. There is good acting, particularly from some of the older characters with small parts.

The performance of the principals is less satisfying. As Michael, Oded Kotler is solid, as the part requires, but no much else.

Efrat Lavie, who plays Hanna, is more effective. But she plays her part from beginning to end with one fixed expression of gloom. Her gloom is a frail and pretty thing to see, but after a while, in its fixity, it makes the whole movie look underexposed.

1976 Mr 16, 29:2

THE SCAR OF SHAME, directed by Frank Peregini; written by David Starkman; produced by Sherman Dudley; director of photography, Al Liguori; a production of the Colored Players Film Corporation of Philadelphia. Running time: 90 minutes. At the Whitney Museum of American Art.
Alvin Hillyard ....Harry Henderson
Louise Howard ......Lucia Lynn Moses
Spike Howard ......Norman John Stone
Lucretia Green ....Ann Kennedy
Eddie Blake ....William E. Pettus
Miss Hathaway ......Perm MacCormick
Mr. Hathaway ....Lawrence Chenault

By VINCENT CANBY

"Scar of Shame," which opened yesterday at the Whitney Museum of American Art, is the first program in the museum's two-part series devoted to the early black American cinema—films made in the silent and early sound eras, by black film makers as well as white, for black audiences, that otherwise saw themselves portrayed in movies only as servants or buffoons.

Produced in 1927 by the Colored Players Film Corporation of Philadelphia, "Scar of Shame" is a fascinating footnote to the story of black aspirations in this country. Though produced on a limited budget, it is technically no better or worse than hundreds of conventional "white" silents of the period. As history, however, it is a devastating reminder of the obstacles that black Americans had to overcome before they could begin to identify the goals of social progress.

A little card at the beginning of "Scar of Shame" promises that the theme of the film will be the effects of environment, how "the childhood training" and "the companions" of one's youth determine whether or not one spends his "useful time on this earth" in pursuit of "the higher things in life." All this sounds harmless enough, but the film that follows demonstrates a system of contradictions that have only recently—in the last 30 years—been hooted and jeered into oblivion.

"Scar of Shame" is the story of a poor, beautiful slavey named Louise who is saved from her wicked stepfather when a rich young concert pianist, Alvin Hill-

yard, marries her. A few months later Louise learns that Alvin has never told his socialite mother of his marriage, and Alvin, who is meant to be a sympathetic character most of the time, explains, "caste is one of the things mother is very determined about, and you don't belong in out set."

In a fight with a gangster, Alvin accidentally shoots Louise in such fashion that, according to a newspaper account, it "left a hideous scar on her neck which completely marred her beauty." Alvin is sent to jail. Louise takes up the life of a night club hostess, wearing a scarf to hide her hideous scar, which could easily be covered by a small Band Aide. Alvin escapes, falls in love with a girl of his set, and Louise, distraught because she still loves him, commits suicide, paving the way for Alvin's future happiness.

•

It's necessary to go into the plot in this detail to appreciate the odd things the film is doing as it attempts to meet the fantasy needs of its black audiences while providing them with uplift.

The black caste system we see is simply an extention of the white burgeoisie's: white is perfect, light-skinned is acceptable, black is ugly. The values and the manners, "the higher things in life," have been borrowed from white society with no questions asked. Louise's sin is not that she does anything wrong, or that she had evil companions in her childhood, but that she wasn't a member of Alvin's set.

Poor Louise simply didn't measure up. Which is something that ghetto audiences of the time apparently understood and accepted. Militant

blacks have subsequently expressed outrage at this sort of nonsense, but that may be to overlook some of the positive effects of such films. Among other things, they portrayed a black society that was educated, had its own lawyers, doctors, intellectuals and artists. At a time when Hollywood was still getting laughs out of the amount of fried chicken eaten by little Farina in the Our Gang comedies, these fantasies and distortions were comparatively healthy ones.

1976 Mr 18, 50:1

SCARAMOUCHE, directed by Enzo Castellari, written by Tito Carpi and Mr. Castellari; produced by Federico Aicardi; director of photography, Giovanni Bergamini; released by Avco Embassy Pictures. At Deluxe Showcase Theaters. Running time: 93 minutes. This film has been rated PG.
Scaramouche ....Michael Sarrazin
Josephine ....Ursula Andress
Napoleon ....Aldo Maccione
Whistle ....Giancarlo Prete
Danglar ....Michael Forest

By RICHARD EDER

It is the time of the French Revolution, more or less. A mob surges by and the cam-

era shows faces in animated close-up. One face looks strained; the shot lengthens and we see it is being carried on a pike.

Only a few minutes into "The Love and Times of Scaramouche" and we become that face. It is our brother in pain. This tedious, jumpy, inept effort to do still another comic take-off on historical swashbucklery is as bad as impalement.

Scaramouche—no kin to Sabatini's dashing character—is a ropy womanizer who gets tangled up in a plot to assassinate Napoleon. There are battle scenes, bedroom scenes, pratfalls and uninterrupted clowning, all of it coarse and witless. The acting is abysmal; the photography suggests a bad case of air pollution.

Ursula Andress is the best-known figure in this mostly Italian production. She is wooden, but still manages to look good when she takes her shirt off, and to make everything else look cheap.

"Scaramouche" is being shown at Showcase Theaters.

1976 Mr 18, 51:4

FILM VIEW

VINCENT CANBY

Why Wilderness Films Are Wildly Popular

The most passionately political films being made in this country today have nothing to do with government scandals or cover-ups by highly placed public officials who goofed. They contain no references to Watergate, Mao, détente, the CIA, Fanne Fox or even the Bicentennial. They make no pleas on behalf of the underprivileged. They certainly aren't revolutionary threats from some underfed underground cooperative. Instead they are what the writers of irate letters to movie critics call "pure" entertainment, which is usually a euphemism for mindless. They haven't the slightest interest in current affairs or social problems, or, at least, none that shows. They are totally devoid of sex and the only violence shown is nature's way. Apparently because of these things, they are films that parents by the carloads are dragging their children off to see in the fond belief that innocence is being simultaneously protected and served.

I'm talking about the new "wilderness" movies with titles such as "Brother of The Wind," "The Life and Times of Grizzly Adams," "The Adventures of the Wilderness Family," "Challenge to Be Free" and "The Bears and I," all except the last (a Walt Disney production) having been financed and distributed outside the auspices of the major Hollywood companies. The films began appearing a year or so ago as a trickle. The trickle has now become a clearly defined wave that would, if I read the films correctly, carry us back to the glorious 19th century, when a man could be free to live life as he saw fit, when women, blacks, Indians and new arrivals

Patrick Wayne hears the call of the wild in "The Bears and I."

with strange accents knew their places, when there was no pollution, when government was small and taxes even smaller, when all it took to get ahead was faith in God and a willingness to work.

To see one of these films is, perhaps, to enjoy a harmless adventure. To see two of them is to begin to recognize a mode of operation. To see three is to understand that a seemingly sentimental longing for old-fashioned values is, on the other side, a furious cry of frustration and rage with political change, especially with a society that questions the morality of the-survival-of-the-fittest as a national policy. When you come out of one of these films, you're likely to think the country started going downhill the day the Federal Government took over the mails. The "wilderness" films not only glorify private enterprise as individual effort; they endow it with mythic powers.

Here are some of the so-called plots:

In "Brother of The Wind," a hardy old man, in remarkably fine shape for his years, has turned his back on civilization to live as a hermit in the wilds of the Canadian Rockies. Most of the film is devoted to his raising four orphaned wolf puppies who, when they are fully grown and out on their own, are more slavishly grateful to the old man than any human children would be.

"The Life and Times of Grizzly Adams" is about another loner, a man who, when falsely accused of a crime, abandons his small, motherless daughter and strikes out for the wilderness where he learns he can communicate with animals more meaningfully than with people. This fellow raises an orphaned grizzly bear cub. When, years later, his name is cleared, the man elects to stay in the wilderness where the animals are his friends and look up to him, much as if the wilderness had become his private plantation.

"The Adventures of The Wilderness Family" is one of the few such films to acknowledge that its theme is escape from contemporary society. It's about the members of a family who attempt to pioneer today in the Pacific Northwest where they are befriended by some of the fauna (black bears, raccoons) and set upon by others (grizzly bears, a pack of wolves). A Westchester reader has told me that her children were scared out of their wits by one of the animal fights in the film. Though this is a pretty feeble movie, it's the only one of the

five to feature a complete family unit (mother, father, two children). They may be as anti-social as the heroes of the other films, but they are anti-social *together*.

"Challenge To Be Free," directed by the 77-year-old Hollywood filmmaker Tay Garnett ("China Seas," "The Postman Always Rings Twice"), stars Mike Mazurki as a legendary Alaskan character named Trapper, a hermit who exists happily in his mountain cabin in the enriching society of wolves, bears, moose, elk, rams and a live-in lynx. When corrupt civilization intrudes in the persons of some law officers, Trapper accidentally shoots one to death, which triggers a cross-Alaska chase in which Trapper is repeatedly saved by a faithful old timber wolf, whose life had earlier been saved by Trapper. In the pious (and cost-cutting) voice-over narration that is used in most of these films, we are told, "Circumstances had placed a real friendship between them (Trapper and the wolf), the kind only understood by those born to stay free."

Disney's "The Bears and I," the one wilderness film that looks as if it cost more than $5 in out-of-pocket expenses, is about a Vietnam vet, Patrick Wayne (John's son), who goes into the Rockies to live alone and find himself, which he does while raising three orphaned bear cubs. (After seeing almost two of these films, one begins to wonder how wilderness animals survive without saintly hermits to raise the homeless young.) This is also the only wilderness film to acknowledge that there may be some point in social order when the Vietnam vet settles a territorial dispute between some local Indians and the head of the Parks Commission.

Any one of these films seen separately might seem innocent enough, but seen altogether they begin to shape up as propaganda, carefully calculated to give the public the kind of escapism it wants, while calling for a return to the old laissez-faire economy where a man was free to be as paternal as he wanted to people (animals) less fortunate than himself. The true rigors of wilderness existence are never emphasized, while the joys of man-beast relationships are rather overstated.

In an article in the Village Voice Feb. 23, J. Hoberman reported at some length on the elaborate methods employed by Sun Classic Pictures, described as "a part of the right-wing Schick conglomerate" and the producers of "Grizzly Adams" and "Brother of The Wind," to research the market before putting any of its films into release. I would suspect that much more money is spent in hard-sell promotion of these films than is ever spent in making them. There is nothing wrong in that except that the films are so technically tacky one would wish a little more had been spent on production. It just may be, however, that the patrons who turned "Grizzly Adams" into one of the biggest box-office hits last year may have been brainwashed by market research without knowing it. I wonder, too, if they realize that the films' romantic notions about wilderness life are actually the fantasies of people with a very particular political message to sell. Political liberals, so often credited as running Hollywood, seldom get their messages across so loud and clear—and so profitably.

1976 Mr 21, II:1:7

BROKEN STRINGS, directed and produced by Bernard Ray; screenplay by Clarence Muse; an International Roadshow release. Running time: 60 minutes. At the Whitney Museum of American Art.
Arthur Williams .... Clarence Muse

By VINCENT CANBY

In most of the films he made after his debut in 1928, Clarence Muse, a black actor whose face is much more familiar to us than his name, played faithful servants of great dignity but of little dramatic interest except as functions in the white plot. They were exceptions. In "So Red the Rose" (1935), Mr. Muse was cast as the leader of some rebellious slaves. In the 1931 version of "Huckleberry Finn," he played Jim, though the accents of the rural South did not come easily to the college-educated actor.

●

In "Broken Strings," the second program in the Whitney Museum's two-part series devoted to the black American cinema, Mr. Muse plays an immensely dignified concert violinist whose career is interrupted because of injuries suffered in an automobile accident. The film, made in 1940, opened at the museum yesterday.

"Broken Strings" is not much as cinema but it is important as history, one of the last examples of a film produced independently for the ghetto market that wanted to see blacks taken seriously as members of the middle class. Most of the values promoted by "Broken Strings" are simply variations of those of the dominant white culture, yet there are moments that express the beginnings of an awareness of black identity.

In addition to being of interest in connection with the rise of black consciousness, "Broken Strings" has subsidiary value as a mirror image of white conventional pictures of the period. A lot of the conflict in the film concerns the older generation's outrage with swing music, a favorite device of 30's musicals and there is one little girl in the film who is the image of the Judy Garland who used to encourage Mickey Rooney to take their high school show to Broadway, where, as she predicted, it became a smash.

Mr. Muse, incidentally, survived to see the boom in the new black films, in 1972, he played a small role in Sidney Poitier's liberated "Buck and the Preacher."

1976 Mr 25, 41:1

JUVENILE LIAISON, a documentary by Joan Churchill and Nicholas Broomfield; produced by the British Film Institute. Running time: 101 minutes. At the Film Forum, 15 Vandam Street.

By RICHARD EDER

Sergeant Ray of the Lancashire Constabulary hasn't the remotest resemblance to the fictional English detective who wears disgust and weariness as elegantly as his tweeds. Sergeant Ray wears shiny dark jackets with ugly yellow squares, a white shirt, a greasy tie, hair slicked back and thinnish, a black leather coat that makes his bulk look brutal.

His disgust and weariness come out as violence, barely repressed and sometimes not even that; as cunning, quite unrepressed and showing through. He is the head of a three-member squad set up to deal with truant, shoplifting or otherwise unmanageable children in Liverpool. He is the central figure in a moving and distressing documentary, "Juvenile Liaison," being shown at the Film Forum, 15 Vandam Street.

It is a film that is far more intelligent than its viewpoint. This, in a documentary, is praise: It does not restrict the viewer to its own conclusions.

The viewpoint is clear enough. We see the sergeant, huge and menacing, cross-examine an 8-year-old Indian girl at her school. Her teachers say she has a consistent record of pilfering things from her schoolmates' bags and desks. Continually hinting that he can take her down to the police station if she doesn't tell the truth, he badgers her about an apple, about some missing pencils.

●

It is a painful sight: This big, ugly man reducing a frail and lovely little girl to incoherence and tears. And yet she is, as it turns out, a liar and a thief. She has produced, around her, all kinds of small chaos, small injustices: She has embedded them in the minds of the children around her. They have lost apples and pencils, the little securities of childhood, and have found no recourse.

The movie stresses the disproportion between the tiny miscreants and their large and strident pursuers. There is an immensely affecting scene where a policewoman snarls and scolds at a fat adolescent girl who has been shoplifting. She batters at her: Isn't she ashamed? Doesn't she think of her parents? Does she want a criminal record? The great balloon of a girl sits stolidly and silently and then, as the buzz-saw voice goes on, tears squeeze from her eyes. And she admits, most touchingly, to one real ambition: She wants to be a prison warden. "Not a chance," the policewoman says.

There are other, similar scenes. The filmmakers show the threat of brutality rather than real brutality, though at one point Sergeant Ray drags a 15-year-old boy — who has beaten his mother — out of bed by the hair.

The intended message is that the youth squad is a blind and cruel response by society to its errant children. Sergeant Ray's explanation — that by making a show of firmness, by making it clear to the children what will happen if they don't reform, some are saved from later, serious involvement with the law — is treated as a rationalization.

Maybe so. But as we watch these ill-prepared, harassed, unequipped, desperately tired officers go about their job, a troubling sympathy grows up for them. In these working-class, often fatherless homes, Sergeant Ray, coming from the same class, uses far more patience, far less violence than the fathers themselves might have used.

The sergeant and his colleagues believe in what they are trying to do, even though they have no illusions about their success. They are medical corpsmen, sent out to treat the wounds of social dismemberment with splints.

They are rough and sometimes mean, but they are also heroic. The film does not see the heroism, but it lets us see it. It sees the entrapment used by the police officers on the children; it lets us see the entrapment in which the officers find themselves.

In the harshest scene, Sergeant Ray feigns to arrest a little boy and sits with him in a jail cell to show him what it it like. The film stresses the child's terror and the barbarity of the device. But what we really see is two people in jail — the boy and the policeman — companions in frustration and helplessness.

1976 Mr 26, 21:3

MOSES, directed by Gianfranco De Bosio; screenplay by Anthony Burgess, Vittorio Bonicelli and Mr. De Bosio; produced by Vincenzo Labella; music, Ennio Morricone; director of photography, Marcello Gatti; editors, Gerry Hambling, Peter Boita, John Guthridge, Alberto Gallitti and Freddie Wilson; an ITC/RAI co-production, distributed by the Avco Embassy Pictures Corporation dunning time: 141 minutes. At the Ziegfeld Theater, 54th Street near the Avenue of the Americas. This film has been rated PG.
Moses .... Burt Lancaster
Aaron .... Anthony Quayle
Miriam .... Ingrid Thulin
Zipporah .... Irene Pappas
Dathan .... Yousef Shiloah
Joshua .... Aharon Ipale
Eliseba .... Marina Berti
Jethro .... Shmuel Rodensky
Princess Bithia .... Mariangela Melato
Pharaoh Mernefta .... Laurent Terzieff
Young Moses ...... William Lancaster
Young Moses ...... William Lancaster
Narrator .... Richard Johnson

By VINCENT CANBY

"Moses" is a movie that appears to have been made by the yard, a bargain-basement Bibical epic that can be cut and shaped to fit any need.

The film, which opened yesterday at the Ziegfeld Theater, has been put together from a lot of the same footage that went into the six one-hour "Moses" shows presented on CBS-TV last year with Burt Lancaster in the title role, with the Old Testament as source material and with additional dialogue by Anthony Burgess, Vittorio Bonicelli and Gianfranco De Bosio.

Because I did not see the television series, I don't know how much of the film duplicates the small-screen shows, though I assume there are certain obligatory scenes that appear in both versions. You can't very well do six hours of Moses on television and not get around to his Red Sea venture, which is one of the theatrical feature's noisiest and most tepid highlights.

¶The movie at the Ziegfeld makes C. B. DeMille's "The Ten Commandments" look like a work by Eisenstein. It is long and loud and so silly in some scenes that the piety in others is efectively denied. The screenplay covers the life of Moses from his birth and subsequent adoption by an Egyptian princess, to his death years later, after he had successfully led the Israelites to the land of Caanan.

¶At its best moments, the film's style is that of Kipling's "Just So Stories" adapted to Sunday school concerns. Thus we learn how the Passover feast came to be, and we are there when Moses more or less invents the Sabbath. The film displays some power when it demonstrates the ferocity with which Moses punishes the lawbreakers, including executions by stoning, some victims, by hurling others off a cliff, and by pouring molten gold into the mouth of some man who would have had the Israelites worship the golden calf.

These brief but vivid glimpses of a harsh, primitive world are softened and sentimentalized by the drab direction, the woodenness of most of the performances (except Mr. Lancaster's) and by dialogue that sounds as if it had been cut out of a failed Neil Simon play. Mr. Lancester, no longer in first youth, has the elemental physical and emotional strength to make a fine Moses, if this were a better film.

One accepts the childlike nature of Moses' people, who may witness their leader turning the Nile to blood on Monday and a rod into a serpent on Wednesday, but who still may wonder on Friday what he's done for them lately. What one doesn't accept is the language in which these doubts are spoken.

Says a petulant tribesman during the journey through the wilderness when water is running short, "You said you knew this place like the back of your hand." Moses: "Will you people never cease to complain?" Irritation is the spur.

This film, which is a coproduction of RAI, the ItalianGovernment-sponsored radia and television company, and Independent Television Corporation of England, a commercial company, was shot in Israel and Italy and has a cast of dozens and dozens, representing most races and creeds. The English Anthony Quayle plays Aaron, the Swedish Ingrid Thulin is Miriam, and the Greek Irene Pappas is Zipporah. Marinangela Melato, who has since become a star in Lina Wertmuller's films, has a small, sort of glide-on part as the princess who finds Moses in the bullrushes.

In addition to contributing to the screenplay, Gianfranco De Bosio is credited as the film's director, which I take to mean he was the film's traffic manager.

1976 Mr 27, 17:1

SKY RIDERS, directed by Douglas Hickox; screenplay by Jack Dewitt, Stanley Mann and Garry Michael White; based on a story by Hall T. Sprague and Bill McGaw; executive producer, Sandy Howard; director of photography, Ousama Rawi; released by 20th Century-Fox. Running time: 90 minutes. This movie has been rated PG.
McCabe .... James Coburn
Ellen .... Susannah York
Bracken .... Robert Culp
Nikolidis .... Charles Aznavour
No. 1 Terrorist.......... Werner Pochath
No. 6 Terrorist.................... ZouZou

By RICHARD EDER

Hang gliders are pieces of fabric stretched over a frame. Properly manipulated they travel for miles on the air currents, giving the person hanging beneath the sensation of pure birdlike flight.

The hang gliders in this movie fly as beautifully as swallows, but why use swallows to carry concrete?

The money spent on "Sky Riders," which opened yesterday at the RKO 86th Street Twin Two, has obviously gone on the gliding, the photography and the stunning backdrop of the Greek coast. Judging from the results, the scriptwriters and the actors seem to have worked for next to nothing.

The movie is about an American industrialist whose wife and children are kidnapped from their Athens home by a gang of political terrorists. They are taken to an abandoned monastery on a needle-shape crag.

The police can do nothing, but the wife's first husband, played by James Coburn, can. Pondering the problem, he sees a couple of crows flying overhead. His eyes widen, his nostrils dilate.

He finds a flying circus of hang glider riders. In just two or three days they teach him to glide, and he teaches them to fight. On a night of the full moon, they swoop in, and the moonlit swooping is authentic, difficult and lovely.

There is enough shooting for two civil wars, and the terrorists—who wear red T-shirts with terrorist insignia on them — are eventually chomped up. But nothing has happened to make us care much, one way or the other.

●

The dialogue, the motivations, the politics are cardboard. The acting is unalloyed lead. After the flying, "Sky Riders" is one long boring crash; as well as vice versa.

1976 Mr 27, 18:4

W.C. FIELDS AND ME, directed by Arthur Hiller; screenplay by Bob Merrill, based on the book by Carlotta Monti with Cy Rice; produced by Jay Weston; director of photography, David M. Walsh; editor, John C. Howard; music, Henry Mancini; distributed by Universal Pictures. Running time: 110 minutes. At the Criterion Theater, Broadway at 45th Street, Baronet Theater, 34th Street near Second Avenue. This film has been rated PG.

W.C. Fields ....Rod Steiger
Carlotta ....Valerie Perrine
Bannerman ....John Marley
John Barrymore ....Jack Cassidy
Melody ....Bernardette Peters
Dockstedter .... Dana Elcar
Ziegfeld ....Paul Stewart
Ludwig ....Billy Barty
La Cava ....Allan Arbus
Chasen ....Milt Kamen
Gene Fowler ....Louis Zorich
Claude ....Andrew Parks
Edward ....Paul Mantee

By VINCENT CANBY

In his 1937 review of W.C. Fields in "Poppy," Graham Greene wrote "To watch Mr. Fields, as Dickensian as anything Dickens ever wrote, is a form of escape for poor human creatures . . . who are haunted by pity, by fear, by our sense of right and wrong . . . by conscience. . ." This prize of escape is the major thing missing from the dreadful new film "W. C. Fields and Me." It holds up a wax dummy of a character intended to represent the great misanthropic comedian and expects us to feel compassion but only traps us in embarrassment.

"W. C. Fields and Me," which opened yesterday at three theaters, is based on the memoir written by Carlotta Monti, Fields's mistress for the last 14 years of his life. The book, written with Cy Rice, is gushy, foolish and self-serving, which is probably understandable.

To expect it to be anything else, I suppose, would be to look for the definitive analysis of the Cuban missile crisis in a memoir by a White House cook. Yet the movie needn't have been quite as brainless as it is. That took work.

●

First off, Bob Merrill, who has written either the lyrics or music (sometimes both) for some good Broadway shows, including "New Girl in Town," has supplied a screenplay that originally may have been meant as the outline for a musical. It exhibits a tell-tale disregard for facts and the compulsion to make a dramatically shapeless life fit into a two-act form. The mind that attends to this sort of hack business would cast Raquel Welsh in the title role of "The Life and Loves of Bliss Carman."

Then there's Arthur Hiller, a director who makes intelligent films when the material is right ("Hospital," "The Americanization of Emily") and terrible ones when the writers fail.

Most prominent in the mess is Rod Steiger, who has been got up in a false nose and dyed hair in a way meant to make him look like Fields, which he does (sort of though he reminds me much more of the way Fields's one-time co-star, Mae West, looked in "Myra Breckinridge." The exterior is pure plastic, though occasionally one sees a sign of individual life deep inside the two holes that have been cut out for the eyes.

●

The film opens in the 1920's in New York, when Fields was already a big Ziegfeld star, and closes with his death in California in 1946, at the age of 67, when he had become one of Hollywood's most celebrated stars. In between these dates "W.C. Fields and Me" attempts to dramatize—with no conviction—the complex, witty actor-writer as if he were one of his own ill-tempered, suspicious heroes with a suddenly discovered heart of gold.

Mr. Steiger reads all of his lines with the monotonous sing-song manner used by third-rate nightclub comics doing Fields imitations. He also speaks most of them out of the corner of his mouth as if he'd had a stroke.

Valerie Perrine, a spectacularly beautiful woman who may also be a good actress, plays Miss Monti, who, in this film anyway, is an unconvincing combination of intelligence, patience, fidelity, sportsmanship and masochism. Perhaps because the visual style of the entire film is more or less mortuous, Jack Cassidy, who plays a flyweight John Barrymore, wears the kind of makeup that makes him look dead several reels before he actually dies.

The movie contains two halfway funny moments: a scene in which we see Fields taking a broom to a swan that has trespassed his Hollywood lawn, and the sight of Baby Harold (based on Baby Leroy, one of Fields's toughest costars) staggering out of his set-side dressing room after Fields has spiked the kid's orange juice with gin.

1976 Ap 1, 28:3

NOT A PRETTY PICTURE, written, produced and directed by Martha Colidge. Photographed by Don Lenzer and Fred Murphy. At the Whitney Museum of American Art. Through April 11.

Martha .... Michele Manenti
Curly .... Jim Carrington
Anne .... Anne Mundstuk
West Virginia .... John Fedinatz
Mr. Cullen .... Hal Studer
Cindy .... Amy Wright
Brian .... Stephen Laurier

By RICHARD EDER

Martha Coolidge was raped on a high-school date. She grew up to become a documentary film maker, and now she has made a film about the rape.

"Not a Pretty Picture," which opened yesterday for 10 days at the Whitney Museum of American Art, is a strange work. It is two films: one is very poor and the other is complex, brilliant and somewhat unfocused.

The poor part—it is more than poor, in fact, it's awful—is the movie about the rape. A cast has been assembled to play out the story. Martha, played by Michele Manenti, is shown at a coeducational boarding-school; she is taken out on a date by Curly, a handsome, arrogant schoolmate; they go to his brother's apartment, conveniently empty, and he forces her to have sex.

●

The dialogue, the acting, the characterizations are so clumsy and amateurish that they make a true story seem fake and embarrassing. Miss Coolidge almost seems to have made it deliberately bad. She uses, for example, her real school roommate as one of the schoolgirls. But the woman is 28 or 29 and the others are in their teens, and the difference shows up ludicrously.

The more important and interesting part of the film is intercut into the "fictional" re-creation. Miss Coolidge films her actors rehearsing the scenes; she films herself directing them; she films the whole company discussing what they are doing and how they feel about it.

There is tremendous emotional force as well as ambiguity here. Miss Coolidge's rape scarred her badly, she says, and left her unable to have a full, trustful relation with men. And she films herself directing a violent re-creation of what she went through. We see her suffering as she works; we also get a suggestion that somehow she is working out her own violent feelings as the actor on the bed assaults the actress on the bed.

●

But it goes beyond this. The actress, Michele Manenti, was herself raped when a schoolgirl. As she rehearses, as she discusses her feelings real, remembered pain and humiliation come and go, blending with her concentration on her role.

And it goes even further. The actor, Jim Carrington, who plays the rapist, is Miss Manenti's boyfriend. The viewer gets the impression that he is her lover, as well. The violence he acts out—he admits wonderingly during one of the breaks—he really feels. Yet there are tenderness and love as well as anger and violence: After one particularly horrific scene Miss Manenti and Mr. Carrington embrace exhaustedly.

Miss Coolidge is plainly making the fiercest possible denunciation of rape. But her message includes a wrenching and difficult recognition of the complexity with which anger and love can blend in the sexual relationship.

There is too much failure for this to be anything but a badly flawed film. But in its best moments it is troubling, subtle and very affecting.

1976 Ap 1, 28:4

SALSA, a musical film directed by Jerry Masucci and Leon Gast; produced by Mr. Masucci; narration written by Mr. Masucci, Mr. Gast and Jeff Cahn; distributed by Fania Records Inc. At the New Embassy 46th Street theater. Running time: 80 minutes.

WITH Celia Cruz, Manu Dibango, Bobby Cruz, Jose Feliciano, Ricardo Ray, Ray Barretto, Willie Colon, Larry Harlow, Johnny Pacheco, Justo Betancourt, Santos Colon, Geraldo Rivera and others.

By RICHARD EDER

"Salsa" is an 80-minute record jacket.

Fania Records Inc., the biggest name in Latin American pop music in New York, has assembled a number of singers and musicians to perform their Caribbean rhythms—loosely known as "Salsa"—before some underendowed cameras.

Much of the material comes from a live performance at Yankee Stadium; other parts come from a concert in San Juan, P.R. The camera, often blinded by lights, goes back and forth from performers to the enthusiastic faces of the audience.

This is straightforward enough, and when the performances are particularly good, impressive. By all odds, the finest section is a seven-minute number, "Bemba Colora," by Celia Cruz. She is a Caribbean Ella Fitzgerald and Pearl Bailey all in one; she is an empress; she is magnificent.

There is also a subtle and powerful sax solo by Manu Dibango, a Cameroonian who has joined the Caribbean music world. Other numbers seem feebler.

The performers are linked by a pretentious narration, illustrated by old film clips, of how Latin music has always been caricatured and misunderstood by Hollywood. We get Desi Arnaz and Carmen Miranda and they are truly awful. The narration is done by Geraldo Rivera, and it is uninformative and unnecessary, though short.

"Salsa" is playing at the New Embassy 46th Street Theater.

1976 Ap 2, 26:1

Hungarian Work Opens Modern Art Series

By VINCENT CANBY

Kata (Kati Berek) is 42 years old, a widow and in good health. She is a self-reliant woman, not given to sudden enthusiasms or rash decisions. She has adjusted to circumstances over which she has no control and though she is not wildly happy, things could be worse. She might not have any lover at all, for example, instead of Joska, played by Laszlo Szabo, who once a week, is amusing and kind and attentive, and who has never once led her to think he would leave his wife and children for her.

"Adoption," which will be shown at the Museum of Modern Art today at 6 P.M. and Sunday at 8:30 P.M., is the measured, unsentimental story of what happens to Kata as she realizes there may be more to life than adjusting to outside circumstances. Kata decides she wants a baby and she does something about it.

The Hungarian film, directed by Marta Meszaros, is the first of 12 that will be shown at the museum between now and April 13 in the annual New Directors / New Films series, a project jointly sponsored by the museum and the Film Society of Lincoln Center.

"Adoption" is very much a woman's movie. Though its title has specific reference to Kata's actions after her lover refuses to give her a baby, the film has even more to do with surrogate relationships, particularly with the friendship that develops between Kata and a teen-age girl (Gyongyver Vigh) who has been put into a state home by her family. It is also about women without men (or with men who don't quite measure up) in a world still dominated by men.

The style is introspective,

The Cast

ADOPTION (Orokbefogadas), directed by Marta Meszaros; screenplay (Hungarian with English subtitles) by Miss Meszaros and Gyula Hernandi; director of cinematography, Lajos Koltai; music, Gyorgy Kovacs; produced by Hunnia Studio. Running time: 89 minutes. At the Museum of Modern Art, 53d Street, west of Fifth Avenue.
Kata .... Kati Berek
Anna .... Gyongyver Vigh
Joska .... Laszlo Szabo
Doctor.............. Dr. Arpad Perlaky

or, at least, as introspective as it is possible to be in a movie that does not attempt to crash through to the subconscious. In the center of the screen most of the time, in the close-ups favored by the director, is the fine, angular, expressive face of Miss Berek, who may remind you of Annie Girardot minus the mannerisms Miss Girardot has been using lately.

"Adoption," which is Miss Meszaros's fifth feature, never explodes with the unexpected insights that separate great films from good ones. It takes no exciting chances. Rather, it records the details of one woman's life with the kind of deliberate care and intelligence that one can recognize without being especially moved.

1976 Ap 2, 26:1

DUVIDHA (TWO FACES, INDECISION). Written, directed and produced by Mani Kaul. Photography by Navrozo. Based on a story by Vijayadan Detha. In Hindi with English subtitles. At the Museum of Modern Art, Today at 8:30 P.M. and Sunday at 6 P.M. With Ravi Menon, Raisa Padamsee, Hardan Shambudan and others.

Even well-informed moviegoers have the impression that there is only one name in Indian film making: Satyajit Ray. "Duvidha" will do nothing to change that impression. It is a folk tale, related with a mixture of pretentiousness and incompetence and with unmixed tedium. It is being shown today and Sunday at the Museum of Modern Art as part of the New Directors series. It is made by Mani Kaul. Viewers will look forward to Mr. Ray's next film.
RICHARD EDER

1976 Ap 2, 26:2

LIPSTICK, directed by Lamont Johnson; screenplay by David Rayfiel; produced by Freddie Fields; director of photography, Bill Butler; music, Michael Polnareff; editor, Marlon Rothman; a Dino De Laurentiis presentation, distributed by Paramount Pictures. Running time: 90 minutes. At Loews State 2 Theater, Broadway at 45th Street; and Loews Cine Theater, Third Avenue near 86th Street. This film has been rated R.
Chris McCormick .... Margaux Hemingway
Carla Bondi .... Anne Bancroft
Gordon Stuart .... Chris Sarandon
Steve Edison .... Perry King
Nathan Cartright .... Robin Gammell
Martin McCormick .... John Bennett Perry
Kathy McCormick ..... Mariel Hemingway
Francesco .... Francesco
Sister Margaret .... Meg Wylie
Sister Monica .... Inga Swenson

By VINCENT CANBY

"Lipstick" is what might be described as a glamour film about rape. Its victim is a

beautiful, hugely successful photographers' model, played by Margaux Hemingway, in real life a beautiful, hugely successful photographers' model who also happens to be Ernest's granddaughter.

The rapist (Chris Sarandon) is a young man who composes avant-garde music and worships the works of another avant-garde composer, identified in the film as Sean Gage. Sean Gage? I'm sure that's what he says, though why "Lipstick" hesitates to drop the name of John Cage, I've no idea.

It's certainly not because "Lipstick" is too discreet. It is, however, anti-intellectual in the ways that B movies always have been. The message of "Lipstick," if I read it right, is less about the physical and legal vulnerability of women than about the sexual hang-ups of eccentric young men who compose music with synthesizers and laser beams. The movie's subliminal message: Bring back the clavichord.

"Lipstick," which opened Friday at the Loews State 2 and Loews Cine Theaters, was written by David Rayfiel and directed by Lamont Johnson ("The Groundstar Conspiracy," "The Last American Hero"), a shrewd, knowledgeable but not very interesting director, who is touted for his fearless way with controversial subjects. "Lipstick" is occasionally violent and crude, and about as controversial as the March of Dimes.

The film appears to take rape seriously, though — the kind of rape in which the victim, who hasn't been permanently injured, must overcome the prejudices of a society that always suspects that such a rape victim got what she asked for. The only time "Lipstick" is believable is during the trial sequence when Anne Bancroft, appearing as the ferociously determined lawyer for the victim, presents the case not only for Miss Hemingway, but also for all women. It's almost like a training film, but it is effective.

For a little while, anyway. "Lipstick's" heart belongs to an earlier, simpler time. It's no accident, I think, that the heroine is presented as a good Roman Catholic with a priest for a brother. We thus know she is a good girl. Neither is it an accident that the rapist is a composer of what the movie clearly believes to be crackpot music, and that the climactic sequence—a second, even more vicious rape—occurs in a modern glass and steel building that, in a film like this, could be the architectural equivalent to "Sean Gage" music.

Mr. Johnson treats Miss Hemingway very gingerly. She's not much of an actress yet, and there are times he seems to be protecting her by cutting away to other actors, when one would expect the camera to stay on her. Mr. Sarandon, who won

an Oscar nomination for his small but effective role in "Dog Day Afternoon," does as well as can be expected with the role of the rapist.

The revelation of "Lipstick" is another Hemingway, first name Mariel, Margaux's 14-year-old sister, who plays her sister in the film. As the chief witness to the events within the movie, and its ultimate victim, she gives an immensely moving, utterly unaffected performance that shows up everything else as a calculated swindle.

1976 Ap 3, 19:1

MOON OVER THE ALLEY, directed and edited by Joseph Despins; photography, Peter Hannan; music, Galt MacDermot; screenplay and lyrics, William Dumaresq; a British Film Institute Production Board film. Running time: 104 minutes. At the Museum of Modern Art, 53d Street west of Fifth Avenue. WITH Doris Fishwick, Peter Farrell, Erna May, John Gay, Sean Caffrey, Sharon Forester, Patrick Murray, Lesley Roach, Basil Clarke, Bill Williams, Vari Sylvester, Joan Geary, Norman Mitchell, Leroy Hyde, Miguel Sergides and Debbie Evans.

If the artistic vision of "Moon Over the Alley" were as sharply focused as its camera, this British film, playing today at 6 P.M. and Monday at 8:30 P.M. in the New Directors/New Films series at the Museum of Modern Art, might merit some outright praise rather than the benign nod of acknowledgement that seems its proper due.

This is a film with a nice eye for a little piece of London life, centering on an aged rooming house abutting the alley of the title in what is said to be the Notting Hill section. The alley itself is the nightly resting place of a vagabond couple—he a music-playing simpleton; she an elderly woman named Sybil, given to sententiousness and song. The house is owned by a docile husband and a moody, tough German woman, whose teen-age son is in love with the local tobacconist' daughter

The roomers include a black couple with an infant, a reclusive old man with an unspecified interest in little girls, an Irishman who says he is trying to save up enough to transform his 17-year engagement into marriage and a young Californian who is willing to pay an excessive rent to sleep under the stairs because money doesn't matter—singing does.

In the neighborhood, there are pot-smoking hippies, squatters, violent youths, a homesick Indian convinced the world will soon end and the pub where Jack, the Irishman, and Jimmy, the black roomer, work behind the bar. In the world at large, forces are at work to demolish the rooming house and remake the neighborhood despite individual and collective protest.

From a purely pictorial standpoint, "Moon Over the Alley," directed and edited

by the Canadian-born Joseph (Chuck) Despins, and photographed in black and white by Peter Hannan, records its people, their lives and their neighborhood with neither sentimentality nor condescension. The look and the atmosphere are right.

But this film, with music by Galt MacDermot (of "Hair") cannot make up its mind what it wants to be—musical, social document or something that might be called a mystical, given the aptly named Sybil's efforts to impart fateful power to the full moon that is its chief symbol.

As a result, it can be said that some of the characters are interesting; some of the songs are not too bland, and some of the episodes are arresting. But, as a whole, "Moon Over the Alley" is pointless.
LAWRENCE VAN GELDER

1976 Ap 3, 19:1

'Wives,' Norway's Answer to 'Husbands'

"Wives," which will be shown at the Museum of Modern Art today at 8:30 P.M. and on Monday at 6 P.M., looks to be the Norwegian woman's answer to John Cassavetes's "Husbands." It's very much the same kind of movie—apparently the product of a lot of improvisation on the part of the cast with the encouragement of the director. Only the sex of its principals has been changed.

Like "Husbands" it's about the friendship of three people, in this case wives. The young women meet after 10 years at a school reunion, discuss (in guarded tones at first) their disappointments as wives, as women, as people, and then go off on the town on a genteel spree during which they pick up some men, get propositioned and, in liberated fashion, proposition back. At the end, they've reached a new plateau of self-understanding.

A museum program note says that the director, Anja Breien, and her three leading actresses didn't want to make a film that would moralize or preach, adding that "they promised themselves their film would not be yet an-

The Cast

WIVES (Hustruer), directed by Anja Breien; screenplay (Norwegian with English subtitles) by Miss Breien; directors of photography, Halvor Naess and Nils Raknerud; editor, Jan Horne; a Kommunenes Filmcentral-Norsk Film production. Running time: 84 minutes. At the Museum of Modern Art, 53d Street west of Fifth Avenue.
Mie .... Anne Marie Otterson
Holdrun .... Froydis Armand
Kaia .... Katja Medboe
Kaia's mother .... Noste Schwab

other intellectual exercise." It isn't. Rather it looks like an acting exercise, one that means a lot more to the performers than it does to us (which is also a fault of Mr. Cassavetes's films).

As in any improvisation by talented professionals, there are some moments that ring true. However, there are even more that don't, that have the ring of desperation as actors lurch from one semichoreographed bit of stagecraft to the next. The actresses are appealing and, though I sympathize with their concerns, I didn't believe one minute of the film they've put together.

"Wives" is being shown as part of the New Directors/New Films series sponsored by the museum and the Film Society of Lincoln Center.
VINCENT CANBY

1976 Ap 3, 19:1

FILM VIEW

VINCENT CANBY

Anyone Who Hates This Film Can't Be All Bad

Sooner or later, all bad movies declare themselves, not with an outright confession of incompetence but in a scene or a sequence of such compelling wrong-headedness that it amounts to the same thing. It's something that seems to happen spontaneously, as if the movie, having some small residue of self-respect, wanted us to know that it knows just how bad it really is. In "W. C. Fields and Me," based on the memoir by Carlotta Monti, who was Fields's mistress for the last 14 years of his life, this confession comes fairly early in the film.

●   ●   ●

We see how Fields (Rod Steiger), a Ziegfield star on Broadway, is wiped out financially by his business adviser and then must borrow money from his stooge, a dwarf played by Billy Barty, so that the two of them can take off in a broken-down flivver for Hollywood where Fields will try his luck. Once on the Coast, Fields and his friend set up housekeeping in a wax museum in a seaside amusement park. As gawking tourists push their way through the exhibits, Fields sits in a back room pounding out scripts. Their money is running low and there is a sense of desperation when Fields looks up from his typewriter to say, "This one's about a bank dick. . . . It's a sure sale."

That this incident appears to have little relation to fact is not important—according to Robert Lewis Taylor's biography, "W. C. Fields: His Follies and Fortunes," when Fields left New York for Hollywood in 1931 he was driving a brand-new Lincoln and carrying $350,000 in one-thousand dollar bills. What is important is the decision of the filmmakers (director Arthur Hiller and writer Bob Merrill) to set this mythical business in a wax museum, which is by way of announcing that this is very much the kind of movie they have made, and with a leading actor whose face looks very much as if it had been sculpted out of candle droppings.

Considering that the filmmakers were out to create a piece of fiction (and all movies are fiction, whether based on fact or not), what destructive force compelled them to use a wax museum as a setting? Even if it had some basis in reality, it would have been wiser to shift the location to, say, a rundown drugstore or maybe a rundown dentist's office, any place but a wax museum. But truth will out, and it comes out all over the place in this dreary exhibition of incompetence, beside which the recent "Gable and Lombard" becomes one of the towering achievements of world cinema.

In a curious way, though, "W. C. Fields and Me" represents another victory in the great comedian's battle with the Establishment, a locking of horns that began when he started out as a teen-age juggler before the turn-of-the-century and is still going on, nearly 30 years after his death on Christmas Day, 1946, aged 67. Fields, who distrusted women, children, producers, dogs, swans, doctors, lawyers, and anyone he needed, lived a life that totally defies easy or sentimental dramatization. He would have been pleased, I think, that this rip-off, whose profits (if any) he cannot participate in, should be such an embarrassment to everyone who contributed to it.

Though he was a brilliant comic actor, and almost equally brilliant as a comic writer, he was in his private life stingy, mean, bigoted, impossibly egotistic and suspicious to the point of paranoia, even in the recollections of those who not only admired him but loved him. It is one of the odd effects both of the Taylor biography, which is well written and affectionate, and of the Monti book, which is dreadfully written (with Cy Rice) and means to be affectionate, that Fields-the-man emerges as someone you might not want to know at all. It's possible to be informed and sometimes vastly entertained when reading about him in the Taylor book and especially in "W. C. Fields By Himself," a revealing collection of Fields's letters, notes, articles and scripts, edited by his grandson, Ronald J. Fields, and appreciate him for the complicated, prickly genius he was, always keeping the man at a safe distance. Which is just what the film fails to do.

"W. C. Fields and Me," with Steiger in his terrible make-up giving a third-rate nightclub imitation of Fields, has so little appreciation of Fields's genius that it allows us to watch Steiger attempt to do one of Fields's classic routines ("The Dentist") in a "Ziegfeld Follies" sequence. The movie also works hard but fails to give Fields emotional dimension in his dealings with the dwarf, with his drinking cronies Gene Fowler and John Barrymore and especially with Miss Monti (Valerie Perrine), who appears to be either a masochist or mentally deficient to have put up with Fields's treatment of her. As a record of his Hollywood career, the film also fails. It's total confusion.

The problem with the movie—and something I suspect Fields also would have appreciated—is that the real W. C. Fields exists entirely within his films. All we need know, all we want to know, all we can know is in that marvelous series of features and shorts, most of which were made in Hollywood after 1932. At its best, the movie, "W. C. Fields and Me," is superfluous; at worst it's misleading. It diminishes his eccentric talent.

Luckily, the great Fields films survive and are never very long out of circulation. Any two minutes of these films are worth an afternoon with fictitious speculations like "W. C. Fields and Me," which attempts to make comprehensible and humane a kind of misanthropy that is too dark and vicious to be treated so foolishly. The reason that Fields's comedies don't date is because they are as liberating as dreams, allowing us to experience his frustrations, furies and frauds without paying any price except laughter. We can respond with delight to his story about beating up Chicago Molly (in "My Little Chickadee"), to his triumphant encounters with Baby Leroy (in "It's a Gift"), and to his particular vision of family life (in "The Bank Dick"), simply because we aren't burdened with analyses or the sense of ultimate consequence that "W. C. Fields and Me" must—in its dumb way—deal with.

Post-script: the two best Fields books available are not biographies or critical studies but recreations of selected sequences, almost frame-by-frame, from some of his best films. "A Flask of Fields" covers the features and "Godfrey Daniels!" the shorts, not all by any means but enough to evoke the Fields humor as accurately as is possible outside a movie theater. Both books, edited by Richard J. Anobile, are available in Avon paperback editions.

1976 Ap 4, II:19:1

IN HORROR MOVIES, SOME THINGS ARE SACRED

By LEONARD WOLF

Horror-movie madness is in full bloom on TV screens, in movie theaters, at film festivals and on campuses around the country. Every major city seems to have its own chilling variation of TV's "Creature Features," and Hollywood is now at work on what will surely be one of next season's biggest blockbusters, "The Heretic — Exorcist II." At 12 o'clock tonight, the prestigious Los Angeles Film Exposition will conclude its "Midnight Monsters" series—"a tribute to the classic motion pictures that have brought fear to the hearts and minds of millions of American moviegoers" — while on the other coast each Tuesday, at midnight, The Yale Film Society, like many other such campus organizations, presents the eerie likes of "The House That Dripped Blood" and "Vampire Lovers" in its popular "Things That Go Bump in the Night" series.

What is there in the horror film that makes it such attractive fare? Why is there an endless stream of giant ants, creatures from black lagoons, vampires, homemade *homo sapiens*, wolfmen, brain-eaters, mad scientists, and voluptuous sacrificial victims flickering on our movie screens? It is easy enough to say that the films are overtly violent and covertly sexual and therefore give their audiences the twin thrills necessary for success in such ventures. But that answer, though partly true, fails to get at a special dimension of the horror films: the lurking religious content which gives many of them their special power to attract.

It seems bizarrely true that the cinema of horror provides its highly secularized audiences with their last—perhaps their only—opportunity to experience mystery and miracle as if they were *dreadful*; as if they were *aweful*. The great frenzies of chaos, creation, disobedience, disaster, solitude and evil which have been rendered vague or bland in the well-bred church and synagogue services of the 70's are restored to their terrifying proportions in the half-light of the movie theaters. Priests of the horror cinema still recite incantations that count; Satan, in his foul and gorgeous panoply, appears; sacrifices are still offered or refused; and men (or creatures) still die to save the world.

The spirit of the Crusades survives, quite literally, in the hundreds of films that have been based, however fuzzily, on Bram Stoker's 19th-century novel, "Dracula." These films invariably turn on the confrontation between one or another avatar of Dr. Van Helsing, the scientist-priest leading his band of pure young men into com-

Leonard Wolf is a professor of English and Creative Writing at San Francisco State University.

Culver Pictures

In addition to inspiring fear, Dracula satisfies the hunger for religious experience.

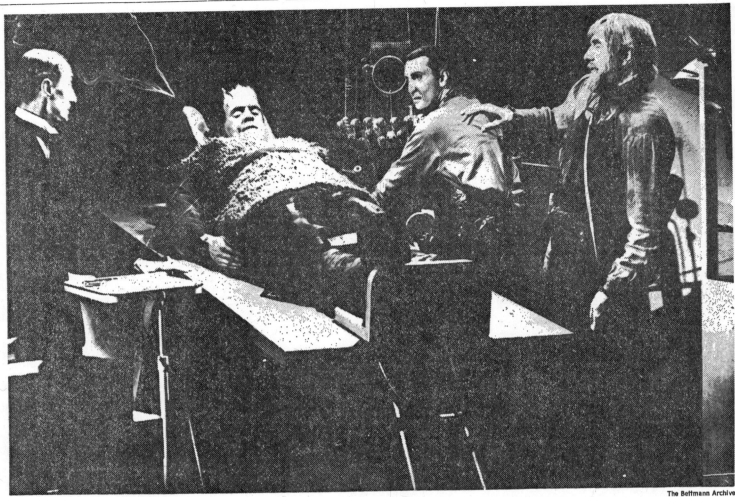

The Bettmann Archive

Frankenstein—"a touching resemblance to Adam awakening in Paradise"

bat against Dracula, the dragon-devil. Van Helsing and his knights triumph, but only with the help of the crucifix, holy water and the communion wafer. In the "Draculas" turned out by England's Hammer Films the vampire's flesh sizzles when touched by the crucifix and holy water. But of course, the sovereign enemy of the vampire is the holy light of the sun, which exposes the vampire for the living dead man that he is, a fiend who survives because he taints the souls of his victims.

The "Frankenstein" films depict the conflict between the ambitions of the scientist and the intellectual limits imposed upon man since his banishment from the garden of Eden; but there is a more poignant theme which recurs in these movies: the tragic innocence of Adam. All but the most feeble of the "Frankenstein" films ("Jessie James Meets Frankenstein's Daughter") have recognized how much the man-made Creature, once he is jolted into life by massive bolts of electricity, bears a touching resemblance to the traditional image of Adam

awakening in Paradise. It is hard to shake the spell of those moments when the huge, misbegotten hulk of stitched-together flesh stirs, opens his eyes and sees the bubbling fluids, the flashing lights, the white-robed scientists and their deformed assistant moving about under the cold, stone vaults of his birth chamber.

It is a moment far different from the one experienced by Adam when he opened *his* eyes in the garden made fragrant by his creator; and the rest of the film (it hardly matters which "Frankenstein" it is) is a bitter exploration of the disparity. The Creature, invariably ugly, innocent and powerful, stumbles through a world that is not equipped to deal with innocence. Though we concede the real world's need to destroy the monster, it is with regret that we consign him to his burning mill, his quicklime grave or to his tomb of ice. Even Adam, we remember, did not stand a chance in Paradise.

"King Kong"—the classic now being remade in Hollywood—is another audacious

jumble, this time of erotic fantasy and religious implication. As any movie buff will recall, Fay Wray, the blonde heroine, is seized by the natives of Skull Island to be offered as a sacrifice to Kong, who is worshipped as a god in their kingdom. Kong is then captured and brought to New York City where he is exhibited and mocked until he breaks loose and wreaks havoc in the streets of Manhattan. At the end, he stands atop the Empire state Building, his body pierced by machine-gun bullets fired from Air Force planes, and he enjoys his moment of triumph. His natural dignity intact, his love for Fay Wray still pure, he stands baffled, mute and bleeding, a precariously noble figure outlined against a skyscrapered sky. Then he falls.

That the scene of Kong's death stirs memories of a similar event on Golgotha we know from the frequency with which the walls of American colleges are scrawled with the message: "King Kong died for our sins."

These are the ways in which the most representative myths of the horror film

genre are able to strike chords of religious feeling. Yet other Biblical themes are threaded throughout these films: the story of Noah, for example, occurs frequently in last-man-on-earth treatments; Sodom and Gomorrah find their fate in the cataclysm (particularly atomic cataclysm) films; and, finally, there is the Book of Revelations, which is certainly the source of the various beast and vampire tales that haunt the screen.

The congregants! They sit before their TV screens or in the popcorn-scented dark of the movie houses, congregants in the unacknowledged cathedrals of the American imagination, participating, as congregants do, in acts of recognition or of witnessing. What do they derive from their participation? For one thing, that most sensuous and most personal of pleasures: the experience of fear in a safe place. The films reiterate, and validate, the continuing presence of fear in the outside world with its vulnerability to cataclysm; as well as fear in the interior world, that pri-

vate life where demons also crouch.

But if the films offer fear, they also mitigate the terror by connecting it to tradition. No doubt the cathedral of horror, as it makes these connections, offers easy allegories and pop profundities. Still, in the welter of beasts and monsters and demons, there is plenty of stuff to stir the soul. Certainly, the films treat the great pageants and the great rituals of human existence as if they were still urgent. The huge antagonisms — light against dark, good against evil, pride against humility, instinct against reason — are portrayed on the screen as still circling each other under the watchful (or baleful) eye of God.

That is no small thing to learn. ■

1976 Ap 4, II:1:6

MAHLER, written and directed by Ken Russell; produced by Roy Baird; director of photography, Dick Bush; Mahler's music played by the Amsterdam Concertgebouw directed by Bernard Haitink. At the D. W. Griffith Theater Running time: 126 minutes.
Mahler .... Robert Powell
Alma Mahler .... Georgina Hale
Max .... Richard Morant
Bernard Mahler .... Lee Montague
Marie Mahler .... Rosalie Crutchley
Hugo Wolfe .... David Collins
Cosima Wagner .... Antonia Ellis

By RICHARD EDER

Ken Russell's "Mahler" is about the Viennese composer in the hallucinatory way that his "The Music Lovers" was about Tchaikovsky and "Lisztomania" was about Liszt.

They are dreams, and as such depict the dreamer much more clearly than they do the figures that appear in them. As far as the audience is concerned, it is almost as if Tchaikovsky, Liszt and Mahler had taken turns making films about Mr. Russell.

The British director shows in his recent swirling, arbitrary films many of the qualities of a creator. But he lacks a major one: He will not relinquish his works. They remain umbilically attached. They do not have heir own life but only his, and he deals with them as capriciously as a child who dyes his kitten pink and knocks if off its feet each time it starts to walk.

"Mahler," which opened yesterday at the D. W. Griffith Theater is somewhat less arbitrary than "Lisztomania," which was made later, although it was shown in New York before. Around the monomaniacal, black-garbed figure of Mahler—whose brilliant portrayal by Robert Powell gives the film some coherence—traveling in a railroad carriage, Mr. Russell builds a series of freely associating fantasies about his life.

The episodes have a basis in the composer's biography. We see him as a boy, bullied by his father and preferring composition to piano lessons; as a young composer making his wife, Alma, copy his scores and ignoring her own efforts at composition. We see the death of his daughter, and his conversion from Judaism to Catholicism to be acceptable for an important musical job in Vienna.

Mr. Russell's intentions in characterizing Mahler are clear up to a point. He presents him as a man consumed with musical ambition, the ambition and the music being quite inseparable. The other passion is Alma—somewhat oddly cast in the person of the blond, round-faced Georgina Hale, but extremely well-played nevertheless.

But this love is submerged in his music, and when she protests that he neglects her, and belittles her own artistic efforts, he replies, "But my music is my love for you."

He goes on to cite a passage in the 8th Symphony, and Russell produces the music for us. When a daughter dies, we hear the "Kindertotenlieder"; when a baby cries, we see him scribbling notes and hear a baby-crying motif.

This verges on the hammy. It crosses over, in fact, recalling the old sentimental musical film biographies. And then Mr. Russell goes off on his dream-extravaganzas.

When Mahler has a heart attack, his fears and jealousies come out in a garish scene where he imagines himself alive in a coffin, while his wife does an obscene dance atop it, and goes off with a Nazi storm trooper. There is a long scene in which the Wagner cult and Nazism are united in a leering and capering Cosima Wagner, and where Mahler shows his renunciation of Judaism by eating a whole pig's head and drinking a glass of milk besides.

There is much too much of this kind of thing. It drowns out the film's real qualities. When Mr. Russell isn't playing campy games his jangling work gives a real sense of the tight-nerved consciousness of a composer to whom all the world was a minefield of noises he had to tread through to pick out a perilous line of music.

1976 Ap 5, 45:4

HARVEST: 3000 YEARS, written, directed, produced and edited by Haile Gerima; Amharic with English subtitles; camera, Elliot Davis; music, Orchestra Ethiopia. Running time: 150 minutes. At the Museum of Modern Art, 53d Street, west of Fifth Avenue.
Grandmother ....Harego-Weyn Tafere
Father ....Melaku Makonen
Mother ....Kasu Astaw
Son ....Adane Melaku
Daughter ....Worke Abraha
Kebebe ....Gebru Dasa

Program notes accompanying "Harvest 3000 Years" indicate that this film about inequity and exploitation in Ethiopia was intended for distribution in third world countries. This bit of background may go a long way toward explaining why audiences viewing this movie on West 53d Street, where it is being exhibited tonight at 6 and tomorrow night at 8:30 as part of the New Directors/New Films series at the Museum of Modern Art, are likely to regard it as a work of rudimentary design and elementary politics.

Both as a movie and as an exercise in consciousness-raising with an eye toward rebellion, its principal flaws—a far too languorous pace, born of an unwillingness or inability to impose concision on its material; an absence of subtlety; and a tone frequently so good-humored as to be at odds with its ultimate purpose—are not likely to be overlooked by audiences familiar with more sophisticated and urgently manipulative techniques.

On the other hand, its exotic setting, its unfamiliar language (Amharic accompanied by English subtitles), its fascinating faces, its vivid sound and excellent photography mitigate the excessive length (two and a half hours) that might otherwise have made "Harvest 3000 Years" a medium of boredom.

"Harvest 3000 Years" was written, directed and produced by Haile Gerima, who was born in Ethiopia and who studied film making at the University of California at Los Angeles. Set in a small town where ownership of an overcoat (even one apparently left over from the Italian invasion of 1936) seems to be a status symbol, it concerns itself mainly with a loathesome landlord, a tenant farmer and his family, and thet local civic gadfly, a man dispossessed of his land and family and possessed of a powerful and ineradicable sense of injustice.

Part-madman, part-saint, part-guru, he is the sole disruptive human force at work in a social order that the title suggests has been fundamentally unchanged for millennia.

Unfortunately, drama and conflict are not the strengths of "Harvest 3000 Years." Attention is its weakness. Exoticism is its strength. And, while showing more than need be seen, it explains less than should be known.

LAWRENCE VAN GELDER

1976 Ap 6, 27:1

FACE TO FACE, directed and produced by Ingmar Bergman; screenplay (Swedish with English subtitles) by Mr. Bergman; director of photography, Sven Nykvist; editor, Siv Lundgren; a Dino De Laurentiis presentation, distributed by Paramount Pictures. Running time: 136 minutes. At the Beekman Theater, Second Avenue at 65th Street. This film has been rated R.
Dr. Jenny Isaksson ....Liv Ullmann
Dr. Thomas Jacobi ....Erland Josephson
Grandpa ....Gunnar Björnstrand
Grandma ....Aino Taube-Henrikson
Maria ....Kari Sylwan
Elizabeth Wankel ....Sif Ruud
Dr. Erik Isaksson ....Sven Lindberg
Lady ....Tore Segelcke
Dr. Helmuth Wankel ......Ulf Johansson
Veronica ....Kristina Adolphson
Mikael Stromberg ....Gösta Ekman
Concert pianist ....Käbi Laretei
Man ....Birger Malmsten
Another man ....Gorman Stangertz
Jenny's mother ......Marianne Aminoff

By VINCENT CANBY

In the first scene of "Face to Face," Ingmar Bergman's beautiful, agonizing new film, Dr. Jenny Isaksson (Liv Ullmann), a psychiatrist with a firm grip on what she takes to be the real world, walks through the newly empty rooms of a house she is moving out of. As she looks about, we share her particular sense of unexpected space. The texture of the wooden floors is seen as if for the first time.The white walls are bright but neutral—simply impersonal backdrops after all. In the void there are echoes of Jenny's footsteps.

Lives—even the most carefully managed—are voids filled with echoes. The echoes accumulate. Sometimes when one least expects it the mind's tuning device, a kind of psychic censor, breaks down and the echoes cannot be sanely controlled. Forgotten moments from the past push into the present. Signals cross, messages overlap. The garble in the void is insupportable. There may be nothing else to do but to turn off.

"Face to Face," which opened last night at the Beekman Theater, traces Jenny's sudden, breathtaking descent into despair, her unsuccessful suicide attempt and her apparent recovery. That is the shape of the film anyway. "Face to Face," like all Bergman films, reaches out to contemplate all sorts of other things, from the more or less fixed, contemporary reality of Jenny's career, her marriage, family and friends, to the emotional anxieties, represented by the echoes from her past, that come out of the dark to overwhelm her.

As Jenny sits on her bed in a room filled with sunlight, and sets about the task of swallowing handfuls of sleeping pills, she tells us she feels neither fear nor sadness. She is instead cheerful, excited as if going on her first train trip.

Why does Jenny do it?

The only reservation I have about "Face to Face" is that Mr. Bergman, perhaps for the first time, is uncharacteristically explicit when it comes to laying out the reasons for Jenny's breakdown. In a series of dreams and waking hallucinations that form important sections of the film he takes us on a guided tour of a house of Jenny's subconscious, a journey through a house of horrors as immaculately tended as a Disneyland funhouse, and carefully laid out to save the biggest surprises for the last few minutes of the ride.

This Freudian literalness is surprising in that Mr. Bergman seems clearly to believe that psychiatry is, at best, a passing fad, something of a shell game, though his feelings are ambivalent. There are times when one suspects that his vision of the decline and fall of Jenny the Psychiatrist, with whom Ingmar Bergman the artist intensely identifies, is really the analysand's ultimate revenge on the analyst. Two things are going on at the same time. The patient is saying, "He's crazier than I," but "I am him."

In his preface to the published screenplay (somewhat expanded from what we see on the screen), Mr. Bergman admits that he's always been "extremely suspicious of dreams, apparitions and visions, both in literature and in films and plays. Perhaps it's because mental excesses of this sort smack too much of being 'arranged.' "

He goes on to say that he thinks of the dreams in this film as being "extensions of reality," and thus, I suppose, not to be taken literally as dreams (if that's not too much of a confusion).

Whatever they are, when fitted together they give us a detailed psychiatric profile of Jenny's childhood when, orphaned as a result of an automobile accident, she was raised by her maternal grandparents, who were loving, strict and, on occasion, stupendously unfeeling.

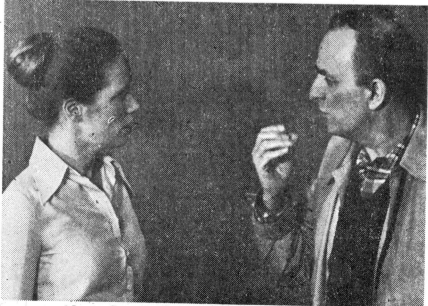

Ingmar Bergman directing Liv Ullmann in "Face to Face"

The power of "Face to Face" is not in its case history. It's in the brilliant drama of an intelligent woman attempting to come to terms with all sorts of disappointments, which will never be made right, and contradictions that have to be reconciled. These are most movingly demonstrated in Jenny's relationship with her grandparents, especially her grandmother, who was an ogre in Jenny's childhood but whom we see, in old age, as a woman of profound gentleness and wisdom, being infinitely kind and patient to a husband who is fighting an angry losing battle with senility.

Almost ignored by the film is Jenny's husband, who is in America during most of the film and who, when we do see him, seems too priggish and dull ever to have interested a woman of Jenny's capabilities—though this may be because we are seeing him through the eyes of the woman who no longer loves him.

"Face to Face" is another tour de force for Miss Ullmann, who is nothing short of immense. I know of no other actress today who has at hand the reserves that enable her to move so effortlessly through such multiple levels of mood and feeling. But then nobody today except Mr. Bergman writes such roles for actresses. Erland Josephson, Miss Ullmann's co-star in "Scenes From a Marriage," is also fine in the much smaller but very affecting role of a man who might have loved Jenny for one small impediment—his homosexuality.

With "Cries and Whispers" and "Scenes from a Marriage," Mr. Bergman's newest film forms a trilogy quite distinct from his earlier though equally fascinating films. In these last three works, Mr. Bergman is more mysterious, more haunting, more contradictory than ever, though the style of the films has never been more precide, clear, level-headed.

1976 Ap 6, 28:1

VERONIQUE, OU L'ETE DE MES 13 ANS (Veronique, or The Summer of My 13th Year), directed by Claudine Guilemain; screenplay (French with English subtitles) by Miss Guilemain; dialogue, Pierre Lartha; director of photography, Jean-Jacques Rochut; music, Jean-Robert Viard; editors, Alfredo Muschietti and Caroline Roulet; executive producer, George Dybman; a production of Films du Losange and Felix Films. Running time: 88 minutes. At the Museum of Modern Art, 53d Street, west of Fifth Avenue.

Veronique ....Anne Teyssedre
Anne ....Anouk Ferjak
Jean ....Michel Peyrelon
Father ....Jean-Pierre Moulin
Mother ....Edith Loria
Michele ....Anne Kerylen
Sylvain ....Christophe Perring

Understatement is to be approved, but some films are so understated that they tend to disappear when you think about them. Like morning mist they evaporate in the sunlight. Claudine Guilemain's "Véronique, ou L'Eté de Mes 13 Ans" (Véronique, or The Summer of My 13th Year) comes dangerously close to being such a film. It is lovely and fragile and understated to the point that the audience must supply many of the details of the interior lives of its characters. If one is willing to do this, as I was, the movie is fascinating. If not, you may wake up screaming.

•

The French film, which will be shown at the Museum of Modern Art today at 9:30 P.M. and tomorrow at 6 P.M., is about the summer vacation of Véronique (Anne Teyssèdre), a pretty, introspective 13-year-old who is on the brink of becoming an intelligent, beautiful, probably passionate woman.

In the meantime she's an outsider, a tireless observer of the curious behavior of others, the adults who surround her and carry on in ways that seem as bizarre to her as might the rituals of a tribe of eskimos.

The eskimos in this instance are Véronique's godmother Anne (Anouk Ferjak) and godfather Jean (Michael Peyrelon), to whom Véronique has been packed off for a summer's tour through southwestern France. Anne and Jean are attractive, affectionate, humorous people, who appear to Véronique to have all of the understanding and sophistication lacking in her parents. As the tour wears on, however, imperfections appear in Anne and Jean.

Véronique studies them solemnly. Has Anne had a quick affair in St. Jean de Luz while Véronique and Jean were off sightseeing? Why does Jean excuse himself at the beach and then go off for some rather particular nude sunbathing? Why the sudden, furious fights, and equally furious reconciliations, between Anne and Jean? Véronique watches them and holds her peace. If she has any speculations, she keeps them to herself.

The one thing she is sure of is her attraction to Jean who, toward the end of the vacation, makes a clumsy pass at her, one that she has been encouraging and that allows her for the first time to participate in adult life by putting him off. In her diary where she records everything in somewhat studious prose, she writes, "He embraced me tenderly," and then turns her mind to her school schedule for the following week.

•

"Véronique" is very funny in a low-key way and beautifully directed by Miss Guilemain who has, I suspect, made exactly the kind of film she set out to—clear and direct, yet full of reserved intelligence and appreciation for the complexities of feelings and motives. Most of the films I've seen in the current New Directors/New Films series, which is presenting "Véronique," don't have enough on their minds to occupy the screen. If they were houses, you might say that half their rooms were empty. "Véronique is completely inhabited.

VINCENT CANBY

1976 Ap 6, 28:1

THE BAD NEWS BEARS, directed by Michael Ritchie; screenplay by Bill Lancaster; produced by Stanley R. Jaffe; director of photography, John A. Alonzo; music, Jerry Fielding; editor, Richard A. Harris; distributed by Paramount Pictures. Running time: 102 minutes. At the Paramount Theater, Broadway at 61st Street, and Sutton Theater, 57th Street near Third Avenue. This film has been rated PG.

Coach Morris Buttermaker.Walter Matthau
Amada Whurlizer ....Tatum O'Neal
Roy Turner ....Vic Morrow
Cleveland ....Joyce Van Patten
Bob Whitewood ....Ben Piazza
Kelly Leak ....Jackie Earle Haley
Ogilvie ....Alfred W. Lutter
Joey Turner ....Brandon Cruz
Tanner Boyle ....Chris Barnes
Ahmad Abdul Rahim..........Erin Blunt
Engelberg ....Gary Lee Cavagnaro
Joe Agilar ....Jaime Escobedo
Regi Tower ....Scott Firestone
Miguel Agilar ....George Gonzales
Jimmy Feldman ....Brett Marx
Rudi Stein ....David Pollock
Timmy Lupus ....Quinn Smith
Toby Whitewood ....David Stambaugh

By VINCENT CANBY

If Neil Simon ever wrote a kiddie comedy it might very well sound like Michael Ritchie's "The Bad News Bears," a wise-cracking, occasionally funny, often foul-mouthed movie about one season in the life of a California sandlot ball club called the Bears.

The Bears, whose ages appear to range from 9 to 13, are more hard luck than bad news until their coach, Morris Buttermaker (Walter Matthau), an over-the-hill ball player who now cleans swimming pools, has the good sense to sign aboard Amanda Whurlizer (Tatum O'Neal), a pitcher with a magic arm.

The predictability of the subsequent rise and rise of the Bears—sparked by their glamorous 12-year-old pitcher—within their mini league is not particularly detrimental to the movie's entertainment value. "The Bad News Bears" relies much more on Mr. Matthau's rich interpretation of the beer-guzzling coach and on an audience that finds something pricelessly funny about kids who can trade one-liners with the best of them.

I really don't. Yet "The Bad News Bears," which opened yesterday at the Paramount and Sutton Theaters, has a number of other virtues that make it a surprisingly painless adventure. Among these are the screenplay by Bill Lancaster, Burt's son, who has the talent and discipline to tell the story of "The Bad News Bears" almost completely in terms of what happens on the baseball diamond or in the dugout.

Mr. Ritchie, whose work ("Smile," "The Candidate," "Downhill Racer") is bound to prompt a lot of boring theses about his vision of what competition means in the American system, keeps the sentimentality in check most of the time and obtains first-rate performers from his miniature cast all of the time.

The star, of course, is Miss O'Neal, in her first film since "Paper Moon." At 12 she has a peculiarly unsettling screen presence, looking, as she does, like a pretty child but possessing the reserve of someone who's been through the wars. She's eerie.

So is Jackie Earle Haley (last seen as the dreadfull child actor who was stomped to death in "The Day of the Locust"), impersonating a juvenile delinquent who smokes, drinks and fools around wtih girls. Like Miss O'Neal he's small, but there's something about him that makes you suspect he may actually be an aged Munchkin, exiled from Oz for crimes that must remain unspeakable.

1976 Ap 7, 28:1

ALL THE PRESIDENT'S MEN, directed by Alan J. Pakula; screenplay by William Goldman, based on the book by Carl Bernstein and Bob Woodward; produced by Walter Coblenz; music, David Shire; director of photography, Gordon Willis; editor, Robert L. Wolfe; a Wildwood production, distributed by Warner Brothers. Running time: 136 minutes. At Loews Astor Plaza, 44th Street West of Broadway, and Loews Tower East, Third Avenue near 72d Street. This film has been rated PG.

Carl Bernstein .... Dustin Hoffman
Bob Woodward .... Robert Redford
Harry Rosenfeld .... Jack Warden
Howard Simons .... Martin Balsam
Deep Throat .... Hal Holbrook
Ben Bradlee .... Jason Robards
Bookkeeper .... Jane Alexander
Debbie Sloan ....Meredith Baxter
Dardis .... Ned Beatty
Hugh Sloan, Jr. ...... Stephen Collins
Sally Aiken .... Penny Fuller
Foreign Editor .... John McMartin
Donald Segretti .... Robert Walden
Frank Wills .... Himself
Bachinski .... David Arkin
Barker .... Henry Calvert
Marinez .... Dominic Chianese
Kay Eddy .... Lindsay Ann Crouse
Miss Milland .... Valerie Curtin
McCord .... Richard Herd
Carolyn Abbot ..... Allyn Ann McLerie
Angry CRP woman .... Neva Patterson
Al Lewis .... Joshua Shelley

By VINCENT CANBY

Newspapers and newspapermen have long been favorite subjects for movie makers—a surprising number of whom are former newspapermen, yet not until "All The President's Men," the riveting screen adaptation of the Watergate book by Carl Bernstein and Bob Woodward, has any film come remotely close to being an accurate picture of American journalism at its best.

"All The President's Men," directed by Alan J. Pakula, written by William Goldman and largely pushed into being by the continuing interest of one of its stars, Robert Redford, is a lot of things all at once: a spellbinding detective story about the work of the two Washington Post reporters who helped break the Watergate scandal, a breathless adventure that recalls the triumphs of Frank and Joe Hardy in that long-ago series of boys' books, and a vivid footnote to some contemporary American history that still boggles the mind.

•

The film, which opened yesterday at Loews Astor Plaza and Tower East Theaters, is an unequivocal smash-hit — the thinking man's "Jaws."

Much of the effectiveness of the movie, which could easily have become a mish-mash of names, dates and events, is in its point of view, which remains that of its two, as yet unknown reporters. Carl Bernstein (Dustin Hoffman), highly competitive and a little more experienced than his partner, and Bob Woodward (Robert Redford), very ambitious and a dog for details.

It's through their eyes—skeptical, hungry, insatiably curious—that "All The President's Men" unfolds. It begins logically on the night of June 17, 1972, when five men were arrested in an apparent break-in at the headquarters of the Democratic National Committee in the Watergate complex in Washington, and continues through the spectacular series of revelations, accusations and admissions of guilt that eventually brought the Nixon Presidency to its conclusion.

Like Bernstein and Woodward in the course of their investigation, the film maintains bifocal vision, becoming thoroughly absorbed in the seemingly unimportant minutiae out of which major conspiracies can sometimes be reconstructed, yet never for long losing sight of the overall relevance of what's going on. Although "All The President's Men" is first and foremost a fascinating newspaper film, the dimensions and implications of the Watergate story obviously give it an emotional punch that might be lacking if, say, Bernstein and Woodward had been exposing corruption in the Junior League.

•

Thus the necessity of the director's use of newsreel footage from time to time—the shots of President Nixon's helicopter making a night landing at the White House, which open the film; the television images of the President entering the House of Representatives, and of other familiar folk including former Attorney General John N. Mitchell, former Vice President Agnew, and, especially, Representative Gerald R. Ford in the course of his nomination of President Nixon at the 1972 Republican National Convention.

Though the film will undoubtedly have some political impact, its strength is the virtually day-by-day record of the way Bernstein and Woodward conducted their investigations, always under the supervision of a kindly avuncular Ben Bradlee (Jason Robards), The Post's managing editor who (in this firm) gives out advice, caution and, occasionally, a "well-done," acting as Dr. Gillespie to their Dr. Kildares.

Mr. Redford and Mr. Hoffman play their roles with the low-keyed, understated efficiency required since they are, in effect, the straight men to the people and the events they are pursuing. The film stays out of their private lives but is full of unexpected, brief, moving glimpses into the private lives of their subjects, including a frightened bookkeeper (Jane Alexander) fo rthe Committee to Re-elect the President, Donald Segretti (Robert Walden), the "dirty tricks" man, and Hugh Sloan Jr. (Stepehn Collins), the committee treasurer, and his wife (Meredith Baxter).

The manners and methods of big-city newspapering, beautifully detailed, contribute as much to the momentum of the film as the mystery that's being uncovered. Maybe even more, since the real excitement of "All The President's Men" is in watching two comparatively inexperienced reporters stumble onto the story of their lives and develop it triumphantly, against all odds.

1976 Ap 8, 42:1

THE DUCHESS AND THE DIRTWATER FOX, directed and produced by Melvin Frank; written by Mr. Frank, Barry Sandler and Jack Rose from a story by Mr. Sandler; director of photography, Joseph Biroc. Released by 20th-Century Fox. At Mann's National, Trans-Lux East, and other theaters. Running time: 105 minutes. This film has been rated PG.

Charlie Malloy	George Segal
Amanda Quaid	Goldie Hawn
Gladstone	Conrad Janis
Widdicombe	Thayer David
Trollop	Jennifer Lee
Bloodworth	Roy Jenson

By RICHARD EDER

This movie is like a roller coaster from which the management has taken all the ups and all the downs and sold them. Flat roller coasters must be cheaper to operate: Hollywood has been using them for years.

It is a gag western. This means it is an action picture in which every bit of action, drama, suspense or whatever, is carefully undermined by what sets itself up to be a whimsical distancing.

•

It is necessary, for instance —it's not only necessary but it happens three times, at least—that when the hero leaps from a window on to his horse, he misses or the horse falls down. When, bound and spread-eagled, the hero roots about with his teeth for some implement to free himself, he pauses to ask his spread-eagled companion, "You haven't got a ham sandwich, have you?"

Nothing is real in "The Duchess and the Dirtwater Fox," which opened yesterday at the National and other theaters, but this kind of self-deprecating gag. Woody Allen does them better, but, even in his movies, by reducing everything to the same deflated horizon, the gags make for monotony. Here the action—there is lots of it—has been polluted for the sake of gags that are rarely even funny in themselves.

The Dirtwater Fox, played by George Segal, is an incompetent cardsharp who gets hold of some loot stolen by bank robbers. He takes up with the Duchess, a honkytonk performer played by Goldie Hawn, and together they get into various adventures trying to keep the money and get away from the robbers.

The adventures are more or less routine: a stagecoach crash: a wedding party to hide out among—in this case a Jewish wedding—shootings, dynamitings and drifting downstream in an oarless boat. We feel not a spark of sympathy with the pair; not because they're not likable—they are, rather—but because they are neither believable nor believing.

•

Both Goldie Hawn and George Segal, properly employed, can do well. Miss Hawn is badly miscast here. She has no skill at brassiness, she can't belt out a song; garters on her look outright embarrassing. Her talent is for being funny and for being sexy, but it is an introspective talent and here it catches cold and dies.

Mr. Segal is not so much miscast as uncast. As in a previous picture, "The Black Bird," he has virtually nothing to do. He has a great face for expressing sharp and funny things, but here it is in dry dock. Someone should put him in the movies.

1976 Ap 8, 43:1

SPARKLE, directed by Sam O'Steen; screenplay by Jol Schumacher; story by Mr. Schumacher and Howard Rosenman; director of photography, Bruce Surtees; file editor, Gordon Scott; music by Curtis Mayfield; produced by Mr. Rosenman; released by Warner Bros. At the Cinerama Theater, Broadway at 47th Street, and neighborhood theaters. Running time: 99 minutes. This film is classified PG.

Stix	Philip M. Thomas
Sparkle	Irene Cara
Siste r.	Lonette McKee
Dolores	Dwan Smith
Mary Alice	Effie

"Sparkle," which opened yesterday at the Cinerama and other theaters, is a melodrama about three black sisters who try to become successful Harlem pop singers. One dies, a victim of drugs and a gangster lover; another leaves town; the third, after all kinds of harassment, finds love and success.

It is a sob story, and a predictable one. There are worse things than being predictable, though. The details strain our patience with their triteness: The mother, for example, is a devoted maid out on Long Island. But the main lines of the story are serious enough, and credible; and this allows the film moments of force and movement.

The acting is awkward, although Irene Cara, as the successful youngest sister, has a persistent charm and conviction that partly compensate for a rough performance.

The picture's minor virtue is a good atmospheric rendering of choked nightclub and street scenes. Its major virtue is some first-rate songs written by Curtis Mayfield and sung with style and power by Lonette McKee, who plays the older sister.

RICHARD EDER

1976 Ap 8, 43:1

ELI NOYES JR. RETROSPECTIVE: CLAY, 8 minutes; IN A BOX, 6 minutes; ALPHABET, 6 minutes; 41 BARKS, 1 minute; SANDMAN, 4 minutes; BAD DOG, 5 minutes; ROACHES' SERENADE, 5 minutes, co-directed by Claudia Weill; LOST AND FOUND, 5 minutes, co-directed by Claudia Weill; THE FABLE OF HE AND SHE, 11 minutes; PEANUT BUTTER AND JELLY, 1 minute; THE DOT, 30 minutes. At the Film Forum, 15 Vandam Street.

Good things, the saying goes, come in small packages. And the small packages that are the films of Eli Noyes Jr. are crammed with wit, beauty, inventiveness and a keen sensitivity to the lunacy and sadness of the human condition.

Eleven of these films—some animated, some live action, one a mixture of the two; some in color, some in black and white—are being shown this weekend and next at the Film Forum in an 82-minute parade that should captivate a great many children, delight adults and disabuse anyone of the notion that when it comes to animation, Walt Disney and his disciples had the last word.

Mr. Noyes is the sort of artist who can take a run through the alphabet with pen and ink in six minutes, stirring up comparisons with Maurice Sendak and Saul Steinberg with his drawing and leaving "Sesame Street" and Richard Scarry in his wake with his humor.

In 8 minutes he can speak volumes about evolution, through — appropriately — a lump of clay transformed with seeming magic into all manner of life. In 60 seconds he can run through a lexicon of barks from a creative kennel full of dogs or make wild sport of the world's peanut-butter-and-jelly addicts. Given a country music background and a few grains of sand, he produces marvelous choreography.

In live action, he transmits a crafty dog's-eye view of singles' life in New York and takes a bold excursion into one of the city's great conflicts — the war against the roach. His most eye-catching clay animation is reserved for "The Fable of He and She," an 11-minute film that suffers, however, from a heavyhanded story about sexual roles that Mr. Noyes did not compose.

His own formidable powers of storytelling and political commentary are strikingly displayed in "The Dot," a 30-minute film that conjures up an eerie, Orwellian world and combines live action and animation to make a statement against repression.

Mr. Noyes is a filmmaker of impressive accomplishment, and his work deserves to be seen.

LAWRENCE VAN GELDER

1976 Ap 9, 26:3

Brazilian Film Studies Tropical Love

By RICHARD EDER

Love is always dangerous but in the tropics it can be mortal. Fertility, a traditionally beneficent notion in the North, becomes a sick joke. Life proliferates and chokes: Too many mosquitoes and snakes. Turn your back on your garden for a minute, and vegetable sex has buried it under fronds and creepers.

"Guerra Conjugal" is a Brazilian film, set in the pastel and languid town of Curitiba, that sees in the relations between men and women the virulence of a poisoned eclair. It is being shown as part of the Museum of Modern Art's New Directors series.

•

Three stories intercut with one another. The first is about a middleaged lawyer who seduces everyone in sight. Finally, in horror and helplessness, he is seduced by an old schoolmate. Don Juan as the repressed homosexual.

The second is about a young man who finds his satisfaction in progressively older women. The last is a horrendous crone of at least 80. Don Juan as the mother-fixated infant.

If the first two episodes dispose of eroticism, the third lays out marital love. An aged couple quarrel more and more violently. He accuses her of thinking of other men; she tells him he disgusts her. Dying, he asks his son to see to it that the wife doesn't kiss his dead face. He dies; she grows miraculously younger.

"Guerra" is Tropical Gothic: It makes Southern Gothic look like cream of wheat. In its violent disgust for the human animal—in this case the human sexual animal—it occasionally reaches the inspired dementia of a Buñuel. There are some brilliantly harsh and funny episodes.

•

Mostly, though, its means —uneven acting, uncertain direction and overblown writing fall a long way short of its intentions. If the eclair is half-baked, there's not much use poisoning it.

1976 Ap 9, 26:2

O THIASSOS (THE TRAVELING PLAYERS). Greek film with English subtitles. Written and directed by Theodor Angelopoulos, produced by Georges Papalios, photography by George Arvanitis and music by Loukianos Kilaidonis. Museum of Modern Art, tonight at 8:30; Wednesday at 7:30 P.M. Running time: 230 minutes.

Elektra	Eva Kotamanidou
Mother	Aliki Georgoulis
Father	Stratos Pachis
Orestes	Petros Zarkadis

By RICHARD EDER

"O Thiassos" is a new Greek film of startling beauty and originality—that is, for the first two hours or so. But it lasts four hours. Length is part of its problem. A much greater problem is that the political message that is only one of the threads in the first part thickens into hawser dimensions, strangling the film and the audience along with it.

Translated as "The Traveling Players," Thiassos is a bloated, spoiled masterpiece. But it is, at the same time, the undoubted high point of the Museum of Modern Art's New Directors series, being shown at the museum today and Wednesday. So far, this year's series has given us a number of fairly dim talents, and sometimes considerably less than that.

Theodor Angelopoulos, whose third film this is, possesses enormous talent; large enough to show clearly through his monstrous lack of restraint and, often, to overcome it. Since restraint is easier to acquire than genius, there is a basis for hoping that we are seeing the work of someone who is destined to become a truly great film maker.

"Thiassos" attempts to tell the story of modern Greece through the wanderings of a band of actors, an unskilled provincial group that sings and dances in front of village theaters to lure audiences inside for a performance of a rough shepherd's play.

The action begins in 1939, goes through World War II and the civil war and ends in 1952. Using flashbacks, flash-forwards and narrated recollections, it manages to suggest a broader time span from the 1920's up to the time of the colonels' coup.

The film's structure is even more complex than its time frame. It is the story of political developments in Greece as they affect the villages visited by the troupe: the right-wing prewar Metaxas dictatorship, the national unity of right and left during the brief fight against the Axis, the civil war and—as the film sees it—the victory of reaction over popular forces.

At the same time it is the story of the troupe itself; the decimation of the company under the stress of personal and political passion. Mr. Angelopoulos manages to blend both things—the jealousies and betrayals within the company and the political divisions of right and left —into a retelling of the Electra tragedy.

There is no space to begin to enumerate the many marvelous things that are accomplished. Over such a sprawling arrangement for example, Mr. Angelopoulos manages a fair unity of mood by shooting virtually the whole film in the cold, milky overcast of Greek winter.

He has some prodigious images. The wartime famine is declared in a tiny scene. A solitary chicken is shown on a snow-covered slope; the members of the troupe advance upon it in black, crablike profile. He has filmed hunger.

Elektra, the young actress, is accosted by a black-shirted member of a pro-Metaxas gang. She takes him to her room and tells him to strip. He does, completely. He takes off his first garments in leering anticipation; then, beneath her contemptuous gaze his movements become less certain. Finally, his total nakedness coincides with total humiliation as she turns and walks out. It is a scene of merciless justness.

There are many scenes of equal brilliance and force. The acting and camera work are flawless. Mr. Agelopoulos takes many risks. He holds camera or characters still for minutes on end; he has scenes that consist of one character addressing the camera at length. Usually these things work, in surprising ways.

But the film begins to flag in the middle. In part, the deliberate pace becomes excessive. Many of the slow gestures begin to seem like affectations.

Furthermore, the message begins to shed its complexity and become simply a tract praising the Communist forces who lost the civil war and attacking and caricaturing the conservative victors and their British and American allies.

The execessive politicization in a work of normal dimensions and equal talent would simply be a flaw. Here it is immensely magnified. The discoveries of the first two hours turn into a relentless pounding during the last two.

1976 Ap 10, 22:1

FAMILY PLOT, directed by Alfred Hitchcock; screenplay by Ernest Lehman, based on the novel "The Rainbird Pattern" by Victor Canning; director of photography, Leonard J. South; editor, J. Terry Williams; music, John Williams; distributed by Universal Pictures. Running time: 120 minutes. At the Rivoli Theater, Broadway at 50th Street, Loew's Orpheum Theater, 86th Street near Third Avenue, Murray Hill Theater, 34th Street near Third Avenue, and other theaters. This film has been rated PG.
Fran ....Karen Black
Lumley ....Bruce Dern
Blanche ....Barbara Harris
Adamson ....William Devane
Maloney ....Ed Lauter
Julia Rainbird ....Cathleen Nesbitt
Mrs. Maloney ....Katherine Helmond
Grandison ....Warren J. Kemmerling
Mrs. Clay ....Edith Atwater
Bishop ....William Prince

By VINCENT CANBY

Not since "To Catch a Thief" and "The Trouble With Harry" has Alfred Hitchcock been in such benign good humor as he is in "Family Plot," the old

master's 56th feature since he began directing films in 1922.

"Family Plot," which opened at theaters all over town yesterday, is a witty, relaxed lark. It's a movie to raise your spirits even as it dabbles in phony ones, especially those called forth by Blanche (Barbara Harris), a sweet, pretty, totally fraudulent Los Angeles medium, who nearly wrecks her vocal cords when possessed by a control whose voice sounds like Sidney Greenstreet's.

But "Family Plot" isn't about anything as esoteric as spiritualism and its sometimes wayward votaries. It's about good old-fashioned greed, or, how to work very, very hard in order to make your fortune illegally. It's one of the many invigorating ironies of "Family Plot" that its con people are so obsessed by their criminal pursuits they never realize the easier way would probably be the lawful one.

Then, of course, there would be no plot, and a high regard for plot is one of the distinguishing joys of both Hitchcock and this new film.

Ernest Lehman's screenplay, based on a novel by Victor Canning, is about the efforts of Blanche and her boyfriend, Lumley (Bruce Dern), a good-natured lug who works as a cab driver but thinks he'd like to be an actor, to track down the missing heir to a huge West Coast fortune. If Blanche's spirits help her to find the fellow, she's been promised $10,000 by the heir's ancient aunt (Cathleen Nesbitt). Although $10,000 isn't exactly beyond our wildest dreams, to Blanche and Lumley it represents a lot of palms that won't have to be read.

The object of their manhunt, though they don't know it for a long time, is a wealthy Los Angeles jeweler named Adamson (William Devane) who, with his girlfriend, Fran (Karen Black), has a passion for oversize diamonds he cannot afford.

To satisfy their passion, Adamson and Fran have perfected the art of kidnapping for ransoms of king-size jewels. When we first meet them, they are just completing the successful abduction of a fabulously rich, seemingly Greek international financier and, before the movie is over, they've had equally good luck with the abduction of a bishop, whom they snatch from the altar of his cathedral during mass.

Hitchcock cross-cuts between the two couples in the course of the film to build a kind of menace-free but very real suspense. Fran and Adamson, who live in a very chic San Francisco town house (though the rest of the movie appears to be set in Los Angeles), are naturally worried when they learn they are being pursued by an eccentric fortuneteller and her taxi driver lover, and they take steps to eliminate the

investigators.

It's not revealing too much, I think, to report that these steps are never completely successful. Blanche and Lumley, merged, make a single bird-brain, but one whom heaven protects and fortune smiles on.

As performed by Miss Harris and Mr. Dern, they are two of the most appealing would-be rascals that Hitchcock has even given us. For that matter so are Adamson and Fran (she has no last name, which leaves her matrimonial state in Old World, gentlemanly doubt). Though Adamson is portrayed as being perfectly willing to murder, when cornered, he never succeeds, and Fran is the kind of kidnapper who prepares gourmet meals for her involuntary guests.

The four are extremely good company, like Hitchcock himself when, in an expansive, genial, storytelling mood, even his digressions have digressions, but always to the point of some higher entertainment truth.

Hitchcock aficionados may well miss signs of the director's often overanalyzed pessimism. "Family Plot" is certainly Hitchcock's most cheerful film in a long time, but it's hardly innocent. One of the things that figure prominently in the plot, though it happens long before the film starts, is the story of a young man who, finding his stepparents boring, pours gasoline all over the house and incinerates the offending pair.

It's a small thing, perhaps, but it continues the master's franchise on the macabre.

1976 Ap 10, 22:1

Only U.S. Film in New Directors' Series

By VINCENT CANBY

"The Long Night," the only American film to be included in this year's generally undistinguished New Directors/New Films series at the Museum of Modern Art, displays more passion for positive thinking than it does for film making, which is what the priorities are when one is primarily concerned with issues.

The film, the first feature to be directed by Woodie King Jr., a major producer on New York's black-theater scene, is an effort to present an accurate picture of Harlem life without exploiting drugs, violence, prostitution or photogenic poverty. It's about gallantry under stress, especially that of Steely Brown (W. Geoffrey King), a young teen-ager whose father a Vietnam vet with a lot of pride and nowhere to put it, walks out on Steely's hard-pressed mother, the sort of woman who wants to survive by making as few waves as possible.

●

In one exceedingly long night, Steely roams the streets of Harlem trying to scrape together the $27 he owes his mother and recalling—in flashbacks—the events that led up to his father's disappearance. "The Long Night" gets high marks for the performance of young Mr. King, who has a winning, unaffected screen presence, and for its good thoughts

The Cast

THE LONG NIGHT, directed by Woodie King Jr.; screenplay by Julian Mayfield and Mr. King, based on the novel by Mr. Mayfield; produced by Mr. King and St. Clair Bourne; director of photography, James Malloy; editors, Joe Staton and Ed McAllister; music, William Daniels and Michael Felder; a production of Woodie King Associates Films. Running time: 85 minutes. At the Museum of Modern Art, 53d Street west of Fifth Avenue.
Fred (Steely) Brown ..W. Geoffrey King
Paul Brown ......Dick Anthony Williams
Mae Brown ....Peggy Kirkpatrick

about black identity and aspirations. As moviemaking it is mechanical and unexciting in almost every respect.

The film is being shown at the museum today at 6 P.M. and again Tuesday at 8:30 P.M. It will be released commercially later this year by Mahler Films.

Being shown at the museum today at 8:30 P.M. is another black film, this one about the exploitation of a poor, hard-working Senegalese farmer by the Marabouts, religious teachers who turn their pupils into professional beggars. The film, "Njangaan," directed by Mahama Johnson Traore, is of primary interest as a report on life from one emerging African nation. It will be shown again

Tuesday at 6 P.M., the last day of the New Directors/New Films series sponsored by the museum and the Film Society of Lincoln Center.

The conclusion of this year's New Directors/New Films program—the fifth in the series sponored by the Museum of Modern Art and the Lincoln Center Film Society — prompts some thoughts about the problems that arise when institutions commit themselves to such "annual" events. Of the 11 films in this year's program (the print of the 12th scheduled film never arrived), only three deserved the attention this sort of festival confers. Those three were the Greek "O Thiassos," the French "Veronique" and the Hungarian "Adoption."

The rest of the films looked suspiciously like program fillers, choices made by the festival's sponsors to keep their annual event going even in a year when they either couldn't obtain new films of remarkable value or couldn't find any worth particular attention.

The New Directors/New Films program last year presented at least three highly original works, and all the rest of the films, except two, were of special interest. The mediocrity of most of this year's selections had a way of diminishing the value of even the several worthy films. Conclusion: There may be some years when the festival sponsors should call the whole thing off.

1976 Ap 11, 45:5

FILM VIEW

VINCENT CANBY

Are Black Films Losing Their Blackness?

It may not actually be a trend as yet—it may simply be a superficial impression, based on several weeks of rather ordinary movie-going—but it does seem as if the bottom has dropped out of the market for black exploitation films. I'm referring to those supercharged, bad-talking, highly romanticized melodramas about Harlem superstuds, the pimps, the private eyes and the pushers who more or less singlehandedly make whitey's corrupt world safe for black pimping, black private-eyeing and black pushing. By next week I may be eating my hat, but right now it seems as if more and more films that once would have been categorized as black films are really films for the general market. They are black films that you don't have to be black to respond to favorably, or to find dreary and pretentious, or foolish and inept.

The most dynamic and entertaining of these "new" black films is a candidly commercial box-office attack called "Sparkle," a story about three young women from Harlem and the high price they pay in their climb to the top as the country's most popular singing-sister act.

It sounds terrible, a sort of retread of "Sally, Irene and Mary" transposed to the never-never land ruled by Barry Gordy and Motown Records. The confusion may well be intentional. The routines performed by the girls in "Sparkle," and the new music provided them by Curtis Mayfield, definitely recall the style and effect of The Supremes and, in Lonette McKee, who plays the sister who goes bad, in the way Lana Turner did in a movie like "Ziegfeld Girl," it has a leading actress whose beauty, talent and verve recall the extraordinary Diana Ross herself.

● ● ●

"Sparkle," like "Mahogany," is a black up-date of the kind of show-biz and glamour movies that were so popular in the 1930's and 1940's. It's fairy-tale stuff, yet in its music and in its performances by Miss McKee and Irene Cara, as the good sister who survives the terrible pressures her talent brings to bear on her, it has so much vitality that one can tolerate its more obvious idiocies. Among these are its melodrama (some obligatory stuff about the mob) and the camerawork of Bruce Surtees who, with what I assume to have been the approval of Sam O'Steen, the director, has so underlit everything that you get the impression that the entire film, not just portions of it, is set in a smokey, dimly lit nightclub.

"Sparkle" is the first theatrical film to be directed by O'Steen, known heretofore as one of Hollywood's most successful editors ("Who's Afraid of Virginia Woolf?," "The Graduate," "Chinatown," etc.) and more recently as a television director. On the basis of one film, it's impossible to tell exactly where his strengths lie, but he appears to have an efficient, no-nonsense way with narrative and the talent to cast properly and then the ability to obtain first-rate performances from his actors.

Another matter of movie is "Boesman and Lena," which is not, strictly speaking, a black film, though when Athol Fugard's original play was done at the Circle in The Square in 1970, it starred James Earl Jones and Ruby Dee. This film version, made in South Africa in 1973 with the white Fugard himself as Boesman, will probably never receive wide commercial release here, and it's easy to understand why. It's virtually a two-character harangue, with much of that harangue spoken in South African accents that make it almost unintelligible to Americans. Though it qualifies as black since it can be played by black actors, it's of less interest as a polemic about South African apartheid than as a Beckett-like meditation upon the human condition.

● ● ●

In "Boesman and Lena" that condition has been effectively reduced to two, to Boesman and his wife, Lena, South African "coloreds," that is, people of mixed blood who are acceptable in neither the white nor black communities. At the beginning of the film when their shanty town is levelled by a bulldozer, Boesman and Lena must take to the road, which, as we learn, is the way they've spent their lives, moving from place to place, carrying on their backs a few essentials and the knowledge that this is the way things always will be. As they move back and forth across the debris-strewn flats on the edge of a large city, they

sustain each other by their mutual hatred and fear. When they sit down to rest, Lena passes the time counting bottles (which they sell back to the bottlers) or bruises, which is how Boesman communicates with her. Boesman, who is the clown in front of whites, is vicious, cruel and slightly mad. Why do they keep going? Because they cannot *not* go on. As Lena says, "I'm on the earth, not in it."

Though Ross Devenish, the director, has filmed the play in recognizably real settings, he has successfully maintained the play's claustrophobic mood. The broad, flat horizon, against which Boesman and Lena endlessly tramp, is broken occasionally by views of the distant city, by a busy highway, or, most menacing, by the silhouette of a huge power plant that will always be for the service of others. In addition to being a record of an extraordinary play by South Africa's leading playwright, "Boesman and Lena" gives us a visual image of human isolation more haunting than any I've ever seen in a motion picture.

"The River Niger" also is a film adaptation of a theater piece—the Joseph A. Walker play that was first done by the Negro Ensemble Company in 1972 and then moved to Broadway where it won a Tony award. It is, essentially, a black variation on the kind of family melodrama that Arthur Miller used to write, but everything that was theatrical and artificial and acceptable on stage now looks gross in this film adaptation, which is unfortunate since the play-wright seems to have a feeling for the way people talk and behave, at least when they aren't under stress.

The cast is headed by James Earl Jones and Cicely Tyson, who are fine actors when they have the material. Here they are left up in the air by the script and by Krishna Shah, the director who might conceivably have imposed some coherence on the work. Even technically, it's a mess.

● ● ●

"Countdown at Kusini" is Ossie Davis's solemn adventure melodrama set in an emerging African nation. It's a movie that wants to be "serious" about African political aspirations while also being entertaining. Though it tries hard, it's neither, but it does recall fond memories of two movies Davis made some years ago—"Cotton Comes to Harlem" and "Gone Are The Days"—when he still had an outrageous sense of humor.

Solemnity and humorlessness also are a problem with "The Long Night," the first theatrical film to be directed by Woody King, Jr., who, as a producer, has been responsible for much of the excitement on New York's black theater scene. The film, about a little Harlem boy's search for his father, is serious but awfully workmanlike, which means it's so busy saying the right things, presenting a picture of Harlem that avoids the melodramatic clichés, that it never allows itself any spontaneity, any sign of the kind of life that distinguishes art from thesis.

The point of these films, good and bad? It's an important one—that filmmakers, black and white, feel there must be alternatives to Shaft, Coffy, Superfly and even Blacula.

1976 Ap 11, II:15:7

FILM VIEW

VINCENT CANBY

Two Exhilarating Thrillers, Plotted by Hitchcock and Nixon

That the strength, excitement, intelligence and perhaps even conscience of the American cinema are more often to be found in its commercial films than in the work of the independents and backroom innovators is not a proposition I'd want to die defending. It wouldn't be an elegant demise—backed into a corner, being simultaneously suffocated and softened into death through repeated

showings of things like "The Exorcist," "Death Wish," "Lipstick" and "W. C. Fields and Me."

Yet this week there are two new films, which, each in its different way, demonstrate the kind of vitality that is unique to American entertainment movies at their best. They are "All The President's Men," a riveting film version of the Watergate book by Washington Post reporters Carl Bernstein and Bob Woodward, directed by Alan J. Pakula and

Dustin Hoffman and Robert Redford in "All the President's Men"—
making "understandable to non-professionals American journalism at its best"

written by William Goldman, and Alfred Hitchcock's supremely droll and graceful "Family Plot," the Old Master's 56th film as a director since he began to practice that particular art in 1922. Each is a film that could not have been made without the existence of the mass market that so often lures moviemakers into the production of outright junk.

"All The President's Men" is being released at what could be an unfortunate time, coinciding, as it does, with the publication of "The Final Days," the Bernstein-Woodward book that recreates in virtually hour-by-hour fashion the collapse of the Nixon Administration. The achievements of "All The President's Men," both as a book and as a film, are too great for them to be diluted or disparaged in the debates that have already begun about the ethics and historical methods employed in writing "The Final Days."

"The Final Days" is a recreation of events composed by writers whose information must inevitably have come to them second- and third-hand, through interviews with persons who either participated in the events or talked immediately to someone who did. "All The President's Men" is a first-person log (though told in the third person) of two young, previously unknown newspaper reporters who came upon what turned out to be the scoop of the decade or maybe century.

It's a mystery story of sorts, and it's about skullduggery and chicanery in high government places, but it's really about the methods, power, responsibilities, pitfalls, drudgery

and, especially, the excitement of being a working journalist. It's the only narrative film I've seen that comes remotely close to dramatizing the kind of journalistic mission personified by I. F. Stone in Jerry Bruck's fine documentary, "I.F. Stone's Weekly."

A Washington Post "staff" meeting in "All the President's Men"

Harris and Devane as a fake medium and a genuine kidnapper in "Family Plot"

"All The President's Men" follows the form of the Bernstein-Woodward book and though it necessarily simplifies a lot of material, it's still so packed with details relating to the many figures involved in the Watergate burglary and the subsequent cover-up that you may think you need a scorecard to follow it. Not really.

•   •   •

Seen in its purest, most cinematic form, what went on at Watergate the night the headquarters of the Democratic National Committee was invaded is the MacGuffin of "All The President's Men." The "MacGuffin," you remember, is what Hitchcock calls the thing—the plan, the formula, the state secret, whatever—that one group of people in an espionage film is either trying to steal from another party, or trying to protect. In a Hitchcock film what the MacGuffin is is never as important as what happens to all the people who are so determined to possess it.

That's not strictly true in "All The President's Men" if the film is viewed as history, as a record of an extraordinary period in our national life, but no film, certainly no narrative entertainment film, could easily dramatize all of the people and events that make up even the Bernstein-Woodward view of the Watergate story. The film is a fascinating footnote to Watergate, and I suppose if one hadn't been living in this country during the whole thing—during the Grand Jury proceedings and the Senate and House hearings—one might walk out of the film with the impression that a couple of young whippersnapping reporters were being given sole credit for Nixon's eventual resignation.

But to criticize the film on those grounds (and I'm sure that a lot of people will try to) will be to miss the point of the movie, which is to make understandable to non-professionals the appeal and the rewards of American journalism at its best. And by rewards, I emphasize, I'm not making subterranean reference to the financial jackpot that Bernstein and Woodward hit with the book that became a best-seller in both hardback and paperback and then went on to prompt a film sale, though, I'm sure, the authors are going to be condemned for that. The popular notion is that crusading journalists, like clergymen, somehow compromise themselves if they don't remain abjectly poor.

"All The President's Men" is such a model of efficient filmmaking that nothing that Alan J. Pakula has heretofore directed (including "Klute") or that William Goldman has written ("Butch Cassidy and The Sundance Kid," "The Great Waldo Pepper") could have prepared us for the success of this picture. "All The President's Men" is as remarkable for its understatement, for the clichés it avoids, for all of the things it doesn't do, as for the things that it does do.

Chief among the latter is the manner in which it utilizes two fine actors, Robert Redford as Woodward and Dustin Hoffman as Bernstein, to tell us all that we need to know about two reporters whose private lives do not impinge on this film, even peripherally. "All The President's Men" is a portrait of life on a large metropolitan daily told entirely in terms of the investigation of a single event. The Bernstein-Woodward characters must emerge from their actions and reactions during this investigation, which means they are roles to which the actors must bring a great deal of baggage containing their own attitudes, insights and observations. They must play straight men to the action, and had they hammed it up at all, the film would have gone out the window.

Good investigative reporters are a very special breed. They must be aggressive enough to ask a grieving widow whether or not she shot her husband, if there's one chance in a million she may say yes. They have to be character-analysts. They have to know when someone who says he can't talk is actually dying to. They have to be able to listen and, if necessary, to be able to record mental notes when the sight of a pad and pen would freeze a source. They must spend endless time on dozens of leads that go nowhere, confident that the next one might pay off. They must care about what they're doing, if only for the time they're doing it, and they must always understand that the story comes first—they exist for it, not the other way around. When this order is reversed it sometimes results in spectacular journalism, but it's usually journalism of a secondary sort.

The investigative journalist's mixture of aggressiveness,

modesty, introspection, and an almost prissy obsession with tiny details, is something "All The President's Men" defines in a way that no other film has ever done in my memory. In a most effective way, too, these characteristics are reflected in the visual style of the film, which Pakula has shot mostly in a series of close-ups and medium close-ups, punctuated every now and then by a slow retreat to a long shot that is the equivalent to the reporter's taking stock of what he's got so far.

It should also be noted that for a film that is imitating a journalistic kind of impartiality, "All The President's Men" contains some individual scenes of surprising feeling. No one who has lived through the Watergate experience is going to watch this movie without having had his responses preconditioned in some fashion. Still one may be suddenly, unexpectedly moved by a scene in which a frightened bookkeeper (Jane Alexander) decides to spill the beans to the reporters, or by another scene in which the conscience-stricken treasurer of the Committee to Re-elect the President begins to cooperate.

We in the audience are in the position of Bernstein and Woodward and these unexpected glimpses into private torments are unsettling. The movie knows, as every investigative reporter knows, that there are times when you'd prefer to respect the other person's privacy. Not all that often, perhaps, but it does happen.

●　　　●　　　●

"Family Plot" is also a mystery, a sort of semi-sweet, after-dinner story involving two pairs of charlatans who have a near-fatal confrontation in a small but intensely serious (to them) matter involving the long-lost heir to a West Coast fortune. The setting is either San Angeles or Los Francisco (Hitchcock shot the film both in Los Angeles and San Francisco, though it's presented as a single city). The story is about a benignly second-rate medium named Blanche (Barbara Harris), Blanche's lover, a taxi driver named Lumley (Bruce Dern), who sometimes loses patience with Blanche and says angrily, "Without my research, Blanche, you'd be about as psychic as a salami," and about Fran (Karen Black) and Adamson (William Devane), a pair of immensely successful kidnappers who, in one of the film's several Hitchcockian highlights, snatch a Roman Catholic bishop from in front of his cathedral's altar.

The film is Hitchcock in the cheerful mood we associate with his appearances as the master-of-ceremonies of his old television series—thoughtful, measured in tone and so courtly that we are well into the performance before we realize just how high he's sending us up, and with what good humor.

Everyone has a right to his own favorite Hitchcock periods. I have two, his middle-class American gothic period ("Shadow of A Doubt," "Strangers on A Train"), and his international high-life period ("North by Northwest," "Rear Window" and "To Catch A Thief"). "Family Plot" doesn't fit easily into any earlier Hitchcock period, though it has the appreciation for the bizarre event set in utterly mundane surroundings that I remember from the best of his TV productions.

The characters are neither the folks next door nor glamorous types who are likely to turn up for the season at Gstaad. They are people shaped to fit the film—odd, quirky, so intensely self-absorbed that they have no idea that what they're doing is at all unusual. Which is what makes them such good company. When was the last time you saw a film in which the kidnap victim, on being informed that the ransom had been paid and that he was being returned, expressed disappointment that he hadn't yet finished his supper?

The film is faultlessly cast. Barbara Harris, who at long last is getting the kind of roles she deserves, is hilarious as the fraudulent seer, as is Karen Black as the kidnapper who cooks gourmet spreads for her temporary house guests.

"Family Plot" has the exhilarating effect of seeing a magic trick performed so smoothly and effortlessly that, at its conclusion, you'd be furious if someone tried to convince you the lady was not, after all, bisected for a harmless interval.

1976 Ap 11, II:1:4

THE SAILOR WHO FELL FROM GRACE WITH THE SEA, written and directed by Lewis John Carlino, based on the novel by Yukio Mishima; produced by by Martin Poll; music by John Mandel; distributed by Avco Embassy Pictures. At the Coronet Theater. Running time: 105 minutes. This movie has been rated R.

Anne Osborne	Sarah Miles
Jim Cameron	Kris Kristofferson
Jonathan Osborne	Jonathan Kahn
Mrs. Palmer	Margo Cunningham
Chief	Earl Rhodes

By RICHARD EDER

The blurred and preposterous foreground of "The Sailor Who Fell From Grace With the Sea" is the activity of a band of Nietzsche-resotted children straight out of "Lord of the Flies." The limpid and beautifully filmed background is the love story of the mother of one of them and a merchant marine officer. The film's climax is the bloody clash between the two stories, a climax that should be tragic but is simply grotesque and unbelievable.

When the main action of a movie is so weak and the background is so strong, a peculiar focus develops. There is a beguilement to "Sailor," which opened yesterday at the Coronet Theater —that of sitting through a movie in a state of irascible unconvincedness while being more than half seduced.

"Sailor" is a radical transplant of a short story by the Japanese writer Yukio Mishima, a writer who gathered around himself a kind of heroic cult and who killed himself to protest the softness of the times. Lewis John Carlino moved it from Yokohama to Dartmouth, a Devon port.

●

With the inspired work of his director of photography, Douglas Slocombe, the transposition is an atmospheric triumph. The sweet but somber English coast, its lowering skies and transforming bursts of sunshine, the clean presence of the sea, the white seaside house where the widowed mother lives and into which

the sailor comes—all these develop a powerful emotional background for their relationship.

It is a relationship that manages to be romantic and erotic. Sarah Miles is spectacular; she makes sensual yearning convincing both in itself and as standing for the whole range of human want. Kris Kristofferson, as the American sailor who gives up the sea to marry her, looks good but doesn't convey much more than puzzled weakness.

But then there is the main story. The widow's 13-year old son, Jonathan, is one of a clique of six boys led by a precocious, mad towhead who has tailored the cult of the superman down into short pants. The boys sit out beside the sea while the chief lectures them on the merciless nobility of the amoeba. They draw up bills of accusation against adults. They sentence a cat to death for being old and fat; they drug it and dissect it alive. Jonathan is ambiguous about his mother's sailor, but the chief concludes that by leaving the sea the sailor has become like the fat cat and deserves the same fate. So the boys go to work on it.

Mishima's implacable mouse-gang had a certain abstract grandness. These round-faced English boys smoking cigars and spouting phrases too large for their mouths simply looked silly. Part of the trouble is the writing; Mishima transposed by Mr. Carlino is not capable, as William Golding or Richard Hughes are, of projecting the local English boy into a primeval childhood.

Furthermore, Mr. Carlino, for all his skill with the adults and the atmosphere, seems to have no idea how to direct children. Their murderous games never convey horror; they get no further than embarrassment.

1976 Ap 12, 36:1

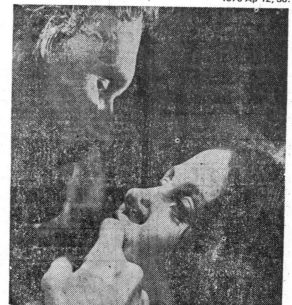

Kris Kristofferson and Sarah Miles

'Virility' By Ponti Arrives

What is a self-respecting and supposedly modern-thinking Sicilian father to do when he knows that the only truthful way to still the townspeople who are calling his London-educated son a homosexual is to reveal that the young man has cuckolded him?

That is the question at the wizened comic heart of "Virility," a Carlo Ponti film that opened yesterday at the 68th Street Playhouse. It isn't that the idea isn't a reasonable updating and extension of the movies' long and occasionally hilarious exploration of the comedic potential of Italian mores.

●

It's simply that "Virility" expends too much time reaching the point where it poses the problem and not enough inventiveness in exploiting the possible answers. Only one scene — of the father, Don Vito, disguised as his son, Roberto, attempting a rape while announcing his assumed identity — begins to hint at what might have been.

The movie can boast sun-washed scenery that is escapist entertainment in itself; the attractions of Agostina Belli as Don Vito's young second wife, and a general air of polish that did not, unfortunately, spread far enough to impart the sparkle of inspiration to the script.

LAWRENCE VAN GELDER

1976 Ap 12, 36:4

THE PHANTOM ENTHUSIAST, a film by Andrew Noren. Running time: 60 minutes. At the Whitney Museum of American Art, Madison Avenue at 75th Street.

"The Phantom Enthusiast," which began a week's run at the Whitney Museum yesterday, is a 60-minute essay on light and shadow by Andrew Noren, the American underground filmmaker. The enthusiast of the title is Mr. Noren. His object here is to turn banal images—curtains blowing in the wind, a bare foot on a wooden floor, a close-up of a curious cat, numerous close-ups of various parts of a female body—into phantom objects that have a kind of heightened reality on film. The effect is soothing for the first 15 minutes, numbing after that.

VINCENT CANBY

1976 Ap 14, 25:5

THE RIVER NIGER, directed by Krishna Shah; screenplay by Joseph A. Walker, based on his play; produced by Sidney Beckerman and Ike Jones; editor, Irving Lerner; director of photography, Michael Margules; music written and performed by members of War; released by Cine Artists Pictures. Running time: 105 minutes. At Loews State 1 Theater, Bway at 45th Street; Fine Arts Theater, 58th Street east of Park Avenue, and UA East Theater, First Avenue at 85th Street. This film has been rated R.

Mattie Williams	Cicely Tyson
Johnny Williams	James Earl Jones
Dr. Dudley Stanton	Lou Gossett
Jeff Williams	Glynn Turner
Big Moe Hayes	Roger E. Mosley
Ann Vanderguild	Jonelle Allen
Grandma Brown	Hilda Haynes
Chips	Theodore Wilson
Skeeter	Charles Weldon
Al	Ralph Wilcox
Gail	Shirley Jo Finney
Police lieutenant	Ed Crick
Policeman	Tony Burton

By VINCENT CANBY

"The River Niger" is the screen version of Joseph A. Walker's award-winning Negro Ensemble Company play that opened off Broadway in 1972 and later went on to have a successful run on Broadway. Now it's virtually an object lesson in how not to make a movie out of a theater piece.

Among other things one should not do is to open up the play to take advantage of the camera's mobility. The people who made "The River Niger" have opened it, all right, then they've left it opened up—exposed and sort of gaping—so that while the actors act, the director directs and the cameraman practices tricks used better by other cameramen, the life of the work has passed on to that great theatrical warehouse in the sky.

"The River Niger" is essentially a black variation of the kind of family play that Arthur Miller once wrote, about fathers and sons and husbands and wives, at a crucial moment of reckoning in their lives. It's about such a moment in the life of Johnny Williams (James Earl Jones), a house painter who writes poetry; his wife, Mattie (Cicely Tyson), and their son Jeff (Glynn Turman), who is coming home after what his parents believe to have been a successful tour of duty as an Air Force navigator.

Jeff, however, has not been entirely truthful with his parents. He was cashiered from officer's training school for refusing to play the role of "Supernigger" for the white officers. Neither has Mattie been entirely truthful to Jeff and her husband. She's dying of cancer, while Johnny, when he isn't painting a house or writing a poem, is a bit of a lush.

There are further problems, especially a subplot involving some old friends of Jeff's who have formed a black revolutionary army of four, one of whom is apparently a police informer.

What really wrecks the screen version of "The River Niger" is not the on-screen melodrama that once was mostly offstage—though it is pretty dopey—but what appears to be a total lack of cohesive style and cinematic intelligence.

I have no idea whether the responsibility is that of Mr. Walker, who adapted his play for the screen, of the director, Krishna Shah, who at times seems to have no idea where his camera should be, or of the editor, Irving Lerner, who may have done the best he could with the footage he was given. Many times two successive shots within a single scene don't match and, worse, characters have a way of leaving a scene without making a conventional exit.

●

The actors have the air of people who've arrived at a party where there's no host. They are on their own. Mr. Jones, one of our finest actors, plays it big, sometimes explosively so, as if he knew things were going on around him that we don't. Miss Tyson carries her nobility around the sets with grim determination, looking like the housewife who says her bulging, 200-pound shopping bag isn't a bit heavy.

Perhaps because he doesn't try so hard, Mr. Turman, who was so effective in "Cooley High," is less offensive, though Hilda Haynes, as the grandmother, is little more than a sight gag, and she doesn't try at all.

Lou Gossett, as the family friend, a doctor whose roots are in the West Indies, is the one cast member not to be compromised by the mess around him.

There are not so many decent black films that the failure of a property like "The River Niger" can be accepted as anything but a major disappointment.

1976 Ap 15, 28:1

COUNTDOWN AT KUSINI, directed by Ossie Davis; written by Mr. Davis, Ladi Ladebo and Al Freeman Jr.; director of photography, Andrew Laszlo; music by Manu Dibango; produced by Mr. Ladebo in association with Tan International Ltd. of Nigeria, Glipp Productions Inc. and Arnold Stone and Bruce Graham; released by Columbia Pictures. At the Penthouse Theater, Broadway and 47th Street, the RKO 59th Street East Twin I Theater, east of Third Avenue and the 86th Street Twin I Theater, west of Lexington Avenue. Running time 101 minutes. This film is rated PG.

"Countdown at Kusini" is the sort of movie that illustrates what happens when achievement falls short of aims.

Conceived as a conventional melodramatic vehicle for the transmission of excitement and as a medium for explanation of the black revolution in Africa to an alien audience, this movie—filmed in and around Lagos, Nigeria—emerges as subpar adventure and less than lucid ideology.

For the most part, it concerns itself with a plot by multinational corporations—the postcolonial villains—to remove a black revolutionary leader through the efforts of a French mercenary and his black and white collaborators. A woman dedicated to the revolution and an American jazz musician, drawn more to the woman than to politics, provide the romantic interest and the effort to thwart the mercenary.

The script is burdened with lamentable lines that require the best efforts of Ossie Davis, Ruby Dee and Greg Morris in the lead roles to overcome and failing that, invite the use of nearly constant music to drown out the dialogue.

Compounding the troubles are the occasional mismatched shots and, in effect, an epilogue that vitiates its educational strivings.

LAWRENCE VAN GELDER

1976 Ap 17, 10:1

The Screen: 'Beanstalk'

In a kind of half-run display—it is being shown in the afternoons but not the evenings—a full-length cartoon version of "Jack and the Beanstalk" opened at neighborhood theaters yesterday.

The lines are blurry, the colors muddy, and the action is blocklike. When the characters' lips move up and down, the words come out sideways. Considerable research discloses that the film was made in Japan and dubbed.

It is the kind of thing grandfathers are sent out to take their grandchildren to. They will sit silently, side by side, and a quiet loathing will spring up between them.

RICHARD EDER

1976 Ap 16, 11:3

Somebody Should Have Put Their Names in Lights

By WALLACE MARKFIELD

Let us now praise not so famous men and women—those timeless small-time sub-stars of the 30's and 40's whose names deserve to be spelled out in bright lights.

The players I have in mind took bullets for Bogart and Robinson and Garfield; lost John Boles to Barbara Stanwyck, George Brent to Bette Davis; chased Frankie Darrow and Billy Halop off their stoops or out of their stores; forced bowls of broth down the throat of Sylvia Sidney; fired, then rehired Fred MacMurray with a fat raise; serviced monster-making machines for Lionel Atwill, racing cars and taxis for Cagney, China Clippers and Flying Fortresses for Pat O'Brien; gunned down Randolph Scott, pistol-whipped Joel McCrea and sold out Alan Ladd to the Syndicate or the Gestapo. Designed for long wear, hard use and instant identity, these studio workhorses, spent much of their prime time supporting the same stars in variations of the same roles. Roughly classified below by way of the things they did best and most often is a bunch of my favorites.

The leading man's Best Pal:

Frank McHugh. He was small, round, had the finest snicker in the business, eyebrows as active and eloquent as Cagney's hands and exuded sweet, spunky decency. A happy worrier, he always had to re-lace a boxer's gloves, make last minute adjustments on carburetors and run into plane hangers with the latest weather reports. All the same, he went down in flames, drove his underpowered overloaded truck off the highway, got himself blinded by gangster acid—though not without the satisfaction of hearing Ann Sheridan, Gale Page, Rosemary Lane say, seconds before they returned his engagement rings, "Ah gee, but you're some swell guy Rockie, Peewee, Fatso, Hunk, Gaffer." The quintessential McHugh can be seen stealing or saving "Boy Meets Girl" (1938), "Dodge City" (1939) and "The Roaring Twenties" (1929).

Allen Jenkins. Chinless, big-nosed, sleepy looking, he had a lovely double-take, a very prolonged slow burn, a heavy, peevish, uninflected voice and blinks or twitches which could carry him from aggravation to genuine anguish. A good-natured lumpen lug, he stood up and got slapped down for such people as the new fish in prison, the wise-guy cub reporter, the widowed waitress with Baby Sandy to raise, the ensign fresh out of Annapolis, the chorine who wanted to be a coed, the coed who wanted to forget she was a princess, a gangster's sister, a crooked politician's daughter. He was a virtuoso of croaky compassion and, at times, something more—as when he bears bad news to Bogart in "Dead End" (1937) or muses on life and death with Joseph Calleia in "Five Came Back" (1939).

Jack Oakie. He looked like the man in the moon, only more benevolent. Among his signature traits: a congested whinny, a Katzenjammer Kid grin, a moan that involved his body up to the metatarsals; a way of barking lines like an exuberant seal; a gait that crossed an uncertain toddle with a cocky pig-trot. Of all screen stooges, he made the finest consoler-cajoler, milking incredible subtleties out of lines like, "Listen, sap she was always crazy about ya — that's why she hadda walk out" . . . "Pop's gotta pull through, honey, conner God is all booked up on singles" . . . "Aw, boss, I begged ya—don't never trust no dame named Dixie." Though I honor his Mussolini in "The Great Dictator" (1940), I still think his best work was done earlier at Paramount—as the dimwitted fullback in "College Humor" (1933), the sorrowful saddle pal in "The Texas Rangers" (1936). Watch him, near the close of "Rangers," playing cards and telling tales with Lloyd Nolan and pretending not to know death is imminent.

Magnificent Brute:

Alan Hale. Big, ruddy, slobbish, bellicose, with a laugh as memorable as Edward Arnold's, he would have made at least a fair Falstaff or an altogether perfect father

Wallace Markfield is writing a secret history of the movies.

for Mickey Rooney's Studs Lonigan. But Warner Brothers did the next best thing by turning him, after his second Porthos, his third Little

John, into a kind of brawling Babbitt who generally wore ill-used union suits, sagging suspenders and one sleeve-garter. As of this writing,

Frank McHugh

Jane Bryan

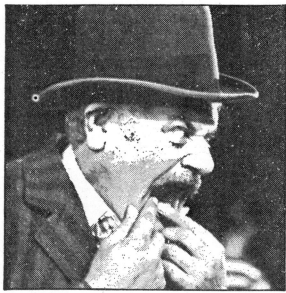

Alan Hale

Ann Dvorak and Barton MacLane

Allen Jenkins

Jack Oakie

I'm still waiting to tire of seeing him spit into each palm, smash both fists down upon the nearest straw skimmer and stand back to back with Cagney ("Strawberry Blonde," 1941) and Flynn ("Gentleman Jim," 1942). And if I could I'd freeze each frame of his stamping dance with Stanwyck in "Stella Dallas" (1937) and move it into a museum.

Barton MacLane. He started as a second banana in silents, made a so-so transition to sound trapping Glenda Farrell into violating her parole, assigning Eddie Woods to the dirtiest job in the prison laundry room and slashing the tires on George E. Stone's cab. Then with "Black Fury" (1935) and "Ceiling Zero" (1936), he had his first good clear shots at what critic Manny Farber calls "the mean, brassy, clawlike soul of the lone American wolf." And for the next two decades, his catfooted bulk, Eskimo eyes and freezing shantytown tenor would be imposing themselves on the pulpiest material, checking and balancing the high-styled histrionic conceits of Davis, Muni and Robinson. To this day, MacLane is so deeply embedded in my memory that I still expect to spot him some night on the 10 o'clock news; he'll be reaching out of a squad car toward the biggest apple in Henry Armetta's pushcart while Gabe Pressman needles him about allegations of police corruption.

Ward Bond. With his Merrie Melodies bulldog face and brawn he was ideally suited to serve all those 25-year hitches in John Ford's cavalry. By my own private poll, though, Bond-buffs were happiest when he played cowtown Caligulas named Buck Lothar and Tim Rasp and Honey Bragg who shamed Victor Jory's squaw, prodded Robert Preston into drawing against Dan Duryea, tossed Charles Winninger into his own jailhouse, landed a haymaker flush on the mouth that Edgar Buchanan had just fitted with brand-new store teeth. Readers looking for profounder pleasures are herewith referred to his great Beery-Dressler act with Edna May Oliver in "Drums Along the Mohawk" (1939) or his death watch soliloquy ("Lord, but she graces me

. . .") in "Joan of Arc" (1948).

Tough Old Hen:

May Robson. Only Helen Westley ever said "Fiddlesticks!" and "Poppycock" more often or as well. But Robson was a shade better, I think, giving hawk-nosed fish-eyed glowers and derisive snorts, and clearly outclassed her at wielding a stout gold-headed cane; with either hand, from the craziest angles, Robson could lay it across the backsides of two fawning relatives simultaneously, sweep medicine bottles from her nightstand, poke a lawyer's paunch, scatter a pack of newshounds, show the door to a defiant ward. Now and then, though, she needed it to flick off a sneaky tear when some kid, fresh from the county orphanage, sang "Ave Maria" alongside her wheel chair. And because she had this weakness for outcasts, guys like Garfield got her to twinkle, beam and do intricate things with an apron. Stay up, then, to watch them in "Four Daughters" (1938) and "They Made Me a Criminal" (1939).

I-Don't-Care Girl:

Ann Dvorak. She was so skinny and her pop-eyes showed such aching fatigue it was a wonder she could talk, let alone fill a sound track with that ferocious sinusey clamor. Yet in a movie era when performers seemed to expend 1,000 calories flaring a nostril, her buzz-saw velocity was phenomenal and a little scary. It made Muni, in "Scarface" (1932) look positively lethargic as he punched her out, conked her with crockery and smashed her Russ Columbo records. Wantons were her specialty; she played them with the kind of down-home herky-jerky "Tillie and Mac" book gusto the early Joan Crawford and the early-middle Bette Davis went after but never quite got. To her everlasting credit, she's the only actress who could convince me that she genuinely wanted a kiss from Warren William. Judge for yourself what she wanted from Cagney in "The Crowd Roars" (1932) and "G-Men" (1933).

Nice Nellie, Tender Comrade:

Jane Bryan. Like Margaret Sullavan, she had one of the very few snub-nosed, apple-cheeked faces that could go from winsome to absolutely adorable without stopping first at cute. It was a powerful asset when she needed to mispronounce "minestrone" in Rose Stradner's kitchen and blush at the mention of "bambini," wheedle William Holden into working for peanuts at John Qualen's one-pump filling station and make Wayne Morris understand that even though their baby was due in October he might still give her bearhugs in March. And because Bryan may have just been the best young actress Warner Brothers ever misused, her sweet-tempered girls named Jo still strike me as tough-minded, muscular and earthbound. She didn't stay in movies long enough to give more than one stunning performance—as the doomed governess in "We Are Not Alone" (1939).

The careers of most of these people ended long ago, along with the studio system itself. Yet I did manage to pick out the late Allen Jenkins' face in the last few feet of Billy Wilder's 1974 remake of "Front Page." He was the telegrapher who wore a green eye shade and got to say "Okay," then "Right," then "Sure." ∎

1976 Ap 18, II:1:5

OTTO MESSMER'S FELIX THE CAT, a program of short cartoons created by Otto Messmer: "Felix Revolts," 1921, 7½ minutes; "The Cold Rush," 1925, 8 minutes; "Eats Are West," 1925, 8½ minutes; "Felix Hits the Deck," 1927, 7½ minutes; "Arabianantics," 1928, 7 minutes; "Switches Witches," 1927, 8 minutes; "Astronomeous," 1928, 7 minutes; "Comicalamities," 1928, 8½ minutes. Total running time: 62 minutes. At the Whitney Museum of American Art, Madison Avenue at 75th Street.

By VINCENT CANBY

The most blithe and buoyant film show in town at the moment is at the Whitney Museum of American Art, where a program titled "Otto Messmer's Felix the Cat" opened a week's run yesterday. It's a tribute not only to one of the first cartoon characters ever to become an international star, but also to Mr. Messmer, who created Felix but whose name never appeared on any of the hundreds of animated shorts that were always identified with Pat Sullivan, who was the producer.

Though Felix made his first appearance in 1919, the Whitney show is composed of eight shorts made between 1921 and 1928, which was Felix's Periclean Age, when the Messmer lines and ink blobs took shape as one of the most dynamic personalities of the silent screen.

In these films Felix is a joyous rediscovery—a truculent, resourceful man-cat

'Designed for long wear, these old-time studio workhorses usually supported the same stars in the same roles'

with a walk that looks like the trudge of a bouncer in a waterfront saloon. As the Messner backgrounds are simple to the point of being philosophic statements (one tree is all trees, one house is all houses, etc.), so too are the stories that were created for Felix. The stories are framing devices for the comic routines, almost any one of which could as conveniently fit into any of the other stories.

For reasons I don't quite understand, there is something immensely liberating about this sort of casual attitude toward narrative. Free form has always been an important quality of animated cartoons, even of the much more sophisticated work of the Disney studios, but in the comparatively primitive Messmer cartoons, the freedom of the form looks almost avant-garde.

Felix doesn't live in a void exactly, like Krazy Kat, but it is a fantasy land that is unadorned by anything except essential props and distinguishing landmarks. It's a place where anything can happen, with profound appreciation for the ridiculous. I particularly like Felix's habit of reaching up to catch the exclamation points that are always issuing from his head and turning them, as needed, into baseball bats, airplane propellers or cart axes. Felix's tail is not only prehensile, it's detachable, so it can be used as a cane or maybe the stalk of an umbrella.

The eight shorts being shown at the Whitney are, of course, silents, and are as full of literary puns as visual ones. In "Felix Hits the Deck" Felix falls through a deck of giant cards into a landscape inhabited by hearts, spades, clubs and diamonds. When Felix, hungry as usual, sees a strange woman. a card reports his thoughts, "Hey that's the king's auntie. I'll work her for some jack."

●

The most inventive and appealing of the Whitney's eight selections is "Comicalamities," made in 1928, in which Felix has trouble with the cartoonist who drew his outlines but forgot to shade his body. Felix rectifies this omission by applying shoe polish. Then, getting the knack of cartooning, he takes it upon himself — with the help of an eraser—to turn an ugly little female cat into a beauty, only to have her snub him at the end. It's "City Lights" three years before Chaplin's.

One of the nicest things about the Whitney show is that Mr. Messmer should be able to enjoy it too. At the age of 83 he lives in the same New Jersey house he's occupied since 1945, with his wife, whom he married 52 years ago.

FILM VIEW

VINCENT CANBY

Bergman Explores The Terrors Of Blandness

There is no war. No foreign troops are massed on the border making threatening gestures. Everyone has enough to eat. Unemployment and discrimination on the basis of race or class are unknown. Something very nearly like the perfect state has been achieved. Yet not long ago the representatives of this perfect state swooped down on Ingmar Bergman, while he was in a theater rehearsing a new play, and carried him off under guard to question him at length about charges that he had defrauded the state of tax monies due. It was front-page news in Stockholm, and here too for a while. Shortly before the charges against Bergman were dropped, Bernard Weinraub, The Times correspondent in London, reported from Stockholm that as much as anything else, many Swedes resented Bergman's talent. He was considered to have gotten too big for his britches. Bergman, the internationally acclaimed filmmaker, had somehow spoiled Swedish symmetry by being a large lump in a flat landscape, by being recognized, critically and financially, for his genius, and genius is something they don't dispense in government-run clinics. It was as if the Swedish national organism automatically was trying to reject him. The aberration had to be excised.

It was a harrowing story, and as much a Bergman story as his new film, "Face to Face," which is about phantoms that come out of the night and almost destroy a woman who is described as a model of mental health. The woman is a closer of doors that have been left ajar. She puts great store by neatness and order and would, if asked, probably tell you that she is as happy as she could ever hope to be in her marriage and in her career (she is a successful psychiatrist). It might not be too much to suggest that the state of nearly perfect control over exterior matters achieved by Dr. Jenny Isaksson (Liv Ullmann) in "Face to Face" is a little like Sweden's. But such perfection, once achieved, demands resources for its successful maintenance that Jenny doesn't have. The interior Jenny is chaos. The overwhelming urge is toward self-destruction.

I don't mean to say that "Face to Face" is an intentional metaphor for Sweden; only that one of the reasons that this Bergman film speaks to us so forcefully is because it is so Swedish. The bland efficiency of the society in which it is set dramatizes the magnitude of the emotional terrors that cause Jenny's breakdown. It isolates those terrors so that they may be seen as what they are. In an American film set in New York or Chicago or Seattle, such a breakdown might conceivably be the result of as many different kinds of exterior pressures as interior confusions.

Sweden—at least the Sweden that Bergman shows us —is that future state in which all social ills have been cured. There are no political or social causes left, no excuses not to tend to the inner self. It's as if mankind had achieved the two-day week and didn't know what to do with the other five days. In an earlier era one might have spent a good deal of that time in church, on one's knees, going through rituals of atonement, supplication and thanksgiving. But now that that has been denied, what is left? The Volvo transports one to the country but not out of oneself.

On its surface "Face to Face" is the painful case history of Jenny Isaksson who, in early summer and at a time of apparent serenity, is suddenly overtaken by doubts and fears that she had thought she had successfully suppressed. Jenny's husband is in Chicago attending a conference. She has taken a lover, whom we never

see and whom she finds boring but necessary. While her new house is being completed, she moves in with her grandmother and grandfather who had raised her as a child, after her parents were killed in an automobile accident.

Once in their apartment, Jenny starts to come apart at the seams. Nightmares and waking hallucinations suggest that Jenny's self-assurance is desperation. Then one Sunday morning she calmly sits on the bed of her childhood and consumes the contents of an entire bottle of sleeping pills. The calm—the bravery—she shows is that of the child in the dark who does not cry out for help (as she says later) for fear no one will come.

The drugged dreams that follow—and that make up important sections of the film—spell out in literal detail Jenny's neuroses. In fact this case history is not as compelling as psychiatry as it is for what it represents, a person trying desperately to make contact with primal emotions that have been either ignored or hidden in order to create a character acceptable to the world. The shock is that Jenny, the most controlled of people, should have been able to fool herself so long but, ultimately, so ineffectually.

This theme is not new to Bergman. This process of self-discovery was an important aspect of "Scenes From A Marriage" as the wife, also played by Miss Ullmann, worked herself free from the character she had created, first for her mother and father and then for her husband, to realize herself. In "Face to Face," as in "Scenes From A Marriage," we witness, in effect, the dispossessed in the act of repossessing.

"Face to Face" has an almost musical shape. The theme is stated, restated with variations, reversed and contradicted, and restated again in terms that have the air of reconciliation.

When we first meet Jenny's grandmother, she seems a handsome, loving, understanding old lady. In Jenny's dreams she is the tyrant who locked her in dark closets and imposed on her a sense of inhibiting propriety. In the last scene the old lady, out of our earshot, is gently tending Jenny's grandfather, a frightened, quarrelsome old man who says of his physical and mental decay, "I'm so ashamed." Jenny watches the two old people together with infinite sadness and something that passes for a new understanding about human relationships, and about love. It's among the most beautiful and affecting scenes Bergman has ever filmed.

Miss Ullmann gives a triumphant performance in what must be one of the greatest roles Bergman has ever written for a woman. Like the film itself, which has such a sense of the sound, light, texture and even the smell of things, the performance is virtually tactile, having about it the kind of excitement one usually experiences only in the theater. Toward the end of the film Jenny huddles against a wall of her hospital room, wearing a hospital gown and white wool socks, her hair matted with sweat, and relives a childhood trauma in her own voice and that of her grandmother. In this scene, more than in any of the dreams, Bergman creates a stunning picture not only of personal anxiety but also of the fury that may exist just below the surface of any perfect state.

CRIME AND PASSION, directed by Ivan Passer; screenplay by Jesse Lasky Jr., and Pat Silver; executive producer, Barney Bernhard; produced by Robert L. Abrams; director of photography, Denis C. Lewiston; music, Vangelis Papathanassiou; editors, John Jympson and Bernard Gribble; a Samuel Z. Arkoff-Gloria Films presentation, distributed by American International Pictures. Running time: 92 minutes. At the Harris Theater, 42d Street west of Broadway, and other theaters. This film has been rated R.

Andre .... Omar Sharif
Susan .... Karen Black
Larry .... Joseph Bottoms

By VINCENT CANBY

The talent of Ivan Passer, the Czechoslovak director-writer who has been living in this country in recent years, is very real but so finely tuned that it can be thrown off by mundane things, like a magnetic compass disoriented by a passing garbage truck. Though Mr. Passer has a poet's eye for unexpected details and associations, and though he's a risk-taker, his is not a fragile talent. When he makes a mistake, it's a whopper.

"Crime and Passion," which opened yesterday at neighborhood theaters, is such a film, a grossly disoriented and disorienting shaggy-dog of a movie that seems to have no point, and no point of view, whatever.

Based on a James Hadley Chase novel that I haven't read, it's a somewhat black comedy about a neurotic international financial consultant (Omar Sharif), who, when things are going bad for him, has seizures of sexual passion the way other men get sweaty palms. It's also about his loyal assistant, played by Karen Black, whom he marries off to an eccentric German millionaire in a scheme to defraud the bridegroom.

The settings include a posh European ski resort and an ancient German castle, while the ghost of a headless knight and an elaborate television monitoring system (in the castle) are among the props.

What it's meant to be, I cannot tell. A comedy, melodrama, spoof? There are moments when you might think you are watching one of those stateless exercises that Roman Polanski likes to make occasionally, a movie that seems peculiarly decadent because it has no discernible national identity. This I suspect to be a false reading because everything that Mr. Passer has ever done, including his American-made "Born to Win" and "Law and Disorder," is the work of a director of profound sensitivity. In "Crime and Passion" the talent has been thrown off—wildly.

1976 Ap 22, 38:3

BOESMAN AND LENA, directed by Ross Davenish; screenplay from his original stage play by Athol Fugard; photographed by David Muir; Produced by Johan Wight. Released by New Yorker Films. At the Film Forum, 15 Vandam St., April [illegible] 25 and April 29 through May 2. This film has not been rated. Running time: 102 minutes.

Lena .... Yvonne Bryceland
Boesman .... Athol Fugard
Outa .... Sandy Tube
Bait-shop owner .... Val David

By RICHARD EDER

It almost seems too confining to refer to Athol Fugard as the great South African playwright—he is one of the most compelling dramatic writers in any part of the English-speaking world—except that his universal images invariably come from the specific local patch of misery in his homeland.

"Boesman and Lena" mines one particular corner of the patch. A Cape colored man and wife are the protagonists. Their mixed blood puts them a bit above the black bottom of exisence, but their wretched shanty-dweller life makes the advantage a tiny and pathetic one.

The action is a day and a night in their life. The day begins with the bulldozer tearing down their shanty, and continues with their painful trek, possessions on their back, across an infernal landscape, half-tropical, half-industrial. The night is a sleepless, harrowing tearing at each other with words and blows, the only interruption being the arrival of an ill black man who huddles with them and dies before morning.

•

Yesterday the Film Forum began a weeklong showing of a film made out of the play by the South African director Ross Devenish. It has two magnificent actors—Yvone Bryceland as Lena and Athol Fugard himself as Boesman. It makes a powerful use of the camera to convert light and landscape into a prison. Its dialogue burns.

To Boesman and Lena the oppression of their lives mean opposite things. In him it becomes anger, violence and bitter rejection. In her it becomes a building-upon the few possibilities they have.

"Do you beat me, Boesman," she asks hopefully, "because you want to touch me?" Or, resignedly, as he trudges ahead of her: "Boesman's back—that's the scenery in my life."

When he does break his silence it is with a magnificently despairing vision. "The white man throws away his rubbish," he says. "We pick it up, we eat it, we wear it. We've become the white man's rubbish."

•

Such an unsparing exposure of existence made "Boesman" one of Fugard's best plays. Unfortunately, the movie doesn't succeed. Film time is different from stage time. The spoken word is not enough to carry it along, and this film—chained to the stage despite the landscape—falters with all its admirable and vivid cargo.

1976 Ap 23, 23:2

THE LAST HARD MEN, directed by Andrew V. McLaglen, screenplay by Guerdon Trueblood from a novel by Brian Garfield, produced by William Belasco, photographed by Duke Callaghan. Released by 20th Century-Fox. At Mann's National and local theaters. Running time: 98 minutes. This movie has been rated R.

Sam Burgade .... Charlton Heston
Zach Provo .... James Coburn
Susan Burgade .... Barbara Hershey
Cesar Menendez .... Jorge Rivero
Sheriff Noel Nye .... Michael Parks

By RICHARD EDER

"The Last Hard Men" is not just a horse opera; it's practically Tristan and Isolde. Only the love-death relation isn't between a man and a woman but between a retired lawman and a half-breed. Navajo who is obsessed with the notion of killing him.

The obsession isn't plain old-fashioned hatred. It is decked out with psychological curlicues. The Navajo cannot simply kill the lawman but has to kill him slowly so as not to lose him all at once.

Charlton Heston is not bad as the retired sheriff who has little but contempt for his technologically minded successor, a young man who relies on the telephone to summon out the cavalry and goes to train robberies in a primitive automobile.

James Coburn is hopeless as the maddened half-breed who leads a gang of convicts into a jailbreak and forces them to follow him on his mission of killing the old sheriff. Mr. Coburn grimaces, shows his teeth, rolls his eyes and gargles his consonants.

The plot moves along with reasonable briskness for a while. The Navajo kidnaps the sheriff's daughter to lure the old man out into chasing him. Mr. Heston does, and there is a shoot-out filmed with the new goriness—viz., each time a bullet goes in the front, sticky red stuff falls out the back. There is also an endless rape scene. It is shot in slow-motion to convey horror, but it only conveys somnolence.

Some of the chases are well done, particularly a night scene when the daughter tries to escape the bandits and is hauled back. I liked the dry performance of Michael Parks as the young sheriff who has more faith in his telephone than in old-fashioned shoot-outs. Otherwise, the film is heavy and pretentious. It is showing at Mann's National and other local theaters.

1976 Ap 24, 16:1

BAMBINA, directed by Alberto Lattuada; screenplay (Italian with English subtitles) by Ottavio Jemma, Mr. Lattuada and Bruno Di Geronimo; director of photography, Lamberto Caimi; music by Fred Bongusto; produced by Silvio Clementelli; released by Buckley Brothers Films Inc. At the Paris Theater, 58th Street west of Fifth Avenue. Running time: 97 minutes. This film is classified R.

Saverio Mazzacolli .... Luigi Proiettei
Donna Raimonda .... Irene Papas
Clotilde .... Teresa Ann Savoy
Peppe .... Bruno Cirino
Don Amilcare .... Mario Scaccia
Concetta .... Lina Polito

By RICHARD EDER

The Italian director Alberto Lattuada has made some splendid movies in his time: "Mafioso," for example, and the odd and interesting "Letters From a Novice." It doesn't seem to be his time any more, judging from "Bambina," which opened yesterday at the Paris Theater. There is a flicker of style in it, but it seems like a dying reflex.

The film is about a scheming young real estate promoter who loses his schemes and most of his wits in a passionate love affair with a mentally retarded 16-year-old girl. A feeble attempt is made to justify it as a kind of innocent Adam and Eve idyll. What is being justified is a lot of fairly explicit sex, aimed — such are the wonders of pornographic specialization — at people with a fetish for imbeciles.

Teresa Ann Savoy never really reaches imbecile level. Luigi Proietti looks as if he could be funny if he were ever to be cast in a funny movie. Irene Papas, as the girl's mother, presides in mournful amazement.

1976 Ap 26, 40:1

STAY HUNGRY, directed by Bob Rafelson; screenplay by Charles Gaines and Mr. Rafelson, based on the novel by Mr. Gaines; produced by Harold Schneider and Mr. Rafelson; director of photography, Victor Kemper; editor, John Link 2d; music, Bruce Langhorne and Byron Berline; an/Outov production, distributed by United Artists. Running time: 103 minutes. At the Trans-Lux East Theater, Third Avenue near 58th Street, and the 86th Street East Theater, 86th Street near Third Avenue. This film has been rated R.

Craig Blake .... Jeff Bridges
Mary Tate Farnsworth .... Sally Field
Joe Santo .... Arnold Schwarzenegger
Thor Erickson .... R. G. Armstrong
Franklin .... Robert Englund
Anita .... Helena Kallianiotes
Newton .... Roger E. Mosley
Craig's uncle .... Woodrow Parfrey
William .... Scatman Crothers
Dorothy Stephens .... Kathleen Miller
Amy Walterson .... Fannie Flagg
Zoe Mason .... Joanna Cassidy

By VINCENT CANBY

"Stay Hungry," the new film directed by Bob Rafelson ("Five Easy Pieces" and "The King of Marvin Gardens"), isn't all bad. It just seems that way when it pretends to be more eccentric than it is and to have more on its mind than it actually does.

From time to time there are some awfully good things in it, including its picture of the "new" go-getting South, in this case Birmingham, Ala., a place where old-money families live side by side in peace and harmony with the new rich, have the same accents, belong to the same country clubs and sometimes share a rapacity that would please the greediest of 19th-century carpetbaggers.

•

There are also good performances by Jeff Bridges as the oddball scion of landed Birmingham gentry, by Sally Field as his something-less-than bluebood mistress and by Arnold Schwarzenegger as a Mr. Universe contestant, a nice, honorable young man who appears to be trapped inside a huge, grotesquely muscled body that has no relation to the conventional head on top of it.

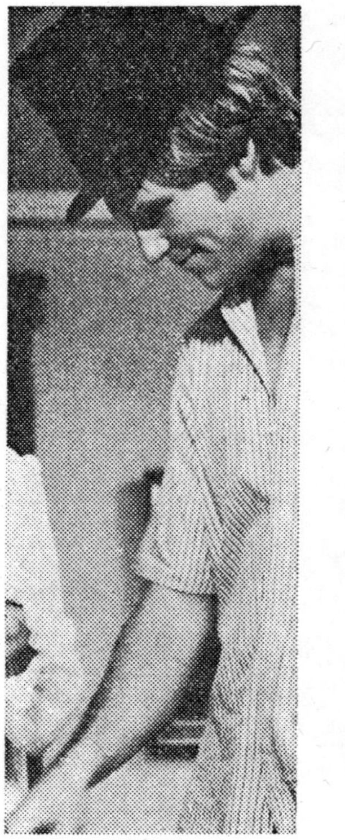

Jeff Bridges

The film, which opened yesterday at the Trans-Lux East and the 86th Street East Theaters, was written by Mr. Rafelson and Charles Gaines, who also wrote the original novel and who, according to the program notes, was ready to make any changes in the novel that Mr. Rafelson wanted. "Frankly," Mr. Gaines is reported to have said, "I just wanted to write a screenplay."

Mr. Rafelson is quoted as saying: "It was more than just adapting a novel to the screen. It meant restructuring the script, bringing new characters to life. [Mr. Gaines's] creative juices flowed as though it was a new project and the whole experience was exhilarating."

•

This, I fear, is just what's wrong with "Stay Hungry." Mr. Gaines was ready to jettison a lot of his novel, on which, I assume, he had worked long and hard, in order to make a movie, any movie, while Mr. Rafelson ran around keping those old creative juices flowing, instead of turning off the taps once in a while. The experience may have been exhilarating for the two of them, but for us it's all clutter.

It is the sort of movie whose vapidity is exposed as soon as the clutter is removed. "Stay Hungry" is essentially a story about a rich kid who betrays his class by playing with the poor kids down the block. However, the consequences aren't especially dire, and we never do understand why he does it, or why he is so fascinated by the society of body builders, whose gym is on the downtown Birmingham property coveted by his erstwhile business associates.

"Stay Hungry" has the air of a story repeated by someone who has forgotten the point he set out to make. Which may be one of the dangers in bringing new characters to life and letting creative juices flow at random.

The film isn't about very much, but the clutter does keep our attention, such as a sequence in which Mr. Schwarzenegger and Mr. Bridges participate in a real down-home fiddling contest, and another in which Helena Kallianiotes (the manic hitchhiker in "Five Easy Pieces") discusses a dentist who keeps his freezer full of doves. R. G. Armstrong creates a wierd, memorable character as the owner of the body builders' gym, an aging body builder himself who sees his potency fading away with his hair.

•

The movie apparently means to respect these body builders, and as long as Mr. Schwarzenegger keeps his clothes on, it does. However, when the camera, at the end of the film, roams over physiques so carefully and lovingly exaggerated they seem about to burst, you suspect the movie of being a freak show that couldn't care less about its freaks.

1976 Ap 26, 41:1

LA CHIENNE (The Bitch), directed by Jean Renoir; screenplay (French with English subtitles) by Mr. Renoir and Andre Girard, based on the novel by Georges de la Fouchardiere; directors of photography, Theodore Sparkuhl and Roger Huburt; editor, Marguerite Renoir; produced by Graunberser-Richebe, print owned by the Cinematheque Francaise. Running time: 100 minutes. At the D. W. Griffith Theater, Second Avenue and 59th Street.
Maurice Legrand ....Michel Simon
Lulu ....Janie Mareze
Dede ....Georgees Flamant
Adele Legrand ....Madeleine Berubet
Alexis Godard ....Gaillard
Dagodet ....Jean Gehret

"La Chienne" (The Bitch), was shown last year at the 13th New York Film Festival. The following excerpt is from Vincent Canby's review, which appeared in The New York Times on Sept. 27.

"This is neither a comedy nor a tragedy. It proves no moral at all. It's simply another story about He and She and The Other Guy."

So says, in effect, the master of ceremonies, the hand puppet that introduces Jean Renoir's 1931 classic, "La Chienne" (The Bitch), whereupon the camera moves across the apron of the miniature stage, through a cloth backdrop and into the world of real-life Paris.

•

Maybe it's not an absolutely real-life Paris. The city we see is familiar in all its physical characteristics, but it is lighted by the unique combination of compassion, wit, amusement and surprise

that this greatest of all French directors has brought to virtually every film he's ever made.

"La Chienne" is Renoir's first full-length sound film. It's based on the novel by Georges de la Fouchardière that was also made into quite a different movie, "Scarlet Street," by Fritz Lang in 1945. The basic story lines of both films are approximately the same, but where the Lang is dark, violent and obsessive, the tone of the Renoir is contemplative and ironic.

It's the not-really-so-sad story of Maurice (Michel Simon), a painter on Sundays and a quiet, self-contained, somewhat comic figure of a bookkeeper the six other days. One night, Maurice, who is married to a perpetually furious shrew, meets a vulgar prostitute named Lulu (Janie Marèze) in the way of such tales, he falls desperately in love with Lulu and sets her up in a flat that is occupied mostly by Lulu and her pimp.

•

"La Chienne" is the tale of Maurice's degradation, his victimization and his ultimate liberation, first through love, followed by violence, then by that curious, benign second sight that Renoir bestows upon characters who have the courage to survive.

Michel Simon

The late Mr. Simon is superb as the bookkeeper who doesn't fit into any stereotype of henpecked husband. His Maurice is a man of many parts, including the will to indulge his pleasures and a remarkable resolution, when necessary. All of the performances are close to flawless, but it's Renoir's unseen presence one remembers most vividly, the man we saw on screen, and recognized immediately, when he introduced the vignettes of his last film, "The Little Theater of Jean Renoir."

1976 My 1, 13:1

FILM VIEW

VINCENT CANBY

Can a Director Grow on Foreign Soil?

Film directors—great film directors—are not as peripatetic as jugglers. Though film directors carry fewer props they are surrounded by baggage that is not always to be packed up and crated without causing certain damage. To anyone in this country who admires Ingmar Bergman's films, which appear to be as much a product of Swedish society, landscape, language, custom, expectation and heritage as of the director's unique sensibility, the news of his decision to leave Sweden and settle abroad must be as disturbing as it is to his countrymen. It's not a matter of sentimentality or even of politics, though Bergman's treatment by the bureaucrats of the Swedish socialism he admired is the material of a 21st century nightmare. One worries about how well the Bergman genius will travel.

The roots of Bergman's genius, more than those of any other important contemporary director, are so deeply embedded in the life of his homeland that it's almost impossible to imagine a non-Swedish Bergman film. Perhaps charming divertissements like "The Magic Flute," but nothing of the order of "Face to Face," "Scenes From A Marriage," "Cries and Whispers," "Persona," or even his seemingly stateless works like "Shame" and the one-hour TV film, "The Ritual."

Film: 'Merry Go Round'

By VINCENT CANBY

"Merry Go Round," which opened at three theaters in Manhattan yesterday, is a German screen version of Arthur Schnitzler's satiric sex-comedy, "Reigan," written in 1902 and filmed at least twice before, by Max Ophuls with great style in 1950 ("La Ronde") and by Roger Vadim with Jane Fonda in 1964 ("Circle of Love").

This version, directed by Otto Schenk, has a rather good cast playing the daisy chain of lovers in a lustful, though not very lusty Vienna at the turn of the century. Whatever virtues the film may once have possessed are obscured by one of the tackiest English dubbing jobs I've heard since Roger Corman and Max Youngstein gave us the once-Japanese "Tidal Wave." The characters

never seem to be speaking their lines but responding to heavenly voices, those of one man and one woman, who sound as if they had dubbed all of the voices, but I may be wrong.

•

Even with a decent soundtrack, though, Schnitzler's caustic wit would probably have been lost in the style that Mr. Schenk has chosen to film his adaptation. The emphasis throughout is on the barrier to sexual intercourse provided not by society but by things like corsets, petticoats and button shoes, which is not, I think, what concerned Schnitzler most.

Sydne Rome and Maria Schneider are among those cast members who are not dishonored by their association with the enterprise, only wasted.

1976 Ap 29, 56:3

Some great directors travel safely. Others don't. Whether they are portable or not has as much to do with their methods as with their concerns, which may well be the same thing ultimately. Only two of Luis Buñuel's extraordinary films, "Viridiana" and "Tristana," were made in the Spain that shaped Buñuel's very particular vision of society, man and the God that is not there. All of the other films were made in either Mexico or France and although each is a uniquely Buñuelian work, it is also indelibly Mexican or French. With hindsight it's possible to attribute Buñuel's success to his being a kind of commentator who would have been an outsider even if he had never left home.

It makes no difference whether Buñuel's characters speak French or Spanish since he is at ease in both languages that share a Latin root. When the chips were down, Buñuel has even been able to direct English language films with honor—"Robinson Crusoe" and "The Young One." Compared to the introverted Bergman, Buñuel is an exuberant extrovert. He travels successfully, though only to those places where he feels a basic kinship.

Federico Fellini, one of Bergman's greatest admirers, is as uniquely Italian as Bergman is Swedish, and though Fellini has such an expansive nature one would assume that he could work anywhere, given a certain amount of shakedown time, Fellini's work is absolutely fused with the Italian scene and the Italian temperament. He got by—just barely—when he used American actors like Anthony Quinn, Broderick Crawford and Richard Basehart in Italian roles, but the practice always represented a compromise for his films. On the basis of her work to date, Lina Wertmuller also would seem to be a talent somehow rooted in a particular region whose gestures and language form the content as well as the shape of her movies.

• • •

In an earlier era when filmmaking was more of an organized industry than it is today, directors were more easily transplantable, even at fairly advanced ages. Fritz Lang was 46 when he first began to work in Hollywood. Ernst Lubitsch was 31, Michael Curtiz 39, Alfred Hitchcock didn't begin his Hollywood career until he was 41, though, of course, there was no language barrier for him.

Hollywood was one of the few beneficiaries of the rise of the Third Reich. Among the men who went to California in the thirties and early forties: Billy Wilder, Otto Preminger, Curt Siodmak, Douglas Sirk, Max Ophuls and the greatest of them all, Jean Renoir, who was 47 when he landed in the United States. Some, like Ophuls and Renoir, returned to Europe when the war was over, but they survived the Hollywood system. Just how Renoir survived is one of the most moving and witty elements in his autobiography, "My Life and My Films."

"My problem," Renoir writes, "was and will always

be the same, arising out of the fact that the calling I seek to practice has nothing to do with the film industry. I have never been able to come to terms with the purely industrial side of films. Hollywood's detractors suppose that the weakness of the industry lies in its anxiety to make money at all costs, and that by catering to the public taste it falls into mediocrity. There is some truth in this, but the desire for gain is not the worst thing about it.

"The real danger, in my opinion, lies in a blind love of so-called perfection, to obtain which a multiplicity of talents is called upon. Such and such a film is based on a literary masterpiece, scripted and revised by half-a-dozen leading script writers and entrusted to a director who is equally celebrated. . . . A big Hollywood film is dished up like a melon, in separate slices."

• • •

In addition to being one of the modern masters, Renoir is a pliant man. During his stay in Hollywood he managed to adapt himself to the system long enough to make several extraordinary "American" films, "The Southerner," "Diary of A Chambermaid" and "Woman on The Beach." Renoir is a social animal as well as a poet.

Roman Polanski has had no trouble adapting to the filmmaking systems in France, England and the United States, but the results ("Repulsion," "Macbeth," "Rosemary's Baby" and "Chinatown") suggest he is a director who was made for the commercial system and not the eccentric talent he was first thought to be on the basis of his Polish-made "Knife in The Water." Milos Forman, this year's Oscar-winner ("One Flew Over The Cuckoo's Nest") seems finally to have found a place in American films, though neither "Cuckoo's Nest" nor "Taking Off," his first film here, has the resonance of his Czech films, "Loves of A Blonde" and "The Firemen's Ball." Ivan Passer, another gifted Czech, whose latest film, the internationally sponsored "Crime and Passion," is a disaster, has made two interesting American films, "Born to Win" and "Law and Disorder," though both are the work of a man who seems to be hanging around America, on a tourist visa, not quite belonging yet.

It may be reasonably argued that every man's life is a succession of exiles, if only the emotional ones that are a part of growing up. That Bergman should have to begin again in a new land at the age of 58 because of some nonsense about income taxes is incredible. How to wish him well?

1976 My 2, II:13:7

Karen Arthur 'Legacy' at Cinema Studio

The Cast

LEGACY, directed and produced by Karen Arthur; screenplay by Joan Hotchkis; director of photography, John Bailey; editor, Carol Littleton; music, Roger Kellaway; released by Kino International Corporation. Running time: 90 minutes. At the Cinema Studio, Broadway at 66th Street. This film has been rated R.

Bissie Hapgood	Joan Hotchkis
Husband	George McDaniel
Lover	Sean Allen
Mother	Dixie Lee

By VINCENT CANBY

Bissie Hapgood has problems. Her mother is senile and calls her on the telephone simply to cry. Bissie's husband does not satisfy her sexually. Her 8-year-old son wets his bed, and her best friend has an annoying habit of wandering away from the telephone when Bissie is in the midst of one of her nonstop, free-association phone calls about her weight, her Japanese gardener or some other self-absorbed topic.

•

When Bissie calls her analyst to describe her latest suicide fantasy, the analyst, apparently bored, suggests that she keep busy.

Bissie tries. God knows she tries. In the day in the life of Bissie Hapgood covered by "Legacy," which opened yesterday at the Cinema Studio, Bissie makes preparations for a formal dinner party.

Busy-ness, however, leads directly to disaster when she finds that she is missing one sterling silver butter knife. Not only has Black, Starr & Gorham discontinued the pattern, there is no longer any Black, Starr & Gorham. Which is enough to send a woman as obsessed with trivia as Bissie is over the edge into lunacy.

"Legacy," which was directed and produced by Karen Arthur (her first feature) and written by Joan Hotchkis, who also plays Bissie, is a most peculiar sort of movie but not a very good one. It also seems uncommonly cruel for a film about a woman made by women. It might, I think, have made a very funny movie if Miss Hotchkis had allowed herself the grace of humor, which is another way of saying compassion, instead of treating Bissie as a foolish, four-star nut.

Bissie has problems, and they are real ones, but "Legacy" only catalogues them without making them seem important or moving. Miss Hotchkis, the actress as well as the writer, displays some talent for satire and none at all for comed yor drama.

The form of the film doesn't help. "Legacy" is said to be based on a play by Miss Hotchkis, which I suspect actually to have been the kind of Ruth Draper-ish monologue that is best delivered from a lecture platform.

Although we do see Bissie's mother briefly (in the film's only arresting sequence) and Bissie's husband and children (in short flashbacks), "Legacy" is still a one-woman movie, a 90-minute monologue that might easily have been reduced to a quarter of an hour. Nothing that either Miss Hotchkis or Miss Arthur does can disguise the awkwardness and artificiality of this monologue form, which finally destroys any serious thoughts the film makers might have about women, the bourgeoisie, sex, America and the difficulty of getting good domestic help in Southern California.

Eventually, the whole thing comes to look like an act of immense vanity.

1976 My 3, 41:1

BIRCH INTERVAL, directed by Delbert Mann, written by Joanna Crawford, produced by Robert B. Radnitz, photographed by Urs B. Furrer, music by Leonard Rosenman. Released by Gamma Three. Running time: 105 minutes. At the 68th Street Playhouse. This film has been rated PG.

Pa	Eddie Albert
Thomas	Rip Torn
Marie	Ann Wedgeworth
Jesse	Susan McClung
Samuel	Brian Part
Esther	Jann Stanley
Charlie	Bill Lucking
Hattie	Margaret Leary
Mrs. Tanner	Anne Revere

By RICHARD EDER

There is no possible way to make a good movie about children if you don't know how to direct children. This is the main reason why "Birch Interval," instead of being a sentimental but effective film about growing-up pains in bucolic America, on the order of "To Kill a Mockingbird," is a painful embarrassment.

Directing children, essentially, is telling them what not to do. They shouldn't, in fact, do anything; they should simply be. They certainly shouldn't act. Children's faces are totally revealing and the camera is terribly sharp; when a child is allowed to act, what we get on the screen is not a child but a child acting.

The central figure in "Birch Interval," which opened yesterday at the 68th Street Playhouse, is a child named Jesse. She is sent to stay with her grandfather's family in the Amish country of Pennsylvania. It is all love and peacefulness, but there are conflict and tragedy underneath.

•

Her beloved Uncle Thomas, a fey eccentric married to a perplexed and unfaithful wife, is manhandled off to an asylum, where he dies. Her grandfather, whom she adores, shows unexpected weakness in letting it happen. Her Amish friends are harassed by the government for not sending their children to school. The neighborhood holds a witch, a mad girl, a band of sadistic children.

The story of a preadolescent girl learning pain and forbearance among the green hills and red barns might have worked, if done with skill and restraint. But there is nothing but excess, self-indulgence and bathos.

Susan McLung, who plays Jesse, is thin and freckled, with a hungry look and expressive dark eyes. She looks fine, but she is never real. She is a catalogue of gestures and expressions.

She pushes her mouth in and out to depict tenderness, anger, grief. She doesn't walk; she strides. Her uncle and grandfather sit on the porch and talk life to her; she assumes an expression of hostessy understanding. There's nothing she doesn't hear, register and react to. What happened to the painfully won dscovery by American directors—the Europeans always knew it—that children look blank most of the time?

The dialogue doesn't help. In quick succession, Jesse has to announce that her uncle, her grandfather and the community of Birch Interval are "the best (uncle/grandfather/place) in the whole world." Her grandfather—played like a wet sunset by Eddie Albert—tells her, "Life is just a bit of eiderdown and a bit of mealy apple."

The photography does some lovely things—there is a good shot of Amish wagons crookedly lined up in the mist—but the loveliness is as excessive as everything else. The camera, almost as self-conscious as Miss McClung, reacts—it all but double-takes, in fact—to every pretty thing it shows.

"Birch Interval" is what the word "icky" has been waiting for all its life. Nobody who sees the film will ever be able to condescend to "icky" again; it rises from cant to lexicographical indispensability.

1976 My 3, 41:2

HURRY TOMORROW, a documentary feature by Richard Cohen and Kevin Rafferty; directed and edited by Mr. Cohen; photography and assistant editor, Mr. Rafferty; sound and additional camera work, Joshua Morton; production assistant, Richard Davis; additional camerawork, Richard Wedler; additional soundwork, Marie Consiglio and Wolf Seberg; produced by Halfway House Films. Running time: 80 minutes. At the Whitney Museum of American Art, Madison Avenue at 75th Street.

By VINCENT CANBY

"Hurry Tomorrow" which opened a week's run yesterday at the Whitney Museum, is a spare, angry documentary feature about the use of various kinds of tranquilizing drugs in the treatment of disturbed patients in a men's ward at Metropolitan State Hospital in Norwalk, Calif. It is a drama of particulars, of individual patients and individual doctors, and it is enough to make you swear off anything stronger than warm milk forever.

The point of the film makers, Richard Cohen (director and editor) and Kevin Rafferty (chief cameraman and assistant editor), is clearly stated within the film by a former patient, a member of an organization called the Network Against Psychiatric Abuse, who sees the administration of any drugs, without the consent of the patient, to be a violation of the body equivalent to rape.

•

This is putting the film makers' case much less emotionally than the film itself does. Though "Hurry Tomorrow" has some technical deficiencies, which are understandable considering the conditions under which it was made, it is an agonizing, involving spectacle to watch, with more bitterness and outrage in any three-minute sequence than in all of "One Flew Over the Cuckoo's Nest."

With the apparent cooperation of the ward's chief doctor, a man who seems so arrogant, vain, self-assured and high on himself that he doesn't realize what sort of film is being made, the cameramen wander the clean but miserably barren halls of the ward, picking up the stories of the patients, some of whom seem much less neurotic than the people treating them.

We watch a young black man being badgered by the doctor, who notes that the patient has a peculiar way of getting angry when he is either hungry or locked up. The patient agrees. "Sometimes you sound just a bit grandiose," says the doctor. "What's grandiose?" says the patient helplessly, which seems to please the doctor. "I want to go home," the young man says. The patient will go home, the doctor tells the film makers, only when he stops asking to—which is this doctor's catch-22.

The film makers attend a get-together of drug salesmen and the doctors where a representative of one company announces fatuously: "No more napalm. We're out of the war business and into the health business." The health business, as the representative of Network Against Psychiatrist Abuse tells us, includes the pushing of tranquilizing drugs that turn patients into zombies, which we see, and that have such possible side effects as dizziness, liver damage and cardiac arrest, which are listed on the drugs themselves.

Nevertheless some things about "Hurry Tomorrow"

bother me. The doctor may well be a first-class creep, but the film makers nudge him along. As he is answering one of their qestions, the camera pans to one side to show us his two Siamese cats lying on a bench covered with imitation leopard skin. What does that tell us? That he's a fur fetishist? His pseudohip jargon is bad enough, we don't have to have a scene in which he proudly shows us his car and the California license plate, M A G I A N, which, he explains, was his second choice, after M A G I. At another point the cameraman, who is never acknowledged by the film, seems to be locked up in solitary with a patient who is being punished.

•

A documentary always has a point of view, sometimes called a bias, and there is nothing wrong with that as long as it is admitted. "Hurry Tomorrow" makes its feelings so apparent, and raises so many important questions, it doesn't need to overstate the nuttiness of the doctor, nor to convince us its cameraman was somehow locked up for hours with a single patient. These are small points, but a documentary as good as this one must be above such things.

1976 My 5, 49:1

BABY BLUE MARINE, directed by John Hancock; screenplay by Stanford Whitmore; produced by Aaron Spelling and Leonard Goldberg; music, Fred Karlin; director of photography, Laszlo Kovacs; editor, Marion Rothman; distributed by Columbia Pictures. Running time: 89 minutes. At the Cinerama Theater, Broadway near 48th Street, and other theaters. This film has been rated PG.

Marion	Jan-Michael Vincent
Rose	Glynnis O'Connor
Mrs. Hudkins	Katherine Helmond
Sheriff Wenzel	Dana Elcar
Mr. Hudkins	Bert Remsen
"Pop" Mosley	B. Kirby Jr.
Marine Raider	Richard Gere
Mr. Elmore	Art Lund
Drill Instructor	Michael Conrad
Barney Hudkins	Michael Le Clair
Capt. Bittman	Allan Miller

"Baby Blue Marine," the first film to be directed by John Hancock since his moving and funny "Bang the Drum Slowly," has the tensile strength of a rubber hot dog.

It's the tastelessly sentimental story of a nice young man named Marion (Jan-Michael Vincent) who, in 1943, has the humiliation of being washed out of a Marine Corps boot camp, for not measuring up, though he's as pretty as a picture of a Norman Rockwell World War II fighting man. Through a series of circumstances too silly to describe, he finds himself hitchhiking home to St. Louis wearing the uniform of a Marine Raider, whose battle ribbons dazzle the folks he meets along the way.

•

Marion has particular success in a small California town that is so idyllically (and mysteriously) set that no matter where you look you see Mount Shasta in the distance. There he meets a family (Mom, Pop, the pretty daughter and her young brother who always has the sniffles) so apple-pie American that one longs for this to be a Hitchcock film, which might mean the family was really a bunch of Nazi spies. No such luck, however,

Mr. Hancock and his screenwriter, Stanford Whitmore, apparently think they can evoke innocence by trafficking in idealizations that weren't convincing even 35 years ago. The film makes no comment on Norman Rockwell's Saturday Evening Post covers that are used behind the opening credits. Rather it adopts their style and then — unwittingly, I assume — he vacuity that lies behind the Rockwell gift for draftsmanship.

Marion, of course, has doubts about the fraud he's pulling on these good honest folks, so would you be struck dumb if you were told that circumstances eventually turn him into an honest-to-gosh hero? Things go bad for him, but then they get better 'n' better.

I can't believe that Mr. Hancock intended to make a movie quite as dopey as this one has turned out to be. Something vital seems to be missing.

•

I also can't understand the PG rating. There is a tiny bit of barracks room language, but nothing you might not hear at a church social if Rover ate the turkey.

VINCENT CANBY

1976 My 6, 45:1

BREAKHEART PASS, directed by Tom Gries; screenplay by Alistair MacLean; produced by Jerry Gershwin; executive producer, Elliot Kastner; director of photography, Lucien Ballard; music, Jerry Goldsmith; editor, Buzz Brandt; distributed by United Artists. Running time: 95 minutes. At the Guild Theater, 50th Street west of Fifth Avenue, and other theaters. This film has been rated PG.

John Deakin	Charles Bronson
Nathan Pearce	Ben Johnson
Richard Fairchild	Richard Crenna
Marica	Jill Ireland
Frank O'Brien	Charles Durning
Maj. Claremont	Ed Lauter
Dr. Molyneux	David Huddleston
Banlon	Roy Jenson
Jackson	Casey Tibbs
Carlos	Archie Moore

By VINCENT CANBY

Either Charles Bronson's movies are getting better or my resistance has worn out. Last year a string of unremarkable but immensely popular Bronson movies was suddenly made interesting with the appearance of "Hard Times," a terse, tough, unsentimental melodrama directed by Walter Hill.

This year we have "Breakheart Pass," a western written by Alistair MacLean and directed by Tom Gries. In between there have been other forgettable items. Though "Breakheart Pass" is not "The Great Train Robbery," it's a highly efficient entertainment of the sort sometimes labeled escapist, a general use of the word that doesn't recognize who's doing the escaping or what's being escaped from. For someone working in a Manhattan laundry, The New York Review of Books could be a month in the country.

"Breakheart Pass," which opened yesterday at the Guild and other theaters, is a western that spends a lot of its time inside a train, a fine smoky antique snaking its way through the snowy mountains of Utah to a date with a destiny that includes outlaws and angry Indians. The time is the virtually mythical 1870's (as someone once wrote, all westerns are set in 1870) and the MacLean story is about gunrunning and a cache of gold.

Time and place require that "Breakheart Pass" be described as a western, though it also contains a few elements that might have been suggested by a close reading of "Murder on the Orient Express." Purists many object to this crossbreeding of genres, but the result is good fun with some spectacular action footage directed by Yakima Canutt, the Hollywood stunt genius who is still playing with dynamite and rolling entire trains off trestles in his 81st year.

The train on which most of the action is set is a special being sent to the relief of a remote mountain fort in the grip on a diphtheria epidemic. On board are a detachment of soldiers, a governor, the daughter of the fort's commander (didn't they ever have sons?), an old-timey sort of Western sheriff (played by Ben Johnson), the train's cook, who's no better than he cooks (layed by Archie Moore) and a mysterious outlaw, a former university lecturer in medicine who's wanted for everything, arson and murder and probably parking tickets.

This fellow, played by Mr. Bronson, seems already to have passed through his own time into history. The great physique is no longer young, but it is more powerful than ever, as if transfused by age with some kind of supervigor that affects brain as well as brawn. Needless to say, he is the film's hero-figure, but how he assumes the role is the point of the screenplay's twists that owe more to Agatha Christie than to Zane Grey.

Mr. Gries, who some years ago directed "Will Penny," a very different kind of western that attempted to recreate a feel for frontier time and place, doesn't permit these mystery-story elements to slow down the film's physical action. "Breakheart Pass" moves, therefore it is.

•

The movie is rated PG, in reference, I suppose, to a couple of fight scenes, and one murder that might possibly upset a very young child who's never had a chance to watch prime-time TV.

1976 My 6, 46:3

Movie Animation, a Starved Art

MOVIE animation is a starved art. All but evicted from the commercial movie theaters—Ralph Bakshi is the rare exception—it survives on commercials, low-grade Saturday morning television cartoons and industrial training films.

But the art is still around, and to prove it the Film Forum has organized a two-part series showing a selection of new and experimental work by film animators.

The first part, which opened yesterday, has its uneven bits. Some of the shorter items—there are 17 in all —are simply pleasant exercises. Three pieces ("Alae," "Kinesis" and "Pictures From a Gallery") representing computer animation—images are constructed or broken up electronically—are toys.

But there's enough originality, excitement and playfullness in the show to suggest that if 10 minutes were cut from every 100-minute feature film now being made, and those minutes were used to show animation, audiences would lose a lot of their stuffed feeling and would have a lot more fun.

Not that the better pieces at the Film Forum are necessarily funny. Most aren't. There is a nightmare of a short, "The Imprint," by the Frenchman Jacques Cardon. In a dead landscape, a mortally oppressed, mortally suffering race of people, great clamps fixed onto their backs, live under jack-booted masters. The use to which the clamps are put is revealed at the end of this seven-minute masterpiece with a blinding and sad shock. "This Is Not a Museum," by John Haugse, is satire rather than horror. The satire is somewhat loose, somewhat trite, somewhat self-indulgent. It presents an art museum as a place of the dead, where the presence of a real live workman is enough to send cracks shooting through the statues and shudders through members of a snooty museum tour.

But its style is fresh and witty: as an art expert leads the tour among canvases and statues, explaining, chalk-line diagrams are left behind. The workman has to scrub them off.

Geoff Dunbar, a British animator, has a film called "Lautrec," in which Toulouse-Lautrec drawings are made to move. The can-can dancers actually dance: Yvette Guilbert actually sings. To tell the truth, Toulouse-Lautrec's works have more life and movement when they are not moving, but Mr. Dunbar's gimmick is cheerfully vulgar.

Then there is Mary Beams, whose "Solo" is enchanting, slightly mysterious and very funny. The sound-track has a woman humming and hooting a waltz while clumping about the house. She seems to be getting undressed.

•

What we see are her thoughts: a series of squiggly lines taking shape. Some are recognizable and sexual; others are abstract and even more sexual. It is a wonderful equivalent of Molly Bloom's soliloquy at the end of "Ulysses," and it only takes two minutes.

There are other good things on the program; an interesting moving perspective, "Autosong," by Al Jarnow. for example. It is only a pity that the opportunity provided by Film Forum is such a rare one.

RICHARD EDER

1976 My 7, C6:3

FILM VIEW

VINCENT CANBY

Worth Waiting For

In 1931 when Jean Renoir's producers were given their first screening of "La Chienne" they were appalled. They had understood that Renoir would deliver a comedy. Instead they saw what they took to be a somber melodrama about a middle-aged, middle-class man, a henpecked husband who murders the prostitute he has fallen in love with and who, after an innocent man is convicted of the crime, winds up as a jolly bum, a clochard of the boulevards surviving on tips handed out by the swells whose car doors he opens, scrambling for their cigarette butts when he happens to get lucky.

A somber melodrama? It may have seemed so then but Renoir knew better, as we do today. "La Chienne" (The Bitch), which was shown at last September's New

York Film Festival and is now being released here for the first time with English titles, is not only one of Renoir's great films, it's one of the greatest film comedies ever made, a forerunner—some people say—of the neo-realist films made after World War II, but only in its insistence that life need not be absolutely, totally, unredeemingly beautiful.

Renoir shot a lot of "La Chienne" on Parisian locations, sometimes having a terrible time obtaining a clean soundtrack (this was his first sound feature) but he is not strictly a social realist. He's a realist most at home in the landscape of the human soul, a twilight place without signposts leading the way to Effect out of Cause, where one is guided not by a compass but by a generosity of spirit that is possessed by very few.

The story of "La Chienne" is not too different from Josef von Sternberg's "The Blue Angel" (1930), a tale of obsession so ferocious and so full of acts of degradation that it becomes a romance entered by a side door. The difference between the two films is the difference in the voices of the two directors—Sternberg being as obsessed in his pursuits as was the Emil Jannings character who gave all for the love of the young, plump Marlene Dietrich, while Renoir is not unlike Maurice Legrand (Michel Simon), the hero of "La Chienne." Legrand survives his obsession with his doxy Lulu (Janie Marèze) not by abject submission to life but by finding within himself an accommodating rhythm. Legrand fights back to the extent that he murders Lulu when she ridicules his love for her and when he allows Lulu's pimp, Dédé (Georges Flamant), whom he believes to be responsible for her treachery, to go to the guillotine. The accommodating rhythm that saves him is his resilience to life's horrors. He doesn't kid himself that life is any less bleak than it seems, but by acknowledging this, by rolling with the punches (but not too far), he maintains some measure of serenity as well as identity.

This, I'm afraid, is the kind of criticism that may put you off one of the most joyous films around at the moment. "La Chienne" is funny, ebullient, a master entertainment, a work of art that imposes on life's chaos an artificial order that isn't, ultimately, any more artificial than, say, the spoken and written language. It's a way of communicating.

Such is the film's opening sequence, a close-up of a puppet theater with a hand puppet announcing gravely that what we're about to see is a drama. He's brushed aside by another puppet who announces that the film to follow is really a comedy. He, in turn, is batted off by a third puppet who straightens everything out: the film we are going to see, he says with just the slightest note of apology in his voice, is neither a comedy nor a drama. It has no moral and it proves nothing whatsoever, he says. Instead it's about He, She and The Other Guy. At which point the scene dissolves into another framed picture, a dining room seen through the opening of a dumb-waiter.

Michel Simon was 36 when he played Maurice Legrand in "La Chienne" but he seems ageless, neither young nor old but an embodiment of particular characteristics, physical as well as emotional. Maurice is moose-jawed, stooped but fastidious in manner. The object of jokes at the lingerie firm where he works as a cashier, he accepts the jibes courteously, as if the most foolish remark might possibly contain wisdom. At home he accepts his wife's insults without actually submitting. Maurice is a weekend painter, something that infuriates his wife who can say, as if genuinely surprised, "What right have you to a pastime?" When she comes in one afternoon and finds him painting, she announces that she hasn't got time for games, that she's been working, "collecting my dividends." "Our dividends," says Maurice firmly as he continues to paint.

Maurice is slightly myopic but not so myopic that when he meets Lulu he doesn't know her profession. He understands but he makes the mistake of trusting her when he sets her up in a tidy apartment that brings out all of her worst petit bourgeois tendencies. Lulu is a bitch though one with her own code of honor. She does everything for Dédé, the pimp whom she loves with the devotion of a mother. "Don't drink too much and don't catch a chill," she says to Dédé as she packs him off to get drunk with the boys. To Lulu there is nothing especially wrong in her supporting Dédé on the money Maurice gives her or in Dédé's selling Maurice's paintings and passing Lulu off as their mysterious American painter,

Clara Wood. Even Maurice doesn't object to this fraud. He only snaps when Lulu reveals that she has never loved him and can't care less about being saved from the wicked Dédé. Though Dédé would certainly blacken both her eyes and perhaps break an arm or two if she lost Maurice, Lulu is the sort of mini-minded but romantic whore who would be happy with Dédé anywhere.

The late Janie Marèze is charming as Lulu, exhibiting what one of the puppets says at the beginning is "a vulgarity all her own," something that is especially hilarious when she goes to a party for art patrons and society folk, to introduce her as "Clara Wood," and acts like a hooker—a very coquettish one. Georges Flamant is superb as the "mec," vain, none too shrewd, arrogant and, finally, the puzzled victim of circumstances he'll never understand. Like Lulu, he has a very small brain. Two other performers must be mentioned, Madeleine Bérubet, who plays Maurice's wife with a mean-tempered conviction that is as funny as anything I've seen in any farce, and Gaillard (no first name) who plays Miss Bérubet's first husband, long thought to be dead but whose reappearance serves to liberate Maurice.

Maurice, of course, is not a victim in any conventional sense. He behaves shockingly but he's no more or less evil than anyone else in "La Chienne." Renoir doesn't point morals. You feel he may have tried it once but kept seeing the other side of every argument. It's the mystery of human behavior that fascinates him. We look with him. We observe. At times we marvel.

1976 My 9, II:13:1

Survivors of 'Village' Bombing Interviewed

By RICHARD EDER

UNDERGROUND, a documentary film by Emile de Antonio, Mary Lampson and Haskell Wexler. Interviews with the following members of the Weather Underground: Billy Ayers, Kathy Boudin, Bernardine Dohrn, Jeff Jones and Cathy Wilkerson. At the Regency Theater. Running time: 88 minutes.

Six years ago, a stock of explosives blew up in a Greenwich Vilalge house, killing three young people and causing five others who escaped to go into hiding.

The eight were members of Weatherman, a small but highly militant segment of the protest movement. From the time of explosion the five survivors, calling themselves the Weather Underground, have eluded the authorities and carried on what they term "armed propaganda." This has consisted of a number of bombings—no injuries occurred; the object was to inflict material damage on symbolic targets — and the publication of a book and a news sheet.

Early last year Emile de Antonio, a documentary film maker who is himself a radical, though scarcely a violent one, managed to get in touch with the Weather Underground. Mr. de Antonio and two associates, Mary Lampson and Haskell Wexler, spent two days in a Los Angeles house with the five, talked with them and filmed the talk.

The result is "Underground," which opened yesterday at the Regency Theater. It suffers from the crippling difficulties under which it was made. It is a film in chains. It is a series of failures, but they are not stupid or careless ones. They are intelligent failures, and if Mr. de Antonio's effort is largely a defeat, it is a defeat that he conducts with skill and integrity.

His intention was to have the five—Kathy Boudin, Bernardine Dohrn, Cathy Wilkerson, Billy Ayers and Jeff Jones—reveal something of themselves. His sympathetic question is: What is a white, middle - class revolutionary group doing in America in the mid-70's?

The answers he gets, despite his efforts, are largely schematic and abstract. The five have schooled themselves to be impersonal. They seem to understand that for a film they must come out a bit, but they rarely manage to.

There are a few breakthroughs. Kathy Boudin recalls her dismay in Havana in 1961 when she found herself—a peace marcher—applauding a parade of Cuban tanks. Bernardine Dohrn gives a curious insight into her long journey from a comfortable middle class to armed concealment: "I was more afraid growing up than I am now. Then it was paranoid; now it's real fear."

There is a hand wielding a coffee pot, and the red ribs of Bernardine Dohrn's sweater. They provide visual life, evidence that in fact we are seeing a film about five people. So do the faces of the three film makers; Mr. de Antonio's eye following that coffee pot has the impact of a cavalry charge.

This is not intended to be facetious. The film makers have done marvelously well with these details, but the fact is, they have hardly anything else to film. The five will not allow their faces to be shown. So the camera shows their backs and their elbows.

Talking faces, used by a film maker of Mr. de Antonoi's skill and sensitivity, would have told us a lot about the five. But without the faces we have only the talk. It is good to have it—Weatherman played a small but significant part in the American radical movement, if only, paradoxically, to weaken it by violence—but the effect is claustrophobic.

The film makers use clips of the war in Vietnam, peace marches and police charges to illustrate the talk and vary its pace. There is also a scene in which the five leave the house and interview people anonymously—we still don't see their faces—at an unemployment center. The unemployed are angry—what else would one expect? — and the five draw encouraging conclusions about an American revolution.

This is naive. It is frail. Weatherman got its name from the Bob Dylan line about not having to be a weatherman to know which way the wind is blowing. Now it has changed its name to Weather Underground. But how do you tell the wind's direction underground?

The film doesn't ask this question, but, despite its sympathy, it doesn't try to conceal it either. That is its honesty.

1976 My 10, 33:1

'Goodby, Norma Jean' About Miss Monroe

GOODBYE, NORMA JEAN, directed and produced by Larry Buchanan; screenplay by Lynn Shubert and Mr. Buchanan; screenplay by Lynn Shubert and Mr. Buchanan; music, Joe Beck; an Austamerican production, distributed by A. Sterling Gold Ltd. Running time: 95 minutes. At the Eastside Cinema, Third Avenue at 55th Street, and other theaters. This film has been rated R.
Norma Jean Baker ......Misty Rowe
Ralph Johnson ....Terrence Locke
Ruth Latimer ....Patch Mackenzie
Hal James ....Preston Hason
Irving Oblach ....Marty Zagon
Sam Dunn ....Andre Philippe

By VINCENT CANBY

"Goodbye, Norma Jean," which is playing at a number of theaters currently, is about Marilyn Monroe before she became a movie star.

It's about those years when she was growing up unhappy in California foster homes that had nothing much going for them except that they were near the movie studios where Norma Jean wanted to work.

"I am going to be a movie star," Norma Jean says more than once. She also says, "I am somebody!" more than once. In the meantime, a lot of dirty old men make passes at her, as well as one dirty old woman. This gives the movie the form, not quite the substance of a soft-core porn work.

"Goodbye, Norma Jean" is a terrible, witless, schlocky movie that Norma Jean Baker might have made in her desperation to be somebody. An actress named Misty Rowe, who looks a lot like Marilyn and may be desperate too, gives a pretty good imitation of the star.

1976 My 11, 26:5

END OF THE GAME, directed by Maximilian Schell; produced by Mr. Schell and Arlene Sellers; screenplay by Mr. Schell and Friedrich Duerrenmatt; photographed by Ennio Guarnieri, Roberto Gerardi and Klaus Koenig; edited by Dagmar Hirtz. Released by 20th-Century Fox; at the Little Carnegie Theater. Running time: 106 minutes. This film has been rated PG.
Walter Tschanz .... Jon Voight
Anna Crawley .... Jacqueline Bisset
Hans Baerlach .... Martin Ritt
Richard Gastmann .... Robert Shaw
Von Schwendi .... Helmut Qualtinger

By RICHARD EDER

"End of the Game" is a metaphysical cuckoo clock of a movie, full of talent and fog. But the mechanism is deranged. Instead of every hour or half-hour, the cuckoo pops out every minute and a half.

It jangles us. There's too much writing, too much acting, too many symbols, too much paradox, too many significant camera angles. The author thinks of lots of clever ways to do each scene; instead of choosing he does them all.

The author, mostly, is Maximilian Schell, who directs, produces and has written the screenplay. The co-writer on the screenplay is Friederich Duerrenmatt, who wrote the original novel, "The Judge and His Hangman," and who also — in more ways than one this movie is like an evening of charades among friends — acts a part.

Other well-known people drop in briefly, as if paying a social call. There's Pinchas Zukerman, a profile swirled in fog, playing for 30 seconds or so on an autumn lawn. Donald Sutherland is even briefer; he is the photograph of a dead man, but when the dead man appears as a corpse some other actor has taken over.

Casualness, sloppiness, excess; yet a lot of "Game" is entertaining, and there is an outrageous vitality to it that gives it a bumpy appeal.

It is half allegory, half mystery. Thirty years ago two young Swiss men sit in a cafe in Istanbul. Gastmann bets Baerlach that he can murder a girl drifter they have picked up without anyone's being able to prove it on him. He pushes her into the Bosphorus.

That is the prologue. When the film proper begins, we are back in Switzerland. Gastmann has become a master businessman-criminal, who wears the Swiss Government around his wrist like a thin watch. Baerlach is a decrepit, ulcer-plagued, cantankerous police detective whose life is a futile effort to catch and punish Gastmann.

Then Schmid, a subordinate of Baerlach, who has been investigating Gastmann, is found murdered. Baerlach brings in Tschanz, a young detective, to help him and the two slowly move in on Gastmann. Gastmann is finally brought down although the death of Schmid is the one crime he didn't commit. The identity of Schmid's killer is the film's one real surprise.

Baerlach is played by Martin Ritt—usually known as a director — Gastmann by Robert Shaw and Tschanz by Jon Voight. All three overact but it is a fine, joyful overacting. Perhaps overacting is appropriate to allegory; in any case their inspired hamminess is the film's real meat.

Mr. Ritt is a fat, shaggy stomach ache. Lethargic and deadly, he is an untidy version of Porfiry in "Crime and Punishment." Mr. Shaw, who lives in a grand mansion complete with two black-coated stranglers, a leopard who prowls loose, and a wheelchaired mother, is bouncily evil.

Mr. Voight is apple-cheeked, righteous and passionate; when the role calls for more complexity he provides it. Jacqueline Bisset, as an Irish dryad whose function is to seduce and confuse, seduces and confuses.

"End of the Game," which opened yesterday at the Little Carnegie Theater, is rated PG

1976 My 13, 41:2

GRIZZLY, directed by William Girdler; screenplay by Harvey Flaxman and David Sheldon; executive producer, Edward L. Montoro; produced by Mr. Sheldon and Mr. Flaxman; music, Robert O. Ragland; editor, Bob Anderson; director of photography, William Anderson; distributed by Film Ventures International. Running time: 92 minutes. At the Rivoli Theater, Broadway and 49th Street, and other theaters. This film has been rated PG.
Kelly .... Christopher George
Don .... Andrew Prine
Scott .... Richard Jaeckel
Allison .... Joan McCall
Kittridge .... Joe Dorsey
Corwin .... Kermit Echols

By VINCENT CANBY

Jean-Luc Godard proposed some years ago that the only adequate way to review one film is to make another in response. A director named William Girdler apparently agrees. He's on his way to the creation of an entire oeuvre of such movies. "Abby," made in 1974, was the repository of the Girdler meditations upon "The Exorcist."

His latest, "Grizzly," is the story of a man-eating grizzly bear that terrozies the campers in a national park. It is Mr. Girdler's answer to "Jaws" and if I had the facilities, I'd review "Grizzly" by making a movie about a teensy-weensy insect walking amok. It would be called "Flea."

"Grizzly," which opened yesterday at the Rivoli and other theaters, is such a blatant imitation of "Jaws" that one has to admire the depth of the flattery it represents, though not the lack of talent involved. In addition to Mr. Girdler, he people behind the film include Edward L. Montoro, the executive producer, and Harvey Flaxman and David Sheldon, who wrote the screenplay and then produced it. Lights like theirs don't fit under bushels.

The national park that is the location of "Grizzly" is never identified, though one would suppose it had to be somewhere in the American Northwest, where one might conceivably find a grizzly bear, and not Georgia, where the movie was actually made. It doesn't help the film that the Georgia forests, while pretty, look somewhat less menacing than Central Park and that the grizzly who plays the lead, though large and probably dangerous, can't quite shake his Winnie-the-Pooh image.

It's one of the curious properties of second-rate fakery that the blood and gore that "Grizzly" deals in are just that much more offensive than they might be in a better-made film, such as "Jaws." "Grizzly" is not only clumsily plotted, photographed and edited, it is also downright rude when it insists on showing us the bear lopping off an arm or decapitating a horse.

Because it's not good enough to earn the right to scare us, I would hope intelligent adults would avoid it and that parents would give it a personal X. Officially it's been rated PG.

1976 My 13, 41:3

THE BLUE BIRD, directed by George Cukor; screenplay by Hugh Whitemore and Alfred Hayes, based on the play by Maurice Maeterlinck; produced by Paul Maslansky; executive producer, Edward Lewis; directors of photography, Freddie Young and Ionas Gritzus; music composed and conducted by Irwin Kostal; songs and ballet music composed by Andrei Petrov; lyrics by Tony Harrison; supervising film editor, Ernest Walter; editors, Tatyana Shapiro and Stanford C. Allen; distributed by 20th Century-Fox. Running time: 99 minutes. At the Radio City Music Hall, Avenue of the Americas at 50th Street. This film has been rated G.
Mother, Maternal Love,
  Witch, Light .... Elizabeth Taylor
Night .... Jane Fonda
Luxury .... Ava Gardner
Cat .... Cicely Tyson
Father Time .... Robert Morley
Oak .... Harry Andrews
Tyltyl .... Todd Lookinland
Myltyl .... Patsy Kensit
Grandfather .... Will Geer
Grandmother .... Mona Washbourne
Dog .... George Cole
Bread .... Richard Pearson
Blue Bird .... Nadejda Pavlova
Sugar .... George Vitzin
Milk .... Margareta Terechova
Fat Laughter .... Oleg Popov
Father .... Leonid Nevedomsky
Mother .. Valentina Ganilaee Ganibalova
Fire .... Yevseny Scherbakov
With members of the Leningrad Kirov Ballet Company.

By VINCENT CANBY

TECHNICALLY "The Blue Bird," the new screen version of Maurice Maeterlinck's old, numbingly high-minded fairy-tale parable, is an American-Soviet co-production—the first—a single film made by the pooling of American and Soviet talents.

The movie was produced entirely in the Soviet Union, mostly in Leningrad and environs, under the direction of an American (George Cukor), with American and English actors (Elizabeth Taylor, Ava Gardner, Jane Fonda, Cicely Tyson, Robert Morley, Harry Andrews), with Soviet performers (Oleg Popov, Nadejda Pavlova, members of the Leningrad Kirov Ballet Company), with one English cameraman and one Soviet, and with dozens of Soviet technicians.

What is being shown at Radio City Music Hall, where "The Blue Bird" opened yesterday, is one movie. Yet as you watch it you keep seeing two films that want to compete but don't, everyone being polite, accepting compromise, effectively neutered.

One of these films is blandly American, like the sort of processed cheese sold in jars that can later be used as water glasses. The other is dimly Russian but without any real Russian character, except for the sets, which aren't great. They look like stuff left over from the Bolshoi Opera's last road tour.

Though the film has about it a kind of lumbering tackiness that I associate with Soviet stage spectacle, I suspect that the Russian version of this co-production might be a lot more interesting than ours. For one thing, Russian audiences apparently love "The Blue Bird," the chef d'oeuvre of the Belgian-born playwright who allowed Stanislavsky to stage the world premiere at the Moscow Art Theater in 1908. This love and familiarity with the work might possibly have inspired Soviet film makers to bring to it a consistency of character and style, as well as a decisive point of view, completely absent from the hyphenated production we have here.

Spectacle for spectacle's sake no longer is the rage in this country. It can still work sometimes if it's put on a large patch of ice, but

Elizabeth Taylor as Maternal Love, right, and, from top; Light, Mother and Witch

the romantic notions that motivate "The Blue Bird" are enough to send most American children, to say nothing of the ancients who may accompany them to the film, into antisocial states beginning with catatonia and ending in armed rebellion.

"The Blue Bird" is the story of Tyltyl and Myltyi, two poor peasant children who are instructed by the Queen of Light to seek the Blue Bird of Happiness. To help them on their quest. Light gives the kids a hat decorated with a magic diamond that permits them to call forth the souls of all things, animate and inanimate. Thus Tyltyl and Myltyl set off on their journey accompanied not only by Light (Miss Taylor in head-to-foot stage jewels) but by people representing Bread, Milk, Water, Sugar, Fire, Cat and Dog.

At this point I'm afraid that I'm going to have to give away the ending of the film: before the children learn that the Blue Bird of Happiness is in their own backyard, they visit the kingdom of the past and the future, and the queendoms of night and luxury, at each stop learning some bit of wisdom. The film is not very old before you're longing to see a nice, self-absorbed Munchkin who wouldn't know an aphorism from a spitball.

Mr. Cukor, a director of wit and immense verve ("Holiday," "Pat and Mike," the Judy Garland "A Star Is Born") seems to have had less chance to direct in this case than to act as the goodwill ambassador who got his actors on and off the sets on time.

The English - language screenplay, by Hugh Whitemore and Alfred Hayes, would tax the inspirations of anyone. What could Mr. Cukor possibly have suggested to Miss Taylor to help her read a line like, "I am the light that makes men see/The radiance in reality"? Keep a straight face, perhaps. The actress has some creditably funny moments as a witch and some not-so-good as a peasant mother who darns socks.

None of the English-speaking actors can do much but behave as if he was in a very unlikely pageant. This includes Miss Gardner (Luxury), Miss Fonda (Night), George Cole (Dog) and Cicely Tyson (Cat). However, the two children—Todd Lookinland as the boy and Patsy Kensit as the girl—are quite charming in situations that make the adults look ridiculous.

The Soviet cast members, who speak in badly dubbed English, are no better except when they are given a chance to dance. Nadejda Pavlova is briefly, truly radiant in a tiny snippet from a ballet in which she dances the Blue Bird, but we see a lot less of it than I'm sure the Soviet audiences will. Members of

the Leningrad Kirov Ballet are also featured in other dances, all of which appear to have been abbreviated for our consumption.

We are also given several dreadful, Disney-esque songs, including one stunner called (I think) "The Blue Halloo."

Why the film suffers from so many technical problems, I have no idea. The color quality of the footage involving the major characters often doesn't match the material shot, I assume, by the Russian cinematographer. Then there are all those blue birds we see from time to time. Some look like black birds and some are simply pigeons dyed blue.

No New Yorker in his right mind would cross a street to look for a pigeon.

1976 My 14, C7:1

ECHOES OF A SUMMER, directed by Don Taylor; written and produced by Robert L. Joseph; director of photography, John Coquillon; edited by Michael F. Anderson; distributed by Cine Artists. At the Columbia Two Theater. Running Time: 99 minutes. This movie has been rated PG.
Eugene Striden..........Richard Harris
Ruth Striden............Lois Nettleton
Deirdre.................Jodie Foster
Sara...................Geraldine Fitzgerald
Dr. Hallett.............William Windom
Phillip Anding..........Brad Savage

By RICHARD EDER

"Echoes of a Summer," about the slow dying of a child, wavers infuriatingly between stoic beauty and sheer foolishness, between wisdom and sententiousness, between wit and archness.

Its virtues, left too long on some vine of creative indecision or second-guessing, have gone badly soft in spots. It could have been a triumph. As it is, endurance, patience and a selective deafness will be needed for the rough parts; the good parts are good enough to make up for the trouble.

The chief good thing is Jodie Foster, who played the barely adolescent hooker of "Taxi Driver." That was a stylish part; gritty, shocking and a natural for an acting tour de force.

"Echoes," made two years earlier, when Miss Foster was still a child, offers no such ease. She must sustain the movie's major role. Her composure, her toughness, her bleak eye that dissolves into a rare but total glee, carry her over bad and embarrassing lines and turn the good ones into arrows.

She plays Deirdre, whose incurabel heart disease has split her parents into opposite and conflicting strategies toward death.

Her mother is consumed by the need to overcome the impossible. She has taken Deirdre to specialist after specialist, in Europe and America, to try to find a cure. ("European doctors look away from you the same as American doctors," Deirdre observes.)

When the movie begins it is her father's turn. A writer, he is convinced that the important thing is to make Deirdre's last year as perfect as possible. No more dragging from city to city; instead he has moved his wife and child to a riverside retreat in Nova Scotia.

He treats Deirdre as his "princess," talks to her in a mixture of child and adult whimsy, makes up stories and fantasies, refuses to talk to her about death. She must end with dignity and grace, he tells his wife. No one dies gracefully, she says.

"Dying is a coming down from the hills," he says cloudily. "Stop that," his wife says, agonized. "How?" he asks. Neither he in his futile whimsy nor she in her futile practicality can accept Deirdre's death.

Deirdre can. She discusses her symptoms pitilessly with a brilliant and rough-mannered doctor—one of the picture's best scenes—and

asks him to soften things a bit for her parents. She indulges her father and plays all his games until pain and weariness exhaust her.

Her only real confidant is a plump, melancholy neighbor boy who is half her size. He lies down beside her on the beach when she asks him to—she wants to feel a man beside her—although he cautions her that he is too young for sex. The scene could be mawkish and coy; it is funny and horribly touching.

If Jodie Foster is the film's main strength—Lois Nettleton as the mother and Brad Savage as the boy are almost as good—its main weakness is Richard Harris.

He is disastrous as the father. He is nothing but the whimsical, sentimental figure he is playing for Deirdre's benefit. And he imparts to the film most of its unbearable softness.

"Echoes," which opened at the Columbia Two Theater, is rated PG. The caution is presumably for some of Deirdre's comments about sex.

1976 My 15, 14:1

FILM VIEW

VINCENT CANBY

This 'Blue Bird' Has a Right To Sing the Blues

Peace treaties and trade pacts are international agreements arrived at through compromise. Movies are not. "The Blue Bird," the first (and possibly the last) American-Soviet motion picture coproduction, isn't good and it isn't a disgrace. It's not much of anything, but movies that are not much of anything are the most difficult to endure. They never give you something truly outrageous to hiss at. There's no opportunity to let off steam. You can't gracefully stomp out of the theater. You have to sit there and squirm. You look at your watch, listen to the fidgets of nearby children and remember with longing getting your adrenaline up while watching something like "The Straw Dogs." "The Blue Bird" isn't a movie. It's a covenant with boredom.

In the early 1960's when French and Italian filmmakers realized that the only way they could survive was through pooling their resources, they quickly learned that the only good coproductions were those films that were, at least to the naked eye and ear, either completely French or completely Italian. They traded stars back and forth, also directors and writers, but the film had to have a dominant national character or it failed to be anything. "The Blue Bird" looks like a movie that had been made on the moon by people communicating through interpreters with walkie-talkies.

The first major compromise seems to have been the source material. The mystical fantasy by Maurice Maeterlinck, the Belgian-born poet and playwright who was so closely identified with the French Symbolists, actually had its

world premiere in 1908 as a Moscow Art Theater production staged by Stanislavsky. Though its appeal has dimmed considerably in this country over the years, it has remained a popular attraction in Russia ever since. Exactly what this tells us about Soviet taste I have no idea, but it should also be pointed out that this same audience supports the best productions of Chekhov in the world. It isn't an audience given exclusively to goo.

Before he got around to writing "The Blue Bird" Maeterlinck was associated with the French theater movement reacting against the naturalism made dogma by Zola. Reality, said these rebels, was more than just measurable externals. It was to be found in what one critic called "fugitive impressions and sensations" that are symbolic of the spirit. Everything has a soul, says Maeterlinck in "The Blue Bird," but it's up to us to discover it. At one point early in his career Maeterlinck was seriously proposing the banishment of live actors from the stage and the substitution of some kind of mechanical actors or life-sized marionettes. The theatrical alternatives that Maeterlinck dreamed of are considerably more interesting than the plays he wrote to demonstrate his ideas, which strike us today as sheerest romantic nonsense.

At least they are in "The Blue Bird," an allegorical fairy tale with characters named Milk, Bread, Water, Fire and so on, about two small peasant children who are sent out on a mission by the Queen of Light to find

Taylor and friends: Their movie is "a covenant with boredom."

the Blue Bird of Happiness, which as Maeterlinck took pains to point out (to us and them), existed all the time in their own backyard. Before they learn this—a piece of information that the queen withholds for no honorable reason—the kids, accompanied by the queen, the walking edibles (Milk, Bread, etc.) as well as by their dog and cat, whose human-like souls have been liberated by magic, journey to such places as the kingdoms of the past and the future, and the queendoms of luxury and night. In a benign mood one can imagine that this would have made a passable libretto for a great romantic composer and a great romantic choreographer. The American-Soviet coproduction has neither and, apparently, didn't even try.

•

What we have is a mostly overweight movie spectacle with some awful pop songs that wouldn't have got beyond the front gate at the Disney studios, plus snippets of ballet by members of the Leningrad Kirov Ballet Company.

The film was shot in Leningrad, in studios and on location, under the direction of George Cukor with a cast that includes Elizabeth Taylor (Light, Mother, Maternal Love and Witch), Ava Gardner (Luxury), Jane Fonda (Night), Cicely Tyson (Cat), Robert Morley (Father Time) and good old Harry Andrews playing a short-tempered tree.

I must say that although I found the film to be the bore of the year to date, I think all of these people did nobly under circumstances that were doomed to fail from the start. Cukor, one of the most elegant directors Hollywood has ever produced, appears to have been locked into his Soviet sets so rigidly that one never feels the film has begun to move. It's like watching a particularly cumbersome stage production in which the scene changes take so long that you know that each new set has got to hang around a while.

While Miss Taylor looks smashing and has a few genuinely raffish moments as the Witch, all of the other performers are squandered, including the Soviet clown, Popov, who is on-screen for maybe two minutes. Hugh Whitemore and Alfred Hayes are credited with the screenplay but when Miss Fonda came on, dressed in modified Barbarella gear as Night, I began to think she had written her lines. Frets Night for no reason that has anything to do with the kiddie-quest for the Blue Bird, "What times we live in. I don't understand these last few years." Night sounds as if she had been moonlighting in the America of the Nixon Administration.

Miss Tyson has some nice moments as the Cat, the the only character whose neck you don't want to wring

at one point or another. She also has the film's single funny line, which reflects the feline ability to dodge platitudes that the other characters have been tossing around like Frizbees for most of the film.

This kind of coproduction does nothing for either party. The elan of the American film talents, particularly Cukor's, is wasted, perhaps inhibited, while the talents of the Soviet participants, particularly those of the Kirov Ballet, are seen so fleetingly that the film could just as easily have been shot in Hoboken.

1976 My 16, II:17:1

THAT'S ENTERTAINMENT, PART 2, an anthology of scenes from M-G-M films; new sequences directed by Gene Kelly; produced by Saul Chaplin and David Melnick; narration written by Leonard Gershe; music arranged and conducted by Nelson Riddle; special lyrics by Howard Dietz and Mr. Chaplin; director of photography, George Folsey; editors, Bud Friedgan and David Blewitt; contributing editors, David Bretherton and Peter C. Johnson, an M-G-M presentation, distributed by United Artists. Running time: 133 minutes. At the Ziegfeld Theater, 54th Street east of Seventh Avenue. This film has been rated G.

By VINCENT CANBY

From the opening credits —Saul Bass's witty montage of various fashions in movie credits—until the closing reprise of the "That's Entertainment" production number from "The Band Wagon," "That's Entertainment, Part 2" is 99 7/10 percent pure magic. The three-tenths that aren't so great are the connectives between the film's individual sequences, which are drawn from 72 M-G-M features (dramas and comedies as well as musicals) and from the studio's short subjects, representing the M-G-M output from 1929 through 1962.

•

Even if you share my feeling that there is something morally wrong about ransacking old movies to make

such anthologies, the objections become academic in the presence of the salutes to the good old days of Metro— "That's Entertainment," released in 1974, and "That's Entertainment, Part 2," which opened yesterday at the Ziegfeld.

If one seriously cares about films (I tell myself piously), one should be wiling to work at them, to sit through all of the films represented here and not rely on excerpts made by someone else. But the 72 features in "Part 2" would require approximately 6½ days of steady viewing with no time out even to go to the refrigerator. If astronauts were provided with In-Flight entertainment, they might be able to survive the lot, but the rest of us, even movie critics, aren't properly trained and equipped.

•

Also, though it may be morally wrong to take movie scenes out of context, most of the films in "That's Entertainment, Part 2" would have a tough time qualifying as moral statements of an order in need of our protection. The greater part of the ma-

terial comes from musicals and, with the exceptions of "Singin' in the Rain," "The Band Wagon," "Meet Me in St. Louis" and a couple of others, none of the musicals is so great that we can't afford to miss the stuff used to bridge the gap between the production numbers.

The straight comedies and dramas are something else. Watching several sequences from "Adam's Rib" and "Pat and Mike," those splendid collaborations of Garson Kanin and Ruth Gordon (the writers), and George Cukor (the director) with Spencer Tracy and Katharine Hepburn, one aches to see the entire films, though the individual scenes hold up beautifully. Mr. Tracy may never have had a finer moment than the one in "Pat and Mike" when he admires Miss Hepburn with the statement, "Not much meat on her, but what's there is cherce."

Such films are too good to be cut up. So is "A Night at the Opera," from which "Part 2" purloins the classic stateroom scene.

Mostly, however, "Part 2" has been compiled with the kind of intelligence and affection that allow us to get some purchase on the Hollywood history made by M-G-M without spending our whole lives at the job. Nelson Eddy and Jeanette MacDonald are not everyone's idea of stars-of-the-ages, but the "Lover Come Back" number from "New Moon" is as much Hollywood operetta as can be stood by those of us not on the gloriously lunatic fringe with the other Eddy-MacDonald buffs.

Other highlights include the great Judy Garland-Gene Kelly "Be a Clown" number from "The Pirate"; Fred Astaire and Cyd Charisse doing Cole Porter's "All of You" from "Silk Stockings" (which just about convinces me she was his best partner); two magnificently manic, almost surreal Busby Berkeley numbers (the finales of "Girl Crazy" and "Easy to Love," shot at Cypress Gardens); a surprisingly little-girlish Lena Horne singing "The Lady Is a Tramp"; a montage of sequences from films about composers composing, climaxed by a virtually classic bit of Hollywood nonsense from "The Great Waltz"; Gene Kelly's fine roller-skating number from "It's Always Fair Weather"; a montage of Frank Sinatra sequences, highlighted by another great Cole Porter number, "You're Sensational," sung to Grace Kelly in "High Society."

The film is so studded with highlights that I suppose we should be grateful for the ordinary contemporary footage that is used to connect the old material. It gives us time to breathe. This new footage features Mr. Astaire, 76 when it was made, and Mr. Kelly, 63, as television-style hosts. They also sing a little, dance a little and kid a little. They are still vital talents, but they should sue the make-up men who have attempted to erase the years of their careers under layers of paint and borrowed hair.

1976 My 17, 40:1

LOOSE ENDS, directed, written and produced by David Burton Morris and Victoria Wozniak; director of photography, Gregory M. Cummins; music, John Paul Hammond; produced by Fat Chance Productions. Running time: 100 minutes. At the Whitney Museum of American Art, Madison Avenue at 75th Street. This film has not been rated.

Billy .... Chris Mulkey
Eddie .... John Jenkins
Jen .... Linda Jenkins

By VINCENT CANBY

Billy (Chris Mulkey) sometimes acts as if he were 14, though he's in his early 20's. Divorced from a wife he never loved, he lives in a one-room apartment, sleeps on a convertible couch, plays the radio too loud and keeps a couple of cats. He seems surprised when he calls a girl for a date at 1 o'clock in the morning and she asks him if he knows what time it is. He does but he's at loose ends.

So is Eddie (John Jenkins), a mechanic who works with Billy at a local garage. Eddie is married, more or less happily, to Jen (Linda Jenkins). They have one child and another on the way. Jen wants to move to the suburbs. Eddie doesn't. Jen wants a dog. Eddie doesn't. They regularly have furious fights, after which Eddie stalks out and joins Billy at a bar called The Club. They play pool and pinball and drink beer. Life for Billy and Eddie is a series of six-packs.

Unlike "Goin' Down the Road," a 1970 Canadian film that ultimately patronized the aimless lives of its two blue-collar friends, "Loose Ends" rides along with Billy and Eddie, seeing just about what they see when they see it without imposing on them heavy sociological significance. The filmmakers let Billy and Eddie speak for themselves, and that's mostly about cars. Says Billy of a woman he's met, "She has this Caprice that's loaded with options," which is what they don't have.

"Loose Ends," which opened a week's run at the Whitney Museum of American Art yesterday, is a remarkably good, level-headed movie about friendship and marriage and the limitations of each when, like Billy and Eddie, the people have never had to develop the means of conceptualizing experience. Neither Billy nor Eddie is dumb. Each is like an underdeveloped country whose highest aim is to become a consumer society. There are plenty of middle-class people with the same dimly realized ambitions.

"Loose Ends" was made on a shoestring in Minneapolis by David Burton Morris and Victoria Wozniak, who wrote, directed and produced the film. They are, I'm told, in their 20's, which is amazing in light of the exceptional discipline in avoiding both overstatement and an easy recourse to jazzy photographic and music techniques.

The performances also are extraordinarily good, especially that of Chris Mulkey as the more loose of the two friends, a guy speeding through life with a transistor radio turned on full and two cats asleep in the back seat. When Billy gets wherever he's going, he won't even recognize it.

"Loose Ends" is the most interesting regional American film I've seen in years.

1976 My 19, 25:5

SMILE ORANGE, Jamaican film directed and written by Trevor Rhone; executive producer, Milton L. Verley, photographed by Dave McDonald. At the Festival and New Yorker Theaters. Running time: 89 minutes. This film has not been rated.

Ringo .... Carl Bradshaw
Busboy .... Glen Morrison
Assistant Manager ..... Vaughn Croskill
Joe .... Stanley Irons

By RICHARD EDER

The tourist is funny and crass; the native who serves and exploits him is crass and funny.

"Smile Orange," a Jamaican film, is based on a play that must have been pungent and witty. The film has some pungency and lilt left in it, but it is terribly awkward.

It is about Ringo, a picaresque hero who works at a tourist hotel, cons the tourists, sleeps with their wives and daughters, doctors the crabs for the crab races that are part of the hotel's slambang entertainment and imparts tactics and a kind of gallows philosophy to a younger colleague.

●

"If you're a black man and won't play a part you're going to starve to death," he counsels his busboy disciple, while giving him lessons in how to be suave and use deodorants.

As Ringo — he played the same role in the extremely successful reggae film "The Harder They Come"—Carl Bradshaw makes a funny and rather noble swindler. He has, not courage but equanimity—that is, grace under pressure under a hot sun.

●

The film makes fun of the lumpiest and palest set of tourists ever to carry plastic shoulder bags. It makes fun of an upwardly mobile hotel manager, married to a lecherous blonde. It makes fun of the blacks' own version of the anti-postcolonial struggle: If you can't beat them, scalp them.

Its best parts are the good lines from the play. Ringo rationalizes his getting his two brothers-in-law jobs as lifeguards, even though they can't swim. "Tourists can all swim," he says. "It's we Jamaicans who are afraid of the water." He scornfully describes the foppish mulatto assistant manager as "a zebra looking over a whitewashed fence."

But there is too much literal carry-over from the play. Head talks to head, back and forth, on and on. The cuts are rough, the photography turns everything to orange and cabbage color. The story goes nowhere, and the humor eventually loses its sharpness and becomes inane and too local.

●

The freshness is like the breeze blowing through a half-built house — enjoyable for a while, but you lose patience with the holes, gaps and splinters.

"Smile Orange," which opened yesterday at the Festival and New Yorker Theaters, is rated PG. It is quite harmless; there's some talk about sex but no action.

1976 My 20, 44:6

Dim 'Premonition'

"The Premonition," which opened yesterday at the National and other theaters, is what might be described as a parapsychological horror film about a deranged woman who attempts to get her natural child back from its adoptive parents and unwittingly unleashes some foolish cinematic special effects.

The movie was photographed in color in Mississippi for no particular purpose except that the state cooperated with the film maker, Robert Allen Schnitzer, a young New Yorker who directed and produced and also collaborated on the screenplay. It includes such lines as "The clairvoyant reality is totally recycled by science," if you know what I mean. It's all pretty dim.

The cast includes Richard Lynch, who is now playing the stranger in "The Lady From the Sea" at the Circle in the Square. He may prefer to forget his participation in this.

The film has been rated PG in the apparent assumption that those youngsters who don't fall asleep immediately will be scared by the kidnapping theme, an unconvincing murder and a lot of artificial blood.

VINCENT CANBY

1976 My 20, 44:6

WHIFFS, directed by Ted Post; written by Malcolm Marmorstein; produced by George Barrie; cinematographer, David Walsh; edited by Robert Lawrence. At the Baronet and Victoria Theaters. Running time: 93 minutes. This film has been rated PG.

Dudley Frapper .... Elliott Gould
Colonel Lockyer .... Eddie Albert
Chops .... Harry Guardino
Dusty .... Godfrey Cambridge
Scottie .... Jennifer O'Neill
Detective Sgt. Poultry...... Alan Manson

If Elliott Gould doesn't stop making awful movies, the notion is going to get around that he is a poorish actor.

A few months ago he was seen here in an awful movie called "I Will, I Will . . . for Now." He played a man who was impotent. Now he is in a movie called "Whiffs," which opened yesterday at the Baronet and Victoria Theaters. He plays a man who is impotent.

"Whiffs" is about a soldier invalided out of the Army after serving as a guinea pig for experiments with gases. He steals gas and uses it to hold up restaurants, bars and eventually a whole town. The experience makes him rich, gets him a girl and restores his potency.

It is a brutally tortured comedy, potholed with intervals of the most embarrassing bad taste.

The rating is PG, which in this case stands for Pathetic Garbage. If Elliott Gould doesn't stop making movies about impotence, the notion is going to get around that he is a poorish actor.

RICHARD EDER

1976 My 20, 44:5

THE MISSOURI BREAKS, directed by Arthur Penn; screenplay by Thomas McGuane; produced by Elliott Kastner and Robert M. Sherman; director of photography, Michael Butler; editors, Jerry Greenberg, Stephen Rotter and Dede Allen; music, John Williams; distributed by United Artists. Running time: 126 minutes. At the Rivoli Theater, Broadway at 49th Street, and other theaters. This film has been rated PG.

Lee Clayton..................... Marlon Brando
Tom Logan..................... Jack Nicholson
Little Tod..................... Randy Quaid
Jane Braxton..................... Kathleen Lloyd
Cary .... Frederic Forrest
Calvin..................... Harry Dean Stanton
David Braxton..................... John McLiam
Si .... John Ryan
Hank Rate..................... Sam Gilman
Lonesome Kid..................... Steve Franken
Pete Marker..................... Richard Bradford
Hellsgate Rancher..................... James Greene
Rancher's Wife .... Luana Anders
Baggage Clerk..................... Danny Goldman

By VINCENT CANBY

"The Missouri Breaks" is a Western set in the fine, high hill country of Montana in the 1880's and is about a rich, literate rancher (he reads "Tristram Shandy" to relax) trying to cope with horse thieves who are stealing him blind. It's about the rancher's pretty, bright exceedingly bored daughter, who quotes Sam Johnson and once seduces an outlaw by suggesting he get down off his horse. "What for? says the outlaw, suddenly prissy "We'll talk about the Wild West, says the girl, "and how to get the hell out of it."

It's about that same outlaw, a horse thief, and his pals, who aren't bad fellows really, nor especially successful, just guys trying to make ends meet under increasingly difficult circumstances. Also about the eccentric "regulator," or private gun, hired by the rancher to bring law and order to his territory.

●

"The Missouri Breaks," which opened yesterday at the Rivoli and other theaters, stars Marlon Brando as the regulator and Jack Nicholson the horse thief and has a cast of superb supporting actors, including Kathleen Lloyd as the rancher's outspoken daughter. Harry Dean Stanton and Randy Quaid as two of Mr. Nicholson's more prominent partners in fumbled crime and John McLiam as the rancher.

More important, "The Missouri Breaks" was directed by Arthur Penn ("Bonnie and Clyde," "Little Big Man") and written by Thomas McGuane. All of the credits associated with "The Missouri Breaks" are impressive. Yet I liked it better when it was called "Rancho Deluxe."

"Rancho Deluxe," which was also written by Mr. McGuane, was a much smaller, similarly wise-talking version of virtually the same story, though set in contemporary Montana. The anachronisms in "Rancho Deluxe" (cattle rustling with a pickup truck, riding the range in a helicopter) were funny and moving partly because they emphasized the disconnection between a romantic past and a motorized present that's lost all ideals, all purpose.

You might think that Mr. McGuane, by setting the same situation in the 1880's, would give us the romantic side of the story. Not at all. In the 1880's of "The Missouri Breaks" the characters are just as bored, confused and directionless as they are in 1975, and they, too, look back to some dimly remembered period when the old days were good. Instead of being elegiac and funny, however, the anachronisms in "The Missouri Breaks" too often seem like camp.

●

This, I suspect, is principally because of the out-of-control performance given by Mr. Brando. He enters the film hidden behind a horse, which he at last peeks around, and then spends the rest of the movie upstaging the writer, the director and the other actors. Nothing he does (affecting the Irish accent he used earlier in "The Nightcomers" and wearing odd costumes, including frontierswoman drag at one point) has any apparent connection to the movie that surrounds him. He grabs our attention but does nothing with it.

In their earlier films both Mr. Penn and Mr. McGuane have demonstrated a fondness for eccentric characters whose impulses have a kind of grandeur about them. There's no grandeur to Mr. Brando's character. Nor much mystery. He behaves like an actor in armed revolt.

One has no way of knowing whether "The Missouri Breaks" would have been a good film without this peculiar presence as its center, but there are so many ar-

Marlon Brando wielding a weapon in hunting expedition during "The Missouri Breaks"

resting things in the rest of the movie that one can speculate — a raucous kangaroo-court sequence in which the defendant, a horse thief, becomes just as giddy and rowdy as the men trying him; a scene in a frontier whorehouse that, for once, looks depressingly grim; a marvelous caper in which several none too bright outlaws steal a corralful of horses from the Royal Canadian Mounties, who are otherwise occupied. They are in church singing "Bringing in the Sheep."

The film conveys a fine sense of place and period, of weather and mood and the precariousness of life, which are things that Mr. Nicholson responds to as an actor. Yet the plot, along with Mr. Brando, keeps intruding and throwing things out of balance. It's one of the film's oddities that as "The Missouri Breaks" proceeds to its bloody climax, with the scenes of violence increasing in intensity until one man slits the throat of another, it becomes increasingly trivial.

•

The killing of a rabbit on screen earlier in the movie (which has been rated PG) is more brutal and more shocking than the climactic confrontation of the two superstars, which doesn't seem important at all.

1976 My 20, 45:1

UNE PARTIE DE PLAISIR (A Piece of Pleasure), directed by Claude Chabrol; screenplay (French with English subtitles) by Paul Gegauff; produced by Andre Genoves; director of photography, Jean Rabier; a co-production of Les Films De La Boetie-Sunchild Productions (Paris) and Gerico Films (Rome), distributed by Joseph Green Pictures. Running time 100: minutes. At the Juliet 1 Theater, Third Avenue near 84th Street. This film has been rated R.
Philippe .... Paul Gegauff
Esther .... Danielle Gegauff
Sylvia .... Paula Moore
Katkof .... Michel Valette
Michel .... Pierre Santini

By VINCENT CANBY

WHEN WE first meet Philippe (Paul Gegauff) and Esther (Danielle Gegauff) they seem an ideally happy couple. They're handsome, healthy, loving, exceedingly well-off. They've been together eight years. They have a bright, sweet daughter, who is 6, and they live in a fine old country house surrounded by lawns, rose hedges and orchards. On weekends friends come out from Paris for good talk and food and companionship.

Even after eight years Philippe and Esther seem to be as sexually excited by each other as they were when they first met. Philippe has the kind of self-absorption carried easily only by the talented or the truly upperclass. His arrogance and conceit have been a form of reassurance for a middleclass girl whom Philippe has transformed into a perfect wife-mistress. Esther listens to everything Philippe says. He listens to her when it amuses him.

•

On its surface Claude Chabrol's "Une Partie de Plaisir," which has opened at the Juliet 1, is the report of what happens when Philippe decides that after eight years both he and Esther should be secure enough in each other's love to have outside affairs. "Preventative medicine," is what Philippe calls them. The film is much more interesting and more haunting, though, as a meditation on love, on the complex system of balances that work in any love relationship, and on the furies that can be let loose within such relationships when the balances are disturbed.

Almost all of Mr. Chabrol's recent films—most importantly "La Femme Infidele" and "Just Before Nightfall" —have dealt with the revelation of hidden flaws in supposedly perfect relationships, but always in the virtually abstract terms of melodrama. I say abstract because unlike the characters in these Chabrol films, few of us are driven to murder, and those few who do don't then go to such extraordinary lengths to hide

Danielle Gegauff in "Une Partie de Plaisir"

the deeds. For most of us murder is a concept as remote as the Pythagorean proposition.

•

"Une Partie de Plaisir" is not a melodrama. Nor is it remote. It's almost a comedy, and it's intensely bitter and cruel. The film focuses mostly on the demonically egocentric Philippe, but it's Esther who emerges as the more interesting character. In the course of the film it's Esther who grows up and away from Philippe, even though torn by her old dependence on him to the point where she actively participates in his humiliation of her.

Not since "Les Biches" has Mr. Chabrol so wittily (and mercilessly) examined the wars that are fought in life's living rooms and bedrooms, in kitchens and over dining room tables with friends as neutral, sometimes amused, sometimes appalled observers. It's a fascinating film and a very harrowing one.

Mr. Gegauff, who has written many of Chabrol screenplays, including those for "Les Biches" and this film, is supremely self-confident and alienating as Philippe, for which he even has the right physique — fastidiously cared for but not so successfully that the first signs of age aren't apparent in the clothes he wears. They are always just a little too tight, a little too young and modish for the fellow he really is. He's a man who would spend more time doing his hair than his wife would.

Miss Gegauff, whom I've never seen before and who is Mrs. Gegauff in private life, is a stunning actress with large gray-green eyes, almost like a cat's, and a beauty that has as much to do with manners and expressions as with nose and jaw lines. That she remains for us someone almost as mysterious as she becomes to her husband— who never has the slightest understanding why she finally leaves him—prevents the film from turning into a predictable treatise on open marriage. "Une Partie de Plaisir" explores emotional territories — dependencies, actually — much closer to home and much more dangerous.

1976 My 21, C7:1

Animated Shorts at Film Forum

NEW ANIMATION: PROGRAM 'II; a collection of recent animated shorts. QUASI AT THE QUACKADERO by Sally Cruikshank; RED BALL EXPRESS by Steve Segal; THE DOODLERS by Kathy Rose; KITSCH IN SYNCH by Adam Beckett; A BRAND NEW DAY by Jane Aaron; THE OWL WHO MARRIED THE GOOSE by Caroline Leaf; B RAE SHEET by John Teton; FACE DANCE by Robert Dvorak; CAT'S CRADLE by Paul Driessen; HOT STUFF by Zlatko Grgic; TOUR D'IVOIRE by Paul Dopff & Bernard Palacios; THE SILVERFISH KING by Pat and John Sauer. At the Film Forum, 15 Vandam Street, through Sunday and May 27 through 30, at 7:30 P.M. Total running time: 76 minutes.

THE SECOND part of the Film Forum's anthology of new cartoons opened yesterday. It shows signs of running out of steam. That could be a tribute to the completeness of the effort, perhaps there was not that much left to show.

There is one marvelous exception: "The Owl Who Married the Goose" by Caroline Leaf for the National Film Board of Canada. It is a misty, sepia film with the delicacy of a Japanese water color. Owl and goose-forms swirl and yearn toward each other, dance and fly off. The goose lightly, the owl heavily.

The goose lights on the water, the owl crashes into the water and goes down. The goose hauls him up— why do we know that the owl is a he?—and the owl floats valiantly for a moment before sinking once more. No second rescue; the owl had his chance; the goose swims away with the geese. It is as laconic as a haiku.

"B Rae Sheet" places side by side, in a sinuous line drawing, the development of a fetus into a baby, and the history of mankind. Wars and harvests follow each other, the fetus develops features, fingers. The idea is not

"Cat's Cradle," one of a series of animated shorts at Film Forum

overly original, and the drawing is not especially interesting.

There is one brilliant note at the end, however. History ends, and we see the baby, now born, his eyes shut. Suddenly the eyes open. The effect is as startling as it is economical.

Another Canadian Film Board production, "Hot Stuff," is more commonplace but thoroughly amusing. It is about fire—its uses and misuses. Man and Woman begin in the cold. They are given fire; the fire turns to toasters and irons and stoves. The toasters, irons and stoves turn to short-circuits—the house burns, the city burns, the world burns.

It is witty and instructive, and at the end bears the appropriate notation that it was made "for the Canadian Fire Commissioner."

The rest of the program is scrappier. One or two items are obscure or pretentious; others are simply feeble. One, "Quasi at the Quackadero," I found stridently obnoxious; a mean, half-campy use of figures and rhythms to tell about a duck who goes to a surreal fun-fair, is pushed into a time-warp booth and ends up with the dinosaurs. Cartooning possesses sharpness to make up for a lack of depth and texture; here the sharpness is tipped with poison.

RICHARD EDER

1976 My 21, C11:1

GUERNICA, written and directed by Fernando Arrabal; produced by Harry Blum and Federico Mueller; director of photography, Ramon Suarez; edited by Renzo Lucidi. At the 68th Street Playhouse, at Third Avenue. Running time: 110 minutes. This film has not been rated.
Vandale . . . . Mariangela Melato
Goya . . . . Ron Faber
Count Cerralbo . . . . Bento Urago
Raphael . . . . Cosimo Cinieri
Onesimo . . . . Franco Ressel
Ramiro . . . . Mario Novelli
Angel . . . . Cyril Spiga
Antonio . . . . Rocco Fontana

By RICHARD EDER

Fernando Arrabal is a precocious 43-year-old child who sits on the floor and tells totally made-up stories about the outside world. They eddy and change color, from ridiculous to obscene to puerile; but stars keep falling into them.

As a playwright, Mr. Arrabal has his own lodging in the Theater of the Absurd: It is called the Theater of Panic. As a novice film maker, he charges the medium head on.

There is a lot of damage any halfway competent movie director could have warned him about; and a measure of splintered brilliance that no halfway competent movie director could have dreamed of.

In "Guernica," which opened at the 68th Street Playhouse yesterday, Mr. Arrabal, an exiled Spaniard, has given us his Civil War. It is grotesque and painful, absurdly obvious in parts, rough and chaotic almost throughout. It is almost totally one-sided—and yet in its own highly personal way it is authentic. It is the Civil War as nightmare, but its obscenity and ferocity are metaphors for tenderness.

The setting is an imaginary village called Villa Romero, set in Extremadura, the most barren and backward of Spain's regions. With no subtlety at all, the film sets out its cast of characters.

Vandale, played by Mariangela Melato, is a beautiful hermit, half-witch. Count Cerralbo is the rural landlord who rails against the Republic and the loss of his authority. He has three brutal sons who ride around assaulting peasant women and meeting in a cellar to plan their part in the Franco uprising.

The fourth son, Goya, is a Surrealist artist who despises politics. He breaks up first-communion services by telling the children the wine is poisoned, paints obscene crucifixion scenes and sits through a scolding by his father while masturbating quietly into his brandy glass.

The Nationalist rising takes place, but in Villa Romero it fails. The landlord's sons flee to join Franco's troops, the landlord climbs into the village school and is hidden by the schoolmaster, a Republican but an advocate of nonviolence.

Vandale and Goya flee separately for France. They meet in the town of Guernica, fall in love instantly (a dove flies in slow motion from one to the other to symbolize it), and are separated when Guernica is bombed.

She returns to Villa Romero and, no longer a hermit, rallies the villagers to fight the oncoming Franco troops. He gets an airplane and machine-guns the besiegers' cannons. Ultimately the village falls, Vandale and Goya are made prisoner, and he is tortured. She manages to escape and free him. They climb to the mountains and against an enormous setting sun, embrace: symbols of a future Spanish liberation.

That is the plot, with all its farfetched melodrama. The film's strength is elsewhere; in images that express the savage yearnings and excesses that were the fuel of a terrible civil war. Many of the villagers are dwarfs: Arrabal uses them to symbolize the oppression of a people. "Now we will be like everyone," one dwarf declares—it is a flash of pain—when the village invades the landlord's castle.

There are other blinding sights. Children move in a slow-motion procession up a hill; the soundtrack alternates their guttural chanting with an anthem; the effect is to bind up in one image churchgoing and church-burning Spain. There is an unbearable but inspired scene after the Republic is defeated: A bullfighter, using all the gestures and postures of his art, fights and kills five dwarfs lashed to wheelbarrows. The audience is the army, the church, the upper classes; the national anthem plays.

These things, intolerable as they may seem, succeed beyond all reasonable expectations. Many other things fail; and the film's technical carelessness (it is filmed in Italy but even the Italian dubbing is sloppy—at one point Miss Melato is speaking Italian and the crowd is answering in Spanish drags it down further.

Miss Melato is a good actress but she doesn't have the force for the role. Her singing of one of the great Civil War songs is almost prim. On the other hand the American actor Ron Faber, playing Goya, makes a first-rate Spaniard.

Rough, ridiculous, arbitrary: "Guernica" is a film designed to make the spectator fight it. The remarkable thing is that it frequently wins.

1976 My 22, 19:3

FILM VIEW

VINCENT CANBY

When Brando Enters The Movie Flops

"The Missouri Breaks" was directed by Arthur Penn, written by Thomas McGuane and stars Marlon Brando and Jack Nicholson. It was produced by Elliott Kastner and Robert M. Sherman and its "production services," according to my credit sheet, "are by Devon/Persky-Bright."

As I write this I have no idea what the phrase, "production services," means, but I mention Devon/Persky-Bright here because they are so prominently featured in the publicity material for "The Missouri Breaks" that I suspect they must be persons of clout. Could they be the people who catered the actors and crew while they were on location in Montana? Probably not. Provided the horses? I doubt it. Helped straighten out legal points during contract talks? Maybe. Raised money? That sounds more like it, if only because "The Missouri Breaks" is one of those movies whose terrific potential appears to have been frittered away by compromises and concessions that may have more to do with economics than art.

Not that the movie looks cheap—far from it. Its settings are authentic and as big as all outdoors, but in spite of all the talents involved it's not the coherent movie it seems to have wanted to be. It's a promise that hasn't been kept. It's a movie that reduces criticism to conjecture.

The person who dominates the movie—though in the wrong way—is Marlon Brando, in his first performance since his extraordinarily successful collaboration with Bernardo Bertolucci in "Last Tango in Paris." Brando doesn't seem to have collaborated with anybody in "The Missouri Breaks," in which he plays something called "a regulator," a hired gun, a killer who is hired by a rich Montana rancher in the late 19th century to put an end to the horse-stealing that threatens to bankrupt the rancher.

• • •

Brando shows up about a quarter of the way through "The Missouri Breaks" looking like an elderly, overweight Indian with Ben Franklin hair and a fondness for peculiar clothes, and the movie, which until that point has been a fascinating collaboration between director Penn and writer McGuane, goes out the window.

Did McGuane write the character that Brando plays? I've no way of knowing. Robert E. Lee Cartwright (Brando) performs as if he were doing a one-man show on the order of "Mark Twain Tonight." For reasons best known to himself he speaks in an Irish accent that destroys most of the scenes he's in with other actors as effectively as if he had painted one of his ears light blue. He mugs in a soft, genteel way, using odd pauses and glances off-screen, that force our attention to him with no relation to the meaning of the scene. At one point, when he's attending to a particularly brutal bit of business (preparing to burn alive a couple of sadly ineffectual horse-thieves), he disguises himself in a sunbonnet and a Mother Hubbard dress, though it's the middle of the night, in the wilderness, and there's no one we can see to be fooled by the disguise.

McGuane, a first-rate novelist ("The Bushwacked Piano," "92 in The Shade") and screenwriter ("Rancho Deluxe," "92 in The Shade"), has a fondness for eccentric characters and it's entirely possible that he created the character Brando plays, down to the last lifted eyebrow and dimly hinted at fetish. I have no way of knowing. I do know that the effect of Brando's performance is not the recognition of a bizarre character but of an actor whose services are very expensive and who is apparently making a movie all by himself.

When an actor costs as much as Brando does today ($1,000,000-plus), he's likely to do pretty much what he wants. The director and writer might have second thoughts but the people financing the film wouldn't want anyone to create a situation that would run the production into overtime—which is what prompted my speculation about Devon/Persky-Bright.

•   •   •

Movies today cost so much that there often isn't time to get things right. Money may not be an auteur but it confers such power on high-priced talent that people like Barbra Streisand and Steve McQueen can be as responsible for what we see on the screen as any of their directors or writers.

"The Missouri Breaks" is a disappointing movie but it's not a boring one. It has a lot of things on its mind and if, at the end, it suddenly seems to have gone nowhere, perhaps we are meant to remember Sterne's "Tristram Shandy," which is mentioned quite early in the movie. "Tristram Shandy" has hardly anything to do with a character called Tristram Shandy. The novel rambles, it digresses, it takes time out, it plays tricks. But it's a work of genius.

"The Missouri Breaks" isn't, but in somewhat the same way the movie makes a method of the non sequitur—Brando's curious performance being the most obvious one. McGuane's screenplay starts out as a rather conventional confrontation of the rancher with the outlaws, a situation that McGuane exploited earlier with irony and great comic effect in "Rancho Deluxe," which was set in the contemporary West. McGuane cannot stick to clichés, though, or to historical periods. He deals in anachronisms. Jack Nicholson's horse thief in "The Missouri Breaks" is actually a city boy at heart. Playing at the outlaw life, he is all butter-fingers. In his one attempt at holding up a train, he makes the mistake of jumping from the mail car as it's crossing a trestle over a gorge. The film's heroine, the rancher's pretty daughter (played by Kathleen Lloyd, a newcomer with a fine sense of the absurd), is about as likely a 19th-century heroine as Gloria Steinem.

•   •   •

The screenplay rambles from one sequence to another with no particular thought of narrative drive but with the browser's delight in coming upon unexpected treasures: a funeral at which it's said of the deceased, "He personified the American West in the days of its rowdy youth" (this being about 1880, remember), a visit to a whore house that is small, cramped, untidy and woefully staffed, a young horse-thief (played by Randy Quaid) struggles to get his thoughts together by a campfire, saying, "Life ain't like anything I ever seen before."

As he did in both "Bonnie and Clyde" and "Little Big Man," Penn looks behind the legends to find truths that are unromantic, occasionally funny and sometimes unspeakably brutal. The first half of "The Missouri Breaks" is full of vivid, provocative things and then, quite late, as it seems to remember that it's supposed to be a mass-market Western with a conventional showdown, the film becomes increasingly violent and so increasingly silly that its conclusion could possibly pass for parody. What went wrong?

1976 My 23, II:17:7

Film: 'Jewish Gauchos' No 'Fiddler' on the Hoof

THE JEWISH GAUCHOS, Argentine film in Spanish with English subtitles. Directed by Juan Jose Jusid; written by Mr. Jusid, Oscar Viale, Alejandro Saderman and Ana Maria Gerchunoff, based on a novel by Alberto Gerchunoff; photographed by Juan Carlos Desanzo; music by Gustavo Beytelmann. Distributed by Julio Tanjeloff Productions. At the Baronet Theater. Running time: 92 minutes. This film has not been rated.
Dr. Naum ....Pepe Soriano
Maria ....Ginamaria Hidalgo
Brene ....Maria Rosa Gallo
Rabbi Simon Liske ..Osvaldo Terranova
Rachel Kelner ....Dora Baret
Gabriel ....Victor Laplace

"The Jewish Gauchos" is an Argentine musical melodrama about Jewish immigrants who settled on the pampas at the turn of the century. Possibly it was inspired by a scratchy print of "Fiddler on the Roof." It opened yesterday at the Baronet Theater.

Ai! Ai!
Oi! Oi!

RICHARD EDER

1976 My 27, 28:5

DRIVE-IN, directed by Rod Amateau, written by Bob Peete; director of photography, Robert Jessup; film editors, Bernard F. Caputo and Guy Scarpitta; produced by Alex Rose and Tamara Asseyev; released by Columbia Pictures. At neighborhood theaters. Running time. 96 minutes. This film has been rated PG.
Glowie Hudson.................Lisa Lemole
Orville Hennigson.........Glen Morshower
Little Bit.................Gary Cavagnaro
Enoch.................Billy Milliken
Alabam.................Lee Newsom
Spoon.................Regan Kee

"Drive-In," which opened yesterday at neighborhood theaters, is two movies for the price of one. And while one is better than the other, both are conceived in mordancy and sent forth with gleeful wickedness at the sort of multidramas made popular by novelists like Arthur Hailey and the disaster movies made profitable by Hollywood.

Like "Hotel" or "Airport," this movie brings together one night in a Texas Panhandle drive-in a pair of bumbling stickup men, two rival youth gangs, a teenage couple perhaps headed for an unfortunate marriage, a pretty girl who has just broken up with one of the gang leaders, the decent but sexually unprecocious boy she is now interested in, his voyeuristic brother, a frightened black doctor and a host of subsidiary characters.

Before the movie on the drive-in screen ends, much will be decided. And what a film it is. Its title is "Disaster '76."

From the occasional glimpses offered, it begins with a dynamite explosion aboard a jetliner, which proceeds to crash into a skyscraper, touching off a major fire. Sometime thereafter, a dam breaks, an ocean liner sinks and a shark menaces both a swimming woman and the ship's captain, who took over the controls of the jetliner after the dynamite went off.

"Disaster '76" is short, sweet and frequently funny. 'Drive-in" posseses the virtue of fresh faces, the drawback of uneven acting, the irritation of occasional overwriting and the limited appeal of what is basically a juvenile story. It may not be "The Last Picture Show," but it may be the last word in the miniaturization of a genre.

•

The PG rating is presumably attributable to a couple of words, a bit of violence and an atmosphere of adolescent prurience.

LAWRENCE VAN GELDER

1976 My 27, 28:7

EMBRYO, directed by Ralph Nelson; screenplay by Anita Doohan and Jack W. Thomas, based on a story by Mr. Thomas; executive producer, Sandy Howard; produced by Arnold H. Orgolini and Anita Doohan; music, Gil Melie; director of photography, Fred Koenekamp; editor, John Martinelli; distributed by Cine Artists. Running time: 104 minutes. At neighborhood theaters. This film has been rated PG.
Dr. Paul Holliston ....Rock Hudson
Martha ....Diane Ladd
Victoria ....Barbara Carrera
Riley ....Roddy McDowall
Helen ....Anne Schedeen
Gordon' ....John Elerick
Dr. Winston ....Jack Colvin
Dr. Brothers ....Dr. Joyce Brothers

If Dr. Charles Brinkman 3d is right, the world as we know it is going to come to an awful end—tomorrow or maybe today. It won't blow up, explode, melt or even bump into another planet. It is Dr. Brinkman's terrifying prophecy that it will turn into a giant B-film, rather like "Embryo," which opened at neighborhood theaters yesterday and whose scientific veracity Dr. Brinkman, the film's technical adviser, guarantees in an opening title card. What we see, he tells us, can happen at any minute.

"Embryo" was directed by Ralph Nelson and is just about as tacky a science-fiction film as you could hope to attend for unintentional laughs. It's about this widower, a brilliant research scientist, played by Rock Hudson, who shoots a three-month old human fetus with a growth-enhancing hormone. Ten days later, Rock has not a fetus but a full-grown ex-model-turned-actress (Barbara Carrera), who comes into the world naked though neatly daubed with eye shadow and mascara, which may be the most practical side-effect of this astonishing hormone.

•

Rock thinks that his big problem with the girl will be solved by passing her off as his research assistant, thus hoping not to stir the jealousy of his live-in sister-in-law (Diane Ladd). Rock is willing to gamble since the stakes are high. (In one of the movie's wilder understatements, he calls the girl the most significant advance in medical research in the last 10 years. Mercy me! (What happened 11 years ago?)

The girl is not only beautiful, brilliant, a natural chess player and a self-assured literary critic, but she also wants Rock to fulfill her. Rock does, but then things begin to go badly, as they did with Frankenstein's monster after awhile.

"Embryo" is an even sillier variation of the Frankenstein theme than Mr. Nelson's "Charly," though both films share the assumption that the public will buy anything if the subject is presented solemnly enough. The acting and direction are dreadful, the screenplay is a joke and a cocktail party sequence features the appearance of someone billed as Dr. Joyce Brothers, playing herself, but it looks more like plastic special effects.

•

"Embryo" is rated PG for what I suppose are any number of valid reasons (a little nudity, some violence) though probably not for degrading a perfectly respectable movie genre.

VINCENT CANBY

1976 My 27, 29:1

WON TON TON, THE DOG WHO SAVED HOLLYWOOD, directed by Michael Winner; written by Arnold Schulman and Cy Howard; director of photography, Richard H. Kline; music by Neal Hefti; editor, Bernard Gribble; produced by David V. Picker, Mr. Schulman and Mr. Winner; released by Paramount Pictures. At the Sutton Theater, Third Avenue and 57th Street and the Paramount Theater, Columbus Circle. Running time: 92 minutes. This film has been rated PG.
Estie Del Ruth ....Madeline Kahn
Grayson Potchuck.........Bruce Dern
J. J. Fromberg.........Art Carney
Murray Fonberg.........Phil Silvers
Dancing Butler.........Stepin Fetchit
Rudy Montague.........Ron Leibman

By RICHARD EDER

"Won Ton Ton, the Dog That Saved Hollywood" is the name of the movie that opened yesterday at the Sutton Theater. What saves the movie, a jumble of good jokes and bad, sloppiness, chaos and apparently any old thing that came to hand, is Madeline Kahn.

Madeline Kahn has eyes like sad soup, a jaw that is both long and vulnerable, and hair like unexplored jungle. Her voice is high and tinny, as though a midget were making a speech inside a beer can.

•

All these things are part of her comic equipment, but they aren't what make her a genuine comedian. What she has—as W. C. Fields and Buster Keaton and Charlie Chaplin had—is a kind of unwavering purpose at right angles to reality, a concentration that she bears, Magoolike, through all kinds of unreasonable events. What is funny is not so much her visible actions as her visible mind.

The movie itself is an untidy, sometimes pleasant mess, a string of sight and situation gags strung along a minimal plot about film-making in Hollywood of the 1920's. The colors and décor look like "Day of the Locust," the jokes about movie-making on a shoestring look like "Hearts of the West."

The gimmick is a trained German shepherd named Won Ton Ton (Rin Tin Tin, believe it or not, is the reference) who makes a fortune and then fades from sight. He is first seen letting himself out of the dog pound, after locking the keepers in his own cage. He meets Estie Del-Ruth (Madeline Kahn), an aspiring starlet, when both are hiding behind some garbage cans. (Never mind the details: It is simply part of a masterly bad day that she begins by walking out of her apartment dragging a whole tablecloth behind her, and continues by causing a monumental chain-collision when she tries to thumb a ride.)

Potchuk, an equally aspiring director who has impractical ideas of making films about a giant shark, a girl possesed by devils and a city destroyed by an earthquake joins up. A teetery and lecherous film-studio chief (Art Carney), who sits at his desk in boxer shorts in order to speed up his interviews with young starlets, spots the dog.

Won Ton Ton's success is phenomenal; he makes both Estie and her director rich. After a while the bubble bursts, the trio is fired, and Won Ton Ton is given away to a traveling dog show. Finally Estie, whose attempts to be an actress are nothing but a comic failure, is spotted as a comedian and makes a second fortune.

There are a number of cheerful things along the way. A torrid romance between Eskimos is being filmed—the director screams at the protagonists to stop sweating.

Bruce Dern is adequate as the young director, but his effectiveness depends on his lines and for long stretches he doesn't get much to contribute. Art Carney's horrendous studio president is funny for a while, but eventually becomes nothing but roaring.

Then there is Miss Kahn. She has some funny things to do and say, but it is in her small moments of comic embroidery that her real talent shows. Some gawky, mindless calisthentics while Mr. Dern, fired, is trying to figure out where they'll go next. A lovely bit where she slumps and rocks in front of a distorting mirror, turning alternately square and oblong.

The dog is all right. But Miss Kahn upstages him. It is because of her that "Won Ton Ton" is something more than a dog.

●

The movie is rated PG. It is quite harmless. Possibly the rating is based on frequent references to sex as the way to get ahead in Hollywood.

1976 My 27, 30:1

MOTHER, JUGS AND SPEED, directed by Peter Yates; screenplay by Tom Mankiewicz, based on a story by Stephen Manes and Mr. Mankiewicz; executive producer, Joseph R. Barbera; produced by Mr. Yates and Mr. Mankiewicz; director of photography, Ralph Woolsey; editor, Frank P. Keller; distributed by 20th Century-Fox. Running time: 98 minutes. At the National Theater, Broadway at 43d Street, and other theaters. This film has been rated PG.

Mother	Bill Cosby
Jugs	Raquel Welch
Speed	Harvey Keitel
Harry Fishbine	Allen Garfield
Murdoch	Larry Hagman
Davey	L. Q. Jones
Leroy	Bruce Davison
Rodeo	Dick Butkus
Barney	Milt Kamen

By VINCENT CANBY

"Mother, Jugs and Speed," a comedy about a supremely schlocky private ambulance service in Los Angeles, begins with a good deal of promise. Playing the president of the F&B Ambulance Company, Allen Garfield, who is to the interpretation of American seediness what Laurence Olivier is to Shakespeare, is giving a pep talk to his drivers.

Harry Fishbine (Mr. Garfield) is drawing a moving portrait of an America on the brink of despair. There are no more frontiers, Harry says in effect. Inflation, unemployment and the general economic depression have sapped the strength of this great nation we all know and love. He pauses for dramatic effect. Then, though it may only be something he ate, hope seems to flicker in his bloodshot eyes. Harry smiles with sudden enthusiasm. "But," he says, "thanks to muggings, malnutrition and disease, we still have a chance to make a buck!"

●

If "Mother, Jugs and Speed," which opened yesterday at the National and other theaters, had more of Harry's deviousness, paranoia and consistently rotten charm, it might have been a most original — and terrifying — comedy. As directed by Peter Yates and written by Tom Mankiewicz, the film comes across as a rude-joke valentine, the sort that's just as soft and sentimental as one decorated with cupids, hearts and paper lace.

It's essentially a fraud, and typical of so many post-"M*A*S*H" comedies that assume that a lunatic juxtaposition of slapstick, brutal realism, obscenities, romance and bad humor automatically make an important statement about the world we live in. Mostly it makes a mess of a film.

"Mother, Jugs and Speed" is a rip-off of vulgarity, poor taste and shock, which, like guns, should be kept away from film makers who don't know how to use them—unlike Ralph Bakshi, Robert Altman and Mel Brooks, film makers who do.

●

It's the erratic tale of three of Harry's employees, Mother (Bill Cosby), who drinks beer while driving his ambulance and likes, to buzz nuns as they cross the street; Jugs (Raquel Welch), who runs the

F&B switchboard, and Speed (Harvey Keitel), a suspended policeman.

It's also about Murdoch (Larry Hagman), whose running gag is his having sexual intercourse in the back of the ambulance with patients, including one unconscious girl who's just taken an overdose of barbiturates. The film's essentially pietistic nature is revealed when Murdoch eventually goes crackers and starts shooting people, which is the films way of showing that he really isn't a very nice fellow.

"Mother, Jugs and Speed" hasn't the courage to stand behind its own outrageousness, though it doesn't hesitate to exploit for laughs or crocodile tears the dismal lives of the people that Mother, Jugs and Speed deal with, including a woman who dies in childbirth after suffering a massive hemorrhage, alcoholics, junkies and the very old and incontinent.

With the exception of Mr. Garfield and Mr. Keitel, the leading actors have the air of people temporarily slumming, which they are.

●

The film has been rated PG in an apparent effort to alert those parents whose children may not be ready for gags about necrophilia.

1976 My 27, 30:1

THE MAN WHO SKIED DOWN EVEREST, produced by F. R. Crawley, James Hager and Dale Hartleben; director of photography, Mitsuji Kanau; written by Judith Crawley, based on the diary of Yuichiro Miura; narrated by Douglas Rain; editors, Bob Cooper and Millie Moore; a Can/Am Ltd. production, distributed by Specialty Films. Running time: 86 minutes. At the D. W. Griffith Theater, 59th Street, west of Second Avenue, and the Regency Theater, Broadway at 67th Street. This film has been rated G.

By VINCENT CANBY

THE MAN Who Skied Down Everest," which opened yesterday at the D. W. Griffith and Regency Theaters, is the filmed record of the 1970 expedition led by Yuichiro Miura, the Japanese skier, sports promoter and television personality whose object was to ski at least partway down Nepal's Mount

Yuichiro Miura on Mount Everest

Everest, the world's highest peak. At times the expedition involved as many as 800 persons. It cost approximately $3 million, as well as the lives of six Sherpa guides.

Yet the film, which was awarded this year's Oscar as the best feature-length documentary, has about as much to do with serious skiing as one of Jim Moran's more famous escapades had to do with bringing relief to the Arctic. Mr. Moran, you may remember, is the man who once sold a refrigerator to an Eskimo.

It makes no difference that the expedition was a dangerous one, that real hardships were experienced in placing Mr. Miura just several thousand feet below Everest's 29,000-foot summit, which was the start of his something more than two-minute descent, or that that descent down sheer ice most of the time required extraordinary skills. The movie makes the whole think look very much like an Evel Knievel stunt that mankind could survive without.

With the exception of the climactic run, which is shown twice, and some footage showing Mr. Miura practicing in conventional, low-altitude snow, most of the film is as doggedly banal and nonskiing as one of those Fitzpatrick travelogues that are kidded in "That's Entertainment, Part 2."

We are shown what seems to be endless footage of the expedition hiking through the pretty Himalayan foothills and stopping at quaint mountain villages. We see Mr. Miura keeping in trim with various exercises, and we see the Japanese members of the expedition astonishing the Sherpas with a videotape showing of "The Seven Samurai."

What's even worse is the virtually nonstop soundtrack narration, spoken in English but said to be based on Mr. Miura's diary. If he had put some of his prose on the bottom of his skis he'd probably still be stuck to the face of Everest. "Skiing is my doorway to adventure," he tells us early on. He looks at an absolutely vertical snowfield and observes without a giggle, "A bit steep, but what

a downhill run."

When the six Sherpas are killed in the cave-in, he has some thoughts about Destiny's way, but he only achieves a truly lyrical nuttiness when he attempts to describe the mysterious compulsion that has brought him all the way to Everest: "I dreamed of skiing on the virgin snows of the Himalayas. It's almost like the beginning of love—you can do anything."

With this kind of buildup, the final two-minute run becomes something of an anticlimax.

It, at least, is well-photographed, but much of the rest of the film isn't. The cameramen never seemed to have got the knack of panning across a wide angle of landscape without creating the impression that the scenery was falling toward the center of the screen.

If this film won the Oscar, how dreary were the contending features?

1976 My 28, C6:6

HAWMPS, produced and directed by Joe Camp; written by William Bickley, Michael Warren and Mr. Camp; music by Euel Box; director of photography, Reddy; edited b yLeon Seith. At the the Guild Theater. Running time: 125 minutes. This movie has been rated G.

Howard Clemmons	James Hampton
Uriah Tibbs	Christopher Connelly
Naman Tucker	Slim Pickens
Colonel Hawkins	Denver Pyle
Hi Jolly	Gene Conforti
Jennifer Hawkins	Mimi Maynard
Bad Jack Cutter	Jack Elam

By RICHARD EDER

"HAWMPS" is a long march on light provisions. Based on a tiny historical curiosity—an experimental use of camels by the United States cavalry in Texas in the mid-19th century—it should have been a nice small movie.

Instead it stretches into an underpopulated two hours and five minutes. Joe Camp, the producer-director, who previously made "Benji," seems to have a neo-Victorian idea of children's entertainment. You give the little things some small toy and they are to enjoy it quietly for a whole afternoon.

●

A plump and febile lieutenant, comfortably stationed in Washington, finds himself arriving at a bleak Texas cavalry outpost to try out somebody's notion that camels would provide ideal military transport for the region. The troops, who have been told only that they will be mounted on "genuine Arabian steeds," greet him enthusiastically. The colonel, an artilleryman who hates his job, greets him sourly.

The arrival of the camels produces universal despair, and some pleasantly ludicrous scenes. The troops learn to love the beasts, the despair abates, and so does the movie. To test the worth of the project, a 300-mile race is set up with a rival horse-mounted detachment. There are tangles with Indians and outlaws, with the camels gaining an eventual, though Pyrrhic, victory.

The jokes, the comic devices, are distended, repeated, italicized. A barroom brawl is stretched out so that it comes to seem longer than the war in Vietnam.

Everybody—James Hampton as the lieutenant Denver Pyle as the commander—overacts. As the leader of the horse detachment, Slim Pickens, who sometimes makes overacting a joy, only manages to make it a chore.

Mr. Camp seems to think that sublety—like properly seasoned food in that hypothetical Victorian household—is unsuitable for children. He feeds them mush: It will occupy them and do them no particular harm, but if they continue on this kind of diet they will grow up awfully boring.

1976 My 28, C9:1

THE MAN WHO FELL TO EARTH, directed by Nicolas Roeg; screenplay by Paul Mayersberg, based on the novel by Walter Tevis; produced by Michael Deeley and Barry Spikings. At the Cinema I and Cinema II Theaters. Running time: 158 minutes. This film has been rated R.
Thomas Jerome Newton.....David Bowie
Nathan Bryce ....Rip Torn
Mary-Lou ....Candy Clark
Oliver Farnsworth ....Buck Henry
Peters ....Bernie Casey

By RICHARD EDER

There are quite a few science-fiction movies scheduled to come out in the next year or so. We shall be lucky if even one or two are as absorbing and as beautiful as "The Man Who Fell to Earth," which opened yesterday at the Cinema I and Cinema II Theaters.

When science-fiction writing enlisted such authors as Ray Bradbury, the emphasis on space machines, time warps and little green men gave way to more philososhical and emotional approaches. It was man or Martian, not as physical but as metaphysical travelers. Space was filled with loss and melancholy as well as gadgets.

•

"The Man Who Fell to Earth" makes some use of far-planetary landscape, of extrahuman physiognomy and even of space machinery. Sparingly, though; as a touch of color. Mainly it is about exile, about being an alien. Its story of an extraterrestrial visitor from another planet is designed mainly to say something about life on this one.

Nicholas Roeg, who made the powerful but grotesque "Don't Look Now," is an elaborate and mannered director. He does nothing simply; he uses indirection and ambiguity paced with sudden shocking effects. His complexity, his baroque style, is redeemed by a considerable though not total precision and control. His idiosyncracies overweighted the story of a grief-hallucinated couple in "Don't Look Now": they are extraordinarily well suited to this space allegory.

Mr. Roeg has chosen the garish, translucent, androgynous-mannered rock-star, David Bowie, for his space visitor. The choice is inspired. Mr. Bowie gives an extraordinary performance. The details, the chemistry of this tall pale figure with black-rimmed eyes are clearly not human. Yet he acquires a moving, tragic force as the stranger caught and destroyed in a strange land.

The story is complicated. It is set up as a near-total mystery that unfolds bit by bit, leaving—it must be said —a few small unexplained gaps. The price paid for this method is a certain confusion; the gain is the spectator's tingling desire to have the puzzle work out.

There is an explosive splash in a Western lake, and soon Newton — David Bowie — is walking into a town. Immediately the film's theme is set. He passes, and is alarmed by a garishly painted fun-park gondola in which a drunkard sits, gibbering. Where is Outer Space? Right here on earth.

Newton pawns an immense collection of gold rings for $10,000. He takes the money and a sheaf of papers to Farnsworth, a top patent lawyer, played by Buck Henry. The papers are nine major electronics inventions. Farnsworth can't believe what he sees: "For starters you can take General Electric, Polaroid and I.B.M.," he tells his strange black-garbed visitor. He is worth hundreds of millions of dollars, he tells him. "Is that all?" Newton asks.

Newton gives Farnsworth complete authority to set up a huge corporation. He takes shelter in a radio-equipped car, then in a motel, then in a lavish lakeside house, then in a desert shack. He is accompanied by a lovely, simple and increasingly tormented woman whom he picks up at the motel. All his contact with the outside world is by telephone through Farnsworth.

•

Newton's empire grows, but is eventually sabotaged by a shadowy, C.I.A.-like group that enlists all those around him—his mistress, his bodyguard and a brilliant, cynical scientist, played by Rip Torn.

Alongside this plot, giving it texture, are the gradually revealed mysteries. Why does Newton drink so much water? Why is he intrigued by railroad trains? Why does he continually watch television? Why does he use all the resources of his vast empire to build a one-man spaceship?

The movie has its incoherences. Sometimes the mannerisms — overlapping shots, for instance—are excessive. Once Newton is broken, and his homeward drive is fully revealed and fully frustrated, the ending drags on for too long.

But it is a first-rate achievement; helped by stunning performances not only by Mr. Bowie, but by Candy Clark, as his mistress. Buck Henry as the lawyer and Rip Torn, the scientist, are subtle and impeccable.

1976 My 29, 13:5

EAT MY DUST, directed and written by Charles Griffith; director of photography, Eric Saarinen; film editor, Tina Hirsch; music by David Grisman; produced by Roger Corman; released by New World Pictures. At the Victoria Theater, Broadway and 46th Street, and UA Columbia I, Second Avenue and 64th Street. Running time: 90 minutes. This film is classified PG.
Hoover ....Ron Howard
Darlene ....Christopher Norris
Harry Niebold ....Warren Kemmerling
Big Bubba Jones ....Dave Madden
Bud ....Robert Broyles

"Eat My Dust," which opened yesterday at neighborhood theaters, is an exuberantly idiotic movie about a chase touched off when the teen-age son of a California sheriff steals the best of stock cars from a race track at the behest of a girl in tight sweater, hot pants and boots.

What follows is a demolition derby with minimal bloodshed in an atmosphere of humor. The music by David Grisman is appropriately bouncy. The photography by Eric Saarinen is suitably pretty. And the cast, directed by Charles Griffith, who wrote the screenplay, acts as though "Eat My Dust" matters. It doesn't. It's simply another slick-looking Roger Corman time-killer for the summer kiddie trade.

•

The PG rating seems to be attributable to the language.
LAWRENCE VAN GELDER

1976 My 29, 13:7

LEADBELLY, directed by Gordon Parks; screenplay by Ernest Kinoy; produced by Marc Merson; executive producer, David Frost; director of photography, Bruce Surtees; music scored and conducted by Fred Karlin; Leadbelly vocals by HiTide Harris; editor, Harry Howard; distributed by Paramount Pictures. Running time: 126 minutes. At Loews State 2, Broadway at 45th Street, and Loews Cine, Third Avenue at 86th Street. This film has been rated PG.
Huddie Ledbetter ....Roger E. Mosley
John Lomax .....James E. Brodhead
Tom Pruitt ....John McDonald
Guard ....Leonard Wrentz
Margaret Judd ......Dana Manno
Wes Ledbetter .....Paul Benjamin
Sally Ledbetter ......Lynn Hamilton
Miss Eula ....Madge Sinclair
Gray Man ....Timothy Pickard
Blind Lemon Jefferson ....Art Evans
Gov. Pat Neff ......John Henry Faulk

By VINCENT CANBY

Huddie Ledbetter, better known as Leadbelly, the great American folk singer and 12-string guitarist who died in 1949 at the age of 60, is evoked in beautiful, soft, dreamlike images in Gordon Park's elegiacal new film, "Leadbelly," which opened

Roger E. Mosley

yesterday at Loews State 2 and Cine Theaters.

Leadbelly's life was hard and violent. He was born black at a time when blacks were "darkies," in the Deep South in which "darkies" were supposed to know their place, which, for Leadbelly's family, was sharecropping. But Leadbelly never did know his place for long.

He served one sentence for murder on a Texas chain gang and another sentence on a Louisiana chain gang. In 1939, after he had gained his reputation as a folk singer (sometime after the period covered by this film), he was once more up against the law, this time in New York, where he was sentenced to a year in prison for a stabbing.

In the meantime he was always refining his music, which provided the order in a life that was in every other respect chaotic, more, perhaps, because of his terrible temper than because of the kind of black militancy that "Leadbelly" suggests.

Mr. Parks and Ernest Kinoy, who wrote the screenplay, have imposed their own very particular kind of order on the Leadbelly story. It's as if the film were a recollection of the legend, rather than of the man. It's done in bold, broad strokes of incident and color that are as carefully balanced as the images in one of the better post-office murals of the 1930's. This Leadbelly is bigger than life —and serenely removed from it. Which is why, I think, one attends to the film carefully and is never very moved.

•

"Leadbelly" is less a failure in execution than a mistake in conception, for if you accept this conception, you must go along with its more or less immaculate vision of triumph over degradation.

You must also accept the performance of Roger E. Mosley in the title role. Mr. Mosley is a big, heavily muscled actor, but the muscles look more as if they came from lifting barbells in some neatly tended gym than from the random heaving of bales of cotton. The performance, like the physique, seems the result of careful study, not the eruption of furious passions. The character is about heroism, not its demonstration.

The film was shot on location in Texas, which the cameraman, Bruce Surtees, often makes to appear so pretty that you can't believe that it's not a stage set by Oliver Smith. This, I suspect, is not because Mr. Parks didn't know exactly what he was doing, because the director has chosen this method, which worked beautifully in "The Learning Tree," Mr. Parks's film about his own idyllic, mostly untroubled childhood, but is at odds with Leadbelly's life.

It's also at odds with the Leadbelly music, sung on the soundtrack by HiTide Harris so effectively that it has no connection to the Leadbelly that we see on the screen. There are vitality, wit, sorrow and joy in this music, but it remains a kind of voice-over commentary to the events we witness.

Two sequences in the film stay in the mind: an early country dance where Leadbelly plays as two dancers whip themselves into a sexual frenzy, and, toward the end, a chance encounter between Leadbelly and a once proud, now exhausted Shreveport madam (Madge Sinclair) who had been an early benefactor. The sequences are not realistic at all, but achieve a legitimate theatricality missing from the rest of the movie.

•

The film has been rated PG, though its scenes of violence are so stylized that the horrors are removed, neutralized.

1976 My 29, 14:1

FILM VIEW

VINCENT CANBY

'Entertainment'—An Eloquent Salute to Show Business

Esther Williams in Busby Berkeley's water ski ballet from "Easy to Love."
"Berkeley was a sculptor whose medium was live people."

After seeing "That's Entertainment" two years ago, M-G-M's first anthological tribute to itself, I couldn't believe that there would be enough first-class material in the studio vaults to make the inevitable sequel. Having now seen the sequel, "That's Entertainment, Part 2," I'm shutting up about the possibilities of "Part 3." It may be that the M-G-M archives are magically replenished. No matter how much material is withdrawn, there still appears to be more where that came from. Certainly "That's Entertainment, Part 2" is as much fun as the first film, and perhaps even more interesting as Hollywood history. It covers more ground in that the 72 features that are represented in "Part 2" include comedies, dramas and melodramas, as well as musicals plus odds and ends of short subjects.

Also, I suspect, my objections to the anthology form are no longer as strong as they once were. It's not an ideal form, of course. It's to original moviemaking what rip-and-read TV newsmen, who use wire service copy, are to journalists who research their own stories. Yet there are good anthology films — the two "That's Entertainments" — and bad. I remember with special horror something called "The Crazy World of Laurel and Hardy" for which the producer ransacked dozens of Laurel and Hardy features and shorts, taking from them only the climaxes of each gag, throwing aside the routines that contained them as if they were of no more importance than tissue paper.

As "That's Entertainment, Part 2" demonstrates, some kind of movie material can be anthologized more easily than others. "Part 2" gives us several scenes from the great Spencer Tracy-Katharine Hepburn comedies, "Adam's Rib" and "Pat and Mike," which are not only good but too good to be treated in this cavalier fashion. They serve to remind us how superlative were those collaborations of Tracy and Hepburn with Garson Kanin and Ruth Gordon, who wrote the screenplays, and George Cukor, who directed them. But reminiscences are not what make "That's Entertainment, Part 2" worth seeing.

● ● ●

The reminiscences are entertaining and sometimes funny—especially a montage from a baker's dozen of old Fitzpatrick travelogues, demonstrating a certain fondness for a severely limited number of clichés, and some clips from a series of Clark Gable films that reveal his public personality depended as much on repetition of attitudes and gestures as Jackie Gleason's Ralph Kramden.

The buoyancy of "Part 2" has nothing to do with what is very loosely called nostalgia but with discoveries, new appreciations and reassessments, some examples of which follow in no particular order of their importance:

Busby Berkeley, represented in "Part 2" by the finales he directed for "Girl Crazy" and "Easy to Love," was less a choreographer than a sculptor whose medium was live people.

Berkeley was a Pop artist long before anyone knew what Pop art was. The Cypress Gardens water ski ballet—the finale of "Easy to Love"—is one of the most breathtaking examples of pure cinematic invention ever realized, and Esther Williams, on her own water skis, taking her own jumps and, finally, being hauled aloft by a helicopter, was the perfect Berkeley star, magnificently formed, fair of face and, apparently, not to be perturbed by air, wind, fire or water. A goddess.

Jack Benny, seen as the master-of-ceremonies in a 1929 M-G-M-short, had already developed the sly mannerisms and the perfect timing that were later to make him one of the greatest comedians in the history of radio and television.

Eleanor Powell, a fixture in M-G-M musicals in the thirties and forties, had marvelous legs, was a good tap dancer and somewhat less sexy than your average, uniformed dental assistant. Tap dancing, unless employed as a kind of Morse code in an Astaire-Rogers flirtation, is a turn-off.

Bob Fosse, featured in an excerpt from "Kiss Me Kate," was dancing dances then—choreographed by Hermes Pan— that look very much like the dances that Fosse has more recently been choreographing for "Sweet Charity," "The Little Prince" and "Chicago."

Fred Astaire, who co-hosts "Part 2" with Gene Kelly, was and still is the greatest. It's not simply the wit and elegance that amaze us, but the continuing variations he worked so successfully for so long. His film, "Belle of New York," may have been a dog but his number from that film, "Stepping Out With My Baby," with Astaire dancing in slow motion in front of a chorus dancing in real time, is a little bit of what great movie musicals are all about.

●　●　●

Cyd Charisse, seen with Astaire in numbers from "Silk Stockings" and "The Band Wagon," was neither a great actress nor comedienne but the most ravishingly beautiful dance partner that Astaire ever had.

Frank Sinatra, seen in a montage of sequences covering his M-G-M career, including the early, unintentionally hilarious "Old Man River" sequence from "Till the Clouds Roll By," not only got better and better as a singer as the years rolled by but his appearance changed considerably, also for the better. Unlike most people who start at the top in movies, this fellow got a chance to grow up on screen.

·"If "That's Entertainment, Part 2" has some moments that are a touch below par, they are easily sat through. They are composed mostly of the new footage in which Astaire and Kelly do rather more hosting than is necessary, providing the bridges between sequences that could have been more efficiently and less intrusively provided by title cards. Otherwise the film is an eloquent salute to M-G-M movies and, through them, to theater or, as it's sometimes called, show business.

1976 My 30, II:11:1

Jab at Male Arrogance

MALE OF THE CENTURY, directed by Claude Berri; screenplay (French with English subtitles) by Claude Berri, with the collaboration of Jean-Louis Richard, based on an idea by Milos Forman; executive producer, Pierre Grunstein; director of photography, Jean-Pierre Baux; music, Claude Morgan; produced by Renn Productions-Les Films Christian Fechner; distributed by Joseph Green Pictures. Running time: 95 minutes. This film has not been rated.

Isabelle .... Juliet Berto
Claude .... Claude Berri
Hubert .... Hubert Deschamps
Ganster .... Laszlo Szabo
Louis Maboul .... Yves Afonso
Son .... Jullen Langmann
Claude's mother .... Mme. Langmann
Isabelle's father .... Jacques Debary
Isabelle's mother ...... Denise Provence
Nurse .... Bernadette Robert

By VINCENT CANBY

The sexual revolution leaves Claude a displaced person in his own house when Isabelle, his wife of six years, admits that she has just had a casual, perfectly satisfying one-night affair on the order of the casual affairs that he has admitted from time to time. Claude wants to kill Isabelle, but he doesn't. Because he loves her he contents himself by knocking her around a bit and then by brooding. As he tells his best friend, as if describing an irretrievable loss, "She was everything to me, a mother, a sister, a wife, a whore. . . ."

All this happens a year before the start of Claude Berri's French comedy, "Male of the Century," but it adds substantially to Claude's worries when Isabelle becomes one of three hostages taken in the course of a bank holdup. Claude worries less that she will come to some physical harm than that she will fall in love with the bank robber.

●

"Male of the Century," which opened yesterday at the Juliet 2 Theater, is so humanely conceived and nicely cast that the principal target of its comedy—male arrogance of an almost prehistoric order—is a lot more genial and fresh than it has any right to be.

Mr. Berri himself plays Claude with an tpically oafish self-assurance that is very funny. Claude is no answer to any maiden's prayer. He's suspicious, pot bellied and mean-tempered, but he somehow transmits his own grand vision of himself to others. It's typical that Claude, who runs a tiny boutique specializing in men's trousers, should describe himself—on the side of his battered delivery truck —as The Pants King.

Juliet Berto, looking more than ever like a young Jeanne Moreau, is equally funny as the resolutely liberated Isabelle, and Hubert Deschamps, who might remind you of a French version of Richard Haydn, has a surprising staunchness as Claude's best friend, a mild-mannered tailor with a ferocious hold on life, no matter what the disappointments.

Unlike such earlier Berri comedies as "The Two of Us" and "Marry Me, Marry Me," "Male of the Century" does not deal in autobiography. It's a sort of humorous "Dog Day Afternoon," though it does display a strong Berri appreciation for family ties. Mr. Berri's mother plays the mother of Claude in the film in such a way that her lack of professional experience is both moving and comic, as when she visits Claude in the hospital and brings him, in her large shopping bag, one small orange and one hardboiled egg. ·

●

Mr. Berri also has a marvelous way of dealing with children, including his small son who plays that role in the film. The children remain un-self-conscious and lighthearted, and as totally self-absorbed as the character that Mr. Berri plays.

"Male of the Century" is not the greatest comedy of the year, but you probably won't see many comedies in the near future. containing a scene as firmly planted in life as the one in which Claude's two sons, eating a dinner consisting entirely of mashed potatoes, look up from their plates suddenly to recognize the television image of their mother in the bank holdup. They are absolutely delighted.

1976 Je 3, 46:1

Film: Football As Joy and Anguish

WE are fairly simple creatures when we bump down into a movie-theater seat. The simplicity can be overcome and educated, but at the price of a certain residual strain. We have an emotional bias toward identifying with what we see on the screen rather than rejecting it. Great satirical and denunciatory films have been made, of course, but they tend to work by linking us with the victim. We experience our anger through him, rather than directly.

●

All of which is prologue to identifying the unreasonable excitement provided by an old documentary brought back by the Film Forum. It is called "Mooney vs. Fowle." It is 54 minutes long and is being shown in tandem with another documentary, "Jane," also 54 minutes long.

The only reason for mentioning the identical lengths is that "Mooney" feels like about 15 minutes, whereas "Jane" lasts every full minute of its 54. To dispose of "Jane": It shows Jane Fonda preparing to play her first starring role on Broadway in "The Fun Couple." It shows the nerves, the doubts, the enthusiasms. The play flopped utterly; the film, made in 1962, has its moments of intelligence, but it is thin stuff and doesn't survive.

"Mooney" is different. It survives magnificently, although the perspective with which many viewers see it will be different from that with which it was made, in 1961.

It is a documentary by Robert Drew, D.A. Pennebaker and Richard Leacock, about two Florida high school football teams preparing for and playing their climactic season's game. It cuts back and forth between equivalent scenes: the hard, harsh final training days of each team, the pep rallies, the pregame locker-room exhortations, the game itself, the shattered dejection of the losers and the amazed, almost diffident exultation of the winners.

The focus is provided by the rival coaches—Haywood Fowle of Edison High, the incumbent title-holders, and Otis Mooney of Miami High, the underdog challengers. Fowle is harder, tighter; he uses a shade more ferocity in psyching his players up to their top destructive edge. Mooney is tough too, but he has thoughtful moments; he seems more human. And—one of those rewards documentary makers stumble into—both men look almost exactly alike.

Some will see it as a small war, and judge the fierceness, the drummed-up competitiveness, the cheerleaders' frenetic rites and their dopey prayers for victory ("because this means so much to Miami High — I think you know that — I think everybody knows that") as a small model of the war disease.

Others — like this writer — will find it moving. These young people are not standing aside; they are staking all their emotion and effort on a victory or a loss, and they catch the joy and the pain squarely. Either way, the film will bind the viewer to the anguish and excitement of game, players and coaches; and it stands as a classic of the documentary art.

RICHARD EDER

1976 Je 4, C11:1

June Is Bombing Out All Over

It's January in June, and the movie industry could be in trouble. With the exception of "That's Entertainment, Part 2," there hasn't been a new film in the last two weeks that looks as if it could become a big hit—whether for the right or wrong reasons—and "That's Entertainment, Part 2" isn't strictly a new film. It's a new appreciation of a lot of old films. All of the other recent openings are also-rans, meaning that people going to the movies in the next month will continue to be paying most of their money to see only three pictures, "All The President's Men," "The Bad News Bears" and "That's Entertainment, Part 2." The rest of the films will have to fight it out for what's left of the public's movie allowance. Hardly a healthy situation.

The successful films are making more money—faster—than ever before, while everything else is dying. If a film is a fair hit, it may make back its distribution costs. Forget the production costs.

I can't remember any June that has begun as bleakly as this one One can't even say that there are a number of films that are failing to do the business they deserve. There aren't. It's like the annual post-Christmas depression when the film companies, having released all of their major productions in December, ride through January on the receipts from those films. The problem this year is that there weren't that many good movies released earlier to carry us through this arid patch. The new stuff is so forgettable that a friend of mine has complained not that they put him to sleep while he was looking at them, but while he was trying to write about them, which is known as the whiplash of boredom.

• • •

"The Missouri Breaks" is not boring. It's a big, fascinating, complicated disappointment, which is the kind of praise "The Blue Bird" might aspire to. "The Blue Bird" *is* boring. It demonstrates boredom as it defines it, from first frame to last. Nicolas Roeg's "The Man Who Fell to Earth," one of the better new films, is not boring. It's worth paying attention to even though it's disappointing. In an earlier time this wouldn't be a problem but today's audiences, who want to classify everything as either a hit or a flop, may not be in the mood to put up with its confusions.

At its best moments "The Man Who Fell to Earth" has the cool, no-nonsense clarity and direction of Kubrick's "2001: A Space Odyssey." It's also funny in a way that refuses to pander to conventional expectations. But by having too much on its mind, it sometimes appears to have nothing. The film is the highly satiric tale of a fellow from outer space, played by David Bowie, the English rock star, who comes to earth seeking water for his own planet. He travels on a British passport and calls himself Thomas Jerome Newton.

Just whether Newton plans to transport earth's water home in some fashion, or bring his planet's people here is not gone into. What is gone into is the way Newton, through some legal hocus-pocus and with the help of what are described as nine basic patents, is able to force corporations like RCA to knuckle under to him and make him the most powerful man in America.

As my colleague Richard Eder has pointed out, "The Man Who Fell to Earth" may be the first of the Howard Hughes movies, Newton being presented by Roeg as the ultimate in eccentric multi-billionaire recluses, whom we see at one point hidden away in a dumpy little New Mexico hotel room, eating candy and watching 12 television sets at once. "Television," he complains, "shows everything but it doesn't tell everything."

"The Man Who Fell to Earth" can also be seen as the story of a very hip, space-age Passion—but one that fails—about a savior who comes to earth not to save us but his own people, and who is, in effect, crucified dead and buried when the members of a competing cartel render him physically incapable of returning home.

The movie has been beautifully cast with the slim, androgynous-looking Bowie in the title role, Candy Clark as the pretty, dim-witted chamber maid he befriends, Rip Torn as a middle-aged scientist with a weakness for 18-year-old girls, and Buck Henry as a legal wizard with a weakness for his weight-lifting male companion.

As long as "The Man Who Fell to Earth" stays on earth, it is terrific, but it keeps taking off into outer space, flashing back to Newton's Planet X family and his bungalow there, which looks not much stranger than a mobile home parked on Route 66. There are also some horrendously arty sex scenes—something that Roeg seems to like—in which, apparently, Newton recalls making love to his wife, an act that on Planet X involves a lot of soap suds.

"The Man Who Fell to Earth" goes wildly silly from time to time, but has the courage to fail in interesting ways, which is more than can be said for the other new films.

• • •

"Mother, Jugs and Speed," directed by Peter Yates and written by him and Tom Mankiewicz, is a grossly witless comedy about the misfortunes of a private ambulance company in Los Angeles. Attractive actors—Bill Cosby, Raquel Welch, Harvey Keitel and Allen Garfield—give nice performances whenever the film's idiocies are not upstaging them. It's a very sleazy endeavor about greed, true love, drugs, sentiment, death and high spirits.

In "Embryo" director Ralph Nelson gives us a variation on his more successful "Charly" film, which was about a retarded man whom science brought up to super intelligence, only to let him relapse. "Embryo" continues the Dr. Frankenstein theme with Rock Hudson as the doc and Barbara Carrera as his monster, a three-month old fetus who, with the injection of a growth-enhancing hormone, turns into the magnificent-looking Barbara in less than two weeks. After Barbara goes off on a murder spree, Rock's son asks his dad why he performed this unnatural experiment. "To give life," says Rock. "To play God," says the son, who is pretty stupid but he does know his late-late shows.

"Leadbelly" is Gordon Parks's idealized biographical film about Huddie Ledbetter, the legendary black blues singer and guitarist. Roger E. Mosley plays the title role, in a series of mostly lifeless recreations of scenes from Leadbelly's life in the cotton fields and on the chain gangs. HiTide Harris sings the Leadbelly songs on the soundtrack so effectively the movie might be best enjoyed with the eyes closed.

CORRECTIONS: (1) Yes, I know the hymn in "The Missouri Breaks" is "Bringing in the Sheaves," not sheep, but I like sheep better, and (2) the great Fred Astaire dance number mentioned last week, "Stepping Out With My Baby," comes from "Easter Parade," not from "Belle of New York." Enough.

1976 Je 6, II:13:7

THE LAST WOMAN, directed by Marco Ferreri; story and screenplay (French with English subtitles) by Mr. Ferreri and Rafael Azcona; produced by Edmondo Amati; director of photography, Luciano Tovoli; editor, Enzo Meniccone; music, Philippe Sarde; a co-production of Productions Jacques Roitfeld (Paris) and Flaminia Produzioni (Rome), distributed by Columbia Pictures. Running time: 111 minutes. At the Fine Arts Theater, 58th Street west of Lexinogn Avenue. This film has been rated X.
Gerard .... Gerard Depardieu
Valerie .... Ornella Muti
Pierrot .... David Biffani
Michel .... Michel Piccoli
Rene .... Renato Salvatori
Gabrielle .... Zouzou
Benoite .... Giuliana Calandra
Anne-Marie .... Carole Lepers
Nathalie .... Nathalie Baye
Michel's friend .... Daniela Silverio

By VINCENT CANBY

It's not chance that Marco Ferreri, the Italian director ("The Ape Woman," "La Grande Bouffe"), has set "The Last Woman," his new French film, in a landscape composed entirely of modern factories, superhighways, shopping centers and handsome high-rise housing developments where each apartment has its own balcony (to overlook other balconies) and where the grass looks as if it

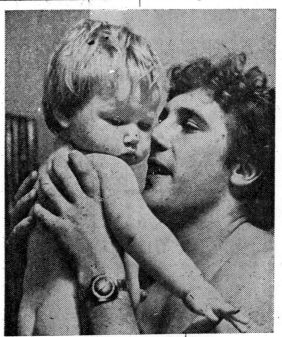

Gérard Depardieu and child

had been installed by a carpet company.

There are no visual references to nature in "The Last Woman." Like a meadow that has been turned into a parking lot, nature has been cemented over, effectively sealed off. But there are cracks, and it's these cracks—terrible crevasses, really—that are the subject of Mr. Ferreri's initially buoyant and erotic comedy that becomes, at the end, a satire of such literal brutality that most people may want to be warned. The film opened yesterday at the Fine Arts.

•

Like "La Grande Bouffe," which was about four bourgeois gentlemen who gorge themselves to death, "The Last Woman" is, finally, easier to talk about than to watch, especially on a full stomach. It may be the year's most ferocious satire, a film that only a very sophisticated society could support, but it's also full of brilliance, especially in the performance of Gérard Depardieu, who has quite suddenly emerged as France's most talented young actor.

As Gérard in "The Last Woman," Mr. Depardieu is the thinking man's lug. Built like a truck driver who drinks too much beer, a slob with a good deal of wit, he is a primal force too powerful to be controlled by the system of checks and balances he's been equipped with. He's not stupid. He's a bunch of outmoded attitudes that can't survive in the kind of concrete landscape that is Mr. Ferreri's comic metaphor.

•

Gérard is a factory engineer by profession and a colossally self-assured male supremacist by nature. He lives with Pierrot, his young son who doesn't yet walk, on a high floor of a spanking-new apartment house in a flat furnished with stereos, hip posters and all sorts of superfluous time-saving gadgets, including an electric carving knife.

Some time before the start of the film Gérard's wife has walked out on him to find her own identity—which is all right with Gérard, who doesn't mind playing mother as well as father to his son and who has no trouble finding temporary mistresses. In fact, he rather likes the temporariness of his sex partners. They don't question his ego nor invade the territory he rules as a father—until the appearance of Valerie.

Valerie (Ornella Muti) is "The Last Woman," a voluptuous green-eyed beauty who teaches in the factory's nursery school. One night when Gérard goes to pick up Pierrot, he also picks up Valerie and takes her home for what he expects will be another limited liaison. But Valerie is different. Between bouts of furious love-making she begins to settle in.

In the way no other woman ever has, she also begins to invade his consciousness, which, to a Narcissus like Gérard, is somehow to diminish him. When she tells him that he never succeeds in giving her an orgasm, she says it matter-of-factly, without accusation, but the effect is eventually devastating.

When she tells him that Pierrot needs to be touched, cuddled and loved, he sees it as a threat to him. "I need to be loved," he yells at her. Finally Valerie, sweet, beautiful, apparently passive, persuades Gérard his sex is the root of his egocentricity. "You are nothing without it," she says, which prompts Gérard to make the ultimate gesture to prove her wrong.

•

What is Mr. Ferreri up to? Sometimes I think I know and sometimes I'm not sure I want to. Then again I suspect that he may be the most passionately wicked satirist since Jonathan Swift. His satire is an electric carving knife that cuts two ways at once. Gérard is part buffoon, part tragic hero. Valerie is Eve, and the film, which begins as an uproariously erotic comedy, concludes as a spectacle so bloody it could send eroticism back to the closet forever.

The film is immaculately played by Mr. Depardieu, Miss Muti, Zouzou (as Gérard's first wife) and David Biffani, a little boy who apparently learned how to act even before he learned how to walk.

1976 Je 7, 35:1

'Deep Red' Is a Bucket of Ax-Murder Cliches

"Deep Red," which opened yesterday at the Cinerama, 86th Street Twin 1 and other theaters, is an English-dubbed Italian-made bucket of ax-murder-movie clichés thoroughly soaked in red paint that seems intended to represent fake blood. I don't think that Dario Argento, the director, meant to distance us from the action in this way. He's simply a director of incomparable incompetence.

In the leading role David Hemmings, the English actor, looks wan and in need of a vacation from Rome's off-screen high life. He plays a music teacher whose friends and acquaintances keep getting hacked up, thus interrupting his composing.

The bill at the RKO 86th Street Twin 1 Theater also includes a terribly self-congratulatory Gulf Oil Corporation industrial film, which is about as boring as industrial films can ever be, and during the intermission the management turns its stereo speakers to radio station WTFM so that the audience can listen to music and commercials for Pepperidge Farm French dinner rolls.

VINCENT CANBY

1976 Je 10, 47:1

JACKSON COUNTY JAIL, directed by Michael Miller; screenplay by Donald Stewart; produced by Jeff Begun; executive producer, Roger Corman; director of photography, Bruce Logan; editor, Caroline Ferrol; music, Loren Newklrk; distributed by New World Pictures. Running time: 85 minutes. At the Embassy Theater, Broadway at 49th Street, and other theaters. This film has been rated R.
Dinah Hunter ....Yvette Mimieux
Coley Blake .... Tommy Lee Jones
Bobby Ray .... Robert Carradine
Hoble .... Frederic Cook
Sheriff Dempsey ..... Severn Darden
David .... Howard Hesseman
Deputy Burt .... John Lawlor
Bartender .... Britt Leach
Alkson .... Nan Martin
Shaw .... Gus Peters
Cassie Anne .... Patrice Rohmer
Poquita .... Amparo Mimieux
Pearl .... Mary Woronov

By VINCENT CANBY

"If you are who you say you are," the small-town sheriff tells the young woman, "you won't have any trouble." The young woman (Yvette Mimieux) is Dinah Hunter, who has just thrown over her job with a Los Angeles advertising agency, as well as her lover of two years, and has been driving back to New York. However, all her identification—along with her money and her car—have been stolen by a pair of pill-popping hitchhikers she picked up earlier in the day, thinking she was doing a good deed.

When the hitchhikers pulled a gun on her and threw her out of the car somewhere in southern Arizona, they dropped Dinah into a nightmare land from which she probably will never emerge. "If you are who you say you are . . ."—the line becomes the theme of a fine, tough little melodrama called "Jackson County Jail," which opened yesterday at the Embassy 49th Street and other theaters in New York.

It isn't the film's very dismal view of Bicentennial America that gives "Jackson County Jail" its vigor. The film lays on the ironies and hypocrisies so heavily that it sometimes seems to be the work of especially snobbish film makers, people who think that everything between Los Angeles and New York is the boondocks.

•

"Jackson County Jail" is film making of relentless energy and harrowing excitement that recall the agit-prop melodramas of the 30's. It's not exactly in a class with Lang's "You Only Live Once," but it possesses the kind of fury that can breathe life into a melodrama even when the point of view is simple-minded.

The film was directed by Michael Miller and written by Donald Stewart, neither of whom I'd heard of before. Roger Corman, sometimes known as the king of the B's, was the executive producer, and it has the drive, movement and economy of narrative that are the marks of Corman films, good and bad. "Jackson County Jail" shows how someone as self-aware, self-assured and secure as its middle-class heroine can, literally overnight, find herself in a land-

Yvette Mimieux
Into nightmare land

scape where nothing she has ever known or believed still holds.

•

Unable to produce identification for the sheriff, Dinah is put into the county lockup for the night. She is raped by the jailer, whom she murders in self-defense, and the next morning is out on the road, sharing a get-away car with a young man who is an accused murderer and admitted truck hijacker.

It's preposterous, and the movie works within its own terms, though one shouldn't overanalyze it for the wrong (political) reasons.

Mr. Miller and Mr. Stewart picture a land of unremitting evil and brutality where everyone is corrupt, from the wise-cracking waitress, who attempts to shortchange Dinah the first morning out, to the policeman-rapist. The only good guy is the truck hijacker who admits to thieving because he likes it and who will rationalize his life only to the extent of saying, "The whole country is a rip-off."

The film manages to stay clear of sentimentality of the conventional sort, though when the hijacker, nicely played by Tommy Lee Jones, says with a shrug just before the final shoot-out, "I was born dead anyway," it's dealing in its own sort of sentimentality.

•

Miss Mimieux is excellent in a role that subjects her to as many bruises, humiliations and indignities as she might get in the boxing ring. All of the performances are fine and to the point. I hesitate to say too much, thus to oversell a movie that is best come upon without great expectations. I would suspect that Mr. Miller and Mr. Stewart are new film makers to watch.

1976 Je 12, 13:1

Is Mankind Ready for 'The Last Woman'?

Warning: This is an X-rated review. It's not even to be read by parents and adult guardians who refuse to believe that there are occasions when it's impossible to write about a film without—in the phraseology of angry letter-writers—giving away the plot. It's not only that one cannot write coherently about "The Last Woman," a new French-language film, without describing it in detail, but one isn't cautioning the reader about matters that, in this case, are the reader's right to know.

In the final scene of "The Last Woman," Gérard (Gérard Dépardieu) sits in the kitchen of his flat in a modern, glass-and-concrete high-rise apartment building, fortifying himself by drinking a bottle of wine. When he is quite drunk, he picks up the electric carving knife that has been a conspicuous prop throughout the earlier scenes of the film. With one quick movement and a cry that mixes horror and anger with indescribable pain, he amputates his penis. His sex has been Gérard's pride and joy, his reason for being, the source of all pleasure, the thing that gave life to his small son and the thing that his latest mistress—the last woman—has convinced him was his obsession, not simply its instrument.

"The Last Woman" is not the work of a mad, militant feminist, nor is it the work of a man who's been co-opted by the movement. It is the work of Marco Ferreri, the Italian-born director who, with this film, becomes the most ferocious satirist at work in movies today.

If you found it difficult to sit through Ferreri's "La Grande Bouffe," about four middle-class men who over-eat themselves to death, you certainly won't have the stamina to watch the graphic butchery that becomes the whole point of "The Last Woman," nor am I convinced that any of us is the less for not being able to.

At this point in our cultural history most of us aren't equipped to be able to accept as an intellectual proposition the pictorial realism with which Ferreri overwhelms us. The shock throws the movie out of kilter. In this instance we may be like the early movie audiences who ducked under their seats when a train on the screen headed straight at them. We haven't yet fixed movies at the remove enjoyed by written fiction. Time still hasn't caught up with the eye-slicing scene in Buñuel's "Un Chien Andalou." I'm not sure it ever will, or that it should.

In the meantime there remain areas of the forbidden, the unspeakable, to be exploited by filmmakers like Ferreri, who are serious, and by entrepreneurs who peddle junk like "Snuff," who aren't.

Until its Grand Guignol finale at the kitchen table, "The Last Woman" is an uproarious, sometimes highly erotic comedy about the efforts of an old-fashioned, sex-obsessed young man trying to survive in a world where women have somehow got the idea that they are people who also have rights. As played by Dépardieu, Gérard is a supremely egotistical but very winning animal, a man who indulges every appetite whenever it occurs to him and sees everything in life as an extension of himself, including his small son, Pierrot, whom he has been raising since his wife left him, and the succession of women who share his apartment.

All has gone along without incident until the appearance of Valerie (Ornella Muti) a phenomenally beautiful young woman with green eyes and a slim but voluptuous figure. Valerie enjoys sex as much as Gérard and after a while begins to think that she and Gérard and Pierrot might share some other pleasures in life. Gérard is not especially interested, but instead of kicking Valerie out then and there, he keeps her around. Little by little she makes Gérard conscious of his failings, which are real and many. He's not that great a lover, she points out quietly, since he's too preoccupied with his own pursuits.

He has absolutely no conception of the sharing of interests, whether it's in sex or in the raising of his child. Once he tries to prove his real love for her by taking a vow of chastity, which lasts for a few terrible days, after which they resume their love-making more furiously than ever. Finally she tells him, less in disgust than in sadness, that all he really is is his sex. If he didn't have that, she suggests, he'd be nothing. Which, of course, leads a man of Gérard's lunatic bravado to make the ultimate gesture.

What is Ferreri telling us? Gérard really is an animal, as impossible and self-centered as everyone says he is, a holdover from some nearly forgotten age when the double-standard worked, when wives stayed at home and tended to the children while husbands won the bread. "We are patriarchs of families that don't exist any more," Gérard says at one point. After ransacking Valerie's trunk and finding nothing to suggest any earlier existence, he accuses her. "You have no memories!" She doesn't, with the exception of an earlier, very casual liaison with another man (Michel Piccoli), who means nothing to her. However, the girl, who is perfectly reasonable and loving, and assertive only when desperate, turns into the instrument of Gérard's destruction. She doesn't hold the knife, but she has given Gérard the idea. Is this Ferreri's view of the modern woman?

Everyone must draw his own conclusion. Ferreri, I suspect, would say that "The Last Woman" is not to be taken as a treatise. Like all fiction, it's a series of possibilities. Is the Last Woman meant to be as destructive as the First Woman? Perhaps. If you can survive the entire film, you will have something to think about.

Male chauvinists also are contemplated in two other new French films, both of more conventional design than the Ferreri work and both directed by men who apparently want to make amends with women.

Claude Chabrol's "Une Partie de Plaisir," written by and starring Paul Gegauff, who has written some of Chabrol's most elegant films, is the beautifully, sorrowfully told tale of a husband who forces his wife (wonderfully played by Danielle Gegauff) into extra-marital adventures, only to become furious later. Claude Berri's "Male of The Century" is a very funny movie about a Lyons pants-maker (played by Berri), who's so obsessed by his masculinity that when his wife is held hostage in a bank robbery, he's less worried that she'll get hurt than that she'll fall in love with the bandit.

If these films were less good it might seem as if the French film industry were dealing with Women's Liberation by quietly taking it over for the industry's own ends. One interesting footnote: though the films are about women's liberation, and seem to be sympathetic, the more flamboyant role in each film goes to the man, who is also more complex though not more romantic or mysterious—in which there may be a sort of sexist difference.

1976 Je 13, II:15:1

THE MARTYR, directed by Aleksander Ford; screenplay by Joseph Gross, based on a story by Alexander Ramati; produced by Artur Brauner; music, Moshe Wilensky; director of photography, Jerzy Lipman; editor, C. O. Bartning; an Israeli-German co-production by CCC-Filmkunst, distributed by Joseph Green Pictures. Running time: 90 minutes. At the Juliet - Theater, Third Avenue near 83d Street. This film has not been rated.

Dr. Janusz Korczak .... Leo Genn
Stefa .... Orna Porat
Ruth .... Efrat Lavi
Yakov .... Ohad Kaplan
Michael .... Benjamin Volz
Adam .... Carlos Werner

By VINCENT CANBY

"The Martyr," which opened yesterday at the Juliet 1 Theater, is a reverential, absolutely stolid, English-speaking Israeli-German co-production based on the heroism of Dr. Janusz Korczak (Leo Genn), the Polish Jewish doctor and novelist who elected to stay with the orphans he was caring for in

the Warsaw ghetto in 1942 rather than go underground to escape the Nazis.

The film, which was made in 1973, was directed by Aleksander Ford, the veteran Polish director who moved to Israel in 1968. As was Mr. Ford's film version of Aleksandr I. Solzhenitsyn's "The First Circle," released here three years ago, this movie is full of good intentions that get smothered by the sentimental, deliberate manners of a cinema style better suited to early sound films.

The only moving portions of the film are provided by Mr. Ford's occasional use of black-and-white still photographs of life in the Warsaw ghetto. They haunt the mind in the way that makes the fictional pieties look almost complacent.

1976 Je 17, 30:1

'WINTERHAWK' FILM ON LOCAL SCREENS

"Winterhawk," now at the Victoria and other theaters, is a mostly slumbrous Western about a Blackfoot Indian chief named Winterhawk and the terrible time he has dealing with white men as he tries to get their remedy for the "white man's disease," which is ravaging Winterhawk's people. They are referred to as Blackfeet when two or more are gathered together, and the disease that afflicts them is smallpox, not syphilis. The film is a tiny mine of information.

Charles B. Pierce wrote, directed and produced "Winterhawk" as if he were making a public service movie on the visual beauty of litterless national parks. (It was filmed in neatly tended parks in Colorado and Montana.)

"Winterhawk," which has been rated PG, is generally discreet about the violence, but it includes one brutal rape that ends in murder and a scene in which the leg of a little boy is speared as if it were a Vienna sausage impaled on a toothpick.

VINCENT CANBY

1976 Je 14, 40:5

A BOY AND HIS DOG, directed and written by L. Q. Jones, based on a novella by Harlan Ellison; producer, Alvy Moore; photographed by John Arthur Morrill; music by Tim McIntire. At the Embassy 46th Street and neighborhood theaters. This movie has been rated R. Running time: 83 minutes.

Vic .... Don Johnson
Quilla June .... Susanne Benton
Lew .... Jason Robards
Fellini .... Ron Feinberg
Voice of Blood .... Tim McIntire

"A Boy and His Dog," a fantasy about the world after a future holocaust, is, more or less, a beginner's movie. It has some good ideas and some terrible ones. The good ideas are marred by awkwardness; the terrible ideas are redeemed somewhat by being, at least, unpredictable.

The world has become one great mudflat, a desert roamed over by armed men, sometimes alone, sometimes in bands. They build shelters out of scrap and old tires, eat stockpiled canned food and also use it for barter, and kill weak strangers. For recreation, they go to outdoor enclosures where pornographic movies are shown on an eight-millimeter projector.

All this comes under the Good Idea heading. It is a spare, miserable world L. Q. Jones, director, has set up; mean, dry and barren, where everyone wears worn and dirty clothes because there is no way to make new ones and no water to wash with. The future is poverty.

Vic, a young man, well-played by Don Johnson, is

the protagonist. His companion is Mr. Jones's main Terrible Idea: Blood, a talking dog. There is nothing that can be done in a movie with a dog that talks. After only a few minutes, the old adage is modified to: He doesn't do it very well, and you're not surprised that he's doing it at all.

Vic meets a woman, makes love to her, and lets her entice him down into the underground society from which she has emerged. Blood advises against it, and he's right.

It is a weird, rural American community, bucolic to all appearances but run as the most savage dictatorship. The dictator is Jason Robards and he's splendid—a kindly, folksy farmer type who gradually becomes as frightening as Heinrich Himmler.

Vic runs into all kinds of trouble before the film ends. The underworld part, brilliantly grotesque as it partly is, breaks the realistic vision of the beginning. The two parts don't really work together; their contrast, and a ridiculous ending, shatter the picture. And the talking dog chews up the pieces.

This is the second film directed by L. Q. Jones, better known as an actor. It is not really a success, but I hope he goes on directing.

RICHARD EDER

1976 Je 17, 32:2

HARRY AND WALTER GO TO NEW YORK, directed by Mark Rydell; screenplay by John Byrum and Robert Kaufman, based on a story by Don Devlin and Mr. Byrum; executive producer, Tony Bill; produced by Mr. Devlin and Harry Gittes; music, David Shire; director of photography, Laszlo Kovacs; supervising film editor, Fredric Steinkamp; editors, David Bretherton and Don Guidice; distributed by Columbia Pictures. Running time: 123 minutes. At Radio City Music Hall, Avenue of the Americas at 50th Street. This film has been rated PG.

Harry Dighby .... James Caan
Walter Hill .... Elliott Gould
Adam Worth .... Michael Caine
Lissa Chestnut .... Diane Keaton
Rufus T. Crisp .... Charles Durning
Gloria Fontaine .... Lesley Ann Warren
Chatsworth .... Val Avery
Mischa .... Jack Gilford
Lewis .... Dennis Dugan
Florence .... Carol Kane
Barbara .... Kathryn Grody
Ben .... David Proval
Billy Gallagher .... Michael Conrad
Warden Durgom .... Burt Young
Guard O'Meara .... Bert Ramsen

By VINCENT CANBY

"HARRY and Walter Go to New York" is a movie based on an original story and screenplay, but it's so implacably cute that you might suspect that it was based on a coloring book based on "The Sting." It's big and blank and so faux naif that you want to hit it over the head in the way that used to bring people to their senses in true farce, of which this is no example.

The time is 1892, which you can roughly guess because the men wear bowler hats and those stiff collars that become partially de-

tached whenever someone is harried. The story is about Harry (James Caan) and Walter (Elliott Gould), a couple of third-rate vaudevillians who become sidetracked as would-be safecrackers.

It's also about Adam Worth (Michael Caine), an elegant, internationally applauded safecracker whom Harry and Walter have met during a brief stay in a Federal pen, and Lissa Chestnut (Diane Keaton), the pretty, passionately committed editor of an anarchist newspaper who decides, for reasons that are perfectly unclear, to rob the Commercial Bank and Trust Company of Lowell, Mass.

There are two funny moments in the entire film: Miss Keaton's stirring declaration that "If that bank has to be robbed, let it be robbed in the name of decency!" and a scene in which she attempts a genteel seduction of Charles Durning, who plays the bank's president, a furiously incompetent lecher.

Miss Keaton, Mr. Caine and Mr. Durning are able farceurs, which means that they lower their sights so that their entire concentration appears to be on a space of approximately one cubic inch. This lunatic enveloping preoccupation with the trivial is one of the things that makes farce funny as well as liberating. It's like watching the combat in an ant palace.

Neither Mr. Caan nor Mr. Gould plays it this way, and I suspect that that was the intention of the director, Mark Rydell, as well as of the script writers, John Byrum and Robert Kaufman. If "Harry and Walter Go to New York" were to work at all—and I'm not sure it could—Harry and Walter would have to be played straight, as believably bumbling innocents, not as a couple of leading men impersonating ineptitude and incompetence. Mr. Gould can be a good comedian, but here he seems to have caught some of Mr. Caan's way of appearing to wink at the audience, as if to disassociate himself from the character.

The two stars don't act, as they are perfectly capable of doing. Instead they cut-up in the desperate manner of performers appearing "live" on television talk shows, or of "guest stars" on television variety shows who can't help cracking up with laughter at jokey ad libs they've already heard 40 times in rehearsal.

Tony Bill, the film's executive producer, was also one of the producers of "The Sting," which makes comparisons between the two films inevitable—and very unfortunate for "Harry and Walter." The new film, which opened yesterday at Radio City Music Hall, features a lot of stylish interior decoration that you will see only in big-budget movies, but the comedy is inconsistent, diluted, the kind that seems to be television's unhappiest gift to theatrical films.

•

"Harry and Walter" has been rated PG, apparently because some of its language is what once was called bold, which isn't the same thing as obscene.

1976 Je 18, C6:5

MIDWAY, directed by Jack Smight; screenplay by Donald S. Sanford; produced by Walter Mirisch; director of photography, Harry Stradling Jr.; editors, Robert Swink and Frank J. Urioste; music, John Williams; a Mirisch Corporation production, distributed by Universal Pictures. Running time, 132 minutes. At the Rivoli Theater, Broadway at 50th Street, and other theaters. This film has been rated PG.
Capt. Matt Garth ...... Charlton Heston
Adm. Nimitz .... Henry Fonda
Capt. Vinton Maddox.......James Coburn
Rear Adm. Spruance........ Glenn Ford
Comdr. Joseph Rochefort.. Hal Holbrook
Adm. Yamamoto .... Toshiro Mifune
Adm. Halsey ....Robert Mitchum
Comdr. Carl Jesson ......Cliff Robertson
Lieut. Comdr. Ernest Blake Robt. Wagner
Rear Adm. Fletcher........Robert Webber
Adm. Pearson ....Ed Nelson
Vice Adm. Nagumo........ James Shigeta
Haruko Sakura ....Christina Kokubo
Comdr. Max Leslie.........Monte Markham
Capt. Miles Browning......Biff McGuire
Ens. George Gay...........Kevin Dobson
Lieut. Comdr. Wade McClusky
                        Christopher George
Lieut. Comdr. John Waldron
                        Glenn Corbett
Capt. Elliott Buckmaster. Gregory Walcott
Lieut. Tom Garth..........Edward Albert

By VINCENT CANBY

"Midway" is a kamikaze attack against one of the greatest sea battles of modern times. The battle—history—survives while the movie blows up harmlessly in a confusion of familiar old newsreel footage, idiotic fiction war movie clichés, and a series of wooden-faced performances by almost a dozen male stars, some of whom appear so briefly that recognizing them is like taking a World War II aircraft-identification test. Is that a single-wing Robert Mitchum? A modified Cliff Robertson? A rebuilt Glenn Ford?

The film, which opened yesterday at the Rivoli and other theaters, attempts to recreate the circumstances leading up to the battle of Midway Island, June 4-5, 1942, when a perilously small United States Navy task force decisively defeated Admiral Yamamoto's - much larger Japanese fleet whose mission had been the invasion and occupation of Midway. It was the turning point of the war against the Japanese who lost four large carriers and never again seriously threatened American sea power in the central Pacific. It was also the battle that established beyond doubt the leading role that carriers were to play in the Pacific war.

Most of these things are reported quite dutifully by the film, but for anyone seriously interested in Midway, I'd recommend a reading of the late Samuel Eliot Morison's fastidiously documented account in his "History of United States Naval Operations in World War II."

As did "Tora Tora Tora," that earlier movie disaster about the Japanese attack on Pearl Harbor, "Midway" sol-

'Musical Holdouts:' Hidden Talent

With one small harmonica tucked into his old hand, Sonny Terry is a swarm of musical bumblebees, three dozen hopping whistling teakettles and a whole bluegrass convention of fiddlers. He plays and he whoops and he clicks and he ticks with the rhythmic precision of a kettle-drum and the tearaway shriek of a steam calliope.

Whether or not he is the world's greatest harmonica player, there is surely nobody like him. A six-minute film, "Shoutin' the Blues," in which he talks a bit with ingratiating fraudulence, and plays one number with total veracity, is the single complete success of the Film Forum's new program, "Musical Holdouts."

The program is made up of three documentaries, which, as the title implies, record performances and performers of a kind that mostly remain outside of commercial promotion.

The centerpiece is "Musical Holdouts" itself — giving the whole program its name—by David Cohen. It moves around the country finding its hidden music.

"Holdouts" films black children on a South Carolina island, playing singing games that are more self-conscious and less remarkable than it would have us believe. It moves on to some old demon banjo player on a Kentucky hills porch; and then to a successful blue-grass singer, who looks and lives like a small businessman. It is an incongruity only to our times and to Mr. Cohen—Bach wore a respectable wig.

The film ends with Comanche Indians chanting, and scenes of street-singers. As a whole it is interesting, but bland. It tries for pungency—a commentary on authenticity versus inauthenticity — but the author's method is indirection and he hasn't the force and aim for it. The music itself mostly lacks attack or conclusiveness.

"Maybe Next Week Sometime" by David Boatwright is the weakest of the three. It wanders through South Carolina, ranging from rock to gospel singing. Some of it works, but it is marred by pretentious inconciusiveness and still more by pretentious camera work.

The Film Forum has had much stronger programs. But six minutes of Sonny Terry lifts this one way above itself.
RICHARD EDER

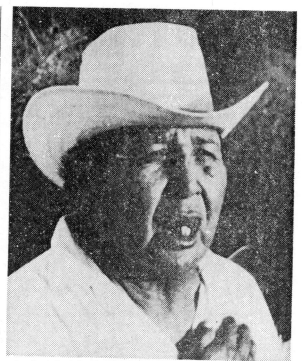

An American Indian in "Musical Holdouts"

1976 Je 18, C6:5

---

emnly cross-cuts between the war councils, chart rooms and communications offices on the American side and those on the Japanese side, with characters, who often have to be identified by subtitles, laboriously trying to give us all of the exposition necessary to make the battle coherent.

There's no way to act such roles, though Henry Fonda as Admiral Nimitz shows a certain amount of ease reading decoded messages and shaking hands with junior officers. Charleston Heston plays a fictional character who might have been stolen from some terrible movie made shortly after World War II—a Navy officer whose Navy pilot son has the bad judgment to fall in love with an American-born Japanese girl.

Mr. Heston is given the movie's silliest lines, though the fact that there really was an Admiral Yamamoto doesn't exactly protect Toshiro Mifune from his share of duds. "Ah," says the movie's Yamamoto when informed of Gen. Jimmy Doolittle's token air raid on Tokyo in early 1942, "this is a blessing in disguise. There'll be no more footdragging by the general staff." Small-talk among flag officers is one of the film's more minor problems.

The major one is the battle, which is a badly edited and badly matched series of scenes made up of studio stuff, miniatures and actual battle footage that was much better used (if my memory serves me) in John Ford's

18-minute documentary, "The Battle of Midway" and Louis De Rochemont's "The Fighting Lady." Jack Smight, the film's director, and his editors also appear to repeat battle footage when it's really good. Maybe not, but it certainly seems that way.

•

At many theaters, the film is being shown with sound effects in Sensurround, the system of low - frequency sound signals (used more effectively in "Earthquake") that are supposed to recreate the sense of the battle but—here—simply annoy the ears. At the beginning of the movie, the producers warn that they will not be responsible for the audience's physical or emotional reactions to Sensurround. They say nothing about the audience's physical or emotional reactions to the movie itself. Producers aren't completely stupid.

•

The film has been rated PG. It would be difficult to make a movie, even a bad one, about a battle like Midway and not show some violence or overhear some of the men using rude words to describe their occasional impatience.

1976 Je 19, 11:1

FILM VIEW
VINCENT CANBY

A Surprise Movie That Charts Our Disintegration

The formula is simple as well as simple-minded and reactionary if you bother to think about it: a young man and a young woman, who is as faithful to the young man as Tonto was to the Lone Ranger, are being pursued by the law. They race down the road in a souped-up automobile following a macadam trail that is eventually revealed to be a large figure eight. Speed, not space, is the medium. The kids land back where they started. The game of flight and pursuit must end badly, a fiery car-crash, perhaps, in which the couple is killed or, at least, a shoot-out in which the young man is killed—it still being a man's world as far as shoot-out deaths are concerned.

Following this formula, several low-budget movies have become astonishingly successful at the box office in the last couple of years, not necessarily at box offices in the large cities but in the smaller towns and rural areas where, for reasons one can only speculate on, audiences respond to this particular kind of hugely romantic, space-age pessimism. What makes the phenomenon so odd is that the films, including "Macon County Line," "Dirty Mary Crazy Larry," "Aloha Bobby and Rose," are often most popular in those parts of the country (the south and southwest) portrayed by these films as being almost mythically iniquitous—hotbeds of corruption, bigotry and hypocrisy.

Each film works its own variations on the formula but in large measure they seem designed for consumption by people with the mentalities of not only the films' putty-brained Romeos and Juliets but also of the red-neck sheriffs and their families and friends, who are the films' nominal villains.

● ● ●

These "road" films have been of some interest in the past if only bcause they are among the successors to the old pre-World War II B-movies—inexpensive formula films ground out in the thirties and forties to play the lower halves of double-bills topped by A-features. They have also occasionally, almost by accident, caught authentic regional sounds and sights, since most of them have been made outside the West Coast studios, which now only television producers and the producers of big-budget theatrical movies can afford.

These thoughts are prompted by the appearance of a new "road" film that by and large follows the formula but is so terse, tough and beautifully put together that it manages to make the entire genre look more interesting than it had any right to earlier. The film is called "Jackson County Jail" and it was directed by Michael Miller and written by Donald Stewart, neither of whose earlier work I'm familiar with. Roger Corman, who has probably directed and/or produced more B-pictures than anyone alive today, was the executive producer. "Jackson County Jail" never for a minute forgets that it's a "road" picture—I'd say that at least half of it takes place either inside a moving vehicle or outside one, that is, looking into it or down onto it, which is one of the genre's prerequisites. What sets the film apart from all the others is not its technical mastery, which can be found in all sorts of films, good and bad, the quality of the casting, which is excellent, nor its fidelity to life (which may be questioned), but the completeness, the consistency, of its nightmare vision by which it details nothing less than the total disintegration of bourgeois America in this bicentennial year. Unsubtle though it is, "Jackson County Jail" is a not unpleasing antidote to the overdoses of self-congratulatory bicentennial nonsense we've been subjected to elsewhere.

It's the story of Dinah Hunter (Yvette Mimieux), a pretty, comparatively sophisticated woman in her early thirties who has thrown over her lover of two years and her job with a Los Angeles ad agency to return to civilization in New York. Driving across the country, Dinah makes a series of almost ludicrously wrong-headed decisions, such as picking up an obviously psychopathic hitchhiker and his pregnant, pill-popping girlfriend who, at the first convenient moment in rural Arizona, pull a gun on Dinah and steal her car, her money and her identification.

When Dinah staggers into an all-night roadside bar, she trusts the drunk bartender and is surprised when he tries to rape her. She also trusts the county policeman who happens onto the scene, who promptly packs her off to the local lock-up because she can't produce evidence to prove she is who she says she is.

One thing leads to another quite swiftly, as it does in films of this sort, and suddenly the comfortably secure, upper-middle-class woman, who quit her ad agency job because of a disagreement about the taste of a TV commercial for sanitary napkins, finds herself in a crude frontier world without identity, without rights of any sort. She is subject to a brutal jail-house rape by the night guard and then, after accidentally killing the guard in self-defense, she is a fugitive from justice in the company of a young man (Tommy Lee Jones), an accused murderer and admitted truck hijacker. Civilization and its values disappear. Dinah is fighting for survival in a country that the young man describes simply as "a rip-off." He's not angry, but he has no illusions. Everything and everybody, he tells her, is crooked—can't she see? She refuses to agree but by the film's violent end, she perceives a glimmer. She has also established, briefly, a relationship (non-sexual) with the young man that is a little like the understanding that two blind people might have for each other, full of direct, unsentimental concern, but perfectly aware of the limitations imposed by fate.

● ● ●

"Jackson County Jail" is, first and foremost, a "road" picture. The precipitous transformation of its heroine from society insider to outsider is detailed in the broad terms of melodrama. Its excitement is visceral, but unlike other "road" films, it doesn't insult the intelligence, which, I think,

has to do with the intelligence of its composition, even of its conception of its characters, who are not in themselves especially intelligent.

"Jackson County Jail" should not be overpraised, but at a time when most movies are either sloppily made, exploitative junk, or expensive, over-produced nightmares about natural disasters, its economy of narrative, its awareness that the mechanics of a movie and the subject are the same, and even its dark view of American life are unexpectedly reassuring and invigorating.

NOTE: Bob Fosse, the director, actor, dancer and choreographer, has written to say that one of the reasons the choreography in a scene from "Kiss Me, Kate" (included in "That's Entertainment, Part 2"), which I identified as looking like his (Fosse's) later choreography, is that he choreographed it, not, as I wrote, Hermes Pan. Which makes sense.

1976 Je 20, II:25:1

THE TENANT, directed by Roman Polanski; screenplay by Gerard Brach and Mr. Polanski, based on the novel by Roland Torpor; produced by Andrew Braunsberg; director of photography, Sven Nykvist; music, Philippe Sarde; editor, Françoise Bonnot; distributed by Paramount Pictures. Running time: 124 minutes. At Loews Tower East, Third Avenue near 72d Street. This film has been rated R.

Trelkovsky	Roman Polanski
Stella	Isabelle Adjani
The concierge	Shelley Winters
Mr. Zy	Melvyn Douglas
Mme. Dioz	Jo Van Fleet
Scope	Bernard Fresson
Mme. Gaderian	Lila Kedrova
Husband	Claude Dauphin
Neighbor	Claude Pieplu
Badar	Rufus
Simon	Romain Bouteille

By VINCENT CANBY

Trelkovsky (Roman Polanski) is a French citizen and he has a carte d'identité to prove it, but he has a foreign accent that puts off Parisian bartenders, concierges, policemen and landlords. Small boned and short—physically vulnerable — Trelkovsky seems to be aware of having put off people all his life. Thus he goes to great lengths to avoid giving offense. He dresses with care—a too-bright necktie might attract the attention of a small talkative child or of a friendly drunk. He answers the unaccountable rudeness of strangers with infinite patience.

●

Trelkovsky exists. He inhabits his own body, but it's as if he had no lease on it, as if at any moment he could be dispossessed for having listened to the radio in his head after 10 P.M. People are always knocking on his walls.

Trelkovsky, the hero of Mr. Polanski's striking new horror film, "The Tenant," is a character who might have been invented by an Edgar Allan Poe who'd had the opportunity to read about Raskolnikov and Josef K. He's a particularly Eastern European kind of late 19th-century outsider set down in contemporary Paris. He is also—by the end of the movie—something of a joke, but an entirely intentional one.

"The Tenant," which opened yesterday at Loews Tower East, is the most successful and most consistently authentic Polanski film in years, and in saying that I realize that a lot of people prefer the Polanski who turns out films more or less tailored to popular tastes,

Roman Polanski
His most authentic film in years.

like "Chinatown" and "Rosemary's Baby."

"The Tenant" displays the clear-eyed narrative discipline of his early "Knife in the Water" and "Repulsion," but without the self-indulgent gimmickry that have made a lot of his later "personal" films, including "The Fearless Vampire Killers" and "What?", almost impossible to sit through even when the idiosyncratic talent behind them was visible.

●

"The Tenant," adapted by Gerard Brach and Mr. Polanski from a novel by Roland Topor, tells the story of the strange series of occupations that take place when Trelkovsky, a filing clerk in what appears to be a library, moves into a two-room Paris apartment made vacant by the attempted suicide of the previous tenant.

The previous tenant, a young woman not yet dead, was unknown to Trelkovsky, but he makes it a point to visit her in the hospital. He is fascinated by what he sees,

a body swathed in bandages, one leg in a cast, only one blackened eye and the mouth visible. He has thoughtfully brought her some oranges to suck.

During this visit he also meets one of the young woman's friends, an apparently sweet but enigmatic girl named Stella (Isabelle Adjani). Leaving the hospital together, they have a drink in a bar and go to a movie where, as best as one can in a theater balcony, they make love, then part.

Little by little Trelkovsky becomes convinced that the other tenants in the building have somehow been responsible for the earlier tenant's suicide attempt. The concierge (Shelley Winters) either ignores him or insults him. The landlord (Melvyn Douglas) monitors his arrivals and departures. The tenants spy on him. One night a mysterious woman (Lila Kedrova) appears at his door with her crippled daughter to report that there's a conspiracy afoot to have her kicked out of the building.

Little by little, too, the other tenants force Trelkovsky, against his will, to assume the identity of the now-dead earlier tenant. One morning he wakes up in full drag, missing the tooth that the dead girl was missing. At a party Trelkovsky says to a friend with a good deal of understatement, "These days relationships with neighbors can get very complicated."

Movies about madness tend to lose me after a certain point. The tension vanishes when one realizes that any absurdity, any trick, is available to the film maker. The director and his audience must share a set of rules for what passes for ordinary behavior if suspense is to be maintained. These rules do not exist in "The Tenant."

●

That "The Tenant" works so well is because it's not strictly about madness, though that is its narrative form. It's about emotional isolation that has become physical. The forces that occupy Trelkovsky's mind were invited in by him, the outsider.

The film is superbly acted by Mr. Polanski, Mr. Douglas and Miss Winters, who might not be entirely convincing as a Parisian concierge in a realistic film, but who fits into this nightmare perfectly. The French actors, including Miss Adjani, sound as if their English dialogue had been dubbed by others—not very intelligently—the result being that the performances no longer seem to be strictly their own.

Mr. Polanski also has a gifted collaborator in Sven Nykvist, the cinematographer whose camera plays the role of narrator, directing our attention to curious details, offering humble asides, as 19th-century authors once felt free to do without embarrassment or excuse.

1976 Je 21, 43:1

VERONIQUE, OU L'ETTE DE MES 13 ANS
(Veronique, or The Summer of My 13th
Year), directed by Claudine Guilemain;
screenplay (French with English sub-
titles) by Miss Guilemain; dialogue,
Pierre Lartha; director of photography,
Jean-Jacques Rochut; music, Jean-Robert
Viard; editors, Alfredo Muschietti and
Caroline Roulet; executive producer,
George Dybman; a production of Films
du Losange and Felix Films. Running
time: 88 minutes. At the 68th Street
Playhouse, at Third Avenue. This film
has not been classified.
Veronique...............Anne Teyssedre
Anne...................Anouk Ferjak
Jean...................Michel Peyrelon
Father.................Jean-Pierre Mouiin
Mother.................Edith Loria
Michele................Anne Keryien
Sylvain................Christophe Perring

VÉRONIQUE, OU L'ETE
DE MES 13 ANS (Véronique,
or The Summer of My 13th
Year), was shown at the
Museum of Modern Art. The
following excerpt is from
Vincent Canby's review,
which appeared April 6. The
film begins today at the 68th
Street Playhouse, at Third
Avenue.

Understatement is to be
approved, but some films are
so understated that they tend
to disappear when you think
about them. Claudine Guilemain's "Véronique, ou L'Eté
de Mes 13 Ans" (Véronique,
or The Summer of My 13th
Year) comes dangerously
close to being such a film. It
is lovely and fragile and understated to the point that
the audience must supply
many of the details of the
interior lives of its characters. If one is willing to do
this, as I was, the movie is
fascinating. If not,' you may
wake up screaming.

The French film is about
the summer vacation of
Véronique (Anne Teyssèdre),
a pretty, introspective 13-
year-old who is on the brink
of becoming an intelligent,
beautiful, probably passionate woman.

In the meantime she's an
outsider, a tireless observer
of the curious behavior of
others, the adults who surround her and carry on in
ways that seem as bizarre
to her as might the rituals of
a tribe of Eskimos.

The Eskimos are Véro-
nique's godmother Anne
(Anouk Ferjak) and godfather,
Jean (Michael Peyrelon), to
whom Véronique has been
packd off for a summer's tour
through southwestern France.
Anne and Jean are attractive,
affectionate, humorous people, who appear to Véronique
to have all of the understanding and sophistication lacking
in her parents. As the tour
wears on, however, imperfections appear in Anne and
Jean.

Véronique studies them
solemnly. Has Anne had a
quick affair in St. Jean de
Luz while Véronique and
Jean were off sightseeing?
Why the sudden, furious
fights, and equally furious
reconciliations, between Anne
and Jean? Véronique watches
them and holds her peace.

The one thing she is sure
of is her attraction to Jean,
who, toward the end of the
vacation, makes a clumsy
pass at her, one that she has
been encouraging and that

allows her for the first time
to participate in adult life by
putting him off. In her diary,
where she records everything
in somewhat studious prose,
she writes, "He embraced me
tenderly," and then turns
her mind to her school
schedule for the following
week.

"Véronique" is very funny
in a low-key way and beautifully directed by Miss Guilemain, who has, I suspect,
made exactly the kind of
film she set out to—clear and
direct, yet full of reserved
intelligence and appreciation
for the complexities of feelings and motives.

1976 Je 21, 43:1

Children of Paradise Is Still Enchanting

By RICHARD EDER

In the 1950's it seemed
wonderfully complex; strange,
and with a most liberating
poetical ambiguity to it. I, for
example, have never talked
quite straight ever since.

"Children of Paradise" was
the quintessential Foreign
Film. Europe wasn't that close
then, anyway; no cheap air
fares—an occasional freighter was the nearest equivalent
—and young people didn't
travel so much. They worked
for master's degrees.

And there, already into its
career of perpetual revival,
came "Children." It was a
"Gone With the Wind" of
cobwebs. Its epic romance,
instead of sweeping over
miles of landscape was
squeezed, Europelike, into
the framework of a stage, the
landscape all inward.

These days some people are
discovering, others rediscov-
ering Marcel Carné's masterpiece. It is going through
still another revival, this time
at the Paris Theater. It looks
to be as perennial as the
Perseids.

Expected and Unexpected

It is in fact, both as expected as seeing a star fall
and as unexpected. There is
the scene where Jean-Louis
Barrault, as the mime Baptiste in his white Pierrot costume, tries to hang himself,
and surrenders his rope successively to a child wanting
it for a skip rope and a woman wanting it for a wash line.
Now that is a famous
scene, quoted and recounted
endlessly. Like some of the
"Magic Flute's" arias it has
a life of its own; and still it
is impossible to watch without the small hairs' trying to
walk off the back of the
neck.
After a quarter-century or
so, a revisit to "Children" is
cheerful and encouraging.
Some things have grown
fust" and cramped in it, but
in general the damage of
time is like the gilt flaking
off a picture frame. It
dates the picture within, but
doesn't harm it.
Some scenes—the opening
street carnival, the drinkers
and dancers in a smoky cafe
—are cluttered and over-
charged. There is a certain
slow and mechanical con-
trivance in setting out some

of the characters.
Not Garance, though, the
fatal woman played by Ar-
letty. We meet her protruding from a barrel filled with
dark liquid. She is indeed
bathing naked, as the sideshow barker has promised,
but all the customers get to
see is her head and shoulders,
comical and stately.

It is part of the film's
lovely alternation of humanity
and fantasy. Arletty is comic
and of a practical sensuality;
she is also a haunting beauty;
at the end, as her carriage
melts into the crowd, she has
acquired some of Baptiste's
elusive transparency.
Baptiste goes the other
way. At the start, as the
drooping Pierrot on the bal-
ustrade, he is pure air. His
rival, Lacenaire, says that to
kill him "would be like killing a ray of moonlight."
Gradually, passion subjects
him to the laws of gravity.
At the end he runs futilely
after Garance's carriage like
any stumbling lover with a
churning gut.
Even the cheerful, earth-
bound Frederic—another rival
—has his moment of rebellious
genius. And Lacenaire, the murderer, thinks of himself as a
literary figure.
The main characters are
both clear and shimmering.
They have their particular attributes, as in any normal
movie, but they also contain
the possibility of being their
own opposites. Reality in this
film is never a matter of
"nothing but."
It is this that makes any
memory of "Children" so
complex. Complexity of this
kind could fall into pretentiousness and incoherence,
but it doesn't—and for a very
simple reason.

Mimes at the Top

"Children" is a perfectly
classical and conventional
story. Garance leaves her
criminal protector to take up
with Baptiste and work at
his mime theater. His love at
this point is tangled in fantasy and he loses her to
Frederic, the talking actor.
(A fascinating motif in the
film is its theatrical hierarchy that places mimes at
the top and speaking actors
lower down—and yet it is
the mimes who are applauded

Jean-Louis Barrault in "Children of Paradise"
To kill him would be like killing a ray of moonlight

by the workers in the cheap
seats high up; the "paradise"
of the title.)
Garance, pressed by the police for her past associations,
marries an aristocratic suitor
for protection. Years pass,
they all prosper, there is a
brief reunion of Garance and
Baptiste—consummated this
time—and Garance leaves.
There are side embellish-
ments, of course, small mysteries and bits of fog. But
they are scrollwork on a perfectly recognizable object. It
is a big stagecoach of a
movie — more than three
hours along — that rumbles
serviceably and creakily on
a perfectly recognizable road.
It is the passengers who
are magic.

1976 Je 22, 30:1

THE GREAT SCOUT AND CATHOUSE
THURSDAY, directed by Don Taylor;
written by Richard Shapiro; produced
by Jules Buck and David Korda; exec-
utive producer, Samuel Z. Arkoff; photo-
graphed by Alex Phillips Jr.; music by
John Cameron. Released by American
International. At the Cinerama and
other Gold Label theaters. Running
time: 102 minutes. This movie is
rated PG.
Sam Longwood..............Lee Marvin
Joe Knox...................Oliver Reed
Jack Colby.................Robert Culp
Nancy Sue.................Elizabeth Ashley
Cathouse Thursday..........Kay Lenz
Billy.....................Strother Martin
Mike......................Sylvia Miles

"The Great Scout and Cat-
house Thursday" begins well
enough, with Lee Marvin
winning a barroom bet by
picking up a rattlesnake and
kissing it. It's not exactly
Gable and Lombard, but the
faces have the same mutual
suitability.
It ends well enough with a

showdown punch-up between
Marvin and the smoothie villain, Robert Culp; lots of
harmless dirty tricks and rolling around in the mud.
Mr. Marvin is good at physical adversity. His features
are shaped by a sandstorm,
and it is in other moments,
when the wind has blown out
and it is time to register
more subtle emotions that he
seems excessive and out of
place, like foul-weather gear
slung over a drawing-room
couch.
The problem with "Great
Scout," which opened yesterday at the Cinerama and
other theaters, is' the long
corrugated road between its
beginning and end. So many
clumsy examples of the funny
western have gouged their
way, square-wheeled, along
it that we set our teeth anticipating each joke as if it
were a pothole.
There were once three partners who prospected a gold
claim. The first, Jack Colby
— played with likable deviousness by Mr. Culp — ab-
sconded with the proceeds,
made a fortune and went into
politics. The other two
bumped along, scavenging a
living.

One is Sam Longwood (Mr.
Marvin). The other, Joe Knox,
is a loud-mouthed Indian half-
breed whose idea of revenge
on the white race is to infect
it with syphilis. Knox, is not
so much played as pillaged
by Oliver Reed. He makes
him winsome.
The plot has these two trying in various ways to steal
their money back from
Colby; one of their schemes
being to kidnap his wife.

The wife has a foul tongue and low sexual habits, but, such is the power of graceful acting, Elizabeth Ashley makes her the movie's closest approach to civil comedy. Kay Lenz, who plays Cathouse Thursday, a young camp-follower of Longwood's, tries hard for the same thing but misses.

•

Rough language, and feet sticking out of beds at non-missionary angles, earn this movie its PG rating.

RICHARD EDER

1976 Je 24, 24:1

LOGAN'S RUN, directed by Michael Anderson; screenplay by David Zelag Goodman, based on the novel by William F. Nolan and George Clayton Johnson; produced by Saul David; director of photography, Ernest Laszlo; editor, Bob Wyman; music, Jerry Goldsmith; a Metro-Goldwyn-Mayer production, distributed by United Artists. Running time: 120 minutes. At the Loews Astor Plaza Theater, 44th Street west of Broadway, and Loews Orpheum Theater, 86th Street near Third Avenue. This film has been rated PG.

Logan .... Michael York
Francis .... Richard Jordan
Jessica .... Jenny Agutter
Box .... Roscoe Lee Browne
Holly .... Farrah Fawcett-Majors
Doc .... Michael Anderson Jr.
Old Man .... Peter Ustinov

It is the dubious premise of "Logan's Run," the science-fiction fantasy that opened yesterday, that by the middle of the 23d century overpopulation and air pollution will have rendered life on the surface of this planet impossible and that the strictly controlled, drastically reduced number of survivors will live near Washington in a city that sort of looks like the Houston Astrodome on the outside but inside is a Hollywood special-effects expert's dream.

Within this huge bubble life is simple, automatic and perfect. Everything is ruled by a computer, including the weather. Babies are born from machines. Pleasure is the principle. At age 30 each citizen goes through "the ritual of the carousel," thus to be reborn in a spectacular display of levitation and laser beams, though it's just a fancy way of executing the old-timers and getting rid of the ashes.

•

If you know your science fiction at all, you know that no perfect world of the future is perfect. This one has a major flaw. A lot of people aren't convinced that the carousel actually renews them, and they try to run away to escape execution. "Logan's Run," written by David Zelag Goodman and directed by Michael Anderson, is the story of one of the city's policemen, a man named Logan (Michael York), who himself becomes one of the "runners" who had earlier been his quarry.

Just why and for what particular purpose Logan makes his run is anything but clear after you've sat through nearly two hours of this stuff. "Logan's Run" is less interested in logic than in gadgets and spectacle, but these are sometimes jazzily effective and even poetic. Had more attention been paid to the screenplay, the movie might have been a stunner.

•

This "Logan's Run," which is quite different from the novel by William F. Nolan and George Clayton, is harmless fun enlivened by a couple of sequences that are

as good as the entire film should have been.

One, early in the movie, shows us the the the carousel ceremony, which is a kind of aerial ballet, fireworks display and skeet shoot. The other is a sequence in which Logan and his girl, played by Jenny Agutter, explore the ruins of Washington, which, though overgrown by vines, could easily be restored to its ancient splendor with the help of a pair of pruning shears, a lawn mower and a little plaster and paint. Peter Ustinov shows up in this sequence giving a benignly fussy performance as a sweet old hermit whose dearest wish is to meet people.

The film's PG rating apparently has reference to some nudity and a very blurry sequence in which Mr. York and Miss Agutter pass in slow-motion through a dimly lit pleasure palace, whose patrons try to persuade the couple to join in. They emerge untampered with.

VINCENT CANBY

1976 Je 24, 25:1

THE DEVIL WITHIN HER, directed by Peter Sasdy; screenplay by Stanley Price, based on a story by Nato De Angelis; executive producer, Mr. De Angelis; music, Ron Grainer; director of photography, Kenneth Talbot; editor, Keith Palmer; distributed by American International Pictures. Running time: 90 minutes. At the Penthouse Theater, Broadway at 48th Street, and other theaters. This film has been rated R.

Lucy .... Joan Collins
Sister Albana .... Eileen Atkins
Dr. Finch .... Donald Pleasence
Gino .... Ralph Bates
Mandy .... Caroline Munro
Mrs. Hyde .... Hilary Mason
Tommy .... John Steiner
Jill .... Janet Key
Hercules .... George Claydon

The week's not yet over but as of yesterday "The

Devil Within Her," which opened at the Penthouse and other theaters, stands a good chance of being the week's worst movie about demonic possession.

The British import, directed by Peter Sasdy, stars Joan Collins as a nightclub stripper who is cursed by a fellow worker, an amorous dwarf (George Claydon) whose advances she has spurned, to bear a devil-child.

One might rightfully hope that all hell would break loose. It doesn't; it just mopes around, although the possessed baby does dispatch his nanny, his mummy, his daddy and his kindly old pediatrician, played by Donald Pleasence.

The film is a smear to dwarfs everywhere.

VINCENT CANBY

1976 Je 24, 26:1

THE BIG BUS, directed by James Frawley; written and produced by Fred Freeman and Lawrence J. Cohen; director of photography, Harry Stradling Jr.; music, David Shire; film editor, Edward Warschilka; released by Paramount Pictures. At Loews State 1, the Sutton and neighborhood theaters. Running time: 88 minutes. This film is rated PG.

Dan Torrance .... Joseph Bologna
Kitty Baxter .... Stockard Channing
Shoulders .... John Beck
Father Kudos .... Rene Auberjonois
Shorty Scotty .... Ned Beatty
Dr. Kurtz .... Bob Dishy
Ironman .... Jose Ferrer
Old Lady .... Ruth Gordon
Professor Baxter .... Harold Gould
Parking Lot Doctor .... Larry Hagman
Sybil Crane .... Sally Kellerman
Claude Crane .... Richard Mulligan
Camille Levy .... Lynn Redgrave

By RICHARD EDER

Movie comedies nowadays are like large airplanes with every conceivable flying feature except aerodynamics. They roar around the runways making the right noises, the jet engines go like a dream, the seat belts and ashtrays are flawless. And none of it lifts as much as an inch from the ground.

For the first few minutes, "The Big Bus" gives every forced sign of being one more gag-stuffed, landbound contraption. Then there is a lurch, a bump and an almost forgotten lifting sensation. For at least three-quarters of an hour it is sparingly, achingly funny.

Then it settles back down on the runway and bumps along more or less predictably. But the glow of startled gratitude lasts for quite a while.

It seems evident from the start that we are in the presence of yet another genre parody or put-on. Not a mock-western or mock-detective movie this time, but a mock-Airport-Hindenberg-Grand Disaster Hotel movie.

The parody involves the creation of a nuclear-powered giant bus that makes the first nonstop run from New York to Denver. Archfiends try to sabotage it, mechanisms fail, the crew is racked with personal and professional problems, the passengers are a menagerie of odd and problematical types.

•

Ruth Gordon

After "50 years of cooking and cleaning and fixing the TV antenna," she's had it.

The conventional parody things start the movie off: the mock portentous announcements of the new invention, the heavy satire on Cape Kennedy-style launching preparations. A bomb goes off, disabling the crew and flooring the scientist in charge. Then comes the fist bump.

The scientist (Harold Gould) lies there attended by a maniacally incompetent doctor. His daughter (Stockard Channing) runs up. "He can't hear you," the doctor says, covering the scientist's face with a sheet. "Of course I can hear you" says a voice from under the sheet. "Oh, I thought he was resting," the doctor says.

A new driver must be found. The scene shifts to a bus drivers' bar. In comes Dan Torrance (Joseph Bologna). "Hello, Whitey," he says to one colleague. "Hello, Blackie," he says to another. "Hello, Reddy, Hello Bluie, Hello, Greenie," he raves on. No one answers; Torrance, the best driver in the business, is ostracized. He is suspected of having eaten 110 passengers when his bus broke down in the desert.

He denies it. "I ate the seats. I boiled the floor mats like they taught us to," he pleads. At most, he insists, he might have eaten one foot by mistake.

He is hired, in any case. The passengers assemble. They include Ruth Gordon as a housewife who has run away from home after "50 years of cooking and cleaning and fixing the TV antenna," a couple celebrating their divorce, a disbarred veterinarian, a failed priest and so on.

The bus—a successfully and comically inflated vehicle—rolls off and the disasters begin. The disasters are of a more or less predictable humor. It is the characters, played with fine lunacy by such actors as Sally Kellerman, Lynn Redgrave and René Auberjonois, that provide the lift.

Richard Jordan, left, stops runaways Michael York and Jenny Agutter
In science fiction, no perfect world of the future is perfect

In their lead roles, both Mr. Bologna and Miss Channing are fine. Miss Channing, who specializes in kooky roles, has the difficult part of straight woman, more or less. Even so, she emanages to be funny just standing still and impersonating Elizabeth Taylor.

The main credit for the picture, though, must go to the writers, Fred Freeman and Lawrence J. Cohen, and the director, James Frawley. They have unearthed a buried truth: Comedies can, in fact, be funny.

"The Big Bus" is playing at the Loews State and the Suttan Theaters. It is rated PG for parental guidance. Parents should take all their children by the shoulders and march them off to see it.

1976 Je 24, 26:1

MURDER BY DEATH, directed by Robert Moore; screenplay by Neil Simon; produced by Ray Stark; music, David Grusin; director of photography, David M. Walsh; supervising film editor, Margaret Booth; editor, John F. Burnett; a Rastar production, distributed by Columbia Pictures. Running time: 94 minutes. At the Baronet Theater, Third Avenue near 59th Street; Little Carnegie Theater, 57th Street near Seventh Avenue; Art Theater, Eighth Street east of Fifth Avenue, and other theaters. This film has been rated PG.

Tess Skeffington	Eileen Brennan
Lionel Twain	Truman Capote
Milo Perrier	James Coco
Sam Diamond	Peter Falk
Bensonmum	Alec Guinness
Jessica Marbles	Elsa Lanchester
Dick Charleston	David Niven
Sidney Wang	Peter Sellers
Dora Charleston	Maggie Smith
Yetta	Nancy Walker
Miss Withers	Estelle Winwood
Marcel	James Cromwell
Willie Wang	Richard Narita

By VINCENT CANBY

The dinner party takes place far from any point of reliable reference, on a foggy night, inside a vast, gloomy old house where one shouldn't trust the wine, the chandeliers, the thunder outside, or the oil portraits, whose eyes tend to follow the action below. The butler is blind and the cook is not only deaf and unable to speak, she also cannot read, which makes the food scarce and communication with and between the domestic help impossible.

What's worse is that the host, an eccentric millionaire named Lionel Twain, is some kind of fiend. In the 1930's he was arrested for attempting to smuggle a truckload of rich white Americans into Mexico to pick melons.

The guests look familiar. Strangely. They include Sidney Wang, the famous Chinese detective and a member of the Catalina police, who starts sentences saying something on the order of "Treacherous fog, like mushrooms. . . ." There are also Sam Diamond, the tough Frisco private eye and his secretary-mistress, Tess; the famous Belgian detective, Milo Perrier, and his chauffeur-companion, Marcel; the tweedy English amateur sleuth, Miss Marbles, and Dick and Nora Charleston, who are elegant, tall and very thin, and who act as if they invented the dry martini.

The occasion is a murder, and the movie, "Murder by Death," is for people who never quite remember who killed Roger Ackroyd. Neil Simon remembers enough to have written one of his nicest, breeziest screenplays, a parody murder mystery that appears to be the cheerful confession of a man who, more often than he should, has sat up until all hours of the night reading to find out who did it, and who has then promptly forgotten.

"Murder by Death," which opened yesterday at the Baronet and other theaters, is Mr. Simon's fond send-up of the work of Agatha Christie, Dashiell Hammett and Earl Derr Biggers. By bringing Sam Spade into the comparatively genteel worlds of Hercule Poirot, Charlie Chan, Miss Marple and Nick and Nora Charles, Mr. Simon might appear to have mixed his genres with unforgivable lack of respect. Yet his creation, Sam Diamond, hilariously mugged by Peter Falk, is one of the principal joys of the film; he's the rude noise that shakes up the drawing room.

All of the performances are good, and if some seem better than others, it may simply be the material. James Coco is very, very funny as the somewhat prissy take-off on Hercule Poirot, his toupée and his eating habits. David Niven and Maggie Smith are marvelous as Dick and Dora Charleston, though they haven't enough to do, and Eileen Brennan is an inspired hybrid of Joan Blondell and Lauren Bacall as Sam Diamond's secretary-mistress. If Peter Sellers is not quite as funny as we expect, it may be because we've seen him do his Oriental bit before. It no longer surprises.

Alec Guinness is most welcome as the blind butler, but Nancy Walker isn't around long enough as the disadvantaged maid, though she almost brings down the house with one magnificent absolutely silent scream. Which leaves Truman Capote, which I suppose I can't because he plays the diabolical Lionel Twain. Mr. Capote possibly is acting, but it looks more as if he's giving us an over-rehearsed impersonation of himself as people see him on unrehearsed TV talk shows.

Considering the tone and manner of "Murder by Death," it would seem to be very much a Neil Simon work, but that may be to underestimate the contributions of Robert Moore, a talented theater director ("The Boys in the Band," "Promises, Promises") who is making his debut as a film director here. Whoever should get the credit, "Murder by Death" is as light and insubstantial as one could wish.

The film has been rated PG. Naughty language did it.

1976 Je 24, 26:1

BUFFALO BILL AND THE INDIANS OR SITTING BULL'S HISTORY LESSON, directed and produced by Robert Altman; story and screenplay by Alan Rudolph and Mr. Altman, based on the play "Indians" by Arthur Koppit; executive producer, David Susskind; music, Richard Baskin, director of photography, Paul Lohmann; editors, Peter Appleton and Dennis Hill; a production of the Dino De Laurentiis Corporation, Lion's Gates Films Inc. and Talent Associates Norton Simon Inc., distributed by United Artists. Running time: 120 minutes. At the Criterion Theater, Broadway at 45th Street; Trans-Lux 85th Street, Madison Avenue; Murray Hill Theater, 34th Street near Lexington Avenue; Eastside Cinema, Third Avenue at 55th Street, and Greenwich Theater, 12th Street near Seventh Avenue. This film has been rated PG.

Buffalo Bill	Paul Newman
Nate Salsbury	Joel Grey
Maj. John Burke	Kevin McCarthy
Col. Prentiss Ingraham	Allan Nicholls
Ed Goodman	Harvey Keitel
Jules Keen	Mike Kaplan
Crutch	Bert Remsen
Ned Buntline	Burt Lancaster
Annie Oakley	Geraldine Chaplin
Frank Butler	John Considine
Chief Sitting Bull	Frank Kaquitts
Interpreter	Will Sampson
Indian Agent McLaughlin	Denver Pyle
Grover Cleveland	Pat McCormick
Mrs. Cleveland	Shelly Duvall
Nina Cavalini	Evelyn Lear
Margaret	Bonnie Leaders
Lucille DuCharmes	Noelle Rogers

By VINCENT CANBY

WHAT are we going to do about Robert Altman? He simply won't stand still so that the movie industdy, movie critics and the movie going public can get a comfortable hold on him. He is praised for doing ine thing right and he takes another direction to try something completely different.

Just about the time we think we've caught up with him, we turn a corner and he's vanished.

Still, there are several continuing factors in his work— an impatience with conventional narrative forms, a fondness for actors and how they think and work and an insatiable interest in the peculiarities of the American experience, past and present, most dramatically evident in "Nashville" and in his newest film, "Buffalo Bill and the Indians or Sitting Bull's History Lesson."

Nothing Mr. Altman does quite matches expectations. Everything seems designed to catch people off guard. Take "Nashville," a film that was received with a lot of critical enthusiasm but never did the business that such enthusiasm is supposed to generate. It made a profit though it was hardly a succès fou. It was more on the order of a succès d'estime, but esteemed successes don't grow on trees and they, too, are occasionally valued in Hollywood.

About the time that "Nashville" came out, Dino De Laurentis, the Italian producer of movies like "Death Wish"

Paul Newman

and "Mandingo," was in need of some esteem to go with his profits. He signed Mr. Altman to a three-picture contract, which was terminated even before the release of "Buffalo Bill." I have no idea why but can only suspect that the producer decided that "Buffalo Bill" wasn't going to deliver the prestige he needed, or that that prestige was being acquired at too high a price.

There were some previews of "Buffalo Bill" a month or so ago, and the early word was that it certainly would not duplicate the success of "Nashville." End contract. Which is too bad but not surprising in a business where each new project has to top the one that went before or you're treated as a terminal illness. Some of the longest and most successful directorial careers have been those of men incapable of making films of any interest whatsoever. Eccentricity is a worse sin in Hollywood than consistent failure if it's dignified.

"Buffalo Bill and the Indians or Sitting Bull's History Lesson," which opened at five theaters yesterday, is nothing if not eccentric, and I can't imagine anyone missing it who is interested in the continuing Altman explorations on the outer edges of commercially acceptable film form or in his preoccupation with Americana. It's a sometimes self-indulgent, confused, ambitious movie that is often very funny and always fascinating.

As in "Nashville," the metaphor in "Buffalo Bill" is "the show business," though this time it's been extended —some will say overextended —to make a sweeping Bicentennial statement about the kind of men who made our country great, which is the way the film's President Grover Cleveland grandly identifies the film's William F. (Buffalo Bill) Cody, a carnival con man, somewhat more successful than most.

The time is 1885 and the world is represented as the setting of Buffalo Bill's Wild West Show, a permanent Western encampment of mov-

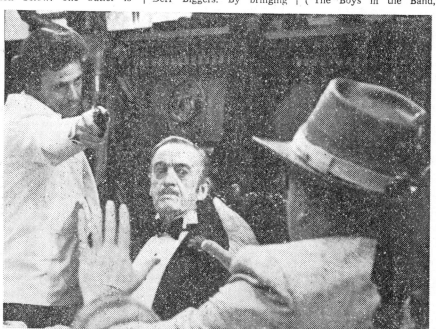

Peter Falk takes aim at Truman Capote, while David Niven recoils
Neil Simon has written one of his nicest, breeziest screenplays

able sets, bunk houses, an arena and souvenir stands where Buffalo Bill puts on shows for tourists, re-enacting the battle of the Little Big Horn, the settling of the West, attacks on stage coaches, bull wrestling, buffalo hunting, etc.

Presiding over this 19th-century fun-fair is Buffalo Bill himself, the aging, wig-wearing producer-star who has come to believe the legends that have been created about his heroic, glorious youth as an Indian fighter.

Paul Newman makes a fine florid, egomaniacal Buffalo Bill, part fraud but also so much a product of time and place that he can't easily be held accountable for having seized the opportunities opened to him. He's the American way.

"Buffalo Bill's Wild West ain't all that different from real life," says Bill as he welcomes the great Hunkpapa Sioux chief Sitting Bull to his company of performers. Sitting Bull (Frank Kaquitts) who stays with Buffalo Bill one season (and five years later was mudered as the last effective leader of his people), never deigns to speak to Bill directly. When the chief negotiates his salary and his rights to all revenues from the sale of his autographed pictures, he does it through an aide. "A man must own his own soul," Sitting Bull says a trifle piously. Is life like show business, or is it the other way around?

Actually this ambiguity is not all that profound, and one of the things that keeps "Buffalo Bill and the Indians" from having more impact is this lack of a decisively dominating theme. The screenplay, by Alan Rudolph and Mr. Altman, is based on Arthur Kopit's play "Indians," which I never saw but I'm told was a series of unequivocal, harrowing variations on the theme of the white American's systematic destruction of the red.

The film touches on this, but so obliquely that you'd hardly notice. There's a rueful exchange between Bill and Sitting Bull's aide when the chief announces that the scene he wants to play will dramatize white men murdering Indian women and children. Bill is appalled. Says Annie Oakley (played with a mixture of great charm and fierce determination by Geraldine Chaplin), "He just wants to show the truth to the people." Answers Bill, "I have a better sense of history." And of show business.

The film that Mr. Altman has made is even more about theater-as-life and about the making of legends (matinee idols, movie stars and Presidents) than it is about genocide. Wandering through the film as a sort of buckskinned Greek chorus of one is Ned Buntline (Burt Lancaster), the dime novelist who was one of Bill's earliest publicists

and Bill's most amused fan. Naturally Bill cannot stand the man.

Some of the film's brightest moments are its evocation of "the show business" that have nothing much to do with metaphors: Annie Oakley doing her sharp-shooting act with her husband, Frank Butler (John Considine), portrayed, as the original, very nervous husband of the star; Bill's home life with a series of opera singers who simply will not shut up; a hilarious reception for President Cleveland (Pat McCormick) and his new wife (Shelley Duvall); the machinations of Bill's producer (Joel Grey) and official publicist (Kevin McCarthy) to hype every chance event into box-office returns.

The film is virtually formless in any way. In place of narrative drive it relies on the momentum created by its visual spectacle, its prodigal way with ideas, its wit and its enthusiasm for the lunatic business of making movies. Mr. Altman makes movies the way other men go on binges — with an abandon that sometimes gets the better of him — and which should be preserved and protected.

•

The film has been rated PG for reasons that I would think have to do with language. There is little real violence or nudity.

1976 Je 25, C8:5

The Screen: 'Omen' Is Nobody's Baby

THE OMEN, directed by Richard Donner; written by David Seltzer; executive producer, Mace Neufeld; producer, Harvey Bernhard; director of photography, Gil Taylor; music by Jerry Goldsmith. Released by 20th Century-Fox. At the National, Loews Cine and other theaters. Running time: 111 minutes. This movie has been rated R.
Robert Thorn .... Gregory Peck
Katherine Thorn .... Lee Remick
Jennings .... David Warner
Mrs. Baylock .... Billie Whitelaw
Damien .... Harvey Stevens
Father Brennan ...... Patrick Troughton
Father Spilletto .... Martin Benson

By RICHARD EDER

The best thing that can be said about "The Omen" is that very few viewers will want to walk out. They will stay, but they will feel foolish.

A member of the "Exorcist" family, it is a dreadfully silly film, which is not to say that it is totally bad. Its horrors are not horrible, its terrors are not terrifying, its violence is ludicrous—which may be an advantage—but it does move along.

•

Movies about Satanic possession do not depend for their effectiveness on making their central device convincing. They should, however, make all the details surrounding this device convincing so plausible that when the Thing appears the audience's skepticism has gone to sleep. It was this peripheral credi-

bility that gave "Rosemary's Baby" its strength.

"The Omen," which opened yesterday at the National, Loews Cine and other theaters, takes its details with no seriousness at all. It is not a put-on—it is terribly solemn, in fact—but it often seems like one.

There are miles of plot. It deals with the problems of a rich and privileged American—he happens to be Ambassador to Great Britain, which is the source of a great deal of the movie's incredibility — whose wife gives birth to a dead baby. A devil - possessed priest slips them another baby who is destined to grow up to rule the world in the name of Satan.

•

The baby becomes a lovely little boy, but when he is 4 years old or so, a mysterious black dog turns up. In quick order the boy's nursemaid hangs herself and a mysterious new nursemaid, a malevolent Mary Poppins, arrives to replace her.

Things begin to go badly wrong and the Ambassador, played by Gregory Peck, can't figure out why. A mad-looking priest arrives—not the one who supplied the

baby —and warns him that the child is the Antichrist. Soon the priest is impaled by a spire falling off a church.

The Ambassador begins to be convinced. Joined by a photographer, played by David Warner, he goes to Italy to try to find the origins of his adopted child, and from that point the disasters begin to mount.

From the moment Mr. Peck comes home after a hard day and tells his wife, played by Lee Remick, that they're off to be Ambassadors, the film's working-level reality is hopelessly scratched. This must be the most unattended American emissary to Great Britain since John Jay. Scenes in which he and his wife look for a house—the United States Ambassador in London has an official residence—or in which he runs around London by himself are quite impossible.

•

Yet the movie is reasonably well-paced. We don't have time to brood about the sillinesses of any particular scene before we are on to the next. There is not a great deal of excitement, but we manage to sustain some curiosity as to how things will work out. "The Omen" is the kind of movie to take along on a long airplane trip.

1976 Je 26, 16:1

FILM VIEW

VINCENT CANBY

When Coyness Becomes a Cop-Out

In a letter dated Aug. 16, 1776, Horace Walpole wrote the Countess of Upper Ossory, "This world is a comedy to those that think, a tragedy to those that feel." One might add, "And a put-on to those that neither think nor feel but still want to make a buck," which some people argue is the only way to deal with contemporary absurdities, though that's more often a cop-out, a way of not taking responsibility for anything at all, not even for a point of view. The dominant manner in television these days is of the put-on, or parody, some of which ("Mary Hartman, Mary Hartman") is better than others: TV newspeople's joshing of the news and of each other, which has the effect of preserving their genial, just-folks "real" personalities and turning the often gloomy events they report into fiction. "Don't blame me," says the stand-up nightclub comic when he's failing utterly, "blame my writers."

This lack of any real commitment to material—this self-conscious separation of the writer, the director or the actor from the work he finds himself engaged in—may one day be seen as a reflection of the current American way in all things, including the country's popular arts. Or it may be simply a fad, like skateboards. In the meantime you and I are being hustled by a lot of people who haven't the courage

to fail honorably in pursuits one might have expected them to be loyal to if not to believe in.

The put-on or, more accurately, put-down way in which a TV talk-show host delivers a commercial for a plumbing aid is not a cause I care to become exercised about, but I don't think it's very different from the curiously disassociated manner in which Marlon Brando behaves in "The Missouri Breaks." Neither Brando nor the talk-show host seems to want to be too closely identified with the product. "Robin and Marian," written by James Goldman and directed by Richard Lester, should have been a fine romance, and it is occasionally, but neither Lester nor Goldman trusted it enough to leave out the gags and the anachronisms that let us know that they know that we shouldn't take it too seriously. Otherwise someone might suspect them of not being hip, which has become the utterly fraudulent, nonprescription existentialism of the our time.

•　•　•

A quite stunning, multimillion-dollar demonstration of this lack of commitment to anything except the desire to be liked as just folks is the new comedy, "Harry and Walter Go to New York," which was directed by Mark Rydell, written by John Byrum and Robert Kaufman, and which would have been better titled "Jimmy (Caan) and Elliott (Gould) Go to New York." The Byrum-Kaufman script, about a pair of third-rate 1892 vaudevillians who attempt new careers at safe-cracking, isn't great. It's a sort of jokey, farcical rip-off of "The Sting," and though it was directed with very little flair for comedy by Rydell, it might possibly have not been offensive since, in addition to Caan and Gould, its contains performances by Diane Keaton, Michael Caine and Charles Durning, all of whom know how to play comedy with absolute conviction.

Where the film goes wildly wrong is in the performances of Caan and Gould, who don't for a minute do anything but cut up in the fashion of a couple of movie personalities doing a sketch on the Carol Burnett Show. It may well be that they thought the material was so terrible that this was the only way to handle it. Sitting in the audience, we have no way of knowing. What we know is what we see: two actors impersonating comic ineptitude in such a way that we won't for a minute confuse it with the public personalities of the actors themselves. It's as if—in this television age of stars who are designed to be "real" people, not the idealized projections that stars used to be—they felt they couldn't afford to act buffoons convincingly. That may be nonsensical speculation, but the movie is so rotten in ways of coy, cute television comedy that it gives one, pause.

Roman Polanski, left to his own devices without the discipline imposed on him by a major American studio when it has a lot of money invested in a project, has been inclined to make his own kind of put-on movies, including "The Fearless Vampire Killers" and "What?", movies that are full of inside jokes and that give every indication that you aren't supposed to take them seriously enough even to sit through them, which may be the ultimate inside joke. In his new film, "The Tenant," Polanski recalls the discipline, style and wit of his earlier, pre-"Rosemary's Baby" and "Chinatown" career.

Polanski is a moviemaker who thinks and thus, to him, the world is a comedy, which isn't to say that you're going to do much laughing as you watch "The Tenant." It's a Poe-like horror story about an odd little Parisian file clerk named Trelkovsky (played by Polanski) who moves into a fourth floor flat made vacant by the suicide of the previous tenant, a young woman who threw herself out the window for reasons no one can fathom.

●   ●   ●

Little by little, Trelkovsky becomes convinced that in moving into the flat he has stumbled onto a shadowy conspiracy, the point of which he cannot learn. It's quite apparent, though, that the landlord (Melvyn Douglas), the concierge (Shelley Winters) and his neighbors (Jo Van Fleet, Lila Kedrova, among others), as well as the dead woman's close friend (Isabelle Adjani), belong to some dark order that is conspiring in his suicide, which means that he must assume the dead woman's identity as well.

There's one moment when you fear that Polanski is going to send up the movie that has been working so beautifully in its own way. It's when Trelkovsky finds himself in full drag, wearing the previous tenant's clothes and a sort of Lola Lane wig. He catches sight of himself in the mirror and says aghast, "I think I'm pregnant!" "The Tenant," however, doesn't traffic in easy jokes. It's the sort of tale of creeping madness that Poe liked, told in a series of tightly controlled revelations about what can only be described as occupancy, first Trelkovsky's occupancy of the flat, and then the occupancy of Trelkovsky's mind and imagination by the spirits around him. This tenant has his own tenants.

Polanski, the director, has not been in as fine and original form since "Knife in the Water" and "Repulsion," and he is superb in the central role, modest, fearful, sometimes immensely knowing. Melvyn Douglas, Shelley Winters and Jo Van Fleet also are excellent, though the English dialogue of the French actors has been so badly dubbed that it sometimes give the movie a very hollow sound. Sven Nykvist, Ingmar Bergman's cameraman, photographed the movie in a manner that is straightforward and without gimmickry as the plan for the movie itself.

"The world is a comedy for those that think, a tragedy for those that feel." Among the major European filmmakers today, only Bergman and Fellini, and sometimes Truffaut, make films that are full of feelings. The others—Chabrol, Ferreri, Wertmuller and Polanski—are primarily filmmakers who intellectualize experiences, with the result that no matter what the forms of their movies, they are essentially comedies. Admittedly they are often cold. We may not slap our knees a lot while watching them, but we know that we are in the presence of artists who are committed to what they're doing, who won't stand aside at the end and say, "Don't blame me, blame my writers."

1976 Je 27, II:15:7

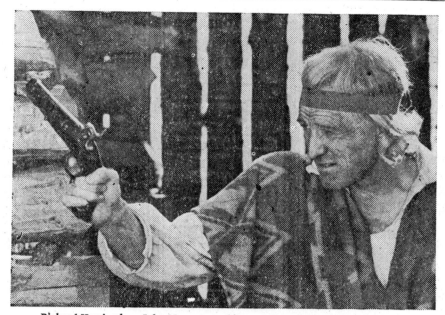

Richard Harris plays John Morgan, a white member of the Yellow Hand tribe

By VINCENT CANBY

Irvin Kershner's "The Return of a Man Called Horse," which opened yesterday at the Ziegfeld Theater, is being shown in 70-millimeter with stereo sound loud enough to drill holes in your back teeth —but you won't feel a thing.

This fancified sequel to Elliot Silverstein's "A Man Called Horse," released six years ago, is so mystical that it effectively numbs the senses much of the time. Not quite all of the time, though, which presents a problem for people who don't have strong stomachs or who aren't stimulated by the spectacle of men solemnly mutilating themselves to purify their souls.

Jack De Witt's screenplay, which is virtually a retread of the one he wrote for the first film, picks up the story of Lord John Morgan, played by Richard Harris, several years later, after the adventuring 19th-century Englishman has returned home, having achieved every small boy's dream of becoming a great Indian warrior. In the first film, you may remember, Morgan was captured by the Yellow Hand, one of the tribes of the Sioux nation, and was eventually adopted by them as one of their own.

While the first film dabbled in American Indian mysticism, "The Return of a Man Called Horse" looks like a cocktail-table book on the subject, full of big, glossy, pretty pictures accompanied by a text of few words and great pretentiousness.

At the start of the film Morgan throws over the easy life of an English country gentleman, not because he's bored but because he's drawn back to his red brothers. In a pretitle sequence that also shows the Yellow Hand being dispossessed by greedy fur trappers, it's apparent that Morgan is receiving extrasensory messages from his adopted people,

The Cast

THE RETURN OF A MAN CALLED HORSE, directed by Irvin Kershner; screenplay by Jack De Witt, based on a character from "A Man Called Horse" by Dorothy M. Johnson; produced by Terry Morse Jr.; executive producer, Sandy Howard; music, Laurence Rosenthal; director of photography, Owen Roizman; editor, Michael Kahn; distributed by United Artists. Running time 125 minutes, Tt the Ziegfeld Theater, 54th Street near the Avenue of the Americas. This film has been rated PG.

John Morgan	Richard Harris
Elk Woman	Gale Sondergaard
Zenas Morro	Geoffrey Lewis
Tom Gryce	Bill Lucking
Running Bull	Jorge Luke
Chemin d'Fer	Claudio Brook
Raven	Enrique Lucero
Blacksmith	Jorge Russek
Moonstar	Ana De Sade
Standing Bear	Pedro Damien
Thin Dog	Humberto Lopez-Pineda
Grey Thorn	Patricia Reyes
Lame Wolf	Regino Herrerra
Owl	Rigoberto Rico
Red Cloud	Alberto Mariscal

Having returned to the Yellow Hand, Morgan must again prove himself worthy in order to help the scattered tribe. This involves a repeat of the flesh-mortifying ritual that seemingly was so popular in the first movie. Small animal bones are inserted into each breast, a line is attached to each bone and the would-be warrior must hang from these lines until he breaks or the lines part. There's also some nonsense with hallucenogenic drugs, some visions and a dandy sequence in which the tribe's medicine man gouges out his own eyes.

Once Morgan and the others have made their peace with the Great Spirit, they go on to take the trappers' fort and reclaim their lands — the substance of the film's action, which is pretty lethargic.

The emphasis that Mr. Kershner and Mr. De Witt very consciously place on mysticism, especially on the need for spiritual rebirth, may be an accurate reflection of Indian belief. However, it makes for a very soggy and at times repellent movie, one that also reflects the faddish mysticism of the 1960's, which, among other things,

helped to make "Billy Jack" so popular.

The character of Morgan is Billy Jack with an English accent, a savior in mufti, and since I'm suspicious of saviors in general, particularly of white saviors among the other races, I found "The Return of a Man Called Horse" more unpleasantly patronizing than uplifting, which also would describe the effect of Mr. Harris's performance. Gale Sondergaard, great actress though she is, plays the Indian woman as if she would be more at home reading tea leaves on Eighth Avenue.

●

"The Return of a Man Called Horse" has been rated PG for very good reasons. Some parents might think that too mild a rating for a film that so painfully and realistically re-creates the Yellow Hand's bloody purification rituals.

1976 Je 29, 19:1

THE CLOCKMAKER, ...cted by Bertrand Tavernier; screenplay (French with English subtitles) by Jean Aurenche and Pierre Bost, adapted from a novel by Georges Simenon; executive producer, Raymond Danon; director of photography, Pierre William Glenn; a Lira Films production, distributed by Joseph Green Pictures. Running time: 109 minutes. At the Embassy 72d Street Theater, Broadway, and Quad 4 Theater, 13th Street west of Fifth Avenue. This film has not been rated.

Michel Descombes	Philippe Noiret
Commissioner Guiboud	Jean Rochefort
Antoine	Jacques Denis
Lawyer	William Sabatier
Madeleine	Andree Tainsy
Bernard Descombes	Sylvain Rougerie
Lilliane	Christine Pascal
Martine	Cecile Vassort

Michel Descombes (Philippe Noiret) is a Lyons clockmaker by trade and by nature an observer of the rules. He waits for the "walk" sign before crossing the street, even when there are no cars and no policemen in sight. When he is asked if he is a widower he considers the question with care. His wife, he says, left him many years earlier, but she is now dead.

Yes, he supposes, he is a widower at least technically. Michel is not a fussy or fearful man, but to the extent that he ponders the inner workings of his life, he values order and accuracy.

"The Clockmaker," which opened yesterday at the Embassy 72d Street and Quad 4 Theaters, is a fine, precise, very moving account of what happens to Michel in a situation where order and accuracy have no application.

●

He wakes up one morning to learn that the son he has raised as a companion has murdered a factory foreman, burned the man's car and run off with a young woman whose existence Michel had never been aware of. Michel cooperates in the police investigation, but it's as if they were searching for a stranger.

The film, an adaptation of the Georges Simenon novel "The Clockmaker of Everton," is a rather startling combination of old and new talents. Maybe reconciliation is the better word. The screenplay is by Jean Aurenche and Pierre Bost—wro wrote the adaptation of "Le Diable au Corps" and are closely identified with the French cinema establishment of the 1940's against which the New Wave was a reaction—but it is the first feature to be directed by Bertrand Tavernier, a young French critic and film scholar who belongs to the post-New-Wave generation.

"The Clockmaker" was produced in 1973 and Mr. Tavernier has since made two more films, but this initial effort is a work of assurance and ease. It is both complex and simple in the way of a film that knows exactly what it's about—which is fathers and sons and the respect that is possible between them under even the worst of circumstances.

When Michel's son (Sylvain Rougerie) and his girl (Christine Pascal) are finally arrested, the young man refuses to give any motive for the crime, refusing even to allow his lawyer to make a point of the murdered man's having been a management spy and responsible for the young woman's having been discharged. "He was a pig," the son says, though not using the word in any political connection, and, "I'm sick of the same ones always winning."

Mr. Tavernier sets the film in an environment that is intensely political though the characters profess not to be. Says a cheery, foolish voice on the radio: "Polls show that 89 percent of all Frenchmen are happy. Are you?" "France is peculiar," Michel is told by the friendly police commissioner (Jean Rochefort) assigned to the case, "Fifty million inhabitants, 20 million informers." Michel's best friend, a Communist, fumes against the complacency of France. Yet the son is no political activist. He has asserted himself in a way that remains mysterious to his father, who nevertheless comes to recognize and respect the boy's identity.

If anything gives away the youth of the director it's his use of quotations—literary quotations (Claudel, Céline), visual quotations from other films, quotations from the news, even reminiscences that are one of the principal ways in which the characters communicate. Events thus recalled establish links to the present and make it if not comprehensible at least tolerable.

Mr. Noiret gives a performance of the high calibre that we now take for granted from him, and Mr. Rochefort and Mr. Rougerie are almost as good in much smaller roles. More important, "The Clockmaker" introduces us to a fine new director.

VINCENT CANBY

1976 Je 29, 19:1

RAPE OF INNOCENCE, directed by Yves Boisset; screenplay (French with English subtitles) by Jean-Pierre Bastid and Michel Martens, adapted by Mr. Boisset and Jean Curtelin; executive producers. Catherine Winter and Gisele Rebillon; director of photography, Jacques Loiseleux, music, Vladimir Coema; a Sofracima production, distributed by New Line Cinema. Running time: 95 minutes. At the Fine Arts Theater 58th Street west of Lexington Aveneue. This film has not been rated-

Georges Lajoie	Jean Carmet
Colin	Pierre Tornade
Boular	Jean Buise
Schumacher	Michel Peyrelon
Ginette Laicie	Ginette Garcia
Mme. Colin	Pascale Roberts
Leo Tartaffione	Jean-Pierre Marielle
Loulou	Robert Castel
Vigerelli	Pino Caruso
Brigitte Colin	Isabelle Huppert

In Yves Boisset's film, "Rape of Innocence," justice, mercy, decency, fair play and a young woman are raped, but not innocence. Innocence is in very short supply in this well-intentioned melodrama, which is so clumsily schematic that you know everything that anyone is going to say or do at least two reels before it happens.

The movie, which opened yesterday at the Fine Arts, is about the lynching of an Arab construction worker by a group of bourgeois vacationers at a French Riviera trailer park. In what I suppose could be interpreted as a hands-across-the-sea gesture, the movie tells us more than once that Frenchmen can be just as bigoted as Americans. Shall we stop the presses?

Jean Carmet, the short, forlorn-faced actor who has been very funny in other French films, is the major villain, a stingy, lecherous owner of a Paris pub. He's effective, but Isabelle Huppert who plays the 16-year-old rape victim, looks older than the woman who plays her mother. Not a major point. Just disconcerting.

VINCENT CANBY

1976 Je 29, 19:2

French Doctor Turns Into Nazi Executioner

In "The Old Gun," a simple and possibly effective story has been ruined by a mass of directional and acting self-indulgence.

A French film, which opened yesterday at the Coronet Theater, it is set in the last months of the German occupation of France. A doctor in a provincial hospital, a comfortable family man whose aid to the Resistance is a matter of careful balancing, turns into a one-man death squad after a group of drunken and demoralized German soldiers murders his wife and daughter.

Prowling through the cellars and back halls of his chateau, where the Germans are bivouacked, the doctor exterminates them messily, one by one. His anguish and desperation are set in a framework of ironic futility: Even while he is going about his mission the Resistance has taken over the village.

●

The movie has a cast, but for all practical purposes it seems to have only one actor in it: Philippe Noiret. Mr. Noiret is a decent actor; his performance as the soft, plump, comfortable doctor whose fire is betrayed only by tiny sparks until it bursts into conflagration is sometimes funny, sometimes moving. It is overdone at times.

It is not, however, as horribly, crushingly overdone as the use of the camera by the director, Robert Enrico, makes it seem. The camera virtually never leaves Mr. Noiret's round, puffing face; when it does, it is only to take in a slightly larger view of his round, puffing figure. We are smothered by him.

Mr. Enrico's major mistake, however, is in using what must be at least a dozen flashbacks to tell his story. Almost at the beginning, we meet Romy Schneider, as the doctor's wife, burned to a cinder. The flashbacks are a way of seeing more of her, but they are no way to make a movie.

●

Once he has come upon his dead family, the doctor can hardly take a few steps or make a move without everything shifting back to scenes that range from a childhood hunt, to the courting of his wife, to a confusing moment during a village festival in which she takes refuge, for no apparent reason, in a cellar.

Whatever coherence or interest the main action might have is shattered by the technique. The intention may be to render even more dreamlike and unreal the doctor's unaccustomed essay into violence; it becomes unreal, all right, and enormously irritating.

RICHARD EDER

1976 Je 30, 25:1

The Cast

THE OLD GUN, directed by Robert Enrico; screenplay (French with English subtitles) by Pascal Jardin, Mr. Enrico and Claude Veillot; original story by Mr. Enrico; photography, Etienne Beckar; music, Francois de Roubaix; a Carmen F. Zollo presentation; a Surrogate release. At the Coronet Theater, Third Avenue at 59th Street. Running time: 104 minutes. This film is not classified.

Julien	Philippe Noiret
Clara	Romy Schneider
Francois	Jean Bouise
Mere de Julien	Madeline Ozeray

SILENT MOVIE, directed by Mel Brooks; screenplay by Mr. Brooks, Ron Clark, Rudy DeLuca and Barry Levinson, based on a story by Mr. Clark; produced by Michael Hertzberg, music, John Morris; director of photography, Paul Lohmann; editors, John C. Howard and Stanford C. Allen; distributed by 20th Century-Fox. Running time: 88 minutes. At the Cinema 1 and 2 Theaters, Third Avenue near 60th Street. This film has been rated PG.

Mel Funn	Mel Brooks
Marty Eggs	Marty Feldman
Dom Bell	Dom DeLuise
Vilma Kaplan	Bernadette Peters
Studio chief	Sid Caesar
Engulf	Harold Gould
Devour	Ron Carey
Pregnant lady	Carol Arthur
News vendor	Lima Dunn
Maitre d'	Fritz Feld
Studio gate guard	Chuck McCann
Studio chief's secretary	Yvonne Wilder
Intensive care nurse	Valerie Currin
Acupuncture man	Anrold Soboloff
Hotel bellhop	Patrick Campbell
Man in tailor shop	Harry Ritz
Blind man	Charlie Callas
Fly-in-soup man	Henry Youngman
British officer	Eddie Ryder

By VINCENT CANBY

You might suspect that Mel Brooks's decision to make a contemporary silent movie titled "Silent Movie," starring himself as a director trying to make a silent movie today, was not the wisest thing he'd ever done, and you'd be right. But having recognized that fact immediately, you can relax and enjoy "Silent Movie" as a virtually uninterrupted series of smiles.

The film, which opened yesterday at the Cinema 1 and 2, doesn't contain a single moment that ever seriously threatens to split the sides, which, I suppose, will strike fanatical Brooks watchers-and-weighers as a statement of dismissal. To the rest of us it's to admit that Mr. Brooks, having given us the lunatic highs of "Blazing Saddles" and "Young Frankenstein," should be allowed to fool around as he sees fit, possibly to extend his talent while discovering its limitations.

●

Actually "Silent Movie" is not silent at all. It has a very busy soundtrack, full of music and of exaggerated noises that accompany such sights as those of a foot crushed in a door, a head bashed against a wall or the collapsing of a Murphy bed.

The only element missing is spoken dialogue, and the written titles, which often adopt a genteel tone as if to spare us the crude reality of the true dialogue, are among the funniest things in the film. I particularly like: "That poor woman is incredibly pregnant. Let's give her a lift." Also the title that appears when a man 15 feet tall rings a stranger's doorbell. "Hi," he says, "I have a glandular condition. May I use your phone?"

●

Politeness is, ultimately, one of the film's problems, especially in the personality of Mel Funn (Mr. Brooks), the reformed boozer who dreams of making his Hollywood comeback by directing a silent film in 1976. Mel Funn is polite, sweet and vulnerable, qualities one associates with some of the old silent film comedians and that fit Mr. Brooks less well than a nun's habit.

The lack of spoken dialogue doesn't disable the character. It's the concept. When you have a Mel Brooks who doesn't allow himself to be rude, testy and master of the low leer, you don't have a funny man. You have an affable floorwalker. He's a suprise and sort of pleasant but not what you were expecting. By being thus prepared, you should be able to appreciate the good things that Mr. Brooks has brought off.

●

These are the sight gags involving Mel Funn and his two staunch associates, Marty Eggs (Marty Feldman) and Dom Bell (Dom DeLuise), as they tootle around Hollywood (identified as "the film capital of Greater Los Angeles") stuffed into a minuscule sports car, signing up real life stars (James Caan, Anne Bancroft, Paul Newman, Burt Reynolds) for the film within the film.

Between the set routines with these stars, who are very funny (particularly Mr. Reynolds and Miss Bancroft), the three indomitable heroes must buck up the failing health of their harried studio chief, played with surprisingly humorless intensity by Sid Caesar. They also have to outwit the corporate and criminal machinations of the New York-based conglomerate, Engulf and Devour ("our fingers are in everything"), which wants to take over the studio.

To this end, Engulf and Devour hires Vilma Kaplan (Bernadette Peters), a night-club performer billed as "a bundle of lust," to lure poor Mel Funn back to his dependency on the bottle.

Everything turns out gloriously, and in something less than 90 minutes, so there's not much time to become impatient with a gag that doesn't build to a boff. As in any good slapstick comedy, some of the most inspired moments are those that have no point whatsoever, such as the "rushes" we are shown of a low-budget picture the studio is then shooting in India.

"Silent Movie" is not the greatest movie Mr. Brooks has made, but if you adjust your expectations, it could be one of the nicest things you'll see all summer.

●

Dom DeLuise, left, Marty Feldman, center, and Mel Brooks in scene from the film

The film, which has been rated PG, contains some visual vulgarisms of the sort that small children find pricelessly funny—such as the sight of a wooden merry-go-round horse doing what live horses do naturally.

1976 Jl 1, 22:1

NO DEPOSIT, NO RETURN, directed by Norman Tokar; screenplay, by Arthur Alsberg and Don Nelson, based on a story by Joe McEveety; produced by Ron Miller with Mr. McEveety as co-producer; director of photography, Frank Phillips; music, Buddy Baker; editor, Cotton Warburton; distributed by Buena Vista. Running time: 112 minutes. At the Festival Theater, 57th Street west of Fifth Avenue, and other theaters. This film has been rated G.

J.W. Osborne	David Niven
Duke	Darren McGavin
Bert	Don Knotts
Sgt. Turner	Herschel Bernardi
Carolyn	Barbara Feldon
Tracy	Kim Richards
Jay	Brad Savage
Jameson	John Williams
Longnecker	Charlie Martin Smith
Big Joe	Vic Tayback
Peter	Bob Hastings

By VINCENT CANBY

"No Deposit, No Return," a new Walt Disney live-action comedy, runs just eight minutes short of two hours, which is lunacy, considering that the members of the audience for whom it is intended can't even concentrate on Donald Duck that long. The film is about two children who blackmail a couple of innocent safecrackers into giving them shelter and attempt to extort $100,000 from their rich grandfather.

According to the brainless plot, the children, played by Kim Richards and Brad Savage, are motivated by loneliness for their widowed mother, who's in Hong Kong and too busy with her career as a roving magazine editor to pay them any attention. A closer reading of their characters suggests that they're

plain spoiled.

●

That the movie goes on so long is no indication that it is especially full of incident, but rather that the director, Norman Tokar, doesn't know when to say cut. Every scene and every gag is allowed too much time, which is too bad, because a couple of routines show promise, especially one in which a small boy attempts to retrieve his pet skunk from the girders of a high-rise building under construction. It's not exactly Harold Lloyd, but it's better than looking at a flying Volkswagen.

As usual, the Disney organization has lined up a group

of actors who are generally much better than the material. They include David Niven (the grandfather), Darren McGarvin and Don Knotts (the safecrackers), Barbara Feldon (the mother), Herschel Bernardi (a police sergeant) and Charlie Martin Smith, who looks startlingly like David Eisenhower, as Mr. Bernardi's over-educated assistant.

"No Deposit, No Return" opened yesterday at the Festival and other theaters on a double bill with the Disney cartoon classic, "Dumbo," which is only 63 minutes long.

1976 Jl 3, 17:1

FILM VIEW

VINCENT CANBY

Robert Altman's American Portrait Gallery

Robert Altman is not 19 or 26 or even 40. He's 51, on the far side of that great half-century divide, but in talent, energy and output he's younger, more independent and more consistently innovative than any other director at work within the commercial film industry today. He's also the most cantankerously critical observer of the current American scene with access to actors, cameras, sound equipment and money.

Looking back over Altman's best films from the vantage point of his new, splendidly overtitled "Buffalo Bill and The Indians or Sitting Bull's History Lesson," we can see that Altman has become increasingly obsessed with the quality of American life as experienced by gallant losers or by people who have made the unfortunate, some-

times fatal mistake of believing our myths — compounds of advertising, publicity, gossip, gullibility, history and wishful thinking. Altman's criticisms sometimes are heavy-handed. Sometimes they fall wide of the mark. The great thing about Altman, though, is his resilience. Instead of fussing too long with one film that doesn't hit the target, he moves on to the next.

In the last eight years while the commercial film industry has been making fewer and fewer films, reducing its perimeters like a wagon train passing through hostile Indian country, Robert Altman has turned out 10 films; Ingmar Bergman has made eight, in addition to directing regularly for the stage and television; François Truffaut has made nine films, including "Pocket Money," which will be released here later

this year under another title; Luis Buñuel four films and Alfred Hitchcock three, but both Buñuel and Hitchcock, being in their seventies, earned the right to take things easy. The Altman output is, I believe, unique among major contemporary filmmakers, certainly among major contemporary American filmmakers, who, more and more, tend to put films together with such deliberation you might think that instead of making movies they were building arks to save mankind.

The prolificity of a filmmaker is no sign of particular talent, except, maybe, the talent to raise money, but when it is evident in filmmakers of special gifts, such as those cited above, it becomes an important aspect of the talent. It's a measure of the need to create, as well as the manner of creation,

which, in Altman's case, is outrageously enthusiastic even when, from time to time, the enthusiasm seems to have leaked out of the finished film, as it had vanished from "Brewster McCloud" and "Images."

More important, the existence of this collection of Altman films has the effect of adding to our knowledge and enriching our appreciation of everything that makes up the collected work. A new film inevitably reshapes our approaches and feelings toward films that came before. Sometimes this process can work to the disadvantage of earlier enthusiasms, as in the case of Sam Peckinpah. The appearances of "The Getaway," "Pat Garrett and Billy The Kid" and "Bring Me The Head of Alfredo Garcia" have made me wonder about the good things I saw in Peckinpah's "The Wild Bunch," "The Ballad of Cable Hogue" and "Junior Bonner," though I think I'd stand by them. As with friends, familiarity breeds contempt at times, and self-doubt, but it can also breed interest, concern, affection, self-assurance, and an awareness that some virtues exist not in spite of but because of some of the faults.

Altman's best films explode with life, sometimes at the expense of form and coherence. He is impatient with a formal screenplay, which he once called "a selling tool" to obtain financing and "not much more than a production schedule." He encourages improvisation to such an extent that life on his set has been compared to psychodrama.

● ● ●

When one of the actresses in "Nashville" asked him several weeks before filming if he wanted her hair to be any special color, he thought a minute and said yes, red. When the actress arrived in Nashville, she found that he'd obviously told all the other actresses the same thing and then had forgotten. There was a lot of rinsing going on before the first cameras could turn.

That Altman was born and raised in Kansas City, Mo., of a mother who was the daughter of Mayflower people and a father who was one of the most successful life-insurance salesmen in the country, has a lot to do with the way he looks at America—literally from the inside out toward the great coasts. Before finally going to Hollywood to stay, he learned his trade in Kansas City in industrial films. Hollywood television production later taught him the value of productivity, meaning that he made his share of claptrap before getting to "M*A*S*H" in 1968.

In the comparatively early "M*A*S*H" Altman was still feeling his way, satirizing service comedies by making one that set new precedents for cruelty, for violence and ultimately for what is and isn't funny, though the film never once assumed an identity as anything but a service comedy. The subversive effect of "M*A*S*H" was achieved largely by shock, which now looks tame, and though Trapper John (Elliott Gould) and Hawkeye (Donald Sutherland) tweak the nose of The System, they are a part of it as top-notch medical doctors and as heros in the same kind of movie that once made Hollywood great.

"Thieves Like Us," Altman's rueful and funny melodrama about three 1930's bankrobbers, and "McCabe and

Mrs. Miller," which becomes more and more interesting within the context of the rest of Altman films, are about losers who are no less gallant for never quite realizing what's happening to them, nor why. If idiotically, they persevere—the bankrobbers because there's no other way out, and McCabe because he believes that the free enterprise system is worth fighting and dying for. Is any other American filmmaker making movies that are simultaneously so sardonic and so physically beautiful, almost voluptuous? I can't think of any. "The Long Goodbye," Altman's update of Raymond Chandler, and "California Split," about a compulsive gambler who has the terrible luck to realize his wildest dream, are both projections of hoary old myths and comments upon them. Altman's Philip Marlowe feels a moral obligation to a friend, and almost gets killed for his trust, while we know that the big winner in "California Split" has thus been robbed of the one thing that made his life worth living from one day to the next. But his dream wasn't good enough.

Nor is the dream of celebrity and stardom good enough in "Nashville," which, I suspect, has suffered more than a little by being accepted as Altman's last word on the quality of All-American life, which it isn't and was never intended to be. It is Altman's most exciting film, a summation of his dazzling methods (narrative, visual, aural) and his foolhardy attempts to make movies about things that are usually left to novelists who, unlike filmmakers, are allowed to create works that are not despised for not being entirely, immediately, absolutely, unequivocally clear. Which leads to "Buffalo Bill and The Indians or Sitting Bull's History Lesson," a film that comes close to creating successfully an epic film form.

"Buffalo Bill and The Indians" is a free-form circus of movie that examines one of America's first great show-business stars, William F. "Buffalo Bill" Cody, when, in 1885, near the zenith of his career, he was presiding over an open-air-and-tent show called "Buffalo Bill's Wild West." The entire film is set in and around this encampment, a sort of late 19th-century Disneyland where tourists come to see re-enactments of the battle of the Little Bighorn, buffalo wrestling, cowboys fighting Indians, fancy-riding demonstrations, hold-ups of the Deadwood stage, and such.

• • •

Unlike "Nashville," which had the drive of its music and the interlocking stories of a dozen or so characters to move it forward, "Buffalo Bill" has little in the way of any narrative at all. It's more like an essay, a very funny and sometimes moving one, on such random subjects as Indians, history, capitalism, mythomania and theater, which is the theme that recurs most often, starting with the opening credits when, in a rehearsal, an Indian is knocked unconscious trying to mount his pony. Says the irritated producer, "Tell Joey he shouldn't get on a horse from the back . . . We're in the authentic business." At the same time we are seeing a log cabin being wheeled off the field.

Buffalo Bill, beautifully played by Paul Newman, is less a fraud than a star, and there are times when the film seems to be Altman's last word on Hollywood. Bill's biggest problem is in not being able to convince the great Hunkpapa Sioux chief Sitting Bull, who joins the show for one season, that show business is serious business. Bill has a fit when Sitting Bull (Frank Kaquitts), a small, taciturn man who smiles once, asks that his act be a dramatization of American soldiers murdering unarmed Indian women and children. "He just wants to show the truth to the people," says a sympathetic Annie Oakley (Geraldine Chaplin). Says Bill, "I have a better sense of history."

If "Buffalo Bill's Wild West Show" is America, as it seems to be in this film, then history—truth—is what Bill and his producer (Joel Grey) make it. "I'm going to Cody-fy the world," the producer announces grandly at one point. When later in the film word comes that Sitting Bull has been killed on his reservation, someone says, "Why bother Bill with a thing like that?" You can hear a protective Presidential advisor at work.

If "Nashville" outraged some people because it had such little regard for story-line, then "Buffalo Bill" is going to have those same people tearing up their seats. I hope not, for though it has its confusions and its self-indulgences, it may turn out to be the most original American film of the year. It might be that if we didn't have those other Altman films leading up to it, it wouldn't be so appealing and full of associations. But we do, so why fight history?

1976 Jl 4, II:1:8

THEY CAME FROM WITHIN, directed and written by David Cronenberg; produced by Ivan Reitman; executive producers, John Dunning, Andre Link and Alfred Pariser; director of photography, Robert Saad; distributed by Trans-American Pictures. Running time: 88 minutes. At the Cinerama II Theater, Broadway near 48th Street. This film has been rated R.

Roger St. Luc ....Paul Hampton
Rollo Linsky ....Joe Silver
Forsythe ....Lynn Lowry
Nicholas Tudor ....Alan Magicovsky
Janine Tudor ....Susan Petrie
Betts ....Barbara Steele
Merrick ....Ronald Mlodzik

and

BOBBIE JO AND THE OUTLAW, directed and produced by Mark W. Lester; screenplay by Vernon Zimmerman; co-producers, Lynn Ross and Steve Brodie; music, Barry De Vorzon; director of photography, Stanley Wright; editor, Michael Luciano; distributed by American International. Running time: 89 minutes. This film has been rated R.

Lyle Wheeler ....Marioe Gortner
Bobbie Jo James ....Lynda Carter
Slick Callahan ....Jesse Vint
Pearl James ....Merrie Lynn Ross
Essie Beaumont ....Belinda Balaski
Sheriff Hicks ....Gene Drew
Hattie James ....Peggie Stewart

By VINCENT CANBY

It's apparent that someone connected with "They Came From Within" has an impertinent sense of humor even though the film is so tackily written and directed, so darkly photographed and the sound so dimly recorded, that it's difficult to stay with it.

The movie is now playing at the Cinerama II and other theaters on a double bill with "Bobbie Jo and the Outlaw," another terrible film about young people on a crime spree in Texas and environs. This one stars Marjoe Gortner, the former child evangelist who is now too weathered to play a young person with much pictorial conviction.

•

"They Came From Within," which was made in Canada, is about a mysterious parasite that attacks the residents of a middle-class apartment complex "12 minutes from downtown Montreal." The parasite looks like a piece of self-propelled calves liver as it slithers about the premises, wantonly attacking young and old and turning its host-victims into sex-mad sybarites for whom the conventional Wednesday night "socials" never end.

1976 Jl 7, 46:4

LE MAGNIFIQUE, directed by Philippe De Brora; screenplay (Frnch with English subtitles) by Mr. De Boca; produced by Alexandre Mnouchkine and Georges Dancigers; director of photography, Maurice Chapiron; music, Tomas Sosa; a production of Les Films Ariane, distributed by Cine III. Running time: 86 minutes. At the Fine Arts Theater, 58th Street west of Lexington Avenue. This film has not been rated.

Bob St. Claire
Francois Mering......Jean-Paul Belmondo
Tatiana
Christine ....Jacqueline Bisset
Karpof
Charron.................Vittorio Capriolo

By VINCENT CANBY

The talent of Philippe De Broca, the French director of "The Love Game," "The Five-Day Lover" and "That Man From Rio," began to melt in the mid-1960's. His last respectable comedy was "King of Hearts" (1967), and that was pretty soft. Mr. De Broca's "Le Magnifique," which opened yesterday at the Fine Arts, is so soft it just sort of sloshes around the ankles like a lukewarm footbath. It's not unpleasant, but it's not much of anything.

The movie is a dual comedy about an impoverished, alimony-ridden writer who turns out pulp novels, and about a glamorous James Bond-type of hero created by the writer. Jean-Paul Belmondo plays both roles with as much verve and style as Mr. De Broca's inspirations allow. Jaqueline Bisset is cast as the spy's sultry assistant as well as the writer's upstairs neighbor, a scholarly young sociology major, while Vittorio Capriolo plays both the writer's stingy publisher and the spy's archenemy.

There is a lot of not very witty cross-cutting between the writer's drab problems in rainy Paris and the spy's extraordinary adventures in sun-drenched Acapulco, and because the scenery is very pretty, the Acapulco footage is more fun. At this point, though, it's impossible to parody the work of Ian Fleming with real enthusiasm, as Mr. De Broca here demonstrates. The good humor that one takes away from "Le Magnifique" will depend entirely on the good humor one takes to it.

1976 Jl 8, 28:3

A SMALL TOWN IN TEXAS, directed by Jack Starrett; screenplay by William Norton; executive producer, Louis S. Arkoff; producer, Joe Solomon; music, Charles Bernstein; director of photography, Bob Jessup; distributed by American International Pictures. Running time: 95 minutes. At the Cinerama 2 Theater, Broadway near 47th Street. This film has been rated PG.

Poke .... Timothy Bottoms
Mary Lee .... Susan George
Duke .... Bo Hopkins
Boogie .... Art Hindle
Lenny .... John Karlen
C.J. Crane .... Morgan Woodward
Cleotus .... Hank Rolike
Bull Parker .... Buck Flower
Junior .... Clay Tanner

By VINCENT CANBY

"A Small Town in Texas," which opened yesterday at the Cinerama 2 and other theaters, is another foolish melodrama about rural life in a fictional state called Texas, where all the county sheriffs are crooked, all the sheriffs' deputies are named either Lenny or Leroy and are slow-witted, and decent young men go wrong because there's nothing else to do.

This one was directed by Jack Starrett. It stars Timothy Bottoms as a fellow who comes home after several years in the slammer (apparently for smoking pot, which is an excessive sentence even in Texas) to pick up his girl, played by Susan George, who is the mother of his illegitimate son. Before they can get out of town there is one political assassination (never explained) and two extended chases in which a lot of police cars are wrecked. Bo Hopkins, who can be a good actor, plays the nasty sheriff.

•

The film has been rated PG, which is a very lenient rating for a film containing so much violence, but perhaps the violence appears to be excessive because none of it seems to be motivated by anything more reasonable than the producers' greed.

1976 Jl 10, 16:1

TUNNELVISION, directed by Brad Swirnoff and Neil Israel; screenplay by Mr. Israel and Michael Mislove; executive producer, Mr. Israel; produced by Joe Roth; music, Dennis Lambert and Brian Potter; director of photography, Don Knight; editors, Roger Parker and Dayle Mustain; an International Harmony-Woodpecker Music Inc. presentation, distributed by Worldwide Films Corp. Running time: 75 minutes. At neighborhood theaters. This film has been rated R.

Christian A. Broder .... Phil Proctor
Senator McManus .... Howard Hesseman
Quant O'Neil .... Ernie Anderson
Melanie Edwards ...... Edwina Anderson

By VINCENT CANBY

"Your mother has passed away, but that's no reason to lose touch," says the television announcer in a commercial for the telephone company. At which point, we see a young man pick up a telephone, dial a number and say, "Hello, mother? What's it like up there?"

If this sketch strikes you as being even dimly amusing, then you might want to see "Tunnelvision," which opened yesterday at theaters around the city. If it doesn't, stay away. The sketch is an accurate indicator of the level of humor of this very wan revue that pretends to give us a sampling of TV programming in 1985. The prediction: it will be just like today's though not as piously, innocently funny.

It's junk like "Tunnelvision" that make one appreciate the mad inspirations of Alan Abel ("Is There Sex After Death?"), the master of a kind of humor often labeled "undergraduate," though its irreverence and fondness for terrible gags can be as liberating as any other kind of humor. There is one catch, however. When undergraduate humor fails, as it does in "Tunnelvision," it doesn't die alone, it threatens to take you with it.

1976 Jl 15, 40:3

RIDE A WILD PONY, directed by Don Chaffey; screenplay by Rosemary Anne Sisson, from the novel "A Sporting Proposition" by James Aldridge; director of photography, Jack Cardiff; editor, Mike Campbell; music by John Addison; produced by Jerome Courtland; released by Buena Vista Distribution Company; a Walt Disney Production. At neighborhood theaters. Running time: 90 minutes. This is classified G.

James Ellison .... Michael Craig
Charles E. Quayle .... John Meillon
Scotty Pirie .... Robert Bettles
Josie Ellison .... Eva Griffith
Bluey Waters .... Graham Rouse
Angus Pirie .... Alfred Bell

It isn't the message that's the trouble with "Ride a Wild Pony," the new film from the Walt Disney organization that opened yesterday at neighborhood theaters on a double bill with a revival of "101 Dalmatians." It's the medium.

The message—or messages,

really—are suitable for the young audiences that can be expected to turn out for "Ride a Wild Pony": respect for the law; facing up, rather than running off.

But the medium turns out to be a fundamentally uneventful and somewhat padded story, set in a small Australian community in the days between world wars, that leads up to a legal contest between a poor boy and a rich but handicapped girl over ownership of a pony.

It may be to the credit of the film makers that neither of the children is sugarcoated. In fact, neither is especially likable. Some children are like that.

But, as a result, it is difficult to care which of the two winds up with the pony and even more difficult to find much suspense in the film's climax. In fact, toward the end some adults might find themseves hoping the horse will declare a pox on both youngsters.

Determined editing might reduce this film to a length appropriate to television, where its essential dullness might be less noticeable. Otherwise, only those youngsters afflicted with rapture at the merest glimpse of horseflesh are likely to mistake "Ride a Wild Pony" for an absorbing movie.

LAWRENCE VAN GELDER

1976 Jl 17, 9:3

THE FOOD OF THE GODS, produced and directed by Bert I. Gordon; screenplay by Mr. Gordon, based on a portion of the novel by H. G. Wells; executive producer, Samuel Z. Arkoff; music, Elliot Kaplan; editor, Corky Ehlers; director of photography, Reg Morris; distributed by American International Pictures. Running time: 89 minutes. At the Cinerama 1 Theater, Broadway near 47th Street, and other theaters. This film has been rated PG.

Morgan .... Marjoe Gortner
Lorna Scott .... Pamela Franklin
Bensington .... Ralph Meeker
Mrs. Skinner .... Ida Lupino
Brian .... Jon Cypher
Rita .... Belinda Belaski
Thomas .... Tom Stovall

On a remote island in Puget Sound, a substance that looks like pancake batter begins to ooze from the earth and not long afterward local animals and insects are growing as big as all outdoors. Chickens stand six-feet tall in their bare claws. Bees grow to the size of turkey buzzards, while rats as large as lions roam the woods, eating everything in sight, including farmers and Volkswagens.

What all this has to do with ecology is never made clear, but the ads for "The Food of the Gods," which opened yesterday at the Cinerama 1 and other theaters, ask ominously, "Has nature finally rebelled?" The answer, I think, is no, but it may be putting us on. Certainly the movie is.

"The Food of the Gods" is a stunningly ridiculous mixture of science-fiction and horror-film clichés, and it's said to be "based on a portion of the H. G. Wells novel" which I've never read. It prattles pieties about clean environment (which would seem to be no big problem in the film's island setting), but it's devoted mostly to showing us Man in the siege of Hollywood Special Effects, though not very good ones.

When the giant rats attack a farmhouse, it's a teeny-tiny miniature farmhouse, and when Marjoe Gortner, the hero of the film, meets them face to face, it's via a split screen, or dummy-rats. There's very little excitement, but quite a few laughs, all provided by the dialogue contributed by Bert I. Gordon, who wrote the screenplay and then produced and directed it. Ida Lupino and Ralph Meeker are among those he conned into appearing in it.

The film has been rated PG, which may be just as well, though it gives the film credit for being scarier than it ever succeeds in being.

VINCENT CANBY

1976 Jl 17, 9:4

THE BINGO LONG TRAVELING ALL-STARS AND MOTOR KINGS, directed by John Badham; screenplay by Hal Barwood and Matthew Robbins; based on the novel by William Brashler; executive producer, Berry Gordy; produced by Rob Cohen; director of photography, Bill Butler; editor, David Rawlins; music, William Goldstein; a Motown production in association with Pan Arts Enterprises, distributed by Universal Pictures. Running time: 111 minutes. At the Cinerama 2 Theater, Broadway near 47th Street; 86th Street Twin 1 Theater, 86th Street near Lexington; 59th Street Twin 2 Theater, 59th Street east of Third Avenue; Murray Hill Theater, 34th Street east of Lexington, and Apollo Theater, 125th Street near Seventh Avenue.

Bingo .... Billy Dee Williams
Leon .... James Earl Jones
Charlie Snow .... Richard Pryor
Willie Lee .... Rico Dawson
Esquire Joe Callaway . Stan Shaw
Rainbow .... DeWayne Jessie
Isaac .... Tony Burton
Sallie Potter .... Ted Ross
Bertha .... Mabel King
The Prostitute .... Anna Capri
Mr. Holland .... Joel Fluellen
Pearline .... Sarina C. Grant

By VINCENT CANBY

The time is 1939. Hitler is moving into Czechoslovakia and making plans to invade Poland. A man in a contemporary newsreel amuses us by eating razor blades. The same newsreel takes us to Yankee Stadium to watch an all-star Negro baseball game.

This is the preface to the genial, slapdash, high-spirited and occasionally moving comedy called "The Bingo Long Traveling All-Stars and Motor Kings," about a barnstorming black baseball team in those long-ago, pre-Jackie Robinson days before the major-league ball clubs admitted black players.

The film, which opened yesterday at five theaters in New York, stars Billy Dee Williams as Bingo Long, the flashiest pitcher in the entire Negro National League, and James Earl Jones as Leon Carter, the catcher with whom Bingo forms his own ball club when it becomes apparent that the owners (black) of the Negro teams are the new slave masters.

For a comedy whose principal mission is to entertain, "The Bingo Long Traveling All-Stars" also manages to provoke a lot of more sober, subsidiary responses that, happily, never get in the way of the show. The film was written by Hal Barwood and Matthew Robbins (who wrote "Sugarland Express"), based on a novel by William Brashler and directed by John Badham, whose earlier credits are in television. It moves in fits and starts of exposition and action, dipping into melodrama from time to time as well as into farce, as it traces the rise and fall and rise of the Bingo Long All-Stars on their travels through the Middle West and South.

The team is a smashing success until the owners of the Negro National League teams put pressure on the owners of the local stadiums not to book the Bingo Long group. This forces the All-stars to seek games with white teams, which, in turn, makes it necessary for the black barnstormers to adapt themselves to the fantasies of the predominantly white audiences.

The All-Stars are required to "shine," to become clowns, in order to reassure the white audiences that they know their places. Bingo at one point pitches a game wearing a gorilla suit. At the same time, though, the black players are dazzling their audiences with extraordinary skills that laughter cannot obscure.

Shining, Bingo says in effect, is simply performance, or theater, or show business. It's a mask. Where Robert Altman's "Buffalo Bill and The Indians" uses show business as a metaphor for American life, "The Bingo Long Traveling All-Stars" acknowledges show business to have been one of the practical means of black survival.

The large, virtually all-black cast is fine, particularly Mr. Williams, Mr. Jones and Richard Pryor, who plays a ballplayer who schemes to get into the major leagues, first as a Cuban, then as an American Indian. Ted Ross, who won a "Tony" for his performance in "The Wiz" on Broadway, is very funny as the most villainous of the ball-club owners, and Stan Shaw is winning, literally, as the Bingo Long rookie who, at long last, breaks the color barrier in the white leagues.

"The Bingo Long All-Stars" has been rated PG. The film includes one razor-cutting scene, which is not funny at all, and a riotous sequence in a whorehouse, which is.

1976 Jl 17, 10:1

FILM VIEW

VINCENT CANBY

How Sci-Fi Films Support The Status Quo

There are currently five science-fiction films in first-run release and another dozen or so in various stages of production, including one called "Puma" for which Anthony Burgess is now writing the original novel so that he can then adapt it for the screen. Science-fiction, paced by the reruns of "Star Trek," is all over television, and if you can believe the Hollywood producer quoted in these pages recently, this renewed interest in the subject reflects the concern of today's young people for "the world of the mind" and their "search for religiosity."

Nonsense.

The evidence provided by the films themselves indicates that the current science-fiction boom is simply another aspect of the new conservatism, which is also a kind of neon-lit, plastic-wrapped anti-intellectualism.

With the exception of Stanley Kubrick's "2001: A Space Odyssey" and "A Clockwork Orange" (adapted from Anthony Burgess's novel), I can't think of any science-fiction films that ever had anything seriously to do with the world of the mind and religiosity. Certainly none of the current films does.

In saying that I exempt for the moment Nicolas Roeg's ambitious, ambiguous "The Man Who Fell to Earth." This film, about an extra-terrestrial visitor played by David Bowie, is too good in many ways to be lumped with the other current sci-fi stuff, though it does share with those other films a concern not for the world of tomorrow but for the world of today. The difference between "The Man Who Fell to Earth" and the rest is that its concerns are the reasons for the film's existence, not the gimmicks that make a creaky plot move forward.

•   •   •

Since the appearance of the first A-bomb at the end of World War II, and especially since the first space flights in the late fifties and early sixties, science-fiction has been increasingly difficult to define. There once was a time when we could always identify science-fiction films by the snappy looking space helmets everyone wore. Today's science-fiction films often don't have any gadgetry at all. Instead they may take place in a contemporary world in which some leap in technology or biology thrusts the characters—you and I—into situations that, in the words

James Earl Jones, left, and Billy Dee Williams

of the people who write this material, could happen tomorrow or (ominous pause) even today. That remark is meant to make us shiver in pleasant anticipation, but the films too often leave us in giggles.

A perfectly ludicrous example is "Embryo," directed by Ralph Nelson ("Lilies of the Field"), a man who should know better. It's about a paunchy research scientist, played by Rock Hudson, who discovers what is described as a growth-enhancing hormone that allows him to take a three-month-old human fetus and, after a couple of weeks of treatment, turn it into a full-grown Barbara Carreras. When Barbara goes on a murder binge (to keep from growing old

Extra-terrestrial visitor David Bowie gets a working-over in "The Man Who Fell to Earth"—"a dampening effect on the impulse toward change."

she needs a steady diet of pituitary glands from unborn but live infants), "Embryo" comes clean with its message: man should not meddle in affairs that are rightfully God's. In other words, don't mess around with the established order of things, which is pretty much what Galileo was told.

The new "The Food of the Gods," the funniest movie of the year so far, is "based on a portion" of the 1904 novel by H. G. Wells, though you wouldn't know to look at it. This one is about a mysterious substance that oozes from the ground and transforms the little animals and insects who eat it into giant-sized carnivores. Though the setting is a remote island in what seems to be Puget Sound, a place that one would think to be fairly unspoiled, the point of "The Food of the Gods" appears to be that the substance is in some way connected to air pollution. For good measure, the movie also suggests that man's greed will be his undoing.

In both "Logan's Run" and "A Boy and His Dog," we are back in more familiar sci-fi territory, a world of the future after a terrible holocaust has destroyed most of the world's population.

"Logan's Run" is set in the 23d century in a large, carefully ordered city inside a plastic bubble. Machines and computers do the work. The citizens laze around all day making love, watching TV or wandering through their handy shopping centers. The catch is that at age 30 each citizen is destroyed.

There's also an underground city in "A Boy and His Dog," set in the year 2024, and it too seems perfect, though it's really a garish facsimile of 19th-century rural America ruled by a folksy dictator.

The method of "Logan's Run" is largely that of the set decorators. It contains some smashing special effects, but the point of the film, as well as of "A Boy and His Dog," whose special effects are much more modest, is to make one think fondly of this world, this society, this time and place—political scandals, social inequities, overpopulation and air pollution notwithstanding.

• • •

Although the hero of "The Man Who Fell to Earth" is an extra-terrestrial visitor, and although the film features some pretty and rather odd flashbacks to that other planet, the film is mostly concerned with life in America today and, unlike the other sci-fi movies out now, it takes anything but a sentimental view of things. Behind the ambiguities of the narrative (some of which must be the result of the film's having been cut 25 minutes for its American release), "The Man Who Fell to Earth" is a picture of a power-corrupted society that depends on its computers—which have usurped the roles once played in science-fiction films by mad scientists.

What sorts of fears and fantasies do these films represent? I'm not sure, but I do think it's interesting that sci-fi writers are always imagining future worlds of perfect order and efficiency that have apparently evolved from our present societies, as if order and efficiency were the worst things we had to put up with. Has any sci-fi writer ever entered into correspondence with Con Ed to try to get the computer to spell his name right, or dealt with The New York Telephone Company on the matter of a call he never made to, say, Recife, Brazil? Such perfect future worlds as they imagine—even though cold and loveless—would seem to contain a certain amount of wishful thinking.

They must also have a certain dampening effect on the impulse toward social change and betterment. I can imagine that someone might emerge from "Logan's Run" thinking that if that's the perfect world of the future, to hell with trying to bring it about.

Thus, most science-fiction films, for all their jazzy special effects, have a vested interest in the status quo. Fritz Lang's 1926 "Metropolis," still one of the most spectacular science-fiction films ever made, is no exception. It portrays a future society run by heartless capitalists and manned by slave-workers who live in an underground city. It would seem to be a perfect Marxist parable except that the point of the film, as it was of Germany at the time the film was made, is compromise and coalition. At the end of the film, after the capitalist-leader has failed in his plan to destroy the workers' city, do the workers shoot him and take over their own destinies? No. They shake hands, each side having learned that love is the great mediator. (Even Lang has gone on record to say he thinks this ending preposterous, though it suited the temper of a Germany then being run by a coalition of Social Democrats and members of various Christian parties.)

Excepting Roeg's "The Man Who Fell to Earth," which is not strictly a science-fiction film, the science-fiction we're getting today is sentimental claptrap. At its nerviest, it will come out firmly against air pollution and other kinds of littering, all the while reminding us that this morally rotten, underfed, unequal old world of ours isn't really so bad after all.

1976 Jl 18, II:11:1

Outrageous Practical Jokes in a Parable

By VINCENT CANBY

Their lives are going nowhere except into loveless middle age. Mascetti (Ugo Tognazzi) has gone through two fortunes (his wife's and his own) and makes a living of sorts in the door-to-door selling of encyclopedias. Melandri (Gastone Moshin) is an architect of no great promise. Perozzi (Philippe Noiret), separated from his wife and father of a maddeningly fastidious son (the sort of fellow who puts a tarpaulin over his car at night), is a crime reporter, a job he's had too long, and Necchi (Duilio Del Prete) runs the local bar where the friends hang out.

Their lives are going nowhere but does it really matter? That's the question that is answered in sometimes uproariously funny terms in "My Friends," a new Italian comedy that was directed by Mario Monicelli ("Big Deal on Madonna Street") after the death of Pietro Germi ("Divorce—Italian Style," "Seduced and Abandoned"), who had collaborated on the screenplay and prepared the production for filming.

"My Friends," which opened yesterday at the 68th Street Playhouse, is a cross between Claude Sautet's "Vincent, François, Paul and the Others" and Federico Fellini's "I Vitelloni." It's a film about supportive male friend-

The Cast

MY FRIENDS, directed by Mario Monicelli; screenplay (Italian with English subtitles) by Pietro Germi, Piero De Barnardi, Leo Benevenuti and Tullio Pinelli; produced by Carlo Nebiolo; director of photography, Luigi Kuveiller; a Rizzoli Films production, distributed by Allied Artists. Running time: 113 minutes. At the 68th Street Playhouse, at Third Avenue. This film has been rated PG.

Mascetti	Ugo Tognazzi
Melandri	Gastone Moshin
Perozzi	Philippe Noiret
Necchi	Duilio Del Prete
Sassaroli	Adolfo Celi
Righi	Bernard Blier
Donatella	Olga Karlatos
Mascetti's wife	Milena Vukotic
Tutti	Angela Goodwin

ship, set in the Italian provinces, and though the milieu is bleak, the comedy is blithe.

•

Singly, each of the men is a failure, with the possible exception of the bar owner, whose life is simply boring. Together, on their occasional "gypsy" outings, they discover a sense of camaraderie that becomes purpose. The friends, who've grown up together and know each other so well they can communicate virtually without talking, devote themselves to the outrageous practical joke.

Sometimes the joke is not elaborate, only a trip to the station where they have a high old time with the passengers on a train just as it's pulling out. The passengers can't respond—the train is carrying them off at mounting speed—and though it's never stated, it may be that in this particular joke, the four friends are doing to strangers what life has done to them. It's as if each man were trying to deal with a

mysterious, totally inexplicable slap in the face.

Sometimes the jokes are terribly elaborate, as when they execute a series of complex charades for the benefit of a stingy old pensioner (Bernard Blier), who believes that the four friends are members of a Mafia drug-selling ring. At least once the joke backfires with curious results.

When Melandri, the architect, thinks he has fallen madly in love with the wife of a local doctor, the friends court her for him with obscene telephone calls that are enormously successful. Melandri wins the wife, as well as her two children, the governess and a giant dog, while the doctor (Adolfo Celi) does not lose a wife, he gains four lunatic friends. It turns out that he is their soul brother.

Before someone writes in to note that "My Friends" appears to take a pretty dim view of women, I should say that may be true, except that isn't the point of the film, which, if I understand it correctly, uses provincial Italian manners to illustrate a parable about self-realization.

The four friends of "My Friends" achieve this only in the company of one another, and always in the performance of the practical joke that is the metaphor of the movie. Having said this, I'm afraid that I've made "My Friends" sound lugubrious. It isn't. Its method is marvelously comic and the mood gallant.

In addition to the actors, who are superb, the film features several performances of equal exuberance by actresses, especially by Angela Goodwin, who plays Mascetti's pretty young mistress, who uses him as he uses her, and Olga Karlatos, as the beauty who is so successfully wooed by telephone.

"My Friends," which carries a PG rating, contains one quick scene of female nudity and a scatological joke that is among the funniest things in the film.

1976 Jl 19, 26:3

French Comedy Opens at the Cinema II

It requires an investment of about 35 minutes to be sure that "The Wild Goose Chase," which opened yesterday at the Columbia II, has settled down on its final course. And once that happens, suspicion becomes certainty: As a product in international trade, this French comedy about the travails of a bank official temporarily elevated to manager and then caught up in a stock theft carried out by a troupe of transvestite performers is unlikely to do much to bolster the health of the franc.

Pierre Richard, who seems doomed forever to be recalled as the star of "The Tall Blond Man With One Black Shoe" and who occasionally resembles Yves Montand trapped in a fright wig, is the bumbling banker who sets out aboard a festive excursion train to pursue the thieves from Paris to Brighton, England. Suspicious that he is rejecting her before she can

The Cast

THE WILD GOOSE CHASE, directed by Claude Zidi; executive producer, Pierre Grunstein; distributed by EDP Films Inc. At the Cinema II theater. This film has not been rated.

Pierre Vidal	Pierre Richard
Jane	Jane Birkin
Bertrand de Revere	Claude Dauphin

reject him, his girlfriend, played by Jane Birkin, trails him. And a French police lieutenant trails them both.

Along the way, the hero is subjected to ordeal by water, by fire and even by his girlfriend, who ties him to a chair and leaves him to become prey to the obtuseness of seaside Britons, who regard his frenzied efforts at freedom as a street performance worthy of their coins. What this brief but successful scene makes clear by contrast is that "The Wild Goose Chase" lacks a truly comic vision of character and life. The result looks like a catalogue of frenzied and familiar situations that exploit the willingness of the performers' flesh on a meager diet of comic spirit.

LAWRENCE VAN GELDER

1976 Jl 22, 25:1

GODZILLA VERSUS MEGALON, directed by Jun Fukuda; screenplay by Mr. Fukuda, based on a novel by Chinchi Skezawa; executive producer, Tomoyuki Tanaka; a production of Toho Eizo Company, distributed by Cinema Shares International. Running time: 85 minutes. At neighborhood theaters. This film has been rated G. WITH Katsuhiko Sasaki, Hiroyuki Kawase, Yutaka Hayashi, Mori Mikita and others.

By VINCENT CANBY

"Godzilla Versus Megalon" completes the canonization of Godzilla, the creature who came from beneath the sea in 1955 (in "Godzilla, King of the Monsters") to destroy

Tokyo and has returned in sequels again and again to protect the land he once loathed. It's been a remarkable transformation of character—the dragon has become St. George.

Godzilla, a Tyrannosaurus except for the tail he sometimes uses as a kangaroo does and the plates of what could be coral growing up his back, swims through the water at supersonic speeds, but he has a less easy time of it on land. With his fat thighs and his chubby knees he totters around perfectly flat surfaces looking like a baby who has just learned how to walk, which is why he is so appealing. Even with all of his impressive defense mechanisms (among other things, he has atomic breath), you know that walking down a flight of stairs would be for him an infinitely complicated task.

There are no flights of stairs to negotiate in "Godzilla Versus Megalon," which takes place mostly in the open air and is about a war launched against Japan by the undersea kingdom of Seatopia. The day is saved by Godzilla with the help of a self-programming robot. Godzilla and the robot, a superman sort whose name I didn't catch, become fast friends to defeat Seatopia's monsters, Megalon and Gigan, but not before most of Tokyo has been destroyed in some rather impressive miniatures, much in the manner of the smashing of sand castles.

The Japanese movie, which opened yesterday at theaters around the city, has been dubbed into an English that would amuse Woody Allen but it's still one of the least offensive comic-book movies I've seen recently. It's wildly preposterous, imaginative and funny (often intentionally). It demonstrates the rewards of friendship, between humans as well as monsters, and it is gentle.

For all of the mayhem nobody is permanently damaged. In a chase the automobiles don't really go very fast so even screeching of tires is gentle, almost soothing. If the Three Bears had tried to catch up with Goldilocks in a Toyota, this is what it would have sounded like.

1976 Jl 22, 26:1

LIFEGUARD, directed by Daniel Petrie; screenplay by Ron Koslow; produced by Ron Silverman; executive producer, Ted Mann; director of photography, Ralph Woolsey; music scored and conducted by Dale Menten; songs by Paul Williams; editor, Argyle Nelson Jr.; distributed by Paramount Pictures. Running time: 96 minutes. At Loews State 1 Theater, Broadway at 45th Street; Loews Tower East, Third Avenue near 72d Street, and other theaters. This film has been rated PG.

Rick	Sam Elliott
Cathy	Anne Archer
Larry	Stephen Young
Chris	Parker Stevenson
Wendy	Kathleen Quinlan

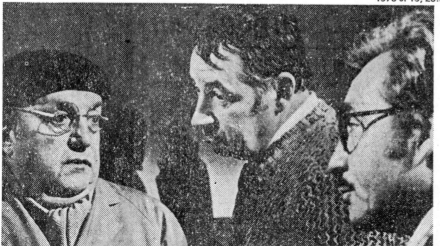

Bernard Blier, left, Philippe Noiret, center, and Ugo Tognazzi

Anne Archer and Sam Elliott

he doesn't feel anything. This bit of analysis is confirmed by the lifeguard's mannerisms and decisions during the rest of the movie, and explains the unintentional laugh that greets his statement that he likes winter duty at the beach best because it gives him time to think.

Thinking would be a totally alien activity to the character written by Mr. Koslow and acted by Mr. Elliott who, consciously or not, moves through the movie—through affairs with a sweet beach-groupie (Kathleen Quinlan) and with a former high-school sweetheart (Anne Archer)—with all of the intellectual and emotional sensitivity of a man holding up a pack of cigarettes in a Marlboro ad.

That Mr. Elliott looks like a successful male model also has the effect of undermining any urgency we may be expected to feel on behalf of the character. After all, if he can't cut it on the beach any longer, he can always go out and make television commercials.

As a film, "Lifeguard" is romantic twaddle, but as sociology it's a spontaneous assault on a very American way of life. People smile a lot, even when they have nothing to smile about. Characters drive to places to commit suicide in expensive sports cars. The interior decoration is the sort that makes every house and apartment look like a motel room. If people read, you know it's TV Guide.

Since I doubt that "Lifeguard" was intended as sociology, one must consider it as entertainment, and as entertainment it ranks somewhat above "Bikini Beach" but below "Godzilla Versus Magalon."

The film has been rated PG. It hasn't a thought in its head, but there are some nudity and rough language, as well as one very ornate love scene photographed in such close-ups that the audience must guess whether a mound of flesh is an elbow, a hip, a nose or a breast. I still don't know.

1976 Jl 24, 12:1

Machine Gun ....Steve Burns
Tina ....Sharon Weber
Mrs. Carlson ....Lenka Peterson
Mr. Carlson...........George D. Wallace

By VINCENT CANBY

"Lifeguard" is the quintessential California "problem" picture. What, it asks, would you do if you were a fine, strong, healthy, handsome Santa Monica lifeguard who finds himself over the hill at the age of 32? Take a job selling Porsches? Stay on with the Parks Department? Shoot yourself?

Only people bred in California could examine this problem in such solemn detail without cracking up, which may be one of the reasons why California fascinates us, and why we sit through a movie as witless as "Lifeguard" experiencing both helpless laughter and undisguised envy. California weather really is great. The beaches are spectacular, the people apparently all beautiful, and sex is everywhere.

The only problem is age, an issue that "Lifeguard" faces unflinchingly. Aging lifeguards are suspect—to themselves as well as to other people—in the California youth culture. Should they be put to sleep? Should they be sent to rehabilitation camps in Nebraska to learn a new trade? Should they be allowed to stay on the job as long as they can perform their duties? Should they be treated with the same respect given 22-year-olds?

The movie that opened yesterday at Loews State 1 and other theaters doesn't mince words. It is the most prolifeguard film ever made. "Lifeguard" looks to be two different movies at the same time. The one directed by Daniel Petrie means to be about freedom and self-realization, while the one written by Ron Koslow and acted by Sam Elliott is about vanity, narcissism.

Quite early in the film, which spends one summer on the Santa Monica sands, Rick Carlson (Mr. Elliott), the lifeguard of the title, is told by one of the young women in his life that though he is great in bed "technically,"

FILM VIEW

VINCENT CANBY

Hollywood Has an Appealing New Star—Old Gooseberry

He's the biggest thing at the box-office this summer no matter what you call him: Satan, Devil, Abaddon, Apollyon, Lucifer, Beelzebub, Ehlis, Tempter, Asmodeus, Belial, Dragon, Serpent, Evil One, God of This World, Prince of Darkness, Prince of The Devils, Prince of The Power of The Air, Prince of This World, Wicked One, Hornie, Nick, Author of Evil, Clootie, Old Harry, Old Ned, Scratch, Azazel, Father of Lies, Foul Fiend, Mephisto, or, my particular favorite, Old Gooseberry.

Not since "Rosemary's Baby" and "The Exorcist" has satanophany paid off as lucratively as it's currently doing with "The Omen" and, to a lesser extent, "The Devil Within Her," both movies of such ceremonious silliness that you may want to see them, if only to get a purchase on a public that this autumn will be exercising its quadrennial Constitutional rights to elect a President. If Old Gooseberry's name were on the ballot, there'd be no contest.

Both in "The Omen," a big-budget American film shot mostly in England with the augustly puzzled presence of Gregory Peck playing the American ambassador to the Court of St. James, and in "The Devil Within Her," a much cheaper English film with Joan Collins playing a frightfully grand ex-Soho stripper, Old Gooseberry is cuddly and cute enough to star in a series of baby-food commercials. Way back when, in the 1920's, the Devil was a woman. Today he's a little boy.

If you care about the welfare of films, of women and of little boys, these movies—to say nothing of the dozens of sequels already planned—represent a long step sideways onto the soft shoulders of puerility.

Satanism has always been an interesting though not very respectable form of movie myth. The subject was usually left to the B-picture makers, who occasionally threw up a first-class producer like Val Lewton, but it was never considered worthy of the attention of the makers of A-films. Roman Polanski's "Rosemary's Baby," which is more a comedy than anything else, started to change that, and all remaining doubts were swept away by the phenomenal success of William Friedkin's "The Exorcist," a movie that seemed pretty dreadful at the time but one that alongside "The Omen" now looks like a work of cinematic art.

It's to overemphasize a point, I suspect, to say that this renewed interest in satanism represents what psychologists and sociologists describe as a need to externalize evil, thus to avoid individual responsibility. The fictional process itself is a way of externalizing ideas and feelings, the better to understand them. The existence of Satan is a part of our mythology. So too—it's now apparent—is our tolerance for solemnly pretentious, superstitious nonsense.

That may be taking "The Devil Within Her" and "The Omen" more seriously than they deserve, but not, I think, the public's gullibility in buying second-rate work.

Before the opening of "The Devil Within Her," Joan Collins has made the mistake of spurning the advances of an amorous dwarf (she doesn't love him "that way") sharing the bill with her in a London nightclub. In his humiliation the dwarf, whose supernatural powers obviously couldn't get him a date at the Palladium, curses Miss Collins, calling upon Old Gooseberry to see that she bears a monster child, which, after her marriage to an antique dealer, she does.

The evil child in "The Devil Within Her" is a devil, not the Devil, but before he is neutralized he manages to do away with dad, mum, the nanny and the pediatrician. The moral of the movie: don't mess around with amorous dwarfs. The point of the movie: the attempt to create suspense as we wait for the characters to realize that the baby is possessed. Joan suspects almost immediately but she acts too late. Salvation comes in the person of Joan's sister-in-law, an Italian nun who is most of the time a research chemist but also an exorcist when the need arises.

"The Devil Within Her" is foolish and probably knows it. "The Omen" is like Gregory Peck's performance—dignified, grave and so hollow-headed it rattles. It takes as its text a bit of hilarious doggerel that David Seltzer, the screenwriter, would have us believe comes right out of the Book of Revelations (sic):

"When the Jews return to Zion/And a comet rips the sky/ And the Holy Roman Empire rises/Then you and I must die/ "From the eternal sea he rises/Creating armies on either shore/Turning man against his brother/'Til man exists no more."/

If you can possibly locate the Book of Revelations (sic), you may possibly locate this quote. It's nowhere to be found in the Book of Revelation, though.

In Seltzer's screenplay, which was directed by Richard Donner, a television director who has a superb way of dismissing any small detail that might give some semblance of

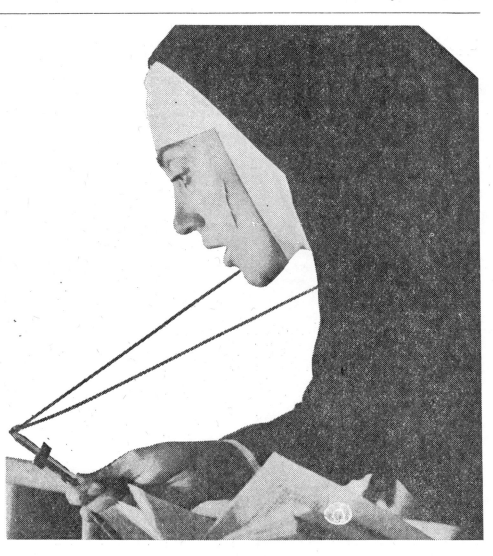

Satanophany is good box office these days as hordes of moviegoers flock to see the likes of Eileen Atkins in "The Devil Within Her" and Harvey Stevens in "The Omen."

conviction to the proceedings, Robert Thorn (Peck) takes it upon himself to adopt an infant boy born in a Rome hospital the same evening that his own son has been born dead. Thorn, who is described in terms that evoke thoughts of the Kennedy family, is terribly regal in his bearing but he doesn't have much upstairs. When a sinister priest suggests the switch in babies, Thorn agrees and explains that his wife Katherine (Lee Remick) should never know. Little does Thorn know that the being he has been conned into taking to his bosom is not just a devil, but Old Gooseberry himself, come to earth to take control, even if it has to be by Constitutional means.

Cut five years into the future when Thorn, Katherine and the boy, Damien, are living in London in splendor untroubled by any of the usual diplomatic duties. After one thing and another (the suicide of a nanny, the impalement of a junkie priest who tried to warn him, Katherine's miscarriage with a second child), Thorn begins to suspect the kid's real identity. The suspicions are confirmed later when the message in Revelations (sic) is interpreted to mean that Old Gooseberry has, indeed, come to earth, now. The Jews *have* returned to Zion, and there *was* a comet. The Holy Roman Empire doesn't mean Holy Roman Empire at all but the Common Market, ("A bit of a stretch," Greg says, but he's convinced), and "the eternal sea," someone else says portentously (and conveniently), is thought to mean "the sea of politics." Greg is not the quickest witted fellow at the Court of St. James but he knows a prognostic augury when he has one interpreted for him. He jumps into action, but. . . . Old Gooseberry triumphs in "The Omen" and well he might, considering the intelligence of the opposition.

It's no contest in movies as nuttily put together as ""The Omen" and "The Devil Within Her," so why should they be so popular? It's to give the films credit for a seriousness they don't possess to suggest that they fill some spiritual needs. Could it be that they provide an outlet for all our pent-up hatred of things like children, dogs, dwarfs and priests? Perhaps. Or, the answer may be much more simple: the reflection of vestigial longings for a *real* change in administration.

1976 Jl 25, II:13:1

Tale of Two Families Possesses a Heart

By VINCENT CANBY

Ludovic (Victor Lanoux), a dance instructor who has also been a mushroom specialist and a horn player in a jazz band, has been married for eight years to Karine (Marie-France Pisier), a pretty, perpetually morose young woman who finds solace in sleep cures and hypnotherapy.

Marthe (Marie-Christine Barrault), a radiant blonde in her early 30's has been married for 11 years to Pascal (Guy Marchand), a classic French bourgeois Casanova. He conquers women (bus drivers, receptionists, sales clerks, family guidance counselors) not because he's especially drawn to them, but because something will have been left unproven if he doesn't.

The Cast

COUSIN, COUSINE, directed by Jean-Charles Tacchella; screenplay (French with English subtitles) by Mr. Tacchella; produced by Bertrand Javal; director of photography, Georges Lendi; editor, Agnes Guilemot; music, Gerard Anfosso; distributed by Libra Films. Running time: 95 minutes. At the Paris Theater, 58th Street west of Fifth Avenue. This film has not been rated.

Marthe	Marie-Christine Barrault
Ludovic	Victor Lanoux
Karine	Marie-France Pisier
Pascal	Guy Marchand
Biju	Ginette Garcin
Diane	Sybil Maas
Sacy	Jean Herbert
Gobert	Pierre Plessis
Nelsa	Catherine Verlor
Thomas	Hubert Gignoux

Jean-Charles Tacchella's completely approving new French comedy, "Cousin, Cousine," which opened yesterday at the Paris Theater, is the story of the growth of the love between Ludovic and Marthe, who are first thrown together at a wedding when Pascal, who can't stop himself, and Karine, who is bored, go off for a quick assignation in the bushes. Ludovic accepts his wife's behavior without panic. Marthe

locks up her feeling.

Some weeks later, long after Pascal and Karine have forgotten their brief affair, Ludovic and Marthe meet again at a family funeral. On the way to the cemetery, Ludovic and Marthe establish their first intimacy. While the new widow sits in the front of the bus weeping and the other members of the funeral party stifle yawns, Ludovic and Marthe sit together in the rear, humming cheerfully and making tentative gestures toward an understanding that will eventually split their two marriages.

●

"Cousin, Cousine," which I believe is the first film by Mr. Tacchella to be released in this country, and which was awarded the Prix Delluc in France, is an exceptionally winning, wittily detailed comedy that is as much about family relationships as it is about love.

Both Marthe and Ludovic belong to large, affectionate families that are infinitely patient and flexible in coping with temporary lapses in behavior, be it a loss of temper, a fit of falling-down drunkenness or blatant adultery.

At first Ludovic and Marthe

meet in secret, being amused by the thought that although their relationship is platonic, no one would believe it. Their mates become worried. Pascal, for whom infidelity is serious self-expression, makes a big point in renouncing all his mistresses. When he breaks with the bus driver, she insults him in the worst way she knows—she makes him get off the bus between designated stops. Karine firmly decides that she will again be amusing.

But it's too late, and since everyone believes them to be lovers already, Ludovic and Marthe oblige.

In a rather startling way, no one seems to get seriously hurt in this film, even though there are deaths and profound disappointments, not because Mr. Tacchella takes a superficially rosy view of things, but because, with the help of his actors, he creates a group of characters who appear either to have inner resources or, like Karine, to be too self-absorbed to feel anything too deeply.

Miss Barrault, who is the niece of Jean-Louis; Miss Pisier, Mr. Lanoux and Mr. Marchand are very good company, especially when they are misbehaving. "Cousin, Cousine" possesses a heart that is both light and generous.

1976 Jl 26, 29:1

Robert Shaw in "Swashbuckler"

SWASHBUCKLER, directed by James Goldstone; screenplay by Jeffrey Bloom, based on a story by Paul Wheeler; executive producer, Elliott Kastner; produced by Jennings Lang; director of photography, Philip Lathrop; editor, Edward A. Biery; music, John Addison; distributed by Universal Pictures. Running time: 101 minutes. At Radio City Music Hall, Ave-minutes. At Radio City Music Hall, Avenue of the Americas at 50th Street. This film has been rated PG.
Ned Lynch .... Robert Shaw
Nick Debrett .... James Earl Jones
Lord Durant .... Peter Boyle
Jane Barnet .... Genevieve Bujold
Major Folly .... Beau Bridges
Cudjo .... Geoffrey Holder
Polonski .... Avery Schreiber
Mr. Moonbeam .... Tom Clancy
Woman of Dark Visage .. Anjelica Huston
Sir James Barnet .... Bernard Behrens
Alice .... Dorothy Tristan
Lute player .... Mark Baker
Willard Culverwell .... Kip Niven

By VINCENT CANBY

THE time is 1718. The place is the island of Jamaica. It is a day of incredible, luminous clarity. In the courtyards of the British fort overlooking the sea an execution by hanging is being prepared. A junior officer sees an ominous spar on the horizon, but his commander won't hear of interruptions. The chaplain coughs. "I find no prayer for a pirate," he says mildly. "The closest I came is something by Peter for fishermen. . . ."

Before the hanging can take place, the ominous spar on the horizon turns out to be the pirate ship Blarney Cock, under the command of Capt. Ned Lynch who has come to cheat the noose of the life of his associate, Nick Debrett. There is a

pitched battle, Nick escapes, and the new pirate adventure, "Swashbuckler," should be off and running. It's not. It's off and sinking.

The film, which opened yesterday at Radio City Music Hall, has hardly anything to recommend it unless, like me, you'll put up with all sorts of gaffes for even the dimmest recollection of a kind of fiction that once made childhood tolerable.

"Swashbuckler," which was directed by James Goldstone and written by Jeffrey Bloom, was photographed largely around Puerto Vallarta, Mexico, on land and seascapes of storybook beauty. Doubling as the Blarney Cock is an exquisitely lovely reproduction of Sir Francis Drake's ship, the Golden Hind, and the cast includes Robert Shaw, James Earl Jones, Genevieve Bujold, Beau Bridges and Peter Boyle, all people of proven talents. Yet the movie is such a mess you might suspect it was tacked together by nearsighted seamstresses.

The screenplay is full of lines that either are arch ("A pirate in love is like a fish out of water") or are failed anachronisms ("We're pirates, Ned, not revolutionaries." "Pirates — revolutionaries—we're all men"). Worse, though, is a plot that is skimpy on incident, acted by people who have been mostly miscast.

As the pirate captain, Mr. Shaw, a good character actor, works extremely hard to create a figure of romantic dash but produces only sweat. He'd have been much better as the wicked governor, a role played by Peter Boyle, who might possibly have been more convincing as an eccentric deckhand

than as an effete fellow who takes hot tubs with his lute player (maie).

Genevieve Bujold is charming as the swordswoman—daughter of a man wrongly imprisoned by the governor, but it's a very, very silly role. Mr. Jones is also wasted as Captain Lynch's best pal. Mr. Jones is a star and looks foolish in what is essentially the Alan Hale part. But then Beau Bridges is also a star, and he's on screen for less time than the opening credits.

A strong director might have imposed some order on the project, but Mr. Goldstone is not such a person. "Swashbuckler" seems to want to be high adventure, but it has no cohesive style, no exuberance. It looks like slogging, joyless hard work.

⬤

"Swashbuckler" has been rated PG, in recognition, I suppose, of a couple of scenes in a busy whorehouse and the dopey reference to the governor's homosexuality, which this mindless film equates with political corruption.

1976 Jl 30, C5:1

SQUIRM, directed and written by Jeff Lieberman; executive producers, Edgar Lansbury and Joseph Berule, produced by George Manasse; director of photography, Joseph Mangine; editor, Brian Smedley-Aston; distributed by American International Pictures. Running time: 92 minutes. At the Cinerama 2 Theater, Broadway near 47th Street, and other theaters. This film has been rated R.
Mick .... John Scardino
Geri .... Patricia Pearcy
Roger .... R. A. Dow
Naomi .... Jean Sullivan
Sheriff .... Peter MacLean
Alma .... Fran Higgins
Quigley .... William Newman
Sheriff's girl .... Barbara Quinn
Willie Grimes .... Carl Dagenhart

"Squirm," the best horror film that opened all day yesterday at the Cinerama 2 and other theaters, seems principally to be about people not paying attention.

The setting is the Georgia coast, where the local power company never thinks to turn off the juice when one of its high-tension towers collapses during a thunderstorm. The electricity pouring into the ground stirs up the local worms, who, shocked and angry, come forth by the millions to eat people. The question asked by "Squirm" is not who will survive, but will anyone?

The film, written and directed by Jeff Lieberman, has two decent performances by John Scardino and Patricia Pearcy and some effectively revolting moments when it deals with real worms photographed in close-up. It sort of goes to pieces, though, in its spectacle scenes. The sight of a young man sinking slowly up to his eyeballs in worms looks no more terrifying than a busboy having an accident at Mama Leone's. It is spaghetti with meat sauce. VINCENT CANBY

1976 Jl 31, 10:4

DRUM, directed by Steve Carver; screenplay by Norman Wexler, based on the novel by Kyle Onstott; produced by Ralph Serpe; director of photography, Lucien Ballard; editor, Carl Kress; music, Charlie Smalls; distributed by United Artists. Running time: 100 minutes. At Loew's State 1, Broadway at 45th Street, and Loew's Orpheum Theater, 86th Street near Third Avenue. This film has been rated R.
Hammond Maxwell ...... Warren Oates
Mariana .... Isela Vega
Drum .... Ken Norton
Regine .... Pam Grier
Blaise .... Yaphet Kotto
Bernard DeMarigny ...... John Colicos
Augusta Chauvet .... Fiona Lewis
Rachel .... Paula Kelly
Zeke .... Royal Dano
Lucretia Borgia .... Lillian Hayman
Calinda .... Brenda Sykes

By VINCENT CANBY

There's more hot air than steam in the overwrought melodrama of "Drum," the sequel to the financially successful "Mandingo" that opened yesterday at the Loew's State 1 and Orpheum Theaters. Life at Falconhurst, the Louisiana slave-breeding plantation introduced in the first film, is just as riotously unpredictable as it was when "Mandingo" ended with the plantation master being shot and his best slave being boiled in oil.

Some years have now passed and the late master's son, Hammond Maxwell (Warren Oates), is running the business as usual, sleeping with pretty slave girls, while his teenage daughter skips through the honeysuckle making indecent proposals to the male slaves, including Drum, played by Ken Norton, who appeared in "Mandingo" as a different character.

⬤

Mr. Norton is a fine figure of a man, but no actor. He walks through the film with the gait of a football star coming off the field after a very long game. He can hear the roar of the crowd that we can't. This seeming lack of interest in anyone except himself doesn't help the melodrama, in which Drum is supposed to be a sort of black Joseph Andrews, a young man of such perfection that both men and women (including his white mom) can't keep their hands off him. Vanity is a far cry from innocence — a small point that isn't understood by people who make exploitation junk like this.

Kyle Onstott's original novel was adapted for the screen by Norman Wexler and directed by Steve Carver, who may be a bad director or may simply be defeated by material that could only be contained in grand opera. Life on the old plantation was horrendous, I agree, but movies like this are less interested in information than titillation, which, in turn, reflects contemporary obsessions rather more than historical truths.

⬤

Not since "Mandingo" have I seen a film so concerned with such methods of humiliation as beating, shooting and castration.

Among the people in the film who don't look totally ridiculous are Mr. Oates; Fiona Lewis, who plays the fiancee he found in a whorehouse, and Pam Grier, who plays a stunningly beautiful slave woman.

1976 Jl 31, 11:1

FILM VIEW

VINCENT CANBY

Two Cheers for Old-Fashioned Adventure

There haven't been so many pirate movies in recent years that one can easily dismiss as ersatz a film like James Goldstone's well-meaning "Swashbuckler," which stars Robert Shaw as an 18th-century Caribbean pirate named Ned Lynch and features as his flagship an exquisite reproduction of Sir Francis Drake's Golden Hind, the vessel in which Drake sailed around the world. The decline and fall into near-extinction of the old-fashioned adventure film is probably inevitable with the increasing sophistication of children who would prefer to see "The Towering Inferno," "Earthquake" and "Young Frankenstein" to most of the children's films being turned out these days by the Walt Disney organization and others.

That decline and fall is sad indeed if, as I sometimes suspect, the place of the adventure movie has been usurped by science-fiction in theatrical films and television series. It could be just a fad but it could also mean that a humanizing if romantic sense of the past has been replaced by an obsession with the future no more profound than an automobile salesman's concern with the looks of next year's model.

If audiences don't take the past seriously, it's little wonder that moviemakers seldom do. Which is why John Huston's "The Man Who Would Be King" was such an enchanting surprise last winter—a story of high adventure and mission told absolutely straight, with respect for old conventions and with no concessions to the comedy that became the dominant method of Richard Lester's two films based on "The Three Musketeers" and seriously threatened the grand romance of his "Robin and Marian."

•   •   •

"Swashbuckler," directed by Goldstone and written by Jeffrey Bloom, would seem to want to take itself seriously as adventure and fails much in the way of a high diver who hasn't learned how to do a full gainer properly. It is willing and athletic and beautiful to look at (it was shot largely on locations near Puerto Vallarta) but it never achieves the exuberance that seemed to come naturally in films like "The Black Swan," "Captain Blood" or "The Man Who Would Be King." Everybody is trying too hard and the efforts show. Even the title, being as much a label as a title, seems to indicate that lack of security. It's as if the filmmakers were afraid of being called square and attached that title to their project in some way to disassociate themselves from such a humiliating tag. Yet, with the exception of only a couple of small details, "Swashbuckler" plays its adventure very straight. Unfortunately, it doesn't do it as well as it might.

The chief problem is the screenplay, which either wasn't good to start with or was fiddled with in the course of filming. Beau Bridges is introduced early in the movie as a dimwitted officer in the employ of the wicked governor (Peter Boyle) of Jamaica, only to disappear for so much of the rest of the movie that it comes as a total surprise when he reappears at the end. Contrary to the business of acting, where less is more, in adventure movies more is more. There isn't enough incident, or plot, in "Swashbuckler." There are two nicely spectacular battle scenes in the film, one at the beginning and one at the end (both of which I'm sure were terrifically expensive to stage in this day and age), but the middle part of the movie is just a lot of horsing around. There's some genuinely amusing stuff, including a duel fought by Ned Lynch with the highborn lady he comes to love (charmingly acted by Genevieve Bujold), but mostly you have the feeling that the director and the actors were trying to think of things to do that wouldn't send the film's budget into the stratosphere. The costs of production these days are such that we should be grateful for what we have been given, but back in the good old days, when pirate films could be made in the studio and we didn't demand the realism of Puerto Vallarta or of the partially disguised Golden Hind II, the derring-do in a pirate movie was more or less non-stop, except for those moments when Errol Flynn made his obligatory grab for Olivia De Havilland.

Which brings us to Robert Shaw in the role that Flynn or Tyrone Power or Burt Lancaster might once have played. Shaw is a fine actor, and because he always appears to be a man who thinks, considers, weighs options and probably sees the darker side of things, he makes a thoroughly bogus pirate hero, the kind of man who, above all, should give the appearance of spontaneous gallantry. Shaw doesn't, which is probably why in this movie he'd probably have been much better as the villain, a role he played with complete credibility in "Robin and Marian."

It may be a further sign of our times that I can't think of one young leading actor today who could play a pirate hero with convincing style. Dustin Hoffman? Al Pacino? Robert Redford, perhaps, but would he want to? It may be that piracy has become a lost movie art.

"The Return of A Man Called Horse," the sequel to the financially successful "A Man Called Horse," released in 1970, can, I suppose, be called an adventure film, but the methods it employs describe the differences between adventure films in the thirties, forties and fifties and now. The innocence has gone. As in the original film, Richard Harris

stars as an English aristocrat who is befriended by a tribe of Sioux Indians who call themselves the Yellow Hands. In the first movie, Harris proved himself by undergoing a ritual of purification consisting largely of bearing up through physical mutilation. In this new adventure, the aristocrat leaves England to return to the Yellow Hands who have been dispossessed by fur trappers. Before they allow him to help them he must undergo all that purification business again. In fact it's the same particular torture (small animal bones are inserted through the skin of each breast, lines are attached to the bones and he must hang from these attachments until the lines break).

The graphic details in which these initiation rites are shown seem to be the major point of the movie, and one that makes it unsuitable for anyone who is squeamish about a lack of imagination or about lovingly detailed mortification of the flesh. "The Return of A Man Called Horse" is, at heart, a variation on the tried and true formulas used by Edgar Rice Burroughs, but its emphasis on physical pain gives it a strictly contemporary S & M twist. If your kids are into bondage, they'll love it. If not, be careful.

The summer has entered its home stretch and I can think of no more than four or five films that might be recommended for children. "Swashbuckler" is okay. "Silent Movie" is fine for the Mel Brooks nuts, no matter how old, but "Murder By Death" is probably too literary for the very young. Teenagers should love the parodies in "The Big Bus," but they'll be bored by "Godzilla Versus Megalon," unless they like instant camp. "The Bingo Long Traveling All-Stars and Motor Kings" is harmless, but "Lifeguard" is not something to take your child to unless he happens to be 32 and facing a change of life. If he can read, this might well be the time to introduce him to "Ivanhoe," "A Tale of Two Cities" and "Treasure Island." There are occasions when it's best to disconnect the television set and stay home.

1976 Ag 1, II:13:1

OBSESSION, directed by Brian De Palma; screenplay by Paul Schrader, based on a story by Mr. De Palma and Mr. Schrader; executive producer, Robert S. Bremson; produced by George Litto and Harry N. Blum; music, Bernard Herrmann; director of photography, Vilmos Zsigmond; editor, Paul Hirsch; distributed by Columbia Pictures. Running time: 98 minutes. At the Coronet Theater, Third Avenue near 59th Street. This film has been rated PG.
Michael Courtland ...... Cliff Robertson
Elizabeth Courtland .. Genevieve Bujold
Sandra Portinari ...... Genevieve Bujold
Robert LaSalle .... John Lithgow
Judy .... Sylvia (Kuumba) Williams
Amy Courtland .... Wanda Blackman
Third Kidnapper ......Patrick McNamara
Inspector Brie .... Stanley J. Reyes
Farber .... Nick Kreiger
Dr. Ellman .... Stocker Fontelieu
Ferguson .... Don Hood
D'Annunzio ....Andrea Esterhazy

By VINCENT CANBY

For slightly more than half its running time, "Obsession" is an entertaining, romantic suspense film of slightly less than transcendental style, a movie conceived (but not executed) in the Hitchcock manner, scored by late Bernard Hermann with what sounds to be enough music to fill an average-sized cathedral and three movies.

Brian De Palma, the director, and Paul Schrader, the writer, have made a mistake, I suspect, in allowing "Obsession" to be identified as an hommage to Hitchcock. It puts a needless strain upon them, and upon us, who thus come to expect something more complex, more terse and more stylish than the film they've made. To be blunt, "Obsession" is no "Vertigo," Hitchcock's witty, sardonic study of obsession that did transcend its material, which wasn't all that bad to start with.

The Schrader screenplay, based on an original story by Mr. Schrader and Mr. De Palma, is most effective when it's most romantic, and transparent when it attempts to be mysterious. Constructing a satisfying mystery is like trying to make up a crossword puzzle that works in three dimensions. One little point doesn't work and the whole thing has to be done over.

Hitchcock's plot aren't always that perfect, but when they aren't he's perceptive enough to know it, and magician enough to distract our attention in a way that is even more satisfying than the identification of logic.

The plot of "Obsession" is such that you'll probably have figured out the mystery very early. No amount of subsequent red herrings can build up one's interest to its original peak. Instead of rising, it goes gently downhill to its climax.

The film, which opened yesterday at the Coronet, requires a lot of exposition to get going, and it's a measure of the movie that the exposition is more entertaining, more moving than most of the drama that follows.

•

"Obsession" is the story of an ambitious young New Orleans businessman, Michael Courtland (Cliff Robertson), who, in 1948, meets and marries the object of his dreams, Elizabeth (Genevieve Bujold), a pretty, chic young woman who shares his success. In 1959, after a party celebrating their 10th

anniversary, Elizabeth and their daughter are kidnapped and, apparently, killed when a police-backed rescue attempt fails.

The movie then cuts to 1975, when Michael, more successful than ever but obsessed by his guilt for having failed his wife and daughter, makes a business trip to Italy, where, in a church that had been a favorite of Elizabeth's, he meets a young Italian girl who is the image of his dead wife. Like the James Stewart character in "Vertigo," Michael sets out to turn the Italian girl, Sandra (also Miss Bujold), into Elizabeth.

•

Logic is not essential in a film of this sort, yet Sandra is such a sensible girl that one wonders how she can participate so wholeheartedly in this scheme of conscious self-deception. Another problem is a cosmetic one. The film, from opening credits until the end, covers almost 30 years, but Mr. Robertson, who otherwise gives one of his best performances, doesn't appear to grow older by a day. He looks serenely ageless in the eerie way of someone made up by a mortician.

Miss Bujold, an extraordinarily intelligent actress as well as a beautiful one, also does not look her best, especially as the Italian girl. This is ironic since almost everything else in the film, shot in New Orleans and Florence by Vilmos Zsigmond, is seen through romanticizing eyes that deny all imperfections.

There is another problem that is difficult to discuss without giving away the plot. I'll say only that I'm not at all sure whether the fate that eventually catches up to Michael is the result of his young-man-on-the-make stinginess or of plot details I didn't catch.

•

Making his film debut in "Obsession" is John Lithgow, a fine New York actor, who plays Michael's best friend and business partner, a fellow of old New Orleans stock that represents the culture that Michael, and all others like him, are in the process of replacing.

With "Obsession" Mr. De Palma is moving into the big time. He's a very talented director and one must be glad for him, though I still prefer those films he made on shoestrings ("Greetings," "Hi, Mom," "Sisters"), when he didn't hesitate to give a Bronx cheer to the Establishment that he now aspires to join.

•

The film has been rated PG. There is nothing terribly shocking by way of nudity, or rough language, but the kidnapping sequence might terrify small children.

1976 Ag 2, 29:1

Albert Finney and Rachel Roberts

ALPHA BETA, directed by Anthony Page, screenplay by E. A. Whitehead based on his play; produced by Timothy Burrill; edited by Tom Priestley; photographed by Charles Stewart; released by Cine III. At the Quad II and Thalia Theaters. Running time: 70 minutes. This film has not been rated.

Frank Elliot .... Albert Finney
Nora Elliot .... Rachel Roberts

By RICHARD EDER

In a sense, it is not a movie. It is a filmed play and filmed plays are usually disastrous. The camera is a restless eye and its restlessness spreads like itching powder.

"Alpha Beta," a contemporary British play about a working-class marriage, is particularly unlikely as a movie. Its two characters confine themselves to a tiny kitchen and living room and spend three acts mutilating each other with words.

But the film, which opened yesterday at the Quad II and Thalia Theaters, is a triumph in chains. The constrictions are a form of discomfort akin to hard seats in a basement theater. The penned-in camera, the talking heads, are insufficient, but it is a relative insufficiency, like that of an opera performed in concert version.

If the singers are good enough, the expedient works. And Rachel Roberts and Albert Finney are so extraordinary as the husband and wife that they make "Alpha," cinematic or not, a startling and wonderful experience.

●

There is no real plot, only a theme. It is that the breakup of a marriage is not a way out, but a playing-out of a joint agony. Inevitable and murderous at the same time, each blow wounds assailant as well as victim.

The passing of time is the dramatic device. "Alpha's" three acts, preserved in the film, take three stages of the breakup, each some five years apart.

At the beginning it is five or six years into the marriage of Frank Elliot, a clerk in a produce-shipping company, and his wife, Nora. From the start, we know exactly where they are. Her hands move quickly, it is to be hoped, incompetently, pasting up hideous white wallpaper in their living room. He stands there stolidly sipping coffee, his incipient estrangement marked equally by his failure to offer her any assistance and to remove his raincoat. He is home from work, but the raincoat is unconscious evidence that he doesn't want to be.

In this first act the despair is Frank's. He is trapped in their narrow life and as they bicker and recriminate he loathes himself for being unable to break out. In the second act he has made the break: They live together under an "arrangement" under which he is virtually a boarder, openly going out with other women. In the third act they are separated and he comes once a week to visit the children.

The agony shifts back and forth. At the end of the first act, Frank, backed into the newly-wallpapered corner, howls at his entrapment. In the second act Frank plays at self-absorbed indifferences, Nora's outrage. Here it is Nora who howls, unable to bear having her husband physically present, but absent in every other sense.

In the last act Nora sits like a stone as Frank, on his weekly visit, chatters compulsively and tidies up the slovenly mess that she has let the house become. The marriage is dead, but not the pain and as they talk there is a faint tenderness but no hope at all.

"Alpha" is unsparingly acute. It is also narrow. Nothing comes in or out the door except Frank E. A. Whitehead, the author, is isolating what may be a universal pain of marriage, but he leaves out the social context, the outside factors that may either help a marriage or destroy it move quickly. He also misses the fact that few people can be so searingly consistent in their suffering.

It is the achievement of Miss Roberts and Mr. Finney to make "Alpha" more universal than it is. Mr. Finney is wrath, anguish, hesitancy and charm in one chunky, seedy package. Miss Roberts is even better: She makes classic tragedy out of this row-house misery. There is authentic pity and terror in the final silences that succeed her first-act flutterings and her second-act vituperation.

"Alpha" is a play forced onto the screen and we see the strain clearly. It didn't have to be a movie: It could, for example, be done quite naturally on television. But the fact is that "Alpha," Miss Roberts and Mr. Finney are here as a movie and that is the only way they can be seen. And they should be seen.

1976 Ag 5, 26:1

THE OUTLAW JOSEY WALES, directed by Clint Eastwood, screenplay by Phil Kaufman and Sonia Chernus; produced by Robert Daley; based on novel "Gone to Texas" by Forrest Carter; director of photography, Bruce Surtees; edited by Ferris Webster. At the Columbia I and other Flagship Theaters. Running time: 137 minutes. This film has been rated PG.

Josey Wales .... Clint Eastwood
Lone Watie .... Chief Dan George
Terrill .... Bill McKinney
Laura Lee .... Sondra Locke
Fletcher .... John Vernon
Grandma Sarah .... Paula Trueman
Jamie .... Sam Bottoms

Each time Clint Eastwood, in "The Outlaw Josey Wales" kills some one, or is about to kill someone, or is on the verge of some other major policy decision, he spits. This is to establish the character.

Mr. Eastwood has established several pints of character by the time he rides off into the sunset fully two hours and 17 minutes after the movie begins. A number of other characters are established by devices every bit as worn and dribbly.

A hard-luck but winsome Indian girl repeatedly gets knocked off her feet or worse; a sneaky boatman cringes and leers; a spry old woman bustles about with a broom, shrills out hymns and grabs a rifle to shoot marauders; a doe-eyed young woman opens her eyes reindeer-size to convey fear, passion or bashfulness; a young follower of the outlaw manages three distinct and radiant deathbed scenes on one bullet hole.

●

The Outlaw Josey Wales," which opened yesterday at various local theaters, is a soggy attempt at a post-Civil War western epic. Josey Wales, a peaceable Missouri farmer, has his farm burned and his wife and child killed by Unionist freebooters. He joins a gang of Confederate maurauders, goes through the war—conveyed briefly by a montage of war shots—mows down a platoon of Union soldiers and flees to Texas with a price on his head and an array of vicious lawmen and bounty-hunters after him.

It is a long exodus, in the course of which Wales kills a great many people and, despite his contention that he wants to travel alone, picks up a whole variegated convoy of stock characters.

They are tedious companions on such a long trip, especially because most of them—Paula Trueman as the old woman, Sondra Locke as the doe-eyed daughter, Sam Bottoms as Wales's dying follower—overact beyond belief. Their lines don't help them. "Clouds are the dreams floating across the sky of your mind," doe-eyes tells Wales.

Will Sampson, who played the Indian in "One Flew Over the Cuckoo's Nest," and another Indian in "Buffalo Bill," does a blue-painted Navajo chieftain and gets to say, among other things: "Your words of death carry iron." Mr. Sampson has specialized in displaced-Indian roles. As a real warrior Indian he seems embarrassed.

Playing a civilized Indian who attaches himself to Wales, Chief Dan George has moments of dry humor and whole stretches of damp whimsy. Mr. Eastwood, as indicated earlier, doesn't act: he spits. He is also the director.

The movie tends to muffle and sell short whatever points it may be trying to make. There seems to be a ghost of an attempt to assert the romantic individualism of the South against the cold expansionism of the North. Every Unionist is vicious and incompetent, whereas Wales, despite his spitting, is really a perfect gentleman.

There is something cynical about this primitive one-sidedness in what is not only a historical context, but happens also to be our own historical context. To the degree a movie asserts history, it should at least attempt to do it fairly.

●

There is one attempted rape, one real rape, some virtually subliminal nudity and a lot of killing. None of it is very graphic, but the combination probably accounts for the PG rating.

RICHARD EDER

1976 Ag 5, 26:1

SURVIVE! directed by Rene Cardona, screenplay by Mr. Cardona; English adaptation by Martin Sherman; produced by Conacine and Rene Cardona Jr.; based on the book "Survive!" by Clay Blair Jr.; music by Gerald Fried; English version edited by Marshall M. Borden; a Robert Stigwood/Alan Carr presentation. Released by Paramount Pictures. At the Loews State 2 and Cine theaters. Running time: 90 minutes. This film has been rated R.

Raul Cardenas .... Pablo Ferrel
Francisco Pedraza .... Hugo Stiglitz
Mrs. Madero ....Luz Maria Aguilar
Mr. Madero ....Fernando Larranaga
Sylvia Pedraza ....Norma Lazareno

Whatever majesty of spirit —forged of ennobled will, faith and intelligence amid death and fierce adversity— enabled the survivors of an Andean airline crash four years ago to endure against all odds is nowhere to be found in "Survive!" which opened yesterday at Loew's State and Loew's Cine theaters.

The makers of this movie might be forgiven had the inextinguishable essence of humanity and the wracking issue of a survival that depended upon cannibalism eluded their talents. Artists for centuries have foundered on great themes that exceeded their grasps.

●

But in the case of "Survive!" which is based not upon Piers Paul Read's bestseller, "Alive," but upon an account by Clay Blair Jr., nobody had aspirations beyond speed and commercialism. While the film based on Mr. Read's book is still to come, the suspicion is that its arrival will establish that "Survive!" has gotten here first with the least.

Made in Mexico, "Survive!" is an irksomely dubbed film of rudimentary exposition with a sometimes tinny musical accompaniment, which attempts by aural flogging to accomplish what the script cannot: engage the intelligence or the emotions. The characters, most of them representing members of a college rugby team, are indistinguishable from one another by appearance or deed.

●

Visually, there are unnecessary scenes of protruding viscera and the lancing of an infected leg. The first butchering of the dead extends beyond the time when its point has ben made. And later scenes, including a brief shot of a flayed corpse in the mountain snow, are wholly gratuitous.

To say that "Survive" is a disaster movie is not to categorize it but to describe it.

LAWRENCE VAN GELDER

1976 Ag 5, 26:1

LET'S TALK ABOUT MEN, written and directed by Lina Wertmüller; produced by Pietro Notarianni; director of photography, Ennio Guarnieri. Released by Allied Artists. At Loews Tower East Theater. Running time: 93 minutes. This film has been rated PG.
The Man .... Nino Manfredi
The Wife (in each episode) ....Luciana Paluzzi, Milena Vukotic, Margaret Lee and Patrizia de Clara

Some authors tear up their juvenile work; others leave it for scholars. Lina Wertmüller has become a fascinating though uneven movie maker, but the public resurrection of one of her first films, made 10 years ago, is probably a mistake.

"Let's Talk About Men," which opened yesterday at Loews Tower East, consists of four vignettes linked for no apparent reason by a sequence dealing with the efforts of a man who has inadvertently locked himself out of his apartment — without clothes — to get back in.

The vignettes, cast in the form of comedy, all seek to demonstrate with underlying anger different ways in which men abuse women. In their mordancy, and in some of their particular touches, there are reflections of things that Miss Wertmüller would do later.

●

The recognition of these things is of some interest, but not enough to make most people pay money to winkle or pay them out of a collection that is three parts bad and one part mediocre.

In the first item, a profiteering businessman whose kittenish wife is a kleptomaniac, suddenly decides to make use of her proclivity when his deals turn sour. In the second, an aging knife-thrower is too vain to heed the pleas of his wife—who is also his badly scarred target—to get a new pair of glasses. The results are predictable.

In the third vignette, a husband's insistence on treating his wife as a cretin stirs her to mutiny. He puts down the mutiny—which takes the form of a complex murder plot—and thus, to his intellectual and erotic satisfaction, proves himself right.

The humor of the first vignette is thin and predictable; the grotesquerie of the knife-throwing and murder-plot vignette is leaden and trite. Nino Manfredi overacts the man's part in each of them.

In the last story, Mr. Manfredi is a farmer who spends the day woolgathering with his cronies while his wife—and theirs—do all the work. At night he comes home drunk and pleased with himself and, despite her reluctance, insists on coupling with her. The man's wastrel existence and his brutal subjection of his wife are familiar material, but Miss Wertmüller does it with some liveliness, and Mr. Manfredi's performance is reasonably convincing.

An occasional line shows some of the strength that Miss Wertmüller developed later. The notion of the knife-thrower hacking up his wife's anatomy bit by bit simply because one day he has an extra drink, another day he decides to use his left hand, and so on, is grandly horrifying. Badly acted and poorly directed, it is no more than weird. In the first vignette there is a telling monologue by the tycoon who tells his wife what it would be like to be poor. "You will grow ugly," he says. "You will grow a mustache."

●

The rating is PG. Possible reasons: two suggested but not demonstrated acts of sexual intercourse. One killing.

RICHARD EDER

1976 Ag 5, 27:1

GUS, directed by Vincent McEveety; screenplay by Arthur Alsberg and Don Nelson, based on a story by Ted Key; director of photography, Frank Phillips; music, Robert F. Brunner; film editor, Robert Stafford; produced by Ron Miller; a Walt Disney Production; distributed by Buena Vista Distribution Company. At the Festival Theater, 57th Street at Fifth Avenue; Kips Bay, Second Avenue and 31st Street; 86th Street Twin 2, at Lexington Avenue, and Loews 83d Street Triplex, on Broadway. Running time: 96 minutes. This film is classified G.
Hank Cooper............... Edward Asner
Coach Venner............... Don Knotts
Andy Petrovic............... Gary Grimes
Crankcase................... Tim Conway
Debbie Kovac........... Liberty Williams
Cal Wilson............... Dick Van Patten

By RICHARD EDER

The great mass of Walt Disney movies over the last dozen years are like airline meals. To be fair, they are like airline meals served on airlines that still make a little effort, providing a piece of fresh fruit, a tube of mustard to adorn the edible cardboard.

The point is that both Disney movies and tray lunches at 20,000 feet have one thing in common. They are not experienced, at least by adults, for their own sake. Nobody, trying to pick a lunch spot, flies to London for the sake of the in-flight pressed meat or even the apple. Very few sane adults would go see even a decently average Disney film such as "Gus" unless they needed to build up moral leverage with an underage domestic pressure group.

●

"Gus," which opened yesterday at the Kips Bay, Festival and other theaters, is about a ludicrously incompetent football team. Some of the incompetencies, such as a pass receiver who looks the other way when the ball finally arrives, are pretty funny. Finally, the team owner hires a Yugoslav mule and its Yugoslav handler.

The mule kicks field goals unerringly and the team gets to the Superbowl on the basis of field goals. This makes a man who has bet against the team very unhappy and he hires two criminals to get in the way. They get the mule drunk and kidnap first the mule handler and then the mule itself. It will destroy no potential spectator's sense of suspense to say that they fail.

●

As I say, this is a decently average Disney film, with a few funny parts and other parts where you would agree to smile if you could. Where the movie tries the hardest, it fails the most, as in a terribly long and trite comedy sequence in a supermarket.

There is a good performance by Edward Asner as the sulphuric team owner and a very good one by Don Knotts as his shrivelled chief coach.

1976 Ag 7, 11:2

FILM VIEW

WALTER GOODMAN

The Man Who Would Be Hitchcock

Like other dramatic forms, the suspense film has its conventions, and like all conventions, these may be ignored or defied by a master, but woe be to the mere journeyman who fails to give them their due. One basic convention calls for a careful balance between the commonplace and the unlikely. Scaring a movie audience is not much of a trick; an assortment of freakish shapes and shadows and sudden screechy sounds can do it. But only when evil intrudes upon ordinary life are deeper reverberations set off. Consider the exemplary scene in the late Fritz Lang's "M," when the horror of the murder of a child—which the audience knows is taking place—is subtly suggested, is slowly created without a touch of violence, as the camera focuses on the mother, waiting with increasing anxiety for her daughter to come home for lunch.

Suspense films are not by nature "realistic." They almost have to be far-fetched—yet never so far-fetched that the viewer loses belief and turns off. A director may, to be sure, try for fantasy, but that is a separate line, with different conventions. At its best, the straight suspense movie introduces evil into our lives for an hour, and compels us to cope with it in some way even as we enjoy it.

But what is a filmmaker to do when he must work with a script that fails to maintain that balance, that overwhelms reality with fabrications, that requires for fullest appreciation a suspension not just of disbelief but of all the viewer's positive faculties as well? Such was the problem confronting Brian De Palma with "Obsession," inspired, he has audaciously announced, by Alfred Hitchcock's "Vertigo." De Palma should know, for in addition to directing, he concocted the plot in cahoots with Paul Schrader.

●   ●   ●

The tale begins in 1959, with the kidnapping of the wife and 10-year-old daughter of a rich New Orleans real estate developer. Instead of paying off the kidnappers, the husband-father calls in the police and, unfortunately for everyone and not least the audience, the victims are lost.

The opening sequences, though improbable, move fast—a quality which the viewer has plenty of time to appreciate during the ensuing hour. This is devoted to the development of the developer's relationship, 16 years after the kidnapping, with a young girl, the spitting image of his late wife, whom he picks up in the very church in Florence where they met. There are hints aplenty from the outset that we are in for some hanky-panky, and no alert mystery fan will

239

fail to catch the identity and motive of the villain, but it's hard to stay alert as the hero's obsession with his late wife turns into love for the girl and their autumn-spring romance drags along for an excrutiating season.

Given a plot that is at once incredible and tedious and characters who are blanks, De Palma resorts to the picturesque. He places his actors in glowing exteriors and sumptuous interiors. His camera, indulgently handled by Vilmos Zsigmond, dotes upon weathered walls and narrow alleys and arches and curving stairways and candlelight and chandeliers and stained glass, often to the accompaniment of a noisy score by the late Bernard Hermann, featuring a band of crazed choristers who go absolutely ape at the sight of a church. If a plane takes off, be assured it will be before a sky streaked by the setting sun. If a gun comes into play, it will be shining silver, taken from the drawer of a desk of burnished wood. If a pair of scissors is required for a stabbing, it will glisten. The De Palma touch fights reality at every point.

When he is not performing travelogue tricks, De Palma relies on star power—Cliff Robertson and Genevieve Bujold drinking deep of one another's eyes—the deepest-drinking eyes you've ever seen; it's a wonder the couple doesn't drown. Robertson is a competent actor within his range, which goes

Bujold and Robertson in "Obsession" —"star power of about 40 watts"

from mild preoccupation to slight indigestion. Bujold is very attractive. The two together generate a star power of about 40 watts.

To compare Alfred Hitchcock, even at his second or third best, with Brian De Palma is not fair sport; it's like putting Muhammad Ali in the ring with Andy Warhol. But De Palma or his publicists have been asking for it, telling interviewers that Hitchcock is his "model". Granted, the Master has employed some of the elements that De Palma employs here. Hitchcock has often played out his tales in exotic settings—but he has typically used the settings to heighten the menace to his characters or to establish a sense of place or of mood, not to divert the audience from the plot. He has not been above plugging into star-power—when he has been lucky or shrewd enough to be working with the likes of Grant and Bergman, Stewart and Kelly. Hitchcock has been properly criticized for overusing the device of having an innocent caught up in machinations beyond his ken, reducing it to a formula, yet even at his weakest, he invariably brings wit to his work, the idiosyncracy that sets a character apart, the throwaway joke, the odd cameo, the playing off his own reputation. Even when he starts with a hokey idea, such as in his recent "Family Plot," he manages to keep things cracking by sheer ingenuity.

To say that "Obsession" is wanting in wit is more courtesy than criticism. This movie takes itself so seriously that just when one ought to be gasping with surprise at the climactic turns on screen, one finds oneself chuckling at the exertions of the moviemakers—fuzzy pictures, wavy pictures, slow motion pictures, and, inevitably, the up-to-the-minute stop-action picture, all put to the service of a preposterous denoument. Whatever shred of credibility the movie retains is dispersed by the final, dead-serious directorial hocus-pocus.

Alfred Hitchcock has been Hollywood's champ tightwirewalker and juggler for a long time. Now Brian De Palma clumps ambitiously onto the wire and has a difficult time just staying there, never mind the juggling. The main suspense about "Obsession" is what Hitchcock is cooking up for De Palma as punishment for dragging his name into this shaky enterprise.

1976 Ag 8, II:11:1

THE SHOOTIST, directed by Don Siegel; screenplay by Miles Hood Swarthout and Scott Hale based on novel by Glendon Swarthout; produced by M. J. Frankovich and William Self; director of photography, Bruce Surtees; music by Elmer Bernstein; edited by Robert Boyle. Released by Paramount. At the Astor Plaza. Running time 100 minutes. This movie has been rated PG.

J. B. Books	John Wayne
Bond Rogers	Lauren Bacall
Gillom Rogers	Ron Howard
Dr. Hostetler	James Stewart
Sweeney	Richard Boone
Pulford	Hugh O'Brian
Cobb	Bill McKinney

By RICHARD EDER

After the climactic shootout the lone survivor marches out of the cafe into the sun's slanting light. It is a beautiful shot, hazy and golden, but it is all wrong. The shootout, we are told, takes place just before noon.

This is pretty symptomatic of the trouble with "The Shootist," third in a wave of geriatric Westerns that have afforded new employment for the wrinkles and creases of John Wayne. It is not so much a question of dishonesty as of a confusion of purposes. Eleven A.M. is a taut High-Noonish time for a showdown, but things look much prettier in the late afternoon. So you have both.

Don Siegel, the director, has used an ironic story about the new and old West, written by Glendon Swarthout, for his own unfocused purposes. Sometimes these run along the same lines of irony and incongruity as the book. Sometimes they are softened or speeded up, either for sentiment or for a traditional Western brand of excitement. The iron comes straight and coated in molasses.

This is not to say that "The Shootist" is a bad picture. It is often funny. It is sometimes telling. And John Wayne, James Stewart and Lauren Bacall all possess that particular mystery of performance that allows them to touch us even when they are ridiculous. But Mr. Siegel's lack of form and fidelity to his own story means that as the movie proceeds, even those things that are charming turn to lead.

With a grizzled mustache, an aged nose and a big stomach, and looking more like a conductor on the old New Haven Railroad than any kind of Western hero, J.B. Books (Mr. Wayne) rides into town. In his prime as a lawman he gunned down 30 villains. What he is after, though, this day in 1902, is medical advice.

He has a backache, he tells the doctor. The doctor —James Stewart, old but apple-voiced — tells him he has terminal cancer. He settles down in a rooming house under an assumed name and waits to die peaceably.

He isn't a peaceable man, though. And the town, which has telephones, sewers, and horsedrawn tramcars, won't let him alone. He represents both the threat and the glamour of the violent past. A young boy adopts him as a hero-figure, a number of old badmen try to kill him, but most of the citizens of the new century figure him for a profit. A sleazy reporter wants to write his memoirs; an old girl friend wants to marry him; an undertaker wants to handle his funeral; a barber sells his hair trimmings.

The doctor, seeing the physical agony that awaits Books, hints diffidently that that he should kill himself. With no diffidence at all the town marshal—grossly overacted by Harry Morgan—gives the same advice, seeing in Books's presence a threat to peace and quiet.

Books devises his own solution — a shootout with three of the region's most sinister characters. The film's irony runs best and sharpest as he prepares himself for battle. He puts on his best suit — newly drycleaned — gets a haircut, orders a tombstone, and heads for the rendezvous. Not by horse, though: by tramcar.

That scene, funny and terrible, is the best thing in the movie. The medical consultation between the aged Messrs. Wayne and Stewart is poignant and near-devastating, though the reasons probably lie less in the film than in our own associations with the two actors. There is a lovely scene where Mr.

Ron Howard and John Wayne in a scene from the motion picture, directed by Don Siegel

Wayne goes for a buggy ride with his landlady — Lauren Bacall—their mutual decrepitude bundled beneath a lap-robe.

These are the film's best points. Its weaknesses drag them down. None of the characters have any real precision, and after the first impact they wither. The attitude of Books toward his own passing—the crucial point in the whole structure —is quite unclear. Is the extinction of his own violent way of life something he accepts or resists? Mr. Siegel allows him to point both ways, and the ambiguity takes the bone out of the movie and it collapses.

"Shootist," which opened yesterday at the Astor Plaza, is rated PG. There is limited violence in the picture, but handled with perfectly good taste.

1976 Ag 12, 38:1

THE RITZ, directed by Richard Lester; screenplay by Terrence McNally, based upon his play; produced by Denis O'Dell; photographed by Paul Wilson; music by Ken Thorne. At the Cinema I. Running time: 91 minutes. This movie has been rated R.

Gaetano Proclo	Jack Weston
Googie Gomez	Rita Moreno
Carmine Vespucci	Jerry Stiller
Vivian Proclo	Kaye Ballard
Chris	F. Murray Abraham
Claude	Paul B. Price
Michael Brick	Treat Williams

By RICHARD EDER

WHEN TERRENCE McNally's "The Ritz," opened on Broadway early last year, the critics and public liked it well enough to give it more than a year's run. It was a farce that laid claim to roughly the same patch of mania the Marx Brothers used to tear up: a scramble of mistaken identities, non sequiturs and people not so much *in* the wrong beds as under them.

It was hung upon a gimmick—a man takes refuge from his murderous brother-in-law inside a bathhouse full

of homosexuals in full orgy— and the gimmick was the occasion for most of the jokes. As a farce though, despite the bumps and caperings, it had an essentially abstract spirit. It didn't dwell on the homosexuality, either the sentiment or the mechanics, any more than a sex farce actually dwells on sex.

In making a movie out of "The Ritz," Mr. McNally and his director, Richard Lester, have succumbed to the failing that has tended to go with screen adaptations of stage comedies ever since the 1930's, when they knew how to do such things. The bubbles don't disappear; on the contrary, they refuse to disappear as proper bubbles should. They are plotted, fixed, sprayed with lacquer.

Still, there are a lot of funny jokes. Most of the principal performers are the same as in the Broadway show, and they are at least serviceably amusing. Rita Moreno, as the female singing star at the bathhouse Saturday night entertainments, is comically incandescent. "The Ritz," which opened yesterday at the Cinema I, might have been a cheerfully lumpy affair. A fallen soufflé can still taste reasonably good, especially if you're hungry and eat it with bread.

And in this sense it does work to some degree. But if the farce suffers mainly from wearing lead shoes, the homosexual gimmick suffers from something more serious.

To have a tolerance, or even an acceptance of homosexuality doesn't rule out having an underlying physical distaste for it. Inevitably perhaps, the camera emphasizes the physical element far more than it was emphasized on the stage. To put it bluntly, it shoves up too close —for most of us, I think—too much pale flesh organized around unshared intentions. There are simply too many male homosexual stomachs,

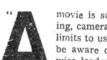

Rita Moreno and Jack Weston in "The Ritz"

arms and faces at too short a range.

•

It spoils the picture. But it is only fair to point out a number of good things that remain in it. There are, as I have said, the jokes. The lineup of weird characters checking into the baths, the fugitive son-in-law among them, is lively and amusing. I particularly like the son-in-law's assumption—he is from out of town—that at such a sleazy establishment he can pay by check. And the fact that—as tends to happen in New York—such an outrageous assumption works.

The acting is often more energetic than funny; particularly in the case of Jack Weston as the fat, puffing son-in-law. On the other hand, Treat Williams is good as a shrill-voiced detective, and F. Murray Abraham manages some comic depth as one of the bathhouse regulars.

1976 Ag 13, C12:4

FUTUREWORLD, directed · by Richard Heffron, written by Mayo Simon and George Schenck; executive producer, Samuel Z. Arkoff; photographed by Howard Schwartz; music by Fred Karlin; edited by James Mitchell. Released by American International Pictures. At showcase theaters. Running time: 104 minutes. This film has been rated PG.

Chuck Browning	Peter Fonda
Tracy Ballard	Blythe Danner
Duffy	Arthur Hill
Gunslinger	Yul Brynner
Schneider	John Ryan
Harry	Stuart Margolin

By RICHARD EDER

"Futureworld" is a film about robots and, evidently, for robots. It is as much fun as running barefoot through Astroturf.

A sequel to "Westworld," the film once again deals with a skeptical reporter who uncovers dirty doings in a great pleasure garden of the future known as Delos.

If they pay a great deal of money, people can go to Delos (by Laker Airways, apparently—a dubious plug in view of what eventually happens there) and live a fantasy life in one of its sections. These are devoted respectively to recreating the Old West, the Middle Ages and space travel. Robots looking exactly like real people provide a variety of services: sex, for instance, or convincing-looking Indians or knights for the clients to kill.

In the earlier film the reporter discovered that some defect in circuitry was causing the robots to kill the customers. In "Futureworld," which opened yesterday at showcase theaters, the same reporter, Chuck Browning, goes back and discovers something far worse: a plot to use the facilities of Delos to get control of all the important people in the world.

•

Browning and his sidekick, Tracy Ballard, go to Delos, accompanied by a planeload of important prospective vic-

tims: a Russian general, an Arab sheik, an influential Japanese. The latter plunge into the fun — the Russian imagines himself a czarist general, the Japanese, a knight-in-armor-with-camera —while Browning and Ballard investigate the plumbing.

After lots of running and hot-breathed pursuit the pair discover what the viewer discovered at least a half-hour earlier: that all these world-leader types are being killed and look-alike robots are being returned in their place. This, as one scientist explains, allows them to be operated by remote-control in the interests of world peace and reason.

•

It is all the most ordinary kind of hardware science fiction, full of computers and empty of thought. It features miles and miles of tubes and pipes and valves and as Tracy—who otherwise mostly says "Let's get out of here"—intelligently observes: "It is about as exciting as a visit to the waterworks."

As the manager of the place, Arthur Hill mugs sleek villainy. Blythe Danner, as Tracy, and Peter Fonda as Chuck have absolutely nothing to do. Starring in "Futureworld" must be the actor's equivalent of going on welfare.

•

The film is rated PG. Parents are advised that there is nothing offensive in it. Offensiveness would help.

1976 Ag 14, 10:1

FILM VIEW

RICHARD EDER

THERE'S A GREAT DEAL MORE TO ACTING THAN MAKING FACES

"A movie is such a tangled entity—direction, writing, camera-work, acting, editing—that there are limits to useful critical dissection. It's possible to be aware of superior photography in an otherwise leaden movie, but often it simply adds to the pain: visual magnificence draped over a dwarf.

Can a director make a good film out of a terrible script? Not really. He can make a good film from a script which in its previous life as a novel may have had little value, but that's not the same thing. It must have shape, purpose, and a fine speaking detail. Or else it must have holes in the right places so that the rare director capable of writing with his camera can supply these elements.

As for acting, its quality or, at any rate, its effect is particularly dependent upon other factors. A screen actor is even more vulnerable to bad lines than a stage actor, who at least can mumble or throw them away. Screen mumbling comes under the category of a grand directorial effect, and lines are almost never thrown away.

• • •

Furthermore, a stage actor can increase or decrease intensity by increasing or decreasing timbre and volume or, visually, by moving down or up stage. A screen actor is more constricted and must depend to a large degree upon the camera—long-shot, medium shot, close-up—to vary the intensity. A reasonably good performance by Philippe Noiret in "The Old Gun" was ruined beyond hope because the camera was kept full upon his face, never lightening its regard. In effect, the camera made him overact.

This said, the most striking cinematic feature of these last soggy weeks has been several spectacular acting performances. There were Rachel Roberts and Albert Finney gutting their marriage and each other in "Alpha Beta." There was the marvelous emotional precision and balance of M. Noiret— this time beautifully complemented by his director, Bernard Tavernier, in "The Clockmaker."

So, with an otherwise dull movie season, it is an appropriate time to talk about film acting. Before getting to the successes, though, it may be useful to go into some of the failures, of which there is always a plentiful supply. In fact, this space being limited, and out of respect for the movie tradition of a cheerful ending, I will talk about the failures first, and leave the triumphs for next week.

As Hamlet told the Players (passionate assertion of the obvious can be an early sign of a mind cracking), bad acting consists of doing either too much or too little. This is true of movie acting, although the proportions are different than on the stage.

For a first example, take last week's long and thoroughly mediocre western, "The Outlaw Josey Wales." The script, alternating between the whimsical and the portentous, casts Clint Eastwood, the outlaw, as an archetype of romantic individualism. He fights a last-ditch stand against the victorious forces of the Union, and retreats to live side by side with the Indians in the southwest.

While secondary characters mug and chatter around him, Mr. Eastwood keeps a total impassivity. Now impassivity can work beautifully on the screen—it rarely does on the stage—but it must be a cover for something else. The camera sees force as an infra-red device sees heat. It can be the force of thought—we see Liv Ullmann thinking in a Bergman film—or the force of emotion, but it must be there. In his best cowboy days John Wayne cultivated impassivity, occasionally broken by a great grin, but what he projected was a ferocious yearning. Mr. Eastwood's one expressive device, a solemn spitting, does not compensate for the fact that he seems to be thinking and feeling nothing, and therefore is all but invisible to the camera. What Stanislavski preached about emotional authenticity the camera enforces.

* * *

Another failure-by-insufficiency can be seen in the screen version of Terrence McNally's "The Ritz." There is a great deal wrong with "The Ritz," even though it has a lot of funny lines but here I would mention the performance of Jack Weston, as the garbageman from Cleveland who takes refuge in a bathhouse full of manic homosexuals.

Mr. Weston is a perfectly agreeable clown. His rotund double and triple takes, his explosive distress might have been enough for broad comic effect on a stage. But again, the camera needs more. Movie clowns must think and feel as well as perform; the camera must be able to register the moral as well as the material consequences of the banana peel. As with Keaton, Chaplin, W. C. Fields. Hardy would have been intolerable without a tender-hearted Laurel. The Marx Brothers would have been sheer noise if the lunatic madness of Groucho and Chico had not been balanced by Harpo's sweet lunar intervals.

Mental and emotional insufficiency is the commonest form of poor movie acting. To be fair to the actors, the aimlessness and foolishness of most movie scripts are partly responsibile. Excessive acting is less common nowadays, but two examples of it can be seen in "The Return of a Man Called Horse."

I liked a good deal in this movie about an English gentleman who goes to live and fight with a tribe of Indians. Irvin Kershner, the director, sought to emphasize the mystical and ritual aspects of the Indians' life. Although it is overlong and overblown—the Parsifal-like music is unbearable—I believe Mr. Kershner has often succeeded extraordinarily well. The opening massacre is a heart-rending masterpiece. The director concentrates on the fleeing, terrified women and children, on the smoke and confusion; and brings back memories of the most tragic Vietnam War footage.

Mr. Kershner's camera draws strength from its long meditations on the faces of the Indians. Not, though, from the faces of the two principal actors, Richard Harris and Gale Sondergaard. Miss Sondergaard is cast as an old Indian squaw. It is not that she is a bad actress, but in trying to catch the slow impassivity possessed by the real Indians in the cast she forces her face in a fashion a camera will not tolerate. Her mouth wants to move, she compresses it, we see the compression; the effect is that of a jawful of novocaine.

The bad actor is Mr. Harris, and his badness does more than any other single thing to spoil the movie. His error is doing too much, screwing his face up into expressions that might have projected across the stage but overload the screen.

When Mr. Harris, still back in England, wants to convey the notion that he is musing about his memories of his first visit to the Indian tribe, he applies musing like make-up. When he comes upon the ruined remains of his tribe's settlement, he applies horror. In a critical situation he casts his eyes upward.

* * *

Instead of simply feeling things, he instructs his face to react to them. We see the instructions. The long initiation scene is hard to bear, but not mainly because of the ritual mutilation. (This, I thought, was handled well. It was painful to watch but it was not gratuitous.)

It is Mr. Harris's mutilation of his own features that hurts: he bulges his eyes, he lets his mouth gape open. Mr. Harris doesn't know that a large part of human pain is borne with a still face, not from bravery but from weariness. But the camera knows it, and tells us.

1976 Ag 15, II:13:1

Harris in "Horse"—"His badness does more than any other single thing to spoil the movie."

Reheated Sex Comedy at Little Carnegie

"Lovers and Other Relatives" is a poorly reheated Italian sex comedy.

A few years ago Salvatore Samperi made a very popular film, "Malizia," about the love affair—half mutual seduction, half moral blackmail—of a 14-year-old boy and his family's beautiful young housekeeper. It was not a great film, but it possessed both humor and sensual force.

•

"Lovers" is an attempt by the same director to cash in on the same theme. In this case the relationship develops between a boy and his sister-in-law. The whole family is on holiday at the beach and the boy's older brother—the sister-in-law's husband—is away most of the week in the city.

As in "Malizia," the peripheral aspects of the story, the details of the life of an upper bourgeois Italian family, are often funny. There is an engaging effort by the father, a retired general, to assassinate his wife's pestilent lapdog. A small, bespectacled boy whose sandcastles are continually smashed by the beach strong-man manages a comically neat revenge.

But the main story is a stale, mechanical and quite

The Cast

LOVERS AND OTHER RELATIVES, directed by Salvatore Samperi; screenplay (Italian with English subtitles) by Ottavio Jemma and Allessandro Parenzo; produced by Silvio Clementelli; released by Crystal Pictures Inc. At the Little Carnegie Theater, 57th Street, east of Seventh Avenue. Running time: 98 minutes. This film is classified R.
Young Wife ....Laura Antonelli
Sandro ....Alessandro Momo
Renzo ....Orazio Orlando
Mother ....Lilla Brignone
Giustino ....Tino Carraro
Contessa ....Monica Guerritore
Beachboy ....Lino Toffolo

unconvincing imitation of the action in "Malizia." Mr. Samperi has used the same actors: the late Alessandro Momo (he died in a motorcycle crash) and Laura Antonelli.

•

Mr. Momo does the same petulant, glowering act that he used last time. Then it seemed motivated: this time it is just monotonous. Miss Antonelli is tremendously sexy, but her part is written flatly and without logic. The love scenes are veiled and droopy: both participants look tired.

"Lovers" is playing at the Little Carnegie Cinema.

RICHARD EDER

1976 Ag 16, 40:1

ODE TO BILLY JOE, directed by Max Baer, written by Herman Raucher; produced by Mr. Baer and Roger Camras; director of photography, Michel Hugo; edited by Frank Morris. Released by Warner Bros. At Loews State II, U.A. Columbia I and other theaters. Running time: 108 minutes. This movie has been rated PG.

Billy Joe McAllister.........Robby Benson
Bobbie Lee Hartley.....Glynnis O'Connor
Anna Hartley................Joan Hotchkis
Glenn Hartley.............Sandy McPeak
Dewey Barksdale...........James Best
James Hartley..........Terence Goodman

By RICHARD EDER

"Ode to Billy Joe" is a movie to lament. Its authors have ruined it. To say so is praise as well as regret. You can only ruin something that has some quality to begin with, and for more than half its length this Southern country romance has a quite individual kind of life and shrewdness.

This first part also has its flaws. Sometimes it is cute where it's supposed to be funny, and sometimes it is soft where it's supposed to be lush. It is too heavily apparent that the director is pleased with what he's doing, and his breath all but fogs the camera. But he has some reason to be pleased, if only he would step back a little. Instead, after an hour or so, he steps forward, grabs his movie with both hands and sinks it.

•

A decade ago the singer Bobby Gentry brought out a song about a Mississippi Delta boy called Billy Joe McAllister who jumped off a Tallahatchie River bridge and died. The song was oblique: It didn't say why he jumped. It hinted at but didn't specify a relationship between Billy Joe and the girl singer/protagonist. Tens of thousands teen-agers stayed up late arguing the gaps.

Max Baer, the director, has extended the song into a two-hour film. Its virtue lies in the setting-out of the two characters — Billy Joe and a girl named Bobby —their timid and then more demanding courtship, the families, the rural background. Its failure comes when Mr. Baer tries to stuff these two, with all their liveliness and appeal, into the song, and invents an answer to the mystery that is grotesquely out of keeping with the life he has established up to then.

The story develops in a perfectly familiar and conventional way. Bobby is the daughter of a hard-working cotton farmer, a strict, religious man saved from dourness by a wary charm and a ghost of humor. These leavening characteristics save him from being simply a stock figure. Here, as in other places, the writing is partly responsible; and so is the impressive acting of the character, played by Sandy McPeak.

•

Bobby is courted by a neighbor boy, an eager, grandiloquent, charming youth who seems to sprout in all directions at once. "He keeps popping up and introducing himself," Bobby's father complains; and at another point, when Billy Joe has come up after church in touching finery—a ginger suit and white shoes, "they look like he's been kicking vanilla ice cream."

The young people are tormented by their pull toward each other. Again, Mr. Baer's writing and the ability of the two actors make it something more than a sentimental cliché: There is. an apt balancing of love and lust.

The two collide with each other, with the grownups around them, with the traditions of their setting. The setting is splendidly done at times; overdone at others. Mr. Baer and his cameraman have captured heat, the sheen of perspiration on the skin, the oppressive greenery, the blue-black stormclouds of the Delta country. They work dramatically as well as pictorially.

This first part develops with an attractive balance of humor, sympathy and perceptive characterization; marred but not invalidated by sentimentality and excessiveness. Glynnis O'Connor, as long as the lines allow, is rebellious, thoughtful and funny as Bobby. Robby Benson, playing Billy Joe, manages his boisterous, wooly-headed role with great charm.

•

But Mr.Baer wants to get the song in, and so Billy Joe has to jump off the bridge. The reason given for his doing so is, as I say, totally arbitrary and without any logical or emotional relation to what has gone before. It drains all the momentum from the film and turns it into ridiculous melodrama.

And after all this comes a long, fatuous epilogue in which Bobby explains that she will keep the real reason for Billy's jump a secret, so as not to spoil the legend. What legend? He has only just finished drowning. The movie drowned some time earlier.

•

The movie is rated PG. Some of the scenes between the lovers are explicit, though emotionally rather than physically. In addition, the rating may rest on the discussion of the particular sexual problem that led to Billy Joe's jump.

1976 Ag 19, 48:1

CORRECTION

In a review of the film "Ode to Billy Joe" in The Times yesterday, a reference was made to Max Baer as the author of the screenplay. Mr. Baer was the director; the screenplay was written by Herman Raucher.

1976 Ag 20, B1:7

'Gumball Rally' Is Film That Loses Own Race

By RICHARD EDER

When the code word "gumball" is passed by a rich young man, two housewives, two stage Englishmen, one Italian Lothario, one bug-eyed motorcyclist a couple of Texans, a girly-magazine model and other assorted types converge upon a New York garage.

"The Gumball Rally," which opened yesterday at the Rivoli, Eastside Cinema and other theaters, opens with a familiar effort at comical mystery. It goes mildly well until the mystery is revealed about a quarter of an hour after the movie starts. All those people are meeting to see which pair can drive a car fastest, in disregard of speed limits and other traffic regulations, from New York to California.

•

After they all start off, and once you get used to the rather handsome speeding-car effects, which is soon, the movie seems to be nothing but one long exhaust pipe. There is only so much that can be done with scenes of cars passing each other.

Some diversions are at-

The Cast

THE GUMBALL RALLY, produced and directed by Chuck Bail; screenplay by Leon Capetanos based on a story by Mr. Capetanos and Mr. Bail; director of photography, Richard C. Glouner; music by Dominic Frontiere. Released by Warner Bros. At the Rivoli, Eastside Cinema and other theaters. Running time: 107 minutes. This film has been rated PG.
Michael Bannon........Michael Sarrazin
Roscoe ....Normann Burton
Gibson ....Gary Busey
Preson ....John Durren
Alice ....Susan Flannery
Lapchick ....Harvey Jason
Kandinsky ....Steven Keats
Franco ....Raul Julia

tempted. The Italian—painlessly played by Raul Julia—keeps stopping to seduce pretty women that he spots along the way. The housewives stop to be seduced. A lot of policemen show up at various points, and all make amiable fools of themselves.

People who pay money to see this effort to find knee-slappers in the 55 mile-an-hour speed limit will also make amiable fools of themselves.

•

The movie is rated PG, for parental guidance. Despite the seductions, all but unseen, it should be harmless for any child who has not had a parent, brother or sister killed or injured in a highway accident.

1976 Ag 21, 13:1

FILM VIEW

RICHARD EDER

And Now for Some Good Actors

Performing and acting have a lot in common—acting is, in part, performing—but there is an important distinction. The essence of performance is delivering a blow. The essence of acting is receiving it. Listening, registering, reacting: these are the heart of stage acting. Never mind the soliloquy; actors must deliver them, of course, but what we remember of actors is not so much the winds they create as the wind they bend to. That is why Hamlet is such an ungrateful role; he reacts to nothing except a ghost and his own insides.

What is true for the stage is even truer for the screen. Movies are about results more than about actions. An example, offered with apology for its obviousness: A war scene may consist of shots both of the soldier with the gun and his target, but the scene's impact lies with the view of the victim staggering and falling, not of the man pulling the trigger.

We think of Bogart as a figure who does something. But the essence of Bogart was his eyes hooding, his head bobbing as Peter Lorre tried to convince him that the moon was made of green cheese and could be sold advantageously in Bucharest.

Last week, discussing examples of bad or non-acting in recent movies, we mentioned the need for the screen actor

Noiret in "The Clockmaker"
—"His intensity is total."

to show that he or she is thinking and listening. With the several instances of splendid acting that follow, this thinking, listening, receiving aspect is particularly important.

Take a small example, first of all. The weaknesses of "The Ritz," a screen version of the stage comedy about a man taking refuge in a bathhouse patronized by homosexuals, have been spelled out by this and other reviewers. It contained a profusion of uninteresting or only mildly interesting performances, notably one by Jack Weston as the hapless heterosexual refugee. There was a very good performance by Rita Moreno as a singing spit-cat. It was performing, not acting.

But there was also a moment of real acting by one of the cast, F. Murray Abramson. Mr. Abramson was one of the bathhouse queens, and for part of the time he puts on a broad and campy performance replete with eyeshadow, strings of beads and floating veils. But in the latter part of the film, as a kind of middleman in the parade of double-takes and mistaken identities, he changes. He becomes the quizzical quiet center of the mock storm: as Mr. Weston booms and Jerry Stiller rants, Mr. Abramson swivels. He is the weird, impassive spectator whose face, moving left-to-right and right-to-left, proclaims the tennis match. It was not a big thing, but it helped a great deal.

We have seen better movies this year than "Alpha Beta" but, with the possible exception of Liv Ullmann's work in "Face to Face," no acting to match the extraordinary duel between Albert Finney and Rachel Roberts.

It is nothing but warfare from beginning to end, this harrowing breakup of a working-class marriage, and enclosed within the space of two rooms. But it is not just the gunfire—if it were, it would be simply two bravura bits of declamation and we couldn't stand it. It is the misfires, the pauses, the false truces, the evacuations, the resupplying, even the war jokes.

Rachel Roberts, her long upper lip lifting and falling like a barometer of internal weather, alternates between quick, optimistic movements as she papers a wall or pulls out a birthday present, and the leaden gestures with which she butters a huge stack of sandwiches while screaming at her husband. Albert Finney, chunky, working-class, with an untutored intellectual hunger, suddenly takes on a physical lightness as he delivers a naïve, moving critique on the institution of marriage. His tension eases, as if theorizing were a rest from the specifics of battle; a soldier discussing Clause-

Finney and Roberts in "Alpha Beta'—Theirs is an "extraordinary duel."

witz in the foxhole.

At one point, they attack each other physically. As they thrash on the floor, each conveys a specific and differing emotion. She claws toward him, not so much aiming to strike as with the gesture of someone trying to tear back possessions scattering in the wind. He hits out, this big man, with tiny mincing blows, as if trying to rid himself of a clinging horror.

• • •

But some of the most telling acting comes when one or the other is not doing or saying something but registering the effect of what is being done or said. Each, attacking, falters and breaks. When he tells her he wants a separation, she, having snatched up her purse to storm out of the room, looks at it as if she didn't recognize it and puts it very slowly back on the table. His self-assurance collapses when she tells him she was on the point of poisoning herself and their two children. The war is total, and yet their awareness of each other is total: It is the ability of the two to register this awareness so constantly that gives greatness to their acting.

And of all the particular achievements the single most grand is silence and motionlessness. Miss Roberts, after her husband has left and comes back only for weekly visits, is destroyed. Up to then she moved and talked constantly. Now she spends her time sunk into an armchair, speaking in monosyllables, chin in hand, one finger playing continually on her mouth. Her face has become a boneyard.

Splendid acting of a very different kind can be seen in Bernard Tavernier's "The Clockmaker." As in any good French film, the actors are so tangible and natural that instead of being cast in their roles they seem to have been harvested from them.

The star is Philippe Noiret as the cautious, thoughtful, comfortable clockmaker whom life gets at through his one vulnerable point: his revolutionary son. The son commits a murder and disappears, and suddenly the whole world—seen by Mr. Tavernier in radical, disaffected terms—seems to crash in on the father. The instruments of state and social power—the police and the press—try to enlist him. He reacts and wavers and reflects until at the end this deliberate man has identified himself deliberately with his son and his son's cause.

M. Noiret, stout, slow, with a long, mournful face, builds his role around his own internal processes. At an early convivial scene with friends in a restaurant the others eat; he seems, rather, to be digesting. After the murder everyone—police, reporters, friends—press ideas and advice on him. He listens, and says little, and lies heavily on his back in bed to think. As if it were a pregnancy, you see him growing and

swelling with his new belief: that instead of being on the side of society he must be on the side of its rebels.

Out of this waiting and listening, his actions gather dramatic force. Indolent, he begins to take walks. In an access of fury, he pursues and beats up two men who have broken his shop window. He has lived by his stomach—the movie is set in Lyons, which is France's stomach—and with small gestures he begins to push away plates of food. Each rejected sausage is an act of dissidence.

Finney and Roberts use a wide range of gesture and color and volume. Noiret uses a very subdued range. Yet, in each case the intensity, directed inward before coming out in particular tones and actions, is total. And the camera, built to see such things, reveals it.

1976 Ag 22, II:11:1

GATOR, directed by Burt Reynolds, written by William Norton; produced by Jules V. Levy and Arthur Gardner; edited by Harold Kress; director of photography, William A. Fraker. Released by United Artists. At the Criterion and other theaters. Running time: 116 minutes. This film has been rated PG.

Gator McCluskey	Burt Reynolds
Irving Greenfield	Jack Weston
Agie Maybank	Lauren Hutton
Bama McCall	Jerry Reed
Emmeline Cavanaugh	Alice Ghostley
Mayor Caffrey	Dub Taylor

By RICHARD EDER

Three years ago a movie called "White Lightning" told the story of a moonshiner, Gator McCluskey, who was let out of jail so that he could catch some real crooks.

Now there is a sequel called "Gator." Again the moonshiner comes out of jail and is set to catch even worse crooks. Again he is played by Burt Reynold, as bland and wholesome as talcum powder and about as interesting.

•

"White Lightning" sold well and that was obviously the reason for taking it up again. There doesn't seem to be much of any other reason. It is not a terrible picture, and it has

some good things in it. But it proceeds like a sleepwalker, perpetually waking and wondering what it is doing, and falling asleep and doing it some more.

Gator, preparing to go back to his illegal still in a Southern swamp, is taken under the fat and bumbling wing of a Federal agent from New York. He is pressured into going to work for a vicious and sadistic thug, Bama McCall, who runs a neighboring county, police, prostitutes and all; the purpose being to develop evidence against him.

Gator does, hates what he sees—despite his years in jail he is upset by shakedown rackets and youthful prostitution—teams up with a beautiful woman reporter and an eccentric old woman with cats, and finally, after a lot of gory beatings and deaths, nails the crook and losses the girls. She, played with nicely lurching eyes by Lauren Hutton, could not love him half so well loved she not honors more.

"I want to win a Pulitzer Prize and make love on the terrace of a New York apartment," she tells him sadly.

•

Miss Hutton could have been quite good had her part been better written. Aside from the preceding quote, there seems to be a complete lack of opinion by the authors as to whether she is to be a wide-eyed companion for Mr. Reynolds or a tough decision-maker.

Again, the Federal agent, played by Jack Weston, starts out as an amusing incompetent. Mr. Weston's clowning begins with some subtlety but becomes broader and broader until he is nothing but sweat and quivers. And then, abruptly, he is a hero and dies horrendously.

Directed by Mr. Reynolds, the movie is racked by indecision and lethargy. Everything seems to happen several times, or, if only once, for a very long time. There is an early scene of Gator's trying to evade the police in a motorboat. He rams police boats not once but what seems like seven or eight times. When he is given a knockout pill in a bar he takes a full 10 minutes to keel over.

•

"Gator" is rated PG. There are several painful deaths of characters who up to that moment play for comic effect and whom we are not prepared to see so nastily disposed of. There are some rough fights and a totally stoned 15-year-old prostitute in scenes that would have very little to offer young children.

1976 Ag 26, 46:3

Hoodlum's Spirit Takes Over Law Student

Summer time can be pretty oppressive on occasion, but there is nothing arduous enough about it to justify running off to see the latest variation on "The Exorcist," which opened yesterday at neighborhood theaters under the title "J. D.'s Revenge."

J. D. Walker is a black hoodlum shot to death in a New Orleans meat-packing house in 1942 in the mistaken belief that he has just slit the throat of his sister. After a lapse of 30 some odd years, his spirit returns to take over the personality of Ike, a hardworking young law student, played by Glynn Turman with more skill than the proceedings merit.

•

Before long, Ike is doing vicious things to the passengers in the taxi that he drives to make ends meet; he is doing terrible things to the divorced young woman he

The Cast

J. D.'s REVENGE, produced and directed by Arthur Marks; screenplay by Jaison Starkes; executive in charge of production, Chuck Stroud; music by Robert Prince; director of photography, Harry May; edited by George Folsey Jr. At neighborhood theaters. An American International Pictures Release. Running time: 95 minutes. This film has been rated R.

Ike .... Glynn Turman
Rev. Bliss .... Lou Gossett
Christella .... Joan Pringle
Tony .... Carl Crudup
Theotis .... Fred Pinkard
Enoch .... Fuddle Bagley

lives with, and there is worse to come before J. D.'s spirit returns, apparently satisfied, to its cemetery vault.

"J. D.'s Revenge" would be bad enough if its only flaws were an excessive reliance on repetitive scenes of gore and a proclivity for mistaking repulsive effects for frightening ones. But it seems to revel in the abuses of women, and when Ike's best friend—who has previously appeared to be rather sensible—seriously counsels the mutual benefits of such conduct, "J. D.'s Revenge" crosses the line from a stupid movie to a potentially harmful one.

LAWRENCE VAN GELDER

1976 Ag 26, 47:2

AT THE EARTH'S CORE, directed by Kevin Connor, written by Milton Subotsky and based on a book by Edgar Rice Burroughs; produced by John Dark; photographed by Derek Browne. Released by American International Pictures. At Gold Medal Theaters. Running time: 90 minutes. This film has been rated PG.

David Innes .... Doug McClure
Abner Perry .... Peter Cushing
Dia .... Caroline Munro
Ra .... Cy Grant
Ghak .... Godfrey James

All the money used to make "At the Earth's Core" seems to have been spent on building monsters with parrotlike beaks that open, close, and emit a steady squawling as if someone were vacuuming next door. Close up, the monsters look like sections of rough concrete wall and the decision to film them in closeup is only one example of the total lack of talent or effort with which the picture is made.

Dealing with the adventures of two English scientists who burrow too far down into the earth and find a lot of disagreeable surprises, the movie is a kind of no-talent competition in which the acting, the script, the direction and the camerawork vie for last place.

•

"Core," which opened here yesterday, is rated PG. The monsters will scare small children. On the other hand they will hardly convince larger children. Perhaps vacuum cleaners would enjoy it.

RICHARD EDER

1976 Ag 28, 9:6

ALICE IN WONDERLAND, directed by Bud Townsend; written by B. Anthony Fredericks, based on the Lewis Carroll story; produced by William Osco; director of photography, Joseph Bardo; edited by Shaun Walsh; music and lyrics by Bucky Searles. Released by General National Enterprises. At the National, UA Eastside Cinema and UA East Theaters. Running time: 75 minutes. This film has been rated X.

Alice .... Kristine de Bell
Rabbit .... Larry Gelman
Mad Hatter .... Allan Novak
Tweedledee .... Tony Tsengoles
Tweedledum .... Sue Tsengoles
King .... John Laurence
Queen .... Julie Graham
Humpty Dumpty ....Bradford Armdexter

By RICHARD EDER

In Porno Chic—such movies as "Emmanuelle" and "The Story of O"—the action is given a lush romantic treatment, and the clothes, no longer on the actors, seem to be draped over the cameras: hence the misty effect.

With "Alice in Wonderland" Porno Chic acquires a subdivision: Porno Cute. Seizing vaguely on several episodes from Lewis Carroll, the film's authors have made an animated version of Playboy magazine. The sex is as as tinkly, the humor as coy and the message as puritanically determined that people must have fun.

Kristine de Bell—who, not coincidentally, is receiving considerable exposure in Playboy—is cast as Alice. After a frigid session with her boyfriend, Alice finds herself following a man dressed up as a white rabbit. He leads her to Wonderland—actually a patch of greenery near Clinton, N. Y. —and there she receives various types of sexual initiation at the hands and other parts of a Mad Hatter, Humpty Dumpty, Tweedledum and Tweedledee, the King and Queen of Hearts and a lewd rock.

The movie has some skill in its silliness. Miss de Bell does innocent depravity with a fine hypocritical glitter in her eyes. Though a lot of the humor is piffle, there are some funny lines, one of which is printable. Alice falls into a pond and is told apologetically by her rescuers: "We had a towel, but a hotel stole it."

The sex scenes, despite a lot of woozy cutting and superimposition, are done with good humor and an appearance of enjoyment. On the other hand, there are just too many camera gimmicks. A long orgy scene is shot in a series of jump cuts; that is, frames are cut out so that the movement appears to jump. The intention, I suppose, is to give a feeling of excitement, but what it looks like is a lot of naked bodies stuttering.

The whole thing comes to an end with Alice back with her boyfriend and headed for a life of jokes and sexual efficiency. As the final message states:

"And so, Alice lived happily ever after in a house with a white picket fence and a family and a little arf-arf puppy."

Arf! Arf!

1976 Ag 28, 11:2

TREASURE OF MATECUMBE, directed by Vincent McEveety; screenplay by Don Tait, based on the book "A Journey to Matecumbe," by Robert Lewis Taylor; director of photography, Frank Phillips; music, Buddy Baker; editor, Cotton Warburton; produced by Bill Anderson; a Walt Disney Production; released by Buena Vista Distribution Company. At neighborhood theaters. Running time: 117 minutes. This film is classified G.

Jim .... Robert Foxworth
Lauriette .... Joan Hackett
Dr. Snodgrass .... Peter Ustinov
Spangler .... Vic Morrow
Davie .... Johnny Doran
Thad .... Billy Attmore

Take two small boys—one white, one black—in quest of buried treasure needed to save the old Kentucky home in the postbellum south. Pursue them down the Mississippi and into the Florida keys with a passel of implacable carpetbagger villians. Throw in an orotund and rotund medicine man whose elixirs are at their most beneficial when used as Molotov cocktails. And an indomitable runaway bride-to-be, a handsome and brave ne'er-do-well, a few Indians, several alligators, a cutpurse and a hurricane, and what you have is a rousing old-time adventure movie, "The Treasure of Matecumbe," which opened yesterday at a multitude of theaters on a double bill with its Walt Disney stablemate, the revival of "Three Caballeros."

Based on a novel by Robert Lewis Taylor, this is a literate movie blessed with good actors—principally Joan Hackett as the runaway bride-to-be, Peter Ustinov as the medicine man and Vic Morrow as the leader of the villains—who seem to be having a good time.

In the midst of its excitement, gunplay, spookiness, music, dancing, gambling and river-boating, "Treasure of Matecumbe" finds time to plant a few ideas about the value of education, the sanctity of the environment, the repugnance of bigots and the consequences of disrespect for the beliefs of others. Cavils? Yes. Some less-than-proficient process of photography.

At a showing yesterday at the Festival Theater, both the adults and the children seemed to be having a high time with "Treasure of Matecumbe." It may be a formula story. But the formula is one that has entranced generations.

LAWRENCE VAN GELDER

1976 Ag 28, 11:2

FILM VIEW

RICHARD EDER

A Little Anticipation Goes a Long Way

The best thing to take into a movie is nothing. A sweater for the air-conditioning; glasses if they are needed for seeing, and possibly dark glasses for looking attentive while asleep.

What is of very little use, and usually harmful, is anticipation. It has ruined any number of movies for people who have gone depending on enthusiastic reviews, word of mouth or a previous happy experience with something made by the same director or with the same actor. If any attitude is to be carried in past the box office, it should be foreboding.

This could be taken simply as saying that most movies are fairly bad and that it is better to be surprised than disappointed. It is true, of course, but I think there's something more. Anticipation and pessimism do different things to the way we register what we are seeing, and by and large expectancy is more likely to put a barrier between the screen and ourselves than gloom.

It could be argued that this is also true of plays and books. But there is something passive about the way we see a movie, much more so than with play-going and infinitely more so than with reading a book. When we advance upon a film, when we pursue and try to seize it, it recedes perversely. A film must inveigle or infiltrate or invade us. We do best starting in with our senses open, our brain, if possible, switched on, but our emotions in neutral. The half-closed eye opening typifies a good experience at the movies; the expectant eye glazing over, a bad one.

Incidentally, the phenomenon sets up a paradox for movie reviewers. To strain it a little way: it could be that the best service to be done for a good movie would be to write discouragedly about it, thus putting prospective spectators into the best possible frame of mind to appreciate it. The trouble, of course, is that they might not go.

Probably the ecstatic reviews given to "Nashville" and to Woody Allen's "Love and Death" contributed to the letdown a great many educated and enthusiastic filmgoers felt when seeing them. I don't suggest that this was the main factor—this column is not Berkeleyan enough to hold that the only reality of a movie is the viewer's frame of mind—but it played a part. More recently, and more trivially, I'm afraid that writing about the immoderate laughter induced in me by "The Big Bus" may have contributed to the immoderate annoyance felt by a number of people who went to see it after reading the review.

•   •   •

All this is a peripheral reflection on the preview of the coming season's films conducted in the neighboring columns. Muffle your hopes: not because they may not be justified, but because having them may stop them from being justified.

As for the predictions themselves, they are utterly reasonable, and carry a proviso about the uncertainty of all such predictions. There is, in fact, a certainty to add: that some which are bound to be good won't be, and that a few others, from which nothing is to be expected, will be extremely good, at least for a while.

For a while. The fact is, movies tend to begin well. Then after five minutes, or 15, or with great luck, 45, most lift and wrinkle around the edges, lose skin tone, shrivel and blow away. It is the opposite of what happens on the stage. There the first thing we are aware of is the artifice and the effort. We see the actors before we see the characters they play, and it takes them a while to move in. It also takes us a while to move in; particularly in those stage pieces that begin in full cry—musicals, Shakespeare and most other classics—while we are just beginning to digest our own presence, the texture of the seats, the distance from the stage, the scenery or the lack of it.

With movies, except for those that experiment with stylized abstraction, we are immediately looking at something. Our eye is curious, itchy, frivolous and unchaste. In the middle of a serious conversation we can't help noticing the odd hat some passer-by is wearing. How many people can resist looking at a lit window, even if it's only to see a man drinking a glass of milk? When the train leaves the tunnel there is a compulsion to look out even if we know it's only the Jersey Meadows. After a while, because it's only the Jersey Meadows, we stop.

The beginning of a movie is exactly like that. Almost anything real the camera shows is compelling, particularly nowadays when directors and cameramen have such skill at setting a scene and a mood. This professional moviegoer can recall all kinds of beginnings of movies that not only had no endings—for all one could remember, or would want to—but no middles either.

Take a nullity like "The Gumball Rally," dealing with the efforts of a variegated band of speed demons to conduct a non-stop car race from New York to California. It begins with one of the most-used movie shots of all time: a panoramic view of Manhattan that gradually zeroes in on one particular office in one particular skyscraper. It is not even particularly well-done, yet the sight of all these familiar buildings continues to please our under-employed eyes, and the very familiarity of the device makes it resemble the "once upon a time'" that began so many stories and always aroused hopefulness. Unfortunately "once upon a time" is followed by something about as gripping as reading a week-old newspaper out loud.

"Gator," a movie that deploys considerably more talent to not a great deal more effect, is another example. It starts well and funny, setting up for us a fat, bumbling but persevering federal agent who is sent from New York to break up organized iniquity in a Deep South swamp county. Jack Weston looks perfect as the disaster-prone agent, a would-be city slicker with not an ounce of slickness in him. Sweating, wearing a tight searsucker suit and tiny hat, he stands in a motorboat crashing through the mangrove swamps and makes it look as if he were trying to keep his balance in a misdirected Seventh Avenue Express. But the movie doesn't aim anywhere in particular—though it has lots of action—and Mr. Weston's talent for clowning and Burt Reynolds' talent for looking kind behind his black mustache all go for very little.

Why do these and so many other movies collapse, immediately or after a while? There are many reasons, different in each case, but what is common to almost all of them is a lack of writing. We tend not to think of movies as a written medium, because so many other elements enter. Yet the great European directors either write their films or are intimately involved in their writing. American directors are often less involved.

In any event, when a movie stops breathing it isn't because the camera stops taking nice pictures or the actors give up. It is because the writing, instead of working to explore a character or even just to tell a story, becomes simply a means to make the picture go on, to provide the actors with something to say, to stuff in gags or action, to give the camera something to look at.

Such movies—the vast majority of those that come to New York each month—start with situations: the New York agent in "Gator," the car fanatics in "Gumball Rally"—but nothing is done with them.

There are better specimens where a little is done. A character or two is created and lives for a while. In "The Shootist" John Wayne gets some initial rounding as the old, sick gunman. In "Ode to Billy Joe" the two young lovers have a very particular and individual kind of charm. But then, with the characters possessing the beginnings of life and movement, the writer doesn't know what to do with them or,

more properly, what it is they would do if they were as real as they started out to be. John Wayne's character is allowed to trail off in a tangle of unresolved motivation. "Billy Joe" is sabotaged by forcing the two characters into an incredible plot line.

We are left with beginnings. If American lives have no second acts, most recent American movies have no second reels.

• • •

In last week's column, discussing examples of good acting, F. Murray Abraham was mentioned for his work in "The Ritz." Unfortunately his name was spelled Abramson. Good acting is not so common that it can afford to be mis-spelled, and we apologize.

1976 Ag 29, II:11:1

The Screen: 'Idi Amin'

Dictator of Uganda Is Star of Documentary

"General Idi Amin Dada" was shown at the Museum of Modern Art. The following is Vincent Canbys review, which appeared April 7, 1975. The film begins today at the RKO 59th Street Twin I, east of Third Avenue.

Barbet Schroeder's feature-length documentary "General Idi Amin Dada" is one of those "authorized" profiles that couldn't be more revealing even if it had been put together in secrecy. The subject of the film, who has been Uganda's dictator since he took power in a coup d'etat in 1971, is not the sort to use bushels to hide lights that would embarrass other men.

"General Idi Amin Dada" was made by Mr. Schroeder and his associates, including the celebrated cameraman Nestor Almendros, in Uganda early in 1974 with the enthusiastic cooperation of the general, who has no fear of making a fool of himself.

To think that General Amin does make a fool of himself, as you sit there watching the movie, which often seems to be funny, is simply a way of insulating yourself to one of the movie's principal points: that modern Africa, lurching toward useful identity, still has a long way to go before it achieves it. In the meantime, extraordinarily complex characters like General Amin bumble along creating lethal chaos along with some measure of self-esteem.

The only fault I'd find with the film, which, according to Mr. Schroeder, was largely directed by the general and afterward submitted for his approval, is that it will seem to be funny, colorful and quaint to sophisticated audiences. Here's a sequence of the general racing some younger associates across his swimming pool and, of course winning. In another

The Program

GENERAL IDI AMIN DADA, a documentary feature directed by Barbet Schroeder; produced by Jean-Pierre Rassam and Charles-Henri Favrod; executive producer, Jean-Francois Chauvel; director of photography, Nestor Almendros; editor, Denise de Casablanca; a production of Mara Film, TV Rencontre and Le Figaro. Running time 90 minutes. This film has not been classified.

he is reminded of his wild telegrams to the heads of other governments (including former President Richard M. Nixon), which strike him (and us) as hugely comic, if only because they are so rude.

•

General Amin, who sees himself as the father both of his country and of black Africa, boasts, struts, plays the accordian, acts as tour guide through a game reserve, lectures his Cabinet on hard work and cautions Uganda's doctors not to drink too much.

Behind it all one sees the general's megalomania, his cruelty, his wit and his charm.

Mr. Schroeder, who made what may be the definitive film about European drop-outs of the 1960's, "More," never intrudes upon the general in this straightforward documentary. The film is virtually a self-portrait—both terrifying and sorrowful.

1976 Ag 31, 21:1

ST. IVES, directed by J. Lee Thompson; screen play by Barry Beckerman; based on the novel "The Procane Chronicle" by Iver Bleeck; produced by Pancho Kohner and Stanley Canter; director of photography, Lucien Ballard; edited by Michael Anderson; music by Lalo Schifrin. Released by Warner Bros. At Loews State II and other theaters. Running time; 94 minutes. This film has been rated PG.

St. Ives	Charles Bronson
Procane	John Houseman
Janet	Jacqueline Bisset
Deal	Harry Guardino
Oller	Harris Yulin
Charlie Blunt	Dana Elcar
Myron Green	Michael Lerner
Hesh	Dick O'Neill
Eddie	Elisha Cook

By RICHARD EDER

It may sound like an extremely modest recommendation, but one of the chief virtues of "St. Ives," a sus-

pense drama about a crime reporter up against a great deal of crime, is its restraint. It transforms an ordinary film into what is now a rarity: an ordinary film that manages to entertain.

The restraint certainly does not lie in the plot, which is packed so full of double and triple dissimulations, reversals and red herrings that by the time it is unraveled at the end we have lost most of the threads we had been trying to hold. It does not lie in the photography, which is over-dramatic, or the music, which is like somebody breathing heavily into your ear.

•

The attraction of "St. Ives," which opened yesterday at Loews State II and other theaters, is that it takes itself neither too seriously nor too lightly. Its occasional wit avoids heavy parody; its action avoids heavy reliance on violence, car chases and other such mechanical paraphernalia.

St. Ives is a swollen, cluttered version of the kind of private-eye role that Humphrey Bogart used to do. The hero, played by Charles Bronson, is a crime writer who finds himself involved in the efforts of a wealthy, highly idiosyncratic crook, played by John Houseman, to steal a bribe that some crooked American businessmen are paying to some crooked Arabs.

The writer more or less works along with the Houseman character and his two associates: a psychiatrist played by Maximilan Schell, and a beautiful woman played by Maximilian Schell. There are innumerable double-crosses. It all comes to an end with most of the principals dead, and with Mr. Bronson throwing Miss Bisset into a swimming pool.

The swimming-pool toss is an example of what I mean by restraint. In a great many films now being made in the genre, the hero would have shot Miss Bisset—who turns out to be not as nice as she seems—instead of dunking her. Similarly, there is a car chase: The car goes about 20 feet before it crashes.

Finally, there is what must be the least explicit sex scene of the year. Miss Bisset sits down on Mr. Bronson's bed, smoldering. She puts one hand to her zipper and, believe it or not, the scene ends. Miss Bisset, who does wonderful things for silly roles and once in a while is allowed to do wonderful things for good ones, makes that unpulled zipper seem like an X-rating all by itself.

Charles Bronson, whose sagging eyes and mustache make him look more and more like Fu Manchu, is not good at a great many things, but he does a few things rather well. He manages a pleasantly tried skepticism while the bodies fall all around. He is like one of

Charles Bronson, unscathed, in "St. Ives"
"While the bodies fall all around, he remains skeptical"

Joan Collins
"A waspish highwaywoman"

the novel. Tom, as a baby, is discovered deposited in the squire's bed; he is brought up as a beloved but illegitimate son; he is snubbed and abused by his nasty half-brother, Blifil, he is pronounced legitimate and marries Squire Western's daughter at the end.

•

The pace is fast enough, and the actors are all more than their roles. Nicky Henson is a pleasant Tom, Trevor Howard and Terry-Thomas, as Squire Western and the tutor Mr. Square, evoke memories of better days and better parts; Georgia Brown is a muscular and straightforward Mrs. Waters, and Joan Collins makes a waspish highwaywoman.

There is absolutely nothing to praise, regret, dwell upon or object to in this movie. Now does anyone remember how Joan Greenwood would curl her lip and droop her eyelids, both at once, heavily, happily, as if both were coated with vanilla ice cream?
RICHARD EDER

1976 S 2, 25:1

those companions on a long trip who become agreeable by not saying very much. "St. Ives" does come to seem rather a long and foolish trip, but Miss Bisset and Mr. Bronson help it pass amiably enough.

•

The frequency of the falling bodies accounts for the PG rating, but otherwise there doesn't seem to be anything here to alarm children.

1976 S 2, 24:1

DEATH PLAY, directed by Arthur Storch; written by Jeff Tambornino; produced by Norman Cohen; photographed by Gerald Colts; edited by Arthur Williams. Released by New Line Cinema. At the Thalia and Cinema Village. Running time 88 minutes. This movie has been rated PG.
Karen .... Karen Leslie
Sam .... Michael Higgins
Steve .... James Keach
Harry .... Hy Anzel
Ernie .... James Catusi
Linda .... Elizabeth Farley
Arthur .... Don Fellows

"Death Play" is a peculiar, lopsided movie that attempts to join two stories done in drastically different modes. Despite one impressive performance it does not succeed.

The main story is a naturalistic account of a young actress who, rehearsing her first big role, becomes increasingly estranged from her lover. The lover, a self-pitying, frustrated writer, vents his resentment of the actress's success by conducting a surreptitious affair with his estranged wife.

The second story, suggestive of the expressionist theme of the 1920's, concerns the insane doorkeeper at the theater where the actress is working. A former Shakespearean actor, he begins to see her as the wife who once

betrayed him. At the movie's end, spouting Othello and Hamlet, he kills her.

Although Michael Higgins does the best he can as the madman, the role simply does not work. The stagy devices that accompany him— the rattling, hissing sound effects, his visions of his wife —are ludicrous.

•

As for the main story, the tensions between the producer, the director and the star hired as the main actor are written with some acuteness, and have moments of liveliness and interest. The lover, on the other hand, played by James Keach, is simply too petulant and unpleasant to arouse the slightest concern.

The one brilliant thing in the movie—pitiably wasted —is a beautiful, high-strung performance by Karen Leslie as the young actress. In her first movie role—she has been seen in various regional theaters—Miss Leslie makes the role not only believable but endearing as well: a shifting prism of high spirits, grief, humor and irrepressible life. She is so good that without being able to believe the murder at the end, we are terribly sorry about it.

•

The PG rating is based, apparently, on the murder and a sex scene between the lover and his estranged wife. The movie, which opened at the Thalia and the Cinema Village, is not likely to draw many children, in any case.
RICHARD EDER

1976 S 2, 24:2

THE BAWDY ADVENTURES OF TOM JONES, directed by Cliff Owen; screenplay by Jeremy Lloyd based on musical by Don MacPherson and Paul Holden; produced by Robert Sadoff; director of photography, Douglas Slocombe; edited by Bill Blunden. At the UA Columbia 2 and other theaters. Running time: 94 minutes. This movie has been rated R.
Tom Jones .... Nicky Henson
Squire Western .... Trevor Howard
Mr. Square .... Terry-Thomas
Dr. Thwackum .... Arthur Lowe
Jenny Jones (Mrs. Waters) .. Georgia Brown
Black Bess .... Joan Collins
Squire Alworthy .... William Mervyn
Blifil .... Murray Melvin
Sophia .... Madeline Smith

This is a starved, tittering imitation of that well-stuffed feast, the "Tom Jones" made 15 years ago by Tony Richardson with a lot of help from his friends.

Those friends happened to be the cream of Britain's movie and theater world: Albert Finney, John Osborne, Hugh Griffith, Diane Cilento, Joan Greenwood, Joyce Redman, Susannah York. Enough. This is supposed to be a review of another picture. But do you remember Albert Finney's Tom and Joyce Redman's Mrs. Waters at lunch: mutual seduction by Gluttony? Or the Welsh gales of Hugh Griffith's Squire Western? Or....

Enough. Here is a movie called "The Bawdy Adventures of Tom Jones," and it opened yesterday at the UA Columbia 2 and other theaters. It is based on a stage musical that opened in Las Vegas and never seems to have made it to New York.

•

When a movie has the word "bawdy" in its title, certain things are guaranteed. Low necklines, sometimes down to the waist. Hiked skirts, sometimes up to the waist. Pinching. Leering. Peruked old men with servant girls on their laps. Leaps into fully occupied beds. Hiding under same.

Entrances and exits through the windows.

"Bawdy Adventures" meets its quotas in every respect. As each sexual score is made —not very explicitly—the Hallelujah Chorus is played or sung. Horses are mounted from the rear. Heroes fall into throughs of manure.

The movie hangs loosely around several episodes from

FILM VIEW

RICHARD EDER

Why This Documentary Is A Work of Art

IN theory the most objective kind of movie, the documentary usually comes across as the most subjective. Documentaries invite us to believe that they are about reality and not just about a story. But stories belong to whoever tells them: reality is our own property and those who plant flags on it risk being cited for trespass and littering.

Unless it manages to be invisibly persuasive, a documentary is apt to become a visible affront. Temporary prisoners—how many people walk out on a movie?—we have a special wariness of sermons over the prison loudspeaker.

Often the most pointedly worked-over effects are the least successful. Cleverness, shock, irony: at some point they seem suddenly to be turned against us as well as the subject. The subject is being manipulated and suddenly we are being manipulated along with it.

"Idi Amin Dada," a full-length study of Uganda's ruler by the French director Barbet Schroeder, is a spectacular instance of a documentary coming perilously close to such a failure and, in the end, avoiding it handsomely. On one level it is a torrent of perceptions of a complex and monstrous figure whose monstrosity is inseparable from a degree of charm, of pathos and of authenticity. No revelation or device is spared to lay the man bare, including that most-abused of documentary tricks, the significant juxtaposition. Amin, for example, declares pompously: "Since I became President the whole country became revolutionary," and immediately there is a shot of carrion birds over a bare field.

Such things are unnecessary. Amin is totally self-revealing and peculiarly vulnerable to the camera. He is a performer who takes over wherever he goes. At a tribal dance he joins in and jumps higher than anyone else. At a swimming pool he splashes in, beats the others to the other side—they swim at the speed of survival—and emerges to announce: "I won." At a meeting of doctors he tells them that the chief thing is not to get drunk.

Physically he towers above everyone. He joins one of the innumerable military parades shown in the film, and his enormous head protrudes over the marchers. In Uganda his bulk is assertion and raw power: to the European camera it is self-betrayal.

Throughout, he displays this uncontained will to dominate the occasion; whether it is dancing, clowning, boasting or telling outrageous lies he knows will not be believed. What he cannot abide is being told something. The one moment of terror in the film is his expression when one of the doctors at the meeting responds to his call for comment and says a few words.

He is in no way disrespectful but the sudden immobility of Amin's face makes it clear that to talk to him is to invade his solipsistic world. He is that terrible figure whose tyranny does not consist in making himself bigger than his surroundings but in shrinking the surroundings.

But the camera is beyond his understanding. He performs to it as if it were an audience. Sometimes the voice of Barbet Schroeder is heard, deferential, amused, a true audience. But that is bait: the camera does not simply listen, it does not simply observe. What it does mainly is declare. Amin thinks he is addressing the camera; in reality the camera is mercilessly addressing him.

If this were all, Barbet Schroeder's film would be brilliant, valuable, amusing—each sequence adds a further sharp facet to the portrait—and deformed. Deformed because at some point one thinks: fine, but what are we missing? Is the whole purpose simply accomplished ridicule, however accurate, however much supplied by the subject himself?

In fact there is more. Barbet Schroeder perceives another dimension to Amin and because he does and manages to let us perceive it, his documentary moves beyond brilliance and becomes important.

His Amin is not just a figure to be caricatured. He himself —and this is more of a suggestion in the film than an assertion—in his excess and outrageousness is a caricature of a great deal that the outside world has brought to Africa.

Amin, once a sergeant in the East African Rifles, elevated and, in a way, demeaned in the colonial hierarchy, responds to all the puffs of political fashion that have blown in the course of his life. By his grotesque applications in his Uganda, he parodies them.

Take the military parades he is constantly attending, fussing over, adjusting. It is ridiculous to see the march steps, the bands and braid and strutting—all according to strict British rules—sweeping past this swollen dictator. But wasn't there something ridiculous—now that we see it deformed—in all this military fanfare brought to Africa, and wasn't there something oppressive about it too?

Take the maneuvers. We see his crack paratroopers jumping off a three-foot scaffolding. We see his crack commandos hurtling down a children's playground slide. The movie is not heavy-handed enough to ask if some of our own military maneuvers may look pretty silly too, but it allows the notion to cross our mind.

Take the shots of one of Amin's most callous acts: the deportation of 80,000 Uganda Asians to Britain. We look at the uprooted families, the litter of children and possessions at the airport, and the thought occurs that our own Western history has also seen forcible mass uprootings.

Amin's parodying—more pointed for being quite involuntary: at least I think it's involuntary—is indiscriminate. As he surges across the swimming pool it is impossible not to think of Mao in the Yellow River. His ludicrous re-staging of the drive on the Golan Heights is a wicked and no doubt unconscious takeoff on the Syrian blitzkrieg of 1974.

None of this, I repeat, is stressed by Barbet Schroeder. The awareness of it grows slowly as we watch, and will vary according to each viewer's perception. This is what makes "Idi Amin Dada" a work of art. It shows us a man who has caught every single disease history has been offering these past 40 years, and it leaves it up to us whether we shall loathe the sick man or meditate on the sickness.

1976 S 5, II:9:1

"Idi Amin Dada" leaves it up to us "whether we shall loathe the sick man or meditate on the sickness."

Film Fete Is a Party

By RICHARD EDER
Special to The New York Times

TELLURIDE, Colo., Sept. 6—The Cannes Film Festival is a manic treasure hunt where only steely organization and inside tips will get you through the industrial din and distraction and into some good movies.

The New York Film Festival is a tour of a modern Rhineland museum: Everything is clear, well-marked and a little impersonal.

The Telluride Festival is a party at which the hosts have put the refreshments somewhere, but everyone is so busy talking and going for midnight walks that nobody passes them around or sets out clean glasses. The guests end up foraging for themselves in a mixture of perplexity and exhilaration.

Winding up its third season in this former boom town and former ghost town—revived recently by dropouts back to exercise a talent for good cooking, the restoration of old houses, some art and an erratic civic energy — this is the smallest, the most original and in many ways the most stimulating of the major film festivals in the United States.

For one thing, it is a festival in the traditional sense of the word. New York, Los Angeles and San Francisco are a collection of films interspersed with cocktail parties and press conferences. In New York and Los Angeles, the selection is bigger and, at least in New York, more important; although each year Telluride comes up with some brilliant surprises.

But for the 500 professionals and addicts who come in from all parts of the country and from abroad, and for a good part of the 1,200 residents, the festival is a pilgrimage and a three-day conversation. It winds its way from breakfast to the two theaters to indoor and outdoor discussions to parties, picnics and jeep rides into the mountains. It mixes new directors and old ones—the venerable King Vidor is here this year—actors, distributors, scholars and the bristly and ardent society of film buffs. Everyone is available to everyone else—names and no-names, young and old—up to the point of exhaustion and past it.

William Pence, one of the three director-founders, describes Telluride as a place where anyone can find Louis Malle or Francis Ford Coppola standing at a bar and talking about his work. True enough, but more to the point is that it is a place where people can go up to Mr. Malle and Mr. Coppola and tell them what they think of their

The New York Times

Jeanne Moreau, now a director, too
"Pretty close to miraculous"

work. They do, incessantly, until the bars close.

Stella Pence, who works with her husband, sums up the lack of barriers or diffidence or silence by saying that "it makes very few people unhappy and many people very happy."

•

Today is the last day of the festival and it began with a few early showers and the first snow appearing on the mountains that wall up the east side of town. Yesterday's session ended around 2 o'clock this morning with the screening of Robert Downey's new "Two Tons of Turquoise to Taos." It is a Monty Pythonesque encyclopedia of fits and starts, including, for example, a baseball game on horseback, two old men fighting over the honor of one of their sisters, and a young man eating underwear for dinner.

Saturday afternoon Mr. Downey had told a large group of people in the town park that plots were dead. Why? asked a young man. "Because we're at a point where if the plot doesn't go, the whole world will go," Mr. Downey said. At 9,000 feet and with a lot of sunshine on the aspens, it sounded all right: but there were a number of desertions at 2 o'clock this morning. They all had to pass ri[...] 'ront of Mr. Downey, who w[...]ling near the popcorn.

Intimacy has its disadvantages. Sometimes the movies themselves get blurred by the unexpected opportunities of seeing Werner Herzog, the German director, and Bar-

bet Schroeder, the French director, playing table football. Sometimes the emphasis on people turns into cozy finger-counting: who came this year (Mr. Malle, Mr. Herzog, Mr. Schroeder, Julie Christie, Bulle Ogier, etc.) and who, for various reasons, didn't (Jeanne Moreau, Luis Buñuel).

But there are great compensations. The demonstration that a love of the art of movies can assemble a community is pretty encouraging and very rare. It is reinforced by seeing Mr. Schroeder, in a black velvet jacket, make his way gamely back to the Sheridan bar, night after night, to be questioned and shown-off to; by seeing Werner Herzog, who makes strange an wonderful pictures and sometimes misses, explain to anyone who asks exactly what he was trying to do at each point of his new film.

It is reinforced by a serio-comical battle between Chuck Jones, the veteran creator of "Road Runner" and "Bugs Bunny," and Stan Brakhage, the experimental filmmaker. Mr. Brakhage, who has an angry manner, was denouncing Walt Disney as an exploiter who abused his audiences and was cruel to animals. He said Disney had cut off the head of a bear to improve a shot. Mr. Jones, who feels that the anti-Disney backlash of these last years obscures his contribution to animation, was goaded into saying that he was sure Disney would never cut a bear's head off, and that "if he had, well, everyone needs a hobby." This allowed Mr. Brakhage to be censorious, and in a way both men managed to make points.

It is reinforced by the sight of Louis Malle, looking tired and unkempt—it is part of the festival's intimacy that everyone says with assurance that Mr. Malle is in the process of breaking up with his actress wife, Alexandra Stewart, who was also there—introduce a showing of a wonderful but neglected old film of his, "The Thief," with Jean-Paul Belmondo. In one sentence, he somehow linked up the movie, the crisis he had just after making it that ended in a divorce and his going to make films in India, and whatever it was he was going through now.

"I thought," he said, "that the character of Belmondo was a lot like me, except that it's more honorable to be a thief than a director."

•

Now for the films. The chief news is that New Yorkers are about to see a magnificent picture, "La Lumière," which is written and directed by Jeanne Moreau. It was not necessarily a surprise that the film, a study of four women, one of them played by Miss Moreau, was good.

But without infringing on the review of the film when it appears shortly at the Women's Film Festival in New York, it can be said that "La Lumière" is pretty close to miraculous. There are absolutely no allowances to be made for the fact that it is the first film Miss Moreau has written and directed. Its study of the four women—actresses of different ages—is so precise, illuminating and beautiful that a fair number of the sophisticated audience was moved to temporary speechlessness. Among the remarks when speech was restored: "The United States should stop making movies." Another (from a

man): "Men should stop making movies."

Another splendid film that came to the festival was the Spanish "Spirit of the Beehive" by Victor Erice. An extraordinary, quite original and delicate study of childhood, the imagination and post-war Spain, it has, among other things, two of the finest children's performances ever seen on the screen. "Spirit" has appeared at festivals here and there, but it has been seen in New York only in a one-day showing at the Museum of Modern Art. Somebody should do something about it.

The new Herzog picture—Mr. Herzog is so enthusiastic about the Telluride Festival that he brought it here for its world premiere—was seen with great expectation. Called "Heart of Glass," it is an allegory set in medieval times, and deals with the human condition in a style reminiscent of "Kaspar Hauser." Although it has moments of force and beauty, it is more confused and less emotionally concentrated than "Kaspar." One of the curiosities bout it is that Mr. Herzog filmed a number of the actors under hypnosis.

Two other films that aroused a mixed response were Rohmer's "Marquise of O" and a film by the Japanese director. Akira Kurosawa, produced in the Soviet Union "Dersu Usala." Both are on the point of being seen at the New York Film Festival.

Another film that New Yorkers will see before long is Barbet Schroeder's "Maîtresse," which closed the festival here this afternoon. It is a coolly done, often shocking but always controlled study of a couple caught in a bizarre and sadistic relationship. It manages to be both chilling and funny, and the audience was somewhat shakily delighted.

The Telluride Festival's program included number of side events. There was one about the movie "King Kong," bringing back some of the people who worked on it. It was interesting for a while, but went on endlessly and suffered from an excessive cherishing of not very much. On the other hand, there was an illuminating retrospective of the work of King Vidor; and the lovely, disenchanted appearance of Viola Dana, a heroine of the silent film era.

"Somebody told me most of my film had disintegrated and I think that's a pretty lousy word for an old person," Mr. Vidor said with a great smile tht hadn't the slightest hint of disintegration about it.

1976 S 7, 38:1

Death Casts Shadow

KASEKI (Fossil), directed by Masaki Kobayashi; screenplay (Japanese with English subtitles) by Shun Inagaki, based on a story by Yasushi Inoue; produced by Masayuki Sato; director of photography, Kouzo Okazaki; music, Touru Takemitsu; distributed by New Yorker Films. Running time: 213 minutes. At the New Yorker Theater, Broadway at 89th Street. This film has not been rated.

Tajihei Itsuki	Shin Saburi
Mme. Marcelin	Keiko Kishi
Funazu	Hisashi Igawa
Kishi	Kei Yamamoto
Mrs. Kishi	Orie Sato
Itsuki's daughters	Komaki Kurihara
	Mayumi Ogawa
Kihara	Shigeru Kouyama
Itsuki's stepmother	Haruko Sugimura
Itsuki's brother	Ichiro Nakatani
Itsuki's friend	Jukichi Uno
Sakagami	Yuusuke Takita
Narrator	Goh Kato

By VINCENT CANBY

MASAKI KOBAYASHI, the Japanese director, makes long, movies. "The Human Condition," his adaptation of the six-volume antiwar novel by Jumpei Gomikawa, ran nine hours in three three-hour segments. It was not the sort of film that would have been easily endured by the late Harry Cohn, the movie mogul, who, when asked how he could tell whether a movie was good or bad, said, though more bluntly, "My backside tells me." Mr. Kobayashi's best film, "Harakiri," ran a mere two hours and 10 minutes. His new (1974) film, "Kaseki" (Fossil), now at the New Yorker, runs close to three hours and is mostly about a man who is dying of cancer.

I say that quickly because, although I think "Kaseki" is a monumental film, not everyone wants to see a monument, and even those who do might want to prepare themselves for the experience. Mr. Kobayashi's method is conventional enough at first. He photographs everything more or less straight on. There are no ornamental dissolves, just plain, clean cuts from one scene to another, and such very conventional devices as shots of airplanes (Pan Am) taking off and landing to let us know that someone who planned a trip has actually made it.

The method seems conventional, but it isn't at all. Mr. Kobayashi has made "Kaseki" the way a novelist writes. He supplies detail upon detail — sometimes visually, sometimes in dialogue, sometimes through the voice of an omniscient narrator — to such an extent that he finally pierces the surface of things that no ordinary, conventionally employed camera ever does. This takes time. To appreciate "Kaseki" you must be ready to pay attention to a director who doesn't bother to smile and say "please." There's no attempt to beguile.

•

"Kaseki" is the story of Itsuki (Shin Saburi), a self-assured, self-made construction-industry tycoon, a widower with two married daughters and self-interested enough to tell his pregnant daughter that she must have a boy. "Your sister has a daughter so I would like to have a son." Itsuki runs a benign autocracy.

As postwar Japan has flourished, so has he until one afternoon, while on a business-pleasure trip in Paris, he feels the first pangs of trouble. When he learns the truth, that he has an inoperable cancer of the stomach, Itsuki locks himself in his hotel room. He considers suicide, but that's not his style. He drinks too much. He pats the place where the pain is as if to soothe the crab within, the cancer that is eating him alive.

"Kaseki" is an almost clinical, hour-by-hour report by a man reassessing his life. On a trip through Burgundy with a young Japanese couple and a beautiful, thirtyish Japanese woman, the wife of a wealthy Frenchman and someone whom Itsuki has come to associate with death, the materialist begins to see a world quite different from any he's known before. He becomes aware of a sense of serenity while walking through an ancient cathedral that has provided continuity for generations.

•

Back in Tokyo he goes about putting his business affairs in order, attempts to re-establish ties with his elderly,

A scene from Masaki Kobayashi's film "Kaseki"
"Thoughtful, contemplative and sometimes beautiful"

addled stepmother, whom he once hated, and has a reunion with an old Army comrade with whom he served in China. Itsuki, who has envied French resistance fighters for being able to die in a just cause, remembers his own service with bitterness. He agrees with the old comrade who say that ever since their war they both have lived on borrowed time.

As played by Shin Saburi, Itsuki initially seems impassive, then a man of such immense, painful sensitivity that when fate changes course and provides a dénouement somewhat different from the one we've expected, what would be a happy ending in any

other film isn't. Mr. Kobayashi isn't interested in such distinctions.

Though "Kaseki" is almost totally humorless, it's not pompous. It is a thoughtful, contemplative film, composed of sometimes beautiful, sometimes banal, sometimes picture-post-card-pretty images that ultimately reveal the profound desolation of one rather ordinary fellow. Itsuki, I suspect, may also be Mr. Kobayashi's image of the Japan of Sony, Toyota, Asahi Pentaxes and those Japanese rice crackers now being exported to the cheese dips of the world.

1976 S 10, C5:1

Museum of Modern Art Film Archives

"Spirit of the Beehive"—"a haunting film about children."

it has one advantage that is unnatural and wrong, and that New York should remedy: the chance to see the best Spanish film ever made. It is also one of the two or three most haunting films about children ever made. It is perhaps one of the two dozen best pictures made anywhere in the past half-dozen years.

● ● ●

"The Spirit of the Beehive," directed by Victor Erice, is shaped by two kinds of repression: the repression of the Spanish society and psyche in the dreadful years just after the Civil War, and the milder but dismal constraint exercised by Spain's censorship of films in 1973 when the picture was made. Its ability to say so many things about Spain, about childhood, about human fragility is a reminder that there is an oddly fertile historic stratum for artistic creation. It is to be found, sometimes, when the grip of a repression begins to weaken, when it still is felt and reckoned with, when the hope of getting past it suddenly produces an explosive imaginative energy.

The way past is usually underneath. We get a picture not of the external aspects of the evil, which is still impossible, but of its internal consequences. In the case of "Spirit," the result is not a movie without flaws but something better: one whose power to move and astonish comes in quite original and magical ways.

It is set in the devastation of post-Civil War Spain. the old Castilian village where it takes place has not seen the war, and the family with which the movie deals belongs to an educated, relatively protected upper middle class. There is shabbiness and scarcity, but the real devastation is human. It is a country of widows and burnt-out survivors. The town cryer is a toothless old woman—her husband had the job and is gone—and there are no young men around. The world in which it was possible or worthwhile to do or say or feel anything has been used up. The family's father keeps bees as a hobby and sits at his cluttered desk all night trying to write something important about them. The mother lives in her own dream, writing letters to a man who disappeared in the war and riding a squeaky bicycle down to the railroad station to mail them.

Ana, 8, and Isabel, 10, live among these shadows. One day, at the village movie house, they see James Whale's classic, "Frankenstein." Ana's eyes open. In bed at night

FILM VIEW

RICHARD EDER

A Great Film We May Never See

TELLURIDE, COLO.

Truth will out, though often too late to do the perpetrator much good. There is no such guarantee for good movies, nor even for great ones. The assertion is something of a self-contradiction: certainly the writer of this column doesn't carry reels of film around in his pocket, nor do they get slipped under his door. To discuss an extraordinary film, as I am about to do, it must come out somewhere or I wouldn't have seen it.

Spain's "The Spirit of the Beehive" has, in fact, come out in a number of places. In Spain, where it did not so much evade the censorship as envelop it, at the London and San Francisco festivals three years ago, and at other spots around Europe. The response was invariably fervent, and nothing happened. Without commercial distribution in this country, the only chance New Yorkers had to see it was at two showings at the Museum of Modern Art a couple of years ago.

Now, in its firefly existence, it has appeared once more; this time at the spirited and admirably unpredictable film festival here in Telluride, a rejuvenated ghost town which has a number of natural advantages over New York. Mile-high walls of aspen and rock, for example, and sunsets that stop the traffic. (The residents gather in the middle of the main street, which handily points due west, to watch them.) But she asks Isabel—the long night dialogues between two children are one of the film's wonders—if the story is true. Isabel is already too old to absorb reality; her impulse is to control it. She tells Ana that the monster is real and can be seen.

The movie is the story of Ana's search; her entrapment in her own imagination and need for mystery. Her tiny figure —black-haired, black-eyed, with two stubby legs protruding from her schoolgirl's cape—wanders through the house, the village, the bleak fields, looking for the monster. With an amazing performance by Ana Torrent—there has probably never been a more extraordinary view of a child on a movie screen—one of the great film images has been created.

•   •   •

With the work of a brilliant photographer, Luis Cuadrado, the film mobilizes all of its elements—the bare, desolate landscape; the grimy trains filled with passengers who, in that time and place, were invariably on errands of misery; the interiors; a stately pillow fight; the long shots of the children wandering over the brown fields; the shifting study of their faces—toward an accumulating dramatic momentum.

Sometimes it accumulates too slowly. The film's middle part is overly deliberate, despite the skill of many of its scenes. Some of the symbolism is confused. At its clearest, the movie's formal meaning is always complex, always allusive. But by the time it ends, it has possessed the viewer completely.

1976 S 12, II:15:4

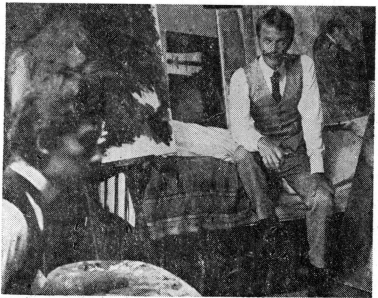

"What matters in the life of an artist is what cannot be eavesdropped upon: the hours alone in the studio."

'Edvard Munch'— A Film Truer to Life Than to Art

By JOHN RUSSELL

It was one of the ambitions of the great Norwegian painter, Edvard Munch (1863-1944), that someday he would change the way in which people looked at art. No longer would people regard painting as a source of polite distraction. "Instead of painting pictures of men reading and women knitting, I shall paint real human beings who breathe, feel, suffer and love. People will realize how sacred that is and they will take off their hats as though they were in church."

Munch—now the subject of a new movie, "Edvard Munch," that opens today at the Walter Reade Festival Theater — succeeded in this over and over again. He brought a new rawness and a revived integrity to the study of personal relations in art. He also managed (above all in a famous painting called "The Cry" of 1893) to make visible to everyone the uncontrollable anxiety which was to characterize European sensibility from Kafka to Samuel Beckett.

He himself was well schooled in that anxiety by his own early experiences. His mother died of tuberculosis when he was 5. His elder sister died of tuberculosis when he was 14. His father, a doctor in a poor section of Oslo, was subject to attacks of religious anxiety which brought him to the edge of in-

sanity and found outlet in terrifying attacks of violence. Munch did not exaggerate when he said later that "Disease and insanity were the black angels beside my cradle."

Clearly, there is much here to tempt the moviemaker. Yet how often have we seen a feature film about a painter that was even passable? A real painter, that is, one who is part of the history of art and can be tested against what we see on the screen.

"Hardly ever" is the answer. Charles Laughton looked right in "Rembrandt" (1936), and he gave of his best; but who's to say how Rembrandt talked? José Ferrer gave of his best as Toulouse-Lautrec in "Moulin Rouge" (1953), and the scenes of Parisian nightlife boiled over quite nicely. But between what we saw and what actually happened, what an abyss! Kirk Douglas as van Gogh and Anthony Quinn as Gauguin took pains over "Lust for Life" (1956), and their scenes together got quite a bit of tension going; but, there too, what a foreshortening of the truth!

So the precedents for Peter Watkins's new film "Edvard Munch" are none too good. What matters in the life of an artist is what cannot be eavesdropped upon: the hours spent alone in the studio. There's just no way of showing that, any more than we can eavesdrop on Einstein formulating the General Theory of Relativity, or on Wittgenstein drafting the "Tractatus."

Peter Watkins's film on Munch is roomy (167 minutes), beautiful to look

at, and very good indeed in its presentation of Munch's childhood and youth. Mr. Watkins takes his time—and to great effect—over the condition of Oslo in the 1860's. We are told just how many people coughed their lungs out and died of it. We learn of the appalling circumstances in which mothers and young children were sent out to work for a pittance and ruined their health as a result. We learn about legalized prostitution and see something of the affronts to human dignity which this involved. The bourgeoisie takes a beating which it doubtless deserved.

There is an unforgettable intensity about Mr. Watkins's presentation of the alternative society of artists and writers who were talking their heads off while Mother died of tuberculosis and Father was thumping his Bible. There is nothing of the studio about those wracked young women, so dedicated to self-definition, or about those odd, haunted and so purely Nordic men. We really believe that the writers can write, and we almost believe that the painters can paint.

When the scene moves to Berlin or to Copenhagen, we go on believing. The faces are right, the text is right, and the mix of languages (Norwegian, German, French and English, subtitled where necessary) gives a real sense of Munch's restless activity. The cameraman, Odd Geir Saether, does a wonderful job of matching up the images on screen with the images that Munch himself produced.

So we get the background—social, political, esthetic—in most memorable detail. We know what was wrong with Munch's childhood and youth, and just why he responded so intensely to his environment. (Geir Westby as Munch could hardly be bettered.) But when the time comes to tackle the art, Mr. Watkins doesn't do quite so well. There is too much of Munch scratching around on the canvas, and there is too much jejune analysis of the pictorial process.

We are left in no doubt that Munch in manhood was still crippled emotionally by his earlier experience. The

themes of death, jealousy and the struggle for freedom of expression are made to overlap with results which, though startling at first, pall with repetition.

It is not in dispute that Munch as a young man had trouble with his family, trouble with women, and trouble with the critics. It is perfectly true that, as the film tells us in its final sequence, he had a nervous breakdown in 1908 and had to go into a clinic. It is true that many of the friends of his youth came to a sad end.

But is also true that eventually Munch could give full and glorious expression to quite other sides of life. As early as 1893 he won the patronage of Walter Rathenau, who later became Foreign Minister of Germany; and in his portrait of Rathenau, as in major paintings like "Girls on the Jetty" (1809) and "Fertility" (circa 1902), he moved far away from his own preoccupations. Moreover, Munch lived to be 80, and although he was never exactly the jester of his set, he ended his life as an upstanding old gentleman who could face isolation in German-occupied Norway with a singular stoicism.

Rather than the elegant diminuendo with which Mr. Watkins brings his film to an end, I for one should have been happy to see at least a foretaste of his undiminished vigor in old age: the Munch who could paint that last self-portrait in the 1940's entitled "Between Clock and Bed." Munch, in his late 70's, stands erect and alone. To his right is a grandfather clock that before long must toll the hour of his death. To his left is the neat single bed, with its brilliant Matisse-like comforter, which has replaced the tossed and rumpled sheets on which so much that was painful or meaningless had gone forward. Even a hint of the undefeated Ancient whom Munch was to become would have added a great deal to Mr. Watkins's engrossing and deeply felt film. ∎

1976 S 12, II:1:5

Geir Westby and Gro Fraas
The multiplicity of factors that work on the artist

EDVARD MUNCH, directed and written by Peter Watkins; director of photography, Odd Geir Saether. A Norsk Rikstringkasting/Sverges Radio AB production. North American distributor. Running time: 167 minutes. At the Fine Arts Theater, 58th Street near Lexington Avenue. This film has not been rated.

Edvard Munch	Geir Westby
Mrs. Heiberg	Gro Fraas
Dr. Christian Munch	Johan Halsbog
Laura Catherine Munch	Gro Jarto
Aunt Karen Bjolstad	Lotte Teig
Inger Munch	Berit Rytter Hasle
Peter Andreas Munch	Gunnar Skjetne
Christian Krohg	Knut Christiansen
Vilhem Krag	Haakon Gundersen
Hans Jaeger	Kars Stormark
August Strindberg	Alf-Kare Strindberg
Dagny Ivell	Isetin von Hanne Bast
Stanislau Przybyszewski	Ladislaw Reznicek

By VINCENT CANBY

Nothing that Peter Watkins, the English director ("The War Game," "Privilege," "Punishment Park"), has done before quite prepares us for the moving, complex, beautifully felt portrait of the great Norwegian artist Edvard Munch (1863-1944), one of the most influential painters in the founding and defining of European Expressionism.

The film "Edvard Munch," which opened yesterday at the Fine Arts Theater, is one of the few ever to dramatize successfully the sensitivity, the profound emotional chaos and the discipline that occasionally combine to produce the special molecular structure of a major artist.

At the heart of this portrait there remains the mystery of the creative process — still unsolved — which is the way it should be. What Mr. Watkins has succeeded in doing is to suggest the multiplicity of psychological and social factors at work on the man, using a narrative form that is simultaneously journalistic and as freely associated as a dream.

In the past, the director's fondness for a simulated cinéma vérité style has resulted in ludicrous anachronisms—facetious television interviews with people on the point of being gunned to death, handheld camera footage of situations unlikely to be recorded even by a secreted Kodak Brownie. The method got in front of the subject and then ridiculed it. Not so this time.

The style is now muted. When members of Munch's family, his friends, associates, critics and contemporaries talk directly to the camera, it's the perfectly acceptable device of fiction that's been used by Bergman, Godard and others. You don't get the queasy "You Are There" feeling that you once got when Walter Cronkite interviewed Julius Caesar on his way to the Forum.

"Edvard Munch" is a long film, just under three hours. It covers the painter's life from his childhood when, as he wrote, "illness, insanity and death were the black angels that kept watch over my cradle," until 1908 when, at the age of 45, he had completed his important "Frieze of Life" paintings and was slipping into nervous collapse.

Art historians may object that this hardly gives a complete picture of the man who, though tormented, perhaps psychotic, continued to work fruitfully with increasing recognition for another 35 years, dying at 80, a substantial age for anyone but especially for someone so ravaged by the demons within.

That may be so, but "Edvard Munch," though it's based upon the life and celebrates the talent of a real artist, is fiction, as are all films except possibly newsreels. The form that Mr. Watkins has imposed on the material illuminates a major part of that life, the obsessions that drove Munch to his seminal attempts to express visually states of mind, including his own anxieties, his fears, his longings to reach to others through love that was was both spiritual and intensely sexual.

●

The two major themes of the film are his death-haunted childhood in Oslo (then Cristiania), when his sister and his mother both died of tuberculosis, and a tumultuous love affair with a still-anonymous married woman identified only as Mrs. Heiberg.

In the manner of an obsessed mind, the film keeps returning to images of his dying sister and to those of later humiliations at the hands of Mrs. Heiberg. At the same time, Mr. Watkins gives us what is virtually a documentary report on the conservative, middle-class, puritan society that shaped his life, a society where (in 1884) prostitution was legalized but there were no laws against child labor.

The movie cuts almost manically back and forth among a half-dozen different periods of time like the thoughts of a man on a couch—from the childhood of disease and death, to disastrous exhibitions in Norway and Germany, to the unhappy love affairs, to youthful discussions in Cristiania's little bohemia, to the later encounters with celebrated contemporaries, including Strindberg.

We see the artist painting and a number of his canvases, woodcuts and lithographs, but the emphasis is on the man and his time, as the director seems to understand that he can't recreate the process by which these extraordinary works came into being.

Geir Westby is fine as the artist whose vision we share in much of the beautiful color-camerawork by Odd Geir Saether. Gro Fraas, whose looks recall Liv Ullmann's, plays Mrs. Heiberg, seeming to be as arbitrary, untrustworthy and tender to us as to Munch. The film, shot in Norway by Mr. Watkins, has Norwegian, Swedish, French and German dialogue, translated by subtitles, as well as English narration based on Munch's own letters and journals.

Admittedly the competition isn't great, but "Edvard Munch" must be one of the few films about a serious artist that can be taken seriously.

1976 S 13, 38:1

'Bugsy Malone' Has Very Short Cast

By JOYCE MAYNARD

At one point in the movie "Bugsy Malone," which had its first New York showing yesterday, Scott Baio, playing Bugsy, asks Florrie Dugger, as his girlfriend, Blousey, how long she has wanted to be a singer. "Since I was a kid," she says.

Scott Baio is 14 years old. Florrie Dugger is the same age. But like everyone else in the film, they play adult roles, often with devastatingly accurate portrayals of their elders. All of this was much to the delight of the audience, most of whom, like most members of the cast, were under 4 feet 10 inches.

The film, which was written and directed by Alan Parker, is set in 1929 New York City. But it is a scaled-down New York, in which the cars and the bar stools and the men's zoot suits and the women's satin gowns are all child-sized. The gangsters carry authentic-looking guns. But what comes out of them are marshmallows. There is not a drop of blood—or an adult face—visible in the entire movie.

Most of the laughter, in the first few minutes of the film, came simply from the sight of children inhabiting a totally child world—a little boy pouring drinks that looked like apple juice at a bar, a girl who looked about 12, in eye shadow, high heels and a training bra, slinking through a chorus line routine. Halfway into the movie, however, the children stopped looking like children, and it would have been the sight of an adult, and not a child, that jarred.

The children in the audience (many of them displaying Fonzie T-shirts and considerable bubble-gum-blowing facility) laughed energetically and often appeared to like the marshmallow-shooting scenes the best.

After the movie ended (with an orgy of pie throwing) there was a press conference and question-and answer session for the audience, with three cast members (Scott Baio, John Cassisi and (Humpty) Albin Jenkins,) along with the director, Alan Parker, and Paul Williams, who wrote the songs for the movie. It opens Wednesday at the Baronet, Third Avenue and 59th Street.

John Cassisi, who is 14 and lives in Bay Ridge, Brooklyn, said he was chosen for the part of Fat Sam when Mr. Parker visited his school and picked him out of a classroom.

"I told my dad, 'I'm going to be in a movie' and he said 'Get

A scene from "Bugsy Malone"
Devastatingly accurate portrayals of their elders

outta here,'" said John, a stocky boy not easily at a loss for words. "We had a great time making the movie. There was a lot of levity on the set."

Scott Baio, wearing a three-piece suit, said being in the movie was "just like any other job I might have done" and added that, "It was frightening to see myself up there on the screen."

Albin Jenkins, who danced to "Raindrops Keep Falling on My Head" at Carnegie Hall when he was 2, seemed pretty cool about the whole thing, as he signed autographs.

During the press conference, some of the adults connected with the film fed questions to the boys and Florrie Dugger were an item on the order of, "I hear that you during the filming." Several writers from an all-child newspaper called The Children's Express, carrying reporter's notebooks and tape recorders, wanted to know about the child actors' salaries (which they said were being handled by their mothers) and asked whether they had any future acting plans. John Cassissi pronounced himself "available" and gave out his phone number.

"To sum it all up," he said. "Luck came knocking on the door, and I answered it."

Robbie Schiller, who is 6, looking on admiringly, said he thought "Bugsy Malone" was very good. "In all the other movies," he said, "they just have adults and people. I like to see a movie with kids."

1976 S 13, 38:1

LOVE UNDER THE CRUCIFIX, directed by Kinuyo Tanaka; screenplay in Japanese, with English subtitles, by Masashize Narusawa; produced by Sennosuke Tsukimori; director of photography, Yoshio Miyajima; a Schochiku Films production. Running time: 104 minutes. At the Festival of Women's Films, Cinema Studio, Broadway at 66th Street. This film has not been rated.
Ukon Takayama ....Tatsuya Nakadai
Ghin ....Imeko Arima
Sen Rikyo ....Ganjiro Nakamura

By VINCENT CANBY

"Being a wife is important, but it's even more important to be a woman," says the spunky heroine of Kinuyo Tanaka's "Love Under the Crucifix," the Japanese film that opened the second International Festival of Women's Films at the Cinema Studio. The heroine goes on to add, rather damply, "A woman must live for love."

That's hardly the gospel according to Erica Jong but those would have been revolutionary words in the late 16th century, which is the period of Miss Tanaka's stately melodrama about a well brought-up young woman, a convert to Christianity, which was then about to be suppressed in Japan, who chooses something other than dishonor when faced with the prospect of becoming the regent's newest concubine.

●

"Love Under the Crucifix" doesn't have very much to do with Christianity, though its heroine wears a cross and has take a vow of chastity because the man she loves, who is Christian, is married. It has more to do with various Japanese interpretations of honor and sacrifice, this time seen largely from a woman's point of view.

Of more interest than the film itself, a sort of feudal soap-opera that was made in 1960, is Kinuyo Tanaka, who is apparently Japan's only woman director. Born in 1910, she was one of the country's leading film actresses during the 30's and 40's and turned to directing in the 50's. Students of Mizoguchi's films will remember her performances in "Life of O-Haru" and "Sansho the Bailiff."

●

The film will be shown again today at 6 P.M. and tomorrow at 8 P.M. The color print is not in the best condition.

Two showings last night of "Lumière," Jeanne Moreau's first film as a director, were the highlight of the opening. That film will be reviewed when it opens its commercial run later in the year.

1976 S 14, 44:3

DAGUERREOTYPES, a documentary directed, produced and written by Agnès Varda; in French with English subtitles and English narration; director of photography, Nurith Aviv; editor, Gordon Swire; a Cine-Tamaris production. Running time: 80 minutes. At the second International Festival of Women's Films at the Cinema Studio, Broadway at 66th Street.

By VINCENT CANBY

The second International Festival of Women's Films, being held at the Cinema Studio, came to glowing life yesterday with the first commercial New York showing of "Daguerreotypes," by Agnès Varda, the French director who made her debut as a director of documentaries, switched to narrative films ("Cleo from 5 to 7," "Le Bonheur,") and combined the two methods with a good deal of comic success in "Lion's Love."

"Daguerreotypes" is Miss Varda's beautiful homage to Louis Jacques Mandé Daguerre, a pioneer in the history of photography. Strictly speaking, the form here is documentary, but the film is more important as a witty, very humane appreciation of Miss Varda's friends and neighbors on a short section of the Rue Daguerre, a lively street of small shops in Paris's 14th Arrondissement, which borders Montparnasse.

The film, which will be shown today at 6 P.M. and tomorrow at 8 P.M., is both a demonstration of the possibilities of the cinema-vérité camera (when the film maker doesn't impose too strict a discipline on the material) and a series of graphic portraits of particular people going about the business of their lives.

The camera's presence is simply accepted by the courtly old man who makes and sells perfume, but it's ignored by his frail, distracted wife of 50 years, who always appears to be listening to voices from the past.

It draws out many of the others —the good-humored, giggly wife of the local baker, the local barber and his wife, who is a beautician, and it is treated quite formally, as if it were a guest, by the tailor and his wife. It is acknowledged and then immediately forgotten by two women who meet on the sidewalk to exchange a small bit of chit-chat about a local marriage going noisily on the rocks.

Miss Varda, in one of her occasional comments on the soundtrack, tells us she is fascinated by "the mysteries of daily trade." The opening part of the film observes this phenomenon and listens to its dialogue. "They took an electro-cardiogram," a woman customer tells the butcher about her ailing husband. Says the butcher, efficiently removing the fat from a beefsteak, "It's just the weather."

In the middle section of the film, the tradespeople talk about their work and their lives, recalling origins often far removed in place and time from the Rue Daguerre in 1975. These recollections of childhoods, meetings and marriages, spoken directly to the camera, sometimes self-consciously, become immensely moving, not because the events are momentous, but because it seems as if we may be sharing the first such assessments ever made.

In the concluding portion of "Daguerreotypes," Miss Varda cuts between an uproarious performance of a magician named Mystag at the local cafe, attended by most of the people we've already met, and scenes from their daily lives she associates with Mystag's tricks. Only here does one suspect that a certain amount of facile intellectualizing is going on. As Miss Varda is fascinated by the mysteries of daily trade, she is also making a point about the daily trade of mysteries.

●

Most of the time, "Daguerreotypes" is content just to look at and to listen to its characters, who are full of splendid mysteries. One scene especially remains in the memory:

It is the end of the day. The old perfumer observes his mute wife looking longingly toward the street. She moves to the door, steps hesitantly outside, appears to have forgotten what was in her mind, and returns. Says her husband, whose love embraces idiosyncrasy without embarrassment, "In the evening . . . . some inner tendency forces her . . . . not to go out . . . . but to want to go out."

1976 S 15, 50:1

Mekas's 'Lost Lost Lost' Opens Whitney Series

By RICHARD EDER

Using techniques that imitate the lack of technique of a home movie, the film maker and critic Jonas Mekas has been taking poetic notes of his adult life ever since he entered the United States as a young Lithuanian refugee in 1949. To open its annual series of American experimental films, the Whitney Museum is showing a three-hour swatch of these notes, under the title "Lost, Lost, Lost."

They are grainy and elliptical, these brief scenes, with Mr. Mekas's voice making a keening, accented commentary upon them. They begin with his first years, living with Lithuanian relatives and friends in Brooklyn; then making a break along with his brother Adolfas, moving to Manhattan and slowly and painfully becoming an experimental film maker and member of an avant-garde that included Allen Ginsberg, Frank O'Hara, Andy Warhol and others.

●

As time passes, the straightforward awkwardness of Mr. Mekas's camera is replaced by a mannered awkwardness, the shots tumbling, blurring and distorting. It is a process the author uses quite deliberately to illustrate the process of pain he is trying to record.

"Sing Ulysses, sing your travels," Mr. Mekas's voice begins, and he goes on to speak of "a man who never wanted to leave his home . . . who was thrown into the world." The movie, from start to finish, is about the damage done by exile; only in the first part it is shown directly, and thereafter, indirectly.

It is the first part that has most of the power: it is an infinitely moving and perceptive record of the exile of a whole community. Mr. Mekas, at the time fully a part of this community, records the meals, the weddings, the Sunday outings. He records the pain of the refugee doctors, lawyers, poets, politicians who suddenly find them-

---

The Program

LOST, LOST, LOST (DIARIES, NOTES & SKETCHES, REELS 1-6). Documentary by Jonas Mekas. New American Filmmakers Series. At the Whitney Museum of American Art. Through Sept. 19, 1 noon and 3 P.M. Also Tuesday at 6:30 P.M. Running time 176 minutes.

selves transplanted as truck drivers, messengers and factory hands.

They meet, they form committees, they dress up for a picnic in the country at the end of which they sit, in rows of garden chairs, to hear a former Cabinet minister talk about the situation. They take all the steps, these educated and decent people, that they have taken all their lives; but suddenly, in the hard soil of a new country, they leave no footprints. The fact that Mr. Mekas used a silent camera strengthens the image of ghosts who gesture, pace, talk and make no sound.

And then Jones, and his brother Adolfas, seeing nothing ahead but a future of Lithuania Day dances, leave this futile reality, move to Manhattan and, as the author puts it, "start from scratch."

Even a futile reality is no so easily replaced. They write, they take odd jobs, they work on film, they make friends in the avant-garde. But there is no center. Mr. Mekas follows and films—sometimes quite beautifully— all the vigils and peace marches of the late 1950's. (How peaceful the demonstrators look from this side of the late 60's; how gentle the police look,) He makes experimental films, makes filmed haikus in the snow.

●

It is pretty, some of it, but dated and pretentious by now. With the novelty long past, the caperings of Mr. Mekas and his friends remind us of children who protest the lack of anything to do by posturing and grimacing. It is a frenetic hopefulness mustered against a real emptiness of exile, and the exile is not just for two Lithuanian brothers from Brooklyn but for their American contemporaries as well.

We get the message, but it does not touch us as the message in the first part does. A dying reality is material for a splendid film; a living emptiness hardly ever is.

1976 S 15, 52:3

BUGSY MALONE, directed and written by Alan Parker; executive producer, David Puttnam; produced by Alan Marshall; words and music by Paul Williams; directors of photography, Michael Seresin and Peter Biziou; editor, Gerry Hambling; a Goodtimes Enterprises production, presented by Robert Stigwood, distributed by Paramount Pictures. Running time: 94 minutes. At the Baronet Theater, Third Avenue at 59th Street. This film has been rated G.

Bugsy	Scott Baio
Blousey	Florrie Dugger
Tallulah	Jodie Foster
Fat Sam	John Cassisi
Dandy Dan	Martin Lev
Leroy Smith	Paul Murphy
Knuckles	Sheridan Russell
Fizzy	"Humpty" Albin Jenkins
Baby Face	Dexter Fletcher

By VINCENT CANBY

"If it were raining brains," says the narrator at the start of "Bugsy Malon," "Roxy Robinson wouldn't even get wet." We then see a close-up of the terrified face of Roxy Robinson as he's pursued down a dark Manhattan alley by the gunmen of a rival gang. Suddenly he's cornered. Roxy pleads for his life. "Hey, fellas . . ." But in vain. Right in front of our eyes Roxy Robinson is executed with gangland's newest secret weapon, the Splurge gun, a machine gun loaded with what looks like Reddi-Whip.

That custard pies can maim and whipped cream should kill are only two of the ways in which some basic laws of the cinema are cheerfully junked in this wildly uneven but imaginative and stylish satire of 1920's gangster movies. The film, which opened yesterday at the Baronet, was written and directed by Alan Parker, an Englishman with a lot of improbable talent.

Jodie Foster
Jean Harlow—plus Twiggy

I mean that only someone with an improbable talent and an emerging death wish would attempt to make such a film, which also includes a first-rate musical score and choreography, along with a cast of kids. They aren't "Our Gang" toddlers by any means, but young teen-agers, some of whom look pre-pubescent and others in their mid-20's, a discrepancy that haunts the film and makes for some uneasy moments.

But discrepancy is virtually the method of the movie, which is at its best when the satire is played straight without cute mannerisms. When one isn't aware that most of the girls look years older than

the boys, and when we don't see that the cars they are driving are propelled by pedals, "Bugsy Malone" has a good deal of the charm of the stage version of Sandy Wilson's "The Boy Friend."

•

In addition to Mr. Parker's very funny screenplay and his apparent ability to tone down the natural stridency of his young actors, the film's chief assets are the 10 Paul Williams songs that are very much of this decade, but presented in orchestrations that wittily recall the sounds of the 1920's.

They are lip-synched by the actors, but sung on the soundtrack with much verve by Mr. Williams and some other uncredited singers, including a young woman who does two Streisand-like numbers, "I'm Feeling Fine" and "Ordinary Fool," as well as the now-comparable Barbra might do them.

Gillian Gregory's choreography, with much emphasis on the Charleston, is the first real choreography we've had on the screen in a couple of years. It has a nice, old-fashioned (by movie standards) directness to it, especially in a song called "Bad Guys," in which five fresh-faced hoodlums sing and dance the pleasures of being absolutely rotten ("We could have been anything we wanted to be.... But we're the very best at being bad").

•

Scott Baio, who looks young in a small, slight, sort of ageless way, plays the title role, that of a good-hearted fellow who joins a gang to get money to send his true love, named Blousey (Florrie Dugger), to fulfill her dreams in Hollywood. I have no idea how old Miss Dugger is, but by being pretty, fat-faced and very, very prissy she is marvelously funny as the ingénue. The star of the show, though, is Jodie Foster who, at 14 (14?), comes across as a combination of Jean Harlow, Twiggy and Glenda Farrell. She is tough, comic, and on her way to becoming one of the screen's great beauties.

The boys in the cast, including Mr. Baio and John Cassissi, who plays Fat Sam, the speakeasy owner and failed ganglord, have a much tougher time because they always look to be in adult masquerade, even when you suspect that they might be older than they look and victims of arrested development. Their performances are good, but their appearances are disorienting, which is not true of the girls because, I suspect, we expect girls to be older for their ages than boys.

"Bugsy Malone" is a picture for Humbert Humbert to see again and again. It is also something of an achievement in the cinema of the G-rated bizarre.

1976 S 16, 54:1

'Take It Like a Man, Madam' Neither Funny nor Moving

"Take It Like a Man, Madam," which was shown yesterday at the second International Festival of Women's Films at the Cinema Studio, is a creditable job of women's lib film making that is likely to leave anyone who hasn't been long dead asking what else is new.

The Cast

TAKE IT LIKE A MAN, MADAM, directed and screenplay (Danish with English subtitles) written by Mette Knudsen, Liv Vilstrup and Elisabeth Rygaard; camera, Katia Forbert Petersen; editing, Ann-Lis Lund; music, Nina Larsen and Gudrun Sten-Andersen; production company, Red Sister. An ASA Film Distribution. Running time: 96 minutes. At the Festival of Women's Films, Cinema Studio, Broadway at 66th Street. This film has not been rated.

Ellen Rasmussen	Tove Maes
Erik Rasmussen	Alf Lassen
Karen, doctor	Berthe Quistgoord
Grethe, designer	Birgit Buel
Harry	Claus Strandberg
Lars	Hans Kragh Jacobsen
Ms. Larsen	Asta Esper Andersen

The 1974 Danish film, communally written and directed by Mette Knudsen, Liv Vilstrup and Elisabeth Rygaard, observes the autumnal plight of

a woman who, at middle age, her children grown up and away, her husband a bit of a boor, demands something better than tranquilizers to get her through menopause.

The woman is played with much intelligence by Tove Maes, but there's not one spontaneously funny or moving moment in the entire film, the centerpiece of which is an extended fantasy in which men and women have reversed roles. It's material for a revue sketch, at best.

The film will be shown again today and tomorrow at 6 P.M.

VINCENT CANBY

1976 S 16, 55:1

Celebrating 'Kate' At the Regency

By WALTER KERR

WHEN THE REGENCY Theater, having finally done with the Brothers Warner, begins its Katharine Hepburn retrospective with a double bill of "Christopher Strong" and "A Woman Rebels" on Sunday, there'll be those who bide their time until they can see their favorite Hepburn films ("Little Women," perhaps, or "African Queen"), and those others who dash off to catch the ones they've never seen, perhaps never even heard of (how about "Sylvia Scarlett," or "Spitfire"?). Twenty-two films, spanning a 30-year stretch from 1932 to 1962, will

arrive at the theater on Broadway near 67th Street in due time, with "Holiday" and "Suddenly Last Summer" wrapping everything up in mid-November.

Me, I'm going back to "Alice Adams" because I always go back to "Alice Adams." (Won't have to wait very long, either, because it's scheduled for Sept. 26-28, scarcely a passionate heart's beat away.) Why am I going yet again to "Alice Adams" when I ought to be making time for James M. Barrie's "Quality Street," a performance I scarcely remember? Possibly because I think it the lady's own best work, possibly because I think it the best film in which she appeared. Possibly. Cer-

The Bettmann Archive

Katharine Hepburn in Dorothy Arzner's 1933 film, "Christopher Strong," which opens the "Kate" festival at the Regency on Sunday.

ainly because it is the most enigmatic, devious, contrary yet ultimately triumphant assertion of self that an extreme-ly self-assertive woman arrived at in a busy, insistent lifetime.

Consider what we're up against in coping with the film. There are two things wrong with it and, mysteriously, both are right. One of them wasn't necessarily wrong in the first place, it's just gone wrong since we got to know Hepburn better. This. In the adaptation of Booth Tarkington's novel, Miss Hepburn plays, as I suppose everyone knows, a lower-middle-class girl of better-than-that pretensions. Her pretensions, indeed, are horrendous because they are so palpably what they are: refinement fabricated out of whole cloth, airs and graces that never were appropriate on land or sea. She is pushy, she is willing to lie about her family social standing, she is—to her knowing neighbors—the town joke, so much the town joke that when she goes to a local dance she is left entirely alone, a wallflower to wipe away the memory of all wallflowers before her. We see her standing there, pitifully trying to attract attention, utterly unattended.

A Ravishing Wallflower

And, looking at the sequence today, we don't believe a frame of it. The girl—no matter what else we may know about her—is so breathtakingly beautiful that the only conceivable next step is for a stag line to form instantly on her left, every male in the room fighting for position up front, and for her to dance, dance, dance all night. Are they idiots? we ask ourselves as we watch the local boys cut this ravishing creature dead.

Curiously, at the time "Alice Adams" was released (1935), this preposterous inversion of all common sense seems to have bothered no one. This newspaper's reviewer found the film at its most poignant during the sequence, speaking of Miss Hepburn as "an unwanted interloper whose pitiful finery is in sad contrast to the resplendent gowns of the other girls." Gowns! Do you realize that that man, instead of looking at Miss Hepburn, was looking at her *clothes*? And what young sporting blood, pray tell, ever danced with the best *dressed* at a party?

Yet the scene held, no doubt for a reason. I suspect that audiences, even after Miss Hepburn had been three years in pictures and made seven earlier films, were able to evade her beauty, or in some way discount it, because they felt insecure with her, unsure of just who and what she was. I think they thought she might bite, that they were in fact afraid of her. I suspect that the fearless John Barrymore was afraid of her when he found himself overwhelmed by this gale of sound, this profile, more indeflectible than his, in her first film, "A Bill of Divorcement" (Regency, Oct. 10). Fortunately, he was playing a man who was mentally ill and so was able to account for his bafflement. Actually, he was fine in the role, and I'm joking, in part; but only in part.

For Miss Hepburn came onto the screen as though she'd been spun from a UFO during a particularly powerful northeaster, an unfathomable force rather than a possible familiar. She didn't look like other people, she didn't talk like other people, and, what is more, she didn't care, Whoosh! Her self-confidence, verging on assault, wasn't based on anything very tangible: a modest Broadway success, a lot of understudying. She was her self-confidence, and, given an open door, she simply charged through it, unstoppable, unassailable, not even bothering to lower her upper lip until she'd shot

whole paragraphs past it. Declaration of independence.

So, when the scene in "Alice Adams" holds, it holds because she *tells* it to, because the audience doesn't dare not believe her. (Today we love her more, which means we are able to take a second, less cautious, look.) The other flaw in "Alice Adams" never was a flaw, though some counted it one at the time. The happy ending. Mr. Tarkington's novel had ended with her losing the young man she'd never really leveled with. Logical. If the film had ended that way, I think audiences

Culver Pictures

Katharine Hepburn in Mark Sandrich's 1936 film "A Woman Rebels"

would have torn RKO down, sound stage by sound stage. I confess I'd have helped. For the personality we'd been inthralled to, however imperious her behavior, *had* to be vulnerable somewhere. We couldn't see it, we just knew it. The more she grated on us the more we ached for what was hidden inside her. She had to have a man, for our sake, not for hers. She commanded the frames, we demanded the ending. The emotional line of the film led us to it; there would have been no complexity without.

Labeled as 'Box-Office Poison'

But, as Miss Hepburn went on having both successes and failures, an uncertainty developed. If she was vulnerable, couldn't that be shown, possibly with tears? She tried that, crying a lot, in "Mary of Scotland," and it didn't work. Belied the steel that was in her. But the steel, unrelieved, was becoming a problem, too: In "Holiday," still beloved by many, critic Frank Nugent called her mannish and overly precise, concluding that her intensity was apt to be too much for "even so sanguinary a temperament as Cary Grant's." Her career shot up and down, erratically,

and a group of less than prophetic exhibitors took out a trade-paper ad labeling her "box office poison." The independence and the vulnerability still hadn't quite come into balance. The lady remained hard to *place*.

Also to lick. Off she went to New York, up she came with a big fat hit in Philip Barry's "Philadelphia Story," back to the coast to make a successful film of it (Regency, Nov. 3). But, strangely, two more years would elapse before she had another film in release. Wouldn't even *hits* put her permanently on tap?

The next one did, and the solution turned out to be simple. Cast with Spencer Tracy in "Woman of the Year" (Regency Nov. 10), she found herself playing opposite a leading man even more independent than she. Eureka! 'Twas all that was needed. She could be as willful as she'd seemed to be from birth, he could knock her ears back when absolutely necessary; the twin strains in her temperament could surface together. Done and **done**.

Or so I read the securing of a career, after which all may not have been gravy but there's been caviar constantly on the table. No one has to place Miss Hepburn these days. She's the girl we didn't dance with, and don't we wish we had?

1976 S 17, C1:1

A Look Backward

RISING TARGET, a documentary film about the assassination of Robert F. Kennedy directed and produced by Barbara Frank; camera, James Joanides, Robert Eberlein, Eli Hollander, Joan Churchill and Eric Saarinen; editor, Jean-Claude Lubtchansky; production Company, Joshua Films. At the Second International Festival of Women's Films, Cinema Studio Theater. Will be shown today at 7 P.M. and tomorrow at 9 P.M. Running time: 80 minutes. This film has not been rated.

By RICHARD EDER

A DOCUMENTARY, such as Barbara Frank's film about the killing of Robert F. Kennedy, has a peculiar power to reverse the order of time. It should be used with delicacy or the emotional effects it produces will be fraudulent.

"Rising Target," which is being shown at the International Women's Film Festival at the Cinema Studio Theater, is a decent film, quite straightforward and often affecting, but it does brush occasionally upon such fraudulence.

•

Making a virtue out of necessity, it is an outsider's view of the few days before, during and after the assassination. The camera shows the campaign train in California, Senator Kennedy's flight to Los Angeles, the partylike atmosphere at the hotel as news of his primary victory came in, the confusion when the shots were fired out of everyone's sight, the vigil at the hospital, and finally the airplane flying out of Los Angeles with the body and the mourners.

American political campaigning has a full share of hoopla and nonsense. The camera shows it all: some silly jokes and sillier dance routines by Jerry Lewis and Gene Kelly, respectively, at a rally just before the balloting; Senator Kennedy's own brief and rather lame speech.

But of course we know he is going to be killed and so the more or less harmless silliness becomes sinister and shocking. Tying the two together is not really a legitimate way to comment

either upon the silliness or upon whatever may be more deeply wrong with American politics.

•

Otherwise, Miss Frank makes good use of her outsider's camera. If her machine is often blocked by the bigger machines of the television crews, if she has to crane and squint and stand on tiptoe, this only makes it a more accurate representation of what most participants actually see.

There is the cheering after Senator Kennedy makes his victory speech, thanks his supporters and leaves. The white doors of the pantry close behind him. There are a few seconds when the crowd in the ballroom remains fixed in its celebration, then a few squeaking screams, one voice distinctly shouting "God, God!" and then a turmoil of shoulders, heads, stunned faces and blocked camera views.

A scene from Barbara Frank's film "Rising Target"

There is the heaviness with which everyone moves after the tragedy has sunk in. Frank Mankiewicz, the press secretary, talks about the details of bullet fragments and bone splinters; Pierre Salinger gives the order of departure of the coffin and mourners. We take in the paradox; public life compels these two intimates of the dead man to speak in public, not about grief, but about timetables.

Miss Frank's film works as a record of a tragedy, even if it misses in its ironic overtones. But it does have an insight of another kind: Not into the tragedy, but into the helplessness that follows.

1976 S 17, C8:3

Little Comedy

PAPER TIGER, directed by Ken Annakin; screenplay by Jack Davies; produced by Euan Lloyd; director of photography, John Cabrera; editor, Alan Pattillo; music, Roy Budd; a MacLean film, distributed by Joseph E. Levine. Running time: 99 minutes. At Radio City Music Hall, Avenue of the Americas at 50th Street. This film has been rated PG.

Walter Bradbury	David Niven
Kagoyama	Toshiro Mifune
Koichi	Ando
Gunther Muller	Hardy Kruger
Foreign Secretary	Ivan Desny
Talah	Irene Tsu
Sergeant Forster	Ronald Fraser

David Niven in "Paper Tiger"

By VINCENT CANBY

"Paper Tiger," which opened yesterday at Radio City Music Hall, is a sentimental, fraudulent little comedy about a faint-hearted English schoolmaster, David Niven, who hires himself out as the tutor to the son of the Japanese Ambassador, Toshiro Mifune, to a mythical Southeast Asian country, played by a real country named Malaysia. When the small boy, played by a small boy named Ando, and the schoolmaster are kidnapped by local revolutionaries, the Niven character gets a chance to prove its mettle.

The film was directed by Ken Annakin with so little style that even the scenery in and around Kuala Lumpur is boring.

●

"Paper Tiger" has been rated PG in recognition, I guess, that the no-nonsense violence that erupts near the end, when the kidnappers are caught, has a stronger reality than anything else in this labored daydream.

1976 S 17, C8:3

Comedy About Prostitutes Much Less Than Funny

"Zig Zig," the 1974 French comedy that opened yesterday at the 72d Street Embassy and 59th Street Twin 1 Theaters, is so heavy with undigested ideas that its ankles collapse in the first 15 minutes. Almost everything afterward is pure pain.

It's about two Pigalle hookers who call themselves "love's little nurses" and dream of building a house in the forest with their earnings. It's also about a police inspector who talks philosophically of his relationship to his tapeworm, a kidnapper who turns himself into a human torch (I think) to

make the police feel sorry, and a man who says cheerily of his wife's kidnapping, "Women are so easily carried away."

The film is the work of Laszlo Szabo, the Hungarian actor-director—a filmmaker who hasn't yet found how to

The Cast

ZIG ZIG, directed by Laszlo Szabo; screenplay (French with English subtitles) by Mr. Szabo; director of photography, Jean-Pierre Baux; music by Karl-Heinz Schafer, a Renn-Productions/Les Films de la Citrouille (Paris)/F.R.A.L. (Rome) co-production; released by Peppercorn and Wormser. At the Embassy 72d Street Theater, at Broadway, and the 59th Street Twin 1 Theater, east of Third Avenue. Running time: 87 minutes. This film is classified R.

Marie	Catherine Deneuve
Pauline	Bernadette Lafont
Mr. Jean	Hubert Deschamps
Walter	Walter Chiari
Inspector Bruyere	Stephen Shandor
Drummer	Jean-Pierre Kalfon
Singer	Georgette Anys
Edelweiss	Jean-Pierre Maud

recycle bad jokes into good ones and how to blend slapstick comedy with melodrama in the manner of something like "Shoot the Piano Player."

"Zig Zig" is chaotic. It also forces Catherine Deneuve and Bernadette Lafont to make idiots of themselves trying simultaneously to be funny and touching as the hookers, who also sing and dance in a Pigalle nightclub numbers that one feel embarrassed for them. That's impolite film-making.

VINCENT CANBY

1976 S 18, 24:5

STREET PEOPLE, directed by Maurice Lucidi; screenplay by Ernest Tidyman and Randall Kleiser; music, Luis Enriquez; art director, Gastogne Carsetti; an American International Release. At the Lyric 42d Street, between Seventh and Eighth Avenues, 86th Street Twin I, at Lexington Avenue, 83d Street Triplex, at Broadway and other theaters. Running time: 92 minutes. This film is classified R.

Ulysses	Roger Moore
Phil	Stacy Keach
Salvatore Francesco	Ivo Garrani
Bishop Lopetri	Entore Manni
Continenza	Ennio Balbo
Nicoletta	Fausto Tozzi

The fact that a half-dozen names are flashed on screen as the writers of "Street People" goes a long way toward explaining why this movie of Mafia fratricide has the look of having been stitched together by script doctors who couldn't manage to close all the seams.

As a result, "Street People," which opened yesterday at neighborhood theaters, suffers from a plot that seems to be pushed along, willy-nilly, despite an inclination toward collapse; from relationships never quite clarified; from characters developed for a while, then allowed to drop; from injections of what must have been hoped were cinematic wonder drugs—car chases reminiscent of "Bullitt," flashbacks reminiscent of "The Godfather, Part II."

None of it helps to cultivate much interest in finding out who smuggled narcotics with a street value of $3 million into San Francisco inside a crucifix imported from Sicily, thanks to the generosity of a Mafioso.

Although the real mystery in "Street People" is the whereabouts of the police during all the shooting, the unraveling of the movie's putative mystery is entrusted to Roger Moore, who plays an Anglo-Sicilian Mafia counselor, and to Stacy Keach, whom he employs to assist him. They play it so cool that they congeal long before most of the blood.

LAWRENCE VAN GELDER

1976 S 18, 24:5

RIDDANCE, directed by Marta Meszaros; screenplay (Hungarian with English subtitles), by Miss Meszaros; director of photography, Laios Koltai; music, Levente Szorenyi; distributed by New Yorker Films. Running time: 84 minutes. At the Second International Festival of Women's Films at the Cinema Studio Theater, Broadway at 66th Street.

Jutka	Erzsebet Kutvolgyi
Andras	Gabor Nagy
Zsuzsu	Mariann Moor
Jutka's father	Ferenc Kallai
Jutka's mother	Mari Szemes
Andras' father	Laszlo Szabo
Andras' mother	Teri Foldi

By VINCENT CANBY

There may no longer be easily recognizable social classes in Communist Hungary, but there remain class distinctions that can be as malignant as any under the old order.

"Riddance," the 1973 Hungarian film directed by Marta Meszaros, is the rueful account of the love affair of a pretty, spirited young woman who works in a textile factory and a young university student whose parents are grossly more equal than other people. Having just emerged from the working class, his mother and father guard their bourgeois status not tenaciously, but primly, as if it were their bookcase full of fragile, unspeakably awful knickknacks.

●

"Riddance," which was shown yesterday at the Second International Festival of Women's Films at the Cinema Studio, will be repeated Monday at 6 P.M. and Tuesday at 8 P.M.

The film is the second by Miss Meszaros, whose "Adoption," was one of the better selections shown this spring at the Museum of Modern Art's New Directors/New Films series.

On the basis of these two films, Miss Meszaros is a director of real sensitivity with an affection for characters who pursue unpopular causes, including honesty, to lunatic lengths. Although the heroines in both films are women of fine backbone and wit, the movies themselves look deceptively austere. It's not that the director is without humor, but rather that she prefers to let it surface so perfectly surrounded by unhappy circumstances that it's easy to overlook. The humor has the effect of a joke remembered in tranquillity. It's lonely

●

Thus, though "Riddence" is a serious film, it's likely to seem more solemn than it actually is. In addition, Miss Meszaros's characters don't share happy or funny moments with the audience. When they occur, it's as if they are simply meant to be a measure of the extent of some future loss. Miss Meszaros does not believe in leaving us laughing or crying, only, if possible, more thoughtful.

Erzsebet Kutvolgyi, as the young woman, a sort of Hungarian Alice Adams whose family doesn't come up to the snobbish standards of her suitor's, is pretty and lithe and as close to being funny as anything in the film. Gabor Nagy is good as the young man whose bourgeois affection and respect for his bourgeois parents are stronger

Erzsebet Kutvolgyi
"A Hungarian Alice Adams"

than his love for the girl. A coincidence: Laszlo Szabo, who plays the young man's father, is the director of the French film "Zig Zig," which also opened yesterday.

1976 S 18, 25:1

ALOISE, directed by Liliane de Kermadec; written by Liliane de Kermadec and Andre Techne; produced by Alain Dahan; photographed by Jean Penzer, the Second International Festival of Women's Films, Cinema Studio Theater. Today at 6 P.M. and tomorrow at 8 P.M. Running time: 117 minutes. This film has not been rated.

Young Aloise	Isabelle Huppert
Adult Aloise	Delphine Seyrig
Father	Marc Heyraud
Singing teacher	Roger Blin
Chaplain	Hans Werner

By RICHARD EDER

"Aloise" is a very static and occasionally very beautiful movie that suffers mainly from not being about as much as it attempts to be about.

It is the story of a repressed, grave girl with lopsided angers who goes from Switzerland to Germany as a governess, falls in love with her employer, is sent back to Switzerland when World War I breaks out, goes mad, and spends the rest of her life in an asylum.

In her old age and the film's, her clogged, mismatched gifts find a sudden channel. Aloise—the protagonist—makes a remarkable series of paintings: bright-colored, Chagall-like figures with a rocketing sexuality and, invariably, closed eyes.

"Aloise," which was shown yesterday in the Second International Festival of Women's Films at the Cinema Studio, is divided by its director, Liliane de Kermadec, into two very distinct sections. The first is an elliptical series of scenes, filmed with deliberate stillness and a white light, showing the protagonist as a young girl.

She is the daughter of a Swiss railroad employee; she lives with him and her sister. Her mother is dead. "My name," she says, "has every vowel except 'u.' I wish I were called 'Lulu.'" She is sure she is a singer; she takes lessons, practices, glares at other less-determined singers at church. But her voice won't serve; it is tuneful, but hard and reedy.

As played by Isabella Huppert, the

adolescent Aloise is, in her unvarying gravity, a figure of some mystery. What is this frustrated effort, this self-delusion building toward?

The scene shifts suddenly, and so does the actress. She arrives in Germany for her job as a governess; almost at once the role is taken over by another actress, Delphine Seyrig. She falls in love hysterically, is sent home, and breaks down.

The mystery of the child is resolved: All those nuances were preparation for madness. But this is asserted, not demonstrated. There is no real link: First she was sad as Isabelle Huppert, then she was mad as Delphine Seyrig.

The bulk of the film, then, is Miss Seyrig in the asylum. We see the doctors talking, the other patients, Aloise serself. It is most painfully and well observed, and Miss Seyrig's perform-

ance is breathtaking. But for quite a while we are never really sure why we are seeing it.

The ending puts things together to some extent. Aloise begins to paint on wrapping paper, the doctors encourage her, and her work is put on exhibition in a big-city gallery. There is one splendid scene: She inspects the display, this aged sparrow of a woman, still quite mad, hopping by those evidences of a life that lives only on the wall and that she only faintly recognizes. And making banal comments such as this one, in front of a picture of two lovers: "This is a little vulgar; pretty, but not my cup of tea."

A startling image of disassociation, it almost makes up for the long, long passages that precede it.

1976 S 21, 30:5

FILM VIEW

VINCENT CANBY

The Surprise Hit of the Movie Season

The surprise box office hit of the New York summer season has not been the lugubriously silly exorcize of demonology, "The Omen," nor Mel Brooks's non-stop smile, "Silent Movie," nor Brian De Palma's soft-focus he-done-it, "Obsession," nor Don Siegel's "The Shootist," which, having John Wayne in the foreground of the Old West, could only have been a surprise had it been a flop. The surprise of the season was—and continues to be—a wise, gentle, supremely romantic French comedy that came into this country with absolutely nothing in the way of the usual build-up going for it, including a director unknown in this hemisphere and some actors whose names might have been slightly familiar though it would have been difficult to place their faces.

Jean-Charles Tacchella's "Cousin, Cousine" is only the director's second feature film (his first, "Voyage en Grande Tartarie," made in 1974, hasn't been released here) but because he has been writing screenplays since 1955 and was, with the late André Bazin and others, a co-founder of the film magazine, "Objectif 49," he can't easily be described as a young Turk or a young anything else. He's been around, which is not the best thing to have been in a business that consumes youth in the manner of Count Alucard draining a maiden at the neck.

Yet "Cousin, Cousine," now in its ninth week at the Paris Theater and still going strong, is setting records that go all the way back to 1966 and Claude Lelouch's "A Man and a Woman," with which "Cousin, Cousine" is being compared, though to me that's to underrate the substance of the new film, if not to underrate its appeal to sentiment that never slops over into the sentimental. "Cousin, Cousine" comes close. Every time disaster threatens Tacchella brings his film and us back from never-never-land by exposing an honest nerve, sometimes painful, more often funny.

● ● ●

"Cousin, Cousine" is a love story of the kind that not many people have made since the golden age of Hollywood's screwball comedies, and though "Cousin, Cousine" is hardly a screwball comedy, it shares with those films—"My Man Godfrey," "It Happened One Night," "The Awful Truth" and "Twentieth Century" — a frank, direct, lyrically comic, thoroughly healthy approach to love. In those Hollywood films a thoroughly transparent, artificial pride was the thing that kept the lovers apart, though there was never any doubt, if only from the casting of the star roles, about who loved whom. "Cousin, Cousine" charts the growth into fully committed sexual love of something that begins as mutual ap-

preciation, evolves into interest, turns into delight and then into a mutually acknowledged love that is maintained for a while in a platonic affair, not because of any particular moral scruples but because the lovers want to have this final joke on their families and friends who immediately assume the affair to be a steamily sexual one.

The lovers of "Cousin, Cousine," Marthe (Marie-Christine Barrault) and Ludovic (Victor Lanoux) are not separated by artificial barriers. When they first meet at the wedding of Marthe's mother to Ludovic's uncle, Marthe and Ludovic are very much married to other spouses, though not happily. Marthe's husband is a compulsive philanderer and Ludovic's wife is a pretty, bird-brained neurotic who takes periodic sleep cures. Marthe and Ludovic are drawn together when Marthe's husband zeros in on Ludovic's wife simply because she's there, but with no more interest than he has in the bus driver, the sales clerk, the family councillor and all the other women with whom he's maintaining liaisons more dopey than dangerous. However, the only real barrier to Marthe and Ludovic is the determination that each must discover within in order to take decisive action.

● ● ●

As written by Tacchella, Marthe and Ludovic are immensely winning characters, rigorously honest, kind without being stupid, witty, each completely in charge of himself/herself and thus in no need to rush into affairs or into sleep cures to cope with or avoid the world outside. They are so practically perfect that they might be impossibly saintlike without the humor, intelligence and revivifying spite that Miss Barrault and Mr. Lanoux bring to their roles. She is a radiant blonde with a firm will and he gives every impression of being the sort of man who has seen most of life's idiocies, identified them and refused to despair if only because he wants to see what new idiocy will turn up next. Actors and characters are so beautifully matched that it's no-contest with anyone else in the film. There's no doubt about what will happen, only how.

Mr. Tacchella's method is steadfastly sunny. Most of "Cousin, Cousine" takes place in spring and summer in the verdant banlieue of Paris. The autumn days we see are brisk and clean, and when the season turns wintry, it's not just any winter day but Christmas Eve. The affair of Marthe and Ludovic is not isolated but contained within a large, loving, tightly knit family group that is prepared to forgive all trespasses. These are the details by which such romantic comedies are created, but if the film were not so essentially comic, the details would be merely decorative.

When it opened in July, "Cousin, Cousine" received favorable notices, but so have a number of other imported films —equally unknown to the general public—which have gone on to die fast deaths at the box offices. It's apparent that audiences are keeping this one alive, a factor that's almost as refreshing as the film itself. It should give backbone to movie distributors and theater owners who, like producers, are inclined to read their balance sheets and think that the only way to stay in business is to show machine-made schlock. Not so.

Not all the films coming in from abroad these days are great, but people who have given up on the domestic stuff should give consideration not only to "Cousin, Cousine," but to another French import, Bertrand Tavernier's "The Clockmaker" featuring Phillipe Noiret's extraordinary performance, Peter Watkins's "Edvard Munch," a fine, very socially conscious biography of an artistic temperament, that of the great Norwegian Expressionist painter, and, from Japan, Masaki Kobayashi's "Kaseki," a dour but monumental film about a man, and a nation, to whom fate hands a queen of spades.

1976 S 19, II:15:1

Miss Dreyfus's Cogent Work
Is Marred by Banal Ending

By VINCENT CANBY

It is late summer in the south of France. The setting is a comfortable old fieldstone farmhouse that has been made suitable, at great expense, for people who want to flee Paris in August in style. One can see the heat rising from the surrounding fields. Days are halcyon.

The children get up at dawn and play almost nonstop so that by evening there are short fits of exhausted tears, ravenous appetites, hysterical giggles at the slightest jokes, followed by bed and the immediate sleep of the innocents, or the drugged.

●

Beside the swimming pool a beautiful woman, Agnes, lies braless, staring at the sun through closed lids and having erotic fantasies about the young gardener. Her husband sits nearby in the shade, going fat around the mid-

The Cast

FEMMES AU SOLEIL (Women In The Sun), directed, produced and written in French with English subtitles by Liliane Dreyfus; director of photography, Nestor Almendros; editor, Claudine Bouche; music, Bookie Brinkley; produced by Bethsebee Films and Sunchild Productions. Running time: 93 minutes. At the Second International Festival of Women's Films at Cinema Studio Theater, Broadway at 66th Street. This film has not been rated.

Emma .... Juliette Maynial
Agnes .... Genevieve Fontanel
Perla .... Nathalie Chantrel

dle. Another young woman, Perla, who feels very much in love, teases her lover, who wants to be left in peace to finish reading a sci-fi novel.

The hostess, Emma, somewhat older than the rest, watches over the company with such serenity that at first we don't realize that the man in the T-shir is her husband, nor that she seriously anticipates leaving him that day for a younger lover.

This is the mood of the beginning of Liliane Dreyfus's "Femmes au Soleil," a beautiful, composed and civilized French movie that was shown yesterday at the Second International Festival of Women's Films at the Cinema Studio. It will be shown again today at 6 P.M. and tomorrow at 8 P.M.

"Femmes au Soleil" is so good for so much of the way that it's a disappointment when it turns comparatively polemical. Near the close of the day covered by the film, Emma, Agnes and Perla gather at the far end of the lawn and begin to tick off the woes of womanhood. The feeling of humor, spontaneous ease and informed indolence that has characterized the film to that point vanishes, to be replaced by what sounds like testimony given at a consciousness raising seminar.

Perhaps I'm overreading this section of the film because of the auspices under which it's being presented in New York, though I doubt it. The quality of the talk in "Femmes Au Soleil" goes suddenly banal, something for which Miss Dreyfus cannot easily avoid responsibility by having Emma say drearily: "I am banal. My words are banal." Banality cannot thus be transformed into something else. Nor is it a bad dream to be neutralized by being identified. When a character makes such an admission, and it's true, the writer surrenders a sacred position to ask our sympathy.

•

Until this point, "Femmes au Soleil" is, as the festival program describes it, "Rohmeresque," at least to the extent that it recalls the mood and the wit of Eric Rohmer's "Claire's Knee," which was also superlatively photographed by Nestor Almendros. Juliette Mayniel, Geneviève Fontanel and Nathalie Chantrel are fine as the unhappy women, though I think Miss Dreyfus ultimately shortchanges them.

Much more moving than talk about fidelity, identity, abortions or the time at which a woman leaves "the age of illusion" to enter "the age of acceptance" of defeat (which is not a problem uniquely woman's), are moments such as the one in which Emma and her small daughter wrestle with the New Math and we are able to see a new mind awakening.

1976 S 22, 29:1

Medical Project and Poverty Are Topics at Whitney

By RICHARD EDER

Two poorly made documentaries on serious subjects make up the second program in the Whitney Museum's cycle on New American Filmmakers.

One, "Tuskegee Subject #626," deals with one of he grimmer stories to come out of the South in recent years. This was the disclosure hat over a period of 40 years, ending in 1972, about 400 black men with syphilis were he subject of a medical-research study in which the directors saw no reason either to tell these men of their illness or make any attempt o cure them.

•

Leroy McDonald, a black filmmaker, has done a fictional account of one subject, an old farmer named Clarence Obadiah Washington. A kindly, cheerful man who has taken part happily in what he thinks is a harmless medical study, he, along with his wife, is shattered when he learns the truth.

The film, intended as denunciation, turns a shocking event into something like bad soap opera, with all the parts

The Program

TUSKEGEE SUBJECT #626, produced, directed, written and edited by Leroy McDonald. Music by Taj Mahal. With Robertearle Jones as Clarence Washington and Pauline Myers as Emma Washington. Running time: 52 minutes.

BLOOD'S WAY, produced, directed, edited and written by Stan Taylor. With Tracy Reed, Leroy McDonald and Ted Wilson. Running time: 18 minutes.

Both films are part of the New American Filmmakers Series at the Whitney Museum of American Art. Through Sunday.

badly written and most of them ludicrously acted. The two principals, the old man and his wife, are played by good actors — Robertearle Jones and Paulene Myers — but the lines they have to speak are so wooden and soft, simultaneously, that the effect is of bad acting.

•

The second film, by Stan Taylor, is sketchier, but about as equally inept. It consists of a couple of scenes between a black teacher and her unemployed husband, who mocks her, degrades her, takes money from her and generally tries to drag her down.

The situation represents one much-documented aspect of black urban poverty, but the film is the equivalent of an undergraduate paper on the subject. It is schematic and forced, and its two characters are merely statistics with faces.

1976 S 22, 38:5

THE WHITE WALL, written and directed by Stig Bjorkman; produced by Bengt Forslund; photographed by Peter Davidsson; edited by Mr. Bjorkman and Margit Nordqvist. At the Cinema Studio Theater tonight at 6 P.M. and tomorrow at 9 P.M. Running time: 80 minutes. This film has not been rated.

Monika .... Harriet Andersson
Berit .... Lena Nyman
Kjell .... Sven Wollter
Arne .... Tomas Ponten

By RICHARD EDER

Stockholm has rarely looked so bleak as it does in Stig Bjorkman's "The White Wall," which was shown yesterday at the International Festival of Women's Films. Except for the protagonist, the streets are all but empty and the few people in sight pass like fish swimming 1,000 feet below the surface of a cold sea.

This numbness, this uncommunicating despair is intended to be the message and consequence we draw from one day and night in the life of a lonely woman. Instead it is applied beforehand, as it were; it flows into the story rather than flowing from it.

•

Monika, played by Harriet Andersson, is divorced and lives with her son. She is looking for a job and picks up men for company. When the film opens, she sits up in bed, climbs over the stranger sleeping beside her, totters into the next room, takes a pill, looks at a newspaper and sends her son off to school. She is wearing white, the bed coverlet is white, the walls are white; the whiteness is a symbol of isolation and sterility.

The man, who has picked her up the night before at one of the dances she regularly goes to for that purpose, comes out to dress. He is perfectly nice, they are both civilized and wry, and they have nothing whatever to say to each other.

She teeters through the day—job-hunting unsuccessfully, buying a skirt, bickering over the telephone with her ex-husband, visiting a friend and going to another dance with her and picking up still one more stranger.

•

Lank, dispirited, numb; she is, or is intended to be, the symbol of the modern urban woman as victim of an impersonal society and of men who are victims too. Men and women are rival gangs: The men gather in knots at the dance hall and plan their attack; the women sit in pairs and mock the attackers. The transactions take place, from sheer need; but they are hostile transactions.

"White Wall," which will be repeated at the Cinema Studio Theater tonight and tomorrow night, has force but it lacks life. Monica's depression, her inability to give or receive anything, her selfishness—these are meant to be wounds but in fact they are knives. Our sympathy is never aroused; and our sense of distance from her and the film may be a pity, but it is a fact.

1976 S 23, 52:1

AMERICA AT THE MOVIES, a documentary composed of scenes from 83 films; produced by George Stevens, Jr.; designed by James R. Silke; narration written by Theodore Strauss and spoken by Charlton Heston; associate producer, Harrison Engle; editor, David Saxon; associate editors, Joseph Parker and Ana Luisa Corley Perez; an American Film Institute production, distributed by Cinema 5. Running time: 116 minutes. At the Beekman Theater, Second Avenue at 66th Street; Paramount Theater, on Columbus Circle; Plaza Theater, 58th Street east of Madison Avenue; and Murray Hill Theater, 34th Street at Third Avenue. This film has been rated PG.

By VINCENT CANBY

In recognition of our Bicentennial year, the American Film Institute, an agency supported by the film industry, private foundations and the National Endowment for the Arts, and the institute's head, George Stevens Jr., have labored long and deliberately to bring forth upon this continent a new genre: the coffee-table movies.

"America at the Movies," which opened at four theaters yesterday, would make the perfect Christmas gift for the person who has everything, including his own screening room and a live-in projectionist. It's not a movie you should feel compelled to look at from beginning to end at one sitting. Like "Life Goes to the Movies," a coffee-table book, it's something to be dipped into at random. It's a movie searching unsuccessfully for a theme, recalling things we already know and never once revealing an original or surprising insight.

•

"America at the Movies" is not really boring. It's just not necessary. Like the most expensive, beautifully designed, high-toned coffee-table book, it's something we would never have missed but, once having it, would hesitate to throw out.

"America at the Movies" is a handsome, glossy anthology-film made up of 92 scenes from 83 movies that date from 1915 ("The Birth of a Nation") to 1974 ("The Godfather, Part II"), though the vast majority of the material is from the sound era. What it means to be is something else. According to Mr. Stevens, "It's not a film about American history and it's not about the movies. Rather it's about the American people and spirit as we've seen it on the screen."

But even that last statement, as vague and general as it is, has the effect of putting a burden on Hollywood filmmakers they never intended to carry, so that although it's upbeat and optimistic, "America at the Movies" winds up a sort of vacant-eyed, solemn-voiced, completely unknowing indictment of the films and film makers it thinks it's celebrating.

For the most part, the American people and spirit we see on the screen here suddenly make us realize how limited and how artificial the terms in which, over the years, Hollywood has interpreted our dreams and given them back to us. That is true but it's also beside the point of the many great individual films that have been ransacked for the material that has gone into "America at the Movies."

The film is divided into a prologue and five sections: "The Land," "The Cities," "The Families," "The Wars" and "The Spirit." Though Mr. Stevens, who produced the film, and James R. Silke, who is credited with having "designed" it, are not frivolous, the effect of their work is.

America's 19th-century preoccupation with its frontiers and land is seen almost entirely in terms of westerns. Twenty of the 23 films in this section are westerns, which means, in the vision of Hollywood, America had no New England, no Virginia, no Louisiana. Instead it was all Monument Valley, real and metaphoric.

What land has meant to Americans is so magnificently summed up in the several scenes we see from John Ford's "The Grapes of Wrath," that you might want to see the rest of that one film and not a lot of tidbits from others.

The remaining sections of "America at the Movies" are equally revealing, and equally silly. It's fun seeing Woody Allen's holdup scene from "Take the Money and Run," but what, really, does this have to do with "The Cities"? "The Families" is considerably brightened by a clip of W. C. Fields threatening his dimwitted daughter (from "The Pharmacist"), which also makes a comment on family relationships totally missing from most of the other clips.

"The Wars" section gives one the impression that the only intelligent movie Hollywood ever made about war was "Patton," if only because the clips from "The Birth of a Nation," "Dr. Strangelove," "Catch 22" and "M*A*S*H," among others, are so unsatisfactory.

The concluding section, "The Spirit," contains some marvelous material—James Cagney singing the title number from "Yankee Doodle Dandy," Buster Keaton in "Steamboat Bill Jr.," Walter Huston in "The Treasure of the Sierra Madre"—but none of them do justice to the films from which it has been taken.

In having failed to give shape to their material, Mr. Stevens and his associates have produced the world's longest coming attraction.

"America at the Movies" has been rated PG ("parental guidance suggested") because, I assume, some of the more recent clips from R-rated films such as "Patton" may contain offensive language.

1976 S 23, 52:1

MAD DOG; directed by Philippe Mora; screenplay by Mr. Mora, based on the book "Morgan the Bold Bushranger" by Margaret Carnegie; director of photography, Mike Molloy; editor, John Scott; music, Patrick Flynn; produced by Jeremy Thomas; released by Cinema Shares International Distribution Corporation. At Loews State I, Broadway and 45th Street; Loews Tower East, Third Avenue and 72d Street, and the 34th Street-East Theater, east of Third Avenue. Running time: 93 minutes. This film is rated R.

Daniel Morgan	Dennis Hopper
Billy	David Gulpilil
Superintendent Cobham	Frank Thring
Detective Manwaring	Jack Thompson
Macpherson	Wallas Eaton
Sergeant Smith	Bill Hunter

A bleak view of mankind is contrasted with the lushness of nature in "Mad Dog." a film about Daniel Morgan, a 19th-century Australian outlaw, that opened yesterday at Loews State I, Loews Tower East and the 34th Street East Theaters.

Like the English highwaymen celebrated by poets and the American gunslingers of the Old West, Daniel Morgan was a man whose exploits as a bushranger—in the gold-rush days when Australia was in the throes of transition from penal colony to what was to be British Commonwealth status —lent themselves both to ugly distortion and mitigating legend. This movie purports to set the record straight, concentrating on the Australian-born Morgan's life during his last dozen years.

It is a period in which Morgan proceeds from having been a volatile, vengeful and unsuccessful inhabitant of a mining camp in which bigots massacre Chinese, through his first holdups, capture and a prison sentence that subjects him to branding, homosexual rape, brutal guards and hard labor; to parole, horse thievery, wounding, nursing at the hands of his only friend—a youth who appears to be an aborigine but is in fact the outcast son of a white father—and a criminal career that makes Morgan the object of relentless police pursuit and the instrument of numerous police deaths.

"Mad Dog" is a film that eyes with deep love the sprawling Australian landscaped and, with matching devotion, its inhabitants. The "civilized" people who hunt down and mutilate Morgan are depicted as no better educated and no more moral than the thief and killer who, toward the end, describes himself as a mad dog.

With its massacres, ambushes, hunts, holdups and frequent bloodlettings, as well as a portrayal of Morgan by Dennis Hopper that ranges from explosive to endearing, "Mad Dog" will bore few searchers for violent escapist entertainment. But this is a film with higher aspirations. And here it turns out to be a movie of odd prissiness and narrative shortcoming.

Here is a film that—to put it kindly —is unflinching about gore and brutality. Heads are blown away. Gouts of blood drench shooters, victims, furnishings. Animal entrails are draped over people. And yet, when Morgan robs people, the victims are rarely seen, unless he is being kind to them for one reason or another.

If this is an effort to shield Morgan, it falls short. Unlike some film outlaws, he remains a basically unsympathetic character which is acceptable, What is unacceptable is that he remains unrevealed. Mad dogs have their explanations. It is all right for "Mad Dog" to stay on the surface of the Australian landscape; but it succumbs to failure by its disinclination to mine character.

LAWRENCE VAN GELDER

1976 S 23, 52:4

Isabel Telleria and Ana Torrent in Victor Erice's "The Spirit of the Beehive"

Fantasy in Ruins

EL ESPIRITU DE LA COLMENA (The Spirit of The Beehive), directed by Victor Erice; screenplay (Spanish with English subtitles) by Francisco J. Querejeta, from an idea by Mr. Erice and Angel Fernandez Santos; director of photography, Luis Cuadrado; editor, Pablo G. del Amo; music, Luis de Pablo; a Janus release, distributed by Kino International. Running time: 98 minutes. At the D. W. Griffith Theater, 59th Street west of Second Avenue. This film has not been rated.

Ana	Ana Torrent
Isabel	Isabel Telleria
Fernando	Fernando Fernan Gomez
Teresa	Teresa Gimpera
Monster	Jose Villasante
Milagros	Lally Soldevilla
The fugitive	Juan Margallo
The doctor	Miguel Picazo

By VINCENT CANBY

LIVING in a city devastated by war can be as pernicious for the survivors as war was for the victims. The daily, weekly, monthly, yearly contact with civilization's debris changes expectations, dulls some senses and sharpens others. The smells are particular—rot and kerosene and, eventually, newly poured concrete. In a place where nothing comes easily, nothing is freely given. Citizens may be seen in groups. They live together as before, but each is a clandestine hermit.

Something of the same sort happens to people in a land long under an unbudgeable tyranny. Even to its artists. That's the effect of Victor Erice's 1973 Spanish film, "The Spirit of The Beehive," which opened yesterday at the D. W. Griffith Theater.

Secretive, deliberately paced, haunted and beautifully sorrowful, the movie is a ruined city, and I'm not sure that those of us who come to it for the first time, fresh from the airport, in effect, can adjust to it quickly enough to be able to see thrugh its various shades of twilight. It's not disorder that makes us uneasy here but the resolute way life goes on.

"The Spirit of the Beehive" is set in a remote Castillian village in 1940, shortly after the end of the Spanish Civil War. Although the village was untouched, the reminders of war are everywhere. When the traveling movie exhibitor arrives to give the villagers

a showing of "Frankenstein," the audience at the city hall is composed entirely of old women and children.

The center of the film is an upper middle-class family—a father, a mother and two small daughters—that has fled to the village with what few possessions they could bring from another home that is never identified. They live in a beautiful, austere old farmhouse that once was a place they may have come to for vacations.

They are clandestine hermits. The mother writes letters of longing to a lover who is probably dead. The father tends his bees and has a journal in which he tries to sort out the unsortable facts of mankind's existence. He keeps life away by dealing in metaphors, pondering at length a quotation from Maeterlinck's "Life of the Bee."

Their daughters, Isabel, 10 years old, and Ana, 8, go to the village school and occupy free time roaming the countryside, going to the occasional movie, making up laws for a universe no one would think they'd be interested in. They fill a void by playing on the railroad tracks, around bonfires, often on the edge of self-destruction.

More out of boredom than maliciousness, Isabel, after the screening of "Frankenstein," makes up a long, convoluted story for Ana about how the monster was not killed in the film ("The movie is a lie") and that, in fact, she (Isabel) knows him quite well. He is, she says, a spirit who comes whenever she calls him.

"The Spirit of The Beehive" is mostly about Ana's search for Frankenstein's monster, the spirit, who, at one point, she thinks she's found in a perfectly ordinary fugitive she discovers in an abandoned farmhouse. Faith, superstition and emotional desolation then take their toll of Ana, played by a little girl named Ana Torrent, who may or may not be an actress, but who responds to the director and the demands of the film with remarkable feeling.

Not since René Clement's "Forbidden Games" has any movie entered so deeply into the perilous country

of children's nightmares and fantasies, which, I suppose, have metaphorical meaning to Mr. Erice, though the film is best taken without too much interpretation.

Mr. Erice's style is eliptical. We always want to know more than he's willing to tell us, which is better than the other way around. The photography is carefully underlit, so that even sunny days have a darkening quality about them. Everything is a bit chilly at first, but as the film goes on, we realize it's because it has so much. It's as if Mr. Erice thought it would be rude to spell it out, and that, indeed, it would not do justice to the experience that haunts him.

1976 S 24, C8:3

BRANDED FOR LIFE, written and directed by Maria do Rosario; produced by Ricardo Moreira; photographed by Renato Neumann; edited by Sergio Sanz and Ruy Guerra; in Brazilian with English subtitles. International Festival of Women's Films, at the Cinema Studio today at 11 p.m. and Saturday at 9 p.m. This film has not been rated. Running time 88 minutes.

Jojo	Tessy Callado
Rosa	Rose Lacreta
Eduardo	Sergio Otero
Branquinho	Waldir Onofre

By RICHARD EDER

"Branded for Life" is an attempt to make a critique of modern Brazilian society through a story of three young drifters. One is a small-time thug, the second a prostitute and the third a street urchin, a girl just past puberty. They meet, move into the same apartment, take up a three-way sexual relationship, and undertake a series of amateurish stickups, with dismal results.

Their small life of crime is intended as a denunciation of a larger crime: the organization of their country's life. But the film, shown at the International Festival of Women's Films at the Cinema Studio Theater, is turgid, wooden and clumsy.

Tessy Callado, who looks somewhat like Maria Schneider, plays the urchin with a tough and eccentric appeal that occasionally becomes self-indulgent. The sex scenes are extraordinarily well done: They show the real passion and real awkwardness — cracker-crumbs in the sheets—of physical love.

But these things are not enough to make up for the film's heavy texture and trite melodrama. It is grotesque without being illuminating.

1976 S 24, C8:4

The Drug Problem

THE GOLDEN TRIANGLE, a documentary film directed by Marianne Lamour. Commentary by Catherine Lamour. Produced by SFP/Flory 100. Distributed by Sygma. At the Cinema Studio Theater, Broadway at 66th Street, tomorrow at 11 A.M. Running time: 52 minutes.

"The Golden Triangle" is a 52-minute, no-nonsense, French-made documentary arguing persuasively that the opium trade that produces 80 percent of the heroin from Southeast Asia is not a police problem, but a political problem.

But even more forcefully, this film defeats the bias of anyone who may still harbor the notion that only men are capable of undertaking and carrying out adventures of great peril and physical hardship in remote corners of the world.

"The Golden Triangle," which will be shown again tomorrow at 11 A.M. at the International Festival of Women's Films at the Cinema Studio, is chiefly the work of Marianne and Catherine Lamour, who made the trip into the distant, anarchic fastness where Laos, Thailand and Burma come together in the shadow of China.

The shape of the area and the value of its produce among the heroin addicts of the world give the film its name. Not the least of its achievements is to revive the excitement of a time when movies were capable of engrossing us by taking us to dangerous places that we could never hope to see.

The Golden Triangle is the redoubt of the Shan rebel army, warring against the Burmese Government, and of the Kuomintang, the remnants of the Chinese nationalist army forced out of its homeland by the victorious Communists more than a quarter of a century ago. The two forces exist in fragile accommodation amidst poppy-growing tribesman who receive a pittance for their harvests. And all exist in peril of Government forces.

The Lamour sisters and their crew, accompanied by Shan troops, made the journey into this area to show the poppy growers, buyers, caravans, refineries and skirmishes along a trail that led eventually to the old warlord who leads the Kuomintang force.

●

And this general, who has received suport from the United States, admits both to abandoning thoughts of overthrowing the Communists and to assisting in the opium traffic.

Not all journeys are worthwhile. But there is no question that the arduous trek of the Lamour sisters is to be valued for the light it sheds on the intricacies of the opium trade and, more enduringly, for the statement it makes on behalf of the capabilities of women.

LAWRENCE VAN GELDER

1976 S 24, C8:6

FILM VIEW

VINCENT CANBY

Killing For Kids

If custard maims and whipped cream kills, is mayhem less brutal or death less final? This is one of the questions posed to the adult by Alan Parker's very curious English film, "Bugsy Malone," a musical parody, enacted by what department stores classify as "young adults," of those American gangster films produced mostly in the thirties about big-city crime in the twenties. When you first learn that "Bugsy Malone" is acted by kids, your stomach has every right to turn over. The heart can miss a beat. The mind bends under the awful weight of memories of radio's old Horn & Hardart Children's Hour, when four-year-old tots with oddly formed vocal chords did imitations of Sophie Tucker, Harry Lauder, Helen Kane, Al Jolson and Lillian Roth. Perhaps, like me, you can also remember being forced to sit through some dreadful nonsense, made, I suppose, for children, in which chimpanzees wearing little suits and dresses and sunbonnets waddled through an entire feature film that was supposed to be a comic Western. My friends and I gave that one a group-cringe. I suppose some kids liked it but at the age of nine or ten, the members of my group thought it was over-cooked rhubarb. When we spent our money on a Western, we wanted Hopalong Cassidy or Buck Jones or even Ken Maynard, not midget apes. It's not that we objected to midget apes, only to the ones who attempted to act like people. We took our movie illusions seriously.

I don't know how many nine- or 10-year-olds today are so severe in their judgments about movies, but I suspect most children are much more logical than adults—sometimes tenaciously so—in demanding not realism but consistency in whatever crazy world they find themselves. They are perfectly willing to accept as a fact in fiction that one special Volkswagen can fly, but then they want to know why a Volkswagen that is able to fly can't change its own tire. If you don't have a satisfactory explanation, be prepared for the interest to flag. It's only when we grow older that we learn that there are times when consistency and logic may be freely abandoned in the cause of some greater truth, like the Marx Brothers'.

The world that Alan Parker has created in "Bugsy Malone" is very peculiar indeed, but he is remarkably successful considering the terrible odds against such a stunt in the first place. The New York City streets, nightclubs, rooms-let-by-the-week and Bowery missions are scaled down to the size of the cast, whose members range in age from what looks to be about 10 to the late teens. The film is the story of a gang war that erupts when a mobster named Dandy Dan, who looks a lot like a Zachary Scott, who's been reduced the way chicken stock is, attempts to take over the rackets of Fat Sam, played by a tubby boy with a raspy voice that's not been too long changed. The hero, Bugsy Malone, played by Scott Baio, who could be older than he looks or else prematurely aged for his years, is a loner who, for the love of his ambitious girlfriend, a singer, throws in with Fat Sam to earn the loot to take them to Hollywood.

The movie opens with a splat, not a bang, in a ritualized gangland execution. Roxy Robinson, one of Fat Sam's soldiers, is rubbed out when Dandy Dan's associates catch him in an alley, place him against the brick wall, and turn their Splurge guns on him. Roxy Robinson is eliminated by gangland's newest secret weapon, the gun that shoots whipped cream. Thereafter, for the rest of the film, the war between Dandy Dan and Fat Sam is punctuated by ambushes, St. Valentine's Day-like massacres, and ridetakings in which the lethal cartridges contain whipped cream. At first it seems funny, sort of cartoon-like, but then when favorite characters wind up among the missing after having been surprised by a lucky hit with a custard pie, one becomes uncomfortable. What is being sent up besides custard and cream? Movie violence?

I'm not sure violence is being parodied as much as displaced, even though the tone of "Bugsy Malone" is consistently cheerful and often intelligently mocking. Yet if custard maims and whipped cream kills, hasn't Mr. Parker simply substituted one form of ammo for another? The characters in "Bugsy Malone" are not like cartoon characters who, after falling from the top of a tall building to cut holes in their own body sizes 30-feet deep in the cement, immediately emerge unscathed to carry on the joke. When Knuckles, Fat Sam's trusted, dim-witted lieutenant, "buys it" in an ambush, he doesn't return. It makes one wonder for whom the G-rated film is intended.

A lot of it is too foolishly cute for words. The cars the characters drive are scaled down models of real cars, but though the characters live in buildings with electric light and running water, the cars are without engines. The driver pedals, which would suggest that "Bugsy Malone" is (at least part of the time) designed for children who have outgrown their kiddie cars but aren't yet allowed to drive bump-o-cars at Coney Island.

Two of the film's strongest assets are its score (10 songs) by Paul Williams and the choreography by Gillian Gregory, which are witty in the manner of the stage production of Sandy Wilson's "The Boy Friend." But how many tykes do you know who will tap their feet and slap their thighs in appreciation of a comic, almost Frank Loesser-like turn of musical phrase? At which point one begins to suspect that maybe Mr. Parker made a mistake in not attempting to film a straight parody, acted not by young adults in scaled-down sets but by adults who really are young. They could also be talented enough, or at least old enough, so

A gangland battle fought by kids with Reddi-Whip guns.

that one's ear isn't put on edge by hearing a fully-developed adult singing voice emerging from the mouth of a babe. His material is so good it could have been staged without gimmickry.

The consistency of the film's illusions gets further tangled up in the physical appearances of the young actors, which makes s-e-x a bit of a problem for the movie. Jodie Foster, the girl who played the teenage hooker in "Taxi Driver," is superbly funny and strikingly beautiful as Fat Sam's girl friend. Though she was reportedly 14 when she made the film, she could pass for 20, while the boy playing Fat Sam looks to be about 12. When we watch Jodie slink around the stage in one of the film's best production numbers, "Tallulah," you get to wondering what this Runyon-esque doll is doing hanging out with the milkshake-and-sasparilla crowd. You suspect she has deep emotional problems, which shatters the illusion of the simple cream-puff world substituted for the real world we think we know.

In the final gangland showdown, staged as a huge custard pie-and-whipped cream battle at Fat Sam's speakeasy, Mr. Parker suddenly suspends the laws that have governed the universe of "Bugsy Malone" until that minute. Everybody gets liberally plastered with splurge, but no one seems to get hurt. That's all very nice, and I really prefer a suspension in laws to seeing a screenful of Reddi-Whipped corpses, but I think that if I were still 10, I'd feel more cheated than I do now.

I admire Mr. Parker's nerve and talent, yet I hope "Bugsy Malone" is not so successful he'll be tempted to go on to do a kiddie "King Lear" or a "Seagull" for shavers. Children's Lib should be kept in its place. ■

1976 S 26, 11:15:1

Dutch 'Keetje Tippel'

Sentiment Fairly Abounds at the 68th St. Playhouse

"Keetje Tippel" is doubtless one of the most gorgeous movies of the year, which is by no means to declare it one of the best. But giving this Dutch film its due is a little like making sport of "Cinderella."

"Keetje Tippel," which opened yesterday at the 68th Street Playhouse, comes to us so coated with the sugar of its splendid costuming, its meticulously re-created late 19th-century Amsterdam atmosphere and the classicism of its improbable, happy ending that the temptation is not so much to advise prospective audiences to check their critical faculties at the door as to check their teeth for fresh cavities upon departing.

•

There is little mitigation in the knowledge that the story told in "Keetje Tippel" is described as being based on fact—the memoirs of a woman named Neel Doff. With her name changed in this film to Keetje (pronounced Kate-yuh), she is one of the children in an impoverished, oversized rural family that, like many others, migrated in 1881 to Amsterdam in search of food and work.

A raw, coarse, naïve and irrepressibly spirited girl, she fights against hazing by her fellow workers in a lethal wool factory, is subjected to rape at the hands of a milliner, submits to a doctor who names sex as his price for saving her from death from tuberculosis and becomes a whore under the chaperonage of her mother before her life takes a sudden turn for the better.

The events of "Ketje Tippel" take place amid the terrible poverty of Keetje's family and others like it. One of her sisters is a prostitute. Her young brother takes money from a homosexual. People steal bread. Water floods their homes. Wooden shoes are used for firewood. Warmth and a little food represent dreams come true.

Present in "Keetje Tippel" are the ingredients for powerful social commentary, but the collaboration of the director, Paul Verhoeven, and the cinematographer, Jan de Bont, has produced a movie that is romantic about adversity. From time to time, as though having pangs about the lavish patina they have imposed on such crushing poverty, the movie-makers inject a burst of revolutionary song, an artist who paints revolutionary pictures, though romantic ones; and a confrontation between workers and the police.

•

As Keetje, Monique van de Ven has a field day, making the most of a role that enables her to undergo a transformation from hoyden to lady, playing by turns the coarse peasant, the innocent shop girl and the reluctant prostitute before blossoming into a radiant woman despite everybody and everything that might have destroyed her.

By and large, her indestructible spirit is admirable. But it comes to us in a context that makes it seem like one more ingredient in a very well made commercial designed to make hideous social inequality appear appetizing and acceptable.

LAWRENCE VAN GELDER

1976 S 27, 41:1

The Cast

KEETJE TIPPEL, directed by Paul Verhoeven; screenplay (Dutch with English subtitles) by Gerard Goetman, based on the writings of Neel Doff; cinematography, Jan de Bont; music, Roger van Oterloo; film editor, Jane Speer; produced by Bob Houwer; released by Cinema National Corporation. At the 68th Street Playhouse, at Third Avenue. Running time: 104 minutes. This film has not been rated.

Keetje Tippel .... Monique van de Ven
Mother .... Andrea Domburg
Father .... Jan Blaaser
Sister Minna .... Hannah De Leeuwe
Andre .... Eddie Brugman
Hugo .... Rutger Hauer
George .... Peter Faber

THE SUNDAY WOMAN, directed by Luigi Comencini; written by Age & Scarpelli; director of photography, Luciano Tovoli; edited by Antonio Siciliano; released by 20th Century-Fox. At the Fine Arts Theater, 130 East 58th Street. Running time: 110 minutes. This movie has been rated R.

Santamaria .... Marcello Mastroianni
Ana Maria .... Jacqueline Bisset
Massimo .... Jean-Louis Trintignant
Lello Rivera .... Aldo Reggiani
De Palma .... Pino Caruso
Virginia Tabusso .... Maria Teresa Albani
Benito .... Omero Antonutti
Vollero .... Gigi Ballista
Nicosia .... Renato Cecilia
Garrone .... Claudio Gora

By RICHARD EDER

A plot is the pretext for a good detective story, not its point. The characters and the setting are the point. The plot serves to display the characters in a conventional kind of motion, as a model's walk displays her clothes. It serves as a vehicle for making tours of the setting; the more rambling and full of holes it is, the better the view.

The plot of the new Italian film, "Sunday Woman," is as full of holes as a plateful of macaroni. It creaks and rambles but it takes us through a dry and lovely comedy of manners, with Marcello Mastroianni, Jacqueline Bisset and Jean-Louis Trintignant all making the most of parts that allow them to show their gifts for stylishness and subtlety.

•

It is set among the rich and bored—a favorite predeliction of Italian films—this time, in Turin. It is a society of busy industrialists and wives who have plently of time and means for odd games and exotic relationships. For example, Ana Maria Dosio, wife of a rich businessman, spends a lot of time with Massimo Campi, the idle son of a rich family. The relationship is more or less platonic—Massimo has a young man as a lover—and is occupied mostly by a search for style. Massimo, for example, decides that it would be equally vulgar to own an expensive car and a cheap one, so he takes taxis. As the movie opens, the two of them are engaged in an interminably reasoned quarrel over whether pronouncing "Boston" with a Bostonian rather than an Italian intonation is the intelligent or the pretentious thing to do.

Into this cobweb life two things erupt. Somebody smashes the head of Garrone, an unlikable crumb attached to Turin's upper crust. The weapon is one of the counterfeit ancient stone phalluses that he sells to foreigners. Quite a few members of Turinese high society, including Ana Maria and Massimo, had reason to dislike Garrone. So, with the greatest reluctance, the authorities put Inspector Santamaria on the case. Hiss assignment, in effect, is to solve the crime without catching anybody.

Santamaria is the most winning and nuanced role that Mastrioanni has had for some time. He is a serious man of the middle class. He has aspirations to the good life, dresses in sport clothes that are a little too careful, and has an eye for women; but he is a moralist.

He is sanely apprehensive about his mission. "Dsio. *Dsio.* Campi. *Campi,*" he mutters, the emphasis acknowledging the trouble he will have with his glittering list of suspects. But he pursues it with tenacity.

The encounters of this naïve, sensitive but purposeful man with the sophisticated and purposeless Beautiful People of Turin are the film's heart. There is a marvelous first encounter with Massimo, played by Trintignant. Santamaria offers American cigarettes; Massimo insists on cheap local ones. Santamaria quotes an appropriate Latin tag; Massimo says he doesn't know Latin. Santamaria is after the good things; Massimo, who has them all, rejects them as vulgar.

The comedy turns serious when Santamaria discovers Massimo's young lover. The two poses crack — Santamaria is deadly serious about the crime; Massimo is deadly serious about his lover — and the two are suddenly shouting at each other. Trintignant makes his jaded sophisticate both funny and affecting, a man teetering on the edge of a crackup.

•

Santamaria's encounters with Ana Maria are even better. Again, seriousness — this time in the form of mutual attraction—breaks through the comical and mannered fencing. Jacqueline Bisset, a beautiful and most skilled actress who is usually starved on silly parts, is a battleground of real feeling and decadent detachment, a tempest in a crystal wine glass.

There is a whole gallery of minor characters, some of them trite but most with at least a few moments of comic inspiration. Aldo Reggiani is particularly good as Massimo's young lover; a mixture of dopiness and moonstruck passion.

The ending of "The Sunday Woman," which opened yesterday at the Fine Arts Theater, is a surprise, but it is a distant surprise and irrelevant. A mystery villain should be under our noses all the time. It is the final creak in the plot, but I was too pleased by the scenery to mind the destination.

1976 S 27, 41:1

HOW FUNNY CAN SEX BE? (Sesso Matto), directed by Dino Risi; screenplay (Italian with English subtitles) by Mr. Risi and Ruggero Maccari; director of photography, Alfio Contini; music, Armando Trovaioli, Alberto Gallitti; produced by Dean Films and Cinetirrena; distributed by In-Frame Films. Running time: 97 minutes. At the Trans-Lux East Theater, Third Avenue at 58th Street. This film has been rated R.

A butler, a young executive, a groom, a laborer, a donor, a provincial man, a corpse, an employee .... Giancarlo Giannini
A rich woman, an 'gnored wife, a bride, a laborer's wife, a nun .... Laura Antonelli
Gilda .... Alberto Lionello

By VINCENT CANBY

Watching Dino Risi's "How Funny Can Sex Be?" (Italian title: "Sesso Matto") is to be on the point of death and to have every Italian comedy ever made pass in front of your eyes instead of your life. It's a disappointment not easily remedied.

The film, which opened yesterday at the Trans-Lux East, stars Giancarlo Giannini and Laura Antonelli in eight sketches that parody Italian sexual manners in ways that run the gamut from harmless to painfully predictable to slightly nasty, as in the sketch in which he plays a young man hopelessly attracted to elderly women, the older and uglier the better.

With the kind of witty material that Lina Wertmuller gives him, Mr. Giannini is an immensely gifted character actor. In this Risi film, we can see remnants of some of those other performances in the Groucho-like walk, the dainty pursuit of lust, the radar-like eyes that can detect and chart a fine bust at a distance of 50 feet.

The material written by Mr. Risi and his partner, Ruggero Maccari, is so exhausted, though, that long before we get through a pointless sketch called "Wild Gooseberries," spoken in imitation Swedish, we notice that the film has become a series of masquerades that allow Mr. Giannini to wear a lot of supposedly funny hair-pieces and glasses.

Among the topics touched on but never successfully sent up are the impotence of a village Romeo, a premeditated murder effected by overindulgence in sex, and artificial insemination.

Laura Antonelli, a stunning beauty and a talented comedienne, also wastes her talents, though the unadorned sight of her helps the time pass more quickly.

1976 S 29, 30:3

NORMAN . . . IS THAT YOU? produced and directed by George Schlatter; screenplay by Mr. Schlatter, Ron Clark, and Sam Bobrick, based upon play by same name by Mr. Clark and Mr. Bobrick; director of photography, Gayne Rescher; edited by George Folsey; music by William Goldstein. At the Criterion, 86th Street East, Appollo and other theaters. Running time: 91 minutes. This film has been rated PG.

Ben	Redd Foxx
Beatrice	Pearl Bailey
Garson	Dennis Dugan
Norman	Michael Warren
Audrey	Tamara Dobson
Melody	Vernee Watson

By RICHARD EDER

It is possible to imagine "Norman . . . Is That You?" on television some rainy afternoon, seen through the rising steam of a pile of ironing, and with the sound turned all the way down. Otherwise—unless customers sneak ironing-boards and tubs of wet-wash into the Criterion, Apollo and other theaters where it opened yesterday—"Norman" is very hard to imagine, let alone see.

As a stage play, which ran 12 performances on Broadway, "Norman" was about the antics of one owner of a dry-cleaning shop who discovers simultaneously that his wife has run off with his partner and that his son is a homosexual. It was a comedy, not a tragedy except, perhaps, for those who bought tickets.

•

The movie version, produced and directed by George Schlatter, substitutes a black family for a Jewish family. It helps matters not at all. It is a series of bad jokes about homosexuality, strung upon trite situation comedy and collapsing into what is meant to be an uplifting message about people being allowed to do their own thing.

Well, Redd Foxx—he plays the dry-cleaner—is a capable performer and he isn't doing his own thing. Pearl Bailey—the wife—is a splendid performer and she isn't doing her own thing. They are both doing Mr. Schlatter's thing, and a poor, small thing it is.

•

"Norman is rated PG A "Parental Guidance Suggested"). It is all talk and no action, but the film's message is that if your children grow up to be homosexuals, don't worry; and presumably this is what the guidance is suggested for.

1976 S 30, 36:1

BURNT OFFERINGS, directed and produced by Dan Curtis; screenplay by William F. Nolan and Mr. Curtis, based on the novel by Robert Marasco; cinematographer, Jacques Marquette; editor, Dennis Virkler; released by United Artists Corporation. At the National Theater, Broadway at 43d Street, Trans-Lux 85th Street, at Madison Avenue, Columbia 2, Second Avenue at 64th Street, and other theaters.

Marian	Karen Black
Ben	Oliver Reed
Brother	Burgess Meredith
Roz	Eileen Heckart
David	Lee Montgomery
Walker	Dub Taylor
Aunt Elizabeth	Bette Davis

Enter Ben and Marian with their 12-year-old boy, checking out the advertisement for a summer rental home. The isolated house is magnificent but decrepit Victoriana, not beyond the power to attract—especially Marian. And the price is right. Nine hundred dollars. Not a month. But for the whole season.

Ben thinks there must be a catch, and what about the housework? "The house takes care of itself," says the woman who, with her rather dotty brother, is offering it for rent. There is, of course, octogenarian mom at the top of the house. But she's no trouble. Just leave a tray outside her room at mealtimes. Marian agrees. She'll care for mom herself.

And so begin the events of "Burnt

Offerings," which opened yesterday at a number of theaters, an excursion into eeriness led with admirable though not perfect assurance by the director, Dan Curtis.

Here is the house as vampire—alluring, renewing itself on injury, violence and death; capable of menace, vengeance, outrage and murder.

To it, in all innocence, come such solid actors as Karen Black as Marian; Lee Montgomery as her son, David; Bette Davis as Ben's old Aunt Elizabeth, and Oliver Reed, as Ben, who is subject to nightmares about a childhood funeral, one of those old-fashioned glass-sided hearses and a chauffeur (Anthony James) whose face is going to haunt a lot of dreams for months to come.

Director Curtis times his audience immersions into the ice bath of terror with such skill that moviegoers will scarcely have the leisure to ask why some of the renters aren't a bit more observant and curious about their dwelling.

Only at the end does Mr. Curtis falter. Part of the climax is predictable; and, in another part, he relinquishes his deftness in favor of violence and gore on a scale that clashes with his earlier restraint.

Nevertheless, such is his ability that, at the approach of the denouement during a preview of "Burnt Offerings," members of the audience began murmuring and shouting nervous jokes in a vain effort to break the undeniable tension.

Rental agents hereabouts should get down on their knees and give thanks that "Burnt Offerings" is opening now. It's the kind of movie that does for summer homes what "Jaws" did for a dip in the surf.

The PG rating ("Parental Guidance Suggested") seems attributable to one long shot of Marian diving nude into a swimming pool; to a couple of scenes indicating the state of Ben's and Marian's sex life, and, perhaps, to the climactic gore.

LAWRENCE VAN GELDER

1976 S 30, 36:1

WHERE THE RED FERN GROWS, directed by Norman Tokar; screenplay by Douglas Stewart and Eleanor Lamb, based on the novel by Wilson Rawls; songs written by the Osmonds; music by Lex De Azevdo; produced by Lyman D. Dayton; released by Cinema Shares. At the Guild Theater, 50th Street and Rockefeller Plaza. Running time: 90 minutes. This film is rated G.

Grampa	James Whitmore
Mother	Beverly Garland
Father	Jack Ging
Sheriff	Lonny Chapman
Billy	Stewart Peterson
Alice	Jill Clark
Sara	Jeanna Wilson
Sam Bellington	Bill Thurman
Ben Kyle	Bill Dunbar

"Where the Red Fern Grows," a children's movie about an Ozarks boy and his two raccoon-hunting hounds, opened yesterday at the Guild Theater. Almost everyone in it—the boy, his parents, grandfather and sisters, and the other hunters—is totally nice. The only ones who aren't nice are two boys who taunt the hero and chew tobacco. One dies from falling upon a hatchet. The movie has some straightforward coon chases that are interesting but murkily photographed. The actors, though not very skillful, are restrained and sometimes appealing. They contend with an excessively treacly plot which stops for minutes on end, sometimes to admire itself, sometimes to weep softly.

RICHARD EDER

1976 S 30, 36:4

Ghost Writer

THE FRONT, directed and produced by Martin Ritt; screenplay, Walter Bernstein; executive producer, Charles Joffe; music, Dave Grusin; director of photography, Michael Chapman; editor, Sidney Levin; distributed by Columbia Pictures. Running time: 94 minutes. At the Coronet Theater, Third Avenue at 59th Street. This film has been rated PG.

Howard Prince	Woody Allen
Hecky Brown	Zero Mostel
Phil Sussman	Herschel Bernardi
Alfred Miller	Michael Murphy
Florence Barrett	Andrea Marcovicci
Hennessey	Remak Ramsay
Meyer Prince	Marvin Lichterman
Delaney	Lloyd Gough
Phelps	David Margulies
Sam	Joshua Shelley
Howard's attorney	Norman Rose
Committee counselor	Charles Kimbrough
Committee chairman	M. Josef Sommer

By VINCENT CANBY

USING a conventional comedy form older than Bob Hope's girdle and an actor whose scope has been defined mostly by the method of his one-liners, Martin Ritt, the director, and Walter Bernstein, the writer, have made a moving, haunted film about the panic that swept this country during the late 1940's and early 50's, the period to which the late Senator Joseph R. McCarthy gave his name.

"The Front," which opened yesterday at the Coronet Theater, makes no attempt to examine the ideological debris of those years. It doesn't deal in ideas but in plights. It dramatizes the experiences of some of the victims of that time when, on charges that never had to be substantiated, successful writers, directors, actors, producers could be blacklisted and thus denied employment in television and motion pictures.

•

As much as an entertainment film can be, "The Front" is about what it was like when to be a member of the Communist Party, or to have been a member at some earlier time, or to have associated with people who might have been members, or to have had

left-wing sympathies, or to have been sympathetic to people who might have had such sympathies, was enough to destroy one's career, to turn old friends into stool pigeons, to humiliate the codes by which men professed to live morally.

The film's inspiration is the casting of Woody Allen in the pivotal role of Howard Prince, a quintessential Woody Allen rat, an unsuccessful, amateur bookmaker who works in a bar as a cashier and has absolutely nothing on his mind except small schemes doomed to fail.

"The Front" looks at the McCarthy period through the eyes of this epically self-absorbed coward, who, as is the way of cowards in such comedies, slips upon his finest hour as if it were a banana peel and slides to unexpected nobility.

•

Through an old schoolmate, a highly paid television writer who has been blacklisted, Howard Prince gets into the business of being a "front." He puts his name on scripts written by others and submits them to the networks. Howard's success is immediate and, to him, mind-boggling. As a front he turns into a mini-corporation. What had begun as a good deed that wouldn't cost him anything becomes, instead, a career with its own particular goals.

Chief among these is a pretty young woman, an assistant producer who falls in love with Howard Prince the successful writer. Because fraudulence has always been one of the most prominent aspects of the public Woody Allen character, the sequences in which Howard Prince tries to ape the manners of a successful writer are very funny.

Pressed for details about his background, Howard says, rather desperately, "I was a boxer and a seaman and all those things you gotta do to be a writer." He basks in his celebrityhood

Woody Allen in "The Front," Martin Ritt's film about the McCarthy era
"Recreates the awful noise of ignorance that can still be heard"

at network cocktail parties, where, of course, his muddle-mindedness is completely safe.

Later his rat instincts emerge. Howard gets finicky about the scripts to which he'll attach his name. He returns them to the authors for rewrites. The more money he makes, the more he wants. His greed exceeds his grasp.

Mr. Ritt and Mr. Bernstein tell the basically comic story of Howard Prince's rise, fall and rise against an authentically grim background of deceit, blackmail, injustice and personal tragedy.

The film evokes that time obliquely through supporting characters like Hecky Brown (Zero Mostel), a blacklisted television star who winds up playing the Catskills for a tenth of his former fee; Phil Sussman (Herschel Bernardi), the producer who plays the blacklisting game, and a mysterious man named Hennessey (Remak Ramsay), to whom the networks turn for "clearance" on politically suspect employees. "I don't do the hiring," says Hennessey at one point. "I only advise on Americanism."

Mr. Allen, Michael Murphy (who plays his blacklisted friend), Mr. Mostel, Andrea Marcovicci (the girl Howard Prince lusts after), are all fine. It's not to disparage Mr. Allen's contributions to say that in this so-called "straight" role, he is simply carrying the familiar Allen character into another context of experience, which endows the character with unexpected and real humanity.

"The Front" is not the whole story of an especially unpleasant piece of American history. It may be faulted for over simplification. Mr. Ritt and Mr. Bernstein, both veterans of the blacklist, are not interested in subtleties. Yet even in its comic moments "The Front" works on the conscience. It re-creates the awful noise of ignorance that can still be heard.

•

The film has been rated PG ("Parental Guidance Suggested") because of the occasional use of obscenities.

1976 O 1, C7:1

Enfants de Truffaut

SMALL CHANGE (L'Argent de Poche), directed by François Truffaut; screenplay (French with English subtitles) by Mr. Truffaut and Suzanne Schiffman; director of photography, Pierre-William Glenn; music, Maurice Jaubert; editors, Yann Dedet, Martine Barraque, Jean Gargonne, Stephanie Granel, Muriel Zeleny; a co-production of Les Films du Crrosse and Les Productions Artistes Associes; distributed by New World Pictures. Running time: 104 minutes. At the New York Film Festival at Alice Tully Hall, Broadway at 65th Street. This film has been rated PG.

Patrick	Geory Desmouceaux
Julian	Philippe Goldman
Mathieu Deluca	Claudio Deluca
Franck Deluca	Franck Deluca
Richard Golfier	Richard Golfier
Laurent Riffle	Laurent Devlaeminck
Bruno Rouillard	Bruno Staab
Oscar	Sebastien Marc
Sylvie	Sylvie Grezel
Martine	Pascale Bruchon
Corinne	Corinne Boucart
Patricia	Eva Truffaut
Jean-François Richet	Jean-François Stevenin
Chantal Petit	Chantal Mercier
Monsieur Riffle	Francis Devlaeminck
Nadine Riffle	Tania Torrens
Lydie Richet	Virginie Thevenet
Madeleine Doinel	Laura Truffaut

CHILDREN—so long, so sentimentally, so horrendously and so profitably exploited by movies as inadequate, miniature imitations of adults—are rediscovered, their lost language intact, in François Truffaut's "Small Change," the lilting, marvelously funny and wise re-creation of childhood that will be shown twice tonight to open the 14th New York

Vernon L. Smith from Scope

François Truffaut

His latest is "an original, a major work on minor keys."

Film Festival at Alice Tully Hall.

"Small Change" is not a wholly satisfying translation of the film's French title, "L'Argent de Poche," but because "Pocket Money" was used for a 1972 Paul Newman film, "Small Change" is probably as good as one can do, though there is nothing secondrate or of minor importance about it.

•

"Small Change" is an original, a major work in minor keys. It's a labor of love that ignores precedent with splendid verve and a film with so many associations to other Truffaut films that watching it is like meeting a previously unknown relative, someone both familiar and utterly new and surprising.

All of Mr. Truffaut's films—not just the obvious ones like the Antoine Doinel cycle that began with "The 400 Blows" and concluded with "Bed and Board"—are full of intimations of childhood. "The Story of Adèle H." is as much about Adèle Hugo's furious, ecstatic, guilt-ridden life as her father's little girl as it is about a young woman's obsession. Jules, Jim and Catherine are adults who have not lost the capacity for extravagances and deceptions, though they no longer live in that state of grace that, says the young mother in "Small Change," is the special blesing of childhood.

Every major character in a Truffaut film, whether or not the film makes particular reference to the past, carries within him the vestiges of the fears and fantasies of growing up. It's not that Mr. Truffaut is the sort of film maker who draws boringly overdetailed psychological profiles of his characters, but that characters, poetically conceived and appreciated, are thus complete.

•

How to describe "Small Change" adequately, and the way in which it manages to make serious assessments with such a blithe spirit?

The film, photographed in Thiers in South Central France, is a series of interlocking vignettes about the world as seen by children from 2 weeks of age to approximately 14.

There is Sylvie, 7, who has a Renoir face but a flinty will when it comes to knowing what purse she wants to take when on a luncheon outing with her parents. The purse is a small, badly scrubbed wool elephant with a zippered stomach. The parents make a fuss. Sylvie remains firm. They leave her at home, at which point Sylvie goes to the window and announces to the world at large, through her father's electric bullhorn, that she's hungry.

There are also Oscar, a little boy who whistles instead of talking, and Gregory, 2, who rejoices in messiness, which, to children, is not to be confused with disorder.

•

Most prominent are Julien Leclou and Patrick Desmouceaux, both 12½, who are immediately identifiable to any student of Truffaut films as two aspects of Antoine Doinel. Julien, dark-eyed, truculently self-reliant, is the delinquent, and experienced thief, a scavenging wild child in the midst of bourgeois plenty. Patrick is fairhaired, shy, a companion to his paralyzed father and hopelessly in love with the beautician-mother of a school friend.

"Small Change" has the air of a child's Saturday afternoon when no special activities have been planned. It ambles through the lives of these children, observing them in school, at home, going to the movies, making do on a Sunday morning when parents sleep late, trying to pawn some textbooks, making painful and hilarious discoveries that, by the time we reach the end, have encompassed most of the ordinary expressions of childhood in ways not possible in the conventional fiction film.

Though it doesn't look like it, "Small Change" is fiction, and the wonder is how Mr. Truffaut allied himself with his cast to capture performances with such a lack of self-consciousness or, when a certain self-consciousness is apparent, without any coy mechanics.

•

Everyone will find his own favorite sequences in the film. Mine are one in which a 10-year-old boy attempts to tell his friends a dirty story that he hasn't yet understood and another in which two older boys attempt to save a friend some money by giving him a haircut. "That's my side," says one of the amateur barbers testily. "Watch out for the ears," says the other.

The children are incomparably funny and affecting. The adult actors, including Jean-François Stevenin and Chantal Mercier, who play teachers, are equally good, I suspect, because the children, not being savvy stage monsters, are performers to whom they can respond.

"Small Change" is Mr. Truffaut's 15th feature and one of the most personal, idiosyncratic films in a body of work that now matches the work of any director active today. It will be opening its regular commercial engagement Sunday at the Cinema II.

•

The film has been rated PG ("Parental Guidance Suggested") because of some obscenities that will not, I think, surprise any parent, or any child who has ever ridden on the subway.

VINCENT CANBY

1976 O 1, C11:1

Sexual Obsession Is Theme of Movie From Japan

By RICHARD EDER

It's impossible to see a painting if your nose is squashed right up against the canvas. Even with the contemporary pleasure in turned-up volume, there is a point at which music is so loud it can't be heard. Excessive visual shock will turn an audience's attention from any other quality a movie may possess and center it exclusively on its own pain.

Nagisa Oshima's film about sexual obsession, "In the Realm of the Senses," was not, in fact, doing very well when, in the last couple of minutes, he turned the volume up. It had become tedious and repetitious; its limited strengths had long since been exhausted from overuse. And in those last couple of minutes a trying film became an intolerable one.

•

I am using the word "intolerable" as a critic. The action of the United States Custom in seizing the film does not spare audiences a the New York Film Festival, where it was to have been shown, anything that has not been available in hard-core porn houses around Manhattan. Except an undeniable—though I think poorly used—artistic imagination.

"Senses" is about the literally consuming passion of a man and a woman. He is married to the owner of a geisha house; she is a newly arrived geisha. The film consists of virtually nothing but their love-making. He is a man of infinite capacity and she is a woman of infinite desire—her doctor's term is "hypersensitive," she delicately explains—and so the sex is incessant. It takes place furtively at first, then more and more openly, alone and in company.

The Cast

IN THE REALM OF THE SENSES (L'EMPIRE DES SENS), directed by Nagisa Oshima; screenplay (Japanese with English subtitles) by Nagisa Oshima; photography, Kenichi Okamofo and Hideo Ito; editor, Keiichi Uraoka; music, Minoru Miki and traditional Japanese songs; produced by Anatole Dauman; production companies Argos Films (Paris)/Oshima Productions (Tokyo). Running time: 115 minutes. This film has not been rated. Previewed at the New York Film Festival, Alice Tully Hall.

Sada	Eiko Matsuda
Kichizo	Tatsuya Fuji
Tramp	Taiji Tonoyama

The sex scenes, totally explicit, are much more than gymnastics. Both actors are good. Eiko Matsuda is appealing and even touching in her insatiability; Tatsuya Fuji has a haunting gentleness and passivity as he comes to recognize his destiny: to be literally loved to death.

The sex is never divorced from emotion, and this, for such a graphic presentation, is a novelty. Mr. Oshima is an artist. The movie, though, is not a work of art; at most, it is an artistic blunder.

Any life outside that of the couple is shadowy. The sex becomes an abstraction; so do the two lovers. Their lovemaking becomes more and more knotted, more and more obsessed with death.

For the viewer, there is little to do but wait the obsession out. It is a mathematical development. It is quite clear that she will kill him, and she does.

•

What is not, perhaps, forseeable is the particularly repulsive form that the killing takes. After strangling her lover, the woman cuts off his sexual organs and displays them, prolongedly and bloodily.

There is some logical justification for the act—a final barbaric rite in a deadly sexual ritual. But there's no real emotional justification for it. The movie was dying anyway; now, after pretty well stupefying, it wounds.

1976 O 2, 14:1

JONAH WHO WILL BE 25 IN THE YEAR 2000, directed by Alain Tanner; screenplay (French, with English subtitles) by John Berger and Alain Tanner; produced by Yves Gasser and Yves Peyrot; director of photography, Renato Berta; music, Jean-Marie Senia; editor, Brigitte Sousselier; a co-production of Action Films, Citel Films, Societe Francaise de Production and SSR-Swiss Television, distributed by New Yorker Films. Running time* 115 minutes. At the New York Film Festival, Alice Tully Hall, Broadway at 65th Street.

Max	Jean-Luc Bideau
Mathilde	Myriam Boyer
Marco	Jacques Denis
Marcel	Roger Jendly
Marguerite	Dominique Labourier
Madeleine	Myriam Meziere
Marie	Miou-Miou
Mathieu	Rufus
Old Charles	Raymond Bussieres

By VINCENT CANBY

All but two of the characters in Alain Tanner's witty, cerebrally playful new Swiss film, "Jonah Who Will Be 25 in the Year 2000," are French-speaking Swiss. The other two are French citizens who live just over the border in France. Yet each of the characters is, in his or her own way, as surrounded as Switzerland, hemmed in, denied access to something essential.

Max (Jean-Luc Bideau), a former political activist, no longer writes for his newspaper. Since 1968 he has worked as a proofreader. Marco (Jacques Denis) is a teacher of history, but his methods are so bizarre that he keeps getting bounced from one school after another. Marie (Miou-Miou) is a cashier in a Geneva supermarket who, being French, is not allowed to sleep in Switzerland. Mathieu (Rufus), fired from his job as a printer because of his union activities, returns to the land as a farm helper.

Miou-Miou and Raymond Bussières in "Jonas"
Characters that talk incessantly but with enthusiasm and humor

"Jonah Who Will Be 25 in the Year 2000" is less the story of nine friends and acquaintances than a highly comic, politicized accounting of their states of mind and their talk. They are surrounded and hemmed in, all right, but they have not been anesthetized by mediocrity into dreamless boredom. They rant and they carry on, like Charles (Raymond Bussières), the retired railroad engineer for whom Marie steals provisions from the supermarket.

At one point, Charles recalls the difference between riding on a train and sitting in the engineer's cab. "When you are a passenger," he says, "the landscape slides past you. When you are the engineer, you are always entering it, approaching that point where the rails meet, but they always open up for you."

"Jonah" is Mr. Tenner's fifth film to be released in this country, and like his two best films ("La Salamandre" and "The Middle of the World"), it has a screenplay written by him in collaboration with John Berger, the English novelist and critic. They make one of the most interesting film-making teams in Europe today.

Their line is Marxist, but their method is exuberantly humane, always aware of the comic aspects to the accommodations being made by characters who, in Mr. Tanner's words, are "metaphors on two legs." That, I think, undercuts the compassion of the film.

The characters may be metaphors, but they are also recognizable individuals, whether determinedly, hilariously steeped in Hindu mysticism, like the beautiful Madeleine (Myriam Mezière), who believes the mind can be fertilized by particular sex practices; or, like the lantern-jaw Mathieu, who is dedicated to shaping a better future for his new son, Jonah.

Mr. Tanner's characters talk incessantly, sometimes, as in the case of Marco, they lecture, playing with theories of history, time, revolution, education and capitalism with such enthusiasm that the spirit of the talk has the effect of giving comic perspective to metaphors not of the first freshness ("the highway of capitalism is collapsing").

●

The stories of the individual characters, which connect casually, gracefully, are punctuated by fantasies that, in contrast to the rest of the color film, are photographed in black and white. They are short, mischievous, sometimes sad, occasionally erotic, always informed, as in the entire film, by Mr. Tanner's awareness that these people, whether two-legged metaphors or not, inhabit a specific society in a particular time.

The performances are so thoroughly integrated with the material that I'm not sure where performances begin and the work of the director and the writers leaves off. The entire cast is splendid.

"Jonah," which will be shown at the 14th New York Film Festival today at 6 P.M. and tomorrow at 9 P.M., will open here at the Fine Arts Theater within the next several weeks. It's a window on a European political-intellectual world seldom seen in films—and never seen with such an appreciation of cinematic style.

1976 O 2, 15:1

OSSESSIONE (Obsession), directed by Luchino Visconti; screenplay (Italian with English subtitles) by Mario Alicata, Antonio Pietrangeli, Gianni Puccini, Giuseppe de Santis and Mr. Visconti; directors of photography, Aldo Tonti and Domenico Scala; editor, Mario Serandrei; executive producer, Liberto Solaroli; a production of ICI (Rome). Running time: 135 minutes. At the New York Film Festival at Alice Tully Hall, Broadway at 65th Street.

Giovanna	Clara Calamai
Gino	Massimo Girotti
The husband	Juan de Landa
The "Spaniard"	Elia Marcuzzo
Anita	Dhia Cristani
Lorry driver	Vittorio Duse

Although there are almost as many definitions of Italian neo-Realism as there are Italian neo-Realist films, Luchino Visconti's first feature, "Ossessione," made in 1942, is generally accepted as having launched the movement whose name was later applied to the work of Antonioni, Rossellini, De Sica and others.

●

The film, which will be presented today at 3 P.M. at the New York Film Festival at Alice Tully Hall and again on Tuesday at 6:15 P.M., is being shown here in a 35-mm. print, for the first time. Earlier showings in the United States had been prohibited because Mr. Visconti had, without permission, helped himself to James M. Cain's novel, "The Postman Always Rings Twice," the rights to which were owned by M-G-M, the studio that later filmed in 1946 with John Garfield and Lana Turner under Tay Garnett's direction.

Comparing the Visconti "Ossessione" with the Garnett "Postman" is to stand a production of "Traviata" next to a McDonald's television commercial, which is not meant to underrate the American film that is as effectively steamy, tough and terse as the Hollywood law allowed in those days.

Mr. Visconti follows with remarkable fidelity the Cain story about the handsome young drifter and the youngish wife who, driven by their sexual passion and greed, murder the woman's old husband to get his money and his business, a combination hamburger stand and filling station.

●

"Ossessione" today looks to be an extraordinarily majestic, elegant and romantic movie to have started anything labeled neo-Realism. There is even something grand about the bleakness of the Italian landscapes, to say nothing of the mood. When the illicit lovers, Gino (Massimo Girotti) and Giovanna (Clara Calamai), are exchanging lustful glances at the dinner table, the soundtrack rumbles with the sounds of distant thunder and frantic cries of caged farm animals. Under these circumstances, one is disappointed that the characters don't sing.

"Ossessione," which also launched the late Mr. Visconti's remarkable film career, may be slow-going to the uninitiated, but its historical importance is not to be denied.

VINCENT CANBY

1976 O 2, 15:1

DIAMONDS, produced and directed by Menahem Golan; screenplay by David Paulsen and Mr. Golan, released by Avco Embassy Pictures. At neighborhood theaters. Running time: 108 minutes. This film is rated PG.

Charles and Earl Hodgson	Robert Shaw
Archie	Richard Roundtree
Sally	Barbara Seagull
Zelda Shapiro	Shelley Winters
Moshe	Shai K. Ophir
Gaby	Gadi Yageel

"Diamonds," which opened yesterday at neighborhood theaters, is the caper movie to end all caper movies. That's not by way of praise, but by way of description of a film that revives a dormant genre only to assure its burial deeper than ever.

Total nonsense from beginning to end, with neither the wit nor idiosyncracy of character that distinguished "Topkapi," which it occasionally apes, "Diamonds" deals with an assault on the security system of the diamond exchange in Tel Aviv. The real asault is on the sensibilities of anyone who has ever had the slightest affection for such movies.

Among them whose consciences should bother them for appearing in this film are Robert Shaw, playing twins, no less; Richard Roundtree as a safecracker; Barbara Seagull as Mr. Roundtree's girl, and Shelley Winters, present for no discernible reason.

At the end of it all, Robert Shaw looks out from the screen and laughs at the audience. Forewarned is forearmed.

●

The PG rating is presumably attributable to a glimpse of Miss Seagull's bare bosom, some of the language and a portrait of a nude that hangs in the home of the character played by Mr. Shaw.

LAWRENCE VAN GELDER

1976 O 2, 15:2

KINGS OF THE ROAD, from West Germany, written, directed and produced by Wim Wenders; photographed by Robbie Mueller, Martin Schafer and Peter Przygodda; music by Axel Linstadt. At the New York Film Festival, at Alice Tully Hall, today at 5 P.M., and tomorrow at 9 P.M. Thereafter at the Embassy 72d Street Theater. Running time: 176 minutes. This film has not been rated.

Bruno .... Ruediger Vogler
Robert .... Hanns Zischler
Cashier .... Lisa Kreuzer
Robert's father .... Rudolf Schuendler
Man who lost his wife .... Marquard Bohm

By RICHARD EDER

Roads have usually been thought of as destinations; they were built to go somewhere and that's what people mostly have used them for. But destinations have been in decline these last few decades, at least as a subject for the imagination. "On the Road," "Easy Rider," these were about leaving, not about arriving.

In "Kings of the Road," by the West German director Wim Wenders, there is nothing but the road, or a series of roads. They run through the North German plain, overcast most of the time, with fog and rain erupting continually and with a sunlight that manages to look dark. The world, whether as a point of departure or a destination, has all but finished—the road remains as a kind of Limbo of our time.

"Kings," which is being shown today and tomorrow at the New York Film Festival and will open Tuesday at the Embassy 72d Street Theater, focuses upon two citizens of the road, one permanent and one temporary.

The first is Bruno, who makes his home in a moving-van and drives from town to town fixing the projectors in the local movie house. He is loose, sleepy, shrewd, good-humored and totally unattached. He longs for women, is attractive to them, but lacks the power of concentration—permanent or temporary—to settle on any particular one.

Bruno has accepted aimlessness and unattachment. He drives through the dour countryside and visits the dour towns, whose streets are virtually unpopulated and whose gas stations seem to be always closed. It's not that aimlessness doesn't hurt him: It does, but so deeply that he doesn't show it.

He has, in fact, only one commitment: to the proper projection of motion pictures and the proper maintenance of the machinery. It is a solitary ideal; the projectionists he deals with are slipshod and indifferent, and more and more villages are are shutting their cinemas down.

Bruno has withdrawn from the world, then, or perhaps it is the other way around. Into his solitude, propelled at full speed, comes a temporary refugee, Robert. Robert is an intellectual who engages actively with society—ne studies children's speech—but his recent encounters have been shattering. His wife has left him, for example.

Two meet, comically: Robert, full of anger and distraction, drives his car into a lake by mistake and it sinks. Bruno and his van are parked nearby. They join forces.

It is a long, slow, wandering they embark upon. Robert becomes Bruno's assistant. He can't face his own world, for the time being; but every time he spots a telephone he tries to call his wife, and every time he sees a newspaper on the ground he reads it.

There are a series of encounters in which each, in his own way, enacts the difficulty of communication. Bruno spends a night with the cashier of a movie house. There is a lovely tenderness, but all he can do, literally, is sleep with her.

Robert visits his father, editor of a small newspaper, and tries to speak of his childhood resentments. But he can't get the words out so finally, as the old man sleeps at his desk, the son goes to work on the linotype. By morning, he has printed a two-page denunciation of his father's treatment of his mother. He finishes, hands the pages to his father; they embrace delicately and part.

Eventually, Robert goes back. His nature is to commit himself, even to an imperfect, half-dead world. He takes a train, that most constrained and committed form of transportation. Bruno, the idealist, wanders on in his lumpy van, whose mournful pace and elephantine presence make a lovely unifying symbol for the film.

It needs one badly. "Kings" is often fascinating. It has a number of compelling and witty scenes, and its imagery is harshly apt. But it is three hours long, which is at least an hour too much; and its successes are scattered like meager raisins through a mass of gray dough.

It moves like silence and sleep, and with a great parsimony of things to look at. Nothing happens but what is happening, and it happens one thing at a time, and one or two people at a time. Our peripheral vision is starved, and we are ready to take the train some time before Robert does.

1976 O 3, 53:1

FILM VIEW

VINCENT CANBY

Our Films Are Better Than This

"The nation," says Charlton Heston, who delivers the pious narration for the American Film Institute's anthology film, "America At The Movies," "endured not by its power and wealth but by its spirit." Yet when one recalls the 82 films that have supplied "America At The Movies" with 93 scenes designed, in the words of George Stevens, Jr., to show "the American people and spirit as we've seen it on the screen," the one fairly obvious common denominator they all share is a concern for power—the desire for, acquisition of, perversions of, corruption by, loss of. This is true whether the film is a Western like John Ford's "Cheyenne Autumn," a gangster melodrama like Mervyn Le Roy's "Little Caesar," a screwball comedy like Frank Capra's "It Happened One Night," or a W.C. Fields short like "The Pharmacist" which provides "America At The Movies" with one of its few highlights when Fields tries—unsuccessfully—to do civilized combat with his shrewish wife and a daughter somewhat large and overaged to be the brat she is.

"America At The Movies" is a most peculiar piece of self-congratulatory, myth-making nonsense that does a disservice to the hustling, ebullient, wonder-working industry it means to celebrate in this Bicentennial year. Divided into a prologue and five sections ("The Land," "The Cities," "The Families," "The Wars" and "The Spirit"), the film is a hodge-podge of scenes that seldom do justice even to the movies from which they've been purloined, to say nothing of Hollywood in general. "America At The Movies" has the effect of trivializing Hollywood's extraordinary contributions to the American civilization by attempting to impose—after the fact—a structure of meaning on approximately 60 years of film-making that had no continuing structure at all, except the need to make a profit. Within such a context the amazing thing is that so many great filmmakers were able to work so productively, though to realize such a thing while watching "America At The Movies" you'll have to squint at the screen and read the footnotes at the back of your own head.

By including in the section titled "The Families" sequences from Shirley Temple's "Bright Eyes" (1934) and from "Love Finds Andy Hardy" (1938), in which a goshgolly Mickey Rooney goes all over hysterical when he sees Judy Garland in an evening dress, "America At The Movies" defines what it's really up to, that is, recalling fashions and fads of the times. This is especially true in a sequence from "Father of The Bride" (1950), included in the same section. What we respond to is not Spencer Tracy's comically timed, middle-of-the-night monologue as a father of a daughter who's just become engaged, but to the fact (dictated by the Production Code then in effect) that Tracy and his wife, played by Joan Bennett, are sleeping separately in twin beds separated by a night table wide enough to insure the celibacy of a satyr.

The sequence from "Father of The Bride," however, does have something to do with family living, which cannot be said of the scenes clipped from "A Streetcar Named Desire," "Carnal Knowledge" and "A Place in the Sun." The latter features the youthful Elizabeth Taylor and Montgomery Clift making their first vows to each other at a dance, and might, with a tiny stretch of the imagination, have been included in the section called "The Cities" or, better yet, in a new section called "The Stars."

Although Mr. Stevens, who produced "America At The Movies" and is the head of the American Film Institute, says that the film is not intended to be about American history or movies, one cannot watch "America At The Movies" without becoming aware of how superficially and in what limited terms Hollywood dealt with American life most of the time. Even when "America At The Movies" includes scenes from such fine and/or eccentric films as "Dr. Strangelove," "Patton," "The Birth of A Nation," "Catch 22" and "M*A*S*H," one gets the impression that no Hollywood films possessed a mentality higher than one would find in a comic-book. This is not true, of course, but it is one of the dangers when one sets about to make what is, in effect, a promotional film bland enough not to upset anyone at home in Hollywood.

In general Hollywood films over the decades have been more interesting for what they omitted, ignored or avoided than for what they fearlessly exposed, with the exception of a film like Ford's fine adaptation of "The Grapes of Wrath," several scenes of which are included in "America At The Movies" in the section called "The Land." Mr. Stevens and his associates, however, haven't attempted to make any sociological points in their anthology. But though they want to recall "the American people and spirit as it appeared on the screen," all they do is recall actors and movies without connection to any real life except the moviegoer's memory of movies.

This doesn't seem good enough for something put out under the auspices of an agency called the American Film Institute, which is funded by the National Foundation for the Arts, private foundations as well as by the film industry. The way Hollywood has depicted American life in the last 60 years is worth serious study, especially by something like the A.F.I.

Instead of the collection of random scenes we have in this anthology, which looks like an endless trailer for the Late Show, how much more interesting and valuable might be a study, in almost this same form, of the Western film, or the gangster film or some such genre, of the politics implicit in these movies, of their attitudes towards power, government, sex, etc. It's a measure of how "America At The Movies" worked on me that when we were given a pointless long-shot of pretty scenery from "True Grit" my first association was to the curious way that film made a convincing argument on behalf of authoritarianism on the American frontier. Might makes right in the Old West when John Wayne is holding the gun, though it's impossible to accept when he plays a contemporary police officer in Seattle, as he did in "McQ."

To say, as does narrator Charlton Heston, that "the nation endured not by its power and its wealth but by its spirit," is to deny the content of most of the films recalled by "America At The Movies," as well as to attempt to invest the entire American experience with magical roots. This may be in keeping with the Bicentennial mood but it's not worthy of the kind of scholarship that the American Film Institute should be engaged in.

1976 O 3, II:15:1

ALEX AND THE GYPSY, directed by John Korty; written by Lawrence B. Marcus; based on the novella "The Bailbondsman" by Stanley Elkin; produced by Richard Shepherd; director of photography, Bill Butler; music by Henry Mancini; edited by Donn Cambern. Released by 20th-Century-Fox. At the Sutton Theater. Running Time: 98 minutes. This film has been rated R.
Alexander Main .... Jack Lemmon
Maritza .... Genevieve Bujold
Crainpool .... James Woods
The Golfer .... Gino Ardito
Judge Ehrlinger .... Robert Emhardt
Treska .... Tito Vandis
Public Defender .... Bill Cort
Roy Blake .... Todd Martin

By RICHARD EDER

Genevieve Bujold is standing in the garden, dressed in a red nightgown. She is looking fiercely at the moon and saying:

"Jowl, jowl."

Why is she saying that?

Because, in the new movie, "Alex and the Gypsy," which opened yesterday at the Sutton Theater, she plays a gypsy. And "jowl, jowl," we are told, is what gypsies say when they want to get pregnant.

It is a small point, but it is fair sample of the kind of ludicrousness that repeatedly overtakes "Alex," a movie that works away at being wonderful, funny and romantic. Once in a while it succeeds, but more often it is like the star English pupil in a Borneo grammar school reciting the witches' lines from "Macbeth." The sounds are there, more or less, but the emphases are wildly off.

●

"Alex" is about a bail bondsman, a man who puts up surety that people facing a trial will show up for it, and protects his risk by keeping a close watch on them. Alex, played by Jack Lemmon, is a crabby, cynical man whose pride in his peculiar work is masked by a flood of black humor.

Alex's carefully controlled life was knocked askew just once. Maritza, running away from her arranged gypsy wedding, attached herself to him. Her unreserved and enthusiastic passion foundered on his cragginess, and she walked out. When the movie opens, Maritza is back, this time awaiting sentencing for stabbing her thuggish husband.

She begs Alex to bail her out for the four days before sentencing;

Genevieve Bujold
Why does she say "jowl?"

gypsies die in jail, she tells him. He hesitates, then puts up the bail. The balance of the movie is devoted to the four days they spend together. He is a watchdog gradually defanged by love: she, the defanger, turns the watchdog into something like a racing whippet.

Except for an awkward use of flashbacks showing the earlier relationship of Alex and Maritza, the film is well constructed and well paced. There are some lovely details: for example, Alex's disenchanted grilling of a potential customer, a horrendous young maniac arrested for setting fire to someone who annoyed him. "Arson," Alex decides. "That's a bailable offense."

The central relationship, the dismantling of a sour principle of order by black-haired, black-eyed Life Force, is hardly a novelty, but it has possibilities and sometimes it is touching.

●

But neither of the principals brings it off. Miss Bujold is a good actress if she has a compelling energy on the screen. But she is quite wrong in the part. It's not merely her catered accent; as if "jowl, jowl" and an erratic deletion of the definite article were enough to establish the gypsy. More seriously, her tumultuousness is only flamboyance. It lacks the stolidity, the reserve that is essential to any representation of gypsy passion. She comes close to resembling the American tourist shown dancing Flamenco in sherry ads, her arms raised a fatal 3

inches too high.

and vulnerable, has a role that is modeled on a Sam Spade or a Philip Marlowe. The object is to be a Noble Wreck. But Mr. Lemmon lacks the assurance, the self-denial for wrecked nobility. He keeps letting the shlemiel in, and the tension out. There is an essential difference between irony and clowning, but Mr. Lemmon doesn't manage it.

1976 O 4, 16:1

Ophuls Sets Standards for Monumental Documentaries

By VINCENT CANBY

Like his earlier "The Sorrow and the Pity," which examined the behavior of the French during the Nazi occupation, Marcel Ophul's "The Memory of Justice" expands the possibilities of the documentary motion picture in such a way that all future films of this sort will be compared to it. "The Sorrow and the Pity" and "The Memory of Justice" have set standards and created expectations that even Mr. Ophuls himself may not always meet, as in "A Sense of Loss," his film about Northern Ireland, that was just as illusive as its subject. Mr. Ophuls doesn't deal in paltry material.

"The Memory of Justice" is monumental, though not only because it goes on for a demanding 4 hours and 38 minutes, plus an intermission. It also marks off, explores, calls attention to and considers, tranquilly, without making easy judgments, one of the central issues of our time: collective versus individual responsibility.

The starting point is an evocation of the 1946-47 Nuremberg war crimes trials, through newsreels and interviews with surviving defendants, prosecutors, defending attorneys, and witnesses, that leads to a consideration of French tactics in the fight to keep Algeria and America in action in Vietnam.

"I go on the assumption," says Yehudi Menuhin early in the film, "that everyone is guilty." But that sort of readiness to accept responsibility, simply by being a member of mankind, evades the truth that Mr. Ophuls seeks here.

The ethical questions are timeless but the subject is particular, and it's through the accumulation of particularities that "The Memory of Justice" makes its impact. More than 40 persons

are interviewed by Mr. Ophuls, and a dozen more key figures are seen speaking for themselves in old newsreel footage.

Hermann Göring and Rudolf Hess whisper on the prisoners' bench in the Nuremberg courtroom. A United States Army psychiatrist recalls that their small talk in court could, indeed, be small, such as comparing the marks they'd received on their Army I.Q. tests.

An old farmer in Schleswig-Holstein remembers the Nazi era fondly. It was a time of law and order in the land. When reminded of the concentration camps and the mass murder of the Jews, he pauses, says: "Oh, that was not right. That was something else." Gen. Telford Taylor discusses his role in preparing the Allied case at Nuremberg, setting precedents he still believes in, then talks about Vietnam and "the degeneration of standards under the pressure of war."

Adm. Karl Dönitz, to whom Hitler bequeathed the Third Reich in its death throes, today denies any knowledge of anything "dark" about Hitler, and describes as "politics" a speech in which he parrotted the official anti-Semitic line.

Albert Speer, urbane, still handsome, has survived to become a kind of professional guilt-assumer. He confesses

The Program

THE MEMORY OF JUSTICE, directed and produced by Marcel Ophuls; chief editor, Inge Behrens; director of photography, Mike Davis; sound recording, Anthony Jackson; executive producers, Max Palevsky and Hamilton Fish 3d, in co-production with Polytel International; distributed by Paramount Pictures. Running time: 278 minutes. At the New York Film Festival at Alice Tully Hall, Broadway at 65th Street. This film has been rated PG.

easily in best-selling books and to movie cameras, but is the confession any less genuine for sounding slick? I'm not sure. When he says, "Long before the Jews were killed, it was all expressed in my buildings," "The Memory of Justice" becomes the memory of guilt. That hs's so glib need not lessen the sincerity. After all, we can remember feeling pain but we don't again. experience it as we remember. Perhaps some such protective device is at work in Speer.

Some people accept responsibility. They embrace it, like Mr. Speer. Others refuse to acknowledge anything but ignorance. Of the average German, one young German woman says of her parents' generation, "They deliberately didn't try to find out what was going on." Daniel L. Ellsberg, talking about "American war criminals" of Vietnam, sounds almost as glib as Mr. Speer.

Others are accidental victims. An aging German actress recalls life as a Nazi exile in Hollywood. The widow

Hitler, accompanied by Goering, during one of his triumphal processions
The ethical questions are timeless but the subject is particular.

of a German general tells how her husband committed suicide rather than sign the death sentence of a group of Catholic priests. Barbara Keating talks proudly, with great feeling, of her husband, who was killed in Vietnam, and Mr. and Mrs. Robert Ransom, with the same feeling, regret that they hadn't urged their son, who was also killed there, to refuse to serve.

•

There is absolutely no way to condense this material. Its effect is cumulative. People who are equally sincere totally disagree. Discussions of moral positions suddenly turn into narratives-within-narratives of the most personal sort, as when someone like Col. Anthony Herbert, now retired, recalls how he finally refused to be a part of a war he considered immoral. Individual responsibility still exists. It still counts.

Mr. Ophuls is very much a presence in "The Memory of Justice," sometimes on the screen as the interviewer, shaping the film by his commitment to search through the past to discover the present. Perhaps because he himself was an exile from Nazi Germany, the son of an exile (Max Ophuls), and is married to a German woman who (in the course of this film) recalls her membership in the Hitler youth, "The Memory of Justice" seems an especially personal, urgent work.

"The Memory of Justice" is long but it rivets the mind and the emotions so consistently that I can think of a dozen 90-minute movies far more difficult to endure. It will be shown at the New York Film Festival at Alice Tully Hall today at 6:30 P.M. and again Saturday at 12:30 P.M. It opens its commercial engagement at the Beekman Theater on Sunday.

•

The film which has been rated PG ("Parental Guidance Suggested"), contains German concentration camp footage of a sort that may well be beyond the comfortable comprehension of small children.

1976 O 5, 54:1

DERSU UZALA, directed by Akira Kurosawa; screenplay by Mr. Kurosawa and Yuri Nagibin, based on story by Vladimir Arseniev; photographed by Asakadru Nakai, Yuri Gantman and Fyodor Dobronavov; A Soviet-Japanese co-production, in Russian with English subtitles. Shown at the Ziegfeld Theater today at 6:15 and 9:30 P.M., as part of the New York Film Festival Running time: 137 minutes.

Dersu Uzala .... Maxim Munzuk
Captain .... Juri Solomine

By RICHARD EDER

When Akira Kurosawa, the gifted Japanese director, takes the unusual step of making a movie in co-production with the Soviet film industry, and when the first half is delicate and haunting and the second half is numb and ponderous, it is hard not to jump to conclusions about who did what.

In any event, "Dersu Uzala," which will be shown twice today at the Ziegfeld Theater as part of the New York Film Festival, seems to be not so much co-produced as partitioned. Unequally.

•

Essentially, "Dersu Uzala" is a Tolstoian parable about the encounter of the blind and deaf power of civilization with the perceiving and magical helplessness of nature. Set in the Asian forests of Imperial Russia around the turn of the century, it tells of the relationship between a military mapping expedition and an old Tungus trapper who acts as its guide.

The soldiers sit in the winter forest at night, uncomfortable, alien, scared. There is a rustle in the bushes and, mastering the temptation to flee, they grab the intruder. He is Dersu, a short, stocky, aging tribesman. He sits by the fire with them, and when a log crackles he speaks sharply to it.

"Fire is a man," he tells them. "Water is a man, too." The captain, a sensitive intermediary between the brutal confidence of the soldier-surveyors and the mystical trapper, hires him as guide. In a series of episodes, told flatly and some with obviousness, but with accumulating force, we see Dersu, through the captain's eyes, reveal his total communication with the world he lives in.

Seeing footprints, he knows that men have been by two days before, and that they are Chinese. Seeing trees with the bark off, he predicts that they will find a shelter, and they do. When the party is about to leave the shelter, he insists on repairing the roof first: for anyone else who may come along.

Dersu, marvelously played by Maxim Munzzuk, a Soviet Asian, draws his wisdom from his complete openness to the natural world. The openness means vulnerability as well. The captain, whose relation to the old man is a growing reverence, discovers him one night, broken with grief by the fire. He is remembering his family, dead of smallpox; and he has no barriers against remembered pain—it is as real as a tree falling upon him.

In the climactic scene of this first part, Dersu and the captain go out to chart a frozen lake. Kurosawa films the cold as it has rarely, if ever, been filmed. It is a visible, red-eyed enemy, visibly terrifying. The two are lost and Dersu, seeing death, is in total fear. The captain has his civilized schooling to constrain him; he also has a compass. When the compass fails, though, Dersu saves them both.

•

Then this beautiful first part recedes. The detachment prepares to return to the city. Dersu declines the captain's offer to come with them. He would die in the city, he says, but as he trudges off through the snow we see he is older and is simply following his own road to death. The soldiers march down a railroad track, singing; Dersu reaches the top of a hill. Just before he crosses, he turns and waves. "Dersu!" the captain cries. "Captain!" Dersu calls back.

It is complete, or should be. If "Dersu Uzala" ended there is would be an odd marvel. But it goes on, repeating the cycle. The captain returns some years later, this time in the summer. He meets Dersu, who displays his powers once more, but with diminishing effect. He has grown too old for the forest; finally he goes to the city with the captain, can't adapt to it, and returns to the forest for the last time.

The episodes in this second part go on endlessly, loosely, obviously. They lack the revelations of the winter scenes and they do little but belabor at length the points already made. They wreck the film's balance and make its achievements dull.

1976 O 5, 54:1

ILLUSTRIOUS CORPSES (Cadaveri Eccellenti), directed by Francesco Rosi; screenplay (Italian with English subtitles) by Mr. Rosi, Tonino Guerra and Lino Januzzi, based on the novel, "The Context," by Leonardo Sciascia; executive producer, Alberto Grimaldi; director of photography, Pasquale De Santis; editor, Ruggero Mastroianni; music, Piero Piccioni and Astor Piazzolla; a co-production of Produzioni Europea Associate (Rome) and Les Artistes Associes (Paris) Running time: 121 minutes. At the New York Film Festival at Alice Tully Hall, Broadway at 65th Street.

Inspector Rogas .... Lino Ventura
Procura Varga .... Charles Vanel
Minister of Security .... Fernando Rey
Chief Justice .... Max Von Sydow
Police Chief .... Tino Carraro
Unemployed man .... Marcel Bozzuffi
Dr. Maxia .... Paolo Bonacelli
Judge Rasto .... Alain Cuny
Mrs. Cres .... Maria Carta
Cusan .... Luigi Pistilli
Prostitute .... Tina Aumont
Police Commissioner .... Renatn Salvatori
Galano .... Paolo Graziosi

By VINCENT CANBY

More and more, Francesco Rosi, the Italian director of such politically conscious films as "Salvatore Giuliano," "Hands Upon the City" and the recent "The Mattei Affair," has come to constructs his movies as if they were jig-saw puzzles from which key pieces must remain missing. This is not because he hasn't a very good idea what the missing pieces are, but because he thinks that to supply them would dampen the speculation he means to stir up.

Sometimes, as in the case of "The Mattei Affair," this works. But then "The Mattei Affair" was based on the life of an Italian industrialist who died under circumstances that have never been satisfactorily explained. In the newest Rosi film, "Illustrious Corpses" ("Cadaveri Eccellenti"), the method is self-defeating. It stirs up not speculation but suspicions that the completed picture is artificially made more complex and provocative than its missing pieces would have revealed it to be.

•

Until one realizes that one has been manipulated to rather predictable ends, "Illustrious Corpses" is a dazzling example of fashionably radical Italian film making—elegantly composed, breathlessly paced, photographed in the beautiful, drained colors of a landscape in mourning for the sun. It's all so beautiful, in fact, that when you see a long shot of a Sicilian piazza in which everything, including the sky, is the same matching beige, you wouldn't be at all surprised to see a high-fashion model, dressed to the scarlet nines, posing amid beige urchins.

The setting of "Illustrious Corpses" seems to be Sicily, though it's never identified, which allows the director to create a fictitious capitalistic social-political structure that cannot be immediately criticized for not being accurately Italian. Wherever it is, corruption and conspiracies are rampant, the poor are getting poorer, the rich are getting richer and the paranoid power élite, when it isn't listening to wiretaps and watching movies made by hidden cameras, attends parties where there are women and food to enchant every taste-bud.

•

The film begins effectively enough. A prominent prosecutor is murdered. Several days later, a prominent judge is similarly assassinated. Later another judge, and another. The country is thrown into disorder. Inspector Rogas (Lino Ventura), a creased, tired policeman from a more conventional mystery melodrama, investigates and becomes convinced that a man, who was once wrongly convicted and sent to prison, is carrying out a campaign of revenge.

The inspector's superiors, however, don't want to hear his evidence. More assassinations occur. The inspector then stumbles on a conspiracy that involves all of his superiors, who are apparently using one man's private vengeance to effect a plot involving the fate of the nation.

Lino Ventura stars in the film
Art spent on knicknack

"Illustrious Corpses" is full of individually arresting details, such as a sequence shot in an ancient catacomb and a scene in which Max Von Sydow, as the mad chief justice, explains that when a judge "celebrates the law," he is like a priest celebrating mass and thus incapable of error. I particularly liked Alain Cuny as another rotten judge, a man completely, almost beatifically composed except for his wayward left hand. It keeps wanting to misbehave and has to be slapped in punishment.

•

All of these arresting details and bizarre characters don't eventually add up to much more than an indictment of government that's so broad, so general, it has no particular force. The end effect is trivial. This is not to say that "Illustrious Corpses" is boring. Rather it's acutely disappointing. The art of so many people, including that of Mr. Rosi and his actors, has been lavishly spent on a knick-knack.

"Illustrious Corpses" will be shown at the New York Film Festival at Alice Tully Hall tonight at 9:30 P.M. and tomorrow at 6:15 P.M.

1976 O 6, 34:1

RITES OF PASSAGE, three short American films, New York Film Festival at Alice Tully Hall, today at 6:15 P.M. and Saturday at 9 P.M.:

SUNDAY FUNNIES, written, directed, edited and produced by Ray Karp, photographed by Roberto Quiroga. With Bette Anderson as Connie, Buddy Anderson as Jeff, and others. Running time: 21 minutes.

IN THE REGION OF ICE, directed and written by Peter Werner; produced by Andre Guttfreund; photographed by Stephen Posey; edited by Michael Goldman. Based on story by Joyce Carol Oates. With Flonnouala Flanagan as Sister Irene; Peter Lempert as Alan Weinstein; Malachi Throne as Mr. Weinstein; Shirley Slater as Mrs. Weinstein, and others. Running time: 37 minutes.

BERNICE BOBS HER HAIR, directed and written by Joan Micklin Silver from story by F. Scott Fitzgerald; produced by Robert Geller; photographed by Ken Van Sickle; edited by Ralph Rosenbaum. With Shelley Duvall as Bernice, Veronica Cartwright as Marjorie, Bud Cort as Warren, and others. Running time: 45 minutes.

By RICHARD EDER

The past tense of "comedy of manners" is "mannered comedy." The short film "Bernice Bobs Her Hair," shown today and Saturday at the New York Film Festival in Alice Tully Hall, is not a revival of F. Scott Fitzgerald's wry story about pre-flappers. It is an embalming, though an elegant and sometimes a funny one.

Joan Micklin Silver, author of "Hester Street," wrote and directed "Bernice" as an exercise in style. She is imitating the literary manner in which a certain period viewed itself rather than re-creating the period itself. Her imitation is so lavish, so thorough, so precise that the effect, paradoxically, is of chilly distance.

Bernice is an awkward, inhibited country cousin who comes to spend a summer vacation in St. Paul with her more advanced cousin, Marjorie. Bernice clings to her wet blanket for a while; then she asks Marjorie for lessons on how to flirt with the young men home on vacation from Yale and Princeton. She is such a good pupil that she threatens to deprive Marjorie of her boyfriend. Marjorie mousetraps her into carrying out her announced, but not seriously meant, intention of bobbing her hair. This is too much, even for St. Paul's fast crowd, and Bernice is brutally isolated; until, that is, she takes her own ingenious revenge.

The pastiche is flawless. We see the girls primping for a dance by crushing jelly beans to dye their lips red; the big houses with porches, maids and lots of dark, polished wood; the mixture of slanginess and formality that belonged to the years just after World War I.

It is all too careful and lifeless. But the performances of the two actresses who play the principals makes up for a good deal. Shelley Duvall, as Bernice, is long, gawky, with watery eyes, frizzy hair and an unhappy mouth. And yet she manages allure when she begins to practice it. The gape becomes a pout; the discouraged slump becomes a languorous slump. As Marjorie, Veronica Cartwright does her small-time femme fatale with a steely practicality: it is obvious she'll grow up to manage the P.T.A.

"Bernice" is the longest of the three short films that make up the Film Festival program, collectively entitled "Rites of Passage."

"In the Region of Ice," directed and written by Peter Werner from a short story by Joyce Carol Oates, is more awkward and less skillful in every way. It is also much more affecting.

The Oates story is about a nun who is troubled and shaken, almost to the depths of her commitment, by a brilliant and unbalanced Jewish student in her Shakespeare class. She holds him off stiffly at first, then warms gradually to his enthusiasm. He has a breakdown, goes off to a mental hospital; comes back and demands from her more help than she can give.

The awkwardness, the constriction and patness of some of the scenes are redeemed partly by the fact that the screenplay is based on some very sound writing; partly by the fact that the film believes in itself. Most important is a wrenching performance by Fionnouala Flanagan as the constricted but flickering nun.

The shortest film in "Rites" is "Sunday Funnies," by Ray Karp. It is a sad attempt to be funny by injecting sex and sadism into a 1950's story about a girl going to a prom. "Garbage!" one man shouted at a preliminary screening, and he was right.

1976 O 6, 35:1

MARATHON MAN, directed by John Schlesinger; screenplay by William Goldman, based on his novel; produced by Robert Evans and Sidney Beckerman; director of photography, Conrad Hall; editor, Jim Clark; music, Michael Small; distributed by Paramount Pictures. Running time: 125 minutes. At Loews State 1, Broadway at 45th Street, and Loews Tower East, Third Avenue near 72d Street. This film has been rated R.

Dustin Hoffman aims at Sir Laurence Olivier in "Marathon Man."

Babe	Dustin Hoffman
Szell	Laurence Olivier
Doc	Roy Scheider
Janeway	William Devane
Elsa	Marthe Keller
Prof. Biesenthal	Fritz Weaver
Karl	Richard Bright
Erhard	Marc Lawrence
Babe's father	Allen Joseph
Melendez	Tito Goya
Szell's brother	Ben Dova
Rosenbaum	Lou Gilbert
LeClerc	Jacques Marin
Chen	James Wing Woo

By VINCENT CANBY

If you were forced at gunpoint to swallow at $16,000 diamond, what would you do? Stall for time by asking for a glass of water? Say you were allergic? Cry? It's not a problem most of us are likely to face. It would seem to be too special to engage our interest at gut level. It's like worrying about what to do with a case of empty Dom Perignon bottles.

Yet when Laurence Olivier, who plays a sadistic ex-Nazi war criminal in "Marathon Man," confronts such a situation, it becomes a matter of universal concern and immense wit in spite of the desperate circumstances.

Szell (Olivier) places the diamond in his mouth and holds it between his front teeth as if it were an unpleasant pill. His eyes glaze slightly at the affront to his position. He pauses. His tongue tentatively touches the gem, but diamonds have no taste. He frowns. He is ordered to swallow. He would sneer but there's a gun aimed at his heart. Like a man forced to jump from the Empire State Building, he closes his eyes and does the deed. The diamond disappears into his gullet. Gulp and gone. What will it do to his ulcer?

Lord Olivier, one of the great ornaments of the English-speaking theater and cinema, helps to make John Schlesinger's "Marathon Man" a film that you won't want to miss, given a strong stomach for bloodshed and graphic torture that includes dental interference of an especially unpleasant sort.

In addition to Lord Olivier's superb performance, "Marathon Man" has several other superior things going for it: Dustin Hoffman as a moody, guilt-ridden, upper-West Side New Yorker, a haunted innocent obsessed with running, pursued by an unknown evil; Roy Schneider and William Devane as members of some sort of super-super Central Intelligence Agency, and the direction of Mr. Schlesinger, who has made a most elegant, bizarre, rococo melodrama out of material that, when you think about it, makes hardly any sense at all.

That's to say that when the lights come up at the end of "Marathon Man" and you start going through the plot, back to front, you're likely to suspect that you've been had. And you have if your only criterion is logic. The William Goldman screenplay, based on his novel, is built upon double-, triple-, and quadruple-crosses that finally cancel themselves out. Instead of logic, the film presents us with a literally breathtaking nightmare that turns out to be, within the film, absolutely true.

The nightmare is that of Babe (Mr. Hoffman), a Columbia graduate student who, for reasons he can't know, is kidnapped by mysterious parties with strange accents who torture him for information he doesn't have. The chief inquisitor is Szell, a notorious former Nazi with a degree in dentistry. "Is it safe?" Szell asks. "What safe?" asks Babe. "Is it safe?" the old Nazi asks again, and starts fiddling with the live nerve in one of Babe's teeth.

When the explanations do start coming, you may feel that "Marathon Man" is a kind of thriller that has run its course. High-level conspiracies really aren't that interesting unless we can get a fix on who is doing what to whom, which is never clear here. Yet the individual details of "Marathon Man," the performances, and the attention given to its physical settings—in New York, Paris and South America—keep one's belief willingly suspended by a wickedly thin thread.

For the first third of the film, Mr. Schlesinger manages to cross-cut between two different narratives so effectively that it's almost a disapointment when they come together, but though the plot is ridiculous, the film is richly fleshed out by character and and an intensifying sense of menace that doesn't rely on tricks. When a fellow, lying back in his hot tub relaxing, is suddenly disturbed by someone trying to break down the door, it's an assassin, not a steam-induced dream.

Which, I suspect, is why "Marathon Man" leaves one feeling comfortably exhausted and not cheated, as does a more serious but equally paranoid political thriller like Francesco Rosi's "Illustrious Corpses." "Marathon Man" hasn't a real idea in its head. It just wants to scare the hell out of you —and it does.

1976 O 7, 62:1

SOLARIS, directed by Andrei Tarkovsky; screenplay by Friedrich Gorenstein and Mr. Tarkovsky from the novel by Stanislaw Lem; photography by Vadim Yusov; music by Eduard Artemyev; in Russian with English subtitles. Released by Magna Distributing Corporation. Running time: 132 minutes. This film has not been rated.

Christ Kelvin	Donatis Banior
Hari	Natalya Bondarch
Snouth	Yuri Jar
Also with Nicolai Grinko, Vladislav Dvorzhetski a Anatoli Solonitsyn.	

By RICHARD EDER

A nation's image of outer space reflects itself. Jules Verne's moon train was a small wagon-lit. American science-fiction movies stress the gleaming pipes and dials, a kind of hi-waterworks. Andrei Tarkovsky's "Solaris," which opened yesterday at the Ziegfeld Theater, gives us Russian outer space.

I say Russian rather than Soviet because this complex and sometimes very beautiful film is about hunmanity but hardly at all about politics.

In any case, the space station on the planet Solaris has an obsent-minded ⅞ neglect about it that could have come straight out of Dostoyevsky's study. There is a suspicion of rust on the pipes, and the furniture would look at home in the Omsky railroad station. One has the feeling that wrappers of half-eaten sausage are lying just out of sight and that a samovar is at work. Outer space is shabbiness, lots of tea and urgent philosophical discussion that leave no time for shaving.

Nothing that's visible matters very much—except for nature: shots of a pond, of water weeds, of a hunning horse—and life's surface are quite unimportant. Because of it, the blockish camera work, the egg-like colors and the general visual poverty are almost irrelevant. What matters is the conversations, the problems they raise, the faces that reflect them, seen blurrily as if at the end of an all-night session.

Mr. Tarkovsky, who is known here for a truncated version of "Andrei Rublev," made "Solaris" from the novel by the Polish writer Stanislaw Lem. It is science-fiction in the formal sense of the word; in substance, it is a parable about the nature of mankind.

Set in some future time, it is about the voyage of Chris Kelvin to the space station on the planet Solaris. The Academy of Sciences has found no profit in the long studies made of the planet. Chris's mission is to talk with the three scientists at the station and to report on closing it down.

The surface of Solaris is something like a sea, a great pulsating mass. A previous scientist, Burton, has come back in severe nervous shock; he believes that it may not be a sea but a superior order of consciousness, a great brain, in fact. Chris, a haunted but practical man, a missioner of human progress, is prepared to order a final experiment: a massive infusion of radiation into the "sea."

Burton, now older, is horrified. "You must not destroy what you don't understand," he says. Chris's father, a solitary, severe man, is also appalled. "Space is too fragile for your kind," he says.

The whole long, strange trip develops the theme. Mankind, with its aggressive expansionism — intellectual as well as material — destroys more than it finds. Chris is the practical man who, by the film's end, will be converted.

He finds that the space station, that summit of technology, is a heart of darkness. All three scientists there have been shattered by encountering the mystery of the planet. Solaris is, in fact, a great consciousness. Thought is made reality there, including the deepest thoughts of its visitors.

One has killed himself, leaving behind an obscure message on videotape for Chris. As he explores the decrepit space station—almost visibly rusted by the presence of a greater reality—Chris finds the other two. Sartorius, who will not accept what he can't understand, barricades himself in his laboratory surrounded by dwarfs—his thoughts made substance. Snouth, more innocent and hopeful, drinks a lot, but his visitors are children.

Chris has arrived with the suicide of his wife, Hari, on his conscience. Hari begins, nevertheless, to visit him. She is not an apparition; she is a yearning that thee Solarian sea has given substance and built—the other scientists explain—of neutrinos. But she becomes more and more human until, in an act of abnegation, she asks to be destroyed so Chris can return to earth.

•

Put in summary, the plot may seem ludicrous. "Solaris" has its problems. Its rhythm is slow, and sometimes is extinguished altogether. The narrative can be difficult to grasp. Finally, as the film draws into conclusion, the parable seems to unclothe; the sense of wonder that Mr. Tarkovsky has created yields to a certain didacticism.

All of these drawbacks must be cited provisionally. "Solaris," whose mystical, totally nonmaterialistic character has won it no other favor in the Soviet Union than the permission to exist, is here in a severely truncated form. The original was reportedly four hours long; a second version, shown in Cannes and elsewhere, was 2 hours and 47 minutes. The version we are seeing is down to 2 hours and 12 minutes and the distributors, who received it that way, say they don't know whether Mr. Tarkovsky supervised the cuts.

•

Obviously it is impossible to judge the pace, the rhythms and the clarity of a film that is cut nearly in half. It is like a fresco partly eaten away by rising damp.

The result must be viewed actively and with some effort. But if it is, the result is extraordinary enough to compensate. The film's great metaphors—the faces of Donatis Banionis as Chris, Natalya Bondarchuk as Hari and Yuri Jarvet as Snouth—involve us totally in the difficult mysteries. Like his Solarian sea, Mr. Tarkovsky has made ideas walk, breathe and move us.

1976 O 7, 63:2

STORY OF SIN (DZIEJE GRZECHU); directed by Walerian Borowczyk; screenplay (Polish with English subtitles) by Mr. Borowczyk from a novel by Stefan Zeromski; produced by Polish Corporation for Film Production, "TOR" Film Unit; director of photography Zygmunt Samosiuk; art director Teresa Barsko; music, Felix Mendelssohn Violin Concerto in E-minor, Johann Pachelbel Prelude in D minor; distributed by TINC Productions. Running Time: 128 minutes. At the New York Film Festival, Alice Tully Hall, Broadway at 65th Street. This film has been rated R.
Eva .... Grazyna Dlugolecka
Count Szczerbic .... Olgierd Lukaszewicz
Lucas .... Jerzy Zelnik

By A. H. WEILER

If sin, like truth and beauty, is in the eye of the beholder, then "Story of Sin," the Polish entry at the New York Film Festival tonight and tomorrow night, is a delight to the eye. But Walerian Borowczyk, the Polish director who previously worked in France, is enamored of a saga that is, in essence, a cross between grand and soap opera.

His principals may be true to themselves, Victorian moralities and their vintage settings but, despite the dedication of the director and his cast, their "Story of Sin" evolves more as a quaint, visually engrossing album of a faded past than as a gripping motion picture.

In fashioning his script from an old Polish novel, Mr. Borowczyk, and an English prologue and subtitles, make it plain that turn-of-the-century Czarist-dominated Warsaw was rough on the staunchly Catholic, disenfranchised Polish petit bourgeois. And our pure, religiously proper young heroine is no exception. She is quickly caught up in the throes of first love with a lodger in her parents' apartment who, it happens, is seeking a divorce. As might be guessed, this is the start of a convoluted, bitter romance indicating that sin isn't necessarily simple.

As was the case in Mr. Borowczyk's "Immoral Tales," seen here early this year, eroticism, costuming, settings and photography are artistically detailed. Lovers engulfed in newly found ecstacy in cramped village quarters or in a baroque Riviera suite leave little to the imagination.

And lust and murder are made equally specific in rich, red damask rooms filled with bibelots and the sounds of a raucous ancient gramophone.

The primal drive of love and the beastliness of sinners in our heroine's life make for a complex plot with some seemingly abrupt transitions. But Mr. Borowczyk's fascination with his subject appears to have rubbed off on his willing players. If he is precise in dealing with action in the boudoir, he is just as careful in maintaining a fast narrative pace.

•

(In a largely unbilled cast that contributes to that momentum, Grazyna Dlugolecka is outstanding as the pretty, driven outcast. She is curvaceous, but more importantly, genuinely winning and realistic, both as the virgin introduced to love and sex amid swirling white petticoats or nude or in black corsets as the seemingly callous streetwalker.

If Jerzy Zelnik's portrait of her beleaguered student dover is merely a profile, others, including Olgierd Lucaszewicz, vigorously project sincere if sometimes-postured portrayals.

Mr. Borowczyk and his actors colorfully evoke the people and places of a restrictive society with the dedication of historians. There inspection of the complexities of sin, however, is as obvious and colorful as a vintage snapshot.

"Story of Sin" is slated to start an engagement at the RKO Twin 1 Theater on East 59th Street next Thursday.

1976 O 7, 63:2

Looking Back

A MATTER OF TIME, directed by Vincente Minnelli; screenplay by John Gay, based on the novel "Film of Memory," by Maurice Druon; executive producers, Samuel Z. Arkoff and Giulio Sbarigia; produced by Jack H. Skirball and J. Edmund Grainger; director of photography, Geoffrey Unsworth; music, Nino Oliviero; editor, Peter Taylor; distributed by American International Pictures. Running time: 97 minutes. At Radio City Music Hall, Avenue of the Americas at 50th Street. This film has been rated PG.
Nina .... Liza Minnelli
The Contessa .... Ingrid Bergman
Count Sanziani .... Charles Boyer
Mario Morello .... Spiros Andros
Valentina .... Tina Aumont
Jeanne Blasto .... Anna Proclemer
Antonio Vicaria .... Gabriele Ferzeti
Pavelli .... Arnolda Foa
Gabriele .... Orso Maria Guerrini
Charles Van Maar .... Fernando Rey
Nun .... Isabella Rossellini

By VINCENT CANBY

IF you can imagine a feature-film equivalent to a Radio City Music Hall stage show, it might look very much like Vincente Minnelli's "A Matter of Time," which opened yesterday—appropriately—at Radio City

'Shadow of the Hawk'

A threshold of fright so minimal that it is bestirred by a jack-in-the-box or a Halloween mask seems to be the prerequisite for enjoyment of "Shadow of the Hawk," now playing at an assortment of local theaters.

To make a long and rather tedious story short, this seems to be the Indian version of "The Exorcist," with chief Dan George as the old medicine man who journeys to the big city to bring back his grandson, played by Jan-Michael Vincent, to apply the strength of youth against a wily evil sorceress named Dsonoqua.

At no time is there any question about the outcome of this 200-year-old family feud. But as grandfather and grandson proceed, accompanied by a freelance woman journalist, masks come out of the woods and mist, snakes and bears attack, Indians with white-painted faces appear and disappear, humans take on animal form and cars do strange things. There are incantations and machinations with tiny dolls.

The director, George McCowan, tends to be better at conveying eeriness with cinematic devices, such as a car that appears and disappears and finally crashes into an invisible wall, than he is at conjuring up terror with the myriad Indian props at his disposal. Dsonoqua is too ill-defined to be taken seriously as a match for the old medicine man and the new. "Shadow of the Hawk" settles for minor intermittent surprises instead of cumulative horror.

•

The PG rating may be attributable to the general intent of the film, rather than to any particular excesses of language, violence or sexual activity.

LAWRENCE VAN GELDER

1976 O 8, C8:4

Liza Minnelli and Ingrid Bergman in Vincente Minnelli's "A Matter of Time"
An operetta from which the music has been removed

Music Hall, where Mr. Minnelli began his career years ago as a designer and producer. It is full of glittery costumes and spectacular props. It is performed by talented, sophisticated people who adopt the faux-naif gestures of an earlier show-biz tradition, and though it is expensive, it sounds peculiarly tacky.

"A Matter of Time" might better have retained the title of the Maurice Druon novel from which John Gay adapted his screenplay—"Film of Memory." "A Matter of Time" is a jumbo-size pousse-café of memories in the form of a fairy tale about a little girl from the Italian provinces who comes to Rome and becomes a big, glamorous movie queen.

•

Its principal star is none other than Liza Minnelli, Mr. Minnelli's daughter by Judy Garland and a screen personality whose appearance recalls her father and whose voice and mannerisms recall her mother. She has talent of her own, but it comes to us through the remembered presence of others.

"A Matter of Time" is not only composed of memories, it is about memory as a mysteriously enriching human capacity, though it never realizes the poetic potential of its subject. Playing opposite Miss Minnelli is Ingrid Bergman as a dotty old contessa, once the toast of Europe and now reduced to living in poverty in the rundown hotel where Liza takes a job as a chambermaid.

As the contessa spins tales about her turn-of-the-century conquests,

little Liza, whose eyes seem to have been widened surgically to play this part, relives the memories on screen, providing Mr. Minnelli with an opportunity for some fancy, romantic fooling of the sort that distinguished the regression sequences in "On a Clear Day You Can See Forever."

Only one sequence, however, comes off with the anticipated élan: Liza, as the contessa, is the hostess at one of those gala, pre-World War I Venice masquerades. She bids good night on the Grand Canal to the Kaiser ("Please call me Wilhelm"), walks back into her palazzo, knee-deep in confetti, discarding her costume as she goes. By the time she reaches the far end of the ballroom, she has returned to mid-20th century. There, backed by five black musicians who had been packing to leave, she drifts into a sort of elegiacal rendition of the great Gershwin number, "Do It Again."

No other moment in the film comes anywhere near to capturing this sort of ghostly, romantic elegance. In addition to "Do It Again," Miss Minnelli sings two new Fred Ebb-John Kander songs, yet the film has the air of an operetta from which the music has been removed. It's even acted that way.

When Miss Minnelli's chambermaid enters a room, it's the way chambermaids enter rooms in operettas. She opens the door breezily, twirls around to close the door with her back to the audience, thus making it possible for her to be struck with dumb surprise or shock when she turns again to see what's going on. It's all a teeny, tiny bit arch.

So is the casting of Charles Boyer in the small role of the contessa's long-lost husband, recalling the teaming of Miss Bergman and Mr. Boyer in "Gaslight." Mr. Boyer has such weight that, after he has been on the screen, the film seems even flimsier than it need be when he disappears.

A further family note: Isabella Rossellini, Miss Bergman's daughter by Roberto Rossellini, shows up at the end of the film as a nun, looking meltingly beautiful, much the way her mother did when she first came to Hollywood.

The English dialogue of the European actors has apparently been post-synchronized, which contributes to the effect of overall hollowness of the movie. Because "A Matter of Time" has moments of real visual beauty, and because what the characters say to each other is mostly dumb, it may be a film to attend while wearing your earplugs.

•

"A Matter of Time" has been rated PG ("Parental Guidance Suggested") for reasons that may have to do with the merest soupçon of discreet nudity, but I'm not sure. It seems totally harmless to me.

1976 O 8, C8:3

SCORCHY, directed, written and produced by Hikmet Avedis; executive producer, Marlene Schmidt; director of photography, Laszlo Pal; editor, Michael Luciano; distributed by American International Pictures. Running time: 99 minutes. At the Cinerama Theater, Broadway near 47th Street, and other heaters. This film has been rated R.

Jackie Parker .... Connie Stevens
Phillip Bianco .... Cesare Danova
Claudia Bianco .... Marlene Schmidt
Carl Henrich .... William Smith
Chief O'Brien .... Norman Burton
Nicky .... John David Chandler
Mary Davis .... Joyce Jameson
Alan .... Greg Evigan
Steve .... Nick Dimitri

"Scorchy" is a stupid, brutal, horribly acted melodrama that is set in Seattle and stars Connie Stevens, who is pretty, though she looks like last year's Debbie Reynolds retread, as a narcotics detective. It was written, directed and produced by Hikmet Avedis ,which if it's a pseudonym, is the only indication of good sense connected with the movie. It opened around town yesterday at a number of theaters, including the Cinerama, where they sometimes forget to lower the lights when the movie starts.

VINCENT CANBY

1976 O 9, 9:4

FIGHTING MAD, directed and produced by Jonathan Demme; music, Bruce Langhorne; produced by Roger Corman; released by 20th Century-Fox Film Corp. At neighborhood theaters. Running time: 88 minutes. This film is rated R.

Tom Hunter .... Peter Fonda
Lorene .... Lynn Lowry
Jeff Hunter .... John Doucette
Crabtree .... Philip Carey

Given a determined effort at self-delusion, it is possible to believe that "Fighting Mad," which opened Friday at neighborhood theaters, is just another good guys versus bad guys movie. The bad guys in this case are a strip miner-land developer, his henchmen, corrupt politicians and inertia-ridden policemen, and the good guys are the sort of farm folk that we know are determined to cleave to their land because they have the sort of faces that made nimble the brush hands of Grant Wood and Norman Rockwell.

•

The truth is that "Fighting Mad," starring Peter Fonda, is a little less than just another good guys versus bad guys movie. The holes in its story line occasionally yawn wide enough to admit six abreast the bulldozers that evil, murderous Crabtree is using in the strip-mining and land-development schemes that are consuming and menacing the farmers' land.

One of the landowners is the father of Tom Hunter, played by Fonda. He has come home to the family horse ranch from the city with his little boy after the breakup of his marriage only to find the clean rustic life he seeks imperilled by men who will stop at nothing to impose their vision of progress on the farmers. So he takes up the cudgels or whatever else is handy.

•

The result is a film so determined to stir the viscera that it overlooks the nourishment of the brain. The real lesson of this sort of movie doesn't seem to be that right wins out in the end. Not so bad comes through. Villains and peripheral characters suffer and die when injured and shot. The protagonist's gunshot wounds don't hurt too much and heal fast. And the law doesn't seem to mind vigilantes.

Well, it isn't life. And, heaven knows, it isn't art.

LAWRENCE VAN GELDER

1976 O 9, 9:5

STRONGMAN FERDINAND, written and directed by Alexander Kluge; produced by Kairos-Film/Reitz-Film; photographed by Thomas Mauch; edited by Heidi Genee. In German with English subtitles. New York Film Festival at Alice Tully Hall, today at 6 P.M. and tomorrow at 9 P.M. Running time: 98 minutes. This film has not been rated.

Ferdinand Rieche .... Heinz Schubert
Gertie Kahlmann .... Verena Rudolph
Kniebeling .... Joachim Hackethal
Ganter .... Heinz Schimmelpfenning
Wilutzki .... Gert Guenther Hoffmann

By RICHARD EDER

The morning is sour and dark. Ferdinand Rieche, a security policeman demoted for overzealousness, is having breakfast. With a mournful countenance, a prominent nose and a face that resembles both mousetrap and mouse, he devours raisin cake. The radio announces a tropical storm approaching Wiesbaden.

Ferdinand grabs his atlas, locates Wiesbaden, assesses its distance from the East German frontier, road routes, rivers. He chews and ponders: who can be behind this storm?

•

This is part of the prologue of Alexander Kluge's "Strongman Ferdinand," a satire on West German society that is being shown in the New York Film Festival at Alice Tully Hall today and tomorrow. It is obsessively narrow in its focus and drawn out too far, but in its better moments—and there are a lot of them—it is original, apt and very, very funny.

Nothing is so troublesome to a society as a man who follows its principles literally. To Kluge, West Germany is a society that maintains a fat complacency by making an idol of order and resistance to change.

Rieche is the dangerous total believer. He pursues order to the point where it becomes outlawry, mad yet oddly logical. Security is his profession and his obsession. When a superior at the factory where he has become chief of security—after leaving the police force—questions the usefulness of his elaborate measures, he retorts: "With security, it's not a question of usefulness." It is a question of the whole purpose of life.

•

"Strongman Ferdinand" is the tragicomic story of what happens when Rieche—50, in poor health, his career broken by his tendency to harangue his police superiors on the need to arrest people *before* they break the law—gets a last chance.

The factory security post becomes vacant. The previous chief was discharged for placing snipers to shoot workers who break plant discipline. The press had got on to the story, and so the bosses—bland, hypocritical men—hire Rieche. They order him to do "enough, but not too much" but they have hired a one-man disaster.

Within 48 hours, Rieche has knocked down his office walls with a sledgehammer to make it bigger, turned it into an advanced communications post, begun drilling the middle-aged factory guards as an élite commando force, and put in so many locks that the washroom attendant is locked in.

Obstacles are put in the way of this small figure with the enormous head who storms around in a green trenchcoat, upsetting everything. He has to take a medical exam: his solution is to force a young woman employee caught pilfering to give him her urine sample. "Very young urine," the doctor congratulates him. "In fact, if you were a woman, I'd say you were three months pregnant."

More seriously, the factory bosses keep cracking down on him for excess; as when he and his guards raid another factory for a training exercise, or when he insists on body-searching a group of visiting American industrialists. It become a mounting war between Rieche and management and eventually, as the battles become more and more comically outrageous, between Rieche and a society that can't understand his efforts to defend it.

•

The movie is done in short, clipped sequences — there are too many of them, though — each like a brief stanza in the ballad of Rieche. The dry, deadpan style of this social fantasy is counterpointed beautifully by a camera that becomes lyrical: focusing on a full moon wrinkled by chimney smoke, or showing the security guards drilling on the beach at dawn and lit up in profile like a line of long-legged wading-birds.

The harshness is redeemed even more by the character of Ferdinand himself, memorably played by Heinz Schubert. He is a small man who sometimes totters under the weight of his big mission. He is fond of cake and his blonde taxi-driving girlfriend, Gertie. They celebrate birthdays at midnight feast in cheap restaurants, and go on a winter trailer trip to practice for Christmas.

"Christmas needs training or it won't work," Rieche says. He is something like Chaplin; something like Hitler played by Chaplin. The combination is unforgettable.

1976 O 9, 10:1

TOUCH OF ZEN (Sha-Nu), directed by King Hu; screenplay (Chinese with English subtitles) by Mr. Hu from a collection of classical Chinese short stories; photography, Hua Hui-Ying; editor, Mr. Hu; music, Ng Tai-Kwong; art direction and costumes by Mr. Hu; presented by Agape Productions. At the New York Film Festival, Alice Tully Hall, Lincoln Center. Running time: 180 minutes. This film is not rated.

Yang Hui-chen .... Hsu Feng
Shih Wen-chiao .... Pai Ying
Monk .... Roy Chiao Hung
Ku Sheng-chai .... Shih Chun
Ou-yang Nien .... Tien Peng
Men Ta .... Wan Jei

By A. H. WEILER

Bruce Lee, as his saddened fans know, is gone. But the frenzied, largely incredible kung fu action fare he popularized is still being churned out in familiar style by the Orient's busy moviemakers. However, "Touch of Zen," the Taiwanese feature on view this afternoon and tomorrow night at the New York Film Festival, is proof that familiarity can also breed a touch of annoyance with a standard approach to the genre.

Its unfamiliar writer-director, King Hu, has not ignored traditional mayhem here, but he has demonstrated that pictorial artistry, Zen mysticism and the stylized martial arts, can make a fascinating mix.

There is more than a touch of Zen and mystery in this period piece, despite its English subtitles. Program notes are necessary in fixing the time and locale as 14th-century China. But it is slowly made evident that a murderous warlord is out to eliminate a fugitive young lady loyal to the Ming Emperor, whose father he has aready dispatched; her two trusted aides and her country-bumpkin lover.

•

Our renegade brunette beauty, it should be stressed, is no demure flower arranger. She is, it turns out, a prize pupil and acolyte of Zen Buddhist monks, who are as adept at weaponless, defensive kung fu as they are devoted to pacifism. As befits a grand myth, she and her equally expert cohort eventually eliminate those bloodthirsty pursuers in a succession of clanging swordplays and hand-to-hand clashes.

As a Renaissance man also credited with the film's art direction and costumes, King Hu, who reportedly spent several years on this king-sized (three-hour) project, is obviously as dedicated to visual beauty and meditative Zen concepts as he is to action. And his views of gloomy bamboo forests, sun-dappled, green or rocky mountain crevasses and rushing rivers and waterfalls make truly spectacular backgrounds to both the peaceful and warring moods of the monks and the combatants.

The confrontations between our heroine and her monks and the glaring villains are, of course, ludicrous and impossible. But King Hu and his cinematographer, Hua Hui-Ying, have staged all the prodigious leaps, the sparring and sword swinging with eye-catching, balletic effect.

•

Aside from the almost mandatory posturing called for in these bouts, the performances are naturalistic, if flamboyant on occasion. As the saffron-robed monk-abbot, Roy Chiao Hung is a monolithic figure who not only is impressive as an imperturbable, unbeatable karate-chopper but also is fairly convincing as a contemplative type. Hsu Feng is animated and appealing as the harried lady sword swinger who sadly forsakes her lover and baby and chooses peace and sanctuary in his monastery. Shih Chun is properly trusting and helpful as her lover and Tien Peng makes a handsome, if menacing, secret-police official.

1976 O 10, 75:3

FILM VIEW

VINCENT CANBY

Grown-Up Movies About Children

Because most performances by professional child actors are dopey adult idealizations of how children should behave, childhood remains the cinema's last dark continent, the one remaining territory of experience to be explored and charted by moviemakers with the sort of obsessive seriousness they have recently devoted to freaks of nature in disaster films and to sex in pornographic films. It's not that children haven't been underfoot, metaphorically speaking, ever since the silent days of movies. Mary Pickford held off her majority until she was almost an old lady. Shirley Temple tap-tap-tap-danced her way into our hearts for far longer than many of us care to remember, Margaret O'Brien, it was reported breathlessly in Silver Screen or some such publication, could cry large, salty, certifiably real tears on cue simply by thinking of something sad, like the loss of a puppy or the possibility that M-G-M wouldn't pick up her option.

Children have been all over movies for as long as movies have been made, yet the recognizable experiences of childhood have largely been ignored except for isolated films like Carol Reed's "The Fallen Idol," René Clement's "Forbidden Games," Fred Zinnemann's "A Member of The Wedding," Morris Engel's "The Little Fugitive" and one or two others. Just why, I'm not sure. Maybe because by the time the professional child actor climbs to the position of having his name in the credits, some important filament has burnt out. They are lightbulbs that rattle. Though it may be true that all children are, to some extent, actors, the rather special demands of show business make them different no matter how carefully they've been treated.

I shall never forget seeing the late Brandon De Wilde, age approximately 10, shortly after he made "Shane," stopping in front of a mirror in the Paramount offices here to examine his bite, looking for traces of malocclusion as solemnly as Marilyn Monroe might have searched for her first gray hair.

* * *

Tatum O'Neal gave a remarkable performance in "Paper Moon," but what made it remarkable was not its associations to childhood but the eerie way in which she seemed to have adopted as her own a whole range of adult gestures and attitudes. Her child was to other children what Godzilla is to the creatures at the Central Park Zoo.

Children as imitation adults have long been big business and a source of unending interest to the media hustlers. Several years ago I wrote what I thought was a fairly blatant parody in the form of a furious polemic by a fictitious 10-year-old child, identified as the founder and president of the Federated Children's Film Societies of Long Island, and as a consultant to a Madison Avenue ad agency. The day after the piece appeared, the kid, who threatened to take his fellows to the streets unless children were treated more truthfully by filmmakers, was invited to appear on two national television shows.

* * *

A kid who parrots the very different vocabularies of Rap Brown and Gloria Steinem is sought out for TV appearances, I suspect, because he might tell adults something about adults, not about children. For one reason or another adults aren't much interested in children, at least in children taken at their own level.

The point in making that statement is to recognize three most unusual exceptions to the rule. François Truffaut's "Small Change" (L'Argent de Poche), which opened the current New York Film Festival at Lincoln Center, Dyan Cannon's first film, "Number One," which was shown at the recently concluded Festival of Women's Films, and Victor Erice's 1973 Spanish film, "The Spirit of The Beehive," which is now playing first-run in New York.

Of the three, Mr. Erice's "The Spirit of the Beehive" is the most complex intellectually and the most conventional, having a more or less fixed beginning, middle and end, and being concerned by a lot of other things in addition to childhood. The heart of the film is in the performances of two little girls, Ana Torrent, 8, and Isabel Telleria, 10, who play the children of comparatively well-to-do, upper-middle class parents living in a small, unscarred Castillian village a year after the end of the Spanish civil war.

The children are anything but conventional in film terms. Left pretty much to their own devices, with only their imaginations to guide them, they create experiences for themselves that are the distorted mirror images of the adult world. Isabel amuses herself by telling wild lies to Ana, who believes everything. At one point Isabel, being bored, toys with the idea of strangling her cat. She doesn't, but the thought was there. They literally play with fire, are always on the edge of disaster.

"The Spirit of the Beehive" looks into the murky depths of children's minds that most of us prefer to forget are there. It is harrowing and touching, and it is played by the two little girls without a moment's self-consciousness. How Mr. Erice got these performances, I have no idea. Is this, truly, acting? Or is it responding?

The same questions can be asked of Miss Cannon's "Number One," a 43-minute film made by the actress with the help of a grant by the American Film Institute. "Number One" is both very, very funny and the most serious American film about children's behavior I've seen in years. Using several professional actors, including Allen Garfield, and two little boys and two little girls who seem to be about nine or 10, and who are, I assume, completely nonprofessional, Miss Cannon recalls the commonplace but dizzying (to kids) childhood experience of finding out what the other sex looks like. The four children meet by accident in the school bathroom, exchange challenges and giggles, then disrobe partially as one little girl, whose parents are obviously given to reading sane-sex books, insists that no one need be ashamed of his body. "Your body is beautiful," she says cheerfully while her skeptical girlfriend undresses with all of the enthusiasm of someone about to receive a giant penicillin shot.

"Number One" enters a children's world as it is seen by them. It is discreet, compassionate and witty without being patronizing, a fine little film that just happens to be the actress's first.

* * *

"Small Change" is the "Gone With the Wind" of this sort of filmmaking—Mr. Truffaut's feature-length meditation upon childhood as experienced by a dozen children whose interlocking stories make up one of the year's most appealing, ebullient comedies. The situations are improvised by the children—non professionals—with an intensity of concentration that matches the seriousness with which Truffaut takes their problems. The mood is debonair and the effect is to have been gifted briefly with an insider's view of that dark continent where everybody and everything is somehow bigger than you are.

"Small Change" is often hilarious and looks to have been composed with magical ease. Yet its concerns are profoundly serious. When a school teacher, toward the end of the film, tells his students that he understands that childhood is a kind of slavery from which there's no emancipation except through age, he's not talking to them—they think he's a bit nuts—but to us. Look at children carefully, he's saying. They aren't imitation adults. They are physically, emotionally, psychologically different—gloriously so.

In the context of most of the stuff turned out by the commercial cinema, these three films are nothing less than revolutionary.

1976 O 10, II:17:1

THE MIDDLEMAN, directed by Satyajit Ray; screenplay (Bengali with English dialogue) by Mr. Ray, based on a story by Shankar; executive producer, Subir Guha; director of photography, Soumendu Ray; editor, Dulal Dutta; music, Satyajit Ray; an Indus Films production. Running time: 134 minutes. At the New York Film Festival at Alice Tully Hall, Broadway at 65th Street.
Somnath .... Pradip Mukherjee
Father .... Satya Banerjee
Brother .... Dipankar Dev
His wife .... Lily Chakravorty
Bishu .... Utpal Dutt
Mr. Mitter .... Rabi Ghosh
Kuana .... Sudeshna Das Sharma
Somnath's fiancee .... Aparna Sen

By VINCENT CANBY

Satyajit Ray's "The Middleman," which will be shown at the New York Film Festival tonight at 9:30 and tomorrow at 6:15 P.M., may well turn out to be the most sorrowful chapter in this extraordinary director's ongoing body of work about life in contemporary India.

More than any other Ray film I've seen, "The Middleman" defines hopelessness. Although the director's political outrage is apparent within this chronicle of despair, it seems to be the outrage of someone exhausted, who's given up all thoughts of solutions or who fears the solutions are so radical he can't bring himself to mention them.

•

Seen in the context of the Ray Calcutta trilogy—"The Adversary," "Simabaddha" and "Days and Nights in the Forest"—"The Middleman," I'm sure, would simply be another view of a society going through tumultuous changes. Seen by itself, "The Middleman" is sternly bleak and pessimistic, as if the director were saying, "This is all there is."

The film is about Somnath (Pradip Mukherjee) who shares a Calcutta apartment with his retired Brahmin father, his older brother and his sister-in-law. Everything seems to be wearing out in this wolrd. The telephone works only intermittently. There are power outages. When Somnath graduates from the university, he misses getting the history honors he deserves because his professor, who needs new spectacles, becomes impatient trying to read the small script of Somnath's thesis.

Calcutta is clogged, figuratively and literally. Too many people, too little space. There are hundreds of applicants for every suitable job. Finally Somnath decides to "do business," to become a middleman, a sort of all-purpose agent who buys and sells eveything from office stationery to industrial chemicals.

•

It isn't quite that simple, though. The middleman needs his own middleman. In Somnath's case this turns out to be a dapper, fast-talking fellow who describes himself as a public-relations expert, which means he finds out who can be bribed and for how much. Little by little Somnath abandons his Brahmin principles until, to survive in the world of business, he has become a pimp.

Mr. Ray's screenplay is so schematic that the course of the film —including a not very surprising twist ending—is fixed within the first half-hour. Plot, however, is not why one attends a Ray film. "The Middleman" is as bitterly satirical as any film Mr. Ray has ever made as it details the curious etiquette, the pretentions and the tackiness of the Calcutta business world. It's capitalism of feverish, totally dehumanizing pettiness.

Pradip Mukherjee is the essential Ray hero-sensitive, observant, and honorable until he must decide how much he's willing to compromise himself. Among the supporting performers, Rabi Ghosh is outstanding as the cheeky little public-relations man who rationalizes—as we suspect Somnath will also rationalize one day—"I don't consider myself dishonest, no matter what people say."

1976 O 12, 45:1

BRUCE CONNER FILMS: A MOVIE, 12 minutes; COSMIC RAY, 4 minutes; REPORT, 13 minutes; THE WHITE ROSE, 7 minutes; CROSSROADS,36 minutes; TAKE THE 5:10 TO DREAMLAND, 6 minutes. At the Whitney Museum of American Art.

Taken collectively, the six short works that opened yesterday at the Whitney Museum of American Art reveal Bruce Conner to be a film maker with a gift for montage, impeccable musical taste and a preoccupation with the signal tragedies and disasters of this century.

The motion pictures, ranging in length from the six minutes of his latest work, the somewhat eerie fantasy called "Take the 5:10 to Dreamland," to the 36 minutes of "Crossroads," a hypnotic and reiterative examination of the film footage of the nuclear explosion at Bikini atoll 30 years ago, constitute the fourth program in thsi season's New American Filmmakers Series at the museum.

•

Only one of the films, "The White Rose," dealing with the removal of a massive accretive painting from the wall of a small apartment and its subsequent removal from the premises, is composed of original footage. By its conrast to the rest of the films, it reveals Mr. Connor to be at his best when manipulating the footage of others.

Although he is given to dealing with such subjects as atomic clouds and the assassination of President Kennedy, as in "Report," Mr. Conner is not without the capacity for humor and irony.

These qualtties are best displayed in the assortment of image — mounted Indians thundering across a plain, covered wagons drawing into a circle, charging elephants, cars hurtling off embankments or over cliff, acrobats on high wires, falling bridges—that are among the elements of the aptly named opening short, "A Movie."

•

Employing to a great extent footage with sure emotional impact—mushroom clouds, the Dallas motorcade, the Hindenburg aflame, the Tacoma Narrows bidge in its sinuous death throes, men at war, Mr. Conner augments its force through excellent use of sound. He s not beyond leaving the otherwse blank screen to pulsate grayly to light generated by a sound track carrying a radio reporter's account of the events of Nov. 22, 1963, in Dallas. And he employs music from Respighi to Ray Charles (in "Cosmic Ray," with its topless and nude dancers, flashing lighs, cartoons, wartime clips and rockets) to heighten the effect of his images.

Mr. Conner knows how to assemble film that plucs at the emotions of an audience. Like many others, he ponders, over and over again, the significance of his time, tossing its images like ancestral bones in the hope that from patterns will emege meanings. He seems not to have found it yet. But then again, who has?

LAWRENCE VAN GELDER

1976 O 13, 36:1

Rivalry of Gorgons Remains Obscure to the Audience

By RICHARD EDER

The valve of myths is resonance; to make a perspective for some contemporary problem or at least some contemporary sensibility. We don't follow these demigods or gorgons for their own sakes but because they give us a far view of a near condition.

The mortal defect of Jacques Rivette's "Duelle" is not its slow pace or mannered style or even its obscurities. It is its failure—deliberate, apparently—to cross over to its audience at any point or to inveigle its audience across to it.

•

"Duelle," which is showing today and tomorrow at the New York Film Festival in Alice Tully Hall, is about the struggle between a Sun spirit and a Moon spirit, in the course of which several ordinary people are badly chewed up. It is simply about itself, despite its contemporary references and setting. It spills over into nothing of ours but décor, and even the décor is an airless, garish, 1930's affair.

The whole thing is filmed inside a Tiffany lamp. As the characters stand at the far end of significant perspectives, they resemble nothing so much as show-window mannequins draped portentiously in the foreground of some nonexistent intrigue—sheikhs seducers or beached Rolls-Royces in the background.

Bulle Ogier and Juliet Berto are, respectively, the Sun and Moon spirits. They duel for possession of a large diamond that will permit the victor to remain on earth for more than the allotted 40 days annual terrestrial leave. Both are fine actresses and it is interesting to see what different effects their inchoate roles have upon them.

Miss Berto has mobile features and the wooliness of her part results in

The Cast

DUELLE, directed by Jacques Rivette; written by Eduardo de Gregorio and Marilu Parolini; produced by Stephane Tchalgadjieff; photographed by William Lubtchansky; edited by Nicole Lubtchansky; music by Jean Wiener. In French with English subtitles. At the New York Film Festival, Alice Tully Hall, today at 9:30 P.M. and tomorrow at 6:15 P.M. Running time: 120 minutes. This film has not been rated.

Viva, Sun Goddess	Bulle Ogier
Leni, Moon Goddess	Juliet Berto
Pierrot	Jean Babilee
Lucie	Hermine Karagheuze
Jeanne/Elsa	Nicole Garcia
Sylvia Stern	Claire Nadeau

our not being quite sure, for a long way into the film, whether she is one or several characters. Miss Ogier, an actress of very pronounced character, is always Bulle Ogier; sometimes dressed up in a Sun-spirit wig.

Their rivalry has them interfering in the lives of several people — Lucie, a hotel night clerk; Elsa. a tax dancer, and Pierrot, a man of no defined profession who variously possess or know the whereabouts of the talisman. The rival spirits maneuver these humans back and forth. All three end up damager, two of them mortally.

The episodes, and some of the speeches, drift off at times into substantial obscurity; although their general meaning is not hard to grasp. Rivette and his screenwriter, Eduardo de Gregorio, have set out the two spirits with a deliberate, prosaic harshness. There is nothing suggestive or allusive about them.

•

Their virtue, at most and only rarely, is to be funny. There is an amusing scene where they gossip through pastry and champagne in what looks like a corner of the Hotel Ritz, before taking up their duel.

There are one or two places where Rivette takes the momentum of the duel's climax and makes something visually affecting out of it: a confrontation, for instance, on a Metro platform between the Moon spirit and Pierrot. But these moments come far too late in a long, elaborate and profoundly unnecessary movie.

1976 O 13, 36:3

PART 2 SOUNDER, directed by William Graham; written by Lonne Elder 3d based on novel by William H. Armstrong; executive producer, Robert B. Radnitz; director of photography, Urs B. Furrer; Music, Taj Mahal. Released by Gamma III. At showcase theaters. Running time: 92 minutes. This film has been rated G.

Nathan Leen Morgan	Harold Sylvester
Rebecca Lee Morgan	Ebony Wright
Ike Phillips	Taj Mahal
Camille Johnson	Annazette Chase
David Lee Morgan	Darryl Young

By RICHARD EDER

Every dog has his day, and apparently the hound-type dog that gave his name to the movie "Sounder" five years ago had had his.

In "Part 2 Sounder" the dog is hardly to be seen: He's just part of the barnyard background. It's like making something called "King Kong 2" with only a view or two of an ape in long shot.

•

The original "Sounder" was a sentimental, immensely popular film about the maturing of a small black farm boy under various types of adversity. The sequel has more maturing, more adversity and enough unleavened sentimentality to give a rhinoceros heartburn.

"Part 2 Sounder" is about the same Louisiana farm family as the original. David, the boy, sets his heart on getting a school for the neighborhood. His father, Nathan, takes up the cause, enlists his neighbors, and works day and night to get a schoolhouse built so that the local teacher—who planned to go North—will stay.

•

It is a depressed kind of film, with a lot of gloominess and teeth-gritting. It is unrelievedly didactic—about the need of working hard and persevering and believing—and lets in as little life or liveliness as a McGuffey's Reader. As the mother, dubious about the school-building effort, Ebony Wright gives a performance that is strong and modulated and above its material. As the father, Harold Sylvester does an obvious rendition of gloom and resolution. The children, particularly Darryl Young as David, are allowed to overact painfully.

"Part 2 Sounder," which opened yesterday at showcase theaters, has Robert B. Radnitz as executive producer and Lonne Elder 3d as screenplay-writer. They were the authors of the original "Sounder"; on the other hand, Mr. Radnitz has chosen a new director, William Graham, to replace Martin Ritt, as well as a new cast. The changes doesn't seem to be an improvement.

1976 O 14, 43:6

NANA, directed by Jean Renoir; screenplay by Piere Lestringuez, based on the Emile Zola novel as adapted by Mr. Renoir; directors of photography, Edmund Corwin and Jean Bachelet; editor, Mr. Renoir; produced by Films Jean Renoir. Running time: 160 minutes. At the New York Film Festival at Alice Tully Hall, Broadway at 65th Street.

Nana	Catherine Hessling
Count de Vandeuvres	Jean Angelo
Count Muffat	Werner Krauss
Georges Hugon	Raymond Guerin-Catelain
Countess Muffat	Jacqueline Forzane
Zoe	Valeska Gert
Francis	Harbacher
Bordenave	Pierre Lestringuez
Fauchery	Claude Autant-Lara
Satin	Nita Romani
Rose Mignon	Jacqueline Ford
La Faloise	Pierre Champagne
Fontan	Rene Koval
Gaga	Marie Prevost
The Tiger	Andre Cerf

By VINCENT CANBY

Jean Renoir's pre-eminence as a film artist is again being acknowledged this year by the New York Film Festival with a retrospective showing of one of his great early works, "Nana," produced in 1925-26 and never before (as far as I can learn) seen here in as complete a version as the one that the festival is presenting. The film, being projected from a fine new 35 mm print with piano accompaniment by Arthur Kleiner, will be presented at Alice Tully Hall tonight at 9:15 and Saturday at 2:30 P.M.

"Nana" was Renoir's second film as a director. (The first was "La Fille de L'Eau, 1924). It's an extraordinary achievement that now seem to fit perfectly into the Renoir oeuvre though at the time of its release in France it was a financial and critical disaster. When The New York Times originally reviewed it on July 30, 1929, the anonymous critic was appalled by the extravagant acting by Catherine Hessling (Renoir's first wife, who played the title role) and suggested rather prissily that the Zola novel would outlive the film.

•

For us today, with hindsight illuminated by all the remarkable Renoir films that came after, seeing "Nana" is like discovering a long lost diary. Though Renoir's "Nana" has never been lost, the two-hour and 40-minute version the festival is presenting is a fully packed treasure trove compared to various cut-down versions that had running times of 98 minutes, 120 minutes and 135 minutes.

It's not difficult to understand why early audiences were confused and turned off by this immensely elaborate screen incarnation of the Zola novel about the Second Empire bit actress who became the most famous courtesan of her day. It moves from realism to expressionism to romanticism, all the while being somewhat comic and cool.

Miss Hessling, her face a white mask containing a tiny black-bow of the mouth and magnificent, pale eyes outlined by kohl, virtually dances through the film, miming attitudes and gestures that suggest those of a haunted performer in a ballet, though the actors around her remain more or less realistic.

•

Her Nana is a nonstop performance, whether she's on-stage or off, which is something that Renoir often seeks to emphasize by photographing scenes as if the camera were sitting in the orchestra of a theater. Yet Renoir, who at this time was strongly influenced by the films of Von Stroheim, was fascinated by naturalistic detail, not only by the contrasts between the elegant and the seedy, but by the contrasts between the true and the make-believe.

The film, which Renoir coproduced with German interests and financed largely himself by selling his father's paintings, is stunningly set and costumed from designs by Claude Autant-Lara, who went on to direct his own films. The backstage settings are wonderfully bleak, while those of Nana's town house have a fairy tale grandeur about them. A final sequence, set in a Montmartre bal, predates by 50 years the exuberance of Renoir's 1955 "French Can-Can."

Renoir himself regards "Nana" as his first important film, an estimate that the festival appreciates not only by presenting it in this expanded version but also by projecting it from a good print and at a speed that preserves the film's original beauty.

1976 O 14, 44:1

Perfectly Sculpted

FEAR OF FEAR (Angst vor der Angst), directed by Rainer Werner Fassbinder; screenplay (German with English subtitles) by Mr. Fassbinder; directors of photography, Jurgen Jurges and Ulrich Prinz; editors, Liesgrett Schmitt-Klink and Beate Fischer-Welskirch; music, Peer Rabin; executive producer, Peter Marthesheimer; a production of Westdeutscher Rundfunk of Cologne, West Germany. Running time: 88 minutes. At the New York Film Festival at Alice Tully Hall, Broadway at 65th Street. This film has not been rated.

Margot	Margit Carstensen
Kurt	Ulrich Faulhaber
Mother	Brigitte Mira
Lore	Irm Hermann
Karli	Amin Meier
Dr. Merck	Adrian Hoven
Mr. Bauer	Kurt Raab
Edda	Ingrid Caven
Mrs. Schall	Lilo Pempeit

By VINCENT CANBY

THE most terrifying fear is the fear that has no discernable cause. It simply exists. Like an air plant, it requires no soil to flourish and grow, only a host.

Margot (Margit Carstensen), the heroine in Rainer Werner Fassbinder's spare, spooky, always sunlit new film, "Fear of Fear" (Angstvor der Angst), knows that the anxieties she began to feel in the last months of her pregnancy, and that have become more and more frequent since the birth of her child, have no particular source.

•

Margot is beautiful, with the perfect features of a department-store mannequin. She has a husband and two small children she loves. They have a car, a comfortable apartment, an idealized middle-class existence. Her mother-in-law and sister-in-law are continually prying into Margot's life and disapproving, but they can be dealt with. Yet something is decidedly wrong.

There are times Margot feels as if she were existing under water. Communication is dulled. Movements are slow. To hear music she must turn up the stereo so high it shakes her brain cells. When she looks at that perfect face in the mirror she isn't sure she knows whose it is, though she realizes that's crazy. Crazy? She takes a couple of Valiums or a swig of brandy and she calms down. For a little while, anyway.

"Fear of Fear," which Mr. Fassbinder made last year for West German television, is about the autumn of materialism in the form of an intensely personal case history of a schizophrenic. As in the world where she lives, everything is perfect for Margot, yet nothing works. Something important is missing. Just what is never stated. The direction of the film is straightforward, blunt, but its meanings and associations are manifest obliquely.

•

Mr. Fassbinder ("The Bitter Tears of Petra Von Kant," "The Merchant of Four Seasons," "Ali—Fear Eats the Soul" and "Fox") continues to be—at the age of 31—the most fascinating, talented, prolific, original young film maker in West Germany and, for that matter, one of the most exciting in Western Europe today.

Compared to a full-scale portraitist like Bernardo Bertolucci, he is a sketch artist, but the sketches are singular, and in their abundance they reveal a film maker of broad and original visions. His work is so rich that I'm sure not even he is always aware of the interpretations that can be read into them, nor that he much cares. He's already moved on to a new project.

"Fear of Fear" is a small film, as perfectly sculpted as Miss Carstensen's features, which, in turn, were as much a part of the decor as the settings and costumes of "Petra Von Kant." The film looks realistic, but these looks are deceiving. Like all Fassbinder films, "Fear of Fear" presents us with a distillation of reality—a dream in which everything counts—rather than photographed reportage on the way things are. Mr. Fassbinder is a major artist and one of the principal discoveries of the 14-year-old New York Film Festival.

"Fear of Fear" will be shown today at the festival at Alice Tully Hall at 6:15 P.M. and tomorrow at 9 P.M.

1976 O 15, C8:3

Underground

HARLAN COUNTY, U.S.A., documentary film directed and produced by Barbara Kopple; photographed by Hart Perry, Kevin Keating, Phil Parmet, Flip McCarthy and Tom Hurwitz; edited by Nancy Baker, Mary Lampson, Lora Hays and Mirra Bank; music by Hazel Dickens, Merle Travis and others. At the New York Film Festival, Alice Tully Hall, today at 9:30 P.M. and tomorrow at 6 P.M. Running time: 103 minutes.

By RICHARD EDER

COAL MINERS are a permanent underground in more than the literal sense. They trouble any society they support: like feet, the more they are weighed down by their owners the more pain they give.

In East Germany and Poland the authorities treat them with a special deference. Even in its harsher times the Franco regime was never able to stop them from striking. Laws against assembly were useless. A hammer would stop a mile below ground; the man in the next chamber would go to see what the matter was; the silence would spread and a line of stubborn, blackened men came to the surface and stayed until the Government could figure out some way of getting them back down.

•

Miners' strength, their assertiveness and solidarity are based largely on their economic power; and where coal-mining becomes marginal to the economy of a region, they lose much of their ability to fight. There is another factor, though. Miners in their tunnels, vulnerable to explosions, cave-ins and destroyed lungs, weigh on a society's conscience as well as its economy. Their grievances command an instinctive respect.

One of the reasons for the defeat of Prime Minister Edward Heath in Britain two years ago was a widespread feeling that in choosing the miners as the target for his austerity fight he had picked just the wrong target.

"Harlan County, U.S.A.," to be shown tonight and tomorrow at the New York Film Festival in Alice Tully Hall, is a full-length documentary of the year-long strike carried on by the miners at the Brookside works in eastern Kentucky. It has flaws, some of them considerable, but it is a fascinating and moving work. Its strength lies chiefly in its ability to illuminate the peculiar frightfulness and valor of coal-mining, and made it clear just why coal-miners can never be rightly treated as a less than a very special case.

•

Barbara Kopple and her photographers have got right inside the life of the miners and their families in their long struggle against the operators of the Brookside mine and its parent company, the Duke Power Company. It is a brilliantly detailed report from one side of a battle that caused one death, several shootings and a flood of violent bitterness; and that brought back to Harlan County memories of the much-bloodier coal strikes of the early 1930's.

•

The strike began after the miners voted to join the United Mine Workers of America—which had lost its hold in eastern Kentucky—and the owners refused to sign a standard U.M.W. contract. It was not until more than a yaer later—after the violence had claimed the life of one striker — that Duke Power, under strong pressure from Federal mediators, agreed to sign.

•

The film shows the picketing, the use of state troopers to keep the road open for nonstrikers, the confrontations, a shooting, the efforts of the strikers and their families to remain organized and united through the long year. It intercuts old footage from the 1931 strike, where five miners were killed. It also details the successful battle of reformers to oust the old national leadership of the U.M.W.; and the support given to the Harlen County strike by the new leadership under Arnold R. Miller.

Some of the thematic interweaving is awkward, but this is more than made up for by the extraordinary intimacy Miss Kopple has achieved with the strikers and with the bitter life o fthe strike. There is an old miner, lungs torn by coal dust, who makes our chests hurt as h etalks. There are frightening scenes of tight-lipped strikebreakers, guns openly displayed rushing through the pickets. There is a terrifying night scene where shots are fired and we see the leader of the strike-breakers brandishing a pistol in the cab of his pick-up truck. There is a heartbreaking scene where the mother of the slain miner collapses at his wake. There is much more, equally good.

The film is entirely partisan. Considering that the company's refusal to sign a contract was condemned by the National Labor Relations Board as a pretext not to recognize the union and considering that the film itself is forthrightly an effort to see the struggle through the miners' own eyes, this is no real drawback. Perhaps there is some skimping: it is something of a cinematic trick to film the President of Duke Power in such tight closeup that his face completely fills the screen.

More serious are the sometimes questionable ways in which the film advances its message: that the Harlan strike is only part of a struggle, and that the miners must go on struggling and striking. The instance I am thinking of comes in its suggestion that the reformist leadership of the U.M.W. may ave sold out in 1974—afte rthe Harlan County strike was over—by recommending acceptance of a national mine contract that curtails local strikes.

•

The film does not call this a sell-out —it uses no narration at all and conveys its message by its editing—but all reactions of individual miners that it shows before the vote are negative. Yet the membership ratified the contract by 44,000 to 34,000. The film states this, to be sure; yet somehow all the faces we have learned to admire during the long Harlan County struggle seem to push us to feel toward Mr. Miller the same way we felt toward the recalcitrant mine owners.

1976 O 15, C8:3

DEADLY HERO, directed by Ivan Nagy; written by George Wislocki; cinematographer, Andrzej Bartkowiak; film editor, Susan Steinberg; music, Brad Fiedel and Tommy Mandel; produced by Tom McGrath; released by Avco Embassy Pictures. At neighborhood theaters. Running time: 102 minutes. This film is rated R.

Lacy	Don Murray
Sally	Diahn Williams
Rabbit	James Earl Jones
Mrs. Broderick	Lilia Skala
Reilly	George S. Irving
Billings	Treat Williams
Baker	Charles Siebert
Buckley	Hank Garrett
D. A. Winston	Dick A. Williams
Arco	Mel Berger

By A. H. WEILER

"These are troubled times," Don Murray, the troubled, titular cop of "Deadly Hero," intones while rehearsing a speech to be made before a right-wing group. It's an augury of the rough but simplistic things to come in this fairly derivative Manhattan melodrama that crashed into local theaters yesterday.

As a youthful 18-year veteran with bravery commendations, our hero has been demoted from detective to patrol cars as a dangerously quick-on-the-trigger, law-and-order type. So it's not surprising that, seething with anger and four-letter epithets, he'll shoot a black mugger-shakedown artist who's been terrorizing a young woman at knifepoint in her West Side apartment.

Hero? Not quite. On second, sober thought, the lady, a schoolteacher and conductor of an avant-garde musical, changes her testimony to implicate our tough cop as a cold-blooded killer. And, of course, threats, tragedy and terror follow in his frenzied steps to extricate himself from the mess.

Mr. Murray's characterization of a blatant bigot forced into bloody desperation to save himself and his career may be workmanlike, but it is mostly superficial talk and action. Diahn Williams is attractive, but not especially forceful as the constantly threatened woman. And several topflight performers, including Lilia Skala, as her solicitous neighbor; James Earl Jones, as the malicious mugger, and George S. Irving, as an oily mayoral candidate, seem wasted in brief, broad portrayals.

Graffiti-besmirched streets, a schoolroom, a rehearsal hall and a precinct station house bear the lively, mood-filled authenticity of a color film shot in New York. But the script and unimaginative direction by Ivan Nagy, a comparative newcomer to the movies, do little to enhance this thin, common-place "Deadly Hero."

1976 O 16, 11:4

CAR WASH, directed by Michael Schultz; screenplay by Joel Schumacher; produced by Art Linson and Gary Stromberg; director of photography, Frank Stanley; music, Norman Whitraphy, Frank Stanley; music, Norman Whitby Universal Pictures. Running time: 97 minutes. At Loew's State 2, Broadway at 45th Street; Loew's Cine, Third Avenue near 86th Street; Columbia 1 Theater, Second Avenue at 64th Street, and Eighth Street Playhouse, Eighth Street west of Fifth Avenue. This film has been rated PG.

T.C.	Franklin Ajaye
Mr. B.	Sully Boyar
Irwin	Richard Brestoff
Taxi driver	George Carlin
Mad Bomber	Prof. Irwin Corey
Lonnie	Ivan Dixon
Duane	Bill Duke
Lindy	Antonio Fargas
Calvin	Michael Fennell
Charlie	Arthur French
Hysterical lady	Lorraine Gary
Lloyd	DeWayne Jessie
Hooker	Lauren Jones
Scruggs	Jack Kehoe
Goody	Henry Kingi
Marsha	Melanie Mayron
Slide	Garrett Morris
Snapper	Clarence Muse
Justin	Leon Pinkney
The Wilson Sisters	The Pointer Sisters
Daddy Rich	Richard Pryor
Mona	Tracy Reed
Chuco	Pepe Serna
Hippo	James Spinks
Geronimo	Ray Vitte
Loretta	Ren Woods

By VINCENT CANBY

It is early morning in the Los Angeles civilization of thruways, service stations, used-car lots, quick-lunch spots and portable swimming pools sold at discount. The start of another day much like any other, the dawn coming up with the voice of a manic disk jockey whose spiel is so fast that the last syllable of one word becomes the first syllable of the next. The sentences are nonstop and, like the records the disk jockey plays, they don't have endings. No record is ever allowed to finish. It is dismissed. The volume is lowered until it is overwhelmed by the record following. It's a glorious, unending river of sound, a Far Western metaphor for life measured in decibels.

Thus begins "Car Wash," a cheerful, somewhat vulgar, very cleverly executed comedy about what goes on in a single 10-hour period in a Los Angeles car wash. Written by Joel Schumacher, who wrote "Sparkle," and directed by Michael Schultz, who was responsible for "Cooley High," "Car Wash" dips into and out of the lives of more than two dozen characters. It demobilizes the old service comedy and returns it to civilian life in blithely free form.

Lonnie (Ivan Dixon), the ex-con; Duane (Bill Duke), the black activist; Lindy, (Antonio Fargas), the

Richard Pryor
An outstanding "cameo"

homosexual whose wrist is limp and whose mouth is loud, and all the other workers at the car wash are updated G.I.'s out of uniform. Mr. B., (Sully Boyar), the harried owner of the car wash, would once

have been the C.O. and his nitwit son, played by Richard Brestoff, who carries Mao's little red book around, wears a Mao T-shirt and wants to liberate the workers, is the commandant's overeducated offspring who is, of course, no match for the enlisted men.

But "Car Wash," which opened at four theaters here yesterday, is more than an old comedy genre recycled. It's a terrifically shrewd piece of movie-making.

Mr. Schumacher, Mr. Schultz and the members of the large, mostly black cast have created a cohesive comedy out of dozens of tiny pieces of narratives and one outstanding "cameo." This is the appearance of Richard Pryor as "Daddy" Rich, the founder-head of the Church of Divine Economic Spirituality, a fellow who drives a

gold limousine with a license plate that spells T-I-T-H-E.

Some of the others who turn up in the course of the day are Lauren Jones as a down-on-her-luck hooker with a sullen disposition and a different wig for every occasion, and Melanie Mayron, who plays the car-wash secretary, a moony young woman who spends more time on her nail polish than on the accounts and who at one point—though how I don't remember—manages to drop one contact lens into a jar of cold cream.

There are also a mad bomber, played by Prof. Irwin Corey, as well as a ratty little boy who terrorizes the neighborhood by being so good on a skate board, a woman who's fearful that her son's having been sick on her car door will

ruin its finish, a would-be hold-up man and on and on.

Nothing terribly dramatic happens, and some of the comedy gets a bit forced, but the wonder of the film is how it manages to succeed so much of the time. "Car Wash" has the rhythm, beat and drive of the rock songs that are playing throughout the film, virtually nonstop, all reflecting a certain mindless contemporary mood without saying anything whatsoever about it. If "Car Wash" makes no comment on our pop culture, it's because it's a piece of it.

●

The film, which has been rated PG ("Parental Guidance Suggested"), contains some mildly obscene words and rude gestures.

1976 O 16, 13:1

FILM VIEW

VINCENT CANBY

Explicit Violence Overwhelms Every Other Value On the Screen

In the very first sequence of "Scorchy," an inept, mindless little melodrama about cops and narcotics smugglers, one hoodlum corners another, sticks the muzzle of his revolver into the victim's mouth and says, "You talk too much." There was a time when the camera would have discreetly glanced away at that point. No longer. When the hoodlum pulls the trigger in "Scorchy," the camera appears to have moved in closer, the better for us to see how a man looks as the back of his head is blown off. His brains smear the camera lens.

It was 11:35 on an otherwise ordinary, perfectly acceptable morning when I witnessed the above scene on the screen of a scroungy Broadway movie theater. I had a strong desire to say to-hell-with-it right then and leave. I didn't. I'm a creature of habit and so I stayed with "Scorchy" to the end. It's my job. As I've told myself in the past, I'm paid to watch and, after all, it's only a movie. But "it's only a movie" no longer reassures as it once did. It's not that such random viciousness and graphically detailed violence are not properly distanced. They are. That's not the problem. I don't think that many adults mistake screen fiction for fact. The "Scorchy" actor wasn't actually killed. That's not what makes these films so aggressively abrasive. Rather, it's the assumption of the movie makers that we are all so jaded by this time that only mayhem, masterfully recreated by all sorts of technical tricks and the clever use of cosmetics, can grab and keep our interest. At the same time there is the lurking suspicion that perhaps the movie makers are right.

As pop music is now being magnified to the point where we can barely hear it, the volume of screen violence is being raised close to the point where we no longer see it. Our thresholds for hearing and seeing continue to rise, but for how much longer?

In Martin Scorsese's "Taxi Driver," one of the more seriously intentioned American films of the year, we are presented with the vividly photographed spectacle of a number of people being shot with a high-powered gun at point-blank range so that blood, guts and bone become the medium as well as the message of the movie. Marco Ferreri's "The Last Woman," which begins as a brilliant satire about a male supremacist, concludes with its hero trying to make amends by using an electric carving knife

to remove his penis—on camera. Nagisa Oshima's "In The Realm of The Senses," the Japanese film that was seized by United States Customs officers before it could be shown officially at the just ended New York Film Festival, concludes with its heroine, who has loved her lover to death, slicing off his sexual organs. Pier Paolo Pasolini's last film, "Salo," based on the Marquis de Sade's "The 120 Days of Sodom," is an attempt to make political point out of scenes of systematized rape, castration and other forms of amputation, disembowelment, defecation, and such.

"Grizzly," an unabashed copy of "Jaws" that features a rampaging bear instead of a shark, shows us a man's arm being ripped off and a horse being decapitated. In "The Omen" David Warner is very efficiently decapitated before our eyes and Lee Remick, who plays the devil's mum, is tossed out a window to her death. In "Burnt Offerings," a dad, played by Oliver Reed, is tossed out a window to his death, landing face down, his head pushing through the windshield of the car where his young son is waiting for him, the child thus being appropriately splattered with glass and dad's remains.

And on it goes, in films made by gifted, intelligent people as well as by hacks. Violence, which, I suppose, is the sensation most easily communicated by films, may not be more prevalent today that it ever was in movies, but because the means by which it is represented have become increasingly graphic, it begins to dominate all other circumstances. Are audiences so bloodthirsty that they demand this realism, or are they simply bored?

Each of us has a different tolerance for screen violence, a tolerance that varies according to the mood of the viewer and the content of the film containing it. Because I found Sam Peckinpah's "The Wild Bunch" a serious and moving film about the last days of the western frontier, I accepted without question the so-called "blood ballet" that concluded the film. Yet the violence in the same director's "The Straw Dogs" was intolerable—the film itself was so simpleminded that the climactic mayhem and murder looked to be nothing more than an exercise in brutality.

Serious artists can argue persuasively that violence is a metaphor for our times, but serious artists need serious audiences, and when I saw a screening of "The Wild Bunch" at a Times Square theater, where the audience hooted and howled with pleasure at the blood-letting, I must admit to having had some reservations about my earlier defense of the picture. Are the audiences at Loew's State 1, who cheer and laugh during some of the rougher moments of "Marathon Man," reacting to a metaphor or to violence as style? The latter, I suspect. After all, violence—including the dental torture that provides "Marathon Man's" most terrifying sequence—may be defined as nothing more than an extreme form of rudeness, and rudeness is more or less how New Yorkers live.

Because "Marathon Man" is a beautifully acted and directed thriller, I find its violence bearable. Yet in more and more films like "Scorchy" and "Drum" and "Lipstick" —movies made without any art and with no purpose except to shock—violence of the graphic sort that is now possible becomes the point of the movie, instead of a means to some other end. This is what separates today's violent films from those of earlier decades (the 1930's gangster films) that were in their own times thought to have gone too far. Explicit violence is as much the point of a film like "Scorchy" as explicit sex is the point of "The Devil in Miss Jones." It's no coincidence that as the public has come to accept the existence of pornographic films in the last decade, so has it come to acccept films that are more and more brutally violent. They are part of the same movement.

By that I don't mean to confuse the run-of-the-mill porn films with films dealing in decapitation, torture and the like, only to emphasize that both kinds of films, in their explicitness and lack of reticence, are being directed at audiences that don't (or won't) think, and that have neither the time nor interest to be emotionally touched. They are looking for immediate sensations, which, in the case of violent films, are not unlike the cheap thrills one gets when riding a roller-coaster.

Unless one has a bad heart, roller coaster riding is harmless. The stomach settles down just as soon as one steps out of the car. The effects of movie violence accumulate. The more violent that films become in order to shock, the more violent they must become to continue to be shocking. The same graphic scenes of violence that penetrate dull brains, make those brains duller, more impervious to shock, so that succeeding films must go even further. The volume of screen violence must continue to be raised.

As it is, the audience's other expectations are lowered. Never, I think, have reason and coherence appeared to be in such short supply in films made for the mass American audience. And never, if the big Broadway movie theaters are representative of first-run theaters elsewhere in the country, has that mass audience been so tolerant of poor management, sloppy projection, high prices and ridiculous programming. On a recent Friday night the audience at the National Theater on Broadway sat through an unscheduled 30-minute intermission between programs, only to be subjected to a short epic of sentimental baloney, "Spike, A Montana Horseman," sponsored by Mobil, and the start of the feature ("Burnt Offerings") without sound.

The creeping second-rateness, which is as much responsible as anything else, including blood-lust, for films of sensation and violence, is as apparent in the theaters that show the schlock as in the schlock they show.

1976 O 17, II:1:1

THE MARQUISE OF O. . . . (Die Marquise von O. . . .), directed by Eric Rohmer; screenplay (German with English subtitles) by Mr. Rohmer adapted from the story by Heinrich von Kleist; director of photography, Nestor Almendros; editor, Cecile Decugis; a co-production of Janus Films (Frankfurt), Artemis (Berlin), Les Films du Losange (Paris) and Gaumont (Neuilly), distributed by New Line Cinema. Running time: 102 minutes. At the New York Film Festival at Alice Tully Hall, Broadway at 65th Street. This film has not been rated.

Marquise	Edith Clever
Count	Bruno Ganz
Father	Peter Luhr
Mother	Edda Seippel
Brother	Otto Sander
Midwife	Ruth Drexel
Doctor	Eduard Linkers
Porter	Hesso Huber
Russian General	Erich Schachinger
Russian Officer	Richard Rogner
Courier	Thomas Straus
Priest	Volker Prachtel

By VINCENT CANBY

"The Marquise of O. . . ." (Die Marquise von O. . . .), Eric Rohmer's German-language screen version of Heinrich von Kleist's 19th-century short story, should be to the new film season what Ingmar Bergman's "The Magic Flute" was to the last. It's a dazzling testament to the civilizing effects of several different arts, witty, joyous and so beautiful to look at that it must seem initially suspect to those of us who have begun to respond to spray-painted subway graffiti as the fine art of our time.

The film was shown twice last night at Alice Tully Hall to end this year's New York Film Festival. It will open its commercial engagement Sunday at the 68th Street Playhouse.

●

Kleist died early, a suicide at the age of 34, in 1811, leaving a small body of work that is little known in this country, aside from "Michael Kolhass." His play, "The Prince of Homburg," will have its American premiere tomorrow night at Brooklyn's Chelsea Theater Center.

"The Marquise of O. . . ." which was awarded the Special Jury Prize at the Cannes Film Festival this year, was mostly patronized by critics there as being, in the words of one reporter, "simply likable." This, I suppose, is probably the way someone might have described "Cosi fan tutte" had it had the odd fortune to have its premiere at a music festival along with 199 other operas.

The association to "Cosi" is not accidental, although "The Marquise of O. . . ." hasn't a bar of music in it. It's a comedy of manners (early 19th century), precisely observed, romantic in mood and put into perspective by the disciplined intelligence of Mr. Rohmer, who follows the Kleist German text as if it were a screenplay.

As he was in the films constituting his "Six Moral Tales"—including "My Night at Maud's," "Claire's Knee" and "Chloe in the Afternoon"—Mr. Rohmer continues to be fascinated by characters ensnared by moral principles that, as often as not, are at complete variance to their passions. The crucial issue is the reconciliation of passion with principle, the space between the two being the arena where the comedy is played.

I've not read the Kleist story, but if Mr. Rohmer has followed it as faithfully as he reports, it would seem that one of the reasons "The Marquise of O. . . ." is so successful is that the French director shares with Kleist an appreciation for a most benign sort of irony.

The time is the late 18th century and the setting a small garrison

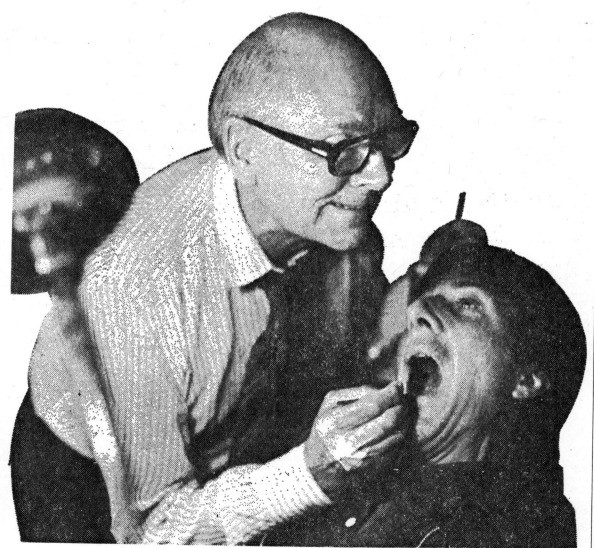

Olivier and Hoffman in "Marathon Man's" "terrifying" dental torture scene

M. Childers/Sygma

Edith Clever and a child in "The Marquise of O."

Characters who talk from the heart

town in northern Italy where the Marquise of O (Edith Clever), a beautiful, virtuous young widow lives with her two small children in the fortress where her father is the commandant. The night the Russians take the town, the highly principled marquise is saved from a brutal rape by a handsome, courtly Russian officer, the count (Bruno Ganz), who, as it turns out, is just as highly principled as the marquise. Almost, that is.

A month or so later, the marquise suspects she may be pregnant, but the idea is so absurd she and her mother laugh at the idea. A few more days pass. The marquise becomes worried. She swears to her mother that she has a clear conscience, but also asks her mother to bring a midwife to examine her. Sniffs her mother, "A clear conscience and a midwife?"

What is apparent to the audience from the start is that the count, who had so honorably saved the marquise from rape by fellows of lesser rank and station, had himself, that same evening, taken advantage of her after she'd been put to sleep with some poppy-seed tea.

Without acknowledging his slip from grace, the count almost immediately has sought to marry the marquise, but the marquise had vowed on the death of her husband never to remarry. She dismisses him. The count suffers. The marquise suffers.

The pregnancy continues. The marquise's father and mother, scandalized, banish their wayward daughter to her country estate, where she plans to live in seclusion. After a while, though, she publishes a public notice to the effect that "the Marquise of O . . ., having become pregnant without her knowing how," will marry the father "for family reasons, if he will present himself."

●

Though "The Marquise of O . . . ." has the shape of a fairy tale, Mr. Rohmer treats his characters with compassion for the predicaments

that, to them, are profoundly serious—and to us profoundly absurd. He never mocks attitudes and choices. He illuminates them by accepting that vanished society on its own terms, and by evoking it in a production of breathtaking images that recall how the world looked to Jacques Louis David, whose "Madame Recamier" seems to have been the principal inspiration for Nestor Almendros, Mr. Rohmer's cameraman.

The German actors—none of whom I've seen before—perform with the kind of grace I associate with stylish Restoration comedy, though the comedy here is of an entirely different sensibility. It's not brittle or bitchy. Characters don't talk from the head but from the heart, and one of the things that makes "The Marquise of O. . . ." much more than simply likable is our awareness that their feelings are earnestly—possibly fatally—sincere.

1976 O 18, 36:1

DINEH: THE PEOPLE, a documentary feature directed by Steven Hornick and Jonathan Reinis; director of photography, Mr. Hornick; produced by Mr. Reinis. Running gtime; 77 minutes. At the Whitney Museum of American Art, Madison Avenue at 75th Street.

"Dineh: the People," which opened a five-day run yesterday at the Whitney Museum of American Art, is an earnest, artless documentary about the plight of approximately 5,000 Navajo Indians who face eviction from their Arizona lands as a result of pressures the film makers identify with large coal and oil interests.

"Dineh," which is what the Navajos call themselves, was directed by Steven Hornick and Jonathan Reinis, who lived with the Navajos for almost a year recording tribal meetings, interviews with tribal leaders and legal representatives, the members of one Indian family as well as with representatives of the Federal Bureau of Indian Affairs.

Though hugely sympathetic to the Navajo cause, the film never takes on a life of its own. It seldom discovers its subject but, instead, has the appearance of recording only authorized moments. This has the unfortunate effect of diminishing and trivializing a problem that is urgent and real.

VINCENT CANBY

1976 O 20, 52:1

Zeppelin's Rock Pulverizes Eardrums at Cinema I

By RICHARD EDER

"The Song Remains the Same" is a movie to listen to the Led Zeppelin by. If you want to listen to the Led Zeppelin. If you don't, there's no point going.

If you do, it's still a dubious proposition. Certainly the sound system at the Cinema I Theater, where it opened yesterday, does full justice to the decibels. Even using the squashed-up balls of paper napkin recommended by a knowledgeable member of this newspaper's music staff, it was loud. Powered eardrum floated about.

Presumably, though, putting this British rock group in a movie was in-

The Program

THE SONG REMAINS THE SAME, directed by Peter Clifton and Joe Massot; photographed by Ernie Day; edited by Mr. Clifton; sound by Jimmy Page; released by Warner Bros. With John Bonham, John Paul Jones, Jimmy Page, Robert Plant, Peter Grant and others. At the Cinema I Theater. Running time: 136 minutes. This film has been rated PG.

tended to be the equivalent not of listening to their records but of attending one of their concerts. This is very hard to do on film: We miss the immediacy, the sense of physical presence and even, to an extent, physical peril. The power of a mass audience to communicate excitement is absent.

To make up for this, the film intercuts a variety of scenes while each of the 13 numbers is being performed. A few are more or less realistic — a sequence outside Madison Square Garden, an argument between the group's manager and a Garden official — and others are fantasy. Members of the group put on cloaks, ride around on horses,

stand in the moonlight.

They are pseudodreams, like the unconvinced artwork on rock record jackets. The scenes showing the group performing are more informative though not much more powerful.

They are dominated by the singer, Robert Plant. A great mass of yellow curls tumbling around his shoulders, Mr. Plant sashays around the stage, posturing, pouting and conducting a meaningful relationship with the microphone. It looks like a sheep trying to seduce a telephone pole.

*

Possibly this is what led to a PG (Parental Guidance Suggested) rating. For the first two-thirds — which was all this reviewer stayed—there seemed to be no other particular threat to the future adults in a stone-deaf civilization.

1976 O 21, 45:5

FILM VIEW

VINCENT CANBY

Who Says There Aren't Any Good Movies Around?

People who go to movies very seldom, if ever, are the first ones to swoop down, pigeon-like, when you're in an exposed social situation to tell you how awful movies are these days and how - we - just - never - go - anymore - because - there's - nothing - to - see - is - there? At least that's what happens to me, and if it's been a long day I find the best way to avoid being mouse-trapped is to say yes. It's not a fool-proof defense against boredom, though. Such people feel very strongly about their ignorance and they will defend to the death their right to agree with you at endless length. Sometimes the only way out is to announce an acute case of stomach cramps, but that means you have to leave the party.

This week I'm going to experiment by disagreeing. The fact is that there are a number of interesting new films, not all equally good and not all for all audiences, but one or two each for almost every kind of audience, including those people who never go anymore and who, I've found, respond most favorably to the movie equivalents to mystery stories or suspense novels one reads when one doesn't care much about reading, only about going to sleep. The following seven films, listed in alphabetical order, either are now in national release or will be soon:

● ● ●

"Car Wash," directed by Michael Schultz and written by Joel Schumacher, is a juke-box of a movie, and just the sort of movie that people who never go to movies should stay away from. Watching it would only confirm their suspicions that American movies are vulgar, in poor taste and pander to the tastes of an anti-intellectual public. Yet "Car Wash" also happens to be very funny most of the time, a shrewdly conceived slice not of life but of popular American entertainment. It's a comic-book variation on "Nashville," which means that it has a couple of dozen characters, but it's not about anything at all except 10 hours in a day in the life of a Los Angeles car wash, about the men (mostly black) who work in the car wash and the people who bring their status symbols in for servicing. The pop songs are loud and non-stop and echo the basic beat and drive of the picture. The exuberant, talented cast includes Ivan Dixon, Sully Boyar, Prof. Irwin Corey, Melanie Mayron, and Richard Pryor as "Daddy" Rich, the founder and leading beneficiary of the Church of Divine Economic Spirituality.

"The Front" is a moving send-up of the McCarthy era by writer Walter Bernstein and director Martin Ritt, both of whom were blacklisted in the fifties, who recall the horrors of that time in what is basically the sort of comedy format that served Bob Hope in films like "Paleface" and "My Favorite Blonde." Woody Allen plays a self-serving, apolitical rat who becomes "the front" through which a number of black-listed writers are able to continue to sell their scripts to TV executives during the "red scare." The movie is not about ideas but about persecution and the perversions of justice, which being unattached to argument, attack the emotions at gut level. Woody is fine in a role that is not quite as serious as you might have feared.

"Jonah Who Will Be 25 in The Year 2000," directed by Alain Tanner and written by him and John Berger, is a terrifically intelligent, witty Swiss comedy (in French) that should also be avoided by people who don't go to movies anymore. It would confirm their suspicions that European films are always Marxist and talky, with characters who are casually promiscuous without ever being sorry. "Jonah" is about eight friends who were young enough to have hoped that the political disturbances of 1968 would have resulted in political and social improvements. They didn't but these people haven't become bored or inactive. They are a larky, eccentric group, extremely pleasant and stimulating to be around, slightly mad and full of compassion. Chief among them are Jean-Luc Bideau, an activist who can't give up, Miou-Miou, a supermarket cashier who steals food for needy customers, and Rufus, whose son Jonah will be 25 in the year 2000.

"Marathon Man," directed by John Schlesinger from William Goldman's adaptation of his suspense novel, is the movie for those who don't go anymore. Its labyrinthian plot, which numbs that part of the brain that copes with plausibility, has to do with an innocent Columbia graduate student (Dustin Hoffman) who falls in love with a mysterious Swiss girl (Marthe Keller) who may or may not be in the service of a notorious ex-Nazi dentist (Laurence Olivier) who kidnaps Dustin and fiddles with his teeth, trying to extract not molars but information. The violence is fairly awful, so you may want to look away much of the time, but when you do look you'll see two superb performances by Olivier and Hoffman and a production so rich in bizarre detail and rococo settings (among other places, the Paris Opera) that sense doesn't seem important.

"The Marquise of O. . . ." is French director Eric Rohmer's elegant, stunningly beautiful German-language adaptation of Heinrich von Kleist's early 19th century story about an exquisite young widow who finds herself mysteriously pregnant and advertises for the unknown father to present himself. But when he does, she refuses on moral principle. The film is a poignant comedy of manners, played absolutely straight by the German cast using the Kleist dialogue, seen in gestures and images suggested by paintings of the period, particularly those of neo-classicist Jacques Louis David. Nestor Almendros ("Claire's Knee") was the cameraman.

"The Memory of Justice" is Marcel Ophuls' magnificent meditation about collective versus individual responsibility in modern society, the take-off point being the Nuremberg trials of the Nazi war criminals but also embracing the French war to retain Algeria and United States involvement in Vietnam. The film is composed of dozens of contemporary interviews, conducted by Ophuls, plus newsreel footage, the effect of which is to make each of us examine not only the past but our present relationship to the political state we inhabit. It runs four hours and 38 minutes and it's spell-binding.

"Small Change" is Francois Truffaut's lyrically funny tribute to children who, in one improvisation and another, deal with a world they did not make and, more often than not, will survive. Although there is no dominant story line, the film moves effortlessly into and out of the lives of a dozen children, from 14 years of age down to two weeks, several of whom may be recognized as variations on characters in other Truffaut films. One of the nicest things to be said about "Small Change" is that children themselves find it hilarious.

1976 O 24, II:15:1

addiction. Alan Arkin is the good Dr. Freud at the beginning of his career, somewhat shy of manner, immensely kind, and a little self-conscious about discussing the latest theories that have been getting him into hot water all over Vienna.

Laurence Olivier is marvelous as Professor Moriarty, an extremely tentative, timid old fellow to be such a tycoon of crime, and Vanessa Redgrave as the unfortunate lady whose beauty drives mad those men who are rich and powerful.

●

The particular revelation of "The Seven-Per-Cent Solution" is Robert Duvall, one of America's best actors, who plays the English Dr. Watson with such wit and control that it's difficult to believe he's ever played an American with equal conviction. It's a very funny performance, and very important to the overall shape and cohesion of the film.

Not since John Huston's "The Man Who Would Be King" and Sidney Lumet's "Murder on the Orient Express" has there been a new film that manages so successfully to recall the innocent qualities one associates with pre-World War II movies without being simple-minded or instant camp. The initial credit must go to Mr. Meyer, whose novel is a fine piece of literary fooling, but Mr. Ross has been equally clever and disciplined in ealizing its screen potential. It's by far the best work he's done to date.

●

"The Seven-Per-Cent Solution" has been rated PG ("Parental Guidance Suggested"), which is a way of alerting parents of small children to a fuzzily photographed primal-scene conclusion, some slightly nightmarish scenes involving Holmes's cocaine cure, and a sequence in a Viennese bordello that, when I was 5 years old, I would have instantly recognized as a lively, eccentric hotel.

1976 O 25, 42:1

An Exhilarating Collector's Item

By VINCENT CANBY

After two months in virtual seclusion, Sherlock Holmes summons his old friend and biographer, Dr. Watson, to his rooms in Baker Street. Dr. Watson, settled family man that he has become, is shocked by both the manner and the appearance of Holmes. He has always been thin but he is now rail-like. Worse, though, is Holmes's behavior. Either he has become a lunatic or he has stumbled onto the grandest criminal conspiracy of his career.

His door bolted against the evil lurking outside, Holmes strides about his untidy, gas-lit study talking in disjointed fashion about a certain Professor Moriarty, a genius, a philosopher, an abstract thinker, a fiend of fiends whose existence Holmes has been in the process of deducing for the last two months. The name of Moriarty means nothing to Watson.

●

"There's the genius and the wonder of the thing," exclaims Holmes, his eyes lighting up like the windows in an empty house one suddenly discovers to be haunted. "The man pervades London, the Western world, even," he says, "and no one has ever heard of him!" At which point Watson notices the empty syringe on Holmes's desk. His friend has passed into the uncharted outer reaches of cocaine madness. Watson must act at once.

The adventure is called "The Seven-Per-Cent Solution," which,

Alan Arkin as Sigmund Freud
Discussing his latest theories.

The Cast

THE SEVEN-PER-CENT SOLUTION, directed and produced by Herbert Ross; screenplay by Nicholas Meyer, based on his novel; executive producers, Alex Winitsky and Arlene Sellers; director of photography, Oswald Morris; music, John Addison; editor, Chris Barnes; distributed by Universal Pictures. Running time: 113 minutes. At the Plaza Theater, 58th Street east of Madison Avenue. This film has been rated PG.

Sherlock Holmes	Nicol Williamson
Sigmund Freud	Alan Arkin
Dr. Watson	Robert Duvall
Lola Deveraux	Vanessa Redgrave
Prof. Moriarty	Laurence Olivier
Lowenstein	Joel Grey
Mary Watson	Samantha Eggar
Baron von Leinsdorf	Jeremy Kemp
Mycroft Holmes	Charles Gray
Mrs. Freud	Georgia Brown
Madame	Regine
Freda	Anna Quayle
Mrs. Holmes	Jill Townsend
Berger	John Bird
Mrs. Hudson	Alison Leggatt
Marker	Frederick Jaeger

as adapted by Nicholas Meyer from his best-selling novel and directed and produced by Herbert Ross, is nothing less than the most exhilarating entertainment of the film year to date. Mr. Meyer and Mr. Ross have taken a few small liberties with the book (which are all to the good) but the essential conceit remains.

That is that Watson, in a desperate effort to save Holmes's life, must somehow get Holmes to Vienna for treatment by a new young doctor named Sigmund Freud, and that Holmes and Freud, two of the greatest minds of their time, join forces to solve a diabolical plot involving a beautiful, red-haired musical comedy star, an arrogant, dishonorable German baron, an amorous Turkish pasha and a great train chase through Austria to the very borders of the Ottoman Empire.

●

The film, which opened yesterday at the Plaza Theater, is popular movie-making at its most stylish. It's simultaneously contemporary in its sensibility and faithful to the courtly mood and decent spirit of the Sir Arthur Conan Doyle originals. It's also one of the most handsome evocations of a vanished period (circa 1890) since "Murder on the Orient Express," and a collector's item in terms of performances.

Nicol Williamson creates an entirely new Sherlock Holmes within our memories of all the old ones, a man of incomparable mental brilliance who walks the world pursued by the hallucinations of his

Tribal Fate

THE LAST OF THE CUIVA, directed and produced by Brian Moser; running time: 65 minutes. A CLEARING IN THE JUNGLE, directed by Charles Nairn; produced by Brian Moser; running time: 38 minutes. Both films distributed by Granada Television International. At the Film Forum, 15 Vandam Street.

The new Film Forum program, which opened yesterday and will play this weekend and next, is composed of two documentaries about primitive South American tribes that face extinction in the near future. Both were produced for Granada Television's "Disappearing World" series in England.

"The Last of the Cuiva," the better of he two, treats in straightforward fashion the life of Colombia's 600 remaniing Cuiva Indians who are slowly being evicted from their lands and pushed into the Creole or peasant culture that suits them not at all.

"A Clearing in the Jungle" deals with Venezuela's Panare Indians who, perhaps because they don't take kindly to strangers, force the film makers and their accompanying anthropologist into making statements that sound like material from a Monty Python show. "If they have food," says the slemn narrator, "they eat breakfast," or, when we are seeing a bunch of Panare dancing around a campfire: "What sort of ritual is this? Unfortunately they often didn't answer our questions or simply laughed at us. We never did find out." There's material here for a first-class parody.

VINCENT CANBY

1976 O 29, C8:3

DEATH COLLECTOR, directed and written by Ralph De Vito; produced by William N. Panzer; a John B. Kelly film, distributed by Goldstone Enterprises. Runningtime: 90 minutes. This film has been rated R.
Jerry Bolante........................Joseph Cortese
Anthony................................Lou Criscuola
THEVOLENT PROFESSIONALS, directed by Sergio Martino; screenplay by Giancarlo Ferrando; a Carlo Ponti film, distributed by Scotia American Pictures. Running time: 93 minutes. This film has been rated R. Both films at the Cinerama, Broadway at 47th Street, and other theaters.
With: Richard Conte, Luke Meranda and others.

"Death Collector," filmed entirely at the other end of the Lincoln Tunnel in New Jersey, is an effective little melodrama about a fast-talking young punk who aspires to get ahead in the local Mafia but hasn't the brains to operate successfully.

Seedy is the word for the world through which this punk moves, often with the towers of Manhattan in the distance and as far removed from him as the moon. Ralph De Vito, who wrote and directed the film, displays a good deal of talent for the kind of movie-making in which action (a lot of it very violent) is exposition and the portrait of a character's soul is the physical landscape that surrounds him. Joseph Cortese and Lou Criscuola are exceedingly good as, respectively, the punk and the local don who befriends him.

"Death Collector" opened yesterday at the Cinerama and other theaters on a double bill with a bad, hollow-sounding, English-dubbed Italian melodrama called "The Violent Professionals." It's about a good cop who feels hamstrung by law-and-order types and a conspiracy to bring down the Italian Government, which in this film apparently represents the law-and-order types. It's very, very mixed up. Old-timer Richard Conte plays a villain, a Fascist who dyes his hair and whose skin has the translucent look of a newly unwrapped mummy.

VINCENT CANBY

1976 O 30, 14:3

PEOPLE OF THE WIND, a documentary feature directed by Anthony Howarth; written by David Koff; produced by Mr. Howarth and Mr. Koff; executive producer, Elizabeth E. Rogers; director of photography, Mike Dodds; sound, Ivan Sharrock; music composed, directed and performed by G. T. Moore and Shusha; editor, Carolyn Hicks, distributed by Carolyn Films. Running time: 127 minutes. At the D. W. Griffith Theater, 59th Street west of Second Avenue. This film has not been rated.
With the voice of James Mason.

By VINCENT CANBY

In 1925 Merian C. Cooper and Ernest P. Schoedsack (who hit the jackpot eight years later with "King Kong") released their well-received documentary feature called "Grass," which recorded the semiannual migration of the Bakhtiari tribes of Persia (now Iran) between their winter and summer grazing lands.

It was an arduous journey then—herding sheep, cattle, donkeys, wives, children, colorful costumes and exotic customs across mountains said to be as high as the Alps and a territory as broad as Switzerland—and it still is, according to "People of the Wind," a documentary record of a similar migration made 50 years later by Anthony Howarth.

The world was somewhat more mysterious in 1925 than it is now, and "Grass" was one of a number of documentaries that catered to the public's interest in what were then strange, romantic peoples and places. The passage of time and World War II, Korea, television, jet travel and Vietnam have changed our outlook and expectations so that a film like "People of the Wind," though well photographed and made with great physical effort, looks peculiarly, calculatingly naïve.

With his camera and sound crews Mr. Howarth went to southern Iran and made the spring migration with the Babadi, one of the Bakhtiari tribes, whose chief is more or less the central figure of the movie Mr. Howarth has made from his footage, which also provided him with a one-hour British Broadcasting Corporation show:

On the soundtrack James Mason speaks an accompanying narration that is intended to be the chief's innermost thoughts as he watches his tribe cross rivers, push donkeys up slopes, run after straying sheep. On one occasion, he admits fatigue. "I'm tired of this coming and going," which, under the circumstances, is funny even though it's not meant to be.

•

It's all so pretty and bland one's mind begins to wander. Questions arise. What place do these people have in the Shah's scheme of things? The chief, via Mr. Mason's voice, notes that his own children now make the migration by automobile and that, in the near future, the entire migration may be made by trucking the animals between their winter and summer lands. But who will pay for the trucks? The Government? Or are the tribes that rich?

"People of the Wind," which opened yesterday at the D. W. Griffith Theater attempts to celebrate the Bakhtiari's ancient ways but it does so by assuming that we are as innocent as they are. Unless you are hopelessly addicted to very long travelogues filled largely with sheep, you may feel, as I do, that "People in the Wind" is a bore.

1976 O 30, 14:6

FILM VIEW

VINCENT CANBY

Sherlock Holmes Should Go On Forever!

In 1893 Arthur Conan Doyle attempted to rid himself of his most popular literary creation by allowing Sherlock Holmes to disappear into the falls at Reichenbach, but Holmes's soul would not be still. Conan Doyle himself reluctantly recalled him from his literary grave and in 1899, when William Gillette sought permission to write a play about Holmes, one in which Holmes would get married, Conan Doyle said, in effect, do what you will — I couldn't care less. Since that time Englishmen, Americans, Danes, Frenchmen and Germans have been doing what they would to Holmes and to his doughty friend and biographer, Dr. Watson, and to the legends that Conan Doyle spawned they've felt no hesitation to add further ones of their own invention.

I can't believe that any other fictional creation has been at once so adaptable, so impervious to change and so capable of accommodating the audiences of such different eras as this remarkable eccentric who, I'm sure, still lives at 221B Baker Street. Holmes has survived all sorts of trials and tribulations but now is the test. Can he survive analysis by a young, not-yet-sure-of-himself Dr. Sigmund Freud? Will a brief peep at his neuroses somehow destroy his appeal by making him seem less mythic and more mortal? That's the question that was first posed by Nicholas Meyer in his novel, "The Seven-Per-Cent Solution," and that is now the heart of the stylish film adaptation written by Mr. Meyer, directed by Herbert Ross, and starring, among others, Nicol Williamson (Holmes), Robert Duvall (Dr. Watson), Alan Arkin (Dr. Freud) and Laurence Olivier (Prof. Moriarty). It's a very pleasant problem to worry about and the prognosis is good.

• • •

As far as I can learn with the help of Leslie Halliwell's "The Filmgoer's Companion," Holmes and Watson have already survived seven decades of movie-making. The first Sherlock Holmes films were American one-reelers made in 1903, 1905 and 1908. The Danes produced a series of Holmes one-reelers in 1908 starring Forrest Holger-Madsen. In the next several years there were two different Sherlock Holmes series made in France, two German films, and in 1913, an American two-reeler with Harry Benham playing Holmes in "The Sign of Four." During World War One there were two-reel versions of "A Study in Scarlet" and "Valley of Fear" made in England, a German adaptation of "The Hound of The Baskervilles," and William Gillette's 1916 screen adaptation of his hugely successful play, "The Adventures of Sherlock Holmes," which was revived on Broadway last season.

In the 1920's and early 1930's Sherlock Holmes appeared on screen in the persons of John Barrymore, Eille Norwood, Carlyle Blackwood, Clive Brook, Arthur Wontner, Raymond Massey, Robert Rendel and Reginald Owen, who had played Watson to Clive Brook's Holmes in "Sherlock Holmes" in 1932 and the following year took over the star part in another adaptation of "A Study in Scarlet." In 1939 Basil Rathbone and Nigel Bruce began their association with the Holmes-Watson stories that, after two films, were abruptly updated to World War II Washington where Holmes became the Roosevelt administration's favorite secret weapon.

Peter Cushing played Holmes in still another remake of "The Hound of The Baskervilles" in 1959 and Christopher Lee, sometime monster to Cushing's Dr. Frankenstein, played Holmes in two German-made films in 1960-1961. Since then John Neville and Donald Houston have been seen as Holmes and Watson in "A Study in Terror" (1965), Billy Wilder examined the relationship between Holmes and Watson in "The Private Life of Sherlock Holmes" (1970), and last year, Gene Wilder presented us with his very funny, sometimes slapstick variation on the theme, "Sherlock Holmes's Smarter Brother."

• • •

You might get the impression that Holmes should be allowed to retire. Not at all. The Sherlock Holmes conceived by Mr. Meyer and played by Mr. Williamson in the new Ross film is the practically perfect hero for our addled, skeptical, neurotic times, a fellow who's sinking fast but who is still salvageable with some help from his friends and particularly from the good doctor in Vienna. Mr. Meyer's novel is literary fooling of rare wit and imagination, both of which have been preserved in a film that succeeds in being faithful to the style and spirit of Conan Doyle while exploring regions of Holmes's subconscious that might have shaken Conan Doyle down to his boots. It's not that Conan Doyle didn't know, but there are some things gentlemen don't discuss.

The adventure of "The Seven-Per-Cent Solution" gets underway when Dr. Watson realizes that he must do something immediately to save his friend Holmes from the certain death that his cocaine addiction holds in store. There's only one man in the world who can help, a young Viennese doctor named Sigmund Freud who has cured himself of the same damnable vice. The hitch: Holmes will not go willingly to Vienna. Says Watson to Sherlock's brother Mycroft, "He feels it generates an unhealthy excitement in the criminal classes when he leaves London."

Their plan is to persuade timid old Prof. Moriarty, whom the maddened Holmes has begun to believe is the arch-criminal of the Western world, to go to Vienna and to allow Holmes to believe that he is tracking this arch-criminal to his lair, which, indeed, will turn out to be Freud's consulting room. With the assistance of a bloodhound named Toby, who once trailed an orangutan through the sewers of Marseilles, the plan works, although, after Holmes, Watson and Toby arrive in Vienna, and after Holmes has submitted to Freud's treatment, they all become embroiled in a mystery that only the combined powers of Holmes and Freud can solve.

• • •

Among other elements this part of the adventure involves a beautiful, red-haired musical-comedy star (Vanessa Redgrave) who has thrown herself into the Danube (I wonder what the real Freud would have to say about the frequency with which Conan Doyle women leap from bridges), an unscrupulous German baron, a Turkish pasha with more money and concubines than are good for him, and, finally, a whiz-bang of a train chase through the Austrian countryside.

Mr. Meyer and Mr. Ross know their Sherlock Holmes and their Sigmund Freud well enough to be able to kid them both royally in a manner that is immensely respectful to their individual but aligned geniuses. The performers also are in notable form. Williamson, Duvall, Arkin and Olivier seem to be having the times of their lives. Ken Adam, who designed the turn-of-the-century settings, Oswald Morris, the cinematographer, and John Addison, who composed the score, are some of the talents behind the scenes.

"The Seven-Per-Cent Solution" is entertainment of such high, intelligent order that I see no reason why Sherlock Holmes shouldn't go on forever, as long as there are sensibilities like Mr. Meyer's around to realize just how accommodating Conan Doyle's creations really are.

1976 O 31, II:17:1

Miss Rainer's Intellectualized Impulse Is at the Whitney

By VINCENT CANBY

Most bad movies are just bad as movies. The awful dividend of bad movies made in the wake of Jean-Luc Godard is that they're also dreadful as written literature. This is what makes watching, reading and listening to Yvonne Rainer's "Kristina Talking Pictures" such a painful experience. It's like being stuck in a tiny elevator with someone who insists on reciting Edgar Guest. It's puerile and pushy. The film opened yesterday at the Whitney Museum of American Art.

Miss Rainer, a figure on New York's modern dance and art scenes, has here given in to an unfortunate impulse to make a film without having anything to make a film about except herself and her friends, who treat themselves with the sort of high-minded seriousness that telephone supervisors adopt when you suggest a mistake has been made in your bill. They are boringly patient with a world that doesn't appreciate them.

Miss Rainer apparently has no idea

The Program

KRISTINA TALKING PICTURES, directed, written and edited by Yvonne Rainer; directors of photography, Roger Dean and Babette Mangolte; distributed by Castelli-Sonnabend Tapes and Films Inc. Running time: 90 minutes. At the Whitney Museum of American Art, Madison Avenue at 75th Street. WITH Yvonne Rainer, Ivan Rainer and others.

that making good movies, especially good movies that break conventional modes, requires discipline, wit and talent. All that we see here is an intellectualized impulse and a superficial knowledge of some of Mr. Godard's favorite techniques, including monologues, written material, jump cuts, fractured images and monotoned narration accompanying a blank screen.

•

The film contains glimpses of a narrative about a young woman named Kristina, a former lion tamer and now a dancer, and her unhappy affair with someone named Raoul. "I was pretty happy doing the lion act for a while," she tells us, "but I'm afraid that Virginia Woolf and Emma Goldman ruined me for the circus." She also blames Martha Graham and Mr. Godard for

having pushed her toward films. As a work of its own, "Kristina Talking Pictures" is a prime example of the ordinary art of implication, another way of saying con game.

1976 N 3, 62:1

DIRTY HANDS, directed and written by Claude Chabrol, based on a story, "Damned Innocents," by Richard Neely; produced by Andre Genoves; director of photography, Jean Rabier; music, Pierre Jansen; editor, Jacques Gaillard; distributed by New Line Cinema. Running time: 102 minutes. At the Forum Theater, Broadway at 47th Street, and other theaters. This film has been rated R.
Julie .... Romy Schneider
Louis .... Rod Steiger
Jeff .... Paolo Giusti
Legal .... Jean Rochefort
Lamy .... Francois Maistre
Villon .... Pierre Santini
Thorent .... FranCois Perrot

By VINCENT CANBY

The peculiar state in which its American distributor has seen fit to release Claude Chabrol's "Dirty Hands" in New York prompts me to wonder whether I should review it or search for its pulse. It's alive but unwell, having been cut from its original 120 minutes to 102 and as poorly dubbed into English as anything I can remember seeing, though I do have a short memory for botch-jobs.

When it opened in Paris in March 1975, it was called "Les Innocents aux Mains Sales," literally "Innocents With Dirty Hands," which has now been shortened to confuse it with the Jean-Paul Sartre play, which is another thing entirely.

The film is set mostly in an elegant house just outside St. Tropez and is about an alcoholic husband (Rod Steiger), his younger wife (Romy Schneider) and the wife's lover (Paolo Giusti), who persuades the wife to join him in putting the old boy out of his misery, for their own fun and profit.

•

When you watch Romy calmly (and idiotically, if you know your crime stories) bludgeon her husband's blanketed form in the bed, without checking to see if he's actually in the bed, you may correctly suspect that Mr. Chabrol is having an off-day and probably an off-picture.

Mr. Chabrol's best films are never exactly what they seem. They have elaborately intellectual superstructures that illuminate the action below and are there for consideration if one cares to climb. "Dirty Hands" (at least in this version) has nothing upstairs, but more plot and, long before the twists start coming, one has stopped being interested in even who is doing what to whom. Forget why.

•

The performances are of a piece —uniformly atrocious. Mr. Steiger surpasses his own earlier records for lumbering busyness. Within his first few minutes on screen he (1) gets drunk, (2) whines, (3) pleads for understanding, (4) weeps and (5) goes to bed alone. Going to bed alone is no big deal in most films, but when Mr. Steiger goes to bed alone, it's Napoleon the night after Waterloo.

Miss Schneider, who was apparently filmed speaking English part of the time and French part of the time, is a beautiful woman, but even her beauty looks faked in this picture, as if she'd been preserved with wax.

I have no idea how much the English dubbing and editing have damaged the original, but the "Dirty Hands" that opened yesterday at the Forum and other theaters is a junk movie.

1976 N 4, 49:1

A Weekend (or so) With Garbo

By JOHN RUSSELL

Greta Garbo made, in all, 32 films. Twelve of the best of them will be shown at a Garbo Festival that begins at the Quad Cinema, 34 West 13th Street, this Sunday and goes on through Nov. 27. They range in date from "Flesh and the Devil" (1927) to "Two-Faced Woman" (1941), and they come two at a time.

It is a wonderful experience to see these films. Garbo has not made a film since "Two-Faced Woman," and not too many of those who were addicted filmgoers at every stage in her career are still around today. (How many of us can boast that we saw all five of the films she made in 1929 at the time of their first appearance?) Often their films demand a leap of the historical imagination, in that they are ridiculous, by any standard: badly written, badly directed, grotesque in their general assumptions, wretchedly acted by almost everyone but herself. Waiting for her to come on, we wonder why on earth we are there. Yet when she does appear, we should hate to be anywhere else.

A good example of this is "Flesh and the Devil," the only one of her silent films to be shown at the Quad, it opens the series on Sunday with her first talkie, "Anna Christie." "Flesh and the Devil" begins as a comedy of barracks life, with John Gilbert and Lars

Garbo with Charles Bickford in the 1930 "Anna Christie"
A creature from another world who is on loan to us for an hour or two

The Bettmann Archive

Hanson as two handsome and high-spirited cadets who are united by the kind of brotherly love that was taken as chivalric in 1927 but looks distinctly more ambiguous today. The Austrian background is quite deft—small-town parade-ground, stallions flicking their tails, local trains that stop at every station, lakes that even Ludwig of Bavaria would have thought romantic—and there is a nice sense of young lives waiting to take shape.

And what young lives! John Gilbert at that time was one of the best-looking men in America. (He was also the star of the movie. His name was in big letters above the title; Garbo's was in small ones a long way below.) Lars Hanson could have been Pushkin's Eugene Onegin come back on earth. The two men were like explosives that functioned on a very short fuse.

Two Leading Men

Garbo in "Flesh and the Devil" was, for once, ideally partnered, with not one but two actors who could manage that high romantic style that is as remote from today's manners as are the conventions of the Kabuki theater. She herself was unsurpassed in the unleisured shorthand of the silent film, and "Flesh and the Devil" holds us captive all the way to the great final scene, in which the two young men call off their duel and gaze into one another's eyes while Garbo, the cause of all the trouble, falls, unnoticed, to her death through a hole in the ice.

It helps not to hear what they have been saying, of course. The silent film was a dream world in which nothing was explained, nothing was justified, nothing was led up to. One look from Garbo, and the two mettlesome young cadets with their startlingly heavy eye makeup were fit to be trussed and tied. And Garbo herself, at 22, had already that complete assurance which makes us watch her as we watch no one else on the screen.

Accident of History

It is a mysterious thing, this continuing thraldom. Fascination can be a generational matter: this year's fascinators are next year's frumps. It can spring from a national need: we can all think of English actresses, French actresses and German actresses whose careers bear the stamp "Not for Export." It can spring from a sudden shift in manners, of which one man or woman is the incarnation. And when fascination goes out of style, we look with pity, or at best with a detached historical interest, on the people who once exerted it.

But none of these things is true of Garbo. Generation, country and class play no part in her enduring success. In only one respect was she favored by history: her career dates entirely from the period during which a moving picture was something that you had to get out of the house to see. In the 1920's and 30's, there was a ceremonial element about "going to the movies" that has evaporated now that everyone can have movies of one kind or another in the house all round the clock.

The now-distant primacy of the movies gave the industry a certain corporate self-assurance. People say hard things about M-G-M in the days of Irving Thalberg, and it is certainly true that we should have liked to have seen Garbo in more films directed by G. W. Pabst and not quite so many directed by Clarence Brown, just as we should have liked to have seen her act more often with the great professionals of the European stage who were with her in "Joyless Street" in 1925 and less often with such actors as Lewis Stone and Lew Ayres. None of this affects (or affected then) the armored assurance with which Hollywood went about its business in the 1930's.

An important part of the genius of Garbo lay in the quality of insubordination which lay somewhere within everything that she did. Sometimes it was in the script: we remember, for instance, the great moment when Charles Bickford orders her a glass of milk in "Anna Christie" and Garbo allows herself just a subliminal grimace when the dreaded liquid comes along. More often it wasn't: we also remember the equivocal by-play that she smuggled into her scenes with Freddie Bartholomew, who acted her young son in "Anna Karenina." It is for this demonic mischief, as much for force and wholeness of feeling, musicality of gesture and a most insinuating way with words that people still roll up to see Garbo.

An unsurpassed beauty of feature also has much to do with it, of course, as does the element of Rimbaudlike renunciation that made her withdraw in mid-career. But the definitive astonishment lies elsewhere. It is that for all her down-to-earthness—don't miss, in the Quad's opening program, the imperious grip with which she enfolds John Gilbert in their first kiss—she really does come across as something that we don't expect to see outside the romantic ballets of the 19th century: a creature from another world who is on loan among us for no more than an hour or two.

1976 N 5, C8:3

Princes Into Frogs

THE SLIPPER AND THE ROSE THE STORY OF CINDERELLA, directed by Bryan Forbes; screenplay by Mr. Forbes and Robert B. Sherman; executive producer, David Frost; producer, Stuart Lyon; music and lyrics, Robert B. Sherman and Richard M. Sherman; director of photography, Tony Imi; editor, Timothy Gee; a Paradine Coproductions Ltd. presentation, distributed by Universal Pictures. Running time: 128 minutes. At the Radio City Music Hall, Avenue of the Americas at 50th Street. This film has been rated G.

Prince	Richard Chamberlain
Cinderella	Gemma Craven
Fairy Godmother	Annette Crosbie
Dowager Queen	Edith Evans
John	Christopher Gable
King	Michael Hordern
Stepmother	Margaret Lockwood
Chamberlain	Kenneth More
Montague	Julian Orchard
Queen	Larry Bowers
Palatine	Sherrie Hewson
Isobella	Rosalind Ayres

By VINCENT CANBY

There've been times of tranquility quillity and ease, without pressures, when I've thought to myself how pleasant it would be anticipating a new Hitchcock film, or a new Buñel, or an Astaire-Rogers revival, or a classy new stage production of "The Importance of Being Earnest." Familiarity can breed fondness with expectation.

But never—except possibly during a fever dream—have I ever thought how great it would be to see an all-new, very lengthy, very elaborate musical version of the story of Cinderella, a movie with music and lyrics by Robert B. and Richard M. Sherman, the songwriting brothers who did "Mary Poppins" and "Bedknobs and Broomsticks," with Richard Chamberlain as the Prince, Gemma Craven as Cinderella and the late Edith Evans shoehorned in as the Prince's old granny.

•

This is not idle talk. It's something every parent should consider before accompanying the children to see the film that opened yesterday at the Radio City Music Hall. Kids, we know, will sit through almost anything, from awful made-in-Yugoslavia cartoons shown on Saturday morning television to the classic "Wizard of Oz" and, if they have to, "Claire's Knee." If there's an image moving on the screen, children will continue to stare at it. It's adults who need to be protected.

"The Slipper and the Rose: The Story of Cinderella" is a movie to turn a prince into a frog.

There aren't that many films one can take small children to these days that "The Slipper and the Rose" should be dismissed. It's harmless, I guess, but it goes on so long — 128 minutes — with so little suspense—there's only so much that can be done about that unwearable glass slipper — that it may well outlast the staying power of children who stuff themselves with popcorn and then drink to excess.

"The Slipper and the Rose," a collaboration of the Shermans and Bryan Forbes, the director, was filmed partially in and around the "Sound of Music" country of Salzburg, Austria, an association that comes naturally enough during the film as one begins to long for a bit of Julie Andrews's chic and sophistication.

The castles are pretty, the costumes are suitably candy-colored and the supporting actors excellent, including Michael Hordern, as the Prince's bubble-headed father; Annette Crosbie, as a most practical fairy godmother, and Margaret Lockwood, as the wicked stepmother.

As the young lovers, Mr. Chamberlain and Miss Craven have impossible roles that are less like characters in a fairy tale than pictures on a jar of peanut butter.

Mr. Forbes and Robert Sherman, authors of the screenplay, have stretched the fable without mercy, largely to accommodate a whole bunch of forgettable songs by the Shermans, who did very well by "Mary Poppins" and "Tom Eawyer," but who, when off stride, as here, sound as if they're parodying the worst of the Broadway musical theater of the 50's. Like Ross Hunter, they're devoted to an earlier tradition they've worn out.

1976 N 5, C8:3

Pain and Pleasure

MAITRESSE, directed by Barbet Schroeder; screenplay (French with English subtitles), by Mr. Schroeder and Paul Voujargol, director of photography, Nestor Almendros; editor, Denise de Casabianca; music, Carlos d'Alessio; a co-production of Les Films du Losange-Gaumont, distributed by TINC Productions. Running time: 112 minutes. At the Baronet Theater, Third Avenue near 59th Street. This film has not been rated.

Olivier	Gerard Depardieu
Ariane	Bulle Ogier
Mario	Andre Rouyer
Lucienne	Nathalie Keryan
Man in cage	Roland Bertin
Emile	Tony Taffin
Gautier	Holger Lowenadler
Secretary	Anny Bartanovsky

One night while burglarizing a Paris apartment he thinks is empty, Olivier (Gérard Dépardieu), a healthy young man with no scruples about breaking and entering, is caught by Ariane (Bulle Ogier), the apartment's mistress, a sweet, gentle thing who runs a high-class parlor devoted to the needs of well-heeled masochists. It's the sort of place a fellow goes after a difficult day at the office, where he can rid himself of the tensions of being happy and successful by hanging from a cross, being put into a cage, beaten or having his penis nailed to a plank.

Olivier is a modern youth—basically unflappable. When Ariane presses him, figuratively, of course, into helping with one of her customers, he goes along with the game. The truth is, he is falling in love with her.

•

He admires the way Ariane goes about her tasks with the spunky dedication of a modern-day, whip-toting, leather-clad Florence Nightingale. She is indefatigable. For Ariane, it's work, work, work. When Olivier suggests it must be exhausting, she says, "Not at all . . . it's fabulous to be able to get into people's craziness, especially in such an intimate way."

Because other people's hang-ups always are balmy to someone who doesn't share them, Barbet Schroeder's "Maîtresse," which opened yesterday at the Baronet, is likely to seem either unintentionally hilarious or disgusting to audiences who are not themselves into fancy S-M. Mr. Schroeder is a serious film maker ("More," "General Idi Amin Dada") but I'm not sure it's possible to be serious about sado-masochism in a medium as graphic as film.

The explicitness of the scenes of flagellation and nailing (performed, says a program note, by a "professional 'maîtresse'") are so bizarre that their place in a metaphor about all love relationships is completely forgotten. The shock effect prevents the film from being about anything more than what we see on the screen, which is a pretty little hustler who makes good money catering to the nutty fantasies of people who can afford to pay.

•

It may be, as Mr. Schroeder suggests in another program note, that there's some S-M in all of us, but there's a big difference between people who must act out their fantasies in elaborately contrived theatrics and those who simply want to torment a cab driver or who make an important appointment they know they can't keep.

Mr. Dépardieu and Miss Ogier are two of France's most appealing young performers. Each also suggests a level-headed intelligence and comic self-awareness that are completely out of place in "Maîtresse" except in those sequences that have to do with their own love affair. The ecstasy, anger, suspicion and helplessness of that affair makes the ritualized torture scenes seem not a projection of extreme psychological needs but clips from a different movie.

VINCENT CANBY

1976 N 5, C8:6

THE INCREDIBLE SARAH, directed by Richard Fleischer; screenplay by Ruth Wolff; produced by Helen M. Strauss; music, Elmer Bernstein; director of photography, Christopher Challis; editor, John Jympson; a Reader's Digest Films Limited presentation. Running time: 106 minutes. At the Festival Theater, 57th Street west of Fifth Avenue. This film has been rated PG.

Sarah Bernhardt	Glenda Jackson
Sardou	Daniel Massey
Montigny	Douglas Wilmer
Duc De Morny	David Langton
Hendi De Ligne	Simon Williams
Damala	John Castle

By VINCENT CANBY

"The Incredible Sarah," which opened yesterday at the Festival Theater, is a foolishly romantic movie about the young Sarah Bernhardt as played by Glenda Jackson, who isn't foolish, romantic or remarkably young. Other things being equal, this might have damaged the film, but they aren't.

Miss Jackson, striding about the screen in that firm, authoritative, brainy way that can sometimes be quite sexy, finding readings for unreadable lines that may be unexpectedly funny, is the only reason to put up with the clichéd lunacies of "The Incredible Sarah" for more than five minutes. In every other respect, the movie is a disaster seemingly calculated to send women back to the kitchen forever.

•

Women were apparently in charge of this movie and all they have shown is that, given the opportunity, they can make movies as rottenly as any group of men. "The Incredible Sarah" was produced by Helen M. Strauss, who, I assume, didn't have to have her arm twisted to hire Richard Fleischer as the director or to accept Ruth Wolff's screenplay. This is no more than a series of talking

Glenda Jackson
Best in curtain calls

tableaux that begin when Miss Jackson, impersonating a stage-struck teen-ager circa 1860, wins a Comédie Française audition, vowing, "I shall be the greatest actress who ever lived."

Thereafter the movie records without comment some of the more bizarre details of the legendary career—how Sarah had a nobleman's son out of wedlock, slept in a coffin, had temper tantrums and insisted on being paid after every performance in gold. There are ups and downs in her career and Mr. Fleischer and Miss Jackson, without offering us tangible proof, ask us to believe the divine Sarah was the greatest actress of her century. Most publicized, maybe, but greatest? We have only the words of the screenplay to go on.

We are shown bits and pieces of Bernhardt performances in "Le Passant," "Phédre," "La Dame aux Camélias" and "King Lear," in all of which Miss Jackson behaves more like Miss Jackson doing educational television than the most startling, most galvanizing actress of her age. No one makes any attempt to recapture the particular Bernhardt style that, some years later, prompted George Bernard Shaw to write several of his most scathing notices as he compared Bernhardt with Duse—very unfavorably.

"The Incredible Sarah" is an incredibly low-brow variation on the story of the actress who must make horrendous personal sacrifices in the name of her art. Considering the lightweight dopiness of the men around Sarah, though, the sacrifices are not all that great. Daniel Massey plays the admiring Sardou, less as a successful playwright than as the hair-dressing member of an actress's entourage. John Castle, who is the fellow Sarah marries, plays a very bad actor badly. Without exception, all the men in the cast are awful.

Miss Jackson is never uninteresting to watch, but her best moments — and I'm not kidding — are her curtain calls, when, exhausted, somewhat dazed, she stands in front of the curtain to acknowledge her audience. One recognizes a real actress even if the bows, considering the movie that contains them, are unseemly.

1976 N 6, 11:1

FILM VIEW

VINCENT CANBY

The Daze and Nights of a Movie Critic

In some weeks it's as if the brain had gone on a diet. After five days it's tired, measurably thinner. The following diary of one such week is less a report on the quality of contemporary film-making (some of the films seen are several years old) than a reflection on the state of contemporary exhibition. With fewer and fewer films being made, theaters are increasingly desperate for material to show.

Monday: The week promises to begin pleasantly enough with a trip downtown to the Film Forum at 15 Vandam Street for a program of anthropological films, "The Last of The Cuiva" and "A Clearing in The Jungle." In the last several years the Film Forum has established itself as the most adventurous and reliable of the Off Off Broadway non-commercial movie operations. Unlike the Whitney Museum of American Art, whose programs are usually restricted to the work of American filmmakers, the Film Forum is free to show innovative work from all points of the compass—South Africa (Athol Fugard's "Boesman and Lena"), Germany (Rainer Werner Fassbinder's "The American Soldier"), the Bronx (films by the Kuchar Brothers). This particular morning, though, is less than memorable. "The Last of The Cuiva" (65 minutes) and "A Clearing in The Jungle" (38 minutes), both produced by Brian Moser for Britain's Granada Television, are solemn, artless studies of two vanishing cultures, those of the Cuiva Indians of Colombia and the Panare of Venezuela. Both films demonstrate the comic dangers when the images on the screen showing primitive Indians going about their lives (lying in hammocks, fishing, lying in hammocks, prancing around bonfires, lying in hammocks, etc.) don't say as much as the soundtrack narrators, who are desperately stumped in their attempts to be informative. At one point we watch a young Indian man, whose wife has just given birth, throwing up. The new father has taken an emetic, the narrator tells us, admitting he has no idea why. The narrator adds wistfully, "Perhaps it might be a symbol of inner cleansing. . . ." At another point, when we see the Indians moving around with blankets over their faces, or standing with their backs to the camera, the off-screen fellow says apologetically, "After 18 months, they began to shun us. . . ." After 60 minutes one's mind is apt to turn to problems closer to home.

In the afternoon I stop by Loew's 83d Street Theater to catch Richard Lester's "The Ritz," which opened when I was away in August. The auditorium is eerie it's so empty. Terrence McNally's farce, set in a gay bathhouse has some funny lines, and Lester's direction minds the manners of farce. He doesn't chop up and isolate the gags as he did to ruin his screen version of "A Funny Thing Happened on The Way To The Forum." Yet it's not very funny. The movie is as bleak and empty as the Loew's auditorium.

•   •   •

Tuesday: Off to the D.W. Griffith Theater at 9:30 A.M. to see a special screening of English documentary filmmaker Anthony Howarth's "People of the Wind," about the semi-annual migration of Iran's Bakhtiari tribes between their winter and summer grazing lands—the same migration that was documented by Merian C. Cooper and Ernest P. Schoedsack in their 1925 film, "Grass." This one is in color. The scenery is pretty, possibly too pretty, and it's more than two hours of watching sheep, being pushed across rivers and pulled up and down mountains ("as high as the Alps," we're told). We are meant to respect these people and their sheep but it's all so bland and cheerful it had the effect of making me suspicious. Where does the Shah figure in all this? Was this one of the movies Mrs. Marion Javits was said to be working on when she was doing p.r. work for Rudder and Finn? Who put up the money for it? Later I learn the benefactor was a Chicagoan, Mrs. Elizabeth E. Rogers who has never before been connected with films and maybe never will be again. That story sounds more interesting than the film.

•   •   •

Wednesday: To see an evening screening of "Maitresse," by Barbet Schroeder, the talented young French director ("More," "Idi Amin Dada") and producer ("My Night at Maud's," "Claire's Knee" and "The Marquise of O," among others). "Maitresse" is a lugubrious romance about the business and the pleasures of masochism. Bulle Ogier is the madame of an S-M establishment and Gérard Dépardieu is the healthy young fellow who comes by to rob the place one night and stays on to love Bulle and help out with the chores. There may be a metaphor for all love relationships here but it is snuffed by the graphic images showing Bulle's customers getting exactly what they pay for (being caged, hung from crosses, needles stuck through breasts, penises nailed to boards, and so on). In case you might wonder, as I did, what a nice girl like Bulle was doing performing such tasks, a program note states: "A professional 'maitresse' performed the scenes of heavy flagellation and nailing." That's a relief, but the real relief is to stay home unless it's your scene.

Thursday: an early evening screening of "The Incredible Sarah" with Glenda Jackson as the young Sarah Bernhardt under the direction of Richard Fleischer, whose feel for place and period suggests he wears down-filled mittens. The film, a Reader's Digest production, is as barren of ideas and excitement as a Con Ed bill. It tells the story of saucy Sarah in such a way that it may remind you of Hayley Mills as Pollyana. There are snippets of Miss Jackson playing in "Phedre," "King Lear," "La Dame Aux Camélias" and "Le Passant." They are no more than talking tableaux but Miss Jackson takes curtain calls that look most authentic. Without exception the men in the film are idiots. Are Miss Jackson, the star, Helen M. Strauss, the producer, and Ruth Wolff, who wrote the screenplay, trying to get even? If so, they have.

Friday: A very long day. In the morning to a screening of a 1974 Claude Chabrol film titled (in English) "Dirty Hands," though it has nothing to do with the Sartre play. This seems to be bottom-drawer Chabrol. I say that tentatively. It's hard to tell in this English-dubbed monstrosity. The story is about a triple- and quadruple-crossing husband (Rod Steiger) and wife (Romy Schneider) and the wife's lover. The acting appears to be ferociously bad. The principal setting—a house just outside St. Tropez—would be a great place to spend a vacation if you could make sure these characters wouldn't return, but "Dirty Hands" is the sort of melodrama in which people keep coming back from the dead.

In the afternoon to a double-feature at the Cinerama on Broadway where the ushers stand in the lobby just outside the auditorium and talk so loudly it's sometimes difficult to hear the screen. They often know something we don't. The first feature, though, is not at all bad. It's "Death Collector," a low-budget, modest Mafia melodrama shot entirely just across the bridge in New Jersey by Ralph DeVito.

It's terse, violent and very well acted by Joseph Cortese and Lou Criscuola. The other film is a badly English-dubbed Italian melodrama that fails in its aspirations to be a kind of untalented director's "Death Wish." Its meaningless title: "The Violent Professionals."

I can't remember a film week in recent history that was both so active and so without real sustenance. It's eating at a fast-food counter while slowly starving to death. Could that be the true American dream?

1976 N 7, II:13:1

A Positive Movie on Blacks

By VINCENT CANBY

Bobby Roth's "Independence Day," which opened yesterday at the Whitney Museum of American Art, is about Fred (Mel Rosier) and Delores (Gammy Burdett), a young black couple who move from Memphis to Los Angeles in hopes of finding a better life.

Fred takes a job in a foundry. Delores first works as a domestic, goes to night school, and then lands a job in an office. They live in a nice apartment, have all the usual appliances, including a Princess telephone, and, even during the strike at Fred's foundry, there's always enough Scotch to drink and a roast in the oven. Fred and Delores fight and part and eventually obtain some sense of individual identity.

Mr. Roth, who wrote and directed "Independence Day," describes it as an attempt to make "a positive film about black working people . . . an alternative to the commercial exploitation films."

I guess it is, but good intentions aren't enough. "Independence Day" is a movie without any real emotional or intellectual momentum. Fred and Delores are essentially nice, decent people but because the writing, directing and acting are solemnly commonplace, their lives amount to little more than the acquisition of liberated attitudes that, like their appliances, are mass-produced.

1976 N 10, C21:5

'Next Man' Plays on Paranoia

By VINCENT CANBY

"The Next Man," which opened at the Rivoli and other theaters yesterday, is a suspense melodrama made by people whose talent for filmmaking and knowledge of international affairs would both fit comfortably into the left nostril of a small bee.

It's about a visionary Saudi Arabian minister of state named Kahlil Abdul-Muhsen, played by the very Scots-sounding Sean Connery, who proposes to defuse the Middle East by signing a mutual assistance pact with Israel and by making petroleum and petroleum by-products available virtually at cost to poor nations.

"The Next Man" is the story of the attempt by various vested interests in this country, the Soviet Union and the Middle East, acting separately, to put an end to this dreadful scheme by putting an end to Khalil.

Like a lot of other films these days, "The Next Man" is obsessed with political assassination but it never really identifies its villains, preferring, instead, to cop out by playing on natural paranoia that assumes that everyone everywhere is on the take from someone somewhere. This attitude is too easy to represent true cynicism. It's simple laziness.

In "The Next Man" the forces of reaction are represented entirely by a mysterious, exceedingly well-dressed young woman named Nicole Scott, said to be the daughter of a former American ambassador to Great Britain, a Bryn Mawr graduate, and a girl who apparently slays not for pay but for thrills of a sort you don't get in the Junior League.

This character is played by Cornelia Sharpe, a new actress who is well on her way to becoming the actress producers will hire when they can't get Faye Dunaway. Miss Sharpe is stunning looking and model-skinny, and you don't for a minute believe her to be an international assassin any more than you believe Mr. Connery to be an Arab anything.

The movie appears to agree. As if to take our minds off such matters, "The Next Man" moves rootlessly around the world like a fretful tourist, from New York to the Middle East, the south of France, London, Ireland, Bavaria, and the Bahamas, though nothing much happens in any one of these places that couldn't as easily happen somewhere else.

The Cast

THE NEXT MAN, directed by Richard C. Sarafian; screenplay by Mort Fine, Alan Trustman, David M. Wolf and Mr. Sarafian, based on a story by Martin Bregman and Mr. Trustman; produced by Mr. Bregman; director of photography, Michael Chapman; editors, Aram Avakian and Robert Lovett; music, Michael Kamen; an Artist's Entertainment Complex film, distributed by Allied Artists. Running time: 108 minutes. At the UA Rivoli, Broadway at 49th Street; Loews Cine, Third Avenue near 86th; Reade's 34th Street East, 34th Street near Second Avenue, and other theaters. This film has been rated R.
Khalil Abdul-Muhsen .... Sean Connery
Nicole Scott .... Cornelia Sharpe
Hamid .... Albert Paulsen
Al Sharif .... Adolfo Celi
Justin .... Marco St. John
Dedario .... Ted Beniades
Fouad .... Charles Cioffi

The characters are always getting in and out of jets and coming upon colorful local festivals (including the Macy's Thanksgiving Day parade in New York), and if there's no parade to look at, the script will arbitrarily have someone decide to climb into a helicopter to go sight-seeing. "The Next Man" is the first film I've ever seen that is so acutely bored with itself that it tries to go away.

Who is responsible for mindless movie-making of this magnitude I've no idea, though it was produced by Martin Bregman, who also shares credit for the film's "original story" with Alan Trustman, who himself shares the screenplay credit with Mort Fine, David M. Wolf and Richard C. Sarafian, who directed the film. It looks as if too many people got into the act.

There have been more expensive films this year, and more foolish ones, but "The Next Man" must be the most foolish film of such expense.

1976 N 11, 52:1

LOVING COUSINS, directed by Sergio Martino; written by Mr. Martino, Savro Scavocini and Fernando Poli; edited by Eugenio Alabiso; produced by Carlo Ponti. Released by Independent International Pictures. At the Trans-lux 86th Street and Flagship theaters. Running time: 87 minutes. This film has been rated R.
Sonia .... Susan Player
Nico .... Alfredo Pea
Professor .... Riccardo Cucciola
Baron Roccadura .... Hugh Griffiths

"Loving Cousins" is a dull, unwholesome Italian film that aims at being soft-core, but is only soft. It has as much erotic energy as two slugs coupling. It tells of the interminably slow seduction of an inhibited boy—he looks like Pinocchio—by his liberated girl-cousin. The hot weather is emphasized. The camera takes close-ups of mouths untidily eating fruit and salad, and of bare legs crossing. The film, which opened yesterday at the Trans-Lux 86th Street and other theaters, is opaque and blotchy. It looks as if it had been knitted.

RICHARD EDER

1976 N 11, 54:3

BEWARE OF A HOLY WHORE, directed by Rainer Werner Fassbinder; screenplay (German with English subtitles by Mr. Fassbinder; director of photography, Michael Ballhaus; distributed by New Yorker Films. Running time: 103 minutes. At the Film Forum, 15 Vandam Street.
WITH Lou Castel, Werner Schroeter, Eddie Constantine, Hanna Schygulla, Margarethe von Trotta, Ulli Lommel, Marquard Bohm, Hannes Fuchs and Mr. Fassbinder.

By VINCENT CANBY

IN 1969, when he was 23, Rainer Werner Fassbinder made his first feature film, "Love Is Colder Than Death," and three more besides that one. In 1970, he stopped fooling around. He made seven features, including "The American Soldier" and "Recruits in Ingolstadt," both of which have already been seen in this country. He also made "Beware of a Holy Whore" (Warnung vor Einer Heiligen Nutte), which opened yesterday at the Film Forum and is as fascinating and dissonant as might be wished by anyone who admires this young German film maker as I do.

"Beware of a Holy Whore" has the informal manner of a practice exercise but it leaves the kind of wounds one receives in a knife fight.

"Beware of a Holy Whore" is Mr. Fassbinder's comic, self-consciously absurd, slightly dizzy "Contempt," "Day for Night" and "The Last Tycoon," made in the manner of the post-"Eat," pre-"Trash" Andy Warhol.

A dozen people, including Eddie Constantine as Eddie Constantine, are hanging around the lobby of a none-too-posh Spanish seaside hotel waiting to start a film. Until the director of the film shows up, the production manager, played by Mr. Fassbinder, is in charge, which means he can be rude and sarcastic and more or less removed from the small intrigues that take place at the bar.

The virile speech coach makes a tentative play for the director's young boyfriend. A young German actress is wrapped up in a German technician until Eddie Constantine looks her way. Another German crew member drinks so many Cuba libres he becomes confused about the love he is drinking to forget. When the director finally arrives, he treats the production manager as badly as the production manager has treated everyone else, and makes his point by taking the production manager's wife away from him. The director is bored with his boyfriend.

"Beware of a Holy Whore" is not really about movie making at all. It's about connections and disconnections. The members of Mr. Fassbinder's movie company spend most of the time moving about the large, gloomy hotel lobby like people trying to make trans-Atlantic calls to one another when the atmospheric condictions are terrible. No sooner has contact been made than there is an inexplicable interruption. Sentences are arbitrarily splintered. Syllables are lost. Wires are crossed.

The Fassbinder view of the world is very special. His images contain not

A scene from Rainer Werner Fassbinder's "Beware of the Holy Whore"

reflections of vital reality but of psychological stress. Mr. Fassbinder's characters are never fully revealed. They are hinted at. The movie, thus, is impossible to enjoy in the conventional sense of a narrative film that has an easily recognzable beginning, middle and end. All of the images are part of a single image, which, in this case, has a number of uproarious funny details though the overall tone is one of despair.

"Beware of a Holy Whore" is the work of a very young, very gifted film maker. In a movie by a director of lesser talent and natural exuberance, some of Mr. Fassbinder's showy, often Godardian effects would be impediments we look around or beyond to appreciate a major career that is erupting with the force of a natural phenomenon.

1976 N 12, C8:3

In Eye of Camera

A CHILD IS A WILD YOUNG THING, produced, written and directed by Peter Skinner; edited by Mr. Skinner and Vincent Suprynowicz; music by Derek Wadsworth; lyrics by Mr. Skinner. At the Quad Cinema. Running time 88 minutes. This film has not been rated.
Miette.........................Marie Antoinette Skinner
Adam................................Himself
Professor's voice.................George S. Irving
Miette's voice.....................Paulette Rubinstein

By RICHARD EDER

THERE are television commercials that take perfectly lovely shots of children running across fields, all tangled up in light. But we aren't moved. The intention cancels the beauty.

Peter Skinner's "A Child Is a Wild Young Thing" is often quite beautiful to look at. Considering it is his first movie—he wrote, directed, produced and photographed it—it is made with some skill. But it is a dreadful and wrongheaded vision of its subject, a wrenched picture of childhood.

Set on a Brittany island, the movie centers upon Adam, a curly haired 2-year-old. Ostensibly — the level of reality shifts somewhat at the end—it is a record made by the narrator, a psychologist who is Adam's father, of the child and the child's mother.

To be exact, the form isn't precisely narration. As the camera shows Adam moving about, playing, eating, crying, prancing, and the mother and three teen-age girls who have come along as vacation baby sitters, what we hear is an interminable argument.

It is the psychologist and his wife tearing at each other. She resents his project, his cold and hidden stance behind the camera in an effort to try out theses about animal behavior on his son. Beyond that, she appears to resent his position as a male, his domination, his philandering.

For his part, he is jealous of her total absorption in the child, her insistence on letting him run around naked and do whatever he pleases, her continual fondling and nuzzling of him.

At one point, the mother lies naked on the beach and holds Adam on top of her in a posture of simulated intercourse. It is not especially shocking, but it isn't healthily natural, either. It is, simply, inappropriate: One more instance of the film's projecting adult ideas of childhood onto this child.

The language of the parents is stilted and exaggerated. They hurl clichés about child development at each other.

Each filmed sequence of Adam calls up a stream of the most banal and irritating comment. Occasionally—in one of the film's most depressing devices—what are presumed to be Adam's thoughts are rendered by songs.

In some sense, it seems to be an attempt at psychodrama—real or fictional or a mixture of both—to try to purge the tensions between husband and wife. At one point, Adam is represented as dying, and one of the movie's genuinely charming bits comes when he refuses to stay out of camera range and is seen skipping about at his own "funeral."

But what ultimately is least real in this movie is what should be most real: the child himself. He is an instrument, an occasion for the interminable acrimony of the parents.

The camera virtually never leaves him, and the movie virtually never thinks of him. Children are not meant to be watched so persistently, so intensely. If they are, they are not seen. They change, they act up, they are distorted by the eye and thoughts of the person who watches them. The only way to look at children is with peripheral vision. Adam, so beautiful, so expressive, is virtually invisible in "A Child Is a Wild Young Thing." It opened yesterday at the Quad Cinema.

1976 N 12, C8:3

TWO MINUTE WARNING, directed by Larry Peerce; screenplay by Edward Hume based on novel by George LaFountaine; produced by Edward S. Feldman; director of photography, Gerald Hirschfeld; music by Charles Fox. Released by Universal. At Loews Astor Plaza, Orpheum and Murray Hill Theaters. Running time: 112 minutes. This movie has been rated R.
Holly ....Charlton Heston
Button ....John Cassavetes
McKeever ....Martin Balsam
Mike Ramsay ....Beau Bridges
Lucy ....Marilyn Hassett
Steve ....David Janssen
Sandman ....Jack Klugman
Janet ....Gena Rowlands
Pickpocket ....Walter Pidgeon

By RICHARD EDER

"Two Minute Warning," about a mad sniper in a crowded football stadium, has the suspense, the compassion, the human vision and the individual nuance you would expect in a movie about a foot stepping on an anthill.

But why, you may ask, would anybody make a movie about a foot stepping on an anthill?

Exactly.

"Warning," which opened yesterday at several local theaters, is more or less of the genre of "Towering Inferno," "Juggernaut," "Jaws," "Hindenburg" and so on. Something terrible is happening, that is, and will somebody stop it, and how are we going to get out of here? And, by contrast, it makes any of them—even "Hindenburg" —look like cinematic poetry.

It assembles its characters in a familiar series of cameos. There is the killer, or rather bits of him: hands, feet, eyeball—we only see all of him once, blurredly, near the very end. He shoots a passing cyclist for practice before placing himself in the top tower of the Los Angeles Memorial Coliseum.

There are the police, or rather there are two groups of the police. The first is the good guys—good, but ineffective, that is—led by a captain, Charlton Heston, who worries about people getting hurt and is dubious about the methods of the second police. These, in overalls and looking like homicidal plumb-

Charlton Heston
A good guy . . . but ineffective

ers, are a tactical commando group. They are mean, violent and messy.

Finally, there are the selected spectators—a quarrelsome middle-age noncouple, a gambler who will be dropped out of a high window if Los Angeles doesn't beat Baltimore, a girl switching boyfriends in midpass, as it were, a harried

young father with wife and children, a pickpocket and so on.

Except for the gambler, who is played with comic but touching desperation by Jack Klugman, none of them have the slightest dimension. They could be placards. Some of them, it's obvious, will die, and the spectator is mildly sorry and mildly curious but that's all.

Curiosity is not suspense. For suspense, some involvement is required. Through almost the whole length of the movie we know nothing about the threat—who he is, what he wants—and nothing about who is threatened or why. It is an abstract threat—at some point somebody is going to begin shooting and some people will be killed and that's all we have.

•

And because it is all so unspecific, the efforts of the police to catch the sniper—all their ladder-climbing and maneuvering—are no more exciting than watching a group of linesmen at work up a telephone pole.

The movie is a blank, in other words, until the end. And then, suddenly, a lot of people are killed very gorily; and there is a mass stampede, and the football crowd becomes a panicked, murderous mob. And even the panic lacks emotion. It has momentum—lots of feet stepping on faces—and viciousness. Nothing more.

1976 N 13, 12:1

FILM VIEW

VINCENT CANBY

It's Time to Hold Glenda Jackson Accountable

It's been accepted critical practice for years to express pity for actors who appear in bad movies or plays. Everybody else is responsible —never the actors. I grew up reading lofty condolences on the order of, ". . . . and Sophie Lewis, one of our most talented, dazzling actresses, was trapped in the proceedings, along with everyone else in the flawless cast." Or, "Robert Forgan does the best he can with the idiotic material, though no one could have saved it." Admittedly, actors and actresses must eat. They have to support families. They have dentist bills and school tuitions to meet, and there aren't that many films or plays that they can always be choosy. Also, there are plenty of films that don't succeed in spite of the talent, taste, imagination and discipline of the people involved. Yet there comes a time when actors who've reached a certain status must share the blame. Should we shake our heads in sorrow when Gene Hackman turns up in a multi-million-dollar bore like "Lucky Lady" and suggest it's not his fault? No more. Gene Hackman was paid a bundle to make that movie and for us to feel sorry for him is ridiculous. You might as well send a CARE package to Nelson Rockefeller. Hackman made that film because he wanted to. No one held a gun to his head.

A current case in point in Glenda Jackson. Watching her as she attempts to fit her driving, powerhouse intelligence to that of a small-minded, make-believe Sarah Bernhardt in "The Incredible Sarah" is to see a film career going up in smoke. It's difficult to believe that the actress who was so affecting, witty and surprising in "Sunday Bloody Sunday," "Hedda" and "The Maids" could not have had an inkling that this match-box of a movie was not going to be as lightweight and flimsy as it turned out to be. All she had to do was to scan a synopsis and check the credits of the people involved.

In six years Miss Jackson has appeared in 12 films and won two Academy Awards, which, one would think, would give her enough room in which to maneuver so that she wouldn't be forced to prop up something like "The Incredible Sarah" in order to pay the rent. Failures come in two basic styles, honorable and totally inexcusable. Joseph Losey's "The Romantic Englishwoman" was an honorable failure. So, even, was Ken Russell's ludicrous "The Music Lovers," in which Miss Jackson played Mrs. Tchaikovsky pretty much on a bass fiddle.

However, there's no way to alibi movies like "Mary Queen of Scots" or "The Nelson Affair," great moments in history made small, or "The Devil Is A Woman," an awful Italian joke about a psychotic nun, the sort of movie that could not have lost anything in the bad English dubbing. It's time to hold Miss Jackson accountable. She isn't having a run of bad luck. She's accepting roles in junk movies that can't even be rationalized for meeting some peculiar popular taste. The movies are duds.

Something is happening to her touch. Is it dire financial need, greed, a woeful lack of judgment? Unless she pulls herself together, a serious career could be heading for the rocks. In the palmy post-"Cleopatra" days Richard Burton and his famous friend attempted to cash in on their temporary box-office appeal by seeming to accept every third script that was offered them. It nearly ruined him as well as Elizabeth Taylor, though Burton, being a great actor, had a hidden resource he couldn't easily hock. She hasn't been as lucky. It wasn't over-exposure that diluted the $1,000,000-plus per-picture fees each of the Burtons received for a while. It was over-exposure in lousy films.

Acting is a terrible business as a business. The professional life can be only slightly longer than the life of a common house fly. One can understand an actor's impulse to cash in quickly when he becomes a hot property, which is apparently what Gene Hackman did the unlucky year he appeared in "French Connection II," "Night Moves," "Bite The Bullet" and "Lucky Lady." Actually both "Night Moves" and "French Connection II" were honorable films, but Hackman is not the sort of idiosyncratic star who can expose his personality that frequently, in that short a time, without having the mediocrity of films like "Bite The Bullet" and "Lucky Lady" rub off on him.

Miss Jackson has a tougher public presence. I've never really been bored by any of her performances, even in something as silly as "The Devil Is A Woman," but her strength is beginning to look strained. Or perhaps we're starting to lose patience. I, for one, am tired of toting a lot of high expectations to a Jackson film only to wind up having to make excuses for her.

All of which leads me to a conclusion that I'd just as soon wasn't true. That is, that the $2,000,000 and $3,000,000 fees reportedly being asked by people like Steve McQueen, Paul Newman, Robert Redford and a few others may, in the long run, be the best things they ever did. It keeps them from being over-exposed, which they don't need at these junctures in their careers, and it may prompt the producers who hire them to take more care with the films these actors go into. That's never a guarantee, of course. "Lucky Lady" was a movie with big-salaried stars and it was a mistake. "The Missouri Breaks," with Marlon Brando and Jack Nicholson was, in the words of a Hollywood friend of mine, not conceived as a movie but as a production deal. Most of the effort expended in the making of "The Missouri Breaks" came from the agents and lawyers who drew up the contracts.

Even with her two Oscars, Miss Jackson is not in that salary range. If her agent should ask for $2,000,000 for a film, it's likely that no one would return his phone calls. That being the case, she, her agent, her best friend, her hairdresser, someone should suggest that she slow down, read a script before signing a commitment, and make bloody sure that she can trust the talent around her. Otherwise, curtains.

1976 N 14, II:15:4

Jeanne Moreau's 'Lumière'

Film on Women Written and Directed by the Actress, Who Stars

By RICHARD EDER

It's a mark of the quality of Jeanne Moreau's "Lumière" that its defects are exaggerations of virtues. There is no fumbling or uncertainty in the first movie that she has written and directed and in which she gives, additionally, a splendid performance.

On the contrary, there is great control. Often it leads to marvelous perceptions. Sometimes, in the too-studied décor of a scene or the overly purposeful marshaling of a character or a dramatic sequence, it gives a sense of contrivance and airlessness.

"Lumière," which opened yesterday at the Beekman Theater, is Miss Moreau's own penetrating vision of what it means to be a woman. It is as autobiographical and personal as a first novel, and as deliberately limited in scope. Miss Moreau's women are not farmers or office workers or sociologists. They are four actresses of different ages, inhabiting a particular, affected, high-pressured world.

If the narrow focus seems precious, it is made up for by the insight with which we are shown the four women's relations with men, with their careers, with time—the almost visible enemy—and with one another. At its best, "Lumière" is subtle, funny and moving. And its ending is so powerful as to make an extraordinarily good movie seem, for these last minutes, close to a perfect one.

●

The form of the picture is something like one of those traditional tales where four characters come out of a storm and into a quiet inn. In this case the meeting is at the country house of Sarah (Miss Moreau), the eldest of the four and the film's central figure. The women swim, sing snatches of childhood songs, lie in hammocks, fly kites, talk.

It is an interval of peace and Miss Moreau uses it to establish her vision of feminine intimacy. It is composed of affection and a simultaneous understanding and restraint. The women see one another's loneliness and tend it with small attentions: presents, caresses, a kind of mutual adornment. They are soldiers resting before setting out for solitary campaigns. All they can do for one another is help with the bandages, not the fighting; and talk around, not through, one another's suffering.

●

The movie then shifts to the four lives. Each is torn in some different way between the traditional feminine needs—stability, the nurture of some fixed situation—and the compulsion to appear and move in the light. This light, the "lumière" of the title, is limelight, the world's attention, the regard not of one person or family but of a series of strangers. Lovers, an audience: for these actresses they are aspects of the same compulsion. "To dream on the stage and to take your audience with you," says Julienne, (Francine

The Cast

LUMIERE, written and directed by Jeanne Moreau; director of photography, Ricardo Aronovich; music by Astor Piazzola; edited by Albert Jurgenson; produced by Claire Duval. In French with English subtitles. Released by New World Pictures. At the Beekman Theater, 65th Street at Second Avenue. Running time: 95 minutes. This film has been rated R.

Sarah .... Jeanne Moreau
Julienne .... Francine Racette
Laura .... Lucia Bose
Caroline .... Caroline Cartier
Gregoire .... Francois Simon
Heinrich Grun .... Bruno Ganz
Thomas .... Francis Huster
Nano .... Niels Arestrup
David .... Keith Carradine
Saint-Loup .... Jacques Spiesser

Racette), one of the younger women.

It is Sarah who is most firmly in the light. Aging — Miss Moreau displays her sagging lines as if they were rewards given for beauty — she is at the height of her career, with a string of younger lovers Yet she clings to a loving friendship with Gregoire, an older man, a medical researcher who lives quietly and could, perhaps, have been her mate. "There is nothing I like so well as talking with you and being silent with you," she tells him. He is the stability she loves and cannot accept.

Laura has gone a different way. A successful Italian actress — played by Lucia Bose, she recalls Sophia Loren — she has married a rich man and thinks of herself mainly as a wife and mother. She has lost the "light" in favor of normality, and the loss gnaws at her strength and serenity.

Julienne is a young star, new to success. She seems feather-headed and flighty, but that is largely because she has only recently arrived from the other side. The other side is her estranged husband and child. When she goes to visit, her clothes and her demeanor suddenly recall the young matron she was on the point of becoming.

For Caroline, the youngest, the light is still a glimmer. She nibbles at it—dinner with a producer, the offer of a bit part without clothes —but is held back by the spoiled young man she lives with. They quarrel continually, but quarreling is a form of stability that she is not prepared to cut away from.

The film cuts from life to life. Sarah is discarding a petulant young film worker and acquiring a German writer. The reject is explosive, funny and futile; the writer—well-played by Bruno Ganz— is tentative and dreamy. Laura, staying with Sarah, is shaken by the discovery that her husband may leave her. Julienne is comically interviewed by a mawkish woman reporter who asks her about her feelings, and comically seduced by a young American film star.

Amid all this, Gregoire discovers he is dying of cancer. He goes to Sarah, possibly—it is only suggested—to ask some act of real if temporary commitment from her. But she is too distracted to give him a chance to talk; he swallows pills and dies quietly.

●

The movie's climax comes when Laura wakes Sarah with breakfast and word of Gregoire's suicide. "I must go there at once," Sarah says, and huddles in bed. "I should take a bath," she saiys, and then:

Francois Simon and Jeanne Moreau in "Lumiere"
The endless striving for the world's attention

"There is too much light." She dresses and goes—to work. We see her surrounded by technicians, posing, performing, using herself as a photographer uses his camera or a carpenter his tools.

At an age when life for most people is cherishing the living and burying the dead, Sarah remains fixed in her world of light. Miss Moreau neither praises the choice nor condemns it, but the achievement of "Lumière" 's extraordinarily moving finale is to make us see its rigor.

1976 N 15, 39:1

NETWORK, directed by Sidney Lumet; screenplay by Paddy Chayefsky; produced by Howard Gottfried; director of photography, Owen Roizman; editor, Alan Heim; music, Elliott Lawrence; a Metro-Goldwyn-Mayer presentation, distributed by United Artists. Running time: 120 minutes. At the Sutton Theater, 57th Street east of Third Avenue. This film has been rated R.
```
Diane Christensen ...................... Faye Dunaway
Max Schumacher ................ William Holden
Howard Beale ...................... Peter Finch
Frank Hackett .................... Robert Duvall
Nelson Chaney ................... Wesley Addy
Arthur Jensen .................... Ned Beatty
Great Ahmend Kahn .......... Arthur Burghardt
Bill Herron ..................... Darryl Hickman
Edward George Ruddy .......... William Prince
Helen Miggs ................. Sasha von Scherler
Louise Schumacher .......... Beatrice Straight
Laureen Hobbs ........... Marlene Warfield
```

By VINCENT CANBY

After a long and rewarding career with the UBS Television network as one of America's most respected news commentators, Howard Beale (Peter Finch) is being given the sack. Because his ratings have begun to slip and his show's share of the national audience is nil, this heir to the ideals of Edward R. Murrow has been found wanting. He's obsolete. The night after receiving the bad news, Howard signs off the air by urging his viewers to tune in to his final show next week. He will, he says cheerily, commit suicide on camera.

The next night, against the better judgment of his employers, Howard is allowed to go back on the air to apologize. Instead, he launches into a tirade full of ob-

scenities about the dreary quality of American life in general and corporate television's inhumanity in particular. More apoplexy in the UBS board room, but Howard Beale has just catapulted himself into a new career as television's biggest new star. He's also flipped, being certifiably insane.

"Network," written by Paddy Chayefsky and directed by Sidney Lumet, is about the fall, rise and fall of Howard Beale and about television's running horrendously and hilariously amok. It's about dangerous maneuvers in the executive suites and about old-fashioned newsmen like Max Schumacher (William Holden), who have scruples and are therefore impotent. It's also about Arab oil, conglomerates and new-fashioned hucksters like Diana Christensen (Faye Dunaway), a television executive whose sensitive reading of the viewing audience ("the American people are turning sullen") prompts her to put

a seeress on the 11 o'clock news (to predict what will happen tomorrow) and to promote the lunatic coming-apart of Howard Beale as America's most popular personality since Will Rogers.

"Network," which opened yesterday at the Sutton Theater, is, as its ads proclaim, outrageous. It's also brilliantly, cruelly funny, a topical American comedy that confirms Paddy Chayefsky's position as a major new American satirist. Paddy Chayefsky? Major? New? A satirist? Exactly.

Mr. Chayefsky, who made his name initially as television's poet of the small and everyday, has evolved through work like "The Latent Heterosexual" and "The Hospital" into one of our very very few, card-carrying satirists with access to the mass market.

His humor is not gentle or generous. It's about as stern and apocalyptic as it's possible to be without alienating the very audience for which it is intended.

Which leads me to wonder what it will mean when "Network" becomes—as I'm sure it will—a huge commercial hit with, one assumes, the same audiences whose tastes supposedly dictate the lunacies that Mr. Chayefsky describes in "Network." Could it be that Mr. Chayefsky has not carried his outrage far enough or that American audiences are so jaded that they will try anything once, say, "Network" or Russian roulette? I'm not sure.

●

I expect that a lot of people will sniff at the film on the ground that a number of the absurdities Mr. Chayefsky and Mr. Lumet chronicle so carefully couldn't happen, which is to miss the point of what they're up to. These wickedly distorted views of the way television looks, sounds and, indeed, is, are the satirist's cardiogram of the hidden heart, not just of television but also of the society that supports it and is, in turn, supported.

"Network" has soft moments. A scene in which the aging, philandering Mr. Holden finally walks out on Miss Dunaway, predicting emotional disaster for such a heartless creature, is of a dopey sentimentality that belongs to another movie, even though both characters are completely credible. Miss Dunaway, in particular, is successful in

making touching and funny a woman of psychopathic ambition and lack of feeling.

●

Robert Duvall, the superb Dr. Watson in "The Seven-Per-Cent Solution," is fine as the network hatchet man, subservient only to the head of the conglomerate that owns the network. This fellow, a folksy messiah beautifully played by Ned Beatty, is the mouthpiece for some of Mr. Chayefsky's bluntest thoughts about the current state of the wealth of nations.

"Network" can be faulted both for going too far and not far enough, but it's also something that very few commercial films are these days. It's alive. This, I suspect, is the Lumet drive. It's also the wit of performers like Mr. Finch, Mr. Holden and Miss Dunaway. As the crazy prophet within the film says of himself, "Network" is vivid and flashing. It's connected into life.

1976 N 15, 39:1

Elegant Mess

CARRIE, directed by Brian de Palma; written by Lawrence D. Cohen from a novel by Stephen King; produced b Paul Monash; edited by Paul Hirsch; music by Pino Donaggio. Released by United Artists. At the Criterion, Columbia I and Red Carpet Theaters. Running time: 98 minutes. This film has been rated R.
```
Carrie .................... Sissie Spacek
Margaret White .................... Piper Laurie
Tommy Ross .................... William Katt
Billy Nolan .................... John Travolta
Sue Snell .................... Amy Irving
Chris Hargenson .................... Nancy Allen
Miss Collins .................... Betty Buckley
```

By RICHARD EDER

CARRIE is an elegant box lunch that got dropped. The wine is all over the rolls. Caviar is embedded in the turkey, and there is lettuce in the mousse. It is a mess, with bits of salvage floating usefully around in it.

The newest film by Brian de Palma, who is often wrong but not dull, "Carrie" is billed as a horror movie. But it is sometimes funny in a puzzling kind of way, it is generally overwrought in an irritating kind of way, and once in a while it is inappropriately touching. It isn't frightening at all until the very end, and then it is briefly and extremely frightening.

Carrie—Sissy Spacek—is a Charles Addams-like teen-ager who lives with her mother in a Charles Addams-like house. The mother, played as a cracked belle by Piper Laurie, is a religious maniac. She hangs a picture of "The Last Supper" over the dining room table, and fills the house with candles and hysterical prayers.

Carrie turns out friendly but strange. Her schoolmates loathe her strangeness. When she menstruates for the first time in the locker room and becomes hysterical—the only advice she gets from her mother is that menstruation is a sign of sexual impurity—the other girls shriek and mock her and pelt her with Tampax. They turn hysteria into something close to an epileptic seizure.

In the process, however, Carrie discovers that, by concentrating, she can break ashtrays, make people fall off bicycles and worse. It's telekinesis, the movie explains.

Well, this changes things. In a pretty funny scene, Carrie tells her mother, who had been shutting her in closets and tries to stop her from going to the prom, that she's in charge now. To underline the point, she makes all the windows in the house bang shut.

Peter Finch in "Network"
Confirms Paddy Chayesky's position as a major American satirist.

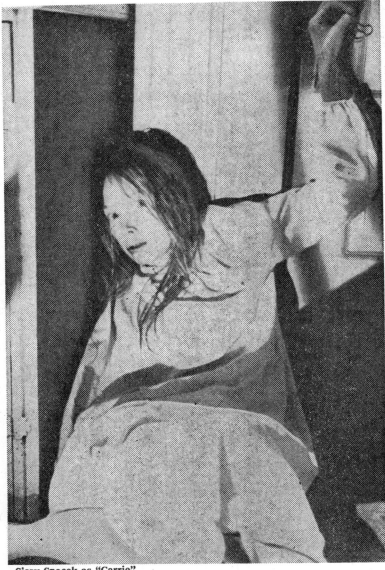

Sissy Spacek as "Carrie"

20's and 30's, Irving Thalberg could. Thalberg, the production chief at M-G-M, a "boy genius" until his death at the age of 37 in 1936, appeared to be able to divine successful films as mysteriously as other people found water with a forked stick of witch hazel.

The equation he held in his head told him how much a certain kind of picture would gross, which, in turn, told him how much could be profitably spent on its production. He knew whose brains to rent. The capacities of directors, writers and actors were as apparent to him as labeled contents. He could cut four minutes from a dreary 100-minute movies in such a way to make it seem a single, breathless experience of 60 minutes. In those days, movies — pictures — didn't waste time getting to points.

Thalberg was responsible for good films and bad. Though his genius was made possible by the period, when Hollywood and its public were one, he was regarded with awe, as if he possessed not simply a knack for pictures but the secret of life.

All of these things are contained in the muted and thoughtful, sad but unsentimental film version of "The Last Tycoon" about Fitzgerald's Thalberg-like hero named Monroe Stahr. Written by Harold Pinter, and directed by Elia Kazan, the movie attempts to take Hollywood seriously, without hoopla and grotesqueries, and especially to take Thalberg-Stahr seriously.

Fitzgerald didn't live to finish "The Last Tycoon," so that the version published in 1941, edited by Edmund Wilson with Fitzgerald's notes, is technically a fragment, yet it's a very complete satisfying fragment, a quality that the film preserves through an abrupt kind of editing style and a narrative that's without conventional shape.

Thalberg died before being overtaken by defeat. In the film, Monroe Stahr does not. Stahr, who is played with reticent passion by Robert De Niro, whose lean, dark good looks seem an idealization of Thalberg's, becomes a casualty of the "new" Hollywood of Wall Street investors, bankers and union organizers that Fitzgerald could see in the future.

"The Last Tycoon," which opened opened yesterday at the Cinema I, is a very low-key movie, and so full of associations—to Thalberg, to the stories one knows of Hollywood in the 30's, to Fitzgerald's own life and career—that it's difficult to differentiate between what one is seeing on the screen and what one is bringing to it.

"The Last Tycoon" doesn't really build to any climax. We follow it horizontally, as if it were a landscape being surveyed by a camera in a long pan-shot. The background is Hollywood in the Golden Thirties, when studios turned out 30 to 40 pictures a year and every backlot could simultaneously contain pictures set in New York, Africa, the South pole and Montmartre.

In the foreground are scenes from the curious life of Monroe Stahr as he edits several films at once, deals with neurotic actors and directors, maneuvers in corporate battles, and carries on an affair with a mysterious English girl whom he loves and loses.

In one of his final notes for "The Last Tycoon," Fitzgerald wrote in capital letters, "Action Is Character." It is one of the achievements of Messrs. Kazan, Pinter and De Niro that so much of Monroe Stahr succeeds in coming through in the film. Other characters that are so vivid in the book simply don't have enough time on screen, though both Robert Mitchum—as Stahr's studio adversary—and Jack Nich-

The prom is a trick, however. Carrie's classmates have been punished for harassing her; to get even, they make a grisly plan whereby she—the wallflower—is taken to the prom by the class football star, elected beauty queen and then doused in pigs' blood. Her reprisals, via telekinesis, are as violent and devastating as an air raid. And there is one final bit—the movie's one real fright—when she gets even with one of the girls who instigated the prom trick.

Until this last bit, our reactions are in a constant state of short-circuitry. Mr. de Palma is our only Pre-Raphaelite director. His apocalyptic scenes, bloody as they theoretically are, too mannered and elegantly draped to be scary. It's Burne-Jones illustrating Dracula, and the result hovers between being ridiculous and making us smile because it is ridiculous.

Mr. de Palma has ordered universal overacting. Piper Laurie does it with considerable grace—the wicked witch in a children's pantomime. The marvel, though, is Sissy Spacek. She makes us perfectly aware that she is overacting, and yet she is very effective. Her hysteria is far too hysterical. Her delight in being taken to the prom is far too radiant. But it moves us; and, in truth, the main horror in Carrie isn't the real bloodshed but our apprehension that

her pleasure as well as her dress will be ruined by that bucket of pig blood.

"Carrie" opened yesterday at the Criterion and other theaters.

1976 N 17, C24:1

THE LAST TYCOON, directed by Elia Kazan; screenplay by Harold Pinter, based on the novel by F. Scott Fitzgerald; produced by Sam Spiegel; director of photography, Victor Kemper; music, Maurice Jarre; editor, Richard Marks; distributed by Paramount Pictures. Running time 125 minutes. At the Cinema I Theater, Third Avenue near 60th Street. This film has been rated PG.

Monroe Stahr	Robert De Niro
Rodriguez	Tony Curtis
Pat Brady	Robert Mitchum
Didi	Jeanne Moreau
Brimmer	Jack Nicholson
Boxley	Donald Pleasence
Kathleen Moore	Ingrid Boulting
Fleishacker	Ray Milland
Red Ridingwood	Dana Andrews
Cecilia Brady	Theresa Russell
Wylie	Peter Strauss
Popolos	Tise Andrews
Marcus	Morgan Farley
Guide	John Carradine
Doctor	Jeff Corey
Stahr's secretary	Diane Shalet
Seal trainer	Seymour Cassell
Edna	Angelica Huston

By VINCENT CANBY

"Not half a dozen men have been able to keep the whole equation of pictures in their heads," says the narrator of F. Scott Fitzgerald's "The Last Tycoon."

For a brief period in the late

Ingrid Boulting and Robert De Niro
Hollywood without hoopla

olson — as the union organizer — are extremely effective. Jeanne Moreau and Tony Curtis make brief, flashy appearances as idols of the old-time silver screen.

•

Ingrid Boulting, who plays Stahr's mysterious English love, is beautiful in an eccentrically large-eyed way, and there are times when she doesn't seem to know how to read a line or where to put her hands. At other moments she is totally, serenely sure of herself, which may or may not be acting but does suggest the odd quality that drew Stahr to her. I also liked another new actress, Theresa Russell, who plays the Hollywood-born, Bennington - educated girl

who narrates the novel but is simply a supporting character in the film.

None of the changes that Mr. Pinter has made in the novel seem to me to damage the style or mood of the book. More than any other screen adaptation of a Fitzgerald work—with the exception of Joan Micklin Silver's fine adaptation of the short story "Bernice Bobs Her Hair"—"The Last Tycoon" preserves original feeling and intelligence. The movie is full of echoes. We watch it as if at a far remove from what's happening, but that too is appropriate: Fitzgerald was writing history as it happened.

1976 N 18, 59:1

Screen: James Dean Dimly Seen

"He remains as relevant today as 20 years ago," says the portentous narrator at the end of "James Dean—The First American Teenager." These patchwork sequences from Dean's three movies and interviews with acquaintances make no case for his relevance, then or now.

If anything, the film excerpts from "East of Eden," "Rebel Without a Cause" and "Giant" leave one to wonder what the fuss was about. The aura

has left the image, and only the pout remains.

The interviews amount to a number of people saying that actually they didn't know him all that well. Among the unrevealing reminiscences are contributions from Carroll Baker, Natalie Wood, Sammy Davis Jr., Dennis Hopper and an unwell-looking Nicholas Ray. "James Dean" opened yesterday at the RKO 59th Street Theater; but why?

RICHARD EDER

1976 N 19, C10:5

FILM VIEW

VINCENT CANBY

Cynical Cinema Is Chic

In an early sequence in Paddy Chayefsky's savagely funny new film, "Network," Faye Dunaway, playing a high-priestess of television, an executive whose job it is to know what the public will take, announces with authority, "The American people are turning sullen." The members of her staff make dutiful notes as she continues in the self-assured manner of someone used to dealing with people in batches of no less than 10-million each. "I want angry shows," she says, "I want counter-culture."

The character goes on to score two of the biggest coups of the new television season by developing (1) a weekly dramatic series based on the adventures of the Ecumenical Liberation Army, a small group of nuts who hold-up banks and kidnap heiresses, and (2) a nightly news show that features the muddled monologues of a certifiable lunatic and news reports by a fortune teller. (The reasoning being that we already know what happened today.)

The cheapjack cynicism that Chayefsky and Sidney Lumet, the director, send up with such high spirits in "Network" is scarcely a failing exclusive to television. It's always been a part of show biz, and television, including television news reporting as we've all watched it evolve, is as much show biz as the medicine show, burlesque, the circus and movies. Such cynicism is now almost the entire point of what virtually amounts to a whole new subcategory of con-

temporary suspense melodrama—the film that deals with a dread, unnamed and unnameable conspiracy of such magnitude that the film's hero-victim goes through the picture like someone who has awakened to find himself in a public place without his pants. It's a bad dream but it's all true. If these films expressed any thoughts or feelings, or if they prompted serious examination of the human condition, one might risk calling them Kafka-esque. Since they don't, they seem merely to be an expression of a new-fashioned pessimism. Some notable examples:

● "The Next Man," an elaborately produced and ludicrously plotted film in which Sean Connery plays the Saudi Arabian minister of state who proposes to sign a mutual assistance pact with Israel and to sell Saudi oil and petroleum by-products to needy nations at cost, thus to free those nations from the East-West conflict, and thus marking himself for assassination by American oil interests, Russian political interests, Middle-East oil interests and Palestinian fanatics. We never really know who has the inside track, only that the track is occupied by a gorgeous young woman, played by Cornelia Sharpe, described as a Bryn Mawr grad and shown to be an accomplished assassin.

● "Marathon Man," a film that is beautifully acted (by Dustin Hoffman and Laurence Olivier) and directed (by John Schlesinger) and seems to be about a conspiracy of some unnamed super-Washington agency to get a load of diamonds collected over the years by a Nazi war criminal living in South America. That's only a guess. Though the film is effectively scary, it never makes the remotest sense.

● "Three Days of The Condor," in which Robert Redford plays a nice, bookish CIA researcher who becomes the target of a Washington agency even more ruthless and high-handed than the CIA. Like Hoffman in "Marathon Man," Redford must run for his life, never really knowing why.

● "Illustrious Corpses." Francesco Rosi's Italian film that was shown at this year's New York Film Festival, about a hard-working police inspector (Lino Ventura) who, in the course of an investigation into the murders of three judges, uncovers a top-level government conspiracy involving everyone except, apparently, Lino and the local Communist Party chief. The point of the conspiracy is never revealed.

● "The Parallax View," based on the idea that somewhere in this country there is a large, efficiently run corporation, complete with trainees and keys to the executive washroom, devoted to the training and promotion of assassins available to anyone with the right price. The conspiracy in this film is not all that mysterious. It's simply to make money through political murder.

None of these films, taken separately, is especially worrisome. Yet considered together, they demonstrate the extent to which the political events in this country in the sixties, for which Watergate was the grand finale, have shaped hopelessness as a perfectably acceptable, popular attitude. When I say hopelessness I don't mean anything as tough and positive as a tragic sense, or even reasoned despair. Just light-hearted, lazy hopelessness. The shrugged shoulder. The street corner sage who avoids thinking, avoids making judgments or any commitments by saying that everybody's crooked, so what's the use?

Unlike "All The President's Men," which, of course, was about an investigation into a real conspiracy, and which movingly depicted the triumph of right over might, these films, with perhaps one exception, depict the exact opposite. Total failure. Death. The triumph of the princes of darkness who, more often than not, are plain-clothed civil servants. It's curious that a public that has witnessed the disgrace of a United States President is so willing to believe—if these films are an accurate indicator—that such fanciful conspiracies are so easily successful and will go undetected. Do we want to accept that? Or are they demonstrations of a kind of collective paranoia, systematized delusions, expressions of all sorts of personal conflicts disguised and projected onto Big Government, which then acts out those terrible desires we can't recognize in ourselves?

Movies like "The Next Man," "Marathon Man" and "Three Days of The Condor" package doom in carry-home cartons. It's not only portable, it's fun. And if it's impossible to find out who's doing what to whom or why, there's no reason to try to correct the situation. Relax. Have a beer. The most we can hope for is to have some excitement before meeting a violent, utterly meaningless end.

1976 N 21, II:13:1

Ringside Story

ROCKY, directed by John G. Avildsen; screenplay by Sylvester Stallone; produced by Irwin Winkler and Robert Chartoff; executive producer, Gene Kirkwood; director of photography, James Crabe; editor, Richard Halsey; music, Bill Conti; distributed by United Artists. Running time: 121 minutes. At the Cinema II Theater, Third Avenue near 60th Street. This film has been rated PG.

Rocky	Sylvester Stallone
Adrian	Talia Shire
Paulie	Burt Young
Apollo	Carl Weathers
Mickey	Burgess Meredith
Jergens	Thayer David
Gazzo	Joe Spinell
Mike	Jimmy Gambina

By VINCENT CANBY

NOT SINCE "The Great Gatsby" two years ago has any film come into town more absurdly oversold than "Rocky," the sentimental little slum movie that opened yesterday at the Cinema II. As a former head of Paramount Pictures said to me with some irritation at the time "Gatsby" came out, movies shouldn't be penalized for being effectively promoted. That's true. Yet the sort of highpowered publicity (most of it free, it seems) that's been attending the birth of "Rocky" must, in turn, subject the movie to impossible expectations that can boomerang. Be warned.

Sylvester Stallone, who had a role in "The Lords of Flatbush," another "sleeper" that never quite measured up as a hit, both wrote the original screenplay and plays the title role. Rocky is a young man who, by day, is a small-time Mafia collector, the sort of fellow who shows his heart of gold by hesitating to break a client's thumbs, and at night pursues a third-rate boxing career in fleabag sporting arenas.

Under the none too decisive direction of John G. Avildsen ("Joe," "Save the Tiger"), Mr. Stallone is all over "Rocky" to such an extent it begins to look like a vanity production. His brother composed one of the film's songs and appears briefly, as does his father, while his dog, a cheerful mastiff named Butkus, plays Rocky's dog. It's as if Mr. Stallone had studied the careers of Martin Scorsese and Francis Ford Coppola and then set out to copy the wrong things.

The screenplay of "Rocky" is purest Hollywood make-believe of the 1930's, but there would be nothing wrong with that, had the film been executed with any verve.

It's the story of Rocky and his girl-friend Adrian (Talia Shire) when Rocky, due to circumstances too foolish to go into, is granted the opportunity of his lifetime. He is given a chance to fight the heavyweight champion of the world, a black fighter named Apollo Creed (Carl Weathers), modeled on Muhammad Ali so superficially as to be an almost criminal waste of character. It's not good enough to be libelous, though by making the Ali-like fighter such a dope, the film explores areas of latent racism that just may not be all that latent.

That Mr. Weathers is no actor doesn't help things, though there are some very good actors in other supporting roles, and they don't help in any significant way. Burt Young is effective as Rocky's best friend, a beer-guzzling mug, as is Burgess Meredith as Rocky's ancient trainer.

The person who comes off best is Miss Shire, Mr. Coppola's sister who made brief, effective appearances in the two "Godfather" films. She's a real actress, genuinely touching and funny

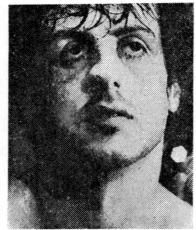
Sylvester Stallone as Rocky

as an incipient spinster who comes late to sexual life. She's so good, in fact, that she almost gives weight to Mr. Stallone's performance, which is the large hole in the center of the film.

Mr. Stallone's Rocky is less a performance than an impersonation. It's all superficial mannerisms and movements, reminding me of Rodney Dangerfield doing a nightclub monologue. The speech patterns sound right, and what he says is occasionally lifelike, but it's a studied routine, not a character.

It's the sort of performance that could have been put together by watching other actors on television. Most of the film was photographed on location in seedy, Philadelphia neighborhoods, and it's one of the film's ironies that a production that has put such emphasis on realism should seem so fraudulent.

The problem, I think, comes back to Mr. Stallone. Throughout the movie we are asked to believe that his Rocky is compassionate, interesting, even heroic, though the character we see is simply an unconvincing actor imitating a lug.

"Rocky," which has been rated PG ("parental guidance suggested"), contains some barroom language and a climactic boxing match that is effectively brutal.

1976 N 22, C19:1

SHOUT AT THE DEVIL, directed by Peter Hunt; screenplay by Wilbour Smith, Alistair Reid and Stanley Price, from the novel by Mr. Smith, music by Maurice Jarre; editor, Michael Duthie; produced by Michael Klinger; released by American International Pictures. At neighborhood theaters. Running time: 128 minutes. This film has been rated PG.

Flynn	Lee Marvin
Sebastian	Roger Moore
Rosa	Barbara Parkins
Fleischer	Rene Kolldehoff
Mohammed	Ian Holm
Von Kleine	Karl Michael Vogler
Kyller	Horst Janson
Braun	Gernoi Endemann

By RICHARD EDER

At the start of "Shout at the Devil" the viewers, who are about to see a lot of elephant hunting, are told that "not a single animal was injured." The collapsing beasts were shot with stupefying darts.

The audience at "Shout," an adventure film that opened yesterday at showcase theaters, is treated with similar humaneness. No injuries, a thorough use of stupefying darts and some mild entertainment. There are about 60 minutes of mild entertainment, along with a few first-rate effects, in a film that

is an incredible 128 minutes long.

The movie is set in East Africa—although, in fact, it was shot in South Africa—just before and during World War I. It is divided into fairly distinct parts. In the first, we follow the adventures of Flynn (Lee Marvin), an alcoholic ivory poacher who lives on a plantation in Mozambique with his daughter, Rosa (Barbara Parkins), and does his ivory hunting across the border in Tanganyika, then held by the Germans.

Flynn, joined by an expatriate Englishman, Sebastian, has some rough encounters with the local German district commissioner, Fleischer, who likes to shoot and hang people. In between sorties, Sebastian marries Rosa after a protracted and mock-comic fistfight with her father.

In the second part, war is declared and Fleischer crosses the border, sets fire to Flynn's house, and kills Sebastian and Rosa's baby. This turns Rosa into a woman with the single obsession of killing Fleischer; meanwhile the three are sent by the British Navy to scout out a German battle-cruiser hidden up a river, and then to blow it up. These things are eventually accomplished.

The movie has too much plot. All that action, conducted by characters without character—except for Fleischer, whose childlike joy in hurting people is almost appealing—produces lethargy. Roger Moore is rather good as Sebastian, a muted Errol Flynn type, but Miss Parkins plays her part with the verve of a damp rope. And Lee Marvin, who does toughness well enough, is insufferable when he is trying to be the comic Irishman. His doubletakes come like delayed mail.

All this said, the movie has its compensations. Rene Kolldehoff, as Fleischer, manages to be entertaining in his exaggerated villainy, and there is a lovely slow chase when, in an ancient paddle-boat steamer, he pursues Marvin, in a sailing dhow, down a winding jungle river. There is a good head-on charge by a crocodile, and the blowing-up of the warship has moments of interest and excitement. The movie is a passable midget in absurdly long pants.

"Shout" has been rated PG ("Parental Guidance Suggested"). There are some fairly graphic scenes of natives being shot, and one that depicts, although we don't actually see it, a baby being thrown into a fire. Nevertheless, the film seems suitable for all but very young children.

1976 N 25, 38:1

A PROGRAM OF SHORT FILMS BY WERNER HERZOG: "Precautions Against Fanatics" (12 minutes), "Last Words" (12 minutes), "The Great Ecstasy of the Sculptor Steiner" (45 minutes), plus "Introduction to an Accompaniment to a Cinematic Scene by Arnold Schoenberg" (15 minutes) by Jean-Marie Staub. All distributed by New Yorker Films. Total running time: 84 minutes. At the Film Forum, 15 Vandam Street.

By VINCENT CANBY

ONE OF THE MOST BEAUTIFUL, moving and exhilarating films available in New York this weekend and next is most cer-

Werner Herzog
Film maker with an instinctive passion

tainly Werner Herzog's "The Great Ecstasy of the Sculptor Steiner," a 45-minute documentary on Walter Steiner, the champion German ski jumper who describes what he does as ski-flying, which it is.

The film occupies the major part of the current program at the Film Forum, 15 Vandam Street, where it may be seen tonight through Sunday evening at 7:30, and at the same time next week, Thursday through Sunday. Making up the rest of the program are two other shorts by Mr. Herzog, "Precautions Against Fanatics" and "Last Words" (each 12 minutes) and Jean-Marie Straub's "Introduction to an Accompaniment to a Cinematic Scene by Arnold Schoenberg" (15 minutes), which was first shown at the 1975 New York Film Festival with Mr. Straub's screen adaptation of Schoenberg's "Moses and Aaron."

On the evidence of such feature films as "Signs of Life," "Even Dwarfs Started Small" and "Every Man for Himself and God Against All" (titled "The Mystery of Kaspar Hauser" for its commercial release here), Werner Herzog is one of West Germany's most vital young film makers. Yet as original as those films have been, they've also suffered from acute over-intellectualism, a disease that has denatured so many young European film makers. Ideas are all very well and good, but a film maker who doesn't also have an instinctive passion, something not quite understood or predictable, might as successfully write textbooks. "The Great Ecstasy of the Sculptor Steiner," made in 1974, reveals for the first time that passion in Mr. Herzog, and in so doing it becomes a kind of key to the three feature films that have already been seen here. Mr. Steiner, who sculpts wood part-time and most of the time is obsessed by ski jumping, is a real-life Herzog hero, a fellow whose particular circumstances set him apart from everyone else.

Most of Mr. Herzog's heroes appear to have been gifted by being deprived of something—normal height or intelligence, for example—the rest of us take for granted. Mr. Steiner is deprived of an ordinary man's peace of mind by being possessed by his talent, the demonstrations of which in this film are as spectacular as anything I've seen on the screen.

"The Great Ecstasy of the Sculptor Steiner" has the shape and manner of a sport film as it records the preparations that Mr. Steiner makes for a competition in Yugoslavia, and then records the competition itself. The things that separate it from other films are the personality of the ski jumper himself and Mr. Herzog's extraordinary slow-motion footage of the ski jumper at work. You have the feeling that on any one of these jumps, Mr. Steiner is going to take off and never again set foot on earth. At least, not alive.

⚫

As a ski jumper, Mr. Setiner is an artist, and though specific jumps can be measured, those measurements have as little to do with his art as do the measurements of a painter's canvas. "The Great Ecstasy of the Sculptor Steiner" is, like "Edvard Munch," really concerned with the mystery of the creative impulse.

The two other Herzog shorts on the Film Forum program are the kind of avant-garde practice films that look as if they had been made for the principal appreciation of the film maker's friends and associates.

1976 N 26, C4:5

FILM VIEW

VINCENT CANBY

'A Surreal Attack on American Life'

Several years ago Patricia Hearst was removed from her apartment against her will and some months later convicted of a bank-robbery that —everyone seems to agree— she would never have participated in if she hadn't been kidnapped in the first place. People who get mugged in the park shouldn't have been walking there. They were asking for it. So do rape victims—everyone knows that. At one time or another in their history, all religions have managed to suggest that the successful man has been smiled upon by God, meaning, of course, that the poor wretch with nine children, no income and a terminal disease is being suitably punished. Sometimes it's called the Protestant ethic: Victims are guilty. Lewis Carroll put it this way:

"Speak roughly to your little boy,
And beat him when he sneezes;
He only does it to annoy,
Because he knows it teases."

When the kid gets a cold, give him a swat—it's his own fault. The Freudians have tried to persuade us that guilty persons are themselves victims but that concept doesn't have the force of time's momentum behind it. Also it involves a lot of hair-splitting. That victims are guilty in some fashion allows us to be righteously stingy with our money, our intelligence and our feelings.

⚫　⚫　⚫

When a film comes along that neither defers to Freud nor subscribes to the idea that victims are guilty, it tends to make us uncomfortable. Every movie should have buried within it somewhere a neat little lodestone that will give us our directions. If not we become disoriented. There's no lodestone in Paddy Chayefsky's "Network," a satiric send-up of commercial television that contains only one decent, upstanding honorable, moral fellow of recognizable strength in the cast of characters—that is, Chayefsky, who doesn't appear on the screen at all but is the dominant presence in the film.

In "Network," Chayefsky, who made a name for himself and a good deal of money (I assume) writing for television in the fifties, takes a long, hilariously jaundiced look at contemporary TV and finds it to be a nightmare and, by inference, the public that supports it (and is supported by it) to be composed of ghouls. He also takes sideswipes at conventional conceptions of capitalism as practiced by conglomerates, the ethics of power and, for good measure, the power of Arab oil.

There are some soft moments in "Network" but it is, most of the time, a non-stop, surreal attack on the quality of American life in the form of a mad tale of one TV network and the way it goes berserk in its search for ratings and audience shares. Though Sidney Lumet has directed it as if we were there and it was happening now, "Network" is not meant to be realistic, a movie-a-clé. It's a rollercoaster ride through Chayefsky's fantasies as he imagines what television might do if given the opportunity.

⚫　⚫　⚫

I can understand people simply not finding this sort of thing as funny as I do. It's a bit masochistic, like sitting on the stern of the Titanic and giggling all the way until you finally slide under the water. But to be morally outraged by Chayefsky's moral outrage, on the grounds that Chayefsky (1) offers no solutions, (2) finds no redeeming factors, or (3) sets himself up as judge and jury, seems to me to be missing the point of satire, which is to be as sweepingly stern as an Old Testament prophet, intelligently concerned and bitterly comic. Satirists have no obligation to be fair to the enemy, or especially accurate.

For that matter no fiction is under any obligation to be fair and accurate in the way that journalism should be. If someone comes along and makes a film supposedly set in New York City where all the citizens are orangutangs, no one, I trust, would have to say that the movie doesn't work because New York City is, observably, not inhabited by orangutangs. If that's the way the filmmaker sees New York City—the way he feels about it—that's enough. We either leave it or make an effort to understand what he's saying.

Satire of any heft is in such short supply in this country that we can't afford to turn it aside lightly. Until the appearance of "Network" this year the sum total of American satire in films and television would have been "Mary Hartman, Mary Hartman" and perhaps a few kindly sketches on "The Carol Burnett Show," and both of those programs deal less in satire than in parody, which ultimately has the effect of certifying the thing being parodied. The satirist is angry. He wants to destroy. The only things that "Mary Hartman" and "Carol Burnett" want to destroy are the opposing shows in the same time slots.

⚫　⚫　⚫

When "The Hospital" came out several years ago I remember being surprised that Chayefsky, whose best television plays ("Marty," "The Catered Affair" and "The Bachelor Party," all made into films) deal with life in ways one accepted to be realistic, could have had such a successful flight of fancy. Yet now it's apparent that Chayefsky's satires succeed not in spite of his talent for accurate observation but because of it. What is new in "The Hospital" and "Network" is not the Chayefsky ear for dialogue and eye for visual detail, but the courage that he exhibits in taking the ordinary and, with a few turns of agile mind, stretches it into the fantastic. One of the pleasures of "Network" is watching Chayefsky's imagination go through the roof as he questions not only television but the entire American system.

Though "Network" specifically aims at a couple of TV program executives and network officers, the buck never stops anywhere. Is the public's wantonness responsible for the desperate acts of the network people? Should the network people resist the economic pressures put on them? Chayefsky doesn't say exactly. If Chayefsky clearly laid these things out I'm sure that "Network" wouldn't be as funny and important as it is. It would be reassuring if we could piously blame TV's ills on a few isolated people. It might also be the same as blaming Patty Hearst for having had the poor form to allow herself to be kidnapped.

1976 N 28, II:17:6

BIM, directed and produced by Hugh A. Robertson; screenplay by Raoul Pantin; director of photography, Bruce Sparks; music, Andre Tanker; editor, Paul L. Evans; distributed by Dennis Bryant. Runnng time: 103 minutes. At the Quad Theater, 13th Street west of Fifith Avenue. This film has not been rated.
Bim (adult) .... Ralph Maharaj
Bim (child) .... Anand Maharaj
Captain .... Hamilton Parris
Whabam .... Wilbert Holder
Jalwat .... Joseph Gilbert
Baba Charlie .... William Harrypaulsingh
Police Commissioner .... Laurie Goldstraw
Governor .... Vernon Lloyd
Father .... Dennis Mahabir
Black politician .... Errol Jones
Constable Joseph .... Neville Delabastide
Commissioner's wife .... Anne Hilton

By VINCENT CANBY

By no conventional standards is "Bim" very good, but it's still vastly more interesting than lots of other movies you're likely to stumble on.

The film, which opened yesterday at the Quad Cinema, is an ambitious attempt by its director-producer, Hugh A. Robertson, to dramatize some aspects of life in Trinidad shortly before the island gained independence.

Mr. Robertson, an American director ("Melinda"), worked with a largely Trinidadian crew and an entirely Trinidadian cast to shape a film that is intended primarily to speak to Trinidadians and to other Caribbean people, and only incidentally to others, who, when they watch it, are in the position of eavesdroppers.

●

The film spins a long, rambling tale that is almost Dickensian in its dependence on coincidences and in its habit of jumping from one narrative climax to the next without fooling around with structural niceties. It's the story of Bim (Ralph Maharaj), a young Trinidadian of East Indian descent whose father was the autocratic leader of the sugar workers union.

After his father is murdered by rivals, Bim is sent off to live in Port of Spain, where he experiences the prejudice of black Trinidadians for the first time and turns to a life of petty crime. Eventually, in about five minutes of film time, Bim succeeds his father as a union power. It becomes something of an anti-climax after all this, then, when Bim's undoing results not from crime, politics, ambition, black rivalries or independence. Once he gets to the top, Bim starts to drink, neither well nor wisely.

●

Too much technology goes into the production of a film for it ever to qualify as truly primitive. There is no movie equivalent to finger-painting, but "Bim" comes close.

Its power is not the result of sophisticated choice, but in the accumulation of the raw, accurate details of the Trinidadian experience. The actors are overwrought, the continuity is dim and a lot of the dialogue unintelligible to an ear not accustomed to West Indian speech rhythms. Yet it's not dull, and it regards Trinidad's racial problems and political aspirations in a way that is unsentimental to the point of being merciless.

1976 D 2, 57:1

LOVE COMES QUIETLY, directed by Nikolai van der Heyde; screenplay (in English and in Dutch with English subtitles) by Mr. van der Heyde; produced by Henk Bos and Andre Thomas; director of photography, Jorgen Persson; editor, Gust Verschueren; music, Georges Delerue; distributed by Libert Films International. Running time: 103 minutes. At the RKO 59th Street Twin 2 Theater, 59th Street east of Third Avenue. This film has been rated R.

Angela .... Barbara Hershey
Harm Wouter .... Sandy van der Linder
Ben .... Ralph Meeker
Menno Dijkstra .... Ward de Ravet
Louise .... Kitty Janssen

"Love Comes Quietly" is a movie that. sets great store by feeling instead of thinking, by hopping boxcars barefoot, by walking in the rain, by skinny-dipping and by having absolutely no sense of humor, fun, beauty or poetry it can call its own. Everything in it is borrowed or stolen.

The Dutch film, which opened yesterday at the RKO 59th Street Twin 2, is set in the Netherlands in the mid-20's and is mostly about the tentative love affair between a repressed young Dutchman, played by Sandy van der Linden, and a carefree, extremely pregnant young American woman, played by Barbara Hershey, who attempt to run away from society only to be destroyed by it.

This is a third-rate retread of "Elvira Madigan" with a dollup of "Easy Rider" pasted on. The Frisian countryside is pretty enough, but no place to get a rest if bird-chirping gets on your nerves.

VINCENT CANBY

1976 D 2, 57:3

SERAIL (Surreal), directed by Eduardo de Gregorio; screenplay (French with English subtitles) by Mr. Gregorio and Michael Graham; photography, Ricardo Aronovich; editor Alberto Yaccelini; music, Michal Portal; production companies, Filmoblic/Openfilm/Institut National de l'Audiovisual/Lusofrance; presented by Irwin Meyer, Stephen R. Friedman and Peter Crane; a Caribou Films release. At the Fine Arts Theater, 58th Street between Park and Lexington Avenues. Running time: 90 minutes. This film is rated R.
Celeste .... Leslie Caron
Ariane .... Bulle Ogier
Agathe .... Marie-France Pisier
Eric .... Corin Redgrave

"Sérail" was shown at the last New York Film Festival. The following is Richard Eder's review, which appeared Oct. 8. The film begins today at the Fine Arts Theater.

There are a number of good names involved in "Sérail" but the movie doesn't so much use them as drop them.

Eduardo de Gregorio, who has done a number of screenplays for Jacques Rivette, and who wrote Bernardo Bertolucci's "The Spider's Strategem," makes his debut as a director with "Sérail," and was one of the screenwriters. He uses two of Europe's best young actresses, Bulle Ogier and Marie-France Pisier. And nothing much happens beyond a certain stylish sifting. You can't make an omelette without lighting a fire.

"Sérail" is a hazy story about an English writer who buys a big old French country house and acquires, in the bargain, two strange and beautiful residents—Misses Ogier and Pisier—and a strange and sinister housekeeper, played by Leslie Caron.

Some of them are ghosts, and it isn't clear which. They undo him thoroughly by the time the film is over and it isn't clear how. Nor do we particularly care. None of the characters are interesting in any way except in terms of their plight; and since we aren't told just what the plight is, there's not much point.

1976 D 4, 17:1

The Unscariest Horror Film

In his new film, "Carrie," a self-styled horror movie, Brian De Palma is having his revenge on a public that hasn't, until now, sufficiently appreciated him by making a lot of us critics look as if we'd become totally unhinged. I don't believe critics are all-powerful, but when we become light-headed, audiences get the hangovers. De Palma has dazzled one of my colleagues to the point of describing "Carrie" as "trash" in admiration, not meaning to call it rubbish. In an effort to pin down qualities the film may or may not have, critics have made associations between "Carrie" and more than two dozen other films, including "Jaws," "The Wizard of Oz," "The Exorcist," "Alice Adams," "The Last Laugh," "Psycho," "Marathon Man," "Taxi Driver," "Splendor in The Grass," "Zabriskie Point," "Great Expectations," "American Graffiti," as well as De Palma's own earlier films, "Greetings," "Hi, Mom," "Get To Know Your Rabbit," "Sisters," "The Phantom of The Paradise" and "Obsession." To my knowledge no one has yet brought up Ray's Apu Trilogy.

Because of an accident of fate and a collision of time schedules I was not able to see "Carrie" until after it had opened and the first reviews had appeared, allowing me the rather rare privilege of seeing an important film under circumstances more or less comparable to those faced by the paying public. Ordinarily when a film opens I've already seen it and written my review and thus I don't bother reading the others. It's too easy to get hung up debating colleagues. This time, however, I hadn't seen the film and because I've long been a De Palma admirer I was interested in what had been written. Should I rush to the theater or take my time? The reviews indicated I should rush, although the associations to all of those other films made me feel that perhaps I might be inadequate. I mean, I simply don't remember "Splendor in The Grass" all that well, and if I don't, won't I be missing something? No.

●　　●　　●

In "Carrie," De Palma, whose first films were marvelously free-form comedies about con-artistry, has adopted the practice himself. "Carrie" is a supremely silly movie about nothing at all that's been so cannily and stylishly constructed that to object to it seriously is to risk banishment to what passes for Siberia in New York's private screening rooms—the first row where images on the screen look like Pointillist billboards. I think I now admire De Palma more than ever, if only because I believe he's getting away with murder . . . not much of it on screen.

"Carrie" may be the most benignly unscary horror film ever made. It's a teeny-tiny screenplay about a sweetly repressed high school girl named Carrie (Sissy Spacek) who has somehow managed to reach the late age of 16 without picking up one fact of life that would prepare her for her first menstrual period, which occurs one afternoon after gym in the school shower room. Carrie is horrified. She believes she's bleeding to death. The other girls, who've always thought her to be a bit of a dope, turn on her hysterically, battering her with Tampaxes, which all of them carry in limitless supply.

In her humiliation Carrie discovers her power—telekinesis, the ability to move or change objects by simple concentration. She first makes an ash tray fall off a desk, almost as if she were doodling, but she discovers the practical uses of the power when her mother, a religious freak played by Piper Laurie, attempts to prevent her from attending the senior prom. "They'll laugh at you," her mother sneers. Carrie thinks a moment. The doors and windows of their little house suddenly bang shut, and Carrie announces, "I'm in charge now."

The problem is that her nutty mom is absolutely right. When Carrie goes to the prom, the students have prepared an elaborate joke: Carrie is elected prom queen as a hoax and at the moment of her triumph, she is splattered with a bucket of pig's blood. When this happens, Carrie literally sees red and destroys the gymnasium and everybody in it in a holocaust that either was intended to be non-frightening or has been rendered so by having been badly photographed and edited.

• • •

De Palma's approach to his guignol material is so boldly and—I think—wrong-headedly lyrical that the spectacle of Carrie destroying her tormentors has all the dramatic punch of a small child swatting buttercups. Quite consciously, I suspect, De Palma has defused what might have been suspense by shooting a lot of the senior prom in such slow motion that by the time the holocaust happens, it has absolutely no dramatic effect, one way or the other. Though Miss Spacek, with her Rubens face and coloring, is a charming actress, we believe neither her predicament (which belongs in a real horror film) nor her passionate longings for love and acceptance (which belong in a movie that wouldn't dream of bringing up telekinesis).

Perhaps I'm more of a purist than I ever realized. I like horror films that keep me on the edge of my seat. A horror film that lulls me to the edge of sleep is innovative, all right, but in the wrong way. Just as it's impossible to have artistic porn (it's either art or porn), I think it's impossible to pull off what De Palma was attempting in "Carrie," to make a horror film about a violent revenge of a character we are meant to take as seriously as we do Carrie.

In the way "Carrie" squanders the talents of everyone involved—De Palma's, Miss Spacek's and particularly Miss Laurie's, whose finely controlled, full-throttle power here suggests she'd be a riveting stage actress—it would seem to confirm the suspicions of non-moviegoers that movies are, by nature, foolish and self-destructive. One can't take them seriously if they don't.

"Carrie" is a joke, but a wan one. It's possible to go through it and find all sorts of little homages to other films, a practice that in the work of someone on the order of Truffaut is tolerated as a kind of exuberance—though in "Carrie" they appear to be no more than dramatic cul-de-sacs. "Carrie" doesn't unreel. It unravels. It was instructive to watch it with a paying audience that may have read reviews comparing it to "Jaws." There is a grand total of one shock in the entire film, and it's a mini-one that is immediately taken back by the following scene.

In his early films, De Palma showed himself to be a fine, anarchic humorist. In the opening sequence of "Obsession" and in a few scenes in "Carrie" he reveals a talent for headlong romanticism. "Carrie" is the work of a highly intelligent filmmaker fooling around, going nowhere, though with a certain amount of undeniable style that prompts favorable notices. For any one except the film buff, "Carrie" is a waste of time.

1976 D 5, II:13:4

that remains clear is that to get to the dream city of the title, one goes to Munich and books a flight to the Near East on Lufthansa. At least that's how the people in the movie do it.

VINCENT CANBY

1976 D 6, 46:6

BOUND FOR GLORY, directed by Hal Ashby; screenplay by Robert Getchell, based on Woody Guthrie's autobiography; produced by Robert F. Blumofe and Harold Leventhal; director of photography, Haskell Wexler; music adapted and conducted by Leonard Rosenman; editors, Robert Jones and Pembroke J. Herring; distributed by United Artists. Running time: 148 minutes. At the Coronet Theater, Third Avenue near 59th Street. This film has been rated PG.

Woody Guthrie	David Carradine
Ozark Bule	Ronny Cox
Mary Guthrie	Melinda Dillon
Pauline	Gail Strickland
Locke	John Lehne
Slim Snedeger	Ji-Tu Cumbuka
Luther Johnson	Randy Quaid
Liz	Elizabeth Macey
Memphis Sue	Melinda Dillon

By VINCENT CANBY

Like the guests of honor who won't be allowed entrance until the proper moment, the presence of Woody Guthrie hovers for a long time—felt but unheard—outside "Bound for Glory," the film biography that Hal Ashby has made of one of America's greatest folk singers and composers. Then, at the film's end, as the final credits are unreeling, the slightly raspy voice of the real Woody Guthrie is invited in via the soundtrack.

The movie, which until that moment has solemnly recorded selected events of Woody's life in Depression America, comes suddenly to life in a medley of Guthrie songs sung by him and others. The songs are buoyant, funny, mocking. They are full of feelings that somehow elude the rest of the film, even though "Bound for Glory" has apparently been made with love and care and is virtually stricken by its social conscience.

•

The film, which opened yesterday at the Coronet, has a number of very good things going for it, in particular David Carradine's dry, haunted performance as the young Woody Guthrie who passes through the film more or less as if he were a camera, storing away impressions and emotions that only occasionally are allowed to erupt with dramatic force. Mr. Carradine may be taller and huskier than the real Woody, but he has the right look and manner — the reserve, skeptical squint, the texture of the countryman's skin.

Mr. Ashby and Haskell Wexler, his cameraman, have also been immensely successful in recreating the look of place and period from the drought-ridden Texas Panhandle of the 1930's, when rural America appeared to be returning to dust even before it had actually died, to the California fruit ranches and the "Hoovervilles" where Woody sang and attempted to organize the migrant workers.

What the film doesn't have much of is a screenplay. At least, it doesn't have a screenplay that matches with dramatic conviction the intensity and drive of its largely mysterious central character.

Woody Guthrie was a very odd duck, and certainly not easy to live with. At the height of the Depression, he abandoned his wife and two small daughters in Texas and took to the road, heading for California on foot and freight car. When he began to receive a little recognition as a country singer on a California radio station, he retrieved his family but abandoned them again. His feelings for "the people" never quite extended far enough to include his wife and children.

Robert Getchell, who wrote the screenplay based on Woody's autobiography, doesn't permit the screen Woody to sound any more articulate than your average,

David Carradine and Melinda Dillon in "Bound for Glory"
The film has a number of very good things going for it

Schaaf's 'Dream City' Has Fuzzy Quality in Its Plot

DREAM CITY, directed by Johannes Schaaf; screenplay (German with English subtitles) by Mr. Schaaf, based on the novel, "The Other Side," by Alfred Kubin; executive producer, Raymond R. Homer; produced by Heinz Angermeyer; director of photography, Gerard Vandernberg; music, Eberhard Schoener; distributed by Peppercorn-Wormser. Running time: 96 minutes. At the Festival Theater, 57th Street west of Fifth Avenue. This film has not been rated.

Florian Sand	Per Oscarsson
Anna Sand	Rosemarie Fendel
Das Madchen	Olimpia
Frau Lampenbogen	Eva Marie Meineke
Dr. Lampenbogen	Alexander May

"Dream City," which opened yesterday at the Festival Theater, is Johannes Schaaf's German - language screen adaptation of "The Other Side," the only novel ever written by the Austrian graphic artist Alfred Kubin (1877-1959), who has been variously described as an Expressionist, a Symbolist, a proto-Surrealist and a latter-day Romantic of the German school.

I have not read the novel, which was published in Austria in 1909 and here in 1968. Yet I would suspect that Mr. Schaaf, by updating it, may have disconnected the logic that compelled

Kubin to create his fantasy about a dream city, an allegorical place that probably owes more to conditions in the middle Europe that Kubin shared with Kafka than it does to those in today's world.

Mr. Schaaf's movie is an interior decorator's dream, full of bizarre sets, costumes and make-up, about a Munich artist (Per Oscarsson) and his wife (Rosemarie Fendel) who, for reasons they never know, are invited to take up residence in a mysterious city where everything is allowed as long as other individuals are respected. Actually this is a rather large, dampening qualification for life in any real dream city, but the movie is so profoundly fuzzy that it doesn't make too much difference.

The film is a vaguely Kafkaesque nightmare that can't make up its mind whether its interests are psychological or political, though it seems to be certain that utopia would drive most people mad. Much of the film was photographed in the old Czechoslovak town of Krumlov, which is very picturesque, maybe just a bit too much so.

The only other detail about the film

tongue-tied man-in-the-street interviewee.

"Seems to me something ought to be done about this," says the film's Woody early on, commenting on the disastrous conditions in the Texas dust bowl. Later, to explain why he had run away from home again, he says, "I had to touch the people again. . . . The worst that can happen to a guy is to cut himself off from the folks."

Had this sort of talk been combined with more of Woody's music as the film unfolds, the result might not have seemed as ultimately barren and trivial as it now does, but Mr. Ashby didn't want "Bound for Glory" to be a musical. That's understandable, though to separate Woody from his music, as the film does to a great extent, is to separate us from a major portion of his experience.

Woody's music is galvanizing, upbeat, convinced of the possibilities for a better society, committed to change. Like Woody's impatience with social and political injustice, the music is unequivocal, decisive. The movie isn't.

It ambles through conventionally pitiful scenes of dust-bowl poverty and union-busting, and shows us Woody refusing to compromise his ideals to get along in show business. On only two occasions, however, do we have some sense of what drove the man.

One is an old-fashioned hoedown with a group of fruit pickers and the other is a sequence in which Woody, attempting to organize workers in a canning plant, is beaten up by company thugs. Both sequences make their points as much through music as through anything that happens.

Though Mr. Carradine's performance is almost the entire film, he receives fine support from the other actors, including Melinda Dillon, who plays both his abandoned wife and a singing partner named Memphis Sue, and Ronny Cox, who plays a fictionalized version of one of Woody's real-life sidekicks and mentors.

●

"Bound for Glory," which has been rated PG ("Parental Guidance Suggested"), contains some mildly rough dialogue.

1976 D 6, 47:1

SILVER STREAK, directed by Arthur Hiller; screenplay by Colin Higgins; executive producers, Frank Yablans and Martin Ransohoff; produced by Edward K. Milkis and Thomas L. Miller; music, Henry Mancini; director of photography, David M. Walsh; editor, David Bretherton; distributed by 20th Century-Fox. Running time: 104 minutes. At the National Theater, Broadway at 44th Street, and Loews Tower East Theater, Third Avenue near 72d Street. This film has been rated PG.
George Caldwell .... Gene Wilder
Hilly Burns .... Jill Clayburgh
Grover Muldoon .... Richard Pryor
Roger Devereau .... Patrick McGoohan
Sweet .... Ned Beatty
Sheriff Chauncey .... Clifton James
Mr. Whiney .... Ray Walston
Johnson .... Stefan Gierasch
Chief .... Len Birman
Plain Jane .... Valerie Curtin
Reace (Goldtooth) .... Richard Kiel
Rita Babtree .... Lucille Benson
Ralston .... Scatman Crothers

By VINCENT CANBY

"Silver Streak" is the sort of comedy that leaves you exhausted, though not from laughing.

The film, which is set mostly aboard a Los Angeles-to-Chicago train and has to do with art forgers, cops and innocent bystanders,

works its cast so relentlessly, with so little real good humor and at such apparent expense and trouble, that it wears you out with the tension that comes from watching good people make idiots of themselves.

●

Among these are a skinny-looking Gene Wilder, who plays a more or less straight romantic role that suits him not at all, and Jill Clayburgh, an actress of too much intelligence to be able to fake identification with a role that is essentially that of a liberated ingenue.

Richard Pryor
His genial moments are undercut

Richard Pryor, a very funny man, who turns up in the last third of the film, has some genial moments that are immediately undercut by what appears to be either thoughtless editing or direction. I don't think I've ever before seen an actor at the end of a movie scene adopt that slightly desperate look we have come to associate with television performers when the camera stays on them too long after they've finished their schtiks.

This sort of sloppiness is a measure of "Silver Streak," which appears to be looking for a dominant style as it lumbers along over mountains, deserts and prairies. Colin Higgins's screenplay is not witty or rambunctious or mysterious, nor does it have the courage to parody a disaster film like "Airport 1975," an idea that seems to pass through its mind from time to time, though it's never acted upon. Bring back "The Big Bus."

"Silver Streak" was directed by Arthur Hiller, a man whose work defies generalization. He's made good films ("The Hospital"), dreadful ones ("Plaza Suite") and one gold mine ("Love Story"). "Silver Streak" is one he may want to forget as quickly as possible.

●

"Silver Streak," which has been rated PG ("Parental Guidance Suggested"), contains some mildly racy dialogue and one love scene that is made vulgar more as a result of the leering behavior of the actors than because of anything that's shown on the screen.

1976 D 9, 61:1

Heavy Judgments

CHICK STRAND, a selection of her films. Includes ANSELMO, MOSORI MONIKA, GUACAMOLE, COSAS DE MI VIDA, MUJER DE MILFUEGOS and ELASTICITY. Total running time: 94 minutes. At the Film Forum, 15 Vandam Street, through Sunday and Dec. 16 through 19.

By RICHARD EDER

CHICK STRAND is a fine photographer and takes good-looking pictures, but her films are so heavy in judgment that they fall out of the screen.

In the Film Forum's survey of Miss Strand's work, the two main items are absurdly pedantic intrusions on some lovely material. One tells of an Indian mission in the Orinoco Delta; the other is the story of a poor Mexican musician who achieves some prosperity.

●

The author flaps in like a great cuckoo bird. She deposits her particular cultural assumptions in these alien nests, and they hatch out with a lot of inappropriate squawking.

Her thesis is that primitive cultures are good and that developed cultures come in and spoil them. The thesis has some legitimacy but it's not a matter for rawboned assertion. Miss Strand's command of nuance is a far remove from Lévi-Strauss: Levi Strauss is more like it.

In "Mosori Monika," her camera alternates between shots of the Indians in their natural habitat—fishing, pounding manioc, sitting in hammocks—and views of a missionary station. There they are clothed in suits and dresses,

and taught sanitation, cooking with aluminum pots, and the catechism.

In the forest, the Indians look extraordinarily beautiful. Dressed in Western clothes, they look stiff and sad, and the nuns in their white habits, brandishing pots, inevitably look a bit silly. And two voices are invented: a nun's voice saying patronizing things about the Indians, and an Indian woman recalling the beauty of the natural life.

In "Cosas de mi Vida," there is a lot of perceptive and appealing footage showing the hard rise of Anselmo Aguascalientes from barefoot Indian boy to successful leader of a band. But the camera dwells heavily on his stereo, his television set, his flush toilet. His Indian nature, the message goes, has been denatured.

This is both cheap and ruinous. Using a camera to make points this way is like using a pistol to make points.

●

The other films are not much more successful. There is an attempt to evoke the old blood-and-death theme of bullfighting in "Guacamolo," and a blackgowned young woman carries stones—intended to symbolize the Latin American woman's plight, apparently—in "Mujer de Milfuegos." Both are as pretentious and contrived as an old-fashioned dance-school pageant.

The other films—a long montage of film clips from the 1940's and 50's—run forward and then backward; and a very short one showing a man carrying a tuba—complete the program.

1976 D 10, C9:1

FILM VIEW

VINCENT CANBY

In Films, Acting Is Behavior

Acting of any kind is difficult enough to judge rationally but film acting is the most illusive, being so dependent on things that have nothing to do with the talent or the craft or the intelligent options exercised by the actor. A good performance on the stage or screen can be shaped as much by what God gave the actor for a nose, a voice or a general physique as by the things the actor does with those original resources. The screen performance is at the further mercy of the director, the lighting cameraman and the editor, all or any of whom can ruin a good performance—as well as they can create a great performance out of what is virtually found material.

Because of the nature of the camera and its ability to crawl into an actor's eyeball if required, a lot of moving acting isn't acting at all in the ordinary sense. It's what Alexander Knox once called "behaving," the simulation of being natural, of being devoid of irrelevant mannerisms that, if magnified a couple of hundred times on the screen, could suggest psychosis rather than an incipient sneeze.

Over the years we've come to recognize the real art that lay behind the apparent "behaving" of such great old stars as Gable, Tracy, Cooper, Wayne, Cagney and Stewart. It took time, though. We had to live with those actors for decades before we knew that what they were doing had as much to do with screen acting as the wildest impersonations by Lon Chaney or the ponderously historical recreations by

Paul Muni who, every now and then, would show us that he could "behave" with the best of them.

These thoughts are prompted by two exceptionally good performances on view in current films—David Carradine's portrayal of Woody Guthrie in Hal Ashby's "Bound For Glory," a biographical film about America's Great Depression poet and balladeer, and Robert De Niro's Monroe Stahr, the title character in the Elia Kazan-Harold Pinter adaptation of F. Scott Fitzgerald's "The Last Tycoon." Each is a "behavioral" performance of a rigor and a depth that might well be overlooked because of the role's position in the film that contains it.

Both Woody Guthrie and Monroe Stahr remain as largely mysterious at the end of their films as they were at the beginnings. Although neither is a passive character, they are passive in terms of the structures of their stories. Unlike the flamboyant, flashy and, to me, skin-deep performance of Sylvester Stallone as the plug-ugly fighter in "Rocky," neither Carradine nor De Niro is allowed to "act" in any easily identifiable way, but each behaves with the kind of assurance that gives weight, urgency and conviction to their films.

What, actually, are they doing? Compared to Stallone, not much.

Stallone's Rocky is a character composed entirely of bizarre mannerisms, the sort of things that impersonators seize on when they do imitations—particular ways of walking and talking that create a character by exaggeration. The problem is that the characterization has such a busy surface one inevitably suspects there's nothing much below.

Carradine's Woody Guthrie is something else. He has an Okie drawl but other than that it is difficult to describe what Carradine does in any vivid way, principally, I suspect, because he's the eyes and ears of the film. He doesn't seem to be acting at all as he moves through the movie's re-creation of Depression America, storing up experiences and feelings that are later to be expressed in Woody Guthrie's music.

•   •   •

As Woody observes the plight of the dust-bowl farmers of Texas and the injustices dealt migrant workers on California's fruit ranches, we observe Carradine and we are aware that Woody's impassive surface is barely containing the outrage that is accumulating within.

Why do we believe? I'm not sure. It has something to do with Carradine's looks and the eyes that seem to be in a perpetual squint against dust and glare. It also has to do with the reserved manner. As Carradine's Woody doesn't waste his energies on mannerisms, so, by extension, would he not waste his time on foolish pursuits.

Carradine's Woody Guthrie is a character who takes his time, a liberty that is granted him by the director and thus might not be counted as an actor's contribution to the role except for the fact that Carradine makes the most of the time he takes.

Early in "Bound for Glory" there's a marvelously effective scene that under other circumstances could have been horrendous. Woody is asked to talk to a farm woman who, in her grief over the death of a child, has refused to eat or drink. She's a cat who's climbed far out onto a branch of sorrow and can't find her way back.

Carradine/Woody seems embarrassed to have healing powers attributed to him. As he looks at the worn woman, we see what he sees, a personification of desolation that he will not accept. He talks to the woman in homely fashion, saying something about her mind and God's having given it to her—eventually she listens to him. She responds not necessarily to his truisms but to his concern, not to panic but to patience.

•   •   •

Heroic film actors have always taken their time. The screen allows actors a license in this regard. Unlike the stage where it's difficult to simulate the passage of time without actually passing time (and putting the audience to sleep), the screen can suggest long, intense interior debate through something as simple (and technical) as a camera movement.

The actor, however, must be able to present the camera with a presence to which we can respond. In the cases of Carradine and De Niro they register something one might label "alertness" for lack of a better word. They register it not by saying anything in particular, not by allowing their jaws to drop open in stupefaction, but by doing virtually nothing.

Screen acting may well defy intelligent analysis by outsiders. I think it was Rouben Mamoulian who, when asked

how he obtained a certain especially esthetic response from Garbo in "Queen Christina," said that he simply told her to sit still and not think of anything. Garbo was a remarkable actress. In addition, her face was a magnificently planed, cheeked and lighted blank on which directors could realize their most romantic fancies.

In spite of her deserved success in the Lubitsch comedy, "Ninotchka," Garbo was never very versatile, nor were Gable and Tracy and Cooper when you study their performances. They remained largely the same—the films that framed them changed. A tendency to overrate versatility was, I think, the reason that these great "behaviorists" were so often overlooked in their own time.

Their talent was not in being able to portray a western hero in one film and a cockney fishmonger in the next, but in being able to convince us, time and time again, that here were figures of larger-than-life moral and psychological moment. Which is what is accomplished by De Niro in "The Last Tycoon" and Carradine in "Bound for Glory."

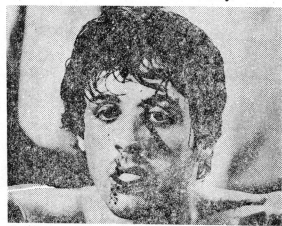

Stallone: "Such a busy surface that one suspects there's nothing much below."

"Bound for Glory" has its problems. It never really explodes with the upbeat force of Woody's music, at least, not until the final credits are unreeling on screen, which is somewhat late to make the film as moving as it might have been.

The fascinating thing about De Niro's Monroe Stahr is how little De Niro seems to be doing to keep our attention. It helps, of course, that other characters keep telling us how brilliant and powerful and successful he is, but not very much of this is demonstrated for us. We must take the character on faith, and on De Niro's presence, which manages to be completely convincing. De Niro's Monroe Stahr is like the fellow at an orgy who succeeds in attracting all eyes by not doing anything.

•   •   •

Watching De Niro in this film is given added dimension by the memory of the seething performance he gave in "Taxi Driver," which is a brilliant example of a flamboyant performance that didn't get in the way of the character the performance meant to reveal. That's a performance that Stallone and other would-be actors might profitably study.

Though there aren't that many good films around at the moment, there are some other noteworthy performances that make the films more interesting than otherwise would be the case. "Lumière," Jeanne Moreau's debut as a film director, begins as if it intended to be a parody of some of those Antonioni films of the sixties, but it's deadly serious, unfortunately. It also takes the problems of four successful and/or beautiful actresses somewhat more solemnly than I can. Yet Moreau herself redeems it with her central performance as the older actress. It's an expansive, witty performance that doesn't stint on details, and by being so magnanimous, it succeeds in making relevant and touching at least one of the four stories the film covers.

"Maîtresse," Barbet Schroeder's "comedy" about a sweet-natured young woman who runs a S-M parlor and the fellow who loves her, is more often grizzly than funny, but it gives us the opportunity to watch Bulle Ogier and Gerard Dépardieu, who are elegantly comic actors even when the circumstances are not. The point, simply stated: if you can't find a film you want to see, look for the performance.

1976 D 12, II:1:1

Haunting, but Also Dull

A DREAM CAN BE RIGGED, but the results are uncertain. Children do it sometimes: perching a teddy bear near the bed, or focusing on the notion of ice cream or a picnic, in the hope that it will be dreamed. Often it is, but not necessarily as hoped. The teddy bear attacks, the ice cream becomes icebergs, the picnic turns into a wake.

"The Apparition," by the experimental film maker Larry Jordan, is something of a rigged dream. It is erratic, sometimes haunting, sometimes comic, and a lot of it dull; dull in the way somebody else's dream—real or rigged—is dull.

•

In "The Apparition," which is being shown at the Whitney Museum's New American Filmmakers series, Mr. Jordan sets up a central figure to whom the dream belongs, and the figure simultaneously constructs it and dreams it. The figure is Paul, a maker of experimental films and commercials, and seemingly Mr. Jordan's alter ego.

Paul lives with Sue, a free spirit just beginning to age. The relationship is uncertain, but deepening, a mixture of hope, guilt and rebellion. He has a casual affair with a younger woman, after their filmed roles as orgiasts in a grape commercial turn real. He visits a California hill family in one of those houses where everything, even the haircuts and eyeglass frames, is handicraft.

Paul films everything, obsessively. He films his two women, a young son of the family, the son's drawing of a sacrifice in a Greek temple, a stuffed owl on a bureau. Gradually, jogged by Paul's tensions and depressions, these real things begin to move in and out of a dream state.

•

An outdoor festival held by the family and friends begins with singing, wine drinking and a beautiful moment in which the children ride up on horses and lead the participants in a circle dance. Paul is in the middle of the circle, shooting frenziedly; and drifting away. He sees a figure in a toga and follows her into the woods.

At another point he is driving alone in his car when a hand reaches from the back seat and touches him on the neck. The figure in the toga reappears, dies, comes to life, tries to talk, dies again. There are columns, the owl, sacrifices.

Hallucination and reality shift back and forth. We see Paul experiencing his visions, telling about them afterward, and—he is a film maker, after all—setting them up.

There is a charming openness in the way Mr. Jordan blurs the lines between fantasy and reality, and between fantasy and fraud. This openness, however, doesn't do much to relieve the ponderousness of some of the visions. In a way, it undercuts the visions.

Along with "Apparition" the museum is showing an earlier, more abstract short work by Mr. Jordan, "Triptych in Four Parts." It is pretty much a film about Mr. Jordan's desire to express something by making a film.

RICHARD EDER

1976 D 15, C24:3

Pink Panther Team Unflappable In Fourth High-Spirited Caper

THE PINK PANTHER STRIKES AGAIN, directed and produced by Blake Edwards; written by Frank Waldman and Mr. Edwards; music by Henry Mancini; director of photography, Harry Waxman; animation and titles by Richard Williams; editor, Alan Jones; distributed by United Artists. Running time: 103 minutes. At the Forum Theater, Broadway at 47th Street, and other theaters. This film has been rated PG.

Inspector Clouseau	Peter Sellers
Dreyfus	Herbert Lom
Alec Drummond	Colin Blakely
Quinlin	Leonard Rossiter
Olga	Lesley-Anne Down
Cato	Burt Kwouk
Francois	Andre Maranne
Deputy Commissioner	Marne Maitland
Dr. Fassbender	Richard Vernon
Jarvis	Michael Robbins
Margo Fassbender	Briony McRoberts
President	Dick Crockett
Secretary of State	Byron Kane

By VINCENT CANBY

Though "The Pink Panther Strikes Again" is the fourth Inspector Clouseau comedy to come from the collaboration of Peter Sellers, the star, and Blake Edwards, the director-producer and co-author, there are no signs that anyone's spirits are flagging or that sanity is in any way imminent.

Ineptitude again triumphs—gloriously. Bungling is rewarded, and Clouseau goes blithely on demonstrating that what he doesn't know, which is everything, can't possibly do him permanent damage.

•

To be near Clouseau is to be at the edge of the hurricane's eye, to risk annihilation, which is pretty much what actually happens to Clouseau's former superior in the French Sûreté, the once-sane Chief Inspector Dreyfus (Herbert Lom), in "The Pink Panther Strikes Again," which opened at Broadway and neighborhood theaters yesterday.

The new film, written by Mr. Edwards and Frank Waldman, picks up Clouseau and Dreyfus several years after we left them in "The Return of the Pink Panther," with Dreyfus, apparently cured after a nervous breakdown brought on by Clouseau, preparing to leave his psychiatric clinic near Paris. One get-well-visit by Clouseau, though, and Dreyfus is pushed over the brink forever, turning into a mad, Goldfinger-like supercrook whose gift for ultimate failure is as certain a law of metaphysics as Clouseau's for success.

They were made for each other, Clouseau and Dreyfus, and I can't believe that a little matter like Dreyfus's having been rendered forever invisible at the end of the new film will prevent Mr. Edwards from reuniting the two sometime in the future.

I'm not sure why Mr. Sellers and Mr. Lom are such a hilarious team, though it may be because each is a fine comic actor with a special talent for portraying the sort of all-consuming, epic self-absorption that makes slapstick farce initially acceptable—instead of alarming—and finally so funny.

There is, too, something most winningly seedy about Mr. Sellers' Clouseau, a fellow who, when he attempts to tear off his clothes in the heat of passion, gets tangled up in his necktie, and who, when he masquerades—for reasons never gone into—as Quasimodo, overinflates his hump with helium.

•

Archfiend Herbert Lom out to get Peter Sellers
"Free-form comedy that goes where its gags lead it"

Both Mr. Sellers and Mr. Edwards delight in old gags, and part of the joy of "The Pink Panther Strikes Again" is watching the way they spin out what is essentially a single routine, such as one fellow's trying, unsuccessfully, to help another fellow out of a lake. And how long has it been since you've seen a crazy dentist routine involving laughing gas and the wrong tooth? For me, too long.

I'm also partial to the Sellers-Clouseau French accent that is always discovering new words, such as "bimp" (as in "You have a nasty bimp on your head"), "rust" (as in "You can rust assured") and "rheuem" (as in "I would like to have a rheuem for the night").

"The Pink Panther Strikes Again," which is more or less about Clouseau's search for archfiend Dreyfus, moves all over the map, from Paris to London and Bavaria—where Dreyfus lives in a neo-Dracula castle — and back again, with a couple of detours to Washington, and a White House inhabited by a President who stumbles on rugs' edges.

It's not, I suspect, a movie to attend looking for reason. It has arid patches, but I couldn't care less. The film is free-form comedy that goes where its gags lead it. That's not to say that it's formless, only that its structure has less to do with narrative than with the comic exuberance of the collaborators, which, after four films, is undiminished.

•

"The Pink Panther Strikes Again," which has been rated PG ("Parental Guidance Suggested"), contains a couple of bedroom scenes that have less to do with sex than with the confusion that can be caused by unexpected visitors.

1976 D 16, 66:1

'King Kong' Bigger, Not Better, In a Return to Screen of Crime

By VINCENT CANBY

When it is played as a straight adventure-fantasy, Dino De Laurentiis's $25-million remake of "King Kong" is inoffensive, uncomplicated fun, as well as a dazzing display of what the special-effects people can do when commissioned to construct a 40-foot-tall ape who can walk, make fondling gestures, is slightly cross-eyed, and smiles a lot.

It's something to make you cringe with embarrassment, though, when it attempts to disarm all criticism by kidding itself (proclaim the ads, "the most exciting original motion picture event of all time") in lines of dialogue that are intended as instant camp ("You goddamned male chauvinist ape!"). I suppose that when you spend as much as Mr. De Laurentiis did on this, you've got to have something for everybody, including the witless.

•

The nicest thing about the 1933 "King Kong," made by Merian C. Cooper and Ernest B. Schoedsack, was that it was no big deal. One could marvel at the wizardly special effects created by Willis O'Brien and not be overwhelmed by an awareness of the terrific time and expense that went into them. Its heart was genuinely light. Not this time.

Why, I think we have a right to ask, would anyone want to remake it? "King Kong" is a classic, but it's not "Hamlet." There's only one way to do it, and that's been done. Having acknowledged these biases, one might as well relax and let it happen.

John Guillermin, the director, and Lorenzo Semple Jr., the writer, display real affection for old-time movie magic and nonsense that come through in spite of a physical production only slightly less elaborate than that of Elizabeth Taylor's "Cleopatra."

Especially effective are the opening sections of the film that lay out —with a respectful gravity that is truly comic—the scientific mumbo jumbo that softens us for the make-believe to come: a team of oil experts from a cartel named Petrox sets out to find a mysterious uncharted South Pacific island that is perpetually enclosed in a cloud of carbon dioxide, indicating that the earth beneath is a virtually bottomless reservoir of petroleum. There's talk about the worldwide energy crisis, and we are shown satellite photographs meant to allay suspicions that even if such an island could have remained undiscovered throughout all of World War II, our spy-in-the-sky system, which can apparently read the fine print on Kremlin documents, would certainly have chanced upon it long before this.

It may well be that we don't need such explanations. Part of the appeal of "King Kong" today, as it was in 1933, is based on the wish to believe that there may still be places in this world unpenetrated by Petrox, Pepsico, General Motors, Sony and the Clubs Mediterranee.

•

The film builds well to Kong's initial appearance, after we are almost an hour into the story, when he comes clomping out of the jungle to claim his monthly sacrifice, who is not, of course, Fay Wray, but Jessica Lange, a beautiful New York model who plays a would-be actress named Dwan. Though Dwan sets Kong's heart aflame, she's more likely to set everyone else's teeth on edge.

This is no reflection on Miss Lange. It's the script. In their attempt to update a fairy tale, the film makers have turned a conventional heroine into a pseudo-Mar-

King Kong
"Something for everybody, including the witless"

ilyn Monroe character who seems less dizzy than certifiably daft, aggressively unpleasant and out of place in this sort of movie.

What sort, exactly, is this movie? It's a series of big, foolish but entertaining spectacle scenes, such as the natives of that uncharted Pacific island prancing around, doing pagan fertility dances that suggest 1950's Broadway musicals. It's the sight of the mighty Kong picking up Dwan in the palm of his hand and washing her off under a jungle waterfall, then fiddling curiously with her bra. It's Kong going amok in New York City, looking for Dwan, grabbing up a subway car and rattling it like a gourd, then trudging south to the World Trade Center, where he ultimately meets his fate.

One of my objections to the film is the substitution of the twin towers of the Trade Center for the Empire State Building, used in the original film. The World Trade Center is a very boring piece of architecture. The Empire State Building is not. Though Kong's last fight with Army helicopters is beautifully (and bloodily) done, the setting trivializes it.

There are other actors in the film beside Miss Lange. They include very good actors such as Jeff Bridges (as a professor of primate paleontology from Princeton) and Charles Grodin (as a vicious, ambitious Petrox executive), but they are supporting characters to the various pieces of machinery (and one man in an ape suit) that portray Kong in his changing moods.

The real auteurs of this "King Kong" are not the producers, the director or the writer, but Carlo Rambaldi, Glen Robinson and Rick Baker, who are credited with hav-

The Cast

KING KONG, directed by John Guillermin; screenplay by Lorenzo Semple Jr., based on a story by Edgar Wallace and Merian C. Cooper; produced by Dino De Laurentiis; executive producers, Federico De Laurentiis and Christian Ferry; director of photography, Richard H. Kline; music, John Barry; editor, Ralph E. Winters; distributed by Paramount Pictures. Running time: 135 minutes. At Loew's State I, Broadway at 45th Street, Loew's Orpheum, 86th Street near Third Avenue, and other theaters. This film has been rated PG.

Jack Prescott	Jeff Bridges
Fred Wilson	Charles Grodin
Dwan	Jessica Lange
Captain Ross	John Randolph
Bagley	Rene Auberjonois
Boan	Julius Harris
Joe Perko	Jack O'Halloran
Sunfish	Dennis Fimple
Carnahan	Ed Lauter
Garcia	Jorge Moreno

ing been responsible for designing, constructing and engineering the mechanisms.

●

"King Kong," which has been rated PG ("parental guidance suggested"), includes some vulgar language, some partial nudity, some violence at the end, and some intimations of unrealizable bestiality that small children everywhere will recognize as simple friendliness.

1976 D 18, 16:1

Charming Tale of the West Will Delight Youngsters

By A. H. WEILER

Stewart Raffill, the writer-director, and Arthur R. Dubs, the producer of last year's Christmas bauble, "Adventures of the Wilderness Family," are not the ones to let a simple, profitable formula lie.

The Cast

ACROSS THE GREAT DIVIDE; written and directed by Stewart Raffill; produced by Arthur R. Dubs; music by Gene Kauer and Douglas Lackey; released by Pacific International Enterprises. Running time: 95 minutes. This film has been classified G. At the Guild and Embassy Theaters.

Zachariah Coop	Robert Logan
Holly Smith	Heather Rattray
Jason Smith	Mark Hall
Indian Chief	George (Buck) Flower

Like kids ever ready to have a go at a second candy cane, they've tackled another innocents-versus-the-wilds confection in "Across the Great Divide," which arrived yesterday at the Guild and Embassy Theaters. And it's safe to say that their new holiday treat is as harmless, say, as that second candy cane, and it should charm the youngsters and even some indulgent grown-ups.

●

If moviegoers with retentive memories detect similarities between "Wilderness Family" and "Great Divide" it is hardly important. Only an urban misogynist would sneer at the idea that once again the focus is on naïve pioneers, the wilderness and such predators as a grizzly and cougars. But the Pacific Northwest and its fauna are still eye-fillingly photogenic and the principals are cheerful and endearing, if amazingly indomitable.

A cynic might question this fiction about a youthful, self-reliant, orphaned sister and brother adrift in the forested high country in 1876, who, with the aid of a resourceful young con-man gambler, finally make it to the lush Oregon acres they've inherited.

But action, a touch of humor and nonmarauding Indians give the proceedings a fair portion of realism. Our handsome gambler and our wandering pre-teen-agers are always on the run. If the youngsters are slow to accept his blarney, they grudgingly do come to trust him. But there's always that grizzly and the cougars who deprive them of their horses, as well as a snarling wolf pack to threaten them, and a band of dissolute, if comic, frontiersmen to keep them and the film moving at a fast clip.

●

The Indians, led by George (Buck) Flower, are decent, family types who appreciate their help in driving off that man-eating grizzly. If some oddly Dickensian dialogue by a pair of newcomers, Heather Rattray and Mark Hall, can be overlooked, they emerge as natural and attractive kids. Robert Logan (one of the leads in "Wilderness Family") is properly stalwart as their knowledgeable protector. And they all blend well with the spectacular Utah and British Columbia landscapes in which "Great Divide" was shot.

1976 D 21, 44:1

MIKEY AND NICKY, directed and written by Elaine May; produced by Michael Hausman; executive producer, Bud Austin; director of photography, Victor J. Kemper; editor, John Carter; music, John Strauss; distributed by Paramount Pictures. Running time: 118 minutes. At the Little Carnegie Theater, 57th Street, east of Seventh Avenue. This film has been rated R.

Mikey	Peter Falk
Nicky	John Cassavetes
Kinney	Ned Beatty
Annie	Rose Arrick
Nell	Carol Grace
Sid Fine	William Hickey
Dave Resnick	Sanford Meisner
Jan	Joyce Van Patten
Bus Driver	M. Emmet Walsh

By VINCENT CANBY

Elaine May's first two films, "A New Leaf" and "The Heartbreak Kid," were comedies of sometimes inspired and often touching lunacy, mostly about the uncertain progress of romantic love between men and women. Her third film

"Mikey and Nicky," which opened yesterday at the Little Carnegie, is something else entirely.

It's a melodrama about male friendship told in such insistently claustrophobic detail that to watch it is to risk an artificially induced anxiety attack. It's nearly two hours of being locked in a telephone booth with a couple of method actors who won't stop talking, though they have nothing of interest to say, and who won't stop jiggling around, though they plainly aren't going anywhere.

"Mikey and Nicky," which Miss May wrote as well as directed, takes place in one approximately 12-hour period. It involves a lot of self-conscious exposition that never quite succeeds in telling us all we have a decent right to know.

It's about a couple of small-time Los Angeles hoods who've grown up together, joined the same mob and now, on this particular night, find their lifelong relationship passing in front of our eyes in aggressive close-up.

Nicky (John Cassavetes), convinced that his bosses have put out a contract on his life, summons Mikey (Peter Falk) to his hideout in a fleabag hotel. Nicky needs help. He's scared out of his wits. He's coming apart at the seams. He's afraid of being murdered but his ulcer is killing him anyway. He isn't sure he can trust Mikey, but if he can't trust Mikey, he can't trust anybody.

When Mikey arrives at the hotel, Nicky at first refuses to let him in, but then he relents. The two men embrace. They are in tears. They clutch each other. They laugh. They cry. They argue. They reconcile. Mikey tries to be reasonable with his distraught friend.

Mikey: "Who told you [there was a contract out on you]?"

Nicky: "Someone I know told me."

Mikey: "How do you know it's true?"

Nicky: "How do you know it's not true?"

Later in the evening, Mikey angrily accuses Nicky of having nicknamed him "the echo" for always saying everything twice. But so do Nicky and everyone else in the film. Miss May used to write that kind of dialogue to be funny. This time she means to be serious but the method isn't good enough.

"Mikey and Nicky" follows the friends as they wander in aimless desperation around a neonlit city, and as we learn eventually that Mikey is, in fact, the finger man.

By this time, though, it's too late to retrieve the film from the kind of busy banality that Mr. Cassavetes' own films, including his recent "The Killing of a Chinese Bookie," fall into when actors take over from the director, apparently with the director's full approval.

Though we are told more than once that the Cassavetes character is a charmer and that he has always treated his friends rottenly, including Mikey, there's no evidence in the performance that Nicky is charming in any way. Nor do we believe that Mikey is a jerk, as he's supposed to be. Both actors are, in fact, as interchangeable in their characters as are their character names. It's significant, I think, that as I write this review I have to keep referring to my notes to remember which actor plays which part.

John Cassavetes, at left, and Peter Falk.
Much ado about little

Short portions of the film come to vivid life, especially toward the end. There's a very funny, typically urban confrontation between Mr. Cassavetes and an officious lady on a bus who doesn't want to start up with his "element," and a fine sequence in an all-black bar whose patrons take Mikey and Nicky for white cops. Not so good is a sequence in a neighborhood bar where Miss May's camera keeps panning across the great faces of the real-life (I'm sure) customers as if she were showing us Hindu temple carvings).

Several supporting actors have some good moments, including Ned Beatty, who plays the hired murderer who worries about the cost of the gasoline he's using up, and Carol Grace, who is superb a slightly dimwitted girlfriend of Mr. Cassavetes. What Mr. Cassavetes and Mr. Falk do, though, exists beyond the fringe of film criticism. They just seem to be carrying on—making elaborate actorish fusses—in front of the camera.

Miss May is a witty, gifted, very intelligent director. It took guts for her to attempt a film like this, but she failed.

1976 D 22, 34:4

NICKELODEON, directed by Peter Bogdanovich; written by Mr. Bogdanovich and W.D. Richter; produced by Irwin Winkler and Robert Chartoff; director of photography, Laszlo Kovacs; edited by William Carruh. Released by Columbia Pictures. At the Columbia I and II Theaters. Running time: 122 minutes. This film has been rated: PG.

Leo Harrigan........................Ryan O'Neal
Buck Greenway....................Burt Reynolds
Alice Forsyte.......................Tatum O'Neal
H.H. Cobb.............................Brian Keith
Marty Reeves.......................Stella Stevens
Franklin Frank.......................John Ritter
Kathleen Cooke....................Jane Hitchcock

By RICHARD EDER

Peter Bogdanovich knows a great deal about movies, including how they are made. Perhaps he doesn't know why they are made. In any case, knowing how something is made isn't the same as making it. "Nickelodeon" is two hours and two minutes of impersonations.

Some of them are very good impersonations—deft and funny—but they lack a life to string them together. The effect is like a vaudevillian imitating a Frenchman making a speech. The imitation is fine but there is no speech.

Despite its length, which is one of its problems, there isn't much movie in "Nickelodeon," which opened yesterday at the Columbia I and II Theaters.

Its subject has been pretty heavily treated of late. It is about the early days of movie-making. Slapstick in style and picaresque in form, it is closer to such spoofs as "Hearts of the West" and "Won Ton Ton the Dog Who Saved Hollywood" than to "Day of the Locust" or "The Last Tycoon."

It is not really a spoof though. At the end Mr. Bogdanovich has his raggle-taggle band of movie makers, given a contract after many reverses, pass a lighted sound-stage. "They're making a movie," says Ryan O'Neal, as their director, in a near-choked voice.

Mr. Bogdanovich mistreats his love for the vitality of American movie-making by proclaiming it so breathily. He mistreats his love for the tricks of the trade, especially the slapstick comic trade, by virtually italicizing each trick as he trots it out.

Harrigan—Mr. O'Neal—is an incompetent lawyer who meets up with Cobb, a manic film producer who is battling the big companies. Some meaningless remark leads Cobb first to hire him as a writer, then to send him out West to take over a band of actors and technicians whose director has decamped. Harrigan gets entagled with an unskilled hoofer—played by Jane Hitchcock—and an unskilled rodeo rider—Burt Reynolds—adds them to the company, and begins to make movies.

It's easy, the cameraman tells them "These are the actors. This is the ccamera. You tell me where to place it, and when you have enough you tell me 'cut.' "

•

It is a nice rendering of the casual improvisation of early movie-making—parodied, but only marginally. Mr. Bogdanovich arranges for some good things to happen. There is a fine trolley-car scene where Cobb's film company rides to the set inventing the script along the way. Not only is the idea-man subject to fits, he also produces ideas only when he has them.

There are any number of sight gags. Some—notably one involving two monocled Germans who make movies clandestinely at the back of a pastry shop—are very funny.

Too many, though, are obvious quotes from old slapstick routines. the shock of recognition, such as it is, quite overpowers the impulse to laugh.

Mr. Bogdanovich lets his routines run on too long. There is an endless fight between Mr. O'Neal and Mr. Reynolds. It is choreographed as a comic ballet: It is infinitely familiar, infinitely slick and not at all funny. Rather than giving us a sense that the movie is going somewhere, the routines succeed one another endlessly. They are a parade that totally interrupts any traffic that might be around.

•

Mr. Reynolds is appealing, and sometimes quite funny as the cowhand who becomes a reluctant star. Miss Hitchcock, with wide cheeks and a pointed chin, seems to have comic potential but the point is never really proved. Tatum O'Neal plays a sarcastic but useful brat as if she'd been there before and too often.

Mr. O'Neal is a major mistake. He has very little talent for comedy. The way to be funny is not to try intensely to be funny. It is to be yourself so single-mindedly as to be funny. If Mr. O'Neal has a self he has left it at home.

An opening day "Nickelodeon" was charging a nickel admission. That's underpricing it; 75 cents would be about right.

•

The film has been rated PG ("Parental Guidance Suggested"). It's hard to see why any such caution is put in. There is nothing that could conceivably be objectionable in it.

1976 D 22, 34:4

REGROUPING; a film by Lizzie Borden. Running time: 75 minutes. At the Whitney Museum of American Art, Madison Avenue and 75th Street, through Sunday.

By A. H. WEILER

Lizzie Borden, who is described as a writer and critic in program notes and obviously is not the late, historic cutup, is indecisive as a film maker in "Regrouping," which opened yesterday at the Whitney Museum of American Art. Her documentation of a sodality of four, young liberated women seeking mutuality and identity and their eventual disenchantment and breakup, is, despite its pointed honesty, blunted by diffuse filming and narrative techniques.

Because there is a conflict of interests in their approaches to art, politics, love, homosexuality, etc., their initially collaborative association appears to be rickety at best. And, it is not surprising that it disintegrates completely with the movie maker's taking over on her own to include a new group, fictional footage and her own commentary. Needless to say, the original quartet, who are fearful of the effects of this intrusion on their privacy, Miss Borden's alleged domination and other things, do state and restate their opposition to the showing of the completed film.

As stated, the honesty is there. But "Regrouping" is marked by a plethora of fragmentary, unrelated information —scenes on city streets, a supermarket, a ladies shower room, a couple dancing, two women making love — that make no specific points. And the sound track includes often confused, clipped or overlapping conversations by unnamed individuals that add to the fuzziness of this admittedly manipulated project.

Of course, there is little doubt as to the altruism of the movie maker and her questioning collaborators. But they are beclouded by disparate, unresolved views of the real issues and problems of these authentically concerned people. Their "Regrouping" is a sincere effort but it merely has the effect of a rough-hewn work in progress.

1976 D 22, 39:1

VOYAGE OF THE DAMNED, directed by Stuart Rosenberg; screenplay by Steve Shagan and David Butler, based on the book by Gordon Thomas and Max Morgan Witts; produced by Robert Fryer; director of photography, Billy Williams; music, Lalo Schifrin; editor, Tom Priestly; an ITC Entertainment Film production, distributed by Avco Embassy Pictures. Running time: 158 minutes, At Loews Astor Plaza Theater, 44th Street west of Broadway; Loews Cine Theater, Third Avenue near 86th Street and Reade's 34th Street East Theater, near Second Avenue. This film has been rated PG.

Denise Kreisler ....Faye Dunaway
Capt. Schroeder ....Max Von Sydow
Dr. Kreisler ....Oskar Werner
Max Gunter ....Malcolm McDowell
Estedes ....Orson Welles
Remos ....James Mason
Lilian Rosen ....Lee Grant
Morris Troper ....Ben Gazzara
Mira Hauser ....Katharine Ross
Prof. Weiler ....Luther Adler
Clasing ....Michael Constantine
Adm Canaris ....Denholm Elliott
Benitez ....Jose Ferrer
Anna Rosen ....Lynne Frederick
Schiendick ....Helmut Griem
Alice Feinchild ....Julie Harris
Rebecca Weiler ....Wendy Hiller
Dr. Glauner ....Donald Houston
Aaron Pozner ....Paul Koslo
Mr. Hauser ....Nehemiah Persoff
President Bru ....Fernando Rey
Commander von Bonin............Leonard Rossiter
Mrs. Hauser ....Maria Schell
Dr. Max Strauss...................Victor Spinetti
Leni Strauss ....Janet Suzman
Carl Rosen ....Sam Wanamaker
Joseph Manasse ....Jonathan Pryce

By VINCENT CANBY

In May 1939 the Hamburg-America liner St. Louis sailed from Hamburg headed for Havana, carrying 937 Jews who had paid Hitler's government dearly in the hope of finding refuge from the Nazis in Cuba. Hitler's strategy was simple: if, indeed, the Cuban Government accepted the refugees (and there was doubt about that, even when they sailed), then Germany was well rid of them and a little bit richer, too.

If Cuba did not accept them, and if the United States and other countries followed suit, then Hitler would have proven his point that Jews were unwanted by the very countries that were so loudly criticizing his anti-Semitic policies while proclaiming their own humanitarian principles.

•

The story of that voyage is a harrowing footnote to the history of World War II. As carefully researched by Gordon Thomas and Max Morgan Witts in their book "The Voyage of the Damned," it is, further, a revealing commentary on how opportunism could dictate policies of friendly governments, including that of the United States.

It also seems to be excellent source material for a film, though you'd never know it from the alternately sluggish and hysterical movie that opened at three New York theaters yesterday. Stuart Rosenberg, the director, and Steven Shagan and David Butler, who wrote the screenplay, appear to have been attracted to the project because of the almost limitless ways in which they could make history look like a bad, all-star movie. to start with, they use a dozen or so too many stories even to fit conveniently into a running time inflated to 158 minutes.

Their touch is so surely banal that they turn potentially moving episodes into second-rate melodrama, while adding some third-rate melodramatics of their own, including a Romeo-and-Juliet suicide pact. It's the kind of movie in which someone says, quite seriously, "Vee Chermans har hallvays hon time" (We Germans are always on time).

•

The cast includes good actors and bad, but even the good actors are inclined to be awful. Faye Dunaway and Oskar Werner are all

Faye Dunaway, above, and Lee Grant
Cast in a movie that is worse than merely boring.

right as a rather posh Berlin doctor and his wife who are carrying their marital problems into exile intact. They travel first-class. Malcolm McDowell plays the role of a cabin boy who appears to be old enough to qualify for Social Security. When we weren't looking, his youth fled. Max von Sydow survives with his reputation undamaged as the liner's humane skipper, but Katharine Ross, who looks like a Rose Bowl parade queen, is a joke as a humane Havana whore.

Orson Welles, James Mason, Denholm Elliott and Jose Ferrer are on and off faster than it takes to type this sentence, while Lee Grant, Julie Harris, Wendy Hiller and Luther Adler might wish they had been so lucky.

Movies as clumsy, tasteless and self-righteous as this are worse than merely boring. By exploiting the tragedies of real people, some wildly fictionalized, "The Voyage of the Damned" attempts to turn them to profit without giving them any measure of the respect that is due.

"Voyage of The Damned," which has been rated PG ("parental guidance suggested", contains nothing of an even mildly suggestive nature except the title, which might mislead children to think they are about to see a disaster film—and a child who wants to see a disaster film and sees this, instead, will be an angry child.

1976 D 23, 18:1

THE ENFORCER, directed by James Fargo; written by Stirling Silliphant and Dean Reisner from a story by Gail Morgan Hickman and S. W. Schurr; produced by Robert Daley; director of photography, Charles W. Short. Released by Warner Bros. At the Criterion and Flagship theaters. Running time: 96 minutes. This film has been rated R.
Harry Callahan ....Clint Eastwood
Lieut. Bressler ....Harry Guardino
Capt. McKay ....Bradford Dillman
DiGeorgio ....John Mitchum
Bobby Maxwell ....DeVeren Bookwalter
Mayor ....John Crawford
Kate Moore ....Tyne Daly

By RICHARD EDER

There's a basic weakness in the movie business' assumption that if you have a big suspense or action picture with lots of movement and thrills, you don't need writing or acting or character in it.

Because what happens? The climax comes. Good and bad are stalking each other around some monstrous hangar, Zoroastrian rest-home or abandoned maple-sugar factory. Music. Suspenseful lighting. Tension. And a face peers around the corner. But by this time, who cares about the face? It might as well be Donald Duck's.

Money, the big name of Clint Eastwood, a lot of gore and howling sirens and the urge to rail at various liberal notions are not enough to make even a passable movie out of "The Enforcer."

The movie, which opened yesterday at the Criterion and other theaters, is the third in the series— "Dirty Harry" and "Magnum Force" were the first two—about a mean though righteous San Francisco cop. It has been billed as "the dirtiest Harry of them all," but it is simply the surliest. It is the same barroom drunk railing at weirdos and pinkos, and four or five glasses farther into his theme.

The movie begins with the killing of two gas-company drivers by the Revolutionary Strike Force. The half-dozen young people in the force need the gas truck to break into an arms depot guarded by one (1) old watchman. They kill him and use the arms and detonators to kidnap the mayor, whom they hold for ransom. The killings are unnecessary, but this is explained by the fact that the leader—who is really in it for the money—is a homicidal madman. We know this because his jaws quiver when he stabs people.

Out comes Harry Callahan (Mr. Eastwood) of the homicide division. That is, he's sometimes of the homicide division. He starts out by driving his car through the window of a liquor store to break up a stickup and kills the three gunmen. He is busted to personnel for roughness, reinstated when the Revolutionary Strike Force begins work, is busted again when he goes after them too vigorously, but manages to get them all anyway when they hole up in what used to be Alcatraz prison.

•

The action is reasonably fast and competently photographed. The picture doesn't exactly drag. But it is maggoty with non-ideas. These non-ideas come in the form of a whole gallery of corrupt or foolish liberal types who interfere with Harry's mission.

There is a progressive priest who shelters the assault gang until one of them, dressed as a nun, tries to shoot Harry. There is a weaselly police captain who says Harry's shooting the liquor-store holdup men was offensive to the city's minorities. "The hoods, you mean,"

Clint Eastwood and Tyne Daly
Lots of non-ideas

Harry says brightly. "They're Americans, too," the captain answers.

That—the movie tells us—is how knee-jerk liberals think. The politicians are corrupt and pathetically eager to appease the thugs/radicals/pornographers.

Feminism is also some kind of conspiracy. Harry is reluctantly saddled with a woman police officer as his partner. Played by Tyne Daly, who is good-hearted and plucky, but she is also a whole shopping list of alleged feminine incompetences.

She runs with her arms flapping all anyhow, holds a pistol as if it were a chamberpot, asks stupid questions, goes around with her mouth gaping, and talks in a high-pitched quack. That is Miss Daly peering around a corner in the climactic scene, not Donald Duck. But, as stated earlier, it might as well be.

1976 D 23, 18:1

New-Style Frontier

PIPE DREAMS, directed, written and produced by Stephen Verona; executive producer, Barry Hankerson; musical director, Dominick Frontiere; editor, Robert L. Estrin; distributed by Avco Embassy Pictures. Running time: 89 minutes. At the RKO Cinerama 2, Broadway and 47th Street; RKO 86th Street Twin 2, near Lexington Avenue, and Apollo 125th Street, near Eighth Avenue. This film has been rated PG.
Maria Wilson ....Gladys Knight
Rob Wilson ....Barry Hankerson
The Duke ....Bruce French
Loretta ....Sherry Bain
Mike Thompson ....Wayne Tippit

By VINCENT CANBY

GLADYS KNIGHT, the recording star, makes a nice, low-keyed movie debut in "Pipe Dreams," the first film I've seen that uses the building of the Alaskan pipeline as an essential part of its action. The film, which also stars Miss

Knight's real-life husband, Barry Hankerson, as her husband, within-the-film, is set in Valdez, Alaska, effectively portrayed as a frozen frontier community of well-heeled, lonely construction workers and the whores and confidence artists who are after their loot.

Stephen Verona, the writer and director of the film, displays little apparent talent in either capacity, but at least he doesn't dwell too long on the foolishness of a plot that includes one plane crash of absolutely no surprise and the inept attempts of a crooked entrepreneur to delay the pipeline's completion. The movie pays no attenkerson, as her husband within-the-fraud involving the pipeline.

•

Mostly it's about Miss Knight's attempts to win back her husband who had earlier left her in Atlanta to make his fortune as an Alaskan bush pilot. Miss Knight and Mr. Hankerson are not great actors by any means, but they play well together, creating some genuinely moving and comic moments of a sort one didn't often see in old-fashioned "B" pictures about lumber camps and gold-strike towns, which "Pipe Dreams" faintly resembles.

Miss Knight doesn't sing on screen but, with the Pips, she's never long off the soundtrack. A lot of the movie is used up sightseeing by air, accompanied by Miss Knight and the Pips singing a batch of songs, some of which have more plot relevance than others. The film opened yesterday at four theaters.

•

"Pipe Dreams," which has been rated PG ("Parental Guidance Suggested"), makes no attempt to disguise the fact that all the women in the film, except its star, are whores, though nothing in the way of explicit sex is shown.

1976 D 24, C10:5

Merger of Hearts

THE PINK TELEPHONE, directed by Edouard Molinaro; produced by Alain Poire; written by Francis Veber; edited by Gerard Hameline; released by S.J. International. At the Fine Arts Theater. Running time: 95 minutes. This film has been rated R.
Benoit Castenjac ....Pierre Mondy
Mrs. Casteniac ....Francoise Prevost
Christine ....Mireille Darc
American Company President ....Michel Lonsdale
Public Relations Director ....Daniel Ceccaldi

By RICHARD EDER

HE PINK TELEPHONE" is a depressing little French soap-opera with various more or less fashionable preoccupations tagged on. It is soft at the center and musty on the surface.

"Telephone," which opened yesterday at the Fine Arts theater, is about a provincial factory owner who sells his factory to a big, American-controlled enterprise. The owner, who plays rugby with his workers on weekends and personifies the old humanity of France, comes up to Paris to discuss the sale.

•

The purchasers, sleek to a fault and inhabiting a faceless glass building, sweeten the talks by providing a call girl who pretends to be somebody's niece and pretends to fall in love with the factory owner. After their night together, he is smitten, and dreams of a new life, of leaving his wife and setting up with the young woman.

He finds out the truth, is disillusioned, the factory sale is put in doubt, the workers protest, he leaves his wife. Meanwhile, he conducts a running argument with the young woman. She asserts the economic advantages of being a call girl. He argues for love. Finally she gets on a plane to meet a client in Italy and then, at the very end, turns back. Presumably they will live somewhere in the country and grow tomatoes.

•

The wildly romantic, implausible ending is reminiscent of "Cousin, Cousine," but nothing else in the film is. Pierre Mondy tries to play the factory owner with the warm impassiveness of the late Jean Gabin; he simply looks sorry for himself. Mireille Darc as the call girl is cool, blonde and—judging by the amount of life she contributes—on strike. Michel Lonsdale is sometimes amusing as the American capitalist.

1976 D 24, C10:5

THE MONKEY HUSTLE, directed by Arthur Marks; screenplay by Charles Johnson; story by Odie Hawkins; director of photography, Jack L. Richards; film editor, Art Seid; music, Jack Conrad; producer, Mr. Marks; released by American International Pictures. At the Cinerama 1, Broadway at 47th Street, and neighborhood theaters. Running time: 90 minutes. This film is classified PG.

Daddy Foxx	Yaphet Kotto
Goldie	Rudy Ray Moore
Mama	Rosalind Cash
Win	Randy Brooks
Vi	Debbi Morgan
Player	Thomas Carter
Tiny	Donn Harper
Jan-Jan	Lynn Caridine
Shirl	Patricia McCaskill

"The Monkey Hustle" is a movie of jellied brain and idiot eyes, like the defective product of combining an old Andy Hardy movie and modern black urban life. The result is something that peers through a haze of moral confusion at street kids, pimps, hustlers, hookers, crooked cops, spaghetti-spined politicians and corrupt businessmen and decides they are lollipops.

The truth is that most of the principal characters, including many of the youngsters, are dishonest or brutal, and the "heroes" are distinguishable only by being slightly less dishonest or brutal than the villains. Reigning at the summit of "The Monkey Hustle's" distorted hagiocracy—apparently by virtue of the fact that he smiles brilliantly and contents himself with small swindles and the immoral upbringing of small children—is Yaphet Kotto as a petty con man named Daddy Foxx.

Aside from concerning itself with the virtues of small-time crime as opposed to numbers and pimping, this movie also busies itself with young love, an expressway that threatens the Chicago neighborhood in which it is set, and an effort to obtain the money for the set of drums to play at the big community block party to oppose the expressway.

This movie's major hustle will be to separate from their money and time the adolescents who might logically be "The Monkey Hustle's" audience—if it merited one.

The PG ("parental guidance suggested") rating is presumably attributable to the movie's street language and its recognition that adolescents are sexual explorers.

LAWRENCE VAN GELDER

1976 D 25, 8:1

A Film Is Reborn

A STAR IS BORN, directed by Frank Pierson; screenplay by John Gregory Dunne and Joan Didion, and Mr. Pierson, based on a story by William Wellman and Robert Carson; produced by Jon Peters; executive producer, Barbra Streisand; director of photography, Robert Surtees; editor, Peter Zinner; music and live recordings produced by Phil Ramone; musical concepts by Miss Streisand; a First Artists presentation, distributed by Warner Brothers. Running time: 140 minutes. At the Ziegfeld Theater, 54th Street near the Avenue of the Americas, and Baronet Theater, Third Avenue near 59th Street. This film has been rated R.

Esther Hoffman	Barbra Streisand
John Norman Howard	Kris Kristofferson
Bobby Ritchie	Gary Busey
Gary Danziger	Oliver Clark
The Oreos	Vanetta Fields
	Clyde King
Quentin	Marta Heflin
Bebe Jesus	M. G. Kelly
Photographer	Sally Kirkland
Freddie	Joanne Linville
Mo	Uncle Rudy
Brian	Paul Mazursky

By VINCENT CANBY

SHE'S A LIKABLE KID, loaded with talent, and still unknown at the start of her career. He's a star, not just any star, but a superstar, at the end of his. They meet and ignite. For an all-too-brief instant as time is computed in the galaxies, their love flares —how should I put it?—incandescently. Then the momentum of their lives separates them as she goes on to become the brightest new star in the firmament while he, has-been that he's about to become, slides back down fame's ladder into oblivion soup. He implodes.

When this was made as "What Price Hollywood?" in 1932, it was based on a story credited to Adela Rogers St. John, directed by George Cukor, and starred Constance Bennett as the ingenue. What with one thing and another, it inspired The New York Time's film critic to write, "Once you have been divorced by a polo player and have had your director commit suicide in your home, there is nothing left but rural France."

•

Things improved with the 1937 remake (as "A Star Is Born") that starred Janet Gaynor and Fredric March and was directed by William Wellman, by which time the original story was being credited to Mr. Wellman and Robert Carson. Things peaked, though, in the 1954 remake, again directed by Mr. Cukor, which had a screenplay by Moss Hart and starred James Mason and Judy Garland in what was probably the greatest performance of her career.

The latest version, which opened Saturday at the Ziegfield and Baronet Theaters, is a transistorized remake, louder than ever, but very small in terms of its being about anything whatsoever. The setting is no longer Hollywood and movie-making, but the contemporary rock scene. Its stars are Barbra Streisand, who plays an unknown singer as if she were the wolf disguised as Red Riding Hood's grandmother, and Kris Kristofferson, who plays the fading rock star whose last decent act, you might say, is passing on the torch of fame to Barbra, who, of course, looks perfectly capable of knocking him down and taking it away from him anyway.

•

According to the credits, the film was directed by Frank Pierson, who won an Oscar for his screenplay for "Dog Day Afternoon," and it was written by John Gregory Dunne and Joan Didion, who worked on it as a team, and by Mr. Pierson. The dominant personality of the production, however, is Miss Streisand's. In addition to being the film's star, she is its executive producer, takes credit for its "musical concepts," contributed her own wardrobe and collaborated on two of its best songs, "Evergreen" and "Lost Inside of You."

As long as this "A Star Is Born" attends to music, it is not at all bad. There is souped-up excitement when it is recording the stars' recording sessions, their giant rock concerts and their benefit performances, and when it is getting them into and out of hysterical crowds via limousine, ambulance and sometimes helicopter. The excitement is suddenly genuine when Miss Streisand sings, but the drama that contains it is as bogus as the star's performance when she pretends to be Esther Hoffman, unknown singer.

•

There's also something completely bogus in the pairing of Miss Streisand and Mr. Kristofferson, who, as lovers, are less exciting than King Kong and Jessica Lange. It would be easy to say that it's not Mr. Kristofferson's fault, but I'm not sure it isn't. He walks through the film looking very bored.

Miss Streisand, at least, attempts to act, delivering with much simulated passion a line such as, "You can trash your life, but you aren't going to trash mine!" Or, when Mr. Kristofferson discovers her at the piano and asks what she's playing, "Just a little something I wrote, hoping it will be a sonata when it grows up." Now that she's her own executive producer she can't blame lines like that on Ray Stark.

•

What Miss Streisand does is not acting. She's a queen condescending to her own court cameraman, which explains, I suspect, why even a couple of semi-nude love scenes have the effect of being anti-erotic. One suspects she, not the director, is the one who yelled "cut" just before the camera would have glimpsed a bare Streisand breast.

She never plays to or with the other actors. She does "A Star Is Born" as a solo turn. Everybody else is a back-up musician, which is okay when she's belting out a lyric, but distinctly odd when other actors come into the same frame.

1976 D 27, C16:5

War Amalgam

ALL THIS AND WORLD WAR II, documentary footage set to rock music, directed by Susan Winslow; produced by Sandy Lieberson and Martin J. Machat; words and music by John Lennon and Paul McCartney; a Lou Reizner Production; a Martin J. Machat/Eric Kronfeld presentation; released by 20th Century-Fox. At the Trans-Lux Theater, Third Avenue and 58th Street. Running time: 98 minutes. This film has been rated PG.

By A. H. WEILER

"All This and World War II," which arrived at the Trans-Lux East yesterday, is, like war, eye-and ear-filling, but confusing. As an amalgam of newsreel and fictional film footage from 20th Century-Fox vaults and a background score of John Lennon and Paul McCartney rock hits, neither the war nor the songs emerge victorious or especially memorable.

Call it a tribute to a well-meant concept and the editing of a vast store of material. But this kaleidoscopic succession of vignettes from the appeasement era to V-J Day are reminders of history that momentarily meld and then just as quickly fade away. A shot of Nazi phalanxes goose-stepping before the hostilities that is coupled with a funny clip about Hitler's "Mein Kampf" from the unnamed Hitchcock classic, "The Lady Vanishes," may be vaguely related, but do not stick in memory.

Some popular World War II slogans painted on a young woman's legs.

One is reminded of the slightly glamorous aspects of war with scenes of the actual inductions into the armed forces of James Stewart, Clark Gable and Tyrone Power. And views of Hitler, President Roosevelt, Churchill, Field Marshal Montgomery and General Eisenhower, Bob Hope, De Gaulle (entering Paris), bombings, evacuated children, the Battle of Midway and scrap drives, among many others, indicate the reality and some of the concomitant levity of the period.

The bombing of Pearl Harbor to the accompaniment of "I Am the Walrus" seems a dubious sort of irony. But G.I.'s reading letters from home to the background singing of "Yesterday" is genuinely effective and poignant. One can't fault the artistry of the composers of "Yesterday" or "Fool on the Hill" or such artists as Helen Reddy or Elton John or the London Symphony and the Royal Philharmonic Orchestras. But their identities here, like the film's fictional movie excerpts, remain fairly mysterious to the untutored.

The producers' intentions, as noted, appear to be good. But their collage of conflict and music evolves as an unresolved tussle between realism, seemingly weak satire and the tunes so dear to the Woodstock generation.

This film has been rated PG ("Parental Guidance Suggested"), probably because of World War II bombings and the like, none of which, in all likelihood, have not been seen before by the small fry on their television screens.

1976 D 27, C17:1

Biblical Journey

IN SEARCH OF NOAH'S ARK, directed by James L. Conway; screenplay by Mr. Conway and Charles E. Sellier, Jr., from a book by David Balsiger and Mr. Sellier; director of photography, George Stapleford; editor, Sharron Miller; produced by Mr. Sellier; released by Sun Classic Pictures Inc. At neighborhood theaters. This film has been rated G.

"In Search of Noah's Ark," now docked at about 100 theaters in the metropolitan area, is, like some quests, ideally motivated but frustrating.

Since the account in Genesis is somewhat minimal, this documentation and re-enactment serves as a fairly reasonable attempt to explain questions that have plagued biblical and scientific scholars for thousands of years. But this delving into records and places in proof of the reality of Noah and his epic Ark adventure is largely a leisurely, pedantic but picturesque journey that lacks the conviction of incontrovertible proof.

That "search" starts, of course, with a dramatization of Noah—here a benign, white-bearded patriarch—his family and that Ark of "gopher" (oak?) wood, a 450-foot leviathan, the largest wooden ship ever built by man, it says here.

While researchers present facts substantiating the possibility of such an accomplishment; that feat done by so few still troubles a viewer.

Before the film wends its way to the 17,000-foot, glacier-crowned, storm and suspicion-ridden Mount Ararat on the Turkish-Soviet border where the Ark landed, we encounter a succession of scholars and varied places such as Turkish villages and the American Earth Resources Satellite Center.

Bits of timber found by Sir James Bryce and those discovered by the French explorer Fernand Navarra on Ararat, as well as some controversial tests on the antiquity of the semi-petrified wood, are presented as evidence of the existence of the Ark. And various expeditions, as well as photographs of their findings by U-2 planes, among others, are presented to indicate the presence of part of the Ark, a black hull stuck in a 15,000-foot glacier.

Unfortunately, the creation of such an immense vessel, its seaworthiness, the ability of Noah to gather thousands of animals and feed them over many months, the possibility of such a flood's occurring some 5,000 years ago, may be presented with seemingly scientific sincerity.

But these data, along with the final statement that the hulk on Ararat cannot be extricated entire because it would cause political havoc between Turkey and the Soviet Union, remain, despite the apparent seriousness of this "Search," arguable points.

A. H. WEILER

1976 D 27, C20:5

THE SHAGGY D. A.; screenplay by Don Tait; suggested by "The Hound of Florence" by Felix Salten; directed by Robert Stevenson; director of photography, Frank Phillips; music by Buddy Baker; dog character voices by George Kirby; edited by Bob Bring and Norman Palmer; produced by Bill Anderson with Ron Miller as executive producer; released by Buena Vista Distribution Company. At local theaters. Running time: 91 minutes. This film has been rated G.

Wilby Daniels .... Dean Jones
Betty Daniels .... Suzanne Pleshette
John Slade .... Keenan Wynn
Brian Daniels .... Shane Sinutko
Tim .... Tim Conway
Katrinka Musselberg .... Jo Anne Worley
Admiral Brenner .... John Myhers
Eddie Roschak .... Vic Tayback
Prof. Whatley .... Hans Conried
Bartender .... Pat McCormick

Now is the time, of course, for all good men to be kind to man and dumb animals. But "The Shaggy D.A.," which bounded into local theaters on Christmas Day, puts that wonderful concept to a severe test. As the sequel to "The Shaggy Dog," Walt Disney's 1959 moneymaker, "The Shaggy D.A." is a farce with all the witless energy of an unrestrained Great Dane puppy and, thankfully, a cast and director who generally avoid taking themselves or the free-wheeling plot seriously.

●

You may recall that "Shaggy Dog" involved a teen-ager who was turned into a sheepdog fairly regularly because of the magical power of a "Borgia" scarab ring. This time, as a married man, father and lawyer in the person of Dean Jones, he again is being transformed into that woolly canine while campaigning for the district attorney's office against that dastard, Keenan Wynn.

Naturally, the story line is incredible and convoluted enough to give an uninhibited cast plenty of opportunities to clown for, unfortunately, a minimum of real laughs. However, between continuous chases, pie-throwing binges and dogs that talk like James Cagney, Edward G. Robinson and Mae West, Dean Jones manages to make the dog-harried D.A. candidate a mildly comic, if improbable, gent. Suzanne Pleshette, in her first film role in five years, plays his wife in amiably tongue-in-cheek style and Shane Sinutko is impish as their pre-teen son.

●

Keenan Wynn is, let's say, an outrageously broad villain who gets his just deserts, animal style. And, among many others, Tim Conway does his shtick as a fairly droll, dead-panned ice-cream vendor who naïvely thinks his pet has suddenly become a talking sheepdog.

"You can't go through life not knowing when you'll turn into a dog," an exasperated Miss Pleshette exclaims at one point. She's right. Despite all the athletic goings-on, "The Shaggy D.A." does turn into a dog too often for comfort.

A. H. WEILER

1976 D 27, C18:1

THE LIFE AND DEATH OF FRIDA KAHLO, a documentary film by Karen and David Crommie; distributed by the Serious Business Company. Running time: 40 minutes.
CHULAS FRONTERAS (Beautiful Borders), a documentary film by Les Blank; produced and conceived by Chris Strachwitz; distributed by Brazos Films. Running time: 58 minutes.
Both films in English and Spanish (with English subtitles). At the Film Forum, 15 Vandam Street.

By VINCENT CANBY

THE LIFE AND DEATH of Frida Kahlo," which is slightly less than half of the new program at the Film Forum, is an exquisite film of its kind. It's a short, moving, vivid recollection of the life and work of the woman who was Diego Rivera's third wife (as well as his fourth), a painter being recognized in her own right—though she remains largely unknown outside her native Mexico—a being haunted by illness from childhood until she died in 1954 at the age of 44. til she died in 1954 at the age of 44.

The film is the work of Karen and David Crommie, the San Francisco film makers who made the movie 10 years ago, although it is only now receiving its well-deserved New York premiere.

It opened yesterday at the Film Forum on a bill with "Chulas Fronteras," Les Blank's 58-minute documentary on Mexican-American music. The program will be seen tonight, tomorrow and Sunday nights at 7:30 o'clock, and at the same time next week, Thursday through Sunday.

Mr. and Mrs. Crommie evoke Miss Kahlo's life through still photographs, pictures of her paintings and, on the soundtrack, the recorded recollections of people who knew her in Mexico and this country. The Crommies' achievement is to have produced such an emotionally charged film at such a far remove in time from their subject, which is testimony, I suspect, not only to their taste and talent as film makers, but also to the vitality of Miss Kahlo and her work.

●

The woman they recall had polio as a child and then in her early teens was in an automobile accident in which her back was broken in two places. For the rest of her life, she was in and out of hospitals for operations that never were successful and that, at the end, after the amputation of one leg, left her an invalid unable to paint.

She was, as a friend remembers and as we see in photographs and self-portraits, "almost beautiful," with fine, dark eyes and what appears to be "a single eyebrow" that passed from one side of here face to the other with virtually no break. After meeting Rivera when she was 14 years old, she told a friend that more than anything else she wanted to have his child. At 19 she married him though he was more than 40, and began a life that seems to have been a classic blend of ecstasy and pain.

The pain was emotional as well as physical. Rivera, according to these old friends and associates, was a monster and an egomaniac, and though he encouraged her painting, he never acknowledged her needs. In 1939 they were divorced, only to remarry a year later.

While Rivera was out decorating public buildings with huge panoramas of the great new Communist society, she was creating small, fantastic paintings of her life, using brilliant, raw colors and realistic but contradictory images of a kind that earned her a reputation as a Surrealist, though critics debate that point.

●

Having never seen any of her work except in this film, I've no idea where to place it. Within the film, though, these sometimes nightmarish and brutal self-portraits, juxtaposed with photographs of the elegant, handsome woman who painted them, help to create a

Frida Kahlo, central figure of the film at the Film Forum

memorable personality—witty, staunch, full of benign feelings and merciless self-appraisal.

"The Life and Death of Frida Kahlo" runs only 40 minutes, but it is more affecting than most features. "Chulas Fronteras," directed by Mr. Blank, is at heart solemnly picturesque, though the Mex-Tex music it studies is lively enough. Mr. Blank's approach is sincerely appreciative and just a bit condescending, like that of the anthropologist who refuses to panic even as his subjects prepare to put him in a kettle of boiling chicken stock.

1976 D 31, C10:1

The Year in Films, From 'Rocky' to Renoir

Any film year is more than simply the best films of the year. It's also people, events, trends, affirmations of old truths, exceptions to rules. The following is 1976 decimalized, including my choices for the best films of the year, though not in any particular order of chronology or importance.

1. Show biz is no biz. They call it an industry but the making of movies remained the biggest crap game in the world in 1976. Dino De Laurentiis has between $22 million and $25 million riding on a bet that says a large proportion of the world's population can't wait to see a remake of "King Kong." It's still too early to tell how he'll make out, though De Laurentiis knows as well as anybody that nothing in movies is a sure thing. The low-budget "Rocky" will probably make a far greater percentage of profit than "The Missouri Breaks," which starred Marlon Brando and Jack Nicholson. "Harry and Walter Go To New York" (Elliott Gould, James Caan and a script in the mode of "The Sting") died upon delivery at theaters, while "Cousin Cousine," a small French comedy that opened here without benefit of star names or publicity, has become a smash. I have faith that good movies will survive even if this is The Year of The Ape.

2. Lina Wertmuller. The phenomenal critical success of—as well as box office support for—Lina Wertmuller's "Seven Beauties" not only announces the arrival of a fine new Italian directorial talent but also the beginning of the end of our prejudice against women-as-directors. Wertmuller's films are so complex, so full of life, that it's not simply unnecessary to read them as the Statements of A Woman, but inadequate to the task. We no longer have to wonder that Wertmuller, Elaine May, Jeanne Moreau, Marguerite Duras, Shirley Clarke, Dyan Cannon and Dorothy Arzner have directed films without suffering fainting fits. We look at their movies for what they are. Some are fine. Some are stinkers, and a lot are what most movies are—somewhere in-between.

3. "All The President's Men." In adapting the fascinating Watergate book by Carl Bernstein and Bob Woodward, the Washington Post reporters, director Alan J. Pakula, writer William Goldman, and stars Dustin Hoffman and Robert Redford have successfully brought off what no folksy, seven o'clock TV news team has ever done. They've made contemporary history seem urgent and the practice of journalism important. And even though all of us knew the end of the story, they made a film as exciting and as full of suspense as any conventional caper film.

4. Ingmar Bergman's "Face to Face." Having completed "Face to Face," the sorrowful and resonant study of the suicidal breakdown of a perfectly composed woman (a psychiatrist magnificently played by Liv Ullmann), Bergman went into self-imposed exile from his native Sweden, the result of a traumatic confrontation with bureaucracy in a perfectly composed socialist state. The film, which could be the last Bergman will ever make in Sweden, may not have been conceived as political though all its implications are. Bergman is now completing a film in Germany. We wait to see how his artistry will survive outside the particular Swedish environment through which his films have always reached us.

5. Jean Renoir. He is 82 and hasn't made a film since 1969 ("The Little Theater of Jean Renoir") yet Renoir, who now lives in California, being a master, is able to make us marvel still. One of the joys of this film season was Renoir's 1931 "La Chienne," his first sound film but which was released here for the first time with English titles. In "La Chienne" Renoir transforms a rather banal story about a prissy, middle-aged bookkeeper (Michel Simon) who falls in love with a two-timing tart whom he murders in a rage of humiliation, into a nearly epic human comedy. Although heroes, rascals, shrews and cheats can be recognized in the landscape, Renoir doesn't take sides to point a moral. He appreciates all of his characters and their curious circumstances too much to be anything but generous, and in so doing, he persuades us to be generous too.

6. "Network." There is nothing generous at all about Paddy Chayefsky's views on American television—the

Ullmann in Bergman's "Face to Face"— "magnificently played"

people who dish it out and the people who swallow it whole —in this flamboyant satire directed in galvanizing style by Sidney Lumet. Like vodka, it leaves you breathless and a bit giddy. The film's method is to celebrate lunacy by forcing us to look at ourselves in the act of celebrating this film, which is eccentric, very, very sure of itself, and hugely funny. Satire, which used to be described as something that closes on Saturday night, is in this case one of the major hits of the year.

7. Sherlock Holmes. The only elementary thing about A. Conan Doyle's remarkable detective is the way he inspires the imaginations of each new generation that comes along. At this point we may be allowed to take for granted that in eight or 10 years there may be another Holmes incarnation on the screen. Right now we have the extraordinarily witty and winning "The Seven-Per-Cent Solution," directed by Herb Ross and adapted by Nicholas Meyer from his best-selling literary conceit that purports to reveal for the first time what happened when Holmes (Nicol Williamson) met the young Dr. Sigmund Freud (Alan Arkin). Movies like "The Omen" and the "King Kong" remake prompt suspicions that movies still are being made for 12-year-olds of all ages. Movies like "The Seven-Per-Cent Solution" restore our faith in the possibilities of mass entertainment movies. Among other things this one offers performances by Laurence Olivier and Robert Duvall that are as fine as any you've seen all year.

8. "The Memory of Justice." Marcel Ophuls's nearly five-hour meditation upon collective and individual political responsibility, using the Nuremberg trials as the starting point, is just as dramatically involving as his "The Sorrow and The Pity," but it may be tougher to take because the questions we must ask ourselves are beyond easy answers— and they still are there at the end. Ophuls has created a virtually new kind of documentary by allowing himself to pile up detail (in dozens of interviews) that simply cannot be accommodated in films of shorter length. Spellbinding.

9. Rainer Werner Fassbinder. He lives in West Germany, he's 30 and he's already made a couple of dozen feature films since his first in 1969, including four ("The American Soldier," "Beware of A Holy Whore," "Fox and His Friends" and "Fear of Fear"), which received limited showings in New York this year. Fassbinder hasn't yet had a commercial hit here, and I'm not sure when he will, but he's one of the most exciting and original new talents at work today. Attention must be paid. The post-Godard generation is at hand.

10. Martin Scorsese's "Taxi Driver." The point of this film—that a psychosis can be successfully purged by running murderously amok for a few minutes—is, I think, debatable, but not the vivid talents of Scorsese, who directed "Taxi Driver," nor of Robert De Niro, who plays the title role. The best comment I heard about his film was

'All President's Men' Wins Critics' Award

Giancarlo Giannini in Wertmuller's "Seven Beauties"—"complex, full of life"

that of a real-life taxi driver who told me that people who make slanderous movies about taxi drivers, like "Taxi Driver," should be taken out and shot.

1976 D 26, II:1:5

By A. H. WEILER

"All the President's Men" won three of the seven awards for 1976 voted yesterday in the 42d annual meeting of the New York Film critics Circle. The dramatization of the newspaper exposé of the Watergate scandal was judged the best film and Alan J. Pakula and Jason Robards took top honors as director and supporting actor, respectively.

Liv Ullmann proved once again to be the critics' favorite by scoring handily as outstanding actress for her sensitive performance as the sorely tried psychiatrist in Ingmar Bergman's Swedish drama "Face to Face." She was a winner for her efforts in two previous Bergman dramas, "Cries and Whispers" (1971) and "Scenes From a Marriage" (1974).

Robert De Niro was an easy victor as the top actor for his portrayal of the psychotic cabbie in Martin Scorsese's "Taxi Driver." Mr. De Niro was also nominated for his role as the movie producer in "The Last Tycoon."

Talia Shire Wins on Third Ballot

Talia Shire emerged the winner as best supporting actress for her role as the touchingly spinsterish and funny girl friend of Sylvester Stallone in "Rocky." In voting that went to an unusual third ballot, she won over Josie Foster, the youthful hooker in "Taxi Driver."

The screen-writing accolade went to the original script of "Network," a bitingly satiric view of the backstage world of television by Paddy Chayefsky. Its 38 votes topped the runner-up script for "The Last Tycoon." The adaptation by Harold Pinter of F. Scott Fitzgerald's last novel got 20 votes. Mr. Chayefsky's "Marty" was named the critics' choice as best film of 1955.

The critics, who cast their tallies at the New York Newspaper Guild headquarters at 133 West 44th Street, voted in a secret, two-ballot system with a simple majority winning on the first ballot. The second, and, when necessary, third ballots allowed each critic to give three, two and one points to each of his three choices.

18 Films in the Running

Although there were 18 films in the running, "All the President's Men" outdistanced the opposition by registering 40 votes on the second ballot to 26 for "Network." Lina Wertmüller's Italian drama, "Seven Beauties," followed with 18 votes. Runners up were "Taxi Driver," 14; "The Memory of Justice," the French documentary, 10; "The Marquise of O," the German period comedy, 7, and "Rocky," 6.

Mr. Pakula's directorial work on "All the President's Men" led the other 13 entries on the second ballot by recording 37 votes to 22 for Mr. Scorsese's direction of "Taxi Driver." However, "Taxi Driver" just managed to fight off other entries including Miss Wertmüller with 21 for "Seven Beauties," and Sidney Lumet with 20 for "Network."

Among others in the field were Marcel Ophuls, "Memory of Jus-

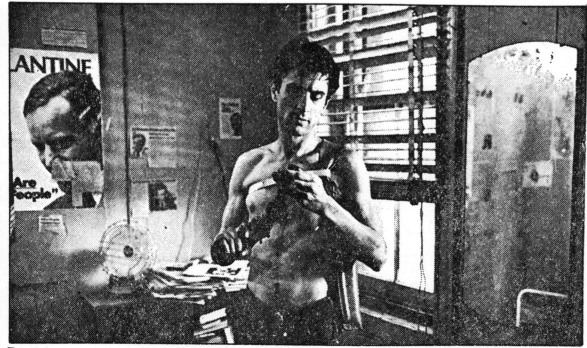

De Niro in Scorsese's "Taxi Driver"—Star and director are "vivid talents"

BEST ACTOR: Robert De Niro in "Taxi Driver."

BEST ACTRESS: Liv Ullmann in "Face to Face."

BEST MOVIE: "All the President's Men," with Dustin Hoffman and Robert Redford.

BEST DIRECTOR: Alan Pakula, for "All the President's Men."

BEST WRITER: Paddy Chayefsky, for "Network."

tice"; Nicholas Roeg, "Man Who Fell to Earth"; Eric Rohmer, "Marquise of O"; Alfred Hitchcock, "Family Plot," and Brian De Palma, "Carrie" and "Obsession."

14 Contenders in Actor Category

While Mr. De Niro's delineation of the "Taxi Driver" was judged the best of 1976 with 33 votes on the second ballot, David Carradine's portrait of the famed folk singer Woody Guthrie in "Bound for Glory" was strong enough to garner 19 votes for second place. Others among the 14 candidates were William Holden, "Network"; Philippe Noiret, "The Clockmaker," and Giancarlo Giannini, "Seven Beauties," with 12 votes each.

Seventeen actresses vied for honors on the second ballot with Faye Dunaway emerging second best to Miss Ullmann with 28 votes for her portrayal of a career-driven executive in "Network." Sissie Spacek collected 24 votes as the youngster with spooky powers in "Carrie" and Miss Shire also received 14 votes for "Rocky" in the starring-actress category.

Miss Shire's 41 votes on the third ballot earned her the victory in the supporting-actress classification over Miss Foster, who received 32.

Among the runners-up of the 25 entries were Marie-France Pisier, "Cousin Cousine," 21 votes; Beatrice Straight, "Network," 9 votes, and Shelley Winters, "Next Stop, Greenwich Village," 7 votes.

The supporting-actor race, with 24 in the running on the second ballot, proved a hands-down win for Mr. Robards, with 37 votes. But some of the runners battled for position, with Harvey Keitel, the pimp in "Taxi Driver," second with 12 votes; Richard Pryor, "Silver Streak," 11 votes; Laurence Olivier, "Marathon Man," 9 votes, as well as 8 votes for "The Seven-Per-Cent Solution"; Robert Duvall, "Network," 9 votes, and 3 votes for "The Seven-Per-Cent Solution."

Mr. Pinter's 20 votes for "The Last Tycoon" was far behind Mr. Chayefsky's 38 votes in the screenwriting contest, which included 17 choices on the second ballot. Others prominent in the running were: "Seven Beauties," Miss Wertmüller, 16; "All the President's Men,"

William Goldman, 13; "Jonah Who Will Be 25 in the Year 2000," John Berger and Alain Tanner, 10, and "Rocky," Sylvester Stallone, 9.

The critics, representing newspapers and magazines, will present plaques to the winners at a reception at Sardi's Restaurant on Sunday, Jan. 30.

Those voting were:

Joy Gould Boyum, chairman of the Critics Circle of The Wall Street Journal; Kathleen Carroll, Ann Guarino, Jerry Oster and Rex Reed of The Daily News; Joseph Gelmis and John Cashman of Newsday; Judith Crist of The Saturday Review/World; Pauline Kael of The New Yorker; John Simon of New York magazine; Roger Greenspun of Penthouse magazine; Andrew Sarris and Molly Haskell of The Village Voice; Richard Schickel of Time; Jack Kroll of Newsweek; Frank Rich of The New York Post; Bernard Drew of the Gannett Newspapers; Frances Taylor of The Long Island Daily Press; William Wolf and Donald Mayerson of Cue; Bruce Williamson of Playboy; Howard Kissel of Women's Wear Daily, and Vincent Canby, Richard Eder, Howard Thompson and A. H. Weiler of The New York Times.

1977 Ja 4, 22:1

'All the President's Men' Makes It 2 in a Row

"All the President's Men," the film based on the best-selling Watergate book by Bob Woodward and Carl Bernstein, was named the best film of 1976 by the National Society of Film Critics at its annual meeting yesterday at the Algonquin Hotel. Participating in the voting were 27 critics who represent newspapers and magazines in New York, Boston, Chicago, Washington, Los Angeles and San Francisco.

The New York Film Critics Circle,

which represents New York-based critics, including many who also belong to the national society, named "All the President's Men" the best picture of the year at its annual meeting on Monday.

Runners-up to "All the President's Men" in the national society's voting were Martin Scorsese's "Taxi Driver" and Marcel Ophuls's "The Memory of Justice."

Mr. Scorsese was named by the society's members as the best director of the year for "Taxi Driver," and his star, Robert De Niro, was voted best actor for his performance as the psychotic cab driver. Alan J. Pakula, the director of "All the President's Men," placed second to Mr. Scorsese, and Eric Rohmer, director of "The Marquise of O . . .," was third.

Mr. De Niro won his award on the first ballot, an unusual event in the national society's voting procedures. He received 16 of the 27 votes cast.

Sissie Spacek, who plays the spooky title role in "Carrie," that of a girl who can move objects or change their shapes simply by thinking hard, was named best actress of the year over her two closest competitors, Faye Dunaway, for her performance in "Network," and Liv Ullmann for her performance in "Face to Face."

The award for best supporting actress went to Jodie Foster, who plays the teen-age prostitute in "Taxi Driver." Placing second and third were Talia Shire (for "Rocky") and Marie-France Pisier (for "Cousin Cousine").

Jason Robards, who plays Ben Bradlee, the managing editor of The Washington Post, was voted best supporting actor of 1976 over Harvey Keitel, who appeared last year in "Taxi Driver," "Buffalo Bill and the Indians" and "Mother, Jugs and Speed." He also won over Robert Duvall, who appeared in "The Seven-Per-Cent Solution" and "Network."

Sissie Spacek
"Best Actress"

Alain Tanner and John Berger, who wrote the French-language screenplay for the Swiss comedy, "Jonah Who Will Be 25 in the Year 2000," were cited by the society for the year's best screenplay. Runners-up in this category were Paddy Chayefsky ("Network"), Paul Mazursky ("Next Stop Greenwich Village") and Harold Pinter ("The Last Tycoon").

The society's best cinematographer award went to Haskell Wexler for "Bound for Glory." Mr. Wexler's closest competitors were Nestor Almendros ("The Marquise of O . . .") and Michael Chapman ("Taxi Driver").

The members of the society made the following recommendation: "Taking cognizance of the death in 1976 of

Luchino Visconti, the society expresses its hope that the legal difficulties, which have for over 30 years prohibited American distribution of Mr. Visconti's 'Ossessione,' will at last be resolved."

"Ossessione," which was shown at last year's New York Film Festibal, has never been commercially released here, because of copyright problems. The film is an Italian adaptation of James M. Cain's "The Postman Always Rings Twice," made in Italy during World War II.

Frank Rich, the film critic of The New York Post, was elected chairman of the society for 1977, succeeding Vincent Canby, the film critic of The New York Times,

1977 Ja 5, C18:5

As was the case in Hollywood last year when the American Academy Awards were passed out, Jack Nicholson and his movie "One Flew Over the Cuckoo's Nest" cut a wide swath through Britain's equivalent of the Oscars this year. Mr. Nicholson was named best actor. Louise Fletcher best actress, Brad Dourf best supporting actor, and Milos Foreman best director. The movie itself received the best picture award. Princess Anne presented the award.

1977 Mr 26, 17:2

'Rocky' Gets Oscar as Top Film; Finch, Dunaway Win for Acting

By JON NORDHEIMER
Special to The New York Times

LOS ANGELES, Mach 28—The Academy Award for best actor went tonight to the late British film star Peter Finch, the first time in the history of the Oscars that an acting award was made posthumously.

It was Mr. Finch's performance as a deranged television anchorman in "Network" that won the award, which was accepted by his widow, her voice breaking with brief remarks that moved the audience.

Mr. Finch's "Network" co-star, Faye Dunaway, took the best-actress award for her portrayal of a callous programming executive in a film that broadly satirized and attacked an old Hollywood nemesis, the television industry. Paddy Chayefsky, who had first found fame in writing for television, was given the award for best original screen play for the movie..

But it was "Rocky," the film about an underdog boxer's shot for the championship, that knocked out the opposition and was named best film of the year at the 49th annual ceremony of the Academy of Motion Pictures Arts and Sciences.

The low-budget film also took best directing honors for John G. Avildsen.

Audience Favorite

"Rocky" was a clear favorite with the audience that applauded each time the title was mentioned during the evening. However, the film's star, Sylvester Stallone, who also had been nominated for writing the screenplay, lost in both categories against other challengers.

Jason Robards won the award for best supporting actor for his performance in "All the President's Men" as a newspaper editor caught in a historic test of will with an American President. Hollywood's elite turned out on a cool, breeze-swept night for the annual awards ritual that can make or break careers.

Mr. Robards, whose acting career has had its finest moments previously on the Broadway stage, said he was going to be unemployed

Sylvester Stallone, left, with Carl Weathers in scene from "Rocky"

Faye Dunaway
Best Actress

Peter Finch
Best Actor

soon and had no set plans for the future or promise of work. "I don't know what I'll do," he told interviewers after receiving his first Oscar.

Portrayed Editor

The actor had portrayed Washington Post editor Ben Bradlee in

the filmed version of the events that set in motion the Watergate disclosures that ultimately led to the resignation of President Richard M. Nixon.

"It was a beautiful picture but a terrible subject," he remarked dryly, gripping the $100 gold-plated statuette that held the attention of the celebrities attending the ceremony at the Los Angeles Music Center and an estimated television audience of 250 million people in 44 countries.

Faye Dunaway was awarded the Oscar as the year's top starring actress for her portrayal of the designing, success-hungry TV executive in "Network." She was previously nominated for Oscars in 1967 for "Bonnie and Clyde" and in 1974 for "Chinatown."

Mr. Avildsen received an Oscar for his direction of "Rocky," the poignantly effective study of a prizefighter who gets a shot at the heavyweight crown. Like Lina Wertmuller and Alan J. Pakula, his competitors, this was his first nomination in this category.

In the United States, the presentations were seen by an estimated 75 million television viewers. The almost-three-hour tradition was broadcast by ABC minus some of the usual on-stage glitter.

William Friedkin, himself an Oscar winner, and producer of this year's awards, was determined to "bone down" the presentations and make the show less "tacky."

A Surprise Winner

The supporting-actress category produced a surprise when the award went to Beatrice Straight for her role as the deserted wife of a television executive in "Network." The actress had appeared in the film for only a scene or two, and was not considered one of the leading prospects in the match-up with other actresses such as Jane Alexander, Lee Grant, Piper Laurie and Jodie Foster.

Miss Straight appeared as stunned as some of those in the audience when she went up to receive the award. "I'm the dark horse and this was very unexpected."

Lone Presenters

Special achievement awards for visual effects were given to Carolo Rambaldi, Glen Robinson and Frank Van der Veer for "King Kong," and L. B. Abbott, Glen Robinson and Matthew Yuricich for "Logan's Run."

Jason Robards after winning best supporting actor award.

Cicely Tyson introduced a brief film celebrating 50 years of sound movies and clips outlining the career of the producer Pandro S. Berman, winner of the Irving Thalberg Memorial award.

The ceremonies' new look, under the guidance of Mr. Friedkin, used lone presenters to open the envelopes and hand out the awards, helping the show to escape some of the mindless chitchat between stars that used to bog down the proceedings.

There were also other departures.

Marty Feldman, the goggle-eyed, stringy-haired British comic, maniacally smashed one Oscar to the stage floor instead of handing it to a recipient.

Sylvester Stallone, who in the movie "Rocky" played a club boxer who fights a black, heavyweight champion to a brutal standoff, was ostensibly moving toward a presentation when Muhammad Ali, the real heavyweight champion, strode challengingly out of the wings.

"You stole my script," the champion shouted accusingly. "I watched that movie . . . You stole my script! Now show me what

Associated Press

Beatrice Straight after receiving best supporting actress award.

you can really do."

The two men then engaged in feigned fisticuffs across the stage, drawing laughs but no blood.

Another surprise occurred when "Black and White in Color" was named best foreign-language film over two movies that had appeared to have an edge in the balloting, "Cousin, Cousine" and "Seven Beauties."

"I feel a little bit like Harry Truman holding up the newspaper saying Dewey had won the election," remarked its elated producer, Arthur Cohn.

Other awards included:

Short Subject—animated: "Leisure," produced by Suzanne Baker for Film Australia.

Short Subject—live: "In the Region of Ice," an Andre Guttfreund Production. Andre Guttfreund and Peter Werner, producers.

Costume Design: Danilo Donati for "Fellini's Casanova."

Art Direction: "All the President's Men," George Jenkins and George Gaines.

Editing: Richard Halsey and Scott Conrad for "Rocky."

Sound Recording: Arthur Piantadosi, Les Fresholtz, Dick Alexander and Jim Webb for "All the President's Men."

John Avildsen
Best Director

Cinematography: Haskell Wexler for "Bound For Glory."

Original Song Score and Its Adaptation or Best Adaptation Score: "Bound for Glory," adapted by Leonard Ronenman.

Original score: "The Omen," Jerry Goldsmith.

Documentary Short Subject: "Number Our Days," produced by Lynee Littman for Community Television of Southern California.

Documentary feature: "Harlan County, U.S.A.," produced by Barbara Kopple for Cabin Creek Films.

Song: "Evergreen" from "A Star Is Born." Music by Barbra Streisand. Lyrics by Paul Williams.

Screenplay Based on Material From Another Medium: William Goldman's adaptation of the book by Carl Bernstein and Bob Woodward for "All the President's Men."

Script Based on Factual or Story Material Not Previously Published or Produced: Paddy Chayefsky for "Network."

1977 Mr 29, 38:1

How To Use Index

This index covers all the film reviews included in this volume. It is divided into three sections: Titles, Persons, and Corporations.

The Title Index lists each film reviewed by title. The Persons Index lists by name every performer, producer, director, screenwriter, etc. mentioned in the reviews, with the function in parentheses following the name, and the titles of the movies with which the person was connected, in chronological order. The Corporations Index lists all producing, distributing and otherwise participating companies mentioned in the reviews by name, again with the function in parentheses following the name, and the titles of the movies with which they were associated, in chronological order.

Citations in this index are by year, month, day, section of newspaper (if applicable), page and column; for example, 1975 Ja 11, II: 12:1. Since the reviews appear in chronological order, the date is the key locator. The citations also serve to locate the reviews in bound volumes and microfilm editions of The Times.

In the citations, the months are abbreviated as follows:

Ja—January	My—May	S—September
F—February	Je—June	O—October
Mr—March	Jl—July	N—November
Ap—April	Ag—August	D—December

TITLE INDEX

All films reviewed are listed alphabetically by title. Titles are inverted only if they begin with an article ("Doctor Glas" is listed under D, not G; but "The Graduate" is listed under G, not T). Titles beginning with a number are alphabetized as though the number were spelled out. Wherever possible, foreign films are entered under both the English and foreign-language title. Titles given incorrectly in the review appear correctly here. Films reviewed more than once and films with identical titles are given multiple listings.

PERSONS INDEX

All persons included in the credits are listed alphabetically, last name first. Their function in the films is listed after the name in parentheses, such as director, producer, screenwriter, etc. In entries where no such qualifier appears, the person was a performer (actor, actress, singer). A person with multiple functions will have multiple entries; for example, an actor who later turned producer or director will have two listings. A person having two functions in the same film will also have two listings. Functions that are very uncommon or are given imprecisely in the reviews are designated miscellaneous (misc).

Names beginning with Mc are alphabetized as though spelled Mac.

Entries under each name are by title of film, in chronological order.

CORPORATIONS INDEX

All companies mentioned in reviews as involved in the production or distribution of the film or in some other major function connected with it are listed here alphabetically. Company names are not inverted unless they start with a personal surname (for example, J Arthur Rank Organization is listed as Rank, J Arthur, Organization). The function of the company is given in parentheses after the name, abbreviated as follows:

Prod—Producer
Distr—Distributer
Misc—Miscellaneous

Misc is used when the function is uncommon or not precisely defined in the review. A company that has more than one function is given more than one listing; thus a user who has completed scanning a long listing under RKO (Distr) will then find an additional listing under RKO (Prod).

Abbreviations in names are alphabetized as though they were words (RKO as Rko).

Entries under each company name are by title of film, in chronological order.

4

Brown, Georgia—Cont
  Bawdy Adventures of Tom Jones, The
    1976,S 2,25:1
  Seven-Per-Cent Solution, The 1976,O 25,42:1
Brown, Henry
  Man in the Glass Booth, The 1975,My 20,46:4
Brown, Jack
  Nothing by Chance 1975,Ja 31,25:2
Brown, Jim
  Take a Hard Ride 1975,O 30,52:2
Brown, Larry (Composer)
  Mitchell 1975,S 11,35:1
Brown, Nacio Herb (Composer)
  Singin' in the Rain 1975,My 4,II,15:1
Brown, O Nicholas (Miscellaneous)
  Nickel Ride, The 1975,Ja 30,26:4
  White Line Fever 1975,Ag 29,14:1
Brown, Timothy
  Nashville 1975,Je 12,32:1
  Nashville 1975,S 11,1:7
Brown, William F (Producer)
  Hiding Place, The 1975,N 6,51:2
Browne, Coral
  Drowning Pool, The 1975,Je 26,34:1
  Drowning Pool, The 1975,Jl 6,II,9:1
Browne, Derek (Cinematographer)
  At the Earth's Core 1976,Ag 28,9:6
Browne, Howard (Screenwriter)
  Capone 1975,Ap 17,48:6
Browne, Roscoe Lee
  Logan's Run 1976,Je 24,25:1
Broyles, Robert
  Eat My Dust 1976,My 29,13:7
Bruant, Joshua
  Framed 1975,O 2,47:1
Bruce, Lenny
  Lenny Bruce Without Tears 1975,Mr 19,59:1
Bruce, Nigel
  Hounds of the Baskervilles, The 1975,Jl 22,23:1
Bruchon, Pascale
  Small Change (L'Argent de Poche)
    1976,O 1,III,11:1
Bruckheimer, Jerry (Producer)
  Farewell, My Lovely 1975,Ag 14,39:1
Bruckmann, Clyde (Screenwriter)
  Sherlock Jr 1975,Jl 22,23:1
Brugman, Eddie
  Keetje Tippel 1976,S 27,41:1
Bruhl, Heidi
  Eiger Sanction, The 1975,My 22,32:1
Bruhne, Lothar (Composer)
  Comedians (Komodianten) 1975,Ja 3,13:2
Brundin, Bo
  Great Waldo Pepper, The 1975,Mr 14,24:1
  Russian Roulette 1975,Ag 21,44:2
Brunner, Robert F (Composer)
  Gus 1976,Ag 7,11:2
Brunner, Robert L (Composer)
  Strongest Man in the World, The 1975,Jl 10,19:1
Bruno S
  Jeder Fur Sich Und Gott Gegen Alle (Every Man
    for Himself and God Against All) 1975,S 28,57:1
Bruns, Philip
  Great Waldo Pepper, The 1975,Mr 14,24:1
Bryant, Dennis (Miscellaneous)
  Bim 1976,D 2,57:1
Bryant, William
  Other Side of the Mountain, The 1975,N 15,20:1
Bryceland, Yvonne
  Boesman and Lena 1976,Ap 23,23:2
Brynner, Yul
  Futureworld 1976,Ag 14,10:1
Buchanan, Larry (Director)
  Goodbye, Norma Jean 1976,My 11,26:5
Buchanan, Larry (Producer)
  Goodbye, Norma Jean 1976,My 11,26:5
Buchanan, Larry (Screenwriter)
  Goodbye, Norma Jean 1976,My 11,26:5
Buck, Jules (Producer)
  Man Friday 1976,Mr 6,22:1
  Great Scout and Cathouse Thursday, The
    1976,Je 24,24:1
Buckley, Betty
  Carrie 1976,N 17,III,24:1
Buckley, David (Director)
  Saturday Night at the Baths 1975,Je 12,33:1
Buckley, David (Producer)
  Saturday Night at the Baths 1975,Je 12,33:1
Buckley, David (Screenwriter)
  Saturday Night at the Baths 1975,Je 12,33:1
Budd, Roy (Composer)
  Destructors, The 1975,Je 12,30:6
  Paper Tiger 1976,S 17,III,8:3
Buel, Birgit
  Take It Like a Man, Madam 1976,S 16,55:1
Buell, John (Original Author)
  Act of Aggression (L'Agression) 1975,D 4,50:1
Buffett, Jimmy (Composer)
  Rancho Deluxe 1975,N 24,28:1
Bugliosi, Vincent T
  Manson 1976,Ja 31,20:4
Buise, Jean
  Rape of Innocence 1976,Je 29,19:2

Bujold, Genevieve
  Kamouraska 1975,Jl 14,21:1
  Swashbuckler 1976,Jl 30,III,5:1
  Swashbuckler 1976,Ag 1,II,13:1
  Obsession 1976,Ag 2,29:1
  Obsession 1976,Ag 8,II,11:1
  Alex and the Gypsy 1976,O 4,16:1
Bulgakova, Maia
  Crime and Punishment 1975,My 15,48:1
Bulut, Tarik (Miscellaneous)
  Reflections (Dry Summer) 1975,Je 12.30:1
Bunuel, Joyce (Screenwriter)
  Black Moon 1975,S 30,31:1
Bunuel, Luis (Director)
  Discreet Charm of the Bourgeoisie, The
    1976,Ja 18,II,13:1
  Daughter of Deceit 1976,Ja 18,II,13:1
  Criminal Life of Archibaldo De La Cruz, The
    (Ensayo De Un Crimen) 1976,Ja 18,II,13:1
  Illusion Travels By Streetcar (Ilusion Viaja En
    Tranvia, La) 1976,Ja 18,II,13:1
  Mexican Bus Ride (Subida Al Cielo)
    1976,Ja 18,II,13:1
  Tristana 1976,Ja 18,II,13:1
  Gran Calavera, El (Great Madcap, The)
    1976,Ja 18,II,13:1
  Great Madcap, The (Gran Calavera, El)
    1976,Ja 18,II,13:1
  Abismos De Pasion 1976,Ja 18,II,13:1
Buono, Victor
  Arnold 1975,Mr 22,36:1
Burckhardt, Jacob (Director)
  Yaknetuma 1975,D 12,53:1
Burckhardt, Rudy (Director)
  City Pasture 1975,D 12,53:1
Burdett, Gammy
  Independence Day 1976,N 10,III,21:5
Burgess, Anthony (Screenwriter)
  Moses 1976,Mr 27,17:1
Burghardt, Arthur
  Network 1976,N 15,39:1
Burke, Paul
  Psychic Killer 1976,F 7,9:1
Burnett, John F (Miscellaneous)
  Sunshine Boys, The 1975,N 7,28:1
  Murder By Death 1976,Je 24,26:1
Burns, Fred (Director)
  Roll 'Em, Lola 1975,O 19,II,1:3
Burns, Fred (Miscellaneous)
  Roll 'Em, Lola 1975,O 19,II,1:3
Burns, George
  Sunshine Boys, The 1975,N 7,28:1
  Sunshine Boys, The 1975,N 9,II,17:1
Burns, Ralph (Composer)
  Lucky Lady 1975,D 26,47:3
Burns, Ralph (Miscellaneous)
  Lucky Lady 1975,D 26,47:3
Burns, Steve
  Lifeguard 1976,Jl 24,12:1
Burrell, Fred
  Shoot It: Black Shoot It: Blue 1975,Jl 10,19:1
Burrill, Christine (Cinematographer)
  Susan: April to June 1975,Ap 17,48:3
Burrill, Timothy (Producer)
  Alpha Beta 1976,Ag 5,26:1
Burroughs, Edgar Rice (Original Author)
  At the Earth's Core 1976,Ag 28,9:6
Burstyn, Ellen
  Alice Doesn't Live Here Anymore 1975,Ja 30,28:1
  Alice Doesn't Live Here Anymore 1975,F 2,II,13:3
  Alice Doesn't Live Here Anymore
    1975,Mr 30,II,1:1
Burton, Norman
  Reincarnation of Peter Proud, The 1975,Ap 26,14:1
  Gumball Rally, The 1976,Ag 21,13:1
  Scorchy 1976,O 9,9:4
Burton, Tony
  River Niger, The 1976,Ap 15,28:1
  Bingo Long Traveling All-Stars and Motor Kings,
    The 1976,Jl 17,10:1
Busey, Gary
  Gumball Rally, The 1976,Ag 21,13:1
  Star is Born, A 1976,D 27,III,16:5
Bush, Billy Green
  Alice Doesn't Live Here Anymore 1975,Ja 30,28:1
Bush, Dick (Cinematographer)
  In Celebration 1975,Mr 18,30:1
  Tommy 1975,Mr 20,48:1
  Mahler 1976,Ap 5,45:4
Bussieres, Raymond
  Jonah Who Will Be 25 in the Year 2000
    1976,O 2,15:1
Butkus, Dick
  Mother, Jugs and Speed 1976,My 27,30:1
Butler, Artie (Composer)
  Rafferty and the Gold Dust Twins 1975,F 3,32:1
Butler, Artie (Miscellaneous)
  At Long Last Love 1975,Mr 7,22:1
Butler, Bill (Cinematographer)
  Jaws 1975,Je 21,19:2
  Lipstick 1976,Ap 3,19:1
  Bingo Long Traveling All-Stars and Motor Kings,
    The 1976,Jl 17,10:1

Butler, Bill (Cinematographer)—Cont
  Alex and the Gypsy 1976,O 4,16:1
Butler, Bill (Miscellaneous)
  One Flew Over the Cuckoo's Nest 1975,N 20,52:1
Butler, David (Screenwriter)
  Voyage of the Damned 1976,D 23,18:1
Butler, Michael (Miscellaneous)
  Brannigan 1975,Mr 27,37:1
Butler, Michael (Screenwriter)
  Brannigan 1975,Mr 27,37:1
Butler, Michael C (Cinematographer)
  92 in the Shade 1975,Ag 22,42:1
  Missouri Breaks, The 1976,My 20,45:1
Buttons, Red
  Gable and Lombard 1976,F 12,42:1
Buzzance, Lando
  Homo Eroticus 1975,Mr 29,10:5
Byrd, Caruth C (Producer)
  Murph the Surf 1975,Je 12,30:6
Byrum, John (Director)
  Inserts 1976,F 28,15:1
  Inserts 1976,Mr 7,II,13:1
Byrum, John (Miscellaneous)
  Harry and Walter Go to New York
    1976,Je 18,III,6:5
Byrum, John (Screenwriter)
  Mahogany 1975,O 9,54:1
  Inserts 1976,F 28,15:1
  Inserts 1976,Mr 7,II,13:1
  Harry and Walter Go to New York
    1976,Je 18,III,6:5
  Harry and Walter Go to New York
    1976,Je 27,II,15:7

C

Caan, James
  Funny Lady 1975,Mr 12,30:1
  Funny Lady 1975,Mr 16,II,17:1
  Rollerball 1975,Je 26,34:1
  Rollerball 1975,Je 29,II,15:7
  Killer Elite, The 1975,D 18,62:1
  Harry and Walter Go to New York
    1976,Je 18,III,6:5
  Harry and Walter Go to New York
    1976,Je 27,II,15:7
  Silent Movie 1976,Jl 1,22:1
Cabot, Christopher
  Man Friday 1976,Mr 6,22:1
Cabrera, John (Cinematographer)
  Paper Tiger 1976,S 17,III,8:3
Cady, Frank
  Hearts of the West 1975,O 4,14:1
Caern, Ingrid
  Fox and His Friends (Fist-Right of Freedom)
    (Faustrecht der Freiheit) 1976,F 3,24:1
Caesar, Sid
  Silent Movie 1976,Jl 1,22:1
Cafarel, Jose Maria
  Passenger, The 1975,Ap 10,46:1
Caffrey, Sean
  Moon Over the Alley 1976,Ap 3,19:1
Cagan, Alex (Composer)
  My Michael 1976,Mr 16,29:2
Cagle, Chris
  Nothing by Chance 1975,Ja 31,25:2
Cahan, Abraham (Original Author)
  Hester Street 1975,O 20,44:1
Cahn, Jeff (Screenwriter)
  Salsa 1976,Ap 2,26:1
Caine, Michael
  Destructors, The 1975,Je 12,30:6
  Wilby Conspiracy, The 1975,S 4,31:1
  Romantic Englishwoman, The 1975,N 27,46:1
  Romantic Englishwoman, The 1975,D 14,II,15:7
  Man Who Would Be King, The 1975,D 18,62:1
  Romantic Englishwoman, The 1976,Ja 18,II,13:7
  Harry and Walter Go to New York
    1976,Je 18,III,6:5
  Harry and Walter Go to New York
    1976,Je 27,II,15:7
Caine, Shakira
  Man Who Would Be King, The 1975,D 18,62:1
Calamai, Clara
  Ossessione (Obsession) 1976,O 2,15:1
Calandra, Giuliana
  All Screwed Up (Tutto a Posto e Niente in
    Ordine) 1976,Ja 15,28:1
  Last Woman, The 1976,Je 7,35:1
Callado, Tessy
  Branded for Life 1976,S 24,III,8:4
Callaghan, Duke (Cinematographer)
  Last Hard Men, The 1976,Ap 24,16:1
Callahan, Gene (Miscellaneous)
  Stepford Wives, The 1975,F 13,43:1
Callan, Michael
  Lepke 1975,My 24,12:1
Callas, Charlie
  Silent Movie 1976,Jl 1,22:1
Callender, Ray
  Sweet Movie 1975,O 10,32:3
Calmi, Lamberto (Cinematographer)
  Bambina 1976,Ap 26,40:1

E

Eymesz, Theat (Miscellaneous)—Cont
Fox and His Friends (Fist-Right of Freedom)
(Faustrecht der Freiheit) 1976,F 3,24:1
Eymon, Florence (Miscellaneous)
Xala 1975,O 1,62:1
Eyre, Peter
Hedda 1976,Ja 26,29:1

F

Faber, Peter
Keetje Tippel 1976,S 27,41:1
Faber, Ron
Guernica 1976,My 22,19:3
Fabian, Francoise
Down the Ancient Stairs 1975,O 18,22:1
Salut L'Artiste (Hail Artist) 1976,F 23,20:1
Salut L'Artiste (Hail Artist) 1976,Mr 7,II,13:1
Fahmy, Abdel Aziz (Cinematographer)
Night of Counting the Years, The 1975,O 23,48:3
Faith, Adam
Stardust 1975,N 13,52:5
Falcon, Andre
Where There's Smoke (Il n'y-a pas de Fumee Sans
Feu) 1975,D 11,59:1
Icy Breasts (Les Seins de Glace) 1975,D 11,59:1
Falk, Peter
Murder By Death 1976,Je 24,26:1
Mikey and Nicky 1976,D 22,34:4
Falla, Raymond, Sir
Story of Adele H, The (L'Histoire d'Adele H)
1975,O 13,36:1
Story of Adele H, The (L'Histoire d'Adele H)
1975,D 23,15:2
Fancher, Hampton
Other Side of the Mountain, The 1975,N 15,20:1
Fargas, Antonio
Cornbread, Earl and Me 1975,My 22,34:1
Next Stop, Greenwich Village 1976,F 5,24:1
Next Stop, Greenwich Village 1976,F 8,II,19:3
Car Wash 1976,O 16,13:1
Fargo, James (Director)
Enforcer, The 1976,D 23,18:1
Farkas, Zoltan (Miscellaneous)
Elektreia 1975,S 30,31:2
Farley, Elizabeth
Death Play 1976,S 2,24:2
Farley, Morgan
Last Tycoon, The 1976,N 18,59:1
Farr, Bobby
Land That Time Forgot, The 1975,Ag 14,39:1
Farrell, Peter
Moon Over the Alley 1976,Ap 3,19:1
Farrow, Robbie (Composer)
Abduction 1975,O 25,17:1
Fassbinder, Rainer Werner
Fox and His Friends (Fist-Right of Freedom)
(Faustrecht der Freiheit) 1975,S 27,21:4
American Soldier, The 1976,Ja 30,18:1
Fox and His Friends (Fist-Right of Freedom)
(Faustrecht der Freiheit) 1976,F 1,II,1:3
Fox and His Friends (Fist-Right of Freedom)
(Faustrecht der Freiheit) 1976,F 3,24:1
Beware of a Holy Whore 1976,N 12,III,8:3
Fassbinder, Rainer Werner (Director)
Fox and His Friends (Fist-Right of Freedom)
(Faustrecht der Freiheit) 1975,S 27,21:4
Fox and His Friends (Fist-Right of Freedom)
(Faustrecht der Freiheit) 1975,O 5,II,15:1
American Soldier, The 1976,Ja 30,18:1
American Soldier, The 1976,F 1,II,1:3
Fox and His Friends (Fist-Right of Freedom)
(Faustrecht der Freiheit) 1976,F 1,II,1:3
Fox and His Friends (Fist-Right of Freedom)
(Faustrecht der Freiheit) 1976,F 3,24:1
Fear of Fear (Angst vor der Angst)
1976,O 15,III,8:3
Beware of a Holy Whore 1976,N 12,III,8:3
Fassbinder, Rainer Werner (Screenwriter)
Fox and His Friends (Fist-Right of Freedom)
(Faustrecht der Freiheit) 1975,S 27,21:4
American Soldier, The 1976,Ja 30,18:1
Fox and His Friends (Fist-Right of Freedom)
(Faustrecht der Freiheit) 1976,F 3,24:1
Fear of Fear (Angst vor der Angst)
1976,O 15,III,8:3
Beware of a Holy Whore 1976,N 12,III,8:3
Faulhaber, Ulrich
Fear of Fear (Angst vor der Angst)
1976,O 15,III,8:3
Faulk, John Henry
Leadbelly 1976,My 29,14:1
Faulkner, James
Conduct Unbecoming 1975,O 6,42:1
Favrod, Charles-Henri (Producer)
General Idi Amin Dada 1975,Ap 7,40:1
General Idi Amin Dada 1976,Ag 31,21:1
Fawcett-Majors, Farrah
Logan's Run 1976,Je 24,25:1
Fedinatz, John
Not a Pretty Picture 1976,Ap 1,28:4
Feinberg, Ron
Boy and His Dog, A 1976,Je 17,32:2

Feingold, Ken (Director)
Subject 1975,My 9,19:3
Feld, Fritz
Silent Movie 1976,Jl 1,22:1
Felder, Michael (Composer)
Long Night, The 1976,Ap 11,45:5
Feldman, Edward S (Producer)
Other Side of the Mountain, The 1975,N 15,20:1
Two Minute Warning 1976,N 13,12:1
Feldman, Marty
Adventure of Sherlock Holmes' Smarter Brother,
The 1975,D 15,42:1
Silent Movie 1976,Jl 1,22:1
Feldman, Phil (Producer)
Posse 1975,Je 5,48:1
Feldon, Barbara
Smile 1975,S 28,II,13:1
Smile 1975,O 9,52:1
Smile 1975,O 19,II,13:7
No Deposit, No Return 1976,Jl 3,17:1
Feliciano, Janna Merlyn (Composer)
Aaron Loves Angela 1975,D 26,46:4
Feliciano, Janna Merlyn (Miscellaneous)
Aaron Loves Angela 1975,D 26,46:4
Feliciano, Jose
Salsa 1976,Ap 2,26:1
Feliciano, Jose (Composer)
Aaron Loves Angela 1975,D 26,46:4
Feliciano, Jose (Miscellaneous)
Aaron Loves Angela 1975,D 26,46:4
Fell, Norman
Cleopatra Jones and the Casino of Gold
1975,Jl 12,16:4
Fellini, Federico (Director)
Dolce Vita, La 1976,Ja 18,II,1:2
Fellous, Maurice (Cinematographer)
Man in the Trunk, The 1975,D 6,22:5
Icy Breasts (Les Seins de Glace) 1975,D 11,59:1
Where There's Smoke (Il n'y-a pas de Fumee Sans
Feu) 1975,D 11,59:1
Fellows, Don
Death Play 1976,S 2,24:2
Fenady, Andrew J (Producer)
Arnold 1975,Mr 22,36:1
Fenady, Georg (Director)
Arnold 1975,Mr 22,36:1
Fendel, Rosemarie
Dream City 1976,D 6,46:6
Feng, Hsu
Touch of Zen 1976,O 10,75:3
Fenn, Suzanne (Miscellaneous)
Saturday Night at the Baths 1975,Je 12,33:1
Fennell, Michael
Car Wash 1976,O 16,13:1
Ferjak, Anouk
Veronique, ou L'Ete de Mes 13 Ans (Veronique, or
The Summer of My 13th Year) 1976,Ap 6,28:1
Veronique, ou L'Ete De Mes 13 Ans (Veronique, or
The Summer of My 13th Year) 1976,Je 21,43:1
Fernandez, Emilio
Lucky Lady 1975,D 26,47:3
Fernandez, Joao (Cinematographer)
Abduction 1975,O 25,17:1
Ferrando, Giancarlo (Screenwriter)
Violent Professional, The 1976,O 30,14:3
Ferrel, Pablo
Survive! 1976,Ag 5,26:1
Ferrer, Jose
Big Bus, The 1976,Je 24,26:1
Voyage of the Damned 1976,D 23,18:1
Ferrer, Mel
Brannigan 1975,Mr 27,37:1
Ferreri, Marco (Director)
Last Woman, The 1976,Je 7,35:1
Last Woman, The 1976,Je 13,II,15:1
Last Woman, The 1976,O 17,II,1:1
Ferreri, Marco (Screenwriter)
Last Woman, The 1976,Je 7,35:1
Ferrol, Caroline (Miscellaneous)
Jackson County Jail 1976,Je 12,13:1
Ferry, Christian (Producer)
King Kong 1976,D 18,16:1
Ferzeti, Gabriele
Matter of Time, A 1976,O 8,III,8:3
Fetchit, Stepin
Won Ton Ton, The Dog Who Saved Hollywood
1976,My 27,30:1
Fiedel, Brad (Composer)
Deadly Hero 1976,O 16,11:4
Field, Sally
Stay Hungry 1976,Ap 26,41:1
Fielder, John
Fortune, The 1975,My 21,49:1
Fielding, Jerry (Composer)
Black Bird, The 1975,D 26,43:1
Bad News Bears, The 1976,Ap 7,28:1
Fields, Freddie (Producer)
Lipstick 1976,Ap 3,19:1
Fields, Vanetta
Star is Born, A 1976,D 27,III,16:5
Fields, Verna (Miscellaneous)
Jaws 1975,Je 21,19:2

Fields, Virginia
Super Spook 1975,Jl 10,19:1
Figurovsky, Nikolai (Screenwriter)
Crime and Punishment 1975,My 15,48:1
Filiatrault, Denise
Once Upon a Time in the East (Il Etait une Fois
Dans l'Est) 1975,Ap 14,41:1
Filon, Daniel
Brannigan 1975,Mr 27,37:1
Fimple, Dennis
King Kong 1976,D 18,16:1
Finch, Peter
Network 1976,N 15,39:1
Findlay, Seaton (Director)
Janis 1975,F 13,43:3
Findlay, Seaton (Miscellaneous)
Janis 1975,F 13,43:3
Fine, Mort (Screenwriter)
Next Man, The 1976,N 11,52:1
Finlay, Frank
Four Musketeers, The 1975,Mr 20,48:1
Finney, Albert
Alpha Beta 1976,Ag 5,26:1
Alpha Beta 1976,Ag 22,II,11:1
Finney, Shirley Jo
River Niger, The 1976,Ap 15,28:1
Fiore, Elena
Seven Beauties 1976,Ja 22,42:1
Firestone, Scott
Bad News Bears, The 1976,Ap 7,28:1
Fischer-Welskirch, Beate (Miscellaneous)
Fear of Fear (Angst vor der Angst)
1976,O 15,III,8:3
Fish, Hamilton 3d (Producer)
Memory of Justice, The 1976,O 5,54:1
Fisher, Carrie
Shampoo 1975,F 12,47:1
Shampoo 1975,Ap 13,II,15:1
Fisher, Gerry (Cinematographer)
Romantic Englishwoman, The 1975,N 27,46:1
Adventure of Sherlock Holmes' Smarter Brother,
The 1975,D 15,42:1
Romantic Englishwoman, The 1976,Ja 18,II,13:7
Fisher, Morgan (Director)
Production Stills 1975,My 9,19:3
Fisher, Morgan (Miscellaneous)
Eadweard Muybridge, Zoopraxographer
1975,S 30,31:1
Fishwick, Doris
Moon Over the Alley 1976,Ap 3,19:1
Fitzgerald, F Scott (Original Author)
Bernice Bobs Her Hair 1976,O 6,35:1
Last Tycoon, The 1976,N 18,59:1
Last Tycoon, The 1976,D 12,II,1:1
Fitzgerald, Geraldine
Echoes of a Summer 1976,My 15,14:1
Fiuzat, Allen
Benji 1975,Je 27,25:1
Flagg, Fannie
Stay Hungry 1976,Ap 26,41:1
Flamand, Didier
India Song 1975,O 8,24:1
Flamant, Georges
Chienne, La (Bitch, The) 1975,S 27,21:4
Chienne, La (Bitch, The) 1976,My 1,13:1
Chienne, La (Bitch, The) 1976,My 9,II,13:1
Flanagan, Flonnouala
In the Region of Ice 1976,O 6,35:1
Flannery, Susan
Gumball Rally, The 1976,Ag 21,13:1
Flaxman, Harvey (Producer)
Grizzly 1976,My 13,41:3
Flaxman, Harvey (Screenwriter)
Grizzly 1976,My 13,41:3
Fleischer, Richard (Director)
Mandingo 1975,My 9,19:1
Incredible Sarah, The 1976,N 6,11:1
Incredible Sarah, The 1976,N 7,II,13:1
Fletcher, Dexter
Bugsy Malone 1976,S 16,54:1
Fletcher, Diane
Autobiography of a Princess 1975,O 5,60:7
Fletcher, Louise
One Flew Over the Cuckoo's Nest 1975,N 20,52:1
One Flew Over the Cuckoo's Nest 1975,N 23,II,1:1
One Flew Over the Cuckoo's Nest
1975,D 21,II,17:5
Flick, Vic (Composer)
Autobiography of a Princess 1975,O 5,60:7
Flower, George (Buck)
Small Town in Texas, A 1976,Jl 10,16:1
Across the Great Divide 1976,D 21,44:1
Floyd, Calvin (Composer)
In Search of Dracula 1975,My 16,24:1
Floyd, Calvin (Director)
In Search of Dracula 1975,My 16,24:1
Floyd, Calvin (Producer)
In Search of Dracula 1975,My 16,24:1
Floyd, Yvonne (Screenwriter)
In Search of Dracula 1975,My 16,24:1
Fluellen, Joel
Bingo Long Traveling All-Stars and Motor Kings,
The 1976,Jl 17,10:1

Jutra, Claude (Screenwriter)
Kamouraska 1975,Jl 14,21:1
Jympson, John (Miscellaneous)
Dove, The 1975,F 20,38:2
Crime and Passion 1976,Ap 22,38:3
Incredible Sarah, The 1976,N 6,11:1

K

Kachanov, R (Director)
Heron and the Crane, The 1975,O 19,II,1:3
Kadar, Jan (Director)
Lies My Father Told Me 1975,O 13,36:1
Kagan, Alex (Composer)
Daughters, Daughters! 1975,Mr 10,40:2
Kahn, Jonathan
Sailor Who Fell From Grace With the Sea, The
1976,Ap 12,36:1
Kahn, Madeline
At Long Last Love 1975,Mr 7,22:1
At Long Last Love 1975,Mr 16,II,17:1
Adventure of Sherlock Holmes' Smarter Brother,
The 1975,D 15,42:1
Won Ton Ton, The Dog Who Saved Hollywood
1976,My 27,30:1
Kahn, Michael (Miscellaneous)
Devil's Rain, The 1975,Ag 8,11:1
Return of a Man Called Horse, The 1976,Je 29,19:1
Kahn, Sheldon (Miscellaneous)
One Flew Over the Cuckoo's Nest 1975,N 20,52:1
Kalaho
Milestones 1975,O 8,24:1
Kalaroglou, Stavros
Engagement of Anna, The 1975,Ap 8,32:1
Kallai, Ferenc
Riddance 1976,S 18,25:1
Kallianiotes, Helena
Drowning Pool, The 1975,Je 26,34:1
Stay Hungry 1976,Ap 26,41:1
Kalton, Jean-Pierre
Zig Zig 1976,S 18,24:5
Kamen, Michael (Composer)
Next Man, The 1976,N 11,52:1
Kamen, Milt
W C Fields and Me 1976,Ap 1,28:3
Mother, Jugs and Speed 1976,My 27,30:1
Kamp, Irene (Screenwriter)
Mr Quilp 1975,N 8,22:5
Kamp, Louis (Screenwriter)
Mr Quilp 1975,N 8,22:5
Kanaly, Steve
Wind and the Lion, The 1975,My 23,22:1
Kanau, Mitsuji (Cinematographer)
Man Who Skied Down Everest, The
1976,My 28,III,6:6
Kander, John (Composer)
Funny Lady 1975,Mr 12,30:1
Funny Lady 1975,Mr 16,II,17:1
Kander, John (Miscellaneous)
Lucky Lady 1975,D 26,47:3
Kane, Byron
Pink Panther Strikes Again, The 1976,D 16,66:1
Kane, Carol
Dog Day Afternoon 1975,S 22,41:1
Hester Street 1975,O 20,44:1
Hester Street 1975,N 2,II,15:6
Harry and Walter Go to New York
1976,Je 18,III,6:5
Kane, Michael
Three Days of the Condor 1975,S 25,60:1
Kanin, Garson (Screenwriter)
That's Entertainment, II 1976,My 30,II,11:1
Kaplan, Adi
Nurith 1975,Je 12,30:4
Kaplan, Chad
Martyr, The 1976,Je 17,30:1
Kaplan, Elliot (Composer)
Food of the Gods, The 1976,Jl 17,9:4
Kaplan, Jonathan (Director)
White Line Fever 1975,Ag 29,14:1
Kaplan, Jonathan (Screenwriter)
White Line Fever 1975,Ag 29,14:1
Kaplan, Joseph (Director)
White Line Fever 1975,S 7,II,7:1
Kaplan, Joseph (Screenwriter)
White Line Fever 1975,S 7,II,7:1
Kaplan, Mike
Buffalo Bill and the Indians or Sitting Bull's History
Lesson 1976,Je 25,III,8:5
Kaplan, Sol (Composer)
Lies My Father Told Me 1975,O 13,36:1
Kaquitts, Frank
Buffalo Bill and the Indians or Sitting Bull's History
Lesson 1976,Je 25,III,8:5
Buffalo Bill and the Indians or Sitting Bull's History
Lesson 1976,Jl 4,II,1:8
Kara, Irene
Aaron Loves Angela 1975,D 26,46:4
Karagheuze, Hermine
Duelle 1976,O 13,36:3
Karalashvili, M (Miscellaneous)
Pirosmani 1975,Ap 5,34:1

Karlatos, Olga
My Friends 1976,Jl 19,26:3
Karlen, John
Small Town in Texas, A 1976,Jl 10,16:1
Karlin, Fred (Composer)
Baby Blue Marine 1976,My 6,45:1
Futureworld 1976,Ag 14,10:1
Karlin, Fred (Miscellaneous)
Leadbelly 1976,My 29,14:1
Karlowa, Elma
Fox and His Friends (Fist-Right of Freedom)
(Faustrecht der Freiheit) 1975,S 27,21:4
Fox and His Friends (Fist-Right of Freedom)
(Faustrecht der Freiheit) 1976,F 3,24:1
Karlson, Phil (Director)
Framed 1975,O 2,47:1
Karmitz, Marin (Producer)
Blow for Blow (Coup Pour Coup) 1975,Mr 3,37:3
Karp, Ray (Director)
Sunday Funnies 1976,O 6,35:1
Karp, Ray (Miscellaneous)
Sunday Funnies 1976,O 6,35:1
Karp, Ray (Producer)
Sunday Funnies 1976,O 6,35:1
Karp, Ray (Screenwriter)
Sunday Funnies 1976,O 6,35:1
Karraz, Gaby
Night of Counting the Years, The 1975,O 23,48:3
Kasatkina, Natalya
World's Young Ballet, The 1975,Jl 10,19:1
Kastner, Elliott (Producer)
Rancho Deluxe 1975,N 24,28:1
92 in the Shade 1976,Ja 22,42:1
92 in the Shade 1976,F 1,II,13:1
Breakheart Pass 1976,My 6,46:3
Missouri Breaks, The 1976,My 20,45:1
Missouri Breaks, The 1976,My 23,II,17:7
Swashbuckler 1976,Jl 30,III,5:1
Kato, Goh
Kaseki (Fossil) 1976,S 10,III,5:1
Katselas, Milton (Director)
Report to the Commissioner 1975,F 6,25:1
Katsouridis, Dinos (Miscellaneous)
Engagement of Anna, The 1975,Ap 8,32:1
Katsouridis, Dinos (Producer)
Engagement of Anna, The 1975,Ap 8,32:1
Katsu, Shintaro (Producer)
Ali the Man 1975,S 18,50:1
Katt, William
Carrie 1976,N 17,III,24:1
Katz, Gloria (Screenwriter)
Lucky Lady 1975,D 14,II,1:2
Lucky Lady 1975,D 26,47:3
Katz, Sid (Miscellaneous)
Rancho Deluxe 1975,N 24,28:1
Katz, Walter (Miscellaneous)
Broken Treaty at Battle Mountain 1975,Ja 16,49:1
Katzav, Tova
Nurith 1975,Je 12,30:4
Kauer, Gene (Composer)
Brother of the Wind 1975,Ja 9,49:1
Adventures of the Wilderness Family, The
1975,D 20,16:1
Across the Great Divide 1976,D 21,44:1
Kaufman, Phil (Screenwriter)
Outlaw Josey Wales, The 1976,Ag 5,26:1
Kaufman, Robert (Screenwriter)
Harry and Walter Go to New York
1976,Je 18,III,6:5
Harry and Walter Go to New York
1976,Je 27,II,15:7
Kaul, Mani (Director)
Duvidha (Two Faces, Indecision) 1976,Ap 2,26:2
Kaul, Mani (Producer)
Duvidha (Two Faces, Indecision) 1976,Ap 2,26:2
Kaul, Mani (Screenwriter)
Duvidha (Two Faces, Indecision) 1976,Ap 2,26:2
Kavanaugh, Dorrie
Hester Street 1975,O 20,44:1
Kavoukidis, Nikos (Cinematographer)
Engagement of Anna, The 1975,Ap 8,32:1
Kawabata, Yasunari (Screenwriter)
Page of Madness 1975,F 4,26:4
Kawase, Hiroyuki
Godzilla Versus Megalon 1976,Jl 22,26:1
Kawkins, Odie (Miscellaneous)
Monkey Hustle, The 1976,D 25,8:1
Kay, Suzan (Miscellaneous)
Kamouraska 1975,Jl 14,21:1
Kaye, John (Screenwriter)
Rafferty and the Gold Dust Twins 1975,F 3,32:1
Kazan, Elia (Director)
Last Tycoon, The 1976,N 18,59:1
Last Tycoon, The 1976,D 12,II,1:1
Kazan, Sandra
Dog Day Afternoon 1975,S 22,41:1
Kaznin, Anatoli (Cinematographer)
World's Young Ballet, The 1975,Jl 10,19:1
Keach, James
Death Play 1976,S 2,24:2
Keach, Stacy
Conduct Unbecoming 1975,O 6,42:1
Street People 1976,S 18,24:5

Kean, E Arthur (Screenwriter)
Murph the Surf 1975,Je 12,30:6
Kean, Marie
Barry Lyndon 1975,D 19,52:4
Keating, Kevin (Cinematographer)
Harlan County, USA 1976,O 15,III,8:3
Keaton, Buster
Sherlock Jr 1975,Jl 22,23:1
Keaton, Buster (Director)
Sherlock Jr 1975,Jl 22,23:1
Keaton, Diane
Love and Death 1975,Je 11,48:1
Love and Death 1975,Je 22,II,1:7
I Will, I Will... For Now 1976,F 19,45:1
Harry and Walter Go to New York
1976,Je 18,III,6:5
Harry and Walter Go to New York
1976,Je 27,II,15:7
Keaton, Joseph
Sherlock Jr 1975,Jl 22,23:1
Keats, Steven
Hester Street 1975,O 20,44:1
Gumball Rally, The 1976,Ag 21,13:1
Kedrova, Lila
Undercovers Hero 1975,O 23,48:3
Tenant, The 1976,Je 21,43:1
Kee, Regan
Drive-In 1976,My 27,28:7
Kehlau, Marianne
Confrontations 1976,Mr 9,26:1
Kehoe, Jack
Car Wash 1976,O 16,13:1
Keiko, Kishi
Yakuza, The 1975,Mr 20,48:1
Keitel, Harvey
Alice Doesn't Live Here Anymore 1975,Ja 30,28:1
Alice Doesn't Live Here Anymore 1975,F 2,II,13:3
Alice Doesn't Live Here Anymore
1975,Mr 30,II,1:1
Taxi Driver 1976,F 8,36:1
Taxi Driver 1976,F 15,II,1:5
Mother, Jugs and Speed 1976,My 27,30:1
Mother, Jugs and Speed 1976,Je 6,II,13:7
Buffalo Bill and the Indians or Sitting Bull's History
Lesson 1976,Je 25,III,8:5
Keith, Brian
Yakuza, The 1975,Mr 20,48:1
Wind and the Lion, The 1975,My 23,22:1
Wind and the Lion, The 1975,Je 15,II,17:7
Nickelodeon 1976,D 22,34:4
Kellaway, Roger (Composer)
Legacy 1976,My 3,41:1
Keller, Frank P (Miscellaneous)
Mother, Jugs and Speed 1976,My 27,30:1
Keller, Marthe
And Now My Love 1975,Mr 22,36:1
Down the Ancient Stairs 1975,O 18,22:1
Marathon Man 1976,O 7,62:1
Marathon Man 1976,O 24,II,15:1
Kellerman, Sally
Rafferty and the Gold Dust Twins 1975,F 3,32:1
Big Bus, The 1976,Je 24,26:1
Kellin, Mike
Next Stop, Greenwich Village 1976,F 5,24:1
Kellogg, Marjorie (Miscellaneous)
Rosebud 1975,Mr 25,24:1
Kelly, Gene
Singin' in the Rain 1975,My 4,II,15:1
That's Entertainment, II 1976,My 30,II,11:1
Kelly, Gene (Director)
Singin' in the Rain 1975,My 4,II,15:1
That's Entertainment, II 1976,My 17,40:1
Keily, Jim
Take a Hard Ride 1975,O 30,52:2
Kelly, M G
Star is Born, A 1976,D 27,III,16:5
Kelly, Martine
Story of O, The 1975,N 15,20:1
Kelly, Paula
Drum 1976,Jl 31,11:1
Kelly, Sharon
Supervixens 1975,Ag 9,9:1
Hustle 1975,D 26,37:1
Kemeny, John (Producer)
White Line Fever 1975,Ag 29,14:1
Kemmerling, Warren
Framed 1975,O 2,47:1
Family Plot 1976,Ap 10,22:1
Eat My Dust 1976,My 29,13:7
Kemp, Jeremy
Seven-Per-Cent Solution, The 1976,O 25,42:1
Kemper, Victor J (Cinematographer)
Reincarnation of Peter Proud, The 1975,Ap 26,14:1
Stay Hungry 1976,Ap 26,41:1
Last Tycoon, The 1976,N 18,59:1
Mikey and Nicky 1976,D 22,34:4
Kemplen, Willy (Miscellaneous)
Destructors, The 1975,Je 12,30:6
Cleopatra Jones and the Casino of Gold
1975,Jl 12,16:4
Ken, Takakura
Yakuza, The 1975,Mr 20,48:1

Lathrop, Philip (Cinematographer)—Cont
Black Bird, The 1975,D 26,43:1
Swashbuckler 1976,Jl 30,III,5:1
Latoni, Bernadette
Zig Zig 1976,S 18,24:5
Lattuada, Alberto (Director)
Bambina 1976,Ap 26,40:1
Lattuada, Alberto (Screenwriter)
Bambina 1976,Ap 26,40:1
Lau, Wesley (Miscellaneous)
Lepke 1975,My 24,12:1
Lau, Wesley (Screenwriter)
Lepke 1975,My 24,12:1
Lauber, Ken (Composer)
Hearts of the West 1975,O 4,14:1
Laughlin, Frank (Director)
Master Gunfighter, The 1975,O 10,32:4
Laughlin, Kathleen (Director)
Susan Through Corn 1976,F 13,19:1
Some Will Be Apples 1976,F 13,19:1
Laughlin, Tom
Master Gunfighter, The 1975,O 10,32:4
Lauler, Ed
Family Plot 1976,Ap 10,22:1
Laura, Ana (Miscellaneous)
Children of Rage 1975,My 29,29:2
Laure, Carol
Sweet Movie 1975,O 10,32:3
Laurence, Caroline
Emmanuelle the Joys of a Woman 1976,F 12,41:3
Laurence, John
Alice in Wonderland 1976,Ag 28,11:2
Laurent, Patrick (Screenwriter)
Cher Victor (Dear Victor) 1976,F 13,19:1
Laurie, Piper
Carrie 1976,N 17,III,24:1
Carrie 1976,D 5,II,13:4
Laurier, Stephen
Not a Pretty Picture 1976,Ap 1,28:4
Lauter, Ed
Breakheart Pass 1976,My 6,46:3
King Kong 1976,D 18,16:1
Lautner, Georges (Director)
Man in the Trunk, The 1975,D 6,22:5
Icy Breasts (Les Seins de Glace) 1975,D 11,59:1
Lautner, Georges (Screenwriter)
Icy Breasts (Les Seins de Glace) 1975,D 11,59:1
Lavia, Gabriele
Devil is a Woman, The 1975,O 27,23:1
Lavie, Efrat
My Michael 1976,Mr 16,29:2
Martyr, The 1976,Je 17,30:1
Lawford, Peter
Rosebud 1975,Mr 25,24:1
Lawlor, John
Jackson County Jail 1976,Je 12,13:1
Lawrence, Elliott (Composer)
Network 1976,N 15,39:1
Lawrence, Marc
Marathon Man 1976,O 7,62:1
Lawrence, Robert (Miscellaneous)
Whiffs 1976,My 20,44:5
Laws, Sam
White Line Fever 1975,Ag 29,14:1
Lawson, Tony (Miscellaneous)
Barry Lyndon 1975,D 19,52:4
Lazare, Carole
Lies My Father Told Me 1975,O 13,36:1
Lazareff, Serge
Sidecar Racers 1975,O 11,24:1
Lazareno, Norma
Survive! 1976,Ag 5,26:1
Le Clair, Michael
Baby Blue Marine 1976,My 6,45:1
Le Mat, Paul
Aloha, Bobby and Rose 1975,Ap 30,24:1
Le Mesurier, John
Adventure of Sherlock Holmes' Smarter Brother,
The 1975,D 15,42:1
Le Noire, Rosetta
Sunshine Boys, The 1975,N 7,28:1
Le Roux, Maurice (Composer)
Immoral Tales (Contes Immoraux) 1976,Mr 11,43:1
Le Roy, Gloria
Day of the Locust, The 1975,My 8,48:1
Leach, Britt
Jackson County Jail 1976,Je 12,13:1
Leacock, Richard (Director)
Mooney vs Fowle 1976,Je 4,III,11:1
Leaders, Bonnie
Buffalo Bill and the Indians or Sitting Bull's History
Lesson 1976,Je 25,III,8:5
Leaf, Caroline (Director)
Owl Who Married the Goose, The
1976,My 21,III,11:1
Lear, Evelyn
Buffalo Bill and the Indians or Sitting Bull's History
Lesson 1976,Je 25,III,8:5
Leary, Margaret
Birch Interval 1976,My 3,41:2
Leavitt, Sam (Cinematographer)
Man in the Glass Booth, The 1975,My 20,46:4
Lebedev, Yevgeni
Crime and Punishment 1975,My 15,48:1

LeCompte, Elizabeth
Tooth of the Crime, The 1975,S 18,49:1
Lecomte, Claude (Cinematographer)
Love at the Top (Le Mouton Enrage)
1975,Ja 27,18:1
L'Ecuyer, Guy
Bar Salon 1975,Ap 12,14:4
Ledoux, Fernand
Donkey Skin (Peau d'Ane) 1975,Mr 24,39:1
Lee, Barbara
Boss Nigger 1975,F 27,30:2
Lee, Christopher
Four Musketeers, The 1975,Mr 20,48:1
In Search of Dracula 1975,My 16,24:1
Killer Force 1976,Mr 11,43:1
Lee, Dixie
Legacy 1976,My 3,41:1
Lee, Jennifer
Duchess and the Dirtwater Fox, The
1976,Ap 8,43:1
Lee, Margaret
Let's Talk About Men 1976,Ag 5,27:1
Lefebvre, Jean
Man in the Trunk, The 1975,D 6,22:5
Legrand, Michel (Composer)
Donkey Skin (Peau d'Ane) 1975,Mr 24,39:1
Touch and Go 1975,Ap 25,24:1
Sheila Levine is Dead and Living in New York
1975,My 17,14:2
F For Fake 1975,S 28,57:1
Gable and Lombard 1976,F 12,42:1
Lehman, Ernest (Screenwriter)
Family Plot 1976,Ap 10,22:1
Lehne, John
Bound for Glory 1976,D 6,47:1
Lehner, Jim (Screenwriter)
Reflections (Dry Summer) 1975,Je 12,30:1
Leibman, Ron
Won Ton Ton, The Dog Who Saved Hollywood
1976,My 27,30:1
Leighton, Margaret
Galileo 1975,Ja 28,26:1
From Beyond the Grave 1976,Mr 4,24:1
Lelouch, Claude (Director)
And Now My Love 1975,Mr 22,36:1
Lelouch, Claude (Screenwriter)
And Now My Love 1975,Mr 22,36:1
Lem, Stanislaw (Original Author)
Solaris 1976,O 7,63:2
Lemmon, Jack
Prisoner of Second Avenue 1975,Mr 15,18:1
Alex and the Gypsy 1976,O 4,16:1
Lemole, Lisa
Drive-In 1976,My 27,28:7
Lempert, Peter
In the Region of Ice 1976,O 6,35:1
Lendi, Georges (Cinematographer)
Cousin, Cousine 1976,Jl 26,29:1
Lennon, John (Composer)
All This and World War II 1976,D 27,III,17:1
Lennon, John (Miscellaneous)
All This and World War II 1976,D 27,III,17:1
Lensky, Leib
Love and Death 1975,Je 11,48:1
Lenz, Kay
White Line Fever 1975,Ag 29,14:1
White Line Fever 1975,S 7,II,7:1
Great Scout and Cathouse Thursday, The
1976,Je 24,24:1
Lenzer, Don (Cinematographer)
Not a Pretty Picture 1976,Ap 1,28:4
Leotard, Philippe
Middle of the World, The 1975,Mr 29,10:5
Middle of the World, The 1975,Ap 27,II,1:1
Kamouraska 1975,Jl 14,21:1
Pas Si Mechant Que Ca (Not Really That Bad)
(Wonderful Crook, The) 1975,O 1,59:1
Lepers, Carole
Last Woman, The 1976,Je 7,35:1
Leporinne, Marjatta (Miscellaneous)
Earth is a Sinful Song, The 1975,N 19,22:3
Leprince, Solange (Miscellaneous)
India Song 1975,O 8,24:1
Lerner, Irving (Miscellaneous)
River Niger, The 1976,Ap 15,28:1
Lerner, Michael
St Ives 1976,S 2,24:1
LeRoux, Maurice (Composer)
Kamouraska 1975,Jl 14,21:1
Leslie, Karen
Death Play 1976,S 2,24:2
Leslie, Robert Franklin (Original Author)
Bears and I, The 1975,Jl 17,21:1
Lester, Mark W (Director)
Bobbie Jo and the Outlaw 1976,Jl 7,46:4
Lester, Mark W (Producer)
Bobbie Jo and the Outlaw 1976,Jl 7,46:4
Lester, Richard (Director)
Four Musketeers, The 1975,Mr 20,48:1
Royal Flash 1975,O 11,23:1
Three Musketeers, The 1975,N 23,II,15:1
Robin and Marian 1976,Mr 12,26:1
Robin and Marian 1976,Mr 14,II,1:1

Lester, Richard (Director)—Cont
Robin and Marian 1976,Je 27,II,15:7
Ritz, The 1976,Ag 13,III,12:4
Ritz, The 1976,N 7,II,13:1
Lester, Tom
Benji 1975,Je 27,25:1
Lestringuez, Pierre
Nana 1976,O 14,44:1
Lestringuez, Pierre (Screenwriter)
Nana 1976,O 14,44:1
Lev, Martin
Bugsy Malone 1976,S 16,54:1
Leventhal, Harold (Producer)
Bound for Glory 1976,D 6,47:1
Levey, Chuck (Cinematographer)
Broken Treaty at Battle Mountain 1975,Ja 16,49:1
Levin, Ira (Original Author)
Stepford Wives, The 1975,F 13,43:1
Levin, Sidney (Miscellaneous)
Nashville 1975,Je 12,32:1
Front, The 1976,O 1,III,7:1
Levine, Joseph E (Miscellaneous)
Paper Tiger 1976,S 17,III,8:3
Levins, John W (Miscellaneous)
Brother of the Wind 1975,Ja 9,49:1
Levinson, Barry (Screenwriter)
Silent Movie 1976,Jl 1,22:1
Levinson, Richard (Miscellaneous)
Hindenberg, The 1975,D 26,46:1
Levitt, Amy
Dog Day Afternoon 1975,S 22,41:1
Levitt, Helen (Director)
In the Street 1975,Je 6,14:1
Levy, Jules (Producer)
Brannigan 1975,Mr 27,37:1
Gator 1976,Ag 26,46:3
Lewin, Albert E (Screenwriter)
I Will, I Will... For Now 1976,F 19,45:1
Lewis, Arthur (Producer)
Killer Elite, The 1975,D 18,62:1
Lewis, Edward (Producer)
Blue Bird, The 1976,My 14,III,7:1
Lewis, Fiona
Lisztomania 1975,O 11,23:1
Drum 1976,Jl 31,11:1
Lewis, Geoffrey
Macon County Line 1975,Ja 16,49:1
Great Waldo Pepper, The 1975,Mr 14,24:1
Wind and the Lion, The 1975,My 23,22:1
Smile 1975,O 9,52:1
Lucky Lady 1975,D 26,47:3
Return of a Man Called Horse, The 1976,Je 29,19:1
Lewis, Joseph H (Director)
Gun Crazy 1975,Ag 3,II,1:1
Lewis, Michael J (Composer)
Russian Roulette 1975,Ag 21,44:2
92 in the Shade 1976,Ja 22,42:1
Lewiston, Denis C (Cinematographer)
Crime and Passion 1976,Ap 22,38:3
L'homme, Pierre (Cinematographer)
Sweet Movie 1975,O 10,32:3
Lichterman, Marvin
Front, The 1976,O 1,III,7:1
Lichtig, Renee (Miscellaneous)
Kamouraska 1975,Jl 14,21:1
Lieberman, Jeff (Director)
Squirm 1976,Jl 31,10:4
Lieberman, Jeff (Screenwriter)
Squirm 1976,Jl 31,10:4
Lieberson, Sandy (Producer)
Brother, Can You Spare a Dime? 1975,Ag 8,10:2
Stardust 1975,N 13,52:5
All This and World War II 1976,D 27,III,17:1
Lifshitz, Avi (Miscellaneous)
Nurith 1975,Je 12,30:4
Lightfoot, Gordon (Composer)
Paperback Hero 1975,Ja 20,23:3
Lightstone, Marilyn
Lies My Father Told Me 1975,O 13,36:1
Ligouri, Al (Cinematographer)
Scar of Shame, The 1976,Mr 18,50:1
Lindberg, Sven
Face to Face 1976,Ap 6,28:1
Linden, Jennie
Old Dracula 1976,Ja 15,30:1
Hedda 1976,Ja 26,29:1
Linder, Stu (Miscellaneous)
Fortune, The 1975,My 21,49:1
Lindsay, John V
Rosebud 1975,Mr 25,24:1
Link, Andre (Producer)
They Came From Within 1976,Jl 7,46:4
Link, John (Miscellaneous)
Race With the Devil 1975,Jl 10,19:3
Stay Hungry 1976,Ap 26,41:1
Link, William (Miscellaneous)
Hindenberg, The 1975,D 26,46:1
Linkers, Eduard
Marquise of O..., The 1976,O 18,36:1
Linkevitch, Barbara
Devil's Cleavage, The 1975,N 29,20:1
Linson, Art (Producer)
Rafferty and the Gold Dust Twins 1975,F 3,32:1
Car Wash 1976,O 16,13:1

27

M

McDowell, Curt (Director)
Nudes (A Sketchbook) 1975,My 10,18:5
McDowell, Malcolm
Royal Flash 1975,O 11,23:1
Voyage of the Damned 1976,D 23,18:1
McEnery, John
Galileo 1975,Ja 28,26:1
Land That Time Forgot, The 1975,Ag 14,39:1
McErlane, Thomas J (Producer)
Give 'Em Hell, Harry! 1975,S 23,30:1
McEveety, Bernard (Director)
Bears and I, The 1975,Jl 17,21:1
McEveety, Joe (Miscellaneous)
No Deposit, No Return 1976,Jl 3,17:1
McEveety, Joe (Producer)
No Deposit, No Return 1976,Jl 3,17:1
McEveety, Joseph L (Screenwriter)
Strongest Man in the World, The 1975,Jl 10,19:1
McEveety, Vincent (Director)
Strongest Man in the World, The 1975,Jl 10,19:1
Gus 1976,Ag 7,11:2
Treasure of Matecumbe 1976,Ag 28,11:2
Macey, Elizabeth
Bound for Glory 1976,D 6,47:1
McGavin, Darren
No Deposit, No Return 1976,Jl 3,17:1
McGavin, Dick
Smile 1975,S 28,II,13:1
McGaw, Bill (Original Author)
Sky Riders 1976,Mr 27,18:4
McGee, Vonetta
Eiger Sanction, The 1975,My 22,32:1
McGinn, Walter
Three Days of the Condor 1975,S 25,60:1
McGinnis, Carol
Gable and Lombard 1976,F 12,42:1
McGiver, John
Arnold 1975,Mr 22,36:1
McGivern, William P (Screenwriter)
Brannigan 1975,Mr 27,37:1
McGoohan, Patrick
Silver Streak 1976,D 9,61:1
McGrath, Joseph (Director)
Great McGonagall, The 1975,Ag 16,10:3
McGrath, Joseph (Screenwriter)
Great McGonagall, The 1975,Ag 16,10:3
McGrath, Tom (Producer)
Deadly Hero 1976,O 16,11:4
McGreevey, Michael
Strongest Man in the World, The 1975,Jl 10,19:1
McGuane, Thomas (Director)
92 in the Shade 1976,Ja 22,42:1
92 in the Shade 1976,F 1,II,13:1
McGuane, Thomas (Screenwriter)
Rancho Deluxe 1975,N 24,28:1
Rancho Deluxe 1975,D 7,II,17:1
92 in the Shade 1976,Ja 22,42:1
92 in the Shade 1976,F 1,II,13:1
Missouri Breaks, The 1976,My 20,45:1
Missouri Breaks, The 1976,My 23,II,17:7
McGuire, Biff
Midway 1976,Je 19,11:1
McGuire, Dennis (Director)
Shoot It: Black Shoot It: Blue 1975,Jl 10,19:1
McGuire, Dennis (Screenwriter)
Shoot It: Black Shoot It: Blue 1975,Jl 10,19:1
McGuire, Katheryn
Sherlock Jr 1975,Jl 22,23:1
McGuire, Michael
Report to the Commissioner 1975,F 6,25:1
Hard Times 1975,O 9,54:2
Machat, Martin J (Producer)
All This and World War II 1976,D 27,III,17:1
Machiavelli, Nicoletta
Icy Breasts (Les Seins de Glace) 1975,D 11,59:1
McIntire, John
Rooster Cogburn 1975,O 18,22:1
McIntire, Tim
Aloha, Bobby and Rose 1975,Ap 30,24:1
Boy and His Dog, A 1976,Je 17,32:2
McIntire, Tim (Composer)
Boy and His Dog, A 1976,Je 17,32:2
Macintosh, Joan
Tooth of the Crime, The 1975,S 18,49:1
McKee, Lonette
Sparkle 1976,Ap 8,43:1
Sparkle 1976,Ap 11,II,15:7
Mackenzie, Patch
Goodbye, Norma Jean 1976,My 11,26:5
McKern, Leo
Adventure of Sherlock Holmes' Smarter Brother,
The 1975,D 15,42:1
Mackey, John (Cinematographer)
Great McGonagall, The 1975,Ag 16,10:3
McKinney, Bill
Outlaw Josey Wales, The 1976,Ag 5,26:1
Shootist, The 1976,Ag 12,38:1
McKnight, Sam
Super Spook 1975,Jl 10,19:1
McLaglen, Andrew V (Director)
Mitchell 1975,S 11,35:1
Last Hard Men, The 1976,Ap 24,16:1

MacLaine, Shirley (Director)
Other Half of the Sky, The: A China Memoir
1975,Mr 13,45:1
Other Half of the Sky, The: A China Memoir
1975,Mr 23,II,1:1
MacLaine, Shirley (Producer)
Other Half of the Sky, The: A China Memoir
1975,Mr 13,45:1
Other Half of the Sky, The: A China Memoir
1975,Mr 23,II,1:1
MacLaine, Shirley (Screenwriter)
Other Half of the Sky, The: A China Memoir
1975,Mr 13,45:1
Other Half of the Sky, The: A China Memoir
1975,Mr 23,II,1:1
MacLean, Alistair (Screenwriter)
Breakheart Pass 1976,My 6,46:3
McLean, Michael (Miscellaneous)
Mr Ricco 1975,Ja 30,26:4
MacLean, Peter
Squirm 1976,Jl 31,10:4
McLerie, Allyn Ann
All The President's Men 1976,Ap 8,42:1
McLiam, John
Dove, The 1975,F 20,38:2
Lucky Lady 1975,D 26,47:3
Missouri Breaks, The 1976,My 20,45:1
McMartin, John
All The President's Men 1976,Ap 8,42:1
McNally, Terrence (Original Author)
Ritz, The 1976,Ag 13,III,12:4
McNally, Terrence (Screenwriter)
Ritz, The 1976,Ag 13,III,12:4
Ritz, The 1976,Ag 15,II,13:1
Ritz, The 1976,N 7,II,13:1
McNamara, Patrick
Obsession 1976,Ag 2,29:1
McPeak, Sandy
Ode to Billy Joe 1976,Ag 19,48:1
MacPherson, Don (Original Author)
Bawdy Adventures of Tom Jones, The
1976,S 2,25:1
Macpherson, Stu
Nothing by Chance 1975,Ja 31,25:2
Macreading, James (Miscellaneous)
Abduction 1975,O 25,17:1
McRoberts, Briony
Pink Panther Strikes Again, The 1976,D 16,66:1
Madame Louise
Story of Adele H, The 1975,O 13,36:1
Story of Adele H, The (L'Histoire d'Adele H)
1975,D 23,15:2
Madaras, Jozsef
Elektreia 1975,S 30,31:2
Madden, Dave
Eat My Dust 1976,My 29,13:7
Maeder, Fritz (Cinematographer)
Confrontations 1976,Mr 9,26:1
Maes, Tove
Take It Like a Man, Madam 1976,S 16,55:1
Maeterlinck, Maurice (Original Author)
Blue Bird, The 1976,My 14,III,7:1
Blue Bird, The 1976,My 16,II,17:1
Magee, Patrick
Galileo 1975,Ja 28,26:1
Barry Lyndon 1975,D 19,52:4
Magicovsky, Alan
They Came From Within 1976,Jl 7,46:4
Mahabir, Dennis
Bim 1976,D 2,57:1
Mahal, Taj
Part 2 Sounder 1976,O 14,43:6
Mahal, Taj (Composer)
Part 2 Sounder 1976,O 14,43:6
Maharaj, Anand
Bim 1976,D 2,57:1
Maharaj, Ralph
Bim 1976,D 2,57:1
Mahon, John (Producer)
Brother of the Wind 1975,Ja 9,49:1
Mahon, John (Screenwriter)
Brother of the Wind 1975,Ja 9,49:1
Maier, Brigitte
Sensations 1975,N 23,II,1:1
Maile, Vincent (Producer)
Sweet Movie 1975,O 10,32:3
Maimberg, Urban
Magic Flute, The 1975,N 12,50:1
Mainka-Jellinghaus, Beate (Miscellaneous)
Jeder Fur Sich Und Gott Gegen Alle (Every Man
for Himself and God Against All) 1975,S 28,57:1
Maistre, Francois
Special Section (Section Speciale) 1975,D 8,42:1
Dirty Hands 1976,N 4,49:1
Maitland, Marne
Pink Panther Strikes Again, The 1976,D 16,66:1
Major, Anthony (Director)
Super Spook 1975,Jl 10,19:1
Major, Anthony (Miscellaneous)
Super Spook 1975,Jl 10,19:1
Major, Anthony (Screenwriter)
Super Spook 1975,Jl 10,19:1

Makaveiev, Dusan (Director)
Sweet Movie 1975,O 10,32:3
Mako
Killer Elite, The 1975,D 18,62:1
Makonen, Melaku
Harvest: 3000 Years 1976,Ap 6,27:1
Malina, Judith
Dog Day Afternoon 1975,S 22,41:1
Malle, Louis (Director)
Lacombe, Lucien 1975,Ja 12,II,1:3
Human, Too Human (Humain, Trop Humain)
1975,F 14,28:1
Black Moon 1975,S 30,31:1
Black Moon 1975,O 3,40:1
Black Moon 1975,O 5,II,15:1
Malle, Louis (Producer)
Human, Too Human (Humain, Trop Humain)
1975,F 14,28:1
Malle, Louis (Screenwriter)
Black Moon 1975,S 30,31:1
Mallet, Jane
Sweet Movie 1975,O 10,32:3
Malloy, James (Cinematographer)
Long Night, The 1976,Ap 11,45:5
Malmsten, Birger
Face to Face 1976,Ap 6,28:1
Malone, Dorothy
Abduction 1975,O 25,17:1
Maloney, Peter
Capone 1975,Ap 17,48:6
Manasse, George (Producer)
Squirm 1976,Jl 31,10:4
Manchette, Jean-Patric (Screenwriter)
Act of Aggression (L'Agression) 1975,D 4,50:1
Mancini, Henry (Composer)
Great Waldo Pepper, The 1975,Mr 14,24:1
Return of the Pink Panther, The 1975,My 22,32:1
Jacqueline Susann's Once is Not Enough
1975,Je 19,28:5
W C Fields and Me 1976,Ap 1,28:3
Alex and the Gypsy 1976,O 4,16:1
Silver Streak 1976,D 9,61:1
Pink Panther Strikes Again, The 1976,D 16,66:1
Mandel, John (Composer)
Escape to Witch Mountain 1975,Jl 3,21:1
Sailor Who Fell From Grace With the Sea, The
1976,Ap 12,36:1
Mandel, Tommy (Composer)
Deadly Hero 1976,O 16,11:4
Manduke, Joe (Director)
Cornbread, Earl and Me 1975,My 22,34:1
Manduke, Joe (Producer)
Cornbread, Earl and Me 1975,My 22,34:1
Manenti, Michele
Not a Pretty Picture 1976,Ap 1,28:4
Manes, Stephen (Miscellaneous)
Mother, Jugs and Speed 1976,My 27,30:1
Manfredi, Nino
Let's Talk About Men 1976,Ag 5,27:1
Mangano, Silvana
Conversation Piece (Gruppo di Famiglia in un
Interno) 1975,S 27,21:2
Conversation Piece 1975,O 5,II,15:1
Mangine, Joseph (Cinematographer)
Squirm 1976,Jl 31,10:4
Mangolte, Babette (Cinematographer)
What Maisie Knew 1976,Ja 15,30:1
Kristina Talking Pictures 1976,N 3,62:1
Mangolte, Babette (Director)
What Maisie Knew 1976,Ja 15,30:1
Mangolte, Babette (Screenwriter)
What Maisie Knew 1976,Ja 15,30:1
Manheim, Kate
What Maisie Knew 1976,Ja 15,30:1
Mankiewicz, Don (Miscellaneous)
Black Bird, The 1975,D 26,43:1
Mankiewicz, Tom (Miscellaneous)
Mother, Jugs and Speed 1976,My 27,30:1
Mankiewicz, Tom (Producer)
Mother, Jugs and Speed 1976,My 27,30:1
Mankiewicz, Tom (Screenwriter)
Mother, Jugs and Speed 1976,My 27,30:1
Mother, Jugs and Speed 1976,Je 6,II,13:7
Mann, Abby (Screenwriter)
Report to the Commissioner 1975,F 6,25:1
Mann, Claude
India Song 1975,O 8,24:1
French Provincial (Souvenir's d'en France)
1975,O 9,52:1
French Provincial (Souvenir d'en France)
1976,F 28,14:3
Mann, Delbert (Director)
Birch Interval 1976,My 3,41:2
Mann, Stanley (Screenwriter)
Russian Roulette 1975,Ag 21,44:2
Sky Riders 1976,Mr 27,18:4
Mann, Ted (Producer)
Lifeguard 1976,Jl 24,12:1
Manni, Entore
Street People 1976,S 18,24:5
Manning, Stacey
Apple Dumpling Gang, The 1975,Jl 24,17:3

Maysles, David (Producer)—Cont
 Grey Gardens 1976,F 22,II,15:1
Mazurki, Mike
 Challenge To Be Free 1976,Mr 21,II,1:7
Mazursky, Paul
 Star is Born, A 1976,D 27,III,16:5
Mazursky, Paul (Director)
 Next Stop, Greenwich Village 1976,F 5,24:1
 Next Stop, Greenwich Village 1976,F 8,II,19:3
Mazursky, Paul (Producer)
 Next Stop, Greenwich Village 1976,F 5,24:1
Mazursky, Paul (Screenwriter)
 Next Stop, Greenwich Village 1976,F 5,24:1
McDonald, Leroy
 Blood's Way 1976,S 22,38:5
McLiam, John
 Rafferty and the Gold Dust Twins 1975,F 3,32:1
Meacham, Anne
 Seizure 1975,Mr 23,II,15:1
Mead, Margaret (Miscellaneous)
 Learning to Dance in Bali 1975,My 3,41:3
Meader, Vaughn
 Lepke 1975,My 24,12:1
Medboe, Katia
 Wives (Hustruer) 1976,Ap 3,19:1
Medioli, Enrico (Miscellaneous)
 Conversation Piece (Gruppo di Famiglia in un
  Interno) 1975,S 27,21:2
Medioli, Enrico (Screenwriter)
 Conversation Piece (Gruppo di Famiglia in un
  Interno) 1975,S 27,21:2
Meeker, Ralph
 Jeopardy 1975,Ag 3,II,1:1
 Food of the Gods, The 1976,Jl 17,9:4
 Love Comes Quietly 1976,D 2,57:3
Mehdi
 Catherine & Co 1976,F 26,23:1
Meier, Amin
 Fear of Fear (Angst vor der Angst)
  1976,O 15,III,8:3
Meillon, John
 Sidecar Racers 1975,O 11,24:1
 Ride a Wild Pony 1976,Jl 17,9:3
Meineke, Eva Marie
 Dream City 1976,D 6,46:6
Meisner, Sanford
 Mikey and Nicky 1976,D 22,34:4
Mekas, Jonas (Director)
 Lost, Lost, Lost (Diaries, Notes & Sketches, Reels
  1-6) 1976,S 15,52:3
Melaku, Adane
 Harvest: 3000 Years 1976,Ap 6,27:1
Melato, Mariangela
 Lulu the Tool 1975,My 12,39:1
 Swept Away (By an Unusual Destiny in the Blue
  Sea of August) 1975,S 18,48:1
 Swept Away (By an Unusual Destiny in the Blue
  Sea of August) 1975,S 21,II,15:1
 Moses 1976,Mr 27,17:1
 Guernica 1976,My 22,19:3
Mell, Marisa
 Mahogany 1975,O 9,54:1
Melle, Gil (Composer)
 Embryo 1976,My 27,29:1
Melnick, David (Producer)
 That's Entertainment, Part 2 1976,My 17,40:1
Melniker, Benjamin (Producer)
 Mitchell 1975,S 11,35:1
Melsel, Myron (Screenwriter)
 I'm a Stranger Here Myself 1975,Ja 17,20:1
Melton, Sid
 Sheila Levine is Dead and Living in New York
  1975,My 17,14:2
Melvin, Murray
 Barry Lyndon 1975,D 19,52:4
 Barry Lyndon 1975,D 21,II,1:7
 Bawdy Adventures of Tom Jones, The
  1976,S 2,25:1
Mendelssohn, Felix (Composer)
 Story of Sin (Dzieje Grzechu) 1976,O 7,63:2
Menez, Bernard
 Don't Cry With Your Mouth Full (Pleure Pas la
  Bouche Pleine) 1975,Ap 14,41:1
Menicone, Enzo (Miscellaneous)
 Last Woman, The 1976,Je 7,35:1
Menon, Rayi
 Duvidha (Two Faces, Indecision) 1976,Ap 2,26:2
Menten, Dale (Miscellaneous)
 Lifeguard 1976,Jl 24,12:1
Meranda, Luke
 Violent Professional, The 1976,O 30,14:3
Mercanton, Victoria Spiri (Miscellaneous)
 Charlotte 1975,Je 23,33:2
Merchant, Ismail (Producer)
 Autobiography of a Princess 1975,O 5,60:7
Merchant, Vivien
 Maids, The 1975,Ap 22,41:1
Mercier, Chantal
 Small Change (L'Argent de Poche)
  1976,O 1,III,11:1
Mercouri, Melina
 Jacqueline Susann's Once is Not Enough
  1975,Je 19,28:5

Jacqueline Susann's Once is Not Enough
  1975,Jl 6,II,9:1
Meredith, Burgess
 Day of the Locust, The 1975,My 8,48:1
 Day of the Locust, The 1975,My 11,II,1:1
 Hindenberg, The 1975,D 26,46:1
 92 in the Shade 1976,Ja 22,42:1
 92 in the Shade 1976,F 1,II,13:1
 Burnt Offerings 1976,S 30,36:1
 Rocky 1976,N 22,III,19:1
Meredith, Lee
 Sunshine Boys, The 1975,N 7,28:1
Merin, Eda Reiss
 Hester Street 1975,O 20,44:1
Merli, Adalberto-Maria
 Night Caller 1975,N 20,52:2
Merrifield, Dick
 Sheba, Baby 1975,Mr 27,37:1
Merrill, Bob (Screenwriter)
 W C Fields and Me 1976,Ap 1,28:3
 W C Fields and Me 1976,Ap 4,II,19:1
Merson, Marc (Producer)
 Leadbelly 1976,My 29,14:1
Mervyn, William
 Bawdy Adventures of Tom Jones, The
  1976,S 2,25:1
Merzin, Leonid
 King Lear 1975,Ag 7,39:3
Messina, Emilio
 Icy Breasts (Les Seins de Glace) 1975,D 11,59:1
Messmer, Otto (Director)
 Arabianantics 1976,Ap 21,21:1
 Astronomeous 1976,Ap 21,21:1
 Comicalamities 1976,Ap 21,21:1
 Eats are West 1976,Ap 21,21:1
 Felix Revolts 1976,Ap 21,21:1
 Switches Witches 1976,Ap 21,21:1
 Cold Rush, The 1976,Ap 21,21:1
 Felix Hits the Deck 1976,Ap 21,21:1
Meszaros, Marta (Director)
 Adoption (Orokbefogadas) 1976,Ap 2,26:1
 Riddance 1976,S 18,25:1
Meszaros, Marta (Screenwriter)
 Adoption (Orokbefogadas) 1976,Ap 2,26:1
 Riddance 1976,S 18,25:1
Metin, Ismail (Director)
 Reflections (Dry Summer) 1975,Je 12,30:1
Metz, Rexford (Miscellaneous)
 Jaws 1975,Je 21,19:2
Meyer, Andrew (Director)
 Tidal Wave 1975,S 16,53:1
Meyer, Andrew (Screenwriter)
 Tidal Wave 1975,S 16,53:1
Meyer, Emile
 Macon County Line 1975,Ja 16,49:1
Meyer, Muffie (Director)
 Grey Gardens 1975,S 27,21:2
 Grey Gardens 1976,F 20,15:2
Meyer, Muffie (Miscellaneous)
 Grey Gardens 1975,S 27,21:2
 Grey Gardens 1976,F 20,15:2
Meyer, Nicholas (Original Author)
 Seven-Per-Cent Solution, The 1976,O 25,42:1
 Seven-Per-Cent Solution, The 1976,O 31,II,17:1
Meyer, Nicholas (Screenwriter)
 Seven-Per-Cent Solution, The 1976,O 25,42:1
 Seven-Per-Cent Solution, The 1976,O 31,II,17:1
Meyer, Richard (Miscellaneous)
 Capone 1975,Ap 17,48:6
Meyer, Russ (Cinematographer)
 Supervixens 1975,Ag 9,9:1
Meyer, Russ (Director)
 Supervixens 1975,Ag 9,9:1
Meyer, Russ (Miscellaneous)
 Supervixens 1975,Ag 9,9:1
Meyer, Russ (Producer)
 Supervixens 1975,Ag 9,9:1
Meyer, Russ (Screenwriter)
 Supervixens 1975,Ag 9,9:1
Meziere, Myriam
 Jonah Who Will Be 25 in the Year 2000
  1976,O 2,15:1
Middlemass, Frank
 Barry Lyndon 1975,D 19,52:4
Mifune, Toshiro
 Midway 1976,Je 19,11:1
 Paper Tiger 1976,S 17,III,8:3
Mikael, Ludmilla
 Vincent, Francois, Paul and the Others
  1976,Mr 8,32:1
Miki, Minoru (Composer)
 In the Realm of the Senses (L'Empire des Sens)
  1976,O 2,14:1
Mikita, Mori
 Godzilla Versus Megalon 1976,Jl 22,26:1
Miles, Christopher (Director)
 Maids, The 1975,Ap 22,41:1
Miles, Christopher (Screenwriter)
 Maids, The 1975,Ap 22,41:1
Miles, Joanna
 Bug 1975,S 18,50:1

Miles, Sarah
 Sailor Who Fell From Grace With the Sea, The
  1976,Ap 12,36:1
Miles, Sylvia
 Farewell, My Lovely 1975,Ag 14,39:1
 92 in the Shade 1976,Ja 22,42:1
 92 in the Shade 1976,F 1,II,13:1
 Great Scout and Cathouse Thursday, The
  1976,Je 24,24:1
Milius, John (Director)
 Wind and the Lion, The 1975,My 23,22:1
 Wind and the Lion, The 1975,Je 15,II,17:7
Milius, John (Screenwriter)
 Wind and the Lion, The 1975,My 23,22:1
 Wind and the Lion, The 1975,Je 15,II,17:7
Milkis, Edward K (Producer)
 Silver Streak 1976,D 9,61:1
Millan, Robyn
 Murph the Surf 1975,Je 12,30:6
Milland, Ray
 Escape to Witch Mountain 1975,Jl 3,21:1
 Last Tycoon, The 1976,N 18,59:1
Millar, Stuart (Director)
 Rooster Cogburn 1975,O 18,22:1
 Rooster Cogburn 1975,O 26,II,15:1
Miller, Allan
 Baby Blue Marine 1976,My 6,45:1
Miller, Hal
 Distance 1975,D 22,44:1
Miller, Jason
 Nickel Ride, The 1975,Ja 30,26:4
Miller, Kathleen
 Stay Hungry 1976,Ap 26,41:1
Miller, Michael (Director)
 Jackson County Jail 1976,Je 12,13:1
 Jackson County Jail 1976,Je 20,II,25:1
Miller, Norman (Producer)
 3 Anthropological Films (Afghan Nomads: The
  Maldar; Wheat Cycle; Naim and Jabar)
  1975,F 16,65:1
Miller, Ron (Producer)
 Escape to Witch Mountain 1975,Jl 3,21:1
 No Deposit, No Return 1976,Jl 3,17:1
 Gus 1976,Ag 7,11:2
 Shaggy D A, The 1976,D 27,III,18:1
Miller, Sharron (Miscellaneous)
 In Search of Noah's Ark 1976,D 27,III,20:5
Miller, Thomas L (Producer)
 Silver Streak 1976,D 9,61:1
Milligan, Spike
 Great McGonagall, The 1975,Ag 16,10:3
Milligan, Spike (Screenwriter)
 Great McGonagall, The 1975,Ag 16,10:3
Milliken, Billy
 Drive-In 1976,My 27,28:7
Millot, Charles
 French Connection II 1975,My 19,24:4
Mills, Brooke
 Part 2 Walking Tall 1975,S 29,37:7
Mills, Donna
 Murph the Surf 1975,Je 12,30:6
Mills, James (Original Author)
 Report to the Commissioner 1975,F 6,25:1
Mills, John
 Human Factor, The 1975,N 20,50:4
Mills, Juliet
 Beyond the Door 1975,Jl 24,17:4
Mimieux, Amparo
 Jackson County Jail 1976,Je 12,13:1
Mimieux, Yvette
 Jackson County Jail 1976,Je 12,13:1
 Jackson County Jail 1976,Je 20,II,25:1
Minazzoli, Christiane
 Story of O, The 1975,N 15,20:1
Minnelli, Liza
 Lucky Lady 1975,D 14,II,1:2
 Lucky Lady 1975,D 26,47:3
 Matter of Time, A 1976,O 8,III,8:3
Minnelli, Vincente (Director)
 Matter of Time, A 1976,O 8,III,8:3
Miou-Miou
 Jonah Who Will Be 25 in the Year 2000
  1976,O 2,15:1
 Jonah Who Will Be 25 in the Year 2000
  1976,O 24,II,15:1
Mira, Brigitte
 Jeder Fur Sich Und Gott Gegen Alle (Every Man
  for Himself and God Against All) 1975,S 28,57:1
 Fear of Fear (Angst vor der Angst)
  1976,O 15,III,8:3
Mirisch, Walter (Producer)
 Midway 1976,Je 19,11:1
Misenheimer, Mike (Original Author)
 Framed 1975,O 2,47:1
Mishima, Yukio
 Rite of Love and Death 1975,F 21,13:1
Mishima, Yukio (Director)
 Rite of Love and Death 1975,F 21,13:1
Mishima, Yukio (Original Author)
 Sailor Who Fell From Grace With the Sea, The
  1976,Ap 12,36:1
Mishima, Yukio (Producer)
 Rite of Love and Death 1975,F 21,13:1

Mishima, Yukio (Screenwriter)
  Rite of Love and Death 1975,F 21,13:1
Mislove, Michael (Screenwriter)
  Tunnelvision 1976,Jl 15,40:3
Mitchell, Adrian (Screenwriter)
  Man Friday 1976,Mr 6,22:1
Mitchell, James (Miscellaneous)
  Futureworld 1976,Ag 14,10:1
Mitchell, Joseph (Screenwriter)
  Sherlock Jr 1975,Jl 22,23:1
Mitchell, Norman
  Moon Over the Alley 1976,Ap 3,19:1
Mitchum, John
  Enforcer, The 1976,D 23,18:1
Mitchum, Robert
  Yakuza, The 1975,Mr 20,48:1
  Farewell, My Lovely 1975,Ag 14,39:1
  Midway 1976,Je 19,11:1
  Last Tycoon, The 1976,N 18,59:1
Mitrani, Michel (Director)
  Black Thursday (Les Guichets du Louvre)
    1975,Ja 12,II,1:3
Miura, Yuichiro (Original Author)
  Man Who Skied Down Everest, The
    1976,My 28,III,6:6
Miyajima, Yoshio (Cinematographer)
  Love Under the Crucifix 1976,S 14,44:3
Mizrachi, Moti
  My Michael 1976,Mr 16,29:2
Mizrahi, Moshe (Director)
  Daughters, Daughters! 1975,Mr 10,40:2
Mizrahi, Moshe (Screenwriter)
  Daughters, Daughters! 1975,Mr 10,40:2
Mlodzik, Ronald
  They Came From Within 1976,Jl 7,46:4
Mnouchkine, Alexandre (Producer)
  Touch and Go 1975,Ap 25,24:1
  Pain in the A--, A (L'Emmerdeur) 1975,Ag 11,33:2
  Magnifique, Le 1976,Jl 8,28:3
Mnouchkine, Georges (Producer)
  Pain in the A--, A (L'Emmerdeur) 1975,Ag 11,33:2
Molinaro, Edouard (Director)
  Pain in the A--, A (L'Emmerdeur) 1975,Ag 11,33:2
  Pink Telephone, The 1976,D 24,III,10:5
Mollberg, Rauni (Director)
  Earth is a Sinful Song, The 1975,N 19,22:3
Mollberg, Rauni (Producer)
  Earth is a Sinful Song, The 1975,N 19,22:3
Mollberg, Rauni (Screenwriter)
  Earth is a Sinful Song, The 1975,N 19,22:3
Molloy, Mike (Cinematographer)
  Mad Dog 1976,S 23,52:4
Momo, Alessandro
  Scent of a Woman 1976,Ja 26,28:4
  Lovers and Other Relatives 1976,Ag 16,40:1
Monash, Paul (Producer)
  Carrie 1976,N 17,III,24:1
Mondy, Pierre
  Pink Telephone, The 1976,D 24,III,10:5
Monicelli, Mario (Director)
  My Friends 1976,Jl 19,26:3
Monnier, Philippe (Director)
  Algerian War, The 1975,Ja 24,19:1
Monnier, Philippe (Producer)
  Algerian War, The 1975,Ja 24,19:1
Montague, Lee
  Mahler 1976,Ap 5,45:4
Montanari, Sergio (Miscellaneous)
  Homo Eroticus 1975,Mr 29,10:5
Montand, Yves
  Delusions of Grandeur (Folie des Grandeurs, La)
    1975,N 27,45:1
  Vincent, Francois, Paul and the Others
    1976,Mr 8,32:1
Monte, Eric (Screenwriter)
  Cooley, High 1975,Je 26,35:1
Montgomery, Belinda J
  Other Side of the Mountain, The 1975,N 15,20:1
Montgomery, Lee
  Burnt Offerings 1976,S 30,36:1
Monti, Carlotta (Original Author)
  W C Fields and Me 1976,Ap 1,28:3
  W C Fields and Me 1976,Ap 4,II,19:1
Montomorency, Andree
  Once Upon a Time in the East (Il Etait une Fois
    Dans l'Est) 1975,Ap 14,41:1
Montoro, Edward L (Producer)
  Grizzly 1976,My 13,41:3
Moon, Keith
  Tommy 1975,Mr 20,48:1
  Tommy 1975,Mr 30,II,13:1
  Stardust 1975,N 13,52:5
Moon, Keith (Composer)
  Tommy 1975,Mr 20,48:1
Mooney, Michael M (Original Author)
  Hindenberg, The 1975,D 26,46:1
Mooney, Otis
  Mooney vs Fowle 1976,Je 4,III,11:1
Moonjean, Hank (Producer)
  Fortune, The 1975,My 21,49:1
Moor, Mariann
  Riddance 1976,S 18,25:1

Moorcock, Michael (Screenwriter)
  Land That Time Forgot, The 1975,Ag 14,39:1
Moore, Allen (Director)
  Playgrounds 1975,D 12,53:1
Moore, Alvy (Producer)
  Boy and His Dog, A 1976,Je 17,32:2
Moore, Archie
  Breakheart Pass 1976,My 6,46:3
Moore, G T (Composer)
  People of the Wind 1976,O 30,14:6
Moore, G T (Miscellaneous)
  People of the Wind 1976,O 30,14:6
Moore, Joanna
  Hindenberg, The 1975,D 26,46:1
Moore, Millie (Miscellaneous)
  Man Who Skied Down Everest, The
    1976,My 28,III,6:6
Moore, Paula
  Partie de Plaisir, Une (Piece of Pleasure, A)
    1976,My 21,III,7:1
Moore, Robert (Director)
  Murder By Death 1976,Je 24,26:1
Moore, Robin (Miscellaneous)
  Happy Hooker, The 1975,My 9,22:2
  Happy Hooker, The 1975,My 18,II,19:1
Moore, Roger
  Street People 1976,S 18,24:5
  Shout at the Devil 1976,N 25,38:1
Moore, Roy (Screenwriter)
  Black Christmas 1975,O 20,45:1
Moore, Rudy Ray
  Monkey Hustle, The 1976,D 25,8:1
Moore, Thomas (Original Author)
  Dog Day Afternoon 1975,S 22,41:1
Mor, Ester (Screenwriter)
  My Michael 1976,Mr 16,29:2
Mora, Philippe (Director)
  Brother, Can You Spare a Dime? 1975,Ag 8,10:2
  Brother Can You Spare a Dime? 1975,Ag 17,II,11:7
  Mad Dog 1976,S 23,52:4
Mora, Philippe (Screenwriter)
  Brother, Can You Spare a Dime? 1975,Ag 8,10:2
  Mad Dog 1976,S 23,52:4
Morant, Richard
  Mahler 1976,Ap 5,45:4
Moraz, Patrick (Composer)
  Middle of the World, The (Le Mileu du Monde)
    1975,Mr 29,10:5
  Invitation, The 1975,Ap 28,34:4
More, Kenneth
  Slipper and the Rose: The Story of Cinderella, The
    1976,N 5,III,8:3
Moreau, Jeanne
  French Provincial (Souvenir's d'en France)
    1975,O 9,52:1
  French Provincial (Souvenir's d'en France)
    1975,O 19,II,13:7
  French Provincial (Souvenir's d'en France)
    1976,F 28,14:3
  Lumiere, La 1976,S 7,38:1
  Lumiere, La 1976,N 15,39:1
  Last Tycoon, The 1976,N 18,59:1
  Lumiere, La 1976,D 12,II,1:1
Moreau, Jeanne (Director)
  Lumiere, La 1976,S 7,38:1
  Lumiere, La 1976,N 15,39:1
  Lumiere, La 1976,D 12,II,1:1
Moreau, Jeanne (Screenwriter)
  Lumiere, La 1976,S 7,38:1
  Lumiere, La 1976,N 15,39:1
Moreira, Ricardo (Producer)
  Branded for Life 1976,S 24,III,8:4
Moreno, Jorge
  King Kong 1976,D 18,16:1
Moreno, Rita
  Ritz, The 1976,Ag 13,III,12:4
  Ritz, The 1976,Ag 22,II,11:1
Morgan, Claude (Composer)
  Male of the Century 1976,Je 3,46:1
Morgan, Debbi
  Monkey Hustle, The 1976,D 25,8:1
Morgan, Donald M (Cinematographer)
  Sheila Levine is Dead and Living in New York
    1975,My 17,14:2
  Let's Do It Again 1975,O 15,45:7
Morgan, Horace
  Sherlock Jr 1975,Jl 22,23:1
Moriarty, Michael
  Report to the Commissioner 1975,F 6,25:1
  Shoot It: Black Shoot It: Blue 1975,Jl 10,19:1
Moriconi, Enrico (Composer)
  Human Factor, The 1975,N 20,50:4
Moritani, Shiro (Director)
  Tidal Wave 1975,S 16,53:1
Moritz, Louise
  Death Race 2000 1975,Je 6,17:1
  One Flew Over the Cuckoo's Nest 1975,N 20,52:1
Morley, Robert
  Blue Bird, The 1976,My 14,III,7:1
  Blue Bird, The 1976,My 16,II,17:1
Morricone, Ennio (Composer)
  Secret, The (Le Secret) 1975,My 9,19:1
  Devil is a Woman, The 1975,O 27,23:1

Morricone, Ennio (Composer)—Cont
  Night Caller 1975,N 20,52:2
  Moses 1976,Mr 27,17:1
Morrill, John Arthur (Cinematographer)
  Boy and His Dog, A 1976,Je 17,32:2
Morris, David Burton (Director)
  Loose Ends 1976,My 19,25:5
Morris, David Burton (Producer)
  Loose Ends 1976,My 19,25:5
Morris, David Burton (Screenwriter)
  Loose Ends 1976,My 19,25:5
Morris, Frank (Miscellaneous)
  Ode to Billy Joe 1976,Ag 19,48:1
Morris, Garrett
  Cooley, High 1975,Je 26,35:1
  Car Wash 1976,O 16,13:1
Morris, Greg
  Countdown at Kusini 1976,Ap 17,10:1
Morris, John (Composer)
  Adventure of Sherlock Holmes' Smarter Brother,
    The 1975,D 15,42:1
  Silent Movie 1976,Jl 1,22:1
Morris, Oswald (Cinematographer)
  Man Who Would Be King, The 1975,D 18,62:1
  Seven-Per-Cent Solution, The 1976,O 25,42:1
Morris, Reg (Cinematographer)
  Black Christmas 1975,O 20,45:1
  Food of the Gods, The 1976,Jl 17,9:4
Morrison, Glen
  Smile Orange 1976,My 20,44:6
Morrow, Vic
  Bad News Bears, The 1976,Ap 7,28:1
  Treasure of Matecumbe 1976,Ag 28,11:2
Morse, Terry Jr (Producer)
  Return of a Man Called Horse, The 1976,Je 29,19:1
Morshed, Mohamed
  Night of Counting the Years, The 1975,O 23,48:3
Morshower, Gien
  Drive-In 1976,My 27,28:7
Morton, Joshua (Miscellaneous)
  Hurry Tomorrow 1976,My 5,49:1
Moser, Brian (Director)
  Last of the Cuiva, The 1976,O 29,III,8:3
Moser, Brian (Producer)
  Clearing in the Jungle, A 1976,O 29,III,8:3
  Last of the Cuiva, The 1976,O 29,III,8:3
  Last of the Cuiva, The 1976,N 7,II,13:1
  Clearing in the Jungle, A 1976,N 7,II,13:1
Moses, Lucia Lynn
  Scar of Shame, The 1976,Mr 18,50:1
Moshin, Gastone
  My Friends 1976,Jl 19,26:3
Mosley, Roger E
  Darktown Strutters 1975,O 9,54:4
  River Niger, The 1976,Ap 15,28:1
  Stay Hungry 1976,Ap 26,41:1
  Leadbelly 1976,My 29,14:1
  Leadbelly 1976,Je 6,II,13:7
Mostel, Zero
  Front, The 1976,O 1,III,7:1
Moulin, Jean-Pierre
  Veronique, ou L'Ete de Mes 13 Ans (Veronique, or
    The Summer of My 13th Year) 1976,Ap 6,28:1
  Veronique, ou L'Ete De Mes 13 Ans (Veronique, or
    The Summer of My 13th Year) 1976,Je 21,43:1
Mouvin, Catherine (Miscellaneous)
  Arthur Rubinstein-Love of Life 1975,F 10,20:4
Mozart, Wolfgang Amadeus (Composer)
  Jeder Fur Sich Und Gott Gegen Alle (Every Man
    for Himself and God Against All) 1975,S 28,57:1
  Magic Flute, The 1975,N 9,II,1:1
  Magic Flute, The 1975,N 16,II,15:1
Mozart, Wolfgang Amadeus (Original Author)
  Magic Flute, The 1975,N 12,50:1
Muehl, Otto
  Sweet Movie 1975,O 10,32:3
Mueller, Cookie
  Female Trouble 1975,F 13,43:1
Mueller, Federico (Producer)
  Guernica 1976,My 22,19:3
Mueller, Robbie (Cinematographer)
  Kings of the Road 1976,O 3,53:1
Muheriee, Pradip
  Middleman, The 1976,O 12,45:1
Muir, David (Cinematographer)
  Boesman and Lena 1976,Ap 23,23:2
Mukeril, Romesh
  Distant Thunder (Ashani Sanket) 1975,O 27,21:4
Mukka, Timo K (Original Author)
  Earth is a Sinful Song, The 1975,N 19,22:3
Mulkey, Chris
  Loose Ends 1976,My 19,25:5
Mulligan, Richard
  Big Bus, The 1976,Je 24,26:1
Mulligan, Robert (Director)
  Nickel Ride, The 1975,Ja 30,26:4
Mulligan, Robert (Producer)
  Nickel Ride, The 1975,Ja 30,26:4
Mulvehill, Chuck
  Passenger, The 1975,Ap 10,46:1
Mundstuk, Anne
  Not a Pretty Picture 1976,Ap 1,28:4
Munro, Caroline
  Devil Within Her, The 1976,Je 24,26:1

Provence, Denise
Male of the Century 1976,Je 3,46:1
Prucani, Ann
Sweet Movie 1975,O 10,32:3
Pruzelius, Gosta
Magic Flute, The 1975,N 12,50:1
Pryce, Jonathan
Voyage of the Damned 1976,D 23,18:1
Pryor, Nicholas
Happy Hooker, The 1975,My 9,22:2
Smile 1975,S 28,II,13:1
Smile 1975,O 9,52:1
Pryor, Richard
Bingo Long Traveling All-Stars and Motor Kings,
The 1976,Jl 17,10:1
Car Wash 1976,O 16,13:1
Car Wash 1976,O 24,II,15:1
Silver Streak 1976,D 9,61:1
Przygodda, Peter (Cinematographer)
Kings of the Road 1976,O 3,53:1
Przygodda, Peter (Miscellaneous)
Lost Honor of Katharina Blum, The (Die Verlorene
Ehre Der Katharina Blum) 1975,O 3,41:1
Puccini, Gianni (Screenwriter)
Ossessione (Obsession) 1976,O 2,15:1
Puttnam, David (Producer)
Brother, Can You Spare a Dime? 1975,Ag 8,10:2
Lisztomania 1975,O 11,23:1
Stardust 1975,N 13,52:5
Bugsy Malone 1976,S 16,54:1
Pyle, Denver
Hawmps 1976,My 28,III,9:1
Buffalo Bill and the Indians or Sitting Bull's History
Lesson 1976,Je 25,III,8:5

Q

Quaid, Randy
Missouri Breaks, The 1976,My 20,45:1
Missouri Breaks, The 1976,My 23,II,17:7
Bound for Glory 1976,D 6,47:1
Qualtinger, Helmut
End of the Game 1976,My 13,41:2
Quayle, Anna
Seven-Per-Cent Solution, The 1976,O 25,42:1
Quayle, Anthony
Moses 1976,Mr 27,17:1
Quenaud, Daniel
Brief Vacation, A 1975,F 10,20:1
Querejeta, Francisco J (Screenwriter)
Spirit of the Beehive, The (Espiritu de la Colmena,
El) 1976,S 24,III,8:3
Quick, Diana
Private Enterprise, A 1975,Ap 12,14:4
Quigley, Geoffrey
Barry Lyndon 1975,D 19,52:4
Quilligan, Veronica
Lisztomania 1975,O 11,23:1
Quinlan, Kathleen
Lifeguard 1976,Jl 24,12:1
Quinn, Anthony
Destructors, The 1975,Je 12,30:6
Quinn, Barbara
Squirm 1976,Jl 31,10:4
Quintins, Tadito Val (Producer)
Alma 1975,Ap 14,41:1
Quiroga, Roberto (Cinematographer)
Sunday Funnies 1976,O 6,35:1
Quistgord, Berthe
Take It Like a Man, Madam 1976,S 16,55:1

R

Raab, Kurt
Fox and His Friends (Fist-Right of Freedom)
(Faustrecht der Freiheit) 1975,S 27,21:4
American Soldier, The 1976,Ja 30,18:1
Fox and His Friends (Fist-Right of Freedom)
(Faustrecht der Freiheit) 1976,F 3,24:1
Fear of Fear (Angst vor der Angst)
1976,O 15,III,8:3
Rabal, Francisco
Devil is a Woman, The 1975,O 27,23:1
Raben, Peer (Composer)
Fox and His Friends (Fist-Right of Freedom)
(Faustrecht der Freiheit) 1975,S 27,21:4
American Soldier, The 1976,Ja 30,18:1
Fear of Fear (Angst vor der Angst)
1976,O 15,III,8:3
Rabier, Jean (Cinematographer)
Breakup, The (Rupture, Le) 1975,Ja 31,20:2
Just Before Nightfall (Juste Avant la Nuit)
1975,S 10,37:4
Partie de Plaisir, Une (Piece of Pleasure, A)
1976,My 21,III,7:1
Dirty Hands 1976,N 4,49:1
Racette, Francine
Lumiere, La 1976,N 15,39:1
Radjiniya, Kasem (Miscellaneous)
Simple Event, A 1975,Ap 8,33:1

Radjiniya, Kasem (Producer)
Simple Event, A 1975,Ap 8,33:1
Radnitz, Robert B (Producer)
Birch Interval 1976,My 3,41:2
Part 2 Sounder 1976,O 14,43:6
Radzins, Elsa
King Lear 1975,Ag 7,39:3
Rafelson, Bob (Director)
Stay Hungry 1976,Ap 26,41:1
Rafelson, Bob (Producer)
Stay Hungry 1976,Ap 26,41:1
Rafelson, Bob (Screenwriter)
Stay Hungry 1976,Ap 26,41:1
Rafferty, Kevin (Cinematographer)
Hurry Tomorrow 1976,My 5,49:1
Rafferty, Kevin (Miscellaneous)
Hurry Tomorrow 1976,My 5,49:1
Raffill, Stewart (Director)
Adventures of the Wilderness Family, The
1975,D 20,16:1
Across the Great Divide 1976,D 21,44:1
Raffill, Stewart (Screenwriter)
Adventures of the Wilderness Family, The
1975,D 20,16:1
Across the Great Divide 1976,D 21,44:1
Raffin, Deborah
Dove, The 1975,F 20,38:2
Jacqueline Susann's Once is Not Enough
1975,Je 19,28:5
Rafikov, Mahmud (Cinematographer)
World's Young Ballet, The 1975,Jl 10,19:1
Ragland, Robert O (Composer)
Return to Macon County 1975,S 4,31:1
Sharks' Treasure 1975,S 11,35:1
Grizzly 1976,My 13,41:3
Rahman, Nazruh
Autobiography of a Princess 1975,O 5,60:7
Rain, Douglas (Narrator)
Man Who Skied Down Everest, The
1976,My 28,III,6:6
Rainer, Ivan
Kristina Talking Pictures 1976,N 3,62:1
Rainer, Yvonne
Kristina Talking Pictures 1976,N 3,62:1
Rainer, Yvonne (Director)
Kristina Talking Pictures 1976,N 3,62:1
Rainer, Yvonne (Miscellaneous)
Kristina Talking Pictures 1976,N 3,62:1
Rainer, Yvonne (Screenwriter)
Kristina Talking Pictures 1976,N 3,62:1
Raines, Cristina
Nashville 1975,Je 12,32:1
Russian Roulette 1975,Ag 21,44:2
Rajala, Panu (Screenwriter)
Earth is a Sinful Song, The 1975,N 19,22:3
Raknerud, Nils (Cinematographer)
Wives (Hustruer) 1976,Ap 3,19:1
Ramati, Alexander (Original Author)
Martyr, The 1976,Je 17,30:1
Ramone, Phil (Composer)
Star is Born, A 1976,D 27,III,16:5
Ramone, Phil (Miscellaneous)
Star is Born, A 1976,D 27,III,16:5
Rampling, Charlotte
Farewell, My Lovely 1975,Ag 14,39:1
Ramsay, Remak
Front, The 1976,O 1,III,7:1
Ramsen, Bert
Harry and Walter Go to New York
1976,Je 18,III,6:5
Ramsey, Logan
Part 2 Walking Tall 1975,S 29,37:7
Randolph, John
King Kong 1976,D 18,16:1
Randolph, Lillian
Jacqueline Susann's Once is Not Enough
1975,Je 19,28:5
Randone, Salvo
Lulu the Tool 1975,My 12,39:1
Ransohoff, Martin (Producer)
Silver Streak 1976,D 9,61:1
Rapisarda, Sara
All Screwed Up (Tutto a Posto e Niente in
Ordine) 1976,Ja 15,28:1
Rasof, Richard
Man in the Glass Booth, The 1975,My 20,46:4
Rassam, Jean-Pierre (Producer)
General Idi Amin Dada 1975,Ap 7,40:1
Lancelot of the Lake (Lancelot du Lac)
1975,Je 5,50:1
General Idi Amin Dada 1976,Ag 31,21:1
Rasulala, Thalmus
Mr Ricco 1975,Ja 30,26:4
Bucktown 1975,Jl 3,21:1
Friday Foster 1975,D 26,38:1
Rathbone, Basil
Hounds of the Baskervilles, The 1975,Jl 22,23:1
Rathkowitz, Ed (Miscellaneous)
92 in the Shade 1976,Ja 22,42:1
Rattray, Heather
Across the Great Divide 1976,D 21,44:1

Rauber, Francois (Miscellaneous)
Jacques Brel is Alive and Well and Living in Paris
1975,F 25,31:1
Raucher, Herman (Screenwriter)
Ode to Billy Joe 1976,Ag 19,48:1
Rawi, Ousama (Cinematographer)
Human Factor, The 1975,N 20,50:4
Sky Riders 1976,Mr 27,18:4
Rawlins, David (Miscellaneous)
Bingo Long Traveling All-Stars and Motor Kings,
The 1976,Jl 17,10:1
Rawls, Wilson (Original Author)
Where the Red Fern Grows 1976,S 30,36:4
Ray, Aldo
Psychic Killer 1976,F 7,9:1
Ray, Bernard (Director)
Broken Strings 1976,Mr 25,41:1
Ray, Bernard (Producer)
Broken Strings 1976,Mr 25,41:1
Ray, Nicholas
I'm a Stranger Here Myself 1975,Ja 17,20:1
Ray, Ricardo
Salsa 1976,Ap 2,26:1
Ray, Satyajit (Composer)
Distant Thunder (Ashani Sanket) 1975,O 27,21:4
Middleman, The 1976,O 12,45:1
Ray, Satyajit (Director)
Distant Thunder (Ashani Sanket) 1975,O 27,21:4
Middleman, The 1976,O 12,45:1
Ray, Satyajit (Screenwriter)
Distant Thunder (Ashani Sanket) 1975,O 27,21:4
Middleman, The 1976,O 12,45:1
Ray, Soumendu (Cinematographer)
Middleman, The 1976,O 12,45:1
Ray, Tony (Producer)
Next Stop, Greenwich Village 1976,F 5,24:1
Rayfiel, David (Screenwriter)
Three Days of the Condor 1975,S 25,60:1
Lipstick 1976,Ap 3,19:1
Raynal, Jackie (Miscellaneous)
Saturday Night at the Baths 1975,Je 12,33:1
Reage, Pauline (Original Author)
Story of O, The 1975,N 15,20:1
Rebillon, Gisele (Producer)
Rape of Innocence 1976,Je 29,19:2
Reddy, Don (Cinematographer)
Benji 1975,Je 27,25:1
Hawmps 1976,My 28,III,9:1
Redfield, Dennis
Wild McCullochs, The 1975,S 4,31:1
Redfield, William
One Flew Over the Cuckoo's Nest 1975,N 20,52:1
Redford, Robert
Great Waldo Pepper, The 1975,Mr 14,24:1
Great Waldo Pepper, The 1975,Mr 16,17:1
Three Days of the Condor 1975,S 25,60:1
Three Days of the Condor 1975,S 28,II,1:1
All The President's Men 1976,Ap 8,42:1
All The President's Men 1976,Ap 11,II,1:4
Three Days of the Condor 1976,N 21,II,13:1
Redgrave, Corin
Serail (Surreal) 1976,D 4,17:1
Redgrave, Lynn
Happy Hooker, The 1975,My 9,22:2
Happy Hooker, The 1975,My 18,II,19:1
Big Bus, The 1976,Je 24,26:1
Redgrave, Vanessa
Seven-Per-Cent Solution, The 1976,O 25,42:1
Seven-Per-Cent Solution, The 1976,O 31,II,17:1
Reed, Bob
Super Spook 1975,Jl 10,19:1
Reed, Jerry
W W and the Dixie Dancekings 1975,Jl 24,18:1
Gator 1976,Ag 26,46:3
Reed, Michael (Cinematographer)
Galileo 1975,Ja 28,26:1
Hiding Place, The 1975,N 6,51:2
Reed, Oliver
Four Musketeers, The 1975,Mr 20,48:1
Tommy 1975,Mr 20,48:1
Tommy 1975,Mr 30,II,13:1
Ten Little Indians 1975,Ap 24,43:1
Royal Flash 1975,O 11,23:1
Great Scout and Cathouse Thursday, The
1976,Je 24,24:1
Burnt Offerings 1976,S 30,36:1
Burnt Offerings 1976,O 17,II,1:1
Reed, Tracy
Blood's Way 1976,S 22,38:5
Car Wash 1976,O 16,13:1
Rees, Charles (Miscellaneous)
Private Enterprise, A 1975,Ap 12,14:4
Reggiani, Aldo
Sunday Woman, The 1976,S 27,41:1
Reggiani, Serge
Vincent, Francois, Paul and the Others
1976,Mr 8,32:1
Regine
Seven-Per-Cent Solution, The 1976,O 25,42:1
Reichenbach, Francois
F For Fake 1975,S 28,57:1
Reichenbach, Francois (Director)
Arthur Rubinstein-Love of Life 1975,F 10,20:4

Smoktunovsky, Innokenti
Crime and Punishment 1975,My 15,48:1
Sneed, Janey
Devil's Cleavage, The 1975,N 29,20:1
Snell, Peter (Producer)
Hennessy 1975,Ag 1,13:1
Soboloff, Arnold
Silent Movie 1976,Jl 1,22:1
Sohlberg, Kari (Cinematographer)
Earth is a Sinful Song, The 1975,N 19,22:3
Sokolova, Liubov
Crime and Punishment 1975,My 15,48:1
Solaroli, Liberto (Producer)
Ossessione (Obsession) 1976,O 2,15:1
Soldevilla, Lally
Spirit of the Beehive, The (Espiritu de la Colmena, El) 1976,S 24,III,8:3
Solf, Suie
Milestones 1975,O 8,24:1
Solms, Kenny (Screenwriter)
Sheila Levine is Dead and Living in New York 1975,My 17,14:2
Solomine, Juri
Dersu Uzala 1976,O 5,54:1
Solomon, Joe (Producer)
Small Town in Texas, A 1976,Jl 10,16:1
Solonitsyn, Anatoli
Solaris 1976,O 7,63:2
Sommer, Elke
Ten Little Indians 1975,Ap 24,43:1
Sommer, M Josef
Front, The 1976,O 1,III,7:1
Sondergaard, Gale
Return of a Man Called Horse, The 1976,Je 29,19:1
Return of a Man Called Horse, The 1976,Ag 15,II,13:1
Sorbas, Elge
American Soldier, The 1976,Ja 30,18:1
Soriano, Pepe
Jewish Gauchos, The 1976,My 27,28:5
Sorokina, Nina
World's Young Ballet, The 1975,Jl 10,19:1
Sorvino, Paul
Shoot It: Black Shoot It: Blue 1975,Jl 10,19:1
I Will, I Will... For Now 1976,F 19,45:1
Sosa, Geo Anne
Master Gunfighter, The 1975,O 10,32:4
Sosa, Tomas (Composer)
Magnifique, Le 1976,Jl 8,28:3
Sousselier, Brigitte (Miscellaneous)
Jonah Who Will Be 25 in the Year 2000 1976,O 2,15:1
Sousseller, Brigitte (Miscellaneous)
Middle of the World, The (Le Mileu du Monde) 1975,Mr 29,10:5
South, Leonard J (Cinematographer)
Family Plot 1976,Ap 10,22:1
Spaak, Catherine
Take a Hard Ride 1975,O 30,52:2
Spacek, Sissy
Carrie 1976,N 17,III,24:1
Carrie 1976,D 5,II,13:4
Sparks, Bruce (Cinematographer)
Bim 1976,D 2,57:1
Sparkuhl, Theodore (Cinematographer)
Chienne, La (Bitch, The) 1975,S 27,21:4
Chienne, La (Bitch, The) 1976,My 1,13:1
Speed, Carol
Abby 1975,Mr 23,II,15:1
Speer, Jane (Miscellaneous)
Keetje Tippel 1976,S 27,41:1
Spelling, Aaron (Producer)
Baby Blue Marine 1976,My 6,45:1
Spiegel, Sam (Producer)
Last Tycoon, The 1976,N 18,59:1
Spielberg, David
Hustle 1975,D 26,37:1
Spielberg, Steven (Director)
Jaws 1975,Je 21,19:2
Jaws 1975,Je 29,II,15:7
Jaws 1975,Ag 24,II,1:1
Spiers, Jack (Screenwriter)
Bears and I, The 1975,Jl 17,21:1
Spiesser, Jacques
Slap, The 1976,Ja 19,25:3
Lumiere, La 1976,N 15,39:1
Spiga, Cyril
Guernica 1976,My 22,19:3
Spikings, Barry (Producer)
Conduct Unbecoming 1975,O 6,42:1
Man Who Fell to Earth, The 1976,My 29,13:5
Spinell, Joe
Taxi Driver 1976,F 8,36:1
Spinetti, Victor
Great McGonagall, The 1975,Ag 16,10:3
Voyage of the Damned 1976,D 23,18:1
Spinks, James
Car Wash 1976,O 16,13:1
Spinnell, Joe
Next Stop, Greenwich Village 1976,F 5,24:1
Rocky 1976,N 22,III,19:1
Spottiswoode, Roger (Miscellaneous)
Hard Times 1975,O 9,54:2

Sprague, Hall T (Original Author)
Sky Riders 1976,Mr 27,18:4
Springer, Gary
Dog Day Afternoon 1975,S 22,41:1
Staab, Bruno
Small Change (L'Argent de Poche) 1976,O 1,III,11:1
Stacy, James
Posse 1975,Je 5,48:1
Stafford, Robert (Miscellaneous)
Escape to Witch Mountain 1975,Jl 3,21:1
Gus 1976,Ag 7,11:2
Stallings, Rex
Undercovers Hero 1975,O 23,48:3
Stallone, Sylvester
Capone 1975,Ap 17,48:6
Death Race 2000 1975,Je 6,17:1
Rocky 1976,N 22,III,19:1
Rocky 1976,D 12,II,1:1
Stallone, Sylvester (Screenwriter)
Rocky 1976,N 22,III,19:1
Rocky 1976,D 12,II,1:1
Stambaugh, David
Bad News Bears, The 1976,Ap 7,28:1
Stamp, Christopher (Producer)
Tommy 1975,Mr 20,48:1
Stander, Lionel
Black Bird, The 1975,D 26,43:1
Stanford, Thomas (Miscellaneous)
Yakuza, The 1975,Mr 20,48:1
Stangerz, Gorman
Face to Face 1976,Ap 6,28:1
Stanley, Florence
Prisoner of Second Avenue 1975,Mr 15,18:1
Fortune, The 1975,My 21,49:1
Stanley, Frank (Cinematographer)
Mr Ricco 1975,Ja 30,26:4
Eiger Sanction, The 1975,My 22,32:1
Car Wash 1976,O 16,13:1
Stanley, Jann
Birch Interval 1976,My 3,41:2
Stanton, Harry Dean
Rafferty and the Gold Dust Twins 1975,F 3,32:1
Farewell, My Lovely 1975,Ag 14,39:1
Rancho Deluxe 1975,N 24,28:1
92 in the Shade 1976,Ja 22,42:1
92 in the Shade 1976,F 1,II,13:1
Missouri Breaks, The 1976,My 20,45:1
Stanwyck, Barbara
Jeopardy 1975,Ag 3,II,1:1
Stapleford, George (Cinematographer)
In Search of Noah's Ark 1976,D 27,III,20:5
Starger, Martin (Producer)
Nashville 1975,Je 12,32:1
Stark, Ray (Producer)
Funny Lady 1975,Mr 12,30:1
Funny Lady 1975,Mr 16,II,17:1
Sunshine Boys, The 1975,N 7,28:1
Murder By Death 1976,Je 24,26:1
Starkes, Jaison (Screenwriter)
J D's Revenge 1976,Ag 26,47:2
Starkman, David (Screenwriter)
Scar of Shame, The 1976,Mr 18,50:1
Starr, Ringo
Lisztomania 1975,O 11,23:1
Lisztomania 1975,O 19,II,1:4
Starrett, Jack (Director)
Race With the Devil 1975,Jl 10,19:3
Small Town in Texas, A 1976,Jl 10,16:1
Starshov, Boris (Screenwriter)
World's Young Ballet, The 1975,Jl 10,19:1
Staton, Joe (Miscellaneous)
Long Night, The 1976,Ap 11,45:5
Staub, Jean-Marie (Director)
Introduction to an Accompaniment to a Cinematic Scene by Arnold Schoenberg 1976,N 26,III,4:5
Steel, Anthony
Story of O, The 1975,N 15,20:1
Steele, Anna
Romantic Englishwoman, The 1975,N 27,46:1
Steele, Barbara
They Came From Within 1976,Jl 7,46:4
Steiger, Rod
Hennessy 1975,Ag 1,13:1
Hennessy 1975,Ag 3,II,11:1
W C Fields and Me 1976,Ap 1,28:3
W C Fields and Me 1976,Ap 4,II,19:1
Dirty Hands 1976,N 4,49:1
Dirty Hands 1976,N 7,II,13:1
Stein, Sarah (Miscellaneous)
Broken Treaty at Battle Mountain 1975,Ja 16,49:1
Shoot It: Black Shoot It: Blue 1975,Jl 10,19:1
Steinberg, Susan (Miscellaneous)
Deadly Hero 1976,O 16,11:4
Steiner, John
Devil Within Her, The 1976,Je 24,26:1
Steinkamp, Fredric (Miscellaneous)
Three Days of the Condor 1975,S 25,60:1
Harry and Walter Go to New York 1976,Je 18,III,6:5
Stell, Aaron (Miscellaneous)
Cornbread, Earl and Me 1975,My 22,34:1

Sten-Andersen, Gudrun (Composer)
Take It Like a Man, Madam 1976,S 16,55:1
Stephan, Aram
French Provincial (Souvenir's d'en France) 1975,O 9,52:1
French Provincial (Souvenir's d'en France) 1976,F 28,14:3
Stephan, Bruno (Cinematographer)
Comedians (Komodianten) 1975,Ja 3,13:2
Stephano, Tony
Reincarnation of Peter Proud, The 1975,Ap 26,14:1
Stevenin, Jean-Francois
Small Change (L'Argent de Poche) 1976,O 1,III,11:1
Stevens, Connie
Scorchy 1976,O 9,9:4
Stevens, George Jr (Producer)
America at the Movies 1976,S 23,52:1
America at the Movies 1976,O 3,II,15:1
Stevens, Harvey
Omen, The 1976,Je 26,16:1
Omen, The 1976,Jl 25,II,13:1
Stevens, Stella
Arnold 1975,Mr 22,36:1
Cleopatra Jones and the Casino of Gold 1975,Jl 12,16:4
Nickelodeon 1976,D 22,34:4
Stevenson, Parker
Lifeguard 1976,Jl 24,12:1
Stevenson, Robert (Director)
One of Our Dinosaurs is Missing 1975,Ag 7,39:1
Shaggy D A, The 1976,D 27,III,18:1
Steward, Ernest (Cinematographer)
Hennessy 1975,Ag 1,13:1
Stewart, Alexandra
Destructors, The 1975,Je 12,30:6
Black Moon 1975,S 30,31:1
Stewart, Charles (Cinematographer)
Alpha Beta 1976,Ag 5,26:1
Stewart, Donald (Screenwriter)
Jackson County Jail 1976,Je 12,13:1
Jackson County Jail 1976,Je 20,II,25:1
Stewart, Douglas (Screenwriter)
Where the Red Fern Grows 1976,S 30,36:4
Stewart, James
Shootist, The 1976,Ag 12,38:1
Stewart, Patrick
Hedda 1976,Ja 26,29:1
Stewart, Paul
Day of the Locust, The 1975,My 8,48:1
Murph the Surf 1975,Je 12,30:6
Bite the Bullet 1975,Je 27,22:1
F For Fake 1975,S 28,57:1
W C Fields and Me 1976,Ap 1,28:3
Stewart, Peggie
Bobbie Jo and the Outlaw 1976,Jl 7,46:4
Stiglitz, Hugo
Survive! 1976,Ag 5,26:1
Stigwood, Robert (Producer)
Tommy 1975,Mr 20,48:1
Bugsy Malone 1976,S 16,54:1
Stiller, Jerry
Ritz, The 1976,Ag 13,III,12:4
Ritz, The 1976,Ag 22,II,11:1
Stine, Clifford (Miscellaneous)
Hindenberg, The 1975,D 26,46:1
Stirling, Geoff (Miscellaneous)
Waiting for Fidel 1975,N 16,II,15:7
Stockdale, Terry (Composer)
Shoot It: Black Shoot It: Blue 1975,Jl 10,19:1
Stoker, Austin
Sheba, Baby 1975,Mr 27,37:1
Stokes, Simon (Composer)
Ali the Man 1975,S 18,50:1
Stole, Mink
Female Trouble 1975,F 13,43:1
Stoler, Shirley
Seven Beauties 1976,Ja 22,42:1
Seven Beauties 1976,Ja 25,II,1:4
Seven Beauties 1976,Mr 7,II,1:4
Stone, Arnold (Producer)
Countdown at Kusini 1976,Ap 17,10:1
Stone, Barbara (Producer)
Milestones 1975,O 8,24:1
Milestones 1975,N 2,II,1:2
Stone, David C
Milestones 1975,O 8,24:1
Milestones 1975,N 2,II,1:2
Stone, David C (Producer)
Milestones 1975,O 8,24:1
Milestones 1975,N 2,II,1:2
Stone, Elly
Jacques Brel is Alive and Well and Living in Paris 1975,F 25,31:1
Stone, Harold J
Mitchell 1975,S 11,35:1
Stone, Norman John
Scar of Shame, The 1976,Mr 18,50:1
Stone, Oliver (Director)
Seizure 1975,Mr 23,II,15:1
Stoppard, Tom (Screenwriter)
Romantic Englishwoman, The 1975,N 27,46:1
Romantic Englishwoman, The 1976,Ja 18,II,13:7

A

ABC Entertainment (Prod.)
Nashville 1975,Je 12,32:1
Man Friday 1976,Mr 6,22:1
Action Films (Prod.)
Middle of the World, The (Le Mileu du Monde) 1975,Mr 29,10:5
Pas Si Mechant Que Ca (Not Really That Bad) (Wonderful Crook, The) 1975,O 1,59:1
Jonah Who Will Be 25 in the Year 2000 1976,O 2,15:1
Agape Productions (Prod.)
Touch of Zen 1976,O 10,75:3
Age & Scarpelli (Misc.)
Sunday Woman, The 1976,S 27,41:1
Allied Artists (Distr.)
Brief Vacation, A 1975,F 10,20:1
Mitchell 1975,S 11,35:1
Conduct Unbecoming 1975,O 6,42:1
Story of O, The 1975,N 15,20:1
Man Who Would Be King, The 1975,D 18,62:1
My Friends 1976,Jl 19,26:3
Let's Talk About Men 1976,Ag 5,27:1
Next Man, The 1976,N 11,52:1
American Film Institute (Prod.)
America at the Movies 1976,S 23,52:1
American Film Theater (Distr.)
Maids, The 1975,Ap 22,41:1
American Film Theater (Prod.)
Galileo 1975,Ja 28,26:1
Jacques Brel is Alive and Well and Living in Paris 1975,F 25,31:1
In Celebration 1975,Mr 18,30:1
Man in the Glass Booth, The 1975,My 20,46:4
American International Pictures (Distr.)
Destructors, The 1975,Je 12,30:6
Friday Foster 1975,D 26,38:1
Killer Force 1976,Mr 11,43:1
Great Scout and Cathouse Thursday, The 1976,Je 24,24:1
Bobbie Jo and the Outlaw 1976,Jl 7,46:4
Street People 1976,S 18,24:5
Macon County Line 1975,Ja 16,49:1
Arnold 1975,Mr 22,36:1
Sheba, Baby 1975,Mr 27,37:1
Reincarnation of Peter Proud, The 1975,Ap 26,14:1
Cornbread, Earl and Me 1975,My 22,34:1
Murph the Surf 1975,Je 12,30:6
Cooley High 1975,Je 26,35:1
Bucktown 1975,Jl 3,21:1
Hennessy 1975,Ag 1,13:1
Land That Time Forgot, The 1975,Ag 14,39:1
Return to Macon County 1975,S 4,31:1
Wild McCullochs, The 1975,S 4,31:1
Part 2 Walking Tall 1975,S 29,37:7
Old Dracula 1976,Ja 15,30:1
Crime and Passion 1976,Ap 22,38:3
Devil Within Her, The 1976,Je 24,26:1
Small Town in Texas, A 1976,Jl 10,16:1
Food of the Gods, The 1976,Jl 17,9:4
Squirm 1976,Jl 31,10:4
Futureworld 1976,Ag 14,10:1
At the Earth's Core 1976,Ag 28,9:6
Matter of Time, A 1976,O 8,III,8:3
Scorchy 1976,O 9,9:4
Shout at the Devil 1976,N 25,38:1
Monkey Hustle, The 1976,D 25,8:1
American Universities Field Staff (Misc.)
3 Anthropological Films (Afghan Nomads: The Maldar; Wheat Cycle; Naim and Jabar) 1975,F 16,65:1
AmeriEuro (Prod.)
Lepke 1975,My 24,12:1
Amsterdam Concertgebouw (Misc.)
Mahler 1976,Ap 5,45:4
Argos Films (Paris) (Prod.)
In the Realm of the Senses (L'Empire des Sens) 1976,O 2,14:1
Arie Filma, Ltd (Prod.)
Nurith 1975,Je 12,30:4
Arkoff, Samuel Z (Prod.)
Crime and Passion 1976,Ap 22,38:3
Artco Films (Prod.)
Pas Si Mechant Que Ca (Not Really That Bad) (Wonderful Crook, The) 1975,O 1,59:1
Artemis (Berlin) (Prod.)
Marquise of O..., The (Die Marquise von O...) 1976,O 18,36:1

Artistes Associes (Paris) (Prod.)
Illustrious Corpses (Cadaveri Eccellenti) 1976,O 6,34:1
Artists Entertainment Complex, Inc (Prod.)
Dog Day Afternoon 1975,S 22,41:1
Next Man, The 1976,N 11,52:1
Artkino Pictures, Inc (Distr.)
Crime and Punishment 1975,My 15,48:1
World's Young Ballet, The 1975,Jl 10,19:1
King Lear 1975,Ag 7,39:3
ASA Film Distribution (Distr.)
Take It Like a Man, Madam 1976,S 16,55:1
Atlantica Cinematografica-Rome Productions (Prod.)
Homo Eroticus 1975,Mr 29,10:5
Austamerican (Prod.)
Goodbye, Norma Jean 1976,My 11,26:5
Avco Embassy Pictures (Distr.)
And Now My Love 1975,Mr 22,36:1
Ten Little Indians 1975,Ap 24,43:1
Farewell, My Lovely 1975,Ag 14,39:1
Russian Roulette 1975,Ag 21,44:2
Psychic Killer 1976,F 7,9:1
Man Friday 1976,Mr 6,22:1
Scaramouche 1976,Mr 18,51:4
Moses 1976,Mr 27,17:1
Sailor Who Fell From Grace With the Sea, The 1976,Ap 12,36:1
Diamonda 1976,O 2,15:2
Deadly Hero 1976,O 16,11:4
Voyage of the Damned 1976,D 23,18:1
Pipe Dreams 1976,D 24,III,10:5
Avco Embassy Pictures (Prod.)
Mr Quilp 1975,N 8,22:5

B

Baker, Fred, Films, Ltd (Distr.)
Lenny Bruce Without Tears 1975,Mr 19,59:1
Bavaria Films (Prod.)
Comedians (Komodianten) 1975,Ja 3,13:2
Bernsen-Ludwig-Bercovici (Prod.)
Take a Hard Ride 1975,O 30,52:2
Bethsabee Films (Prod.)
Femmes au Soleil (Women in the Sun) 1976,S 22,29:1
Biograph Films (Distr.)
Sweet Movie 1975,O 10,32:3
Bioscop (Munich) (Prod.)
Black Moon 1975,S 30,31:1
Braunberger-Richebe (Prod.)
Chienne, La (Bitch, The) 1975,S 27,21:4
Brazos Films (Distr.)
Chulas Fronteras (Beautiful Borders) 1976,D 31,III,10:1
British Film Institute (Prod.)
Juvenile Liaison 1976,Mr 26,21:3
British Film Institute Production Board (Prod.)
Private Enterprise, A 1975,Ap 12,14:4
Moon Over the Alley 1976,Ap 3,19:1
British Lion (Prod.)
Conduct Unbecoming 1975,O 6,42:1
Brut Productions (Distr.)
Hedda 1976,Ja 26,29:1
Bryanston Distributors, Inc (Distr.)
Devil's Rain, The 1975,Ag 8,11:1
Bryanston Films (Distr.)
Human Factor, The 1975,N 20,50:4
Bryanston Pictures (Distr.)
Coonskin 1975,Ag 21,44:1
Bryna Company (Prod.)
Posse 1975,Je 5,48:1
Buckley Brothers Films Inc (Distr.)
Bambina 1976,Ap 26,40:1
Buena Vista Distribution Company (Distr.)
Escape to Witch Mountain 1975,Jl 3,21:1
Strongest Man in the World, The 1975,Jl 10,19:1
Bears and I, The 1975,Jl 17,21:1
Apple Dumpling Gang, The 1975,Jl 24,17:3
One of Our Dinosaurs is Missing 1975,Ag 7,39:1
No Deposit, No Return 1976,Jl 3,17:1
Ride a Wild Pony 1976,Jl 17,9:3
Gus 1976,Ag 7,11:2
Treasure of Matecumbe 1976,Ag 28,11:2
Shaggy D A, The 1976,D 27,III,18:1

C

Can/Am Ltd (Prod.)
Man Who Skied Down Everest, The 1976,My 28,III,6:6
Cannon Group (Distr.)
Happy Hooker, The 1975,My 9,22:2
Canyon Cinema Cooperative (Distr.)
Images of Asian Music 1975,Ap 7,40:1
Tibet Paths of Cessation 1975,Ap 7,40:1
Capra, Claude Productions (Prod.)
Charlotte 1975,Je 23,33:2
Caribou Films (Distr.)
Serail (Surreal) 1976,D 4,17:1
Carolyn Films (Distr.)
People of the Wind 1976,O 30,14:6
Castelli-Sonnabend Tapes and Films, Inc (Distr.)
Pine Barrens 1975,O 23,49:1
Swamp 1975,O 23,49:1
Pursuit 1975,O 23,49:1
Kristina Talking Pictures 1976,N 3,62:1
CCC (Prod.)
Martyr, The 1976,Je 17,30:1
Central Film Office of the Iranian Ministry of Culture /(Misc.)
Simple Event, A 1975,Ap 8,33:1
Charter Film Productions, Ltd (Prod.)
Undercovers Hero 1975,O 23,48:3
Cientifilm Aurora (Prod.)
Chac 1975,Ap 5,34:3
CinAmerica Released, Inc (Distr.)
Ali the Man 1975,S 18,50:1
Cine Artists (Distr.)
River Niger, The 1976,Ap 15,28:1
Echoes of a Summer 1976,My 15,14:1
Embryo 1976,My 27,29:1
Cine Artists International (Prod.)
Aloha, Bobby and Rose 1975,Ap 30,24:1
Cine Bright (Distr.)
Distance 1975,D 22,44:1
Cine-Films, Inc (Prod.)
Maids, The 1975,Ap 22,41:1
Cine III (Distr.)
Magnifique, Le 1976,Jl 8,28:3
Alpha Beta 1976,Ag 5,26:1
Cine-Tamaris (Prod.)
Daguerrotypes 1976,S 15,50:1
Cinegai (Prod.)
Just Before Nightfall (Juste Avant la Nuit) 1975,S 10,37:4
Cinema National Corporation (Distr.)
Keetje Tippel 1976,S 27,41:1
Cinema National Films (Distr.)
Secret, The (Le Secret) 1975,My 9,19:1
Cinema Services, Paris (Prod.)
Blow for Blow (Coup Pour Coup) 1975,Mr 3,37:3
Cinema Shares (Distr.)
Where the Red Fern Grows 1976,S 30,36:4
Cinema Shares International (Distr.)
No Way Out 1975,N 6,51:2
Godzilla Versus Megalon 1976,Jl 22,26:1
Cinema Shares International Distribution Corporation /(Distr.)
Mad Dog 1976,S 23,52:4
Cinema V (Distr.)
Swept Away (By An Unusual Destiny in the Blue Sea of August) 1975,S 18,48:1
Autobiography of a Princess 1975,O 5,60:7
Seven Beauties 1976,Ja 22,42:1
Cinema 5 (Distr.)
Monty Python and the Holy Grail 1975,Ap 28,34:4
America at the Movies 1976,S 23,52:1
Cinemagic Productions (Distr.)
Nurith 1975,Je 12,30:4
Cinematheque Francaise (Misc.)
Chienne, La (Bitch, The) 1975,S 27,21:4
Chienne, La (Bitch, The) 1976,My 1,13:1
Cinepix (Prod.)
Kamouraska 1975,Jl 14,21:1
Cinerama (Distr.)
Part 2 Walking Tall 1975,S 29,37:7
Cinerama (Prod.)
Reincarnation of Peter Proud, The 1975,Ap 26,14:1
Cinetirrena (Prod.)
How Funny Can Sex Be? (Sesso Matto) 1976,S 29,30:3
Cinevideo, Inc (Prod.)
Jacques Brel is Alive and Well and Living in Paris 1975,F 25,31:1

Property of
HARRISBURG AREA
COMMUNITY COLLEGE LIBRARY
Harrisburg, Pa.